Excel 2007 VBA Programming with XML and ASP

Julitta Korol

Wordware Publishing, Inc.

Library of Congress Cataloging-in-Publication Data

Korol, Julitta.
Excel 2007 VBA programming with XML and ASP / by Julitta Korol.
p. cm.
Includes index.
ISBN-13: 978-1-59822-043-8
ISBN-10: 1-59822-043-8 (pbk.)
1. Microsoft Excel (Computer file) 2. Microsoft Visual Basic for applications. 3. Electronic spreadsheets. 4. XML (Document markup language). 5. Active server pages. 6. Computer software--Development. I. Title.
HF5548.4.M523K6842 2008
005.54--dc22 2008045789
CIP

1100 Summit Ave., Suite 102
Plano, Texas 75074

Printed in the United States of America

ISBN-13: 978-1-59822-043-8
ISBN-10: 1-59822-043-8
10 9 8 7 6 5 4 3 2 1
0811

All inquiries for volume purchases of this book should be addressed to Wordware Publishing, Inc., at the above address. Telephone inquiries may be made by calling:

(972) 423-0090

Be sure to check out our other books at www.wordware.com.

Contents

Part II — Controlling Program Execution

Part III — Keeping Track of Multiple Values

Part IV — Error Handling and Debugging

Part V — Manipulating Files and Folders with VBA

Part VII — Enhancing the User Experience

Part VIII — Programming Excel Special Features

Part IX — Excel and Web Technologies

Acknowledgments

I would like to express my grateful appreciation to all the people involved in the creation of this book. Special thanks go to Beth Kohler, editor at Wordware Publishing, Inc., for her help, comments, and thorough review of this book. It is always a pleasure to work with Beth on a book project.

Thanks to Tana-Lee Rebhan from Hawaii, an Excel power user, for devoting a great deal of her free time to reviewing this book's chapters as they were written. Tana-Lee's comments helped make this step-by-step Excel 2007 programming tutorial more useful and comprehensive.

Many thanks go to Publisher Tim McEvoy for doing such a great job in coordinating this project. To the production team of Wordware Publishing, Inc. — Martha McCuller, Denise McEvoy, and Alan McCuller — a big thank you for all the hard work and expertise in the area of editing, design, and desktop publishing.

Introduction

This book shows you what's doable with Microsoft Excel 2007 beyond the standard user interface. If you ever wanted to open a new worksheet without using built-in commands or create a custom, fully automated form to gather data and store the results in a spreadsheet, you've picked up the right book. This book shows you how to delegate many time-consuming and repetitive tasks to Excel by using its built-in language, VBA (Visual Basic for Applications). By using special commands and statements and a number of Excel's built-in programming tools, you can work smarter than you ever thought possible.

When I first started programming in Excel (circa 1990), I was working in a sales department and it was my job to calculate sales commissions and send the monthly and quarterly statements to our sales representatives spread all over the U.S. As this was a very time-consuming and repetitive task, I became immensely interested in automating the whole process. In those days it wasn't easy to get started in programming on your own. There weren't as many books written on the subject, so all I had was the built-in documentation that was difficult to understand. Nevertheless, I succeeded; my first macro worked like magic. It automatically calculated our sales folks' commissions and printed out nicely formatted statements. And while the computer was busy performing the same tasks over and over again, I was free to deal with other more interesting projects. Many years have passed since that day and Excel is still working like magic for me and a great number of other people who took time to familiarize themselves with its programming interface.

If you'd like to join these people and have Excel do magical things for you as well, this book provides an easy, step-by-step introduction to VBA and other hot technologies that work nicely with Microsoft Excel. One is ASP (short for Active Server Pages) and the other is XML (or Extensible Markup Language). Besides this book, there is no other cost; all the tools you need are built in to Excel. If you have not yet discovered them, *Excel 2007 VBA Programming with XML and ASP* will lead you through the process of creating your first macros, VBA procedures, VBScripts, ASP pages, and XML documents, from start to finish. Along the way, there are detailed, practical "how-to" examples and plenty of illustrations. The book's approach is to learn by doing. There's no better way than step by step. Simply turn on the computer, open this book, read, and follow the steps.

Here's what Tana-Lee Rebhan has to say about the previous edition of this book:

Aloha,

I am sitting here at Starbucks with a bookstore copy of Julitta's "Excel 2003 VBA Programming with XML and ASP" (which, of course, I have at home on my own bookshelf, too) trying to create an Excel UserForm to improve redundant data input for my work supervisor. I am an occasional monkey-see-monkey-do user who finds Julitta's books immeasurably useful when I need to accomplish a task in Access or Excel.

While I have had both the pleasure and the privilege of proofreading Julitta's Excel and Access VBA programming books since her 2002 editions, I don't often have the opportunity to use her work to do my own infrequent projects. But when I have a project to work on, I keep on grabbing her books because they are the most easy-to-follow, hands-on texts to assist me in any of my programming tasks.

While Julitta's books are always an excellent resource, particularly for the beginning VBA programmer, they also contain a wealth of information for those who are more experienced and are trying to keep current on Microsoft's latest updates. If you are serious about getting into Excel programming and need a book to work with at your own pace, I encourage you to purchase this book and start working though its hands-on exercises. If you already have, I think you'll be glad you did!

Tana-Lee Rebhan, Hawaii

Excel 2007 VBA Programming with XML and ASP is divided into nine parts (30 chapters) that progressively introduce you to programming Microsoft Excel 2007 as well as controlling other applications with Excel.

Part I introduces you to Excel 2007 VBA programming. Visual Basic for Applications (VBA) is the programming language for Microsoft Office Excel. In this part of the book you acquire the fundamentals of VBA by recording macros and examining the VBA code behind the macro using the Visual Basic Editor. Here you'll also learn about different VBA components, the use of variables, and VBA syntax. With these topics covered, you begin writing and executing VBA procedures.

Part I consists of the following five chapters:

Chapter 1: Automating Spreadsheet Tasks with Macros — In this chapter you learn how you can introduce automation into your spreadsheets by simply using the built-in macro recorder. You also learn about different phases of macro design and execution and about macro security.

Chapter 2: Exploring the Visual Basic Editor (VBE) — In this chapter you learn almost everything you need to know about working with the Visual Basic Editor window, commonly referred to as VBE. Some of the programming tools that are not covered here are discussed and put to use in Chapter 10.

Chapter 3: Excel VBA Fundamentals — In this chapter you are introduced to basic VBA concepts such as the Microsoft Excel object model and its objects, properties, and methods. You also learn about many tools that will assist you in writing VBA statements quicker and with fewer errors.

Chapter 4: Using Variables, Data Types, and Constants — In this chapter you are introduced to basic VBA concepts that allow you to store various pieces of information for later use.

Chapter 5: VBA Procedures: Subroutines and Functions — In this chapter you learn how to write two types of VBA procedures: subroutines and functions. You also learn how to provide additional information to your procedures before they are run. You are introduced to working with some useful built-in functions and methods that allow you to interact with your VBA procedure users.

While the Excel macro recorder can get you started with VBA, it does not allow you to incorporate complex logic into your program. In Part II of this book you'll find out how the knowledge of decisions and looping enables you to control program flow and create useful VBA procedures and functions.

There are two chapters in Part II:

Chapter 6: Decision Making with VBA — In this chapter you learn how to control your program flow with a number of different decision-making statements.

Chapter 7: Repeating Actions in VBA — In this chapter you learn how you can repeat the same actions by using looping structures.

Although you can use individual variables to store data while your VBA code is executing, many advanced VBA procedures will require that you implement more efficient methods of keeping track of multiple values. In Part III of this book you'll learn about working with groups of variables (arrays) and storing data in collections.

Again, there are two chapters in Part III:

Chapter 8: Working with Arrays — In this chapter you learn about static and dynamic arrays, which you can use for holding various values. You also learn about built-in array functions.

Chapter 9: Working with Collections and Class Modules — In this chapter you learn how to create and use your own VBA objects and collections of objects.

While you may have planned to write a perfect VBA procedure, there is always a chance that incorrectly constructed or typed code or perhaps logic errors will cause your program to fail or produce unexpected results. In Part

IV of this book you'll learn about various methods of handling errors, and testing and debugging VBA procedures.

Part IV contains two chapters:

Chapter 10: VBE Tools for Testing and Debugging — In this chapter you begin using built-in debugging tools to test your programming code and trap errors.

Chapter 11: Conditional Compilation and Error Trapping — In this chapter you learn how to run the same procedure in different languages, and how you can test the ways your program responds to run-time errors by causing them on purpose.

While VBA offers a number of built-in functions and statements for working with the file system, you can also perform file and folder manipulation tasks via objects and methods included in the Windows Script Host installed by default on Windows 98 and later versions of Microsoft Windows. In addition, you can open and manipulate files directly via the low-level file I/O functions. In Part V of the book you discover various methods of working with files and folders, and learn how to programmatically open, read, and write three types of files.

Part V consists of the following three chapters:

Chapter 12: File and Folder Manipulation with VBA — In this chapter you learn numerous VBA statements used in working with Windows files and folders.

Chapter 13: File and Folder Manipulation with Windows Script Host (WSH) — In this chapter you learn learn how the Windows Script Host works together with VBA and allows you to get information about files and folders.

Chapter 14: Using Low-Level File Access — In this chapter you learn how to get in direct contact with your data by using the process known as low-level file I/O (input/output). You also learn about various types of file access.

The VBA programming language goes beyond Excel. It is used by other Office applications such as Word, PowerPoint, Outlook, and Access, and is also supported by a growing number of non-Microsoft products. The VBA skills you acquire in Excel can be used to program any application that supports this language. In Part VI of the book you learn how other applications expose their objects to VBA.

Part VI consists of the following two chapters:

Chapter 15: Using Excel VBA to Interact with Other Applications — In this chapter you learn how you can launch and control other applications from within VBA procedures written in Excel. You also learn how to establish a reference to a type library and use and create Automation objects.

Chapter 16: Using Excel with Microsoft Access — In this chapter you learn about accessing Microsoft Access data and running Access queries and functions from VBA procedures. If you are interested in learning more about Access programming with VBA using a step-by-step approach, I recommend my recent book *Access 2007 Programming by Example with VBA, XML, and ASP* (Wordware Publishing, 2008).

Extensive changes have been made to the user interface (UI) in Excel 2007. The menus and toolbars are replaced with a new navigation tool called the Ribbon that provides a task-oriented method of performing spreadsheet activities — whether it's formatting or analyzing data. In Part VII of the book you learn how to create desired interface elements for your users via Ribbon customizations and the process of creating dialog boxes and custom forms. You will also learn how to format spreadsheets with VBA and control Excel with event-driven programming.

In Part VII there are five chapters:

Chapter 17: Event-Driven Programming — In this chapter you learn the types of events that can occur when you are running VBA procedures in Excel. You get a working knowledge of writing event procedures and handling various types of events.

Chapter18: Using Dialog Boxes — In this chapter you learn about working with Excel's built-in dialog boxes programmatically.

Chapter 19: Creating Custom Forms — In this chapter you learn how to use various controls for designing user-friendly forms. This chapter has two complete hands-on applications you build from scratch.

Chapter 20: Formatting Worksheets with VBA — In this chapter you learn how to perform worksheet formatting tasks with VBA by applying new visual features such as data bars, color scales, and icon sets. You also learn how to produce consistent looking worksheets by using new document themes and styles.

Chapter 21: Shortcut Menu Programming and Ribbon Customizations — In this chapter you learn how to add custom options to Excel's built-in shortcut menus and how to work programmatically with the new Ribbon interface that replaces the old style menus and toolbars.

Some Excel 2007 features are used more frequently than others; some are only used by Excel power users and developers. In Part VIII of the book you start by writing code that automates printing and e-mailing. Next, you gain experience in programming advanced Excel features such as PivotTables, PivotCharts, and Excel tables. You are also introduced to a number of useful Excel 2007 objects and learn how to program the Visual Basic Editor (VBE) itself.

Part VIII has the following five chapters:

Chapter 22: Printing and Sending E-mail from Excel — In this chapter you learn how to control printing and e-mailing your workbooks via VBA code.

Chapter 23: Programming PivotTables and PivotCharts — In this chapter you learn how to work with two powerful Microsoft Excel objects that are used for data analysis: PivotTable and PivotChart. You will learn how to use VBA to manipulate these two objects to quickly produce reports that allow you or your users to easily examine large amounts of data pulled from an Excel worksheet range or from an external data source such as a Microsoft Access database.

Chapter 24: Using and Programming Excel Tables — In this chapter you learn how to work with Excel tables. You will learn how to retrieve information from a Microsoft Access database, convert it into a table, and enjoy database-like functionality in the spreadsheet. You will also learn how tables are exposed through Excel's object model and manipulated via VBA.

Chapter 25: Programming Special Features — In this chapter you learn about a number of useful objects from the Excel 2007 object library and get a feel for what can be accomplished by calling upon them.

Chapter 26: Programming the Visual Basic Editor (VBE) — In this chapter you learn how to use numerous objects, properties, and methods from the Microsoft Visual Basic for Applications Extensibility 5.3 Object library to control the Visual Basic Editor (VBE) to gain full control over Excel.

Thanks to the Internet and intranets, your spreadsheet data can be easily accessed and shared with others 24/7. Excel 2007 is capable of both capturing data from the web and publishing it to the web. In Part IX you are introduced to using Excel with web technologies. You learn how to retrieve live data into worksheets with web queries and use Excel VBA to create and publish HTML files. You also learn how to retrieve and send information to Excel via Active Server Pages (ASP). Programming XML and Smart Tags is also thoroughly discussed and practiced.

Part IX consists of the following four chapters:

Chapter 27: HTML Programming and Web Queries — In this chapter you learn how to create and publish HTML files using VBA. You also learn how to create and run various types of web queries (dynamic, static, and parameterized).

Chapter 28: Excel and Active Server Pages (ASP) — In this chapter you learn how to use the Microsoft-developed Active Server Pages (ASP) technology to write ASP pages that open worksheets in the Microsoft Excel 2007 application, and how to get data entered in your browser into Excel.

You also learn how to create charts dynamically based on data pulled from an Access database.

Chapter 29: Using XML in Excel 2007 — In this chapter you learn how to use Extensible Markup Language (XML) with Excel. You learn about enhanced XML support in Excel 2007 and many objects and technologies that are used to process XML documents.

Chapter 30: Using and Programming Smart Tags — In this chapter you learn how smart tags can help Excel users get instant, context-sensitive access to information stored in external sources such as web pages or databases.

Who This Book Is For

This book is designed for Excel users who want to know how to quickly expand their knowledge and learn what's possible to accomplish with Excel worksheets beyond the provided user interface.

Consider this book as a sort of private course that you can attend in the comfort of your office or home. Some courses have prerequisites, and this is no different. *Excel 2007 VBA Programming with XML and ASP* does not explain how to select options from the Ribbon or use shortcut keys. The book assumes that you can easily locate options that are required to perform any of the tasks preprogrammed by the Microsoft team. With the basics mastered, this book will take you to the next learning level where your custom requirements and logic are rendered into the language that Excel can understand. Let your worksheets perform magical things for you, and you won't regret it.

The Companion Files

The example files for all the hands-on activities are available to be downloaded at www.wordware.com/files/excel2007. For more information, please see the ReadThisFirst link included on the web page.

Part I

Introduction to Excel 2007 VBA Programming

Visual Basic for Applications (VBA) is the programming language for Microsoft Office Excel.

In this part of the book, you acquire the fundamentals of VBA by recording macros and examining the VBA code behind the macro using the Visual Basic Editor. Here you'll also learn about different VBA components, the use of variables, and VBA syntax. With these topics covered you begin writing and executing VBA procedures.

Chapter 1

Automating Spreadsheet Tasks with Macros

Are you ready to build intelligence into your Microsoft Office Excel 2007 spreadsheets? By automating routine tasks, you can make your spreadsheets run quicker and more efficiently. This first chapter walks you through the process of speeding up spreadsheet tasks with macros. You learn what macros are, how and when to use them, and how to write and modify them. Getting started with macros is easy. Creating them requires nothing more than what you already have — a basic knowledge of Microsoft Office Excel 2007 commands and spreadsheet concepts. Are you ready to begin? Make sure you are seated at a computer and launch Microsoft Office Excel 2007.

What Are Macros?

Macros are programs that store a series of commands. When you create a macro, you simply combine a sequence of keystrokes into a single command that you can later "play back." Because macros can reduce the number of steps required to complete tasks, using macros can significantly decrease the time you spend creating, formatting, modifying, and printing your worksheets. You can create macros by using Microsoft Excel's built-in recording tool (macro recorder), or you can write them from scratch by using the Visual Basic Editor. Microsoft Office Excel 2007 macros are created with the powerful programming language Visual Basic for Applications, commonly known as VBA.

Common Uses for Macros

Microsoft Office Excel 2007 comes with dozens of built-in, timesaving features that allow you to work faster and smarter. Before you decide to automate a worksheet task with a macro, make sure there is not already a built-in feature that you can use to perform that task. Consider creating a macro when you find yourself performing the same series of actions over and over again or when Excel does not provide a built-in tool to do the job. Macros enable you to automate just about any part of your spreadsheet.

For example, you can automate data entry by creating a macro that enters headings in a worksheet or replaces column titles with new labels. Macros also enable you to check for duplicate entries in a selected area of your worksheet. With a macro, you can quickly apply formatting to several worksheets, as well as combine different formats, such as fonts, colors, borders, and shading. Even though Excel has an excellent chart facility, macros are the way to go if you wish to automate the process of creating and formatting charts. Macros will save you keystrokes when it comes to setting print areas, margins, headers, and footers, and selecting special options for printouts.

VBA — The Common Macro Language in Office

Excel 5 was the first application on the market to feature Visual Basic for Applications. Since then, VBA has made its way into all Microsoft Office applications. This means that what you learn about VBA in this book can be used in programming other Microsoft Office products such as Word, PowerPoint, Outlook, and Access.

Microsoft Excel 4.0 Macro Sheets (.xlm)

In Excel 4, programmers and power users relied heavily on the XLM macro language to automate Excel. Macros had to be programmed manually using Excel 4.0 macro sheets that were saved in a file with an .xlm extension. In Excel 2007 you can continue to use and maintain Excel 4.0 macros; however, this book only covers macros recorded or written in the VBA macro language. (To insert an XLM macro sheet into a workbook, right-click any sheet tab and choose Insert. In the Insert dialog box, select MS Excel 4.0 Macro, and click OK.)

Excel 2007 Versions and File Formats

This book focuses on programming in Excel 2007, and only Excel 2007 should be used for working with this book's Hands-On exercises. Because the Excel menu system has been replaced with an entirely new Ribbon interface, the Hands-On instructions in this book will not work for previous versions of Excel. If you own or have access to Excel 2003 or Excel 2002 and would like to learn Excel programming, check out my previous programming books available from Wordware Publishing: *Excel 2003 VBA Programming with XML and ASP* or *Learn Microsoft Excel 2002 VBA Programming with XML and ASP*.

The default Office Excel 2007 file format is XML-based (.xlsx). However, this file format does not allow storing VBA macro code or Microsoft Excel 4.0 macro sheets (.xlm). The formats suitable for storing your programming code in Excel 2007 are as follows:

- Excel Macro-Enabled Workbook (.xlsm)
- Excel Binary Workbook (.xlsb)
- Excel Macro-Enabled Template (.xltm)

Macro Security Settings

Because macros can contain malicious code designed to put a virus on a user's computer, it is important to understand different security settings that are available in Microsoft Excel 2007. It is also critical that you run up-to-date antivirus software on your computer.

If a workbook file you are attempting to open contains macros and there is antivirus software installed on your computer, the workbook file is scanned for known viruses before it is opened.

The default Excel 2007 macro security setting is to disable all macros with notification, as shown in Figure 1-1.

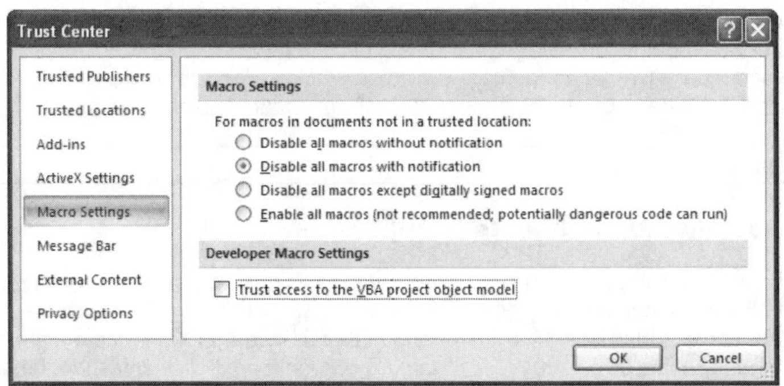

Figure 1-1: By disabling all macros with notification, Excel will prompt you whether or not to run potentially unsafe macros upon opening a workbook.

If macros are present in a workbook you are trying to open you will receive a security warning message just under the Ribbon, as shown in Figure 1-2.

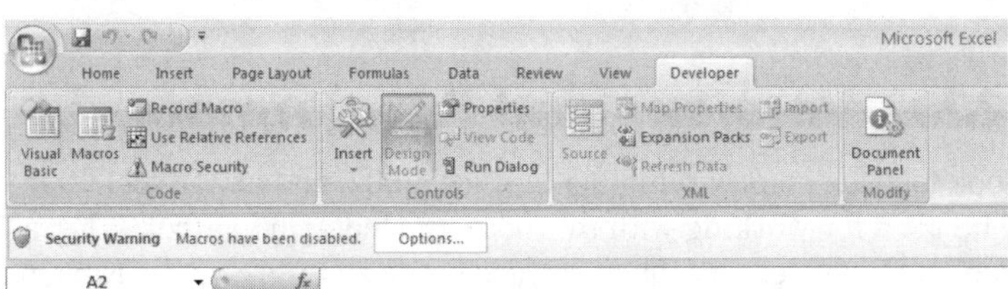

Figure 1-2: The security warning message in Excel 2007.

To use the disabled components, a user must click the Options button on the message bar. This will bring up the Security Alert – Macro dialog box (Figure 1-3). By default the Help protect me from unknown content (recommended) option button is selected. To enable the disabled macro content only for the current session, users need to select the Enable this content option button and then click OK. These steps will need to be repeated each time the workbook is opened. If users select not to trust the workbook content, they will still be able to view the data in the workbook; however, they will not be able to view or run macros.

Figure 1-3: The Security Alert – Macro dialog box allows you to temporarily enable macro content.

To make it easy to work with macro-enabled workbooks (or with the binary file format that may contain VBA code), you will not want to bother with enabling the macro content each time you open your practice workbook. To permanently trust your workbooks with recorded macros or VBA code, you can place the workbooks in a trusted location — a folder on your local or a network drive that you mark as trusted. Notice the Open the Trust Center hyperlink at the bottom of the Security Alert - Macro dialog box in Figure 1-3. This hyperlink will open a Trust Center where you can set up a trusted folder. You can also access the Trust Center from the Microsoft Office button as demonstrated in Hands-On 1-1.

Before you read more about macro security, let's take a few minutes to set up your Excel application so you can easily run macros on your computer.

Hands-On 1-1: Setting up Excel 2007 for Macro Development

1. Create a folder on your hard drive named **C:\Ex07_ByExample**.
2. If you haven't yet done so, start up Microsoft Excel 2007.
3. Click the **Microsoft Office** button, and then click **Excel Options**.
4. Click **Popular**, and select the **Show Developer tab in the Ribbon** box (Figure 1-4).
5. Click **OK**.

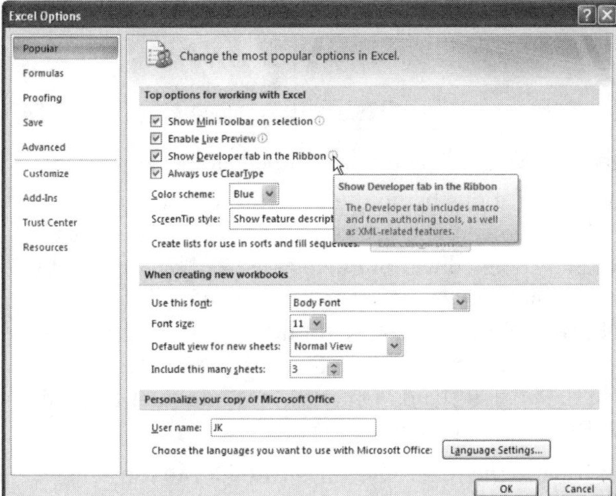

Figure 1-4: The Developer tab on the Ribbon makes it easy to write and run macros. You should enable this tab via the Excel Options dialog box.

6. Select the **Developer** tab on the Ribbon and click the **Macro Security** button (Figure 1-5).

   The Trust Center dialog box opens up, as depicted earlier in Figure 1-1.

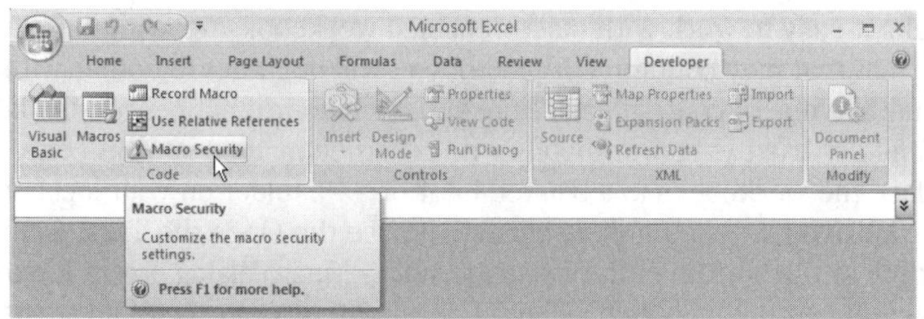

Figure 1-5: The Developer tab must be activated via the Excel Options (see Figure 1-4 above).

7. In the left pane of the Trust Center dialog box, click **Trusted Locations.**

   The Trusted Locations dialog box already shows several predefined trusted locations that were created when you installed Office 2007. For the purpose of this book, we will add a custom location to this list.

8. Click the **Add new location** button.
9. In the Path text box, type the path and folder name of a location on your local hard drive that you want to set up as a trusted source for opening files. Let's enter **C:\Ex07_ByExample** to designate this folder as a trusted location for this book's Excel programming exercises (Figure 1-6).

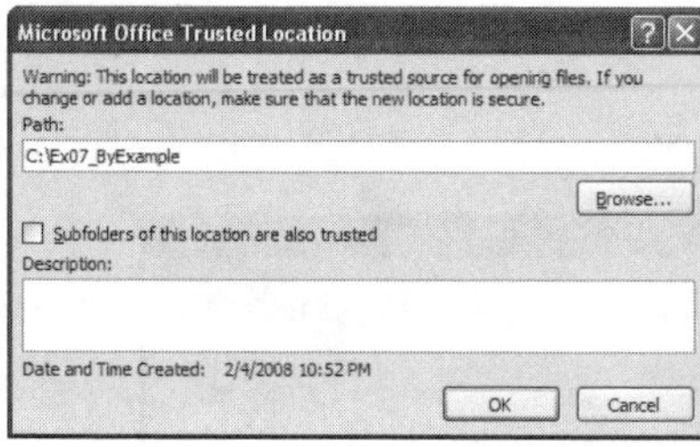

Figure 1-6: Setting a Trusted Location folder for this book's programming examples.

10. Click **OK** to close the Trusted Location dialog box.
11. The Trusted Locations list in the Trust Center now includes the C:\Ex07_ByExample folder as a trusted source. Files placed in a trusted location can be opened without being checked by the Trust Center security feature. Click **OK** to close the Trust Center dialog box.

    Your Excel application is now set up for easy macro development as well as opening files containing macros. You should save all the files created in the book's Hands-On exercises into your trusted C:\Ex07_ByExample folder.

Now let's get back to the Macro Settings category in the Trust Center (Figure 1-1).

The first option in this category, *Disable all macros without notification*, will cause the workbook to load with all macros and other add-in programs disabled. You will not be notified about the existence of macros in the workbook. When macros are disabled you can still view and edit those macros, but you cannot run them.

The second option, *Disable all macros with notification*, was discussed earlier in this chapter. This default setting will cause Excel to display a message bar security alert (see Figures 1-2 and 1-3) each time you open a workbook that contains macros or other executable code.

The third option, *Disable all macros except digitally signed macros*, depends on whether a macro is digitally signed. A macro that is digitally signed is referred to as a *signed macro*. A *digital signature* on a macro is similar to a handwritten signature on a printed letter. This signature confirms that the macro has been signed by the creator and the macro code has not been altered since then. To digitally sign macros you must install a digital certificate (see Chapter 2 for more information). A signed macro provides information about its signer and the status of the signature. If you open a workbook containing executable code and that workbook has been digitally signed, Excel checks whether you have already trusted the signer. If the signer can be found in the Trusted Publishers list (Figure 1-7), the workbook will be opened with macros enabled. If the Trusted Publishers list does not have the name of the signer, you will be presented with a security dialog box that allows you to either enable or disable macros in the signed workbook.

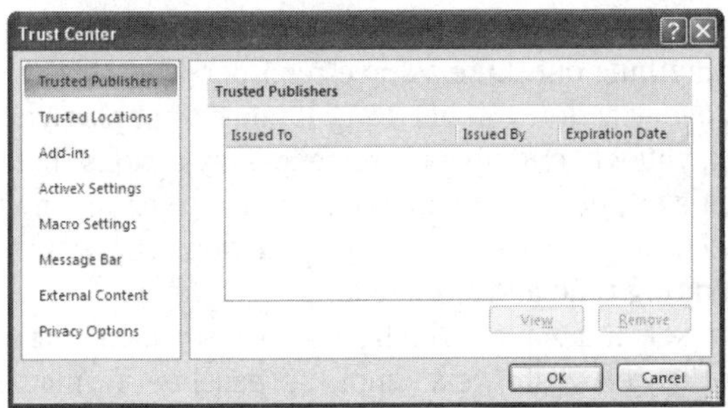

Figure 1-7: Trusted Publishers are developers who have signed their code project with a valid and current digital signature issued by a reputable certificate authority (CA).

The fourth option, *Enable all macros (not recommended; potentially dangerous code can run)*, enables all macros and other executable code in all workbooks. This option is the least secure; it does not display any notifications.

The setting in the Developer Macro Settings category, *Trust access to the VBA project object model*, is for developers who need to programmatically access and manipulate the VBA object model and the Visual Basic Editor environment (VBE). This check box should be left unchecked to prevent unauthorized programs from accessing the VBA project of any workbook or add-in. We will come back to this setting in Chapter 26 when we tackle programming the Visual Basic Editor.

More about Signed/Unsigned Macros

Sometimes a signed macro may have an invalid signature because of a virus, incompatible encryption method, or a missing key, or its signature cannot be validated because it was made after the certificate expired or was revoked. Signed macros with invalid signatures are automatically disabled, and users attempting to open workbooks containing macros are warned that the signature validation was not possible.

An unsigned macro is a macro that does not bear a digital signature. Such macros could potentially contain malicious code. Upon opening a workbook containing unsigned macros, you are presented with a security warning (Figure 1-2). You can ignore this message if you need to use the workbook without the macro features, or you can decide whether to allow the macros for this session by clicking the Options button.

Planning a Macro

Before you create a macro, take a few minutes to consider what you want to do. Because a macro is a collection of a fairly large number of keystrokes, it is important to plan your actions in advance. The easiest way to plan your macro is to manually perform all the actions that the macro needs to do. As you enter the keystrokes, write them down on a piece of paper exactly as they occur. Don't leave anything out. Like a voice recorder, Microsoft Excel's macro recorder records every action you perform. If you do not plan your macro prior to recording, you will end up with unnecessary actions that will slow it down. Although it's easier to edit a macro than it is to erase unwanted passages from a voice recording, performing only the actions you want recorded will save you editing time and trouble later.

Suppose you want to see at a glance which areas of a worksheet are text, numbers, and formulas. Figure 1-8 shows a simple spreadsheet formatted with distinct font colors and styles to help identify the contents of the underlying cells.

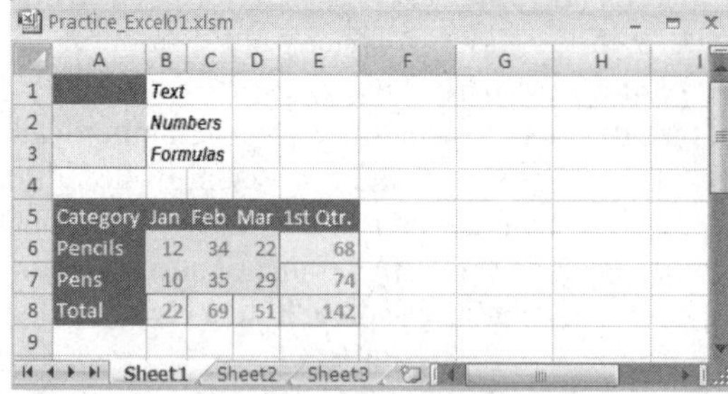

Figure 1-8: Finding out "what's what" in a spreadsheet is easy with formatting applied by an Excel macro.

Hands-On 1-2: Creating a Worksheet for Data Entry

1. Open a new workbook and save it as **C:\Ex07_ByExample\Practice_Excel01.xlsm.**

   Make sure that you save the workbook in the macro-enabled format (.xlsm).

2. Starting in cell A1, enter the text, numbers, and formulas shown in Figure 1-9:

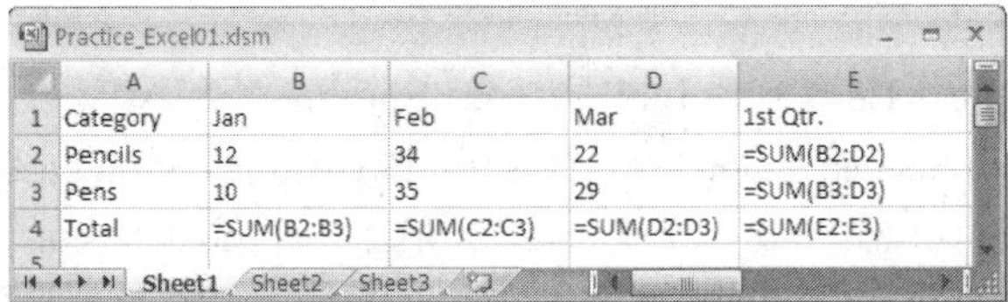

Practice_Excel01.xlsm

	A	B	C	D	E
1	Category	Jan	Feb	Mar	1st Qtr.
2	Pencils	12	34	22	=SUM(B2:D2)
3	Pens	10	35	29	=SUM(B3:D3)
4	Total	=SUM(B2:B3)	=SUM(C2:C3)	=SUM(D2:D3)	=SUM(E2:E3)

Sheet1 Sheet2 Sheet3

Figure 1-9: This sample worksheet will be automatically formatted with a macro.

3. Save the changes in the Practice_Excel01.xlsm workbook file.

To produce the formatting results shown in Figure 1-8, perform Hands-On 1-3.

Hands-On 1-3: Applying Custom Formatting to the Worksheet

This Hands-On relies on the worksheet that was prepared in Hands-On 1-2.

1. Select any cell in the Practice_Excel01.xlsm file. Make sure that only one cell is selected.
2. Select **Home | Find & Select | Go To Special**.
3. In the Go To Special dialog box, click the **Constants** option button and then remove the check mark next to Numbers, Logicals, and Errors. Only the Text check box should be checked.
4. Click **OK** to return to the worksheet. Notice that the cells containing text are now selected. Be careful not to change your selection until you apply the necessary formatting in the next step.
5. With the text cells still selected, choose **Home | Cell Styles** and click on the **Accent4** style under Heading 4.

   Notice that the cells containing text now appear in a different color.

Steps 1 to 5 allowed you to locate all the cells that contain text. To select and format cells containing numbers, perform the following actions:

6. Select a single cell in the worksheet.
7. Select **Home | Find & Select | Go To Special**.
8. In the Go To Special dialog box, click the **Constants** option button and remove the check mark next to Text, Logicals, and Errors. Only the Numbers check box should be checked.
9. Click **OK** to return to the worksheet. Notice that the cells containing numbers are now selected. Be careful not to change your selection until you apply the necessary formatting in the following step.
10. With the number cells still selected, choose **Home | Cell Styles** and click on the **Neutral** style.

    Notice that the cells containing numbers now appear shaded.

In steps 6 to 10 you located and formatted cells with numbers. To select and format cells containing formulas, perform the following actions:

11. Select a single cell.
12. Select **Home | Find & Select | Go To Special.**
13. In the Go To Special dialog box, click the **Formulas** option button.
14. Click **OK** to return to the worksheet. Notice that the cells containing numbers that are results of formulas are now selected. Be careful not to change your selection until you apply the necessary formatting in the next step.
15. With the formula cells still selected, choose **Home | Cell Styles** and click on the **Calculation** style in the Data and Model section.

In steps 11 to 15 you located and formatted cells containing formulas. To make it easy to understand all the formatting applied to the worksheet's cells, you will now add the color legend.

16. Select cells **A1:A3** and choose **Home | Insert | Insert Sheet Rows**.
17. Select cell **A1**.
18. Choose **Home | Cell Styles**, and click on the **Accent4** style under Heading 4.
19. Select cell **B1** and type **Text**.
20. Select cell **A2**.
21. Choose **Home | Cell Styles**, and click on the **Neutral** style.
22. Select cell **B2** and type **Numbers**.
23. Select cell **A3**.
24. Choose **Home | Cell Styles**, and click on the **Calculation** style in the Data and Model section.
25. Select cell **B3** and type **Formulas**.
26. Select cells **B1:B3** and right-click within the selection. Choose **Format Cells** from the shortcut menu.
27. In the Format Cells dialog box, click the **Font** tab. Select **Arial Narrow** font, **Bold Italic** font style, and **10** font size, and click **OK** to close the dialog box.

After completing steps 16 to 27, cells A1:B3 will display a simple color legend, as shown in Figure 1-8 earlier.

As you can see, no matter how simple your spreadsheet task appears at first, many steps may be required to get exactly what you want. Creating a macro that is capable of playing back your keystrokes can be a real time-saver, especially when you have to repeat the same process for a number of worksheets.

Before you go on to the next section in which you will record your first macro, let's remove the formatting from the example worksheet.

Hands-On 1-4: Removing All Formatting from the Worksheet

To remove all the formatting from your worksheet, perform the following steps:

1. Press **Ctrl+A** to select the entire worksheet.
2. In the Home tab's Editing group, click the **Clear** button's drop-down arrow, and then select **Clear Formats**.
3. Select cells **A1:A4** and in the Home tab's Cells group, click the **Delete** button's drop-down arrow, and then select **Delete Sheet Rows**.
4. Select cell **A1**.

Recording a Macro

Now that you know what actions you need to perform, it's time to turn on the macro recorder and create your first macro.

Hands-On 1-5: Recording a Macro that Applies Formatting to a Worksheet

To create your first macro, follow these steps:

1. Select any single cell in your Practice_Excel01.xlsm workbook.

   Before you record a macro, you should decide whether or not you want to record the positioning of the active cell. If you want the macro to always start in a specific location on the worksheet, turn on the macro recorder first and then select the cell you want to start in. If the location of the active cell does not matter, select a single cell first and then turn on the macro recorder.
2. Choose **View | Macros | Record Macro.**
3. In the Record Macro dialog box, enter the name **WhatsInACell** for the sample macro, as depicted in Figure 1-10. Do not dismiss this dialog box until you are instructed to do so.

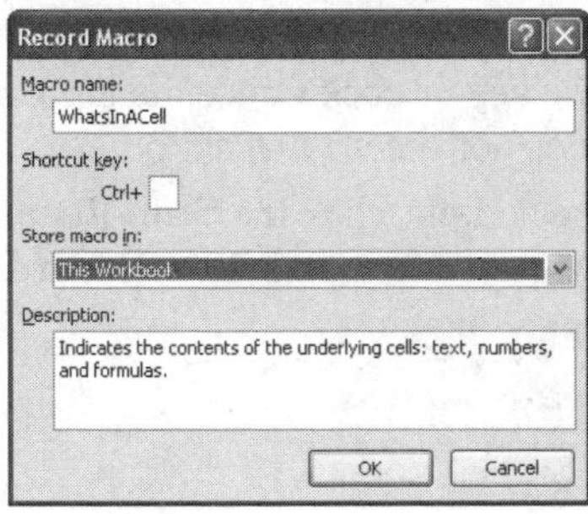

Figure 1-10: When you record a new macro, you must name it. In the Record Macro dialog box you can also supply a shortcut key, the storage location, and a description for your macro.

Macro Names

If you forget to enter a name for the macro, Excel assigns a default name such as Macro1, Macro2, and so on. Macro names can contain letters, numbers, and the underscore character, but the first character must be a letter. For example, Report1 is a correct macro name, while 1Report is not. Spaces are not allowed. If you want a space between the words, use the underscore. For example, instead of WhatsInACell, enter Whats_In_A_Cell.

4. Select **This Workbook** in the Store macro in list box.

Storing Macros

Excel allows you to store macros in three locations:

- Personal Macro Workbook — Macros stored in this location will be available each time you work with Microsoft Excel. Personal Macro Workbook is located in the XLStart folder. If this workbook doesn't already exist, Excel creates it the first time you select this option.
- New Workbook — Excel will place the macro in a new workbook.
- This Workbook — The macro will be stored in the workbook you are currently using.

5. In the Description box, enter the following text: **Indicates the contents of the underlying cells: text, numbers, and formulas.**
6. Choose **OK** to close the Record Macro dialog box and begin recording.

   The Stop Recording button (Figure 1-11) appears in the status bar. Do not click on this button until you are instructed to do so. When this button appears in the status bar, the workbook is in the recording mode.

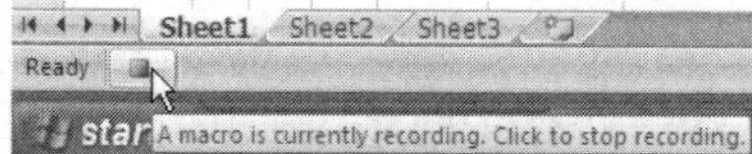

Figure 1-11: The Stop Recording button in the status bar indicates that the macro recording mode is active.

7. Perform the actions you tried out manually in the previous section (see Hands-On 1-3, steps 1-27).

   The Stop Recording button remains in the status bar as you record your macro. Only the actions finalized by pressing Enter or clicking OK are recorded. If you press the Esc key or click Cancel before completing the entry, the macro recorder does not record that action.
8. When you have performed all the actions, click the **Stop Recording** button in the status bar or choose **View | Macros | Stop Recording**.

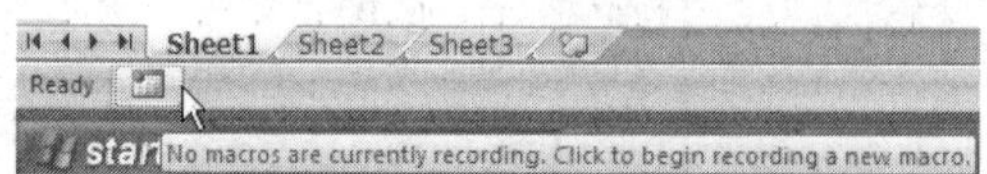

Figure 1-12: When you stop the macro recorder, the status bar displays a button that allows you to record another macro.

Using Relative or Absolute References in Macros

- If you want your macro to execute the recorded action in a specific cell, no matter what cell is selected during the execution of the macro, use absolute cell addressing. Absolute cell references have the following form: $A$1, $C$5, etc. By default, the Excel macro recorder uses absolute references. Before you begin to record a new macro, make sure the Use Relative References option is not selected when you click the Macros button (see Figure 1-13).
- If you want your macro to perform the action in any cell, be sure to select the Use Relative References option before you choose the Record Macro option. Relative cell references have the following form: A1, C5, etc. Bear in mind, however, that Excel will continue recording using the relative cell references until you exit Microsoft Excel or click the Use Relative References option again.
- During the process of recording your macro, you may use both methods of cell addressing. For example, you may select a specific cell (e.g., $A$4), perform an action, then choose another cell relative to the selected cell (e.g., C9, which is located five rows down and two columns to the right of the currently active cell $A$4). Relative references automatically adjust when you copy them, and absolute references don't.

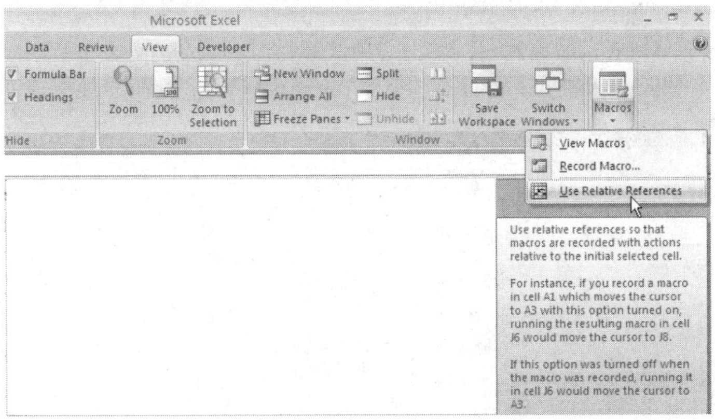

Figure 1-13: Excel's macro recorder can record your actions using absolute or relative cell references.

Before we try out the newly recorded macro, let's record another macro that will remove the formatting that we've applied to our worksheet.

Hands-On 1-6: Recording a Macro that Removes Formatting from a Worksheet

To remove the formatting from the worksheet depicted in Figure 1-8, perform the following steps:

1. Choose **View | Macros | Record Macro** (or you may click the **Begin recording** button located in the status bar).
2. Enter **RemoveFormats** as the name for your macro.
3. Ensure that **This Workbook** is selected in the Store macro in list box.

4. Click **OK.**
5. Press **Ctrl+A** to select the entire worksheet.
6. In the Home tab's Editing group, click the **Clear** button's drop-down arrow, and then select **Clear Formats**.
7. Select cells **A1:A4** and in the Home tab's Cells group, click the **Delete** button's drop-down arrow, and then select **Delete Sheet Rows**.
8. Select cell **A1**.
9. Click the **Stop Recording** button in the status bar, or choose **View | Macros | Stop Recording.**

We will run this macro the next time we need to clear the worksheet.

Executing Macros

After you create a macro, you should run it at least once to make sure it works correctly. Later in this chapter you will learn other ways to run macros, but for now, we will use the Macro dialog box.

Hands-On 1-7: Running a Macro

1. Make sure that the Practice_Excel01.xlsm workbook is open and Sheet1 with the example worksheet is active.
2. Choose **View | Macros | View Macros.**
3. In the Macro dialog box, click the **WhatsInACell** macro name.

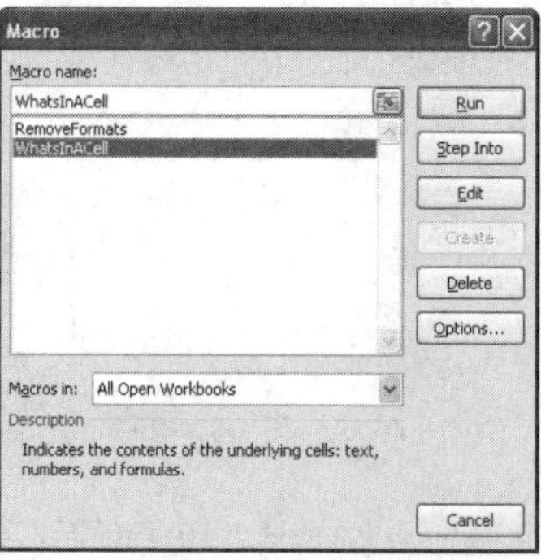

Figure 1-14: In the Macro dialog box you can select a macro to run, edit, or delete.

4. Click **Run** to execute the macro.

The WhatsInACell macro applies the formatting you have previously recorded.

Now, let's proceed to remove the formatting with the RemoveFormats macro:

5. Choose **View | Macros | View Macros**.
6. In the Macro dialog box, click the **RemoveFormats** macro name.
7. Click **Run** to execute the macro.

```
' Indicates the contents of the underlying cells: text, numbers, and
' formulas.
'
'
    Selection.SpecialCells(xlCellTypeConstants, 2).Select
    Selection.Style = "Accent4"
    Range("C2").Select
    Selection.SpecialCells(xlCellTypeConstants, 1).Select
    Selection.Style = "Neutral"
    Range("C3").Select
    Selection.SpecialCells(xlCellTypeFormulas, 23).Select
    Selection.Style = "Calculation"
    Range("A1:A4").Select
    Selection.EntireRow.Insert
    Range("A1").Select
    Selection.Style = "Accent4"
    Range("B1").Select
    ActiveCell.FormulaR1C1 = "Text"
    Range("A2").Select
    Selection.Style = "Neutral"
    Range("B2").Select
    ActiveCell.FormulaR1C1 = "Numbers"
    Range("A3").Select
    Selection.Style = "Calculation"
    Range("B3").Select
    ActiveCell.FormulaR1C1 = "Formulas"
    Range("B1:B3").Select
    With Selection.Font
        .Name = "Arial Narrow"
        .FontStyle = "Bold Italic"
        .Size = 10
        .Strikethrough = False
        .Superscript = False
        .Subscript = False
        .OutlineFont = False
        .Shadow = False
        .Underline = xlUnderlineStyleNone
        .ThemeColor = xlThemeColorLight1
        .TintAndShade = 0
        .ThemeFont = xlThemeFontNone
    End With
End Sub
```

For now, let's focus on finding answers to two questions:

- How do you read the macro code?
- How can you edit macros?

Notice that the macro code that you have recorded is located between the Sub and End Sub keywords. You read the code line by line from top to bottom. Lines that begin with a single quote will not execute when you run your macro. These lines are comments, which are discussed in the next section. Editing macros boils down to deleting or modifying existing code, or typing new instructions in the Code window.

Macro Comments

Take a look at the recorded macro code. Notice the lines that begin with a single quote. These lines denote comments. By default, comments appear in green. When the macro code is executed, Visual Basic ignores the comment lines. Comments are often placed within the macro code for documenting the meaning of certain lines that aren't obvious. Comments can also be used to temporarily disable certain blocks of code that you don't want to execute. This is often done while testing and debugging your macros.

Let's add some comments to the WhatsInACell macro to make the code easier to understand.

Hands-On 1-9: Adding Comments to the Macro Code

1. Make sure that the Visual Basic Editor screen shows the Code window with the WhatsInACell macro.
2. Click in front of "Selection.SpecialCells(xlCellTypeConstants, 2).Select" and press **Enter**.
3. Move the pointer to the empty line you just created and type the comment shown below. Be sure to start with a single quote.

```
' Find and format cells containing text
```

4. Click in front of "Selection.SpecialCells(xlCellTypeConstants, 1).Select" and press **Enter**.
5. Move the pointer to the empty line and type the following comment:

```
' Find and format cells containing numbers
```

6. Click in front of "Selection.SpecialCells(xlCellTypeFormulas, 23).Select" and press **Enter**.
7. Move the pointer to the empty line and add the following comment:

```
' Find and format cells containing formulas
```

8. Click in front of "Range("A1:A4").Select" and press **Enter**.
9. Move the pointer to the empty line and add the following comment:

```
' Create a legend
```

10. Press **Ctrl+S** to save the changes in Practice_Excel01.xlsm, or choose **File | Save Practice_Excel01.xlsm**.

About Comments

In the VBE Code window, every line that begins with a single quote is a comment. The default comment color is green. You can change the color of comments in the Options dialog box (Tools | Options | Editor Format tab). You can also add a comment at the end of the line of code. For example, to add a comment following the line .Size = 10, click at the end of this line, press Tab, type a single quote, and then type the text of your comment.

The comment lines don't do anything except provide information to the user about the purpose of a macro or macro action. When you write your own VBA procedures, don't forget to include comments. Comments will make your life easier if you need to return to the macro procedure several months later. They will also allow others to understand various parts of your procedure.

Analyzing the Macro Code

All macro procedures begin with the keyword Sub and end with the keywords End Sub. The Sub keyword is followed by the macro name and a set of parentheses. Between the keywords Sub and End Sub are statements that Visual Basic executes each time you run your macro. Visual Basic reads the lines from top to bottom, ignoring the statements preceded with a single quote (see the previous section on comments) and stops when it reaches the keywords End Sub. Notice that the recorded macro contains many periods. The periods appear in almost every line of code and are used to join various elements of the Visual Basic for Applications language. How do you read the instructions written in this language? They are read from the right side of the last period to the left.

Here are a few statements from the WhatsInACell procedure and a description of what they mean:

Range("A1:A4").Select	Select cells A1 to A4.
Selection.EntireRow.Insert	Insert a row in the selected area. Because the previous line of code selects four cells, Visual Basic will insert four rows.
ActiveCell.FormulaR1C1 = "Text"	Let the formula of the active cell be "Text." Because the previous line of code, Range("B1").Select, selects cell B1, B1 is currently the active cell, and this is where Visual Basic will enter the text.

With Selection.Font .Name = "Arial Narrow" .FontStyle = "Bold Italic" .Size = 10 .Strikethrough = False .Superscript = False .Subscript = False .OutlineFont = False .Shadow = False .Underline = xlUnderlineStyleNone .ThemeColor = xlThemeColorLight1 .TintAndShade = 0 .ThemeFont = xlThemeFontNone End With	This is a special block of code that is interpreted as follows: Set the name of the font to "Arial Narrow" for the currently selected cells, set the Font Style to "Bold Italic", etc. The block of code that starts with the keywords With and ends with the keywords End With speeds up the execution of the macro code. Instead of repeating the instruction "Selection.Font" for each of the font settings, the macro recorder uses a shortcut. It places the repeating text, Selection.Font, to the right of the keyword With and ends the block with the keywords End With.

Cleaning Up the Macro Code

As you review and analyze your macro code line by line, you may notice that Excel recorded a lot of information that you didn't intend to include. For example, after selecting cells containing text, in addition to setting the font style to bold italic and the size to 10, Excel also recorded the current state of other options on the Font tab — strikethrough, superscript, subscript, outline font, shadow, underline, theme color, tint and shade, and theme font. Take a look at the following code fragment:

```
With Selection.Font
    .Name = "Arial Narrow"
    .FontStyle = "Bold Italic"
    .Size = 10
    .Strikethrough = False
    .Superscript = False
    .Subscript = False
    .OutlineFont = False
    .Shadow = False
    .Underline = xlUnderlineStyleNone
    .ThemeColor = xlThemeColorLight1
    .TintAndShade = 0
    .ThemeFont = xlThemeFontNone
End With
```

When you use dialog boxes, Excel always records all the settings. These additional instructions make your macro code longer and more difficult to understand. Therefore, when you finish recording your macro, it is a good idea to go over the recorded statements and delete the unnecessary lines. Let's do some code cleanup in the WhatsInACell macro.

Hands-On 1-10: Cleaning up the Macro Code

1. In the Code window with the WhatInACell macro, locate the following block of code and delete the lines that are crossed out:

```
With Selection.Font
    .Name = "Arial Narrow"
    .FontStyle = "Bold Italic"
    .Size = 10
```

```
        .Strikethrough = False
        .Superscript = False
        .Subscript = False
        .OutlineFont = False
        .Shadow = False
        .Underline = xlUnderlineStyleNone
        .ThemeColor = xlThemeColorLight1
        .TintAndShade = 0
        .ThemeFont = xlThemeFontNone
    End With
```

After the cleanup, only three statements should be left between the keywords With and End With. These statements are the settings that you actually changed in the Format Cells dialog box when you recorded this macro:

```
With Selection.Font
    .Name = "Arial Narrow"
    .FontStyle = "Bold Italic"
    .Size = 10
End With
```

2. Locate the following two lines of code:

```
Range("A1:A4").Select
Selection.EntireRow.Insert
```

3. Replace the above two lines of code with the following line:

```
Range("A1:A4").EntireRow.Insert
```

4. Save your changes by clicking the Save icon on the Standard toolbar.

Testing the Modified Macro

When you modify a recorded macro, it is quite possible that you will introduce some errors. For example, you may delete an important line of code, or you may inadvertently remove or omit a necessary period. To make sure that your macro continues to work correctly after your modifications you need to run it again.

Hands-On 1-11: Testing the Modified Macro Code

1. In the Visual Basic Editor Code window, place the cursor in any line of the WhatsInACell macro code, and choose **Run | Run Sub/UserForm**.

   If you didn't introduce any problems during the modification of your macro, the macro will run smoothly and no errors will be reported.

2. To see the result of your macro, you must switch to the Microsoft Excel window. To do this, press **Alt+F11**.

   If the Visual Basic Editor encounters an error during the execution of your macro, you will see a dialog box displaying the type of error found. Before you run macros, you must make sure that your macro can run in the worksheet that is currently selected. For example, if you try to run the WhatsInACell macro when a blank sheet is selected, you will get the "Run time error '1004' — No Cells were found" error message. Click the End button, and make sure that you select the correct worksheet before you try to run the macro again.

If the selected worksheet contains only cells with text and you try to run the WhatsInACell macro, Visual Basic will encounter a problem when attempting to select cells with numbers. The same "No cells found" message will be displayed.

If you omit the period in With Selection.Font, on running this line of code, Visual Basic will generate the "Run time error '424' — Object required" message. Click the Debug button in the message box, and you will be placed in the Code window. At this time, Visual Basic will enter into break mode and will use the yellow highlighter to indicate the line that it had trouble executing. As soon as you correct your error, Visual Basic may announce "This action will reset your project, proceed anyway?" Click OK to this message. Although you can edit code in break mode, some edits prevent continuing execution. After correcting the error, run the macro again, as there may be more errors to be fixed before the macro can run smoothly.

3. Switch back to the Visual Basic Editor screen by pressing **Alt+F11**.

Two Levels of Macro Execution

You can run your macros from either the Microsoft Excel window or the Visual Basic Editor window. When you execute the WhatsInACell macro from the VBE screen, Visual Basic executes the macro behind the scenes. You can't see when Visual Basic selected and applied formatting to the text cells or when it inserted four empty rows for the color legend. To watch Visual Basic at work, you must run your macro from the Macro dialog box as demonstrated earlier, or arrange your screen in such a way that the Microsoft Excel and Visual Basic windows can be viewed at the same time.

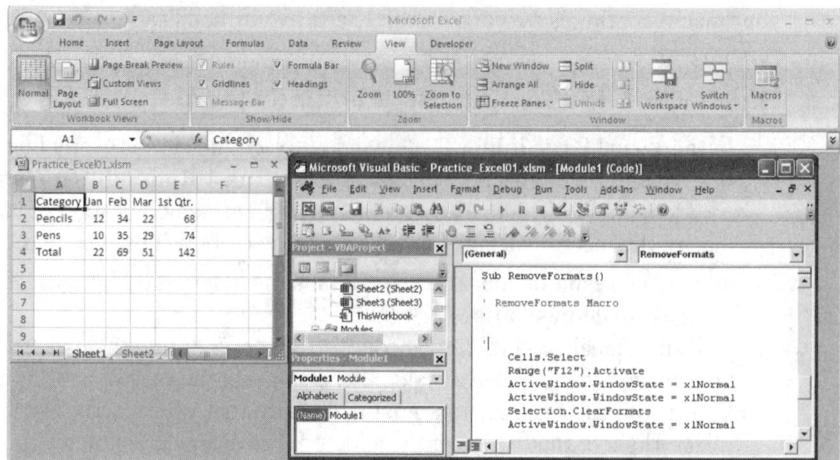

Figure 1-16: If you want to watch the execution of your macro from the level of the Visual Basic Editor, you must position the Microsoft Excel and VBE windows side by side.

Improving Your Macro

After you record your macro, you may realize that you'd like the macro to perform additional tasks. Adding new instructions to the macro code is not very difficult if you are already familiar with the Visual Basic language. In most situations, however, you can do this more efficiently when you delegate the extra tasks to the macro recorder. You may argue that Excel records more instructions than are necessary. One thing is for sure, however — the macro recorder does not make mistakes, and you can rely fully on it. If you want to add additional instructions to your macro using the macro recorder, you must record a new macro, copy the sections you want, and paste them into the correct location in your original macro. Suppose you would like to include a thick border around cells A1:B3 when you format your worksheet with the WhatsInACell macro. Let's see how this can be achieved with the macro recorder.

Hands-On 1-12: Recording Additional Features for the Existing Macro in a New Macro

1. Activate the Microsoft Excel window with the sample worksheet you created in this chapter.
2. Choose **View | Macros | Record Macro.**
3. In the Record Macro dialog box, click **OK** to accept the default macro name.
4. Select cells **A1:B3.**
5. Click the drop-down arrow on the **Border** tool in the Font group of the Home tab, and select **Thick Box Border.**
6. Click cell **A1.** Notice the thick border around cells A1:B3.
7. Click the **Stop Recording** button in the status bar, or choose **View | Macros | Stop Recording.**
8. Remove the thick border from your worksheet by clicking the **Undo** button in the Office Quick Access toolbar.
9. To view the recorded macro code, switch to the Visual Basic Editor window and locate the new macro in the Code window. The recorded macro is shown below:

```
Sub Macro3()
'
' Macro3 Macro
'

'
    Range("A1:B3").Select
    Selection.Borders(xlDiagonalDown).LineStyle = xlNone
    Selection.Borders(xlDiagonalUp).LineStyle = xlNone
    With Selection.Borders(xlEdgeLeft)
        .LineStyle = xlContinuous
        .ColorIndex = 0
```

```
            .TintAndShade = 0
            .Weight = xlMedium
        End With
        With Selection.Borders(xlEdgeTop)
            .LineStyle = xlContinuous
            .ColorIndex = 0
            .TintAndShade = 0
            .Weight = xlMedium
        End With
        With Selection.Borders(xlEdgeBottom)
            .LineStyle = xlContinuous
            .ColorIndex = 0
            .TintAndShade = 0
            .Weight = xlMedium
        End With
        With Selection.Borders(xlEdgeRight)
            .LineStyle = xlContinuous
            .ColorIndex = 0
            .TintAndShade = 0
            .Weight = xlMedium
        End With
        Selection.Borders(xlInsideVertical).LineStyle = xlNone
        Selection.Borders(xlInsideHorizontal).LineStyle = xlNone
        Range("A1").Select
    End Sub
```

Let's analyze the above code. Do you think you can get rid of some instructions? Before you start deleting unnecessary lines of code, think of how you can use the comment feature that you've recently learned. You can comment out the unwanted lines and run the macro with the commented code. If the Visual Basic Editor does not generate errors, you can safely delete the commented lines. If you follow this path, you will never find yourself recording the same keystrokes more than once. And if the macro does not perform correctly, you can remove the comments from the lines that may be needed after all.

When you create macros with the macro recorder, you can quickly learn the VBA equivalents for the Excel commands and dialog box settings. Then you can look up the meaning and the usage of these Visual Basic commands in the online help. It's quite obvious that the more instructions Visual Basic needs to read, the slower the execution of your macro will be. Eliminating extraneous commands will speed up your macro. However, to make your macro code easier to understand, you may want to put on your detective hat and search for a better way to perform a specific task. For example, take a look at the code the macro recorder generated for placing a border around selected cells. It appears that the macro recorder handled each line separately. It seems hard to believe that Visual Basic does not have a simple one-line command that places a border around a selected range of cells.

Learning the right word or expression in any language takes time. If you look long enough, you will find that Visual Basic has a BorderAround method that allows you to add a border to a range of cells and set the Color, LineStyle, and Weight for the new border. Using Visual Basic for

Applications, the quickest way to create the thick border around a selection of cells is with the following statement:

```
Range("A1:B3").BorderAround Weight:=xlThick
```

The above instruction uses the BorderAround method of the Range object. It uses the thick line to create a border around cells A1:B3. (You'll learn about Visual Basic objects, properties, and methods in Chapter 3.)

Now that you know what instruction is needed to produce a thick border around selected cells, let's add it to the WhatsInACell macro.

Hands-On 1-13: Adding Additional Code to the Existing Macro

1. Activate the Code window with the WhatsInACell macro.
2. Add a new line after ActiveCell.FormulaR1C1 = "Formulas".
3. In the blank line, enter the following instruction:

   ```
   Range("A1:B3").BorderAround Weight:=xlThick
   ```

4. Place the cursor anywhere in the macro code and press **F5** to run the modified macro.
5. Press **Alt+F11** to switch to the Microsoft Excel window to see the formatting changes applied by the macro to the worksheet.

Including Additional Instructions

To include additional instructions in the existing macro, add empty lines in the required places of the macro code by pressing Enter, and type in the necessary Visual Basic statements.

If the additional instructions are keyboard actions or menu commands, you may use the macro recorder to generate the necessary code and then copy and paste these code lines into the original macro.

Want to add more improvements to your macro? Why not add a message box to notify you when Visual Basic has finished executing the last macro line. This sort of action cannot be recorded, as Excel does not have a corresponding Ribbon command or shortcut menu option. However, using the Visual Basic language, you can add new instructions to your macro by hand. Let's see how this is done.

Hands-On 1-14: Adding Visual Basic Statements to the Recorded Macro Code

1. In the Code window containing the code of the WhatsInACell macro procedure, click in front of the End Sub keywords and press **Enter**.
2. Place your cursor on the empty line and type the following statement:

   ```
   MsgBox "All actions have been performed."
   ```

   MsgBox is one of the most frequently used VBA functions. You will learn more about its usage in Chapter 5.

3. Make sure the cursor is located anywhere in the WhatsInACell macro code, and press **F5**.
4. Click **OK** when Visual Basic completes the last recorded instruction and displays the message.

You now know for sure that the macro has finished running.

Renaming the Macro

When you add additional actions to your macro, you may want to change the macro name to better indicate its purpose. The name of the macro should communicate its function as clearly as possible. To change the macro name, you don't need to press a specific key. In the Code window, simply delete the old macro name and enter the new name following the Sub keyword.

Other Methods of Running Macros

So far, you have learned three methods of running macros. You already know how to run a macro by choosing View | Macros | View Macros. Unfortunately, this method of running a macro is not convenient if you need to run your macro often. You also tried to run the macro in the VBE Code window with the keyboard shortcut F5 or by choosing Run | Run Sub/UserForm. In addition, you can run a macro from the Visual Basic Editor window by clicking a button on the Standard toolbar (see Figure 1-17) or by choosing Tools | Macro | Macros.

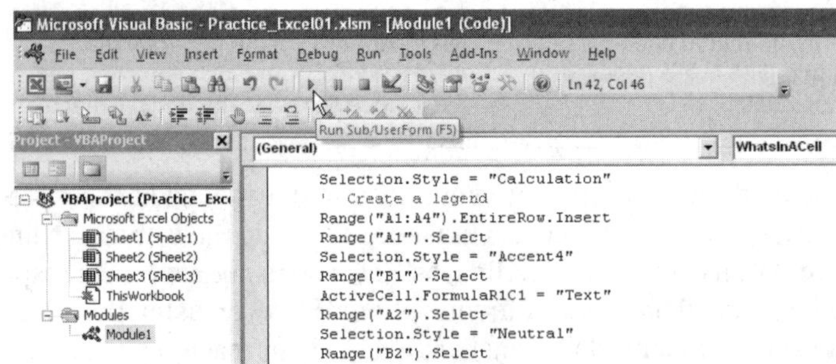

Figure 1-17: The Visual Basic procedure can be run from the toolbar button.

In this section you will learn three cool methods of macro execution that will allow you to run your macros using a keyboard shortcut, toolbar button, or worksheet button. Let's get started.

Running the Macro Using a Keyboard Shortcut

A popular method to run a macro is by using an assigned keyboard shortcut. It is much faster to press Ctrl+Shift+I than it is to activate the macro from the Macro dialog box. Before you can use the keyboard shortcut, you must assign it to your macro. Let's learn how this is done.

Hands-On 1-15: Assigning a Macro to a Keyboard Shortcut

1. Press **Alt+F8** to open the Macro dialog box.
2. In the list of macros, click the **WhatsInACell** macro, and then choose the **Options** button.
3. When the Macro Options dialog box appears, the cursor is located in the Shortcut key text box.
4. Hold down the **Shift** key and press the letter **I** on the keyboard. Excel records the keyboard combination as Ctrl+Shift+I. The result is shown in Figure 1-18.

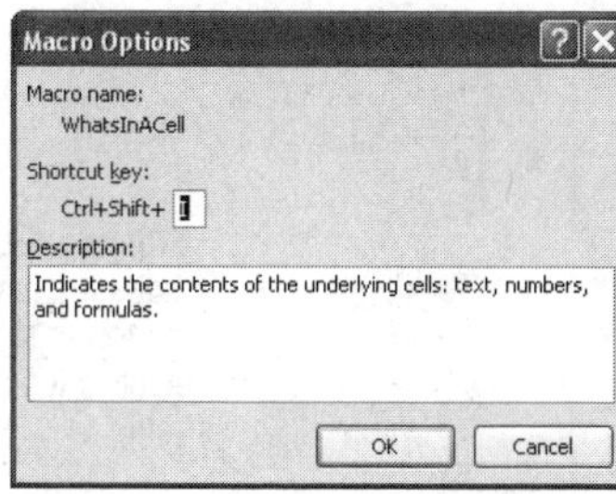

Figure 1-18: Using the Macro Options dialog box, you can assign a keyboard shortcut for running a macro.

5. Click **OK** to close the Macro Options dialog box.
6. Click **Cancel** to close the Macro dialog box and return to the worksheet.
7. On your own, assign the **Ctrl+Shift+L** keyboard shortcut to the **RemoveFormats** macro.
8. To run your macros using the newly assigned keyboard shortcuts, make sure the Microsoft Excel window is active and press **Ctrl+Shift+L** to remove the formats and then press **Ctrl+Shift+I** to run the second macro to format the worksheet.

   Your macros go to work and your spreadsheet is now formatted.
9. Press **Ctrl+Shift+L** to run the RemoveFormats macro again.

Avoid Shortcut Conflicts

If you assign to your macro a keyboard shortcut that conflicts with a Microsoft Excel built-in shortcut, Excel will run your macro if the workbook containing the macro code is currently open.

Running the Macro from the Quick Access Toolbar

In Office 2007 applications, users can add their own buttons to the built-in Quick Access toolbar. Let's see how it is done from Excel.

Hands-On 1-16: Running a Macro from the Quick Access Toolbar

1. In the Microsoft Excel window, click the **Customize Quick Access Toolbar** button (the downward-pointing arrow in the title bar) and choose **More Commands.**

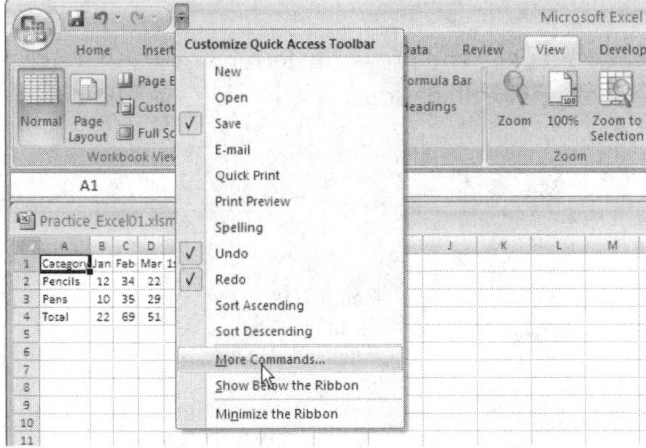

Figure 1-19: Adding a new button to the Quick Access toolbar (step 1).

The Excel Options dialog box appears with the page titled Customize the Quick Access Toolbar.

2. In the **Choose commands from** drop-down list box, select **Macros.**
3. In the **Customize Quick Access Toolbar** drop-down list box, select **For Practice_Excel01.xlsm.**
4. Select **WhatsInACell** in the list box on the left-hand side.

   The current selections are shown in Figure 1-20.

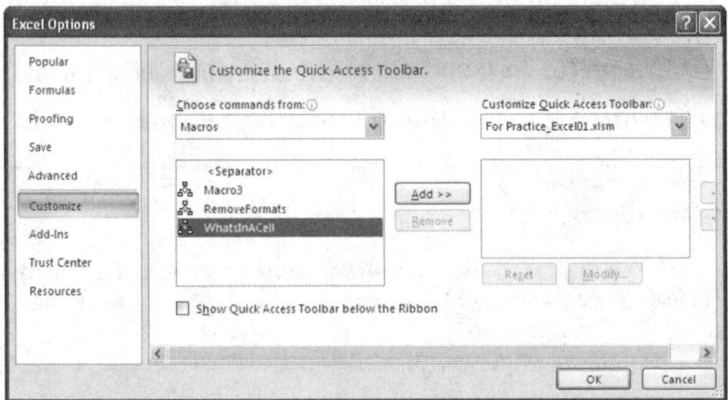

Figure 1-20: Adding a new button to the Quick Access toolbar (step 2).

5. Click the **Add** button to move the WhatsInACell macro to the list box on the right-hand side.
6. To change the button image for your macro, click the **Modify** button.
7. Select the blue square button in the button gallery, and click **OK.**

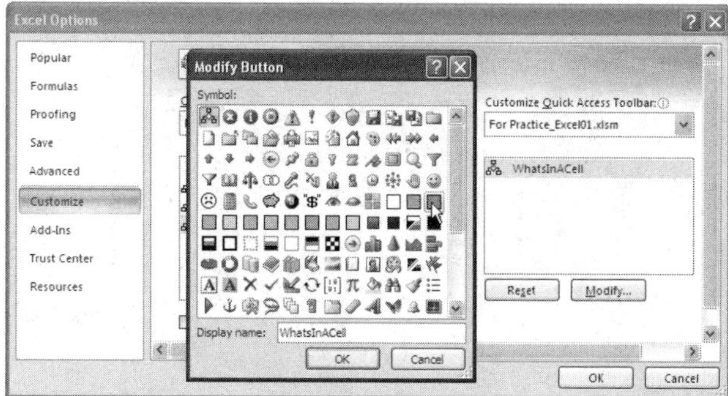

Figure 1-21: Adding a new button to the Quick Access toolbar (step 3).

8. After closing the gallery window, make sure that the image to the left of the macro name has changed. Click **OK** to close the Excel Options dialog.

   You should now see a new button on the Quick Access toolbar. This button will be available whenever the Practice_Excel01.xlsm workbook is active. It will disappear when you activate another workbook.

Figure 1-22: A custom button placed on the Quick Access toolbar will run the specified macro.

9. Make sure the Sheet1 worksheet with the sample data is now active, and click the blue square button you've just added to run the macro assigned to it.

   Again, your macro goes to work and your spreadsheet is now formatted. Let's remove the formatting you just applied by running the RemoveFormats macro that you recorded earlier in this chapter.

10. Press **Alt+F8** to open the Macro dialog box. Select the **RemoveFormats** macro and click the **Run** button (or just press **Ctrl+Shift+L**).

Running the Macro from a Worksheet Button

Sometimes it makes most sense to place a macro button right on the worksheet where it cannot be missed. Let's go over the steps that will attach the WhatsInACell macro to a worksheet button.

Hands-On 1-17: Running a Macro from a Button Placed on a Worksheet

1. Activate Sheet1 with the example worksheet you prepared in this chapter.
2. Choose **Developer | Insert**. The Forms toolbar appears, as shown in Figure 1-23.

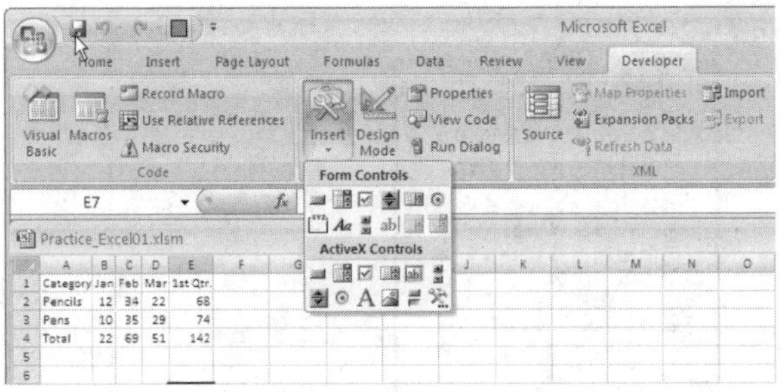

Figure 1-23: Adding a button to a worksheet (step 1).

3. In the Form Controls area, click the first image, which represents a button.
4. Click anywhere in the empty area of the worksheet. When the Assign Macro dialog box appears, choose the **WhatsInACell** macro and click **OK**.
5. To change the button's label, highlight the default text on the button, and type **Format Cells.** If the text does not fit, do not worry. You will resize the button in step 7. When the button is selected, it looks like the one shown in Figure 1-24. If the selection handles are not displayed, right-click **Button 1** on the worksheet and choose **Edit Text** on the shortcut menu. Select the default text and enter the new label.

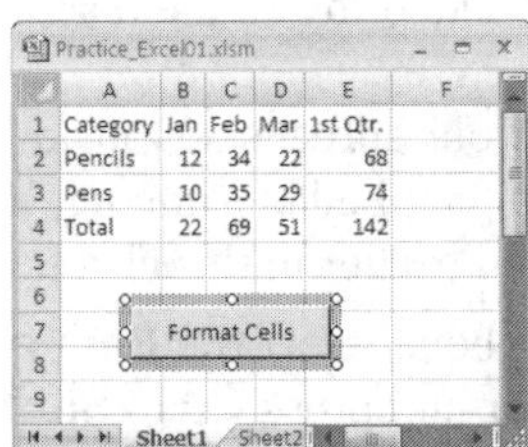

Figure 1-24: A button with an attached macro.

6. When you're done renaming the button, click outside the button to exit the edit mode.

   Since the text you entered is longer than the default button text, let's resize the button so that the entire text can be viewed.
7. Right-click the button you've just renamed, point to one of the tiny circles that appear in the button's right edge, and drag right to expand the button until you see the complete entry, Format Cells.
8. When you're done resizing the button, click outside the button to exit the selection mode.
9. To run your macro, click the button you just created.

   Again, your macro goes to work and your worksheet is now formatted. Let's remove the formatting you just applied by running the RemoveFormats macro.
10. Press **Alt+F8** to open the Macro dialog box. Select the **RemoveFormats** macro and click the **Run** button.

11. On your own, create another button on this worksheet that will be used for running the RemoveFormats macro.

Adding Controls to a Worksheet

You can add controls to a worksheet by choosing the Insert button on the Developer tab. This gives you access to two types of controls: Form controls and ActiveX controls (see Figure 1-23 earlier). The Form controls are compatible with earlier versions of Excel and can be used on chart sheets, old XLM macro sheets, and worksheets when all you want to do is run a macro by clicking a control. The ActiveX controls can be placed on worksheets or custom forms that you create in the Visual Basic Editor window. While the Form controls can only respond to the Click event, the ActiveX controls have many different actions, or events, that can occur when you use the control. When you use a Form control, you assign a macro to it that is stored in a module of This Workbook, New Workbook, or Personal Macro Workbook. When you use an ActiveX control, you write macro code that is stored with the control itself.

In addition to assigning macros to a button in the Form controls or a command button in the ActiveX controls, you can assign a macro to any drawing object on a worksheet. Excel 2007 has a large selection of ready-made shapes under the Shapes button on the Insert tab. Simply place the desired shape on the worksheet, right-click it, and choose Assign Macro.

You can also run macros from a hyperlink or a button placed in the Ribbon. These techniques will be introduced in Chapter 21.

Saving Macros

The WhatsInACell and RemoveFormats macros that you created in this chapter are located in a Microsoft Excel workbook. To save the macro to disk, all you need to do is save the open workbook.

Hands-On 1-18: Saving Macros and Running Macros from Another Workbook

1. Save your practice workbook and then close it.
2. Open a brand new workbook.

   Notice that your custom macro button no longer appears on the Quick Access toolbar. Recall that we told Excel to associate the macro with the Practice_Excel01.xlsm workbook. Also, there is no trace of your macros in the Macro dialog box. If you'd like to run the macros you recorded earlier in this chapter in another workbook, you need to open the file that stores these macros. But before you do this, let's enter some data into the worksheet.
3. In the new workbook that you just opened, activate Sheet1 and enter the text **Addition** in cell A1, the number **2** in cell A2, the number **4** in cell A3, and **=Sum(A2:A3)** in cell A4.

4. Save this workbook as **C:\Ex07_ByExample\Practice_Excel01Calc.xlsx.** We will not have any macros in this workbook, so you can save it in the Excel 2007 default file format.
5. Open the **C:\Ex07_ByExample\Practice_Excel01.xlsm** workbook file.
6. Activate **Sheet1** in the Practice_Excel01Calc.xlsx workbook.
7. Press **Alt+F8** to activate the Macro dialog box. Notice that Excel displays macros in all open workbooks. The name of each macro is preceded with the workbook name where it is located.
8. Select the **Practice_Excel01.xlsm!WhatsInACell** macro and click **Run.**

   The macro goes to work again. You should see your new worksheet formatted in the same way the formatting was applied in the Practice_Excel01.xlsm workbook.
9. Close the **Practice_Excel01Calc.xlsx** workbook file. Do not save the changes. Do not close the Practice_Excel01.xlsm workbook file. We will need it in the next section.

Printing Macros

If you want to document your macro or perhaps study the macro code when you are away from the computer, you can print your macros. You can print the entire module sheet where your macro is stored or indicate a selection of lines to print. Let's print the entire module sheet that contains your WhatsInACell macro.

Hands-On 1-19: Printing Macro Code

1. Switch to the Visual Basic Editor window and double-click **Module1** in the Project Explorer window to activate the module containing the WhatsInACell macro.
2. Choose **File | Print.**
3. In the Print - VBAProject dialog box, the Current Module option button should be selected.
4. Click **OK** to print the entire module sheet.

If you'd like to only print a certain block of programming code, perform the following steps:

1. In the module sheet, highlight the code you want to print.
2. Choose **File | Print.**
3. In the Print - VBAProject dialog box, the Selection option button should be selected.
4. Click **OK** to print the highlighted code.

Storing Macros in the Personal Macro Workbook

When you record a macro, you can specify to store the macro code in the Personal macro workbook. When you store a macro in the Personal macro workbook, Excel creates a file named Personal.xlsb and places it in one of the following locations:

- \Documents and Settings\username\Application Data\Microsoft\Excel\XLStart
- \Program Files\Microsoft Office\Office12\XLStart

Any file saved to the XLStart folder is loaded automatically each time you start Excel. The Personal macro workbook is a convenient place to store general-purpose macros like the FormulasOnOff macro recorded in the next Hands-On. The purpose of this macro is to toggle the display of worksheet formulas.

Hands-On 1-20: Recording a Macro in the Personal Macro Workbook

1. Make sure you are in the Microsoft Excel application window.
2. Choose **View | Macros | Record Macro.**
3. In the Record Macro dialog box, enter **FormulasOnOff** in the Macro name box.
4. Choose **Personal Macro Workbook** from the Store macro in the drop-down list.
5. Click in the Shortcut key text box, and press **Shift+F**.
6. Choose **OK** to exit the Record Macro dialog box.
7. Choose **Formulas | Show Formulas.**

   Because you have now turned on the display of formulas, the worksheet cells show the formulas instead of the values that the formulas produce.
8. Click the **Stop Recording** button in the status bar, or choose **View | Macros | Stop Recording.**
9. To see the macro code, choose **Developer | View Code.** This activates the Visual Basic Editor window. Notice that the Project Explorer window now shows an additional VBA project (Personal.xlsb).
10. To open Personal.xlsb, click the plus sign (+) to the left of the project name.

    The VBA project contains two folders: Microsoft Excel Objects and Modules.
11. Click the plus sign next to the Modules folder to open it and then double-click **Module1**.

The Code window shows the code of the FormulasOnOff macro, as shown in Figure 1-25.

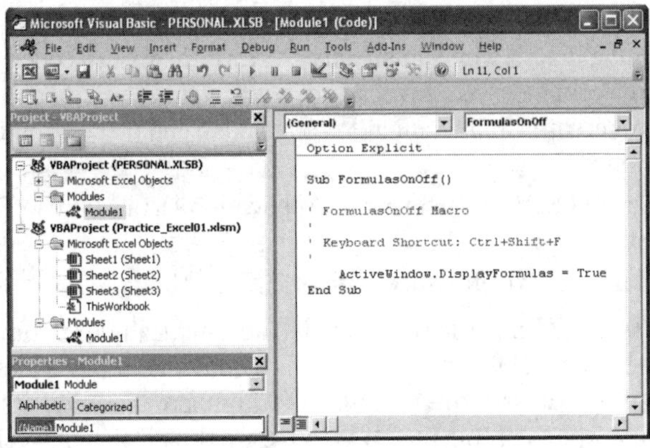

Figure 1-25: Because the FormulasOnOff macro was recorded in the Personal.xlsb workbook it will be accessible from any workbook.

Notice that each Excel workbook contains a single project. The first time you record a macro, Excel creates a Modules folder and places your macro code in Module1. If you record another macro in the same workbook, Excel places it below the previously recorded macro in the same Module1 sheet. All macros recorded in the same work session are stored in the same module. If you close Excel, reopen the same workbook, and record a new macro, Excel will store it in a new module.

When you recorded your macro, you turned on the display of formulas. The macro name suggests that the macro can toggle the formulas. To make the macro behave this way, you must edit it. The following recorded macro line sets the display of formulas in the active window to True:

```
ActiveWindow.DisplayFormulas = True
```

The setting that will turn off the display of formulas looks like this:

```
ActiveWindow.DisplayFormulas = False
```

12. To make a toggle in VBA, you need to connect the statements shown in the previous step in the following way:

```
ActiveWindow.DisplayFormulas = Not ActiveWindow.DisplayFormulas
```

13. Replace the recorded macro line with the statement above.

    The revised macro code is shown below:

```
Sub FormulasOnOff()
'
' FormulasOnOff Macro
'
' Keyboard Shortcut: Ctrl+Shift+F
'
ActiveWindow.DisplayFormulas = Not ActiveWindow.DisplayFormulas
End Sub
```

14. Choose **Run | Run Sub/UserForm** to execute the macro.

15. Switch back to the Microsoft Excel application window by pressing **Alt+F11** and press **Ctrl+Shift+F** to run the macro again.
    No matter how many times you run this macro, it always knows what to do. You can use the same idea to create macros that toggle the display of gridlines and other Microsoft Excel features.
16. Close the Practice_Excel01.xlsm workbook file and click **OK** when prompted to save changes.
17. Exit Microsoft Excel. You will be prompted to save the changes you made to the Personal macro workbook. Click **Yes** to save the changes.
18. Restart Excel.
    When you restart Excel, the Personal macro workbook will automatically load in the background.
19. To run the FormulasOnOff macro right now, press **Ctrl+Shift+F**. Because the workbook does not contain any data, all you will see is the change in the width of the worksheet columns.
20. Press **Ctrl+Shift+F** again to turn off the display of formulas.
21. Press **Alt+F11** to switch to the Visual Basic Editor window.
    Notice that the Personal.xlsb file is listed in the Project Explorer window as a separate project.
22. Press **Alt+F11** to switch back to the Microsoft Excel application window.
23. Exit Microsoft Excel. Click **No** when prompted to save changes in Book1.

Storing Other Macros in the Personal Workbook

If you want to store other macros in the Personal macro workbook, you can take one of the following routes:

- Record a new macro and choose the Personal macro workbook for its storage location.
- Switch to the Visual Basic Editor and open the project that contains the macro you want to move to the Personal macro workbook. Cut the macro code from the current location and open the Personal macro workbook project. Paste the macro code into the existing module in the Personal macro workbook, or create a new module prior to pasting.
- In the Visual Basic Editor window, choose File | Import File to bring the macro code from a text file or another Visual Basic project file (*.frm, *.bas, *.cls).

Chapter Summary

In this chapter you have learned how to create macros by recording your selections in the Microsoft Excel application window. You also learned how to view, read, and modify the recorded macros in the Visual Basic Editor window. In addition, you tried various methods of running macros. This chapter has also explained macro security issues that you should be aware of when opening workbooks containing macro code.

The next chapter introduces you to various windows that are available in the Visual Basic Editor screen.

Chapter 2

Exploring the Visual Basic Editor (VBE)

Understanding the Project Explorer Window ■ Understanding the Properties Window ■ Understanding the Code Window ■ Other Windows in the Visual Basic Editor Window ■ Assigning a Name to the VBA Project ■ Renaming the Module ■ Understanding Digital Signatures ■ Creating a Digital Certificate ■ Signing a VBA Project ■ Chapter Summary

Now that you know how to record, run, and edit macros, let's spend some time in the Visual Basic Editor window and become familiar with its features.

With the tools located in the Visual Basic Editor window, you can:

- Write your own VBA procedures.
- Create custom forms.
- View and modify object properties.
- Test VBA procedures and locate errors.

The Visual Basic Editor window can be accessed in the following ways:

- Choose Developer | Visual Basic.
- Choose Developer | View Code.
- Press Alt+F11.

Understanding the Project Explorer Window

The Project Explorer window displays a hierarchical list of currently open projects and their elements.

A VBA project can contain the following elements:

- Worksheets
- Charts
- ThisWorkbook — The workbook where the project is stored
- Modules — Special sheets where programming code is stored
- Classes — Special modules that allow you to create your own objects
- Forms
- References to other projects

With the Project Explorer you can manage your projects and easily move between projects that are currently loaded into memory. You can activate the Project Explorer window in one of three ways:

- From the View menu by selecting Project Explorer.
- From the keyboard by pressing Ctrl+R.
- From the Standard toolbar by clicking the Project Explorer button (see Figure 2-1).

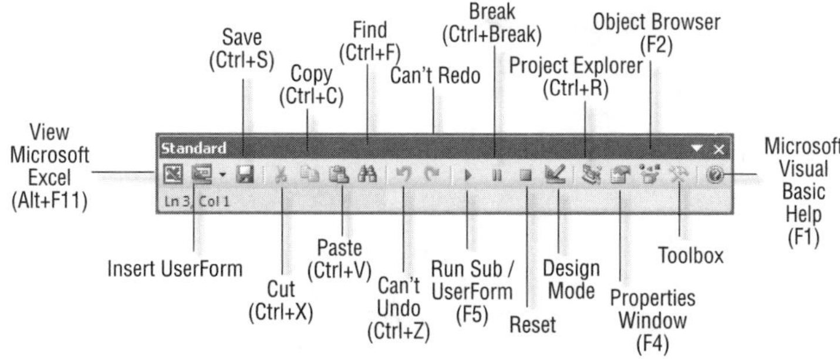

Figure 2-1: Buttons on the Standard toolbar provide a quick way to access many of the Visual Basic features.

The Project Explorer window contains three buttons (see Figure 2-2 in the next section). The first button from the left (View Code) displays the Code window for the selected module. The middle button (View Object) displays the selected sheet in the Microsoft Excel Object folder, or a form located in the Forms folder. The button on the right (Toggle Folders) hides and unhides the display of folders in the Project Explorer window.

Understanding the Properties Window

The Properties window allows you to review and set properties of various objects in your project. The name of the currently selected object is displayed in the Object box located just below the Properties window's title bar. Properties of the object can be viewed alphabetically or by category by clicking on the appropriate tab (see Figure 2-2).

- Alphabetic tab — Lists alphabetically all properties for the selected object. You can change the property setting by selecting the property name and typing or selecting the new setting.
- Categorized tab — Lists all properties for the selected object by category. You can collapse the list so that you see the categories, or you can expand a category to see the properties. The plus sign (+) icon to the left of the category name indicates that the category list can be expanded. The minus sign (–) indicates that the category is currently expanded.

The Properties window can be accessed in three ways:

- From the View menu by selecting Properties Window.
- From the keyboard by pressing F4.
- From the toolbar by clicking the Properties Window button (see Figure 2-1).

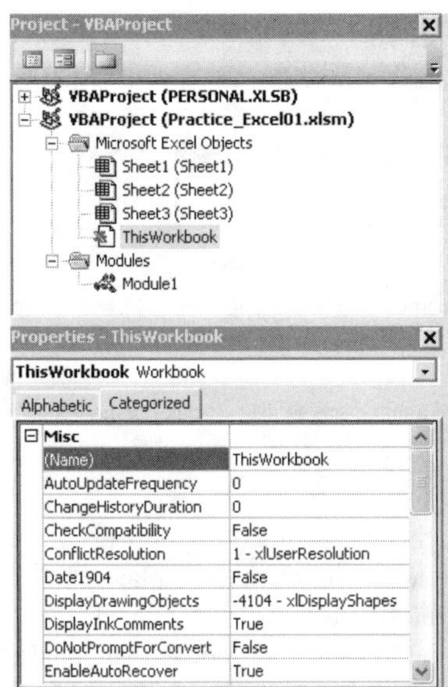

Figure 2-2: (Top) The Project Explorer window displays a list of currently open projects. (Bottom) The Properties window displays the settings for the object currently selected in the Project Explorer.

Understanding the Code Window

The Code window is used for Visual Basic programming as well as for viewing and modifying the code of recorded macros and existing VBA procedures. Each module can be opened in a separate Code window.

There are several ways to activate the Code window:

- From the Project Explorer window, choose the appropriate UserForm or module, and click the View Code button.
- From the menu bar, choose View | Code.
- From the keyboard, press F7.

At the top of the Code window, there are two drop-down list boxes (see Figure 2-3) that allow you to move quickly within the Visual Basic code. In the Object box on the left side of the Code window, you can select the object whose code you want to view. The box on the right side of the Code window lets you quickly choose a particular procedure or event procedure to view. When you open this box, the names of all procedures located in a module are sorted alphabetically. If you select a procedure in the Procedures/Events box, the cursor will jump to the first line of this procedure.

By dragging the split bar (see Figure 2-3) down to a selected position in the Code window, you can divide the Code window into two panes (see Figure 2-4). You can then view different sections of a long procedure or a different procedure in each pane. Setting up the Code window for the two-pane display is often used for copying or cutting and pasting sections of code between procedures of the same module.

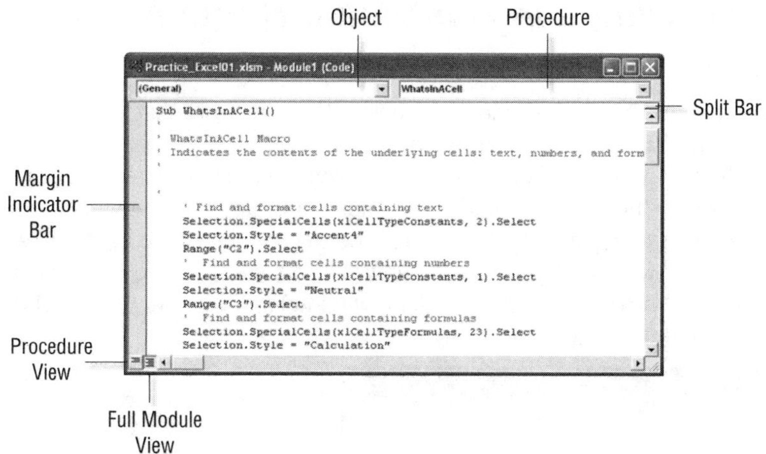

Figure 2-3: The Visual Basic Code window has several elements that make it easy to locate procedures and review the VBA code.

To return to the one-window display, simply drag the split bar all the way to the top of the Code window.

At the bottom of the Code window, there are two icons. The Procedure View icon displays one procedure at a time in the Code window. To select another procedure, use the Procedures/Events box. The Full Module View icon displays all the procedures in the selected module. Use the vertical scroll bar to scroll through the module's code.

The margin indicator bar is used by the Visual Basic Editor to display helpful indicators during editing and debugging. If you'd like to take a quick look at some of these indicators, skim through Chapter 10.

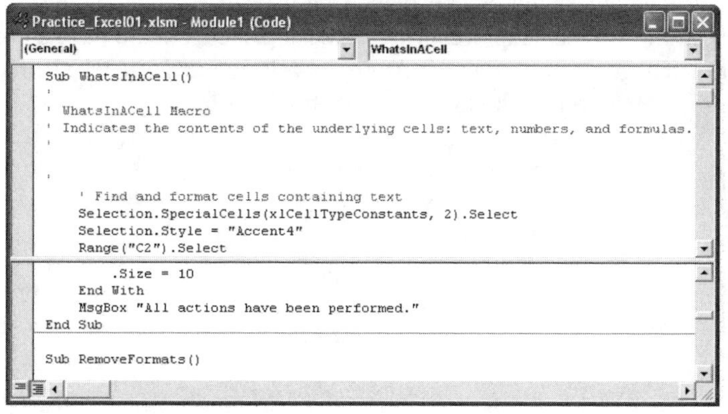

Figure 2-4: For reviewing longer procedures, you can divide the Code window into two panes by dragging down the split bar (see Figure 2-3).

Other Windows in the Visual Basic Editor Window

In addition to the Code window, there are other windows that are frequently used in the Visual Basic environment.

The Form window is used for creating custom dialog boxes and user forms. You will learn how to do these things in Chapter 18.

Figure 2-5 displays the list of windows that can be docked in the Visual Basic Editor window. You will learn how to use some of these windows in Chapter 3 (Object Browser, Immediate window) and Chapter 10 (Locals window, Watch window).

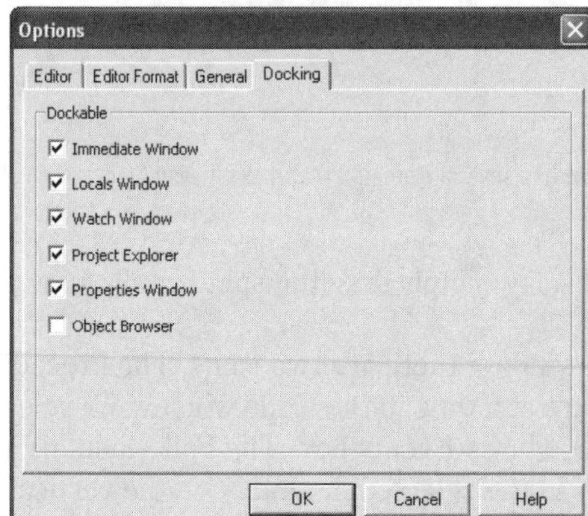

Figure 2-5: The Docking tab in the Options dialog box allows you to choose which windows you want to be dockable in the Visual Basic Editor screen.

Assigning a Name to the VBA Project

A *project* is a set of Microsoft Excel objects, modules, forms, and references. Instead of the default name, VBAProject, that precedes the name of the workbook in the Project Explorer window, each project should have a unique name. Let's assign names to the VBA projects (Practice_Excel01.xlsm and Personal.xlsb) that you worked with in Chapter 1.

Avoid Naming Conflicts

To avoid naming conflicts between your VBA projects, give your projects unique names. You can change the name of the project in one of the following ways:

- In the Project Explorer window, select the name of the project, double-click the (Name) property in the Properties window, and enter a new name.
- In the Project Explorer window, right-click the name of the project and select ProjectName Properties, where ProjectName is the name of the highlighted project. The Project Properties dialog box appears, as shown in Figure 2-6. Type the new project name in the Project Name text box and click OK.

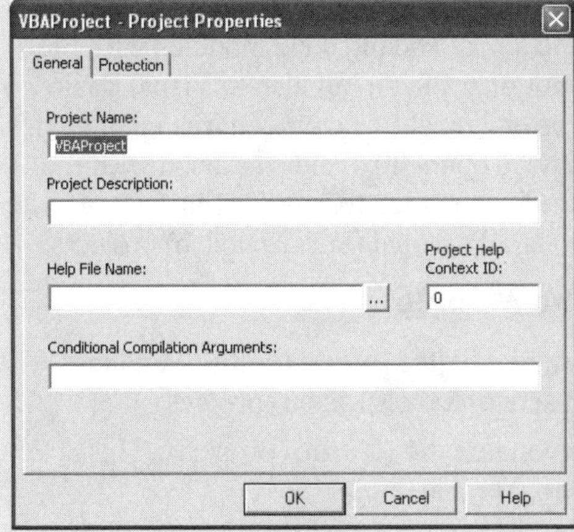

Figure 2-6: The Project Properties dialog can be used for changing the name and description of the selected VBA project that is highlighted in the Project Explorer window.

Hands-On 2-1: Renaming the VBA Project

1. Start Microsoft Excel, and open **C:\Ex07_HandsOn\Practice_Excel01.xlsm** where your WhatsInACell macro code is stored. Recall that the Personal macro workbook where you recorded the FormulasOnOff macro will be automatically loaded when you start Excel.
2. Press **Alt+F11** to switch to the Visual Basic Editor window.
3. In the Project Explorer window, highlight **VBA project (Practice_Excel01.xlsm).**
4. In the Properties window, double-click the **(Name)** property. This action selects the default project name VBAProject.
5. Type **FirstSteps** for the name of the VBA project and press **Enter**. Notice that the Project Explorer window now displays FirstSteps (Practice_Excel01.xlsm) as the name of the VBA project.
6. In the Project Explorer window, highlight **VBAProject (Personal.xlsb).**
7. In the Properties window, double-click the **(Name)** property.

8. Type **Personal** for the name of the VBA project and press **Enter**. Notice that the Project Explorer window now displays Personal (Personal.xlsb) as the name of the VBA project.

Renaming the Module

When you record a macro or create a new procedure from scratch, Visual Basic stores your VBA code in special sheets called Module1, Module2, and so on. The code modules are placed in the Modules folder that can be accessed from the Project Explorer window. When you open up a new workbook and create VBA procedures, code modules in the new VBA project are again named Module1, Module2, and so on. Having code modules with the same name can be very confusing not only to you but also to Visual Basic since it tries to execute your macros or Visual Basic procedures in an environment where several projects may be open. To avoid confusion with the names of the modules, let's assign unique names to Module1 in the FirstSteps (Practice_Excel01.xlsm) and Personal (Personal.xlsb) projects.

Hands-On 2-2: Renaming the Module

1. In the Project Explorer window, highlight **Module1** in the Modules folder under the FirstSteps (Practice_Excel01.xlsm) project.
2. In the Properties window, double-click the **(Name)** property. This action selects the default module name, Module1.
3. Type **WorksheetFormatting** for the name of Module1 and press **Enter**.

   Notice that the Project Explorer window now displays WorksheetFormatting as the name of the module (see Figure 2-7).
4. In the Project Explorer window, highlight **Module1** in the Modules folder under the Personal (Personal.xlsb) project.
5. In the Properties window, double-click the **(Name)** property. This action selects the default module name, Module1.
6. Type **Switches** for the name of Module1 and press **Enter**.

   Notice that the Project Explorer window now displays Switches as the name of the module (see Figure 2-7).

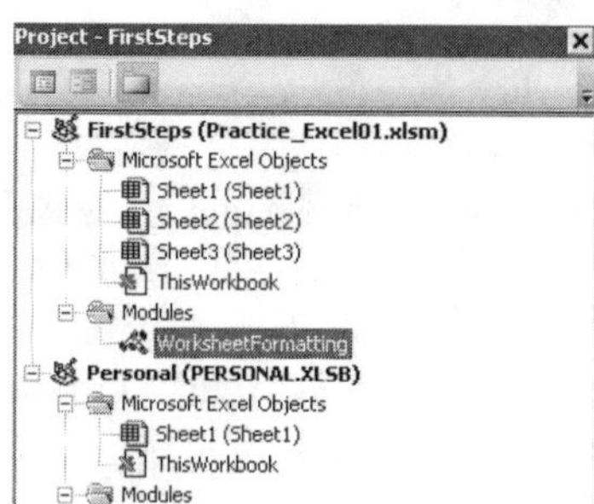

Figure 2-7: The Project Explorer window now shows the unique names that were assigned to VBA projects and modules using the Name property in the Properties window.

Understanding Digital Signatures

You already know from Chapter 1 that Excel macros can be signed or unsigned. By default, macros are unsigned and disabled. To avoid the security prompt when opening workbooks with macros, you can digitally sign your VBA projects.

A digital signature confirms that the programming code comes from a specific author and that it has not been tampered with or altered in any way since the VBA project was signed. When you (or others) open a workbook file containing signed macros, you will be able to see who the author is and you can decide whether to always trust the macros from that publisher.

Because the digital signature is overwritten when the file is saved, adding a digital signature should be the last step before the workbook file is ready for distribution. Also, it is a good idea to lock the VBA project before digitally signing it so that users will not accidentally modify your VBA code and invalidate your signature by attempting to save the code changes. Before you can sign your macros, you must purchase a digital certificate from a trusted organization called a Certification Authority (CA), such as VeriSign, Inc., or create a digital certificate for your own use as described in the next section. Let's start by taking a look at a list of trusted certificate authorities that you could contact.

Hands-On 2-3: Viewing Digital Certificates on Your Computer

1. Open the Control Panel and double-click **Internet Options**.
2. In the Internet Properties dialog box, click the **Content** tab.
3. Click the **Certificates** button.
4. In the Certificates dialog box, click the **Trusted Root Certification Authorities** tab.

   You should see a list of trusted authorities as shown in Figure 2-8.
5. Click **Close** to close the Certificates dialog box.
6. Click **Cancel** to close the Internet Properties dialog box and then close the Control Panel.

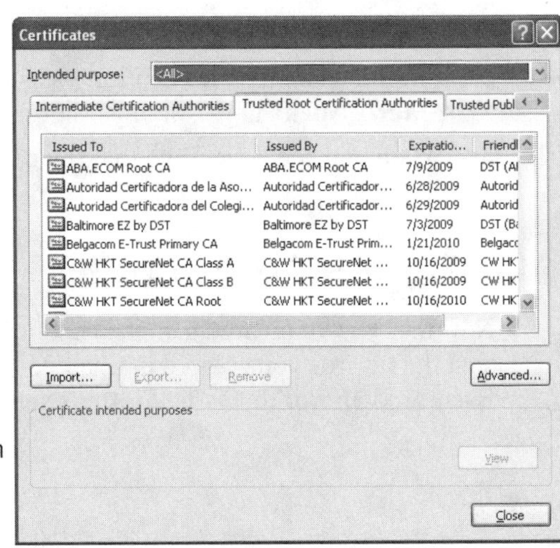

Figure 2-8: A listing of trusted certification authorities can be accessed via Internet Options (in the Control Panel) or Tools | Options (in Internet Explorer).

Creating a Digital Certificate

A digital certificate from a CA can cost several hundred dollars a year. If you simply want to avoid the security warning message when running your own macros, you can create a digital certificate yourself. This certificate will only be valid on the machine where it was created. Let's take a few minutes and create one right now.

Hands-On 2-4: Creating a Digital Certificate for Personal Use

1. Open the Start menu in Windows and select **All Programs | Microsoft Office | Microsoft Office Tools | Digital Certificate for VBA Projects.** This executes the SelfCert.exe program. You should see the Create Digital Certificate dialog box shown in Figure 2-9.

Note: If you cannot locate the SelfCert.exe file on your computer, you may download it from Microsoft.

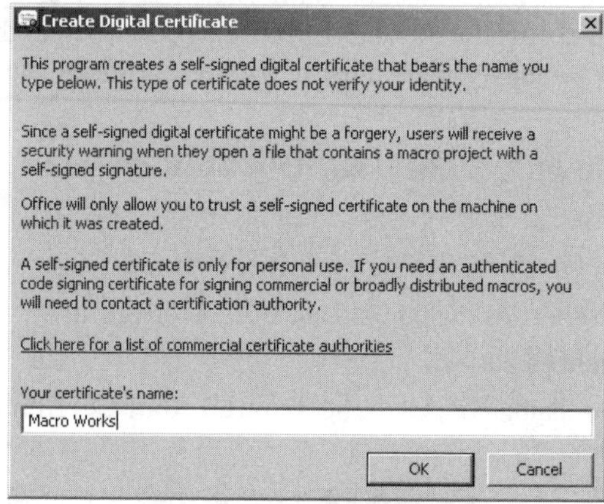

Figure 2-9: Creating a digital certificate for personal use.

2. Enter a name for the certificate as shown in Figure 2-9 (we are using **Macro Works** here), or any other name you'd like, and click **OK.**
3. When you see a message that the certificate was successfully created, click **OK.**

Signing a VBA Project

Now that you've created a digital certificate on your machine, let's use it to sign the macros you created in Chapter 1. We will use the Practice_Excel01.xlsm workbook file for this exercise.

Hands-On 2-5: Using a Digital Certificate to Sign a VBA Project

1. Make sure the Practice_Excel01.xlsm workbook is open.
2. Press **Alt+F11** to switch to the Visual Basic Editor.
3. In the Project Explorer, right-click the **FirstSteps (Practice_Excel01.xlsm)** project and click **FirstSteps Properties** on the shortcut menu.
4. Click the **Protection** tab and select the **Lock project for viewing** check box.
5. Enter **secret** for the password and re-enter it in the Confirm password box, then click **OK**.

   The next time you open this workbook and decide to view the code, you'll need to provide the password you typed in this step.

Note: Although you don't need to lock the project from yourself, steps 4 to 5 demonstrate how you can prevent others from viewing and altering your code.

A locked VBA project does not prevent you from replacing the current digital signature with another. You may want to replace the signature for the following reasons:

- You purchased an approved signature from a Certification Authority (CA) and you'd like to use it instead of the self-issued signature.
- The current signature has expired.

6. Select **Tools | Digital Signature.**

   You should see the Digital Signature dialog box, as shown in Figure 2-10.

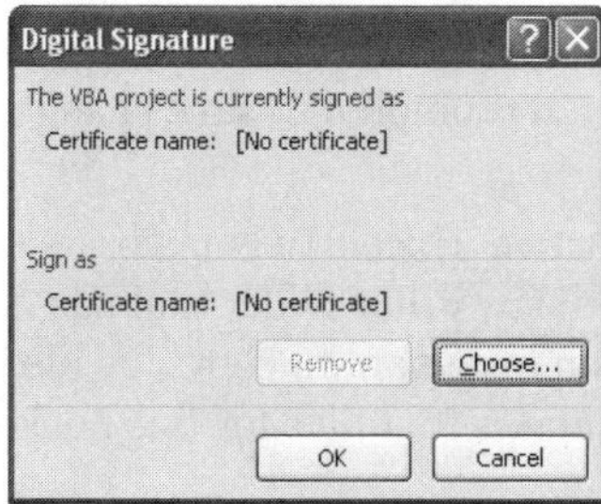

Figure 2-10: Signing a VBA project.

7. Click on the **Choose** button in the Digital Signature dialog box. Visual Basic displays a dialog box with the list of certificates installed on your computer.

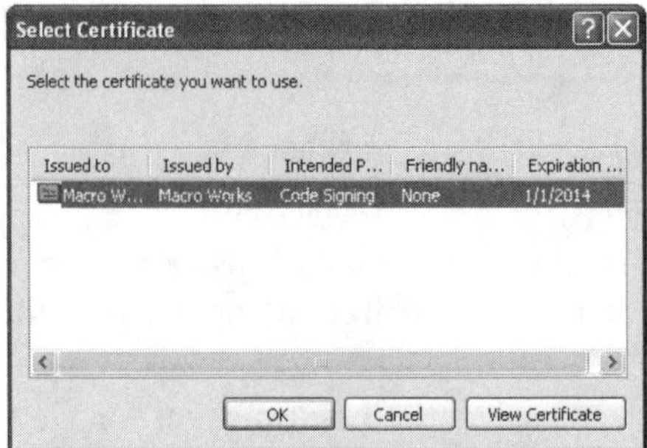

Figure 2-11: Selecting a digital certificate.

8. Click the **Macro Works** certificate that you've created for yourself and click **OK**.

   You will be returned to the Digital Signature dialog box, which now displays Macro Works as the name of the selected certificate (see Figure 2-12).

Figure 2-12: After selecting a digital certificate, its name appears in the Digital Signature dialog box.

9. Click **OK** to finish signing your VBA project.
10. Press **Alt+11** to switch to the Microsoft Excel application window.
11. Close the **Practice_Excel01.xlsm** workbook. Click **Yes** when prompted to save the changes.
12. Exit Microsoft Excel. Click **Yes** when prompted to save changes in the Personal macro workbook.
13. In Windows Explorer, copy the Practice_Excel01.xlsm workbook file from the Ex07_ByExample folder to any other folder that has not been designated as a trusted location. You may want to copy this file to the **C:\Ex07_HandsOn** folder that contains text files for this book's Hands-On exercises.
14. Double-click on the **Practice_Excel01.xlsm** file located in the Ex07_HandsOn folder to open the file in Excel.

    Excel displays the security warning message that macros have been disabled.
15. Click the **Options** button in the Security Warning message bar.

    Since this is the first time you are using the certificate, Excel will prompt you what to do (see Figure 2-13).

Figure 2-13: The Security Alert - Macro dialog box now displays the name of your digital signature.

16. Click the **Show Signature Details** link in the Security Alert - Macro dialog box.

    This displays the certificate details, as shown in Figure 2-14.

Figure 2-14: General information about a digital signature.

17. Click **OK** to exit the Digital Signature Details dialog box.
18. In the Security Alert - Macro dialog box, select the option button to **Trust all documents from this publisher**, and then click **OK**.
19. Press **Alt+F11** to switch to the Visual Basic Editor screen.
20. Double-click the **FirstSteps (Practice_Excel01.xlsm)** project in the Project Explorer window.

    Because this VBA project is locked you will be asked to enter the password.
21. Enter **secret** for the password and click **OK**.

Now the VBA project is unlocked for your eyes only. Do not make any changes to the code as this will invalidate the digital signature. You can, however, make changes to the contents of your worksheet at any time, even if the VBA project is locked and signed.

22. Press **Alt+F11** to switch back to the Excel application window.
23. Close the **Practice_Excel01.xlsm** workbook.
24. Reopen the **C:\Ex07_HandsOn\Practice_Excel01.xlsm** workbook.

    Notice that the workbook file now opens without the Security Alert - Macro dialog.
25. Close the **Practice_Excel01.xlsm** workbook and exit Excel.

Note: If the VBA project contains Excel 4.0 macro sheets, you must remove all XLM macros before you can sign the VBA project.

Chapter Summary

This chapter has given you a quick tour of the Visual Basic Editor window so that you are ready to start working with it in the next chapter. You also learned how to sign a VBA project with a self-issued digital certificate and how to protect your macros from others by locking a VBA project.

The next chapter introduces you to the fundamentals of Visual Basic for Applications. You will acquire a useful VBA vocabulary that will let you delegate a great many tedious tasks to Excel.

Chapter 3

Excel VBA Fundamentals

Language study is a long-term activity during which you pass through various stages of proficiency. The same is true about learning how to program in Visual Basic for Applications. There are no shortcuts. Before you can customize Microsoft Excel with VBA, you need to acquire new vocabulary and grammar. How do you say in Visual Basic, "Add a new worksheet to a workbook," "Delete the contents of cell A5," "Copy the formula from cell A1 to cell B1"? You may already know the individual words, but do you know how to combine them correctly so that Excel can carry out these tasks? In this chapter, you will learn the terms and rules of VBA.

Understanding Instructions, Modules, and Procedures

In Chapter 1, you learned that Microsoft Excel's macro recorder creates a series of instructions that are the exact equivalents of the actions you perform. These instructions are automatically placed in a workbook sheet called a *module*. Excel stores the module in a Modules folder located in the current workbook, a new workbook, or the Personal macro workbook. To review the recorded macro code, you must activate the Visual Basic Editor window and double-click the Modules folder in the Project Explorer window. When the module sheet opens up in the Code window, you are able to analyze your procedure's code.

A VBA *procedure* contains all of the recorded instructions. Each line in a procedure is an *instruction*. There are various types of instructions, such as keywords, operators, and calls to other procedures.

Let's start with keywords. These words carry a special meaning in Visual Basic. In Chapter 1, you already learned the most popular VBA keywords — the words Sub and End Sub, which begin and end a procedure. By default, keywords appear in blue. Because keywords are reserved by Visual Basic, don't use these words for other purposes.

In addition to keywords, Visual Basic instructions can contain operators. There are four types of operators: arithmetic, string concatenation, logical, and comparison. *Operators* allow you to combine, join, and manipulate certain values. For example, the division operator (/) can be used to calculate the percentage of the total. In this book, you get many opportunities to see how operators are used in VBA procedures.

Another type of Visual Basic instruction is a call to a procedure. Calls to procedures allow you to quickly jump to other procedures and execute other sets of instructions. Is it hard to picture this? Let's take the WhatsInACell macro you recorded in Chapter 1. Suppose you want to include the statement you entered in the FormulasOnOff macro inside the WhatsInACell macro. How can you do this? Without knowing any better, you could copy the required line of code from one procedure to another. However, there is an easier and quicker way. Instead of copying instructions between procedures, you can call the procedure by specifying its name. For example, if you want to process the FormulasOnOff macro instructions while Visual Basic executes the WhatsInACell macro, enter FormulasOnOff on a separate line within this procedure. When Visual Basic reaches this line, it will jump right into the FormulasOnOff procedure and execute its code. Next, it will return to the WhatsInACell macro to continue on with the remaining code, stopping when it reaches the End Sub keywords. Before you can try out an example of this, you must learn how to call procedures from different projects.

Calling a Procedure from Another Project

You can call a procedure located in any module in the same project by specifying the procedure name. Let's suppose that the procedure FormulasOnOff is located in another module but in the same VBA project as the WhatsInACell macro. To call the procedure FormulasOnOff from the WhatsInACell macro, all you need to do is specify the procedure name, as shown in the following example:

```
Sub WhatsInACell()
    Instructions...
    FormulasOnOff
End Sub
```

However, if two or more modules contain a procedure with the same name, in addition to the procedure name you must also include the module name. Let's suppose that the FirstSteps (Practice_Excel01.xlsm) project has three modules. The WorksheetFormatting module contains the WhatsInACell macro, while the Switches module and Formulas module both contain the FormulasOnOff macro. To call FormulasOnOff (located in the Switches module) from the WhatsInACell macro, you need to precede the procedure name with the module name, as shown in the following example:

```
Sub WhatsInACell()
    Instructions...
    Switches.FormulasOnOff
End Sub
```

To call a procedure from a different project, begin by setting up the reference to that project. You do this in the References dialog box, as shown in the following example. Let's see how you can call the FormulasOnOff macro, located in the Personal (Personal.xlsb) project, from the WhatsInACell macro.

Hands-On 3-1: Running a VBA Procedure from Another Procedure

1. Start Microsoft Excel and open the **C:\Ex07_ByExample\Practice_Excel01.xlsm** workbook file you created in Chapter 1.
2. Press **Alt+F11** to switch to the Microsoft Visual Basic Editor window.

3. In the Project Explorer window, double-click **FirstSteps (Practice_ Excel01.xlsm)**. If you are prompted for a password, enter **secret** and click **OK**.

Note: If a VBA project is locked for viewing, the References command on the Tools menu is disabled.

4. Choose **Tools | References.**
5. In the References dialog box, click the check box next to **Personal** (see Figure 3-1). Then click **OK.**

Note: If Personal is not listed in the Available References area of the References dialog box, click the Browse button and look for the Personal.xlsb file in one of the following locations:

- C:\Documents and Settings\username\Application Data\Microsoft\Excel\XLStart
- C:\Program Files\Microsoft Office\Office12\XLStart

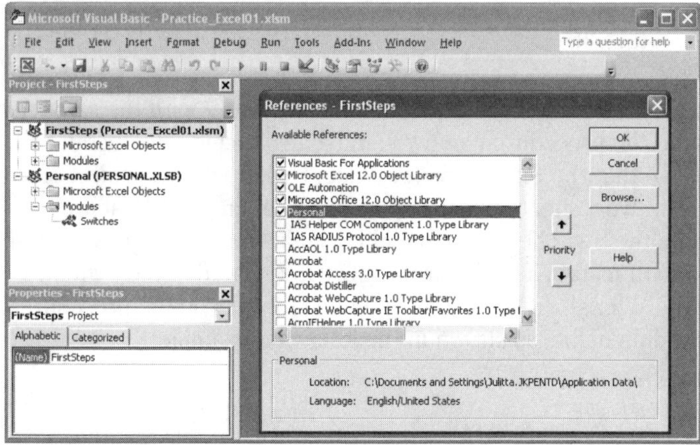

Figure 3-1: The References dialog box lists all the references available to your project. If you want to execute a procedure located in a different project, you must establish a reference to the other project.

After you have set up a reference to another VBA project, the Project Explorer window displays the References folder with the name of the created reference, as shown in Figure 3-2.

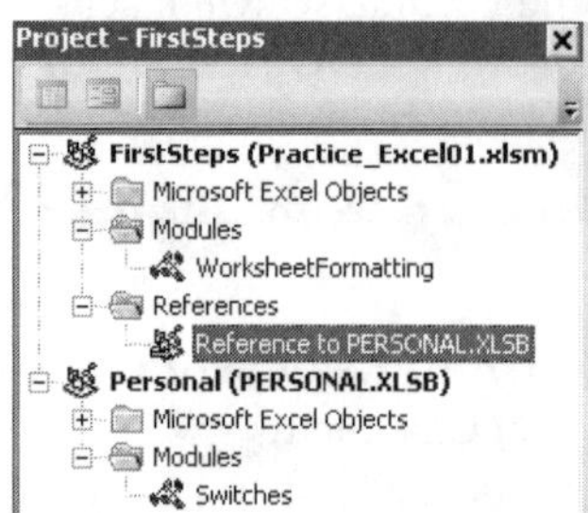

Figure 3-2: A reference has been established to the Personal.xlsb workbook.

Now that the reference to the Personal project has been established, let's call the FormulasOnOff macro from the WhatsInACell procedure.

Hands-On 3-2: Calling One Macro from Another Macro

1. In the Project Explorer window, double-click **WorksheetFormatting** in **FirstSteps (Practice_Excel01.xlsm).**
2. In the WhatsInACell macro, enter a new line just before MsgBox "All actions have been performed" and type **FormulasOnOff.**
3. Press **Alt+F11** to return to the Microsoft Excel window and make sure that Sheet1 contains the example spreadsheet.
4. Run the WhatsInACell macro using any of the techniques you learned in Chapter 1. After you run this macro Sheet1 should be formatted as shown in Figure 3-3.

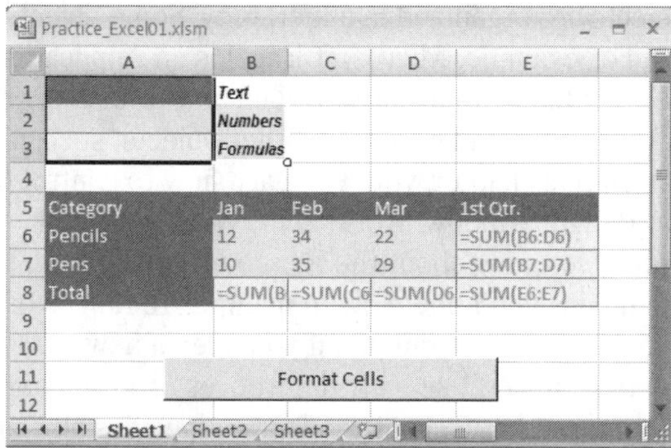

Figure 3-3: This worksheet has been formatted in one step using the following two macros: WhatsInACell and FormulasOnOff.

How Visual Basic Locates the Called Procedure

When you call a procedure, Visual Basic first looks for it in the same module where the calling procedure (WhatsInACell) is located. If the called procedure (FormulasOnOff) is not found in the same module, Visual Basic searches other modules in the same project. If the procedure still can't be found, Visual Basic checks the references to other projects.

Setting up a Reference to Another VBA Project

If you want to call a procedure from another VBA project and that project is currently closed, perform the following steps to establish the project reference:

1. Choose Tools | References.
2. In the References dialog box, click the Browse button and open the folder where the project is located. By default, the Add Reference dialog box lists Library Files (*.olb, .tlb, .dll).
3. Choose Microsoft Excel Files (*.xlsm, *.xlam, *.xls) from the Files of Type drop-down list.
4. Select the file that contains the procedure you want to set the reference to.
5. Click the Open button. The name of the project will be added as the last entry in the References dialog box.
6. Click OK to close the References dialog box.

Understanding Objects, Properties, and Methods

Using Visual Basic for Applications, you can create procedures that control many features of Microsoft Excel. You can also control a large number of other applications. The power of Visual Basic comes from its ability to control and manage various objects. But what is an object?

An *object* is a thing you can control with VBA. Workbooks, a worksheet, a range in a worksheet, a chart, or a toolbar are just a few examples of things you may want to control while working in Excel. These things are objects. Excel contains a multitude of objects that you can manipulate in different ways. All of these objects are organized in a hierarchy. Some objects may contain other objects. For example, Microsoft Excel is an Application object. The Application object contains other objects, such as workbooks or command bars. The Workbook object may contain other objects, such as worksheets or charts. In this chapter, you will learn how to control the following Excel objects: Range, Window, Worksheet, Workbook, and Application. You begin by learning about the Range object. You can't do much work in spreadsheets unless you know how to manipulate ranges of cells.

Certain objects look alike. For example, if you open a new workbook and examine its worksheets, you won't see any differences. A group of like objects is called a *collection*. A Worksheets collection includes all worksheets in a particular workbook, while the CommandBars collection contains all the toolbars and menu bars. Collections are also objects. In Microsoft Excel, the most frequently used collections are:

- Workbooks collection — Represents all currently open workbooks.
- Worksheets collection — Represents all the Worksheet objects in the specified or active workbook. Each Worksheet object represents a worksheet.
- Sheets collection — Represents all the sheets in the specified or active workbook. The Sheets collection can contain Chart or Worksheet objects.
- Windows collection — Represents all the Window objects in Microsoft Excel. The Windows collection for the Application object contains all the windows in the application, whereas the Windows collection for the Workbook object contains only the windows in the specified workbook.

When you work with collections, you can perform the same action on all the objects in the collection.

Each object has some characteristics that allow you to describe the object. In Visual Basic, the object's characteristics are called *properties*. For example, a Workbook object has a Name property, and the Range object has such properties as Column, Font, Formula, Name, Row, Style, and Value. The object properties can be set. When you set an object's property, you control its appearance or its position. Object properties can only take on one specific value at any one time. For example, the active workbook can't be called two different names at the same time.

The most difficult part of Visual Basic is understanding the fact that some properties can also be objects. Let's consider the Range object. You can change the appearance of the selected range of cells by setting the Font property. But the font can have a different name (Times New Roman, Arial, ...), different size (10, 12, 14, ...), and different style (bold, italic, underline, ...). These are font properties. If the font has properties, then the font is also an object.

Properties are great. They let you change the look of the object, but how can you control the actions? Before you can make Excel carry out some tasks, you need to know another term. Objects have methods. Each action you want the object to perform is called a *method*. The most important Visual Basic method is the Add method. Using this method, you can add a new workbook or worksheet. Objects can use various methods. For example, the Range object has special methods that allow you to clear the cell contents (ClearContents method), formats (ClearFormats method), and both contents and formats (Clear method). Other methods allow the objects to be selected, copied, or moved.

Methods can have optional parameters that specify how the method is to be carried out. For example, the Workbook object has a method called Close. You can close any open workbook using this method. If there are changes to the workbook, Microsoft Excel will display a message prompting you to save the changes. You can use the Close method with the SaveChanges parameter set to False to close the workbook and discard any changes that have been made to it, as in the example below:

```
Workbooks("Practice_Excel01.xls").Close SaveChanges:=False
```

Microsoft Excel Object Model

When you learn new things, theory can give you the necessary background, but how do you really know what's where? The majority of people think in pictures. To make it easy to understand the Microsoft Excel object hierarchy, the Visual Basic online help offers a diagram of the object model, a portion of which is shown in Figure 3-4.

Working with the Excel 2007 Object Model

To work with the Excel 2007 object model interactively, choose Help | Microsoft Visual Basic Help in the Visual Basic Editor window. In the Table of Contents, click Excel Object Model Reference | Excel Object Model Map | Object Model Map.

The object that represents Microsoft Excel is called Application. This object allows you to specify application-level properties and execute application-level methods. Analyzing the object model is a great way to learn about Excel objects and collections of objects. The time you spend here will pay big dividends later when you start writing VBA procedures from scratch.

Figure 3-4: The partial listing of the Microsoft Excel object model. To see the entire object model diagram see the online help.

VBA and Prior Versions of Microsoft Excel

Microsoft Excel online help lists changes made to the Microsoft Excel object model in prior versions of Excel. Many objects, properties, and methods have been replaced with new and improved features. To provide backward compatibility, replaced objects have been hidden. For more information, activate the online help from the Visual Basic Editor window. Hidden objects can also be located in the Object Browser. If you right-click in the Object Browser window, you can choose the option Show hidden members. You will learn how to use the Object Browser later in this chapter.

Writing VBA Statements

Suppose you want to delete the contents of cell A4. To do this manually, you would select cell A4 and press the Delete key on your keyboard. To perform the same operation using Visual Basic, you first need to find out how to make Excel select an appropriate cell. Cell A4, like any other worksheet cell, is represented by the Range object. Visual Basic does not have the Delete method for deleting contents of cells. Instead, you should use the ClearContents method, as in the following example:

```
Range("A4").ClearContents
```

Notice the dot operator between the name of the object and its method. This instruction removes the contents of cell A4. However, how do you make Excel delete the contents of cell A4 located in the first sheet of the Practice_Excel03.xlsm workbook? Let's also assume that there are several workbooks open. If you don't want to end up deleting the contents of cell A4 from the wrong workbook or worksheet, you must write a detailed instruction so that Visual Basic knows where to locate the necessary cell:

```
Application.Workbooks("Practice_Excel03.xlsm").Worksheets("Sheet1").Range
("A4").ClearContents
```

The above instruction should be written on one line and read from right to left as follows: Clear the contents of cell A4, which is part of a range located in a worksheet named Sheet1 contained in a workbook named Practice_Excel03.xlsm, which in turn is part of the Excel application. Notice the letter "s" at the end of the collection names: Workbooks and Worksheets. All references to the names of workbooks, worksheets, and cells must be enclosed in quotation marks.

Syntax Versus Grammar

Now that you know the basic elements of VBA (objects, properties, and methods), it's time to start using them. But how do you combine objects, properties, and methods into correct language structures? Every language has grammar rules that people follow in order to make themselves understood. Whether you communicate in English, Spanish, French, or another language, you apply certain rules to your writing and speech. In programming, we use the term *syntax* to specify language rules. You can look up the syntax of each object, property, or method in the online help or in the Object Browser window.

To make sure Excel always understands what you mean, just stick to the following rules:

■ Rule #1: Referring to the property of an object

If the property does not have arguments, the syntax is as follows:

```
Object.Property
```

Object is a placeholder. It is where you should place the name of the actual object that you are trying to access. Property is also a placeholder. Here you place the name of the object's characteristics. For example, to refer to the value entered in cell A4 on your worksheet, you can write the following instruction:

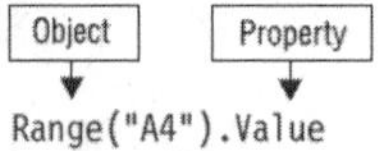

Notice that there is a period between the name of the object and its property.

When you need to access the property of an object that is contained within several other objects, you must include the names of all objects in turn, separated by the dot operator, as shown below:

```
ActiveSheet.Shapes(2).Line.Weight
```

The example above references the Weight property of the Line object and refers to the second object in the collection of Shapes located in the active worksheet.

Some properties require one or more arguments. For example, when using the Offset property, you can select a cell relative to the active cell. The Offset property requires two arguments. The first argument indicates the row number (rowOffset), and the second one determines the column number (columnOffset).

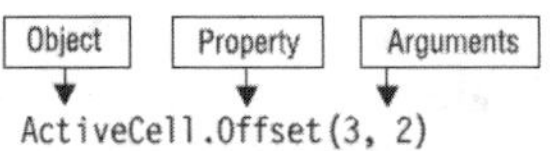

In the example above, assuming the active cell is A1, Offset(3, 2) will reference the cell located three rows down and two columns to the right of cell A1. In other words, cell C4 is referenced. Because the arguments placed between parentheses are often difficult to understand, it's common practice to precede the value of the argument with its name, as in the following example:

```
ActiveCell.Offset(rowOffset:=3, columnOffset:=2)
```

Notice that a colon and an equal sign always follow the named arguments. When you use the named arguments, you can list them in any order. The above instruction can also be written as follows:

```
ActiveCell.Offset(columnOffset:=2, rowOffset:=3)
```

The revised instruction does not change the meaning; you are still referencing cell C4 assuming that A1 is the active cell. However, if you transpose the arguments in a statement that does not use named arguments, you will end up referencing another cell. For example, the statement ActiveCell.Offset(2, 3) will reference cell D3 instead of C4.

- **Rule #2: Changing the property of an object**

```
Object.Property = Value
```

Value is a new value that you want to assign to the property of the object. The value can be:

- A number. The following instruction enters the number 25 in cell A4.

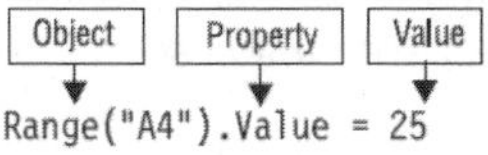

```
Object      Property    Value
Range("A4").Value = 25
```

- Text entered in quotes. The following instruction changes the font of the active cell to Times New Roman.

```
ActiveCell.Font.Name = "Times New Roman"
```

- A logical value (True or False). The following instruction applies bold formatting to the active cell.

```
ActiveCell.Font.Bold = True
```

- **Rule #3: Returning the current value of the object property**

```
Variable = Object.Property
```

Variable is the name of the storage location where Visual Basic is going to store the property setting. You will learn about variables in Chapter 4.

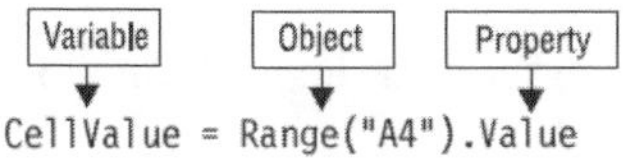

```
Variable    Object      Property
CellValue = Range("A4").Value
```

The above instruction saves the current value of cell A4 in the variable named CellValue.

- **Rule #4: Referring to the object's method**

If the method does not have arguments, the syntax is as follows:

```
Object.Method
```

Object is a placeholder. It is where you should place the name of the actual object that you are trying to access. Method is also a placeholder. Here you place the name of the action you want to perform on the object. For example, to clear the contents in cell A4, use the following instruction:

```
Object      Method
Range("A4").ClearContents
```

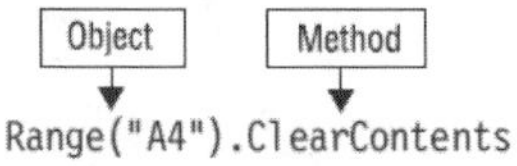

If the method requires arguments, the syntax is as follows:

```
Object.Method (argument1, argument2, ... argumentN)
```

For example, using the GoTo method, you can quickly select any range in a workbook. The syntax of the GoTo method is shown below:

```
Object.GoTo(Reference, Scroll)
```

The Reference argument is the destination cell or range. The Scroll argument can be set to True to scroll through the window or to False to not scroll through the window. For example, the following VBA statement selects cell P100 in Sheet1 and scrolls through the window:

```
Application.GoTo _
    Reference:=Worksheets("Sheet1").Range("P100"), _
    Scroll:=True
```

The above instruction did not fit on one line, so it was broken into sections using the special line continuation character (the underscore), as described in the next section.

Breaking Up Long VBA Statements

You can break up a long VBA statement into two or more lines to make your procedure more readable. Visual Basic has a special line continuation character that can be used at the end of a line to indicate that the next line is a continuation of the previous one, as in the following example:

```
Selection.PasteSpecial _
   Paste:=xlValues, _
   Operation:=xlMultiply, _
   SkipBlanks: =False, _
   Transpose:=False
```

The line continuation character is the underscore (_). You must precede the underscore with a space.

You can use the line continuation character in the following locations in your code:

- Before or after operators; for example: &, +, Like, NOT, AND
- Before or after a comma
- Before or after a colon and an equal sign (:=)
- Before or after an equal sign

You cannot use the line continuation character between a colon and equal sign. For example, the following use of the continuation character is not recognized by Visual Basic:

```
Selection.PasteSpecial Paste: _
     =xlValues, Operation: _
     =xlMultiply, SkipBlanks: _
     =False, Transpose: _
     =False
```

Also, you may not use the line continuation character within the text enclosed in quotes. For example, the following usage of the underscore is invalid:

```
MsgBox "To continue the long instruction, use the _
   line continuation character."
```

The above instruction should be broken up as follows:

```
MsgBox "To continue the long instruction, use the " & _
       "line continuation character."
```

Understanding VBA Errors

In the course of writing or editing VBA procedures, no matter how careful you are, you're likely to make some mistakes. For example, you may misspell a statement, misplace a comma or quote, or forget a period or ending parenthesis. These kinds of mistakes are known as syntax errors. Fortunately, Visual Basic is quite helpful in spotting this kind of error. To have Visual Basic automatically check for correct syntax after you enter a line of code, choose Tools | Options in the Visual Basic Editor window. Make sure the Auto Syntax Check setting is checked on the Editor tab (see Figure 3-5).

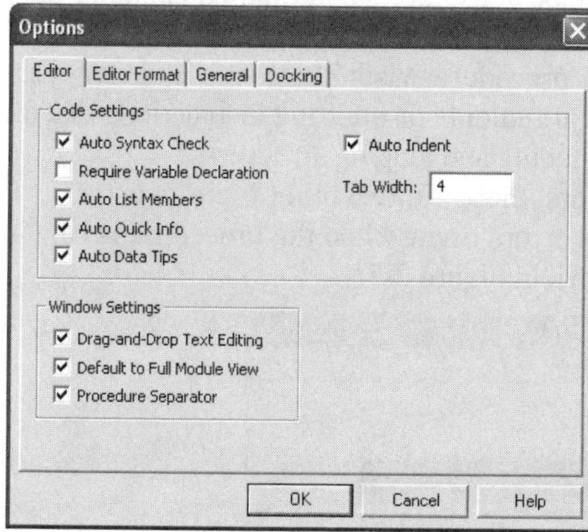

Figure 3-5: The Auto Syntax Check setting on the Editor tab of the Options dialog box allows you to find typos in your VBA procedures.

When Visual Basic finds a syntax error, it displays an error message box and changes the color of the incorrect line of code to red (see Figure 3-6) or another color as indicated on the Editor Format tab in the Options dialog box.

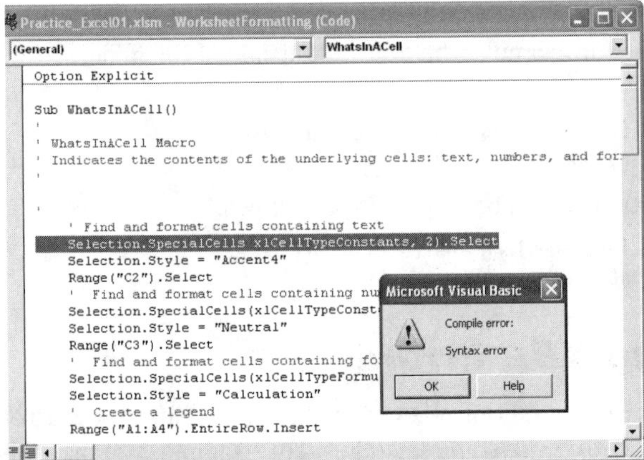

Figure 3-6: This error message was caused by a missing beginning parenthesis in front of xlCellTypeConstants.

If the explanation in the error message isn't clear, you can always click the Help button for more information. And, if the Visual Basic online help cannot point you in the right direction, return to your procedure and carefully examine the offending instruction for missed letters, quotes, periods, colons, equal signs, and beginning and ending parentheses.

Finding syntax errors can be aggravating and time-consuming. Certain syntax errors can be caught only during the execution of the procedure. While attempting to run your procedure, Visual Basic can find errors that were caused by using invalid arguments or omitting instructions that are used in pairs, such as If statements and looping structures.

In addition to syntax errors, there are two other types of errors: run-time and logic. Run-time errors occur while the procedure is running. A typical run-time error is shown in Figure 3-7.

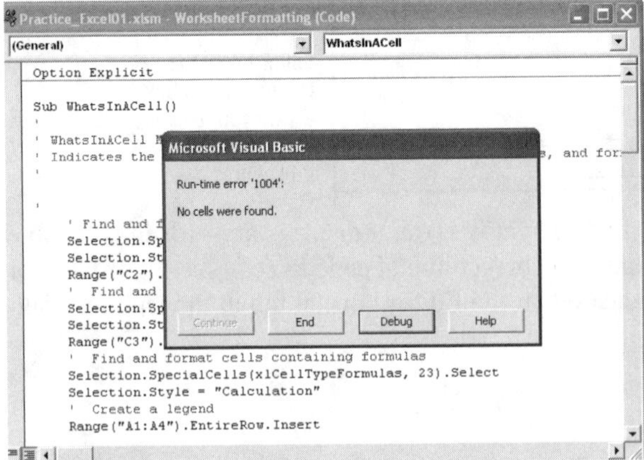

Figure 3-7: When Visual Basic tries to select text cells when none exist in the selected worksheet or range of cells, a run-time error occurs.

Run-time errors are often caused by those unexpected situations that the programmer did not think of while writing the code. These occur, for example, when the program is trying to access a drive or a file that does not exist on a user's computer or copy a file to a CD or other media without first checking whether the media was available.

Program Bugs

You've probably heard more than once that "computer programs are full of bugs." In programming, errors are called bugs, and debugging is the process of eliminating errors from your programs. The first step in debugging a procedure is to correct all syntax errors. Visual Basic provides a myriad of tools with which to track down and eliminate bugs. In this chapter, you will find out how you can use Visual Basic's assistance in writing code with a minimum amount of errors. In Part IV, you will learn how to use special debugging tools to trap errors in your VBA procedures.

The third type of error, a logic error, often does not generate a specific error message. The procedure may have no flaws in its syntax and may even run without errors, yet it produces incorrect results. Logic errors are usually very difficult to locate, and those that happen intermittently are so well concealed that you can count on spending long hours, and even days, trying to locate the source of the error.

In Search of Help

When you use the macro recorder, all your actions are translated into VBA instructions and placed in a module. When studying the recorded procedure, don't forget that help is within your reach. While the meaning of some of the instructions may be pretty straightforward, you will probably find some of them less obvious. This is the time to ask for help. When you're working alone, your VBA tutor is just a click or keypress away. You can quickly get to the necessary help page from the Visual Basic Code window. Let's take a few minutes to examine how, with the help of the built-in VBA tutor, you can make the first instruction in the WhatsInACell procedure a part of your VBA vocabulary:

```
Selection.SpecialCells(xlCellTypeConstants, 2).Select
```

The above instruction can be broken into three parts. What parts? Is Selection an object or a property? What is SpecialCells? What is Select? To answer these questions, perform the following exercise.

Hands-On 3-3: Dissecting the Meaning of a VBA Statement

1. In the Visual Basic Editor window, activate the Code window with the WhatsInACell procedure.
2. Position the cursor anywhere within the word Selection in the following statement:

   ```
   Selection.SpecialCells(xlCellTypeConstants, 2).Select
   ```

3. Press **F1**.

The help system opens up and since the cursor was located within the word Selection, the screen tells you that Selection is a property of an Application or a Window object. If you position the cursor within the next unknown term (SpecialCells) and again follow the steps above, you end up on the SpecialCells help screen and find out that SpecialCells is a method that returns a Range object (see Figure 3-8).

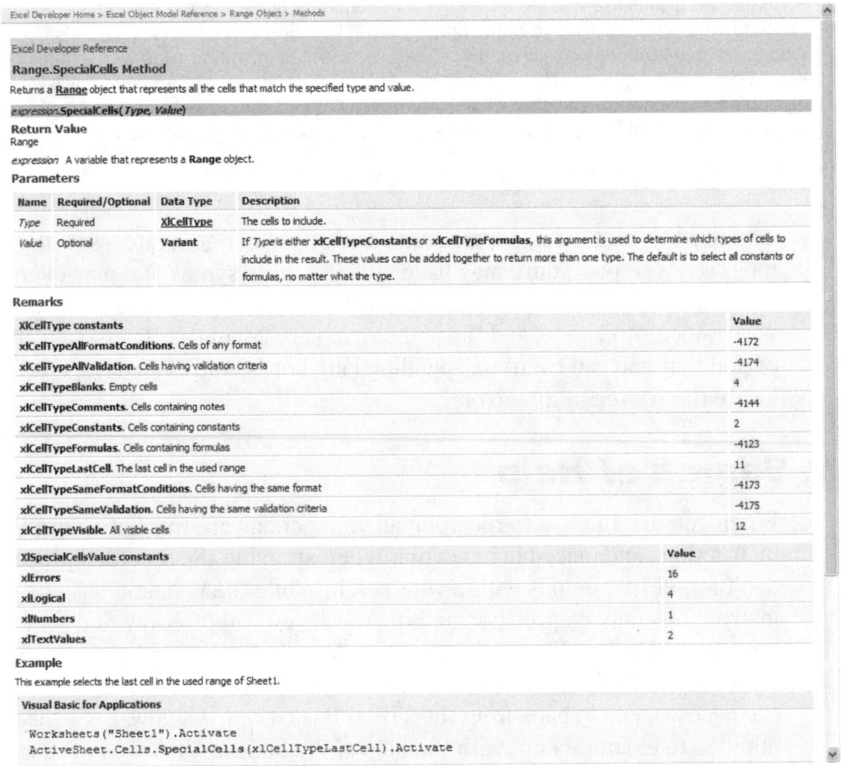

Excel Developer Home > Excel Object Model Reference > Range Object > Methods

Excel Developer Reference

Range.SpecialCells Method

Returns a **Range** object that represents all the cells that match the specified type and value.

expression.**SpecialCells(*Type*, *Value*)**

Return Value

Range

expression A variable that represents a **Range** object.

Parameters

Name	Required/Optional	Data Type	Description
Type	Required	XlCellType	The cells to include.
Value	Optional	**Variant**	If *Type* is either **xlCellTypeConstants** or **xlCellTypeFormulas**, this argument is used to determine which types of cells to include in the result. These values can be added together to return more than one type. The default is to select all constants or formulas, no matter what the type.

Remarks

XlCellType constants	Value
xlCellTypeAllFormatConditions. Cells of any format	-4172
xlCellTypeAllValidation. Cells having validation criteria	-4174
xlCellTypeBlanks. Empty cells	4
xlCellTypeComments. Cells containing notes	-4144
xlCellTypeConstants. Cells containing constants	2
xlCellTypeFormulas. Cells containing formulas	-4123
xlCellTypeLastCell. The last cell in the used range	11
xlCellTypeSameFormatConditions. Cells having the same format	-4173
xlCellTypeSameValidation. Cells having the same validation criteria	-4175
xlCellTypeVisible. All visible cells	12

XlSpecialCellsValue constants	Value
xlErrors	16
xlLogical	4
xlNumbers	1
xlTextValues	2

Example

This example selects the last cell in the used range of Sheet1.

Visual Basic for Applications

```
Worksheets("Sheet1").Activate
ActiveSheet.Cells.SpecialCells(xlCellTypeLastCell).Activate
```

Figure 3-8: Objects, properties, and methods of Visual Basic for Applications are explained in detail in the online help.

Notice that each Help screen contains lots of information. You can find out what a particular expression returns and what parameters it takes. Additional information can be found in the Remarks area. The Example section shows example statements or procedures that use the particular object, method, or property. You can easily copy the code from the example into your own procedure. Simply highlight the lines you want to copy and press Ctrl+C, or right-click the selection and choose Copy from the shortcut menu. Switch to the Visual Basic Code window, click in the location where you want to paste the code example, and press Ctrl+V or choose Edit | Paste.

On-the-fly Syntax and Programming Assistance

The Edit toolbar in the Visual Basic Editor window contains several buttons that let you enter correctly formatted VBA instructions with speed and ease. If the Edit toolbar isn't currently docked in the Visual Basic Editor window, you can turn it on by choosing View | Toolbars.

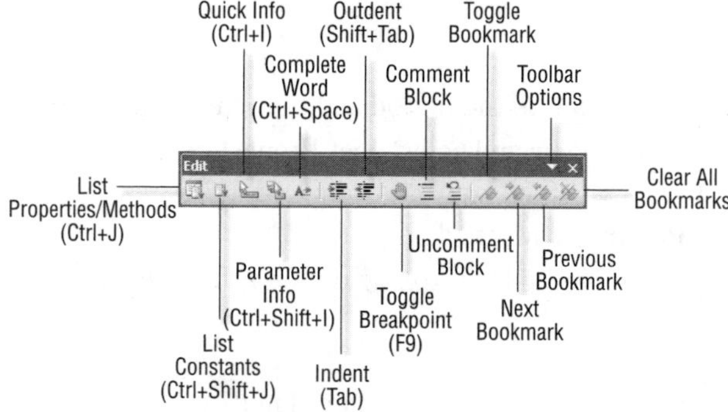

Figure 3-9: Buttons located on the Edit toolbar make it easy to write and format VBA instructions.

Writing procedures in Visual Basic requires that you use hundreds of built-in instructions and functions. Because most people cannot memorize the correct syntax of all the instructions that are available in VBA, the IntelliSense technology provides you with syntax and programming assistance on demand during the course of entering instructions. While working in the Code window, you can have special windows pop up and guide you through the process of creating correct VBA code.

List Properties/Methods

Each object can contain a number of properties and methods. When you enter the name of the object and a period that separates the name of the object from its property or method in the Code window, a pop-up menu may appear. This menu lists the properties and methods available for the object that precedes the period (see Figure 3-10). To turn on this automated feature, choose Tools | Options. In the Options dialog box, click the Editor tab, and make sure the Auto List Members check box is selected.

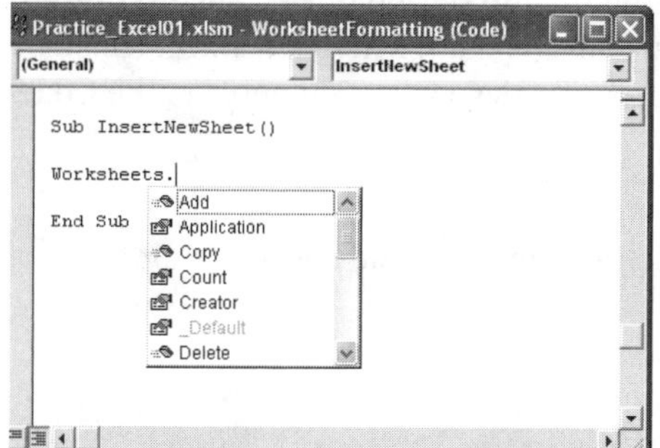

Figure 3-10: While entering the VBA instructions, Visual Basic suggests properties and methods that can be used with the particular object.

To choose an item from the pop-up menu shown above, start typing the name of the property or method that you want to select. When Excel highlights the correct item name, press Enter to insert the item into your code and start a new line. Or, if you want to continue writing instructions on the same line, press the Tab key instead. You can also double-click the item to insert it in your code. To close the pop-up menu without inserting an item, simply press Esc. When you press Esc to remove the pop-up menu, Visual Basic will not display it again for the same object. To display the Properties/Methods pop-up menu again, you can:

- Press Ctrl+J.
- Use the Backspace key to delete the period and type the period again.
- Right-click in the Code window and select List Properties/Methods from the shortcut menu.
- Choose Edit | List Properties/Methods.
- Click the List Properties/Methods button on the Edit toolbar.

List Constants

Earlier in this chapter, you learned that to assign a value to a property, you need to use the following rule:

```
Object.Property = Value
```

If there is a check mark next to the Auto List Members setting on the Editor tab in the Options dialog box, Excel displays a pop-up menu listing the constants that are valid for the property that precedes the equal sign.

A *constant* is a value that indicates a specific state or result. Excel and other member applications of the Microsoft Office suite have a number of predefined, built-in constants. You will learn about constants, their types, and usage in Chapter 4.

Suppose you want your program to turn on the Page Break Preview of your worksheet. In the Microsoft Excel application window the View tab lists five different types of workbook views. The Normal View is the default view for most tasks in Excel. Page Layout View allows you to view the document as it will appear on the printed page. Page Break Preview allows you to see where pages will break when the document is printed. Custom Views allows you to save the set of display and print settings as a custom view. Full Screen allows you to see the document in the full screen mode. The first three view options are represented by a built-in constant. Microsoft Excel constant names begin with the characters "xl". As soon as you enter in the Code window the instruction:

```
ActiveWindow.View =
```

a pop-up menu will appear with the names of valid constants for the property, as shown in Figure 3-11.

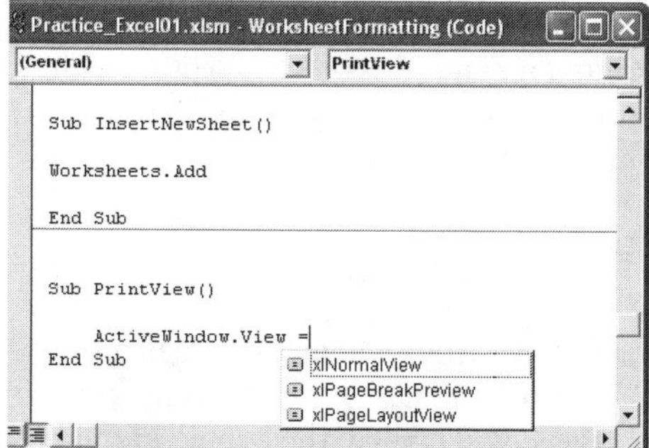

Figure 3-11: The List Constants pop-up menu displays a list of constants that are valid for the property entered.

To work with the List Constants pop-up menu, use the same techniques as for the List Properties/Methods pop-up menu outlined in the preceding section.

The List Constants pop-up menu can be activated by pressing Ctrl+Shift+J or clicking the List Constants button on the Edit toolbar.

Parameter Info

If you've had a chance to work with Excel worksheet functions, you already know that many functions require one or more arguments (or *parameters*). For example, here's the syntax for the most common worksheet function:

```
SUM(number1,number2, ...)
```

Where number1, number2, ... are 1 to 30 arguments which you can add up.

Similar to functions, Visual Basic methods may require one or more arguments. If a method requires an argument, you can see the names of required and optional arguments in a tooltip box that appears just below the cursor as soon as you type the beginning parenthesis (see Figure 3-12). In the tooltip, the current argument is displayed in bold. When you supply the first argument and enter the comma, Visual Basic displays the next argument in bold. Optional arguments are surrounded by square brackets [ ].

You can open the Parameter Info tooltip using the keyboard. To do this, enter the method or function name, follow it with the left parenthesis, and press Ctrl+Shift+I. You can also click the Parameter Info button on the Edit toolbar or choose Edit | Parameter Info.

Figure 3-12: A tooltip displays a list of arguments utilized by a VBA method.

The Parameter Info feature makes it easy for you to supply correct arguments to a VBA method. In addition, it reminds you of two other things that are very important for the method to work correctly: the order of the arguments and the required data type of each argument. You will learn about data types in Chapter 4.

Quick Info

When you select an instruction, function, method, procedure name, or constant in the Code window and then click the Quick Info button on the Edit toolbar (or press Ctrl+I), Visual Basic will display the syntax of the highlighted item, as well as the value of a constant. The Quick Info feature can be turned on or off using the Options dialog box. To use the feature, click the Editor tab and choose the Auto Quick Info option.

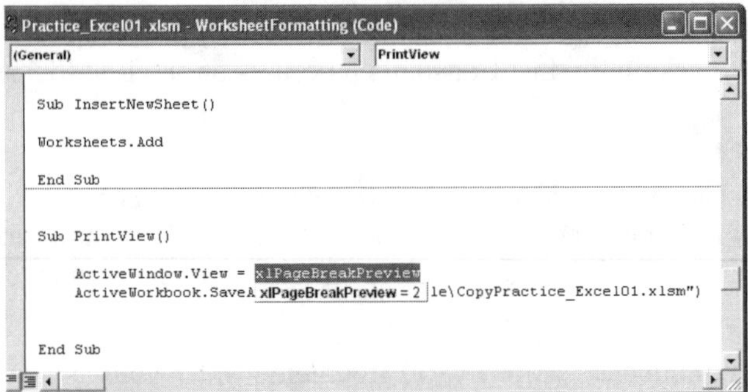

Figure 3-13: The Quick Info feature can provide you with a list of arguments required by a selected method or function, a value of a selected constant, or the type of the selected object or property.

Complete Word

Another way to increase the speed of writing VBA procedures in the Code window is with the Complete Word feature. As you enter the first few letters of a keyword and press Ctrl+Spacebar, or click the Complete Word button on the Edit toolbar, Visual Basic will save you time entering the remaining letters by completing the keyword entry for you. For example, when you enter the first four letters of the keyword Application (Appl) in the Code window and press Ctrl+Spacebar, Visual Basic will complete the rest of the word, and in the place of Appl, you will see the entire word Application.

If there are several VBA keywords that begin with the same letters, Visual Basic will display a pop-up menu listing all the keywords when you press Ctrl+Spacebar. Select the appropriate keyword from the pop-up menu and press Enter.

Indent/Outdent

As you saw earlier in Figure 3-5, the Editor tab in the Options dialog box contains a number of settings that you can turn on to make many automated features available in the Code window. If the Auto Indent option is turned on, you can automatically indent the selected lines of code by the number of characters specified in the Tab Width text box. The default entry for Auto Indent is four characters. You can easily change the Tab Width by typing a new value in the text box.

Why would you want to use indentation in your code? When you indent certain lines in your VBA procedures, you make them more readable and easier to understand. Indenting is especially recommended for entering lines of code that make decisions or repeat actions. You will learn how to create these kinds of Visual Basic instructions in Chapters 6 and 7. Let's spend a few minutes to learn how to apply the indent and outdent features to the lines of code in the WhatsInACell macro.

Hands-On 3-4: Indenting/Outdenting Visual Basic Code

1. In the Project Explorer window, select the **FirstSteps (Practice_Excel01.xlsm)** VBA project and activate the WorksheetFormatting module that contains the code of the WhatsInACell macro.
2. Select the block of code beginning with the keyword With and ending with the keywords End With.
3. Click the **Indent** button on the Edit toolbar, or press **Tab** on the keyboard. The selected block of instructions will move four spaces to the right if you are using the default setting in the Tab Width box in the Options dialog box (Editor tab).
4. Click the **Outdent** button on the Edit toolbar, or press **Shift+Tab** to return the selected lines of code to the previous location in the Code window.

The Indent and Outdent options are also available from the Edit menu.

Comment Block/Uncomment Block

In Chapter 1 you learned that a single quote placed at the beginning of a line of code denotes a comment. Not only do comments make it easier to understand what the procedure does, but they are also very useful in testing and troubleshooting VBA procedures.

For example, when you execute a procedure, it may not run as expected. Instead of deleting the lines that may be responsible for encountered problems, you may want to skip those lines of code for now and return to them later. By placing a single quote at the beginning of the line you want to avoid, you can continue checking the other parts of your procedure. While commenting one line of code by typing a single quote works fine for most people, when it comes to turning entire blocks of code into comments, you'll find the Comment Block and Uncomment Block buttons on the Edit toolbar very handy and easy to use.

- To comment a few lines of code, simply select the lines and click the Comment Block button .
- To turn the commented code back into VBA instructions, select the lines and click the Uncomment Block button .

If you don't select text and click the Comment Block button, the single quote is added only to the line of code where the cursor is currently located.

Using the Object Browser

If you want to move easily through the myriad of VBA elements and features, examine the capabilities of the Object Browser. This special built-in tool is available in the Visual Basic Editor window.

To access the Object Browser, use any of the following methods:

- Press F2.
- Choose View | Object Browser.
- Click the Object Browser button on the toolbar.

The Object Browser allows you to browse through the objects that are available to your VBA procedures, as well as view their properties, methods, and events. With the aid of the Object Browser, you can move quickly between procedures in your own VBA projects, as well as search for objects and methods across object type libraries.

The Object Browser window is divided into three sections (see Figure 3-14). The top of the window displays the Project/Library drop-down list box with the names of all libraries and projects that are available to the currently active VBA project. A library is a special file that contains information about the objects in an application. New libraries can be added via the References dialog box (Tools | References). The entry for <All Libraries> lists the objects of all libraries that are installed on your computer. When you select the library called Excel, you will only see the names of the objects that are exclusive to Microsoft Excel. In contrast to the Excel library, the VBA library lists the names of the objects that are common to Visual Basic for Applications.

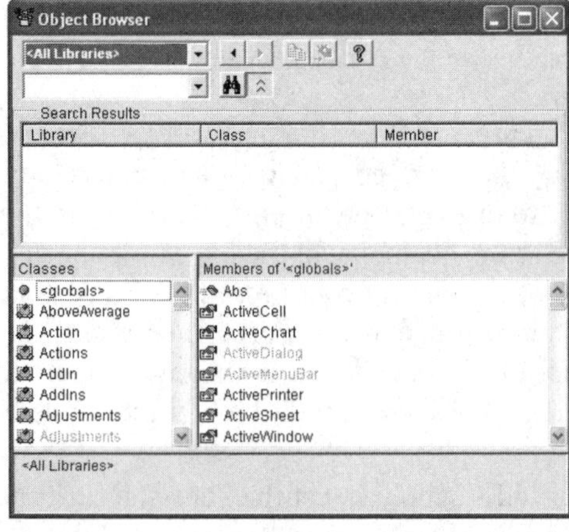

Figure 3-14: The Object Browser window allows you to browse through all the objects, properties, and methods available to the current VBA project.

Below the Project/Library drop-down list box is a Search text box that allows you to quickly find information in a particular library. This field remembers the last four items for which you searched. To find only whole words, you can right-click anywhere in the Object Browser window and choose Find Whole Word Only from the shortcut menu.

The Search Results section of the Object Browser displays the library, class, and member elements that met the criteria entered in the Search text box (see Figure 3-15).

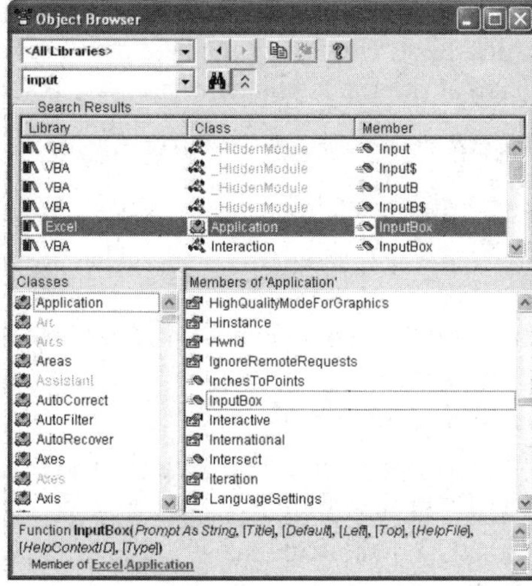

Figure 3-15: Searching for answers in the Object Browser.

When you type the search text and click the Search button, Visual Basic expands the Object Browser dialog box to show the Search Results area. You can hide or show the Search Results by clicking the button located to the right of the binoculars icon.

The Classes list box displays the available object classes in the selected library. If you select a VBA project, this list shows objects in the project. In Figure 3-15 the Application object class is selected. When you highlight a class, the list on the right-hand side (Members) shows the properties, methods, and events available for that class. By default, members are listed alphabetically. You can, however, organize the members list by group type (properties, methods, or events) using the Group Members command from the Object Browser shortcut menu.

If you select a VBA project in the Project/Library list box, the Members list box will list all the procedures available in this project. To examine the code of a procedure, simply double-click its name. If you select a VBA library, you will see a listing of Visual Basic built-in functions and constants. If you need more information on the selected class or a member, click the question mark button at the top of the Object Browser window.

The bottom of the Object Browser window displays a code template area with the definition of the selected member. If you click the green hyperlink text in the code template, you can quickly jump to the selected member's class or library in the Object Browser window. Text displayed in the code template area can be copied to the Windows clipboard and then pasted to a

Code window. If the Code window is visible while the Object Browser window is open, you can save time by dragging the highlighted code template and dropping it into the Code window.

You can easily adjust the size of the various sections of the Object Browser window by dragging the dividing horizontal and vertical lines.

Now that you've discovered the Object Browser, you may wonder how you can put it to use in VBA programming. Let's assume that you placed a text box in the middle of your worksheet. How can you make Excel move this text box so that it is positioned at the top left-hand corner of the sheet?

Hands-On 3-5: Writing a VBA Procedure to Move a Text Box on the Worksheet

1. Open a new workbook.
2. Choose **Insert | Text Box.**
3. Now draw a box in the middle of the sheet and enter any text (see Figure 3-16).
4. Select any cell outside the text box area.
5. Press **Alt+F11** to activate the Visual Basic Editor window, and select **Personal (Personal.xlsb)** in the Project Explorer window.
6. Choose **Insert | Module** to add a new module sheet to the Personal Workbook.
7. In the Properties window, enter the new name for this module: **Manipulations**.
8. Choose **View | Object Browser** or press **F2**.
9. In the Project/Library list box, click the drop-down arrow and select the **Excel** library.
10. Enter **textbox** as the search text in the Search box and click the **Search** button. Make sure you don't enter a space in the search string.

    Visual Basic searches the Excel library and displays the search results. It appears that the Shapes object is in control of our text box operations (see Figure 3-17). Looking at the members list, you can quickly determine that the AddTextbox method is used for adding a new text box to a worksheet. The code template at the bottom of the Object Browser shows the correct syntax for using this method. If you select the AddTextbox method and press F1, you will see the Help window with more details on how to use this method (see Figure 3-18).

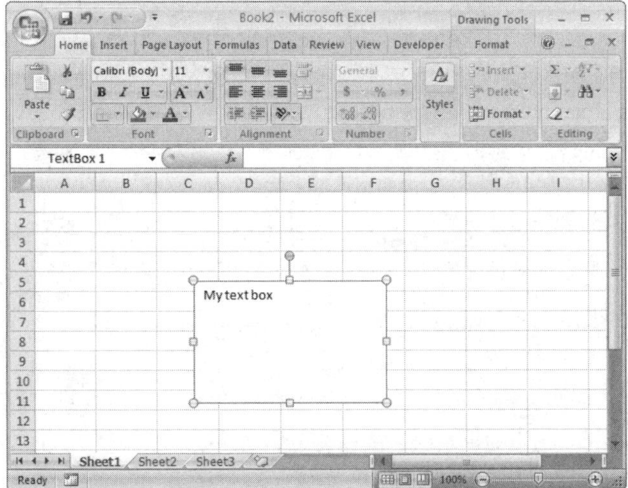

Figure 3-16: Excel displays the name of the inserted object in the Name box above the worksheet.

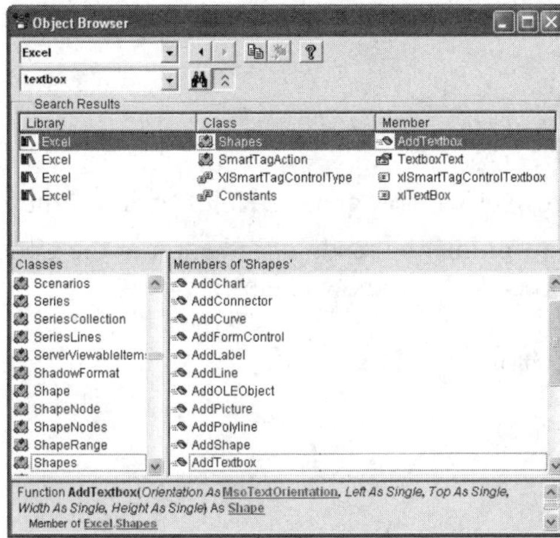

Figure 3-17: Using the Object Browser window, you can find the appropriate VBA instructions for writing your own procedures.

When you examine the parameters of the AddTextbox method and their explanations in the Help window, you can quickly figure out that the Left and Top properties determine the position of the text box in a worksheet. All you have to do now is return to the Code window and write the procedure to move the text box to the upper left-hand corner.

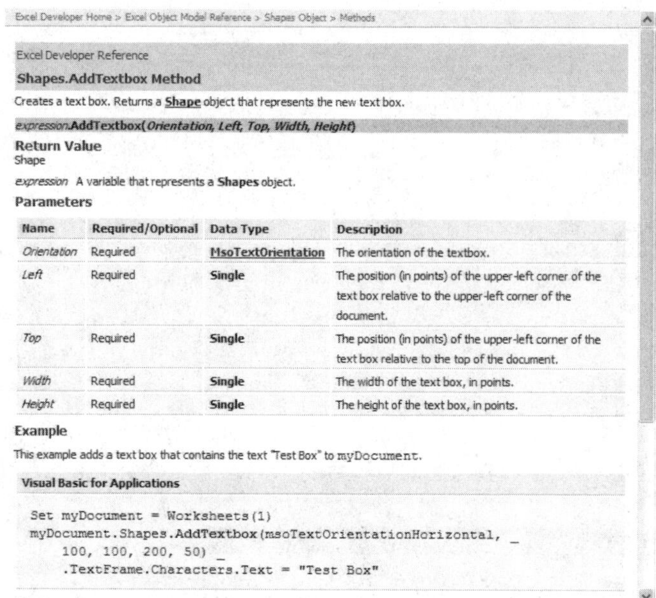

Excel Developer Home > Excel Object Model Reference > Shapes Object > Methods

Excel Developer Reference

Shapes.AddTextbox Method

Creates a text box. Returns a **Shape** object that represents the new text box.

expression.**AddTextbox**(*Orientation, Left, Top, Width, Height*)

Return Value
Shape

expression A variable that represents a **Shapes** object.

Parameters

Name	Required/Optional	Data Type	Description
Orientation	Required	**MsoTextOrientation**	The orientation of the textbox.
Left	Required	**Single**	The position (in points) of the upper-left corner of the text box relative to the upper-left corner of the document.
Top	Required	**Single**	The position (in points) of the upper-left corner of the text box relative to the top of the document.
Width	Required	**Single**	The width of the text box, in points.
Height	Required	**Single**	The height of the text box, in points.

Example

This example adds a text box that contains the text "Test Box" to `myDocument`.

Visual Basic for Applications

```
Set myDocument = Worksheets(1)
myDocument.Shapes.AddTextbox(msoTextOrientationHorizontal, _
    100, 100, 200, 50) _
    .TextFrame.Characters.Text = "Test Box"
```

Figure 3-18: To get detailed information on any item found in the Object Browser, select the item and press F1.

11. Close the Object Browser window and the Help window if they are open.
12. Double-click the **Manipulations** module, and enter in the Code window the MoveTextBox procedure, as shown below:

```
Sub MoveTextBox()
    With ActiveSheet.Shapes("TextBox 1")
        .Select
        .Left = 0
        .Top = 0
    End With
End Sub
```

The MoveTextBox procedure selects TextBox 1 in the collection of Shapes. TextBox 1 is the default name of the first object placed in the worksheet. Each time you add a new object to your worksheet, Excel assigns a new number (index) to it. Instead of using the object name, you can refer to the member of a collection by its index. For example, instead of:

```
With ActiveSheet.Shapes("TextBox 1")
```

enter:

```
With ActiveSheet.Shapes(1)
```

13. Choose **Run | Run Sub/UserForm** to execute this procedure.
14. Press **Alt+F11** to switch to the Microsoft Excel application window.

Notice that the text box is now positioned at the top left-hand corner of the worksheet.

Let's manipulate another object with Visual Basic.

Hands-On 3-6: Writing a VBA Procedure to Move a Circle on the Worksheet

1. Place a small circle in the same worksheet where you originally placed the text box in Hands-On 3-5. Use the **Oval** shape in the Basic Shapes area of the **Insert | Shapes** tool. Hold down the Shift key while drawing on the worksheet to create a perfect circle.
2. Click outside the circle to deselect it.
3. Press **Alt+F11** to activate the Visual Basic Editor screen.
4. In the Manipulations module's Code window write a VBA procedure that will place the circle inside the text box. Keep in mind that Excel numbers objects consecutively. The first object is assigned a number 1, the second one a number 2, and so on. The type of object — whether it is a text box, a circle, or a rectangle — does not matter.

   The MoveCircle procedure shown below demonstrates how to move a circle to the top left-hand corner of the active worksheet:

```
Sub MoveCircle()
    With ActiveSheet.Shapes(2)
        .Select
        .Left = 0
        .Top = 0
    End With
End Sub
```

Moving a circle is similar to moving a text box or any other object placed in a worksheet. Notice that instead of referring to the circle by its name, Oval 2, the procedure uses the object's index.

Using the VBA Object Library

In the previous examples, you used the properties of objects that are members of the Shapes collection in the Excel object library. While the Excel library contains objects specific to using Microsoft Excel, the VBA object library provides access to many built-in VBA functions grouped by categories. These functions are general in nature. They allow you to manage files, set the date and time, interact with users, convert data types, deal with text strings, or perform mathematical calculations. In the following exercise, you will see how to use one of the built-in VBA functions to create a new Windows subfolder without leaving Excel.

Hands-On 3-7: Writing a VBA Procedure to Create a Folder in Windows

1. Return to the Manipulations module where you entered the MoveTextBox and MoveCircle procedures.
2. Enter on a new line the name of the new procedure: **Sub NewFolder()**.
3. Press **Enter**. Visual Basic will enter the ending keywords End Sub.

4. Press **F2** to activate the Object Browser.
5. Click the drop-down arrow in the Project/Library list box and select **VBA**.
6. Enter **file** as the search text in the Search box and press **Enter**.
7. Scroll down in the Members list box and highlight the **MkDir** method (see Figure 3-19).

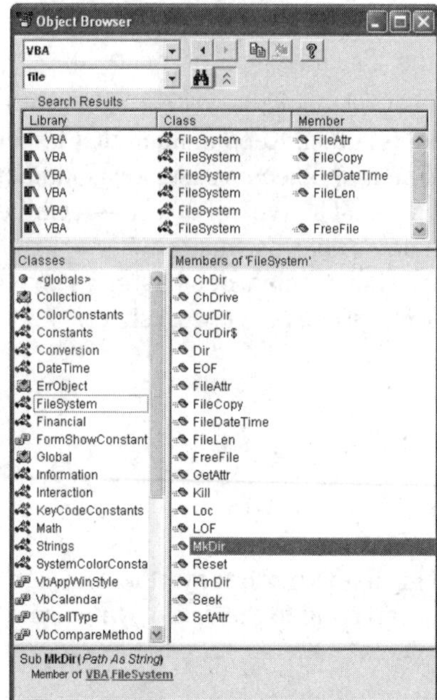

Figure 3-19: When writing procedures from scratch, consult the Object Browser for names of the built-in VBA functions.

8. Click the **Copy** button in the Object Browser window to copy the selected method name to the Windows clipboard.
9. Return to the Manipulations Code window and paste the copied instruction inside the procedure NewFolder.
10. Enter a space, followed by "**C:\Study**". Be sure to enter the name of the entire path in quotes. The NewFolder procedure should look like this:

```
Sub NewFolder()
    MkDir "C:\Study"
End Sub
```

11. Choose **Run | Run Sub/UserForm** to execute the NewFolder procedure.

    When you run the NewFolder procedure, Visual Basic creates a new folder on drive C. To see the folder, activate Windows Explorer.

    After creating a new folder, you may realize that you don't need it after all. Although you could easily delete the folder while in Windows Explorer, how about getting rid of it programmatically? The Object Browser displays many other methods that are useful for working with folders and files. The RmDir method is just as simple to use as the MkDir method.

12. To remove the Study folder from your hard drive, you could replace the MkDir method with the RmDir method, and then rerun the NewFolder procedure. However, let's write in the Manipulations Code window a new procedure called RemoveFolder, as shown here:

```
Sub RemoveFolder()
   RmDir "C:\Study"
End Sub
```

    The RmDir method allows you to remove unwanted folders from your hard disk.

13. Choose **Run | Run Sub/UserForm** to execute the RemoveFolder procedure.

    Check Windows Explorer to see that the Study folder is gone.

Locating Procedures with the Object Browser

In addition to locating objects, properties, and methods, the Object Browser is a handy tool for locating and accessing procedures written in various VBA projects. The following example demonstrates how you can see, at a glance, which procedures are stored in the Personal Workbook.

Hands-On 3-8: Using Object Browser to Locate VBA Procedures

1. In the Object Browser, select **Personal** from the Project/Library drop-down list (see Figure 3-20).

    The left side of the Object Browser displays the names of objects that are included in the selected project. The Members list box on the right shows the names of all the available procedures.

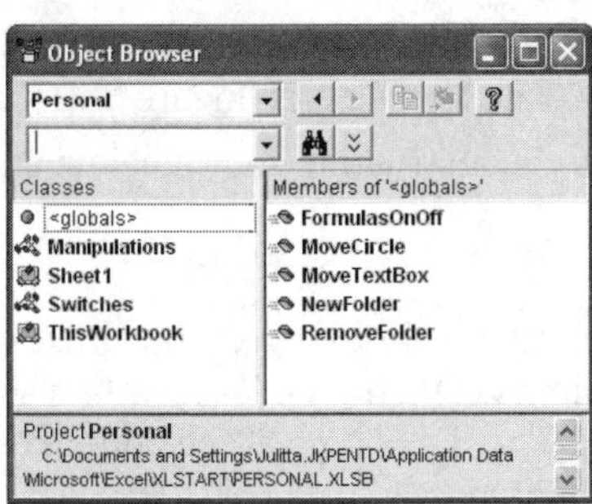

Figure 3-20: The Object Browser lists all the procedures available in a particular VBA project.

2. Double-click the **NewFolder** procedure.

    Visual Basic positions the cursor in the first line of the selected procedure.

Using the Immediate Window

Before you start creating full-fledged VBA procedures (this awaits you in the next chapter!), begin with some warm-up exercises to build up your VBA vocabulary. How can you do this quickly and painlessly? How can you try out some of the newly learned VBA statements? Here is a short, interactive language exercise: Enter a simple VBA instruction and Excel will check it out and display the result in the next line. Let's begin by setting up your exercise screen.

Hands-On 3-9: Entering and Executing VBA Statements in the Immediate Window

1. In the Visual Basic Editor window, choose **View | Immediate Window**.

   The Immediate window is used for trying out various instructions, functions, and operators present in the Visual Basic language before deciding to use them in your own VBA procedures. It is a great tool for experimenting with your new language. Instructions that you enter in this window immediately display results.

   The Immediate window allows you to type VBA statements and test their results immediately without having to write a procedure. The Immediate window is like a scratch pad. Use it to try out your statements. If the statement produces the expected result, you can copy the statement from the Immediate window into your procedure (or you can drag it right onto the Code window if it is visible).

   The Immediate window can be moved anywhere on the Visual Basic Editor screen or it can be docked so that it always appears in the same area of the screen. The docking setting can be turned on and off on the Docking tab in the Options dialog box (Tools | Options).

   To quickly access the Immediate window, simply press Ctrl+G while in the Visual Basic Editor screen. To close the Immediate window, click the Close button in the top right-hand corner of the window.

2. Arrange the screen so that both the Microsoft Excel window and the Visual Basic window are placed side by side (see Figure 3-21).
3. In the Immediate window, type the instruction shown below, and press **Enter**:

   ```
   Worksheets("Sheet2").Activate
   ```

   When you press the Enter key, Visual Basic gets to work. If you entered the above VBA statement correctly, VBA activates a second sheet in the current workbook. The Sheet2 tab at the bottom of the workbook should now be highlighted.

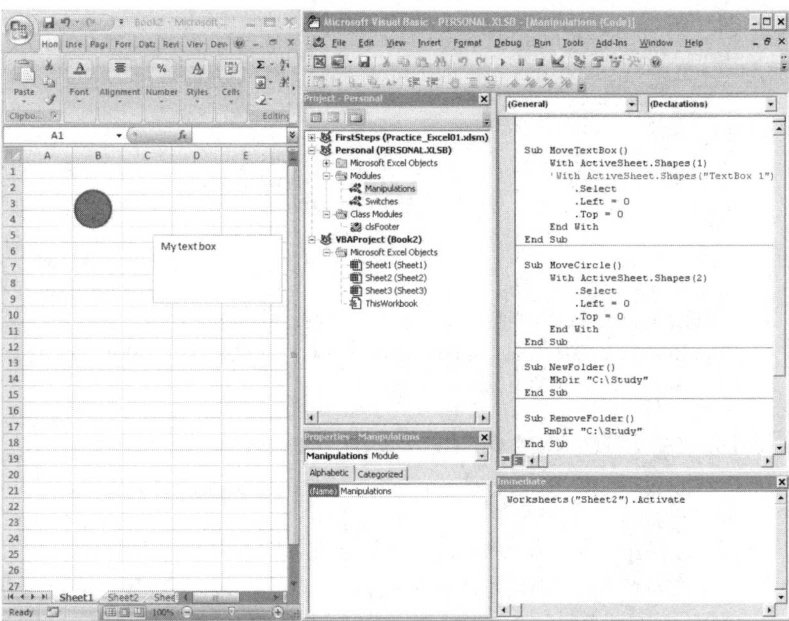

Figure 3-21: By positioning the Microsoft Excel and Visual Basic windows side by side you can watch the execution of the instructions entered in the Immediate window.

4. In the Immediate window, type another VBA statement and be sure to press **Enter** when you're done:

   ```
   Range("A1:A4").Select
   ```

   As soon as you press **Enter**, Visual Basic highlights the cells A1, A2, A3, and A4 in the active worksheet.

5. Enter the following instruction in the Immediate window:

   ```
   [A1:A4].Value = 55
   ```

   When you press **Enter**, Visual Basic places the number 55 in every cell of the specified range, A1:A4. The above statement is an abbreviated way of referring to the Range object. The full syntax is more readable:

   ```
   Range("A1:A4").Value = 55
   ```

6. Enter the following instruction in the Immediate window:

   ```
   Selection.ClearContents
   ```

   When you press **Enter**, VBA deletes the results of the previous statement from the selected cells. Cells A1:A4 are now empty.

7. Enter the following instruction in the Immediate window:

   ```
   ActiveCell.Select
   ```

   When you press **Enter**, Visual Basic makes cell A1 active.

Figure 3-22 shows all the instructions entered in the Immediate window in this exercise. Every time you pressed the Enter key, Excel executed the statement on the line where the cursor was located. If you want to execute the same instruction again, click anywhere in the line containing the instruction and press Enter.

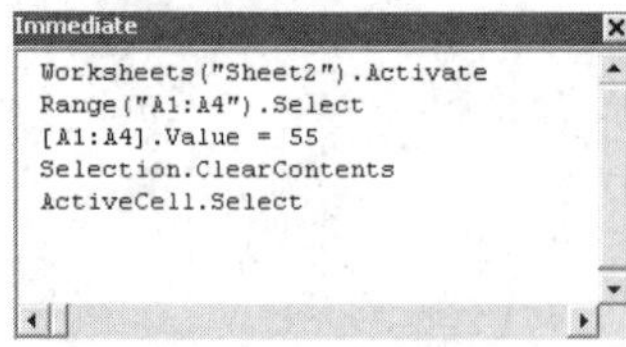

Figure 3-22: Instructions entered in the Immediate window are executed as soon as you press the Enter key.

For more practice you may want to rerun the statements shown in Figure 3-22. Start from the instruction displayed in the second line of the Immediate window. Execute the instructions one by one by clicking in the appropriate line and pressing the Enter key.

Obtaining Information in the Immediate Window

So far you have used the Immediate window to perform actions. These actions could have been performed manually by clicking the mouse in various areas of the worksheet and entering data.

Instead of simply performing actions, the Immediate window also allows you to ask questions. Suppose you want to find out which cells are currently selected, the value of the active cell, the name of the active sheet, or the number of the current window. When working in the Immediate window, you can easily get answers to these and other questions.

In the preceding exercise, you entered several instructions. Let's return to the Immediate window to ask some questions. Excel remembers the instructions entered in the Immediate window even after you close this window. The contents of the Immediate window are automatically deleted when you exit Microsoft Excel.

Hands-On 3-10: Obtaining Information in the Immediate Window

1. Click the mouse in the second line of the Immediate window where you previously entered the instruction Range("A1:A4").Select.
2. Press **Enter** to have Excel reselect cells A1:A4.
3. Click in the new line of the Immediate window, enter the following question, and press **Enter**:

   ```
   ?Selection.Address
   ```

   When you press Enter, Excel will not select anything in the worksheet. Instead, it will display the result of the instruction on a separate line in the Immediate window. In this case, Excel returns the absolute address of the cells that are currently selected ($A$1:$A$4).

   The question mark (?) in the above statement tells Excel to display the result of the instruction in the Immediate window. Instead of the question mark, you can use the Print keyword, as shown in the next step.

4. In a new line in the Immediate window, enter the following statement and press **Enter**:

```
Print ActiveWorkbook.Name
```

Excel enters the name of the active workbook on a new line in the Immediate window.

How about finding the name of the application?

5. In a new line in the Immediate window, enter the following statement and press **Enter**:

```
?Application.Name
```

Excel will reveal its full name: Microsoft Excel.

The Immediate window can also be used for a quick calculation.

6. In a new line in the Immediate window, enter the following statement and press **Enter**:

```
?12/3
```

Excel shows the result of the division on the next line. But what if you want to know right away the result of 3+2 and 12*8?

Instead of entering these instructions on separate lines, you can enter them on one line, as in the following example:

```
?3+2:?12*8
```

Notice the colon separating the two blocks of instructions. When you press the Enter key, Excel displays the results 5, 96 on separate lines in the Immediate window.

Below are all the instructions you entered in the Immediate window including Excel's answers to your questions:

```
Worksheets("Sheet2").Activate
Range("A1:A4").Select
[A1:A4].Value = 55
Selection.ClearContents
ActiveCell.Select
?Selection.Address
$A$1:$A$4
Print ActiveWorkbook.Name
Book2
?Application.Name
Microsoft Excel
?12/3
 4
?3+2:?12*8
 5
 96
```

To delete the instructions from the Immediate window, press Ctrl+A to highlight all the lines, and then press Delete.

Learning about Objects

Creating custom applications in Excel requires a working knowledge of common objects or collections of objects such as Range, Workbook (Workbooks), Worksheet (Worksheets), Window (Windows), and Application. In preceding sections, you explored several methods of learning about Visual Basic. Here's a summary of when to use a specific tool:

- When in doubt about objects, properties, or methods in an existing VBA procedure, fire up the online help by pressing F1.
- If you need a quick listing of properties and methods for every available object or have trouble locating a hard-to-find procedure, go with the Object Browser.
- If you want to experiment with VBA and see the results of the VBA commands immediately, activate the Immediate window.

To help you better understand the VBA syntax, the remaining pages of this chapter contain a number of VBA language drills. You will get the most out of these drills if you take the time to work through them in the Immediate window.

Working with Worksheet Cells

When you are ready to write your own VBA procedure to automate a particular spreadsheet task, you will most likely begin searching for instructions that allow you to manipulate worksheet cells. You will need to know how to select cells, how to enter data in cells, how to assign range names, how to format cells, and how to move, copy, and delete cells. Although these tasks can be easily performed with the mouse or keyboard, mastering these techniques in Visual Basic for Applications requires a little practice. You must use the Range object to refer to a single cell, a range of cells, a row, or a column. There are three properties that allow you to access the Range object: the Range property, the Cells property, and the Offset property.

Using the Range Property

The Range property returns a cell or a range of cells. The reference to the range must be in an A1-style and in quotation marks (for example, "A1"). The reference can include the range operator, which is a colon (for example, "A1:B2"), or the union operator, which is a comma (for example, "A", "B12").

Hands-On 3-11: Practice Using the Range Property to Select Worksheet Cells

To render this into VBA:	Enter this in the Immediate window:
Select a single cell (e.g., A5).	Range("A5").Select
Select a range of cells (e.g., A6:A10).	Range("A6:A10").Select
Select several non-adjacent cells (e.g., A1, B6, C8).	Range("A1, B6, C8").Select
Select several non-adjacent cells and cell ranges (e.g., A11:D11, C12, D3).	Range("A11:D11, C12, D3").Select

Using the Cells Property

You can use the Cells property to return a single cell. When selecting a single cell, this property requires two arguments. The first argument indicates the row number, and the second one is the column number. Arguments are entered in parentheses. When you omit arguments, Excel selects all the cells in the active worksheet.

Hands-On 3-12: Practice Using the Cells Property to Select Worksheet Cells (Part I)

To render this into VBA:	Enter this in the Immediate window:
Select a singe cell (e.g., A5).	Cells(5, 1).Select
Select a range of cells (e.g., A6:A10).	Range(Cells(6, 1), Cells(10, 1)).Select
Select all cells in a worksheet.	Cells.Select

Notice how you can combine the Range property and the Cells property:

```
Range(Cells(6, 1), Cells(10, 1)).Select
```

In the above example, the first Cells property returns cell A6, while the second one returns cell A10. The cells returned by the Cells properties are then used as a reference for the Range object. As a result, Excel will select the range of cells where the top cell is specified by the result of the first Cells property and the bottom cell is defined by the result of the second Cells property.

A worksheet is a collection of cells. You can also use the Cells property with a single argument that identifies a cell's position in the collection of a worksheet's cells. Excel numbers the cells in the following way: Cell A1 is the first cell in a worksheet, cell B1 is the second one, cell C1 is the third one, and so on. Cell 16384 is the last cell in the first spreadsheet row. You may recall that there are 16,384 columns in the Microsoft Excel 2007 worksheet. Previous version of Excel allowed only 256 columns in a worksheet.

Hands-On 3-12: Practice Using the Cells Property to Select Worksheet Cells (Part II)

To render this into VBA:	Enter this in the Immediate window:
Select cell A1.	Cells(1).Select or Cells.Item(1).Select
Select cell C1.	Cells(3).Select or Cells.Item(3).Select
Select cell XFD.	Cells(16384).Select or Cells.Item(16384).Select
Select cell A2.	Cells(16385).Select or Cells.Item(16385).Select

Notice that the word Item is a property that returns a single member of a collection. Because Item is the default member for a collection, you can refer to a worksheet cell without explicitly using the Item property.

Now that you've discovered two ways to select cells (Range property and Cells property), you may wonder why you should bother using the more complicated Cells property. It's quite obvious that the Range property is more readable; after all, you used the Range references in Excel formulas and functions long before you decided to learn about VBA. Using the Cells property is more convenient, however, when it comes to working with cells as a collection. Use this property to access all the cells or a single cell from a collection.

Using the Offset Property

Another very flexible way to refer to a worksheet cell is with the Offset property. Quite often when automating worksheet tasks, you may not know exactly where a specific cell is located. How can you select a cell whose address you don't know? The answer: Have Excel select a cell based on an existing selection.

The Offset property calculates a new range by shifting the starting selection down or up a specified number of rows. You can also shift the selection to the right or left a specified number of columns. In calculating the position of a new range, the Offset property uses two arguments. The first argument indicates the row offset, and the second one is the column offset. Let's try out some examples.

Hands-On 3-13: Selecting Cells Using the Offset Property

To render this into VBA:	Enter this in the Immediate window:
Select a cell located one row down and three columns to the right of cell A1.	Range("A1").Offset(1, 3).Select
Select a cell located two rows above and one column to the left of cell D15.	Range("D15").Offset(–2, –1).Select
Select a cell located one row above the active cell. If the active cell is located in the first row you will get an error message.	ActiveCell.Offset(–1, 0).Select

In the first example above, Excel selects cell D2. As soon as you enter the second example, Excel chooses cell C13.

If cells A1 and D15 are already selected, you can rewrite the first two statments in the following way:

```
Selection.Offset(1, 3).Select
Selection.Offset(-2, -1).Select
```

Notice that the third example in the practice table above displays zero (0) in the position of the second argument. Zero entered as a first or second argument of the Offset property indicates a current row or column. The instruction ActiveCell.Offset(–1, 0).Select will cause an error if the active cell is located in the first row.

When working with the Offset property, you may occasionally need to change the size of a selection of cells. Suppose that the starting selection is A5:A10. How about shifting the selection two rows down and two columns to the right and then changing the size of the new selection? Let's say the new selection should highlight cells C7:C8. The Offset property can only take care of the first part of this task. The second part requires another property. Excel has a special Resize property. You can combine the Offset property with the Resize property to answer the above question. Before you combine these two properties, let's learn how you can use them separately.

Hands-On 3-14: Writing a VBA Statement to Resize a Selection of Cells

1. Arrange the screen so that the Microsoft Excel window and the Visual Basic window are side by side.
2. Activate the Immediate window and enter the following instructions:

```
Range("A5:A10").Select
Selection.Offset(2, 2).Select
Selection.Resize(2, 4).Select
```

The first instruction above selects range A5:A10. Cell A5 is the active cell. The second instruction shifts the current selection to cells C7:C12. Cell C7 is located two rows below the active cell A5 and two columns to the right of A5. Now the active cell is C7.

The last instruction resizes the current selection. Instead of range C7:C12, cells C7:F8 are selected.

Like the Offset property, the Resize property takes two arguments. The first argument is the number of rows you intend to include in the selection, and the second argument specifies the number of columns. Hence, the instruction Selection.Resize(2, 4).Select resizes the current selection to two rows and four columns.

The last two instructions can be combined in the following way:

```
Selection.Offset(2, 2).Resize(2, 4).Select
```

In the example above, the Offset property calculates the beginning of a new range, the Resize property determines the new size of the range, and the Select method selects the specified range of cells.

Recording a Selection of Cells

By default, the macro recorder selects cells using the Range property. If you turn on the macro recorder and select cell A2, enter any text, and select cell A5, you will see the following lines of code in the Visual Basic Editor window:

```
Range("A2").Select
ActiveCell.FormulaR1C1 = "text"
Range("A5").Select
```

You can have the macro recorder use the Offset property if you tell it to use relative references. To do this, click View | Macros | Use Relative References, and then choose Record Macro. The macro recorder produces the following lines of code:

```
ActiveCell.Offset(-1,
   0).Range("A1").Select
ActiveCell.FormulaR1C1 = "text"
ActiveCell.Offset(3,
   0).Range("A1").Select
```

When you record a procedure using the relative references, the procedure will always select a cell relative to the active cell. The first and third lines in the first set of instructions reference cell A1, even though nothing was said about cell A1. As you remember from Chapter 1, the macro recorder has its own way of getting things done. To make the above instructions less complex, you can delete the reference to Range("A1"):

```
ActiveCell.Offset(-1, 0).Select
ActiveCell.FormulaR1C1 = "text"
ActiveCell.Offset(3, 0).Select
```

After recording a procedure using the relative reference, make sure Use Relative References is not selected if your next macro does not require the use of relative addressing.

Other Methods of Selecting Cells

If you often have to quickly access certain remote cells in your worksheet, you may already be familiar with the following keyboard shortcuts: End+Up Arrow, End+Down Arrow, End+Left Arrow, and End+Right Arrow. In VBA, you can use the End property to quickly move to remote cells.

Hands-On 3-15: Selecting Cells Using the End Property

To render this into VBA:	Enter this in the Immediate window:
Select the last cell in any row.	ActiveCell.End(xlToRight).Select
Select the last cell in any column.	ActiveCell.End(xlDown).Select
Select the first cell in any row.	ActiveCell.End(xlToLeft).Select
Select the first cell in any column.	ActiveCell.End(xlUp).Select

Notice that the End property requires an argument that indicates the direction you want to move. Use the following Excel built-in Direction Enumeration constants to jump in the specified direction: xlToRight, xlToLeft, xlUp, xlDown.

Selecting Rows and Columns

Excel uses the EntireRow and EntireColumn properties to select the entire row or column.

Hands-On 3-16: Selecting Entire Rows and Columns

To render this into VBA:	Enter this in the Immediate window:
Select an entire row where the active cell is located.	Selection.EntireRow.Select
Select an entire column where the active cell is located.	Selection.EntireColumn.Select

When you select a range of cells you may want to find out how many rows or columns are included in the selection. Let's have Excel count rows and columns in Range("A1:D15").

1. Type the following VBA statement in the Immediate window and press **Enter**:

   ```
   Range("A1:D15").Select
   ```

   If the Microsoft Excel window is visible, Visual Basic will highlight the range A1:D15 when you press Enter.

2. To find out how many rows are in the selected range, enter the following statement:

   ```
   ?Selection.Rows.Count
   ```

   As soon as you press **Enter**, Visual Basic displays the answer on the next line. Your selection includes 15 rows.

3. To find out the number of columns in the selected range, enter the following statement:

   ```
   ?Selection.Columns.Count
   ```

   As soon as you press **Enter**, Visual Basic tells you that the selected Range("A1:D15") occupies the width of four columns.

4. In the Immediate window, position the cursor anywhere within the word Rows or Columns and press **F1** to find out more information about these useful properties.

Obtaining Information about the Worksheet

How big is an Excel worksheet? How many columns and rows does it contain? If you ever forget the details, use the Count property.

Hands-On 3-17: Counting Rows and Columns

To render this into VBA:	Enter this in the Immediate window:
Find out the total number of rows in an Excel worksheet.	?Rows.Count
Find out the total number of columns in an Excel worksheet.	?Columns.Count

A Microsoft Excel 2007 worksheet has 1,048,576 rows and 16,384 columns.

Entering Data in a Worksheet

The information entered in a worksheet can be text, numbers, or formulas. To enter data in a cell or range of cells, you can use either the Value property or the Formula property of the Range object.

Using the Value property:

```
ActiveSheet.Range("A1:C4").Value = "=4 * 25"
```

Using the Formula property:

```
ActiveSheet.Range("A1:C4").Formula = "=4 * 25"
```

In both examples shown above, cells A1:C4 display 100 — the result of the multiplication 4 * 25.

Hands-On 3-18: Using VBA Statements to Enter Data in a Worksheet

To render this into VBA:	Enter this in the Immediate window:
Enter in cell A5 the following text: Amount Due	Range("A5").Formula = "Amount Due"
Enter the number 123 in cell D21.	Range("D21").Formula = 123 or Range("D21").Value = 123
Enter in cell B4 the following formula: = D21 * 3	Range("B4").Formula = "=D21 * 3"

Returning Information Entered in a Worksheet

In some Visual Basic procedures you will undoubtedly need to return the contents of a cell or a range of cells. Although you can use either the Value or

Formula property, this time the two Range object's properties are not interchangeable.

- The Value property displays the result of a formula entered in a specified cell. If, for example, cell A1 contains a formula = 4 * 25, then the instruction

  ```
  ?Range("A1").Value
  ```

  will return the value of 100.

- If you want to display the formula instead of its result, you must use the Formula property:

  ```
  ?Range("A1").Formula
  ```

  Excel will display the formula = 4 * 25 instead of its result (100).

Finding Out about Cell Formatting

A frequent spreadsheet task is applying formatting to a selected cell or a range. Your VBA procedure may need to find out the type of formatting applied to a particular worksheet cell. To retrieve the cell formatting, use the NumberFormat property:

```
?Range("A1").NumberFormat
```

Upon entering the above statement in the Immediate window, Excel displays the word "General," which indicates that no special formatting was applied to the selected cell. To change the format of a cell to dollars and cents using VBA, enter the instruction shown below:

```
Range("A1").NumberFormat = "$#,##0.00"
```

If you enter 125 in cell A1 after it has been formatted with the above VBA instruction, cell A1 will display $125.00. You can look up the available format codes in the Format Cells dialog box in Microsoft Excel (see Figure 3-23).

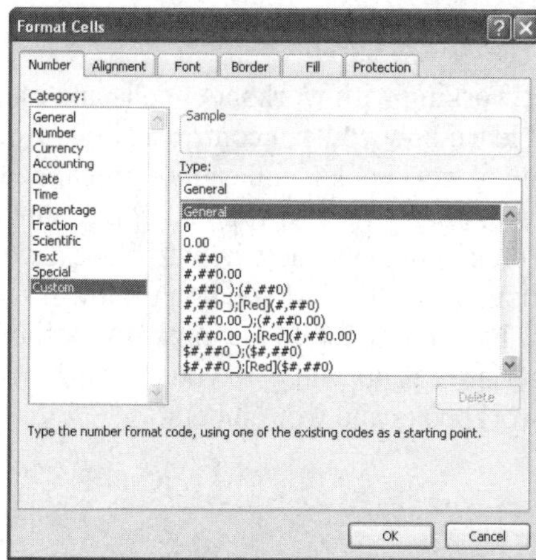

Figure 3-23: You can apply different formatting to selected cells and ranges using the format codes, as displayed in the Custom category in the Format Cells dialog box.

If the format you want to apply is not listed in the Format Cells dialog box, refer to the online help for guidelines on creating user-defined formats.

Moving, Copying, and Deleting Cells

In the process of developing a new worksheet model, you often find yourself moving and copying cells and deleting cell contents. Visual Basic allows you to automate these worksheet editing tasks with three simple-to-use methods: Cut, Copy, and Clear.

Hands-On 3-19: Moving, Copying, and Deleting Cells

To render this into VBA:	Enter this in the Immediate window:
Move the contents of cell A5 to cell A4.	Range("A5").Cut Destination:=Range("A4")
Copy a formula from cell A3 to cells D5:F5.	Range("A3").Copy Destination:=Range("D5:F5")
Delete contents of cell A4.	Range("A4").Clear or Range("A4").Cut

Notice that the first two methods in the table require a special argument called Destination. This argument specifies the address of a cell or a range of cells where you want to place the cut or copied data. In the last example, the Cut method is used without the Destination argument to remove data from the specified cell.

The Clear method deletes everything from the specified cell or range, including any applied formats and cell comments. If you want to be specific about what you delete, use the following methods:

- ClearContents — Clears only data from a cell or range of cells.
- ClearFormats — Clears only applied formats.
- ClearComments — Clears all cell comments from the specified range.

Working with Workbooks and Worksheets

Now that you've got your feet wet working with worksheet cells and ranges, it's time to move up one level and learn how you can control a single workbook, as well as an entire collection of workbooks. You cannot prepare a new spreadsheet if you don't know how to open a new workbook. You cannot remove a workbook from the screen if you don't know how to close a workbook. You cannot work with an existing workbook if you don't know how to open it. These important tasks are handled by the following VBA methods: Add, Open, and Close. The next series of drills will give you the language skills necessary for dealing with workbooks and worksheets.

Hands-On 3-20: Working with Workbooks

To render this into VBA:	Enter this in the Immediate window:
Open a new workbook.	Workbooks.Add
Find out the name of the first workbook.	?Workbooks(1).Name
Find out the number of open workbooks.	?Workbooks.Count
Activate the second open workbook.	Workbooks(2).Activate
Close the Practice_Excel01.xlsm workbook and save the changes.	Workbooks("Practice_Excel01.xlsm").Close SaveChanges:=True
Open the Practice_Excel01.xlsm workbook. Type the correct path to the file location on your computer.	Workbooks.Open "C:\Ex07_ByExample\ Practice_Excel01.xlsm"
Activate the Practice_Excel01.xlsm workbook.	Workbooks("Practice_Excel01.xlsm").Activate
Save the active workbook as NewChap.xlsm.	ActiveWorkbook.SaveAs Filename:= "NewChap.xlsm"
Close the first workbook.	Workbooks(1).Close
Close the active workbook without saving recent changes to it.	ActiveWorkbook.Close SaveChanges:=False
Close all open workbooks.	Workbooks.Close

If you worked through the last example in Hands-On 3-20, all workbooks are now closed. Before you experiment with worksheets, make sure you have opened a new workbook.

When you deal with individual worksheets, you must know how to add a new worksheet to a workbook, select a worksheet or a group of worksheets, name a worksheet, and copy, move, and delete worksheets. In Visual Basic, each of these tasks is handled by a special method or property.

Hands-On 3-21: Working with Worksheets

To render this into VBA:	Enter this in the Immediate window:
Add a new worksheet.	Worksheets.Add
Find out the name of the first worksheet.	?Worksheets(1).Name
Select a sheet named Sheet3.	Worksheets(3).Select
Select sheets 1, 3, and 4.	Worksheets(Array(1,3,4)).Select
Activate a sheet named Sheet1.	Worksheets("Sheet1").Activate
Move Sheet2 before Sheet1.	Worksheets("Sheet2").Move Before:=Worksheets("Sheet1")
Rename worksheet Sheet2 to Expenses.	Worksheets("Sheet2").Name = "Expenses"
Find out the number of worksheets in the active workbook.	?Worksheets.Count
Remove the worksheet named Expenses from the active workbook.	Worksheets("Expenses").Delete

Notice the difference between the Select and Activate methods:

- The Select and Activate methods can be used interchangeably if only one worksheet is selected.
- If you select a group of worksheets, the Activate method allows you to decide which one of the selected worksheets is active. As you know, only one worksheet can be active at a time.

Sheets Other than Worksheets

In addition to worksheets, the collection of workbooks contains chart sheets. To add a new chart sheet to your workbook, use the Add method:

```
Charts.Add
```

To count the chart sheets, use:

```
?Charts.Count
```

Working with Windows

When you work with several Excel workbooks and need to compare or consolidate data or when you want to see different parts of the same worksheet, you are bound to use the options available from the Microsoft Excel Window menu: New Window and Arrange.

Let's see how you can arrange your screen with Visual Basic for Applications.

Hands-On 3-22: Working with Windows

To render this into VBA:	Enter this in the Immediate window:
Show the active workbook in a new window.	ActiveWorkbook.NewWindow
Display on screen all open workbooks.	Windows.Arrange
Activate the second window.	Windows(2).Activate
Find out the title of the active window.	?ActiveWindow.Caption
Change the active window's title to My Window.	ActiveWindow.Caption = "My Window"

When you display windows on screen, you can decide how to arrange them. The Arrange method has many arguments. The argument that allows you to control the way the windows are positioned on your screen is called ArrangeStyle. If you omit the ArrangeStyle argument, all windows are tiled.

Constant	Value	Description
xlArrangeStyleTiled	1	Windows are tiled (the default value).
xlArrangeStyleCascade	7	Windows are cascaded.
xlArrangeStyleHorizontal	2	Windows are arranged horizontally.
xlArrangeStyleVertical	3	Windows are arranged vertically.

Instead of the names of constants, you can use the value equivalents shown above.

To cascade all windows, use the following VBA instruction:

```
Windows.Arrange ArrangeStyle:=xlArrangeStyleCascade
```

Or simply:

```
Windows.Arrange ArrangeStyle:=7
```

Managing the Excel Application

At the beginning of this chapter, you learned that objects are organized in a special structure called the object model. The Application object represents the Excel application itself. By controlling the Application object, you can perform many tasks, such as saving the way your screen looks at the end of a day's work or quitting the application. As you know, Excel allows you to save the screen settings by using the Save Workspace button on the View tab. The task of saving the workspace can be easily performed with VBA:

```
Application.SaveWorkspace "Project"
```

The above instruction saves the screen settings in the workspace file named Project. The next time you need to work with the same files and arrangement of windows, simply open the Project.xlwx file, and Excel will bring up the correct files and restore your screen with those settings.

Hands-On 3-23: Working with the Excel Application

To render this into VBA:	Enter this in the Immediate window:
Check the name of the active application.	?Application.Name
Change the title of the Excel application to My Application.	Application.Caption = "My Application"
Change the title of the Excel application back to Microsoft Excel.	Application.Caption = "Microsoft Excel"
Find out what operating system you are using.	?Application.OperatingSystem
Find out the name of a person or firm to whom the application is registered.	?Application.OrganizationName
Find out the name of the folder where the Excel executable file (Excel.exe) resides.	?Application.Path
Quit working with Microsoft Excel.	Application.Quit

Chapter Summary

In this chapter you learned many basic VBA terms and how to use some built-in tools that make it easier to write and troubleshoot VBA statements. You should now have a good idea of how the most common Microsoft Excel objects are organized and controlled. This chapter focused on teaching you how to use these new language skills to gain control over Microsoft Excel immediately without writing complete VBA procedures. For this reason, we focused on the Immediate window.

Visual Basic procedures usually contain more than one line of code. In fact, they can become quite complex. Before you can start creating complete VBA procedures, you still need to learn a couple of things. For example, how can you save information returned by Excel so that your procedures can use it later? While entering instructions in the Immediate window, you learned how to question Excel for the vital information. You got answers to questions such as "How many worksheets are in the active workbook?" or "What are the contents of cell A4?" Excel did not mind any of your "nosy" questions. As long as you phrased your question by following the strict VBA syntax rules, Excel gave you the answer. When you start writing your own procedures, you will need to know how to save Excel answers. In the next chapter, you will learn how to save this kind of information for later use by using variables. You will also explore data types and constants.

Chapter 4

Using Variables, Data Types, and Constants

Saving Results of VBA Statements ■ What Are Variables? ■ Data Types ■ How to Create Variables ■ How to Declare Variables ■ Specifying the Data Type of a Variable ■ Assigning Values to Variables ■ Forcing Declaration of Variables ■ Understanding the Scope of Variables ■ Procedure-Level (Local) Variables ■ Module-Level Variables ■ Project-Level Variables ■ **Lifetime of Variables ■ Understanding and Using Static Variables ■ Declaring and Using Object Variables ■** Using Specific Object Variables ■ **Finding a Variable Definition ■ Using Constants in VBA Procedures ■** Built-in Constants ■ **Chapter Summary**

In programming, just as in life, certain things need to be done at once while others can be put off until later. When you postpone a task, you may enter it in your mental or paper "to-do" list. The individual entries on your list are often classified by their type or importance. When you delegate the task or finally get around to doing it yourself, you cross it off the list. This chapter shows you how your VBA procedures can memorize important pieces of information for use in later statements or calculations. You will learn how a procedure can keep a "to-do" entry in a variable, how variables are declared, and how they relate to data types and constants.

Saving Results of VBA Statements

In Chapter 3, while working in the Immediate window, you tried several Visual Basic instructions that returned some information. For example, when you entered ?Rows.Count, you found out that there are 1,048,576 rows in a worksheet. However, when you write Visual Basic procedures outside of the Immediate window, you can't use the question mark. When you omit the question mark and enter Rows.Count in your procedure, Visual Basic won't stop suddenly to tell you the result of this instruction. If you want to know the result after executing a particular instruction, you must tell Visual Basic to memorize it. In programming, results returned by Visual Basic instructions can be written to variables.

What Are Variables?

A *variable* is simply a name that is used to refer to an item of data. Each time you want to remember a result of a VBA instruction, think of a name that will represent it. For example, if the number 1,048,576 has to remind you of the total number of rows in a worksheet (a very important piece of information when you want to bring external data into Excel 2007), you can make up a name such as AllRows, NumOfRows, or TotalRows, and so on. The names of variables can contain characters, numbers, and some punctuation marks, except for the following: , # $ % & @ !

The name of a variable cannot begin with a number or contain a space. If you want the name of the variable to include more than one word, use the underscore (_) as a separator. Although the name of a variable can contain as many as 254 characters, it's best to use short and simple variable names. Using short names will save you typing time when you need to refer to the variable in your Visual Basic procedure. Visual Basic doesn't care whether you use uppercase or lowercase letters in variable names, but most programmers use lowercase letters in variable names, and when the variable names are comprised of one or more words, they use the title case, as in the names NumOfRows and First_Name.

Reserved Words Can't Be Used for Variable Names

You can use any label you want for a variable name, except for the reserved words that VBA uses. Visual Basic statements and certain other words that have a special meaning in VBA cannot be used as names of variables. For example, words such as Name, Len, Empty, Local, Currency, or Exit will generate an error message if used as a variable name.

Meaningful Variable Names

Give variables names that can help you remember their roles. Some programmers use a prefix to identify the type of a variable. A variable name that begins with "str" (for example, strName) can be quickly recognized within the code of your procedure as the one holding the text string.

Data Types

When you create Visual Basic procedures, you have a purpose in mind: You want to manipulate data. Because your procedures will handle different kinds of information, you should understand how Visual Basic stores data. The term *data type* determines how the data is stored in the computer's memory. For example, data can be stored as a number, text, date, object, etc. If you forget to tell Visual Basic the type of your data, it assigns the Variant data type. The Variant type has the ability to figure out on its own what kind of data is being manipulated and then take on that type.

The Visual Basic data types are shown in Table 4-1. In addition to the built-in data types, you can define your own data types. You will see an example of a user-defined data type in Chapter 14 (see Hands-On 14-6 and "Understanding the Type Statement"). Because data types take up different amounts of space in the computer's memory, some of them are more expensive than others. Therefore, to conserve memory and make your procedure run faster, you should select the data type that uses the least amount of bytes and, at the same time, is capable of handling the data that your procedure has to manipulate.

Table 4-1: The VBA data types

Data Type (Name)	**Size** (Bytes)	**Description**
Boolean	2	Logical value of True or False
Byte	1	Integer from 0 to 255
Integer	2	Integer from –32,768 to 32,767
Long	4	Integer from –2,147,483,648 to 2,147,483,647
Single	4	Single-precision floating-point real number. Negative numbers: –3.402823E38 to –1.401298E–45 Positive numbers: 1.401298E–45 to 3.402823E38

Data Type (Name)	Size (Bytes)	Description
Double	8	Double-precision floating-point real number. Negative numbers: –1.79769313486231E308 to –4.94065645841247E–324 Positive numbers: 4.94065645841247E–324 to 1.79769313486231E308
Currency	8	(scaled integer) Used in fixed-point calculations: –922,337,203,685,477.5808 to 922,337,203,685,477.5807
Decimal	14	+/–79,228,162,514,264,337,593,543,950,335 with no decimal point; +/–7.9228162514264337593543950335 with 28 places to the right of the decimal; smallest non-zero number is +/–0.0000000000000000000000000001
Date	8	Date from January 1, 100 to December 31, 9999
String (variable-length)	10 bytes + string length	A variable-length string can contain up to approximately 2 billion characters.
String (fixed-length)	Length of string	A fixed-length string can contain 1 to approximately 65,400 characters.
Object	4	Object variable used to refer to any Excel object
Variant (with numbers)	16	Any numeric value up to the range of a Double
Variant (with characters)	22 bytes + string length	Same range as for variable-length string
User-defined (using Type)	Number required by elements	The range of each element is the same as the range of its data type.

How to Create Variables

You can create a variable by declaring it with a special command or by just using it in a statement. When you declare your variable, you make Visual Basic aware of the variable's name and data type. This is called *explicit variable declaration*. There are several advantages to explicit variable declaration:

- Explicit variable declaration speeds up the execution of your procedure. Since Visual Basic knows the data type, it reserves only as much memory as is absolutely necessary to store the data.
- Explicit variable declaration makes your code easier to read and understand because all the variables are listed at the very beginning of the procedure.
- Explicit variable declaration helps prevent errors caused by misspelled variable names. Visual Basic automatically corrects the variable name based on the spelling used in the variable declaration.

If you don't let Visual Basic know about the variable prior to using it, you are implicitly telling VBA that you want to create this variable. Variables declared implicitly are automatically assigned the Variant data type (see

Table 4-1). Although implicit variable declaration is convenient (it allows you to create variables on the fly and assign values without knowing in advance the data type of the values being assigned), it can cause several problems, as outlined below:

- If you misspell a variable name in your procedure, Visual Basic may display a run-time error or create a new variable. You are guaranteed to waste some time troubleshooting problems that could have been easily avoided had you declared your variable at the beginning of the procedure.
- Since Visual Basic does not know what type of data your variable will store, it assigns it a Variant data type. This causes your procedure to run slower because Visual Basic has to check the type of data every time it deals with your variable. Because a Variant can store any type of data, Visual Basic has to reserve more memory to store your data.

How to Declare Variables

You declare a variable with the Dim keyword. Dim stands for dimension. The Dim keyword is followed by the name of the variable and then the variable type.

Suppose you want the procedure to display the age of an employee. Before you can calculate the age, you must feed to the procedure the employee's date of birth. To do this, you declare a variable called DateOfBirth, as follows:

```
Dim DateOfBirth As Date
```

Notice that the Dim keyword is followed by the name of the variable (DateOfBirth). This name can be anything you choose, as long as it is not one of the VBA keywords. Specify the data type the variable will hold by placing after its name the As keyword followed by one of the data types from Table 4-1. The Date data type tells Visual Basic that the variable DateOfBirth will store a date. To store the employee's age, declare the age variable as follows:

```
Dim age As Integer
```

The age variable will store the number of years between today's date and the employee's date of birth. Since age is displayed as a whole number, this variable has been assigned the Integer data type.

You may also want your procedure to keep track of the employee's name, so you declare another variable to hold the employee's first and last name:

```
Dim FullName As String
```

Since the word "Name" is on the VBA list of reserved words, using it in your VBA procedure would guarantee an error. To hold the employee's full name, call the variable FullName and declare it as the String data type since the data it will hold is text.

Declaring variables is regarded as a good programming practice because it makes programs easier to read and helps prevent certain types of errors.

Informal Variables

Variables that are not explicitly declared with Dim statements are said to be implicitly declared. These variables are automatically assigned a data type called Variant. They can hold numbers, strings, and other types of information. You can create a variable by simply assigning some value to a variable name anywhere in your VBA procedure. For example, you will implicitly declare a variable in the following way: DaysLeft = 100.

Now that you know how to declare your variables, let's take a look at a procedure that uses them:

```
Sub AgeCalc()
    ' variable declaration
    Dim FullName As String
    Dim DateOfBirth As Date
    Dim age As Integer

    ' assign values to variables
    FullName = "John Smith"
    DateOfBirth = #01/03/1967#

    ' calculate age
    age = Year(Now())-Year(DateOfBirth)

    ' print results to the Immediate window
    Debug.Print FullName & " is " & age & " years old."
End Sub
```

The variables are declared at the beginning of the procedure in which they are going to be used. In the procedure above, the variables are declared on separate lines. If you want, you can declare several variables on the same line, separating each variable name with a comma, as shown in the example below:

```
Dim FullName As String, DateOfBirth As Date, age As Integer
```

Notice that the Dim keyword appears only once at the beginning of the variable declaration line.

When Visual Basic executes the variable declaration statements, it creates the variables with the specified names and reserves memory space to store their values. Then specific values are assigned to these variables.

To assign a value to a variable, begin with a variable name followed by an equal sign. The value entered to the right of the equal sign is the data you want to store in the variable. The data you enter here must be of the type determined by the variable declaration. Text data should be surrounded by quotation marks and dates by the # characters.

Using the data supplied by the DateOfBirth variable, Visual Basic calculates the age of an employee and stores the result of the calculation in the age variable. Then the full name of the employee as well as the age is printed to the Immediate window using the instruction Debug.Print. When the Visual Basic procedure has executed, you must open the Immediate window to see the results.

Let's see what happens when you declare a variable with the incorrect data type. The purpose of the following procedure is to calculate the total number of rows in a worksheet and then display the results to the user in a dialog box.

```
Sub HowManyRows()
    Dim NumOfRows As Integer

    NumOfRows = Rows.Count
    MsgBox "The worksheet has " & NumOfRows & " rows."
End Sub
```

A wrong data type can cause an error. In the procedure above, when Visual Basic attempts to write the result of the Rows.Count statement to the variable NumOfRows, the procedure fails and Excel displays the message "Run-time error 6 — Overflow." This error results from selecting an invalid data type for that variable. The number of rows in a spreadsheet does not fit the Integer data range. To correct the problem, you should choose a data type that can accommodate a larger number:

```
Sub HowManyRows2()
    Dim NumOfRows As Long

    NumOfRows = Rows.Count
    MsgBox "The worksheet has " & NumOfRows & " rows."
End Sub
```

You can also correct the problem caused by the assignment of the wrong data type in the first example above by deleting the variable type (As Integer). When you rerun the procedure, Visual Basic will assign to your variable the Variant data type. Although Variants use up more memory than any other variable type and also slow down the speed at which your procedures run (because Visual Basic has to do extra work to check the Variant's context), when it comes to short procedures, the cost of using Variants is barely noticeable.

What Is the Variable Type?

You can quickly find out the type of a variable used in your procedure by right-clicking the variable name and selecting Quick Info from the shortcut menu.

Concatenation

You can combine two or more strings to form a new string. The joining operation is called concatenation. You have seen examples of concatenated strings in the AgeCalc and HowManyRows2 procedures above. Concatenation is represented by an ampersand character (&). For instance, "His name is " & FirstName will produce the following string: His name is John. The name of the person is determined by the contents of the FirstName variable. Notice that there is an extra space between is and the ending quote: "His name is ". Concatenation of strings also can be represented by a plus sign (+). However, many programmers prefer to restrict the plus sign to operations on numbers to eliminate ambiguity.

Specifying the Data Type of a Variable

If you don't specify the variable's data type in the Dim statement, you end up with an untyped variable. Untyped variables in VBA are always Variant data types. It's highly recommended that you create typed variables. When you declare a variable of a certain data type, your VBA procedure runs faster because Visual Basic does not have to stop to analyze the Variant variable to determine its type.

Visual Basic can work with many types of numeric variables. Integer variables can only hold whole numbers from –32,768 to 32,767. Other types of numeric variables are Long, Single, Double, and Currency. Long variables can hold whole numbers in the range –2,147,483,648 to 2,147,483,647. Unlike the Integer and Long variables, the Single and Double variables can hold decimals. String variables are used to refer to text. When you declare a variable of String data type, you can tell Visual Basic how long the string should be. For instance:

```
Dim extension As String * 3
```

declares a fixed-length String variable named extension that is three characters long. If you don't assign a specific length, the String variable will be dynamic. This means that Visual Basic will make enough space in computer memory to handle whatever amount of text is assigned to it.

After you declare a variable, you can only store the type of information in it that you determined in the declaration statement. Assigning string values to numeric variables or numeric values to String variables results in the error message "Type mismatch" or causes Visual Basic to modify the value. For example, if your variable was declared to hold whole numbers and your data uses decimals, Visual Basic will disregard the decimals and use only the whole part of the number. When you run the MyNumber procedure shown below, Visual Basic modifies the data to fit the variable's data type (Integer) and instead of 23.11 the variable ends up holding a value of 23.

```
Sub MyNumber()
    Dim myNum As Integer
```

```
    myNum = 23.11
    MsgBox myNum
End Sub
```

If you don't declare a variable with a Dim statement, you can still designate a type for it by using a special character at the end of the variable name. To declare the FirstName variable as String, you can append the dollar sign to the variable name, as shown below:

```
Dim FirstName$
```

The above declaration is the same as Dim FirstName As String. Other type declaration characters are shown in Table 4-2.

Table 4-2: Type declaration characters

Data Type	Character
Integer	%
Long	&
Single	!
Double	#
Currency	@
String	$

Notice that the type declaration characters can only be used with six data types. To use the type declaration character, append the character to the end of the variable name.

In the AgeCalc2 procedure below we use two type declaration characters shown in Table 4-2.

```
Sub AgeCalc2()
    ' variable declaration
    Dim FullName$
    Dim DateOfBirth As Date
    Dim age%

    ' assign values to variables
    FullName$ = "John Smith"
    DateOfBirth = #1/3/1967#

    ' calculate age
    age% = Year(Now()) - Year(DateOfBirth)

    ' print results to the Immediate window
    Debug.Print FullName$ & " is " & age% & " years old."
End Sub
```

Declaring Typed Variables

The variable type can be indicated by the As keyword or a type symbol. If you don't add the type symbol or the As command, the variable will be the default data type. VBA defaults to the Variant type.

Assigning Values to Variables

Now that you know how to name and declare variables and have seen examples of using variables in complete procedures, let's gain experience using them. We will begin by creating a variable and assigning it a specific value.

Hands-On 4-1: Writing a VBA Procedure with Variables

1. Open a new workbook and save it as **Practice_Excel04.xlsm.**
2. Activate the Visual Basic Editor window.
3. In the Project Explorer window select the new project and change the name of the project in the Properties window to **Chapter4.**
4. Choose **Insert | Module** to add a new module to the Chapter4 (Practice_Excel04.xlsm) VBA project.
5. In the Properties window change the name of Module1 to **Variables.**
6. In the Code window, enter the CalcCost procedure shown below:

```
Sub CalcCost()
    slsPrice = 35
    slsTax = 0.085

    Range("A1").Formula = "The cost of calculator"
    Range("A4").Formula = "Price"
    Range("B4").Formula = slsPrice
    Range("A5").Formula = "Sales Tax"
    Range("A6").Formula = "Cost"
    Range("B5").Formula = slsPrice * slsTax
    cost = slsPrice + (slsPrice * slsTax)

    With Range("B6")
        .Formula = cost
        .NumberFormat = "0.00"
    End With

    strMsg = "The calculator total is $" & cost & "."
    Range("A8").Formula = strMsg
End Sub
```

The above procedure calculates the cost of purchasing a calculator using the following assumptions: The price of a calculator is 35 dollars and the sales tax equals 8.5%.

The procedure uses four variables: slsPrice, slsTax, cost, and strMsg. Because none of these variables have been explicitly declared, they all have the same data type — Variant. The variables slsPrice and slsTax were created by assigning some values to variable names at the beginning of the procedure. The cost variable was assigned a value that is a result of a calculation: slsPrice + (slsPrice * slsTax). The cost calculation uses the values supplied by the slsPrice and slsTax variables. The strMsg variable puts together a text message to the user. This message is then entered as a complete sentence in a worksheet cell. When you assign values to variables, place an equal sign after the name of the variable. After the equal sign, you should enter the value of the variable. This can be a number, a formula, or text surrounded by quotation marks. While the values assigned to the variables slsPrice, slsTax, and cost are easily understood, the value stored in the strMsg variable is a little more involved. Let's examine the contents of the strMsg variable.

```
strMsg = "The calculator total is $" & cost & "."
```

- The string "The calculator total is " is surrounded by quotation marks. Notice that there is an extra space before the ending quote.
- The dollar sign inside the quotes is used to denote the type of Currency. Because the dollar symbol is a character, it is surrounded by the quotes.
- The & character allows appending to the string another string or the contents of a variable. The & character must be used every time you want to append a new piece of information to the previous string.
- The cost variable is a placeholder. The actual cost of the calculator will be displayed here when the procedure runs.
- The & character attaches yet another string.
- The period is surrounded by quotes. When you require a period at the end of a sentence, you must attach it separately when it follows the name of the variable.

Variable Initialization

When Visual Basic creates a new variable, it initializes the variable. Variables assume their default value. Numerical variables are set to zero (0), Boolean variables are initialized to False, String variables are set to the empty string (""), and Date variables are set to December 30, 1899.

Now let's execute the CalcCost procedure.

7. Position the cursor anywhere within the CalcCost procedure and choose **Run | Run Sub/UserForm.**

   When you run this procedure, Visual Basic may display the following message: "Compile error: Variable not defined." If this happens, click **OK** to close the message box. Visual Basic will select the slsPrice variable and highlight the name of the Sub CalcCost procedure. The title bar displays "Microsoft Visual Basic – Practice_Excel04.xlsm [break]." The Visual Basic break mode allows you to correct the problem before you continue. Later in this book, you will learn how to fix problems in break mode. For now, exit this mode by choosing **Run | Reset.** Now go to the top of the Code window and delete the statement Option Explicit that appears on the first line. The Option Explicit statement means that all variables used within this module must be formally declared. You will learn about this statement in the next section. When the Option Explicit statement is removed from the Code window, choose **Run | Run**

Sub/UserForm to rerun the procedure. This time, Visual Basic goes to work with no objections.

8. After the procedure has finished executing, press **Alt+F11** switch to Microsoft Excel.

   The result of the procedure should match Figure 4-1.

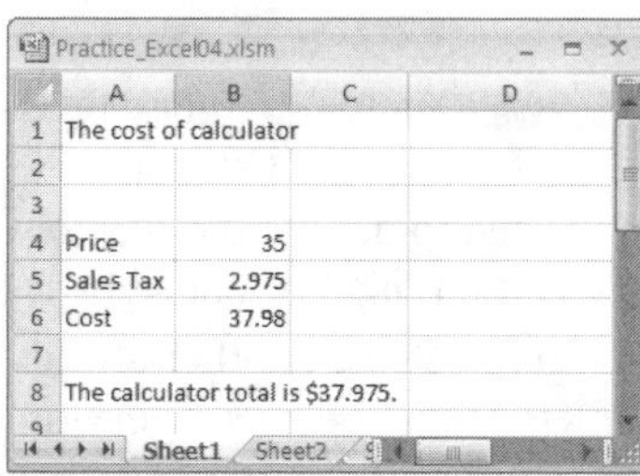

Figure 4-1: The VBA procedure can enter data and calculate results in a worksheet.

   Cell A8 displays the contents of the strMsg variable. Notice that the cost entered in cell B6 has two decimal places, while the cost in strMsg displays three decimals. To display the cost of a calculator with two decimal places in cell A8, you must apply the required format not to the cell but to the cost variable itself.

   VBA has special functions that allow you to change the format of data. To change the format of the cost variable, you will now use the Format function. This function has the following syntax:

```
Format(expression, format)
```

   Where expression is a value or variable that you want to format, and format is the type of format you want to apply.

9. Change the calculation of the cost variable in the CalcCost procedure:

```
cost = Format(slsPrice + (slsPrice * slsTax), "0.00")
```

10. Replace the With...End With block of instructions with the following:

```
Range("B6").Formula = cost
```

11. Replace the statement Range("B5").Formula = slsPrice * slsTax with the following instruction:

```
Range("B5").Formula = Format((slsPrice * slsTax), "0.00")
```

12. Rerun the modified procedure.

    Notice that now the text displayed in cell A8 shows the cost of the calculator formatted with two decimal places.

After trying out the CalcCost procedure, you may wonder why you should bother declaring variables if Visual Basic can handle undeclared variables so well. The CalcCost procedure is very short, so you don't need to worry about how many bytes of memory will be consumed each time Visual Basic uses the Variant variable. In short procedures, however, it is not the memory that matters but the mistakes you are bound to make when typing variable names. What will happen if the second time you use the cost variable you omit the "o" and refer to it as cst?

```
Range("B6").Formula = cst
```

What will you end up with if instead of slsTax, you use the word Tax in the formula?

```
Cost = Format(slsPrice + (slsPrice * Tax), "0.00")
```

The result of the CalcCost procedure after introducing the above mentioned mistakes is shown in Figure 4-2.

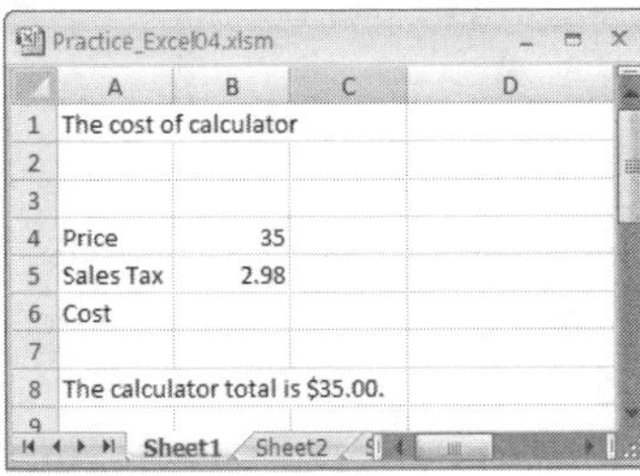

Figure 4-2: Mistakes in the names of variables can produce incorrect results.

Notice that in Figure 4-2 cell B6 does not show a value because Visual Basic does not find the assignment statement for the cst variable. Because Visual Basic does not know the sales tax, it displays the price of the calculator (see cell A8) as the total cost. Visual Basic does not guess. It simply does what you tell it to do. This brings us to the next section, which explains how to make sure errors of this kind don't occur.

Note: If you have made changes in the variable names as described above, before you continue, be sure to replace the names of the variables cst and tax with cost and slsTax in the appropriate lines of the VBA code.

Forcing Declaration of Variables

Visual Basic has the Option Explicit statement that automatically reminds you to formally declare all your variables. This statement has to be entered at the top of each of your modules. The Option Explicit statement will cause Visual Basic to generate an error message when you try to run a procedure that contains undeclared variables.

Hands-On 4-2: Writing a VBA Procedure with Explicitly Declared Variables

This Hands-On requires prior completion of Hands-On 4-1.

1. Return to the Code window where you entered the CalcCost procedure.
2. At the top of the module window (in the first line), type **Option Explicit** and press **Enter**. Excel will display the statement in blue.
3. Run the CalcCost procedure. Visual Basic displays the error message "Compile error: Variable not defined."
4. Click **OK** to exit the message box.

Visual Basic highlights the name of the variable slsPrice. Now you have to formally declare this variable. When you declare the slsPrice variable and rerun your procedure, Visual Basic will generate the same error as soon as it encounters another variable name that was not declared.

5. Enter the following declarations at the beginning of the CalcCost procedure:

```
' declaration of variables
Dim slsPrice As Currency
Dim slsTax As Single
Dim cost As Currency
Dim strMsg As String
```

The revised CalcCost procedure is shown below:

```
Sub CalcCost()

    ' declaration of variables
    Dim slsPrice As Currency
    Dim slsTax As Single
    Dim cost As Currency
    Dim strMsg As String

    slsPrice = 35
    slsTax = 0.085
    Range("A1").Formula = "The cost of calculator"
    Range("A4").Formula = "Price"
    Range("B4").Formula = slsPrice
    Range("A5").Formula = "Sales Tax"
    Range("A6").Formula = "Cost"
    Range("B5").Formula = Format((slsPrice * slsTax), "0.00")
    cost = Format(slsPrice + (slsPrice * slsTax), "0.00")

    Range("B6").Formula = cost
    strMsg = "The calculator total is $" & cost & "."
    Range("A8").Formula = strMsg
End Sub
```

Option Explicit in Every Module

To automatically include Option Explicit in every new module you create, follow these steps:

1. Choose Tools | Options.
2. Make sure that the Require Variable Declaration check box is selected in the Options dialog box (Editor tab).
3. Choose OK to close the Options dialog box.

From now on, every new module will be added with the Option Explicit statement in line 1. If you want to require variables to be explicitly declared in a previously created module, you must enter the Option Explicit statement manually by editing the module yourself.

Option Explicit forces formal (explicit) declaration of all variables in a particular module. One big advantage of using Option Explicit is that any mistyping of the variable name will be detected at compile time (when Visual Basic attempts to translate the source code to executable code). If included, the Option Explicit statement must appear in a module before any procedures.

Understanding the Scope of Variables

Variables can have different ranges of influence in a VBA procedure. The term *scope* defines the availability of a particular variable to the same procedure, other procedures, or other VBA projects.

Variables can have the following three levels of scope in Visual Basic for Applications:

- Procedure-level scope
- Module-level scope
- Project-level scope

Procedure-Level (Local) Variables

From this chapter, you already know how to declare a variable by using the Dim keyword. The position of the Dim keyword in the module sheet determines the scope of a variable. Variables declared with the Dim keyword placed within a VBA procedure have a *procedure-level scope*.

Procedure-level variables are frequently referred to as *local variables*. Local variables can only be used in the procedure in which they were declared. Undeclared variables always have a procedure-level scope. A variable's name must be unique within its scope. This means that you cannot declare two variables with the same name in the same procedure. However, you can use the same variable name in different procedures. In other words, the CalcCost procedure can have the slsTax variable, and the ExpenseRep procedure in the same module can have its own variable called slsTax. Both variables are independent of each other.

Module-Level Variables

Local variables help save computer memory. As soon as the procedure ends, the variable dies, and Visual Basic returns the memory space used by the variable to the computer. In programming, however, you often want the variable to be available to other VBA procedures after the procedure in which the variable was declared has finished running. This situation requires that you change the scope of a variable. Instead of a procedure-level variable, you want to declare a module-level variable. To declare a module-level variable, you must place the Dim keyword at the top of the module sheet before any procedures (just below the Option Explicit keyword). For instance, to make the slsTax variable available to any other procedure in the Variables module, declare the slsTax variable in the following way:

```
Option Explicit
Dim slsTax As Single
```

```
Sub CalcCost()
...Instructions of the procedure...
End Sub
```

In the example above, the Dim keyword is located at the top of the module, below the Option Explicit statement. Before you can see how this works, you need another procedure that uses the slsTax variable. Let's write a new VBA procedure named ExpenseRep.

Hands-On 4-3: Writing Another VBA Procedure with a Module-Level Variable

1. In the Code window, cut the declaration line Dim slsTax As Single in the Variables module from the CalcCost procedure and paste it at the top of the module sheet below the Option Explicit statement.
2. In the same module where the CalcCost procedure is located, enter the code of the ExpenseRep procedure as shown below:

```
Sub ExpenseRep()
    Dim slsPrice As Currency
    Dim cost As Currency

    slsPrice = 55.99

    cost = slsPrice + (slsPrice * slsTax)
    MsgBox slsTax
    MsgBox cost
End Sub
```

   The ExpenseRep procedure declares two Currency type variables: slsPrice and cost. The slsPrice variable is then assigned a value of 55.99. The slsPrice variable is independent of the slsPrice variable that is declared within the CalcCost procedure.

   The ExpenseRep procedure calculates the cost of a purchase. The cost includes the sales tax stored in the slsTax variable. Because the sales tax is the same as the one used in the CalcCost procedure, the slsTax variable has been declared at the module level.

3. Run the ExpenseRep procedure.

   Because you have not yet run the CalcCost procedure Visual Basic does not know the value of the slsTax, so it displays zero in the first message box.

4. Run the CalcCost procedure.

   After Visual Basic executes the CalcCost procedure that you revised in the earlier exercise, the contents of the slsTax variable equals 0.085. If slsTax were a local variable, the contents of this variable would be empty upon the termination of the CalcCost procedure.

   When you run the CalcCost procedure, Visual Basic erases the contents of all the variables except for the slsTax variable, which was declared at a module level.

5. Run the ExpenseRep procedure again.

As soon as you attempt to calculate the cost by running the ExpenseRep procedure, Visual Basic retrieves the value of the slsTax variable and uses it in the calculation.

Private Variables

When you declare variables at a module level, you can use the Private keyword instead of the Dim keyword. For instance:

```
Private slsTax As Single
```

Private variables are available only to the procedures that are part of the module where they were declared. Private variables are always declared at the top of the module after the Option Explicit statement.

Keeping the Project-Level Variable Private

To prevent a project-level variable's contents from being referenced outside its project, you can use the Option Private Module statement at the top of the module sheet, just below the Option Explicit statement and before the declaration line. For example:

```
Option Explicit
Option Private Module
Public slsTax As Single

Sub CalcCost()
...Instructions of the procedure...
End Sub
```

Project-Level Variables

Module-level variables that are declared with the Public keyword (instead of Dim) have project-level scope. This means that they can be used in any Visual Basic for Applications module. When you want to work with a variable in all the procedures in all the open VBA projects, you must declare it with the Public keyword. For instance:

```
Option Explicit
Public slsTax As Single
Sub CalcCost()
...Instructions of the procedure...
End Sub
```

Notice that the slsTax variable declared at the top of the module with the Public keyword will now be available to any other procedure or VBA project.

Lifetime of Variables

In addition to scope, variables have a lifetime. The *lifetime* of a variable determines how long a variable retains its value. Module-level and project-level variables preserve their values as long as the project is open. Visual Basic, however, can reinitialize these variables if required by the program's logic. Local variables declared with the Dim statement lose their values when a procedure has finished. Local variables have a lifetime as long as a procedure is running, and they are reinitialized every time the program is run. Visual

Basic allows you to extend the lifetime of a local variable by changing the way it is declared.

Understanding and Using Static Variables

A variable declared with the Static keyword is a special type of local variable. Static variables are declared at the procedure level. Unlike local variables declared with the Dim keyword, static variables do not lose their contents when the program is not in their procedure. For example, when a VBA procedure with a static variable calls another procedure, after Visual Basic executes the statements of the called procedure and returns to the calling procedure, the static variable still retains the original value. The CostOfPurchase procedure shown below demonstrates the use of the static variable named allPurchase. Notice how this variable keeps track of the running total.

Hands-On 4-4: Writing a VBA Procedure with a Static Variable

1. In the Code window of the variable's module, write the following procedure:

```
Sub CostOfPurchase()
    ' declare variables
    Static allPurchase
    Dim newPurchase As String
    Dim purchCost As Single

    newPurchase = InputBox("Enter the cost of a purchase:")
    purchCost = CSng(newPurchase)
    allPurchase = allPurchase + purchCost

    ' display results
    MsgBox "The cost of a new purchase is: " & newPurchase
    MsgBox "The running cost is: " & allPurchase
End Sub
```

The above procedure begins with declaring a static variable named allPurchase and two other local variables: newPurchase and purchCost. The InputBox function used in this procedure displays a dialog box and waits for the user to enter the value. As soon as you input the value and click OK, Visual Basic assigns this value to the variable newPurchase.

The InputBox function is discussed in detail in Chapter 5. Because the result of the InputBox function is always a string, the newPurchase variable was declared as the String data type. You can't, however, use strings in mathematical calculations. That's why the next instruction uses a type conversion function (CSng) to translate the text value into a numeric variable of the Single data type. The CSng function requires one argument — the value you want to translate. The number obtained as the result of the CSng function is then stored in the variable purchCost.

The next instruction, allPurchase = allPurchase + purchCost, adds to the current purchase value the new value supplied by the InputBox function.

2. Position the cursor anywhere within the CostOfPurchase procedure and press **F5**. When the dialog box appears, enter a number. For example, enter **100** and click **OK** or press **Enter**. Visual Basic displays the message "The cost of a new purchase is: 100." Click **OK** in the message box. Visual Basic displays the second message "The running cost is: 100."

   When you run this procedure for the first time, the content of the allPurchase variable is the same as the content of the purchCost variable.

3. Rerun the same procedure. When the input dialog appears, enter another number. For example, enter **50** and click **OK** or press **Enter**. Visual Basic displays the message "The cost of a new purchase is: 50." Click **OK** in the message box. Visual Basic displays the second message "The running cost is: 150."

   When you run the procedure the second time, the value of the static variable is increased by the new value supplied in the dialog box. You can run the CostOfPurchase procedure as many times as you want. The allPurchase variable will keep the running total for as long as the project is open.

Type Conversion Functions

To find out more about the CSng function (and other type conversion functions), position the insertion point anywhere within the word CSng and press F1.

Declaring and Using Object Variables

The variables that you've learned about thus far are used to store data. Storing data is the main reason for using "normal" variables in your procedures. In addition to the normal variables that store data, there are special variables that refer to the Visual Basic objects. These variables are called *object variables*. In Chapter 3, you worked with several objects in the Immediate window. Now, you will learn how you can represent an object with the object variable.

Object variables don't store data; instead, they tell where the data is located. For example, with the object variable you can tell Visual Basic that the data is located in cell E10 of the active worksheet. Object variables make it easy to locate data. When writing Visual Basic procedures, you often need to write long instructions, such as:

```
Worksheets("Sheet1").Range(Cells(1, 1), Cells(10, 5).Select
```

Instead of using long references to the object, you can declare an object variable that will tell Visual Basic where the data is located. Object variables are declared similarly to the variables you already know. The only difference is that after the As keyword, you enter the word Object as the data type. For instance:

```
Dim myRange As Object
```

The statement above declares the object variable named myRange.

Well, it's not enough to declare the object variable. You also have to assign a specific value to the object variable before you can use this variable in your procedure. Assign a value to the object variable by using the Set keyword. The Set keyword must be followed by the equal sign and the value that the variable will refer to. For example:

```
Set myRange = Worksheets("Sheet1").Range(Cells(1, 1), Cells(10, 5))
```

The above statement assigns a value to the object variable myRange. This value refers to cells A1:E10 in Sheet1. If you omit the word Set, Visual Basic will display an error message — "Run-time error 91: Object variable or With block variable not set."

Again, it's time to see a practical example. The UseObjVariable procedure shown below demonstrates the use of the object variable called myRange.

Hands-On 4-5: Writing a VBA Procedure with Object Variables

1. In the Code window of the Variables module, write the following procedure:

```
Sub UseObjVariable()
    Dim myRange As Object
    Set myRange = Worksheets("Sheet1").Range(Cells(1, 1), Cells(10, 5))
    myRange.BorderAround Weight:=xlMedium

    With myRange.Interior
    .ColorIndex = 6
    .Pattern = xlSolid
    End With

    Set myRange = Worksheets("Sheet1").Range(Cells(12, 5), Cells(12, 10))
    myRange.Value = 54

    Debug.Print IsObject(myRange)
End Sub
```

Let's examine the code of the UseObjVariable procedure line by line. The procedure begins with the declaration of the object variable myRange. The next statement sets the object variable myRange to the range A1:E10 on Sheet1. From now on, every time you want to reference this range, instead of using the entire object's address, you'll use the shortcut — the name of the object variable. The purpose of this procedure is to create a border around the range A1:E10. Instead of writing a long instruction:

```
Worksheets("Sheet1").Range(Cells(1, 1), Cells(10, 5)).BorderAround
Weight:=xlMedium
```

you can take a shortcut by using the name of the object variable:

```
myRange.BorderAround Weight:=xlMedium
```

The next series of statements changes the color of the selected range of cells (A1:E10). Again, you don't need to write the long instruction to reference the object that you want to manipulate. Instead of the full object name, you can use the myRange object variable. The next statement assigns a new reference to the object variable myRange. Visual Basic forgets the old reference, and the next time you use myRange, it refers to another range (E12:J12).

After the number 54 is entered in the new range (E12:J12), the procedure shows you how you can make sure that a specific variable is of the Object type. The instruction Debug.Print IsObject(myRange) will enter True in the Immediate window if myRange is an object variable. IsObject is a VBA function that indicates whether a specific value represents an object variable.

2. Position the cursor anywhere within the UseObjVariable procedure and press **F5**.

Advantages of Using Object Variables

- They can be used instead of the actual object.
- They are shorter and easier to remember than the actual values to which they point.
- You can change their meaning while your procedure is running.

Using Specific Object Variables

The object variable can refer to any type of object. Because Visual Basic has many types of objects, it's a good idea to create object variables that refer to a particular type of object to make your programs more readable and faster. For instance, in the UseObjVariable procedure (see the previous section), instead of the generic object variable (Object), you can declare the myRange object variable as a Range object:

```
Dim myRange As Range
```

If you want to refer to a particular worksheet, then you can declare the Worksheet object:

```
Dim mySheet As Worksheet
Set mySheet = Worksheets("Marketing")
```

When the object variable is no longer needed, you can assign Nothing to it. This frees up memory and system resources:

```
Set mySheet = Nothing
```

Finding a Variable Definition

When you find an instruction in a VBA procedure that assigns a value to a variable, you can quickly locate the definition of the variable by selecting the variable name and pressing Shift+F2 or choosing View | Definition. Visual Basic will jump to the variable declaration line. To return your mouse pointer to its previous position, press Ctrl+Shift+F2 or choose View | Last Position. Let's take a look how this works in the following Hands-On.

Hands-On 4-6: Finding a Variable Definition in the Code Window

1. Locate the code of the CostOfPurchase procedure.
2. Locate the statement purchCost = CSng(newPurchase).
3. Right-click the variable name and choose **Definition** from the shortcut menu.
4. Return to the previous location by pressing **Ctrl+Shift+F2**.
5. Try finding definitions of other variables in other procedures created in this chapter. Each time use a different way to jump to the variable definition.

What Type Is This Variable?

You can find out the type of a variable by using one of the Visual Basic built-in functions. See Chapter 5 for a sample usage of the VarType function.

Using Constants in VBA Procedures

The contents of a variable can change while your procedure is executing. If your procedure needs to refer to unchanged values over and over again, you should use constants. A *constant* is like a named variable that always refers to the same value. Visual Basic requires that you declare constants before you use them. Declare constants by using the Const statement, as in the following examples:

```
Const dialogName = "Enter Data" As String
Const slsTax = 8.5
Const ColorIdx = 3
```

A constant, like a variable, has a scope. To make a constant available within a single procedure, declare it at the procedure level, just below the name of the procedure. For instance:

```
Sub WedAnniv()
Const Age As Integer = 25
...instructions...
End Sub
```

If you want to use a constant in all the procedures of a module, use the Private keyword in front of the Const statement. For instance:

```
Private Const dsk = "B:" As String
```

The Private constant has to be declared at the top of the module, just before the first Sub statement.

If you want to make a constant available to all modules in the workbook, use the Public keyword in front of the Const statement. For instance:

```
Public Const NumOfChar = 255 As Integer
```

The Public constant has to be declared at the top of the module, just before the first Sub statement.

When declaring a constant, you can use any one of the following data types: Boolean, Byte, Integer, Long, Currency, Single, Double, Date, String, or Variant.

Like variables, several constants can be declared on one line if separated by commas. For instance:

```
Const Age As Integer = 25, City As String = "Denver", PayCk As Currency = 350
```

Using constants makes your VBA procedures more readable and easier to maintain. For example, if you refer to a certain value several times in your procedure, use a constant instead of the value. This way, if the value changes (for example, the sales tax goes up), you can simply change the value in the declaration of the Const statement instead of tracking down every occurrence of that value.

Built-in Constants

Both Microsoft Excel and Visual Basic for Applications have a long list of predefined constants that do not need to be declared. These built-in constants can be looked up using the Object Browser window. Let's open the Object Browser to take a look at the list of Excel constants.

Hands-On 4-7: Viewing Excel Constants in the Object Browser

1. In the Visual Basic Editor window, choose **View | Object Browser**.
2. In the Project/Library list box, click the drop-down arrow and select **Excel**.
3. Enter **constants** as the search text in the Search box and press **Enter** or click the **Search** button. Visual Basic shows the result of the search in the Search Results area.
4. Scroll down in the Classes list box to locate and then select **Constants** (see Figure 4-3). The right side of the Object Browser window displays a list of all built-in constants that are available in the Microsoft Excel object library. Notice that the names of all the constants begin with the prefix "xl."

5. To look up VBA constants, choose **VBA** in the Project/Library list box. Notice that the names of the VBA built-in constants begin with the prefix "vb."

Figure 4-3: Use the Object Browser to look up any built-in constant.

The best way to learn about predefined constants is by using the macro recorder. Let's take a few minutes to record the process of minimizing the active window.

Hands-On 4-8: Learning about Constants Using the Built-in Macro Recorder

1. In the Microsoft Excel window, choose **View | Macros | Record Macro**.
2. Type **MiniWindow** as the name of the macro. Under Store macro in, select **This Workbook**. Then click **OK**.
3. Click the **Minimize** button. Make sure you minimize the document window and not the Excel application window.
4. Choose **View | Macros | Stop Recording**.
5. Maximize the minimized document window.
6. Switch to the Visual Basic Editor window and double-click **Module1** in the Project Explorer window. The Code window displays the following procedure:

```
Sub MiniWindow()
'
' MiniWindow Macro
'
```

```
'
    ActiveWindow.WindowState = xlMinimized
End Sub
```

Sometimes you may see VBA procedures that use values instead of built-in constant names. For example, the actual value of xlMaximized is –4137, xlMinimized has a value of –4140, and xlNormal has a value of –4143 (see Figure 4-4).

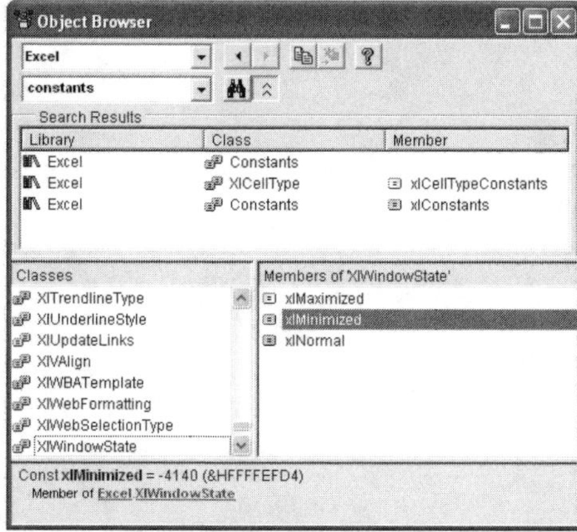

Figure 4-4: You can see the actual value of a constant by selecting its name in the Object Browser.

Chapter Summary

This chapter introduced several new VBA concepts such as data types, variables, and constants. You learned how to declare various types of variables and define their types. You also saw the difference between a variable and a constant. Now that you know what variables are and how to use them, you are capable of creating VBA procedures that can manipulate data in more meaningful ways than you saw in previous chapters.

In the next chapter, you will expand your VBA knowledge by learning how to write procedures with arguments as well as function procedures. In addition, you will learn about built-in functions that will allow your VBA procedure to interact with users.

Chapter 5

VBA Procedures: Subroutines and Functions

Earlier in this book you learned that a procedure is a group of instructions that allows you to accomplish specific tasks when your program runs. VBA has three types of procedures:

- **Subroutine procedures** (*subroutines*) perform some useful tasks but don't return any values. They begin with the keyword Sub and end with the keywords End Sub. Subroutines can be recorded with the macro recorder (as you did in Chapter 1) or written from scratch in the Visual Basic Editor window (see Chapters 3 and 4). In Chapter 1, you learned various ways to execute this type of procedure.
- **Function procedures** (*functions*) perform specific tasks that return values. They begin with the keyword Function and end with the keywords End Function. In this chapter, you will create your first function procedure. Function procedures can be executed from a subroutine or accessed from a worksheet just like any Excel built-in function.
- **Property procedures** are used with custom objects. With property procedures you can set and get the value of an object's property or set a reference to an object. You will learn how to create custom objects and use property procedures in Chapter 9.

In this chapter, you will learn how to create and execute custom functions. In addition, you find out how variables (see Chapter 4) are used in passing values to subroutines and functions. Later in the chapter, you will take a thorough look at the two most useful VBA functions: MsgBox and InputBox.

About Function Procedures

With the hundreds of built-in Excel functions you can perform a wide variety of calculations automatically. However, there will be times when you may require a custom calculation. With VBA programming, you can quickly fulfill this special need by creating a function procedure. You can build any functions that are not supplied with Excel.

Among the reasons for creating custom VBA functions are the following:

- To analyze data and perform calculations
- To modify data and report information
- To take a specific action based on supplied or calculated data

Creating a Function Procedure

Like Excel functions, function procedures perform calculations and return values. The best way to learn about functions is to create one, so let's get started. After setting up a new VBA project, you will create a function procedure that sums two values.

Hands-On 5-1: Writing a Simple Function Procedure

1. Open a new Excel workbook and save it as **C:\Ex07_ByExample\Practice_Excel05.xlsm**.
2. Switch to the Visual Basic Editor window and select **VBAProject (Practice_Excel05.xlsm)**.
3. In the Properties window, change the name of the project name to **ProcAndFunctions**.
4. Select the **ProcAndFunctions (Practice_Excel05.xlsm)** project in the Project Explorer window, and choose **Insert | Module**.
5. In the Properties window, change the Module1 name to **Sample1**.
6. In the Project Explorer window, highlight **Sample1** and click anywhere in the Code window. Choose **Insert | Procedure**. The Add Procedure dialog box appears.
7. Make the following entries in the Add Procedure dialog box (see Figure 5-1):

   Name: **SumItUp**
   Type: **Function**
   Scope: **Public**

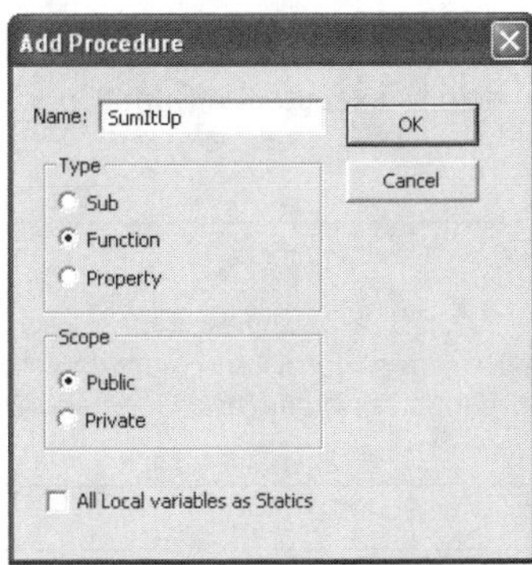

Figure 5-1: When you use the Add Procedure dialog box, Visual Basic automatically creates the procedure type you choose.

8. Click **OK** to close the Add Procedure dialog box. Visual Basic enters an empty function procedure that looks like this:

```
Public Function SumItUp()
End Function
```

9. Modify the function declaration as follows:

```
Public Function SumItUp(m,n)
End Function
```

   The purpose of this function is to add two values. Instead of passing the actual values to the function, you can make the function more flexible by providing it with the arguments in the form of variables. By doing this, your custom function will be able to add any two numbers that you specify. Each of the passed variables (m, n) represents a value. You will supply the values for each of these variables when you run this function.

10. Type the following statement between the Public Function and End Function statements:

```
SumItUp = m + n
```

This statement instructs Visual Basic to add the value stored in the n variable to the value stored in the m variable and return the result to the SumItUp function. To specify the value that you want the function to return, type the function name followed by the equal sign and the value you want it to return. In the statement above, set the name of the function equal to the total of m + n. The completed custom function procedure is shown below:

```
Public Function SumItUp(m,n)
    SumItUp = m + n
End Function
```

The first statement declares the name of the function procedure. The Public keyword indicates that the function is accessible to all other procedures in all other modules. The Public keyword is optional. Notice the keyword Function followed by the name of the function (SumItUp) and a pair of parentheses. In the parentheses, you will list the data items that the function will use in the calculation. Every function procedure ends with the End Function statement.

Note: Check out Hands-On 5-2 to see how to execute the SumItUp function.

About Function Names

Function names should suggest the role that the function performs and must conform to the rules for naming variables (see Chapter 4, "Using Variables, Types, and Constants").

Scoping VBA Procedures

In the previous chapter you learned that the variable's scope determines which modules and procedures it can be used in. Like variables, VBA procedures have scope. A procedure scope determines whether it can be called by procedures in other modules. By default, all VBA procedures are public. This means they can be called by other procedures in any module. Since procedures are public by default, you can skip the Public keyword if you want. And if you replace the Public keyword with the Private keyword, your procedure will be available only to other procedures in the same module, not to procedures in other modules.

Executing a Function Procedure

Congratulations! In the previous section you created your first function. However, a function procedure is useless unless you know how to execute it. This section shows you how to put your new function to work.

As you already know, Visual Basic provides you with various ways of executing a subroutine procedure. Unlike a subroutine, a function procedure can be executed in just two ways. You can use it in a worksheet formula or you can call it from another procedure. Function procedures that you create in VBA cannot be accessed by choosing Developer | Macros in the Microsoft Excel window. And they cannot be run by pressing the F5 key when the mouse pointer is located inside the code of the function procedure. In the following sections, you will learn special techniques for executing functions.

Running a Function Procedure from a Worksheet

A custom function procedure is like an Excel built-in function. If you don't know the exact name of the function or its arguments, you can use the Formula palette to help enter the required function in a worksheet as shown below.

Hands-On 5-2: Executing a Function Procedure from within an Excel Worksheet

1. Switch to the Microsoft Excel window, and select any cell.
2. Click the **Insert Function** (*fx*) button on the Formula bar. Excel displays the Insert Function dialog box. The lower portion of the dialog box displays an alphabetical listing of all the functions in the selected category.
3. In the category drop-down box, select **User Defined.** In the function name box, locate and select the **SumItUp** function that was created earlier in this chapter. When you highlight the name of the function in the function name box, the bottom part of the dialog box displays the function's syntax: SumItUp(m,n).

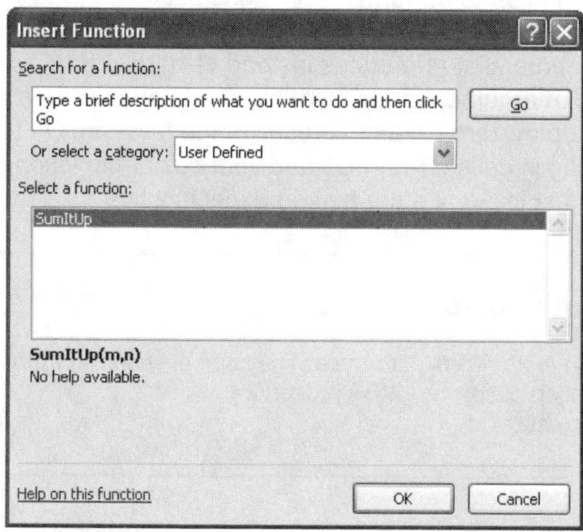

Figure 5-2: VBA custom function procedures are listed under the User Defined category in the Insert Function dialog box. They also appear in the list of all Excel built-in functions when you select All in the category drop-down.

4. Click **OK** to begin writing a formula. The Function Arguments dialog box appears, as shown in Figure 5-3. This dialog displays the name of the function and each of its arguments: m and n.
5. Enter the values for the arguments as shown in Figure 5-3, or enter your own values. As you type the values in the argument text boxes, Excel displays the values you entered and the current result of the function. Because both arguments (m and n) are required, if you skip either one of the arguments, the function will return an error.

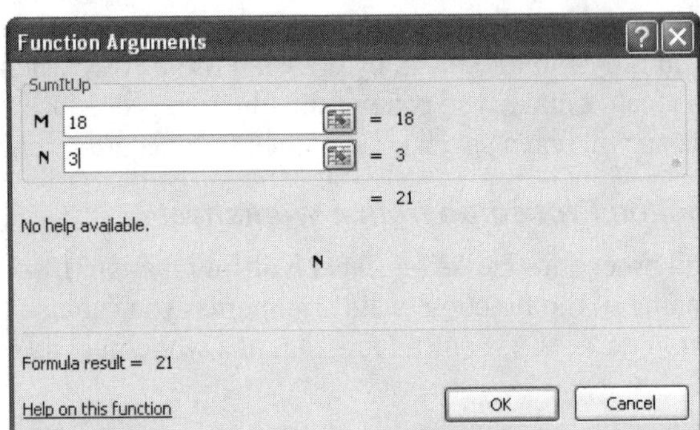

Figure 5-3: The Formula palette feature is helpful in entering any worksheet function, whether built-in or custom-made with VBA programming.

6. Click **OK** to exit the Function Arguments dialog.

   Excel enters the SumItUp function in the selected cell and displays its result.
7. To edit the function, select the cell that displays the function's result and click the **Insert Function** (*fx*) button to access the Function Arguments dialog box. Enter new values for the function's m and n arguments and click **OK**.

Note: To edit the arguments' values directly in the cell, double-click the cell containing the function and make the necessary changes. You may also set up the SumItUp function to perform calculations based on the values entered in cells. To do this, in the Function Arguments dialog box (Figure 5-3 above) simply enter cell references instead of values. For example, enter C1 for the m argument and C2 for the n argument. When you click OK, Excel will display zero (0) as the result of the function. On the worksheet, enter the values in cells C1 and C2 and your custom function will recalculate the result just like any other built-in Excel function.

Private Functions Are Not Visible to Users

Functions declared with the Private keyword do not appear in the Insert Function dialog box. Private functions cannot be used in a formula. They can only be run from another VBA procedure.

Quick Access to Custom Functions

As soon as you create your first VBA function with Public scope, Excel adds a User Defined category in the Insert Function dialog box. By selecting this category, you can gain quick access to your custom VBA functions.

Running a Function Procedure from Another VBA Procedure

As mentioned earlier, you cannot run a function procedure from the Visual Basic Editor window by placing the mouse pointer within the code of the function procedure and pressing F5. Nor can you choose Run | Run Sub/UserForm. To run a function, you must call the function name from another procedure. To execute a custom function, write a VBA subroutine and call the function when you need it. The following procedure calls the SumItUp function and prints the result of the calculation to the Immediate window.

Hands-On 5-3: Executing a Function from a VBA Procedure

1. In the same module where you entered the code of the SumItUp function procedure, enter the RunSumItUp procedure. You may copy the procedure code from **C:\Ex07_HandsOn\Ex07_Chapter05.txt.**

```
Sub RunSumItUp()
    Dim m As Single, n As Single
    m = 370000
    n = 3459.77

    Debug.Print SumItUp(m,n)
    MsgBox "Open the Immediate window to see the result."
End Sub
```

   Notice how the above subroutine uses one Dim statement to declare the m and n variables. These variables will be used to feed the data to the function. The next two statements assign the values to those variables. Next, Visual Basic calls the SumItUp function and passes the values stored in the m and n variables to it. When the function procedure statement SumItUp = m + n is executed, Visual Basic returns to the RunSumItUp subroutine and uses the Debug.Print statement to print the function's result to the Immediate window. Finally, the MsgBox function informs the user where to look for the result. You can find more information about using the MsgBox function later in this chapter.

2. Place the mouse pointer anywhere within the RunSumItUp procedure and press **F5** to run it.

Ensuring Availability of Your Custom Functions

Your custom VBA function is only available as long as the workbook where the function is stored is open. If you close the workbook, the function is no longer available. To make sure that your custom VBA functions are available every time you work with Microsoft Excel, you can do one of the following:

- Store your functions in the Personal macro workbook.
- Save the workbook with your custom VBA function in the XLStart folder.
- Set up a reference to the workbook containing your custom functions. (See Chapter 3 for information about setting up a reference to another project.)

A Quick Test of a Function

After you write your custom function, you can quickly try it out in the Immediate window. To display the value of a function, open the Immediate window and type a question mark (?) followed by the function name. Remember to enclose the function's arguments in parentheses. For example, type:

```
? SumItUp(54, 367.24) and press Enter.
```

Your function procedure runs, using the values you passed for the *m* and *n* arguments. The result of the function appears on a line below:

```
421.24
```

Passing Arguments

So far you've created simple VBA procedures that carried out specific tasks. These procedures did not require that you provide additional data before they could be run. However, in real life, procedures (both subroutines and functions) often take arguments. *Arguments* are one or more values needed for a procedure to do something. Arguments are entered between parentheses. Multiple arguments are separated with commas.

Having used Excel for a while, you already know that Excel's built-in functions can produce different results based on the values you supply to them. For example, if cells A4 and A5 contain the numbers 5 and 10, respectively, the Sum function =SUM(A4:A5) will return 15, unless you change the values entered in the specified cells. Just like you can pass any values to Excel's built-in functions, you can pass values to custom VBA procedures.

Let's see how you can pass some values from a subroutine procedure to the SumItUp function. We will write a procedure that collects the user's first and last name. Next, we will call the SumItUp function to get the sum of characters in a person's first and last names.

Hands-On 5-4: Passing Arguments to Functions (Example 1)

1. Type the following NumOfCharacters subroutine in the same module (Sample1) where you entered the SumItUp function:

```
Sub NumOfCharacters()
    Dim f As Integer
    Dim l As Integer
```

```
    f = Len(InputBox("Enter first name:"))
    l = Len(InputBox("Enter last name:"))

    MsgBox SumItUp(f,l)
End Sub
```

2. Place the mouse pointer within the code of the NumOfCharacters procedure and press **F5**. Visual Basic displays the input box asking for the first name. This box is generated by the following function: InputBox("Enter first name:"). For more information on the use of this function, see the section titled "Using the InputBox Function" later in this chapter.
3. Enter any name, and press **Enter** or click **OK**. Visual Basic takes the text you entered and supplies it as an argument to the Len function. The Len function calculates the number of characters in the supplied text. Visual Basic places the result of the Len function in the f variable for further reference. After that, Visual Basic displays the next input box, this time asking for the last name.
4. Enter any last name, and press **Enter** or click **OK.**

   Visual Basic passes the last name to the Len function to get the number of characters. Then that number is stored in the l variable. What happens next? Visual Basic encounters the MsgBox function. This function tells Visual Basic to display the result of the SumItUp function. However, because the result is not yet ready, Visual Basic jumps quickly to the SumItUp function to perform the calculation using the values saved earlier in the f and l variables. Inside the function procedure, Visual Basic substitutes the m argument with the value of the f variable and the n argument with the value of the l variable. Once the substitution is done, Visual Basic adds up the two numbers and returns the result to the SumItUp function.

   There are no more tasks to perform inside the function procedure, so Visual Basic returns to the subroutine and provides the SumItUp function's result as an argument to the MsgBox function. Now a message appears on the screen displaying the total number of characters.
5. Click **OK** to exit the message box.

   You can run the NumOfCharacters procedure as many times as you'd like, each time supplying different first and last names.

Now, let's look at another example of passing arguments using variables.

Hands-On 5-5: Passing Arguments to Functions (Example 2)

1. Add a new module to the ProcAndFunctions (Practice_Excel05.xlsm) project and change the module's name to **Sample2**.
2. Activate the Sample2 module and enter the EnterText subroutine as shown below:

```
Sub EnterText()
    Dim m As String, n As String, r As String
```

```
    m = InputBox ("Enter your first name:")
    n = InputBox("Enter your last name:")
    r = JoinText(m, n)

    MsgBox r
End Sub
```

3. Enter the following function procedure:

```
Function JoinText(k,o)
    JoinText = k + " " + o
End Function
```

As Visual Basic executes the statements of the procedure, it collects the data from the user and stores the values of the first and last names in the variables m and n. Then these values are passed to the JoinText function. Visual Basic substitutes the variables' contents for the arguments of the JoinText function and assigns the result to the name of the function (JoinText). When Visual Basic returns to the EnterText procedure, it stores the function's value in the r variable. The MsgBox function then displays the contents of the r variable in a message box. The result is the full name of the user (first and last names separated by a space).

4. Place the cursor anywhere inside the code of the EnterText procedure and press **F5** to run it.

Note: You can call the JoinText function directly from the MsgBox function like this:

```
MsgBox JoinText(m, n)
```

What Function Procedures Cannot Do

Functions cannot perform any actions. For instance, they cannot include statements for inserting, deleting, or formatting data in a worksheet; opening files; or changing the way the screen looks.

If you don't specify the data type, Visual Basic assigns the default type (Variant data type) to your function's result. When you specify the data type for your function's result, you get the same advantages as when you specify the data type for your variables: Your procedure uses memory more efficiently, and therefore it runs faster.

To pass a specific value from a function to a subroutine, assign the value to the name of the function. For example, the NumOfDays function shown below passes the value of 7 to the subroutine DaysInAWeek.

```
Function NumOfDays()
    NumOfDays = 7
End Function

Sub DaysInAWeek()
    MsgBox "There are " & NumOfDays & " days in a week."
End Sub
```

Specifying Argument Types

In the preceding section, you learned that functions perform some calculations based on data received through their arguments. When you declare a function procedure, you list the names of arguments inside a set of parentheses. Argument names are like variables. Each argument name refers to whatever value you provide at the time the function is called. When a subroutine calls a function procedure, it passes the required arguments as variables to it. Once the function does something, the result is assigned to the function name. Notice that the function procedure's name is used as if it were a variable.

Like variables, functions can have types. The result of your function procedure can be String, Integer, Long, etc. To specify the data type for your function's result, add the keyword As and the name of the desired data type to the end of the function declaration line. For example:

```
Function MultiplyIt(num1, num2) As Integer
```

Let's take a look at an example of a function that returns an Integer number, although the arguments passed to it are declared as Single data types in a calling subroutine.

Hands-On 5-6: Passing Arguments to Functions (Example 3)

1. Add a new module to the ProcAndFunctions (Practice_Excel05.xlsm) project and change the module's name to **Sample3**.
2. Activate the Sample3 module and enter the HowMuch subroutine as shown below:

```
Sub HowMuch()
    Dim num1 As Single
    Dim num2 As Single
    Dim result As Single

    num1 = 45.33
    num2 = 19.24

    result = MultiplyIt(num1, num2)
    MsgBox result
End Sub
```

3. Enter the following function procedure below the HowMuch subroutine:

```
Function MultiplyIt(num1, num2) As Integer
    MultiplyIt = num1 * num2
End Function
```

Because the values stored in the variables num1 and num2 are not whole numbers, to ensure that the result of multiplication is a whole number, you may want to assign the Integer data type to the result of the function. If you don't assign the data type to the MultiplyIt function's result, the HowMuch procedure will display the result in the data type specified in the declaration line of the result variable. Instead of 872, the result of the multiplication will be 872.1492.

To make the MultiplyIt function more useful, you can pass different values each time you run the procedure. Instead of hard coding the values to be used in the multiplication, use the InputBox function to ask the user for the values at run time.

Passing Arguments by Reference and Value

In some procedures, when you pass arguments as variables Visual Basic can suddenly change the value of the variables. To ensure that the called function procedure does not alter the value of the passed arguments, you should precede the name of the argument in the function's declaration line with the keyword ByVal. Let's look at the following example.

Hands-On 5-7: Passing Arguments to Functions (Example 4)

1. Add a new module to the ProcAndFunctions (Practice_Excel05.xlsm) project and change the module's name to **Sample4.**
2. Activate the Sample4 module and type the procedures shown below:

```
Sub ThreeNumbers()
    Dim num1 As Integer, num2 As Integer, num3 As Integer
    num1 = 10
    num2 = 20
    num3 = 30

    MsgBox MyAverage(num1, num2, num3)
    MsgBox num1
    MsgBox num2
    MsgBox num3
End Sub

Function MyAverage(ByVal num1, ByVal num2, ByVal num3)
    num1 = num1 + 1

    MyAverage = (num1 + num2 + num3) / 3
End Function
```

To prevent the function from altering values of arguments, use the keyword ByVal before the arguments' names.

The ThreeNumbers subroutine assigns values to three variables and then calls the MyAverage function to calculate and return the average of the numbers stored in these variables. The function's arguments are the variables num1, num2, and num3. Notice that all variable names are preceded with the keyword ByVal. Also, notice that prior to the calculation of the average, the MyAverage function changes the value of the num1 variable. Inside the function procedure, the num1 variable equals 11 (10 + 1). Therefore, when the function passes the calculated average to the ThreeNumbers procedure, the MsgBox function displays the result as 20.3333333333333 and not 20, as expected. The next three MsgBox functions show the contents of each of the variables. The values stored in these variables are the same as the original values assigned to them — 10, 20, and 30.

What will happen if you omit the keyword ByVal in front of the num1 argument in the MyAverage function's declaration line? The function's result will still be the same, but the contents of the num1 variable displayed by MsgBox num1 is now 11. The MyAverage function has not only returned an unexpected result (20.3333333333333 instead of 20) but has also modified the original data stored in the num1 variable. To prevent Visual Basic from permanently changing the values supplied to the function, use the ByVal keyword.

Know Your Keywords: ByRef and ByVal

Because any of the variables passed to a function procedure (or a subroutine) can be changed by the receiving procedure, it is important to know how to protect the original value of a variable. Visual Basic has two keywords that give or deny permission to change the contents of a variable — ByRef and ByVal. By default, Visual Basic passes information into a function procedure (or a subroutine) by reference (ByRef keyword), referring to the original data specified in the function's argument at the time the function is called. So, if the function alters the value of the argument, the original value is changed. You will get this result if you omit the ByVal keyword in front of the num1 argument in the MyAverage function's declaration line. If you want the function procedure to change the original value, you don't need to explicitly insert the ByRef keyword, since passed variables default to ByRef. When you use the ByVal keyword in front of an argument name, Visual Basic passes the argument by value. It means that Visual Basic makes a copy of the original data. This copy is then passed to a function. If the function changes the value of an argument passed by value, the original data does not change — only the copy changes. That's why when the MyAverage function changed the value of the num1 argument, the original value of the num1 variable remained the same.

Using Optional Arguments

At times you may want to supply an additional value to a function. Let's say you have a function that calculates the price of a meal per person. Sometimes, however, you'd like the function to perform the same calculation for a group of two or more people. To indicate that a procedure argument is not always required, precede the name of the argument with the Optional keyword. Arguments that are optional come at the end of the argument list, following the names of all the required arguments.

Optional arguments must always be the Variant data type. This means that you can't specify the Optional argument's type by using the As keyword. In the preceding section, you created a function to calculate the average of three numbers. Suppose that sometimes you'd like to use this function to calculate the average of two numbers. You could define the third argument of the MyAverage function as optional.

To preserve the original MyAverage function, let's create the Avg function to calculate the average for two or three numbers.

Hands-On 5-8: Writing Functions with Optional Arguments

1. Add a new module to the ProcAndFunctions (Practice_Excel05.xlsm) project and change the module's name to **Sample5**.
2. Activate the Sample5 module and enter the function procedure shown below:

```
Function Avg(num1, num2, Optional num3)
    Dim totalNums As Integer

    totalNums = 3

    If IsMissing(num3)Then
        num3 = 0
        totalNums = totalNums - 1
    End If

    Avg = (num1+num2+num3)/totalNums
End Function
```

   Let's take a few minutes to analyze the Avg function. This function can take up to three arguments. The arguments num1 and num2 are required. The argument num3 is optional. Notice that the name of the optional argument is preceded with the Optional keyword. The optional argument is listed at the end of the argument list. Because the type of the num1, num2, and num3 arguments is not declared, Visual Basic treats all of these arguments as Variants. Inside the function procedure, the totalNums variable is declared as an Integer and then assigned a beginning value of 3. Because the function has to be capable of calculating an average of two or three numbers, the handy built-in function IsMissing checks for the number of supplied arguments. If the third (optional) argument is not supplied, the IsMissing function puts in its place the value of zero (0), and at the same time it deducts the value of 1 from the value stored in the totalNums variable. Hence, if the optional argument is missing, totalNums is 2. The next statement calculates the average based on the supplied data, and the result is assigned to the name of the function.

   The IsMissing function allows you to determine whether or not the optional argument was supplied. This function returns the logical value true if the third argument is not supplied, and it returns false when the third argument is given. The IsMissing function is used here with the decision-making statement If...Then. (See Chapter 6 for a detailed description of decision-making statements used in VBA.) If the num3 argument is missing (IsMissing), then (Then) Visual Basic supplies a zero for the value of the third argument (num3 = 0) and reduces the value stored in the argument totalNums by one (totalNums = totalNums – 1).

3. Now call this function from the Immediate window like this:

```
?Avg(2,3)
```

As soon as you press **Enter**, Visual Basic displays the result: 2.5. If you enter the following:

```
?Avg(2,3,5)
```

This time the result is 3.3333333333333.

As you've seen, the Avg function allows you to calculate the average of two or three numbers. You decide which values and how many values (two or three) you want to average. When you start typing the values for the function's arguments in the Immediate window, Visual Basic displays the name of the optional argument enclosed in square brackets.

How else can you run the Avg function? On your own, run this function from a worksheet. Make sure you run it with two and then with three arguments.

Testing a Function Procedure

To test whether a custom function does what it was designed to do, write a simple subroutine that will call the function and display its result. In addition, the subroutine should show the original values of arguments. This way, you'll be able to quickly determine when the values of arguments were altered. If the function procedure uses optional arguments, you'll also need to check those situations in which the optional arguments may be missing.

Locating Built-in Functions

VBA comes with many built-in functions. These functions can be looked up easily in the Visual Basic online help. To access an alphabetical listing of all VBA functions, choose Help | Microsoft Visual Basic Help in the Visual Basic Editor window. In the Table of Contents, choose Visual Basic for Applications Language Reference. Next, click Visual Basic Language Reference and then Functions.

Take, for example, the MsgBox or the InputBox function. One of the features of a good program is its interaction with the user. When you work with Microsoft Excel, you interact with the application by using various dialog boxes. When you make a mistake, a dialog box comes up and displays a message informing you of the error. When you write your own procedures, you can also inform the users about an unexpected error or the result of a specific calculation. You do this with the help of the MsgBox function. So far you have seen a simple implementation of this function. In the next section, you will find out how to control the way your message looks. You will also learn how to get information from the user with the InputBox function. But before we go on to discuss these functions in detail, let's take a look at one VBA function that can be especially useful to you now that you have familiarized yourself with variables and their data types.

Visual Basic has the VarType function that returns an integer indicating the type of a variable. Figure 5-4 displays the VarType function's syntax and the values it returns.

Now let's see how you can use the VarType function in the Immediate window.

Hands-On 5-9: Using the Built-in VarType Function

1. In the Visual Basic Editor window, choose **View | Immediate Window**.
2. Type the following statements that assign values to variables:

```
age = 18
birthdate = #1/1/1981#
firstName = "John"
```

3. Now ask Visual Basic what type of data each of the variables holds:

```
?VarType(age)
```

When you press **Enter**, Visual Basic returns 2. As shown in Figure 5-4, the number 2 represents the Integer data type. If you type:

```
?VarType(birthdate)
```

Visual Basic returns 7 for Date. If you make a mistake in the variable name (let's say you type birthday, instead of birthdate), Visual Basic returns zero (0). If you type:

```
?VarType(firstName)
```

Visual Basic tells you that the value stored in the variable firstName is a String type (8).

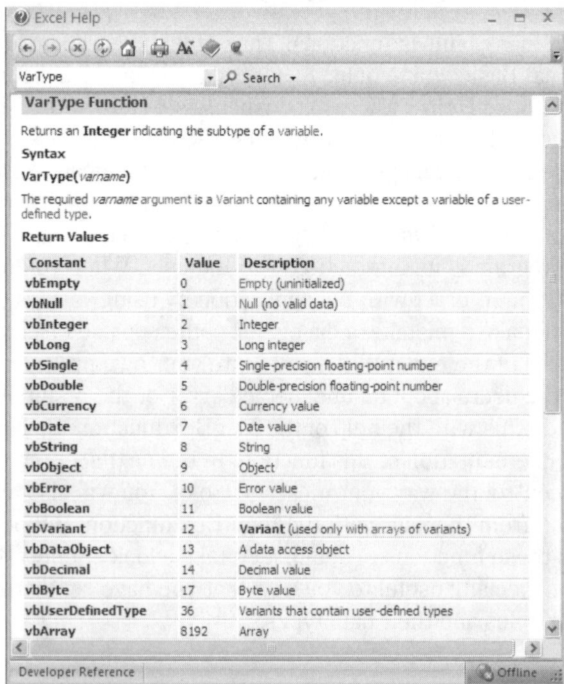

Constant	Value	Description
vbEmpty	0	Empty (uninitialized)
vbNull	1	Null (no valid data)
vbInteger	2	Integer
vbLong	3	Long integer
vbSingle	4	Single-precision floating-point number
vbDouble	5	Double-precision floating-point number
vbCurrency	6	Currency value
vbDate	7	Date value
vbString	8	String
vbObject	9	Object
vbError	10	Error value
vbBoolean	11	Boolean value
vbVariant	12	**Variant** (used only with arrays of variants)
vbDataObject	13	A data access object
vbDecimal	14	Decimal value
vbByte	17	Byte value
vbUserDefinedType	36	Variants that contain user-defined types
vbArray	8192	Array

Figure 5-4: With the built-in VarType function, you can learn the data type the variable holds.

Using the MsgBox Function

The MsgBox function that you have used thus far was limited to displaying a message to the user in a simple, one-button dialog box. You closed the message box by clicking the OK button or pressing the Enter key. You create a simple message box by following the MsgBox function with the text enclosed in quotation marks. In other words, to display the message "The procedure is complete." you write the following statement:

```
MsgBox "The procedure is complete."
```

You can quickly try out the above instruction by entering it in the Immediate window. When you type this instruction and press Enter, Visual Basic displays the message box shown in Figure 5-5.

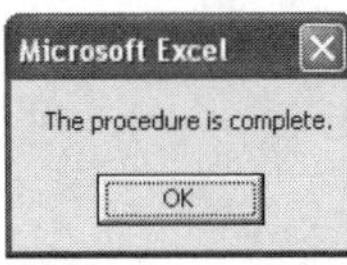

Figure 5-5: To display a message to the user, place the text as the argument of the MsgBox function.

The MsgBox function allows you to use other arguments that make it possible to determine the number of buttons that should be available in the message box or change the title of the message box from the default, Microsoft Excel. You can also assign your own help topic.

The syntax of the MsgBox function is shown below:

```
MsgBox (prompt [, buttons] [, title], [, helpfile, context])
```

Notice that while the MsgBox function has five arguments, only the first one, prompt, is required. The arguments listed in square brackets are optional. When you enter a long text string for the prompt argument, Visual Basic decides how to break the text so it fits the message box. Let's do some exercises in the Immediate window to learn various text formatting techniques.

Hands-On 5-10: Formatting Text for Display in the MsgBox Function

1. Enter the following instruction in the Immediate window. Be sure to enter the entire text string on one line, and then press **Enter**.

```
MsgBox "All done. Now open your workbook file and place an empty disk in
the diskette drive. The following procedure will copy this file to the
disk."
```

As soon as you press **Enter**, Visual Basic shows the resulting dialog box.

Figure 5-6: This long message will look more appealing when you take the text formatting into your own hands.

When the text of your message is particularly long, you can break it into several lines using the VBA Chr function. The Chr function requires one argument and a number between 0 and 255, and it returns a character represented by this number. For example, Chr(13) returns a carriage return character (this is the same as pressing the Enter key), and Chr(10) returns a linefeed character (this is useful for adding spacing between the text lines).

2. Modify the instruction entered in the previous step in the following way:

```
MsgBox "All done." & Chr(13) & "Now open your workbook file and place" &
Chr(13) & "an empty disk in the diskette drive." & Chr(13) & "The
following procedure will copy this file to the disk."
```

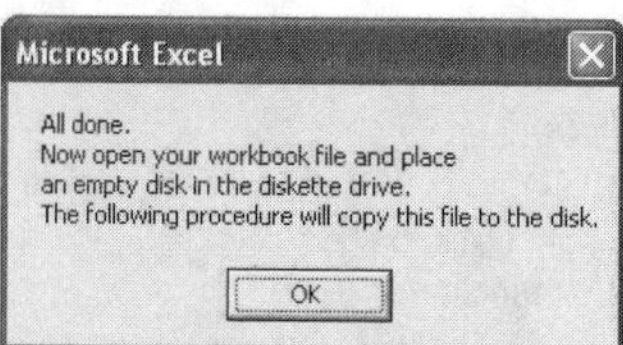

Figure 5-7: You can break a long text string into several lines by using the Chr(13) function.

You must surround each text fragment by quotation marks. Quoted text embedded in a text string requires an additional set of quotation marks:

```
MsgBox "All done." & Chr(13) & "Now open your workbook file
(""SalesAnalysis.xls"") and place" & Chr(13) & "an empty disk in the
diskette drive." & Chr(13) & "The following procedure will copy this file
to the disk."
```

The Chr(13) function indicates a place where you'd like to start a new line. The string concatenation character (&) is used to add a carriage return character to a concatenated string.

When you enter exceptionally long text messages on one line, it's easy to make a mistake. As you recall, Visual Basic has a special line continuation character (an underscore _) that allows you to break a long VBA statement into several lines. Unfortunately, the line continuation character cannot be used in the Immediate window.

3. Add a new module to the ProcAndFunctions (Practice_Excel05.xlsm) project and change the module's name to **Sample6**.

4. Activate the Sample6 module and enter the MyMessage subroutine as shown below. Be sure to precede each line continuation character (_) with a space:

```
Sub MyMessage()
    MsgBox "All done." & Chr(13) _
      & "Now open your workbook file and place" & Chr(13) _
      & "an empty disk in the diskette drive." & Chr(13) _
      & "The following procedure will copy this file to the disk."
End Sub
```

When you run the MyMessage procedure, Visual Basic displays the same message as the one shown in Figure 5-7. As you can see, the text entered on several lines is more readable, and the code is easier to maintain.

To improve the readability of your message, you may want to add more spacing between the text lines by including blank lines. To do this, use two Chr(13) or two Chr(10) functions, as shown in the following step.

5. Enter the following MyMessage2 procedure:

```
Sub MyMessage2()
    MsgBox "All done." & Chr(10) & Chr(10) _
       & "Now open your workbook file and place" & Chr(13) _
       & "an empty disk in the diskette drive." & Chr(13)& Chr(13) _
       & "The following procedure will copy this file to the disk."
End Sub
```

Figure 5-8 displays the message box generated by the MyMessage2 procedure.

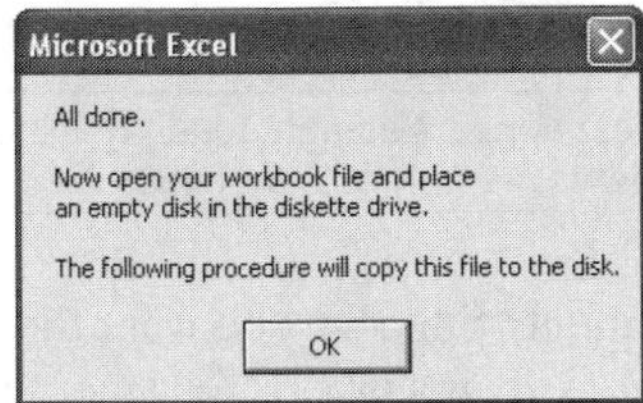

Figure 5-8: You can increase the readability of your message by increasing spacing between the selected text lines.

Now that you've mastered the text formatting techniques, let's take a closer look at the next argument of the MsgBox function. Although the buttons argument is optional, it's frequently used.

The buttons argument specifies how many and what types of buttons you want to appear in the message box. This argument can be a constant (see Table 5-1) or a number. If you omit this argument, the resulting message box includes only the OK button, as you've seen in the preceding examples.

Table 5-1: Settings for the MsgBox buttons argument

Constant	Value	Description
Button settings		
vbOKOnly	0	Displays only an OK button. This is the default.
vbOKCancel	1	OK and Cancel buttons
vbAbortRetryIgnore	2	Abort, Retry, and Ignore buttons
vbYesNoCancel	3	Yes, No, and Cancel buttons
vbYesNo	4	Yes and No buttons
vbRetryCancel	5	Retry and Cancel buttons
Icon settings		
vbCritical	16	Displays the Critical Message icon
vbQuestion	32	Displays the Question Message icon
vbExclamation	48	Displays the Warning Message icon
vbInformation	64	Displays the Information Message icon

Constant	Value	Description
Default button settings		
vbDefaultButton1	0	The first button is the default.
vbDefaultButton2	256	The second button is the default.
vbDefaultButton3	512	The third button is the default.
vbDefaultButton4	768	The fourth button is the default.
Message box modality		
vbApplicationModal	0	The user must respond to the message before continuing to work in the current application.
vbSystemModal	4096	All applications are suspended until the user responds to the message box.
Other MsgBox display settings		
vbMsgBoxHelpButton	16384	Adds Help button to the message box
vbMsgBoxSetForeground	65536	Specifies the message box window as the foreground window
vbMsgBoxRight	524288	Text is right aligned.
vbMsgBoxRtlReading	1048576	Text appears as right-to-left reading on Hebrew and Arabic systems.

When should you use the buttons argument? Suppose you want the user of your procedure to respond to a question with Yes or No. Your message box may then require two buttons. If a message box includes more than one button, one of them is considered a default button. When the user presses Enter, the default button is selected automatically. Because you can display various types of messages (critical, warning, information), you can visually indicate the importance of the message by including in the buttons argument the graphical representation (icon) for the chosen message type.

In addition to the type of message, the buttons argument can include a setting to determine if the message box must be closed before a user switches to another application. It's quite possible that the user may want to switch to another program or perform another task before responding to the question posed in your message box. If the message box is application modal (vbApplication Modal), the user must close the message box before continuing to use your application. On the other hand, if you want to suspend all the applications until the user responds to the message box, you must include the vbSystemModal setting in the buttons argument.

The buttons argument settings are divided into five groups: button settings, icon settings, default button settings, message box modality, and other MsgBox display settings (see Table 5-1). Only one setting from each group can be included in the buttons argument. To create a buttons argument, you can add up the values for each setting you want to include. For example, to display a message box with two buttons (Yes and No), the question mark icon, and the No button as the default button, look up the corresponding values in Table 5-1 and add them up. You should arrive at 292 (4+32+256).

Let's go back to the Immediate window for more testing of the capabilities of the MsgBox function.

Hands-On 5-11: Using a Built-in MsgBox Function with Arguments (Example 1)

1. To quickly see the message box using the calculated message box argument, enter the following statement in the Immediate window, and press Enter:

   ```
   MsgBox "Do you want to proceed?", 292
   ```

   The resulting message box is shown in Figure 5-9.

   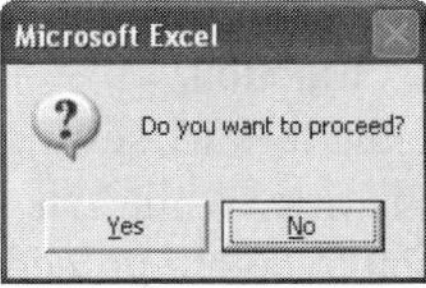

   Figure 5-9: You can specify the number of buttons to include in the message box by using the optional buttons argument.

   When you derive the buttons argument by adding up the constant values, your procedure becomes less readable. There's no reference table where you can check the hidden meaning of 292. To improve the readability of your MsgBox function, it's better to use the constants instead of their values.

2. Now enter the following revised statement in the Immediate window:

   ```
   MsgBox "Do you want to proceed?", vbYesNo + vbQuestion + vbDefaultButton2
   ```

   The above statement produces the same result as shown in Figure 5-9 and is more readable.

The following example shows how to use the buttons argument inside the Visual Basic procedure.

Hands-On 5-12: Using a Built-in MsgBox Function with Arguments (Example 2)

1. Add a new module to the ProcAndFunctions (Practice_Excel05.xlsm) project and change the module's name to **Sample7**.
2. Activate the Sample7 module and enter the MsgYesNo subroutine shown below:

   ```
   Sub MsgYesNo()
       Dim question As String
       Dim myButtons As Integer

       question = "Do you want to open a new workbook?"
       myButtons = vbYesNo + vbQuestion + vbDefaultButton2

       MsgBox question, myButtons
   End Sub
   ```

In the above subroutine, the question variable stores the text of your message. The settings for the buttons argument is placed in the myButtons variable. Instead of using the names of constants, you can use their values, as in the following:

```
myButtons = 4 + 32 + 256
```

However, by specifying the names of the buttons argument's constants, you make your procedure easier to understand for yourself and others who may work with this procedure in the future.

The question and myButtons variables are used as arguments for the MsgBox function. When you run the procedure, you see the result displayed, as shown earlier in Figure 5-9. Notice that the No button is selected. It's the default button for this dialog box. If you press Enter, Excel removes the MsgBox from the screen. Nothing happens because your procedure does not have any more instructions following the MsgBox function.

To change the default button, use the vbDefaultButton1 setting instead.

The third argument of the MsgBox function is title. While this is also an optional argument, it's very handy, as it allows you to create procedures that don't provide visual clues to the fact that you programmed them with Microsoft Excel. Using this argument, you can set the title bar of your message box to any text you want.

Suppose you want the MsgYesNo procedure to display in its title the text "New workbook." The following MsgYesNo2 procedure demonstrates the use of the title argument:

```
Sub MsgYesNo2()
    Dim question As String
    Dim myButtons As Integer
    Dim myTitle As String

    question = "Do you want to open a new workbook?"
    myButtons = vbYesNo + vbQuestion + vbDefaultButton2
    myTitle = "New workbook"

    MsgBox question, myButtons, myTitle
End Sub
```

The text for the title argument is stored in the variable myTitle. If you don't specify the value for the title argument, Visual Basic displays the default text, "Microsoft Excel."

Notice that the arguments are listed in the order determined by the MsgBox function. If you would like to list the arguments in any order, you must precede the value of each argument with its name, as shown below:

```
MsgBox title:=myTitle, prompt:=question, buttons:=myButtons
```

The last two optional arguments — helpfile and context — are used by programmers who are experienced with using help files in the Windows environment.

The helpfile argument indicates the name of a special help file that contains additional information you may want to display to your VBA procedure user. When you specify this argument, the Help button will be added to your message box. When you use the helpfile argument, you must also use the context argument. This argument indicates which help subject in the specified help file you want to display.

Suppose HelpX.hlp is the help file you created, and 55 is the context topic you want to use. To include this information in your MsgBox function, you would use the following instruction:

```
MsgBox title:=mytitle, _
    prompt:=question _
    buttons:=mybuttons _
    helpFile:= "HelpX.hlp", _
    context:=55
```

The above is a single VBA statement, broken down into several lines with the line continuation character.

Returning Values from the MsgBox Function

When you display a simple message box dialog with one button, clicking the OK button or pressing the Enter key removes the message box from the screen. However, when the message box has more than one button, your procedure should detect which button was pressed. To do this, you must save the result of the message box in a variable. Table 5-2 shows values that the MsgBox function returns.

Table 5-2: Values returned by the MsgBox function

Button Selected	Constant	Value
OK	vbOK	1
Cancel	vbCancel	2
Abort	vbAbort	3
Retry	vbRetry	4
Ignore	vbIgnore	5
Yes	vbYes	6
No	vbNo	7

Let's take time to revise the MsgYesNo2 procedure to show which button the user has chosen.

Hands-On 5-13: Using a Built-in MsgBox Function with Arguments (Example 3)

1. Activate the Sample7 module and enter the MsgYesNo3 subroutine as shown below:

```
Sub MsgYesNo3()
    Dim question As String
    Dim myButtons As Integer
    Dim myTitle As String

    Dim myChoice As Integer

    question = "Do you want to open a new workbook?"
    myButtons = vbYesNo + vbQuestion + vbDefaultButton2
```

```
    myTitle = "New workbook"
    myChoice = MsgBox(question, myButtons, myTitle)

    MsgBox myChoice
End Sub
```

In the above procedure, we assigned the result of the MsgBox function to the variable myChoice. Notice that the arguments of the MsgBox function are now listed in parentheses:

```
myChoice = MsgBox(question, myButtons, myTitle)
```

2. Run the MsgYesNo3 procedure.

   When you run the MsgYesNo3 procedure, a two-button message box is displayed. By clicking on the Yes button, the statement MsgBox myChoice displays the number 6. When you click the No button, the number 7 is displayed.

In the next chapter you will learn how to make your procedure carry out a task depending on a button's selection (see Hands-On 6-6).

> **MsgBox Function — With or Without Parentheses?**
>
> Use parentheses around the MsgBox function's argument list when you want to use the result returned by the function. By listing the function's arguments without parentheses, you tell Visual Basic that you want to ignore the function's result. Most likely, you will want to use the function's result when the MsgBox contains more than one button.

Using the InputBox Function

The InputBox function displays a dialog box with a message that prompts the user to enter data. This dialog box has two buttons — OK and Cancel. When you click OK, the InputBox function returns the information entered in the text box. When you select Cancel, the function returns the empty string (""). The syntax of the InputBox function is as follows:

```
InputBox(prompt [, title] [, default] [, xpos] [, ypos] [, helpfile, context])
```

The first argument, prompt, is the text message that you want to display in the dialog box. Long text strings can be entered on several lines by using the Chr(13) or Chr(10) functions (see examples of using the MsgBox function earlier in this chapter). All of the remaining InputBox arguments are optional.

The second argument, title, allows you to change the default title of the dialog box. The default value is "Microsoft Excel."

The third argument of the InputBox function, default, allows the display of a default value in the text box. If you omit this argument, the empty edit box is displayed.

The following two arguments, xpos and ypos, let you specify the exact position where the dialog box should appear on the screen. If you omit these arguments, the box appears in the middle of the current window. The xpos argument determines the horizontal position of the dialog box from the left edge of the screen. When omitted, the dialog box is centered horizontally. The ypos argument determines the vertical position from the top of the screen. If you omit this argument, the dialog box is positioned vertically approximately one-third of the way down the screen. Both xpos and ypos are measured in special units called twips. One twip is equivalent to approximately 0.0007 inches.

The last two arguments, helpfile and context, are used in the same way as the corresponding arguments of the MsgBox function discussed earlier in this chapter.

Now that you know the meaning of the InputBox function's arguments, let's look at some examples of using this function.

Hands-On 5-14: Writing a Procedure with the Built-in InputBox Function (Example 1)

1. Add a new module to the ProcAndFunctions (Practice_Excel05.xlsm) project and change the module's name to **Sample8**.
2. Activate the Sample8 module and enter the Informant subroutine shown below:

```
Sub Informant()
    InputBox prompt:="Enter your place of birth:" & Chr(13) _
       & " (e.g., Boston, Great Falls, etc.) "
End Sub
```

   The above procedure displays the following dialog box with two buttons. The input prompt is displayed on two lines.

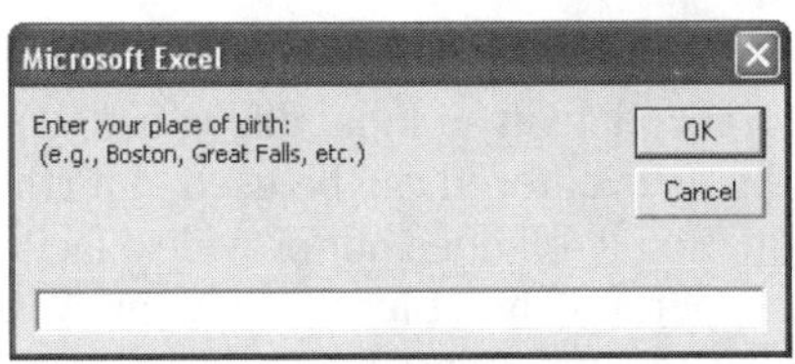

Figure 5-10: A dialog box generated by the Informant subroutine.

   As with the MsgBox function, if you plan on using the data entered by the user in the dialog box, you should store the result of the InputBox function in a variable.

3. Type the Informant2 procedure shown below to assign the result of the InputBox function to the variable town:

```
Sub Informant2()
    Dim myPrompt As String
    Dim town As String

    Const myTitle = "Enter data"
```

```
    myPrompt = "Enter your place of birth:" & Chr(13) _
       & "(e.g., Boston, Great Falls, etc.)"
    town = InputBox(myPrompt, myTitle)

    MsgBox "You were born in " & town & ".", , "Your response"
End Sub
```

Notice that this time the arguments of the InputBox function are listed between parentheses. Parentheses are required if you want to use the result of the InputBox function later in your procedure. The Informant2 subroutine uses a constant to specify the text to appear in the title bar of the dialog box. Because the constant value remains the same throughout the execution of your procedure, you can declare the input box title as a constant. However, if you'd rather use a variable, you still can. When you run a procedure using the InputBox function, the dialog box generated by this function always appears in the same area of the screen. To change the location of the dialog box, you must supply the xpos and ypos arguments, as explained earlier.

4. To display the dialog box in the top left-hand corner of the screen, modify the InputBox function in the Informant2 procedure as follows:

   ```
   town = InputBox(myPrompt, myTitle, , 1, 200)
   ```

   Notice that the argument myTitle is followed by two commas. The second comma marks the position of the omitted default argument. The next two arguments determine the horizontal and vertical position of the dialog box. If you omit the second comma after the myTitle argument, Visual Basic will use the number 1 as the value of the default argument. If you precede the values of arguments by their names (for example, prompt:=myPrompt, title:=myTitle, xpos:=1, ypos:=200), you won't have to remember to place a comma in the place of each omitted argument.

What will happen if you enter a number instead of the name of a town? Because users often supply incorrect data in an input dialog box, your procedure must verify that the data the user entered can be used in further data manipulations. The InputBox function itself does not provide a facility for data validation. To validate user input, you must learn additional VBA instructions that are presented in the next chapter.

Converting Data Types

The result of the InputBox function is always a string. If the user enters a number, before your procedure can use this number in mathematical computations, the string value the user entered should be converted to a numeric value. Visual Basic is capable of converting values from one data type to another.

Let's try out a procedure that suggests what type of data the user should enter by supplying a default value in the InputBox dialog.

Hands-On 5-15: Writing a Procedure with the Built-in InputBox Function (Example 2)

1. Activate the Sample8 module in the MyFunctions (Practice_Excel05.xlsm) project and enter the following AddTwoNums procedure:

```
Sub AddTwoNums()
    Dim myPrompt As String
    Dim value1 As String
    Dim mySum As Single

    Const myTitle = "Enter data"

    myPrompt = "Enter a number:"
    value1 = InputBox(myPrompt, myTitle, 0)
    mySum = value1 + 2

    MsgBox mySum & " (" & value1 & " + 2)"
End Sub
```

   The AddTwoNums procedure displays the dialog box shown in Figure 5-11. Notice that this dialog box has two special features that are obtained by using the InputBox function's optional title and default arguments. Instead of the default title "Microsoft Excel," the dialog box displays a text string defined by the contents of the myTitle constant. The zero entered as the default value in the edit box suggests that the user enter a number instead of text. Once the user provides the data and clicks OK, the user's input is assigned to the variable value1.

```
value1 = InputBox(myPrompt, myTitle, 0)
```

2. Run the AddTwoNums procedure and supply any number when prompted, and then click **OK**.

Figure 5-11: To suggest that the user enter a specific type of data, you may want to provide a default value in the edit box.

   The data type of the variable value1 is String.

3. You can check the data type easily if you follow the above instruction in the procedure code with this statement:

```
MsgBox VarType(value1)
```

   When Visual Basic runs the above line, it will display a message box with the number 8. If you look at Figure 5-4 earlier in this chapter, you will notice that this number represents the String data type.

Define a Constant

To ensure that all the title bars in a particular VBA procedure display the same text, assign the title text to a constant. By following this tip, you will save yourself time by not having to type the title text more than once.

Avoid the Type Mismatch Error

If you attempt to run the AddTwoNums procedure in previous versions of Microsoft Excel (prior to version 2000), you will get the Type mismatch error when Visual Basic tries to execute the following line of code:

```
mysum = value1 + 2
```

To avoid the Type mismatch error, use the built-in CSng function to convert a string stored in the value1 variable to a Single type number. Write the following statement:

```
mysum = CSng(value1) + 2
```

The next line, mySum = value1 + 2, adds 2 to the user's input and assigns the result of the calculation to the variable mySum. Because the value1 variable's data type is String, prior to using this variable's data in the computation, Visual Basic goes to work behind the scenes to perform the data type conversion. Visual Basic understands the need for conversion. Without it, the two incompatible data types (Text and Number) would generate a Type mismatch error. The procedure ends with the MsgBox function displaying the result of the calculation and showing the user how the total was derived.

Using the InputBox Method

In addition to the built-in InputBox VBA function, there is also the Excel InputBox method. If you activate the Object Browser window and type "inputbox" in the search box and then press Enter, Visual Basic will display two occurrences of InputBox — one in the Excel library and the other one in the VBA library (see Figure 5-12).

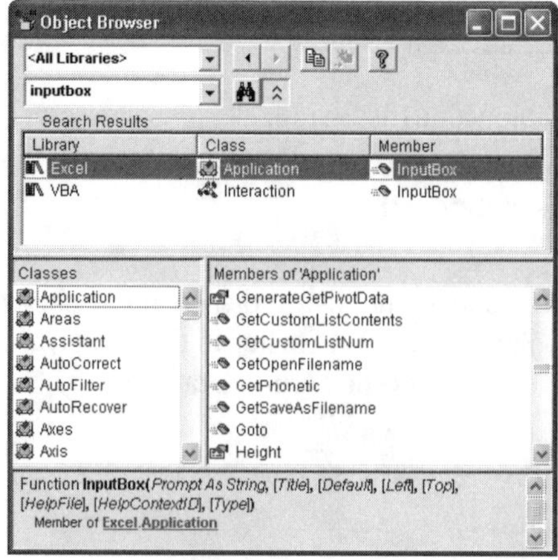

Figure 5-12: Don't forget to use the Object Browser when researching Visual Basic functions and methods.

The InputBox method available in the Microsoft Excel library has a slightly different syntax than the InputBox function that was covered earlier in this chapter. Its syntax is:

```
expression.InputBox(prompt, [title], [default], [left], [top], _
    [helpfile], [helpcontextID], [type])
```

All bracketed arguments are optional. The Prompt argument is the message to be displayed in the dialog box, the Title is the title for the dialog box, and the Default is a value that will appear in the text box when the dialog box is initially displayed.

The Left and Top arguments specify the position of the dialog box on the screen. The values for these arguments are entered in points. Recall that one point equals 1/72 inch. The arguments HelpFile and HelpContextID identify the name of the help file and the specific number of the help topic to be displayed when the user clicks the Help button.

The last argument of the InputBox method, Type, specifies the return data type. If you omit this argument, the InputBox method will return text. The values of the Type argument are shown in Table 5-3.

Table 5-3: Data types returned by the InputBox method

Value	Type of Data Returned
0	A formula
1	A number
2	A string (text)
4	A logical value (True or False)
8	A cell reference, as a Range object
16	An error value (for example, #N/A)
64	An array of values

You can allow the user to enter a number or text in the edit box if you use 3 for the Type argument. This value is obtained by adding up the value for a number (1) and a string (2), as shown in Table 5-3. The InputBox method is quite useful for VBA procedures that require a user to select a range of cells in a worksheet.

Let's look at an example procedure that uses the Excel InputBox method.

Hands-On 5-16: Writing a VBA Procedure with the Excel InputBox Method

1. Close the Object Browser window if you opened it before.
2. In the Sample8 module, enter the following WhatRange procedure:

```
Sub WhatRange()
    Dim newRange As Range
    Dim tellMe As String
    tellMe = "Use the mouse to select a range:"
    Set newRange = Application.InputBox(prompt:=tellMe, _
        Title:="Range to format", _
```

```
          Type:=8)
    newRange.NumberFormat = "0.00"
    newRange.Select
End Sub
```

The WhatRange procedure begins with a declaration of an object variable — newRange. As you recall from Chapter 4, object variables point to the location of the data. The range of cells that the user selects is assigned to the object variable newRange. Notice the keyword Set before the name of the variable:

```
Set newRange = Application.InputBox(prompt:=tellMe, _
    Title:="Range to format", _
    Type:=8)
```

The Type argument (Type:=8) enables the user to select any range of cells. When the user highlights the cells, the next instruction:

```
newRange.NumberFormat = "0.00"
```

changes the format of the selected cells. The last instruction selects the range of cells that the user highlighted.

3. Run the WhatRange procedure.

   Visual Basic displays a dialog box prompting the user to select a range of cells in the worksheet.

4. Use the mouse to select any cells you want. As you drag the mouse to select the cells, Visual Basic enters the selected range reference in the edit box (see Figure 5-13).

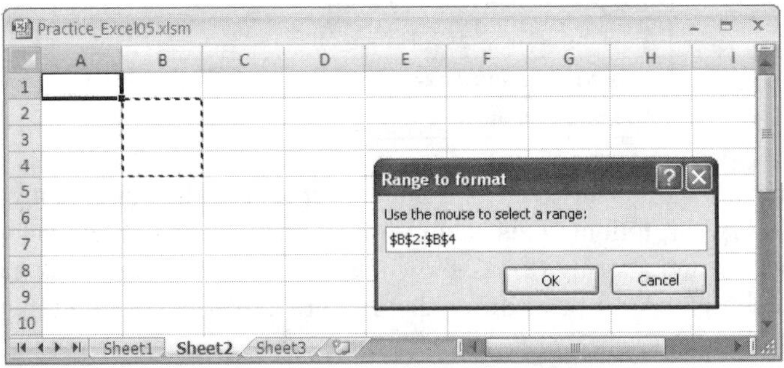

Figure 5-13: Using Excel's InputBox method, you can get the range address from the user.

5. When you're done selecting cells, click **OK** in the dialog box.

   The selected range is now formatted. To check this out, enter a whole number in any of the selected cells. The number should appear formatted with two decimal places.

6. Rerun the procedure, and when the dialog box appears, click **Cancel**.

   The WhatRange procedure works fine if you click OK after selecting a cell or a range of cells. Unfortunately, when you click the Cancel button or press Esc, Visual Basic displays an error message — "Object Required." When you click the Debug button in the error dialog box, Visual Basic will highlight the line of code that caused the error. Because you don't want to select anything when you cancel the dialog box, you must find a way to ignore the error that Visual Basic displays. Using a special statement, On Error GoTo labelname, you can take a detour when an error occurs. This instruction has the following syntax:

```
On Error GoTo labelname
```

This instruction should be placed just below the variable declaration lines. Labelname can be any word you want, except for a Visual Basic keyword. If an error occurs, Visual Basic will jump to the specified label, as shown in step 8 below.

7. Choose **Run | Reset** to cancel out the procedure you were running.
8. Modify the WhatRange procedure so it looks like the WhatRange2 procedure shown below:

```
Sub WhatRange2()
    Dim newRange As Range
    Dim tellMe As String

    On Error GoTo VeryEnd

    tellMe = "Use the mouse to select a range:"
    Set newRange = Application.InputBox(prompt:=tellMe, _
          Title:="Range to format", _
          Type:=8)
    newRange.NumberFormat = "0.00"
    newRange.Select

    VeryEnd:
End Sub
```

Notice that this time the procedure does not generate the error when you cancel the dialog box. When Visual Basic encounters the error, it jumps to the VeryEnd label placed at the end of the procedure. The statements placed between On Error Goto VeryEnd and the VeryEnd labels are ignored. In Chapter 11 you will find other examples of trapping errors in your VBA procedures.

9. Run the modified WhatRange2 procedure, and click **Cancel** as soon as the input box appears.

Subroutines and Functions: Which Should You Use?

Create a subroutine when...	Create a function when...
You want to perform some actions.	You want to perform a simple calculation more than once.
You want to get input from the user.	You must perform complex computations.
You want to display a message on the screen.	You must call the same block of instructions more than once.
	You want to check if a certain expression is True or False.

Using Master Procedures and Subprocedures

When your VBA procedure gets larger, it may be difficult to maintain its many lines of code. To make your program easier to write, understand, and modify, you should use a structured approach. When you create a structured program, you simply break a large problem into small problems that can be solved one at a time. In VBA, you do this by creating a master procedure and one or more subordinate procedures. Because both master procedures and subordinate procedures are subroutines, you declare them with the Sub keyword. The master procedure can call the required subroutines and pass arguments to them. It may also call functions.

The following example shows the AboutUser procedure, which requests the user's first and last names and then extracts the first and last names from the full name string. The last statement displays the user's last name followed by a comma and the first name. As you read further, this procedure will be broken down into several tasks to demonstrate the concept of using master procedures, subprocedures, and functions.

```
Sub AboutUser()
    Dim fullName As String
    Dim firstName As String
    Dim lastName As String
    Dim space As Integer

    ' get input from user
    fullName = InputBox("Enter first and last name:")

    ' get first and last name strings
    space = InStr(fullName, " ")
    firstName = Left(fullName, space - 1)
    lastName = Right(fullName, Len(fullName) - space)

    ' display last name, first name
    MsgBox lastName & ", " & firstName
End Sub
```

The AboutUser procedure can be divided into the following smaller tasks:

Task 1	Obtain the user's full name.
Task 2	Divide the user-supplied data into two strings: last name and first name. These tasks can be delegated to separate functions (for example: GetLast and GetFirst).
Task 3	Display a message showing the reordered full name string.

Now that you know what tasks you should focus on, let's see how you can accomplish each task.

Hands-On 5-17: Writing a Master VBA Procedure

1. Add a new module to your current VBA project and rename it **Sample9**.

2. Enter the following AboutUserMaster procedure in the Sample9 module window:

```
Sub AboutUserMaster()
    Dim first As String, last As String, full As String

    Call GetUserName(full)

    first = GetFirst(full)
    last = GetLast(full)
    Call DisplayLastFirst(first, last)
End Sub
```

   The master procedure shown above controls the general flow of your program by calling appropriate subprocedures and functions. The procedure begins with the declaration of variables. The first statement, Call GetUserName(full), calls the GetUserName subroutine (see step 3) and passes it an argument — the contents of the full variable. Because the variable full is not assigned any value prior to the execution of the Call statement, it has the value of an empty string (""). Notice that the name of the subprocedure is preceded by the Call statement. Although you are not required to use the Call keyword when calling a procedure, you must use it when the call to the procedure requires arguments. The argument list must be enclosed in parentheses.

3. Enter the following GetUserName subroutine:

```
Sub GetUserName(fullName As String)
    fullName = InputBox("Enter first and last name:")
End Sub
```

   The procedure GetUserName demonstrates two very important Visual Basic programming concepts: how to pass arguments to a subprocedure and how to pass values back from a subprocedure to a calling procedure.

   In the master procedure (see step 2), you called the GetUserName procedure and passed it one argument: the variable full. This variable is received by a fullName parameter declared in the GetUserName subprocedure's Sub statement. Because at the time Visual Basic called the GetUserName subprocedure the variable full contained an empty string, the fullName parameter receives the same value — an empty string (""). When Visual Basic displays the dialog box and gets the user's last name, this name is assigned to the fullName parameter. A value assigned to a parameter is passed back to the matching argument after the subprocedure is executed. Therefore, when Visual Basic returns to the master procedure, the full variable will contain the user's last name.

   Arguments passed to a subprocedure are received by parameters. Notice that the parameter name (fullName) is followed by the declaration of the data type (As String). Although the parameter's data type must agree with the data type of the matching argument, different names may be used for an argument and its corresponding parameter.

4. Enter the following GetFirst function procedure:

```
Function GetFirst(fullName As String)
    Dim space As Integer

    space = InStr(fullName, " ")

    GetFirst = Left(fullName, space - 1)
End Function
```

The second statement in the master procedure (see step 2), first = GetFirst(full), passes the value of the full variable to the GetFirst function. This value is received by the function's parameter — fullName. To extract the first name from the user-provided full name string, you must find the location of the space separating the first name and last name. Therefore, the function begins with a declaration of a local variable — space.

The next statement uses the VBA built-in function InStr to return the position of a space character ("") in the fullName string. The obtained number is then assigned to the variable space. Finally, the Left function is used to extract the specified number of characters (space – 1) from the left side of the fullName string. The length of the first name is one character less than the value stored in the variable space. The result of the function (user's first name) is then assigned to the function's name. When Visual Basic returns to the master procedure, it places the result in the variable first.

5. Enter the following GetLast function procedure:

```
Function GetLast(fullName As String)
    Dim space As Integer

    space = InStr(fullName, " ")

    GetLast = Right(fullName, Len(fullName) - space)
End Function
```

The third statement in the master procedure (see step 2), last = GetLast(full), passes the value of the full variable to the GetLast function. This function's purpose is to extract the user's last name from the user-supplied fullName string. The GetLast function uses the built-in Len function to calculate the total number of characters in the fullName string. The Right function extracts the specified number of characters (Len(fullName) – space) from the right side of the fullName string. The obtained string is then assigned to the function name, and upon returning to the master procedure, it is stored in the variable last.

6. Enter the following DisplayLastFirst subroutine:

```
Sub DisplayLastFirst(firstName As String, lastName As String)
    MsgBox lastName & ", " & firstName
End Sub
```

The fourth statement in the master procedure (see step 2), Call DisplayLastFirst(first, last), calls the DisplayLastFirst subroutine and passes two arguments to it: first and last. To receive these arguments, the DisplayLastFirst subprocedure is declared with two matching parameters — firstName and lastName. Recall that different names can be used for arguments and their corresponding parameters. The DisplayLastFirst subprocedure then displays the message box showing the user's last name followed by the comma and the first name.

Arguments Versus Parameters

- An argument is a variable, constant, or expression that is passed to a subprocedure.
- A parameter is simply a variable that receives a value passed to a subprocedure.

Advantages of Using Subprocedures

- It's easier to maintain several subprocedures than one large procedure.
- A task performed by a subprocedure can be used by several other procedures.
- Each subprocedure can be tested individually before being placed in the main program.
- Several people can work on individual subprocedures that constitute a larger procedure.

Chapter Summary

In this chapter you learned the difference between subroutine procedures that perform actions and function procedures that return values. While you can create subroutines by recording or typing code directly in the Visual Basic module, function procedures cannot be recorded because they can take arguments. You must write them manually. You saw examples of function procedures called from a worksheet and from another Visual Basic procedure. You learned how to pass arguments to functions and determine the data type of a function's result. You increased your repertoire of VBA keywords with the ByVal, ByRef, and Optional keywords. You also saw how problems can be broken into simpler and smaller tasks to make your programs easier to understand. Finally, you learned how, with the help of parameters, subprocedures can pass values back to the calling procedures. After working through this chapter, you should be able to create some custom functions of your own that are suited to your specific needs. You should also be able to interact easily with your procedure users by employing the MsgBox and InputBox functions as well as the Excel InputBox method.

Chapter 6 introduces you to decision making. You will learn how to change the course of your VBA procedure based on the results of the conditions that you supply.

Part II

Controlling Program Execution

While the Excel macro recorder can get you started with VBA, it does not allow you to incorporate complex logic into your program.

In this part of the book, you'll find out how decisions and looping enable you to control program flow and create useful VBA procedures and functions.

Chapter 6

Decision Making with VBA

Relational and Logical Operators ■ If ...Then Statement ■ Decisions Based on More Than One Condition ■ If Block Instructions and Indenting ■ If...Then...Else Statement ■ If...Then...ElseIf Statement ■ Nested If...Then Statements ■ Select Case Statement ■ Using Is with the Case Clause ■ Specifying a Range of Values in a Case Clause ■ Specifying Multiple Expressions in a Case Clause ■ **Chapter Summary**

We make thousands of decisions every day. Some decisions are spontaneous; we make them automatically without having to stop and think. Other decisions require that we weigh two or more options or even plan several tasks ahead. Visual Basic for Applications, like other programming languages, offers special statements that allow you to include decision points in your own procedures. But what is decision making? Suppose someone approaches you with the question, "Do you like the color red?" After giving this question some thought, you'll answer "yes" or "no." And, if you're undecided or simply don't care, you might answer "maybe" or "perhaps." In programming, you must be decisive. Only "yes" or "no" answers are allowed. In programming, all decisions are based on supplied answers. If the answer is positive, the procedure executes a specified block of instructions. If the answer is negative, the procedure executes another block of instructions or simply doesn't do anything. In this chapter, you will learn how to use VBA conditional statements to alter the flow of your program. Conditional statements are often referred to as "control structures," as they give you the ability to control the flow of your VBA procedure by skipping over certain statements and "branching" to another part of the procedure.

Relational and Logical Operators

You make decisions in your VBA procedures by using conditional expressions inside the special control structures. A *conditional expression* is an expression that uses a relational operator (Table 6-1), a logical operator (Table 6-2), or a combination of both. When Visual Basic encounters a conditional expression in your program, it evaluates the expression to determine whether it is true or false.

Table 6-1: Relational operators in VBA

Operator	Description
=	Equal to
<>	Not equal to
>	Greater than
<	Less than
>=	Greater than or equal to
<=	Less than or equal to

Table 6-2: Logical operators in VBA

Operator	Description
AND	All conditions must be true before an action can be taken.
OR	At least one of the conditions must be true before an action can be taken.
NOT	Used for negating a condition. If a condition is true, NOT makes it false. If a condition is false, NOT makes it true.

If ...Then Statement

The simplest way to get some decision making into your VBA procedure is to use the If...Then statement. Suppose you want to choose an action depending on a condition. You can use the following structure:

```
If condition Then statement
```

For example, to delete a blank row from a worksheet, first check if the active cell is blank. If the result of the test is true, go ahead and delete the entire row that contains that cell:

```
If ActiveCell = "" Then Selection.EntireRow.Delete
```

If the active cell is not blank, Visual Basic will ignore the statement following the Then keyword.

Sometimes you may want to perform several actions when the condition is true. Although you could add other statements on the same line by separating them with colons, your code will look clearer if you use the multiline version of the If...Then statement, as shown below:

```
If condition Then
    statement1
    statement2
    statementN
End If
```

For example, to perform some actions when the value of the active cell is greater than 50, you can write the following block of instructions:

```
If ActiveCell.Value > 50 Then
    MsgBox "The exact value is " & ActiveCell.Value
    Debug.Print ActiveCell.Adress & ": " & ActiveCell.Value
End If
```

In the above example, the statements between the Then and the End If keywords are not executed if the value of the active cell is less than or equal to 50. Notice that the block If...Then statement must end with the keywords End If.

How does Visual Basic make a decision? It evaluates the condition it finds between the If...Then keywords. Let's try to evaluate the following condition: `ActiveCell.Value > 50`.

Hands-On 6-1: Evaluating Conditions in the Immediate Window

1. Open a new Microsoft Excel workbook.
2. Select any cell in a blank worksheet and enter **50**.
3. Switch to the Visual Basic Editor window.
4. Activate the Immediate window.

5. Enter the following statement, and press **Enter** when you're done:

```
? ActiveCell.Value > 50
```

When you press Enter, Visual Basic writes the result of this test — false. When the result of the test is false, Visual Basic will not bother to read the statement following the Then keyword in your code. It will simply go on to read the next line of your procedure, if there is one. However, if there are no more lines to read, the procedure will end.

6. Now change the operator to less than or equal to, and have Visual Basic evaluate the following condition:

```
? ActiveCell.Value <= 50
```

This time, the test returns true, and Visual Basic will jump to whatever statement or statements it finds after the Then keyword.

7. Close the Immediate window.

Now that you know how Visual Basic evaluates conditions, let's try the If...Then statement in a VBA procedure.

Hands-On 6-2: Writing a VBA Procedure with a Simple If...Then Statement

1. Open a new workbook and save it as **C:\Ex07_ByExample\Practice_Excel06.xlsm.**
2. Switch to the Visual Basic Editor screen and rename the VBA project **Decisions.**
3. Insert a new module in the Decisions (Practice_Excel06.xlsm) project and rename this module **IfThen.**
4. In the IfThen module, enter the following procedure:

```
Sub SimpleIfThen()
    Dim weeks As String
    weeks = InputBox("How many weeks are in a year:", "Quiz")
    If weeks <> 52 Then MsgBox "Try Again"
End Sub
```

The SimpleIfThen procedure stores the user's answer in the variable named weeks. The variable's value is then compared with the number 52. If the result of the comparison is true (that is, if the value stored in the variable weeks is not equal to 52), Visual Basic will display the message "Try Again."

5. Run the SimpleIfThen procedure and enter a number other than 52.
6. Rerun the SimpleIfThen procedure and enter the number **52.**

When you enter the correct number of weeks, Visual Basic does nothing. The procedure simply ends. It would be nice to display a message when the user guesses right.

7. Enter the following instruction on a separate line before the End Sub keywords:

```
If weeks = 52 Then MsgBox "Congratulations!"
```

8. Run the SimpleIfThen procedure again and enter **52**.

   When you enter the correct answer, Visual Basic does not execute the statement MsgBox "Try Again." When the procedure is executed, the statement to the right of the Then keyword is ignored if the result from evaluating the supplied condition is false. As you recall, a VBA procedure can call another procedure. Let's see whether it can also call itself.

9. Modify the first If statement in the SimpleIfThen procedure as follows:

```
If weeks <> 52 Then MsgBox "Try Again": SimpleIfThen
```

   We added a colon and the name of the SimpleIfThen procedure to the end of the existing If...Then statement. If the user enters the incorrect answer, he will see a message, and as soon as he clicks the OK button in the message box, he will get another chance to supply the correct answer — the input box will appear again. The user will be able to keep on guessing for a long time. In fact, he won't be able to exit the procedure gracefully until he supplies the correct answer. If he clicks Cancel, he will have to deal with the unfriendly error message "Type mismatch." You saw in the previous chapter how to use the On Error GoTo label statement to go around the error, at least temporarily until you learn more about error handling in Part IV. For now, you may want to revise your SimpleIfThen procedure as follows:

```
Sub SimpleIfThen()
    Dim weeks As String
    On Error GoTo VeryEnd
    weeks = InputBox("How many weeks are in a year:", "Quiz")
    If weeks <> 52 Then MsgBox "Try Again": SimpleIfThen
    If weeks = 52 Then MsgBox "Congratulations!"
    VeryEnd:
End Sub
```

10. Run the SimpleIfThen procedure a few times by supplying incorrect answers. The error trap that you added to your procedure allows the user to quit guessing without having to deal with the ugly error message.

Two Formats for the If...Then Statement

The If...Then statement has two formats — single line and multiline. The single-line format is good for short or simple statements like:

```
If secretCode <> 01W01 Then MsgBox "Access denied"
```

or

```
If secretCode = 01W01 Then alpha = True : beta = False
```

Here, secretCode, alpha, and beta are the names of variables. In the first example, Visual Basic displays the message "Access denied" if the value of secretCode is not equal to 01W01. In the second example, Visual Basic sets the value of alpha to true and beta to false when the secretCode variable is equal to 01W01. Notice that the second statement to be executed is separated from the first by a colon. The multiline If...Then statement is clearer when there are more statements to be executed when the condition is true or when the statement to be executed is extremely long, as in the following example:

```
If ActiveSheet.Name = "Sheet1" Then
    ActiveSheet.Move after:= Sheets(Worksheets.Count)
End If
```

Here, Visual Basic examines the active sheet name. If it is Sheet1, the condition ActiveSheet.Name = "Sheet1" is true, and Visual Basic proceeds to execute the line following the Then keyword. As a result, the active sheet is moved to the last position in the workbook.

Decisions Based on More Than One Condition

The SimpleIfThen procedure that you worked with earlier evaluated only a single condition in the If...Then statement. This statement, however, can take more than one condition. To specify multiple conditions in an If...Then statement, use the logical operators AND and OR (see Table 6-2 at the beginning of this chapter). Here's the syntax with the AND operator:

```
If condition1 AND condition2 Then statement
```

In the above syntax, both condition1 and condition2 must be true for Visual Basic to execute the statement to the right of the Then keyword. For example:

```
If sales = 10000 And salary < 45000 Then SlsCom = Sales * 0.07
```

In this example:

```
Condition1 sales = 10000
Condition2 salary < 45000
```

When AND is used in the conditional expression, both conditions must be true before Visual Basic can calculate the sales commission (SlsCom). If either of these conditions is false, or both are false, Visual Basic ignores the statement after Then.

When it's good enough to meet only one of the conditions, you should use the OR operator. Here's the syntax:

```
If condition1 OR condition2 Then statement
```

The OR operator is more flexible. Only one of the conditions has to be true before Visual Basic can execute the statement following the Then keyword.

Let's look at this example:

```
If dept = "S" OR dept = "M" Then bonus = 500
```

In the above example, if at least one condition is true, Visual Basic assigns 500 to the bonus variable. If both conditions are false, Visual Basic ignores the rest of the line.

Now let's look at a complete procedure example. Suppose you can get a 10% discount if you purchase 50 units of a product, each priced at $7.00. The IfThenAnd procedure demonstrates the use of the AND operator.

Hands-On 6-3: Writing a VBA Procedure with Multiple Conditions

1. Enter the following procedure in the IfThen module of the Decisions (Practice_Excel06.xlsm) project:

```
Sub IfThenAnd()
    Dim price As Single
    Dim units As Integer
    Dim rebate As Single

    Const strmsg1 = "To get a rebate you must buy an additional "
    Const strmsg2 = "Price must equal $7.00"

    units = Range("B1").Value
    price = Range("B2").Value

    If price = 7 AND units >= 50 Then
        rebate = (price * units) * 0.1
        Range("A4").Value = "The rebate is: $" & rebate
    End If

    If price = 7 AND units < 50 Then
        Range("A4").Value = strmsg1 & 50 - units & " unit(s)."
    End If

    If price <> 7 AND units >= 50 Then
        Range("A4").Value = strmsg2
    End If

    If price <> 7 AND units < 50 Then
        Range("A4").Value = "You didn't meet the criteria."
    End If
End Sub
```

The IfThenAnd procedure shown above has four If...Then statements that are used to evaluate the contents of two variables: price and units. The AND operator between the keywords If...Then allows more than one condition to be tested. With the AND operator, all conditions must be true for Visual Basic to run the statements between the Then...End If keywords. Because the IfThenAnd procedure is based on the data entered in worksheet cells, it's more convenient to run it from the Microsoft Excel window.

2. Switch to the Microsoft Excel application window, and choose **Developer | Macros.**
3. In the Macro dialog box, select the **IfThenAnd** macro and click the **Options** button.
4. While the cursor is blinking in the Shortcut key box, press **Shift+I** to assign the shortcut key Ctrl+Shift+I to your macro, and then click **OK** to exit the Macro Options dialog box.
5. Close the Macro dialog box.
6. Enter the following data in a worksheet:

	A	B
1	Units	234
2	Price	7

7. Press **Ctrl+Shift+I** to run the IfThenAnd procedure.
8. Change the values of cells B1 and B2 so that every time you run the procedure, a different If...Then statement is true.

If Block Instructions and Indenting

To make the If blocks easier to read and understand, use indentation. Compare the following:

```
If condition Then            If condition Then
action                           action
End If                       End If
```

Looking at the If...Then block statement on the right, you can easily see where the block begins and where it ends.

If...Then...Else Statement

Now you know how to display a message or take an action when one or more conditions are true or false. What should you do, however, if your procedure needs to take one action when the condition is true and another action when the condition is false? By adding the Else clause to the simple If...Then statement, you can direct your procedure to the appropriate statement depending on the result of the test.

The If...Then...Else statement has two formats — single line and multiline. The single-line format is as follows:

```
If condition Then statement1 Else statement2
```

The statement following the Then keyword is executed if the condition is true, and the statement following the Else clause is executed if the condition is false. For example:

```
If Sales > 5000 Then Bonus = Sales * 0.05 Else MsgBox "No Bonus"
```

If the value stored in the variable Sales is greater than 5000, Visual Basic will calculate the bonus using the following formula: Sales * 0.05. However, if the variable Sales is not greater than 5000, Visual Basic will display the message "No Bonus."

The If...Then...Else statement should be used to decide which of the two actions to perform. When you need to execute more statements when the condition is true or false, it's better to use the multiline format of the If...Then...Else statement:

```
If condition Then
    statements to be executed if condition is True
Else
    statements to be executed if condition is False
End If
```

Notice that the multiline (block) If...Then...Else statement ends with the End If keywords. Use the indentation shown above to make this block structure easier to read. Here's a code example that uses the above syntax:

```
If ActiveSheet.Name = "Sheet1" Then
    ActiveSheet.Name = "My Sheet"
    MsgBox "This sheet has been renamed."
Else
    MsgBox "This sheet name is not default."
End If
```

If the condition (ActiveSheet.Name = "Sheet1") is true, Visual Basic will execute the statements between Then and Else and ignore the statement between Else and End If. If the condition is false, Visual Basic will omit the statements between Then and Else and execute the statement between Else and End If.

Let's look at the complete procedure example.

Hands-On 6-4: Writing a VBA Procedure with an If...Then...Else Statement

1. Insert a new module into the Decisions (Practice_Excel06.xlsm) project.
2. Change the module name to **IfThenElse**.
3. Enter the following WhatTypeOfDay procedure:

```
Sub WhatTypeOfDay()
    Dim response As String
    Dim question As String
    Dim strmsg1 As String, strmsg2 As String
    Dim myDate As Date

    question = "Enter any date in the format mm/dd/yyyy:" _
         & Chr(13)& " (e.g., 11/22/1999)"
```

```
        strmsg1 = "weekday"
        strmsg2 = "weekend"
        response = InputBox(question)
        myDate = Weekday(CDate(response))
        If myDate >= 2 And myDate <= 6 Then
             MsgBox strmsg1
        Else
             MsgBox strmsg2
        End If
End Sub
```

The above procedure asks the user to enter any date. The user-supplied string is then converted to the Date data type with the built-in CDate function. Finally, the Weekday function converts the date into an integer that indicates the day of the week (see Table 6-3). The integer is stored in the variable myDate. The conditional test is performed to check whether the value of the variable myDate is greater than or equal to 2 (>=2) and less than or equal to 6 (<=6). If the result of the test is true, the user is told that the supplied date is a weekday; otherwise, the program announces that it's a weekend.

Table 6-3: Values returned by the built-in Weekday function

Constant	Value
vbSunday	1
vbMonday	2
vbTuesday	3
vbWednesday	4
vbThursday	5
vbFriday	6
vbSaturday	7

4. Run the procedure from the Visual Basic window. Run it a few times, each time supplying a different date. Check the Visual Basic answers against your desktop or wall calendar.

What Is Structured Programming?

Structured programming requires that all programs have a modular design and use only three types of logical structures: sequences, decisions, and loops. Sequences are statements that are executed one after another. Decisions allow you to execute specific statements based on a test of some condition. Loops make it possible to execute one or more statements repeatedly, as long as a specified condition is true. Loops are the subject of the next chapter. In structured programming, other logical statements, such as GoTo, are not allowed. The code of a structured program is easy to follow — it flows smoothly from top to bottom without jumping around to specified labels. Below are examples of structured and unstructured programs:

Unstructured program	Structured program

Sub GoToDemo()
Dim num As Integer, mystr As String
num = 1
If num = 1 Then GoTo line1 Else GoTo Line2
Line1:
mystr = "Number equals 1"
GoTo LastLine
Line2:
mystr = "Number equals 2"
LastLine:
Debug.Print mystr
End Sub
	Sub Structure()
	Dim num As Integer, mystr As String
	  num = 1
	  If num = 1 Then
	    mystr = "Number equals 1"
	    Debug.Print mystr
	  Else
	    mystr = "Number equals 2"
	  End if
	End Sub

When you write your VBA procedure from scratch and your VBA procedure needs to jump from one line of a program to another, you may be tempted to use the GoTo statement. Don't jump around. Relying on the GoTo statements for changing the course of your procedure leads to confusing code that is referred to as spaghetti code. You can easily arrive at the required destination in your procedure by using structured programming.

Here's another practice procedure to demonstrate the use of the If...Then...Else statement:

```
Sub EnterData()
    Dim cell As Object
    Dim strmsg As String

    On Error GoTo VeryEnd

    strmsg = "Select any cell:"
    Set cell = Application.InputBox(prompt:=strmsg, Type:=8)
    cell.Select

    If IsEmpty(ActiveCell) Then
        ActiveCell.Formula = InputBox("Enter text or number:")
    Else
        ActiveCell.Offset(1, 0).Select
    End If

    VeryEnd:
End Sub
```

The EnterData subroutine shown above prompts the user to select any cell. The cell address is then assigned to the cell object variable. The If...Then... Else structure checks if the selected cell is empty. IsEmpty is the built-in function that is used to determine whether a variable has been initialized. IsEmpty returns true if the variable is uninitialized. Recall that a variable is said to be initialized when it is assigned an initial value. In this procedure, if the activeCell is empty, Visual Basic treats it as a zero-length string ("").

Instead of:

```
If IsEmpty(ActiveCell) Then
```

you can use the following instruction:

```
If ActiveCell.Value = "" Then
```

If the active cell is empty, the statement following Then is executed. This statement prompts the user to enter text or number data, and once the input is provided, the data is entered in the active cell. If the active cell is not empty, Visual Basic will jump to the instruction following the Else clause. This instruction will cause Visual Basic to select the next cell in the same column.

When you run this procedure and the input box prompts you to select a cell, click any cell in the worksheet. The selected cell address will appear in the edit box. Click OK to exit the input box. Visual Basic will check the contents of the selected cell and jump to the true or false section of your procedure (the true section follows Then, and the false section follows Else).

If...Then...ElseIf Statement

Quite often you will need to check the results of several different conditions. To join a set of If conditions together, you can use the ElseIf clause. Using the If...Then...ElseIf statement, you can supply more conditions to evaluate than is possible with the If...Then...Else statement discussed earlier.

Here's the syntax of the If...Then...ElseIf statement:

```
If condition1 Then
    statements to be executed if condition1 is True
ElseIf condition2 Then
    statements to be executed if condition2 is True
ElseIf condition3 Then
    statements to be executed if condition3 is True
ElseIf conditionN Then
    statements to be executed if conditionN is True
Else
    statements to be executed if all conditions are False
End If
```

The Else clause is optional; you can omit it if there are no actions to be executed when all conditions are false. Your procedure can include any number of ElseIf statements and conditions. The ElseIf clause always comes before the Else clause. The statements in the ElseIf clause are executed only if the condition in this clause is true.

Let's look at the following code example:

```
If ActiveCell.Value = 0 Then
    ActiveCell.Offset(0, 1).Value = "zero"
ElseIf ActiveCell.Value > 0 Then
    ActiveCell.Offset(0, 1).Value = "positive"
ElseIf ActiveCell.Value < 0 Then
    ActiveCell.Offset(0, 1).Value = "negative"
End if
```

This example checks the value of the active cell and enters the appropriate label (zero, positive, negative) in the adjoining column. Notice that the Else clause is not used. If the result of the first condition (ActiveCell.Value = 0) is false, Visual Basic jumps to the next ElseIf statement and evaluates its condition (ActiveCell.Value > 0). If the value is not greater than zero, Visual Basic skips to the next ElseIf and the condition ActiveCell.Value < 0 is evaluated.

Let's see how the If...Then...ElseIf statement works in a complete procedure.

Hands-On 6-5: Writing a VBA Procedure with an If...Then... ElseIf Statement

1. Insert a new module into the current VBA project.
2. Rename the module **IfThenElseIf**.
3. Enter the following WhatValue procedure:

```
Sub WhatValue()
    Range("A1").Select
    If ActiveCell.Value = 0 Then
        ActiveCell.Offset(0, 1).Value = "zero"
    ElseIf ActiveCell.Value > 0 Then
        ActiveCell.Offset(0, 1).Value = "positive"
    ElseIf ActiveCell.Value < 0 Then
        ActiveCell.Offset(0, 1).Value = "negative"
    End If
End Sub
```

   Because you need to run the WhatValue procedure several times to test each condition, let's have Visual Basic assign a temporary keyboard shortcut to this procedure.

4. Open the Immediate window and type the following statement:

```
Application.OnKey "^+y", "WhatValue"
```

   When you press **Enter**, Visual Basic runs the OnKey method that assigns the WhatValue procedure to the key sequence Ctrl+Shift+Y. This keyboard shortcut is only temporary — it will not work when you restart Microsoft Excel. To assign the shortcut key to a procedure, use the Options button in the Macro dialog box accessed from Developer | Macros in the Microsoft Excel window.

5. Now switch to the Microsoft Excel window and activate Sheet1.

6. Enter **0** (zero) in cell A1 and press **Ctrl+Shift+Y**. Visual Basic calls the WhatValue procedure and enters "zero" in cell B1.
7. Enter any number greater than zero in cell A1 and press **Ctrl+Shift+Y**.
   Visual Basic again calls the WhatValue procedure. Visual Basic evaluates the first condition, and because the result of this test is false, it jumps to the ElseIf statement. The second condition is true, so Visual Basic executes the statement following Then and skips over the next statements to the End If. Because there are no more statements following the End If, the procedure ends. Cell B1 now displays the word "positive."
8. Enter any number less than zero in cell A1 and press **Ctrl+Shift+Y**.
   This time, the first two conditions return false, so Visual Basic goes to examine the third condition. Because this test returns true, Visual Basic enters the word "negative" in cell B1.
9. Enter any text in cell A1 and press **Ctrl+Shift+Y**.
   Visual Basic's response is "positive." However, this is not a satisfactory answer. You may want to differentiate between positive numbers and text by displaying the word "text." To make the WhatValue procedure smarter, you need to learn how to make more complex decisions by using nested If...Then statements.

Nested If...Then Statements

You can make more complex decisions in your VBA procedures by placing an If...Then or If...Then...Else statement inside another If...Then or If...Then...Else statement.

Structures in which an If statement is contained inside another If block are referred to as nested If statements. The following TestConditions procedure is a revised version of the WhatValue procedure created in the previous section. The WhatValue procedure was modified to illustrate how nested If...Then statements work.

```
Sub TestConditions()
    Range("A1").Select
    If IsEmpty(ActiveCell) Then
        MsgBox "The cell is empty."
    Else
        If IsNumeric(ActiveCell.Value) Then
            If ActiveCell.Value = 0 Then
                ActiveCell.Offset(0, 1).Value = "zero"
            ElseIf ActiveCell.Value > 0 Then
                ActiveCell.Offset(0, 1).Value = "positive"
            ElseIf ActiveCell.Value < 0 Then
                ActiveCell.Offset(0, 1).Value = "negative"
            End If
        Else
            ActiveCell.Offset(0, 1).Value = "text"
        End If
```

```
        End If
End Sub
```

To make the TestConditions procedure easier to understand, each If...Then statement is shown with different formatting. You can now clearly see that the procedure uses three If...Then blocks. The first If block (in bold) checks whether the active cell is empty. If this is true, the message is displayed, and Visual Basic skips over the Else part until it finds the matching End If. This statement is located just before the End Sub keywords. If the active cell is not empty, the IsEmpty (ActiveCell) condition returns false, and Visual Basic runs the single underlined If block following the Else formatted in bold. This (underlined) If...Then...Else statement is said to be nested inside the first If block (in bold). This statement checks if the value of the active cell is a number. Notice that this is done with the help of another built-in function — IsNumeric. If the value of the active cell is not a number, the condition is false, so Visual Basic jumps to the statement following the underlined Else and enters "text" in cell B1. However, if the active cell contains a number, Visual Basic runs the double-underlined If block, evaluating each condition and making the appropriate decision. The first If block (in bold) is called the outer If statement. This outer statement contains two inner If statements (single and double underlined).

Select Case Statement

To avoid complex nested If statements that are difficult to follow, you can use the Select Case statement instead. The syntax of this statement is as follows:

```
Select Case testexpression
    Case expressionlist1
          statements if expressionlist1 matches testexpression
    Case expressionlist2
          statements if expressionlist2 matches testexpression
    Case expressionlistN
          statements if expressionlistN matches testexpression
    Case Else
          statements to be executed if no values match testexpression
End Select
```

You can place any number of Case clauses to test between the keywords Select Case and End Select. The Case Else clause is optional. Use it when you expect that there may be conditional expressions that return false. In the Select Case statement, Visual Basic compares each expressionlist with the value of testexpression.

Here's the logic behind the Select Case statement. When Visual Basic encounters the Select Case clause, it makes note of the value of testexpression. Then it proceeds to test the expression following the first Case clause. If the value of this expression (expressionlist1) matches the value stored in testexpression, Visual Basic executes the statements until another Case clause is encountered and then jumps to the End Select statement. If, however, the expression tested in the first Case clause does not match the testexpression, Visual Basic checks the value of each Case clause until it finds a match. If none of the Case clauses contain the expression that matches the value stored in testexpression, Visual Basic jumps to the Case Else clause and executes the statements until it encounters the End Select keywords. Notice that the Case Else clause is optional. If your procedure does not use Case Else and none of the Case clauses contain a value matching the value of the testexpression, Visual Basic jumps to the statements following End Select and continues executing your procedure.

Let's look at an example of a procedure that uses the Select Case statement. In Chapter 5, you learned quite a few details about the MsgBox function that allows you to display a message with one or more buttons. You also learned that the result of the MsgBox function can be assigned to a variable. Using the Select Case statement, you can now decide which action to take based on the button the user pressed in the message box.

Hands-On 6-6: Writing a VBA Procedure with a Select Case Statement

1. Insert a new module into the current VBA project.
2. Rename the new module **SelectCase**.
3. Enter the following TestButtons procedure:

```
Sub TestButtons()
    Dim question As String
    Dim bts As Integer
    Dim myTitle As String
    Dim myButton As Integer

    question = "Do you want to open a new workbook?"
    bts = vbYesNoCancel + vbQuestion + vbDefaultButton1
    myTitle = "New Workbook"
    myButton = MsgBox(prompt:=question, _
                buttons:=bts, _
                title:=myTitle)
    Select Case myButton
        Case 6
            Workbooks.Add
        Case 7
            MsgBox "You can open a new book manually later."
        Case Else
            MsgBox "You pressed Cancel."
    End Select
End Sub
```

The first part of the TestButtons procedure displays a message with three buttons: Yes, No, and Cancel. The value of the button selected by the user is assigned to the variable myButton. If the user clicks Yes, the variable myButton is assigned the vbYes constant or its corresponding value — 6. If the user selects No, the variable myButton is assigned the constant vbNo or its corresponding value — 7. Lastly, if Cancel is pressed, the contents of the variable myButton will equal vbCancel, or 2. The Select Case statement checks the values supplied after the Case clause against the value stored in the variable myButton. When there is a match, the appropriate Case statement is executed.

The TestButtons procedure will work the same if you use the constants instead of button values:

```
Select Case myButton
    Case vbYes
         Workbooks.Add
    Case vbNo
         MsgBox "You can open a new book manually later."
    Case Else
         MsgBox "You pressed Cancel."
End Select
```

You can omit the Else clause. Simply revise the Select Case statement as follows:

```
Select Case myButton
    Case vbYes
         Workbooks.Add
    Case vbNo
         MsgBox "You can open a new book manually later."
    Case vbCancel
         MsgBox "You pressed Cancel."
End Select
```

4. Run the TestButtons procedure three times, each time selecting a different button.

Using Is with the Case Clause

Sometimes a decision is made based on a relational operator, such as whether the test expression is greater than, less than, or equal to (see Table 6-1). The Is keyword lets you use a conditional expression in a Case clause. The syntax for the Select Case clause using the Is keyword is shown below:

```
Select Case testexpression
    Case Is condition1
         statements if condition1 is True
    Case Is condition2
         statements if condition2 is True
    Case Is conditionN
         statements if conditionN is True
End Select
```

Although using Case Else in the Select Case statement isn't required, it's always a good idea to include one, just in case the variable you are testing has an unexpected value. The Case Else is a good place to put an error message. For example, let's compare some numbers:

```
Select Case myNumber
    Case Is <=10
         MsgBox "The number is less than or equal to 10"
```

```
        Case 11
              MsgBox "You entered eleven."
        Case Is >=100
              MsgBox "The number is greater than or equal to 100."
        Case Else
              MsgBox "The number is between 12 and 99."
    End Select
```

Assuming that the variable myNumber holds 120, the third Case clause is true, and the only statement executed is the one between the Case Is >=100 and the Case Else clause.

Specifying a Range of Values in a Case Clause

In the preceding example you saw a simple Select Case statement that uses one expression in each Case clause. Many times, however, you may want to specify a range of values in a Case clause. Do this by using the To keyword between the values of expressions, as in the following example:

```
    Select Case unitsSold
        Case 1 To 100
              Discount = 0.05
        Case Is <= 500
              Discount = 0.1
        Case 501 To 1000
              Discount = 0.15
        Case Is > 1000
              Discount = 0.2
    End Select
```

Let's analyze the above Select Case block with the assumption that the variable unitsSold currently holds the value 99. Visual Basic compares the value of the variable unitsSold with the conditional expression in the Case clauses. The first and third Case clauses illustrate how to use a range of values in a conditional expression by using the To keyword. Because unitsSold = 99, the condition in the first Case clause is true; thus, Visual Basic assigns the value 0.05 to the variable Discount. How about the second Case clause, which is also true? Although it's obvious that 99 is less than or equal to 500, Visual Basic does not execute the associated statement Discount = 0.1. The reason for this is that once Visual Basic locates a Case clause with a true condition, it doesn't bother to look at the remaining Case clauses. It jumps over them and continues to execute the procedure with the instructions that may be following the End Select statement.

To get more practice with the Select Case statement, let's use it in a function procedure. As you recall from Chapter 5, function procedures allow you to return a result to a subroutine. Suppose a subroutine has to display a discount based on the number of units sold. You can get the number of units from the user and then run a function to figure out which discount applies.

Hands-On 6-7: Writing a Function Procedure with a Select Case Statement

1. Enter the following subroutine in the SelectCase module:

```
Sub DisplayDiscount()
    Dim unitsSold As Integer
    Dim myDiscount As Single
    unitsSold = InputBox("Enter the number of sold units:")
    myDiscount = GetDiscount(unitsSold)
    MsgBox myDiscount
End Sub
```

2. Enter the following function procedure:

```
Function GetDiscount(unitsSold As Integer)
    Select Case unitsSold
          Case 1 To 200
                GetDiscount = 0.05
          Case Is <= 500
                GetDiscount = 0.1
          Case 501 To 1000
                GetDiscount = 0.15
          Case Is > 1000
                GetDiscount = 0.2
    End Select
End Function
```

3. Place the cursor anywhere within the code of the DisplayDiscount procedure and press **F5** to run it. Run the procedure several times, entering values to test each Case statement.

   The DisplayDiscount procedure passes the value stored in the variable unitsSold to the GetDiscount function. When Visual Basic encounters the Select Case statement, it checks whether the value of the first Case clause expression matches the value stored in the unitsSold parameter. If there is a match, Visual Basic assigns a 5% discount (0.05) to the function name, and then jumps to the End Select keywords. Because there are no more statements to execute inside the function procedure, Visual Basic returns to the calling procedure — DisplayDiscount. Here it assigns the function's result to the variable myDiscount. The last statement displays the value of the retrieved discount in a message box.

Specifying Multiple Expressions in a Case Clause

You may specify multiple conditions within a single Case clause by separating each condition with a comma, as shown in the following code example:

```
Select Case myMonth
    Case "January", "February", "March"
          Debug.Print myMonth & ": 1st Qtr."
    Case "April", "May", "June"
          Debug.Print myMonth & ": 2nd Qtr."
    Case "July", "August", "September"
          Debug.Print myMonth & ": 3rd Qtr."
```

```
        Case "October", "November", "December"
            Debug.Print myMonth & ": 4th Qtr."
    End Select
```

Multiple Conditions with the Case Clause

The commas used to separate conditions within a Case clause have the same meaning as the OR operator used in the If statement. The Case clause is true if at least one of the conditions is true.

Nesting Statements

Nesting means placing one type of control structure inside another control structure. You will see more nesting examples with the looping structures discussed in Chapter 7.

Chapter Summary

Conditional statements, which were introduced in this chapter, let you control the flow of your procedure. By testing the truth of a condition, you can decide which statements should be run and which should be skipped over. In other words, instead of running your procedure from top to bottom, line by line, you can execute only certain lines. If you are wondering what kind of conditional statement you should use, here are a few guidelines:

- If you want to supply only one condition, the simple If…Then statement is the best choice.
- If you need to decide which of two actions to perform, use the If…Then…Else statement.
- If your procedure requires two or more conditions, use the If…Then…ElseIf or Select Case statements.
- If your procedure has many conditions, use the Select Case statement. This statement is more flexible and easier to comprehend than the If…Then…ElseIf statement.

Some decisions have to be repeated. For example, you may want to repeat the same actions for each cell in a worksheet or each sheet in a workbook. The next chapter teaches you how to perform the same steps over and over again.

Chapter 7

Repeating Actions in VBA

Now that you've learned how conditional statements can give your VBA procedures decision-making capabilities, it's time to get more involved. Not all decisions are easy. Sometimes you will need to perform a number of statements several times to arrive at a certain condition. On other occasions, however, after you've reached the decision, you may need to run the specified statements as long as a condition is true or until a condition becomes true. In programming, performing repetitive tasks is called *looping*. VBA has various looping structures that allow you to repeat a sequence of statements a number of times. In this chapter, you will learn how to loop through your code.

What Is a Loop?

A *loop* is a programming structure that causes a section of program code to execute repeatedly. VBA provides several structures to implement loops in your procedures: Do...While, Do...Until, For...Next, For...Each, and While...Wend.

Do Loops: Do...While and Do...Until

Visual Basic has two types of Do loop statements that repeat a sequence of statements either as long as or until a certain condition is true. The Do...While loop lets you repeat an action as long as a condition is true. This loop has the following syntax:

```
Do While condition
     statement1
     statement2
     statementN
Loop
```

When Visual Basic encounters this loop, it first checks the truth value of the condition. If the condition is false, the statements inside the loop are not executed. Visual Basic will continue to execute the program with the first statement after the Loop keyword. If the condition is true, the statements inside the loop are run one by one until the Loop statement is encountered. The Loop statement tells Visual Basic to repeat the entire process again, as long as the testing of the condition in the Do While statement is true. Let's now see how you can put the Do...While loop to good use in Microsoft Excel.

In Chapter 6, you learned how to make a decision based on the contents of a cell. Let's take it a step further and see how you can repeat the same decision for a number of cells. The decision is to apply bold formatting to any cell in a column, as long as it's not empty.

Hands-On 7-1: Writing a VBA Procedure with a Do...While Statement (Example 1)

1. Open a new workbook and save it as **C:\Ex07_ByExample\Practice_Excel07.xlsm.**

2. Switch to the Visual Basic Editor screen, and change the name of the new project to **Repetition**.
3. Insert a new module into the Repetition project and change its name to **DoLoops**.
4. Enter the following procedure in the DoLoops module:

```
Sub ApplyBold()
    Do While ActiveCell.Value <> ""
          ActiveCell.Font.Bold = True
          ActiveCell.Offset(1, 0).Select
    Loop
End Sub
```

5. Press **Alt+F11** to switch to the Microsoft Excel application window and activate Sheet1. Enter any data (text or numbers) in cells A1:A7.
6. When finished with the data entry, select cell **A1**.
7. Choose **Developer | Macros**. In the Macro dialog box, double-click the **ApplyBold** procedure (or highlight the procedure name and click **Run**).

   When you run the ApplyBold procedure, Visual Basic first evaluates the condition in the Do While statement — ActiveCell.Value <>"". The condition says: Perform the following statements as long as the value of the active cell is not an empty string (""). Because you have entered data in cell A1 and made this cell active (see steps 5-6 above), the first test returns true. So Visual Basic executes the statement ActiveCell.Font.Bold = True, which applies the bold formatting to the active cell. Next, Visual Basic selects the cell in the next row (the Offset property is discussed in Chapter 2). Because the statement that follows is the Loop keyword, Visual Basic returns to the Do While statement and again checks the condition. If the newly selected active cell is not empty, Visual Basic repeats the statements inside the loop. This process continues until the contents of cell A8 are examined. Because this cell is empty, the condition is false, so Visual Basic skips the statements inside the loop. Because there are no more statements to execute after the Loop keyword, the procedure ends. Let's look at another Do...While loop example.

The next example procedure demonstrates how to display today's date and time in Microsoft Excel's status bar for 10 seconds.

Hands-On 7-2: Writing a VBA Procedure with a Do...While Statement (Example 2)

1. Enter the following procedure in the DoLoops module:

```
Sub TenSeconds()
    Dim stopme

    stopme = Now + TimeValue("00:00:10")

    Do While Now < stopme
         Application.DisplayStatusBar = True
```

```
        Application.StatusBar = Now
    Loop

    Application.StatusBar = False
End Sub
```

In the above procedure, the statements inside the Do...While loop will be executed as long as the time returned by the Now function is less than the value of the variable called stopme. The variable stopme holds the current time plus 10 seconds. (See the online help for other examples of using the built-in TimeValue function.)

The statement

```
Application.DisplayStatusBar
```

tells Visual Basic to turn on the display of the status bar. The next statement places the current date and time in the status bar. While the time is displayed (and this lasts only 10 seconds), the user cannot work with the system (the mouse pointer turns into the hourglass). After the 10 seconds are over (that is, when the condition Now < stopme evaluates to true), Visual Basic leaves the loop and executes the statement after the Loop keyword. This statement returns the default status bar message "Ready."

2. Press **Alt+F11** to switch to the Microsoft Excel application window.
3. Choose **Developer | Macros.** In the Macro dialog box, double-click the **TenSeconds** macro name (or highlight the macro name and click **Run**).

   Observe the date and time display in the status bar. The status bar should return to "Ready" after 10 seconds.

The Do...While loop has an alternative syntax that lets you test the condition at the bottom of the loop in the following way:

```
Do
    statement1
    statement2
    statementN
Loop While condition
```

When you test the condition at the bottom of the loop, the statements inside the loop are executed at least once. Let's take a look at an example:

```
Sub SignIn()
    Dim secretCode As String
    Do
        secretCode = InputBox("Enter your secret code:")
        If secretCode = "sp1045" Then Exit Do
    Loop While secretCode <> "sp1045"
End Sub
```

Notice that by the time the condition is evaluated, Visual Basic has already executed the statements one time. In addition to placing the condition at the end of the loop, the SignIn procedure shows how to exit the loop when a condition is reached. When the Exit Do statement is encountered, the loop ends immediately.

Avoid Infinite Loops

If you don't design your loop correctly, you get an *infinite* loop — a loop that never ends. You will not be able to stop the procedure by using the Escape key. The following procedure causes the loop to execute endlessly because the programmer forgot to include the test condition:

```
Sub SayHello()
    Do
        MsgBox "Hello."
    Loop
End Sub
```

To stop the execution of the infinite loop, you must press Ctrl+Break. When Visual Basic displays the message box that says "Code execution has been interrupted," click End to end the procedure.

Another handy loop, Do...Until, allows you to repeat one or more statements until a condition becomes true. In other words, Do...Until repeats a block of code as long as something is false. Here's the syntax:

```
Do Until condition
    statement1
    statement2
    statementN
Loop
```

Using the above syntax, you can now rewrite the previous ApplyBold procedure in the following way:

```
Sub ApplyBold2()
    Do Until IsEmpty(ActiveCell)
        ActiveCell.Font.Bold = True
        ActiveCell.Offset(1, 0).Select
    Loop
End Sub
```

The first line of this procedure says to perform the following statements until the first empty cell is reached. As a result, if the active cell is not empty, Visual Basic executes the two statements inside the loop. This process continues as long as the condition IsEmpty(ActiveCell) evaluates to false. Because the ApplyBold2 procedure tests the condition at the beginning of the loop, the statements inside the loop will not run if the first cell is empty. You will get the chance to try out this procedure in the next section.

Similar to the Do...While loop, the Do...Until loop has a second syntax that lets you test the condition at the bottom of the loop:

```
Do
    statement1
    statement2
    statementN
Loop Until condition
```

If you want the statements to execute at least once, place the condition on the line with the Loop statement no matter what the value of the condition.

Let's try out an example procedure that deletes empty sheets from a workbook.

Hands-On 7-3: Writing a VBA Procedure with a Do...Until Statement

1. Enter the DeleteBlankSheets procedure, as shown below, in the DoLoops module that you created earlier. You may copy the code from **C:\Ex07_HandsOn\Ex07_Chapter07.txt.**

```
Sub DeleteBlankSheets()
    Dim myRange As Range
    Dim shcount As Integer
    shcount = Worksheets.Count
    Do
          Worksheets(shcount).Select
          Set myRange = ActiveSheet.UsedRange
          If myRange.Address = "$A$1" And _
                Range("A1").Value = "" Then
                Application.DisplayAlerts = False
                Worksheets(shcount).Delete
                Application.DisplayAlerts = True
          End If
          shcount = shcount - 1
    Loop Until shcount = 1
End Sub
```

2. Press **Alt+F11** to switch to the Microsoft Excel window and manually insert three new worksheets into the current workbook. In one of the sheets, enter text or numbers in cell A1. On another sheet, enter some data in cells B2 and C10. Do not enter any data on the third inserted sheet.
3. Run the DeleteBlankSheets procedure.

When you run this procedure, Visual Basic deletes the selected sheet whenever two conditions are true — the UsedRange property address returns cell A1 and cell A1 is empty. The UsedRange property applies to the Worksheet object and contains every non-empty cell on the worksheet, as well as all the empty cells that are among them. For example, if you enter something in cells B2 and C10, the used range is $B$2:$C$10. If you later enter data in cell A1, the UsedRange will be $A$1:$C$10. The used range is bounded by the farthest upper-left and farthest lower-right non-empty cell on a worksheet.

Because the workbook must contain at least one worksheet, the code is executed until the variable shcount equals one. The statement shcount = shcount – 1 makes sure that the shcount variable is reduced by one each time the statements in the loop are executed. The value of shcount is initialized at the beginning of the procedure with the following statement:

```
Worksheets.Count
```

Notice also that when deleting sheets, Excel normally displays the confirmation dialog box. If you'd rather not be prompted to confirm the deletion, use the following statement:

```
Application.DisplayAlerts = False
```

When you are finished, turn the system messages back on with the following statement:

```
Application.DisplayAlerts = True
```

Counters

A counter is a numeric variable that keeps track of the number of items that have been processed. The DeleteBlankSheets procedure shown above declares the variable shcount to keep track of sheets that have been processed. A counter variable should be initialized (assigned a value) at the beginning of the program. This makes sure you always know the exact value of the counter before you begin using it. A counter can be incremented or decremented by a specified value. See other examples of using counters with the For...Next loop later in this chapter.

Watching a Procedure Execute

When you run procedures that use looping structures, it's sometimes hard to see whether the procedure works as expected. Occasionally, you'd like to watch the procedure execute in slow motion so that you can check the logic of the program. Let's examine how Visual Basic allows you to execute a procedure line by line.

Hands-On 7-4: Executing a Procedure Line by Line

1. Insert a new sheet into the current workbook and enter any data in cells A1:A5.
2. Select cell **A1** and choose **Developer | Macros**.
3. In the Macro dialog box, select the **ApplyBold2** procedure and click the **Step Into** button.

   The Visual Basic Editor screen will appear with the name of the procedure highlighted in yellow (see Figure 7-1). Notice the yellow arrow in the margin indicator bar of the Code window.
4. Make the Visual Basic window smaller. To do this, click the **Restore** button in the Visual Basic title bar and arrange the screen as shown in Figure 7-1.
5. Press **F8**. The yellow highlight in the Code window jumps to this line:

   ```
   Do Until IsEmpty(ActiveCell)
   ```
6. Continue pressing **F8** while watching both the Code window and the worksheet window.

Note: You will find more information related to stepping through VBA procedures in Chapter 10.

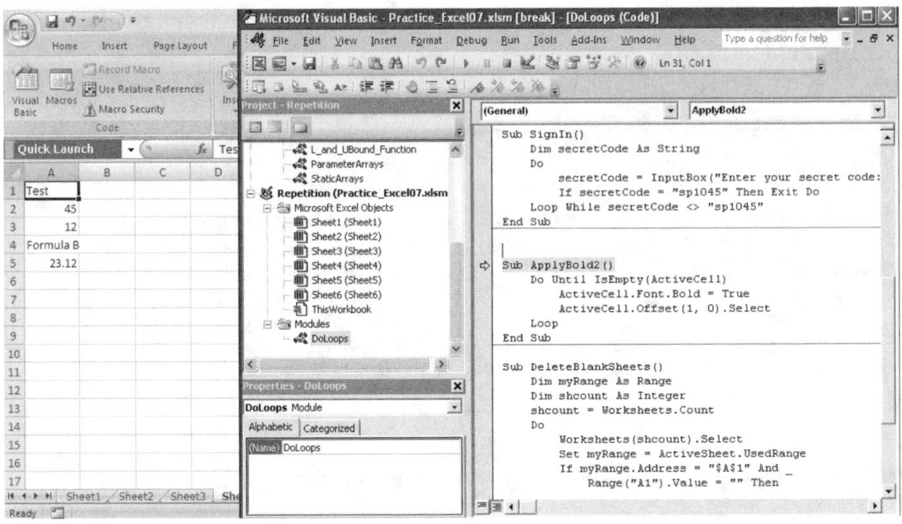

Figure 7-1: Watching the procedure code execute line by line.

While...Wend Loop

The While...Wend loop is functionally equivalent to the Do...While loop. This statement is a carryover from earlier versions of Microsoft Basic and is included in VBA for backward compatibility. The loop begins with the keyword While and ends with the keyword Wend. Here's the syntax:

```
While condition
    statement1
    statement2
    statementN
Wend
```

The condition is tested at the top of the loop. The statements are executed as long as the given condition is true. Once the condition is false, Visual Basic exits the loop.

Let's look at an example of a procedure that uses the While...Wend looping structure. We will change the row height of all non-empty cells in a worksheet.

Hands-On 7-5: Writing a VBA Procedure with a While... Wend Statement

1. Insert a new module into the current VBA project. Rename the module **WhileLoop**.
2. Enter the following procedure in the WhileLoop module. You can copy the code from **C:\Ex07_HandsOn\Ex07_Chapter07.txt**.

```
Sub ChangeRHeight()
    While ActiveCell <> ""
    ActiveCell.RowHeight = 28
```

```
        ActiveCell.Offset(1, 0).Select
        Wend
    End Sub
```

3. Switch to the Microsoft Excel window and enter some data in cells B1:B4 of any worksheet.
4. Select cell **B1** and choose **Developer | Macros.**
5. In the Macro dialog, select the **ChangeRHeight** procedure and click **Run**.

The ChangeRHeight procedure shown above sets the row height to 28 when the active cell is not empty. The next cell is selected by using the Offset property of the Range object. The statement ActiveCell.Offset(1, 0).Select tells Visual Basic to select the cell that is located one row below (1) the active cell and in the same column (0).

For...Next Loop

The For…Next loop is used when you know how many times you want to repeat a group of statements. The syntax of a For…Next loop looks like this:

```
For counter = start To end [Step increment]
    statement1
    statement2
    statementN
Next [counter]
```

The code in the brackets is optional. Counter is a numeric variable that stores the number of iterations. Start is the number at which you want to begin counting, and end indicates how many times the loop should be executed.

For example, if you want to repeat the statements inside the loop five times, use the following For statement syntax:

```
For counter = 1 To 5
    Your statements go here
Next
```

When Visual Basic encounters the Next keyword, it will go back to the beginning of the loop and execute the statements inside the loop again, as long as counter hasn't reached the end value. As soon as the value of counter is greater than the number entered after the To keyword, Visual Basic exits the loop. Because the variable counter automatically changes after each execution of the loop, sooner or later the value stored in counter exceeds the value specified. By default, every time Visual Basic executes the statements inside the loop, the value of the variable counter is increased by one. You can change this default setting by using the Step clause. For example, to increase the variable counter by three, use the following statement:

```
For counter = 1 To 5 Step 3
    Your statements go here
Next counter
```

When Visual Basic encounters the above instruction, it executes the statements inside the loop twice. The first time in the loop, counter equals 1. The second time in the loop, counter equals 4 (3+1). After the second time inside the loop, counter equals 7 (4+3). This causes Visual Basic to exit the loop. Note that the Step increment is optional, and isn't specified unless it's a value other than 1. You can also place a negative number after Step. Visual Basic will then decrement this value from the counter each time it encounters the Next keyword. The name of the variable (counter) after the Next keyword is also optional. However, it's good programming practice to make your Next keywords explicit by including counter.

How can you use the For...Next loop in a Microsoft Excel spreadsheet? Suppose in your sales report you'd like to include only products that were sold in a particular month. When you imported data from a Microsoft Access table, you also got rows with the sold amount equal to zero. How can you quickly eliminate those "zero" rows? Although there are many ways to solve this problem, let's see how you can handle it with a For...Next loop.

Hands-On 7-6: Writing a VBA Procedure with a For...Next Statement

1. In the Visual Basic window, insert a new module into the current project and rename it **ForNextLoop**.
2. Enter the following procedure in the ForNextLoop module:

```
Sub DeleteZeroRows()
    Dim totalR As Integer
    Dim r As Integer

    Range("A1").CurrentRegion.Select
    totalR = Selection.Rows.Count
    Range("B2").Select

    For r = 1 To totalR - 1
        If ActiveCell = 0 Then
            Selection.EntireRow.Delete
            totalR = totalR - 1
        Else
            ActiveCell.Offset(1, 0).Select
        End If
    Next r
End Sub
```

Let's examine the DeleteZeroRows procedure line by line. The first two statements calculate the total number of rows in the current range and store this number in the variable totalR. Next, Visual Basic selects cell B2 and encounters the For keyword. Because the first row of the spreadsheet contains the column headings, decrease the total number of rows by one (totalR – 1). Visual Basic will need to execute the instructions inside the loop six times. The conditional statement (If...Then...Else) nested inside the loop tells Visual Basic to make a decision based on the value of the active cell. If the value is equal to zero, Visual Basic deletes the current row and reduces the value of totalR by one. Otherwise, the condition is false, so Visual Basic selects the next cell. Each time Visual Basic completes the loop, it jumps to the For keyword to compare the value of r with the value of totalR – 1.

3. Switch to the Microsoft Excel window and insert a new worksheet. Enter the data as shown below:

	A	B
1	Product Name	Sales (in Pounds)
2	Apples	120
3	Pears	0
4	Bananas	100
5	Cherries	0
6	Blueberries	0
7	Strawberries	160

4. Choose **Developer | Macros.**
5. In the Macro dialog, select the **DeleteZeroRows** procedure and click **Run.**

   When the procedure ends, the sales spreadsheet does not include products that were not sold.

Paired Statements

For and Next must be paired. If one is missing, Visual Basic generates the following error message: "For without Next."

For Each...Next Loop

When your procedure needs to loop through all of the objects of a collection or all of the elements in an array (arrays are covered in Chapter 8), the For Each...Next loop should be used. This loop does not require a counter variable. Visual Basic can figure out on its own how many times the loop should execute.

Let's take, for example, a collection of worksheets. To remove a worksheet from a workbook, you have to first select it and then choose Edit | Delete Sheet. To leave only one worksheet in a workbook, you have to use the same command several times, depending on the total number of worksheets. Because each worksheet is an object in a collection of worksheets, you can speed up the process of deleting worksheets by using the For Each...Next loop. This loop looks like this:

```
For Each element In Group
    statement1
    statement2
    statementN
Next [element]
```

In the above syntax, the element is a variable to which all the elements of an array or collection will be assigned. This variable has to be of the Variant data type for an array and an Object data type for a collection. Group is the name of a collection or an array.

Let's now see how to use the For Each...Next loop to remove some worksheets.

Hands-On 7-7: Writing a VBA Procedure with a For Each... Next Statement

1. Insert a new module into the current project and rename it **ForEachNextLoop**.
2. Type the following procedure in the ForEachNextLoop module:

```
Sub RemoveSheets()
    Dim mySheet As Worksheet

    Application.DisplayAlerts = False

    Workbooks.Add
    Worksheets("Sheet2").Select

    For Each mySheet In Worksheets
        ActiveWindow.SelectedSheets.Delete
    Next mySheet

    Application.DisplayAlerts = True
End Sub
```

   Visual Basic will open a new workbook and delete all the sheets except for Sheet1. Notice that the variable mySheet represents an object in a collection of worksheets. Therefore, this variable has been declared of the specific object data type Worksheet. The first instruction, Application.DisplayAlerts = False, makes sure that Microsoft Excel does not display alerts and messages while the procedure is running. If you omit this statement, Microsoft Excel will ask you to confirm the deletion of the selected worksheet. Next, the procedure opens a new workbook and selects Sheet2. The For Each...Next loop steps through each worksheet (starting from the selected Sheet2) and deletes it. When the procedure ends, the workbook has only one sheet — Sheet1.

3. Position the insertion point anywhere within the RemoveSheets procedure code and press **F5** to run it.

Here's another example that checks whether a certain sheet is part of a workbook:

```
Sub IsSuchSheet()
    Dim mySheet As Worksheet
    Dim counter As Integer

    counter = 0

    For Each mySheet In Worksheets
        If mySheet.name = "Sheet2" Then
            counter = counter + 1
        End If
    Next mySheet

    If counter = 1 Then
        MsgBox "This workbook contains Sheet2."
    Else
        MsgBox "Sheet2 was not found."
    End if
End Sub
```

Exiting Loops Early

Sometimes you may not want to wait until the loop ends on its own. It's possible that a user has entered the wrong data, a procedure has encountered an error, or perhaps the task has been completed and there's no need to do additional looping. You can leave the loop early without reaching the condition that normally terminates it. Visual Basic has two types of Exit statements:

- The Exit For statement is used to end either a For...Next or a For Each...Next loop early.
- The Exit Do statement immediately exits any of the VBA Do loops.

The following procedure demonstrates how to use the Exit For statement to leave the For Each...Next loop early.

Hands-On 7-8: Writing a VBA Procedure with an Early Exit from a For Each...Next Statement

1. Enter the following procedure in the ForEachNextLoop module:

```
Sub EarlyExit()
    Dim myCell As Range
    For Each myCell in Range("A1:H10")
        If myCell.Value = "" Then
            myCell.Value = "empty"
        Else
            Exit For
        End If
    Next myCell
End Sub
```

The EarlyExit procedure examines the contents of each cell in the specified range — A1:H10. If the active cell is empty, Visual Basic enters the text "empty" in the active cell. When Visual Basic encounters the first non-empty cell, it exits the loop.

2. Open a new workbook and enter a value in any cell within the specified range — A1:H10.
3. Choose **Developer** | **Macros**.
4. In the Macro dialog, select the **EarlyExit** procedure and click **Run**.

Nested Loops

So far in this chapter you have tried out various loops. Each procedure demonstrated the use of each individual looping structure. In programming practice, however, one loop is often placed inside another. Visual Basic allows you to "nest" various types of loops (For and Do loops) within the same procedure. When writing nested loops, you must make sure that each inner loop is completely contained inside the outer loop. Also, each loop has to have a unique counter variable. When you use nesting loops, you can often execute a specific task more effectively.

The following ColorLoop procedure illustrates how one For…Next loop is nested within another For…Next loop.

Hands-On 7-9: Writing a VBA Procedure with a Nested For...Next Statement

1. Enter the following procedure in the ForEachNextLoop module:

```
Sub ColorLoop()
    Dim myRow As Integer
    Dim myCol As Integer
    Dim myColor As Integer

    myColor = 0

    For myRow = 1 To 8
          For myCol = 1 To 7
                Cells(myRow, myCol).Select
                myColor = myColor + 1
                With Selection.Interior
                      .ColorIndex = myColor
                      .Pattern = xlSolid
                End With
          Next myCol
    Next myRow
End Sub
```

The ColorLoop procedure shown above uses two For…Next loops to change the color of each cell located in the first eight rows and seven columns of a worksheet. While the outer loop keeps track of the row number, the inner loop does more than one thing. It determines the current column number, selects the appropriate cell based on the current row and column index, keeps track of the color index, and then applies the color to the selected cell. The inner For...Next loop applies a different color to seven cells in the first spreadsheet row (A1, B1, C1, D1, E1, F1, and G1). When the variable myCol is greater than 7, Visual Basic jumps back to the outer loop to increment the variable myRow by one and returns to the inner loop to color the next set of cells in the second row. When the procedure ends, 56 cells (8*7) are formatted with all the colors available in the current color palette. The first cell, A1, is formatted with a black color (color index number 1). The second cell, B1, is formatted as white (color index number 2). Each time the cell address changes — Cells(myRow, myCol).Select — the contents of the variable myColor change as well — myColor = myColor + 1.

2. Open a new workbook and choose **Developer | Macros.**
3. In the Macro dialog, select the **ColorLoop** procedure and click **Run.**

Exiting Procedures

If you want to exit a subroutine earlier than normal, use the Exit Sub statement. If the procedure is a function, use the Exit Function statement instead.

Chapter Summary

In this chapter you learned how to repeat certain groups of statements using procedure loops. While working with several types of looping statements, you saw how each loop performs repetitions in a slightly different way. As you gain experience, you'll find it easier to choose the appropriate flow control structure for your task. In the following chapters of this book, there are many additional examples of using loops. In the next chapter, for instance, you will see how arrays and nested loops are used in a VBA procedure that picks lottery numbers.

Chapter 8 will show you how arrays are used to work with larger sets of data.

Part III

Keeping Track of Multiple Values

Although you can use individual variables to store data while your VBA code is executing, many advanced VBA procedures will require that you implement more efficient methods of keeping track of multiple values.

In this part of the book, you'll learn about working with groups of variables (arrays) and storing data in collections.

Chapter 8

Working with Arrays

In previous chapters, you worked with many VBA procedures that used variables to hold specific information about an object, property, or value. For each single value that you wanted your procedure to manipulate, you declared a variable. But what if you have a series of values? If you had to write a VBA procedure to deal with larger amounts of data, you would have to create enough variables to handle all of the data. Can you imagine the nightmare of storing in your program currency exchange rates for all the countries in the world? To create a table to hold the necessary data, you'd need at least three variables for each country: country name, currency name, and exchange rate. Fortunately, Visual Basic has a way to get around this problem. By clustering the related variables together, your VBA procedures can manage a large amount of data with ease. In this chapter, you'll learn how to manipulate lists and tables of data with arrays.

What Is an Array?

In Visual Basic an *array* is a special type of variable that represents a group of similar values that are of the same data type (String, Integer, Currency, Date, etc.). The two most common types of arrays are one-dimensional arrays (lists) and two-dimensional arrays (tables). A one-dimensional array is sometimes referred to as a *list*. A shopping list, a list of the days of the week, or an employee list are examples of one-dimensional arrays or, simply, numbered lists. Each value in the list has an index. Below is a diagram of a list that contains six elements (items):

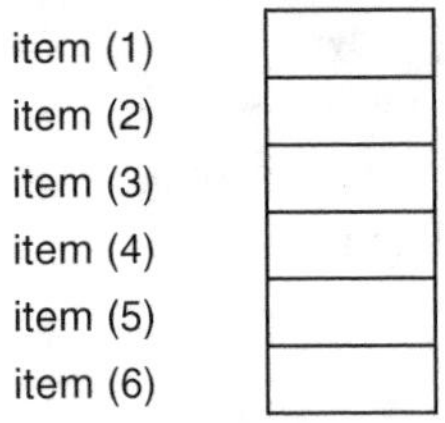

item (1)	
item (2)	
item (3)	
item (4)	
item (5)	
item (6)	

Notice that the column representing the one-dimensional array is currently empty. If you want to fill this array with data, simply use one variable name followed by a number in parentheses instead of six individual labels. In the diagram above, item is a variable name and the numbers in parentheses — (1), (2), (3), (4), (5), and (6) — identify individual elements of the array. All elements of the array must be of the same data type. In other words, one array cannot store both strings and integers. Following are two examples of one-dimensional arrays: a one-dimensional array called cities is populated with text (String data type — $), and a one-dimensional array called lotto contains six lottery numbers (Integer data type — %).

One-dimensional array named cities$ (of String data type)

cities(1)	Baltimore
cities(2)	Atlanta
cities(3)	Boston
cities(4)	Washington
cities(5)	New York
cities(6)	Trenton

One-dimensional array named lotto% (of Integer data type)

lotto(1)	25
lotto(2)	4
lotto(3)	31
lotto(4)	22
lotto(5)	11
lotto(6)	5

As you can see, the contents assigned to each array element match the variable type. If you want to store values of different data types in the same array, you must declare the array as Variant. Two-dimensional arrays are tables of data represented in rows and columns. The position of each element in a table is determined by its row and column number. Below is a diagram of an empty two-dimensional array.

rows ↓	1	2	3	←columns
1	(1,1)	(1,2)	(1,3)	
2	(2,1)	(2,2)	(2,3)	
3	(3,1)	(3,2)	(3,3)	
4	(4,1)	(4,2)	(4,3)	
5	(5,1)	(5,2)	(5,3)	

Notice how items in a two-dimensional array are identified with row and column indices. In this diagram, the first element of the array is located in the first row and the first column (1,1). The last element of the array is positioned in the fifth row and third column (5,3). Let's now populate this array with some values. The two-dimensional array that is shown below stores the name of the country, its currency, and the U.S. dollar exchange rate.

Two-dimensional array named exchange (of Variant data type)

Japan *(1,1)*	Japanese Yen *(1,2)*	108.83 *(1,3)*
Australia *(2,1)*	Australian Dollar *(2,2)*	1.28601 *(2,3)*
Canada *(3,1)*	Canadian Dollar *(3,2)*	1.235 *(3,3)*
Norway *(4,1)*	Norwegian Krone *(4,2)*	6.4471 *(4,3)*
Europe *(5,1)*	Euro *(5,2)*	0.816993 *(5,3)*

Although VBA arrays can have up to 60 dimensions, most people find it difficult to picture dimensions beyond 3D. A three-dimensional array is a collection of tables where each table has the same number of rows and columns. Each element of a three-dimensional array is identified by three pieces of data: row, column, and table.

Declaring Arrays

Because an array is a variable, you must declare it in a similar way that you declare other variables — by using the Dim statement. When you declare an array variable, you set aside the required memory space to hold its values. Let's take a look at some examples of array declarations:

```
Dim cities(6) As String
Dim daysOfWeek(7) As String
Dim lotto(6) As Integer
Dim exchange(5, 3) As Variant
```

Notice that the names of variables are followed by some numbers in parentheses. One-dimensional arrays require one number between parentheses. This number specifies the maximum number of elements that can be stored in a list. The name of a two-dimensional array is always followed by two numbers — the first number is the row index, and the second number is the column index. In the example above, the exchange array can hold a maximum of 15 values (5*3 = 15).

The last part of the array declaration is the definition of the data type that the array will hold. An array can hold any of the following data types: Integer, Long, Single, Double, Variant, Currency, String, Boolean, Byte, or Date.

When you declare an array, Visual Basic automatically reserves enough memory space. The amount of the memory allocated depends on the array's size and data type. When you declare a one-dimensional array named lotto with six elements, Visual Basic sets aside 12 bytes — 2 bytes for each element of the array (recall that the size of the Integer data type is 2 bytes, hence 2 * 6 = 12). The larger the array, the more memory space is required to store the data. Because arrays can eat up a lot of memory and impact your computer's performance, it's recommended that you declare arrays with only as many elements as you think you'll use.

What Is an Array Variable?

An array is a group of variables that have a common name. While a typical variable can hold only one value, an array variable can store a large number of individual values. You refer to a specific value in the array by using the array name and an index number.

Subscripted Variables

The numbers inside the parentheses of the array variables are called subscripts, and each individual variable is called a subscripted variable or element. For example, cities(6) is the sixth subscripted variable (element) of the array cities().

Array Upper and Lower Bounds

By default VBA assigns zero (0) to the first element of the array. Therefore, number 1 represents the second element of the array, number 2 represents the third, and so on. With numeric indexing starting at 0, the one-dimensional array cities(6) contains seven elements numbered from 0 to 6. If you'd rather start counting your array's elements at 1, you can explicitly specify a lower bound of the array by using an Option Base 1 statement. This instruction must be placed in the declaration section at the top of a VBA module before any Sub statements. If you don't specify Option Base 1 in a procedure that uses arrays, VBA assumes that the statement Option Base 0 is to be used and begins indexing your array's elements at 0. You can have the array indexing start at a number other than 0 or 1. To do this, you must specify the bounds of an array when declaring the array variable. The bounds of an array are its lowest and highest indices. Let's take a look at the following example:

```
Dim cities(3 To 6) As Integer
```

The above statement declares a one-dimensional array with four elements. The numbers enclosed in parentheses after the array name specify the lower (3) and upper (6) bounds of the array. The first element of this array has the number 3, the second is 4, the third is 5, and the fourth is 6. Notice the keyword To between the lower and the upper indices.

Using Arrays in VBA Procedures

After you declare an array, you must assign values to its elements. This is often referred to as "filling an array" or "populating an array."

Let's try out a VBA procedure that uses a one-dimensional array to programmatically display a list of six American cities.

Hands-On 8-1: Using a One-Dimensional Array

1. Open a new workbook and save it as **C:\Ex07_ByExample\Practice_Excel08.xlsm**.
2. Switch to the Microsoft Visual Basic Editor window and rename the VBA project **Arrays**.
3. Insert a new module into the Arrays (Practice_Excel08.xlsm) project, and rename this module **StaticArrays**.
4. In the StaticArrays module, enter the following FavoriteCities procedure:

```
' start indexing array elements at 1
Option Base 1

Sub FavoriteCities()
    ' now declare the array
    Dim cities(6) As String

    ' assign the values to array elements
```

```
    cities(1) = "Baltimore"
    cities(2) = "Atlanta"
    cities(3) = "Boston"
    cities(4) = "Washington"
    cities(5) = "New York"
    cities(6) = "Trenton"

    ' display the list of cities
    MsgBox cities(1) & Chr(13) & cities(2) & Chr(13) _
          & cities(3) & Chr(13) & cities(4) & Chr(13) _
          & cities (5) & Chr(13) & cities(6)
End Sub
```

Before the FavoriteCities procedure begins, the default indexing for an array is changed. Notice that the position of the Option Base 1 statement is at the top of the module window before the Sub statement. This statement tells Visual Basic to assign the number 1 instead of the default 0 to the first element of the array. The array cities() is declared with six elements of String data type. Each element of the array is then assigned a value. The last statement uses the MsgBox function to display the list of cities. When you run this procedure, the city names will appear on separate lines in the message box (see Figure 8-1). You can change the order of the displayed data by switching the index values.

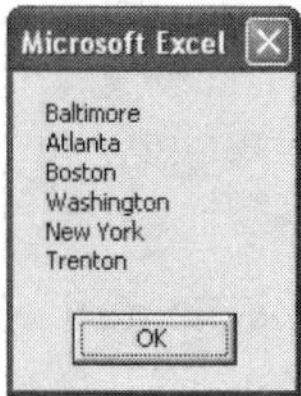

Figure 8-1: You can display the elements of a one-dimensional array with the MsgBox function.

5. Position the insertion point anywhere within the procedure code and press **F5** to run the FavoriteCities procedure.
6. On your own, modify the FavoriteCities procedure so that it displays the names of the cities in the reverse order (from 6 to 1).

The Range of the Array

The spread of the subscripts specified by the Dim statement is called the range of the array (for example: Dim mktgCodes(5 To 15)).

Arrays and Looping Statements

Several looping statements that you learned in Chapter 7 (see the For...Next loop and For Each...Next loop) will come in handy now that you're ready to perform tasks such as populating an array or displaying the elements of an array. It's time to combine the skills you've learned so far.

How can you rewrite the FavoriteCities procedure so that it shows the name of each city in a separate message box? The FavoriteCities2 procedure shown below replaces the last statement of the original procedure with the For Each...Next loop.

Hands-On 8-2: Using For Each...Next Statement to Enumerate the Array Elements

1. In the StaticArrays module, enter the following procedure:

```
Sub FavoriteCities2()
    ' now declare the array
    Dim cities(6) As String
    Dim city As Variant

    ' assign the values to array elements
    cities(1) = "Baltimore"
    cities(2) = "Atlanta"
    cities(3) = "Boston"
    cities(4) = "Washington"
    cities(5) = "New York"
    cities(6) = "Trenton"

    ' display the list of cities in separate messages
    For Each city in cities
         MsgBox city
    Next
End Sub
```

   Notice that the For Each...Next loop uses the variable city of Variant data type. As you recall from the previous chapter, For Each... Next allows you to loop through all of the objects in a collection or all of the elements of an array and perform the same action on each object or element.

2. Run the FavoriteCities2 procedure.

   When you run the FavoriteCities2 procedure, the loop will execute as many times as there are elements in the array.

Let's take a look at yet another variation of the FavoriteCities procedure. In Chapter 5 you practiced passing arguments as variables to subroutines and functions. The FavoriteCities3 procedure demonstrates how you can pass elements of an array to another procedure.

Hands-On 8-3: Passing an Array to Another Procedure

1. In the StaticArrays module, enter the two procedures as shown below:

```
Sub FavoriteCities3()
    ' now declare the array
    Dim cities(6) As String

    ' assign the values to array elements
    cities(1) = "Baltimore"
    cities(2) = "Atlanta"
    cities(3) = "Boston"
    cities(4) = "Washington"
    cities(5) = "New York"
```

```
    cities(6) = "Trenton"

    ' call another procedure and pass the array as argument
    Hallo cities()
End Sub

Sub Hallo(cities() As String)
    Dim counter As Integer

    For counter = LBound(cities()) To UBound(cities())
        MsgBox "Hello " & cities(counter)
    Next
End Sub
```

Notice that the last statement in the FavoriteCities3 procedure calls the Hallo procedure and passes to it the array cities() that holds the names of our favorite cities. Also notice that the declaration of the Hallo procedure includes an array type argument — cities() passed to this procedure as String. In order to iterate through the elements of an array you need to know how many elements the passed array contains. You can easily retrieve this information via two array functions — LBound and UBound. These functions are discussed later in this chapter. In this procedure example, LBound(cities()) will return 1 as the first element of the array; UBound(cities()) will return 6 as the last element of the cities() array. Therefore, the statement "For counter = LBound(cities()) To UBound(cities())" will boil down to "For counter = 1 To 6".

2. Run the FavoriteCities3 procedure.

Passing array elements from a subroutine to a subroutine or function procedure allows you to reuse the same array in many procedures without unnecessary duplication of the program code.

And here's how you can put to work your newly acquired knowledge about arrays and loops in real life. If you're an avid lotto player who is getting tired of picking your own lucky numbers, have Visual Basic do the picking. The Lotto procedure below populates an array with six numbers from 1 and 54. You can adjust this procedure to pick numbers from any range.

Hands-On 8-4: Practical Application of an Array

1. In the StaticArrays module, enter the following procedure:

```
Sub Lotto()
    Const spins = 6
    Const minNum = 1
    Const maxNum = 54

    Dim t As Integer                ' looping variable in outer loop
    Dim i As Integer                ' looping variable in inner loop
    Dim myNumbers As String         ' string to hold all picks
    Dim lucky(spins) As String      ' array to hold generated picks

    myNumbers = ""
```

```
    For t = 1 To spins
        Randomize
        lucky(t) = Int((maxNum - minNum + 1) * Rnd) + minNum

        ' see if this number was drawn before
        For i = 1 To (t - 1)
            If lucky(t) = lucky(i) Then
                lucky(t) = Int((maxNum - minNum + 1) * Rnd) + minNum
                i = 0
            End If
        Next i
        MsgBox "Lucky number is " & lucky(t)
        myNumbers = myNumbers & " - " & lucky(t)
    Next t

    MsgBox "Lucky numbers are " & myNumbers
End Sub
```

The Randomize statement initializes the random number generator. The instruction Int((maxNum – minNum + 1) * Rnd) + minNum uses the Rnd function to generate a random value between the specified minNum and maxNum. The Int function converts the resulting random number to an integer. Instead of assigning constant values for minNum and maxNum, you can use the InputBox function to get these values from the user. The inner For…Next loop ensures that each picked number is unique — it may not be any one of the previously picked numbers. If you omit the inner loop and run this procedure multiple times, you'll likely see some occurrences of duplicate numbers pop up.

2. Run the Lotto procedure.

Initial Value of an Array Element

Until a value is assigned to an element of an array, the element has its default value. Numeric variables have a default value of zero (0), and String variables have a default value of the empty string ("").

Passing Arrays between Procedures

When an array is declared in a procedure, it is local to this procedure and unknown to other procedures. However, you can pass the local array to another procedure by using the array's name followed by an empty set of parentheses as an argument in the calling statement. For example, the statement Hallo cities() calls the procedure named Hallo and passes to it the array cities().

Using a Two-Dimensional Array

Now that you know how to programmatically produce a list (a one-dimensional array), it's time to take a closer look at how you can work with tables of data. The following procedure creates a two-dimensional array that will hold the country name, currency name, and exchange rate for three countries.

Hands-On 8-5: Storing Data in a Two-Dimensional Array

1. In the StaticArrays module, enter the following procedure:

```
Sub Exchange()
    Dim t As String
    Dim r As String
    Dim Ex(3, 3) As Variant

         t = Chr(9)  ' tab
         r = Chr(13) ' Enter

         Ex(1, 1) = "Japan"
         Ex(1, 2) = "Yen"
         Ex(1, 3) = 104.57
         Ex(2, 1) = "Mexico"
         Ex(2, 2) = "Peso"
         Ex(2, 3) = 11.2085
         Ex(3, 1) = "Canada"
         Ex(3, 2) = "Dollar"
         Ex(3, 3) = 1.2028
         MsgBox "Country " & t & t & "Currency" & t & "per US$" _
              & r & r _
              & Ex(1, 1) & t & t & Ex(1, 2) & t & Ex(1, 3) & r _
              & Ex(2, 1) & t & t & Ex(2, 2) & t & Ex(2, 3) & r _
              & Ex(3, 1) & t & t & Ex(3, 2) & t & Ex(3, 3) & r & r _
              & "* Sample Exchange Rates for Demonstration Only", , _
              "Exchange"
End Sub
```

2. Run the Exchange procedure.

   When you run the Exchange procedure, you will see a message box with the exchange information presented in three columns.

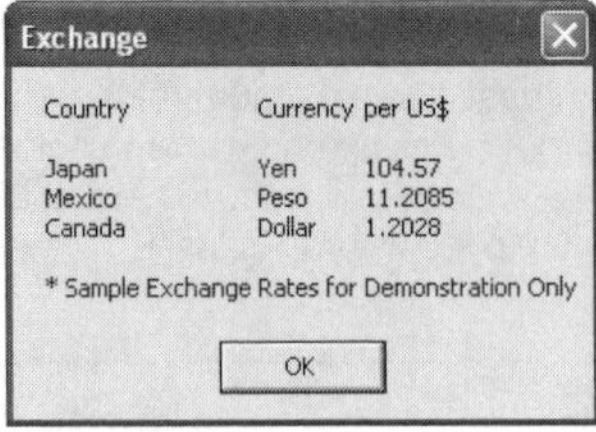

Figure 8-2: The text displayed in a message box can be custom formatted.

Static and Dynamic Arrays

The arrays introduced thus far in this chapter were static. A *static array* is an array of a specific size. Use a static array when you know in advance how big the array should be. The size of the static array is specified in the array's declaration statement. For example, the statement Dim Fruits(10) As String declares a static array called Fruits that is made up of 10 elements.

But what if you're not sure how many elements your array will contain? If your procedure depends on user input, the number of user-supplied elements might vary every time the procedure is executed. How can you ensure that the array you declare is not wasting memory? You may recall that after you declare an array, VBA sets aside enough memory to accommodate the array. If you declare an array to hold more elements than what you need, you'll end up wasting valuable computer resources. The solution to this problem is making your arrays dynamic.

A *dynamic array* is an array whose size can change. You use a dynamic array when the array size is determined each time the procedure is run. To declare a dynamic array, don't place a number inside the parentheses after the array name:

```
Dim Fruits() As String
```

A dynamic array is declared by placing empty parentheses after the array name. Before you use a dynamic array in your procedure, you must use the ReDim statement to dynamically set the lower and upper bounds of the array. The ReDim statement redimensions arrays as the code of your procedure executes and informs Visual Basic about the new size of the array. This statement can be used several times in the same procedure.

Now let's see how your procedure could use a dynamic array.

Hands-On 8-6: Using a Dynamic Array

1. Insert a new module into the current project and rename it **DynamicArrays.**
2. Enter the following DynArray procedure:

```
Sub DynArray()
    Dim counter As Integer

    ' declare a dynamic array
    Dim myArray() As Integer

    ' specify the initial size of the array
    Redim myArray(5)

    Workbooks.Add

    ' populate myArray with values
    For counter = 1 To 5
        myArray(counter) = counter + 1
        ActiveCell.Offset(counter-1, 0).Value = myArray(counter)
```

```
        Next

        ' change the size of myArray to hold 10 elements
        Redim Preserve myArray(10)

        ' add new values to myArray
        For counter = 6 To 10
              myArray(counter) = counter * counter
              With ActiveCell.Offset(counter-1, 0)
                    .Value = myArray(counter)
                    .Font.Bold = True
              End with
        Next counter
    End Sub
```

In the DynArray procedure, the statement Dim myArray() As Integer declares a dynamic array called myArray. Although this statement declares the array, it does not allocate any memory to the array. The first ReDim statement specifies the initial size of myArray and reserves 10 bytes of memory for it to hold its five elements. As you know, every Integer value requires 2 bytes of memory.

The statement Workbooks.Add opens a new workbook, and the For...Next loop populates myArray with data and writes the array's elements to a worksheet. The value of the variable counter equals 1 at the beginning of the loop.

The first statement in the loop:

```
myArray(counter) = counter + 1
```

assigns the value 2 to the first element of myArray.

The second statement,

```
ActiveCell.Offset(counter-1, 0).Value = myArray(counter)
```

enters the current value of myArray's element in the active cell. The active cell is A1.

Because the variable counter equals 1, the statement above results in the following:

```
ActiveCell.Offset(1-1, 0).Value = myArray(1)
```

or

```
ActiveCell.Offset(0,0).Value = myArray(1)
```

The above instruction enters data in cell A1. The statements inside the loop are executed five times. Visual Basic enters data in the appropriate worksheet cells and proceeds to the next statement:

```
ReDim Preserve myArray(10)
```

Normally, when you change the size of the array, you lose all the values that were in that array. The ReDim statement alone reinitializes the array.

However, you can append new elements to an existing array by following the ReDim statement with the Preserve keyword. In other words, the Preserve keyword guarantees that the redimensioned array will not lose its existing data. If you omit it, the new array will be empty. The second For...Next loop assigns values to the sixth, seventh, eighth, ninth, and tenth elements of myArray. This time, the values of the array's elements are obtained by multiplication: counter * counter. Visual Basic enters the additional array's values in the appropriate spreadsheet cells using the bold font style.

3. Set your screen so that the Microsoft Excel application and Visual Basic Editor windows are positioned side by side.
4. Run the DynArray procedure step by step. To do this, place the mouse pointer inside the code of this procedure and press **F8** to execute each statement. The result of the DynArray procedure is shown in the following figure.

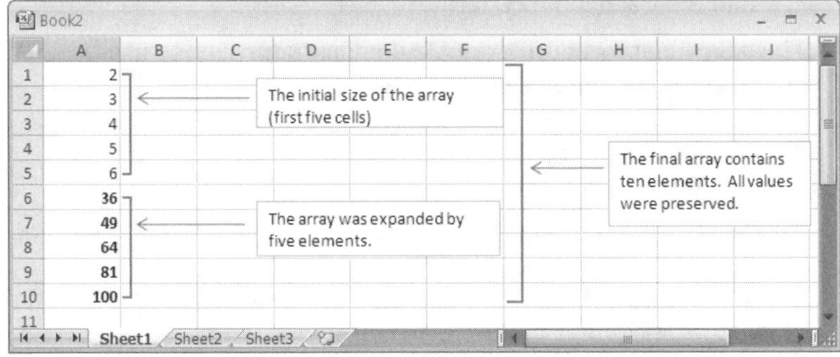

Figure 8-3: An array showing 10 values.

> **Fixed-dimension Arrays**
>
> A static array contains a fixed number of elements. The number of elements in a static array isn't going to change once it has been declared.

Array Functions

You can manipulate arrays with five built-in VBA functions: Array, IsArray, Erase, LBound, and UBound. The following sections demonstrate the use of each of these functions in VBA procedures.

The Array Function

The Array function allows you to create an array during code execution without having to dimension it first. This function always returns an array of Variants. Using the Array function, you can quickly place a series of values in a list.

The CarInfo procedure shown below creates a fixed-size, one-dimensional, three-element array called auto.

Hands-On 8-7: Using the Array Function

1. Insert a new module into the current project and rename it **Array_Function**.
2. Enter the following CarInfo procedure:

```
Option Base 1

Sub CarInfo()
    Dim auto As Variant
    auto = Array("Ford", "Black", "1999")
    MsgBox auto(2) & " " & auto(1) & ", " & auto(3)
    auto(2) = "4-door"
    MsgBox auto(2) & " " & auto(1) & ", " & auto(3)
End Sub
```

3. Run the CarInfo procedure.

The following procedure example demonstrates how to use the Array function to enter column headings in a worksheet:

```
Sub ColumnHeads()
    Dim heading As Variant
    Dim cell As Range
    Dim i As Integer

    i = 1
    heading = Array("First Name", "Last Name", "Position", "Salary")
    Workbooks.Add

    For Each cell in Range("A1:D1")
    cell.Formula = heading(i)
    i = i + 1
    Next

    Columns("A:D").Select
    Selection.Columns.AutoFit
    Range("A1").Select
End Sub
```

Dimensioning Arrays

Arrays must be dimensioned in a Dim or ReDim statement before they are used. This means that you can't assign a value to an array element until you have declared the array with the Dim or ReDim statement.

The IsArray Function

Using the IsArray function, you can test whether a variable is an array. The IsArray function returns either true, if the variable is an array, or false, if it's not an array.

Here's an example.

Hands-On 8-8: Using the IsArray Function

1. Insert a new module into the current project and rename it **IsArray_Function.**
2. Enter the code of the IsThisArray procedure, as shown below:

```
Sub IsThisArray()
    ' declare a dynamic array
    Dim sheetNames() As String
    Dim totalSheets As Integer
    Dim counter As Integer

    ' count the sheets in the current workbook
    totalSheets = ActiveWorkbook.Sheets.Count

    ' specify the size of the array
    ReDim sheetNames(1 To totalSheets)

    ' enter and show the names of sheets
    For counter = 1 to totalSheets
          sheetNames(counter) = ActiveWorkbook.Sheets(counter).Name
          MsgBox sheetNames(counter)
    Next counter

    ' check if this is indeed an array
    If IsArray(sheetNames) Then
          MsgBox "The sheetNames is an array."
    End If
End Sub
```

3. Run the IsThisArray procedure.

The Erase Function

When you want to remove the data from an array, you should use the Erase function. This function deletes all the data held by static or dynamic arrays. In addition, the Erase function reallocates all of the memory assigned to a dynamic array. If a procedure has to use the dynamic array again, you must use the ReDim statement to specify the size of the array.

The example below shows how to erase the data from the array cities.

Hands-On 8-9: Using the Erase Function

1. Insert a new module into the current project and rename it **Erase_Function.**
2. Enter the code of the FunCities procedure shown below:

```
' start indexing array elements at 1
Option Base 1

Sub FunCities()
' declare the array
Dim cities(1 To 5) As String

' assign the values to array elements
cities(1) = "Las Vegas"
```

```
cities(2) = "Orlando"
cities(3) = "Atlantic City"
cities(4) = "New York"
cities(5) = "San Francisco"

' display the list of cities
    MsgBox cities(1) & Chr(13) & cities(2) & Chr(13) _
          & cities(3) & Chr(13) & cities(4) & Chr(13) _
          & cities (5)
Erase cities

' show all that was erased
MsgBox cities(1) & Chr(13) & cities(2) & Chr(13) _
    & cities(3) & Chr(13) & cities(4) & Chr(13) _
    & cities (5)
End Sub
```

After the Erase function deletes the values from the array, the MsgBox function displays an empty message box.

3. Run the FunCities procedure.

The LBound and UBound Functions

The LBound and UBound functions return whole numbers that indicate the lower bound and upper bound indices of an array.

Hands-On 8-10: Using the LBound and UBound Functions

1. Insert a new module into the current project and rename it **L_and_UBound_Function**.
2. Enter the code of the FunCities2 procedure shown below:

```
Sub FunCities2()
    ' declare the array
    Dim cities(1 To 5) As String

    ' assign the values to array elements
    cities(1) = "Las Vegas"
    cities(2) = "Orlando"
    cities(3) = "Atlantic City"
    cities(4) = "New York"
    cities(5) = "San Francisco"

    ' display the list of cities
    MsgBox cities(1) & Chr(13) & cities(2) & Chr(13) _
          & cities(3) & Chr(13) & cities(4) & Chr(13) _
          & cities (5)
    ' display the array bounds
    MsgBox "The lower bound: " & LBound(cities) & Chr(13) _
          & "The upper bound: " & UBound(cities)
End Sub
```

3. Run the FunCities2 procedure.
4. To determine the upper and lower indices in a two-dimensional array, add the following statements at the end of the Exchange procedure that

was prepared in Hands-On 8-5 (add these lines of code just before the End Sub keywords):

```
MsgBox "The lower bound (first dimension) is " _
    & LBound(Ex, 1) & "."
MsgBox " The upper bound(first dimension) is " _
    & UBound(Ex, 1) & "."
MsgBox "The lower bound (second dimension) is " _
    & LBound(Ex, 2) & "."
MsgBox " The upper bound(second dimension) is " _
    & UBound(Ex, 2) & "."
```

Note: When determining the lower and upper bound indices of a two-dimensional array, you must specify the dimension number: 1 for the first dimension and 2 for the second dimension.

Errors in Arrays

When working with arrays, it's easy to make a mistake. If you try to assign more values than there are elements in the declared array, VBA will display the error message "Subscript out of range," as shown in Figure 8-4.

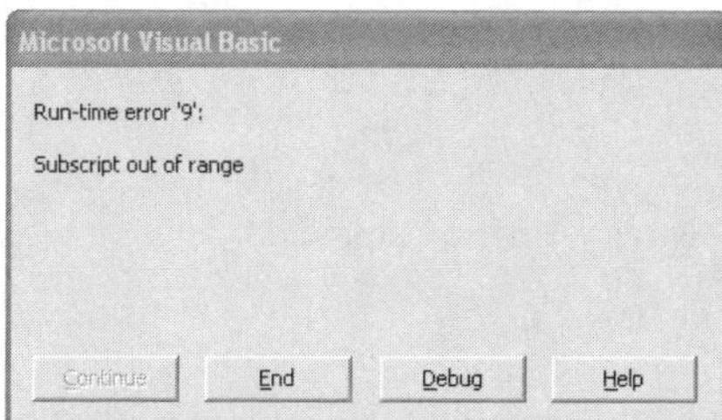

Figure 8-4: This error was caused by an attempt to access a nonexistent array element.

Suppose you declare a one-dimensional array that consists of six elements and you are trying to assign a value to the seventh element. When you run the procedure, Visual Basic can't find the seventh element, so it displays the error message. When you click the Debug button Visual Basic will highlight the line of code that caused the error.

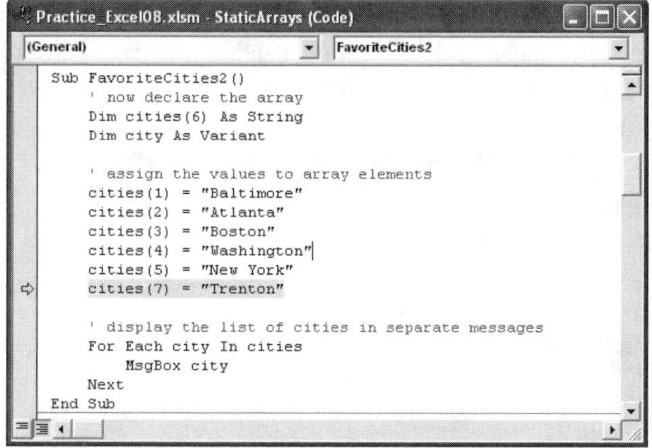

Figure 8-5: When you click the Debug button in the error message, Visual Basic highlights the statement that triggered the error.

To fix this type of error, you should begin by looking at the array's declaration statement. Once you know how many elements the array should hold, it's easy to figure out that the culprit is the index number that appears in the parentheses in the highlighted line of code. In the example shown in Figure 8-5, once we replace the line of code cities(7) = "Trenton" with cities(6) = "Trenton" and press F5 to resume the procedure, the procedure will run as intended.

The error "Subscript out of range" is often triggered in procedures using loops. The procedure Zoo1 shown below serves as an example of such a situation.

Hands-On 8-11: Triggering an Error in an Array

1. Insert a new module into the current project and rename it **Errors_In_Arrays**.
2. In the Errors_In_Arrays module, enter the following procedure:

```
Sub Zoo1()
    ' this procedure triggers an error "Subscript out of range"
    Dim zoo(3) As String
    Dim i As Integer
    Dim response As String
    i = 0

    Do
         i = i + 1
         response = InputBox("Enter a name of animal:")
         zoo(i) = response
    Loop until response = ""
End Sub
```

   Notice that the statements in the loop will be executed until the user cancels out from the input box.

3. Run the Zoo1 procedure.

   While executing this procedure, Visual Basic will not be able to find the fourth element in a three-element array when the variable i equals 4, so the error message will appear.

The modified procedure Zoo2 demonstrates how using the LBound and UBound functions introduced in the preceding section can avoid errors caused by an attempt to access a nonexistent array element.

```
Sub Zoo2()
    ' this procedure avoids the error "Subscript out of range"
    Dim zoo(3) As String
    Dim i As Integer
    Dim response As String
    i = 1

    Do While i >= LBound(zoo) And i <= UBound(zoo)
         response = InputBox("Enter a name of animal:")
         If response = "" Then Exit Sub
         zoo(i) = response
         i = i + 1
```

```
        Loop

        For i = LBound(zoo) To UBound(zoo)
              MsgBox zoo(i)
        Next
    End Sub
```

Another frequent error you may encounter while working with arrays is Type mismatch. To avoid this error, keep in mind that each element of an array must be of the same data type. If you attempt to assign to an element of an array a value that conflicts with the data type of the array declared by the Dim statement, you'll obtain the Type mismatch error during code execution. To hold values of different data types in an array, declare the array as Variant.

Parameter Arrays

In Chapter 5 you learned that values can be passed between subroutines or functions as required or optional arguments. If the passed argument is not absolutely required for the procedure to execute, the argument's name is preceded by the keyword Optional. Sometimes, however, you don't know in advance how many arguments you want to pass. A classic example is addition. You may want to add together two numbers. Later, you may use three, 10, or 15 numbers.

Using the keyword ParamArray, you can pass an array consisting of any number of elements to your subroutines and function procedures.

The following AddMultipleArgs function will add up as many numbers as you require. This function begins with the declaration of an array, myNumbers. Notice the use of the ParamArray keyword. The array must be declared as an array of type Variant, and it must be the last argument in the procedure definition.

Hands-On 8-12: Passing an Array to Procedures Using the ParamArray Keyword

1. Insert a new module into the current project and rename it **ParameterArrays**.
2. In the ParameterArrays module, enter the following AddMultipleArgs function procedure:

```
Function AddMultipleArgs(ParamArray myNumbers() As Variant)
     Dim mySum As Single
     Dim myValue As Variant
     For Each myValue in myNumbers
           mySum=mySum+myValue
     Next
     AddMultipleArgs = mySum
End Function
```

3. To try out the above function, activate the Immediate window and type the following instruction:

```
?AddMultipleArgs(1, 23.24, 3, 24, 8, 34)
```

When you press **Enter**, Visual Basic returns the total of all the numbers in the parentheses: 93.24. You can supply an unlimited number of arguments. To add more values, enter additional values in parentheses and press Enter. Notice that each function argument must be separated by a comma.

Chapter Summary

In this chapter you learned that by creating an array, you can write procedures that require a large number of variables. You worked with examples of procedures that demonstrated how to declare and use a one-dimensional array (list) and a two-dimensional array (table). You also learned the difference between static and dynamic arrays.

This chapter ended by introducing you to five built-in VBA functions that are frequently used with arrays. You also learned how to use a new keyword — ParamArray. You now know all the control structures that can make your code more intelligent: conditional statements, loops, and arrays. In the next chapter you will learn how to use collections instead of arrays to manipulate large amounts of data.

Chapter 9

Working with Collections and Class Modules

Microsoft Excel 2007 offers a large number of built-in objects that you can access from your VBA procedures to automate many aspects of your spreadsheets. You are not by any means limited to using these built-in objects. VBA allows you to create your own objects and collections of objects, complete with their own methods and properties.

While writing your own VBA procedures, you may come across a situation where there's no built-in collection to handle the task at hand. The solution is to create a custom collection object. You already know from the previous chapter how to work with multiple items of data by using dynamic or static arrays. Because collections have built-in properties and methods that allow you to add, remove, and count their elements, they are much easier to work with. In this chapter, you will learn how to work with collections, including how to declare a custom collection object. The usage of class modules to create user-defined objects will also be discussed.

Before diving into the theory and hands-on examples in this chapter, let's get familiar with several terms:

- **Collection** — An object that contains a set of related objects.
- **Class** — A definition of an object that includes its name, properties, methods, and events. The class acts as a sort of object template from which an instance of an object is created at run time.
- **Instance** — A specific object that belongs to a class is referred to as an instance of the class. When you create an instance, you create a new object that has the properties and methods defined by the class.
- **Class module** — A module that contains the definition of a class, including its property and method definitions.
- **Module** — A module containing sub and function procedures that are available to other VBA procedures and are not related to any object in particular.
- **Form module** — A module that contains the VBA code for all event procedures triggered by events occurring in a user form or its controls. A form module is a type of class module.
- **Event** — An action recognized by an object, such as a mouse click or a keypress, for which you can define a response. Events can be caused by a user action or a VBA statement or can be triggered by the system.
- **Event procedure** — A procedure that is automatically executed in response to an event initiated by the user or program code or triggered by the system.

Working with Collections

A set of similar objects is known as a *collection*. In Microsoft Excel, for example, all open workbooks belong to the collection of Workbooks, and all the sheets in a particular workbook are members of the Worksheets collection. In Microsoft Word, all open documents belong to the Documents collection, and each paragraph in a document is a member of the Paragraphs collection. Collections are objects that contain other objects. No matter what collection you want to work with, you can do the following:

- Refer to a specific object in a collection by using an index value. For example, to refer to the second object in the collection of Worksheets, use either one of the following statements:

```
Worksheets(2).Select
Worksheets("Sheet2").Select
```

- Determine the number of items in the collection by using the Count property. For example, when you enter in the Immediate window the statement:

```
?Worksheets.Count
```

  VBA will return the total number of worksheets in the current workbook.

- Insert new items into the collection by using the Add method. For example, when you enter in the Immediate window the statement:

```
Worksheets.Add
```

  VBA will insert to the current workbook a new worksheet. The Worksheets collection now contains one more item.

- Cycle through every object in the collection by using the For Each… Next loop.

  Suppose that you opened a workbook containing five worksheets with the following names: "Daily wages," "Weekly wages," "Bonuses," "Yearly salary," "Monthly wages." To delete the worksheets that contain the word "wages" in the name you could write the following procedure:

```
Sub DeleteSheets()
    Dim ws As Worksheet
    Application.DisplayAlerts = False
    For Each ws In Worksheets
        If InStr(ws.Name, "wages") Then
            ws.Delete
        End If
    Next
End Sub
```

Declaring a Custom Collection

To create a user-defined collection, you should begin by declaring an object variable of the Collection type. This variable is declared with the New keyword in the Dim statement, as shown below:

```
Dim collection_name As New Collection
```

Adding Objects to a Custom Collection

After you've declared the Collection object with the Dim keyword, you can insert new items into the collection by using the Add method. The Add method looks like this:

```
object.Add item[, key, before, after]
```

You are only required to specify the object and the item. The object is the collection name. This is the same name that was used in the declaration of the Collection object. The item is the object that you want to add to the collection.

Although other arguments are optional, they are quite useful. It's important to understand that the items in a collection are automatically assigned numbers starting with 1. However, they can also be assigned a unique key value. Instead of accessing a specific item with an index (1, 2, 3, and so on) at the time an object is added to a collection, you can assign a key for that object. For instance, if you are creating a collection of custom sheets, you could use a sheet name as a key. To identify an individual in a collection of students or employees, you could use Social Security numbers as a key.

If you want to specify the position of the object in the collection, you should use either a before or after argument (do not use both). The before argument is the object before which the new object is added. The after argument is the object after which the new object is added.

The objects with which you populate your collection do not have to be of the same data type.

The GetComments procedure shown below declares the custom collection object called colNotes.

Hands-On 9-1: Using a Custom Collection Object

1. Open a new workbook and save it as **C:\Ex07_ByExample\Practice_Excel09.xlsm**.
2. Right-click any cell in Sheet1 and choose **Insert Comment** from the shortcut menu. Type any text you want. Click outside the comment frame to exit the comment edit mode. Use the same technique to enter two comments in Sheet2. Enter different text for each comment. Add a new sheet (Sheet4) to the workbook, and add a comment in any cell. You should now have four comments in three worksheets.
3. Click the **Microsoft Office** button in the top-left corner of the Microsoft Excel window and choose **Excel Options**. In the Excel Options window's Popular tab, in the area named Personalize your copy of Microsoft Office, you should see a text box with your name. Delete your name and enter **Joan Smith**, then click **OK**. Now, enter one comment anywhere on Sheet2 and one comment anywhere on Sheet4. These comments should be automatically stamped with Joan Smith's name. When you're done entering the comment text, return to the Excel Options window and change the User name text box entry on the Popular tab back to the way it was (your name).
4. Switch to the Visual Basic Editor, and rename the VBA project **ObjColClass**.
5. Add a new module to the current project, and rename it **MyCollection**.

6. In the MyCollection module, enter the GetComments procedure, as shown below:

```
Sub GetComments()
    Dim sht As Worksheet
    Dim colNotes As New Collection
    Dim myNote As Comment
    Dim I As Integer
    Dim t As Integer
    Dim strName As String

    strName = InputBox("Enter author's name:")
    For Each sht In ThisWorkbook.Worksheets
        sht.Select
        I = ActiveSheet.Comments.Count
        For Each myNote In ActiveSheet.Comments
            If myNote.Author = strName Then
                MsgBox myNote.Text
                If colNotes.Count = 0 Then
                    colNotes.Add Item:=myNote, key:="first"
                Else
                    colNotes.Add Item:=myNote, Before:=1
                End If
            End If
        Next
        t = t + I
    Next
    If colNotes.Count <> 0 Then MsgBox colNotes("first").Text
    MsgBox "Total comments in workbook: " & t & Chr(13) & _
        "Total comments in collection:" & colNotes.Count
    Debug.Print "Comments by " & strName
    For Each myNote In colNotes
        Debug.Print Mid(myNote.Text, Len(myNote.Author) + 2, _
            Len(myNote.Text))
    Next
End Sub
```

The above procedure begins by declaring the custom collection object called colNotes. Next, the procedure prompts for an author's name and then loops through all the worksheets in the active workbook to locate this author's comments. Only comments entered by the specified author are added to the custom collection.

The procedure assigns a key to the first comment and then adds the remaining comments to the collection by placing them before the comment that was added last (notice the use of the before argument). If the collection includes at least one comment, the procedure displays a message box with the text of the comment that was identified with the special key argument. Notice how the key argument is used in referencing an item in a collection. The procedure then prints the text of all the comments included in the collection to the Immediate window.

Text functions (Mid and Len) are used to get only the text of the comment without the author's name. Next, the total number of comments in a workbook and the total number of comments in the custom collection are returned by the Count property.

7. Run the GetComments procedure and check its results in the Immediate window.

Removing Objects from a Custom Collection

Removing an item from a custom collection is as easy as adding an item. To remove an object, use the Remove method in the following format:

```
object.Remove item
```

The object is the name of the custom collection that contains the object you want to remove. The item is the object you want to remove from the collection.

To demonstrate the process of removing an item from a collection, let's modify the GetComments procedure that you prepared in the preceding section. At the end of this procedure, we'll display the contents of the items that are currently in the colNotes collection one by one, and ask the user whether the item should be removed from the collection.

Hands-On 9-2: Removing Items from a Custom Collection

1. Add the following lines to the declaration section of the GetComments procedure:

```
Dim response
Dim myID As Integer
```

The first statement declares the variable called response. You will use this variable to store the result of the MsgBox function. The second statement declares the variable myID to store the index number of the Collection object.

2. Locate the following statement in the GetComments procedure:

```
For Each myNote In colNotes
```

Precede the above statement with the following line of code:

```
myID = 1
```

3. Locate the following statement in the GetComments procedure:

```
Debug.Print Mid(myNote.Text, Len(myNote.Author) + 2, _
    Len(myNote.Text))
```

Enter the following block of instructions below the statement:

```
response = MsgBox("Remove this comment?" & Chr(13) _
    & Chr(13) & myNote.Text, vbYesNo + vbQuestion)
If response = 6 Then
    colNotes.Remove Index:=myID
Else
    myId = myID + 1
End If
```

4. Enter the following statements at the end of the procedure before the End Sub keywords:

```
Debug.Print "The following comments remain in the collection:"
For Each myNote in colNotes
Debug.Print Mid(myNote.Text, Len(myNote.Author) + 2, _
    Len(myNote.Text))
Next
```

The revised GetComments procedure named GetComments2 is shown below. Note that this procedure removes the specified comments from the custom collection. It does not delete the comments from the worksheets.

```
Sub GetComments2()
    Dim sht As Worksheet
    Dim colNotes As New Collection
    Dim myNote As Comment
    Dim I As Integer
    Dim t As Integer
    Dim strName As String
    Dim response
    Dim myID As Integer

    strName = InputBox("Enter author's name:")
    For Each sht In ThisWorkbook.Worksheets
          sht.Select
          I = ActiveSheet.Comments.Count
                For Each myNote In ActiveSheet.Comments
                      If myNote.Author = strName Then
                            MsgBox myNote.Text
                            If colNotes.Count = 0 Then
                                  colNotes.Add Item:=myNote, key:="first"
                            Else
                                  colNotes.Add Item:=myNote, Before:=1
                            End If
                      End If
                Next
          t = t + I
    Next
    If colNotes.Count <> 0 Then MsgBox colNotes("first").Text
    MsgBox "Total comments in workbook: " & t & Chr(13) & _
          "Total comments in collection:" & colNotes.Count
    Debug.Print "Comments by " & strName
          myID = 1
          For Each myNote In colNotes
                Debug.Print Mid(myNote.Text, Len(myNote.Author) + 2, _
                      Len(myNote.Text))
                response = MsgBox("Remove this comment?" & Chr(13) _
                      & Chr(13) & myNote.Text, vbYesNo + vbQuestion)
                If response = 6 Then
                      colNotes.Remove index:=myID
                Else
                      myID = myID + 1
                End If
          Next
    MsgBox "Total notes in workbook: " & t & Chr(13) & _
          "Total notes in collection:" & colNotes.Count
    Debug.Print "The following comments remain in the collection:"
          For Each myNote In colNotes
                Debug.Print Mid(myNote.Text, Len(myNote.Author) + 2, _
```

```
                             Len(myNote.Text))
                 Next
    End Sub
```

5. Run the GetComments2 procedure and remove one of the comments displayed in the message box.

Reindexing Collections

Collections are reindexed automatically when an object is removed. Therefore, to remove all objects from a custom collection, you can use 1 for the Index argument, as in the following example:

```
Do While myCollection.Count >0
  myCollection.Remove Index:=1
Loop
```

Creating Custom Objects

Notice that there are two module commands available in the Visual Basic Editor's Insert menu: Module and Class Module. So far, you've used standard modules to create subroutine and function procedures. You'll use the class module for the first time in this chapter to create a custom object and define its properties and methods.

Creating a new, nonstandard VBA object involves inserting a class module into your VBA project and adding code to that module. However, before you do so, you need a basic understanding of what a class is. If you refer back to the beginning of this chapter, you will see that we described a class as a sort of object template.

A frequently used analogy is comparing an object class to a cookie cutter. Just as a cookie cutter defines what a particular cookie will look like, the definition of the class determines how a particular object should look and behave. Before you can actually use an object class, you must first create a new *instance* of that class. Object instances are the cookies. Each object instance has the characteristics (properties and methods) defined by its class. Just as you can cut out many cookies using the same cookie cutter, you can create multiple instances of a class. You can also change the properties of each instance of a class independently of any other instance of the same class.

A class module lets you define your own custom classes, complete with custom properties and methods. Recall that a property is an attribute of an object that defines one of its characteristics, such as shape, position, color, title, and so on. A method is an action that the object can perform. You can create the properties for your custom objects by writing property procedures in a class module. The object methods are also created in a class module by writing the sub or function procedures. After building your object in the class module, you can use it in the same way you use other built-in objects. You can also export the object class outside the VBA project to other VBA-capable applications.

Creating a Class

The remaining sections of this chapter demonstrate the process of creating and working with a custom object called CEmployee. This object will represent an employee. The CEmployee object will have properties such as ID, FirstName, LastName, and Salary. It will also have a method for modifying the current salary. Be sure to perform all the exercises. We will start by creating a class module.

Custom Project 9-1a: Creating a Class Module

1. Select **ObjColClass (Practice_Excel09.xlsm)** in the Project Explorer window and choose **Insert | Class Module.**
2. Highlight the **Class 1** module in the Project Explorer window and use the Properties window to rename the class module **CEmployee.**

Naming a Class Module

Every time you create a new class module, give it a meaningful name. Set the name of the class module to the name you want to use in your VBA procedures using the class. The name you choose for your class should be easily understood and identify the "thing" the object class represents. As a rule, the object class name is prefaced with an uppercase "C".

Variable Declarations

After adding and renaming the class module, the next step is to declare the variables that will hold the data you want to store in the object. Each item of data you want to store in an object should be assigned a variable. Variables in a class module are called data members and are declared with the Private keyword. This keyword ensures that the variables will be available only within the class module. Using the Private keyword instead of the familiar Dim statement hides the data members and prevents other parts of the application from referencing them. Only the procedures within the class module in which the variables were defined can modify the value of these variables.

Because the name of a variable also serves as a property name, use meaningful names for your object's data members. It's traditional to preface the variable names with m_ to indicate that they are data members of a class.

Let's continue with our project by declaring data members for our CEmployee class.

Custom Project 9-1b: Declaring Members of the CEmployee Class

3. Type the following declaration lines at the top of the CEmployee class module:

```
' declarations
Private m_LastName As String
Private m_FirstName As String
Private m_Salary As Currency
Private m_ID As String
```

   Notice that the name of each data member variable begins with the prefix m_.

Defining the Properties for the Class

Declaring the variables with the Private keyword guarantees that the variables cannot be directly accessed from outside the object. This means that the VBA procedures from outside the class module will not be able to set or read data stored in those variables. To enable other parts of your VBA application to set or retrieve the employee data, you must add special property procedures to the CEmployee class module.

There are three types of property procedures:

- Property Let — This type of procedure allows other parts of the application to set the value of a property.
- Property Get — This type of procedure allows other parts of the application to get or read the value of a property.
- Property Set — This type of procedure is used instead of Property Let when setting the reference to an object.

Property procedures are executed when an object property needs to be set or retrieved. The Property Get procedure can have the same name as the Property Let procedure.

You should create property procedures for each property of the object that can be accessed by another part of your VBA application. The easiest of the three types of property statements to understand is the Property Get procedure. Let's examine the syntax of the property procedures by taking a closer look at the Property Get LastName procedure. As a rule, the property procedures contain the following parts:

- A procedure declaration line that specifies the name of the property and the data type:

  ```
  Property Get LastName() As String
  ```

  LastName is the name of the property and As String determines the data type of the property's return value.

- An assignment statement similar to the one used in a function procedure:

  ```
  LastName = m_LastName
  ```

The LastName is the name of the property, and m_LastName is the data member variable that holds the value of the property you want to retrieve or set. The m_LastName variable should be defined with the Private keyword at the top of the class module. If the retrieved value is obtained as a result of a calculation, you can include the appropriate VBA statement:

```
Property Get Royalty()
    Royalty = (Sales * Percent) - Advance
End Property
```

- The End Property keywords that specify the end of the property procedure.

Creating the Property Get Procedures

The CEmployee class object has four properties that need to be exposed to VBA procedures that reside in other modules in the current VBA project. When working with the CEmployee object, you would certainly like to get information about the employee ID, first and last names, and current salary. Let's continue with our project by writing the necessary Property Get procedures.

Custom Project 9-1c: Writing Property Get Procedures for the CEmployee Class

4. Type the following Property Get procedures in the CEmployee class module, just below the declaration section. The code can be copied from **C:\Ex07_HandsOn\Ex07_Chapter09.txt.**

```
Property Get ID() As String
    Id = m_ID
End Property

Property Get LastName() As String
    LastName = m_LastName
End Property

Property Get FirstName() As String
    FirstName = m_FirstName
End Property

Property Get Salary() As Currency
    Salary = m_Salary
End Property
```

Notice that each type of the needed employee information requires a separate Property Get procedure. Each one of the above Property Get procedures returns the current value of the property. The Property Get procedure is similar to a function procedure. Like function procedures, the Property Get procedures contain an assignment statement. As you recall from Chapter 5, to return a value from a function procedure, you must assign it to the function's name.

Immediate Exit from Property Procedures

Just like the Exit Sub and Exit Function keywords allow you to exit early from a subroutine or a function procedure, the Exit Property keywords give you a way to immediately exit from a property procedure. Program execution will continue with the statements following the statement that called the Property Get, Property Let, or Property Set procedure.

Creating the Property Let Procedures

In addition to retrieving values stored in data members (private variables) with Property Get procedures, you must prepare corresponding Property Let procedures to allow other procedures to change the values of these variables as needed. However, you don't need to define a Property Let procedure if the value stored in a private variable is meant to be read-only.

Suppose you don't want the user to change the employee ID. To make the ID read-only, you simply don't write a Property Let procedure for it. Hence, the CEmployee class will only have three properties (LastName, FirstName, and Salary). Each of these properties will require a separate Property Let procedure.

Let's continue with our project and write the required Property Let procedures for our custom CEmployee object.

Custom Project 9-1d: Writing Property Let Procedures for the CEmployee Class

5. Type the following Property Let procedures in the CEmployee class module:

```
Property Let LastName(L As String)
    m_LastName = L
End Property

Property Let FirstName(F As String)
    m_FirstName = F
End Property

Property Let Salary(ByVal dollar As Currency)
    m_Salary = dollar
End Property
```

The Property Let procedures require at least one parameter that specifies the value you want to assign to the property. This parameter can be passed by value (see the ByVal keyword in the Property Let Salary procedure shown above) or by reference (ByRef is the default). If you need a refresher on the meaning of these keywords, see the section titled "Passing Arguments by Reference and Value" in Chapter 5.

The data type of the parameter passed to the Property Let procedure must have exactly the same data type as the value returned from the Property Get or Set procedure with the same name. Notice that the

Property Let procedures have the same name as the Property Get procedures prepared in the preceding section. By skipping the Property Let procedure for the ID property, you created a read-only ID property that can be retrieved but not set.

Defining the Scope of Property Procedures

You can place the Public, Private, or Static keyword before the name of a property procedure to define its scope. For example, to indicate that the Property Get procedure is accessible to other procedures in all modules, use the following statement format:

```
Public Property Get FirstName()
As String
```

To make the Property Get procedure accessible only to other procedures in the module where it is declared, use the following statement format:

```
Private Property Get FirstName()
As String
```

To preserve the Property Get procedure's local variables between procedure calls, use the following statement format:

```
Static Property Get FirstName()
As String
```

If not explicitly specified using either Public or Private, property procedures are public by default. Also, if the Static keyword is not used, the values of local variables are not preserved between the procedure calls.

Creating the Class Methods

Apart from properties, objects usually have one or more methods. A *method* is an action that the object can perform. Methods allow you to manipulate the data stored in a class object. Methods are created with the sub or function procedures. To make a method available outside the class module, use the Public keyword in front of the sub or function definition.

The CEmployee object that you create in this chapter has one method that allows you to calculate the new salary. Assume that the employee salary can be increased or decreased by a specific percentage or amount.

Let's continue with our project by writing a class method that calculates the employee salary.

Custom Project 9-1e: Writing Methods for the CEmployee Class

6. Type the following CalcNewSalary function procedure in the CEmployee class module:

```
Public Function CalcNewSalary(choice As Integer, _
        curSalary As Currency, amount As Long) As Currency
    Select Case choice
        Case 1 ' by percent
            CalcNewSalary = curSalary + ((curSalary + amount)/100)
        Case 2 ' by amount
            CalcNewSalary = curSalary + amount
    End Select
End Function
```

The CalcNewSalary function defined with the Public keyword in a class module serves as a method for the CEmployee class. To calculate a new salary, a VBA procedure from outside the class module must pass three arguments: choice, curSalary, and amount. The choice argument specifies the type of the calculation. Suppose you want to increase the employee salary by 5% or by $5. Choice one will increase the salary by the specified percentage, and choice two will add the specified amount to the current salary. The curSalary argument is the current salary figure for an employee, and amount determines the value by which the salary should be changed.

About Class Methods

- Only those methods that will be accessed from outside of the class should be declared as Public. All others should be Private.
- Methods perform some operation on the data contained within the class.
- If a method needs to return a value, write a function procedure. Otherwise, create a subprocedure. If you don't use the New keyword with the Dim statement (as shown earlier), VBA does not allocate memory for your custom object until your procedure actually needs it.

Creating an Instance of a Class

After typing all the necessary Property Get, Property Let, sub, and function procedures for your VBA application in the class module, you are ready to create a new instance of a class, which is called an object.

Before an object can be created, an object variable must be declared in a standard module to store the reference to the object. If the name of the class module is CEmployee, a new instance of this class can be created with the following statement:

```
Dim emp As New CEmployee
```

The emp variable will represent a reference to an object of the CEmployee class. When you declare the object variable with the New keyword, VBA creates the object and allocates memory for it; however, the object isn't instanced until you refer to it in your procedure code by assigning a value to its property or running one of its methods.

You can also create an instance of the object by declaring an object variable with the data type defined to be the class of the object as in the following:

```
Dim emp As CEmployee
Set emp = New CEmployee
```

You will create an instance of the class as stated above later in this chapter when we proceed to write our application code in a form class module.

Event Procedures in the Class Module

An *event* is basically an action recognized by an object. Custom classes recognize only two events: Initialize and Terminate. These events are triggered when an instance of the class is created and destroyed, respectively. The Initialize event is generated when an object is created from a class (see the preceding section on creating an instance of a class). In the CEmployee class example, the Initialize event will also fire the first time that you use the emp variable in code. Because the statements included inside the Initialize event are the first ones to be executed for the object before any properties are set or any methods are executed, the Initialize event is a good place to perform initialization of the objects created from the class.

As you recall, the ID is read-only in the CEmployee class. You can use the Initialize event to assign a unique five-digit number to the m_ID variable.

Let's continue with our project by adding the Initialize event procedure to our CEmployee class.

Custom Project 9-1f: Writing the Initialize Event Procedure for the CEmployee Class

7. In the CEmployee class module, enter the following Class_Initialize procedure:

```
Private Sub Class_Initialize()
    Randomize
    m_ID = Int((99999 - 10000) * Rnd + 10000)
End Sub
```

The Class_Initialize procedure initializes the CEmployee object by assigning a unique five-digit number to the variable m_ID. To generate a random integer between two given integers where ending_number = 99999 and beginning_number = 10000, the following formula is used:

```
=Int((ending_number - beginning_number) * Rnd + beginning_number)
```

The Class_Initialize procedure also uses the Randomize statement to reinitialize the random number generator. For more information on using the Rnd and Integer functions, as well as the Randomize statement, search the online help.

The Terminate event occurs when all references to an object have been released. This is a good place to perform any necessary cleanup tasks. The Class_Terminate procedure uses the following syntax:

```
Private Sub Class_Terminate()
    [cleanup code goes here]
End Sub
```

To release an object variable from an object, use the following syntax:

```
Set objectVariable = Nothing
```

When you set the object variable to Nothing, the Terminate event is generated. If you have written a Terminate event procedure, any code in this event is executed then.

Creating a Form for Data Collection

Implementing your custom CEmployee object requires that you design a custom form. We will create the form shown in Figure 9-1 and later hook it up with our custom CEmployee object. While creating custom forms is covered in detail later in this book (see Chapter 19), use the following guidelines for a quick introduction to this subject.

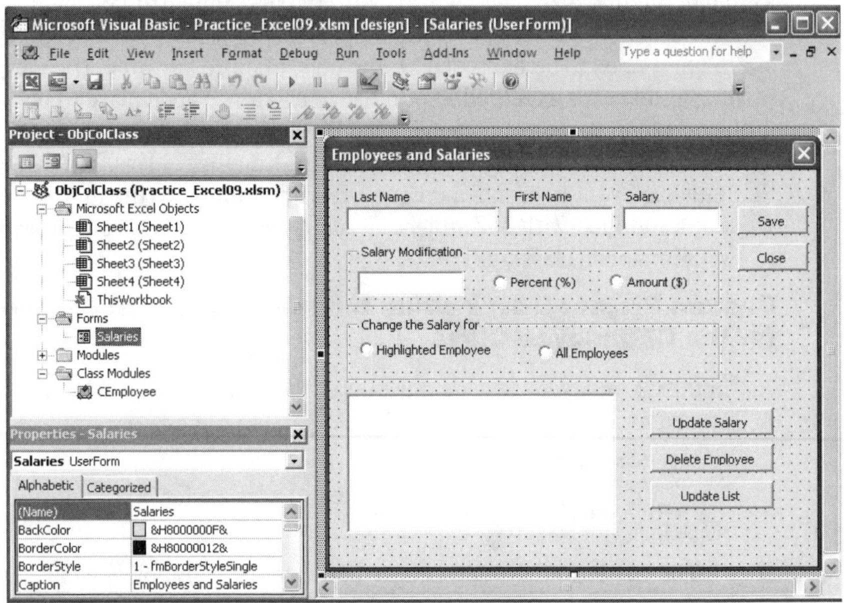

Figure 9-1: This form demonstrates the use of the CEmployee custom object.

Custom Project 9-1g: Creating a User Form for the CEmployee Object

8. Highlight the current VBA project in the Project Explorer window and choose **Insert | UserForm.**

   A blank form should appear with UserForm1 in its title bar.

9. Make the form larger by positioning the mouse on the selection handle in the bottom right-hand corner and dragging it to the right and down. Make the form big enough to hold all the controls and labels shown in Figure 9-1 above.

10. Choose **View | Toolbox.**

    A small toolbox should appear on the screen with standard Visual Basic buttons that can be placed on the user form.

11. Get familiar with the controls in the toolbox by reading the section titled "Tools for Creating User Forms" in Chapter 19.

12. Find out how to place toolbox controls on the user form by reading the section titled "Placing Controls on a Form" in Chapter 19.

13. Now that you've got some background information on working with user forms, click the **Text Box** control in the toolbox and drag it to the form. Drop it at a position shown in Figure 9-1. Use the same technique to add all the remaining controls and labels to the form.
14. Now that all the controls and labels are placed on the form, you need to set the properties for the form and its controls as shown in Table 9-1. To set each of these properties, click on the object listed in the Object column in Table 9-1. Once the object is selected on the form, locate in the Properties window the property name listed in the Property column. Replace the current property setting shown in the second column of the Properties window with the value stated in the Setting column.

Table 9-1: Setting the properties for the custom form

Object	Property	Setting
UserForm1	Name Caption	Salaries Employees and Salaries
label1	Caption	Last Name
text box below the Last Name label	Name	txtLastName
label2	Caption	First Name
text box below the First Name label	Name	txtFirstName
label3	Caption	Salary
text box below the Salary label	Name	txtSalary
frame1	Caption	Salary Modification
text box in the frame titled Salary Modification	Name	txtRaise
option button 1	Name Caption	optPercent Percent (%)
option button 2	Name Caption	optAmount Amount ($)
frame2	Caption	Change the Salary for
option button 3	Name Caption	optHighlighted Highlighted Employee
option button 4	Name Caption	optAll All Employees
list box	Name Height Width	lboxPeople 91.45 180.75
command button 1	Name Caption	cmdSave Save
command button 2	Name Caption	cmdClose Close
command button 3	Name Caption	cmdUpdate Update Salary
command button 4	Name Caption	cmdDelete Delete Employee
command button 5	Name Caption	cmdEmployeeList Update List

Creating a Worksheet for Data Output

Now that the user form is ready, the next step requires the preparation of a data entry worksheet, as shown in Figure 9-2.

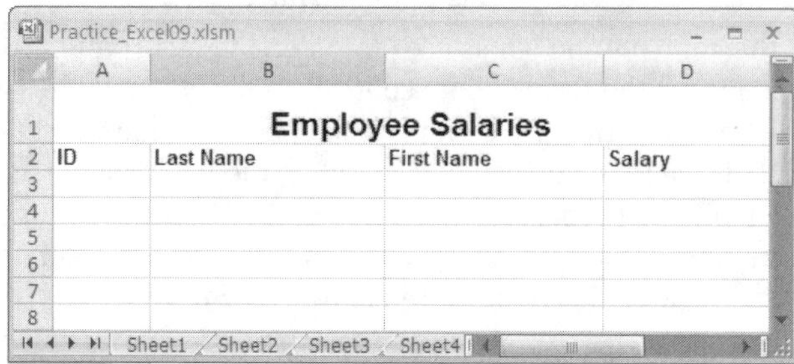

Figure 9-2: Data entered on the Employees and Salaries form will be transferred to the worksheet.

Custom Project 9-1h: Creating a Worksheet for Data Transfer

15. Insert a new worksheet to the current workbook and rename it **Salaries**.
16. Prepare a Salaries data entry worksheet as shown in Figure 9-2.

Writing Code behind the User Form

With the form and worksheet ready, all that is left to do for the CEmployee class implementation is writing the necessary procedures in the form class module. We will need an event procedure to initialize the controls on the form and several click event procedures that will run when users click the form's buttons. We also need to write a function to locate employee data in a worksheet.

Custom Project 9-1i: Writing Code for the UserForm

17. Switch back to the Visual Basic Editor window and double-click the form background to activate the form module. You can also click the **View Code** button in the Project Explorer window when the form is selected.
18. Enter the following variable declarations at the top of the Code window of the Employees and Salaries form just below the Option Explicit statement. You may copy this declaration from **C:\Ex07_HandsOn\Ex07_Chapter09.txt**.

```
Dim emp As New CEmployee
Dim CEmployees As New Collection
Dim index As Integer
Dim ws As Worksheet
Dim extract As String
Dim cell As Range
Dim lastRow As Integer
Dim empLoc As Integer
Dim startRow As Integer
Dim endRow As Integer
```

```
Dim choice As Integer
Dim amount As Long
```

The first statement declares the variable emp as a new instance of the CEmployee class. The second statement declares a custom collection. The CEmployees collection will be used to store employee data. Other variables declared here will be used by VBA procedures assigned to various controls on the form.

19. Type the following UserForm_Initialize procedure to enable or disable controls on the form:

```
Private Sub UserForm_Initialize()
    txtLastName.SetFocus
    cmdEmployeeList.Visible = False
    lboxPeople.Enabled = False
    Frame1.Enabled = False
    txtRaise.Value = ""
    optPercent.Value = False
    optAmount.Value = False
    txtRaise.Enabled = False
    optPercent.Enabled = False
    optAmount.Enabled = False
    Frame2.Enabled = False
    optHighlighted.Enabled = False
    optAll.Enabled = False
    cmdUpdate.Enabled = False
    cmdDelete.Enabled = False
End Sub
```

The statements entered inside the UserForm_Initialize procedure will enable only the desired controls when the form is first loaded.

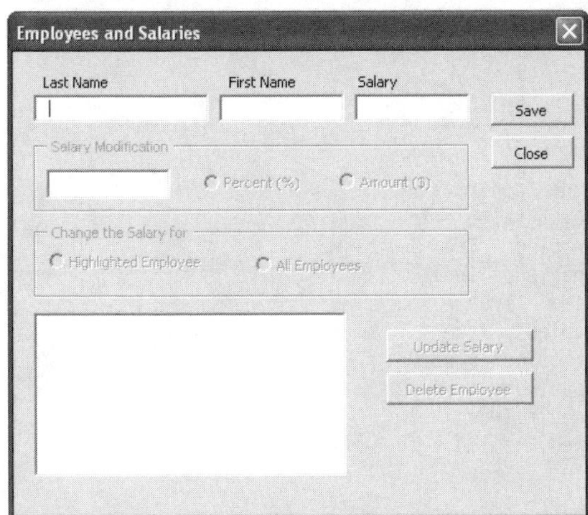

Figure 9-3: The UserForm_Initialize procedure disables certain controls that cannot be used when the form is first loaded.

20. Enter the following cmdSave_Click procedure to transfer the data entered on the form to the spreadsheet:

```
Private Sub cmdSave_Click()
    If txtLastName.Value = "" Or txtFirstName.Value = "" Or _
        txtSalary.Value = "" Then
```

```
                MsgBox "Enter Last Name, First Name and Salary."
                txtLastName.SetFocus
                Exit Sub
    End If

    If Not IsNumeric(txtSalary) Then
          MsgBox "You must enter a value for the Salary."
          txtSalary.SetFocus
          Exit Sub
    End If

    If txtSalary < 0 Then
          MsgBox "Salary cannot be a negative number."
          Exit Sub
    End If

    Worksheets("Salaries").Select
    index = ActiveSheet.UsedRange.Rows.Count + 1
    lboxPeople.Enabled = True

    ' set and enter data into the CEmployees collection
    With emp
          Cells(index, 1).Formula = emp.ID
          .LastName = txtLastName
          Cells(index, 2).Formula = emp.LastName
          .FirstName = txtFirstName
          Cells(index, 3).Formula = emp.FirstName
          .Salary = CCur(txtSalary)
          If .Salary = 0 Then Exit Sub
          Cells(index, 4).Formula = emp.Salary
          CEmployees.Add emp
    End With

    ' delete data from text boxes
    txtLastName = ""
    txtFirstName = ""
    txtSalary = ""

    ' enable hidden controls
    cmdEmployeeList.Value = True
    cmdUpdate.Enabled = True
    cmdDelete.Enabled = True
    Frame1.Enabled = True
    txtRaise.Enabled = True
    optPercent.Enabled = True
    optAmount.Enabled = True
    Frame2.Enabled = True
    optHighlighted.Enabled = True
    optAll.Enabled = True
    txtLastName.SetFocus
End Sub
```

The cmdSave_Click procedure starts off with validating the user's input in the Last Name, First Name, and Salary text boxes. If the user entered correct data, VBA assigns to the variable index the number of the first empty row on the active sheet for the data entry purposes. The next statement enables the form's list box control. When the program reaches the With emp . . . construct, a new instance of the CEmployee class is created. The LastName, FirstName, and Salary properties are set based on the data entered in the corresponding text boxes, and the ID property is set with the number generated by the statements inside the Class_Initialize event procedure. Each time VBA sees the reference to the instanced emp object, it will call the appropriate Property Let procedure located in the class module.

The last section of this chapter demonstrates how to walk through this procedure step by step to see exactly when the property procedures are executed. After setting the object property values, VBA transfers the employee data to the worksheet. The last statement inside the With emp. . . construct adds the user-defined object emp to a custom collection called CEmployees.

Next, Visual Basic removes the current entries from the form's text boxes and enables command buttons that were turned off by the UserForm_Initialize procedure. Notice the first instruction in this block: cmdEmployeeList.Value = True. This statement causes the automatic execution of the cmdEmployeeList_Click procedure attached to the Update List command button. (By the way, this is the only control that the user never sees.) The code for this procedure is shown in step 21.

21. Type the cmdEmployeeList_Click procedure, as shown here:

```
Private Sub cmdEmployeeList_Click()
    lboxPeople.Clear
    For Each emp In CEmployees
         lboxPeople.AddItem emp.ID & ", " & _
         emp.LastName & ", " & emp.FirstName & ", $" & _
         Format(emp.Salary, "0.00")
    Next emp
End Sub
```

The cmdEmployeeList_Click procedure is attached to the Update List command button. This button is controlled by the cmdSave_Click procedure and causes the new employee data to be added to the list box

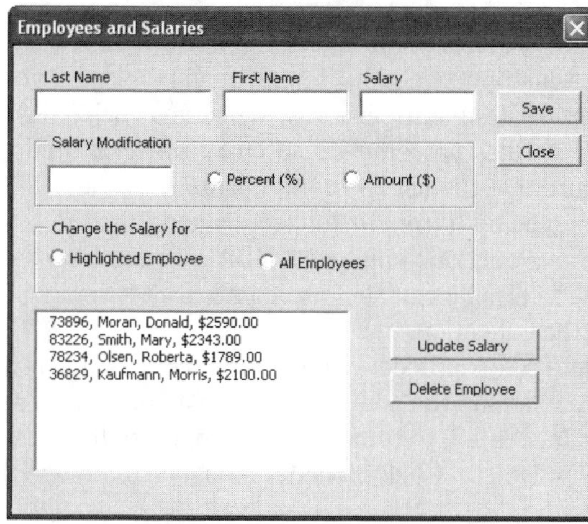

Figure 9-4: The list box control displays employee data as entered in the custom collection CEmployees.

control. The cmdEmployeeList_Click procedure begins with clearing the contents of the list box and then populating it with the items stored in the custom collection CEmployees, as shown in Figure 9-4.

22. Type the following cmdClose_Click procedure:

```
Private Sub cmdClose_Click()
    Unload Me
End Sub
```

The cmdClose_Click procedure allows you to remove the user form from the screen and finish working with the custom collection of employees. When you run the form again, the employees you enter will become members of a new CEmployees collection.

23. Type the following cmdDelete_Click procedure:

```
Private Sub cmdDelete_Click()
    ' make sure that an employee is highlighted in the
    ' list control

    If lboxPeople.ListIndex > -1 Then
         MsgBox "Selected item number: " & lboxPeople.ListIndex
         extract = CEmployees.Item(lboxPeople.ListIndex + 1).ID
         MsgBox extract
         Call FindId
         MsgBox empLoc
         Range("A" & empLoc).Delete (3)
         MsgBox "There are " & CEmployees.Count & _
                " items in the CEmployees collection. "
         CEmployees.Remove lboxPeople.ListIndex + 1
         MsgBox "The CEmployees collection has now " & _
                 CEmployees.Count & " items."
         cmdEmployeeList.Value = True
         If CEmployees.Count = 0 Then
              Call UserForm_Initialize
         End If
    Else
         MsgBox "Click the item you want to remove."
    End If
End Sub
```

The cmdDelete_Click procedure lets you remove an employee from the CEmployees custom collection. To delete an employee, you must click the appropriate item in the list box. When you click a list item, the cmdEmployeeList_Click procedure is automatically executed. This procedure makes sure that the list box contents are refreshed. The employee is removed both from the collection and from the list box. If the list box contains only one employee, VBA calls the UserForm_Initialize procedure to disable certain form controls after removing the last employee from the collection.

The cmdDelete_Click procedure contains several MsgBox statements that allow you to examine the contents of the list box control as you make deletions. In addition to removing the employee from the custom collection, the cmdDelete_Click procedure must also remove the corresponding row of employee information from the worksheet. Locating the employee data in the worksheet is handled by the FindId function. (The code of this procedure is in step 24 below.) This function returns to the cmdDelete_Click procedure the row number that has to be deleted.

24. Type the following function procedure:

```
Private Function FindId()
    Set ws= ActiveWorkbook.Sheets("Salaries")
    startRow = ActiveSheet.UsedRange.Rows.Count + _
          1 - CEmployees.Count
    endRow = ActiveSheet.UsedRange.Rows.Count
    For Each cell In ws.Range(Cells(startRow, 1), _
          Cells(endRow, 1))
          If cell.Value = extract Then
                empLoc = cell.Row
                FindId = empLoc
                Exit Function
          End If
    Next
End Function
```

The FindId function procedure returns to the calling procedure the row number that contains the data of the employee who is currently selected in the form's list box. The search for the data in the worksheet is based on the contents of the variable extract that stores the unique employee number. The search for the employee ID is limited to the first worksheet column and begins with the row in which the first collection item was placed. This approach makes the search faster. You don't want to search the entire used area of the worksheet. Recall that if you use the form more than once, the contents of your custom collection will not include the previously entered employees.

25. Type the following cmdUpdate_Click procedure:

```
Private Sub cmdUpdate_Click()
    If optHighlighted.Value = False And optAll.Value = False Then
          MsgBox "Click the 'Highlighted Employee' or " _
                & " 'All Employees' option button."
          Exit Sub
    End If
    If Not IsNumeric(txtRaise) Then
          MsgBox "This field requires a number."
          txtRaise.SetFocus
          Exit Sub
    End If
    If optHighlighted.Value = True And _
          lboxPeople.ListIndex = -1 Then
                MsgBox "Click the name of the employee."
                Exit Sub
    End If
    If lboxPeople.ListIndex <> -1 And _
          optHighlighted.Value = True And _
          optAmount.Value = True And _
          txtRaise.Value <> "" Then
```

```
            extract = CEmployees.Item(lboxPeople.ListIndex + 1).ID
            MsgBox extract
            Call FindId
            MsgBox empLoc
            choice = 2
            amount = txtRaise
            CEmployees.Item(lboxPeople.ListIndex + 1).Salary = _
                 emp.CalcNewSalary(choice, _
            CEmployees.Item(lboxPeople.ListIndex + 1).Salary, amount)
            Range("D" & empLoc).Formula = CEmployees. _
                 Item(lboxPeople.ListIndex + 1).Salary
            cmdEmployeeList.Value = True
    ElseIf lboxPeople.ListIndex <> -1 And _
         optHighlighted.Value = True And _
         optPercent.Value = True And _
         txtRaise.Value <> "" Then
            extract = CEmployees.Item(lboxPeople.ListIndex + 1).ID
            MsgBox extract
            Call FindId
            MsgBox empLoc
            CEmployees.Item(lboxPeople.ListIndex + 1).Salary = _
                 CEmployees.Item(lboxPeople.ListIndex + 1).Salary _
                 + (CEmployees.Item(lboxPeople.ListIndex + _
                 1).Salary * txtRaise / 100)
            Range("D" & empLoc).Formula = CEmployees. _
                 Item(lboxPeople.ListIndex + 1).Salary
            cmdEmployeeList.Value = True
    ElseIf optAll.Value = True And _
         optPercent.Value = True And _
         txtRaise.Value <> "" Then
            For Each emp In CEmployees
                 emp.Salary = emp.Salary + ((emp.Salary * _
                      txtRaise) / 100)
                 extract = emp.ID
                 MsgBox extract
                 Call FindId
                 MsgBox empLoc
                 Range("D" & empLoc).Formula = emp.Salary
            Next emp
            cmdEmployeeList.Value = True
    ElseIf optAll.Value = True And _
         optAmount.Value = True And _
         txtRaise.Value <> "" Then
            For Each emp In CEmployees
                 emp.Salary = emp.Salary + txtRaise
                 extract = emp.ID
                 MsgBox extract
                 Call FindId
                 MsgBox empLoc
                 Range("D" & empLoc).Formula = emp.Salary
            Next emp
            cmdEmployeeList.Value = True
    Else
         MsgBox "Enter data or select an option."
    End If
End Sub
```

With the cmdUpdate_Click procedure, you can modify the salary by the specified percentage or amount. The update can be done for the selected employee or all the employees listed in the list box control and collection. The cmdUpdate_Click procedure checks whether the user selected the appropriate option buttons and entered the increase value in the text box. Depending on which options are specified, the Salary amount is updated for one employee or all the employees, either by a percentage or amount. The salary modification is also reflected in the worksheet.

Figure 9-5 displays the salary of Roberta Olsen, which has been increased by 10%. By entering a negative number in the text box, you can decrease the salary by the specified percentage or amount.

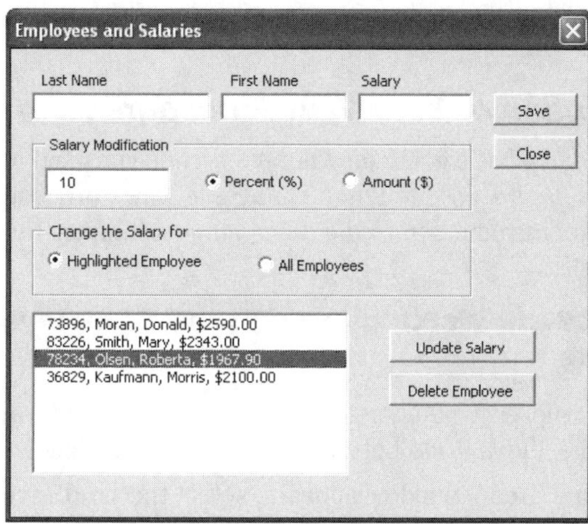

Figure 9-5: The employee salary can be increased or decreased by the specified percentage or amount.

Practice_Excel09.xlsm

	A	B	C	D
1	Employee Salaries			
2	ID	Last Name	First Name	Salary
3	73896	Moran	Donald	$2,590.00
4	83226	Smith	Mary	$2,343.00
5	78234	Olsen	Roberta	$1,967.90
6	36829	Kaufmann	Morris	$2,100.00
7				

Sheet1 Sheet2 Sheet3 Sheet4

Figure 9-6: When you update the employee information in the form the relevant data is also updated in the worksheet.

Working with the Custom CEmployee Class

The application using a custom CEmployee class is now ready. To make it easy to work with the user form, we'll write a one-line procedure in the standard module that shows the form.

Custom Project 9-1j: Writing a Procedure to Display the User Form

26. Insert a standard module into the current project by choosing **Insert | Module.** Rename this module **WorkAndPay.**
27. Type the following procedure in the WorkAndPay module to display the Employees and Salaries form:

```
Sub ClassDemo()
    Salaries.Show
End Sub
```

28. Run the ClassDemo procedure to work with the custom class. You can also display the form by clicking the form's background and pressing **F5**, or you can place a button in a worksheet and assign the ClassDemo procedure to it.

Watching the Execution of Your VBA Procedures

To help you understand what's going on when your code runs and how your custom object works, let's step through the cmdSave_Click procedure. Treat this exercise as a brief introduction to the debugging techniques that are covered in detail in Part IV.

Custom Project 9-1k: Walking through the CEmployee Application Code

29. In the Project Explorer window, select the **Employees and Salaries** form and click the **View Code** button at the top of this window.
30. When the Salaries (Code) window appears, select the **cmdSave** procedure from the combo box at the top left-hand side of the Code window.
31. Set a breakpoint by clicking in the left margin next to the following line of code (see Figure 9-7):

```
If txtLastName.Value = "" Or txtFirstName.Value = "" Or _
    txtSalary.Value = "" Then
```

Practice_Excel09.xlsm - Salaries (Code)

cmdSave | Click

```
Private Sub cmdSave_Click()
    If txtLastName.Value = "" Or txtFirstName.Value = "" Or txtSalary.Value = "" Then
        MsgBox "Enter Last Name, First Name and Salary."
        txtLastName.SetFocus
        Exit Sub
    End If
    If Not IsNumeric(txtSalary) Then
        MsgBox "You must enter a value for the Salary."
    txtSalary.SetFocus
        Exit Sub
    End If
    If txtSalary < 0 Then
        MsgBox "Salary cannot be a negative number."
```

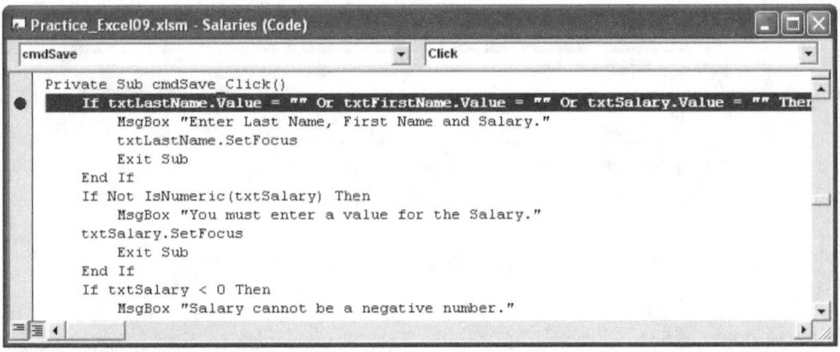

Figure 9-7: A red circle in the margin indicates a breakpoint. When VBA encounters the statement with a breakpoint, it automatically switches to the Code window and displays the text of the line as white on a red background.

32. In the Project Explorer window, highlight the **WorkAndPay** module and click the **View Code** button.
33. Place the cursor anywhere inside the ClassDemo procedure and press **F5**, or choose **Run | Run Sub/UserForm**.
34. When the form appears, enter data in the Last Name, First Name, and Salary text boxes, and click the **Save** button on the form. Visual Basic should now switch to the Code window since it encountered the breakpoint in the first line of the cmdSave_Click procedure.

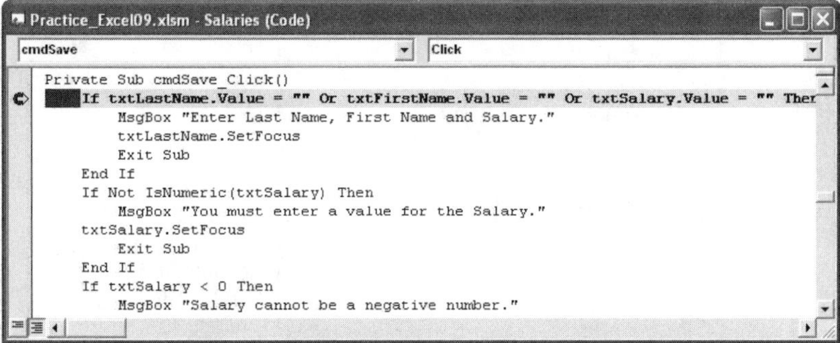

Figure 9-8: When Visual Basic encounters a breakpoint while running a procedure, it switches to the Code window and displays a yellow arrow in the margin to the left of the statement at which the procedure is suspended.

35. Step through the code one statement at a time by pressing **F8.**

    Visual Basic runs the current statement and then automatically advances to the next statement and suspends execution. The current statement is indicated by a yellow arrow in the margin and a yellow background. Keep pressing F8 to execute the procedure step by step. When Visual Basic encounters the With emp statement, it switches to the Class_Initialize procedure.

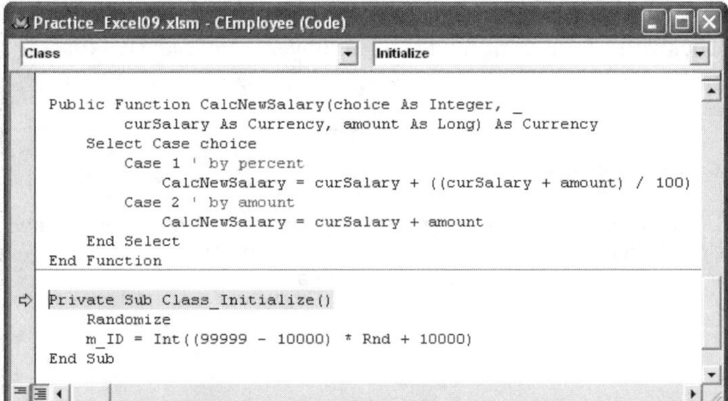

Figure 9-9: When Visual Basic encounters the reference to the object variable emp, it goes out to execute the Class_Initialize procedure. After executing the statements inside this procedure, VBA returns to the cmdSave_Click procedure.

When Visual Basic encounters the statement Cells(Index, 1).Formula = emp.ID, it executes the Property Get ID procedure in the CEmployee class module.

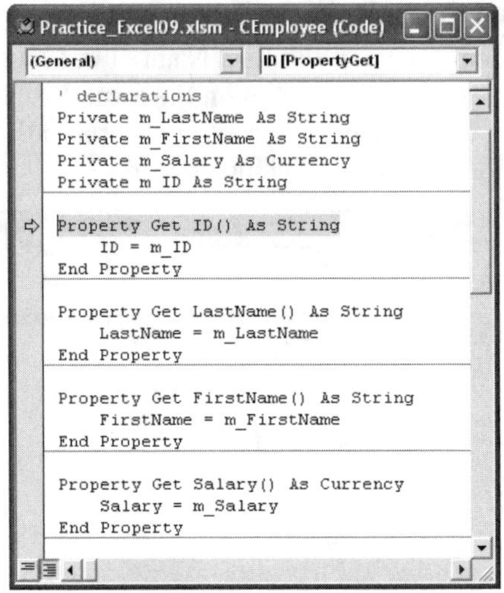

Figure 9-10: Reading properties of your custom object is accomplished through the Property Get procedures.

36. Using the **F8** key, trace the execution of the cmdSave_Click procedure to the end.
37. When VBA encounters the end of the procedure (End Sub), the yellow highlighter is turned off. At this time, either press **Alt+F11** or click the **Microsoft Excel Practice_Excel09.xlsm** button on the Windows taskbar at the bottom of the screen to return to the active form. Enter data for a new employee and click the **Save** button.
38. When Visual Basic displays the Code window, choose **Debug | Clear All Breakpoints.** Now press **F5** to run the rest of the procedure without stepping through it.
39. Click the **Close** button on the Employees and Salaries form to exit the application.

VBA Debugging Tools

Visual Basic provides a number of debugging tools to help you analyze how your application operates, as well as locate the source of errors in your procedures. See the chapters in Part IV for details on working with these tools.

Chapter Summary

In this chapter, you learned how to create and use your own objects and collections in VBA procedures. You used a class module to create a user-defined (custom) object, and you saw how to define your custom object's properties using Property Get and Property Let procedures. You also learned how to write a method for your custom object. Next, you saw how to make the class module available to the user by building a custom form. Finally, you learned how to analyze your VBA application by stepping through its code.

This chapter concludes Part III of this book. In the next chapter, you will learn how to troubleshoot your VBA procedures.

Part IV

Error Handling and Debugging

While you may have planned to write a perfect VBA procedure, there is always a chance that incorrectly constructed or typed code, or perhaps logic errors, will cause your program to fail or produce unexpected results.

In this part of the book, you'll learn about various methods of handling errors, and testing and debugging VBA procedures.

Chapter 10

VBE Tools for Testing and Debugging

Testing VBA Procedures ■ Stopping a Procedure ■ Using Breakpoints ■ When to Use a Breakpoint ■ Using the Immediate Window in Break Mode ■ Using the Stop Statement ■ **Using the Watch Window** ■ Removing Watch Expressions ■ **Using Quick Watch** ■ **Using the Locals Window and the Call Stack Dialog Box** ■ **Stepping through VBA Procedures** ■ Stepping Over a Procedure and Running to Cursor ■ Setting the Next Statement ■ Showing the Next Statement ■ Stopping and Resetting VBA Procedures ■ **Chapter Summary**

It does not take much for an error to creep into your VBA procedure. The truth is that no matter how careful you are it is rare that all of your VBA procedures will work correctly the first time. In Chapter 3 you learned that there are three types of errors in VBA: syntax errors, logic errors, and run-time errors. This chapter introduces you to the Visual Basic Editor tools that are available for you to use in the process of analyzing the code of your VBA procedures and locating the source of errors.

Testing VBA Procedures

Thus far in this book you've created and executed dozens of sample procedures and functions. Because most of these procedures were quite short, finding errors wasn't very difficult. However, when writing longer and more complex procedures, locating the source of errors is more tedious and time consuming. Fortunately, Visual Basic Editor provides a set of handy tools that can make the process of tracking down your VBA problems easier, faster, and less frustrating. Bugs are errors in computer programs and debugging is a process of locating and fixing those errors. Debugging allows you to find out the reason your procedure doesn't work the way it's supposed to work. You can do this by stepping through the code of your procedure or checking the values of variables.

When testing your VBA procedure, use the following guidelines:

- If you want to analyze your procedure, step through your code one line at a time by pressing F8, or choose Debug | Step Into.
- If you suspect that an error may occur in a specific place in your procedure, use a breakpoint.
- If you want to monitor the value of a particular variable or expression used by your procedure, add a watch expression.
- If you are tired of scrolling through a long procedure to get to sections of code that interest you, set up a bookmark to jump quickly to the desired location.

Each of these guidelines is demonstrated in a hands-on scenario in this chapter.

Stopping a Procedure

While testing your VBA procedure you may want to halt its execution. This can be done simply by pressing the Escape key. If you press the Escape key while running a procedure, Visual Basic will stop your program and display the message shown in Figure 10-1. However, in addition to the mighty and very reliable, in most circumstances, Escape key, VBA offers other methods of stopping your procedure. When you stop your procedure you enter into what is called break mode.

To enter break mode, do one of the following:

- Press the Ctrl+Break key combination

- Set one or more breakpoints
- Insert the Stop statement into your procedure code
- Add a watch expression

A break occurs when execution of your VBA procedure is temporarily suspended. Visual Basic remembers the values of all variables and the statement from which the execution of the procedure should resume when the user decides to continue by clicking Run Sub/UserForm on the toolbar (or the Run menu option with the same name) or by clicking the Continue button in the dialog box. The error dialog box shown in Figure 10-1 informs you that the procedure was halted. The buttons in this dialog are described in Table 10-1.

Table 10-1: Error dialog buttons

Continue	Click this button to resume code execution. This button will be grayed out if an error was encountered.
End	Click this button if you do not want to troubleshoot the procedure at this time. VBA will stop code execution.
Debug	Click this button to enter break mode. The Code window will appear, and VBA will highlight the line at which the procedure execution was suspended. You can examine, debug, reset, or step through the code.
Help	Click this button to view the online help that explains the cause of this error message.

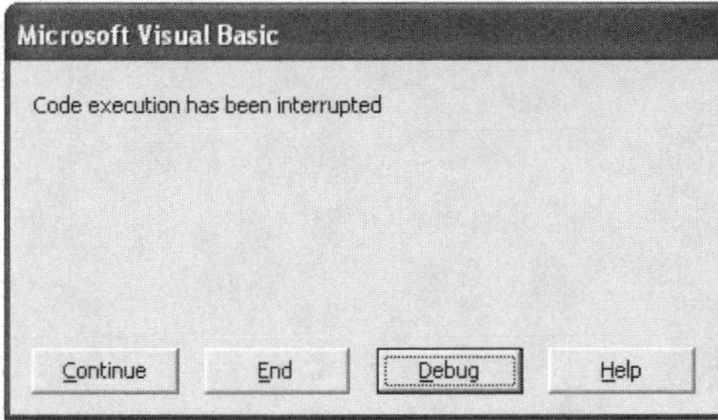

Figure 10-1: This message appears when you press Esc or Ctrl+Break while your VBA procedure is running.

You can prevent application users from halting your procedure by including the following statement in the procedure code:

```
Application.EnableCancelKey = xlDisabled
```

When the user presses Esc or Ctrl+Break while the procedure is running, nothing happens. The Application object's EnableCancelKey property disables these keys.

Using Breakpoints

If you know more or less where you can expect a problem in the code of your procedure, you should suspend code execution at that location (on a given line). Setting a breakpoint boils down to pressing F9 when the cursor is on the desired line of code. When VBA gets to that line while running your procedure, it will immediately display the Code window. At this point, you can step through the code of your procedure line by line by pressing F8 or choosing Debug | Step Into. To see how this works, let's look at the following scenario. Assume that during the execution of the ChangeCode procedure the following line of code could get you in trouble:

```
ActiveCell.FormulaR1C1 = _
   "=VLOOKUP(RC[1],Codes.xlsx!R1C1:R6C2,2)"
```

Hands-On 10-1: Setting Breakpoints in a VBA Procedure

1. Copy the **Practice_Excel10.xlsm** workbook from the **C:\Ex07_HandsOn** folder to your **C:\Ex07_ByExample** folder.
2. Copy the **Codes.xlsx** workbook from the **C:\Ex07_HandsOn** folder to your **C:\Ex07_ByExample** folder.
3. Start Microsoft Excel and open both these files (**Practice_Excel10.xlsm, Codes.xlsx)** from the **C:\Ex07_ByExample** folder.
4. Examine the data in both workbooks (see Figures 10-2 and 10-3).

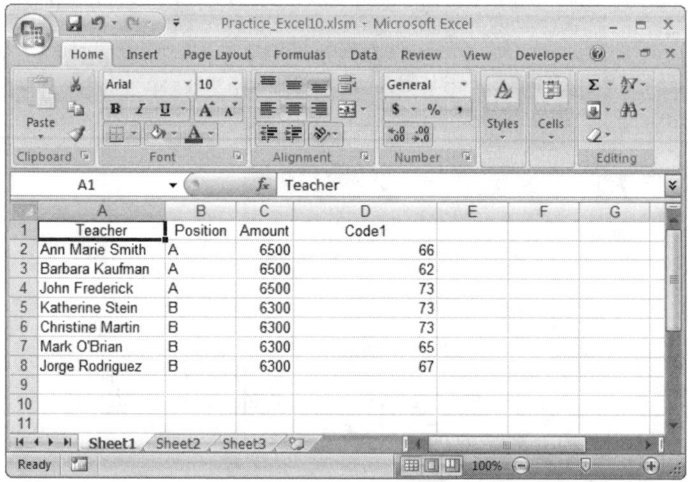

Figure 10-2: The data entered in column D of this spreadsheet will be replaced by the ChangeCode procedure with the data illustrated in Figure 10-3.

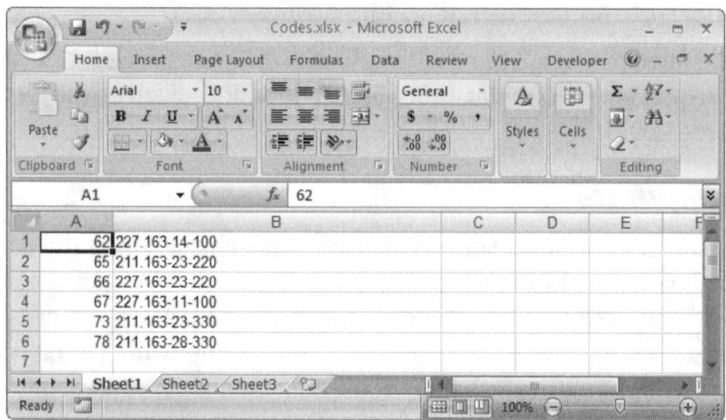

Figure 10-3: The ChangeCode procedure uses this code table for lookup purposes.

5. Close the Codes.xlsx workbook. Leave the other file open.
6. With Practice_Excel10.xlsm active, switch to the Visual Basic Editor window.
7. In the Project Explorer, open the Modules folder in the **Debugging (Practice_Excel10.xlsm)** project and double-click the **Breaks** module.

   The Breaks module Code window lists the following ChangeCode procedure:

```
Sub ChangeCode()
    Workbooks.Open Filename:="C:\Ex07_ByExample\Codes.xlsx"
    Windows("Practice_Excel10.xlsm").Activate
    Columns("D:D").Insert Shift:=xlToRight
    Range("D1").Formula = "Code"
    Columns("D:D").SpecialCells(xlBlanks).Select
    ActiveCell.FormulaR1C1 = "=VLookup(RC[1],Codes.xlsx!R1C1:R6C2,2)"
    Selection.FillDown
        With Columns("D:D")
            .EntireColumn.AutoFit
            .Select
        End With
    Selection.Copy
    Selection.PasteSpecial Paste:=xlValues
    Rows("1:1").Select
        With Selection
            .HorizontalAlignment = xlCenter
            .VerticalAlignment = xlBottom
            .Orientation = xlHorizontal
        End With
    Workbooks("Codes.xlsx").Close
End Sub
```

8. In the ChangeCode procedure, click anywhere on the line containing the following statement:

```
ActiveCell.FormulaR1C1 = "=VLookup(RC[1],Codes.xlsx!R1C1:R6C2,2)"
```

9. Press **F9** (or choose Debug | Toggle Breakpoint) to set a breakpoint on the line where the cursor is located.

   Another way to set a breakpoint is to click in the margin indicator to the left of the line on which you want to pause the procedure. When you set the breakpoint, Visual Basic displays a red circle in the margin. At the same time, the line that has the breakpoint is indicated as white text on a red background (see Figure 10-4). The color of the breakpoint can be changed on the Editor Format tab in the Options dialog box (Tools menu).

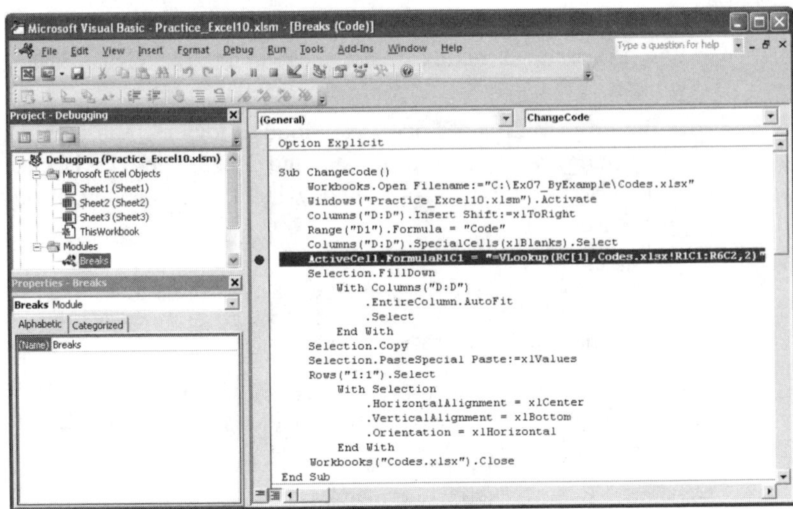

Figure 10-4: The line of code where the breakpoint is set is displayed in the color specified on the Editor Format tab in the Options dialog box.

10. Press **F5** to run the ChangeCode procedure.

    When you run the procedure, Visual Basic will execute all the statements until it encounters the breakpoint. Once the breakpoint is reached, the code is suspended, and the screen displays the Code window (see Figure 10-5). Visual Basic displays a yellow arrow in the margin to the left of the statement at which the procedure was suspended. At the same time, the statement appears inside a box with a yellow background. The arrow and the box indicate the current statement or the statement that is about to be executed. If the current statement also contains a breakpoint, the margin displays both indicators overlapping one another (the circle and the arrow).

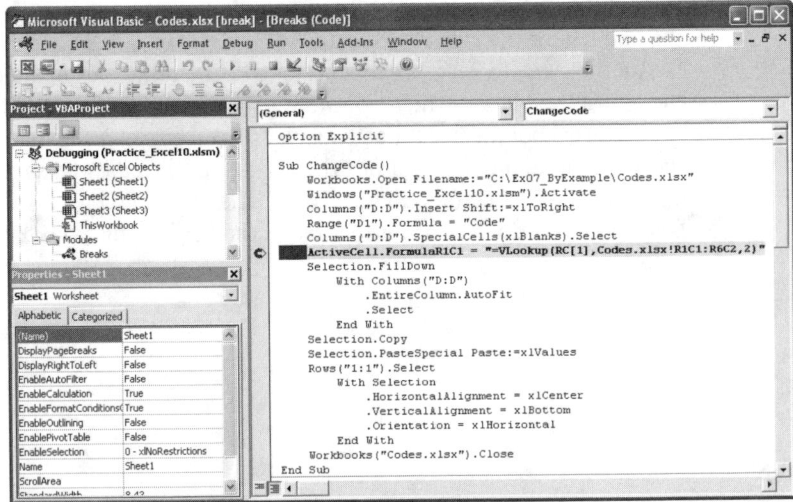

Figure 10-5: When Visual Basic encounters a breakpoint, it displays the Code window and indicates the current statement.

While in break mode, you can change code, add new statements, execute the procedure one line at a time, skip lines, set the next statement, use the Immediate window, and more. When Visual Basic is in break mode, all of the options on the Debug menu are available. If you change certain code while you work in break mode, VBA will prompt you to reset the project by displaying the following error message: "This action will reset your project, proceed anyway?" You can click OK to cease the program's execution and proceed editing your code, or click Cancel to delete the new changes and continue running the code from the point at which it was suspended.

11. Press **F5** (or choose Run Sub/UserForm) to continue running the procedure.

    Visual Basic leaves break mode and continues to run the procedure statements until it reaches the end of the procedure. When the procedure finishes executing, Visual Basic does not automatically remove the breakpoint. Notice that the line of code with the VLookup function is still highlighted.

    In this example you have set only one breakpoint. Visual Basic allows you to set any number of breakpoints in a procedure. This way, you can suspend and continue the execution of your procedure as you please. You can analyze the code of your procedure and check the values of variables while execution is suspended. You can also perform various tests by typing statements in the Immediate window.

12. Remove the breakpoint by choosing **Debug | Clear All Breakpoints** or by pressing **Ctrl+Shift+F9**. You can also click on the red circle in the margin area to remove the breakpoint.

    All the breakpoints are removed. If you had set several breakpoints in a given procedure and would like to remove only one or some of them, click on the line containing the breakpoint that you want to remove and press F9 (or choose Debug | Clear Breakpoint). You should clear the breakpoints when they are no longer needed. The breakpoints are automatically removed when you close the file.

13. Switch to the Microsoft Excel application window and notice that a new column with the looked up codes was added on Sheet1 of the Practice_Excel10.xlsm workbook.

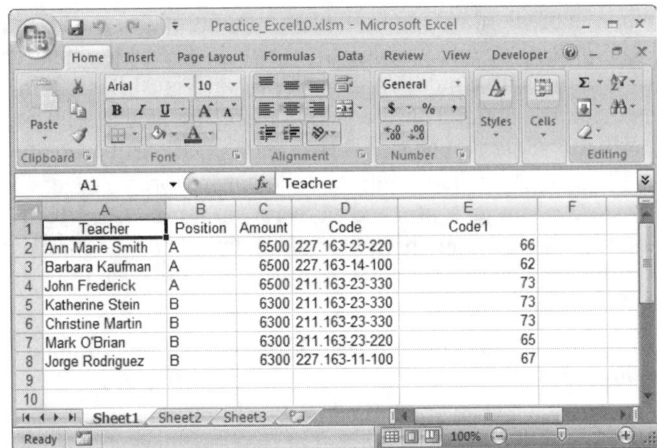

	A	B	C	D	E	F
1	Teacher	Position	Amount	Code	Code1	
2	Ann Marie Smith	A	6500	227.163-23-220	66	
3	Barbara Kaufman	A	6500	227.163-14-100	62	
4	John Frederick	A	6500	211.163-23-330	73	
5	Katherine Stein	B	6300	211.163-23-330	73	
6	Christine Martin	B	6300	211.163-23-330	73	
7	Mark O'Brian	B	6300	211.163-23-220	65	
8	Jorge Rodriguez	B	6300	227.163-11-100	67	
9						
10						

Figure 10-6: This worksheet was modified by the ChangeCode procedure in Hands-On 10-1.

When to Use a Breakpoint

Consider setting a breakpoint if you suspect that your procedure never executes a certain block of code. In break mode, you can quickly find out the contents of the variable at the cursor in the Code window. Simply hold the mouse pointer over any variable in a running procedure to find out the value of that variable. For example, in the VarValue procedure shown in Figure 10-7, the breakpoint has been set on the Workbooks.Add statement. When Visual Basic encounters this statement, the Code window (break mode) appears. Because Visual Basic has already executed the statement that stores the name of ActiveWorkbook in the variable strName, you can quickly find out the value of this variable by resting the mouse pointer over its name. The name of the variable and its current value appear in a tooltip frame.

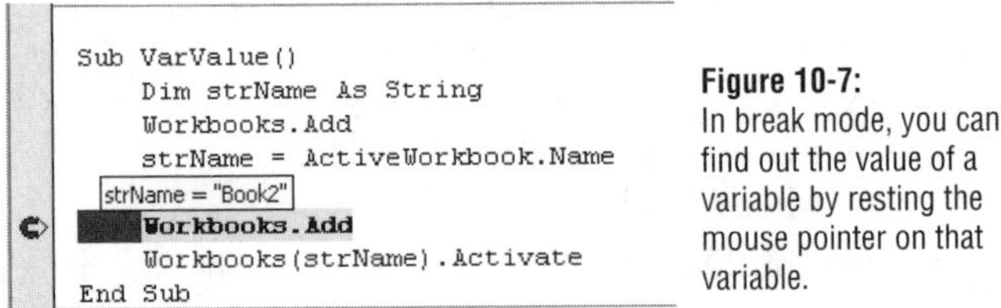

```
Sub VarValue()
    Dim strName As String
    Workbooks.Add
    strName = ActiveWorkbook.Name
 strName = "Book2"
    Workbooks.Add
    Workbooks(strName).Activate
End Sub
```

Figure 10-7: In break mode, you can find out the value of a variable by resting the mouse pointer on that variable.

Note: To show the values of several variables used in a procedure at once, you should use the Locals window, which is discussed later in this chapter.

Using the Immediate Window in Break Mode

Once the procedure execution is suspended and the Code window appears, you can activate the Immediate window and type VBA instructions to find out, for instance, which cell is currently active or the name of the active sheet. You can also use the Immediate window to change the contents of variables in order to correct values that may be causing errors.

Figure 10-8 shows the suspended ChangeCode procedure and the Immediate window with the questions that were asked of Visual Basic while in break mode.

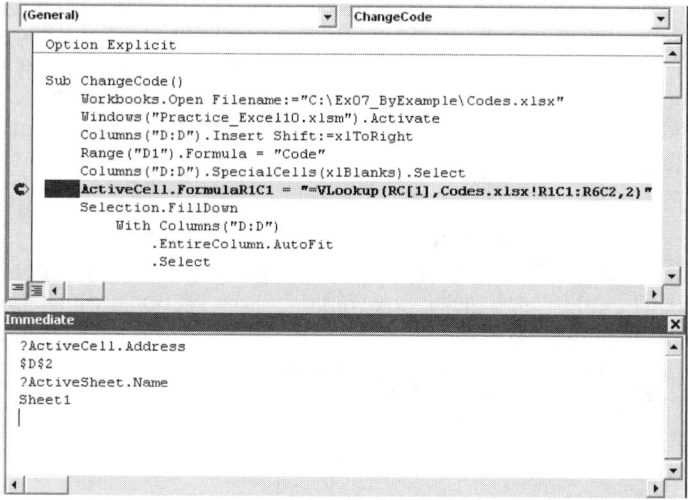
(General)
ChangeCode
Option Explicit
Sub ChangeCode()
Workbooks.Open Filename:="C:\Ex07_ByExample\Codes.xlsx"
Windows("Practice_Excel10.xlsm").Activate
Columns("D:D").Insert Shift:=xlToRight
Range("D1").Formula = "Code"
Columns("D:D").SpecialCells(xlBlanks).Select
ActiveCell.FormulaR1C1 = "=VLookup(RC[1],Codes.xlsx!R1C1:R6C2,2)"
Selection.FillDown
With Columns("D:D")
.EntireColumn.AutoFit
.Select
Immediate
?ActiveCell.Address
$D$2
?ActiveSheet.Name
Sheet1

Figure 10-8: When the code execution is suspended, you can find answers to many questions by entering appropriate statements in the Immediate window.

Using the Stop Statement

Sometimes you won't be able to test your procedure right away. If you set up your breakpoints and then close the file, Excel will remove your breakpoints, and the next time you are ready to test your procedure, you'll have to begin by setting up breakpoints again. If you need to postpone the task of testing your procedure until later, you can take a different approach. Simply insert a Stop statement into your code wherever you want to halt a procedure. Figure 10-9 shows a Stop statement before the For Each...Next loop. Visual Basic will suspend the execution of the StopExample procedure when it encounters the Stop statement. The screen will display the Code window in break mode.

```
Sub StopExample()
    Dim curCell As Range
    Dim num As Integer

    ActiveWorkbook.Sheets(1).Select
    ActiveSheet.UsedRange.Select
    num = Selection.Columns.Count
    Selection.Resize(1, num).Select
    Stop
    For Each curCell In Selection
        Debug.Print curCell.Text
    Next
End Sub
```

Figure 10-9: You can insert a Stop statement anywhere in the code of your VBA procedure. The procedure will halt when it gets to the Stop statement, and the Code window will appear with the line highlighted.

Although the Stop statement has exactly the same effect as setting a breakpoint, it has one disadvantage — all Stop statements stay in the procedure until you remove them. When you no longer need to stop your procedure, you must locate and remove all the Stop statements.

Using the Watch Window

Many errors in procedures are caused by variables that assume unexpected values. If a procedure uses a variable whose value changes in various locations, you may want to stop the procedure and check the current value of that variable. Visual Basic offers a special Watch window that allows you to keep an eye on variables or expressions while your procedure is running.

To add a watch expression to your procedure, perform the following:

1. In the Code window, select the variable whose value you want to monitor.
2. Choose **Debug | Add Watch.**

   The screen will display the Add Watch dialog box, as shown in Figure 10-10. The Add Watch dialog box contains three sections, which are described in Table 10-1.

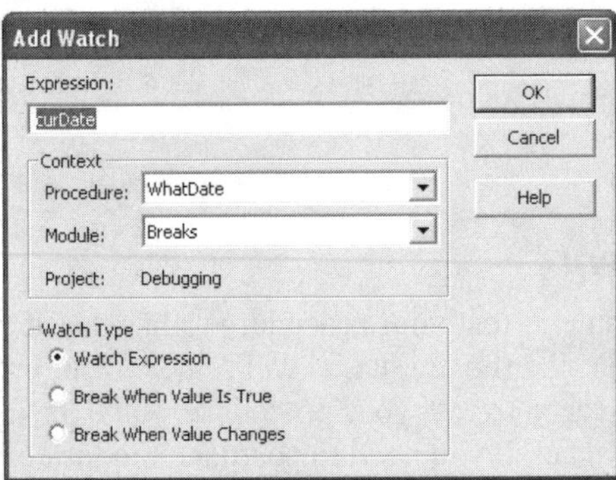

Figure 10-10: The Add Watch dialog box allows you to define conditions that you want to monitor while a VBA procedure is running.

Table 10-2: Add Watch dialog options

Expression	Displays the name of a variable that you have highlighted in your procedure. If you opened the Add Watch dialog box without selecting a variable name, type the name of the variable you want to monitor in the Expression text box.
Context	In this section you should indicate the name of the procedure that contains the variable and the name of the module where this procedure is located.
Watch Type	Specifies how to monitor the variable. If you choose the Watch Expression option button, you will be able to read the value of the variable in the Watch window while in break mode. If you choose Break When Value Is True, Visual Basic will automatically stop the procedure when the variable evaluates to true (nonzero). The last option button, Break When Value Changes, stops the procedure each time the value of the variable or expression changes.

You can add a watch expression before running a procedure or after execution of your procedure has been suspended. The difference between a breakpoint and a watch expression is the breakpoint always stops a procedure in a specified location and the watch stops the procedure only when the specified condition (Break When Value Is True or Break When Value

Changes) is met. Watches are extremely useful when you are not sure where the variable is being changed. Instead of stepping through many lines of code to find the location where the variable assumes the specified value, you can simply put a watch expression on the variable and run your procedure as normal. Let's see how this works.

Hands-On 10-2: Watching the Values of VBA Expressions

1. The Breaks module Code window lists the following WhatDate procedure:

```
Sub WhatDate()
    Dim curDate As Date
    Dim newDate As Date
    Dim x As Integer

    curDate = Date
    For x = 1 To 365
        newDate = Date + x
    Next
End Sub
```

   The WhatDate procedure uses the For...Next loop to calculate the date that is x days in the future. If you run this procedure, you won't get any result unless you insert the following instruction in the code of the procedure:

```
MsgBox "In " & x & " days, it will be " & NewDate
```

   In this example, however, you don't care to display the individual dates, day after day. What if all you want to do is to stop the program when the value of the variable x reaches 211? In other words, what date will be 211 days from now? To get the answer, you could insert the following statement into your procedure:

```
If x = 211 Then MsgBox "In " & x & " days it will be " & NewDate
```

   Introducing new statements into your procedure just to get an answer about the value of a certain variable when a specific condition occurs will not always be viable. Instead of adding MsgBox or other debug statements to your procedure code that you will later need to delete, you can use the Watch window and avoid extra code maintenance. If you add watch expressions to the procedure, Visual Basic will stop the For...Next loop when the specified condition is met, and you'll be able to check the values of the desired variables.

2. Choose **Debug | Add Watch.**
3. In the Expression text box, enter the following expression: **x = 211**. In the Context section, choose **WhatDate** from the Procedure combo box and **Breaks** from the Module combo box. In the Watch Type section, select the **Break When Value Is True** option button.
4. Click **OK** to close the Add Watch dialog box. You have now added your first watch expression.

Visual Basic opens the Watch window and places in it your expression: x = 211. Now let's add another expression to the Watch window that will allow us to track the current date.

5. In the Code window, position the insertion point anywhere within the name of the curDate variable.
6. Choose **Debug | Add Watch** and click **OK** to set up the default watch type with Watch Expression.

   Notice that curDate now appears in the Expression column of the Watch window.

   We will also want to keep track of the newDate variable.
7. In the Code window, position the insertion point anywhere within the name of the newDate variable.
8. Choose **Debug | Add Watch** and click **OK** to set up the default watch type with Watch Expression.

   Notice that newDate now appears in the Expression column of the Watch window. After performing the above steps, the WhatDate procedure contains the following three watches:

   x = 211 — Break When Value is True
   curDate — Watch Expression
   newDate — Watch Expression
9. Position the insertion point anywhere inside the code of the WhatDate procedure, and press **F5**.

   Visual Basic stops the procedure when x = 211 (see Figure 10-11).

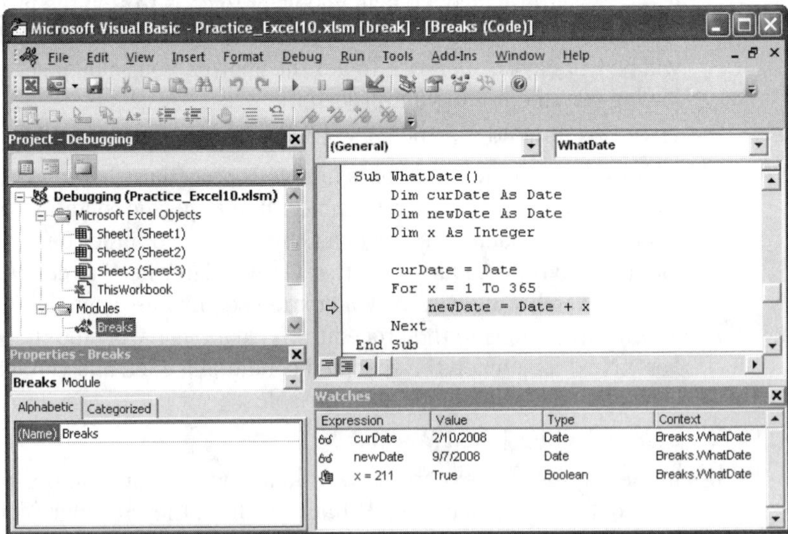

Figure 10-11: Using the Watch window.

Notice that the value of the variable x in the Watch window is the same as the value that you specified in the Add Watch dialog. In addition, the Watch window shows the value of both variables — curDate and newDate. The procedure is in break mode. You can press F5 to continue or you can ask another question, such as "What date will be in 277 days?" The next step shows how to do this.

10. Choose **Debug | Edit Watch**, and enter the following expression: **x = 277**.
11. Click **OK** to close the Edit Watch dialog box.

    Notice that the Watch window now displays a new value for the expression. The x is now False.
12. Press **F5** to continue running the procedure.

    The procedure stops again when the value of x = 277. The value of curDate is the same; however, the newDate variable now contains a new value — a date that is 277 days from now. You can change the value of the expression again or finish running the procedure.
13. Press **F5** to finish running the procedure.

    When your procedure is running and a watch expression has a value, the Watch window displays the value of the watch expression. If you open the Watch window after the procedure has finished, you will see <out of context> instead of the variable values. In other words, when the watch expression is out of context, it does not have a value.

Removing Watch Expressions

To remove the watch expressions, click on the expression in the Watch window that you want to remove and press Delete. You may now remove all the watch expressions you had defined in the preceding example.

Using Quick Watch

In break mode you can check the value of an expression for which you have not defined a watch expression by using the Quick Watch dialog box.

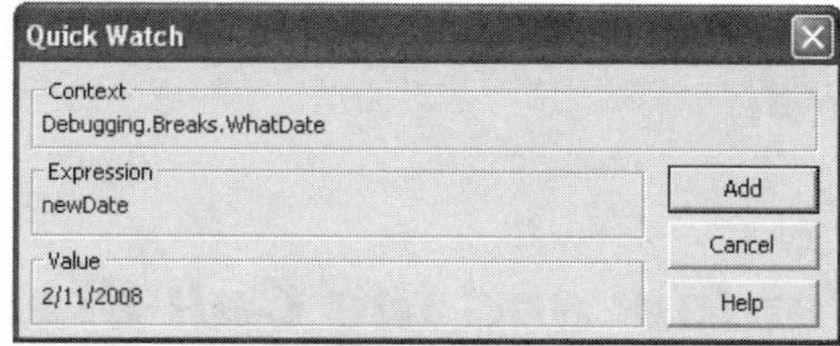

Figure 10-12: The Quick Watch dialog box shows the value of the selected expression in a VBA procedure.

The Quick Watch dialog box can be accessed in the following ways:

- While in break mode, position the insertion point anywhere inside the name of a variable or expression you wish to watch.
- Choose Debug | Quick Watch
- Press Shift+F9

The Add button on the Quick Watch dialog box allows you to add the expression to the Watch window. Let's find out how to work with this dialog box.

Hands-On 10-3: Using the Quick Watch Dialog Box

1. Make sure that the WhatDate procedure you entered in the previous Hands-On exercise does not contain any watch expressions. See the section called "Removing Watch Expressions" for instructions on how to remove a watch expression from the Watch window.
2. In the WhatDate procedure, position the insertion point on the name of the variable x.
3. Choose **Debug | Add Watch.**
4. Enter the following expression: **x = 50.**
5. Choose the **Break When Value Is True** option button, and click **OK.**
6. Run the WhatDate procedure.

   Visual Basic will suspend procedure execution when x = 50. Notice that the Watch window does not contain the newDate or the curDate variable. To check the values of these variables, you can position the mouse pointer over the appropriate variable name in the Code window, or you can invoke the Quick Watch dialog box.
7. In the Code window, position the mouse pointer inside the newDate variable and press **Shift+F9.**

   The Quick Watch dialog shows the name of the expression and its current value.
8. Click **Cancel** to return to the Code window.
9. In the Code window, position the mouse pointer inside the curDate variable and press **Shift+F9.**

   The Quick Watch dialog now shows the value of the variable curDate.
10. Click **Cancel** to return to the Code window.
11. Press **F5** to continue running the procedure.
12. In the Watch window, highlight the line containing the expression x = 50 and press **Delete** to remove it.
13. Close the Watch window.

Using the Locals Window and the Call Stack Dialog Box

If during the execution of a VBA procedure you want to keep an eye on all the declared variables and their current values, make sure you choose View | Locals Window before you run the procedure. While in break mode, Visual Basic will display a list of variables and their corresponding values in the Locals window (see Figure 10-13).

The Locals window contains three columns. The Expression column displays the names of variables that are declared in the current procedure. The first row displays the name of the module preceded by the plus sign. When you click the plus sign, you can check if any variables have been declared at the module level. For class modules, the system variable Me is defined. For standard modules, the first variable is the name of the current module. The global variables and variables in other projects are not accessible from the Locals window.

The second column shows the current values of variables. In this column, you can change the value of a variable by clicking it and typing the new value. After changing the value, press Enter to register the change. You can also press Tab, Shift+Tab, or the up or down arrow, or click anywhere within the Locals window after you've changed the variable value. The third column displays the type of each declared variable.

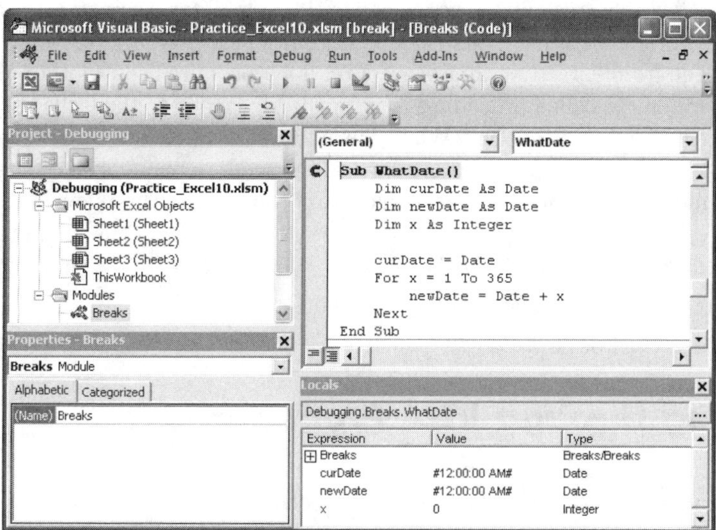

Figure 10-13: The Locals window displays the current values of all the declared variables in the current VBA procedure.

To observe the values of variables in the Locals window, perform the following Hands-On exercise.

Hands-On 10-4: Using the Locals and Call Stack Windows

1. Choose **View | Locals Window.**
2. Click anywhere inside the WhatDate procedure and press **F8.**

   By pressing F8, you place the procedure in break mode. The Locals window displays the name of the current module and the local variables and their beginning values.

3. Press **F8** a few more times while keeping an eye on the Locals window.

   The Locals window also contains a button with three dots. This button opens the Call Stack dialog box (shown in Figure 10-14), which displays a list of all active procedure calls. An active procedure call is a procedure that is started but not completed. You can also activate the Call Stack dialog box by choosing **View | Call Stack**. This option is only available in break mode.

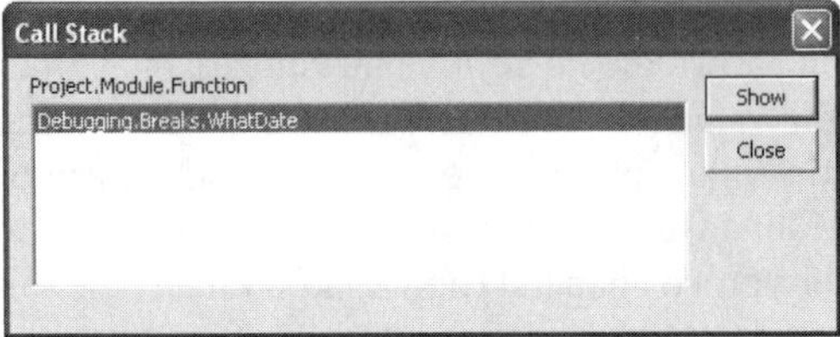

Figure 10-14: The Call Stack dialog box displays a list of the procedures that are started but not completed.

   The Call Stack dialog box is especially helpful for tracing nested procedures. Recall that a nested procedure is a procedure that is being called from within another procedure. If a procedure calls another, the name of the called procedure is automatically added to the Calls list in the Call Stack dialog box. When Visual Basic has finished executing the statements of the called procedure, the procedure name is automatically removed from the Call Stack dialog box. You can use the Show button in the Call Stack dialog box to display the statement that calls the next procedure listed in the dialog box.

4. Press **F5** to continue running the WhatDate procedure.
5. Close the Locals window.

Stepping through VBA Procedures

Stepping through the code means running one statement at a time. This allows you to check every line in every procedure that is encountered. To start stepping through a procedure from the beginning, place the insertion point anywhere inside the code of your procedure and choose Debug | Step Into or press F8. The Debug menu contains several options that allow you to execute a procedure in step mode (see Figure 10-15). When you run a procedure one statement at a time, Visual Basic executes each statement until it encounters the End Sub keywords. If you don't want Visual Basic to step through every statement, you can press F5 at any time to run the rest of the procedure without stepping through it.

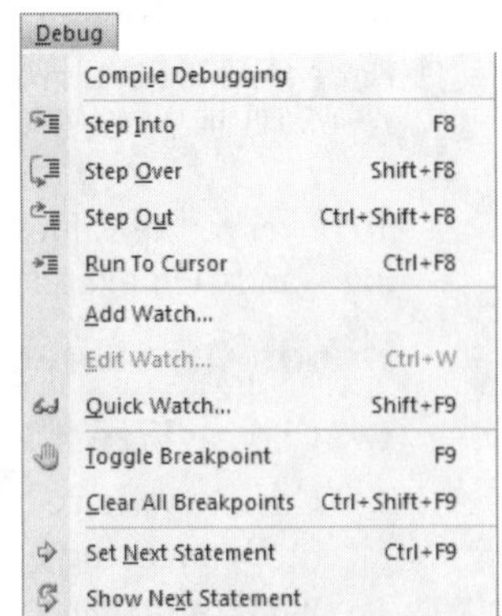

Figure 10-15: The Debug menu offers many commands for stepping through VBA procedures.

Let's step through a procedure line by line.

Hands-On 10-5: Stepping through a VBA Procedure

1. Place the insertion point anywhere inside the code of the procedure whose execution you wish to trace.
2. Press **F8** or choose **Debug | Step Into.**

   Visual Basic executes the current statement and automatically advances to the next statement and suspends execution. While in break mode, you can activate the Immediate window, Watch window, or Locals window to see the effect of a particular statement on the values of variables and expressions. And, if the procedure you are stepping through calls other procedures, you can activate the Call Stack window to see which procedures are currently active.
3. Press **F8** again to execute the selected statement.

   After executing this statement, Visual Basic will select the next statement, and the procedure execution will be halted again.
4. Continue stepping through the procedure by pressing **F8**, or press **F5** to continue the code execution without stopping.

   You can also choose **Run | Reset** to stop the procedure at the current statement without executing the remaining statements. When you step over procedures (Shift+F8), Visual Basic executes each procedure as if it were a single statement. This option is particularly useful if a procedure contains calls to other procedures and you don't want to step into these procedures because they have already been tested and debugged, or you want to concentrate only on the new code that has not yet been debugged.

Stepping Over a Procedure and Running to Cursor

Suppose that the current statement in MyProcedure calls the SpecialMsg procedure. If you choose Debug | Step Over (Shift+F8) instead of Debug | Step Into (F8), Visual Basic will quickly execute all the statements inside the SpecialMsg procedure and select the next statement in the calling procedure (MyProcedure). During the execution of the SpecialMsg procedure, Visual Basic continues to display the Code window with the current procedure.

Hands-On 10-6: Stepping Over a Procedure

1. In the Breaks module Code window, locate the following procedure:

```
Sub MyProcedure()
    Dim strName As String
    Workbooks.Add
    strName = ActiveWorkbook.Name
    ' choose Step Over to avoid stepping through the
    ' lines of code in the called procedure - SpecialMsg
    SpecialMsg strName
    Workbooks(strName).Close
End Sub
```

```
Sub SpecialMsg(n As String)
    If n = "Book2" Then
        MsgBox "You must change the name."
    End If
End Sub
```

2. Add a breakpoint at the following statement:

   ```
   SpecialMsg strName
   ```

3. Place the insertion point anywhere within the code of MyProcedure, and press **F5** to run it.

   Visual Basic halts execution when it reaches the breakpoint.

4. Press **Shift+F8**, or choose **Debug | Step Over**.

   Visual Basic quickly runs the SpecialMsg procedure and advances to the statement immediately after the call to the SpecialMsg procedure.

5. Press **F5** to finish running the procedure without stepping through its code.

6. Remove the breakpoint you set in step 2.

   Stepping over a procedure is particularly useful when you don't want to analyze individual statements inside the called procedure. Another command on the Debug menu, Step Out (Ctrl+Shift+F8), is used when you step into a procedure and then decide that you don't want to step all the way through it. When you choose this option, Visual Basic will execute the remaining statements in this procedure in one step and proceed to activate the next statement in the calling procedure. In the process of stepping through a procedure you can switch between the Step Into, Step Over, and Step Out options. The option you select depends on which code fragment you wish to analyze at a given moment. The Debug menu's Run To Cursor (Ctrl+F8) command lets you run your procedure until the line you have selected is encountered. This command is really useful if you want to stop the execution before a large loop or you intend to step over a called procedure. Suppose you want to execute MyProcedure to the line that calls the SpecialMsg procedure.

7. Click inside the statement SpecialMsg strName.

8. Choose **Debug | Run To Cursor**. Visual Basic will stop the execution of the MyProcedure code when it reaches the specified line.

9. Press **Shift+F8** to step over the SpecialMsg procedure.

10. Press **F5** to execute the rest of the procedure.

Setting the Next Statement

At times, you may want to rerun previous lines of code in the procedure or skip over a section of code that is causing trouble. In each of these situations, you can use the Set Next Statement option on the Debug menu. When you halt execution of a procedure, you can resume the procedure from any statement you want. Visual Basic will skip execution of the statements between the selected statement and the statement where execution was suspended.

Suppose that in MyProcedure (see the code of this procedure in the preceding section) you have set a breakpoint on the statement calling the SpecialMsg procedure. To skip the execution of the SpecialMsg procedure, you can place the insertion point inside the statement Workbooks (strName).Close and press Ctrl+F9 (or choose Debug | Set Next Statement).

You can't use the Set Next Statement option unless you have suspended the execution of the procedure.

While skipping lines of code can be very useful in the process of debugging your VBA procedures, it should be done with care. When you use the Next Statement option, you tell Visual Basic that this is the line you want to execute next. All lines in between are ignored. This means that certain things that you may have expected to occur don't happen, which can lead to unexpected errors.

Showing the Next Statement

If you are not sure from which statement the execution of the procedure will resume, you can choose Debug | Show Next Statement and Visual Basic will place the cursor on the line that will run next. This is particularly useful when you have been looking at other procedures and are not sure where execution will resume. The Show Next Statement option is available only in break mode.

Stopping and Resetting VBA Procedures

At any time, while stepping through the code of a procedure in the Code window, you can:

- Press F5 to execute the remaining instructions without stepping through.
- Choose Run | Reset to finish the procedure without executing the remaining statements.

When you reset your procedure, all the variables lose their current values. Numeric variables assume the initial value of zero, variable-length strings are initialized to a zero-length string (""), and fixed-length strings are filled with the character represented by the ASCII character code 0 or Chr(0). Variant variables are initialized to Empty, and the value of object variables is set to Nothing.

Chapter Summary

In this chapter you learned how to test your VBA procedures to make sure they perform as planned. You debugged your code by stepping through it using breakpoints and watches. You learned how to work with the Immediate window in break mode, and you found out how the Locals window can help you monitor the values of variables and how the Call Stack dialog box can be helpful in keeping track of where you are in a complex program.

By using the built-in debugging tools, you can quickly pinpoint the problem spots in your procedures. Try to spend more time getting acquainted with the Debug menu options and debugging tools discussed in this chapter. Mastering the art of debugging can save you hours of trial and error.

In the next chapter you will learn additional debugging techniques for your VBA procedures.

Chapter 11

Conditional Compilation and Error Trapping

Understanding and Using Conditional Compilation ■ Navigating with Bookmarks ■ Trapping Errors ■ Using the Err Object ■ Procedure Testing ■ **Chapter Summary**

If you've read Chapter 10, you should now know how to debug your code using the built-in VBE debugging tools. With these tools, you can easily set a breakpoint to stop a program while it is running and use step options to run your code one statement at a time. You can review the values of variables by using Watch expressions and the Locals and Immediate windows. And, with more complex procedures, you can use the Call Stack dialog box to view all active procedure calls and trace the execution of nested procedures. This chapter introduces additional techniques that you will find useful for debugging your Visual Basic applications. In particular, you will learn how conditional compilation can help you to include or ignore certain blocks of code, and how you can add effective error-handling code to your procedures.

Understanding and Using Conditional Compilation

When you run a procedure for the first time, Visual Basic converts the VBA statements you used into the machine code understood by the computer. This process is called *compiling*. You can also perform the compilation of your entire VBA project manually before you run your procedure. To do this, simply choose Debug | Compile (your VBA project name) in the Visual Basic Editor window. You can tell Visual Basic to include or ignore certain blocks of code when compiling and running by using so-called *conditional compilation*.

To enable conditional compilation, use special expressions called *directives*. Use the #Const directive to declare a Boolean (True, False) constant. Next, check this constant inside the #If...Then...#Else directive. The portion of code that you want to compile conditionally must be surrounded by these directives. Notice that the If and Else keywords are preceded by a number sign (#). If a portion of code is to be run, the value of the conditional constant has to be set to True (–1). Otherwise, the value of this constant should be set to False (0). Declare the conditional constant in the declaration section of the module like this:

```
#Const User = True
```

This declares the conditional constant named User.

Conditional compilation can be used to compile an application that will be run on different platforms (Windows or Macintosh, Win16-, Win32-, Win64-bit). It is also useful in localizing an application for different languages, or excluding certain debugging statements before the VBA application is sent off for distribution. The program code excluded during the conditional compilation is omitted from the final file; thus it has no effect on the size or performance of the program.

In the procedure that follows, data is displayed in the Polish language when the conditional constant named verPolish is True. The WhatDay procedure calls the DayOfWeek function, which returns the name of the week based on the supplied date. To compile the program in the English language, all you have to do is change the conditional constant to False and Visual Basic will jump to the block of instructions located after the #Else directive.

Hands-On 11-1: Writing a VBA Procedure Using Conditional Compilation

1. Start Microsoft Excel and open a new workbook. Save the workbook file as **C:\Ex07_ByExample\Practice_Excel11.xlsm**.
2. Switch to the Visual Basic Editor window and in the Project Explorer window select **VBAProject (Practice_Excel11.xlsm)**. In the Properties window, rename the project **Testing**.
3. Choose **Insert | Module** to add a new module to the selected project.
4. Use the Properties window to rename Module1 **Conditional**.
5. In the Conditional module Code window, enter the following procedure and functions:

```
' declare a conditional compiler constant
#Const verPolish = True

Sub WhatDay()
    Dim dayNr As Integer

    #If verPolish = True Then
          dayNr = Weekday(InputBox("Wpisz date, np. 10/01/2008"))
          MsgBox "To bedzie " & DayOfWeek(dayNr) & "."
    #Else
          WeekdayName
    #End If
End Sub

Function DayOfWeek(dayNr As Integer) As String
    DayOfWeek = Choose(dayNr, "niedziela", "poniedzialek", "wtorek", _
                "sroda", "czwartek", "piatek", "sobota")
End Function

Function WeekdayName() As String
    Select Case Weekday(InputBox("Enter date, e.g., 10/01/2008"))
          Case 1
                WeekdayName = "Sunday"
          Case 2
                WeekdayName = "Monday"
          Case 3
                WeekdayName = "Tuesday"
          Case 4
                WeekdayName = "Wednesday"
          Case 5
                WeekdayName = "Thursday"
          Case 6
                WeekdayName = "Friday"
          Case 7
                WeekdayName = "Saturday"
    End Select
    MsgBox "It will be " & WeekdayName & "."
End Function
```

6. Run the WhatDay procedure.

   Because the conditional compilation constant (verPolish) is set to True at the top of the module, Visual Basic runs the Polish version of the WhatDay procedure. It asks for the user's input in Polish and displays the result in Polish.

7. To run the English version of the code, set the verPolish constant to False, and rerun the procedure.

   Instead of declaring the conditional compiler constants at the top of a module, you can choose Tools | Testing Properties. When you use the Project Properties dialog box (Figure 11-1), use the following syntax in the Conditional Compilation Arguments text box to enable the English version of the WhatDay procedure:

   ```
   verPolish = 0
   ```

   If there are more conditional compilation constants, each of the constants must be separated by a colon.

8. Comment out the #Const verPolish directive at the top of the module and enter the conditional compilation constant in the Project Properties dialog box as shown in Figure 11-1. Then run the WhatDay procedure to see how the Else branch of your program is now executed for English-speaking users.

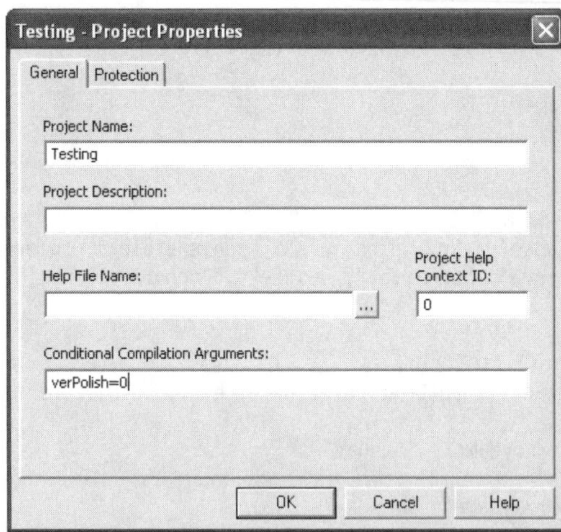

Figure 11-1: The conditional compilation constant can be declared either at the top of the module or in the Project Properties dialog box but never in both places.

Navigating with Bookmarks

In the process of analyzing or reviewing your VBA procedures, you will often find yourself jumping to certain areas of code. Using the built-in bookmark feature, you can easily mark the spots that you want to navigate between.

To set up a bookmark:

1. Click anywhere in the statement that you want to define as a bookmark.

2. Choose **Edit | Bookmarks | Toggle Bookmark**, or click the Toggle Bookmark button on the Edit toolbar (see Figure 11-2).

Visual Basic will place a blue, rounded rectangle in the left margin beside the statement.

Once you've set up two or more bookmarks, you can jump between the marked locations of your code by choosing Edit | Bookmarks | Next Bookmark or simply by clicking the Next Bookmark button on the Edit toolbar. You can remove bookmarks at any time by choosing Edit | Bookmarks | Clear All Bookmarks or by clicking the Clear All Bookmarks button on the Edit toolbar. To remove a single bookmark, click anywhere in the bookmarked statement and choose Edit | Bookmarks | Toggle Bookmark or click the Toggle Bookmark button on the Edit toolbar.

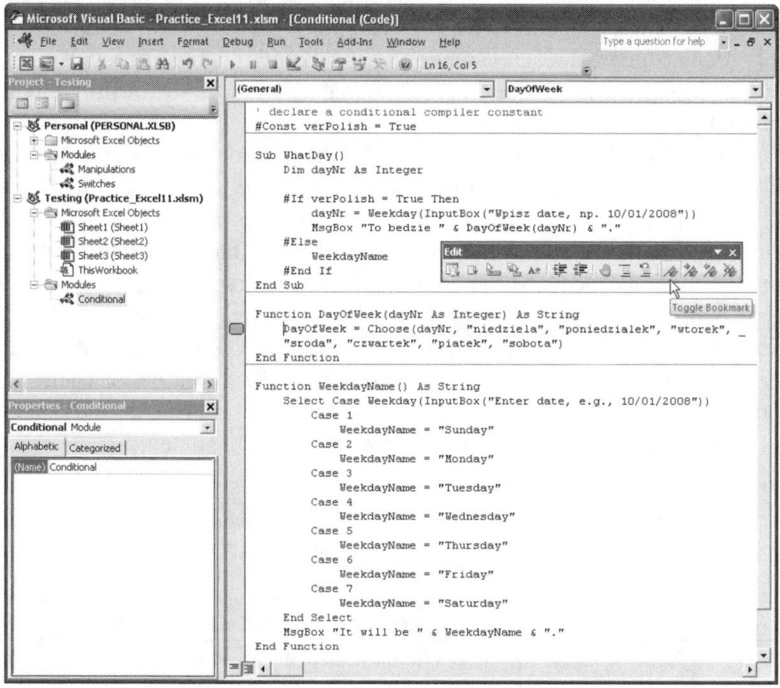

Figure 11-2: Using bookmarks you can quickly jump between often-used sections of your procedures.

Trapping Errors

No one writes bug-free programs the first time. When you create VBA procedures, you have to determine how your program will respond to errors. Many unexpected errors happen during run time. For example, your procedure may try to give a workbook the same name as an open workbook. Run-time errors are often discovered by users who attempt to do something that the programmer has not anticipated. If an error occurs when the procedure is running, Visual Basic displays an error message and the procedure is stopped. Most often, the error message that VBA displays is quite cryptic to the user. You can prevent users from seeing many run-time errors by including error-handling code in your VBA procedures. This way, when Visual Basic encounters an error, instead of displaying a default error message, it will show a much friendlier and more comprehensive error message, perhaps advising the user how to correct the error.

In programming, mistakes and errors are not the same thing. A mistake, such as a misspelled or missing statement, a misplaced quote or comma, or assigning a value of one type to a variable of a different (and incompatible) type, can be removed from your program through proper testing and debugging. But even though your code may be free of mistakes, this does not mean that errors will not occur. An error is the result of an event or an operation that doesn't work as expected. For example, if your VBA procedure accesses a particular file on disk and someone has deleted this file or moved it to another location, you'll get an error no matter what. An error prevents the procedure from carrying out a specific task.

How should you implement error handling into your VBA procedure? The first step is to place the On Error statement in your procedure. This statement tells VBA what to do if an error happens while your program is running. In other words, VBA uses the On Error statement to activate an error-handling procedure that will trap run-time errors. Depending on the type of procedure, you can exit the error trap by using one of the following statements: Exit Sub, Exit Function, Exit Property, End Sub, End Function, or End Property. You should write an error-handling routine for each procedure.

Table 11-1 shows how the On Error statement can be used.

Table 11-1: On Error statement options

On Error GoTo *Label*	Specifies a label to jump to when an error occurs. This label marks the beginning of the error-handling routine. An error handler is a routine for trapping and responding to errors in your application. The label must appear in the same procedure as the On Error statement.
On Error Resume Next	When a run-time error occurs, Visual Basic ignores the line that caused the error, and does not display an error message but continues the procedure with the next line.
On Error GoTo 0	Turns off error trapping in a procedure. When VBA runs this statement, errors are detected but not trapped within the procedure.

The Archive procedure shown below uses an error-handling routine (see the bottom of the procedure). The procedure uses the built-in SaveCopyAs method to save the copy of the current workbook to a file without modifying the open workbook in memory.

Hands-On 11-2: Writing a VBA Procedure with Error-Handling Code (Example 1)

1. Insert a new module into the Testing project and rename it **Traps**.
2. In the Traps module Code window, enter the Archive procedure as shown below:

```
Sub Archive()
    Dim folderName As String
    Dim MyDrive As String
    Dim BackupName As String

    Application.DisplayAlerts = False

    On Error GoTo ErrorHandler

    folderName = ActiveWorkbook.Path

    If folderName = "" Then
        MsgBox "You can't copy this file. " & Chr(13) _
            & "This file has not been saved.", _
            vbInformation, "File Archive"
    Else
        With ActiveWorkbook
            If Not .Saved Then .Save
            MyDrive = InputBox("Enter the Pathname:" & _
             Chr(13) & "(for example: D:\, " & _
              "E:\MyFolder\, etc.)", _
              "Archive Location?", "D:\")
              If MyDrive <> "" Then
                 If Right(MyDrive, 1) <> "\" Then
                    MyDrive = MyDrive & "\"
                 End If
                 BackupName = MyDrive & .Name
                 .SaveCopyAs Filename:=BackupName
                 MsgBox .Name & " was copied to: " _
                 & MyDrive, , "End of Archiving"
              End If
        End With
    End If
    GoTo ProcEnd
ErrorHandler:
    MsgBox "Visual Basic cannot find the " & _
     "specified path (" & MyDrive & ")" & Chr(13) & _
     "for the archive. Please try again.", _
     vbInformation + vbOKOnly, "Disk Drive or " & _
     "Folder does not exist"
ProcEnd:
    Application.DisplayAlerts = True
End Sub
```

After the declaration of variables, the statement Application.DisplayAlerts = False ensures that Visual Basic won't display its own alerts and messages while the procedure is running. The next statement, On Error GoTo ErrorHandler, specifies a label to jump to when an error occurs. The path name where the active workbook was saved is stored in the variable folderName. If Visual Basic can't find the workbook's path, it assumes the file was not saved and displays an appropriate message. Next, Visual Basic jumps to the statement following the End If and executes the instruction GoTo ProcEnd, which directs it to the ProcEnd label located just before the End Sub keywords. Notice that the label name is followed by a colon. Visual Basic executes the statement Application.

DisplayAlerts = True, which restores the system's built-in alerts and messages. Because there are no more statements to execute, the procedure ends. If the active workbook's path is not an empty string, Visual Basic checks whether the recent changes in the workbook have already been saved. If they weren't, VBA uses the If Not .Saved Then .Save statement to save the active workbook. Saved is a VBA property of the Workbook object.

Next, Visual Basic uses the InputBox function to prompt the user for the location of the archive. The specified pathname is then stored in the variable MyDrive. If user cancelled the input box, the procedure will end. If user entered a path, we need to ensure that the specified string ends with the backslash character (\). This is done via the Right function. This function returns a specified number of characters from the right side of a string. If the last character of the supplied pathname is not a backslash, then Visual Basic will append the backslash to the end of the pathname specified in the MyDrive variable. The content of the MyDrive variable is then combined with the name of the active workbook and stored in the variable named BackupName. As you know, all kinds of things can go wrong while copying files. For example, a specified drive/folder may not exist, or a drive may not have sufficient free space left. When Visual Basic detects an error, it jumps to the line of code beginning with the label ErrorHandler and an appropriate message is displayed. If VBA can find the specified pathname, it will copy the active workbook to that location and will notify the user that the copy operation was successful.

3. Run the Archive procedure several times, each time responding differently to the presented options. Be sure to test as many possibilities as you can identify. Use various debugging techniques that you learned in Chapter 10.

Using the Err Object

Your error-handling code can utilize various properties and methods of the Err object. For example, to check which error occurred, check the value of the Err.Number. The Number property of the Err object will tell you the value of the last error that occurred, and the Description property will return a description of the error. You can also find the name of the application that caused the error by using the Source property of the Err object (this is very helpful when your procedure launches other applications). After handling the error, use the Err.Clear statement to reset the error number. This will set Err.Number back to zero.

To test your error-handling code you can use the Raise method of the Err object. For example, to raise the "Disk not ready" error, use the following statement:

```
Err.Raise 71
```

The OpenToRead procedure shown below demonstrates the use of the Resume Next and Error statements, as well as the Err object.

Hands-On 11-3: Writing a VBA Procedure with Error-Handling Code (Example 2)

1. In the Traps module Code window, enter the OpenToRead procedure as shown below:

```
Sub OpenToRead()
    Dim myFile As String
    Dim myChar As String
    Dim myText As String
    Dim FileExists As Boolean

    FileExists = True

    On Error GoTo ErrorHandler

    myFile = InputBox("Enter the name of file you want to open:")
    Open myFile For Input As #1
    If FileExists Then
        Do While Not EOF(1)           ' loop until the end of file
            myChar = Input(1, #1)     ' get one character
            myText = myText + myChar ' store in the variable myText
        Loop
        Debug.Print myText            ' print to the Immediate window
        Close #1                      ' close the file
    End If
    Exit Sub

ErrorHandler:
    FileExists = False
        Select Case Err.Number
            Case 76
                MsgBox "The path you entered cannot be found."
            Case 53
                MsgBox "This file can't be found on the " & _
                    "specified drive."
            Case 75
                Exit Sub
            Case Else
                MsgBox "Error " & Err.Number & " :" & Error(Err.Number)
            Exit Sub
        End Select
        Resume Next
End Sub
```

The purpose of the OpenToRead procedure is to read the contents of the user-supplied text file character by character (working with files is covered in detail in Chapters 12 through 14). When the user enters a filename, various errors can occur. For example, the filename or the path may be wrong, or the user may try to open a file that is already open. To trap these errors, the error-handling routine at the end of the OpenTo-Read procedure uses the Number property of the Err object.

The Err object contains information about run-time errors. If an error occurs while the procedure is running, the statement Err.Number will return the error number. If errors 76, 53, or 75 occur, Visual Basic will display user-friendly messages stored inside the Select...Case block and then proceed to the Resume Next statement, which will send it to the line of code following the one that caused the error. If another (unexpected) error occurs, Visual Basic will return its error code (Err.Number) and error description (Error (Err.Number)). At the beginning of the procedure, the variable FileExists is set to True. This way, if the program doesn't encounter an error, all the instructions inside the If FileExists Then block will be executed. However, if VBA encounters an error, the value of the FileExists variable will be set to False (see the first statement in the error-handling routine just below the ErrorHandler label). This way, Visual Basic will not cause another error while trying to read a file that caused the error on opening. Notice the Exit Sub statement before the ErrorHandler label. Put the Exit Sub statement just above the error-handling routine because you don't want Visual Basic to carry out the error handling if there are no errors.

To test the OpenToRead procedure and better understand error trapping, we will need a text file (see step 2).

2. Use Windows Notepad to prepare a text file. Enter any text you want in this file. When done, save the file as **C:\Ex07_ByExample\Vacation.txt**.
3. Run the OpenToRead procedure three times in step mode (using the F8 key), each time supplying one of the following:
   - Name of the C:\Ex07_ByExample\Vacation.txt file
   - Filename that does not exist on drive C
   - Path that does not exist on your computer (e.g., K:\Test)

Procedure Testing

You are responsible for the code that you produce. This means that before you give your procedure to others to test, you must test it yourself. After all, you will understand how it is supposed to work. Some programmers think that testing their own code is some sort of degrading activity, especially when they work in an organization that has a team devoted to testing. Don't make this mistake. The testing process at the programmer level is as important as the code development itself. After you've tested the procedure yourself, you should give it to users to test. Users will provide you with answers to questions such as: Does the procedure produce the expected results? Is it easy and fun to use? Does it follow the standard conventions? Also, it is usually a good idea to give the entire application not only to power users for their feedback but also to someone who knows the least about using this particular application, and ask him or her to play around with it and try to break it. This is how even the most unsuspected errors can quickly be discovered.

You can test the ways that your program responds to run-time errors by causing them on purpose:

- Generate any built-in error by using the following syntax:

  ```
  Error error_number
  ```

  For example, to display the error that occurs on the attempt to divide by zero, type the following in the Immediate window:

  ```
  Error 11
  ```

  When you press Enter, Visual Basic will display an error message saying: *Run-time error 11. Division by zero.*

- To check the meaning of the generated error, use the following syntax:

  ```
  ?Error(error_number)
  ```

  For example, to find out what error number 7 means, type the following in the Immediate window:

  ```
  ?Error(7)
  ```

  When you press Enter, Visual Basic returns the error description: *Out of memory.*

- To generate the same error at run time in the form of a message box (see Figure 11-3), enter in the Immediate window or in your procedure code:

  ```
  Err.Raise 7
  ```

Figure 11-3: To test the error-handling code, you can use the Raise method of the Err object to generate a run-time error during the execution of your procedure.

When you finish debugging your VBA procedures, make sure you remove all statements that raise errors.

Chapter Summary

In this chapter you've learned how conditional compilation can enable you to run various parts of code based on the specified condition. You also learned how to mark your code with bookmarks so you can easily navigate between various sections of your procedure. This chapter also showed you how to trap errors by including error-handling routines inside your VBA procedures, and how to use the VBA Err object.

This chapter concludes Part IV of this book. In the next chapter, you will learn how to manipulate files and folders with VBA.

Part V

Manipulating Files and Folders with VBA

While VBA offers a number of built-in functions and statements for working with the file system, you can also perform file and folder manipulation tasks via objects and methods included in the Windows Script Host installed by default on Microsoft Windows 98 and later versions. In addition, you can open and manipulate files directly via the low-level file I/O functions.

In this part of the book, you discover various methods of working with files and folders, and learn how to programmatically open, read, and write three types of files.

Chapter 12

File and Folder Manipulation with VBA

Manipulating Files and Folders ■ Finding Out the Name of the Active Folder ■ Changing the Name of a File or Folder ■ Checking the Existence of a File or Folder ■ Finding Out the Date and Time the File Was Modified ■ Finding Out the Size of a File (the FileLen Function) ■ Returning and Setting File Attributes (the GetAttr and SetAttr Functions) ■ Changing the Default Folder or Drive (the ChDir and ChDrive Statements) ■ Creating and Deleting Folders (the MkDir and RmDir Statements) ■ Copying Files (the FileCopy Statement) ■ Deleting Files (the Kill Statement) ■ **Chapter Summary**

In the course of your work, you've surely accessed, created, renamed, copied, and deleted hundreds of files and folders. However, you've probably never performed these tasks programmatically. So here's your chance. This chapter focuses on VBA functions and instructions that specifically deal with files and folders. By using these functions, you'll be able to:

- Find out the name of the current folder (CurDir function)
- Change the name of a file or folder (Name function)
- Check whether a file or folder exists on a disk (Dir function)
- Find out the date and time a file was last modified (FileDateTime function)
- Get the size of a file (FileLen function)
- Check and change file attributes (GetAttr and SetAttr functions)
- Change the default folder or drive (ChDir and ChDrive statements)
- Create and delete a folder (MkDir and RmDir statements)
- Copy and delete a file or folder (FileCopy and Kill statements)

Manipulating Files and Folders

This section discusses a number of VBA functions used to perform operations on files and folders.

Finding Out the Name of the Active Folder

When you work with files, you often need to find out the name of the current folder. You can get this information easily with the CurDir function, which looks like this:

```
CurDir([drive])
```

Note that drive is an optional argument. If you omit drive, VBA uses the current drive. The CurDir function returns a file path as Variant. To return the path as String, use CurDir$ (where $ is the type declaration character for a string).

To see this function in action, let's perform a couple of exercises in the Immediate window.

Hands-On 12-1: Using the CurDir Function

1. Open a new workbook and save it as **Practice_Excel12.xlsm** in your C:\Ex07_ByExample folder.
2. Switch to Microsoft Visual Basic Editor and press **Ctrl+G** to activate the Immediate window. Type the statement shown below, and press **Enter**:

   ```
   ?CurDir
   ```

   When you press Enter, Visual Basic displays the name of the current folder. For example:

```
C:\
```

If you have a second disk drive (or a CD-ROM drive), you can find out the current folder on drive D, as follows:

```
?CurDir("D:\")
```

Note: If you supply a letter for a drive that does not exist, Visual Basic will display the following error message: "Device unavailable."

3. To store the name of the current disk drive in a variable called myDrive, type the statement shown below and press **Enter**:

   ```
   myDrive = Left(CurDir$,1)
   ```

   When you press Enter, Visual Basic stores the letter of the current drive in the variable myDrive. Notice how the CurDir$ function is used as the first argument of the Left function. The Left function tells Visual Basic to extract the leftmost character from the string returned by the CurDir$ function and store it in the myDrive variable.

4. To check the contents of the variable myDrive, type the statement shown below and press **Enter**:

   ```
   ?myDrive
   ```

5. To return the letter of the drive followed by the colon, type the following instructions, pressing **Enter** after each line:

   ```
   myDrive = Left(CurDir$,2)
   ?myDrive
   ```

Changing the Name of a File or Folder

To rename a file or folder, use the Name function, as follows:

```
Name old_pathname As new_pathname
```

Old_pathname is the current path and name of a file or folder that you want to rename. New_pathname specifies the new path and name of the file or folder.

Using the Name function, you can move a file from one folder to another (you can't move a folder). Here are some precautions to consider while working with the Name function:

- The filename in new_pathname cannot refer to an existing file.

  Suppose you'd like to change the name of the system.txt file to test.txt. This is easily done with the following statement:

  ```
  Name "c:\system.txt" As "c:\test.txt"
  ```

  However, if the file c:\test.txt already exists on drive C, Visual Basic will display the following error message: "File already exists." Similarly, the "File not found" error message will appear if the file you want to rename does not exist. Try the above statement in the Immediate window (replace the example names with the actual names of your files).

- If the new_pathname already exists, and it's different from the old_pathname, the Name function moves the specified file to a new folder and changes its name, if necessary.

  ```
  Name "c:\system.txt" As "d:\test.txt"
  ```

  If the test.txt file doesn't exist in the root directory on drive D, Visual Basic moves the c:\system.txt file to the specified drive; however, it does not rename the file.

- If the new_pathname and old_pathname refer to different directories and both supplied filenames are the same, the Name function moves the specified file to a new location without changing the filename.

  ```
  Name "d:\test.txt" As "c:\DOS\test.txt"
  ```

  The above instruction moves the test.txt file to the DOS folder on drive C.

Renaming an Open File

You must close an open file before renaming it. Also note that the filename cannot contain the wildcard characters (*) or (?).

Checking the Existence of a File or Folder

The Dir function, which returns the name of a file or folder, has the following syntax:

```
Dir[(pathname[, attributes])]
```

Notice that both arguments of the Dir function are optional. Pathname is the name of a file or folder. You can use one of the following constants or values for the attributes argument:

Table 12-1: File attributes

Constant	Value	Attribute Name
vbNormal	0	Normal
vbHidden	2	Hidden
vbSystem	4	System
vbVolume	8	Volume Label
vbDirectory	16	Directory or Folder

The Dir function is often used to check whether a file or folder exists on a disk. If a file or folder does not exist, the null string ("") is returned (see step 3 in the Hands-On exercise below).

Let's try out the Dir function in several exercises in the Immediate window.

Hands-On 12-2: Using the Dir Function

1. In the Immediate window, type the following statement and press **Enter**:

```
?Dir("C:\", vbNormal)
```

As soon as you press Enter, Visual Basic returns the name of the first file in the specified folder. A normal file (vbNormal) is any file that does not have a Hidden, Volume Label, Directory, Folder, or System file attribute.

To return the names of other files in the current directory, type the Dir function without an argument and press **Enter**:

```
?Dir
```

2. Enter the following instructions in the Immediate window and examine their results as you press **Enter**:

```
mfile = Dir("C:\", vbHidden)
?mfile
mfile = Dir
?mfile
mfile = Dir
?mfile
```

3. Type the following instruction in the Immediate window and press **Enter**:

```
If Dir("C:\stamp.bat") = "" Then Debug.Print "File was not found."
```

Because the stamp.bat file doesn't exist on your drive C, Visual Basic prints the message "File was not found" in the Immediate window.

4. To find out whether a file exists on a disk, type the following statement on one line in the Immediate window and press **Enter**:

```
If Dir ("C:\autoexec.bat") <> "" Then Debug.Print "This file exists on
your C drive."
```

The Dir function allows you to use the wildcards in the specified pathname — an asterisk (*) for multiple characters and a question mark (?) for a single character. For example, to find all the configuration settings files in the WINDOWS folder, you can look for all the INI files, as shown below (the lines in italics show what Visual Basic might return as you call the Dir function):

```
?Dir("C:\WINDOWS\*.ini", vbNormal)
system.ini
?dir
WIN.INI
?dir
WINFILE.INI
?dir
control.ini
?dir
EQUIP32.INI
?dir
sxpwin32.ini
```

Now let's try out a couple of complete procedures that use the Dir function. How about writing the names of files in the specified directory to the Immediate window and a spreadsheet? We'll make our output consistent by using the LCase$ function, which causes the names of files to appear in lowercase.

Hands-On 12-3: Using the Dir Function in a Procedure

1. Open the Visual Basic Editor window in the **Practice_Excel12.xlsm** workbook.
2. Rename the VBA project **FileMan_VBA**.
3. Insert a new module into the FileMan_VBA (Practice_Excel12.xlsm) project, and rename it **DirFunction**.
4. Enter the MyFiles procedure in the Code window as shown below:

```
Sub MyFiles()
    Dim mfile As String
    Dim mpath As String

    mpath = InputBox("Enter pathname, e.g. C:\Excel")
    If Right(mpath, 1) <> "\" Then mpath = mpath & "\"

    mfile = Dir(mpath & "*.*")
    If mfile <> "" Then Debug.Print "Files in the " & mpath & " folder:"
    Debug.Print LCase$(mfile)
    If mfile = "" Then
         MsgBox "No files found."
         Exit Sub
    End If
    Do While mfile <> ""
         mfile = Dir
         Debug.Print LCase$(mfile)
    Loop
End Sub
```

   The MyFiles procedure shown above asks the user for the pathname. If the path does not end with the backslash, the Right function appends the backslash to the end of the pathname string. Next, Visual Basic looks for all the files (*) in the specified path. If there are no files, a message is displayed. If files exist, the filenames are written to the Immediate window.

5. Run the MyFiles procedure.
6. To output the filenames to a spreadsheet, enter the GetFiles procedure in the same module where you entered the MyFiles procedure, and then run it:

```
Sub GetFiles()
    Dim myFile As String
    Dim nextRow As Integer

    nextRow = 1
    With Worksheets("Sheet1").Range("A1")
         myFile = Dir("C:\", vbNormal)
         .Value = myFile
```

```
            Do While myFile <> ""
                myFile = Dir
                .Offset(nextRow, 0).Value = myFile
                nextRow = nextRow + 1
            Loop
        End With
    End Sub
```

The GetFiles procedure obtains the names of files located in the root directory of drive C and writes each filename into a worksheet.

Finding Out the Date and Time the File Was Modified

If your procedure must check when a file was last modified, use the FileDateTime function in the following form:

```
FileDateTime(pathname)
```

Pathname is a string that specifies the file you want to work with. The pathname may include the drive and folder where the file resides. The function returns the date and time stamp for the specified file. The date and time format depends on the regional settings selected in the Windows Control Panel. Let's practice using this function in the Immediate window.

Hands-On 12-4: Using the FileDateTime Function

1. Enter the following statement in the Immediate window:

   ```
   ?FileDateTime("C:\Config.sys")
   ```

   When you press Enter, Visual Basic returns the date and time stamp in the following format:

   ```
   5/4/2008 10:52:00 AM
   ```

   To return the date and time separately, use the FileDateTime function as an argument of the DateValue or TimeValue functions. For instance:

   ```
   ?DateValue(FileDateTime("C:\Config.sys"))
   ?TimeValue(FileDateTime("C:\Config.sys"))
   ```

2. Enter the following statement in one line in the Immediate window:

   ```
   If DateValue(FileDateTime("C:\Config.sys")) < Date then Debug.Print "This
   file was not modified today."
   ```

   The Date function returns the current system date as it is set in the Date and Time Properties dialog box accessed in the Windows Control Panel.

Finding Out the Size of a File (the FileLen Function)

If you want to check whether a certain file will fit on a diskette, use the FileLen function in the following form:

```
FileLen(pathname)
```

The FileLen function returns the size of a specified file in bytes. If the file is open, Visual Basic returns the size of the file when it was last saved.

Suppose you want to find out the total size of all the files that store the configuration settings in the Windows directory. Let's write a procedure that performs this task.

Hands-On 12-5: Using the FileLen Function

1. Insert a new module into the project FileMan_VBA (Practice_Excel12.xlsm), and rename it **FileLenFunction**.
2. Enter the TotalBytesIni procedure in the module's Code window and run it:

```
Sub TotalBytesIni()
    Dim iniFile As String
    Dim allBytes As Long

    iniFile = Dir("C:\WINDOWS\*.ini")
    allBytes = 0
    Do While iniFile <> ""
        allBytes = allBytes + FileLen("C:\WINDOWS\" & iniFile)
        iniFile = Dir
    Loop
    Debug.Print "Total bytes: " & allBytes
End Sub
```

As the procedure loops through the .ini files located in the Windows folder, the size of each file is stored in the allBytes variable. The Immediate window displays the total number of bytes that the .ini files occupy.

Returning and Setting File Attributes (the GetAttr and SetAttr Functions)

Files and folders can have attributes such as read-only, hidden, system, and archive. To find out the attributes of a file or folder, use the GetAttr function, which returns an integer that represents the sum of one or more of the constants shown in Table 12-2. The only argument of this function is the name of the file or folder you want to work with:

```
GetAttr(pathname)
```

Table 12-2: File and folder attributes

Constant	Value	Attribute
vbNormal	0	Normal (other attributes are not set)
vbReadOnly	1	Read-only (file or folder can't be modified)
vbHidden	2	Hidden (file or folder isn't visible under normal setup)
vbSystem	4	System file
vbDirectory	16	The object is a directory
vbArchive	32	Archive (the file has been modified since it was last backed up)

To find out whether a file has any of the attributes shown above, use the AND operator to compare the result of the GetAttr function with the value of the constant. If the function returns a non-zero value, the file or folder specified in the pathname has the attribute for which you are testing.

What are the attributes of C:\MsDos.sys or another file located on your computer? You can find out quickly in the Immediate window.

Hands-On 12-6: Returning File Attributes with the GetAttr Function

1. Enter the following statements preceded with the question mark in the Immediate window and press **Enter**. Feel free to substitute the filename with an existing file on your computer. Check the return values that you get against Table 12-2.

```
?getattr("C:\MsDos.sys") And vbReadOnly
1
?getattr("C:\MsDos.sys") And vbHidden
2
?getattr("C:\MsDos.sys") And vbSystem
4
?getattr("C:\MsDos.sys") And vbArchive
32
```

   Now let's put this information together in a procedure.

2. Insert a new module into the project FileMan_VBA (Practice_Excel12.xlsm), and rename it **GetAttrFunction**.
3. Enter the following GetAttributes procedure and run it.

```
Sub GetAttributes()
    Dim attr As Integer
    Dim msg As String

    attr = GetAttr("C:\MSDOS.SYS")
    msg = ""

    If attr And vbReadOnly Then msg = msg & "Read-Only (R)"
    If attr And vbHidden Then msg = msg & Chr(10) & "Hidden (H)"
    If attr And vbSystem Then msg = msg & Chr(10) & "System (S)"
    If attr And vbArchive Then msg = msg & Chr(10) & "Archive (A)"
    MsgBox msg, , "MSDOS.SYS"
End Sub
```

   When you run the procedure, you should see the message box shown in Figure 12-1.

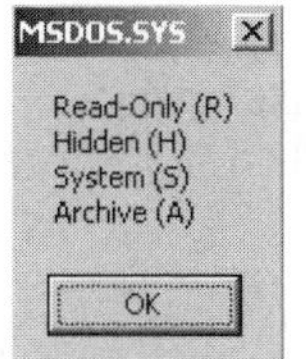

Figure 12-1: You can get the attributes of any file using the GetAttr function.

The opposite of the GetAttr function is the SetAttr function, which allows you to set the attributes for files or folders that are closed. Its syntax is:

```
SetAttr pathname, attributes
```

Pathname is a string that specifies the file or folder that you want to work with. The second argument, attributes, is one or more constants that specify the attributes you want to set. See Table 12-2 earlier in this chapter for the list of available constants.

Suppose you have a file called C:\stamps.txt and you want to set two attributes: read-only and hidden.

Hands-On 12-7: Setting File Attributes with the SetAttr Function

1. To set the file attributes, type the following instruction in the Immediate window, and press **Enter** (replace the C:\stamps.txt with the name of a file that exists on your disk):

   ```
   SetAttr "C:\stamps.txt", vbReadOnly + vbHidden
   ```

2. To find out what attributes were set in step 1, type the following instruction in the Immediate window and press **Enter** (check the returned value against Table 12-2):

   ```
   ?GetAttr("C:\stamps.txt")
   ```

Changing the Default Folder or Drive (the ChDir and ChDrive Statements)

You can easily change the default folder by using the ChDir statement, as follows:

```
ChDir pathname
```

In the statement above, pathname is the name of the new default folder. Pathname may include the name of the disk drive. If pathname doesn't include a drive designation, the default folder will be changed on the current drive. The current drive will not be changed. Suppose the default folder is C:\DOS. The statement:

```
ChDir "D:\MyFiles"
```

changes the default folder to D:\MyFiles; however, the current drive is still drive C.

To change the current drive, you should use the ChDrive statement in the following format:

```
ChDrive drive
```

The drive argument specifies the letter of the new default drive.

For instance, to change the default drive to drive D or E, you can use the following statements:

```
ChDrive "D"
ChDrive "E"
```

If you refer to a nonexistent drive, you will get the message "Device unavailable."

Creating and Deleting Folders (the MkDir and RmDir Statements)

You can create a new folder using the following syntax of the MkDir statement:

```
MkDir pathname
```

Pathname specifies the new folder you want to create. If you don't include the name of the drive, Visual Basic will create the new folder on the current drive.

To delete a folder you no longer need, use the RmDir function. This function has the following syntax:

```
RmDir pathname
```

Pathname specifies the folder you want to delete. Pathname may include the drive name. If you omit the name of the drive, Visual Basic will delete the folder on the current drive if a folder with the same name exists. Otherwise, Visual Basic will display the error message "Path not found."

Let's run through some examples in the Immediate window.

Hands-On 12-8: Creating and Deleting Folders with the MkDir and RmDir Statements

1. Type the following instruction in the Immediate window and press **Enter** to create a folder called Mail on drive C:

   ```
   MkDir "C:\Mail"
   ```

2. To change the default folder to C:\Mail, enter the following statement and press **Enter**:

   ```
   ChDir "C:\Mail"
   ```

3. To find out the name of the active folder, enter the following statement and press **Enter**:

   ```
   ?CurDir
   ```

4. To delete the C:\Mail folder that was created in step 1, enter the following statements and press **Enter**:

   ```
   ChDir "C:\"
   RmDir "C:\Mail"
   ```

> **RmDir Removes Empty Folders**
>
> You cannot delete a folder if it still contains files. You should first delete the files with the Kill statement (discussed later in this chapter).

Copying Files (the FileCopy Statement)

To copy files between folders, use the FileCopy statement shown below:

```
FileCopy source, destination
```

The first parameter of this statement, source, specifies the name of the file that you want to copy. The name may include the drive in which the file resides. The second parameter, destination, is the name of the destination file and may include the drive and folder designation. Both parameters are required.

Suppose you want to copy a file specified by a user to a folder called C:\Abort. The procedure shown below demonstrates how to do this.

Hands-On 12-9: Copying Files with the FileCopy Statement

1. Insert a new module into the project FileMan_VBA (Practice_Excel12.xlsm), and rename it **FileCopyAndKill**.
2. In the module's Code window, enter the following CopyToAbortFolder procedure:

```
Sub CopyToAbortFolder()
    Dim folder As String
    Dim source As String
    Dim dest As String
    Dim msg1 As String
    Dim msg2 As String
    Dim p As Integer
    Dim s As Integer
    Dim i As Long

    On Error GoTo ErrorHandler

    folder = "C:\Abort"
    msg1 = "The selected file is already in this folder."
    msg2 = "was copied to"
    p = 1
    i = 1
    ' get the name of the file from the user
    source = Application.GetOpenFilename
    ' don't do anything if cancelled
    If source = "False" Then Exit Sub
    ' get the total number of backslash characters "\" in the source
    ' variable's contents
    Do Until p = 0
          p = InStr(i, source, "\", 1)
          If p = 0 Then Exit Do
          s = p
          i = p + 1
    Loop
    ' create the destination filename
    dest = folder & Mid(source, s, Len(source))
          ' create a new folder with this name
          MkDir folder
          ' check if the specified file already exists in the
          ' destination folder
```

```
        If Dir(dest) <> "" Then
            MsgBox msg1
        Else
        ' copy the selected file to the C:\Abort folder
            FileCopy source, dest
            MsgBox source & " " & msg2 & " " & dest
        End If
        Exit Sub
    ErrorHandler:
        If Err = "75" Then
            Resume Next
        End If
        If Err = "70" Then
            MsgBox "You can't copy an open file."
        Exit Sub
    End If
End Sub
```

The procedure CopyToAbortFolder uses the Excel application method called GetOpenFilename to get the name of the file from the user. This method causes the built-in Open dialog box to pop up. Using this dialog box, you can choose any file, in any directory, and on any disk drive. If the user cancels, Visual Basic returns the value "False" and the procedure ends. If the user selects a file and clicks Open, the selected file will be assigned to the variable source.

For the purpose of copying you'll only need the filename (without the path), so the Do...Until loop finds out the position of the last backslash (\) in the file stored in the variable source, the first argument of the FileCopy statement. Next, Visual Basic prepares a string of characters and assigns it to the variable dest, the second argument of the FileCopy statement. This variable holds the string obtained by concatenating the name of the destination folder (C:\Abort) with the user-specified filename preceded by a backslash (\).

The MkDir function creates a new folder called C:\Abort if it doesn't exist on drive C. If such a folder already exists, Visual Basic will need to deal with error 75. This error will be caught by the error-handler code included at the end of the procedure. Notice that the error handler is a fragment of code that begins with the label ErrorHandler followed by a colon.

When Visual Basic encounters the Resume Next statement, it will continue to execute the procedure from the instruction following the instruction that caused the error. This means that the statement MkDir folder won't be executed.

Next, the procedure checks whether the selected file already exists in the destination folder. If the file already exists there, the user will get the message stored in the variable msg1. If the file does not exist in the destination folder and the file is not currently open, Visual Basic will copy the file to the specified folder and notify the user with the appropriate message. If the file is open, Visual Basic will encounter run-time error

70 and run the corresponding instructions in the ErrorHandler section of the procedure.

3. Run the CopyToAbortFolder procedure several times, each time selecting files from different folders.
4. Try to copy a file that was copied before by this procedure to the C:\Abort folder.
5. Try to copy an open file while using the CopyToAbortFolder procedure.
6. Run the procedure MyFiles prepared earlier in this chapter to write to the Immediate window the contents of the folder C:\Abort.

Note: Do not delete the C:\Abort folder and files that you have copied to it. You'll delete both the folder and the files in the next section using a VBA procedure.

Deleting Files (the Kill Statement)

You already know from one of the earlier sections in this chapter that you can't delete a folder if it still contains files. To delete the files from any folder, use the following Kill statement:

```
Kill pathname
```

Pathname specifies the names of one or more files that you want to delete. Optionally, pathname may include the drive and folder name where the file resides. To enable quick deletion of files, you can use the wildcard characters (* or ?) in the pathname argument.

You can't delete a file that is open. If you worked through the exercises in the preceding section, your hard drive now contains the folder C:\Abort with several files. Let's write a VBA procedure to dispose of this folder and the files contained in it.

Hands-On 12-10: Deleting Files with the Kill Statement

1. Insert a new module into the project FileMan_VBA(Practice_Excel12.xlsm), and rename it **KillStatement**.
2. Enter the code of the RemoveMe procedure, as shown below:

```
Sub RemoveMe()
    Dim folder As String
    Dim myFile As String

    ' assign the name of folder to the folder variable
    ' notice the ending backslash "\"
    folder = "C:\Abort\"
    myFile = Dir(folder, vbNormal)

    Do While myFile <> ""
        Kill folder & myFile
        myFile = Dir
```

```
    Loop
          RmDir folder
End Sub
```

3. Run the RemoveMe procedure. When the procedure ends, check Windows Explorer to see that the Abort folder was removed.

Chapter Summary

In the course of this chapter, you learned about and tried out VBA functions and statements that allow you to work with the file system. You found out how to manage files and folders by using built-in VBA functions, such as the CurDir function to get the name of the current folder. You wrote code that uses the GetAttr and SetAttr functions to check and change file attributes. And you learned about creating, copying, and deleting files and folders by using the statements MkDir, FileCopy, and RmDir.

In the next chapter, we will look at Windows Script Host (WSH), an invaluable ActiveX tool that lets you control and retrieve information from the Windows operating system environment.

Chapter 13

File and Folder Manipulation with Windows Script Host (WSH)

There is a hidden treasure in your computer called Windows Script Host (WSH), which allows you to create little programs that control the Windows operating system and its applications, as well as retrieve information from the operating system. WSH is an ActiveX control found in the Wshom.ocx file. This file is automatically installed in the Windows\System32 folder if you are running Windows 95, Windows 98, Windows NT 5.0, Windows 2000, Windows XP, or Vista.

WSH is a scripting language. A *script* is a set of commands that can be run automatically. Scripts can be created and run directly from the command prompt by using the Command Script Host (Cscript.exe) or from Windows by using the Windows Script Host (Wscript.exe). In the following sections of this chapter, you will learn how the Windows Script Host works together with VBA.

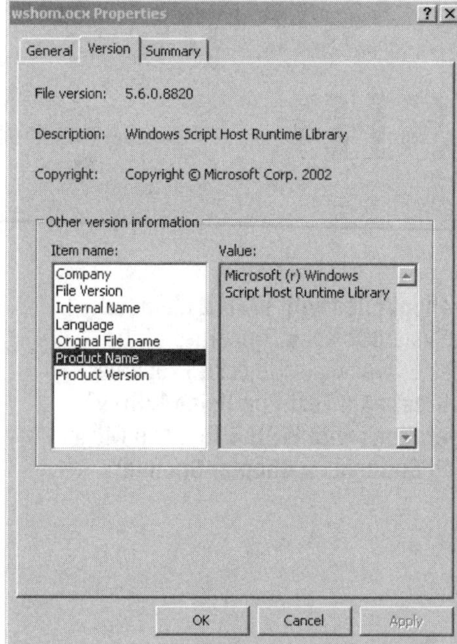

Figure 13-1: Windows Script Host is an ActiveX control used to create scripts that perform simple or complex operations, which previously could only be performed by writing batch files (.bat) in the MS-DOS operating system.

WSH has its own object hierarchy. Using the CreateObject function, you can refer to WSH objects from your VBA procedure. Before you start writing VBA procedures that utilize WSH objects, let's take a look at some of the objects you will be able to control.

Hands-On 13-1: Controlling Objects with Windows Script Host (WSH)

1. Open a new workbook and save it as **C:\Ex07_ByExample\ Practice_Excel13.xlsm**.

2. Switch to the Visual Basic Editor window and choose **Tools | References.** Click the check box next to Microsoft Scripting Runtime, then click **OK** to close the References dialog box.

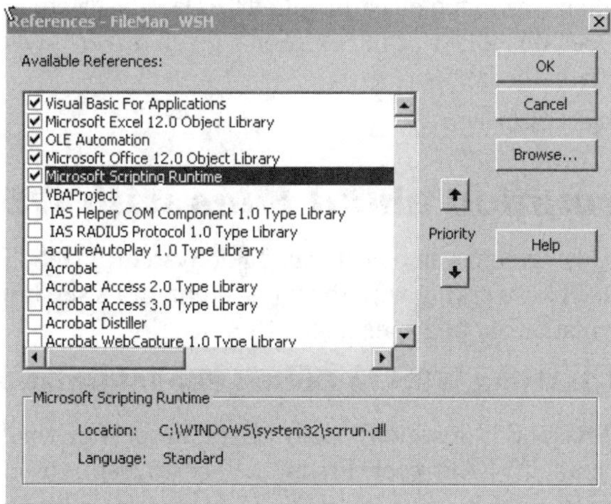

Figure 13-2: Creating a reference to the Microsoft Scripting Runtime.

3. Press **F2** to open the Object Browser.
4. In the <All Libraries> combo box, choose **Scripting.** You will see a list of objects that are part of the Windows Script Host library, as shown in Figure 13-3.

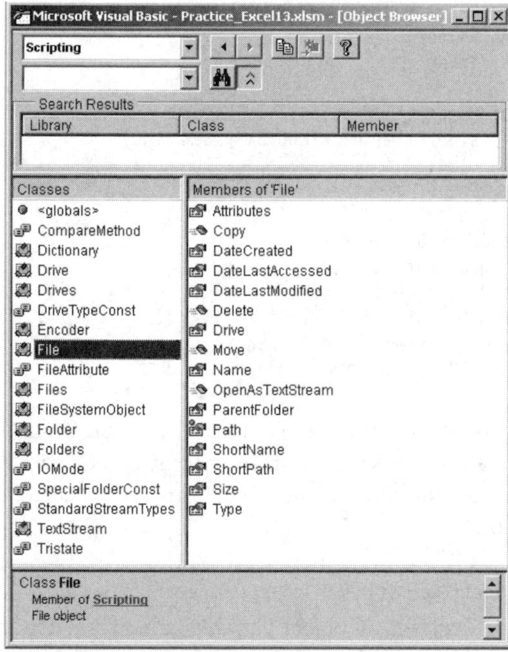

Figure 13-3: After establishing a reference to the Microsoft Scripting Runtime (see Figure 13-2), the Object Browser displays many objects that allow you to work with disks, folders, files, and their contents

Windows Script Host allows you to quickly obtain answers to such questions as "On which disk can I locate a particular file?" (GetDrive method), "What is the extension of a filename?" (GetExtensionName method), "When was this file last modified?" (DateLastModified property), and "Does this folder or file exist on a given drive?" (FolderExists and FileExists methods).

5. Close the Object Browser.

Finding Information about Files with WSH

Windows Script Host exposes an object called FileSystemObject. This object has several methods for working with the file system. Let's see how you can obtain some information about a specific file.

Hands-On 13-2: Using WSH to Obtain File Information

1. In the Visual Basic Editor window, activate the Properties window and change the name of VBAProject (Practice_Excel13.xlsm) to **FileMan_WSH**.
2. Insert a new module into the FileMan_WSH project and rename it **WSH**.
3. In the WSH module's Code window, enter the following FileInfo procedure:

```
Sub FileInfo()
    Dim fs As Object
    Dim objFile As Object
    Dim strMsg As String

    Set fs = CreateObject("Scripting.FileSystemObject")
    Set objFile = fs.GetFile("C:\WINDOWS\System.ini")
    strMsg = "File name: " & _
         objFile.Name & vbCrLf
    strMsg = strMsg & "Disk: " & _
         objFile.Drive & vbCrLf
    strMsg = strMsg & "Date Created: " & _
         objFile.DateCreated & vbCrLf
    strMsg = strMsg & "Date Modified: " & _
         objFile.DateLastModified & vbCrLf
    MsgBox strMsg, , "File Information"
End Sub
```

The FileInfo procedure shown above uses the CreateObject VBA function to create an ActiveX object (FileSystemObject) that is a part of the Windows Script Host library. This object provides access to a computer's file system.

```
Dim fs As Object
Set fs = CreateObject("Scripting.FileSystemObject")
```

The above code declares an object variable named fs. Next, it uses the CreateObject function to create an ActiveX object and assigns the object to an object variable. The statement

```
Set objFile = fs.GetFile("C:\WINDOWS\System.ini")
```

creates and returns a reference to the File object for the System.ini file in the C:\WINDOWS folder and assigns it to the objFile object variable. The File object has many properties that you can read. For example, the statement objFile.Name returns the full name of the file.

The statement objFile.Drive returns the drive name where the file is located. The statements objFile.DateCreated and objFile.DateLastModified return the date the file was created and when it was last modified. This procedure can be modified easily so that it also returns the type of file, its attributes, and the name of the parent folder. Try to modify this procedure on your own by adding the following instructions to the code: objFile.Type, objFile.Attributes, objFile.ParentFolder, and objFile.Size. Check the Object Browser for other things you can learn about the file by referencing the File object.

4. Run the FileInfo procedure.

Methods and Properties of FileSystemObject

You can access the computer's file system using FileSystemObject. This object offers a number of methods, some of which are shown below:

- FileExists — Returns True if the specified file exists.

```
Sub FileExists()
    Dim fs As Object
    Dim strFile As String
    Set fs = CreateObject("Scripting.FileSystemObject")
    strFile = InputBox("Enter the full name of the file: ")
    If fs.FileExists(strFile) Then
        MsgBox strFile & " was found."
    Else
        MsgBox "File does not exist."
    End If
End Sub
```

- GetFile — Returns a File object.
- GetFileName — Returns the filename and path.
- GetFileVersion — Returns the file version.
- CopyFile — Copies a file.

```
Sub CopyFile()
    Dim fs As Object
    Dim strFile As String
    Dim strNewFile As String

    strFile = "C:\Hello.doc"
    strNewFile = "C:\Program Files\Hello.doc"

    Set fs = CreateObject("Scripting.FileSystemObject")
    fs.CopyFile strFile, strNewFile
    MsgBox "A copy of the specified file was created."
    Set fs = Nothing
End Sub
```

- MoveFile — Moves a file.
- DeleteFile — Deletes a file.

```
Sub DeleteFile()
    ' This procedure requires that you set up
    ' a reference to Microsoft Script Runtime
    Dim fs As FileSystemObject
    Set fs = New FileSystemObject

    fs.DeleteFile "C:\Program Files\Hello.doc"
    MsgBox "The requested file was deleted."
End Sub
```

- DriveExists — Returns True if the specified drive exists.

```
Function DriveExists(disk)
    Dim fs As Object
    Dim strMsg As String
    Set fs = CreateObject("Scripting.FileSystemObject")
    If fs.DriveExists(disk) Then
        strMsg = "Drive " & UCase(disk) & " exists."
    Else
        strMsg = UCase(disk) & " was not found."
    End If
    DriveExists = strMsg
' run this function from the worksheet
' by entering the following in any cell : =DriveExists("E:\")
End Function
```

- GetDrive — Returns a Drive object.

```
Sub DriveInfo()
    Dim fs, disk, infoStr, strDiskName
    strDiskName = InputBox("Enter the drive letter:", _
        "Drive Name", "C:\")

    Set fs = CreateObject("Scripting.FileSystemObject")
    Set disk = fs.GetDrive(fs.GetDriveName(strDiskName))
    infoStr = "Drive: " & UCase(strDiskName) & vbCrLf
    infoStr = infoStr & "Drive letter: " & _
        UCase(disk.DriveLetter) & vbCrLf
    infoStr = infoStr & "Drive Type: " & disk.DriveType & vbCrLf
    infoStr = infoStr & "Drive File System: " & _
        disk.FileSystem & vbCrLf
    infoStr = infoStr & "Drive SerialNumber: " & _
        disk.SerialNumber & vbCrLf
    infoStr = infoStr & "Total Size in Bytes: " & _
        FormatNumber(disk.TotalSize / 1024, 0) & " Kb" & vbCrLf
    infoStr = infoStr & "Free Space on Drive: " & _
        FormatNumber(disk.FreeSpace / 1024, 0) & " Kb" & vbCrLf
    MsgBox infoStr, vbInformation, "Drive Information"
End Sub
```

- GetDriveName — Returns a string containing the name of a drive or network share.

```
Function DriveName(disk)
    Dim fs As Object
    Dim strDiskName As String
```

```
    Set fs = CreateObject("Scripting.FileSystemObject")
    strDiskName = fs.GetDriveName(disk)
    DriveName = strDiskName
' run this function from the Immediate window
' by entering ?DriveName("D:\")
End Function
```

- FolderExists — Returns True if the specified folder exists.

```
Sub DoesFolderExist()
    Dim fs As Object
    Set fs = CreateObject("Scripting.FileSystemObject")
    MsgBox fs.FolderExists("C:\Program Files")
End Sub
```

- GetFolder — Returns a Folder object.

```
Sub FilesInFolder()
    Dim fs As Object
    Dim objFolder As Object
    Dim objFile As Object

    Set fs = CreateObject("Scripting.FileSystemObject")
    Set objFolder = fs.GetFolder("C:\")

    Workbooks.Add
    For Each objFile In objFolder.Files
        ActiveCell.Formula = objFile.Name
        ActiveCell.Offset(0, 1).Range("A1").Select
        Selection.Formula = objFile.Type
        ActiveCell.Offset(1, -1).Range("A1").Select
    Next
    Columns("A:B").Select
    Selection.Columns.AutoFit
End Sub
```

- GetSpecialFolder — Returns the path to the operating system folders:
  0 — Windows folder
  1 — System folder
  2 — Temp folder

```
Sub SpecialFolders()
    Dim fs As Object
    Dim strWindowsFolder As String
    Dim strSystemFolder As String
    Dim strTempFolder As String

    Set fs = CreateObject("Scripting.FileSystemObject")
    strWindowsFolder = fs.GetSpecialFolder(0)
    strSystemFolder = fs.GetSpecialFolder(1)
    strTempFolder = fs.GetSpecialFolder(2)

    MsgBox strWindowsFolder & vbCrLf _
          & strSystemFolder & vbCrLf _
          & strTempFolder, vbInformation + vbOKOnly, _
          "Special Folders"
End Sub
```

- CreateFolder — Creates a folder.

```
Sub MakeNewFolder()
    Dim fs, objFolder
    Set fs = CreateObject("Scripting.FileSystemObject")
    Set objFolder = fs.CreateFolder("C:\TestFolder")
    MsgBox "A new folder named " & _
         objFolder.Name & " was created."
End Sub
```

- CopyFolder — Creates a copy of a folder.

```
Sub MakeFolderCopy()
    Dim fs As FileSystemObject
    Set fs = New FileSystemObject
    If fs.FolderExists("C:\TestFolder") Then
         fs.CopyFolder "C:\TestFolder", "C:\FinalFolder"
         MsgBox "The folder was copied."
    End If
End Sub
```

- MoveFolder — Moves a folder.
- DeleteFolder — Deletes a folder.

```
Sub RemoveFolder()
    Dim fs As FileSystemObject
    Set fs = New FileSystemObject

    If fs.FolderExists("C:\TestFolder") Then
         fs.DeleteFolder "C:\TestFolder"
         MsgBox "The folder was deleted."
    End If
End Sub
```

- CreateTextFile — Creates a text file.
- OpenTextFile — Opens a text file.

```
Sub ReadTextFile()
    Dim fs As Object
    Dim objFile As Object
    Dim strContent As String
    Dim strFileName As String

    strFileName = "C:\WINNT\System.ini"
    Set fs = CreateObject("Scripting.FileSystemObject")
    Set objFile = fs.OpenTextFile(strFileName)
    Do While Not objFile.AtEndOfStream
         strContent = strContent & objFile.ReadLine & vbCrLf
    Loop

    objFile.Close
    Set objFile = Nothing
    ActiveWorkbook.Sheets(3).Select
    Range("A1").Select
    Selection.Formula = strContent
End Sub
```

The FileSystemObject has only one property called Drives, which returns a reference to the collection of drives. Using this property you can create a list of drives on a computer, as shown below:

```
Sub DrivesList()
    Dim fs As Object
    Dim colDrives As Object
    Dim strDrive As String

    Set fs = CreateObject("Scripting.FileSystemObject")
    Set colDrives = fs.Drives

        For Each Drive In colDrives
            strDrive = "Drive " & Drive.DriveLetter & ": "
            Debug.Print strDrive
        Next
End Sub
```

Properties of the File Object

The File object allows you to access all of the properties of a specified file. The following lines of code create a reference to the File object:

```
Set fs = CreateObject("Scripting.FileSystemObject")
Set objFile = fs.GetFile("C:\My Documents\myFile.doc")
```

You will find an example of using the File object in the FileInfo procedure that was created earlier in this chapter.

These are the properties of the File object:

- Attributes — Returns file attributes (compare this property to the GetAttr VBA function explained in Chapter 12).
- DateCreated — File creation date.
- DateLastAccessed — File last-access date.
- DateLastModified — File last-modified date.
- Drive — Drive name followed by a colon.
- Name — Name of the file.
- ParentFolder — Parent folder of the file.
- Path — Full path of the file.
- Size — File size in bytes (compare this property to the FileLen VBA function explained in Chapter 12).
- Type — File type. This is the text that appears in the Type column in Windows Explorer, e.g., configuration settings, application, and shortcut.

Properties of the Folder Object

The Folder object provides access to all of the properties of a specified folder. The following lines of code create a reference to the Folder object:

```
Set fs = CreateObject("Scripting.FileSystemObject")
Set objFolder = fs.GetFolder("C:\My Documents")
```

See examples of VBA procedures in the properties list below that access the Folder object:

- Attributes — Folder attributes.
- DateCreated — Folder creation date.
- Drive — Returns the drive letter of the folder where the specified folder resides.
- Files — Collection of files in the folder.

```
Sub CountFilesInFolder()
    Dim fs, strFolder, objFolder, colFiles

    strFolder = InputBox("Enter the folder name:")
    If Not IsFolderEmpty(strFolder) Then
          Set fs = CreateObject("Scripting.FileSystemObject")
          Set objFolder = fs.GetFolder(strFolder)
          Set colFiles = objFolder.Files
          MsgBox "The number of files in the folder " & _
                strFolder & "=" & colFiles.Count
    End If
End Sub
```

  The above procedure calls the IsFolderEmpty function (used in the Size property description example below).

- IsRootFolder — Returns True if the folder is the root folder.
- Name — Name of the folder.
- ParentFolder — Parent folder of the specified folder.
- Path — Full path to the folder.
- Size — Folder size in bytes.

```
Function IsFolderEmpty(myFolder)
    Dim fs, objFolder

    Set fs = CreateObject("Scripting.FileSystemObject")
    Set objFolder = fs.GetFolder(myFolder)
    IsFolderEmpty = (objFolder.Size = 0)
End Function
```

- SubFolders — Collection of subfolders in the folder.
- Type — Folder type, e.g., file folder or Recycle Bin.

Properties of the Drive Object

The Drive object provides access to the properties of the specified drive on a computer or a server. The following lines of code create a reference to the Drive object:

```
Set fs = CreateObject("Scripting.FileSystemObject")
Set objDrive = fs.GetDrive("C:\")
```

You will find several procedure examples that use the Drive object in the following list of properties:

- AvailableSpace — Available space in bytes.
- FreeSpace — Same as AvailableSpace.

- DriveLetter — Drive letter (without the colon).
- DriveType — Type of drive:

  0 — Unknown
  1 — Removable
  2 — Fixed
  3 — Network
  4 — CD-ROM
  5 — RAM disk

```
Sub CDROM_DriveLetter()
    Const CDROM = 4
    Dim fs, colDrives
    Set fs = CreateObject("Scripting.FileSystemObject")
    Set colDrives = fs.Drives
    For Each Drive In colDrives
        If Drive.DriveType = CDROM Then
            MsgBox "The CD-ROM Drive: " & Drive.DriveLetter
        End If
    Next
End Sub
```

- FileSystem — File system such as FAT, NTFS, or CDFS.
- IsReady — Returns True if the appropriate media (CD-ROM disk) is inserted and ready for access.

```
Function IsCDROMReady(strDriveLetter)
    Dim fs, objDrive

    Set fs = CreateObject("Scripting.FileSystemObject")
    Set objDrive = fs.GetDrive(strDriveLetter)

    IsCDROMReady = (objDrive.DriveType = 4) And _
        objDrive.IsReady = True
    ' run this function from the Immediate window
    ' by entering: ?IsCDROMReady("D:")
End Function
```

- Path — Path of the root folder.
- SerialNumber — Serial number of the drive.
- TotalSize — Total drive size in bytes.

Creating a Text File Using WSH

Windows Script Host (WSH) offers three methods for creating text files: CreateTextFile, OpenTextFile, and OpenAsTextStream. The syntax of each of these methods and example procedures are shown below.

- **CreateTextFile** `object.CreateTextFile(filename[, overwrite[, unicode]])`
  - Object is the name of the FileSystemObject or the Folder object.
  - Filename is a string expression that specifies the file to create.
  - Overwrite (optional) is a Boolean value that indicates whether you can overwrite an existing file. The value is True if the file can be

overwritten and False if it can't be overwritten. If omitted, existing files are not overwritten.

- Unicode (optional) is a Boolean value that indicates whether the file is created as a Unicode or ASCII file. The value is True if the file is created as a Unicode file and False if it's created as an ASCII file. If omitted, an ASCII file is assumed.

```
Sub CreateFile_Method1()
     Dim fs, objFile
     Set fs = CreateObject("Scripting.FileSystemObject")
     Set objFile = fs.CreateTextFile("C:\Phones.txt", True)
     objFile.WriteLine ("Margaret Kubiak: 212-338-8778")
     objFile.WriteBlankLines (2)
     objFile.WriteLine ("Robert Prochot: 202-988-2331")
     objFile.Close
End Sub
```

The above procedure creates a text file to store the names and phone numbers of two people. Because there is a Boolean value of True in the position of the Overwrite argument, the C:\Phones.txt file will be overwritten if it already exists in the specified folder.

- **OpenTextFile** `object.OpenTextFile(filename[, iomode[, create[, format]]])`
  - Object is the name of the FileSystemObject.
  - Filename is a string expression that identifies the file to open.
  - Iomode (optional) is a Boolean value that indicates whether a new file can be created if the specified filename doesn't exist. The value is True if a new file is created and False if it isn't created. If omitted, a new file isn't created. The Iomode argument can be one of the following constants:

    ForReading (1)
    ForWriting (2)
    ForAppending (8)
  - Create (optional) is a Boolean value that indicates whether a new file can be created if the specified filename doesn't exist. The value is True if a new file is created and False if it isn't created. If omitted, a new file isn't created.
  - Format (optional) is one of three Tristate values used to indicate the format of the opened file. If omitted, the file is opened as ASCII.

    `TristateTrue` — Open the file as ASCII.
    `TristateFalse` — Open the file as Unicode.
    `TristateUseDefault` — Open the file using the system default.

```
Sub CreateFile_Method2()
     Dim fs, objFile
     Set fs = CreateObject("Scripting.FileSystemObject")
     Set objFile = fs.OpenTextFile("C:\Shopping.txt", _
          ForWriting, True)
```

```
        objFile.WriteLine ("Bread")
        objFile.WriteLine ("Milk")
        objFile.WriteLine ("Strawberries")
        objFile.Close
    End Sub
```

- **OpenAsTextStream** `object.OpenAsTextStream([iomode, [format]])`
  - Object is the name of the File object.
  - Iomode (optional) indicates input/output mode. This can be one of three constants:

    ForReading (1)
    ForWriting (2)
    ForAppending (8)
  - Format (optional) is one of three Tristate values used to indicate the format of the opened file. If omitted, the file is opened as ASCII.

    `TristateTrue` — Open the file as ASCII.
    `TristateFalse` — Open the file as Unicode.
    `TristateUseDefault` — Open the file using the system default.

```
Sub CreateFile_Method3()
    Dim fs, objFile, objText
    Set fs = CreateObject("Scripting.FileSystemObject")
    fs.CreateTextFile "New.txt"
    Set objFile = fs.GetFile("New.txt")
    Set objText = objFile.OpenAsTextStream(ForWriting, _
        TristateUseDefault)
    objText.Write "Wedding Invitation"
    objText.Close
    Set objText = objFile.OpenAsTextStream(ForReading, _
        TristateUseDefault)
    MsgBox objText.ReadLine
    objText.Close
End Sub
```

Performing Other Operations with WSH

WSH makes it possible to manipulate any Automation object installed on your computer. In addition to accessing the file system through FileSystem-Object, WSH allows you to perform such tasks as handling WSH and ActiveX objects, mapping and unmapping printers and remote drives, manipulating the registry, creating Windows and Internet shortcuts, and accessing the Windows NT Active Directory service.

The WSH object model is made of the following three main objects:

- WScript
- WshShell
- WshNetwork

This section demonstrates how you can take advantage of the WshShell object to write procedures to start other applications and create shortcuts.

Running Other Applications

In Chapter 15, you will learn various methods of launching external applications from Excel. You can add to those methods what you are about to find out in this section.

Suppose you want to start up Windows Notepad from your VBA procedure. The procedure that follows shows you how easy it is to run an application using the WshShell object that is a part of Windows Script Host. If you'd rather launch the built-in calculator, just replace the name of the Notepad application with Calc.

Hands-On 13-3: Running Other Applications Using the WSH Object

1. Insert a new module into the project FileMan_WSH (Practice_Excel13.xlsm) and rename it **WSH_Additional**.
2. Enter the RunNotepad procedure in the WSH_Additional module's Code window, as shown below:

```
Sub RunNotepad()
    Dim WshShell As Object
    Set WshShell = CreateObject("WScript.Shell")
    WshShell.Run "Notepad"
    Set WshShell = Nothing
End Sub
```

The above procedure begins by declaring and creating a WshShell object:

```
Dim WshShell As Object
Set WshShell = CreateObject("WScript.Shell")
```

The next statement uses the Run method to run the required application:

```
WshShell.Run "Notepad"
```

Using the same concept, it is easy to run Windows utility applications such as Calculator or Explorer:

```
WshShell.Run "Calc"
WshShell.Run "Explorer"
```

The last line in the procedure destroys the WshShell object because it is no longer needed:

```
Set WshShell = Nothing
```

3. Execute the RunNotepad procedure.

Instead of launching an empty application window, you can start your application with a specific document, as shown in the following procedure:

```
Sub OpenTxtFileInNotepad()
    Dim WshShell As Object
    Set WshShell = CreateObject("WScript.Shell")
    WshShell.Run "Notepad C:\Phones.txt"
    Set WshShell = Nothing
End Sub
```

Creating Shortcuts

When you start distributing your VBA applications, users will certainly request that you automatically place a shortcut to your application on their desktop. VBA does not provide a way to create Windows shortcuts. Luckily for you, you now know how to work with WSH, and you can use its Shell object to create shortcuts to applications or web sites without any user intervention. The WshShell object exposes the CreateShortcut method, which you can use in the following way:

```
Set myShortcut = WshShell.CreateShortcut(pathname)
```

Pathname is a string indicating the full path to the shortcut file. All shortcut files have the .lnk extension, which must be included in the pathname. The CreateShortcut method returns a shortcut object that exposes a number of properties and one method:

- TargetPath — The TargetPath property is the path to the shortcut's executable.

  ```
  WshShell.TargetPath = ActiveWorkbook.FullName
  ```

- WindowStyle — The WindowStyle property identifies the window style used by a shortcut.

  1 — Normal window
  3 — Maximized window
  7 — Minimized window

  ```
  WshShell.WindowStyle = 1
  ```

- Hotkey — The Hotkey property is a keyboard shortcut. For example, Alt+F, Shift+G, Ctrl+Shift+Z, etc.

  ```
  WshShell.Hotkey = "Ctrl+Alt+W"
  ```

- IconLocation — The IconLocation property is the location of the shortcut's icon. Because icon files usually contain more than one icon, you should provide the path to the icon file followed by the index number of the desired icon in this file. If not specified, Windows uses the default icon for the file.

  ```
  WshShell.IconLocation = "notepad.exe, 0"
  ```

- Description — The Description property contains a string value describing a shortcut.

  ```
  WshShell.Description = "Wordware Web Site"
  ```

- WorkingDirectory — The WorkingDirectory property identifies the working directory used by a shortcut.

  ```
  strWorkDir = WshShell.SpecialFolders("Desktop")
  WshShell.WorkingDirectory = strWorkDir
  ```

- Save — Save is the only method of the Shortcut object. After using the CreateShortcut method to create a Shortcut object and set the Shortcut object's properties, the Save method must be used to save the Shortcut object to disk.

Creating a shortcut is a three-step process:

1. Create an instance of a WshShortcut object.
2. Initialize its properties (shown above).
3. Save it to disk with the Save method.

The following example creates a WshShell object and uses the CreateShortcut method to create two shortcuts: a Windows shortcut to the active Microsoft Excel workbook file and an Internet shortcut to the Wordware Publishing web site. Both shortcuts are placed on the user's desktop.

Hands-On 13-4: Creating Shortcuts Using the WshShell Object

1. In the WSH_Additional module created in the previous Hands-On exercise, enter the CreateShortcut procedure as shown below:

```
Sub CreateShortcut()
    ' this script creates two desktop shortcuts
    Dim WshShell As Object
    Dim objShortcut As Object

    Set WshShell = CreateObject("WScript.Shell")
    ' create an Internet shortcut
    Set objShortcut = WshShell.CreateShortcut(WshShell. _
        SpecialFolders("Desktop") & "\Wordware.url")
    objShortcut.TargetPath = "http://www.wordware.com"

    objShortcut.Save

    ' create a file shortcut
    Set objShortcut = WshShell.CreateShortcut(WshShell. _
        SpecialFolders("Desktop") & "\" & ActiveWorkbook.Name & ".lnk")
    With objShortcut
        .TargetPath = ActiveWorkbook.FullName
        .WindowStyle = 7
        .Save
    End With

    Set objShortcut = Nothing
    Set WshShell = Nothing
End Sub
```

   The above procedure uses the SpecialFolders property of the WshShell object to return the path to the Windows desktop.

2. Run the CreateShortcut procedure.
3. Switch to your desktop and click the Wordware shortcut.

Using the SpecialFolders Property

You can find out the location of a special folder on your machine using the SpecialFolders property. The following special folders are available: AllUsersDesktop, AllUsersStartMenu, AllUsersPrograms, AllUsersStartup, Desktop, Favorites, Fonts, MyDocuments, NetHood, PrintHood, Programs, Recent, SendTo, StartMenu, Startup, and Templates. If the requested special folder is not available, the SpecialFolders property returns an empty string.

Chapter Summary

In the course of this chapter, you learned how to use the Windows Script Host (WSH) to access the FileSystemObject and perform other operations, such as launching applications and creating Windows shortcuts with the WshShell object.

In the next chapter, you will learn how to work with three types of files: sequential, random access, and binary.

Chapter 14

Using Low-Level File Access

File Access Types ■ Working with Sequential Files ■ Reading Data Stored in Sequential Files ■ Reading a File Line by Line ■ Reading Characters from Sequential Files ■ Reading Delimited Text Files ■ Writing Data to Sequential Files ■ Using Write # and Print # Statements ■ **Working with Binary Access Files ■ Working with Binary Files ■ Chapter Summary**

In addition to opening files within a particular application, your VBA procedures are capable of opening other types of files and working with their contents. This chapter will put you in direct contact with your data by introducing you to the process known as low-level file I/O (input/output).

File Access Types

There are three types of files used by a computer:

- *Sequential access files* are files where data is retrieved in the same order as it is stored, such as files stored in the CSV format (comma-delimited text), TXT format (text separated by tabs), or PRN format (text separated by spaces). Sequential access files are often used for writing text files such as error logs, configuration settings, and reports. Sequential access files have the following modes: Input, Output, and Append. The mode specifies how you can work with a file after it has been opened.
- *Random access files* are text files where data is stored in records of equal length and fields separated by commas. Random access files have only one mode: Random.
- *Binary access files* are graphic files and other non-text files. Binary files can only be accessed in a Binary mode.

Working with Sequential Files

The hard drive of your computer contains hundreds of sequential files. Configuration files, error logs, HTML files, and all sorts of plain text files are all sequential files. These files are stored on disk as a sequence of characters.

The beginning of a new text line is indicated by two special characters: the *carriage return* and the *line feed*. When you work with sequential files, start at the beginning of the file and move forward character by character, line by line, until you encounter the end of the file. Sequential access files can be easily opened and manipulated by just about any text editor.

Reading Data Stored in Sequential Files

Let's take one of the sequential files already present on your computer and read its contents with VBA straight from the Microsoft Excel Visual Basic Editor window. You can read the Autoexec.bat file or any other text file you want. To read data from a file, you must first open the file with the Open statement. Here's the general syntax of this statement, followed by an explanation of each component:

```
Open pathname For mode[Access access][lock] As [#]filenumber [Len=reclength]
```

The Open statement has three required arguments: pathname, mode, and filenumber. In the syntax shown above, these arguments are preceded by keywords that appear in bold.

- Pathname is the name of the file you want to open. The filename may include the name of a drive and folder.
- Mode is a keyword that determines how the file was opened. Sequential files can be opened in one of the following modes: Input, Output, or Append. Use Input to read the file, Output to write to a file overwriting any existing file, and Append to write to a file by adding to any existing information.
- The optional Access clause can be used to specify permissions for the file (Read, Write, or Read Write).
- The optional Lock argument determines which file operations are allowed for other processes. For example, if a file is open in a network environment, lock determines how other people can access it. The following lock keywords can be used: Shared, Lock Read, Lock Write, or Lock Read Write.
- Filenumber is a number from 1 to 511. This number is used to refer to the file in subsequent operations. You can obtain a unique file number using the Visual Basic built-in FreeFile function.
- The last element of the Open statement, reclength, specifies the buffer size (total number of characters) for sequential files, or the record size for random access files.

Taking the preceding into consideration, to open C:\Autoexec.bat or any other sequential file in order to read its data, you should use the following instruction:

```
Open "C:\Autoexec.bat" For Input As #1
```

If a file is opened for input, it can only be read from. After you open a sequential file, you can read its contents with the Line Input # or Input # statements or by using the Input function. When you use sequential access to open a file for input, the file must already exist.

> **What Is a Sequential File?**
>
> A sequential file is one in which the records must be accessed in the order they occur in the file. This means that before you can access the third record, you must first access record number 1 and then record number 2.

Reading a File Line by Line

To read the contents of Autoexec.bat or any other sequential file line by line, use the following Line Input # statement:

```
Line Input #filenumber, variableName
```

#filenumber is the file number that was used in the process of opening the file with the Open statement. The variableName is a String or Variant variable that will store the line being read. The statement Line Input # reads a single line in an open sequential file and stores it in a variable. Bear in mind that the Line Input # statement reads the sequential file one character at a time, until it encounters a carriage return (Chr(13)) or a carriage return-line-feed sequence (Chr(13) & Chr(10)). These characters are omitted from the text retrieved in the reading process.

The ReadMe procedure that follows demonstrates how you can use the Open and Line Input # statements to read the contents of the Win.ini file line by line. Apply the same method for reading other sequential files.

Hands-On 14-1: Reading File Contents with the Open and Line Input # Statements

1. Open a new workbook and save it as C:\Ex07_ByExample\Practice_Excel14.xlsm.
2. Switch to the Visual Basic Editor and use the Properties window to rename VBAProject (Practice_Excel14.xlsm) **FileMan_IO.**
3. Insert a new module in the FileMan_IO project and rename it **SeqFiles**.
4. In the SeqFiles module's Code window, enter the ReadMe procedure shown below:

```
Sub ReadMe(strFileName As String)
    Dim rLine As String
    Dim i As Integer            ' line number

    i = 0

    On Error GoTo ExitHere

    Open strFileName For Input As #1

    ' stay inside the loop until the end of file is reached
        Do While Not EOF(1)
            i = i + 1
            Line Input #1, rLine
            MsgBox "Line " & i & " in " & strFileName & " reads: " _
                & Chr(13) & Chr(13) & rLine
        Loop
    MsgBox i & " lines were read."
    Close #1
    Exit Sub
ExitHere:
    MsgBox "File " & strFileName & " could not be found."
End Sub
```

The ReadMe procedure opens the specified text file in the Input mode as file number 1 in order to read its contents. If the specified file cannot be opened (because it may not exist), Visual Basic jumps to the label ExitHere and displays a message box.

If the file is successfully opened, we can proceed to read its content. The Do...While loop tells Visual Basic to execute the statements inside the loop until the end of the file has been reached. The end of the file is determined by the result of the EOF function. The EOF function returns a logical value of true if the next character to be read is past the end of the file. Notice that the EOF function requires one argument — the number of the open file you want to check. This is the same number used in the Open statement. Use the EOF function to ensure that Visual Basic doesn't read past the end of the file.

The Line Input # statement stores each line's contents in the variable rLine. Next, a message is displayed that shows the line number and its contents. Visual Basic exits the Do...While loop when the result of the EOF function is true. Before VBA ends the procedure, two more statements are executed. A message is displayed with the total number of lines that have been read, and the file is closed.

5. To run the procedure, open the Immediate window, type the following statement, and press **Enter** to execute:

```
ReadMe "C:\Ex07_HandsOn\TestTextFile.txt"
```

Reading Characters from Sequential Files

Suppose that your procedure needs to check how many commas appear in the Win.ini file. Instead of reading entire lines, you can use the Input function to return the specified number of characters. Next, the If statement can be used to compare the obtained character against the one you are looking for. Before you write a procedure that does this, let's review the syntax of the Input function:

```
Input(number, [#]filenumber)
```

Both arguments of the Input function are required; number specifies the number of characters you want to read, and filenumber is the same number that the Open statement used to open the file. The Input function returns all the characters being read, including commas, carriage returns, end of file markers, quotes, and leading spaces.

Hands-On 14-2: Reading Characters from Sequential Files

1. Enter the CountChar procedure below in the SeqFiles module.

```
Sub CountChar(strFileName As String, srchChar As String)
    Dim counter As Integer

counter = 0
    Open strFileName For Input As #1

    Do While Not EOF(1)
        char = Input(1, #1)
        If char = srchChar Then
          counter = counter + 1
        End If
    Loop
    If counter <> 0 Then
      MsgBox "Characters (" & srchChar & ") found: " & counter
    Else
      MsgBox "The specified character (" & srchChar & _
```

```
                ") has not been found."
    End If
    Close #1
End Sub
```

2. To run the procedure, open the Immediate window, type the following statement, and press **Enter** to execute:

```
CountChar "C:\Ex07_HandsOn\TestTextFile.txt", "."
```

3. Run the procedure again after replacing the period character with any other character you'd like to find.

   The Input function allows you to return any character from the sequential file. If you use the Visual Basic function called LOF as the first argument of the Input function, you'll be able to quickly read the contents of the sequential file without having to loop through the entire file. The LOF function returns the number of bytes in a file. Each byte corresponds to one character in a text file. The following ReadAll procedure shows how to read the contents of a sequential file to the Immediate window:

```
Sub ReadAll(strFileName As String)
    Dim all As String

    Open strFileName For Input As #1
    all = Input(LOF(1), #1)
    Debug.Print all
    Close #1
End Sub
```

4. To execute the above procedure, open the Immediate window, type the following statement, and press **Enter**:

```
ReadAll "C:\Ex07_HandsOn\TestTextFile.txt"
```

Instead of printing the file contents to the Immediate window, you can read it into a text box placed in a worksheet (see Figure 14-1). Let's take a few minutes to write this procedure.

Hands-On 14-3: Printing File Contents to a Worksheet Text Box

1. Enter the WriteToTextBox procedure below in the SeqFiles module.

```
Sub WriteToTextBox(strFileName As String)
    Dim sh As Worksheet
    Set sh = ActiveWorkbook.Worksheets(3)

    On Error GoTo CloseFile:

    Open strFileName For Input As #1
    sh.Shapes.AddTextbox(msoTextOrientationHorizontal, _
        10, 10, 300, 200).Select

    Selection.Characters.Text = Input(LOF(1), #1)
CloseFile:
```

```
    Close #1
End Sub
```

Notice that the statement On Error GoTo CloseFile activates error trapping. If an error occurs during the execution of a line of the procedure, the program will jump to the error-handling routine that follows the CloseFile label. The statement Close #1 will be executed, whether or not the program encounters an error. Before the file contents are placed in a worksheet, a text box is added using the AddTextbox method of the Shapes object.

2. To execute the above procedure, open the Immediate window, type the following statement, and press **Enter**:

```
WriteToTextBox "C:\Ex07_HandsOn\TestTextFile.txt"
```

The result should be similar to Figure 14-1.

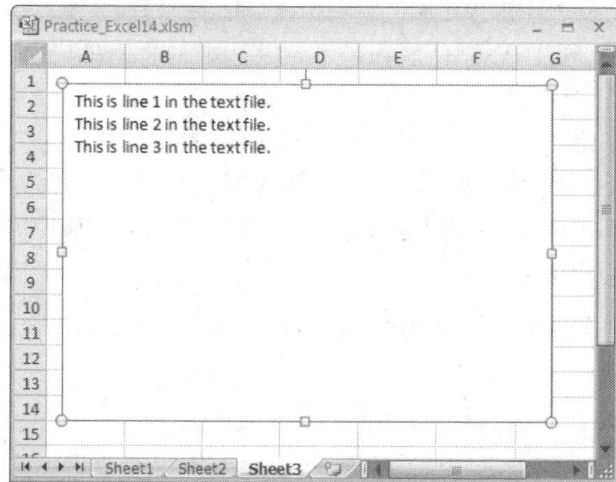

Figure 14-1: The contents of a text file are displayed in a text box placed in an Excel worksheet.

Reading Delimited Text Files

In some text files (usually files saved in CSV, TXT, or PRN format), data entered on each line of text is separated (or delimited) with a comma, tab, or space character. These types of files can be read faster with the Input # statement instead of the Line Input # statement introduced earlier in this chapter. The Input # statement allows you to read data from an open file into several variables. This function looks like the following:

```
Input #filenumber, variablelist
```

The filenumber is the same file number that was used in the Open statement. The variablelist is a comma-separated list of variables that you will want to use to store the data being read. You can't use arrays or object variables. You can, however, use a user-defined variable (this type of variable is explained later in this chapter). An example of a sequential file with comma-delimited values is shown below:

```
Smith,John,15
Malloney,Joanne,28
Ikatama,Robert,15
```

Note that in the example above there are no spaces before or after the commas. To read text formatted in this way, you must specify one variable for each item of data: last name, first name, and age. Let's try it out.

Hands-On 14-4: Reading a Comma-delimited (CSV) File with the Input # Statement

1. Open a new workbook and enter the data shown below in a worksheet:

	A	B	C	D
1	Smith	John	15	
2	Malloney	Joanne	28	
3	Ikatama	Robert	15	

Figure 14-2: You can create a comma-delimited file from an Excel workbook.

2. Click the **Microsoft Office** button, and then click **Save As**. Switch to the **C:\Ex07_ByExample** folder. In the Save as type drop-down box, select **CSV (Comma delimited) (*.csv)**. Change the filename to **Winners.csv** and click **Save**.
3. Excel will display a message that the selected file type does not support workbooks that contain multiple sheets. Click **OK** to save only the current sheet. Click **Yes** to keep the workbook in comma-delimited format.
4. Close the Winners.csv file.
5. Activate the Practice_Excel14.xlsm workbook and switch to the Visual Basic Editor.
6. In the Project Explorer window, double-click the SeqFiles module in the FileMan_IO project and enter the Winners procedure as shown below:

```
Sub Winners()
    Dim lname As String
    Dim fname As String
    Dim age As Integer

    Open "C:\Ex07_ByExample\Winners.csv" For Input As #1
    Do While Not EOF(1)
        Input #1, lname, fname, age
        MsgBox lname & ", " & fname & ", " & age
    Loop
    Close #1
End Sub
```

   The above procedure opens the Winners.csv file for input and sets up a Do...While loop that runs through the entire file until the end of file is reached. The Input #1 statement is used to write the contents of each line of text into three variables: lname, fname, and age. Then a message box displays the contents of these variables. The procedure ends by closing the Winners.csv file.

7. Run the Winners procedure.

Writing Data to Sequential Files

When you want to write data to a sequential file, you should open the file in the Append or Output mode. The differences between these modes are explained below:

- Append mode — This mode allows adding data to the end of an existing text file. For example, if you open the Readme.txt file in Append mode and add to this file the text "Thank you for reading this document," Visual Basic won't delete or alter the text that is currently in the file but will add the new text to the end of the file.
- Output mode — When you open a file in Output mode, Visual Basic will delete the data that is currently in the file. If the file does not exist, a brand-new file will be created. For example, if you open the Readme.txt file in Output mode and attempt to write some text to it, the previous text that was stored in this file will be removed. If you don't back up the file prior to writing the data, this mistake may be quite costly. *You should open an existing file in Output mode only if you want to replace its entire contents with new data.*

Here are some examples of when to open a file in Append mode or Output mode:

- To create a brand-new text file called C:\Ex07_ByExample\Readme.txt, open the file in Output mode as follows:

```
Open "C:\Ex07_ByExample\Readme.txt" For Output As #1
```

- To add new text to the end of C:\Ex07_ByExample\Readme.txt, open the file in Append mode as follows:

```
Open "C:\Ex07_ByExample\Readme.txt" For Append As #1
```

- To replace the contents of an existing file C:\Ex07_ByExample\Winners.csv with a list of new winners, first prepare a backup copy of the original file, then open the original file in Output mode:

```
FileCopy "C:\Ex07_ByExample\Winners.csv","C:\Ex07_ByExample\Winners.old"
Open "C:\Ex07_ByExample\Winners.csv" For Output As #1
```

Can't Read and Write at the Same Time

You cannot perform read and write operations simultaneously on an open sequential file. The file must be opened separately for each operation. For instance, after data has been written to a file that has been opened for output, the file must be closed before being opened for input.

Advantages and Disadvantages of Sequential Files

Although sequential files are easy to create and use, and don't waste any space, they have a number of disadvantages. For example, you can't easily find one specific item in the file without having to read through a large portion of the file. Also, you must rewrite the entire file to change or delete an individual item in the file. And as stated above, sequential files have to be opened for reading, and again for writing.

Using Write # and Print # Statements

Now that you know both methods (Append or Output) for opening a text file with the intention of writing to it, it's time to learn the Write # and Print # statements that will allow you to send data to the file.

When you read data from a sequential file with the Input # statement, you usually write data to this file with the Write # statement. This statement looks like this:

```
Write #filenumber, [outputlist]
```

The filenumber specifies the number of the file you're working with. It is the only required argument of the Write # statement. The outputlist is the text you want to write to the file. The outputlist can be a single text string or a list of variables that contain data that you want to write. If you specify only the filenumber, Visual Basic will write a single empty line to the open file.

To illustrate how data is written to a file, let's prepare a text file with the first name, last name, birthdate, and the number of siblings for three people.

Hands-On 14-5: Using the Write # Statement to Write Data to a File

1. In the SeqFiles module, enter the DataEntry procedure as shown below:

```
Sub DataEntry()
    Dim lname As String
    Dim fname As String
    Dim birthdate As Date
    Dim sib As Integer

    Open "C:\Ex07_ByExample\Friends.txt" For Output As #1
    lname = "Smith"
    fname = "Gregory"
    birthdate = #1/2/1963#
    sib = 3
    Write #1, lname, fname, birthdate, sib

    lname = "Conlin"
    fname = "Janice"
    birthdate = #5/12/1948#
    sib = 1
    Write #1, lname, fname, birthdate, sib

    lname = "Kaufman"
    fname = "Steven"
    birthdate = #4/7/1957#
    sib = 0
    Write #1, lname, fname, birthdate, sib

    Close #1
End Sub
```

The above procedure opens the C:\Ex07_ByExample\Friends.txt file for output. Because this file does not yet exist on your hard disk, Visual Basic creates a brand-new file and writes three records to it. The data written to the file is stored in variables. Notice that the strings are delimited with double quotes ("") and the birthdate is surrounded by pound signs (#).

2. Run the DataEntry procedure.
3. Locate the Friends.txt file created by the DataEntry procedure and open it using Windows Notepad.

   The Friends.txt file opened in Notepad looks as follows:

```
"Smith","Gregory",#1963-01-02#,3
"Conlin","Janice",#1948-05-12#,1
"Kaufman","Steven",#1957-04-07#,0
```

   The Write # statement in the DataEntry procedure automatically inserted commas between the individual data items in each record and placed the carriage return-linefeed sequence (Chr(13) & Chr(10)) at the end of each line of text so that each new record starts in a new line. In the above example, each line of text shows one record — each record begins with the last name and ends with the number of siblings.

   If instead of separating data with commas you'd rather show the contents of a file in columns, write the data with the Print # statement. For example, if you replace the Write # statement in the DataEntry procedure with the Print # statement, Visual Basic will write the data in the following way:

```
Smith Gregory 1/2/63 3
Conlin Janice 5/12/48 1
Kaufman Steven 4/7/57 0
```

Although the Print # statement has the same syntax as the Write # statement, Print # writes data to the sequential file in a format ready for printing. The variables in the list may be separated with semicolons or spaces. To print out several spaces, you should use the Spc(*n*) instruction, where *n* is the number of spaces. Similarly, to enter a word in the fifth column, you should use the instruction Tab(5). Let's look at some formatting examples:

- To add an empty line to a file, use the Write # statement with a comma: Write #1,
- To enter the text "fruits" in the fifth column: Write #1, Tab(5); "fruits"
- To separate the words "fruits" and "vegetables" with five spaces: Write #1, "fruits"; Spc(5); "vegetables"

Working with Random Access Files

When a file contains structured data, open the file in random access mode. A file opened for random access allows you to:

- Read and write data at the same time
- Quickly access a particular record

In random access files, all records are of equal length, and each record has the same number of fixed size fields. The length of a record or field must be determined prior to writing data to the file. If the length of a string that is being written to a field is less than the specified size of the field, Visual Basic automatically enters spaces at the end of the string to fill in the entire size of the field. If the text being written is longer than the size of the field, the text that does not fit will be truncated.

What Is a Random Access File?

A random access file is one in which data is stored in records that can be accessed without having to read every record preceding it.

To find out how to work with random access files, let's create a small database for use in a foreign language study. This database will contain records made up of two fields: an English term and its foreign language equivalent.

Hands-On 14-6: Creating a Random Access Database with a User-defined Data Type

1. Insert a new module into the FileMan_IO project in Practice_Excel14.xls, and rename it **RandomFiles**.
2. Enter the following statements just below the Option Explicit statement at the top of the RandomFiles module:

```
' create a user-defined data type called Dictionary
Type Dictionary
    en As String * 16 ' English word up to 16 characters
    sp As String * 20 ' Spanish word up to 20 characters
End Type
```

   In addition to the built-in data types introduced in Chapter 4 (see Table 4-1), Visual Basic allows you to define a nonstandard data type using a Type…End Type statement placed at the top of the module. This nonstandard data type is often referred to as a user-defined data type. The user-defined data type can contain items of various data types (String, Integer, Date, and so on). When you work with files opened for random access, you often create a user-defined variable because such a variable provides you with easy access to the individual fields of a record.

   The user-defined type called Dictionary that you just defined contains two items declared as String with the specified size. The en item can accept up to 16 characters. The size of the second item (sp) cannot exceed 20 characters. By adding up the lengths of both of these items, you will get a record length of 36 characters (16 + 20).

Understanding the Type Statement

The Type command allows you to create a custom group of mixed variable types called a "user-defined data type." This statement is generally used with random access files to store data as fields within records of a fixed size. Instead of declaring a separate variable for each field, cluster the fields into a user-defined variable using the Type statement. For example, define a record containing three fields in the following way:

```
Type MyRecord
     country As String * 20
     city As String * 14
     rank As Integer
End Type
```

Once the general type is defined, you must give a name to the particular variable that will be of that type:

```
Dim myInfo As MyRecord
```

Access the interior variables (country, city, rank) by using the following format:

```
Variable_name.Interior_variable_name
```

For example, to specify the city, enter:

```
MyInfo.city = "Warsaw"
```

3. Enter the EnglishToSpanish procedure as shown below:

```
Sub EnglishToSpanish()
    Dim d As Dictionary
    Dim recNr As Long
    Dim choice As String
    Dim totalRec As Long

    recNr = 1
    ' open the file for random access
    Open "C:\Ex07_ByExample\Translate.txt" _
        For Random As #1 Len = Len(d)

    Do
        ' get the English word
        choice = InputBox("Enter an English word", "ENGLISH")
        d.en = choice
        ' exit the loop if cancelled
        If choice = "" Then Exit Do
        choice = InputBox("Enter the Spanish equivalent of " _
            & d.en, "SPANISH EQUIVALENT  " & d.en)
        If choice = "" Then Exit Do
        d.sp = choice

        ' write to the record
        Put #1, recNr, d
        ' increase record counter
        recNr = recNr + 1
    'ask for words until Cancel
    Loop Until choice = ""

    totalRec = LOF(1) / Len(d)
    MsgBox "This file contains " & totalRec & " record(s)."
    ' close the file
    Close #1
End Sub
```

The EnglishToSpanish procedure begins with the declaration of four variables. The variable d is declared as a user-defined type called Dictionary. This type was declared earlier with the Type statement (see step 2 above).

After the initial value is assigned to the variable RecNr, Visual Basic opens the Translate.txt file for random access as file number 1. The Len(d) instruction tells Visual Basic that the size of each record is 36 characters. (The variable d contains two elements: sp is 20 characters, and en is 16 characters. Consequently, the total size of a record is 36 characters.) Next, Visual Basic executes the statements inside the Do...Until loop.

The first statement in the loop prompts you to enter an English word, and assigns it to the variable choice. The value of this item is then passed to the first element of the user-defined variable d (d.en). When you cancel or stop entering data, Visual Basic exits the Do loop and executes the final statements in the procedure that calculate and display the total number of records in the file. The last statement closes the file.

If you enter an English word and click OK, you will be prompted to supply a foreign language equivalent. If you do not enter a word, Visual Basic will exit the loop and continue with the remaining statements. If you do enter the foreign language equivalent, Visual Basic will assign it to the variable choice and then pass it to the second element of the user-defined variable d (d.sp). Next, Visual Basic will write the entire record to the file using the following statement:

```
Put #1, recNr, d
```

After writing the first record, Visual Basic will increase the record counter by one and repeat the statements inside the loop. The EnglishToSpanish procedure allows you to enter any number of records into your dictionary. When you quit supplying the words, the procedure uses the LOF and Len functions to calculate the total number of records in the file, and displays the message:

```
"This file contains " & totalRec & " record(s)."
```

After displaying the message, Visual Basic closes the text file (Translate.txt). Creating a random access file is only the beginning. Next, we create the VocabularyDrill procedure to illustrate how to work with records in a file opened for random access. Here you will learn statements that allow you to quickly find the appropriate data in your file.

4. Run the EnglishToSpanish procedure. When prompted, enter data as shown in Figure 14-3. For example, enter the word **mother**. When prompted for a Spanish equivalent of mother, enter **madre**.

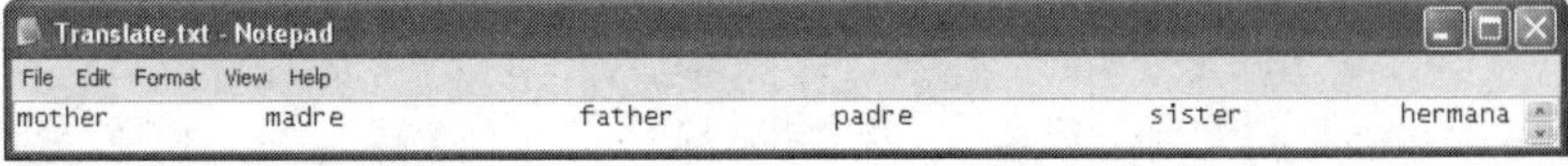

Figure 14-3: The contents of a random access file opened in Notepad.

5. Below the EnglishToSpanish procedure, enter the VocabularyDrill procedure as shown below:

```
Sub VocabularyDrill()
    Dim d As Dictionary
    Dim totalRec As Long
    Dim recNr As Long
    Dim randomNr As Long
    Dim question As String
    Dim answer As String

    ' open a random access file
    Open "C:\Ex07_ByExample\Translate.txt" _
        For Random As #1 Len = Len(d)

    ' print the total number of bytes in this file
    Debug.Print "There are " & LOF(1) & " bytes in this file."

    ' find and print the total number of records
    recNr = LOF(1) / Len(d)
    Debug.Print "Total number of records: " & recNr

    Do
        ' get a random record number
        randomNr = Int(recNr * Rnd) + 1
        Debug.Print randomNr

        ' find the random record
        Seek #1, randomNr

        ' read the record
        Get #1, randomNr, d
        Debug.Print Trim(d.en); " "; Trim(d.sp)

        ' assign answer to a variable
        answer = InputBox("What's the Spanish equivalent?", d.en)

        ' finish if cancelled
        If answer = "" Then Close #1: Exit Sub
        Debug.Print answer
            ' check if the answer is correct
            If answer = Trim(d.sp) Then
                MsgBox "Congratulations!"
            Else
                MsgBox "Invalid Answer!!!"
            End If
    ' keep on asking questions until Cancel is pressed
    Loop While answer <> ""

    ' close file
    Close #1
End Sub
```

After declaring variables, the VocabularyDrill procedure opens a file for random access and tells Visual Basic the length of each record: Len = Len(d). Next, two statements print in the Immediate window the total number of bytes and records in the open file. The number of bytes is returned by the LOF(1) statement. The number of records is computed by dividing the entire file (LOF) by the length of one record — Len(d). Next, Visual Basic executes the statements inside the loop until Esc is pressed or Cancel is clicked.

The first statement in the loop assigns the result of the Rnd function to the variable randomNr. The next statement writes this number to the Immediate window. The instruction:

```
Seek #1, randomNr
```

moves the cursor in the open file to the record number specified by the variable randomNr. The next instruction reads the contents of the found record. To read the data in a file opened for random access, you must use the Get statement.

The instruction:

```
Get #1, randomNr, d
```

tells Visual Basic the record number (randomNr) to read and the variable (d) into which data is being read. The first record in a random access file is at position 1, the second record at position 2, and so on. *Omitting a record number causes Visual Basic to read the next record.* The values of both elements of the user-defined type dictionary are then written to the Immediate window. The Trim(d.en) and Trim(d.sp) functions print the values of the record being read without the leading and trailing spaces that the user may have entered.

Next, Visual Basic displays an input box with a prompt to supply the foreign language equivalent of the word shown in the input box title. The word is assigned to the variable answer. If you press Esc instead of clicking OK, Visual Basic closes the file and ends the procedure. Otherwise, Visual Basic prints your answer to the Immediate window and notifies you whether or not your answer is correct. You can press Esc or click the Cancel button in the dialog box whenever you want to quit the vocabulary drill.

If you decide to continue and click OK, a new random number will be generated, and the program will retrieve the English word and ask you for the Spanish equivalent.

You can modify the VocabularyDrill procedure so that every incorrectly translated word is written to a worksheet. Also, you may want to write all the records from the Translate.txt file to a worksheet so that you always know the contents of your dictionary.

6. Run the VocabularyDrill procedure. When prompted, type the Spanish equivalent of the English word shown in the title bar of the input box. Press **Cancel** to exit the vocabulary drill.
7. Press **Alt+F11** to activate the Microsoft Excel application screen.

   Steps 8-9 demonstrate the process of opening random access files in Excel.

8. Click the **Microsoft Office** button, and then click **Open**. Switch to the **C:\Ex07_ByExample** folder. Select **All Files (*.*)** in the Files of type drop-down box, and double-click the **Translate.txt** file. Excel displays the Text Import Wizard as shown in Figure 14-4.

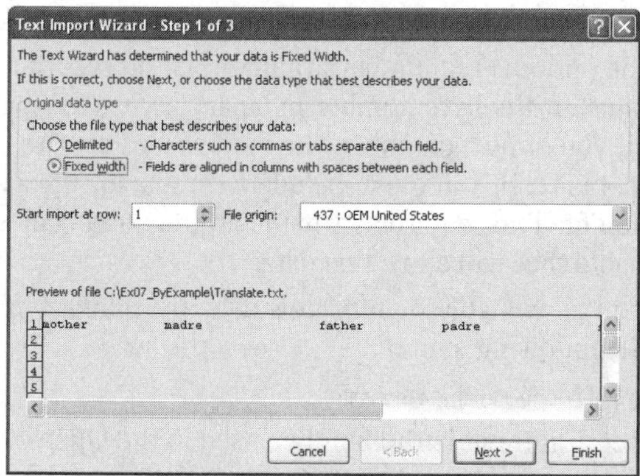

Figure 14-4: The contents of a random access file on attempt to open it with Microsoft Excel. Notice that Excel correctly recognizes the original data type — the data in a random access file is fixed width.

9. Click **Finish** to load your translation data file into Excel.
10. Close the Translate.txt file.

Advantages and Disadvantages of Random Access Files

Unlike sequential files, data stored in random access files can be accessed very quickly. Also, these files don't need to be closed before writing into them and reading from them, and they don't need to be read or written to in order. Random access files also have some disadvantages. For example, they often store the data inefficiently. Because they have fixed-length fields and records, the same number of bytes is used regardless of the number of characters being stored. So if some fields are left blank or contain strings shorter than the declared field size, you may waste a lot of space.

Working with Binary Files

Unlike random access files that store data in records of fixed length, binary files store records with variable lengths. For example, the first record may contain 10 bytes, the second record may have only 5 bytes, while the third record may have 15 bytes. This method of storing data saves a lot of disk space, because Visual Basic doesn't need to add additional spaces to the stored string to ensure that all the fields are of the same length.

Just like random access files, binary files can be opened for simultaneous read and write operations. However, because binary file records are of variable length, it is more difficult to manipulate these files. In order to retrieve the data correctly, you must store information about the size of each field and record.

To work with binary files, you will use the following four statements:

- The Get statement is used to read data. This statement has the following syntax:

  ```
  Get [#]filenumber, [recnumber], varname
  ```

  The filenumber argument is the number used in the Open statement to open a file. The optional recnumber argument is the record number in random access files, or the byte number in binary access files, at which reading begins. If you omit recnumber, the next record or byte after the last Get statement is read. You must include a comma for the skipped recnumber argument. The required varname argument specifies the name of the variable that will store this data.

- The Put statement allows you to enter new data into a binary file. This statement has the following syntax:

  ```
  Put [#]filenumber, [recnumber], varname
  ```

  The filenumber argument is the number used in the Open statement to open a file. The optional recnumber argument is the record number in random access files, or the byte number in binary access files, at which writing begins. If you omit recnumber, the next record or byte after the last Put statement is written. You must include a comma for the skipped recnumber argument. The required varname argument specifies the name of the variable containing data to be written to disk.

- The Loc statement returns the number of the last byte that was read. (In random access files, the Loc statement returns the number of the record that was last read.)

- The Seek statement moves the cursor to the appropriate position inside the file.

To quickly master the usage of the above statements, let's open the Immediate window and enter instructions shown in the left column of the table below. The purpose of this exercise is to enter your first and last name in a binary file called C:\Ex07_ByExample\MyData.txt and then retrieve the information you entered.

Hands-On 14-7: Mastering the Get and Put Statements

Enter in the Immediate window:	Explanation
Open "C:\Ex07_ByExample\MyData.txt" For Binary As #1	Open the file MyData.txt for binary access as file number 1. Be sure to type this statement on one line in the Immediate window.
MsgBox "Total bytes: " & LOF(1)	Show the number of bytes on opening the file. (The file is currently empty.)
fname = "Julitta"	Assign a value to the variable fname.
ln = len(fname)	Assign to the variable ln the length of the string stored in the variable fname.

Enter in the Immediate window:	Explanation
Put #1, , ln	Enter the value of the variable ln in the binary file in the position of the next byte.
MsgBox "The last byte: " & LOC(1)	Display the position of the last byte.
Put #1, , fname	Enter the contents of the variable fname in the next position.
lname = "Korol"	Assign a value to the variable lname.
ln = len(lname)	Assign to the variable ln the length of the string stored in the variable lname.
Put #1, , ln	Enter the value of the variable ln in the binary file in the position of the next byte.
Put #1, , lname	Enter the contents of the variable lname in the next byte position.
MsgBox "The last byte: " & LOC(1)	Display the position of the last byte.
Get #1, 1, entry1	Read the value stored in the position of the first byte and assign it to the variable entry1.
MsgBox entry1	Display the contents of the variable entry1.
Get #1, , entry2	Read the next value and assign it to the variable entry2.
MsgBox entry2	Display the contents of the variable entry2.
Get #1, , entry3	Read the next value and store it in the variable entry3.
MsgBox entry3	Display the contents of the variable entry3.
Get #1, , entry4	Read the next value and store it in the variable entry4.
MsgBox entry4	Display the contents of the variable entry4.
Debug.Print entry1;entry2;entry3;entry4	Print all the data in the Immediate window.
7 Julitta 5 Korol	The result of the previous instruction as displayed in the Immediate window.
Close #1	Close the file.

When entering data to a binary file, use the following guidelines:

- Before writing a string to a binary file, assign the length of the string to an Integer type variable. Usually the following block of instructions can be used:

```
string_length = Len(variable_name)
Put #1, , string_length
Put #1, , variable_name
```

- When reading data from binary files, first read the string length and then the string contents. To do this, use the Get statement and the String function:

```
Get #1, , string_length
variable_name=String(string_length, " ")
Get #1, , variable_name
```

Advantages and Disadvantages of Binary Access Files

In comparison with sequential and random access files, binary files are the smallest of all. Because they use variable-length records, they can conserve disk space. Like files opened for random access, you can simultaneously read and write to a file opened for binary access. One big disadvantage of binary access files is that you must know precisely how the data is stored in the file to retrieve or manipulate it correctly.

Chapter Summary

This chapter has given you a working knowledge of writing to and retrieving data from three types of files: sequential, random access, and binary.

The next chapter introduces you to more automating tasks. You will learn, for example, how to use VBA to control other applications. You will also learn various methods of starting applications, and find out how to manipulate them directly from Microsoft Excel.

Part VI

Controlling Other Applications with VBA

The VBA programming language goes beyond Excel. It is used by other Office applications such as Word, PowerPoint, Outlook, and Access and is also supported by a growing number of non-Microsoft products. The VBA skills you acquire in Excel can be used to program any application that supports this language.

In this part of the book, you learn how other applications expose their objects to VBA.

Chapter 15

Using Excel VBA to Interact with Other Applications

One of the nicest things about the VBA language is that you can use it to launch and control other Office applications. For example, you can create or open a Word document straight from your VBA procedure without ever leaving Excel or seeing the Word user interface. You can also start and manipulate a number of non-Office programs by using built-in VBA functions. This chapter shows you various methods of launching other programs and transferring data between them.

Launching Applications

There's more than one way to launch an application. In fact, there are at least five ways you can manually start a program: via the Start | Programs menu, a shortcut menu, the Run command, the MS-DOS window, or by double-clicking an executable file in Windows Explorer.

This section assumes that you are familiar with the manual techniques of launching applications and that you are anxious to experiment with additional techniques to start applications by writing code.

Let's begin with the simplest of all — the Shell function. This function allows you to start any program directly from a VBA procedure. Suppose that your procedure must open the Windows Notepad application. To launch Notepad, all you need is one statement between the keywords Sub and End Sub. Or better yet, you can type the following statement in the Immediate window and press Enter to see the result immediately:

```
Shell "notepad.exe", vbMaximizedFocus
```

In the above statement, notepad.exe is the name of the program you want to start. This name should include the complete path (the drive and folder name) if you have any concerns that the program may not be found. Notice that the program name is in double quotes. The second argument of the Shell function is optional. This argument specifies the window style (that is, how the program will appear once it is launched). In the above example, Notepad will appear in a maximized window. If the window style is not specified, the program will be minimized with focus (see Table 15-1).

Table 15-1: Window styles used in the Shell function

Window Style Constant	Value	Window Appearance
vbHide	0	Hidden
vbNormalFocus	1	Normal size with focus
vbMinimizedFocus (default setting)	2	Minimized with focus (this is the default setting)
vbMaximizedFocus	3	Maximized with focus
vbNormalNoFocus	4	Normal without focus
vbMinimizedNoFocus	6	Minimized without focus

If the Shell function is successful in launching the specified executable file, it will return a number called a Task ID. This number uniquely identifies the application that has been launched. If the Shell function is unsuccessful (that is, it cannot start the specified program), Visual Basic generates an error. The Shell function works *asynchronously*. That means that Visual Basic starts the program specified by the Shell function, and immediately after launching, it returns to the procedure to continue with the execution of the remaining instructions (therefore not giving you a chance to work with the application). If you want to work with the program launched by the Shell function, do not enter any other statements in the procedure after the Shell function.

Let's see how to use the Shell function to launch the Control Panel.

Hands-On 15-1: Using the Shell Function to Activate the Control Panel

1. Open a new workbook and save it as **C:\Ex07_ByExample\Practice_Excel15.xlsm**.
2. Switch to the Visual Basic Editor window and insert a new module in the Practice_Excel15.xlsm VBA project.
3. Rename the VBA project **WorkWApplets**, and change the module name to **Shell_Function**.
4. In the Shell_Function Code window, enter the StartPanel procedure as shown below:

```
Sub StartPanel()
    Shell "Control.exe", vbNormalFocus
End Sub
```

5. Run the above procedure.

   When you run the StartPanel procedure the Control Panel window is opened automatically on top of any other windows. The Control Panel contains a number of tools represented by individual icons. As you know, there is a program behind every icon that is activated when the user double-clicks the icon or selects the icon with the arrow keys and then presses Enter. As a rule, you can check what filename is driven by a particular icon by looking at the icon's properties. Unfortunately, the icons in the Control Panel have the Properties option disabled. You can, however, find out the name of the Control Panel file by creating a shortcut. For example, before you create a procedure that changes the regional settings in your computer, let's find out the name of the file that activates this tool.

6. In the Control Panel window, right-click the **Regional and Language Options** icon and choose **Create Shortcut** from the shortcut menu.
7. Click **Yes** to place the shortcut on the desktop.
8. Close the Control Panel window.
9. Switch to your desktop and right-click the **Shortcut to Regional and Language Options** icon. Next, choose **Properties** from the shortcut menu.

10. In the Properties window, click the **Shortcut** tab and then click the **Change Icon** button to bring up the Change Icon window.

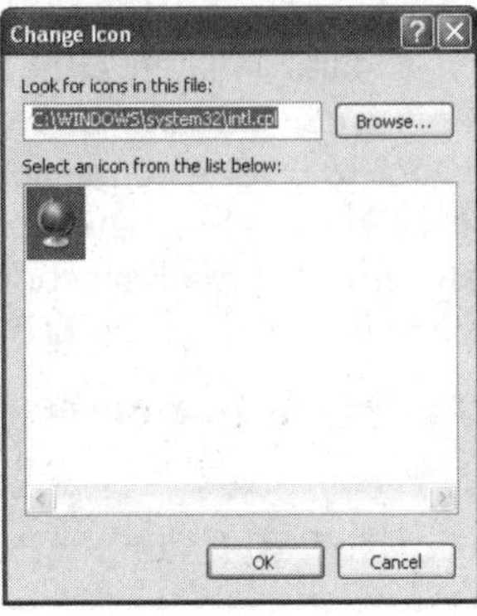

Figure 15-1: Each Control Panel tool icon file has a .cpl extension.

11. Write down the name of the CPL file (Control Panel Library) or DLL file (Dynamic Link Library) listed at the top of the Change Icon window and close all the windows that were opened in this exercise.

Table 15-2: Some of the files that activate Control Panel tools

Icon in the Control Panel	CPL or DLL File
Phone and Modem Options	telephon.cpl or modem.cpl
Add/Remove Programs	appwiz.cpl
Network and Dial-up Connections	netcpl.cpl or netshell.dll
32-Bit ODBC	odbccp32.cpl
System	sysdm.cpl
Mail	mlcfg32.cpl
Users and Passwords	password.cpl or netplwiz.dll
Date/Time	timedate.cpl
Regional Options	intl.cpl
Internet Options	inetcpl.cpl
Sounds and Multimedia Properties	mmsys.cpl
Display	desk.cpl
Mouse	main.cpl

12. In the ShellFunction Code window, enter the ChangeSettings procedure as shown below:

```
Sub ChangeSettings()
    Dim nrTask
    nrTask = Shell("Control.exe intl.cpl", vbMinimizedFocus)
    Debug.Print nrTask
End Sub
```

The ChangeSettings procedure demonstrates how to launch the Control Panel's Regional Settings icon using the Shell function. Notice that the arguments of the Shell function must appear in parentheses if you want to use the returned value later in your procedure.

13. Run the ChangeSettings procedure several times, each time supplying a different CPL file according to the listing presented in Table 15-2 above. You may want to modify the above procedure as follows:

```
Sub ChangeSettings2()
    Dim nrTask
    Dim iconFile As String
    iconFile = InputBox("Enter the name of the control " & _
         "icon CPL or DLL file:")
    nrTask = Shell("Control.exe " & iconFile, vbMinimizedFocus)
    Debug.Print nrTask
End Sub
```

If a program you want to launch is a Microsoft application, it's more convenient to use the Visual Basic ActivateMicrosoftApp method rather than the Shell function. This method is available from the Microsoft Excel Application object. For example, to launch PowerPoint from the Immediate window, all you need to do is type the following instruction and press Enter:

```
Application.ActivateMicrosoftApp xlMicrosoftPowerPoint
```

Notice that the ActivateMicrosoftApp method requires a constant to indicate which program to start. The above statement starts Microsoft PowerPoint if it is not already running. If the program is already open, this instruction does not open a new occurrence of the program; it simply activates the already running application. You can use the constants shown in Table 15-3 with the ActivateMicrosoftApp method.

Table 15-3: ActivateMicrosoftApp method constants

Application Name	Constant
Access	xlMicrosoftAccess
FoxPro	xlMicrosoftFoxPro
Mail	xlMicrosoftMail
PowerPoint	xlMicrosoftPowerPoint
Project	xlMicrosoftProject
Schedule	xlMicrosoftSchedulePlus
Word	xlMicrosoftWord

Moving between Applications

Because the user can work simultaneously with several applications in the Windows environment, your VBA procedure must know how to switch between the open programs. Suppose that in addition to Microsoft Excel, you have two other applications open: Microsoft Word and Windows Explorer. To activate an already open program, use the AppActivate statement using the following syntax:

```
AppActivate title [, wait]
```

Only the title argument is required. This is the name of the application as it appears in the title bar of the active application window or its task ID number as returned by the Shell function.

The wait argument is optional. This is a Boolean value (True/False) that specifies when Visual Basic activates the application. The value of False in this position immediately activates the specified application, even if the calling application does not have the focus. If you place True in the position of the wait argument, the calling application waits until it has the focus. Then it activates the specified application.

For example, here's how you can activate Microsoft Word:

```
AppActivate "Microsoft Word"
```

Notice that the name of the application is surrounded by double quotation marks. You can also use the return value of the Shell function as the argument of the AppActivate statement:

```
' run Microsoft Word
ReturnValue = Shell("C:\Program Files\Microsoft Office\Office12\WinWord.exe",1)
' activate Microsoft Word
AppActivate ReturnValue
```

The AppActivate statement is used for moving between applications and requires that the program is already running. This statement merely changes the focus. The specified application becomes the active window. The AppActivate statement will not start an application running.

Controlling Another Application

Now that you know how to use VBA statements to start a program and switch between applications, let's see how one application can communicate with another. The simplest way for an application to get control of another is by means of the SendKeys statement. This statement allows you to send a series of keystrokes to the active application window. You can send a key or a combination of keys and achieve the same result as if you worked directly in the active application window using the keyboard. The SendKeys statement looks as follows:

```
SendKeys string [, wait]
```

The required argument, string, is the key or key combination that you want to send to the active application. For example, to send a letter "f," use the following instruction:

```
SendKeys "f"
```

To send the key combination Alt+f, use:

```
SendKeys "%f"
```

The percent sign (%) is the symbol used for the Alt key.

To send a combination of keys, such as Shift+Tab, use the following statement:

```
SendKeys "+{TAB}"
```

The plus sign (+) denotes the Shift key.

To send other keys and combinations of keys, see Table 15-4.

The SendKeys statement's second argument, wait, is optional. Wait is a logical value that is True or False. If False (default), Visual Basic returns to the procedure immediately upon sending the keystrokes. If wait is True, Visual Basic returns to the procedure only after the sent keystrokes have been executed.

To send characters that aren't displayed when you press a key, use the codes in Table 15-4. Remember to enclose these codes in quotes. For example:

```
SendKeys "{BACKSPACE}"
```

Table 15-4: Keycodes used with the SendKeys statement

Key	Code
Backspace	{BACKSPACE}{BS}{BKSP}
Break	{BREAK}
Caps Lock	{CAPSLOCK}
Del or Delete	{DELETE}{DEL}
Down Arrow	{DOWN}
End	{END}
Enter	{ENTER} or ~
Esc	{ESC}
Help	{HELP}
Home	{HOME}
Ins or Insert	{INSERT}{INS}
Left Arrow	{LEFT}
Num Lock	{NUMLOCK}
Page Down	{PGDN}
Page Up	{PGUP}
Print Screen	{PRTSC}
Right Arrow	{RIGHT}
Scroll Lock	{SCROLLLOCK}
Tab	{TAB}
Up Arrow	{UP}
F1	{F1}
F2	{F2}
F3	{F3}
F4	{F4}
F5	{F5}
F6	{F6}
F7	{F7}
F8	{F8}
F9	{F9}

Key	Code
F10	{F10}
F11	{F11}
F12	{F12}
F13	{F13}
F14	{F14}
F15	{F15}
F16	{F16}
Shift	+
Ctrl	^
Alt	%

You can only send keystrokes to applications that were designed for the Microsoft Windows operating system.

SendKeys and Reserved Characters

Some characters have a special meaning when used with the SendKeys statement. These keys are: plus sign (+), caret (^), tilde (~), and parentheses ( ). To send these characters to another application, you must enclose them in braces {}. To send braces, enter {{} and {}}.

Earlier in this chapter you learned that CPL files launch various Control Panel icons. Let's create a VBA procedure that locates on your computer all the files with the .cpl extension. The example procedure uses keystrokes that work under Windows XP. For Windows 2000 and Windows Vista, you will need to revise the procedure to make it work.

Hands-On 15-2: Using the SendKeys Statement in a VBA Procedure

1. Insert a new module into the WorkWApplets (Practice_Excel15.xlsm) project and rename it **SendKeysStatement**.
2. Enter the FindCPLFiles procedure, as shown below:

```
Sub FindCPLFiles()
' The keystrokes are for Windows XP
Shell "Explorer", vbMaximizedFocus

' delay the execution by 5 seconds
Application.Wait (Now + TimeValue("0:00:05"))

' Activate the Search window
SendKeys "{F3}", True

' delay the execution by 5 seconds
Application.Wait (Now + TimeValue("0:00:05"))
```

```
    ' move the pointer to All files and Folder in
    ' Search Companion toolbar

    SendKeys "{Tab}{Tab}{ENTER}", True

    ' type in the search string
    SendKeys "*.cpl", True

    ' move to the Look in drop-down box
    SendKeys "{Tab}{Tab}", True

    ' change to the root directory
    SendKeys "C:\", True

    ' execute the Search
    SendKeys "{ENTER}", True

End Sub
```

After activating Windows Explorer with the Shell statement, the procedure uses a number of keystrokes from Table 15-4 to perform operations in the active application.

3. Switch to the Microsoft Excel application window and run the FindCPLFiles procedure (use **Alt+F8** to open the Macro dialog, highlight the name of the procedure, and then click **Run**).

   Observe what happens in the My Documents window as your VBA procedure sends keystrokes that activate the Search function. The result of this procedure is the Search Results window with a list of Control Panel files with the extension .cpl.

SendKeys Statement Is Case Sensitive

When you send keystrokes with the SendKeys statement, bear in mind that you must distinguish between lower- and uppercase characters. Therefore, to send the key combination Ctrl+d, you must use ^d, and to send Ctrl+Shift+d, you should use the following string: ^+d.

Other Methods of Controlling Applications

Although you can pass commands to another program by using the SendKeys statement, to gain full control of another application you must resort to other methods. There are two standard ways in which applications can communicate with one another. The newest method, known as Automation, allows you to access and manipulate the objects of another application. Through Automation you can write VBA procedures that control other applications by referencing another application's objects, properties, and methods. The old data-exchange technology called DDE (Dynamic Data Exchange) is a protocol that allows you to dynamically send data between two programs by creating a special channel for sending and receiving information. DDE is quite slow and difficult to work with. DDE should be used only if you need to communicate with an older application that does not support Automation. DDE is not covered in this book.

In the remaining sections of this chapter, you will learn how to control another application via Automation.

Understanding Automation

When you communicate with another application, you may require more functionality than simply activating it for sending keystrokes. For example, you may want to create and manipulate objects within that application. You can embed an entire Word document in a Microsoft Excel spreadsheet. Because both Excel and Word support Automation, you can write a VBA procedure in Excel to manipulate Word objects, such as documents or paragraphs. The applications that support Automation are called *Automation servers* or *Automation objects*. The applications that can manipulate a server's objects are referred to as *Automation controllers*. Some applications can be only a server or a controller, and others can act in both of these roles. All Microsoft Office 2000/2002/2003/2007 applications can act as Automation servers and controllers. The Automation controllers can be all sorts of ActiveX objects installed on your computer.

Understanding Linking and Embedding

Before you learn how to control other applications from a VBA procedure using Automation, let's take a look at how the manual method is used to link and embed an object. *Object linking and embedding* (OLE) allows you to create *compound documents*. A compound document contains objects created by other applications. For example, if you embed a Word document in a Microsoft Excel worksheet, Excel only needs to know the name of the application that was used to create this object and the method of displaying the object on the screen. Compound documents are created by either linking or embedding objects. When you use the manual method to embed an object, you first need to copy it in one application and then paste it into another. The main difference between a linked object and an embedded object is in the way the object is stored and updated. Let's try this out.

Hands-On 15-3: Experiments with Linking and Embedding

1. Activate Microsoft Word and open any document.
2. Select and copy any text.
3. In a Microsoft Excel worksheet, you can now paste the copied text using one of these four methods:
   - Paste as text. (Right-click on a cell, and choose **Paste** from the shortcut menu.)

     The copied text will appear in the active cell (see Figure 15-2, cell A1).

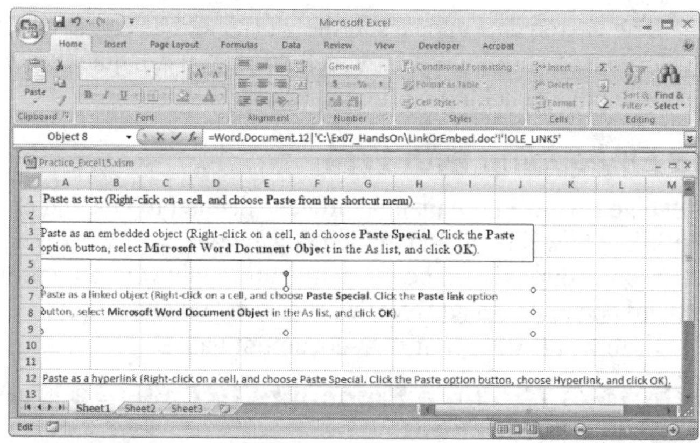

Figure 15-2: A demonstration of linking and embedding.

- Paste as an embedded object. (Right-click on a cell, and choose **Paste Special**. Click the **Paste** option button, select **Microsoft Word Document Object** in the As list, and click **OK**.)

  The text will be pasted into the worksheet as an embedded object (see Figure 15-2, cell A3). The embedded object becomes a part of the destination file. Because the embedded object is not connected with the original data, the information is static. When the data changes in the source file, the embedded object is not updated. To change the embedded data, you must double-click it. This will open the object for editing in the source program. Of course, the source program must be installed on the computer. When you embed objects, all of the data is stored in the destination file. This causes the file size to increase considerably. Notice that when you embed an object, the Formula bar displays:

  ```
  =EMBED("Word.Document.12","")
  ```

- Paste as a linked object. (Right-click on a cell, and choose **Paste Special**. Click the **Paste link** option button, select **Microsoft Word Document Object** in the As list, and click **OK**.)

  Although the destination file displays all of the data, it stores only the address of the data. When you double-click the linked object (see Figure 15-2, cell A7), the source application is launched. Linking objects is a dynamic operation. This means that the linked data is updated automatically when the data in the source file changes. Because the destination document contains only information on how the object is linked with the source document, object linking doesn't increase the size of a destination file. The following formula is used to link an object in Microsoft Excel:

  ```
  =Word.Document.12|'C:\Ex07_HandsOn\LinkOrEmbed.doc'!'!OLE_LINK5'
  ```

- Paste as a hyperlink. (Right-click on a cell, and choose **Paste Special**. Click the **Paste** option button, choose **Hyperlink**, and click **OK**.)

The pasted data appears in the worksheet as single underlined, colored text (see Figure 15-2, cell A12). You can quickly activate the source file by clicking on the hyperlink.

Linking and Embedding with VBA

Now that we've reviewed the manual process needed to link and embed objects, let's see how linking and embedding is done with VBA. The InsertLetter procedure shown below demonstrates how to programmatically embed a Word document in an Excel worksheet. You should replace the reference to C:\Hello.doc with your own document name.

Hands-On 15-4: Writing a Procedure to Embed a Word Document in a Worksheet

1. Insert a new module into the WorkWApplets (Practice_Excel15.xlsm) VBA project and rename it **OLE**.
2. In the OLE module Code window, enter the InsertLetter procedure as shown below:

```
Sub InsertLetter()
    Workbooks.Add
    ActiveSheet.Shapes.AddOLEObject Filename:="C:\Ex07_HandsOn\Hello.doc"
End Sub
```

   The InsertLetter procedure uses the AddOLEObject method. This method creates an OLE object and returns the Shape object that represents the new OLE object. To find additional arguments that the AddOLEObject method can use, look it up in the Visual Basic online documentation.

3. Run the InsertLetter procedure.

   The procedure opens a new workbook and embeds the indicated Word document in it. If you'd rather link a document, you must specify an additional argument, Link, as shown below:

```
ActiveSheet.Shapes.AddOLEObject FileName:="C:\Hello.doc", Link:=True
```

Objects — Linking or Embedding

When you have to make a decision on whether to embed or link an object, use object embedding if:

- You don't mind if the size of a document increases, or you have enough disk space and memory to handle large files.
- You will never need the source file or use source text in other compound documents.
- You want to send the document to other people by e-mail or on a diskette, and you want to make sure that they can read the data without any problems.

COM and Automation

The driving force behind Automation is the Component Object Model (COM), which determines the rules for creating objects by the server application and specifies the methods that both the server and the control application must apply when using these objects. The COM standard contains a collection of functions that are made available as *Automation interfaces*. When a server application creates an object, it automatically makes available an interface that goes along with it. This interface includes properties, methods, and events that can be recognized by the object. The controller application doesn't need to know the internal structure of the object in order to control it; it only needs to know how to manipulate the object interface that is made available by the server application.

Understanding Binding

For a controller application to communicate with the Automation object (server), you must associate the object variable that your VBA procedure uses with the actual Automation object on the server. This process is known as *binding*. There are two types of binding: *late binding* and *early binding*. Your choice of binding will have a great impact on how well your application performs.

Late Binding

When you declare a variable As Object or As Variant, Visual Basic uses late binding. Late binding is also known as *run-time binding*. Late binding simply means that Visual Basic doesn't associate your object variable with the Automation object at design time but waits until you actually run the procedure. Because the declaration As Object or As Variant is very general in nature, Visual Basic cannot determine at compile time that the object your variable refers to has the properties and methods your VBA procedure is using.

The following declaration results in late binding of the specified object:

```
Dim mydoc As Object
```

The advantage of late binding is that all the Automation objects know how to use it. The disadvantage is that there is no support for built-in constants. Because Visual Basic does not know at design time the type library to which your object is referring, you must define constants in your code by looking up the values in the application's documentation. Also, querying an application at run time can slow down the performance of your solution.

Note: Late binding makes it possible to access objects in a type library of another application without first establishing a reference to the object library. Use late binding if you are uncertain that your users will have the referenced type libraries installed on their machines. The main difference between late binding and early binding is how you declare your object variables.

Let's write a VBA procedure that uses late binding. The purpose of this procedure is to print out a Word document. Be sure to modify the filename so that you can actually print a Word document that exists on your hard disk.

Hands-On 15-5: Printing a Word Document with VBA

1. Insert a new module into the WorkWApplets (Practice_Excel15.xlsm) VBA project and rename it **Automation.**
2. In the Automation module Code window, enter the PrintWordDoc procedure as shown below:

```
Sub PrintWordDoc()
    Dim objWord As Object
    Set objWord = CreateObject("Word.Application")

    With objWord
        .Visible = True
        .Documents.Open "C:\Ex07_HandsOn\LinkOrEmbed.doc"
        .Options.PrintBackground = False
        .ActiveDocument.PrintOut
        .Documents.Close
        .Quit
    End With

    Set objWord = Nothing
End Sub
```

3. Run the PrintWordDoc procedure.

   You should get a printed copy of your document.

Early Binding

When you declare object variables as specific object types, Visual Basic uses early binding. Early binding is also known as *compile-time binding*. This means that Visual Basic associates your object variable with the Automation object in the period during which the procedure source code is translated to executable code. The general syntax looks like this:

```
Dim objectVariable As Application.ObjectType
```

In the above syntax, Application is the name of the application as it appears in the Object Browser's Project/Library drop-down list (for example, Word and Excel). ObjectType is the name of the object class type (for example, application, document, workbook, and worksheet). The following declarations result in early binding:

```
Dim mydoc As Word.Document
Dim mydoc As Excel.Worksheet
```

Early binding allows you to take full advantage of many of the debugging tools that are available in the Visual Basic Editor window. For example, you can look up external objects, properties, and methods with the Object Browser. Visual Basic Auto Syntax Check, Auto List Members, and Auto Quick Info (all discussed in Chapter 3) can help you write your code faster and with fewer errors. In addition, early binding allows you to use built-in constants as arguments for methods and property settings. Because these constants are available in the type library at design time, you do not need to define them. The handy built-in syntax checking, IntelliSense features, or support for built-in constants aren't available with late binding. Although VBA procedures that use early binding execute faster, some very old Windows applications can only use late binding.

Note: In order to use early binding, you must first establish a reference to the object library (see the following section). Use early binding when you are certain that your users will have the referenced type libraries installed on their machines.

Establishing a Reference to a Type Library

If you decide to use early binding to connect to another application via Automation, you should start by establishing a reference to the object library whose objects you are planning to manipulate. Follow the steps outlined below to create a reference to the Microsoft Word object library.

Hands-On 15-6: Setting Up a Reference to a Type Library

1. Activate the Visual Basic Editor window.
2. Select the current project in the Project Explorer window, and choose **Tools | References.**
3. In the References dialog box, choose the name of the application in the Available References list box. For this example, click the check box next to **Microsoft Word 12.0 Object Library** or **Microsoft Word 11.0 Object Library** (see Figure 15-3). Scroll down in the Available References list box to locate this object library. If the type library for an object application that is installed on your computer doesn't appear in the list of available references, click the **Browse** button.

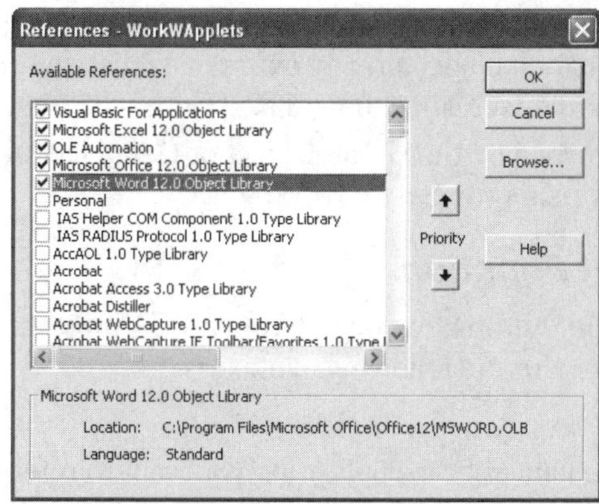

Figure 15-3: In order to manipulate objects of another application, you should set a reference to the required object library.

4. Click **OK** to close the References dialog box.

   The References dialog box lists the names of the references that are available to your VBA project. The references that are not used are listed alphabetically. The references that are checked are listed by priority. For example, in Excel, the Microsoft Excel 12.0 object library has a higher priority than the Microsoft Word 12.0 object library. When a procedure references an object, Visual Basic searches each referenced object library in the order in which the libraries are displayed in the References dialog box. After setting a reference to the required object library, you can browse the object properties and methods by using the Object Browser (see Figure 15-4).

Figure 15-4: All of the Microsoft Word objects, properties, and methods can be accessed from a Microsoft Excel VBA project after adding a reference to the Microsoft Word 12.0 object library (see Figure 15-3).

Creating Automation Objects

To create an Automation object in your VBA procedure, follow these steps:

- Declare an object variable using the Dim…As Object or Dim…As Application.ObjectType clause (see the topics on using late and early binding in the preceding sections).
- If you are using early binding, use the References dialog box to establish a reference to the Application object type library.
- If the Automation object doesn't exist yet, use the CreateObject function. If the Automation object already exists, establish the reference to the object by using the GetObject function.
- Assign the object returned by the CreateObject or GetObject function to the object variable by using the Set keyword.

Using the CreateObject Function

To create a reference to the Automation object from a VBA procedure, use the CreateObject function with the following syntax:

```
CreateObject(class)
```

The argument class is the name of the application you want to reference. This name includes the object class type as discussed earlier (see the section on early binding). The Automation object must be assigned to the object variable by using the Set keyword, as shown below:

```
Set variable_name = CreateObject(class)
```

For example, to activate Word using the Automation object, include the following declaration statements in your VBA procedure:

```
' early binding
Dim wordAppl As Word.Document
Set wordAppl = CreateObject("Word.Application")
```

or

```
' late binding
Dim wordAppl As Object
Set wordAppl = CreateObject("Word.Application")
```

As a rule, the CreateObject function creates a new instance of the specified Automation object. Some applications, however, register themselves as so-called "single instance" applications. This means that you cannot run more than one instance of the application at a time. Microsoft Word and PowerPoint are such single instance applications. Therefore, if Word or PowerPoint is already running, the CreateObject function will simply reference a running instance instead of creating a new instance.

Creating a New Word Document Using Automation

Let's see how you can apply what you have learned in the preceding sections about binding in a real-life example. Sometimes you may be required to open a Word document programmatically and write some data to it straight from Excel. The following example uses early binding.

Hands-On 15-7: Creating a New Word Document with VBA

1. In the Visual Basic Editor screen, select the WorkWApplets (Practice_Excel15.xlsm) VBA project and choose **Tools | References**.
2. If the Microsoft Word 12.0 object library or earlier object library is not selected in the Available References list box, locate this object library and click the check box to select it. Click **OK** when done.
3. In the Automation module Code window, enter the WriteLetter procedure as shown below:

```
Sub WriteLetter()
    Dim wordAppl As Word.Application

    Set wordAppl = CreateObject("Word.Application")
    With wordAppl
        .Visible = True
        .StatusBar = "Creating a new document..."
        .Documents.Add
        .ActiveDocument.Paragraphs(1).Range.InsertBefore "Invitation"
        .StatusBar = "Saving document..."
        .ActiveDocument.SaveAs Filename:="C:\Ex07_ByExample\Invite.doc"
        .StatusBar = "Exiting Word..."
        .Quit
    End With
```

```
    Set wordAppl = Nothing
End Sub
```

The WriteLetter procedure begins with the declaration of the object variable of the specific object type (Word.Application). Recall that this type of declaration (early binding) requires that you establish a reference to the Microsoft Word object library (discussed earlier in this chapter). The Automation object returned by the CreateObject function is assigned to the object variable called wordAppl. Because the applications launched by Automation don't appear on the screen, the statement:

```
wordAppl.Visible = True
```

makes the launched Word application visible so that you can watch the VBA at work.

The remaining statements of this procedure open a new Word document (the Add method), enter text in the first paragraph (the InsertBefore method), save the document in a disk file (the SaveAs method), and close the Word application (the Quit method). Each statement is preceded by an instruction that changes the message displayed in the status bar at the bottom of the Word application window. When the Word application is closed, the instruction:

```
Set wordAppl = Nothing
```

clears the object variable to reclaim the memory used by the object.

As mentioned earlier, Microsoft Word is a *single instance* application. This means that you cannot run more than one instance of Word at a time. In short, the CreateObject function used in the WriteLetter procedure will launch Word if it is not already running; otherwise, it will use the currently active instance of Word.

4. Switch to the Microsoft Excel application window and choose **View | Macros | View Macros**. Select the WriteLetter procedure in the list of macros and click **Run**.

Using the GetObject Function

If you are certain that the Automation object already exists or is already open, consider using the GetObject function. This function looks like this:

```
GetObject([pathname][, class])
```

The GetObject function has two arguments, both of which are optional. Use the first argument to specify the name of the file that you want to open. The full path should be given. If you omit this argument, you have to specify the class argument that indicates the type of object to work with. For example:

```
Excel.Application
Excel.Sheet
Excel.Chart
Excel.Range
Word.Application
Word.Document
PowerPoint.Application
```

To create an Excel object based on the Report.xls spreadsheet and force the object to be an Excel version 5 spreadsheet, you could use the following declaration:

```
' late binding
Dim excelObj As Object
Set excelObj = GetObject("C:\Ex07_HandsOn\Report.xls", Excel.Sheet.5")
```

To set the object variable to a specific Word document, you would use:

```
' early binding
Dim wordObj As Word.Application
Set wordObj = GetObject("C:\Ex07_ByExample\Invite.doc")
```

To access a running Office application object, leave the first argument out:

```
Dim excelObj As Object
Set excelObj = GetObject(, "Excel.Application")
```

When the GetObject function is called without the first argument, it returns a reference to an instance of the application. If the application isn't running, an error will occur.

Opening an Existing Word Document

The CenterText procedure that follows demonstrates the use of the GetObject function to access the Invite.doc file. As you recall, this file was created earlier in this chapter by the WriteLetter procedure. The CenterText procedure will center the first paragraph in the specified Word document.

Hands-On 15-8: Opening and Modifying a Word Document with VBA

This Hands-On uses the Word document file (Invite.doc) created in Hands-On 15-7.

1. In the Automation module Code window, enter the CenterText procedure as shown below:

```
Sub CenterText()
    Dim wordDoc As Word.Document
    Dim wordAppl As Word.Application
    Dim strDoc As String
    Dim myAppl As String

    On Error GoTo ErrorHandler

    strDoc = "C:\Ex07_ByExample\Invite.doc"
    myAppl = "Word.Application"

    ' first find out whether the specified document exists
    If Not DocExists(strDoc) Then
       MsgBox strDoc & " does not exist." & Chr(13) & Chr(13) _
          & "Please run the WriteLetter procedure to create " & _
          strDoc & "."
       Exit Sub
    End If
```

```
    ' now check if Word is running
    If Not IsRunning(myAppl) Then
       MsgBox "Word is not running -> will create " & _
          "a new instance of Word. "
       Set wordAppl = CreateObject("Word.Application")
       Set wordDoc = wordAppl.Documents.Open(strDoc)
    Else
       MsgBox "Word is running -> will get the specified document. "
       ' bind the wordDoc variable to a specific Word document
       Set wordDoc = GetObject(strDoc)
    End If
    ' center the 1st paragraph horizontally on page
    With wordDoc.Paragraphs(1).Range
       .ParagraphFormat.Alignment = wdAlignParagraphCenter
    End With
    wordDoc.Application.Quit SaveChanges:=True
    Set wordDoc = Nothing
    Set wordAppl = Nothing
    MsgBox "The document " & strDoc & " was reformatted."
    Exit Sub
ErrorHandler:
    MsgBox Err.Description, vbCritical, "Error: " & Err.Number
End Sub
```

The CenterText procedure uses a custom function named DocExists (see code in step 2) to check for the existence of the specified document. Another custom function, IsRunning (see code in step 3), checks whether a copy of Microsoft Word is already running. Based on the findings, either the CreateObject or GetObject function is used. If an error occurs, the error number and error description are displayed.

2. In the Automation module Code window, enter the DocExists function procedure as shown below:

```
Function DocExists(ByVal mydoc As String) As Boolean
    On Error Resume Next
    If Dir(mydoc) <> "" Then
          DocExists = True
    Else
          DocExists = False
    End If
End Function
```

3. In the Automation module Code window, enter the IsRunning function procedure as shown below:

```
Function IsRunning(ByVal myAppl As String) As Boolean
    Dim applRef As Object
    On Error Resume Next

    Set applRef = GetObject(, myAppl)
    If Err.Number = 429 Then
          IsRunning = False
    Else
          IsRunning = True
    End If
    ' clear the object variable
    Set applRef = Nothing
```

```
End Function
```

4. In the Visual Basic Editor window, position the pointer anywhere within the code of the CenterText procedure, then choose **Debug | Step Into**.
5. When a yellow highlight appears on the Sub CenterText line, press **F8**. Keep on pressing F8 to execute the procedure step by step. Notice how Visual Basic jumps to the appropriate function procedure to find out whether the specified Word document exists and whether the Word application is running.

Using the New Keyword

Instead of using the CreateObject function to assign a reference to another application, you can use the New keyword. The New keyword tells Visual Basic to create a new instance of an object, return a reference to that instance, and assign the reference to the object variable being declared. For example, you can use the New keyword in the following way:

```
Dim objWord As Word.Application
Set objWord = New Word.Application
Dim objAccess As Access.Application
Set objAccess = New Access.Application
```

Object variables declared with the New keyword are always early bound. Using the New keyword is more efficient than using the CreateObject function. Each time you use the New keyword, Visual Basic creates a new instance of the application. If the application is already running and you don't want to start another instance, you should use the GetObject function.

The New keyword can also be used to create a new instance of the object at the same time that you declare its object variable. For example:

```
Dim objWord As New Word.Application
```

Notice that when you declare the object variable with the New keyword in the Dim statement, you do not need to use the Set statement. However, this method of creating an object variable is not recommended because you lose control over when the object variable is actually created. Using the New keyword in the declaration statement causes the object variable to be created even if it isn't used. Therefore, if you want control over when the object is created, always declare your object variables using the following syntax:

```
Dim objWord As Word.Application
Set objWord = New Word.Application
```

The Set statement can be placed further in your code where you need to use the object. The following section demonstrates how to use the New keyword to create a new instance of Microsoft Outlook and write your contact addresses to an Excel worksheet.

Using Automation to Access Microsoft Outlook

To access Outlook's object model directly from Excel, begin by establishing a reference to the Microsoft Outlook 12.0 or earlier object library. The example procedure that follows will insert your Outlook contact information into an Excel spreadsheet.

Hands-On 15-9: Bringing Outlook Contacts to Excel

1. Establish a reference to the Microsoft Outlook 12.0 (or earlier) object library.
2. In the Automation module Code window, enter the GetContacts procedure as shown below:

```
Sub GetContacts()
Dim objOut As Outlook.Application
Dim objNspc As NameSpace
Dim objItem As ContactItem
Dim r As Integer ' row index
Dim Headings As Variant
Dim i As Integer ' array element
Dim cell As Variant

r = 2
Set objOut = New Outlook.Application
Set objNspc = objOut.GetNamespace("MAPI")

Headings = Array("Full Name", "Street", "City", _
      "State", "Zip Code", "E-Mail")
Workbooks.Add
Sheets(1).Activate
      For Each cell In Range("A1:F1")
            cell.FormulaR1C1 = Headings(i)
            i = i + 1
      Next

For Each objItem In objNspc.GetDefaultFolder _
      (olFolderContacts).Items
      With ActiveSheet
            .Cells(r, 1).Value = objItem.FullName
            .Cells(r, 2).Value = objItem.BusinessAddress
            .Cells(r, 3).Value = objItem.BusinessAddressCity
            .Cells(r, 4).Value = objItem.BusinessAddressState
            .Cells(r, 5).Value = objItem.BusinessAddressPostalCode
            .Cells(r, 6).Value = objItem.Email1Address
      End With
      r = r + 1
Next objItem
Set objItem = Nothing
Set objNspc = Nothing
Set objOut = Nothing
MsgBox "Your contacts have been dumped to Excel."
End Sub
```

The GetContacts procedure starts by declaring an object variable called objOut to hold a reference to the Outlook application. This variable is defined by a specific object type (Outlook.Application); therefore VBA will use early binding. Notice that in this procedure, we use the New keyword discussed earlier to create a new instance of an Outlook

Application object, return a reference to that instance, and assign the reference to the objOut variable being declared.

In order to access contact items in Outlook, you also need to declare object variables to reference the Outlook Namespace and Item objects. The Namespace object represents the message store known as MAPI (Messaging Application Programming Interface). The Namespace object contains folders (Contacts, Journal, Tasks, etc.), which in turn contain items. An item is a particular instance of Outlook data, such as an e-mail message or a contact.

After writing column headings to the worksheet using the For Each...Next loop, the procedure uses another For Each...Next loop to iterate through the Items collection in the Contacts folder. The GetDefaultFolder method returns an object variable for the Contacts folder. This method takes one argument, the constant representing the folder you want to access. After all the contact items are written to an Excel spreadsheet, the procedure releases all object variables by setting them to Nothing.

3. Run the GetContacts procedure.

When you run the GetContacts procedure, you may get a warning message that the program is trying to access e-mail addresses. Choose **Allow access for 1 minute** and click **Yes** to allow the operation. Upon the successful execution of the procedure, click **OK** to the message and switch to the Microsoft Excel application window to view your Outlook contacts in a new workbook file that was created by the GetContacts procedure.

Chapter Summary

In this chapter, you learned how to launch, activate, and control other applications from VBA procedures. You learned how to send keystrokes to another application by using the SendKeys method and how to manually and programmatically link and embed objects. Additionally, you used Automation to create a new Word document from Excel and accessed this document later to change some formatting. You also learned how to retrieve your contact addresses from Microsoft Outlook and place them in an Excel worksheet. You expanded your knowledge of VBA statements with two new functions — CreateObject and GetObject — and learned how and when to use the New keyword.

In the next chapter you will learn various methods of controlling Microsoft Access from Excel.

Chapter 16

Using Excel with Microsoft Access

Object Libraries ■ Setting Up References to Object Libraries ■ **Connecting to Access** ■ **Opening an Access Database** ■ Using Automation to Connect to an Access Database ■ Using DAO to Connect to an Access Database ■ Using ADO to Connect to an Access Database ■ **Performing Access Tasks from Excel** ■ Creating a New Access Database with DAO ■ Opening an Access Form ■ Opening an Access Report ■ Creating a New Access Database with ADO ■ Running a Select Query ■ Running a Parameter Query ■ Calling an Access Function ■ **Retrieving Access Data into an Excel Worksheet** ■ Retrieving Data with the GetRows Method ■ Retrieving Data with the CopyFromRecordset Method ■ Retrieving Data with the TransferSpreadsheet Method ■ Using the OpenDatabase Method ■ Creating a Text File from Access Data ■ Creating a Query Table from Access Data ■ Creating an Embedded Chart from Access Data ■ **Transferring the Excel Spreadsheet to an Access Database** ■ Linking an Excel Spreadsheet to an Access Database ■ Importing an Excel Spreadsheet to an Access Database ■ Placing Excel Data in an Access Table ■ **Chapter Summary**

In Chapter 15 you learned about controlling Microsoft Word and Outlook from Excel via Automation. This chapter shows you how to programmatically use Access from Excel as well as how to retrieve Access data into an Excel spreadsheet by using the following methods:

- Automation
- DAO (Data Access Objects)
- ADO (ActiveX Data Objects)

Before you learn how to use Excel VBA to perform various tasks in an Access database, let's briefly examine the data access methods that Microsoft Access uses to gain programmatic access to its objects.

Object Libraries

A Microsoft Access database consists of various types of objects stored in different object libraries. In this chapter, you will be accessing objects, properties, and methods from several libraries that are listed below.

- The Microsoft Access 12.0 object library

  This library provides objects that are used to display data and work with the Microsoft Access 2007 application. The library is stored in the MSACC.OLB file and can be found in the C:\Program Files\Microsoft Office\Office12 folder. After setting up a reference to this library in the References dialog box (this is covered in the next section), you will be able to look up this library's objects, properties, and methods in the Object Browser.

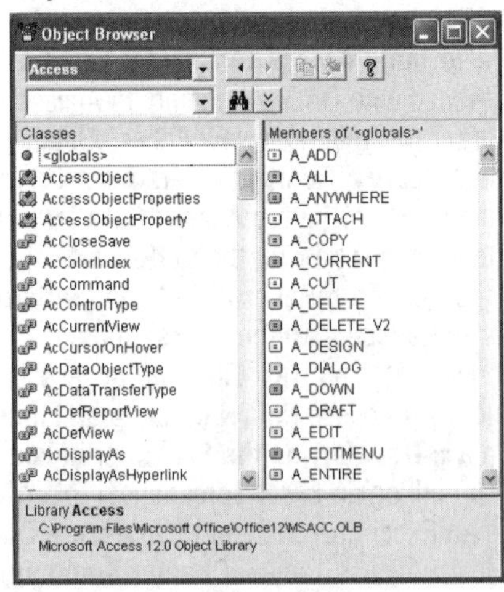

Figure 16-1: The Microsoft Access 12.0 object library.

- The Microsoft DAO 3.6 object library

  Data Access Objects (DAO) that are provided by this library allow you to determine the structure of your database and manipulate data using VBA. This library is stored in the DAO360.DLL file and can be found in the C:\Program Files\Common Files\Microsoft Shared\DAO folder. After setting up a reference to this library in the References dialog box (this is covered in the next section), you will be able to look up the library's objects, properties, and methods in the Object Browser.

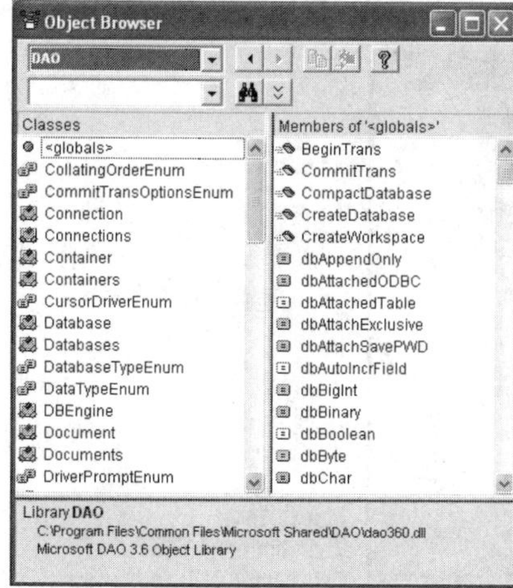

Figure 16-2: The Microsoft DAO 3.6 object library.

- The Microsoft ActiveX Data Objects 2.8 library (ADODB)

  ActiveX Data Objects (ADO) that are provided by this library allow you to access and manipulate data using the OLE DB provider. ADO objects make it possible to establish a connection with a data source in order to read, insert, modify, and delete data in an Access database. This library is stored in MSADO15.DLL and can be found in the C:\Program Files\Common Files\System\ado folder. After setting up a reference to this library in the References dialog, you will be able to access this library's objects, properties, and methods in the Object Browser.

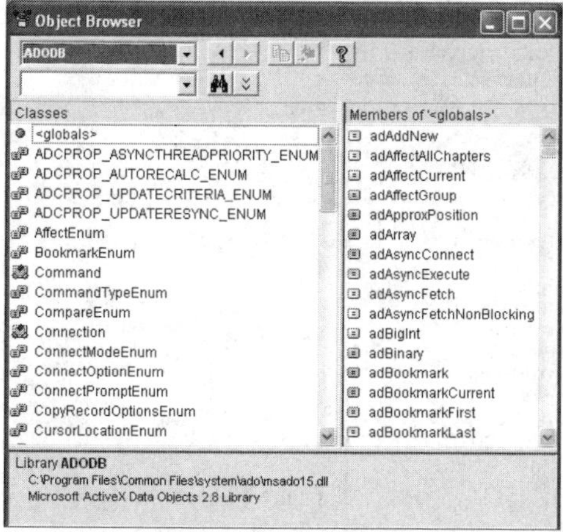

Figure 16-3: The Microsoft ActiveX Data Objects 2.8 library (ADODB).

- The Microsoft ADO Ext. 2.8 for DDL and Security (ADOX)

  Objects that are stored in this library allow you to define the database structure and security. For example, you can define tables, indexes, and relationships, as well as create and modify user and group accounts. This library is stored in MSADOX.DLL and can be found in the C:\Program Files\Common Files\System\ado folder. After setting up a reference to this library in the References dialog box, you will be able to look up this library's objects, properties, and methods in the Object Browser.

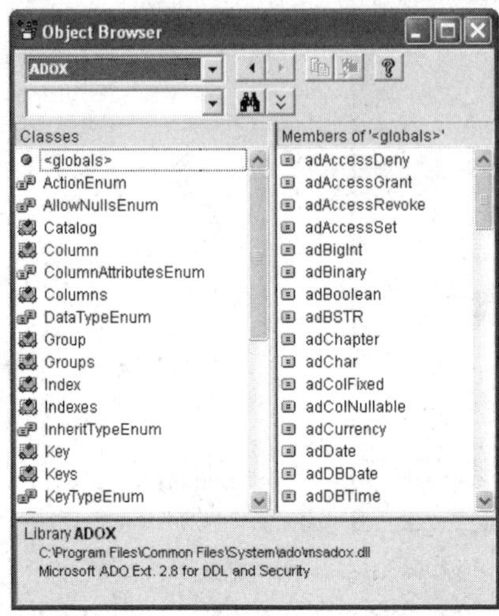

Figure 16-4: The Microsoft ADO Ext. 2.8 for DDL and Security library (ADOX).

- The Microsoft Jet and Replication Objects 2.6 library (JRO)

  Objects contained in this library are used in the replication of a database. This library is stored in MSJRO.DLL and can be found in the C:\Program Files\Common Files\System\ado folder. After setting up a reference to this library in the References dialog box, you will be able to look up this library's objects, properties, and methods in the Object Browser. Please note that database replication is not supported in the new Office Access 2007 .accdb file format.

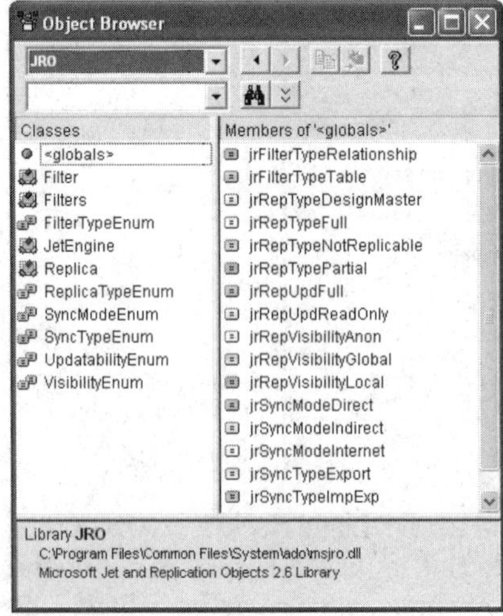

Figure 16-5: The Microsoft Jet and Replication Objects 2.6 library (JRO).

- The Visual Basic for Applications object library (VBA)

  Objects contained in this library allow you to access your computer's file system, work with date and time functions, perform mathematical and financial computations, interact with users, convert data, and read text files. This library is stored in the VBE6.DLL file located in the C:\Program Files\Common Files\Microsoft Shared\VBA\VBA6 folder. The reference to this library is automatically set when you install Office Excel 2007. This library is shared between all Office 2007 applications.

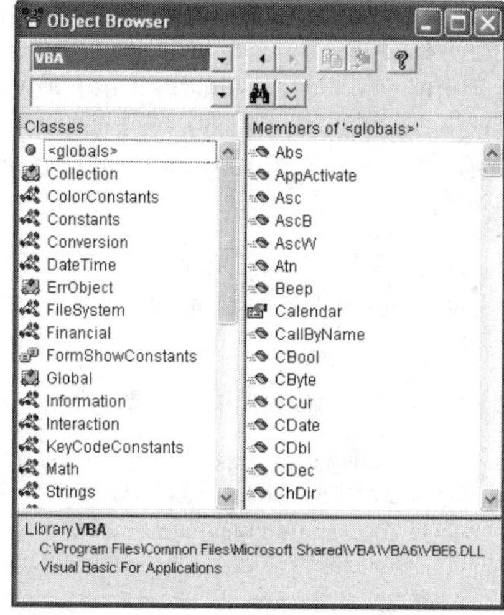

Figure 16-6: The Visual Basic for Applications object library (VBA).

Setting Up References to Object Libraries

To work with Microsoft Access 2007 objects, begin by creating a reference to the Microsoft Access 12.0 object library.

Hands-On 16-1: Establishing a Reference to the Access Object Library

1. Start Microsoft Excel and open a new workbook. Save the file as **C:\Ex07_ByExample\Practice_Excel16.xlsm**.
2. Activate the Visual Basic Editor window, and choose **Tools | References** to open the References dialog box. This dialog displays a list of all the type libraries that are available on your computer based on the applications you have installed.
3. Locate **Microsoft Access 12.0 Object Library** in the list of entries and select its check box.

   To work with previous versions of Microsoft Access, choose Microsoft Access 9.0 Object Library for Access 2000, Microsoft Access 10.0 Object Library for Access 2002, or Microsoft Access 11.0 Object Library for Access 2003.

4. Close the References dialog box.

   Once you've created a reference to the Microsoft Access type library, you can use the Object Browser to view a list of the application's objects, properties, and methods (see Figure 16-1 in the previous section).

5. Use the References dialog box to set up references to other object libraries that will be accessed in this chapter's exercises. You will find the list of libraries at the beginning of this chapter. You can skip setting up the reference to the Microsoft Jet and Replication Objects 2.6 library (JRO), as it will not be used here. If you are interested in database replication, there are many books on Microsoft Access VBA programming that cover this subject, including those of mine that are available from Wordware Publishing: *Access 2003 Programming by Example with VBA, XML, and ASP* (ISBN 1-55622-223-8) and *Access 2007 Programming by Example with VBA, XML, and ASP* (ISBN 1-59822-042-X).

Advantages of Creating a Reference to a Microsoft Access Object Library

When you set a reference to the Microsoft Access object library, you gain the following:

- You can look up Microsoft Access objects, properties, and methods in the Object Browser.
- You can run Microsoft Access functions directly in your VBA procedures.
- You can declare the object variable of the Application type instead of the generic Object type. Declaring the object variable as Dim objAccess As Access.Application (early binding) is faster than declaring it as Dim objAccess As Object (late binding).
- You can use Microsoft Access built-in constants in your VBA code.
- Your VBA procedure will run faster.

Connecting to Access

The example procedures in this chapter use various methods of connecting to Microsoft Access. Each method is discussed in detail as it first appears in the procedure (see the next section titled "Opening an Access Database"). You can establish a connection to Microsoft Access by using one of the following three methods:

- Automation
- Data Access Objects (DAO)
- ActiveX Data Objects (ADO)

Opening an Access Database

In order to access data in a database, you need to open it. How you open a particular database depends largely on which method you selected to establish a database connection.

Using Automation to Connect to an Access Database

When working with Microsoft Access from Excel (or another application) using Automation, you must take the following steps:

1. Set a reference to the Microsoft Access 12.0 object library. (Refer to the section titled "Setting up References to Object Libraries" earlier in this chapter.)
2. Declare an object variable to represent the Microsoft Access Application object:

```
Dim objAccess As Access.Application
```

   In the declaration line above, objAccess is the name of the object variable, and Access.Application qualifies the object variable with the name of the Visual Basic object library that supplies the object.

3. Return the reference to the Application object and assign that reference to the object variable. Return the reference to the Application object using the CreateObject function, GetObject function, or the New keyword as demonstrated below. Notice that you must assign the reference to the object variable with the Set statement.

- Use the CreateObject function to return a reference to the Application object when there is no current instance of the object. If Microsoft Access is already running, a new instance is started and the specified object is created.

```
Dim objAccess As Object
Set objAccess = CreateObject("Access.Application.12")
```

- Use the GetObject function to return a reference to the Application object to use the current instance of Microsoft Access or to start Microsoft Access and have it load a file.

```
Dim objAccess As Object
Set objAccess = GetObject(, "Access.Application.12")
```

or

```
Set objAccess = GetObject("C:\Program Files\" _
    & "Microsoft Office\Office12\Samples\Northwind 2007.accdb")
```

Arguments of the GetObject Function

The first argument of the GetObject function, pathname, is optional. It is used when you want to work with an object in a specific file. The second argument, class, specifies which application creates the object and what type of object it is. When the first argument is optional and the second argument is required, you must place a comma in the position of the first argument, as shown below:

```
Dim objAccess As Object
Set objAccess = GetObject(, "Access.
  Application.12")
```

Because the first argument (pathname) of the GetObject function is omitted, a reference to an existing instance of the Microsoft Access application class is returned.

```
Dim objAccess As Object
Set objAccess = GetObject("C:\Program
    Files\" & _
  "Microsoft Office\Office12\
  Samples\Northwind 2007.accdb")
```

When the first argument of the GetObject function is the name of a database file, a new instance of the Microsoft Access application is activated or created with the specific database.

- Use the New keyword to declare an object variable, return a reference to the Application object, and assign the reference to the object variable, all in one step.

```
Dim objAccess As New Access.Application
```

It is also possible to declare an object variable using the two-step method, which gives more control over the object:

```
Dim objAccess As Access.Application
Set objAccess = New Access.Application
```

Using the New Keyword

- When you declare the object variable with the New keyword, the Access application does not start until you begin working with the object variable in your VBA code.
- When you use the New keyword to declare the Application object variable, a new instance of Microsoft Access is created automatically and you don't need to use the CreateObject function.
- Using the New keyword to create a new instance of the Application object is faster than using the CreateObject function.

Because you may have more than one version of Microsoft Access installed, include the version number in the argument of the GetObject or Create-Object function. The six most recent versions of Microsoft Access are shown below:

Microsoft Access 2007	Access.Application.12
Microsoft Access 2003	Access.Application.11
Microsoft Access 2002	Access.Application.10
Microsoft Access 2000	Access.Application.9
Microsoft Access 97	Access.Application.8
Microsoft Access 95	Access.Application.7

Once you've created a new instance of the Application class by using one of the methods outlined in step 3 above, you can open a database or create a new database with the help of OpenCurrentDatabase. You can close the Microsoft Access database that you opened through Automation by using the CloseCurrentDatabase method.

Now that you know how to create an object variable that represents the Application object, let's take a look at an example procedure that opens an Access database straight from an Excel VBA procedure.

Hands-On 16-2: Opening an Access Database Using Automation

This Hands-On requires that you establish a reference to the Microsoft Access 12 object library (see Hands-On 16-1).

1. Switch to the Visual Basic Editor window and rename VBAProject (Practice_Excel16.xlsm) to **AccessFromExcel.**
2. Insert a new module into the AccessFromExcel project and rename it **Automation.**
3. In the Automation module Code window, enter the AccessViaAutomation procedure as shown below:

```
Sub AccessViaAutomation()
    Dim objAccess As Access.Application
    Dim strPath As String

    On Error Resume Next

    Set objAccess = GetObject(, "Access.Application.12")
    If objAccess Is Nothing Then
        ' Get a reference to the Access Application object
        Set objAccess = New Access.Application
    End If

    strPath = "C:\Ex07_HandsOn\Northwind 2007.accdb"

    ' Open the Employees table in the Northwind database
    With objAccess
        .OpenCurrentDatabase strPath
        .DoCmd.OpenTable "Employees", acViewNormal, acReadOnly
        If MsgBox("Do you want to make the Access " & vbCrLf _
            & "Application visible?", vbYesNo, _
            "Display Access") = vbYes Then
            .Visible = True
            MsgBox "Notice the Access Application icon " _
            & "now appears on the Windows taskbar."
        End If
        ' Close the database and quit Access
        .CloseCurrentDatabase
        .Quit
    End With

    Set objAccess = Nothing
End Sub
```

The above procedure uses a current instance of Access if it is available. If Access isn't running, a run-time error will occur and the object variable will be set to Nothing. By placing the On Error Resume Next statement inside this procedure, you can trap this error. Therefore, if Access isn't running, a new instance of Access will be started. This particular example uses the New keyword to start a new instance of Access.

As mentioned earlier, instead of creating a new object instance with the New keyword, you can use the CreateObject function to start a new instance of an automation server, as illustrated below:

```
Set objAccess = GetObject(, "Access.Application.12")
If objAccess Is Nothing Then
    Set objAccess = CreateObject(, "Access.Application.12")
End If
```

Once Access is opened and the Northwind database is loaded with the OpenCurrentDatabase method, we issue a command to open the Employees table in read-only mode. The procedure then asks the user whether to make the Access application window visible. If the user selects Yes to this prompt, the Visible property of the Access Application object is set to True and the user is prompted to look for the Access icon on the taskbar. After selecting OK in response to the message, the Northwind database is closed with the CloseCurrentDatabase method and the Access Application object is closed with the Quit method. After closing the object, the object variable is set to the Nothing keyword to free the memory resources used by the variable. You can prevent an instance of Microsoft Access from closing by making an object variable a module-level variable rather than declaring it at the procedure level. Under these circumstances, the connection to the database will remain open until you close the Automation controller (Excel) or use the Quit method in your VBA code.

4. Run the above procedure by stepping through its code with the **F8** key. Be sure to check the Access interface before running the statement that closes Access. At the top of the Access window just below the Ribbon you should see a familiar security warning message. Access 2007, like Excel 2007, automatically disables all potentially harmful database content. To let Access know that you trust the database, click the **Options** button and select **Enable this content**. To permanently trust the Northwind database for this chapter's exercises, use the Access Options button in the Office start menu to activate the Trust Center and set up the C:\Ex07_HandsOn folder as a trusted location. (See Chapter 1 for more information on trusted locations.)

Opening a Secured Microsoft Access Database

If the Access database is secured with a password, the user will be prompted to enter the correct password. You must use Data Access Objects (DAO) or ActiveX Data Objects (ADO) to programmatically open a password-protected Microsoft Access database. The following example uses the DBEngine property of the Microsoft Access object to specify the password of the database. For this procedure to work, you must set up a reference to the Microsoft DAO 3.6 object library, as explained in the beginning of this chapter. You should also replace the name of the database file with your own Access database that you have previously secured with password "test".

```
Sub OpenSecuredDB()
    Static objAccess As _
        Access.Application
    Dim db As DAO.Database
    Dim strDb As String

    strDb = "C:\myAccessDb.mdb"
    Set objAccess = New _
        Access.Application
    Set db = objAccess.DBEngine. _
         OpenDatabase(Name:=strDb, _
         Options:=False, _
         ReadOnly:=False, _
         Connect:=";PWD=test")
    With objAccess
        .Visible = True
        .OpenCurrentDatabase strDb
    End With
    db.Close
    Set db = Nothing
End Sub
```

Using DAO to Connect to an Access Database

To connect to a Microsoft Access database using Data Access Objects (DAO), you must first set up a reference to the Microsoft DAO 3.6 object library in the References dialog box (see the section titled "Setting up References to Object Libraries" earlier in this chapter). The example procedure shown below uses the OpenDatabase method of the DBEngine object to open the Northwind database and then proceeds to read the names of its tables.

Hands-On 16-3: Opening an Access Database with DAO

1. Insert a new module into the AccessFromExcel VBA project and rename it **Examples_DAO**.
2. In the Examples_DAO module Code window, enter the DAO_OpenDatabase procedure as shown below:

```
Sub DAO_OpenDatabase(strDbPathName As String)
    Dim db As DAO.Database
    Dim tbl As Variant

    Set db = DBEngine.OpenDatabase(strDbPathName)

    MsgBox "There are " & db.TableDefs.Count & _
      " tables in " & strDbPathName & "." & vbCrLf & _
      " View the names in the Immediate window."

    For Each tbl In db.TableDefs
        Debug.Print tbl.Name
```

```
    Next

    db.Close
    Set db = Nothing
    MsgBox "The database has been closed."
End Sub
```

The DBEngine object allows you to initialize the standard Access database engine known as Jet/ACE, and open a database file. You can open a file in the default Access 2007 file format (.accdb) or an older .mdb format. Once the database is open, the DAO_OpenDatabase procedure retrieves the total number of tables from the TableDefs collection. A TableDefs collection contains all stored TableDef objects in a Microsoft Access database. Next, the procedure iterates through the TableDefs collection, reading the names of tables and printing them out to the Immediate window. All these operations occur behind the scenes; notice that the Access application window is not visible to the user. Finally, the procedure uses the Close method to close the Northwind database.

3. To run the DAO_OpenDatabase procedure, type either of the following statements in the Immediate window and press **Enter**:

```
DAO_OpenDatabase "C:\Ex07_HandsOn\Northwind 2007.accdb"
DAO_OpenDatabase "C:\Ex07_HandsOn\Northwind.mdb"
```

Notice that when the procedure finishes, the Immediate window contains the names of all the Northwind database tables.

Using ADO to Connect to an Access Database

Another method of establishing a connection with an Access database is using ActiveX Data Objects (ADO). You must begin by setting up a reference to the Microsoft ActiveX Data Objects 2.8 library or a lower version. The example procedure ADO_OpenDatabase connects to the Northwind database using the Connection object.

Hands-On 16-4: Opening an Access Database with ADO

1. Insert a new module into the AccessFromExcel VBA project and rename it **Examples_ADO**.
2. In the Examples_ADO module Code window, enter the ADO_OpenDatabase procedure as shown below:

```
Sub ADO_OpenDatabase(strDbPathName)
    Dim con As New ADODB.Connection
    Dim rst As New ADODB.Recordset
    Dim fld As ADODB.Field

    ' Connect with the database

    If Right(strDbPathName, 3) = "mdb" Then
        con.Open _
        "Provider=Microsoft.Jet.OLEDB.4.0;" _
        & "Data Source=" & strDbPathName
```

```
    ElseIf Right(strDbPathName, 3) = "cdb" Then
        con.Open _
        "Provider = Microsoft.ACE.OLEDB.12.0;" _
         & "Data Source=" & strDbPathName
    Else
        MsgBox "Incorrect filename extension"
        Exit Sub
    End If


    ' Open Recordset based on the SQL statement
      rst.Open "SELECT * FROM Employees " & _
        "WHERE City = 'Redmond'", con, _
        adOpenForwardOnly, adLockReadOnly

    ' Print the field values for each
    ' Redmond Employee to the Immediate window
      Do Until rst.EOF
        For Each fld In rst.Fields
          Debug.Print fld.Name & "=" & fld.Value & vbCrLf
        Next
        rst.MoveNext
      Loop

    ' Close the Recordset and connection with Access
    rst.Close
    con.Close

    ' Destroy object variables to reclaim the resources
    Set rst = Nothing
    Set con = Nothing
End Sub
```

In the above procedure we open the Access database via the Open method. The Open method requires a connection string argument that contains the name of the data provider (in this example, it's Microsoft.Jet.OLEDB.4.0 for Access databases in the .mdb file format and Microsoft.ACE.OLEDB.12.0 for databases in the Access 2007 .accdb file format) and the data source name (in this example, it's the full name of the database file you want to open).

After establishing a connection to the Northwind database, you can use the Recordset object to access its data. Recordset objects are used to manipulate data at the record level. The Recordset object is made up of records (rows) and fields (columns). To obtain a set of records, you need to use the Open method. This method requires that you specify information such as the source of records for the recordset. The source of records can be the name of a database table, a query, or the SQL statement that returns records. After specifying the source of records, you also need to indicate the connection with the database (con) and two constants, one of which defines the type of cursor (adOpenForwardOnly) and the other the lock type (adLockReadOnly). The adOpenForwardOnly constant tells VBA to create the forward-only recordset, which scrolls forward in the returned set of records. The second constant, adLockReadOnly, specifies the type of the lock placed on records during editing; the records are read-only, which means that you cannot alter the data.

Next, the procedure iterates through the entire recordset and its Fields collection to print the contents of all the fields to the Immediate window.

After obtaining the data, the Close method closes the recordset and another Close method is used to close the connection with the Access database.

3. To run the ADO_OpenDatabase procedure, type either of the following statements in the Immediate window and press **Enter**:

```
ADO_OpenDatabase "C:\Ex07_HandsOn\Northwind 2007.accdb"
ADO_OpenDatabase "C:\Ex07_HandsOn\Northwind.mdb"
```

4. In the Visual Basic Editor window, press **Ctrl+G** to activate the Immediate window and check the procedure results.

Performing Access Tasks from Excel

After connecting to Microsoft Access from Excel, you can perform different tasks within the Access application. This section demonstrates in particular how to use VBA code to:

- Create a new Access database
- Open an existing database form
- Create a new database form
- Open a database report
- Run an Access function

Creating a New Access Database with DAO

If you want to programmatically transfer Excel data into a new Access database, you may need to create a database from scratch by using VBA code. The following example procedure demonstrates how this is done using Data Access Objects (DAO).

Hands-On 16-5: Creating a New Access Database

1. In the Examples_DAO module Code window, enter the NewDB_DAO procedure as shown below:

```
Sub NewDB_DAO()
    Dim db As DAO.Database
    Dim tbl As DAO.TableDef
    Dim strDb As String
    Dim strTbl As String

    On Error GoTo Error_CreateDb_DAO
    strDb = "C:\Ex07_ByExample\ExcelDump.mdb"
```

```
    strTbl = "tblStates"
    ' Create a new database named ExcelDump
    Set db = CreateDatabase(strDb, dbLangGeneral)

    ' Create a new table named tblStates
    Set tbl = db.CreateTableDef(strTbl)

    ' Create fields and append them to the Fields collection
    With tbl
      .Fields.Append .CreateField("StateID", dbText, 2)
      .Fields.Append .CreateField("StateName", dbText, 25)
      .Fields.Append .CreateField("StateCapital", dbText, 25)
    End With

    ' Append the new tbl object to the TableDefs
    db.TableDefs.Append tbl
    ' Close the database
    db.Close
    Set db = Nothing
    MsgBox "There is a new database on your hard disk. " _
        & "This database file contains a table " _
        & "named " & strTbl & "." & vbCrLf _
        & "Before you activate this database, please close " _
        & "the Excel application."
Exit_CreateDb_DAO:
    Exit Sub
Error_CreateDb_DAO:
    If Err.Number = 3204 Then
        ' Delete the database file if it
        ' already exists
        Kill strDb
        Resume
    Else
        MsgBox Err.Number & ": " & Err.Description
        Resume Exit_CreateDb_DAO
    End If
End Sub
```

The CreateDatabase method is used to create a new database named ExcelDump.mdb. The CreateTableDef method of the Database object is then used to create a table named tblStates.

Before a table can be added to a database, the fields must be created and appended to the table. The procedure creates three text fields (dbText) that can store 2, 25, and 25 characters each. As each field is created, it is appended to the Fields collection of the TableDef object using the Append method.

Once the fields have been created and appended to the table, the table itself is added to the database with the Append method. Because the database file may already exist in the specified location, the procedure includes the error-handling routine that will delete the existing file so the database creation process can go on. Because other errors could occur, the Else clause includes statements that will display the error and its description and allow an exit from the procedure.

2. Run the NewDB_DAO procedure.
3. Exit Microsoft Excel.
4. Launch Microsoft Access and open the **ExcelDump.mdb** file. Next, open the table named **tblStates**. The result of this procedure is shown in Figure 16-7.

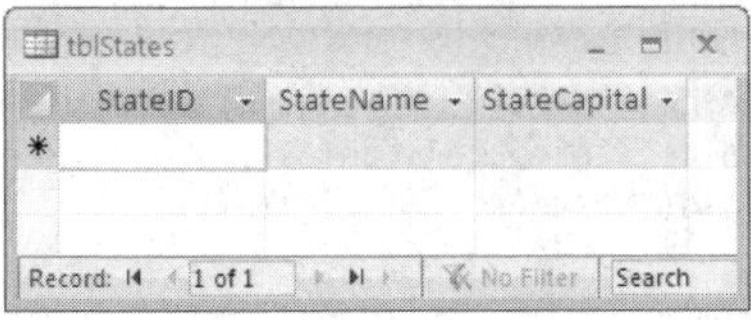

Figure 16-7: This Microsoft Access database table was created by an Excel VBA procedure.

5. Close the Access application.
6. Start Excel and open the **C:\Ex07_ByExample\Practice_Excel16.xlsm** workbook.

Opening an Access Form

You can open a Microsoft Access form from Microsoft Excel. You can also create a new form. The following example uses Automation to connect to Access.

Hands-On 16-6: Opening an Access Form from a VBA Procedure

1. Insert a new module into the AccessFromExcel VBA project and rename it **Database_Forms**.
2. In the Database_Forms module Code window, enter the following module-level declaration and the DisplayAccessForm procedure as shown below:

```
Dim objAccess As Access.Application

Sub DisplayAccessForm()
    Dim strDb As String
    Dim strFrm As String

    strDb = "C:\Ex07_HandsOn\Northwind.mdb"
    strFrm = "Customers"

    Set objAccess = New Access.Application
    With objAccess
        .OpenCurrentDatabase strDb
        .DoCmd.OpenForm strFrm, acNormal
        .DoCmd.Restore
        .Visible = True
    End With
End Sub
```

In the above procedure, the OpenCurrentDatabase method is used to open the sample Northwind database. The Customers form is opened in normal view (acNormal) with the OpenForm method of the DoCmd object. To display the form in design view, use the acDesign constant. The Restore method of the DoCmd object ensures that the form is displayed on the screen in a window and not minimized. The Visible property of the Access Application object (objAccess) must be set to True for the form to become visible.

Notice that the Access.Application object variable (objAccess) is declared at the top of the module. For this procedure to work correctly, you must set up a reference to the Microsoft Access object library.

3. Switch to the Microsoft Excel application window and press **Alt+F8** to display the Macro dialog box. Highlight the **DisplayAccessForm** macro name and click **Run**. Figure 16-8 shows the Customers form after it's been opened.

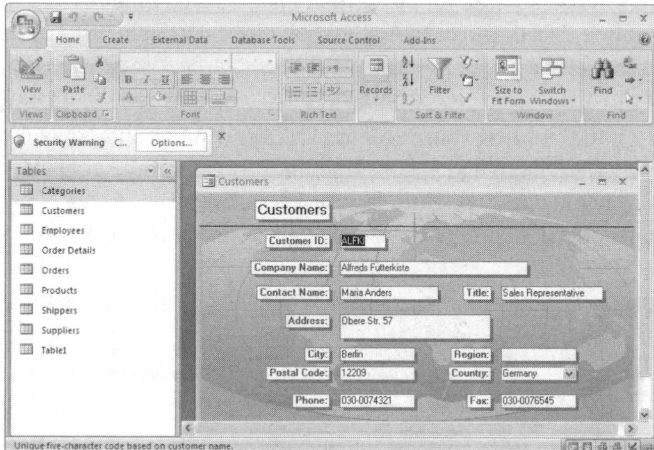

Figure 16-8: A Microsoft Access form can be opened using an Excel VBA procedure.

4. Close the Customers form and exit Microsoft Access.

Opening an Access Report

You can open a Microsoft Access report from Microsoft Excel. The following procedure demonstrates how you can display an existing Access report straight from Excel.

Hands-On 16-7: Opening an Access Report

1. Insert a new module into the AccessFromExcel VBA project and rename it **Database_Reports**.
2. In the Database_Reports module Code window, enter the module-level declaration and the DisplayAccessReport procedure as shown below:

```
Dim objAccess As Access.Application

Sub DisplayAccessReport()
    Dim strDb As String
    Dim strRpt As String
    strDb = "C:\Ex07_HandsOn\Northwind.mdb"
```

```
        strRpt = "Products by Category"

        Set objAccess = New Access.Application
        With objAccess
            .OpenCurrentDatabase (strDb)
            .DoCmd.OpenReport strRpt, acViewPreview
            .DoCmd.Maximize
            .Visible = True
        End With
    End Sub
```

In the above procedure, the OpenCurrentDatabase method is used to open the sample Northwind database. The Products by Category report is opened in print preview mode with the OpenReport method of the DoCmd object. The Maximize method of the DoCmd object ensures that the form is displayed on the screen in a full size window.

Notice that the Access.Application object variable (objAccess) is declared at the top of the module. For this procedure to work correctly, you must set up a reference to the Microsoft Access object library.

3. Switch to the Microsoft Excel application window and press **Alt+F8** to display the Macro dialog box. Highlight the **DisplayAccessReport** macro name and click **Run**. Figure 16-9 shows the Products by Category report after it's been opened and displayed in print preview mode.

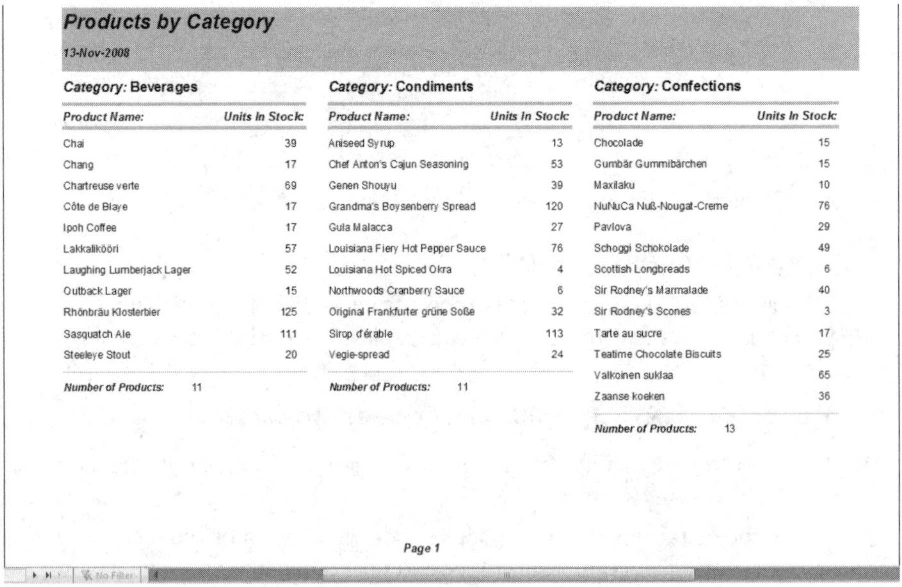

Products by Category

13-Nov-2008

Category: **Beverages**

Product Name:	*Units In Stock:*
Chai	39
Chang	17
Chartreuse verte	69
Côte de Blaye	17
Ipoh Coffee	17
Lakkalikööri	57
Laughing Lumberjack Lager	52
Outback Lager	15
Rhönbräu Klosterbier	125
Sasquatch Ale	111
Steeleye Stout	20

Number of Products: 11

Category: **Condiments**

Product Name:	*Units In Stock:*
Aniseed Syrup	13
Chef Anton's Cajun Seasoning	53
Genen Shouyu	39
Grandma's Boysenberry Spread	120
Gula Malacca	27
Louisiana Fiery Hot Pepper Sauce	76
Louisiana Hot Spiced Okra	4
Northwoods Cranberry Sauce	6
Original Frankfurter grüne Soße	32
Sirop d'érable	113
Vegie-spread	24

Number of Products: 11

Category: **Confections**

Product Name:	*Units In Stock:*
Chocolade	15
Gumbär Gummibärchen	15
Maxilaku	10
NuNuCa Nuß-Nougat-Creme	76
Pavlova	29
Schoggi Schokolade	49
Scottish Longbreads	6
Sir Rodney's Marmalade	40
Sir Rodney's Scones	3
Tarte au sucre	17
Teatime Chocolate Biscuits	25
Valkoinen suklaa	65
Zaanse koeken	36

Number of Products: 13

Page 1

Figure 16-9: A Microsoft Access report can be opened using an Excel VBA procedure.

4. Close the Print Preview window and exit Microsoft Access.

The example procedure below is more versatile, as it allows you to display any Access report in any Access database. Notice that this procedure takes two string arguments: the name of the Access database and the name of the report. Make sure that the following declaration is present at the top of the module:

```
Dim objAccess As Access.Application
Sub DisplayAccessReport2(strDb As String, strRpt As String)

    Set objAccess = New Access.Application

    With objAccess
          .OpenCurrentDatabase (strDb)
          .DoCmd.OpenReport strRpt, acViewPreview
          .DoCmd.Maximize
          .Visible = True
    End With
End Sub
```

You can run the DisplayAccessReport2 procedure from the Immediate window or from a subroutine, as shown below:

- Running the DisplayAccessReport2 procedure from the Immediate window:

```
' type the following statement on one line
' in the Immediate window and press Enter
Call DisplayAccessReport2("C:\Ex07_HandsOn\Northwind.mdb", "Invoice")
```

- Running the DisplayAccessReport2 procedure from a subroutine:

```
' Enter the following procedure in the Code window and run it

Sub ShowReport()
    Dim strDb As String
    Dim strRpt As String

    strDb = InputBox("Enter the name of the database (full path): ")
    strRpt = InputBox("Enter the name of the report:")
    Call DisplayAccessReport2(strDb, strRpt)
End Sub
```

Creating a New Access Database with ADO

In Hands-On 16-5 you created a new database called ExcelDump.mdb by using Data Access Objects (DAO). Creating a new Access database from a VBA procedure is also possible and just as easy by using ActiveX Data Objects (ADO). All you need is the Catalog object of the ADOX object library and its Create method. The Catalog object represents the entire database. This object contains such database elements as tables, fields, indexes, views, and stored procedures.

In the following Hands-On we will create an Access database named ExcelDump2.mdb.

Hands-On 16-8: Creating a New Access Database with ADO

1. In the Visual Basic Editor window, choose **Tools | References** and ensure that the **Microsoft ADO Ext. 2.8 for DDL and Security Library** is selected.
2. Click **OK** to exit the References dialog box.
3. In the Examples_ADO module's Code window, enter the CreateDB_ViaADO procedure as shown below:

```
Sub CreateDB_ViaADO()
    Dim cat As ADOX.Catalog
    Set cat = New ADOX.Catalog

    cat.Create "Provider=Microsoft.ACE.OLEDB.12.0;" & _
        "Data Source=C:\Ex07_ByExample\ExcelDump2.accdb;"

    Set cat = Nothing
End Sub
```

   The above procedure uses the ADOX Catalog object's Create method to create a new Access database. Notice that we created an Access 2007 database. To create a database file in the .mdb format, make sure you change the Provider string and the filename.

4. Run the CreateDB_ViaADO procedure and switch to Window Explorer to check out the database file that this procedure has just created.

Running a Select Query

The most popular types of queries that are executed in the Access user interface are select and parameter queries. You can run these queries easily from within an Excel VBA procedure. To place the data returned by the query into an Excel worksheet, use the CopyFromRecordset method of the Range object. Let's work with a procedure that executes an Access select query.

Hands-On 16-9: Running an Access Select Query

1. Insert a new module into the AccessFromExcel VBA project and rename it **Database_Queries**.
2. Choose **Tools | References** and ensure that the **Microsoft ActiveX Data Objects 2.8** and Microsoft **ADO Ext. 2.8 for DDL and Security** libraries are selected.
3. Click **OK** to exit the References dialog box.
4. In the Database_Queries module Code window, enter the RunAccessQuery procedure as shown below:

```
Sub RunAccessQuery(strQryName As String)
    Dim cat As ADOX.Catalog
    Dim cmd As ADODB.Command
    Dim rst As ADODB.Recordset
    Dim i As Integer
```

```
    Dim strPath As String

    strPath = "C:\Ex07_HandsOn\Northwind.mdb"

    Set cat = New ADOX.Catalog
    cat.ActiveConnection = _
        "Provider=Microsoft.Jet.OLEDB.4.0;" & _
        "Data Source=" & strPath

    Set cmd = cat.Views(strQryName).Command
    Set rst = cmd.Execute

    Sheets(2).Select
    For i = 0 To rst.Fields.Count - 1
        Cells(1, i + 1).Value = rst.Fields(i).Name
    Next
    With ActiveSheet
        .Range("A2").CopyFromRecordset rst
        .Range(Cells(1, 1), _
            Cells(1, rst.Fields.Count)).Font.Bold = True
        .Range("A1").Select
    End With

    Selection.CurrentRegion.Columns.AutoFit
    rst.Close

    Set cmd = Nothing
    Set cat = Nothing
End Sub
```

The example procedure RunAccessQuery begins by creating an object variable that points to the Catalog object. Next the ActiveConnection property of the Catalog object defines the method of establishing the connection to the database:

```
Set cat = New ADOX.Catalog
cat.ActiveConnection = "Provider=Microsoft.Jet.OLEDB.4.0;" & _
    "Data Source=" &strPath
```

The Command object in the ADODB object library specifies the command that you want to execute in order to obtain data from the data source. This procedure attempts to access a specific query in a database whose name will be supplied at run time.

```
Set cmd = cat.Views(strQryName).Command
```

The Views collection, which is a part of the ADOX object library, contains all View objects of a specific catalog. A *view* is a filtered set of records or a virtual table created from other tables or views.

After gaining access to the required query in the database, you can run the query in the following way:

```
Set rst = cmd.Execute
```

The Execute method of the Command object allows you to activate a specific query, an SQL statement, or a stored procedure. The returned set of records is then assigned to the object variable of the type

Recordset using the Set keyword. After creating the set of records, these records are placed in an Excel worksheet using the CopyFromRecordset method (see more information on using this method later in this chapter).

5. To run the above procedure, type the following statement in the Immediate window and press **Enter**:

```
RunAccessQuery("Current Product List")
```

6. Switch to the Microsoft Excel application window to view the results obtained by executing the RunAccessQuery procedure in Sheet 2.

	A	B
1	ProductID	ProductName
2	3	Aniseed Syrup
3	40	Boston Crab Meat
4	60	Camembert Pierrot
5	18	Carnarvon Tigers
6	1	Chai
7	2	Chang
8	39	Chartreuse verte
9	4	Chef Anton's Cajun Seasoning
10	48	Chocolade
11	38	Côte de Blaye
12	58	Escargots de Bourgogne
13	52	Filo Mix
14	71	Fløtemysost

Figure 16-10: The results of running an Access query from an Excel VBA procedure are placed in a worksheet.

Running a Parameter Query

When you want to obtain a different set of data based on the provided criteria, you will want to utilize parameter queries. This section demonstrates how you can run a Microsoft Access parameter query and place the resulting data in a Microsoft Excel spreadsheet. Let's write a procedure to run the Employee Sales by Country query and retrieve records for the period beginning 7/1/96 and ending 7/31/96.

Hands-On 16-10: Running an Access Parameter Query

1. In the Database_Queries module Code window, enter the RunAccessParamQuery procedure as shown below:

```
Sub RunAccessParamQuery()
    Dim cat As ADOX.Catalog
    Dim cmd As ADODB.Command
    Dim rst As ADODB.Recordset
    Dim i As Integer
    Dim strPath As String
    Dim StartDate As String
    Dim EndDate As String

    strPath = "C:\Ex07_HandsOn\Northwind.mdb"
    StartDate = "7/1/96"
    EndDate = "7/31/96"
```

```
    Set cat = New ADOX.Catalog
    cat.ActiveConnection = "Provider=Microsoft.Jet.OLEDB.4.0;" & _
        "Data Source=" & strPath
    Set cmd = cat.Procedures("Employee Sales by Country").Command

    cmd.Parameters("[Beginning Date]") = StartDate
    cmd.Parameters("[Ending Date]") = EndDate

    Set rst = cmd.Execute

    Sheets.Add
    For i = 0 To rst.Fields.Count - 1
        Cells(1, i + 1).Value = rst.Fields(i).Name
    Next
    With ActiveSheet
        .Range("A2").CopyFromRecordset rst
        .Range(Cells(1, 1), Cells(1, rst.Fields.Count)) _
            .Font.Bold = True
        .Range("A1").Select
    End With
    Selection.CurrentRegion.Columns.AutoFit

    rst.Close
    Set cmd = Nothing
    Set cat = Nothing
End Sub
```

To run parameter queries in the Microsoft Access database you need to access the Command object of the Procedures collection of the ADOX Catalog object:

```
Set cmd = cat.Procedures("Employee Sales by Country").Command
```

Because the Microsoft Access Employee Sales by Country query requires two parameters that define the beginning and ending dates, you need to define these parameters by using the Parameters collection of the Command object:

```
cmd.Parameters("[Beginning Date]") = StartDate
cmd.Parameters("[Ending Date]") = EndDate
```

After setting up the parameters, the query is executed using the following statement:

```
Set rst = cmd.Execute
```

The set of records returned by this query is assigned to the object variable of type Recordset and then copied to a worksheet using the CopyFromRecordset method (see more information on using this method later in this chapter).

2. Run the above procedure.

   Because the parameter values are hard-coded in the procedure, you are not prompted for input. On your own, modify the RunAccessParamQuery procedure so that you can provide the parameter values at run time.

3. Switch to the Excel application window to view the results obtained by executing the RunAccessParamQuery procedure.

Calling an Access Function

You can run a built-in Microsoft Access function from Microsoft Excel through Automation. The following example procedure calls the EuroConvert function to convert 1000 Spanish pesetas to Euro dollars. The EuroConvert function uses fixed conversion rates established by the European Union.

```
Sub RunAccessFunction()
    Dim objAccess As Object

    On Error Resume Next
    Set objAccess = GetObject(, "Access.Application")

    ' if no instance of Access is open, create a new one
    If objAccess Is Nothing Then
        Set objAccess = CreateObject("Access.Application")
    End If
    MsgBox "For 1000 Spanish pesetas you will get " & _
        objAccess.EuroConvert(1000, "ESP", "EUR") & _
        " euro dollars. "
    Set objAccess = Nothing
End Sub
```

Retrieving Access Data into an Excel Worksheet

There are numerous ways of bringing external data into Excel. This section shows you different techniques of putting Microsoft Access data into an Excel worksheet. While you have worked with some of these methods earlier in this book, the following sections discuss these methods in greater detail.

- Using the GetRows method
- Using the CopyFromRecordset method
- Using the TransferSpreadsheet method
- Using the OpenDatabase method
- Creating a text file
- Creating a query table

Retrieving Data with the GetRows Method

To place Microsoft Access data into an Excel spreadsheet, you can use the GetRows method. This method returns a two-dimensional array where the first subscript is a number representing the field, and the second subscript is the number representing the record. Record and field numbering begins with 0.

The following example demonstrates how to use the GetRows method in a VBA procedure. We will run the Invoices query in the Northwind database and return records to a worksheet. For this procedure to work correctly, you must first establish a reference to the Microsoft DAO 3.6 object library. Refer to the instructions on setting up a reference to object libraries earlier in this chapter.

Hands-On 16-11: Retrieving Access Data Using the GetRows Method

1. Insert a new module into the AccessFromExcel VBA project and rename it **Method_GetRows**.
2. Choose **Tools | References** and ensure that **Microsoft DAO 3.6 Object Library** is selected.
3. Click **OK** to exit the References dialog box.
4. In the Method_GetRows module Code window, enter the GetData_withGetRows procedure as shown below:

```
Sub GetData_withGetRows()
    Dim db As DAO.Database
    Dim qdf As DAO.QueryDef
    Dim rst As DAO.Recordset
    Dim recArray As Variant
    Dim i As Integer
    Dim j As Integer
    Dim strPath As String
    Dim a As Variant
    Dim countR As Long
    Dim strShtName As String

    strPath = "C:\Ex07_HandsOn\Northwind.mdb"
    strShtName = "Returned records"

    Set db = OpenDatabase(strPath)
    Set qdf = db.QueryDefs("Invoices")
    Set rst = qdf.OpenRecordset

    rst.MoveLast
    countR = rst.RecordCount
    a = InputBox("This recordset contains " & _
        countR & " records." & vbCrLf _
        & "Enter number of records to return: ", _
        "Get Number of Records")

    If a = "" Or a = 0 Then Exit Sub
    If a > countR Then
        a = countR
        MsgBox "The number you entered is too large." & vbCrLf _
            & "All records will be returned."
    End If

    Workbooks.Add
    ActiveWorkbook.Worksheets(1).Name = strShtName
```

```
    rst.MoveFirst
        With Worksheets(strShtName).Range("A1")
            .CurrentRegion.Clear
            recArray = rst.GetRows(a)
            For i = 0 To UBound(recArray, 2)
                For j = 0 To UBound(recArray, 1)
                    .Offset(i + 1, j) = recArray(j, i)
                Next j
            Next i
            For j = 0 To rst.Fields.Count - 1
                .Offset(0, j) = rst.Fields(j).Name
                .Offset(0, j).EntireColumn.AutoFit
            Next j
        End With
    db.Close
End Sub
```

After opening an Access database with the OpenDatabase method, the GetData_withGetRows procedure illustrated above runs the Invoices query using the following statement:

```
Set qdf = db.QueryDefs("Invoices")
```

In the Microsoft DAO 3.6 object library the QueryDefs object represents a select or action query. Select queries return data from one or more tables or queries, while action queries allow you to modify data. (You can add, modify, or delete records using action queries.)

After executing the query, the procedure places the records returned by the query in the object variable of type Recordset using the OpenRecordset method, as shown below:

```
Set rst = qdf.OpenRecordset
```

Next, the record count is retrieved using the RecordCount method and placed in the countR variable. Notice that to obtain the correct record count, the record pointer must first be moved to the last record in the recordset by using the MoveLast method:

```
rst.MoveLast
countR = rst.RecordCount
```

The procedure then prompts the user to enter the number of records to return to the worksheet. You can cancel at this point by clicking the Cancel button in the input dialog box or you can type the number of records to retrieve. If you enter a number that is greater than the record count, the procedure will retrieve all the records.

Before retrieving records, you must move the record pointer to the first record by using the MoveFirst method. If you forget to do this, the record pointer will remain on the last record and only one record will be retrieved.

The procedure then goes on to activate the Returned records worksheet and clear the current region. The records are first returned to the Variant variable containing a two-dimensional array by using the GetRows method of the Recordset object. Next, the procedure loops through both dimensions of the array to place the records in the worksheet starting at cell A2. When this is done, another loop will fill in the first worksheet row with the names of fields and autofit each column so that the data is displayed correctly.

5. Run the GetData_withGetRows procedure. When prompted for the number of records, type **10** and click **OK**. Next, switch to the Microsoft Excel application window to view the results.

The GetRows method can also be used with ActiveX Data Objects as demonstrated in the following GetData_withGetRows_ADO procedure. If you want to try out this procedure, ensure that the References dialog box has the **Microsoft ActiveX Data Objects 2.8** and **Microsoft ADO Ext. 2.8 for DDL and Security** libraries checked.

```
Sub GetData_withGetRows_ADO()
    Dim cat As ADOX.Catalog
    Dim cmd As ADODB.Command
    Dim rst As ADODB.Recordset
    Dim strConnect As String
    Dim recArray As Variant
    Dim i As Integer
    Dim j As Integer
    Dim strPath As String
    Dim a As Variant
    Dim countR As Long
    Dim strShtName As String

    strConnect = "Provider=Microsoft.ACE.OLEDB.12.0;" _
        & "Data Source=C:\Ex07_HandsOn\Northwind 2007.accdb;"

    strShtName = "Returned records"

    Set cat = New ADOX.Catalog
    cat.ActiveConnection = strConnect

    Set cmd = cat.Views("Order Summary").Command
    Set rst = New ADODB.Recordset
    rst.Open cmd, , adOpenStatic, adLockReadOnly

    countR = rst.RecordCount
    a = InputBox("This recordset contains " & _
        countR & " records." & vbCrLf _
        & "Enter number of records to return: ", _
        "Get Number of Records")

    If a = "" Or a = 0 Then Exit Sub
    If a > countR Then
        a = countR
        MsgBox "The number you entered is too large." & vbCrLf _
            & "All records will be returned."
    End If

    Workbooks.Add
    ActiveWorkbook.Worksheets(1).Name = strShtName
    rst.MoveFirst
        With Worksheets(strShtName).Range("A1")
```

```
            .CurrentRegion.Clear
            recArray = rst.GetRows(a)
            For i = 0 To UBound(recArray, 2)
                For j = 0 To UBound(recArray, 1)
                    .Offset(i + 1, j) = recArray(j, i)
                Next j
            Next i
            For j = 0 To rst.Fields.Count - 1
                .Offset(0, j) = rst.Fields(j).Name
                .Offset(0, j).EntireColumn.AutoFit
            Next j
        End With

    Set rst = Nothing
    Set cmd = Nothing
    Set cat = Nothing
End Sub
```

Retrieving Data with the CopyFromRecordset Method

To retrieve an entire recordset into a worksheet, use the CopyFromRecordset method of the Range object. This method can take up to three arguments: Data, MaxRows, and MaxColumns. Only the first argument, Data, is required. This argument can be the Recordset object. The optional arguments, MaxRows and MaxColumns, allow you to specify the number of records (MaxRows) and the number of fields (MaxColumns) that should be returned.

If you omit the MaxRows argument, all the returned records will be copied to the worksheet. If you omit the MaxColumns argument, all the fields will be retrieved.

Let's try out a procedure that uses the ADO objects and the CopyFromRecordset method to retrieve all the records from the Northwind database Products table.

Hands-On 16-12: Retrieving Access Data Using the CopyFromRecordset Method

1. Insert a new module into the AccessFromExcel VBA project and rename it **Method_CopyFromRecordset**.
2. In the Method_CopyFromRecordset module Code window, enter the GetProducts procedure as shown below.

Note: For this procedure to work correctly, you must create a reference to the Microsoft ActiveX Data Objects 2.8 library. (Refer to the instructions on setting up a reference to object libraries earlier in this chapter.)

```
Sub GetProducts()
    Dim conn As New ADODB.Connection
    Dim rst As ADODB.Recordset
    Dim strPath As String
```

```
    strPath = "C:\Ex07_HandsOn\Northwind.mdb"

    conn.Open "Provider=Microsoft.Jet.OLEDB.4.0;" _
        & "Data Source=" & strPath & ";"
    conn.CursorLocation = adUseClient

    ' Create a Recordset from all the records
    ' in the Products table

    Set rst = conn.Execute(CommandText:="Products", _
        Options:=adCmdTable)

    rst.MoveFirst

    ' transfer the data to Excel
    ' get the names of fields first
    With Worksheets("Sheet3").Range("A1")
        .CurrentRegion.Clear
        For j = 0 To rst.Fields.Count - 1
            .Offset(0, j) = rst.Fields(j).Name
        Next j
        .Offset(1, 0).CopyFromRecordset rst
        .CurrentRegion.Columns.AutoFit
    End With
    rst.Close
    conn.Close

    Set rst = Nothing
    Set conn = Nothing
End Sub
```

The above procedure copies all the records from the Products table in the Northwind database into an Excel worksheet. If you want to copy fewer records, use the MaxRows argument as follows:

```
.Offset(1, 0).CopyFromRecordset rst, 5
```

The above statement tells Visual Basic to copy only five records. The Offset method causes the records to be entered in a spreadsheet, starting with the second spreadsheet row. To send all the records to the worksheet using the data from only two table fields, use the following statement:

```
.Offset(1, 0).CopyFromRecordset rst, , 2
```

The above statement tells Visual Basic to copy all the data from the first two columns. The comma between the rst and the number 2 is a placeholder for the omitted MaxRows argument.

3. Run the GetProducts procedure and switch to the Excel application window to view the results.

Retrieving Data with the TransferSpreadsheet Method

It is possible to use the TransferSpreadsheet action of the Microsoft Access DoCmd object to import or export data between the current Access database (.mdb) or Access project (.adp) and a spreadsheet file. Using this method, you can also link the data in an Excel spreadsheet to the current Access database. With a linked spreadsheet, you can view and edit the spreadsheet data with Access while still allowing complete access to the data from your Excel spreadsheet application.

The TransferSpreadsheet method carries out the TransferSpreadsheet action in Visual Basic and has the following syntax:

```
DoCmd.TransferSpreadsheet [transfertype][, spreadsheettype], _
    tablename, filename [, hasfieldnames][, range]
```

The transfertype argument can be one of the following constants: acImport (default setting), acExport, or acLink. These constants define whether data has to be imported, exported, or linked to the database.

The spreadsheettype argument can be one of the constants shown in Table 16-1.

Table 16-1: spreadsheettype argument constants

spreadsheettype Constant Name	Value
acSpreadsheetTypeExcel3 (default setting)	0
acSpreadsheetTypeExcel4	6
acSpreadsheetTypeExcel5	5
acSpreadsheetTypeExcel7	5
acSpreadsheetTypeExcel8	8
acSpreadsheetTypeExcel9	8
acSpreadsheetTypeLotusWK1	2
acSpreadsheetTypeLotusWK3	3
acSpreadsheetTypeLotusWK4	7

It is not difficult to guess that the spreadsheettype argument specifies the spreadsheet name and the version number.

The tablename argument is a string expression that specifies the name of the Access table you want to import spreadsheet data into, export spreadsheet data from, or link spreadsheet data to. Instead of the table name, you may also specify the name of the select query whose results you want to export to a spreadsheet.

The filename argument is a string expression that specifies the filename and path of the spreadsheet you want to import from, export to, or link to.

The hasfieldnames argument is a logical value of True (–1) or False (0). True indicates that the first worksheet row contains the field names. False denotes that the first row contains normal data. The default setting is False (no field names in the first row).

The range argument is a string expression that specifies the range of cells or the name of the range in the worksheet. This argument applies only to importing. If you omit the range argument, the entire spreadsheet will be imported. Leave this argument blank if you want to export, unless you need to specify the worksheet name.

The ExportData example procedure shown below exports data from the Shippers table in the Northwind database to the Shippers.xls spreadsheet using the TransferSpreadsheet method.

Hands-On 16-13: Retrieving Access Data Using the TransferSpreadsheet Method

1. Insert a new module into the AccessFromExcel VBA project and rename it **Method_TransferSpreadsheet**.
2. In the Method_TransferSpreadsheet module Code window, enter the ExportData procedure as shown below:

```
Sub ExportData()
    Dim objAccess As Access.Application
    Set objAccess = CreateObject("Access.Application")

    objAccess.OpenCurrentDatabase filepath:= _
        "C:\Ex07_HandsOn\Northwind.mdb"

    objAccess.DoCmd.TransferSpreadsheet _
        TransferType:=acExport, _
        SpreadsheetType:=acSpreadsheetTypeExcel12, _
        TableName:="Shippers", _
        Filename:="C:\Ex07_ByExample\Shippers.xls", _
        HasFieldNames:=True, _
        Range:="Sheet1"

    objAccess.Quit
    Set objAccess = Nothing
End Sub
```

The ExportData procedure uses Automation to establish a connection to Microsoft Access. The database is opened using the OpenCurrent-Database method. The TransferSpreadsheet method of the DoCmd object is used to specify that the data from the Shippers table should be exported into an Excel spreadsheet named Shippers.xls and placed in Sheet1 of this workbook. The first row of the worksheet is to be used by field headings. When data is retrieved, the Access application is closed and the object variable pointing to the Access application is destroyed.

3. Switch to the Excel application window and choose **View** | **Macros** | **View Macros**. In the Macros dialog box, select the **ExportData** procedure and click **Run**.
4. Open the Shippers.xls file created by the ExportData procedure to view the retrieved data. When asked to verify that the file is not corrupted or is from a trusted source, click **OK**.

Using the OpenDatabase Method

Introduced in Excel 2002, the OpenDatabase method is the easiest way to get database data into a Microsoft Excel spreadsheet. This method, which applies to the workbooks, requires that you specify the name of a database file that you want to open.

The following example procedure demonstrates how to open the Northwind database using the OpenDatabase method of the Workbooks collection.

```
Sub OpenAccessDatabase()
    On Error Resume Next

    Workbooks.OpenDatabase _
        Filename:="C:\Ex07_HandsOn\Northwind.mdb"
    Exit Sub
End Sub
```

When you run the above procedure, Excel will display a dialog box listing all the tables and queries in the database (see Figure 16-11). After making a selection from the list, a new workbook is opened with the worksheet showing data from the selected table or query.

The OpenDatabase method has four optional arguments that you can use to further qualify the data that you want to retrieve.

Table 16-2: Optional arguments for the OpenDatabase method

Optional Argument Name	Data Type	Description
CommandText	Variant	The SQL query string. See the example below for using this argument.
CommandType	Variant	The command type of the query. Specify one of the following constants: xlCmdCube, xlCmdList, xlCmdSql, xlCmdTable, or xlCmdDefault.
BackgroundQuery	Variant	Use True to have Excel perform queries for the report asynchronously (in the background). The default value is False.
ImportDataAs	Variant	Specifies the format of the query. Use xlQueryTable or xlPivotTableReport to generate a query table or a PivotTable report from the retrieved database data.

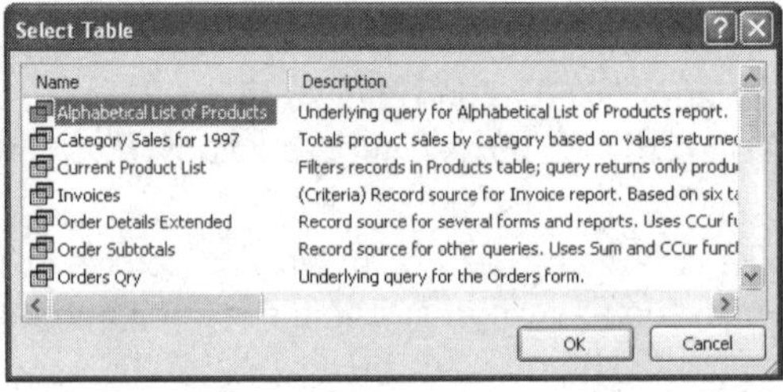

Figure 16-11: Database data stored in a table or query can be easily retrieved into an Excel workbook using the OpenDatabase method.

Let's write a procedure that creates a PivotTable report from the retrieved customer records.

Hands-On 16-14: Retrieving Access Data into a PivotTable Using the OpenDatabase Method

1. Insert a new module into the AccessFromExcel VBA project and rename it **Method_OpenDatabase**.
2. In the Method_OpenDatabase module Code window, enter the CountCustomersByCountry procedure as shown below:

```
Sub CountCustomersByCountry()
    On Error Resume Next

    Workbooks.OpenDatabase _
        Filename:="C:\Ex07_HandsOn\Northwind.mdb", _
        CommandText:="Select * from Customers", _
        CommandType:=xlCmdSql, _
        BackgroundQuery:=True, _
        ImportDataAs:=xlPivotTableReport
    Exit Sub
End Sub
```

3. Switch to the Excel application window and choose **View | Macros | View Macros**. Select the **CountCustomersByCountry** procedure and click **Run**. When you run the procedure, Excel opens a new workbook and displays a PivotTable Field List window listing the fields that are available in the Customers table (see Figure 16-12).

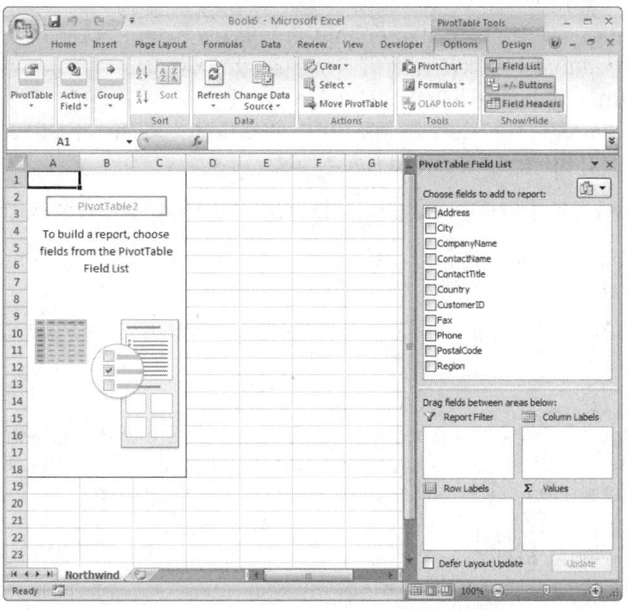

Figure 16-12: Using the OpenDatabase method's optional arguments, you can specify that the database data be retrieved into a specific format, such as a PivotTable report or a query table.

4. Drag the Country and CustomerID fields from the PivotTable Field List and drop them in the Row Labels area. Drag the CustomerID field and drop it in the Values area. Figure 16-13 displays the completed PivotTable report.

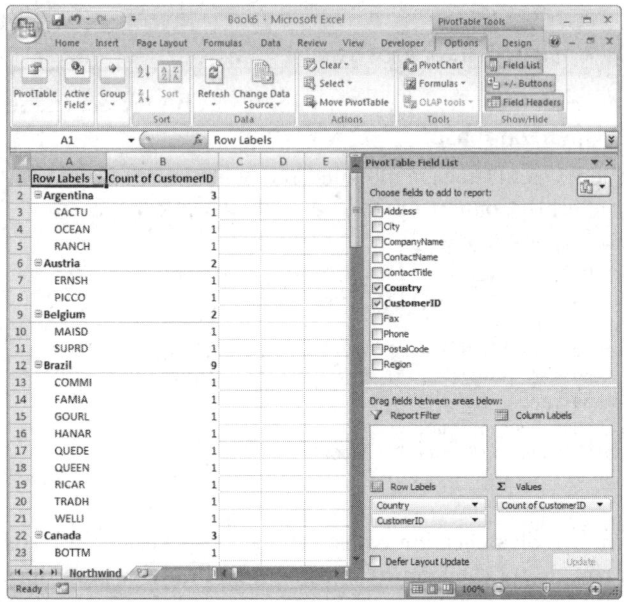

Figure 16-13: A PivotTable report based on the data retrieved from the Northwind database's Customers table.

5. Close the workbook with the PivotTable report.

Creating a Text File from Access Data

You can create a comma- or tab-delimited text file from Access data by using a VBA procedure in Excel. Text files are particularly useful for transferring large amounts of data to a spreadsheet.

The example procedure below illustrates how you can create a tab-delimited text file from an ADO Recordset.

Hands-On 16-15: Creating a Text File from Access Data

1. Insert a new module into the AccessFromExcel VBA project and rename it **TextFiles**.
2. In the TextFiles module Code window, enter the CreateTextFile procedure as shown below.

Note: For this procedure to work correctly, you must create a reference to the Microsoft ActiveX Data Objects 2.8 library. (Refer to the instructions on setting up a reference to object libraries earlier in this chapter.)

```
Sub CreateTextFile()
    Dim strPath As String
    Dim conn As New ADODB.Connection
    Dim rst As ADODB.Recordset
    Dim strData As String
    Dim strHeader As String
    Dim strSQL As String
    Dim fld As Variant
```

```
    strPath = "C:\Ex07_HandsOn\Northwind.mdb"

    conn.Open "Provider=Microsoft.Jet.OLEDB.4.0;" _
        & "Data Source=" & strPath & ";"

    conn.CursorLocation = adUseClient

    strSQL = "SELECT * FROM Products WHERE UnitPrice > 50"
    Set rst = conn.Execute(CommandText:=strSQL, Options:=adCmdText)

    ' save the recordset as a tab-delimited file
    strData = rst.GetString(StringFormat:=adClipString, _
                ColumnDelimeter:=vbTab, RowDelimeter:=vbCr, _
                nullExpr:=vbNullString)

    For Each fld In rst.Fields
        strHeader = strHeader + fld.Name & vbTab
    Next

    Open "C:\Ex07_ByExample\ProductsOver50.txt" For Output As #1
    Print #1, strHeader
    Print #1, strData
    Close #1

    rst.Close
    conn.Close

    Set rst = Nothing
    Set conn = Nothing
End Sub
```

Before the text file can be created we retrieve the necessary records from the Access database using the GetString method of the Recordset object. This method returns a set of records into a string and is faster than looping through the recordset. The GetString method has the following syntax:

```
variant = recordset.GetString(StringFormat, NumRows, ColumnDelimiter, _
     RowDelimiter, NullExpr)
```

The first argument (StringFormat) determines the format for representing the recordset as a string. Use the adClipString constant for this argument. The second argument (NumRows) specifies the number of recordset rows to return. If blank, GetString will return all the rows. The third argument (ColumnDelimiter) specifies the delimiter for the columns within the row (the default is a tab — vbTab). The fourth argument (RowDelimiter) specifies a row delimiter (the default is a carriage return — vbCr). The fifth argument (NullExpr) specifies an expression to represent NULL values (the default is an empty string — vbNullString).

Once we have all the data in a String variable, the procedure loops through the fields in the recordset to retrieve the names of columns. The GetString method can only handle the data requests, so if you need the data with the headings you need to get this info separately. We store the names of fields in a separate String variable.

Next, the procedure creates a text file with the following statement:

```
Open "C:\Ex07_ByExample\ProductsOver50.txt" For Output As #1
```

You should already be familiar with this method of creating text files as it was discussed in detail in Chapter 14.

Next, we use the Print statement to write both the heading and the data string to the text file. Now that the file has the data, we can close it with the Close statement.

3. Run the CreateTextFile procedure. The procedure creates the ProductsOver50.txt file in the root directory of your C drive.
4. Open the ProductsOver50.txt file. In the Open dialog box, select **All Files (*.*)** in the Files of type drop-down list. Next, select the **ProductsOver50.txt** file and click **Open**. The Text Import Wizard (Step 1 of 3) dialog box will open with the Delimited option button selected. Click **Next** to preview the structure of this file. Click **Finish** to show the data in a worksheet.

In Chapter 13, you learned how to work with text files using the FileSystemObject. The procedure below demonstrates how to use this object to create a text file named ProductsOver20.txt:

```
Sub CreateTextFile2()
    Dim conn As New ADODB.Connection
    Dim rst As ADODB.Recordset
    Dim strPath As String
    Dim strData As String
    Dim strHeader As String
    Dim strSQL As String
    Dim fso As Object
    Dim myFile As Object
    Dim fld As Variant

    Set fso = CreateObject("Scripting.FileSystemObject")
    Set myFile = fso.CreateTextFile( _
       "C:\Ex07_ByExample\ProductsOver20.txt", True)

    strPath = "C:\Ex07_HandsOn\Northwind 2007.accdb"

    conn.Open "Provider=Microsoft.ACE.OLEDB.12.0;" _
        & "Data Source=" & strPath & ";"
    conn.CursorLocation = adUseClient
    strSQL = "SELECT * FROM Products WHERE [List Price] > 20"

    Set rst = conn.Execute(CommandText:=strSQL, Options:=adCmdText)

    ' save the recordset as a tab-delimited file
    strData = rst.GetString(StringFormat:=adClipString, _
                ColumnDelimeter:=vbTab, RowDelimeter:=vbCr, _
                nullExpr:=vbNullString)

    For Each fld In rst.Fields
        strHeader = strHeader + fld.Name & vbTab
    Next
```

```
    With myFile
        .WriteLine strHeader
        .WriteLine strData
        .Close
    End With
End Sub
```

Creating a Query Table from Access Data

If you want to work in Excel with data that comes from external data sources and you know that the data you'll be working with often undergoes changes, you may want to create a query table. A *query table* is a special table in an Excel worksheet that is connected to an external data source, such as a Microsoft Access database, SQL Server, web page, or text file. To retrieve the most up-to-date information, the user can easily refresh the query table. Microsoft Excel offers a special option for obtaining data from external data sources: Simply choose Data | From Other Sources | From Microsoft Query.

By querying an external database, you can bring in data that fits your requirements exactly. For example, instead of bringing all product information into your spreadsheet for review, you may want to specify criteria that the data must meet prior to retrieval. Thus, instead of bringing in all the products from an Access table, you can retrieve only products with a unit price greater than $20.

In VBA, you can use the QueryTable object to access external data. Each QueryTable object represents a worksheet table built from data returned from an external data source, such as an SQL Server or a Microsoft Access database. To create a query programmatically, use the Add method of the QueryTables collection object. This method requires three arguments that are explained in the following Hands-On exercise. Let's see how you can use the QueryTable object programmatically.

Hands-On 16-16: Creating a Query Table from Access Data

1. Insert a new module into the AccessFromExcel VBA project and rename it **QueryTable**.
2. In the QueryTable module Code window, enter the CreateQueryTable procedure as shown below:

```
Sub CreateQueryTable()
    Dim myQryTable As Object
    Dim myDb As String
    Dim strConn As String
    Dim Dest As Range
    Dim strSQL As String

    myDb = "C:\Ex07_HandsOn\Northwind.mdb"
    strConn = "OLEDB;Provider=Microsoft.Jet.OLEDB.4.0;" _
        & "Data Source=" & myDb & ";"

    Workbooks.Add
    Set Dest = Worksheets(1).Range("A1")
```

```
    Sheets(1).Select
    strSQL = "SELECT * FROM Products WHERE UnitPrice > 20"
    Set myQryTable = ActiveSheet.QueryTables.Add(strConn, _
            Dest, _
            strSQL)
    With myQryTable
        .RefreshStyle = xlInsertEntireRows
        .Refresh False
    End With
End Sub
```

The CreateQueryTable procedure uses the following statement to create a query table on the active sheet:

```
Set myQryTable = ActiveSheet.QueryTables.Add(strConn, Dest, strSQL)
```

strConn is a variable that provides a value for the first argument of the QueryTables method — Connection. This is a required argument of the Variant data type that specifies the data source for the query table.

Dest is a variable that provides a value for the second argument — Destination. This is a required argument of the Range data type that specifies the cell where the resulting query table will be placed.

strSQL is a variable that provides a value for the third argument — SQL. This is a required argument of the String data type that defines the data to be returned by the query.

When you create a query using the Add method, the query isn't run until you call the Refresh method. This method accepts one argument — BackgroundQuery. This is an optional argument of the Variant data type that allows you to determine whether the control should be returned to the procedure when a database connection has been established and the query has been submitted (True) or to return control to the procedure after the query has been run and all the data has been retrieved into the worksheet (False).

The CreateQueryTable procedure only retrieves from the Northwind database's Products table those products whose UnitPrice field is greater than 20. Notice that the control is returned to the procedure only after all the relevant records have been fetched. The RefreshStyle method determines how data is inserted into the worksheet. The following constants can be used:

- **xlOverwriteCells** — Existing cells are overwritten with the incoming data.
- **xlInsertDeleteCells** — Cells are inserted or deleted to accommodate the incoming data.
- **xlInsertEntireRows** — Entire rows are inserted to accommodate incoming data.

3. Run the CreateQueryTable procedure. When this procedure completes, you should see a new workbook. The first sheet in this workbook will contain the data you specified in the query (Figure 16-14).

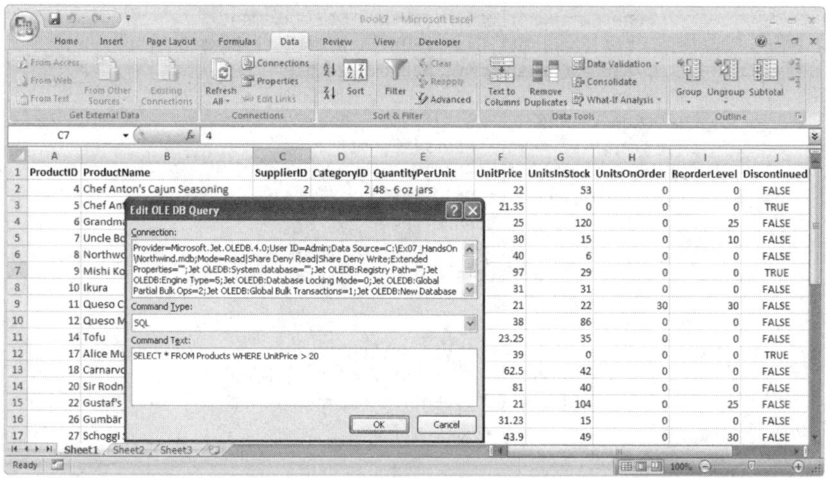

Figure 16-14: To modify the SQL statement for the query table, right-click anywhere within the returned data and choose Edit Query.

Creating an Embedded Chart from Access Data

Using VBA, you can easily create a chart based on the data retrieved from a Microsoft Access database. Charts are created by using the Add method of the Charts collection.

Let's spend some time now creating a procedure that fetches data from the Northwind database and creates an embedded chart.

Hands-On 16-17: Creating an Embedded Chart from Access Data

1. Insert a new module into the AccessFromExcel VBA project and rename it **ChartingData.**
2. In the ChartingData module Code window, enter the ChartData_withADO procedure as shown below:

```
Sub ChartData_withADO()
    Dim conn As New ADODB.Connection
    Dim rst As New ADODB.Recordset
    Dim mySheet As Worksheet
    Dim recArray As Variant
    Dim strQueryName As String
    Dim i As Integer
    Dim j As Integer

    strQueryName = "Category Sales for 1997"

    ' Connect with the database
    conn.Open _
        "Provider=Microsoft.Jet.OLEDB.4.0;" _
        & "Data Source=C:\Ex07_HandsOn\Northwind.mdb;"
```

```
    ' Open Recordset based on the SQL statement
        rst.Open "SELECT * FROM [" & strQueryName & "]", conn, _
        adOpenForwardOnly, adLockReadOnly

    Workbooks.Add
    Set mySheet = Worksheets("Sheet2")
    With mySheet.Range("A1")
        recArray = rst.GetRows()
        For i = 0 To UBound(recArray, 2)
            For j = 0 To UBound(recArray, 1)
                .Offset(i + 1, j) = recArray(j, i)
            Next j
        Next i
        For j = 0 To rst.Fields.Count - 1
            .Offset(0, j) = rst.Fields(j).Name
            .Offset(0, j).EntireColumn.AutoFit
        Next j
    End With

    rst.Close
    conn.Close
    Set rst = Nothing
    Set conn = Nothing

    mySheet.Activate
    Charts.Add
    ActiveChart.ChartType = xl3DColumnClustered
    ActiveChart.SetSourceData _
        Source:=mySheet.Cells(1, 1).CurrentRegion, _
        PlotBy:=xlRows
    ActiveChart.Location Where:=xlLocationAsObject, _
        Name:=mySheet.Name

    With ActiveChart
        .HasTitle = True
        .ChartTitle.Characters.Text = strQueryName
        .Axes(xlCategory).HasTitle = True
        .Axes(xlCategory).AxisTitle.Characters.Text = ""
        .Axes(xlValue).HasTitle = True
        .Axes(xlValue).AxisTitle. _
            Characters.Text = mySheet.Range("B1") & "($)"
        .Axes(xlValue).AxisTitle.Orientation = xlUpward
    End With
End Sub
```

The above procedure uses ActiveX Data Objects (ADO) to retrieve data from an Access database query. The data rows are retrieved using the GetRows method of the Recordset object. As you already know from earlier examples in this chapter, the GetRows method retrieves data into a two-dimensional array. Once the data is placed in an Excel worksheet, a chart is added with the Add method. The SetSourceData method of the Chart object sets the source data range for the chart, like this:

```
ActiveChart.SetSourceData Source:=mySheet.Cells(1, 1).CurrentRegion, _
          PlotBy:=xlRows
```

Source is the range that contains the source data that we have just placed on the worksheet beginning at cell A1. PlotBy will cause the embedded chart to plot data by rows.

Next, the Location method of the Chart object specifies where the chart should be placed. This method takes two arguments: Where and Name. The Where argument is required. You can use one of the following constants for this argument: xlLocationAsNewSheet, xlLocationAsObject, or xlLocationAutomatic. The Name argument is required if Where is set to xlLocationAsObject. In this procedure, the Location method specifies that the chart should be embedded in the active worksheet:

```
ActiveChart.Location Where:=xlLocationAsObject, Name:=mySheet.Name
```

Next, a group of statements formats the chart by setting various properties.

3. Run the ChartData_withADO procedure.

   The resulting chart is shown in Figure 16-15.

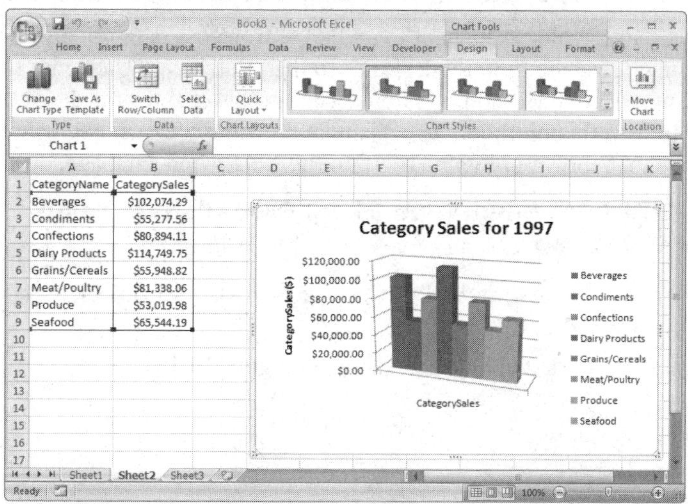

Figure 16-15: You can create an embedded chart programmatically with VBA based on the data retrieved from a Microsoft Access table, a query, or an SQL statement.

Transferring the Excel Spreadsheet to an Access Database

Many of the world's biggest databases began as spreadsheets. When the time comes to build a database application from your spreadsheet, you can resort to a tedious manual method to have the data transferred, or you can use your recently acquired VBA programming skills to automatically turn your spreadsheets into database tables. Once in a database format, your Excel data can be used in advanced company-wide reports or as a stand-alone application (needless to say, the latter requires that you possess database application design skills).

The remaining sections of this chapter demonstrate how to link and import Excel spreadsheets to an Access database. Prior to moving your Excel data to Access, it is a good idea to clean up your data as much as possible so that the transfer operation goes smoothly. Keep in mind that each spreadsheet row you'll be transferring will become a record in a table, and each column will function as a table field. For this reason, the first row of the spreadsheet range that you are planning to transfer to Access should contain field names. There should be no gaps between the columns of data that you want to transfer. In other words, your data should be contiguous. If the data you want to transfer represents a large number of columns, you should print your data first and examine it so that there are no surprises later. If the first column of your data contains the field names, it is recommended that you use the built-in Transpose feature to reposition your data so that the data goes down rather than from left to right. The key to smooth data import is to make your spreadsheet look as close as possible to a database table.

Linking an Excel Spreadsheet to an Access Database

You can link an Excel spreadsheet to a Microsoft Access database by using the TransferSpreadsheet method. (Refer to the "Retrieving Data with the TransferSpreadsheet Method" section earlier in this chapter for the details on working with this method.) The example procedure shown below links the spreadsheet shown in Figure 16-16 to the Northwind database.

Hands-On 16-18: Linking an Excel Spreadsheet to an Access Database

1. Insert a new sheet into the Practice_Excel16.xlsm workbook and rename it **mySheet**.
2. Prepare the worksheet data as shown in Figure 16-16.

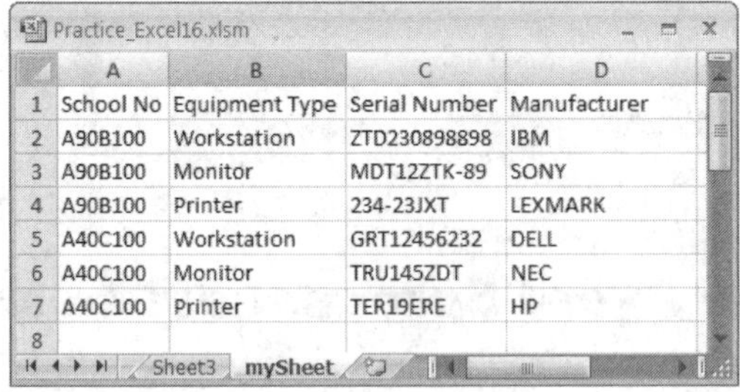

	A	B	C	D
1	School No	Equipment Type	Serial Number	Manufacturer
2	A90B100	Workstation	ZTD230898898	IBM
3	A90B100	Monitor	MDT12ZTK-89	SONY
4	A90B100	Printer	234-23JXT	LEXMARK
5	A40C100	Workstation	GRT12456232	DELL
6	A40C100	Monitor	TRU145ZDT	NEC
7	A40C100	Printer	TER19ERE	HP
8				

Figure 16-16: The LinkExcel_ToAccess VBA procedure links this spreadsheet to the Northwind database in Microsoft Access.

3. Switch to the Visual Basic Editor screen and insert a new module into the AccessFromExcel VBA project. Rename this module **ExcelToAccess.**
4. In the ExcelToAccess module Code window, enter the LinkExcel_ToAccess procedure as shown below:

```
Sub LinkExcel_ToAccess()
    Dim objAccess As Access.Application
    Dim strTableName As String
```

```
    Dim strBookName As String
    Dim strPath As String

    strPath = ActiveWorkbook.Path
    strBookName = strPath & "\Practice_Excel16.xlsm"
    strName = "Linked_ExcelSheet"

    Set objAccess = New Access.Application

    With objAccess
      .OpenCurrentDatabase "C:\Ex07_HandsOn\Northwind 2007.accdb"
      .DoCmd.TransferSpreadsheet acLink, _
             acSpreadsheetTypeExcel12Xml, _
             strName, strBookName, True, "mySheet!A1:D7"
    End With
End Sub
```

After opening the Access database with the OpenCurrentDatabase method, the procedure uses the TransferSpreadsheet method of the Microsoft Access DoCmd object to create a linked table named Linked_ExcelSheet from the specified range of cells (A1:D7) located in the mySheet worksheet in the Practice_Excel16.xls spreadsheet file. Notice that the True argument in the DoCmd statement indicates that the first row of the spreadsheet contains column headings.

Note: You cannot add, change, or delete the data in Access tables that are linked to Excel workbooks in Access 2007/2003/2002. If you need to perform these operations, you should import the Excel data to Access, make the required changes, and then export the data to Excel in the .xls file format.

5. Run the LinkExcel_ToAccess procedure. When the procedure finishes execution, open the Northwind 2007 database and take a look at the linked table.

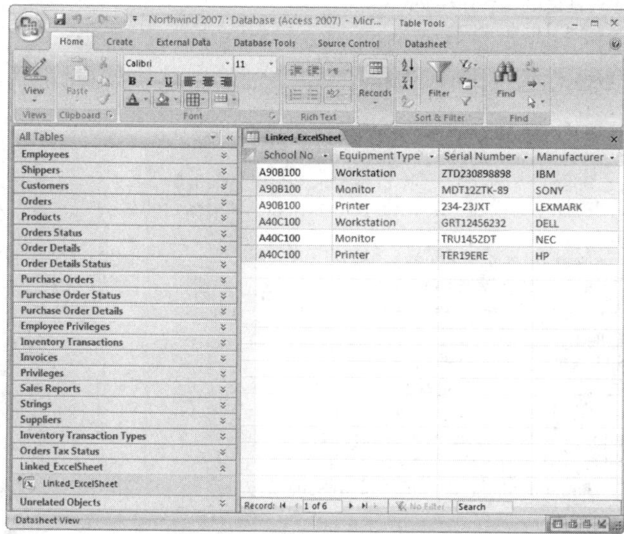

Figure 16-17: The Microsoft Excel spreadsheet is linked to a Microsoft Access database.

6. Close the Linked_ExcelSheet table in Access and exit the application.

Importing an Excel Spreadsheet to an Access Database

In the previous section, you learned how to link your Excel spreadsheet to an Access database. Importing your spreadsheet data is just as easy. You can even use the same VBA procedure you used for linking with only minor changes; simply modify the name, replace the acLink constant with acImport, change the table name, and you are done.

Placing Excel Data in an Access Table

What if, rather than linking or importing your Excel spreadsheet, you wanted to create an Access table from scratch and load it with the data sitting in a worksheet? Using several programming techniques that you've already acquired in this book, you can easily accomplish this task.

Let's write a VBA procedure that dynamically creates an Access table based on the Excel worksheet presented in Figure 16-16 (see "Linking an Excel Spreadsheet to an Access Database").

Hands-On 16-19: Creating an Access Table and Populating It with the Worksheet Data

This Hands-On requires the worksheet data prepared in Hands-On 16-18 (see Figure 16-16).

1. In the ExcelToAccess module Code window, enter the AccessTbl_From_ExcelData procedure as shown below:

```
Sub AccessTbl_From_ExcelData()
    Dim conn As ADODB.Connection
    Dim cat As ADOX.Catalog
    Dim myTbl As ADOX.Table
    Dim rstAccess As ADODB.Recordset
    Dim rowCount As Integer
    Dim i As Integer

    On Error GoTo ErrorHandler

    ' connect to Access using ADO
    Set conn = New ADODB.Connection
    conn.Open "Provider = Microsoft.Jet.OLEDB.4.0;" & _
        "Data Source = C:\Ex07_HandsOn\Northwind.mdb;"

    ' create an empty Access table
    Set cat = New Catalog
    cat.ActiveConnection = conn
    Set myTbl = New ADOX.Table
    myTbl.Name = "TableFromExcel"
    cat.Tables.Append myTbl

    ' add fields (columns) to the table
    With myTbl.Columns
        .Append "School No", adVarWChar, 7
```

```
        .Append "Equipment Type", adVarWChar, 15
        .Append "Serial Number", adVarWChar, 15
        .Append "Manufacturer", adVarWChar, 20
    End With
    Set cat = Nothing

    MsgBox "The table structure was created."

    ' open a recordset based on the newly created
    ' Access table

    Set rstAccess = New ADODB.Recordset
    With rstAccess
        .ActiveConnection = conn
        .CursorType = adOpenKeyset
        .LockType = adLockOptimistic
        .Open myTbl.Name
    End With

    ' now transfer data from Excel spreadsheet range

    With Worksheets("mySheet")
        rowCount = Range("A2:D7").Rows.Count

        For i = 2 To rowCount + 1
            With rstAccess
                .AddNew    ' add a new record to an Access table
                .Fields("School No") = Cells(i, 1).Text
                .Fields("Equipment Type") = Cells(i, 2).Value
                .Fields("Serial Number") = Cells(i, 3).Value
                .Fields("Manufacturer") = Cells(i, 4).Value
                .Update    ' update the table record
            End With
        Next i
    End With

    MsgBox "Data from an Excel spreadsheet was loaded into the table."

    ' close the Recordset and Connection object and remove them
    ' from memory
    rstAccess.Close
    conn.Close
    Set rstAccess = Nothing
    Set conn = Nothing

    MsgBox "Open the Northwind database to view the table."
AccessTbl_From_ExcelDataExit:
    Exit Sub
ErrorHandler:
    MsgBox Err.Number & ": " & Err.Description
    Resume AccessTbl_From_ExcelDataExit
End Sub
```

Notice that this procedure connects to the Access database using ActiveX Data Objects (ADO). After the connection is established, the procedure creates a new Access table by using the Catalog and Table objects from the ADOX object library. Next, the fields are added to the table based on the names of the worksheet columns. Each text field specifies the maximum number of characters that it can accept. If the worksheet cell's length is larger than the specified field size, the error-handling routine will display the Access built-in message appropriate for this error and the procedure will end. The final task in the procedure is the data transfer operation. To perform this task, the procedure opens a recordset based on the newly created table. Because we need to add records to the table, the procedure uses an adOpenKeyset cursor type. The For...Next loop is used to move through the Excel data rows, placing information found in each worksheet cell into the corresponding table field. Notice that a new record is added to an Access table with the AddNew method of the Recordset object. After copying data from all cells in each row, the procedure uses the Update method of the Recordset object to save the table record.

2. Run the AccessTbl_From_ExcelData procedure.
3. Open the Northwind database to view the procedure results.

Chapter Summary

This chapter presented numerous examples of getting Excel data into a Microsoft Access database and retrieving data from Microsoft Access into a worksheet. You learned how to control an Access application from an Excel VBA procedure, performing such tasks as opening Access forms and reports, creating new forms, running select and parameter queries, and calling Access built-in functions. In addition, this chapter has shown you techniques for creating text files, query tables, and charts from the Access data. You also learned how to place Excel data in an Access database by using linked, imported, and dynamic Access tables.

This chapter completes Part VI of this book. In the next chapter, you will learn how event programming can help you build spreadsheet applications that respond to or limit user actions.

Part VII

Enhancing the User Experience

Extensive changes have been made to the Excel 2007 user interface (UI). The menus and toolbars are replaced with a new navigation tool called the Ribbon that provides a task-oriented method of performing spreadsheet activities — whether it's formatting or analyzing data.

In this part of the book, you learn how to create desired interface elements for your users via Ribbon customizations and how to create dialog boxes and custom forms. You will also learn how to format spreadsheets with VBA and control Excel with event-driven programming.

Chapter 17

Event-Driven Programming

Introduction to Event Procedures ■ Writing Your First Event Procedure ■ Enabling and Disabling Events ■ Event Sequences ■ Worksheet Events ■ Worksheet_Activate() ■ Worksheet_Deactivate() ■ Worksheet_SelectionChange() ■ Worksheet_Change() ■ Worksheet_Calculate() ■ Worksheet_BeforeDoubleClick(ByVal Target As Range, Cancel As Boolean) ■ Worksheet_BeforeRightClick(ByVal Target As Range, Cancel As Boolean) ■ **Workbook Events ■** Workbook_Activate() ■ Workbook_Deactivate() ■ Workbook_Open() ■ Workbook_BeforeSave (ByVal SaveAsUI As Boolean, Cancel As Boolean) ■ Workbook_BeforePrint(Cancel As Boolean) ■ Workbook_BeforeClose(Cancel As Boolean) ■ Workbook_NewSheet (ByVal Sh As Object) ■ Workbook_WindowActivate(ByVal Wn As Window) ■ Workbook_WindowDeactivate(ByVal Wn As Window) ■ Workbook_WindowResize(ByVal Wn As Window) ■ **PivotTable Events ■ Chart Events ■** Writing Event Procedures for a Chart Located on a Chart Sheet ■ Writing Event Procedures for Embedded Charts ■ **Events Recognized by the Application Object ■ Query Table Events ■ Chapter Summary**

How do you disable a built-in shortcut menu when a user clicks on a worksheet cell? How do you display a custom message before a workbook is opened or closed? How can you validate data entered in a cell or range of cells?

To gain complete control over Microsoft Excel, you must learn how to respond to events. Learning how to program events will allow you to implement your own functionality in an Excel application. The first thing you need to know about this subject is what an event is. An *event* is an action recognized by an object. An event is something that happens to objects that are part of Microsoft Excel. However, once you learn about events in Excel, you will find it easier to understand events that occur to objects in Word or any other Microsoft Office application.

Events can be triggered by an application user (such as you), another program, or the system itself. So, how can you trigger an event? Suppose you right-clicked a worksheet cell. This particular action would display a built-in shortcut menu for a worksheet cell, allowing you to quickly access the most frequently used commands related to worksheet cells. But what if this particular built-in response isn't appropriate under certain conditions? You may want to entirely disallow right-clicking in a worksheet or perhaps ensure that a custom menu appears on a cell shortcut menu when the user right-clicks any cell. The good news is you can use VBA to write code that can react to events as they occur. The following Microsoft Excel objects can respond to events:

- Worksheet
- Chart sheet
- Query table
- Workbook
- Application

You can decide what should happen when a particular event occurs by writing an event procedure.

Introduction to Event Procedures

A special type of VBA procedure, an *event procedure*, is used to react to specific events. This procedure contains VBA code that handles a particular event. Some events may require a single line of code, while others can be more complex. Event procedures have names, which are created in the following way:

```
ObjectName_EventName()
```

In the parentheses after the name of the event, you can place parameters that need to be sent to the procedure. The programmer cannot change the name of the event procedure.

Before you can write an event procedure to react to an Excel event, you need to know:

- The name of the particular object and event to which you want to respond.

  Objects that can respond to events display a list of events in the Procedure drop-down list in the Code window (see Figure 17-1). Also, you can use the Object Browser to find out the names of the events (see Figure 17-2).

- The place where you should put the event code.

  Some events are coded in a standard module; others are stored in a class module. While workbook, chart sheet, and worksheet events are available for any open sheet or workbook, to create event procedures for an embedded chart, query table, or the Application object, you must first create a new object using the With Events keyword in the class module.

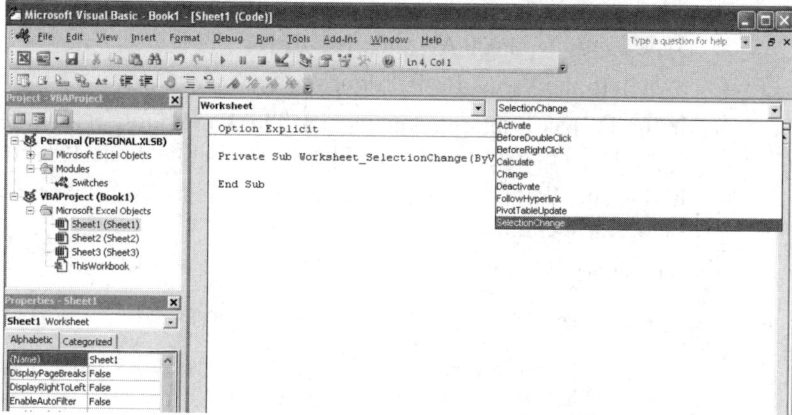

Figure 17-1: You can find out the event names in the Code window.

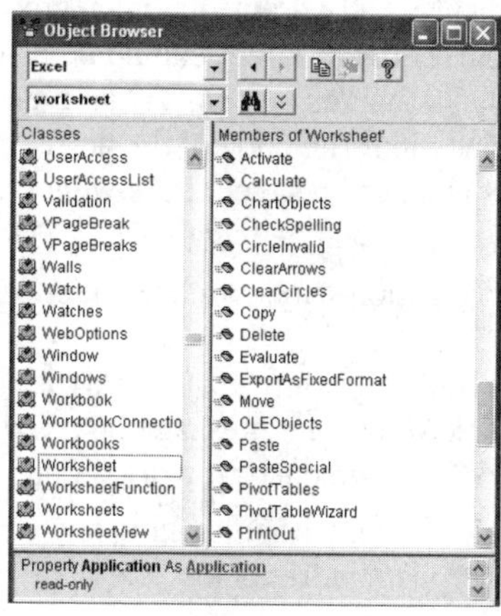

Figure 17-2: You can also find out the event names in the Object Browser.

Writing Your First Event Procedure

The first event procedure you will write in this chapter displays a dialog box prompting the user to copy the active worksheet to another workbook whenever the workbook save operation is requested. Once this event procedure is written, its code will run automatically when a user attempts to save the workbook file in which the procedure is located.

Hands-On 17-1: Writing an Event Procedure

1. Open a new workbook and save it as **C:\Ex07_ByExample\Practice_Excel17.xlsm.**
2. Change the name of Sheet1 in the Practice_Excel17.xlsm workbook to **Test**.
3. Type anything in cell A1 and press **Enter**.
4. Switch to the Visual Basic Editor screen.
5. In the Project Explorer, double-click **ThisWorkbook** in the Microsoft Excel Objects folder under VBAProject (Practice_Excel17.xlsm).
6. In the ThisWorkbook Code window, enter the following Workbook_BeforeSave event procedure:

```
Private Sub Workbook_BeforeSave(ByVal SaveAsUI As Boolean, _
          Cancel As Boolean)
    If MsgBox("Would you like to copy " & vbCrLf _
          & "this worksheet to " & vbCrLf _
          & "a new workbook?", vbQuestion + vbYesNo) = vbYes Then
          Sheets(ActiveSheet.Name).Copy
    End If
End Sub
```

   The above event procedure displays a two-button dialog box asking the user whether a copy of the current worksheet should be placed in another workbook. If the user clicks the Yes button, Visual Basic will open a new workbook and will place in it the copy of the active workbook. The original workbook file will not be saved. If, however, the user clicks No, the Excel built-in save event will be triggered.

7. Switch to the Microsoft Excel application window, click the **Microsoft Office** button, and choose **Save**.

   The Workbook_BeforeSave event procedure that you wrote in step 6 will be triggered at this time. Click **Yes** to the message box. Excel will open a new workbook with the copy of the current worksheet.

8. Close the workbook file created by Excel without saving any changes. Do not close the Practice_Excel17.xlsm workbook.
9. Click the **Microsoft Office** button and choose **Save** to save Practice_Excel17.xlsm.

   Notice that again you are prompted with the dialog box. Click **No** to the message. Notice that the workbook file is now being saved.

But what if you wanted to copy the worksheet file to another workbook and also save the original workbook file? Let's modify our Workbook_BeforeSave procedure to make sure the workbook file is saved regardless of whether the user answered Yes or No to the message.

10. Change the Workbook_BeforeSave procedure as follows:

```
Private Sub Workbook_BeforeSave(ByVal SaveAsUI As Boolean, _
        Cancel As Boolean)

    Dim wkb As Workbook
    Set wkb = ActiveWorkbook

    Cancel = False

    If MsgBox("Would you like to copy " & vbCrLf _
        & "this worksheet to " & vbCrLf _
        & "a new workbook?", vbQuestion + vbYesNo) = vbYes Then
        Sheets(ActiveSheet.Name).Copy
        wkb.Activate
    End If
End Sub
```

To continue with the saving process, all you need to do is set the Cancel argument to False. This will trigger Excel's built-in save event.

Note: If you'd rather call your own saving procedure, set the Cancel property to True and type the name of your custom save procedure. Here's a short event procedure example:

```
Private Sub Workbook_BeforeSave(ByVal SaveAsUI As Boolean, _
        Cancel As Boolean)
    ' abort the built-in save event
    Cancel = True
    ' call your own saving procedure
    MyCustomSaveProcedure
End Sub
```

11. Type anything in the Test worksheet in the Practice_Excel17.xlsm file, then click the **Save** button on the Quick Access toolbar.

    When you click Yes or No in response to the message box, Excel proceeds to save the workbook file (you should see the flashing message in the status bar). If you clicked Yes, Excel also copies the Test worksheet to another workbook. After all these tasks are completed, Excel activates the Practice_Excel17.xlsm workbook.

12. If you answered Yes in the previous step, close the workbook file created by Excel without saving any changes. Do not close Practice_Excel17.xlsm.

    Now that you know how to use the Cancel argument, let's look at the other argument of the Workbook_BeforeSave event — SaveAsUI. This argument allows you to handle the situation when the user chooses the Save As option. Suppose that in our procedure example we want to prompt the user to copy the current worksheet to another workbook only when the Save option is selected. When the user selects Save As, we don't want to bother him with the prompt. The following step takes this situation into consideration.

13. Modify the Workbook_BeforeSave event procedure as follows:

```
Private Sub Workbook_BeforeSave(ByVal SaveAsUI As Boolean, _
        Cancel As Boolean)

    If SaveAsUI = True Then Exit Sub
    Dim wkb As Workbook
    Set wkb = ActiveWorkbook

    Cancel = False

    If MsgBox("Would you like to copy " & vbCrLf _
        & "this worksheet to " & vbCrLf _
        & "a new workbook?", vbQuestion + vbYesNo) = vbYes Then
        Sheets(ActiveSheet.Name).Copy
        wkb.Activate
    End If
End Sub
```

14. Switch to the Practice_Excel17.xlsm application window, click the **Microsoft Office** button, and choose **Save As | Excel Macro-Enabled Workbook.**

    Notice that you are not prompted to copy the current worksheet to another workbook. Instead, Excel proceeds to run its own built-in Save As process. When the Save As dialog box appears, click **Cancel.**

Enabling and Disabling Events

You can use the Application object's EnableEvents property to enable or disable events. If you are writing a VBA procedure and don't want a particular event to occur, set the EnableEvents property to False.

To demonstrate how you can prevent a custom event procedure from running, we will write a procedure in a standard module that will save the workbook after making some changes in the active sheet. We will continue working with the Practice_Excel17.xlsm file because it already contains the Worksheet_BeforeSave event procedure we want to block in this demonstration.

Hands-On 17-2: Disabling a Custom Event Procedure

This Hands-On requires prior completion of Hands-On 17-1.

1. Choose **Insert | Module** to add a standard module to VBAProject (Practice_Excel17.xlsm).
2. In the module's Code window, enter the following EnterData procedure:

```
Sub EnterData()
    With ActiveSheet.Range("A1:B1")
        .Font.Color = vbRed
```

```
        .Value = 15
    End With
    Application.EnableEvents = False
    ActiveWorkbook.Save
    Application.EnableEvents = True
End Sub
```

Notice that prior to calling the Save method of the ActiveWorkbook property, we have disabled events by setting the EnableEvents property to False. This will prevent the Workbook_BeforeSave event procedure from running when Visual Basic encounters the statement to save the workbook. We don't want the user to be prompted to copy the worksheet while running the EnterData procedure. When Visual Basic has completed the saving process, we want the system to respond to the events as we programmed them, so we enable the events with the Application.EnableEvents statement set to True.

3. Switch to the Practice_Excel17.xlsm application window and choose **View | Macros | View Macros**. In the Macro dialog box, select **EnterData** and click **Run**.

   Notice that when you run the EnterData procedure, you are not prompted to copy the worksheet before saving. This indicates that the Workbook_BeforeSave event is not running.

4. Close the Practice_Excel17.xlsm workbook.

Event Sequences

Events occur in response to specific actions. Events also occur in a predefined sequence. The table below demonstrates the sequence of events that occur while opening a new workbook, adding a new worksheet to a workbook, and closing the workbook.

Table 17-1: Event sequences

Action	Object	Event Sequence
Opening a new workbook	Workbook	NewWorkbook ↓ WindowDeactivate ↓ WorkbookDeactivate ↓ WorkbookActivate ↓ WindowActivate
Inserting a new sheet into a workbook	Workbook	WorkbookNewSheet ↓ SheetDeactivate ↓ SheetActivate

Action	Object	Event Sequence
Closing a workbook	Workbook	WorkbookBeforeClose ↓ WindowDeactivate ↓ WorkbookDeactivate ↓ WorkbookActivate ↓ WindowActivate

Worksheet Events

A Worksheet object responds to such events as activating and deactivating a worksheet, calculating data in a worksheet, making a change to a worksheet, and double-clicking or right-clicking a worksheet. Below you will find some of the events to which the Worksheet object can respond.

Table 17-2: Worksheet events

Worksheet Event Name	Event Description
Activate	This event occurs upon activating a worksheet.
Deactivate	This event occurs when the user activates a different sheet.
SelectionChange	This event occurs when the user selects a worksheet cell.
Change	This event occurs when the user changes a cell formula.
Calculate	This event occurs when the user recalculates the worksheet.
BeforeDoubleClick	This event occurs when the user double-clicks a worksheet cell.
BeforeRightClick	This event occurs when the user right-clicks a worksheet cell.

Let's try out the above events to get the hang of them.

Worksheet_Activate()

This event occurs upon activating a worksheet.

Hands-On 17-3: Writing the Worksheet_Activate() Event Procedure

1. Open a new workbook and save it as **Practice_WorksheetEvents.xlsm** in your **Ex07_ByExample** folder.
2. Switch to the Visual Basic Editor window.

3. In the Project Explorer window, double-click **Sheet2** under VBAProject (Practice_WorksheetEvents.xlsm) in the Microsoft Excel Objects folder.
4. In the Sheet2 Code window, enter the code shown below:

```
Dim shtName As String

Private Sub Worksheet_Activate()
    shtName = ActiveSheet.Name
    Range("B2").Select
End Sub
```

   The example procedure selects cell B2 each time the sheet is activated. Notice that the shtName variable type is declared at the top of the module.
5. Switch to the Microsoft Excel application window and activate **Sheet2**.

   Notice that when Sheet2 is activated, the selection is moved to cell B2. Excel also stores the sheet name in the shtName variable that was declared at the top of the module. We will need this value as we work with other event procedures in this section.

Worksheet_Deactivate()

This event occurs when the user activates a different sheet in a workbook.

Hands-On 17-4: Writing the Worksheet_Deactivate() Event Procedure

This Hands-On uses the Practice_WorksheetEvents workbook created in the previous Hands-On exercise.

1. Switch to the Visual Basic Editor window. In the Sheet2 Code window, enter the Worksheet_Deactivate procedure as shown below:

```
Private Sub Worksheet_Deactivate()
    MsgBox "You deactivated " & _
        shtName & "." & vbCrLf & _
        "You switched to " & _
        ActiveSheet.Name & "."
End Sub
```

   The example procedure displays a message when Sheet2 is deactivated.
2. Switch to the Microsoft Excel application window and click the **Sheet2** tab.

   The Worksheet_Activate procedure that you created in Hands-On 17-3 will run first. Excel will select cell B2 and store the name of the worksheet in the shtName global variable declared at the top of the Sheet2 code module.
3. Now click any other sheet in the active workbook.

   Notice that Excel displays the name of the worksheet that you deactivated and the name of the worksheet to which you have switched.

Worksheet_SelectionChange()

This event occurs when the user selects a worksheet cell.

Hands-On 17-5: Writing the Worksheet_SelectionChange() Event Procedure

1. Switch to the Visual Basic Editor window. In the Project Explorer window, double-click **Sheet3** under VBAProject (Practice_WorksheetEvents.xlsm) in the Microsoft Excel Objects folder.
2. In the Sheet3 Code window, enter the Worksheet_SelectionChange procedure as shown below.

```
Private Sub Worksheet_SelectionChange(ByVal Target As Excel.Range)
    Dim myRange As Range

On Error Resume Next
    Set myRange = Intersect(Range("A1:A10"), Target)
    If Not myRange Is Nothing Then
       MsgBox "Data entry or edits are not permitted."
    End If
End Sub
```

   The example procedure displays a message if the user selects any cell in myRange.

3. Switch to the Microsoft Excel application window and activate **Sheet3**. Click on any cell within the specified range A1:A10.

   Notice that Excel displays a message whenever you click a cell in the restricted area.

Worksheet_Change()

This event occurs when the user changes a cell formula.

Hands-On 17-6: Writing the Worksheet_Change() Event Procedure

1. In the Visual Basic Editor window, activate the Project Explorer window and double-click **Sheet1** in the Microsoft Excel Objects folder of Practice_WorksheetEvents.xlsm.
2. In the Sheet1 Code window, enter the Worksheet_Change event procedure as shown below:

```
Private Sub Worksheet_Change(ByVal Target As Excel.Range)
    Application.EnableEvents = False
        Target = UCase(Target)
        Columns(Target.Column).AutoFit
    Application.EnableEvents = True
End Sub
```

   The example procedure changes what you type in a cell to uppercase. The column where the target cell is located is then auto sized.

3. Switch to the Microsoft Excel application window and activate **Sheet1**. Enter any text in any cell.

   Notice that as soon as you press the **Enter** key, Excel changes the text you typed to uppercase, and auto sizes the column.

Worksheet_Calculate()

This event occurs when the user recalculates the worksheet.

Hands-On 17-7: Writing the Worksheet_Calculate() Event Procedure

1. Add a new sheet to the Practice_WorksheetEvents workbook. In cell A2 of this newly added sheet, enter **1**, and in cell B2, enter **2**. Enter the following formula in cell C2: **= A2+B2**.
2. Switch to the Visual Basic Editor window, activate the Project Explorer window and double-click the sheet you added in step 1.
3. In the Code window, enter the code of the Worksheet_Calculate procedure as shown below:

```
Private Sub Worksheet_Calculate()
    MsgBox "The worksheet was recalculated."
End Sub
```

4. Switch to the Microsoft Excel application window and modify the entry in cell B2 on the sheet you added in step 1 by typing any number.

   Notice that after leaving Edit mode, the Worksheet_Calculate event procedure is triggered and you are presented with a custom message.

Worksheet_BeforeDoubleClick(ByVal Target As Range, Cancel As Boolean)

This event occurs when the user double-clicks a worksheet.

Hands-On17-8: Writing the Worksheet_BeforeDoubleClick() Event Procedure

1. Enter any data in cell **C9** on **Sheet2** of the Practice_WorksheetEvents workbook.
2. In the Visual Basic Editor window, activate the Project Explorer window and open the Microsoft Excel Objects folder. Double-click **Sheet2**.
3. In the Sheet2 Code window, type the code of the procedure as shown below:

```
Private Sub Worksheet_BeforeDoubleClick(ByVal _
       Target As Range, Cancel As Boolean)
    If Target.Address = "$C$9" Then
        MsgBox "No double-clicking, please."
        Cancel = True
    Else
        MsgBox "You may edit this cell."
```

```
    End If
End Sub
```

The example procedure disallows in-cell editing when cell C9 is double-clicked.

4. Switch to the Microsoft Excel application window and double-click cell **C9** on Sheet2.

   The Worksheet_BeforeDoubleClick event procedure cancels the built-in Excel behavior, and the user is not allowed to edit the data inside the cell. However, the user can get around this restriction by clicking on the formula bar or pressing F2. When writing event procedures that restrict access to certain program features, write additional code that prevents any workaround.

Worksheet_BeforeRightClick(ByVal Target As Range, Cancel As Boolean)

This event occurs when the user right-clicks a worksheet cell.

Hands-On 17-9: Writing the Worksheet_BeforeRightClick() Event Procedure

1. In the Visual Basic Editor window, activate the Project Explorer window and double-click **Sheet2** in the Microsoft Excel Objects folder.
2. In the Sheet2 Code window, enter the code of the Worksheet_Before-RightClick procedure as shown below:

```
Private Sub Worksheet_BeforeRightClick(ByVal _
    Target As Range, Cancel As Boolean)

    With Application.CommandBars("Cell")
        .Reset
        If Target.Rows.Count > 1 Or _
            Target.Columns.Count > 1 Then
            With .Controls.Add(Type:=msoControlButton, _
                    before:=1, temporary:=True)
                    .Caption = "Print..."
                    .OnAction = "PrintMe"
            End With
        End If
    End With
End Sub
```

   The example procedure adds a Print option to the cell shortcut menu when the user selects more than one cell on the worksheet

3. Insert a new module into the current project and enter the PrintMe procedure as shown below:

```
Sub PrintMe()
    Application.Dialogs(xlDialogPrint).Show arg12:=1
End Sub
```

   The PrintMe procedure is called by the Worksheet_BeforeRightClick event when the user selects the Print option from the shortcut menu.

Notice that the Show method of the Dialogs collection is followed by a named argument: arg12:=1. This argument will display the Print dialog box with the preselected option button "Selection" in the Print area of the dialog box. Excel dialog boxes are covered in the next chapter.

4. Switch to the Microsoft Excel application window and right-click on any single cell in Sheet2.

   Notice that the shortcut menu appears with the default options.

5. Now select at least two cells in the Sheet2 worksheet and right-click the selected area.

   You should see the Print option as the first menu entry. Click the **Print** option and notice that instead of the default "Print active sheet," the Print dialog displays "Print Selection."

Workbook Events

Workbook object events occur when the user performs such tasks as opening, activating, deactivating, printing, saving, and closing a workbook. Workbook events are not created in a standard VBA module. To write code that responds to a particular workbook you can:

- Double-click the ThisWorkbook object in the Visual Basic Editor's Project Explorer.
- In the Code window that appears, open the Object drop-down list on the left-hand side and select the Workbook object.
- In the Procedure drop-down list (the one on the right), select the event you want. The selected event procedure stub will appear in the Code window as shown below:

```
Private Sub Workbook_Open()
    place your event handling code here
End Sub
```

Below you will find some of the events to which the Workbook object can respond.

Table 17-3: Workbook events

Workbook Event Name	Event Description
Activate	This event occurs when the user activates the workbook. This event will not occur when the user activates the workbook by switching from another application.
Deactivate	This event occurs when the user activates a different workbook within Excel. This event does not occur when the user switches to a different application.
Open	This event occurs when the user opens a workbook.
BeforeSave	This event occurs before the workbook is saved. The SaveAsUI argument is read-only and refers to the Save As dialog box. If the workbook has not been saved, the value of SaveAsUI is True; otherwise, it is False.

Workbook Event Name	Event Description
BeforePrint	This event occurs before the workbook is printed and before the Print dialog appears. The example procedure places the full workbook's name in the document footer prior to printing if the user clicks Yes in the message box.
BeforeClose	This event occurs before the workbook is closed and before the user is asked to save changes.
NewSheet	This event occurs after the user creates a new sheet in a workbook.
WindowActivate	This event occurs when the user shifts the focus to any window showing the workbook.
WindowDeactivate	This event occurs when the user shifts the focus away from any window showing the workbook.
WindowResize	This event occurs when the user opens, resizes, maximizes, or minimizes any window showing the workbook.

Let's try out the above events to get the hang of them.

Workbook_Activate()

This event occurs when the user activates the workbook. This event will not occur when the user activates the workbook by switching from another application.

Hands-On 17-10: Writing the Workbook_Activate() Event Procedure

1. Open a new workbook and save it as **Practice_WorkbookEvents.xlsm** in your **C:\Ex07_ByExample** folder.
2. Switch to the Visual Basic Editor window. In the Project Explorer window, double-click **ThisWorkbook** in the Microsoft Excel Objects folder.
3. In the ThisWorkbook Code window, type the Workbook_Activate procedure as shown below:

```
Private Sub Workbook_Activate()
    MsgBox "This workbook contains " & _
        ThisWorkbook.Sheets.Count & " sheets."
End Sub
```

   The example procedure displays the total number of worksheets when the user activates the workbook containing the Workbook_Activate event procedure.
4. Switch to the Microsoft Excel application window and open a new workbook.
5. Activate the Practice_WorkbookEvents workbook. Excel should display the total number of sheets in this workbook.

Workbook_Deactivate()

This event occurs when the user activates a different workbook within Excel. This event does not occur when the user switches to a different application.

Hands-On 17-11: Writing the Workbook_Deactivate() Event Procedure

1. In the Visual Basic Editor window, activate the Project Explorer window and double-click **ThisWorkbook** in the Microsoft Excel Objects folder under VBAProject (Practice_WorkbookEvents.xlsm).
2. In the ThisWorkbook Code window, type the Workbook_Deactivate procedure as shown below:

```
Private Sub Workbook_Deactivate()
    Dim cell As Range
    For Each cell In ActiveSheet.UsedRange
        If Not IsEmpty(cell) Then
            Debug.Print cell.Address & ":" & cell.Value
        End If
    Next
End Sub
```

   The example procedure will print to the Immediate window the addresses and values of cells containing entries in the current workbook when the user activates a different workbook.
3. Switch to the Microsoft Excel application window and make some entries on the active sheet. Next, activate a different workbook.
   This action will trigger the Workbook_Deactivate event procedure.
4. Switch to the Visual Basic Editor screen and open the Immediate window to see what entries were reported.

Workbook_Open()

This event occurs when the user opens a workbook.

Hands-On 17-12: Writing the Workbook_Open() Event Procedure

1. Double-click the **ThisWorkbook** object in the Microsoft Excel Objects folder under VBAProject (Practice_WorkbookEvents.xlsm).
2. In the ThisWorkbook Code window, type the Workbook_Open procedure as shown below:

```
Private Sub Workbook_Open()
    ActiveSheet.Range("A1").Value = Format(Now(), "mm/dd/yyyy")
    Columns("A").AutoFit
End Sub
```

   The example procedure places the current date in cell A1 when the workbook is opened.

3. Save and close Practice_WorkbookEvents.xlsm and then reopen it.

   When you open the workbook file again, the Workbook_Open event procedure will be triggered and the current date will be placed in cell A1 on the active sheet.

Workbook_BeforeSave(ByVal SaveAsUI As Boolean, Cancel As Boolean)

This event occurs before the workbook is saved.

The SaveAsUI argument is read-only and refers to the Save As dialog box. If the workbook has not been saved, the value of SaveAsUI is True; otherwise, it is False.

Hands-On 17-13: Writing the Workbook_BeforeSave() Event Procedure

1. In the Visual Basic Editor screen, activate the Project Explorer window and open the Microsoft Excel Objects folder under VBAProject (Practice_WorkbookEvents.xlsm). Double-click **ThisWorkbook**.
2. In the ThisWorkbook Code window, type the Workbook_BeforeSave procedure as shown below:

```
Private Sub Workbook_BeforeSave(ByVal _
        SaveAsUI As Boolean, Cancel As Boolean)
    If SaveAsUI = True And _
        ThisWorkbook.Path = vbNullString Then
        MsgBox "This document has not yet " _
            & "been saved." & vbCrLf _
        & "The Save As dialog box will be displayed."
    ElseIf SaveAsUI = True Then
        MsgBox "You are not allowed to use " _
            & "the SaveAs option. "
        Cancel = True
    End If
End Sub
```

   The example procedure displays the Save As dialog box if the workbook hasn't been saved before. The workbook's pathname will be a null string (vbNullString) if the file has not been saved before. The procedure will not let the user save the workbook under a different name — the SaveAs operation will be aborted by setting the Cancel argument to True. The user will need to choose the Save option to have the workbook saved.

3. Switch to the Microsoft Excel application window and activate any sheet in the Practice_WorkbookEvents.xlsm workbook.
4. Make an entry in any cell of this workbook, click the **Microsoft Office** button, and choose **Save As | Excel Macro-Enabled Workbook.**

   The Workbook_BeforeSave event procedure will be activated, and the ElseIf clause gets executed. Notice that you are not allowed to save the workbook by using the SaveAs option.

Workbook_BeforePrint(Cancel As Boolean)

This event occurs before the workbook is printed and before the Print dialog appears.

Hands-On 17-14: Writing the Workbook_BeforePrint() Event Procedure

1. In the Visual Basic Editor window, activate the Project Explorer window and double-click the **ThisWorkbook** object in the Microsoft Excel Objects folder under VBAProject (Practice_WorkbookEvents.xlsm).
2. In the ThisWorkbook Code window, type the Workbook_BeforePrint event procedure as shown below:

```
Private Sub Workbook_BeforePrint(Cancel As Boolean)
    Dim response As Integer
    response = MsgBox("Do you want to  " & vbCrLf & _
        "print the workbook's full name in the footer?", _
        vbYesNo)
    If response = vbYes Then
        ActiveSheet.PageSetup.LeftFooter = _
            ThisWorkbook.FullName
    Else
        ActiveSheet.PageSetup.LeftFooter = ""
    End If
End Sub
```

   The example procedure places the workbook's full name in the document footer prior to printing if the user clicks Yes in the message box.
3. Switch to the Microsoft Excel application window and activate any sheet in the Practice_WorkbookEvents.xlsm workbook.
4. Enter anything you want in any worksheet cell.
5. Click the **Microsoft Office** button and choose **Print | Print Preview**.
   Excel will ask you if you want to place the workbook's name and path in the footer.

Workbook_BeforeClose(Cancel As Boolean)

This event occurs before the workbook is closed and before the user is asked to save changes.

Hands-On 17-15: Writing the Workbook_BeforeClose() Event Procedure

1. In the Visual Basic Editor window, activate the Project Explorer window and double-click **ThisWorkbook** in the Microsoft Excel Objects folder under VBAProject (Practice_WorkbookEvents.xlsm).
2. In the ThisWorkbook Code window, type the Workbook_BeforeClose event procedure as shown below:

```
Private Sub Workbook_BeforeClose(Cancel As Boolean)
    If MsgBox("Do you want to change " & vbCrLf _
```

```
        & " workbook properties before closing?", _
            vbYesNo) = vbYes Then
        Application.Dialogs(xlDialogProperties).Show
    End If
End Sub
```

The example procedure displays the Properties dialog box if the user responds Yes to the message box.

3. Switch to the Microsoft Excel application window, and close the Practice_WorkbookEvents.xlsm workbook.

   Upon closing, you should see a message box asking you to view the Properties dialog box prior to closing. After viewing or modifying the workbook properties, the procedure closes the workbook. If there are any changes that you have not yet saved, you are given the chance to save the workbook, cancel the changes, or abort the closing operation altogether.

Workbook_NewSheet(ByVal Sh As Object)

This event occurs after the user creates a new sheet in a workbook.

Hands-On 17-16: Writing the Workbook_NewSheet() Event Procedure

1. Open a new workbook and save it as **Practice_Workbook-Events2.xlsm** in your C:\Ex07_ByExample folder.
2. Switch to the Visual Basic Editor window, and in the Project Explorer window, double-click **ThisWorkbook** in the Microsoft Excel Objects folder under VBAProject (Practice_WorkbookEvents2.xlsm).
3. In the ThisWorkbook Code window, type the Workbook_NewSheet event procedure as shown below:

```
Private Sub Workbook_NewSheet(ByVal Sh As Object)
    If MsgBox("Do you want to place  " & vbCrLf _
        & "the new sheet at the beginning " & vbCrLf _
        & "of the workbook?", vbYesNo) = vbYes Then
                Sh.Move before:=ThisWorkbook.Sheets(1)
    Else
        Sh.Move After:=ThisWorkbook.Sheets( _
             ThisWorkbook.Sheets.Count)
        MsgBox Sh.Name & _
             " is now the last sheet in the workbook."
    End If
End Sub
```

   The example procedure places the new sheet at the beginning of the workbook if the user responds Yes to the message box; otherwise, the new sheet is placed at the end of the workbook.

4. Switch to the Microsoft Excel application window and click the **Insert Worksheet** tab (at the bottom of the screen). Excel will ask where to place the new sheet.

Let's try out some of the events related to operations on workbook windows.

Workbook_WindowActivate(ByVal Wn As Window)

This event occurs when the user shifts the focus to any window showing the workbook.

Hands-On 17-17: Writing the Workbook_WindowActivate() Event Procedure

1. In the Visual Basic Editor window, activate the Project Explorer window and double-click the **ThisWorkbook** object in the Microsoft Excel Objects folder under VBAProject (Practice_WorkbookEvents2.xlsm).
2. In the ThisWorkbook Code window, enter the Workbook_Window-Activate event procedure as shown below:

```
Private Sub Workbook_WindowActivate(ByVal Wn As Window)
    Wn.GridlineColor = vbYellow
End Sub
```

   The example procedure changes the color of the worksheet gridlines to yellow when the user activates the workbook containing the code of the Workbook_WindowActivate procedure.
3. Switch to the Microsoft Excel application window and open a new workbook.
4. To arrange Microsoft Excel workbooks vertically on the screen, choose **View | Arrange All** to open the Arrange Windows dialog. Select the **Vertical** option button and click **OK**. When you activate the worksheet of the workbook in which you entered the code of the Workbook_WindowActivate event procedure, the color of the gridlines should change to yellow.

Workbook_WindowDeactivate(ByVal Wn As Window)

This event occurs when the user shifts the focus away from any window showing the workbook.

Hands-On 17-18: Writing the Workbook_WindowDeactivate() Event Procedure

1. In the Visual Basic Editor window, activate the Project Explorer window and double-click the **ThisWorkbook** object in the Microsoft Excel Objects folder under VBAProject (Practice_WorkbookEvents2.xlsm).
2. In the ThisWorkbook Code window, enter the Workbook_Window-Deactivate procedure as shown below:

```
Private Sub Workbook_WindowDeactivate(ByVal Wn As Window)
    MsgBox "You have just deactivated " & Wn.Caption
End Sub
```

   The example procedure displays the name of the deactivated workbook when the user switches to another workbook from the workbook containing the code of the Workbook_WindowDeactivate procedure.

3. Switch to the Microsoft Excel application window and open a new workbook.

   Excel displays the name of the deactivated workbook in a message box.

Workbook_WindowResize(ByVal Wn As Window)

This event occurs when the user opens, resizes, maximizes, or minimizes any window showing the workbook.

Hands-On 17-19: Writing the Workbook_WindowResize() Event Procedure

1. In the Visual Basic Editor window, activate the Project Explorer window and double-click the **ThisWorkbook** object in the Microsoft Excel Objects folder under VBAProject (Practice_WorkbookEvents2.xlsm).
2. In the ThisWorkbook Code window, enter the Workbook_WindowResize procedure as shown below.

```
Private Sub Workbook_WindowResize(ByVal Wn As Window)
    If Wn.WindowState <> xlMaximized Then
        Wn.Left = 0
        Wn.Top = 0
    End If
End Sub
```

   The example procedure moves the workbook window to the top left-hand corner of the screen when the user resizes it.

3. Switch to the Microsoft Excel application and activate the Practice_WorkbookEvents2.xlsm workbook.
4. Click the **Restore Window** button to the right of the menu bar.
5. Move the Practice_WorkbookEvents2.xlsm window to the middle of the screen by dragging its title bar.
6. Change the size of the active window by dragging the window borders in or out.

   As you complete the sizing operation, the workbook window should automatically jump to the top left-hand corner of the screen.

7. Click the **Maximize** button to restore the Practice_Workbook-Events2.xlsm workbook window to its full size.

An Excel workbook can respond to a number of other events, as shown in Table 17-4.

Table 17-4: Additional workbook events

Workbook Event Name	Event Description
SheetActivate	This event occurs when the user activates any sheet in the workbook. The SheetActivate event occurs also at the application level when any sheet in any open workbook is activated.
SheetDeactivate	This event occurs when the user activates a different sheet in a workbook.
SheetSelectionChange	This event occurs when the user changes the selection on a worksheet. This event happens for each sheet in a workbook.
SheetChange	This event occurs when the user changes a cell formula.
SheetCalculate	This event occurs when the user recalculates a worksheet.
SheetBeforeDoubleClick	This event occurs when the user double-clicks a cell on a worksheet.
SheetBeforeRightClick	This event occurs when the user right-clicks a cell on a worksheet.

PivotTable Events

In Excel, PivotTable reports provide a powerful way of analyzing and comparing large amounts of information stored in a database. By rotating rows and columns of a PivotTable report, you can see different views of the source data or see details of the data that interests you the most. When working with PivotTable reports programmatically, you can determine when a PivotTable report opened or closed the connection to its data source by using the PivotTableOpenConnection and PivotTableCloseConnection workbook events and determine when the PivotTable was updated via the SheetPivotTableUpdate event.

Table 17-5: Workbook events related to PivotTable reports

Workbook Event Name	Event Description
PivotTableOpenConnection	Occurs after a PivotTable report opens the connection to its data source. This event requires that you declare an object of type Application or Workbook using the WithEvents keyword in a class module (see examples of using this keyword near the end of this chapter).
PivotTableCloseConnection	Occurs after a PivotTable report closes the connection to its data source. This event requires that you declare an object of type Application or Workbook using the WithEvents keyword in a class module (see examples of using this keyword near the end of this chapter).

<table>
<tr><th>Workbook Event Name</th><th>Event Description</th></tr>
<tr><td>SheetPivotTableUpdate

The SheetPivotTableUpdate event procedure takes the following two arguments:

Sh — the selected sheet

Target — the selected PivotTable report.</td><td>This event occurs after the sheet of the PivotTable report has been updated. This event requires that you declare an object of type Application or Workbook using the WithEvents keyword in a class module (see examples of using this keyword at the end of this chapter). The example event procedure shown below, along with other procedures related to this event, can be found in the downloadable file Practice_PivotReportEvents.xlsm.<pre>
Private Sub pivTbl_SheetPivotTableUpdate(_
        ByVal Sh As Object, _
        ByVal Target As PivotTable)
    MsgBox Target.Name & _
      " report has been updated." & vbCrLf _
      & "The PivotReport is located in cells " & _
      Target.DataBodyRange.Address
End Sub
</pre></td></tr>
</table>

Chart Events

As you know, you can create charts in Excel that are embedded in a worksheet or located on a separate chart sheet. In this section, you will learn how to control chart events no matter where you've decided to place your chart. Before you try out selected chart events, perform the tasks in Hands-On 17-20.

Hands-On 17-20: Creating Charts for Trying Out Chart Events

1. Open a new Excel workbook and save it as **Practice_Chart-Events.xlsm.**
2. Enter sample data as shown in Figure 17-3.
3. Select cells **A1:D5**, and choose **Insert | Column | Clustered Cylinder.**

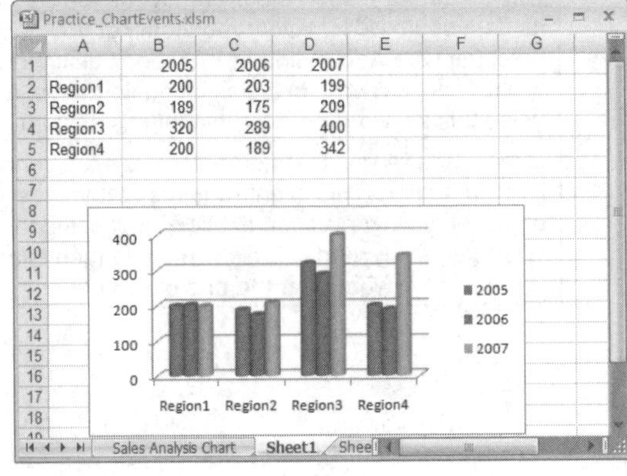

Figure 17-3: Column chart embedded in a worksheet.

4. Size the chart as shown in Figure 17-3.
5. Using the same data, create a line chart on a separate chart sheet, as shown in Figure 17-5. To add a new chart sheet, right-click any sheet tab in the workbook and choose **Insert**. In the Insert dialog box, select **Chart** and click **OK.** On the Design tab in the Data group, click the **Select Data** button. Excel will display the Select Data Source dialog box. At this point, click the **Sheet1** tab and select cells **A1:D5**. Excel will fill in the Chart data range box in the dialog box (Figure 17-4). Click **OK** to complete the chart. Now, change the chart type to Line chart with Markers by choosing the **Change Chart Type** button in the Type group of the Ribbon's **Design** tab. In the Change Chart Type dialog box, select **Line** chart in the left pane, and click the button representing the Line chart with Markers. Click **OK** to close the dialog box.
6. Change the name of the chart sheet to **Sales Analysis Chart**.

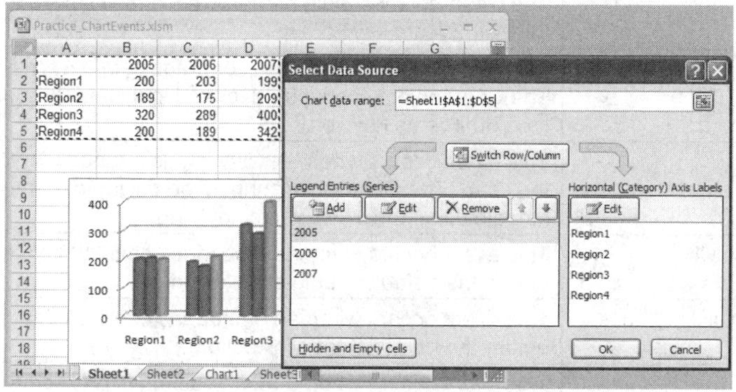

Figure 17-4: Creating a chart in a chart sheet.

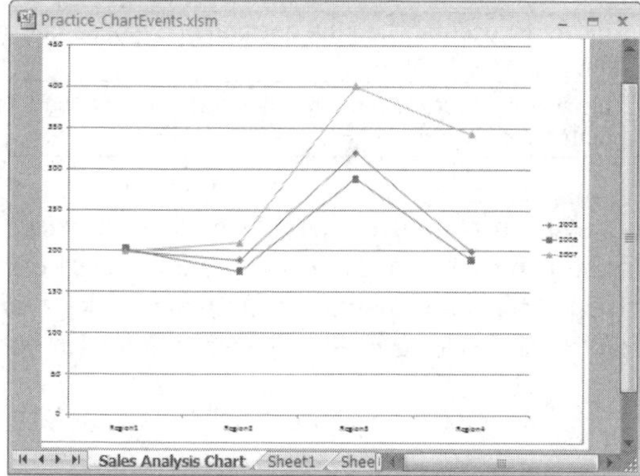

Figure 17-5: Line chart placed in a chart sheet.

Writing Event Procedures for a Chart Located on a Chart Sheet

Excel charts can respond to a number of events, as shown in the table below.

Table 17-6: Chart events

Chart Event Name	Description
Activate	This event occurs when the user activates the chart sheet.
Deactivate	This event occurs when the user deactivates the chart sheet.
Select	This event occurs when the user selects a chart element.
SeriesChange	This event occurs when the user changes the value of a chart data point. The Chart object should be declared in the class module using the WithEvents keyword.
Calculate	This event occurs when the user plots new or changed data on the chart.
Resize	This event occurs when the user changes the size of the chart. The Chart object should be declared in the class module using the WithEvents keyword.
DragOver	This event occurs when the user drags data over the chart. The Chart object should be declared in the class module using the WithEvents keyword.
DragPlot	This event occurs when the user drags a range of cells over the chart. The Chart object should be declared in the class module using the WithEvents keyword.
BeforeDoubleClick	This event occurs when an embedded chart is double-clicked, before the default double-click action.
BeforeRightClick	This event occurs when an embedded chart is right-clicked, before the default right-click action.
MouseDown	This event occurs when a mouse button is pressed while the pointer is over a chart.
MouseMove	This event occurs when the position of a mouse pointer changes over a chart.
MouseUp	This event occurs when a mouse button is released while the pointer is over a chart.

We will start by writing event procedures that control a chart placed on a separate chart sheet as shown in Figure 17-5. Events for a chart embedded in a worksheet (see Figure 17-3) require using the WithEvents keyword and are explained in the section titled "Writing Event Procedures for Embedded Charts."

Chart_Activate()

This event occurs when the user activates the chart sheet.

Chart_Deactivate()

This event occurs when the user deactivates the chart sheet.

Chart_Select(ByVal ElementID As Long, ByVal Arg1 As Long, ByVal Arg2 As Long)

This event occurs when the user selects a chart element.

ElementID returns a constant representing the type of the selected chart element. Arguments Arg1 and Arg2 are used in relation to some chart elements. For example, the chart axis (ElementID = 21) can be specified as Main Axis (Arg1 = 0) or Secondary Axis (Arg1 = 1), while the axis type is specified by Arg2, which can be one of the following three values: 0 – Category Axis, 1 – Value Axis, and 3 – Series Axis.

Chart_Calculate()

This event occurs when the user plots new or changed data on the chart.

Chart_BeforeRightClick()

This event occurs when the user right-clicks the chart.

Chart_MouseDown(ByVal Button As Long, ByVal Shift As Long, ByVal x As Long, ByVal y As Long)

This event occurs when a mouse button is pressed while the pointer is over a chart.

The Button argument determines which mouse button was pressed (MouseDown event) or released (MouseUp event): 1 – left button, 2 – right button, and 4 – middle button.The Shift argument specifies the state of the Shift, Ctrl, and Alt keys: 1 – Shift was selected, 2 – Ctrl was selected, 4 – Alt was selected. The x, y arguments specify the mouse pointer coordinates.

Hands-On 17-21: Writing Event Procedures for a Chart Sheet

1. In the Visual Basic Editor window, activate the Project Explorer window and open the Microsoft Excel Objects folder under VBAProject (Practice_ChartEvents.xlsm).
2. Double-click the chart object **Chart1 (Sales Analysis Chart)**.
3. In the Code window, enter the code of the following event procedures:

```
Private Sub Chart_Activate()
    MsgBox "You've activated the chart sheet."
End Sub

Private Sub Chart_Deactivate()
    MsgBox "It looks like you want to leave the " _
     & "chart sheet."
End Sub

Private Sub Chart_Select(ByVal ElementID As Long, _
            ByVal Arg1 As Long, ByVal Arg2 As Long)
    If Arg1 <> 0 And Arg2 <> 0 Then
        MsgBox ElementID & ", " & Arg1 & ", " & Arg2
    End If
```

```
    If ElementID = 4 Then
        MsgBox "You've selected the chart title."
    ElseIf ElementID = 24 Then
        MsgBox "You've selected the chart legend."
    ElseIf ElementID = 12 Then
        MsgBox "You've selected the legend key."
    ElseIf ElementID = 13 Then
        MsgBox "You've selected the legend entry."
    End If
End Sub

Private Sub Chart_Calculate()
    MsgBox "The data in your spreadsheet has " & vbCrLf _
        & "changed. Your chart has been updated."
End Sub

Private Sub Chart_BeforeRightClick(Cancel As Boolean)
    Cancel = True
End Sub

Private Sub Chart_MouseDown(ByVal Button As Long, _
    ByVal Shift As Long, ByVal x As Long, ByVal y As Long)
    If Button = 1 Then
         MsgBox "You pressed the left mouse button."
    ElseIf Button = 2 Then
        MsgBox "You pressed the right mouse button."
    Else
        MsgBox "You pressed the middle mouse button."
    End If
End Sub
```

4. Activate the chart sheet and perform the actions that will trigger the event procedures that you've written. For example, click the chart legend and notice that this action triggers two events: Chart_MouseDown and Chart_Select.

Writing Event Procedures for Embedded Charts

To capture events raised by a chart embedded in a worksheet, you must first create a new object in the class module using the keyword WithEvents.

The WithEvents keyword allows you to specify an object variable that will be used to respond to events triggered by an ActiveX object. This keyword can only be used in class modules in the declaration section. In the following example procedure, we will learn how to use the WithEvents keyword to capture the Chart_Activate event for the embedded chart you created in Hands-On 17-20.

Hands-On 17-22: Writing the Chart_Activate() Event Procedure for an Embedded Chart

1. Activate the Visual Basic Editor window. In the Project Explorer, select **VBAProject (Practice_ChartEvents.xlsm)**.

2. Choose **Insert | Class Module.**

   In the Class Modules folder, you will see a module named Class1.
3. In the Properties window, rename Class1 to **clsChart**.
4. In the clsChart class module Code window, type the following declaration:

   ```
   Public WithEvents xlChart As Excel.Chart
   ```

   The above statement declares an object variable that will represent the events generated by the Chart object.

   The Public keyword will make the object variable xlChart available to all modules in the current VBA project. Declaring an object variable using the WithEvents keyword exposes all of the events defined for that particular object type. After typing the above declaration, the xlChart object variable is added to the drop-down Object list in the upper-left corner of the Code window, and the events associated with this object variable appear in the Procedure drop-down list box in the upper-right corner of the Code window.
5. Open the Object drop-down list box and select the **xlChart** variable.

   The Code window should now show the skeleton of the xlChart_Activate event procedure:

   ```
   Private Sub xlChart_Activate()

   End Sub
   ```
6. Add your VBA code to the event procedure. In this example, we will add a statement to display a message box. After adding this statement, your VBA procedure should look like the following:

   ```
   Private Sub xlChart_Activate()
       MsgBox "You've activated a chart embedded in " & ActiveSheet.Name
   End Sub
   ```

   After entering the code of the event procedure, you need to inform Visual Basic that you are planning on using it (see step 7).
7. In the Project Explorer window, double-click the object named **ThisWorkbook**, and enter in the first line of the ThisWorkbook Code window the statement to create a new instance of the class named clsChart:

   ```
   Dim myChart As New clsChart
   ```

   This instruction declares an object variable named myChart. This variable will refer to the xlChart object located in the class module clsChart. The New keyword tells Visual Basic to create a new instance of the specified object.

   Before you can use the myChart object variable you must write a VBA procedure that initializes it (see step 8).

8. Enter the following procedure in the ThisWorkbook Code window to initialize the object variable myChart:

```
Sub InitializeChart()

' you must run this procedure before event procedures
' written in clsChart class module can be triggered for
' the chart embedded in Sheet1

' connect the class module with the Excel chart object
    Set myChart.xlChart = _
        Worksheets("Sheet1").ChartObjects(1).Chart
End Sub
```

9. Run the InitializeChart procedure.

   After running this procedure, the event procedures entered in the clsChart class module will be triggered in response to a particular event. Recall that right now the clsChart class module contains the Chart_Activate event procedure. Later on you may want to write in the clsChart class module additional event procedures to capture other events for your embedded chart.

10. Activate the Microsoft Excel application window and click the embedded chart in Sheet1.

    At this time, the xlChart_Activate event procedure that you entered in step 6 above should be triggered.

11. Save and close the Practice_ChartEvents.xlsm workbook file.

Events Recognized by the Application Object

If you want your event procedure to execute no matter which Excel workbook is currently active, you need to create the event procedure for the Application object. Event procedures for the Application object have a global scope. This means that the procedure code will be executed in response to a certain event as long as the Microsoft Excel application remains open.

Events for the Application object are listed in Table 17-7. Similar to an embedded chart, event procedures for the Application object require that you create a new object using the WithEvents keyword in a class module.

Table 17-7: Application events

Application Event Name	Event Description
NewWorkbook	This event occurs when the user creates a new workbook.
WorkbookOpen	This event occurs when the user opens a workbook.
WorkbookActivate	This event occurs when the user shifts the focus to an open workbook.
WorkbookDeactivate	This event occurs when the user shifts the focus away from an open workbook.

Application Event Name	Event Description
WorkbookNewSheet	This event occurs when the user adds a new sheet to an open workbook.
WorkbookBeforeSave	This event occurs before an open workbook is saved.
WorkbookBeforePrint	This event occurs before an open workbook is printed.
WorkbookBeforeClose	This event occurs before an open workbook is closed.
WorkbookAddInInstall	This event occurs when the user installs a workbook as an add-in.
WorkbookAddInUninstall	This event occurs when the user uninstalls a workbook as an add-in.
SheetActivate	This event occurs when the user activates a sheet in an open workbook.
SheetDeactivate	This event occurs when the user deactivates a sheet in an open workbook.
SheetFollowHyperlink	This event occurs when the user clicks any hyperlink in Microsoft Excel.
SheetPivotTableUpdate	This event occurs after the sheet of the PivotTable report has been updated.
SheetSelectionChange	This event occurs when the user changes the selection on a sheet in an open workbook.
SheetChange	This event occurs when the user changes a cell formula in an open workbook.
SheetCalculate	This event occurs when the user recalculates a worksheet in an open workbook.
SheetBeforeDoubleClick	This event occurs when the user double-clicks a worksheet cell in an open workbook.
SheetBeforeRightClick	This event occurs when the user right-clicks a worksheet cell in an open workbook.
WindowActivate	This event occurs when the user shifts the focus to an open window.
WindowDeactivate	This event occurs when the user shifts the focus away from the open window.
WindowResize	This event occurs when the user resizes an open window.
WorkbookPivotTableCloseConnection	This event occurs after a PivotTable report connection has been closed.
WorkbookPivotTableOpenConnection	This event occurs after a PivotTable report connection has been opened.
WorkbookAfterXmlExport (new in 2003)	This event occurs after Microsoft Excel saves or exports data from any open workbook to an XML data file.
WorkbookAfterXmlImport (new in 2003)	This event occurs after an existing XML data connection is refreshed or new XML data is imported into any open Microsoft Excel workbook.

Application Event Name	Event Description
WorkbookBeforeXmlExport (new in 2003)	This event occurs before Microsoft Excel saves or exports data from any open workbook to an XML data file.
WorkbookBeforeXmlImport (new in 2003)	This event occurs before an existing XML data connection is refreshed or new XML data is imported into any open Microsoft Excel workbook.
WorkbookSync (new in 2003)	This event occurs when the local copy of a workbook that is part of a document workspace is synchronized with the copy on the server.

Let's try a couple of event procedures for the Application object.

Hands-On 17-23: Writing Event Procedures for the Application Object

1. Open a new workbook and save it as **Practice_ApplicationEvents.xlsm** in **C:\Ex07_ByExample.**
2. Switch to the Visual Basic Editor window, and in the Project Explorer window select **VBAProject (Practice_ApplicationEvents.xlsm).**
3. Choose **Insert | Class Module.**
4. In the Properties window, change the class module name to **clsApplication.**
5. In the clsApplication Code window, type the following declaration statement:

```
Public WithEvents App As Application
```

   This statement uses the WithEvents keyword to declare an object variable to represent the Application object.

6. Below the declaration statement, enter the event procedures as shown below:

```
Private Sub App_NewWorkbook(ByVal Wb As Workbook)
    Application.DisplayAlerts = False
    If Wb.Sheets.Count = 3 Then
        Sheets(Array(2, 3)).Delete
    End If
    Application.DisplayAlerts = True
End Sub

Private Sub App_WorkbookOpen(ByVal Wb As Workbook)
    If Wb.FileFormat = xlCSV Then
       If MsgBox("Do you want to save this " & vbCrLf _
         & "file as an Excel workbook?", vbYesNo, _
         "Original file format: " _
         & "comma delimited file") = vbYes Then
              Wb.SaveAs FileFormat:=xlWorkbookNormal
        End If
    End If
End Sub
```

```
Private Sub App_WorkbookBeforeSave(ByVal _
        Wb As Workbook, ByVal SaveAsUI As Boolean, _
        Cancel As Boolean)
    If Wb.Path <> vbNullString Then
        ActiveWindow.Caption = Wb.FullName & _
            " [Last Saved: " & Time & "]"
    End If
End Sub

Private Sub App_WorkbookBeforePrint(ByVal _
        Wb As Workbook, Cancel As Boolean)
    Wb.PrintOut Copies:=2
End Sub

Private Sub App_WorkbookBeforeClose(ByVal _
        Wb As Workbook, Cancel As Boolean)
    Dim r As Integer
    Sheets.Add
    r = 1
    For Each p In Wb.BuiltinDocumentProperties
      On Error GoTo ErrorHandle
        Cells(r, 1).Value = p.Name & " = " & _
            ActiveWorkbook.BuiltinDocumentProperties _
            .Item(p.Name).Value
        r = r + 1
    Next
    Exit Sub
ErrorHandle:
        Cells(r, 1).Value = p.Name
        Resume Next
End Sub

Private Sub App_SheetSelectionChange(ByVal Sh _
        As Object, ByVal Target As Range)

    If Selection.Count > 1 Or _
            (Selection.Count < 2 And _
            IsEmpty(Target.Value)) Then
        Application.StatusBar = Target.Address
    Else
        Application.StatusBar = Target.Address & _
            "(" & Target.Value & ")"
    End If
End Sub

Private Sub App_WindowActivate(ByVal _
        Wb As Workbook, ByVal Wn As Window)

    Wn.DisplayFormulas = True
End Sub
```

7. After you've entered the code of the above event procedures in the class module, choose **Insert | Module** to insert a standard module into your current VBA project.
8. In the newly inserted standard module, create a new instance of the clsApplication class and connect the object located in the class module

clsApplication with the object variable App representing the Application object, as shown below:

```
Dim DoThis As New clsApplication

  Public Sub InitializeAppEvents()
  Set DoThis.App = Application
End Sub
```

Recall that you declared the App object variable to point to the Application object in step 5 above.

9. Now place the mouse pointer within the InitializeAppEvents procedure and press **F5** to run it.

   As a result of running the InitializeAppEvents procedure, the App object in the class module will refer to the Excel application. From now on, when a specific event occurs, the code of the event procedures you've entered in the class module will be executed.

   If you don't want to respond to events generated by the Application object, you can break the connection between the object and its object variable by entering in a standard module (and then running) the following procedure:

```
Public Sub CancelAppEvents()
   Set DoThis.App = Nothing
End Sub
```

   When you set the object variable to Nothing, you release the memory and break the connection between the object variable and the object to which this variable refers. When you run the CancelAppEvents procedure, the code of the event procedures written in the class module will not be automatically executed when a specific event occurs.

   Now let's proceed to try triggering the application events you coded in the class module.

10. Switch to the **Practice_ApplicationEvents** workbook in the Excel application window. Click the **Microsoft Office** button and choose **New**. Select **Blank Workbook**, and click **Create**.

    Notice that the newly opened window contains only one sheet. While opening the new workbook the NewWorkbook event procedure has deleted the other two sheets that appear in all new workbooks by default.

11. Click the **Microsoft Office** button and choose **Save As**. Save the workbook opened in step 10 as **TestBeforeSaveEvent.xlsx**.

12. Type anything in Sheet1 of the TestBeforeSaveEvent.xlsx workbook and save this workbook.

    Notice that Excel writes the full name of the workbook file and the time the workbook was last saved in the workbook's title bar as coded in the WorkbookBeforeSave event procedure (see step 6). Every time you save this workbook file, Excel will update the last saved time in the workbook's title bar.

13. Take a look at the code in other event procedures you entered in step 6 and perform actions that will trigger these events.
14. Close the Practice_ApplicationEvents.xlsm file and other workbooks if they are currently opened.

Query Table Events

A query table is a table in an Excel worksheet that represents data returned from an external data source, such as an SQL Server database, a Microsoft Access database, a web page, or a text file. Excel provides two events for the QueryTable object: BeforeRefresh and AfterRefresh. These events are triggered before or after the query table is refreshed. Unlike previous versions, Excel 2007 can create a query table as a standalone object or as a list object whose data source is a query table. The list object is a new feature in Excel 2007 and is discussed in detail in Chapter 24.

When you retrieve data from an external data source such as Access or SQL Server using the controls available on the Excel 2007 Ribbon's Data tab, Excel creates a query table that is associated with a list object. The resulting table is easier to use thanks to a number of built-in data management features available on the Ribbon. The next Hands-On demonstrates how to create a query table associated with a list object and enable the QueryTable object's BeforeRefresh and AfterRefresh events. This exercise assumes that you have Microsoft Access 2007 and its sample Northwind 2007.accdb database installed on your computer.

Hands-On 17-24: Writing Event Procedures for a Query Table

1. Open a new Microsoft Excel workbook and save it as **Practice_QueryTableEvents.xlsm** in your **C:\Ex07_ByExample** folder.
2. Choose the **Data** tab. In the Get External Data group, click the **From Other Sources** button and choose **From Microsoft Query**.
3. In the Choose Data Source dialog box, select **<New Data Source>** and click **OK**.
4. In step 1 of the Create New Data Source dialog box, enter **SampleDb** as the data source name, as shown in Figure 17-6.
5. In step 2 of the Create New Data Source dialog box, select **Microsoft Access Driver (*.mdb, *.accdb)** from the drop-down list.

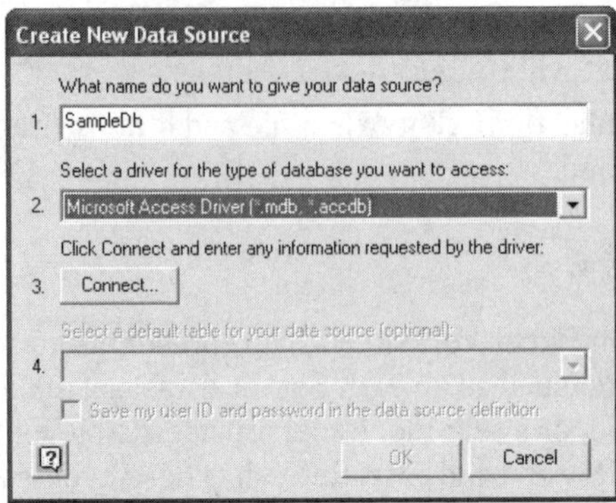

Figure 17-6: Use the Create New Data Source dialog box to specify the data source that will provide data for the query table.

6. In step 3 of the Create New Data Source dialog box, click the **Connect** button.
7. In the ODBC Microsoft Access Setup dialog box, click the **Select** button.
8. In the Select Database dialog box, navigate to the C:\Ex07_HandsOn folder and select the **Northwind 2007.accdb** file, then click **OK** to close the Select Database dialog box.
9. Click **OK** again to exit the ODBC Microsoft Access Setup dialog box.
10. In step 4 of the Create New Data Source dialog box, select the **Order Details** table in the drop-down list box.

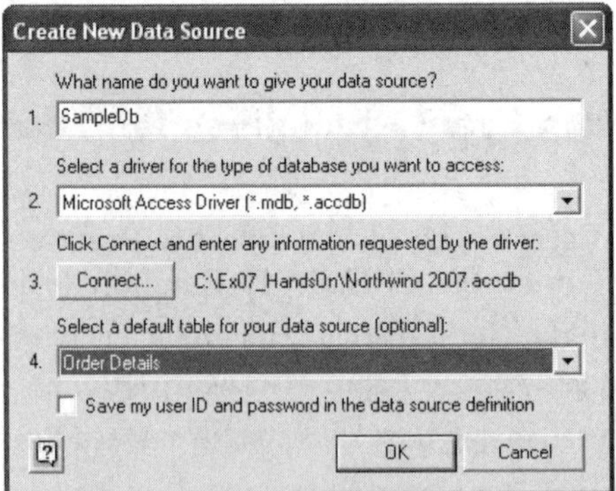

Figure 17-7: Use step 4 of the Create New Data Source dialog to specify a default table for your data source.

11. Click **OK** to close the Create New Data Source dialog box.
12. In the Choose Data Source dialog box, the SampleDb data source name should now be highlighted. Click **OK**.
13. In the Query Wizard – Choose Column dialog box, click the button with the greater than sign (>) to move all the fields from the Order Details table to the Columns in your query box.
14. Click the **Next** button until you get to the Query Wizard – Finish dialog box.
15. In the wizard's Finish dialog box, make sure the Return Data to Microsoft Office Excel option button is selected and click **Finish**.

16. In the Import Data dialog box the current spreadsheet cell is selected. Click cell **A1** in the current worksheet to change the cell reference. Click the **Properties** button. Excel will display the Connection Properties dialog box. Check **Refresh the data when opening the file** and click **OK**. Click **OK** to exit the Import Data dialog box.

    After completing the above steps, the data from the Order Details table in the Northwind 2007 database should be placed in the active worksheet.

    To write event procedures for a QueryTable object, you must create a class module and declare a QueryTable object by using the WithEvents keyword. Let's continue.

17. Save the changes in the **Practice_QueryTableEvents.xlsm** workbook.
18. Switch to the Visual Basic Editor window and insert a class module into VBAProject (Practice_QueryTableEvents.xlsm).
19. In the Properties window, rename the class module **clsQryTbl.**
20. In the clsQryTbl Code window, type the following declaration statement:

    ```
    Public WithEvents qryTbl As QueryTable
    ```

    After you've declared the new object (qryTbl) by using the WithEvents keyword, it appears in the Object drop-down list box in the class module.

21. In the clsQryTbl Code window, enter the two event procedures shown below:

    ```
    Private Sub qryTbl_BeforeRefresh(Cancel As Boolean)
       Response = MsgBox("Are you sure you " _
            & " want to refresh now?", vbYesNoCancel)
        If Response = vbNo Then Cancel = True
    End Sub

    Private Sub qryTbl_AfterRefresh(ByVal Success As Boolean)
      If Success Then
         MsgBox "The data has been refreshed."
      Else
         MsgBox "The query failed."
      End If
    End Sub
    ```

    The BeforeRefresh event of the QueryTable object occurs before the query table is refreshed. The AfterRefresh event occurs after a query is completed or canceled. The Success argument is True if the query was completed successfully.

    Before you can trigger these event procedures, you must connect the object that you declared in the class module (qryTbl) to the specified QueryTable object. This is done in a standard module as shown in step 22.

22. Insert a standard module into VBAProject (Practice_QueryTable-Events.xlsm) and enter the declaration line and the procedure as shown below:

```
Dim sampleQry As New clsQryTbl

Public Sub Auto_Open()
   ' connect the class module and its objects with the Query object

   Set sampleQry.qryTbl = ActiveSheet.ListObjects(1).QueryTable
End Sub
```

The above procedure creates a new instance of the QueryTable class (clsQryTbl) and connects this instance with the first list object on the active worksheet.

Note: A query table associated with a list object can only be accessed through the ListObject.QueryTable property. This query table is not a part of the Worksheet.QueryTables collection, and therefore the statement that worked fine in Excel 2003:

```
Set sampleQry.qrytbl = ActiveSheet.QueryTables(1)
```

will not work in Excel 2007. You will get a run-time error "*Subscript out of range.*" In Excel 2007, to find out whether a query table exists on a worksheet, be sure to check both the QueryTables and ListObjects collections. This can be done easily by entering in the Immediate window the following statements:

```
?ActiveSheet.ListObjects.Count
?ActiveSheet.QueryTables.Count
```

23. Run the Auto_Open procedure.

After you run this initialization procedure, the object that you declared in the class module points to the specified QueryTable object.

Note: In the future when you want to work with the QueryTable object in this workbook file you won't need to run the Auto_Open procedure. This procedure will run automatically upon opening the workbook file.

24. Switch to the Microsoft Excel application window and in the worksheet where you placed the Order Details table from the Microsoft Access database, choose **Data | Refresh All.** Excel will now trigger the qryTbl_BeforeRefresh event procedure and you should see the custom message box. If you click **Yes**, the data in the worksheet will be refreshed with the existing data in the database. Excel will then trigger the qryTbl_AfterRefresh event procedure and another custom message will be displayed.
25. Close the Practice_QueryTableEvents.xlsm workbook.

Chapter Summary

In this chapter you gained hands-on experience with events and event-driven programming in Excel. These are invaluable skills, whether you are planning to create spreadsheet applications for others to use or simply automating your routine daily tasks. Excel provides many events to which you can respond. By writing event procedures, you can change the way objects respond to events. Your event procedures can be as simple as a single line of code displaying a custom message, or more complex with code including decision-making statements and other programming structures that allow you to change the flow of your program when a particular event occurs. When a certain event occurs, Visual Basic will simply run an appropriate event procedure instead of responding in the standard way. You've learned that some event procedures are written in a standard module (workbook, worksheet, and standalone chart sheet), while others (embedded chart, application, and query table) require that you create a new object using the WithEvents keyword in a class module. You've also learned that you can enable or disable events using the EnableEvents property.

The next chapter takes you through the process of accessing Excel dialog boxes with VBA.

Chapter 18

Using Dialog Boxes

Excel Dialog Boxes ■ **File Open and File Save As Dialog Boxes** ■ Filtering Files ■ Selecting Files ■ **GetOpenFilename and GetSaveAsFilename Methods** ■ Using the GetOpenFilename Method ■ Using the GetSaveAsFilename Method ■ **Chapter Summary**

In Chapters 4 and 5 you learned how to use the built-in InputBox function to collect single items of data from the user during the execution of your VBA procedure. But what if your procedure requires more data at run time? The user may want to supply all the data at once or make appropriate selections from a list of items. If your procedure must collect data, you can:

- Use the collection of built-in dialog boxes
- Create a custom form

This chapter teaches you how to display the built-in dialogs from your VBA procedures. In Chapter 19, you will design your own custom forms from scratch.

Excel Dialog Boxes

Before you start creating your own forms, you should spend some time learning how to take advantage of dialog boxes that are built into Excel and are therefore ready for you to use. I'm not talking about your ability to manually select appropriate options, but how to call these dialog boxes from your own VBA procedures.

Microsoft Excel has a special collection of built-in dialog boxes that are represented by constants beginning with xlDialog, such as xlDialogClear, xlDialogFont, xlDialogDefineName, and xlDialogOptionsView. These built-in dialog boxes are Microsoft Excel objects that belong to the built-in collection of dialogs. Each Dialog object represents a built-in dialog box.

Table 18-1: Frequently used built-in dialog boxes

Dialog Box Name	Constant
New	xlDialogNew
Open	xlDialogOpen
Save As	xlDialogSaveAs
Page Setup	xlDialogPageSetup
Print	xlDialogPrint
Fonts	xlDialogFont

To display a dialog box, use the Show method in the following format:

```
Application.Dialogs(constant).Show
```

For example, the following statement displays the Fonts dialog box:

```
Application.Dialogs(xlDialogFont).Show
```

The list of constants identifying Excel built-in dialog boxes is available in the Object Browser window after selecting the Excel library and searching for xlDialog (see Figure 18-1).

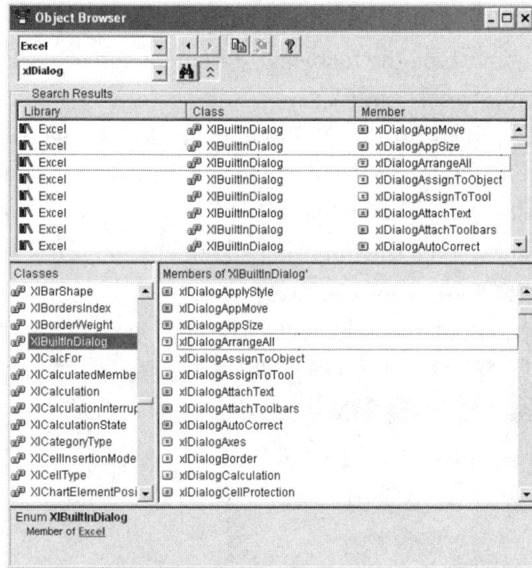

Figure 18-1: Constants prefixed with "xlDialog" identify Excel built-in dialog boxes.

Let's practice displaying some of the Excel dialog boxes straight from the Immediate window.

Hands-On 18-1: Using Excel Dialog Boxes from the Immediate Window

1. Open a new workbook and save it as **C:\Ex07_ByExample\Practice_Excel18.xlsm.**
2. Switch to the Visual Basic Editor window and open the Immediate window.
3. In the Immediate window, type the following statement and press **Enter**:

   ```
   Application.Dialogs(xlDialogFont).Show
   ```

   The above instruction displays the Fonts dialog box.

   After displaying a built-in dialog box, you can select an appropriate option, and Excel will format the selected cell or range, or the entire sheet. Although you can't modify the looks or behavior of a built-in dialog box, you can decide which initial setting the built-in dialog box will display when you show it from your VBA procedure. If you don't change the initial settings, VBA will display the dialog box with its default settings.
4. Press **Cancel** to exit the Fonts dialog box.
5. In the Immediate window, type the following statement and press **Enter**:

   ```
   Application.Dialogs(xlDialogFontProperties).Show
   ```

   The above instruction displays the Format Cells dialog box with the Font tab active.

6. Press **Cancel** to exit the Format Cells dialog box.
7. In the Immediate window, type the following statement and press **Enter**:

```
Application.Dialogs(xlDialogDefineName).Show
```

   The above statement displays the Define Name dialog box where you can define a name for a cell or a range of cells.
8. Press **Close** to exit the Define Name dialog box.
9. In the Immediate window, type the following statement and press **Enter**:

```
Application.Dialogs(xlDialogOptionsView).Show
```

   The above instruction opens the Excel Options dialog box with the Advanced options displayed as shown in Figure 18-2.

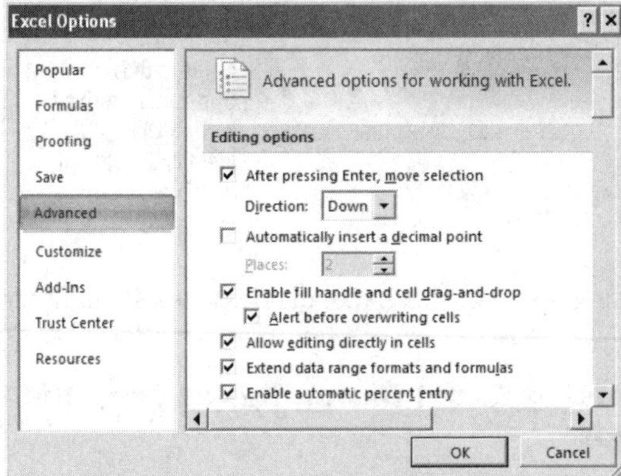

Figure 18-2: The advanced settings available in the Excel Options dialog box are identified by the xlDialogOptionsView constant.

10. Press **Cancel** to exit the Excel Options dialog box.
11. Type the following statement in the Immediate window and press **Enter**:

```
Application.Dialogs(xlDialogClear).Show
```

   Excel shows the Clear dialog box with four option buttons: All, Formats, Contents, and Comments. Normally, the Contents option button is selected when Excel displays this dialog box. But what if you wanted to invoke this dialog with a different option selected as the default? To do this, you can include a list of arguments. Arguments are entered after the Show method. For example, to display the Clear dialog box with the first option button (All) selected, you would enter the following statement.

```
Application.Dialogs(xlDialogClear).Show 1
```

   Excel often numbers the available options. Therefore, All = 1, Formats = 2, Contents = 3, and Comments = 4. The built-in dialog box argument lists are available by searching Excel Help (see Figure 18-3).

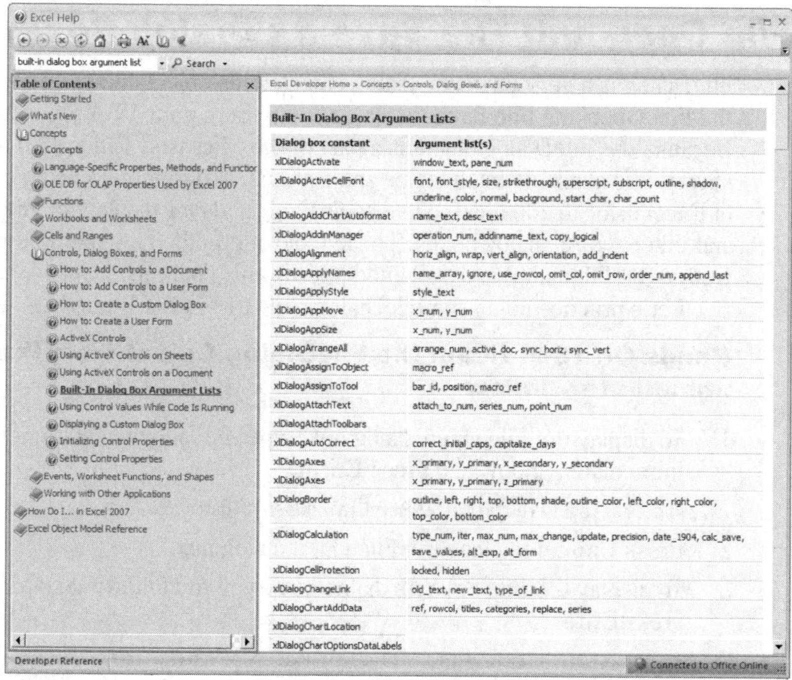

Figure 18-3: Microsoft Excel built-in dialog box arguments list.

12. Press **Cancel** to close the Clear dialog box.
13. To display the Fonts dialog box in which the Arial 14-point font is already selected, type the following instruction in the Immediate window and press **Enter**:

```
Application.Dialogs(xlDialogFont).Show "Arial", 14
```

14. Press **Cancel** to close the Fonts dialog box.
15. To specify only the font size, enter a comma in the position of the first argument:

```
Application.Dialogs(xlDialogFont).Show , 8
```

16. Press **Cancel** to close the Fonts dialog box.
17. Type the following instruction in the Immediate window and press **Enter**:

```
Application.Dialogs(xlDialogDefineName).Show "John", "=$A$1"
```

The above statement displays the Define Name dialog box, enters "John" in the Names in workbook text box, and places the reference to cell A1 in the Refers to box. The Show method returns True if you click OK, and False if you cancel.

18. Press **Close** to close the Define Name dialog box.

File Open and File Save As Dialog Boxes

FileDialog is a very powerful dialog object. This object allows you to display the File Open and File Save As dialog boxes from your VBA procedures. Because the FileDialog object is a part of the Microsoft Office 12.0 object library, it is available to all Office applications. Programmers using versions of Excel prior to 2002 had to use special methods for displaying File Open and File Save As dialog boxes. These older methods (GetOpenFilename and GetSaveAsFilename) are explained later in this chapter.

Let's practice using the FileDialog object from the Immediate window.

Hands-On 18-2: Using the FileDialog Object from the Immediate window

1. To display the File Open dialog box, type the following statement in the Immediate window and press **Enter**:

```
Application.FileDialog(msoFileDialogOpen).Show
```

2. Press **Cancel** to close the File Open dialog box.
3. To display the File Save As dialog box, type the following statement and press **Enter**:

```
Application.FileDialog(msoFileDialogSaveAs).Show
```

4. Press **Cancel** to close the File Save dialog box.

   In addition to File Open and File Save As dialog boxes, the FileDialog object is capable of displaying a dialog box with a list of files (see Figure 18-4) or a list of files and folders (see Figure 18-5). Let's take a quick look at these dialog boxes.

5. Type the following statement in the Immediate window and press **Enter**:

```
Application.FileDialog(msoFileDialogFilePicker).Show
```

   Excel displays a dialog box as shown in Figure 18-4.

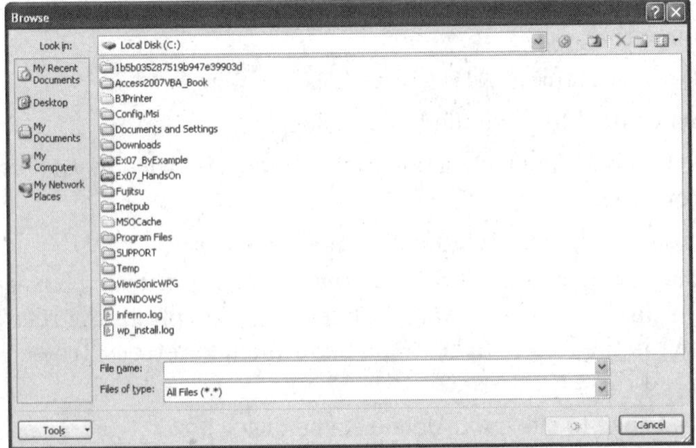

Figure 18-4: The File Picker dialog box lets users select one or more files. This dialog box displays a list of files and folders and shows Browse in the title bar.

6. Press **Cancel** in the dialog box to return to the Immediate window.

7. Type the following statement in the Immediate window and press **Enter**:

```
Application.FileDialog(msoFileDialogFolderPicker).Show
```

Excel displays a dialog box as shown in Figure 18-5.

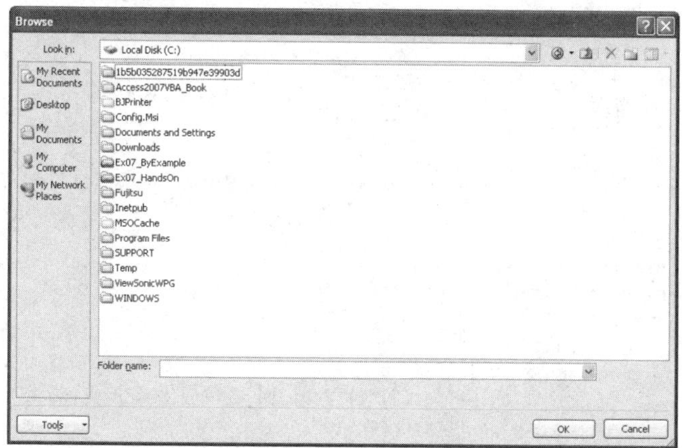

Figure 18-5: The Folder Picker dialog box lets users select a path. This dialog box displays a list of directories and shows Browse in the title bar.

8. Press **Cancel** in the dialog box to return to the Immediate window.

The constants that the FileDialog object uses are listed in Table 18-2. The "mso" prefix denotes that the constant is a part of the Microsoft Office object model.

Table 18-2: FileDialog object's constants

Constant Name	Value
msoFileDialogOpen	1
msoFileDialogSaveAs	2
msoFileDialogFilePicker	3
msoFileDialogFolderPicker	4

Filtering Files

You can control the types of files that are displayed with the FileDialog Filters property. If you open the Files of type drop-down list box at the bottom of the File Open dialog box, you will see quite a selection of preset file filters to choose from. You can also add your own filters to this list. Filters are stored in the FileDialogFilters collection for the FileDialog object.

Let's create a simple procedure that returns the list of default file filters to an Excel worksheet.

Hands-On 18-3: Writing a List of Default File Filters to an Excel Worksheet

1. In the Project Explorer window, select **VBAProject (Practice_Excel18.xlsm)**.
2. In the Properties window, rename the project **VBA_Dialogs**.

3. Insert a new module into the VBA_Dialogs (Practice_Excel18.xlsm) project and rename it **DialogBoxes**.
4. In the DialogBoxes Code window, enter the ListFilters procedure as shown below:

```
Sub ListFilters()
    Dim fdf As FileDialogFilters
    Dim fltr As FileDialogFilter
    Dim c As Integer

    Set fdf = Application.FileDialog(msoFileDialogOpen).Filters

    Workbooks.Add
    Cells(1, 1).Select
    Selection.Formula = "List of Default filters"
    With fdf
        c = .Count
        For Each fltr In fdf
            Selection.Offset(1, 0).Formula = fltr.Description & _
                ": " & fltr.Extensions
            Selection.Offset(1, 0).Select
        Next
    MsgBox c & " filters were written to a worksheet."
    End With
End Sub
```

   The above procedure declares two object variables. The fdf object variable returns a reference to the FileDialogFilters collection of the FileDialog object, and the fltr object variable stores a reference to the FileDialogFilter object. The Count property of the FileDialogFilters collection returns the total number of filters.

   Next, the procedure iterates through the FileDialogFilters collection and retrieves the description and extension of each defined filter.

5. Run the ListFilters procedure.

   When the procedure completes, you should see a list of preset filters in the worksheet of a new workbook.

   Using the Add method of the FileDialogFilters collection, you can easily add your own filter to the default filters. The following modified ListFilters procedure (ListFilters2) demonstrates how to add a filter to filter out temporary files (*.tmp). The last statement in this procedure will open the File Open dialog box so that you can check for yourself that the custom filter Temporary files (*.tmp) has indeed been added to the Files of type drop-down list.

```
Sub ListFilters2()
    Dim fdf As FileDialogFilters
    Dim fltr As FileDialogFilter
    Dim c As Integer

    Set fdf = Application.FileDialog(msoFileDialogOpen).Filters

    Workbooks.Add
    Cells(1, 1).Select
```

```
        Selection.Formula = "List of Default filters"
        With fdf
            c = .Count
            For Each fltr In fdf
                Selection.Offset(1, 0).Formula = fltr.Description & _
                    ": " & fltr.Extensions
                Selection.Offset(1, 0).Select
            Next
            MsgBox c & " filters were written to a worksheet."
            .Add "Temporary Files", "*.tmp", 1
            c = .Count
            MsgBox "There are now " & c & " filters." & vbCrLf _
                & "Check for yourself."
            Application.FileDialog(msoFileDialogOpen).Show
        End With
    End Sub
```

You can remove all the preset filters using the Clear method of the FileDialogFilters collection. For example, you could modify the ListFilters2 procedure to clear the built-in filters prior to adding the custom filter — Temporary files (*.tmp).

Selecting Files

When you select a file in the Open File dialog box, the selected filename and path is placed in the FileDialogSelectedItems collection. Use the SelectedItems property to return the FileDialogSelectedItems collection. By setting the AllowMultiSelect property of the FileDialog object to True, a user can select one or more files by holding down the Shift or Control keys while clicking filenames.

The following procedure demonstrates how to use the above-mentioned properties. This procedure will open a new workbook and insert a list box control. The user will be allowed to select more than one file. The selected files will then be loaded into the list box control, and the first filename will be highlighted.

Hands-On 18-4: Loading Files into a Worksheet List Box Control

1. In the DialogBoxes module Code window, enter the ListSelectedFiles procedure as shown below:

```
Sub ListSelectedFiles()
    Dim fd As FileDialog
    Dim myFile As Variant
    Dim lbox As Object

    Application.FileDialog(msoFileDialogOpen).Filters.Clear
    Set fd = Application.FileDialog(msoFileDialogOpen)
    With fd
        .AllowMultiSelect = True
        If .Show Then
            Workbooks.Add
            Set lbox = Worksheets(1).Shapes. _
```

```
                AddFormControl(xlListBox, _
                Left:=20, Top:=60, Height:=40, Width:=300)
            lbox.ControlFormat.MultiSelect = xlNone
            For Each myFile In .SelectedItems
                lbox.ControlFormat.AddItem myFile
            Next
            Range("B4").Formula = _
                "You've selected the following " & _
                lbox.ControlFormat.ListCount & " files:"
            lbox.ControlFormat.ListIndex = 1
        End If
    End With
End Sub
```

The above procedure uses the following statement to clear the list of filters in the File Open dialog box to ensure that only the preset filters are listed:

```
Application.FileDialog(msoFileDialogOpen).Filters.Clear
```

Next, the reference to the FileDialog object is stored in the object variable fd:

```
Set fd = Application.FileDialog(msoFileDialogOpen)
```

Prior to displaying the File Open dialog, we set the AllowMultiSelect property to True so that users can select more than one file.

Next, the Show method is used to display the File Open dialog. This method does not open the files selected by the user. When the user clicks the Open button, the names of the files are retrieved from the SelectedItems collection via the SelectedItems property and placed in a list box on a worksheet.

2. Run the ListSelectedFiles procedure. When the File Open dialog box appears on the screen, switch to the Ex07_HandsOn folder, select a couple of files (hold down the Shift or Ctrl key to choose contiguous or nonadjacent files), and then click **Open**.

   The selected files are not opened. The procedure simply loads the names of the files you selected in a list box control that has been added to a worksheet (see Figure 18-6).

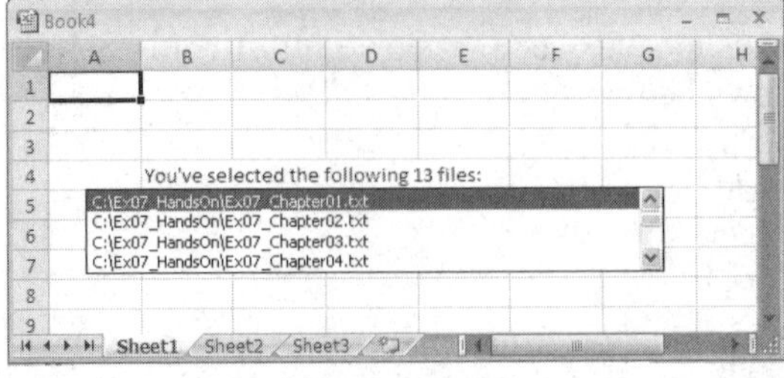

Figure 18-6: User-selected files are loaded into a list box control placed in a worksheet by the ListSelectedFiles procedure.

If you'd like to immediately carry out the File Open operation when the user clicks the Open button, you must use the Execute method of the FileDialog object. The OpenRightAway procedure shown below demonstrates how to open the user-selected files right away.

```
Sub OpenRightAway()
    Dim fd As FileDialog
    Dim myFile As Variant

    Set fd = Application.FileDialog(msoFileDialogOpen)
    With fd
        .AllowMultiSelect = True
        If .Show Then
            For Each myFile In .SelectedItems
                .Execute
            Next
        End If
    End With
End Sub
```

GetOpenFilename and GetSaveAsFilename Methods

For many years now, Excel has offered its programmers two handy VBA methods for displaying the File Open and File Save As dialog boxes: GetOpenFilename and GetSaveAsFilename. These methods are available only in Excel and can still be used in Excel 2007 if backward compatibility is required. The GetOpenFilename method displays the Open dialog box, where you can select the name of a file to open. The second method (GetSaveAsFilename) shows the Save As dialog box. Let's try out these methods from the Immediate window.

Using the GetOpenFilename Method

Let's open a file using the GetOpenFilename method.

Hands-On 18-5: Using the GetOpenFilename Method

1. Type the following statement in the Immediate window and press **Enter**:

   ```
   Application.GetOpenFilename
   ```

   The above statement displays the Open dialog box where you can select a file. The GetOpenFilename method gets a filename from the user without actually opening the specified file. This method has four optional arguments. The most often used are the first and third arguments, shown in Table 18-3.

Table 18-3: Arguments of the GetOpenFilename method

Argument Name	Description
fileFilter	This argument determines what appears in the dialog box's Save as type field. For example, the filter excel files (*.xls), .xls displays the following text in the Save As drop-down list of files: excel files. The first part of the filter, excel files (.xls), determines the text to be displayed. The second part, .xls, specifies which files are displayed. The filter parts are separated by a comma.

Argument Name	Description
title	This is the title of the dialog box. If omitted, the dialog box will appear with the default title "Open."

2. Click **Cancel** to close the dialog box opened in step 1.
3. To see how arguments are used with the GetOpenFilename method, enter the following statement in the Immediate window (be sure to enter it on one line and press **Enter**):

```
Application.GetOpenFilename("excel macro-enabled files(*.xlsm),
*.xlsm"),,"Highlight the File"
```

   Notice that the Open dialog box now has the text "Highlight the File" in the title bar. Also, the Files of type drop-down list box is filtered to display only the specified file type.
4. Click **Cancel** to close the dialog box opened in step 3.

   The GetOpenFilename method returns the name of the selected or specified file. This name can be used later by your VBA procedure to open the file. Let's see how this is done.
5. In the Immediate window, type the following statement and press **Enter**:

```
yourFile = Application.GetOpenFilename
```

   The above statement displays the Open dialog box. The file you select while this dialog box is open will be stored in the yourFile variable.
6. Select an Excel file and click **Open.**

   Notice that Excel did not open the selected file. All it did is remember its name in the yourFile variable. Let's check this out.
7. In the Immediate window, type the following statement and press **Enter**:

```
?yourFile
```

   Excel prints the name of the selected file in the Immediate window. Now that you have a filename you can write a statement to actually open this file (see the next step).
8. In the Immediate window, type the following statement and press **Enter**:

```
Workbooks.Open Filename:=yourFile
```

   Notice that the file you picked is now opened in Excel.
9. Close the file you opened in step 8.

Note: The GetOpenFilename method returns False if you cancel the dialog box by pressing Escape or clicking Cancel.

Using the GetSaveAsFilename Method

Now that you know how to open a file using the GetOpenFilename method, let's examine a similar method that allows you to save a file. We will continue to work in the Immediate window.

Hands-On 18-6: Using the GetSaveAsFilename Method

1. Open a new workbook and switch to the Visual Basic Editor window.
2. In the Immediate window, type the following statement and press **Enter**.

```
yourFile = Application.GetSaveAsFilename
```

   The above statement displays the Save As dialog box. The suggested filename is automatically entered in the File name box at the bottom of this dialog box. The GetSaveAsFilename method is convenient for obtaining the name of the file the workbook should be saved as. The filename that the user enters in the File name box will be stored in the yourFile variable.
3. Type **Test1.xlsx** in the File name box and click **Save.**
   When you click the Save button, the GetSaveAsFilename method will store the filename and its path in the yourFile variable. To actually save the file you have to enter a different statement.
4. In the Immediate window, type the following statement and press **Enter**:

```
ActiveWorkbook.SaveAs yourFile
```

   Now the workbook file opened in step 1 has been saved as Test1.xlsx.
5. To close the Test1.xlsx file, type the following statement in the Immediate window and press **Enter**:

```
Workbooks("Test1.xlsx").Close
```

   When using the GetSaveAsFilename method, you can specify the filename, file filter, and custom title for the dialog box:

```
yourFile = Application.GetSaveAsFilename("Test1.xlsx", "Excel
files(*.xlsx), *.xlsx",,"Name your file")
```

Chapter Summary

In this chapter you learned how to use VBA statements to display various built-in dialog boxes. You also learned how to select files by using the FileDialog object. You ended this chapter by familiarizing yourself with older methods of displaying the File Open and File Save As dialogs that you will encounter often in VBA procedures written in Excel versions prior to 2002.

In the next chapter you will learn how to create and display your custom dialog boxes with user forms.

Chapter 19

Creating Custom Forms

Creating Forms ■ **Tools for Creating User Forms** ■ **Placing Controls on a Form** ■ Setting Grid Options ■ **Sample Application 1: Info Survey** ■ Setting Up the Custom Form ■ Displaying a Custom Form ■ Understanding Form and Control Events ■ Writing VBA Procedures to Respond to Form and Control Events ■ **Sample Application 2: Students and Exams** ■ Using MultiPage and TabStrip Controls ■ Setting Up the Worksheet for the Students and Exams Application ■ Writing VBA Procedures for the Students and Exams Custom Form ■ Using the Students and Exams Custom Form ■ **Chapter Summary**

Creating Forms

Although ready to use and convenient, the built-in dialog boxes will not meet all of your VBA application's requirements. Apart from displaying a dialog box on the screen and specifying its initial settings, you can't control the dialog box's appearance. You can't decide which buttons to add, which ones to remove, and which ones to move around. Also, you can't change the size of a built-in dialog box. Therefore, if you're looking to provide a custom interface, your only solution is to create a user form.

A user form is like a custom dialog box. You can add various controls to the form, set properties for these controls, and write VBA procedures that respond to form and control events. Forms are separate objects that you add to a VBA project by choosing Insert | UserForm from the Visual Basic Editor. Forms can be shared across applications. For example, you can reuse the form you designed in Microsoft Excel in Microsoft Word or any other application that uses Visual Basic Editor.

To create a custom form, follow these steps:

1. Switch to the Visual Basic Editor window.
2. Choose Insert | UserForm.

A new folder called Forms appears in the Project Explorer window. This folder contains a blank UserForm object. The work area automatically displays the form and the Toolbox with the necessary tools for adding controls (see Figure 19-1).

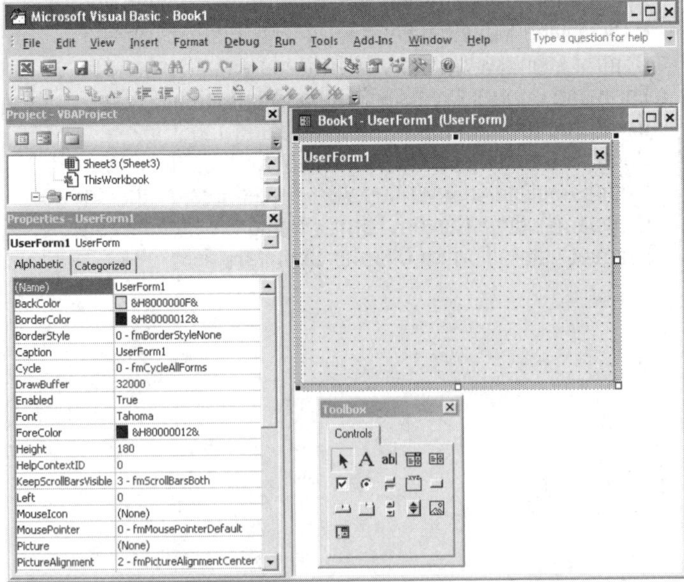

Figure 19-1: A new form can be added to the open VBA project by selecting UserForm from the Insert menu.

The Properties window (see Figure 19-2) displays a number of properties that you can set, depending on your needs. To list form properties by category, click the Categorized tab in the Properties window. The form properties are arranged into seven categories: Appearance, Behavior, Font, Misc, Picture, Position, and Scrolling. To find out information on a specific property, click the property name and press F1. The online help will be launched with the property description topic.

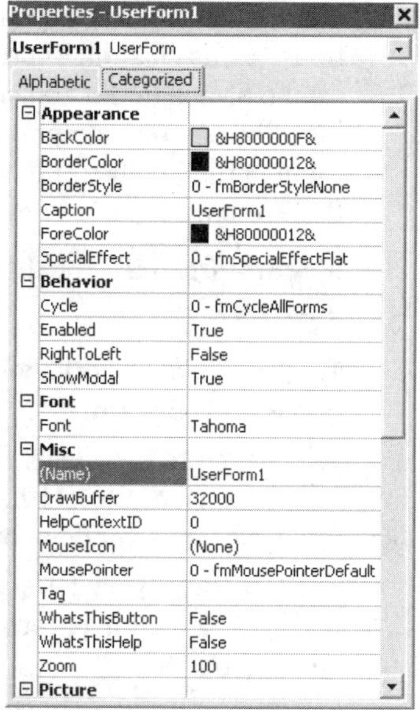

Figure 19-2: Using the Properties window, you can easily change the appearance, behavior, and other features of your custom form.

After adding a new form to your VBA project, you should assign a unique name to it by setting the Name property. In addition to the name, you can set the form's title by using the Caption property.

All VBA applications that use the Visual Basic Editor share features for creating custom forms. You can share your forms by exporting and importing form files or by dragging a form object to another project. To import or export a form file, choose File | Import File or File | Export File. Before you export a form file, be sure to select it in the Project Explorer window. Before dragging a form to a diferent VBA application, arrange the VBE windows so that you can see the Project Explorer window in both applications. Drop the form on the name of another project in the Project Explorer.

Tools for Creating User Forms

When you design a form, you insert appropriate controls on it to make it useful. The Toolbox contains standard Visual Basic buttons for all the controls that you can add to a form. It may also contain additional controls that have been installed on your computer. Controls available in the Toolbox are known as ActiveX controls. These controls can respond to specific user actions, such as clicking a control or changing its value.

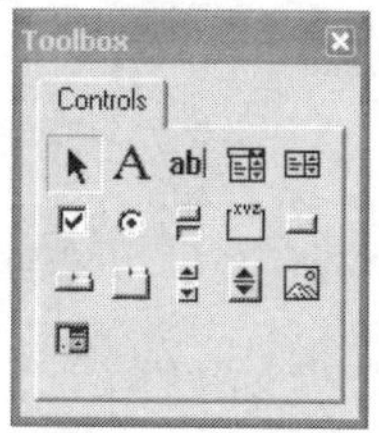

Figure 19-3: The Toolbox displays the controls that can be added to your custom form.

You will learn how to use the Toolbox controls throughout the remaining sections of this chapter. Microsoft Office offers additional ActiveX controls that can be placed in the Toolbox for quick access. If you have other applications installed on your computer that contain ActiveX controls, you can also place them in the Toolbox. Let's take a few minutes and add a Calendar control to the Toolbox.

Hands-On 19-1: Adding an ActiveX Calendar Control to the Toolbox

1. Open a new workbook and save it as **C:\Ex07_ByExample\Practice_Excel19.xlsm.**
2. Switch to the Visual Basic Editor window and select **VBAProject (Practice_Excel19.xlsm)** in the Project Explorer window. Use the Properties window to rename the project **VBA_Forms.**
3. Choose **Insert | UserForm** to add a new form to the selected project.

   A default user form named UserForm1 appears with the accompanying Toolbox.
4. Right-click the **Controls** tab in the Toolbox and choose **New Page** from the shortcut menu.

   A New Page tab appears in the Toolbox.
5. Right-click the **New Page** tab in the Toolbox and choose **Rename.** If this option is not available, make sure you are right-clicking the New Page tab.
6. In the Caption box, type **Extra Controls** as the new name
7. In the Control Tip Text box, type the following description: **Additional ActiveX Controls.**
8. Click **OK** to return to the Toolbox.
9. Right-click anywhere within the new page area and choose **Additional Controls** from the shortcut menu. If this option is not available, make sure you are right-clicking the page area and not the Extra Controls tab itself.
10. When the Additional Controls dialog box appears, click the check box next to **Calendar Control,** as shown in Figure 19-4.
11. Click **OK** to close the Additional Controls dialog box.

The Calendar control now appears on the new tab page of the Toolbox. You will use this control later in this chapter.

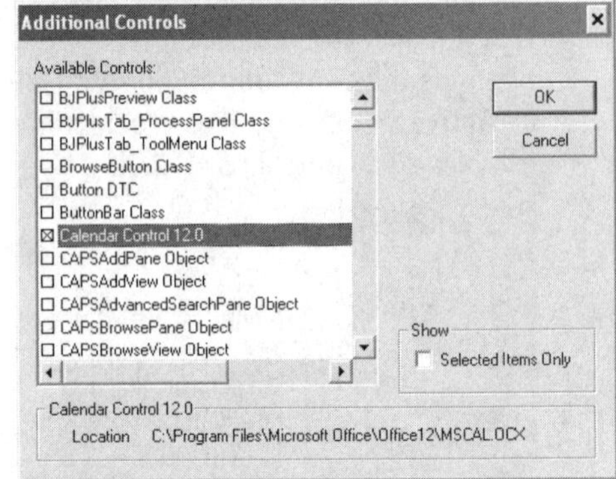

Figure 19-4: You can add to the Toolbox additional ActiveX controls that are installed on your computer.

The standard Visual Basic controls are described below.

Select Objects

Select Objects is the only item in the Toolbox that doesn't draw a control. Use it to resize or move a control that has already been drawn on a form.

Label

Labels allow you to add text to your form. The Label control is often used to add captions, titles, headings, and explanations. You can use the label to assign a title to those controls that don't have the Caption property (for example, text boxes, list boxes, scroll bars, and spin buttons). You can define an accelerator (shortcut) key for the label. For example, by pressing Alt and a specified letter, you can activate the control that was added to the form immediately after adding the Label control and setting its Accelerator property. To add a title or a keyboard shortcut to an existing control, add a Label control and type a letter from its caption in its Accelerator property in the Properties window. Next, choose View | Tab Order, and make sure that the name of the label appears before the name of the control that you want to activate with the assigned keyboard shortcut. You will learn how to use the Tab Order dialog box later in this chapter (see Figure 19-7).

Text Box

Text boxes are the most popular form controls because they can be used to either display or request data from the user. You can enter text, numbers, cell references, or formulas in them. By changing the setting of the MultiLine property, you can enter more than one line of text in a text box. The text lines can automatically wrap when you set the WordWrap property. And if you set the EnterKeyBehavior property to True when the MultiLine property is also set to True, you'll be able to start a new line in the text box by pressing Enter. Another property, EnterFieldBehavior, determines whether the text is selected when the user selects the text field. Setting this property to 0 (fmEnterFieldBehaviorSelectAll) will select the text within the field. Setting this property to 1 (fmEnterFieldBehaviorRecallSelect) will only select the text that the user selected the last time he activated this field. If you want to limit the number of characters the user can enter in a text box, you can do this by specifying the exact number of characters in the MaxLength property.

Frame

Frames allow you to visually organize and logically group various controls placed on the form. When you use the frame control around the option buttons, Visual Basic treats these buttons as mutually exclusive and therefore allows you to select only one of the options. In other words, if a user selects one of the available option buttons, the other option buttons cannot be selected. Later in this chapter, you will find an example of the Info Survey form that uses two frames. One of them organizes Hardware and Software option buttons into one logical group, while the second frame groups the check boxes related to the computer type (see Figure 19-5).

Command Button

A command button carries out a command when it is clicked. In this chapter you will learn how to execute VBA procedures from command buttons.

Option Button

An option button lets you select one of a number of mutually exclusive options. Option buttons usually appear in groups of two or more buttons surrounded by a frame control. Only one option button can be selected. When you select a new option button, the previously selected option button is automatically deselected. To activate or deactivate an option button, set its Value property to True or False. True means that the option is activated; False indicates that the option is deactivated.

Check Box

Check boxes are used for turning specific options on and off. Unlike option buttons, which allow you to select only one option at a time, you can select one or more check boxes. If the check box is selected, its Value property is set to True; if the check box is not selected, its Value property is set to False.

Toggle Button

A toggle button looks like a command button and works similarly to an option button. When you click a toggle button, the button stays pressed. The next click on the button returns it to the normal (unpressed) state. The pressed toggle button has its Value property set to True.

List Box

Instead of prompting the user to enter a specific value in a text box, sometimes it's better to present a list of available choices from which to select. The list box reduces the possibility of data entry errors. The list box entries can be typed in a worksheet, or they can be loaded directly from a VBA procedure using the AddItem method. The RowSource property indicates the source of data displayed in the list box. For example, the reference $A$1:$B$8 will display in the list box the contents of the specified range of cells.

The list box can display one or more columns when you set the ColumnCount property. Another property, ColumnHeads, can be set to True to display the column titles in the list box. The user is not limited to selecting just one option. If the procedure requires that two or more list items be selected, you can set the MultiSelect property to True.

Combo Box

The combo box is a control that combines a text box with a list box. This control is often used to save space on the form. When the user clicks the down arrow located to the right of the combo box, the box will drop open to reveal a number of items from which to choose. If none of the displayed choices is applicable, the user may enter a new value if you set the MatchRequired property to False. The ListRows property determines how many items will appear when the user drops down the list. The Style property determines the type of combo box. To let the user select an item from the list, use 0 (fmStyleDropDownCombo). Set the Style property to 2 (fmStyleDropDownList) to limit the user's selection to the items available in the combo box.

Scroll Bar

This control allows you to place horizontal and vertical scroll bars on your form. Although normally used to navigate windows, scroll bars can be used on your form to enter values in a predefined range. The current value of the scroll bar is set or returned by the Value property. The scroll bar's Max property lets you set its maximum value. The Min property determines the minimum value. The LargeChange property determines by what value the Value property should change when the user clicks inside the scroll bar. When programming the behavior of the scroll bar, don't forget to set the SmallChange property that determines how the Value property changes when you click one of the scroll arrows.

Spin Button

The spin button works similarly to a scroll bar. You can click an arrow to increment or decrement a value. The spin button is often used together with a text box. The user can then type the exact value in the text box or select a value by using the arrows. The technique of using the spin button with a text box is discussed later in this chapter.

Image Control

The image control lets you display a graphical image on a form. This control supports the following file formats: *.bmp, *.cur, *gif, *.ico, *.jpg, and *.wmf. Like other controls in the Toolbox, the image control has a number of properties that you can set. For example, you can control the appearance of the picture with the PictureSizeMode property. This property has three settings:

- 0 (fmPictureSizeModeClip) crops the part of a picture that does not fit within the picture frame
- 1 (fmPictureSizeModeStretch) stretches the picture horizontally or vertically until it fills the entire frame area
- 3 (fmPictureSizeModeZoom) enlarges the picture without distorting its proportions

MultiPage Control

The MultiPage control displays a series of tabs at the top of the form (see Figure 19-9). Each tab acts as a separate page. Using the MultiPage control, you can design forms that contain two or more pages. You can place a different set of controls on each form page. When a form contains a lot of data, it can become less readable. It's much easier to click a form tab than move around in a long form using scroll bars. By default, each MultiPage control appears on your form with two pages. New pages can be added by using the shortcut menu or the Add method from within a VBA procedure. The last

Hands-On exercise in this chapter demonstrates how to use this control to keep track of students' exam grades.

TabStrip Control

Although the TabStrip and MultiPage controls look almost alike, each has a different function. The TabStrip (see Figure 19-10) lets you use the same controls for displaying multiple sets of the same data. Suppose that the form shows students' exams. Each student has to pass an exam in the same subjects. Each subject can be placed on a separate page (tab). Each tab will contain the same controls to collect data, such as the grade received and the date of the exam. When you activate any subject tab, you will see the same controls. Only the data in these controls will change. See the last Hands-On exercise in this chapter for an example of how to use the TabStrip control.

RefEdit Control

This control is specific to forms created in Microsoft Excel, as it allows you to select a cell or a range of cells in a worksheet and pass it to your VBA procedure. You can see how this control works by taking a look at some of the built-in dialog boxes in Excel. For example, the Consolidate dialog accessed from the Data tab's Data Tools group has a RefEdit control labeled Reference that lets you specify the range of data that you want to consolidate. To temporarily hide the dialog box while selecting a range of cells, click the button on the right of the RefEdit control.

Placing Controls on a Form

When you create a custom form, you place various controls that are available in the Toolbox on an empty form. The type of control you select depends on the type of data the control will have to store and the functionality of your form. The Toolbox is always visible when you work with your form. You can move it around on the screen, change its size, or close it when all controls are already on the form and all you want to do is work with their properties. The Toolbox display can be toggled on and off by choosing View | Toolbox. Working with the Toolbox is easy.

To add a new control to a form, first click the control image in the Toolbox and then click the form or draw a frame. Clicking on a form (without drawing a frame) will place a control in its default size. The standard settings of each control can be looked up in the Properties window. For example, the standard text box size is 18 x 72 points (see the Height and Width properties of the text box). After placing a control on a form, the Select Object button (represented by the arrow) becomes the active control in the Toolbox. When you double-click a control in the Toolbox, you can draw as many instances of that control as you want. For example, to quickly place three text boxes on your form, double-click the text box control in the Toolbox and then click three times on the form.

Setting Grid Options

When you drag a control on a form, Visual Basic adjusts the control so that it aligns with the form's grid. You can set the grid to your liking by using the Options dialog box.

To access grid options:

1. Choose **Tools | Options**.
2. Click the **General** tab in the Options dialog box.

The Form Grid Settings area lets you turn off the grid, adjust the grid size, and decide whether you want the controls aligned to the grid.

Sample Application 1: Info Survey

Now that you've read through the theory of creating user forms and understand the differences between various controls available in the Toolbox, you are ready for some hands-on experience. As you already know, the best way to understand a complex feature is to apply it in a real-life project. In this section, you will create a custom form for a coworker who requested that you streamline the tedious process of entering survey data into a spreadsheet. While working with this form (Figure 19-5), you will have the chance to experiment with many controls and their properties. Also, you will learn how to transfer data from your custom form to a worksheet (Figure 19-6).

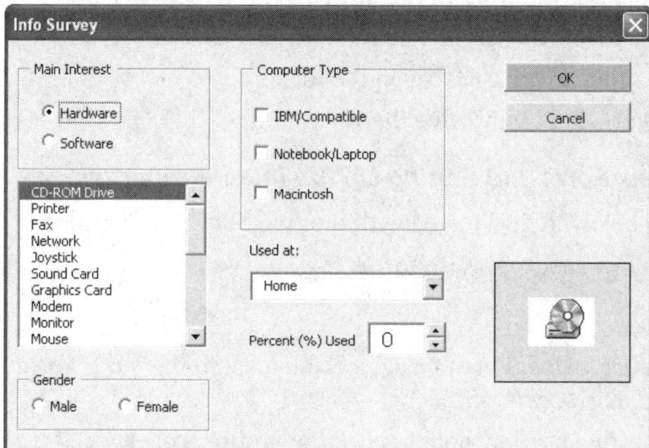

Figure 19-5: The Info Survey custom form allows the user to quickly enter data by making appropriate selections from various controls placed on the form.

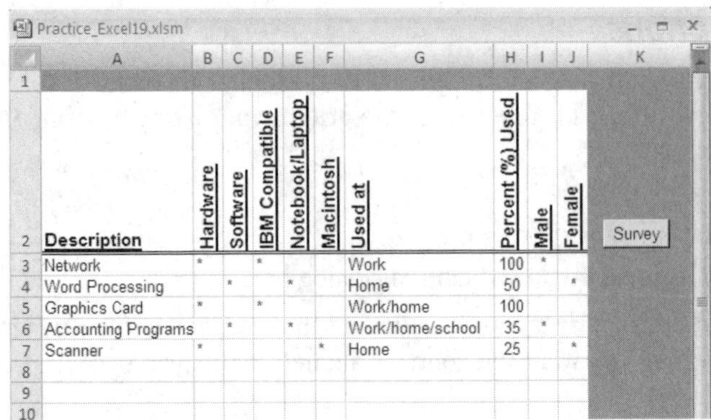

Description	Hardware	Software	IBM Compatible	Notebook/Laptop	Macintosh	Used at	Percent (%) Used	Male	Female
Network	*		*			Work	100	*	
Word Processing		*		*		Home	50		*
Graphics Card	*		*			Work/home	100		
Accounting Programs		*		*		Work/home/school	35	*	
Scanner	*				*	Home	25		*

Figure 19-6: Each time the Info Survey form is used, the user's selections are written to the worksheet.

Setting Up the Custom Form

Before you can begin programming, you need to perform several tasks. The tasks listed below are described in Hands-On 19-2 through 19-7.

1. Insert a new form into your VBA project and set up this form's initial properties like the Name and Caption properties that will allow you to identify the form.
2. Adjust the size of the form so that all controls required by the application can be easily placed on the form and the form does not look crowded.
3. Place the required controls on the form.
4. Adjust other properties of the form and its controls.
5. Set the tab order of the controls on the form.
6. Prepare a worksheet to receive the data.

Inserting a New Form and Setting Up the Initial Properties

Follow the step below to get started with the Info Survey application.

Hands-On 19-2: Inserting a New Form

Step 1

1. Choose **Insert | UserForm** to add a blank form to the VBA_Forms (Practice_Excel19.xlsm) project.
2. In the Properties window, double-click the **Name** property and type **InfoSurvey** to change the default form name.

   We will use this name later on to refer to this UserForm object in VBA procedures.
3. Double-click the **Caption** property and type the new title for the form: **Info Survey**.

   The name Info Survey will appear in your form's title bar.
4. Double-click the **BackColor** property, click the **Palette** tab, and select a color for the form background.

Changing the Size of the Form

When a default form inserted in your project is too large or too small to fit all the controls properly, you can change its size by using the mouse or by setting the form properties in the Properties window.

To resize the form with the mouse, click on an empty part of the form. Notice that several selection handles appear around the form. Place the mouse pointer over any selection handle located in the middle of a side and drag it to the position you want, then release the mouse button.

You can also place the mouse pointer over the selection handle located at the undocked corner and drag the handle to the position you want. Release the mouse button.

To resize the form using the Properties window, you will need to enter new values for the form's Height and Width.

Note that each new form has a default size of 180 x 240. The form's dimensions are in points. One point equals 1/72 inch. Click in the form's title bar. In the Properties window, double-click the Height property and enter a new value. Do the same for the Width property if you need to adjust the form's width as well. To avoid extra work, always resize the form before adding the desired controls.

After setting the initial properties for our custom form Info Survey, we need to adjust the size of the form so that all the controls that we need to place on this form will fit nicely.

Hands-On 19-3: Adjusting the Size of the Form

Step 2

1. Click the form's title bar (where the words Info Survey appear).
2. In the Properties window, double-click the **Height** property and enter the value **252.75**.
3. In the Properties window, double-click the **Width** property and enter the value **405.75**.

Adding Buttons, Check Boxes, and Other Controls to a Form

Now we are ready to proceed with placing the required controls on the Info Survey form. We will model this form after Figure 19-5.

The UserForm toolbar contains a number of useful shortcuts for working with forms, such as making controls the same size, centering a control horizontally or vertically, aligning control edges, and grouping and ungrouping controls. To display this toolbar, choose View | Toolbars | UserForm.

Hands-On 19-4: Adding Buttons, Check Boxes, and Other Controls to a Form

Step 3

1. Click the **Frame** control in the Toolbox.

   The mouse pointer changes to a cross accompanied by the symbol of the selected control.

2. Point to the upper left-hand side of the form, then click and drag the mouse to draw a small rectangle.

   When you release the mouse button, you will see a small rectangle titled Frame1. When the frame is selected, various selection handles will appear in its sides, and the Properties window's title bar will display Properties - Frame1.

3. In the Properties window, double-click the **Caption** property and replace the selected default caption, Frame1, with **Main Interest**.

4. Click the **Option Button** control in the Toolbox. Next, click inside the Main Interest frame that you've just added to your form. Click and drag the mouse to the right until you see a rectangle with the default label OptionButton1.

5. In the Properties window, change the option button's Caption property to **Hardware**.

6. Use the method presented in step 4 to add another option button to the Main Interest frame. Change the Caption property of this option button to **Software**.

   The option buttons are used whenever the user has to select one choice from a group of mutually exclusive choices. If the user can select more than one choice, check boxes are used.

7. Click the **List Box** control in the Toolbox.

   The mouse pointer will change to a cross accompanied by the symbol of the selected control.

8. Click below the Main Interest frame, and drag the mouse down and to the right to draw a list box.

   When you release the mouse button, you will see a white rectangle. Figure 19-5 shows the list box populated with hardware entries.

9. Insert a frame below the list box. Change the frame's Caption property to **Gender**. Add two option buttons inside this frame, and change the first button's Caption property to **Male** and the second one to **Female** (see Figure 19-5).

10. Click the **Frame** control in the Toolbox and draw a rectangle to the right of the frame labeled Main Interest.

11. Change the Caption property of the new frame to **Computer Type**.

12. Click the **Check Box** control in the Toolbox, and click inside the empty frame that you have just added. The CheckBox1 control should appear inside the frame.
13. Change the Caption property of the CheckBox1 control to **IBM/Compatible.**
14. Place two more check boxes inside the frame labeled Computer Type. Use the Caption property to assign the following new titles to these check boxes: **Notebook/Laptop** and **Macintosh**. The final result should match Figure 19-5.

    Unlike option buttons, which are mutually exclusive, check boxes allow the user to activate one or more options simultaneously. The check box can be checked, unchecked, or unavailable at a particular time. An unavailable check box has its label grayed out and is therefore inactive (cannot be selected). The checked box has an x in front of its caption. The check box that has the focus is indicated by a dotted line around the caption.

    Use option buttons when only one option can be selected at a given time. Use check boxes to have the user select any number of options that apply.
15. Click the **Label** control in the Toolbox.
16. Click the empty space below the frame labeled Computer Type. The Label1 control should appear.
17. Change the Caption property of Label1 to **Used at.**
18. Click the **Combo Box** control in the Toolbox.
19. Click the empty space below the Used at label and drag the mouse to draw a rectangle. Release the mouse button.

    The combo box displays a list of available choices only after you click the down arrow placed at the right of this control. The combo box is sometimes referred to as a drop-down list and is used to save valuable space on the screen. Although the user can only see one element of the list at a given time, the current selection can be quickly changed by clicking on the arrow button.
20. Click the **Label** control in the Toolbox.
21. Click on the empty part of the form just below the Used at combo box. A label control will appear. Change the Caption property for this label to **Percent (%) Used.**
22. Click the **Text Box** control in the Toolbox.
23. Click to the right of the Percent (%) Used label control to place a default size text box.
24. Click the **Spin Button** control in the Toolbox, and then click to the right side of the text box control. A default size spin button will appear. The final result is shown in Figure 19-5.

The spin button has two arrows that are used to increment or decrement a value in a given range. The maximum value is determined by the setting of the Max property, and the minimum value is set with the Min property. The spin button has the same properties as the scroll bar, with two differences. The spin button does not have a scroll box, and it lacks the LargeChange property. A text box is usually placed next to the spin button. This allows the user to enter a value directly into the text box or use the spin buttons to determine the value. If the spin button has to work with the text box, your VBA procedure must ensure that the value of the text box and the spin button are synchronized. In this example, you will use the spin button to indicate the percent of interest that the user has in the selected hardware or software product.

25. Double-click the **Command Button** control in the Toolbox. Recall that by double-clicking the control in the Toolbox, you indicate that you want to create more than one control using the selected tool.
26. Click in the top right-hand corner of the form. This will cause CommandButton1 to appear.
27. Click below CommandButton1. CommandButton2 will appear.
28. Change the Caption property of the CommandButton1 to **OK** and the CommandButton2 to **Cancel**.

    Most custom forms have two command buttons, OK and Cancel, which enable the user to accept the data entered on the form or dismiss the form. In this example, the OK button will transfer the data entered on the form to a worksheet. The user will be able to click the Cancel button when he's done inputting the data. To make the buttons respond to user actions, you will write appropriate VBA procedures later in this chapter.
29. Click the **Image** control in the Toolbox.
30. Click the mouse below the Cancel button, and drag the mouse to draw a rectangle. Release the mouse button. The final result is shown in Figure 19-5.

    The form will display a different picture depending on whether the Hardware or Software option button is selected. The images will be loaded by a VBA procedure.
31. Click the title bar, or click on any empty area of the form to select it.
32. Press **F5** or choose **Run | Run Sub/UserForm** to display the form as the user will see it. Visual Basic switches to the active sheet in the Microsoft Excel window and displays the custom form you designed.

    If you forget to select the form, the Macro dialog box will appear. Close the dialog box, and repeat the two steps outlined above.
33. Click the **Close** button (x) in the top right-hand corner of the form to close the form and return to the Visual Basic Editor.

Recall that the OK and Cancel buttons placed on the form aren't functional yet. They require VBA procedures to make them work. After you've added controls to the form, use the mouse or the Format menu commands to adjust the alignment and spacing of the controls.

The Info Survey form design is now completed. From now on you should feel comfortable designing any form you want. When working with controls, you should learn some shortcuts. Here's how you can quickly copy and move controls:

- To copy a control, click the Select Objects tool in the Toolbox and select the control (a selected control will have handles at its sides), hold down the Ctrl key, position the mouse pointer inside the control, and press the left mouse button. Drag the pointer to the position you want, and then release the mouse button. Then change the control's Caption property.
- To select an entire group of controls, click the Select Objects tool in the Toolbox and start drawing a rectangle around the group of controls that you want to move together. When you release the mouse button, all the controls will be selected. (You can also select more than one control by holding down the Control key while clicking each of the controls you want to select — don't just read about it, try it now!)
- To move the selected group of controls to another position on the form, click within the selected area and drag the mouse to the desired position.

Changing Control Names and Properties

After you have placed controls on your form but before you begin to write procedures to control the form, you should assign your own names to the controls. Although Visual Basic automatically assigns a default name to each control (OptionButton1, OptionButton2, and so on), these names are difficult to distinguish in a procedure that may reference objects of the same class that have almost identical names. Assigning meaningful names to the controls placed on your form makes VBA procedures referencing these controls much more readable.

Before you change the Name property, make sure that the title bar of the Properties window displays the correct type of the control. For example, to assign a new name to the frame control, click the frame control on the form. When the Properties window displays "Properties - Frame1," double-click the Name property and type the new name in place of the highlighted default name. Do not confuse the name of the control with the control's title (caption). For example, on the Info Survey form, the default name of the frame control is Frame1, but the title of this control is Main Interest. The control's title can be changed by setting the Caption property. While the control's caption allows the user to identify the purpose of the control and may suggest the type of data expected, it is the name of the control that will be used in the code of your VBA procedures to make things happen.

Let's go back to our form to make adjustments in the controls' properties.

Hands-On 19-5: Naming Form Controls

Step 4

1. Assign names to the controls placed on the Info Survey form as shown in the following table. To assign a new name to a control, perform these steps:
   a. Click the appropriate control on the form.
   b. Double-click the Name property in the Properties window.
   c. Type the corresponding name as shown in the Name Property column in the table below.

Object Type	Name Property
First option button	optHard
Second option button	optSoft
List box	lboxSystems
Third option button	optMale
Fourth option button	optFemale
First check box	chkIBM
Second check box	chkNote
Third check box	chkMac
Combo box	cboxWhereUsed
Text box	txtPercent
Spin button	spPercent
First command button	cmdOK
Second command button	cmdCancel
Image	picImage

The controls that you placed on the Info Survey form are objects. Each of these objects has its own properties and methods. You've just changed the Name property for all the objects that will be referenced later from within VBA procedures. The control properties can be set during the design phase of your custom form or at run time (that is, when your VBA procedure is executed).

Let's now set some properties for selected controls.

2. Change the object properties as shown in the following table.

   To set a property, click a control on the form, locate the desired property in the Properties window, and type the new value in the space to the right of the property name. For example, to set the ControlTipText property of the lboxSystems control, click the list box control on the Info Survey form and locate the ControlTipText property in the Properties window. In the right-hand column of the Properties window, type the text you want to display when the user positions the mouse pointer over the list box control — in this case, **Select only one item**.

Object Name	Property	Change to:
lboxSystems	ControlTipText	Select only one item.
spPercent	Max	100
spPercent	Min	0
cmdOK	Accelerator	O
cmdCancel	Accelerator	C
picImage	PictureSizeMode	0-fmPictureSizeModeClip

The Accelerator property indicates which letter in the object name can be used to activate the control with the keyboard shortcut combination. The specified letter will appear underlined in the object's caption (title). For example, after displaying the form, you will be able to quickly select OK by pressing Alt+O.

The remaining properties of the Info Survey form objects will be set directly from VBA procedures.

Setting the Tab Order

The user can move around a form by using the mouse or the Tab key. Because many users prefer to navigate through the form using the keyboard, it is important to determine the order in which each control on the form is activated. Follow these steps to set the tab order in the Info Survey form.

Hands-On 19-6: Setting the Tab Order in a Form

Step 5

1. In the Forms folder in the Project Explorer window, double-click the **InfoSurvey** form.
2. Choose **View | Tab Order.**

   The Tab Order dialog box appears. This box displays the names of all the controls on the Info Survey form in the order that they were added. The right side of the dialog box has buttons that allow you to move the selected control up or down. To move a control, click its name and click the **Move Up** or **Move Down** button until the control appears in the position you want.
3. Rearrange the controls of the Info Survey form as shown in Figure 19-7.

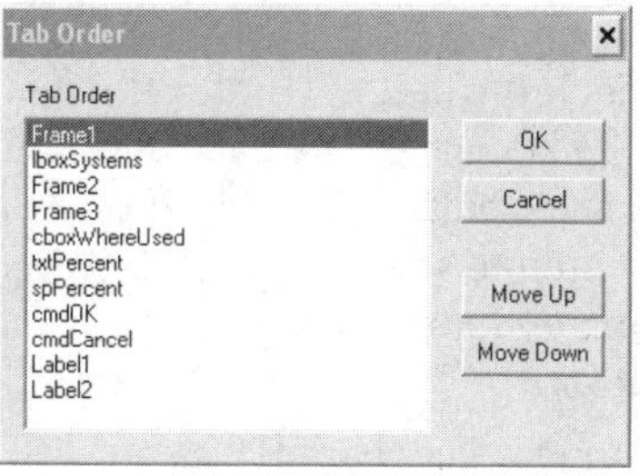

Figure 19-7: The Tab Order dialog box lets you organize the controls on the form in the order you would like to access them.

4. Close the Tab Order dialog box by clicking **OK**.
5. Activate the Info Survey user form and tab through the controls. Press the **Tab** key to move forward. Press **Shift+Tab** to move backward.
6. Close the Info Survey form.

If you'd like to change the order in which the controls are activated, reopen the Tab Order dialog box and make the appropriate changes.

Preparing a Worksheet to Store Custom Form Data

After the user selects appropriate options on the custom form and clicks OK, the selected data will be transferred to a worksheet. However, before this happens, we need to prepare a worksheet to accept the data and give the user an easy interface for launching your form. Follow the steps below to get your worksheet ready.

Hands-On 19-7: Preparing a Worksheet to Store Custom Form Data

Step 6

1. Activate the Microsoft Excel window.
2. Double-click the **Sheet1** tab in the Practice_Excel19.xlsm workbook, and type the new name for this sheet: **Info Survey**.
3. Enter the column headings as shown in Figure 19-6 earlier in this chapter.
4. Select row 1 through column K, and change the background of all cells to your favorite color (use the Fill Color button in the Font section of the Home tab). You may also want to change the background color of column K as shown in Figure 19-6.

   The easiest way to launch a custom form from a worksheet is by clicking a button. The remaining steps walk you through the process of adding the Survey button to your Info Survey worksheet.
5. Choose **Developer | Controls | Insert**.
6. Click the **Button** control on the Form Controls toolbar. Click in cell K2 to place a button. When the Assign Macro dialog box appears, type **DoSurvey** in the Macro name box, and click **OK**. You will write this procedure later.
7. When you return to the worksheet, the button (Button1, if it is your first button) to which you assigned the DoSurvey macro should still be selected. Type the new name for this button: **Survey**. If the button is not selected, use the right mouse button to select it. Choose **Edit Text** from the shortcut menu, and type **Survey** for the button's new name. To exit Edit mode, click outside the button.
8. Save the changes you've made to Practice_Excel19.xlsm.

Displaying a Custom Form

Each UserForm has a Show method that allows you to display the form to the user. In the example below, you will prepare the DoSurvey procedure. Recall that in the previous section you assigned the DoSurvey procedure to the Survey button placed in the Info Survey worksheet.

Hands-On 19-8: Displaying a Custom Form

Step 7

1. In the Visual Basic Editor window, select the **VBA_Forms (Practice_Excel19.xlsm)** VBA project in the Project Explorer window and choose **Insert | Module.**
2. In the Properties window, change the new module's name to **ShowSurvey.**
3. Enter the following procedure to display the custom form:

   ```
   Sub DoSurvey()
       InfoSurvey.Show
   End Sub
   ```

   Notice that the Show method is preceded by the name of the form object as it appears in the Forms folder (InfoSurvey).
4. Save the changes made to the Practice_Excel19.xlsm workbook.
5. Switch to the Microsoft Excel window and click the **Survey** button. The Info Survey form appears.

Note: If an error message appears after you click the Survey button, you have not assigned the required macro to this button as instructed in Step 6 in the previous section. To correct this problem, click OK to the message, right-click the Survey button, and choose Assign Macro from the shortcut menu. Click the DoSurvey macro name in the list box, and click OK. Now click the Survey button to display the form.

6. Close the Info Survey form by clicking the **Close** button (x) in the top right-hand corner of the form.

Before we can utilize this form we need to program in some events.

Understanding Form and Control Events

In addition to having properties and methods, each form and control has a predefined set of events. An *event* is some type of action, such as clicking a mouse button, pressing a key, selecting an item from a list, or changing a list of items available in a list box. Events can be triggered by the user or the system.

To specify how a form or control should respond to events, you write *event procedures*. When you design a custom form, you should anticipate and program events that can occur at run time (while the form is being used). The most popular event is the Click event. Every time a command button is clicked, it triggers the appropriate event procedure to respond to the Click event for that button. A form itself can respond to more than 20 separate events, including Click, DblClick, Activate, Initialize, and Resize. Table 19-1 lists events that are recognized by various form controls. If a control does not recognize a specific event, the table cell displays "N"; otherwise, it is blank. Take a few minutes now to familiarize yourself with the names of the events. For example, take a look at the AddControl event in the table. You can see at a glance that this event is only available for three objects: Frame, MultiPage control, and the UserForm itself. Excel events were covered in detail in Chapter 17.

Table 19-1: Form and control events

Event Name	User Form	Label	Text Box	Combo Box	Check Box	Option Button	Toggle Button	Frame	Command Button	TabStrip Control	MultiPage Control	ScrollBar	Spin Button	Image	RefEdit
Activate		N	N	N	N	N	N	N	N	N	N	N	N	N	N
AddControl		N	N	N	N	N	N		N	N		N	N	N	N
AfterUpdate	N	N						N	N	N	N			N	
BeforeDragOver															
BeforeDropOrPaste															
BeforeUpdate	N	N						N	N	N	N			N	
Change	N	N						N	N					N	
Click			N									N	N		N
DblClick												N	N		
Deactivate		N	N	N	N	N	N	N	N	N	N	N	N	N	N
DropButtonClick	N	N			N	N	N	N	N	N	N	N	N	N	
Enter	N	N												N	
Error															
Exit	N	N												N	
Initialize		N	N	N	N	N	N	N	N	N	N	N	N	N	N
KeyDown		N												N	
KeyPress		N												N	
KeyUp		N												N	
Layout		N	N	N	N	N	N		N	N		N	N	N	N
MouseDown												N	N		
MouseMove												N	N		
MouseUp												N	N		
QueryClose		N	N	N	N	N	N	N	N	N	N	N	N	N	N
RemoveControl		N	N	N	N	N	N		N	N	N	N	N	N	N
Resize		N	N	N	N	N	N	N	N	N		N	N	N	N
Scroll		N	N	N	N	N	N		N	N			N	N	N

Event Name	User Form	Label	Text Box	Combo Box	Check Box	Option Button	Toggle Button	Frame	Command Button	TabStrip Control	MultiPage Control	ScrollBar	Spin Button	Image	RefEdit
SpinDown	N	N	N	N	N	N	N	N	N	N	N	N		N	N
SpinUp	N	N	N	N	N	N	N	N	N	N	N	N		N	N
Terminate		N	N	N	N	N	N	N	N	N	N	N	N	N	N
Zoom		N	N	N	N	N	N		N	N		N	N	N	N

N — indicates control does not recognize that event

Each form you create contains a form module for storing VBA event procedures. To access the form module to write an event procedure or to find out the events recognized by a specific control, you can:

- Double-click a control.
- Right-click the control, and choose View Code from the shortcut menu.
- Click the View Code button in the Project Explorer window.
- Double-click any unused area of the user form.

When you execute any of the above actions, a Code window will open for the form. Figure 19-8 displays the Code window activated by double-clicking a command button placed on a form. Notice the title in the Microsoft Visual Basic title bar: Practice_Excel19.xlsm - [UserForm1(Code)]. A form module contains a general section as well as individual sections for each control placed on the form. The general section is used for declaration of form variables or constants.

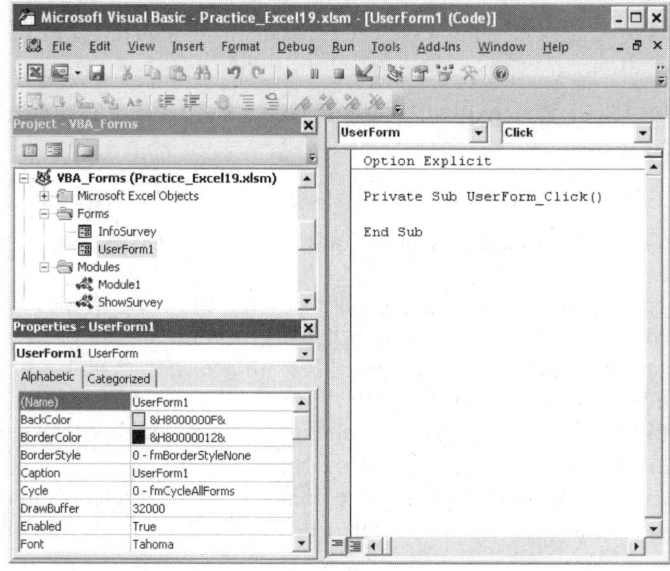

Figure 19-8: The combo box above the Code window lists the available event procedures for the UserForm.

You can access the desired section by clicking the down arrow to the right of the combo box in the upper-right corner. This combo box, the Procedure box, displays the event procedures that are recognized by the control selected in the combo box on the left. Events that already have procedures written for them appear in bold.

Writing VBA Procedures to Respond to Form and Control Events

Before the user can accomplish specific tasks with a custom form, you must usually write several VBA procedures. As mentioned earlier, each form created in the Visual Basic Editor has a module for storing procedures used by that form. Before displaying a custom form, you may want to set initial values for controls. To set the initial values, or default values, that the controls will have every time the form is displayed, write an Initialize event procedure for a user form. The Initialize event occurs when the form is loaded but before it's shown on the screen.

Writing a Procedure to Initialize the Form

Suppose that you want the Info Survey form to appear with the following initial settings:

- The Hardware button is selected in the Main Interest frame.
- The list box below contains the items that correspond to the selected Hardware option button.
- None of the Computer Type check boxes are selected.
- The combo box below the Used at label displays the first available item, and the user cannot add a new item to the combo box.
- The text box next to the spin button displays the initial value of zero (0).
- The image control displays a picture related to the selected Hardware option button.

Hands-On 19-9: Writing a Procedure to Initialize the Form

Step 8

1. In the Project Explorer window, double-click the **InfoSurvey** form.
2. Double-click the background of the form to open the Code window for the active form.

   When you double-click the form or a control, the Code window opens to the form or control's Click event. In the procedure definition, Visual Basic automatically adds the keyword Private before the Sub keyword. Private procedures can be called only from the current form module. In other words, a procedure that is located in another module of the current project cannot call this particular (Private) procedure.

   There are two combo boxes above the Code window. The combo box on the left displays the names of all form objects. The combo box on the right shows the event procedures recognized by the selected form object.

3. Click the down arrow in the Procedure box on the right, and select the **Initialize** event. Visual Basic displays the InfoSurveyUserForm_Initialize procedure in the Code window:

```
Private Sub UserForm_Initialize()

End Sub
```

4. Type the form's initial settings between the Private Sub and End Sub keywords. The complete UserForm_Initialize procedure is shown below:

```
Private Sub UserForm_Initialize()
'select the Hardware option
    optHard.Value = True
'turn off the Software option and all the check boxes
    optSoft.Value = False
    chkIBM.Value = False
    chkNote.Value = False
    chkMac.Value = False
    'display a zero in the text box
    txtPercent.Value = 0
'call ListHardware procedure
    Call ListHardware
'populate the combo box
    With Me.cboxWhereUsed
        .AddItem "Home"
        .AddItem "Work"
        .AddItem "School"
        .AddItem "Work/home"
        .AddItem "Home/school"
        .AddItem "Work/home/school"
    End With
'select the first element in the list box
    Me.cboxWhereUsed.ListIndex = 0
'load a picture file for the Hardware option
    Me.picImage.Picture = LoadPicture("C:\Ex07_HandsOn\cd.bmp")
End Sub
```

To simplify the event procedure code, you can use the Me keyword instead of the actual form name. For example, instead of using the statement:

```
InfoSurvey.cboxWhereUsed.ListIndex = 0
```

you can save time typing by using the following statement:

```
Me.cboxWhereUsed.ListIndex = 0
```

This technique is especially useful when the form name is long. Notice also that the first element of the list box has the index number zero (0). Therefore, if you'd like to select the second item in the list, you must set the ListIndex property to 1.

The UserForm_Initialize procedure calls the outside procedure (ListHardware) to populate its list box control with the hardware items. The code of this procedure is shown in step 5 below.

Notice that the UserForm_Initialize procedure ends with loading a picture into the image control. Make sure that the specified graphics file can be located in the indicated folder. If you don't have this file, enter the complete path of a valid picture file that you want to display.

5. Double-click the **ShowSurvey** module in the Project Explorer window and enter in the Code window the ListHardware procedure as shown below:

```
Sub ListHardware()
    With InfoSurvey.lboxSystems
        .AddItem "CD-ROM Drive"
        .AddItem "Printer"
        .AddItem "Fax"
        .AddItem "Network"
        .AddItem "Joystick"
        .AddItem "Sound Card"
        .AddItem "Graphics Card"
        .AddItem "Modem"
        .AddItem "Monitor"
        .AddItem "Mouse"
        .AddItem "Zip Drive"
        .AddItem "Scanner"
    End With
End Sub
```

Now that you've prepared the UserForm_Initialize procedure and the ListHardware procedure, you can run the form to see how it displays with the initial settings.

6. Launch the form by clicking the **Survey** button in the Info Survey worksheet.

After the form is displayed, the user can select appropriate options or click the Cancel button. When the user clicks the Software option button, the list box should display different items. At the same time, the image control should load a different picture. The next section explains how you can program these events.

Writing a Procedure to Populate the List Box Control

In the preceding section, you prepared the ListHardware procedure to populate the lboxSystems list box with the Hardware items. You can use the same method to load the Software items into the list box.

Hands-On 19-10: Populating the List Box Control

Step 9

1. Activate the ShowSurvey module and enter the code of the ListSoftware procedure, as shown below:

```
Sub ListSoftware()
    With InfoSurvey.lboxSystems
        .AddItem "Spreadsheets"
        .AddItem "Databases"
        .AddItem "CAD Systems"
```

```
        .AddItem "Word Processing"
        .AddItem "Finance Programs"
        .AddItem "Games"
        .AddItem "Accounting Programs"
        .AddItem "Desktop Publishing"
        .AddItem "Imaging Software"
        .AddItem "Personal Information Managers"
    End With
End Sub
```

Writing a Procedure to Control Option Buttons

When the user clicks the Software button in the Info Survey form, the hardware items from the list box should be replaced with the software items and vice versa. Let's write procedures that will control the Hardware and Software buttons in the Main Interest frame.

Hands-On 19-11: Controlling Option Buttons

Step 10

1. Activate the InfoSurvey form, and double-click the **Software** option button located in the Main Interest frame.
2. When the Code window appears with the optSoft_Click procedure skeleton, highlight the code and press **Delete**.
3. Click the down arrow in the upper right-hand combo box, and select the Change event procedure. Visual Basic will automatically enter the beginning and end of the optSoft_Change procedure for you.
4. Enter the code of the optSoft_Change procedure as shown below:

```
Private Sub optSoft_Change()
    Me.lboxSystems.Clear
    Call ListSoftware
    Me.lboxSystems.ListIndex = 0
    Me.picImage.Picture = LoadPicture("C:\Ex07_HandsOn\books.bmp")
End Sub
```

The optSoft_Change procedure begins with a statement that uses the Clear method to remove the current list of items from the lboxSystems list box. The next statement calls the ListSoftware procedure to populate the list box with software items. In other words, when the user clicks the Software button, the procedure removes the hardware items from the list box and adds the software items. If you don't clear the list box prior to adding new items, the new items will be appended to the current list. The statement Me.lboxSystems.ListIndex = 0 selects the first item in the list. The final statement in this procedure loads a picture file to the image control. Be sure to replace the reference to this file with the complete path to a valid picture file that is located in your computer. Because the user may want to reselect the Hardware button after selecting the Software button, you must create a similar Change event procedure for the optHard option button.

5. Enter the following optHard_Change procedure, just below the optSoft_Change procedure:

```
Private Sub optHard_Change()
    Me.lboxSystems.Clear
    Call ListHardware
    Me.lboxSystems.ListIndex = 0
    Me.picImage.Picture = LoadPicture("C:\Ex07_HandsOn\cd.bmp")
End Sub
```

6. Launch the form by clicking the **Survey** button in the Info Survey worksheet and check the results.

   When you click the Software option button, you should see the software items display in the list box below. At the same time, the image control should display the assigned picture. After clicking the Hardware option button, the list box should display the appropriate hardware items. At the same time, the image control should display a different picture.

7. Close the form by clicking the **Close** button in the form's upper-right corner.

Writing Procedures to Synchronize the Text Box with the Spin Button

The Info Survey form has a text box in front of the spin button control. To indicate a percent of time that the selected Hardware or Software item is used, the user can type a value in a text box or use the spin button. The initial value of the text box is set to zero (0). Suppose the user entered 10 in the text box and now wants to increase this value to 15 by using the spin button. To enable this action, the text box and the spin button have to be synchronized. Each of these objects requires a separate Change event procedure.

Hands-On 19-12: Synchronizing the Text Box with the Spin Button

Step 11

1. Right-click the spin button and choose **View Code** from the shortcut menu.
2. Enter the spPercent_Change procedure as shown below:

```
Private Sub spPercent_Change()
    txtPercent.Value = spPercent.Value
End Sub
```

   Using the spin buttons will cause the text box value to go up or down.

3. Working in the same Code window, enter the following txtPercent_Change procedure:

```
Private Sub txtPercent_Change()
    Dim entry As String

    On Error Resume Next

    entry = Me.txtPercent.Value
```

```
        If entry > 100 Then
            entry = 0
            Me.txtPercent.Value = entry
        End If
    spPercent.Value = txtPercent.Value
End Sub
```

The txtPercent_Change procedure ensures that only values from 0 to 100 can be entered into the text box. The procedure uses the On Error Resume Next statement to ignore data entry errors. If the user enters a non-numeric value in the text box (or a number greater than 100), Visual Basic will reset the text box value to zero (0). Each time a spin button is pressed, a text box value is incremented or decremented by one.

Writing a Procedure that Closes the User Form

After displaying the form, the user may want to cancel it by pressing Esc or clicking the Cancel button. To remove the form from the screen, let's prepare a simple procedure that uses the Hide method.

Hands-On 19-13: Writing a Procedure that Closes the Form

Step 12

1. Double-click the **Cancel** button and enter the following cmdCancel_Click procedure:

```
Private Sub cmdCancel_Click()
    Me.Hide
End Sub
```

The Hide method hides the object but does not remove it from memory. This way, your VBA procedure can use the form's objects and properties behind the scenes when the form isn't visible to the user. Use the Unload method to remove the form both from the screen and from memory resources:

```
Unload Me
```

When the form is unloaded, all memory associated with it is reclaimed. The user can't interact with the form, and the form's objects can't be accessed by your VBA procedure until the form is placed in memory again by using the Load statement.

Transferring Form Data to the Worksheet

When the user clicks the OK button, the form's selections should be written to the worksheet. The user can quit using the form at any time by clicking the Cancel button. Let's write a procedure that will copy the form's data to the worksheet when the OK button is clicked.

Hands-On 19-14: Transferring Form Data to the Worksheet

Step 13

1. In the Visual Basic Editor window, double-click the **InfoSurvey** form in the Project Explorer.
2. Double-click the **OK** button on the Info Survey form and enter the cmdOK_Click procedure shown below:

```
Private Sub cmdOK_Click()
    Dim r As Integer
    Me.Hide

    r = Application.CountA(Range("A:A"))
    Range("A1").Offset(r + 1, 0) = Me.lboxSystems.Value

    If Me.optHard.Value = True Then
        Range("A1").Offset(r + 1, 1) = "*"
    End If
    If Me.optSoft.Value = True Then
        Range("A1").Offset(r + 1, 2) = "*"
    End If
    If Me.chkIBM.Value = True Then
        Range("A1").Offset(r + 1, 3) = "*"
    End If
    If Me.chkNote.Value = True Then
        Range("A1").Offset(r + 1, 4) = "*"
    End If
    If Me.chkMac.Value = True Then
        Range("A1").Offset(r + 1, 5) = "*"
    End If
    Range("A1").Offset(r + 1, 6) = Me.cboxWhereUsed.Value
    Range("A1").Offset(r + 1, 7) = Me.txtPercent.Value

    If Me.optMale.Value = True Then
        Range("A1").Offset(r + 1, 8) = "*"
    End If
    If Me.optFemale.Value = True Then
        Range("A1").Offset(r + 1, 9) = "*"
    End If
   Unload Me
End Sub
```

The cmdOK_Click procedure begins by hiding the user form. The statement:

```
r = Application.CountA(Range("A:A"))
```

uses the Visual Basic CountA function to count the number of cells that contain data in column A. The result of the function is assigned to the variable r. The next statement:

```
Range("A1").Offset(r + 1, 0) = Me.lboxSystems.Value
```

enters the selected list box item in a cell located one row below the last used cell in column A (r + 1).

Next, there are several conditional statements. The first one tells Visual Basic to place an asterisk in the appropriate cell in column B if the Hardware option button is selected. Column B is located one column to the right of column A, hence there's a 1 in the position of the second argument of the Offset method. The second If statement enters the asterisk in column C if the user selected the Software option button. Similar instructions record the actual check box values. In column G, the procedure will enter the item selected in the Used at combo box. Column H will show the value entered in the Percent (%) Used text box, and columns I and J will identify the gender of the person who submitted the survey.

Using the Info Survey Application

Your application is now ready for the final test. Take off your programming hat and enjoy the result of your work from the user's standpoint. As you work with the form, think of improvements you would like to make to enhance the user's experience.

Hands-On 19-15: Using the Info Survey Application

Step 14

1. Switch to the Microsoft Excel Info Survey worksheet, and click the **Survey** button.
2. When the form appears, select appropriate options and click **OK.**
3. Activate the form several times, each time selecting different options.
4. Save the changes made to the Practice_Excel19.xlsm workbook.

Sample Application 2: Students and Exams

In recent years, many Windows applications have been relying more and more heavily on tabbed dialog boxes for grouping sets of controls together. Tabbed dialog boxes are very easy and convenient to use. When designing custom forms for more advanced VBA applications, you can take advantage of two special tabbed controls available in the Toolbox: the MultiPage control and the TabStrip control. The Students and Exams application, the subject of the remainder of this chapter, uses these and other advanced controls to keep track of students and their exam grades.

Using MultiPage and TabStrip Controls

The central object of the custom form shown in Figure 19-9 is a MultiPage control that consists of two pages. The first page contains text and combo boxes to gather student data, such as Social Security number (SSN), first and last name, year of study, and major. A pair of option buttons at the top of the form allows you to enter or view data. If the student's data is not available in a worksheet, the View Data option button will be disabled (grayed out). When the form is first loaded, the Data Entry option button is automatically selected. When you want to view data, clicking the View Data option button will display a list box with students' names, as entered on the worksheet.

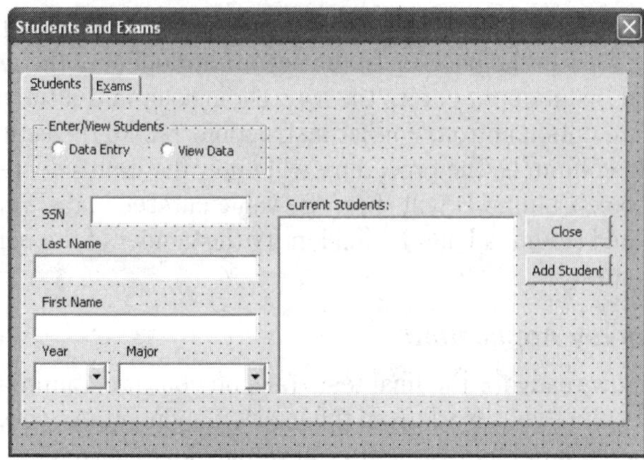

Figure 19-9: The MultiPage control can contain two or more pages. Each page shows a different set of controls.

Let's set up the Students and Exams form as shown in Figures 19-9 and 19-10.

Hands-On 19-16: Using MultiPage and TabStrip Controls

Step 1

1. In the VBE window, choose **Insert | UserForm** to add a new UserForm object into the current project, then rename it **Students**.
2. Change the form's Caption property to **Students and Exams**.
3. Click the **MultiPage** control in the Toolbox, and then click in the upper left-hand corner of the form and drag the mouse down and to the right to draw a large frame.
4. Right-click the **Page1** tab, and choose **Rename** from the shortcut menu. Type **Students** in the Caption text box, and enter **S** in the Accelerator Key field. In the same way, rename the second page **Exams**, and enter **x** in the Accelerator Key field.
5. Click the **Students** tab. Using the controls in the Toolbox, add to the Students page all of the controls shown in Figure 19-9. Follow these guidelines:
   - The Enter/View Students frame in the upper-left corner contains two option buttons. Set the Caption property of these buttons to **Data Entry** and **View Data**. Next, change the Name property of the first button to **optDataEntry** and the second one to **optViewData**. The frame's Caption property should be set to **Enter/View Students.**
   - Text boxes are titled using label controls with their Caption property set to **SSN**, **Last Name**, and **First Name**. Change the Name property of the text box controls to **txtSSN**, **txtLast**, and **txtFirst**.
   - Combo boxes are titled using label controls with their Caption property set to **Year** and **Major**. Set the Name property of the combo box controls to **cboxYear** and **cboxMajor**. To allow the user

to select only one of the specified items, set the following properties for each of the combo boxes: MatchRequired to **True**, MatchEntry to **1–fmMatchEntryComplete**.

- Set the Name property of the list box control to **lboxStudents**. Set the ColumnCount property to **2** to display two columns of data.
- Place the **Current Students:** label above the list box control and set its Name property to **lblNames**.
- Set the Caption property of the command buttons to **Close** and **Add Student**, and set their Name property to **cmdClose** and **cmdAddStudent**.

The second page of the MultiPage control (see Figure 19-10) is used to record and display information related to exams taken. This page contains two objects. The label control has a temporary title, "Last, First." At run time, this label will display the student's name as selected on the previous page. The second object on this page is the TabStrip control. It contains four tabs with the names of the exam subjects. Although this example displays the tabs at the top of the form, Visual Basic also allows you to set the orientation of the tabs to bottom, left, or right. As you navigate from tab to tab, you will see the same controls. Only the data displayed inside each control changes.

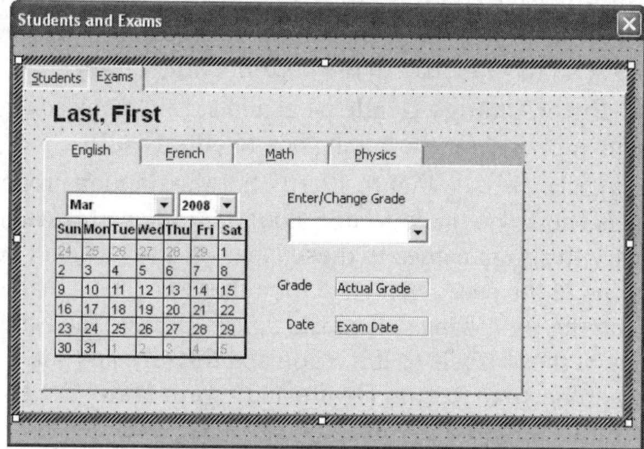

Figure 19-10: The outside frame contains the MultiPage control. The inside frame contains the TabStrip control.

6. Click the **Exams** tab in the MultiPage control.
7. Click the **Label** control in the Toolbox and click in the upper left-hand corner of the Exams page. Drag a rectangle large enough to hold a person's first and last name.
8. In the Properties window, set this label's Name property to **lblWho.** Set the label's Caption property to **Last, First.** Set the Font property to **Arial, Bold, 14 point.**
9. Click the **TabStrip** control in the Toolbox. Click on the form just below the label control, and drag the mouse until the strip is the size and shape

you want (see Figure 19-10). By default, the TabStrip control will display two tabs: Tab1 and Tab2. To add new tab pages, first click inside the TabStrip control to select the TabStrip object. Click again until the hatched frame around the TabStrip object appears in bold. Right-click any tab, and choose **New Page** from the shortcut menu. Visual Basic will add Tab3. Use the same method to add Tab4. Right-click each of the tabs, and choose **Rename** from the shortcut menu. See Figure 19-10 for the names of all the tabs. Notice that each tab name has an underlined letter, which allows the user to access the tab from the keyboard. For example, pressing Alt+E will activate the English tab. In the Rename dialog box, be sure to enter the underlined letter in the Accelerator Key box.

10. Click the **English** tab and begin drawing controls, as explained below:
    - If the Toolbox contains only one page titled Controls, go back to the earlier section in this chapter titled "Tools for Creating User Forms" to find out how to add a Calendar control to the Toolbox. Then place the Calendar control inside the TabStrip control, as shown in Figure 19-10. Set the ShowDateSelectors property for the Calendar control to **True**.

      The best way to set up a TabStrip control is to add it as the first control to the form and then place other controls inside it. However, if you already have controls placed on the form, you can draw the TabStrip control over these controls and use the Send to Back command to send the TabStrip to the bottom of the Z-order.
    - Add the **Enter/Change Grade** label and a combo box control. Set the Name property for the combo box to **cboxGrade**.
    - Create four labels (see Figure 19-10). Set the Caption property of the labels shown on the left-hand side to **Grade** and **Date**. It is not necessary to assign names to these labels as they will not be referenced in the code. Next, add the other two labels that are shown on the right-hand side in the figure. Change the Name property of these labels to **lblGrade** and **lblDate** and set the Caption property to **Actual Grade** and **Exam Date**. Set the SpecialEffect property for lblGrade and lblDate to **3–fmSpecialEffectEtched**.

Setting Up the Worksheet for the Students and Exams Application

The Students and Exams custom form allows you to enter new data or display data as entered in the worksheet. Figure 19-11 shows the worksheet used by this form.

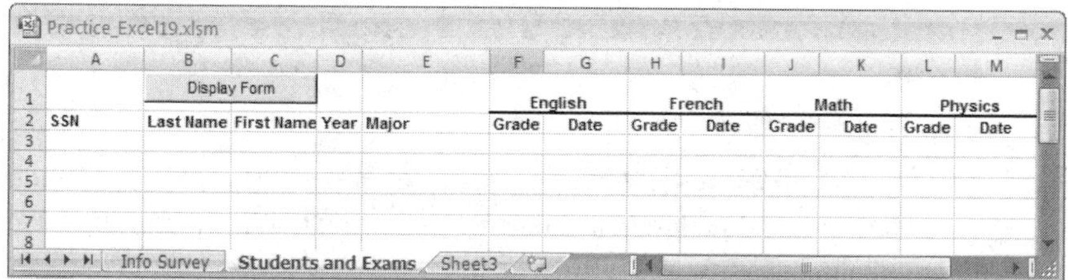

Figure 19-11: Supporting spreadsheet for the Students and Exams application.

Go ahead and prepare the worksheet as shown above using the following steps.

Hands-On 19-17: Preparing a Supporting Worksheet

Step 2

1. In an empty worksheet, type labels as shown in Figure 19-11. Use the Bottom Border setting of the Borders icon located in the Font group of the Home tab to create the horizontal line that runs across columns F-M.
2. Rename this worksheet **Students and Exams.**
3. Add the Display Form button to your worksheet and assign to it the DoStudents procedure. Follow the example of setting up the worksheet for the Info Survey application that was discussed earlier.
4. In the Visual Basic Editor screen, add a new module to the current project, and set the module's Name property to **InfoStudents**.
5. Enter the following DoStudents procedure in the InfoStudents module:

```
Sub DoStudents()
    Students.Show
End Sub
```

6. Return to the worksheet, and click the **Display Form** button to test the DoStudents procedure.
7. Close the form by clicking the **Close** button in the upper right-hand corner of the form.

Writing VBA Procedures for the Students and Exams Custom Form

The custom form Students and Exams contains about a dozen VBA procedures, which are shown below. The code of these procedures has to be entered in the form module. To quickly activate the form module, double-click the form background.

Hands-On 19-18: Writing VBA Procedures for a Custom Form

Step 3

1. Double-click the **Students and Exams** form in the Project Explorer window and double-click the form background to bring up this form's module.
2. From the combo box at the top left-hand side of the Code window, choose (**General**).

   The Procedure selection combo box on the right should display (Declarations).
3. Type the following variable declarations in the Code window:

```
' Global Declarations
Dim r As Integer
Dim nr As Integer
Dim indexPlus As Integer
Dim YesNo As Integer
Dim startRow As Integer
Dim endRow As Integer
```

4. Enter the code of the UserForm_Initialize procedure to set the form's initial settings:

```
Private Sub UserForm_Initialize()
    Me.MultiPage1.Value = 0
    optDataEntry.Value = True
    optViewData.Value = False
    If ActiveSheet.UsedRange.Rows.Count > 2 Then
        optViewData.Enabled = True
    Else
        optViewData.Enabled = False
        lboxStudents.Visible = False
    End If
    lblNames.Visible = False

    With Me.cboxYear
        .AddItem "1"
        .AddItem "2"
        .AddItem "3"
        .AddItem "4"
    End With

    With Me.cboxMajor
        .AddItem "English"
        .AddItem "Chemistry"
        .AddItem "Mathematics"
        .AddItem "Linguistics"
        .AddItem "Computer Science"
    End With

    With Me.cboxGrade
        .AddItem "A"
        .AddItem "B"
        .AddItem "C"
```

```
            .AddItem "D"
            .AddItem "F"
        End With

        Me.Calendar1.Value = Date

        Me.lblDate.Caption = Me.Calendar1.Value
        Me.TabStrip1.Value = 0
        Me.txtSSN.SetFocus
    End Sub
```

5. Enter two procedures to control the option buttons (optDataEntry_Click and optViewData_Click):

```
Private Sub optDataEntry_Click()
    cmdAddStudent.Visible = True
    lblNames.Visible = False
    lboxStudents.Visible = False

    Me.MultiPage1(1).Enabled = False
        If lboxStudents.RowSource <> "" Then
            Me.txtSSN.Text = ""
            Me.txtLast.Text = ""
            Me.txtFirst.Text = ""
            Me.cboxYear.Text = ""
            Me.cboxMajor.Text = ""
            Me.txtSSN.SetFocus
        End If
    Me.txtSSN.SetFocus
End Sub

Private Sub optViewData_Click()
    startRow = 3
    endRow = ActiveSheet.UsedRange.Rows.Count
    If endRow > 2 Then
        lblNames.Visible = True
        lboxStudents.Visible = True
        lboxStudents.RowSource = _
          Range(Cells(startRow, 2), Cells(endRow, 3)).Address
        lboxStudents.ListIndex = 0
        cmdAddStudent.Visible = False
   End If
End Sub
```

6. Enter the code of the lboxStudents_Change procedure that controls the behavior of the list box control placed on the Students page:

```
Private Sub lboxStudents_Change()
    indexPlus = lboxStudents.ListIndex + 3

    With ActiveWorkbook.Worksheets("Students and Exams")
        Me.txtSSN.Text = Range("A" & indexPlus).Value
        Me.txtLast.Text = Range("B" & indexPlus).Value
        Me.txtFirst.Text = Range("C" & indexPlus).Value
        Me.cboxYear.Text = Range("D" & indexPlus).Value
        Me.cboxMajor.Text = Range("E" & indexPlus).Value

     Call TabStrip1_Change
```

```
        Me.MultiPage1(1).Enabled = True
    End With
End Sub
```

7. Enter the code to control the command buttons Add Student (cmdAddStudent_Click) and Close (cmdClose_Click):

```
Private Sub cmdAddStudent_Click()
    If IsFilled = False Then
        MsgBox "Please enter all the data " & _
            "or click Close to exit."
        Me.txtSSN.SetFocus
        Exit Sub
    End If
    If Me.optDataEntry.Value = True Then
        Me.Hide
        ActiveWorkbook.Sheets("Students and Exams").Select
        r = ActiveSheet.UsedRange.Rows.Count
        nr = r + 1
        Range("A" & nr).Value = Me.txtSSN.Text
        Range("B" & nr).Value = Me.txtLast.Text
        Range("C" & nr).Value = Me.txtFirst.Text
        Range("D" & nr).Value = Me.cboxYear.Text
        Range("E" & nr).Value = Me.cboxMajor.Text

        Me.txtSSN.Text = ""
        Me.txtLast.Text = ""
        Me.txtFirst.Text = ""
        Me.cboxYear.Text = ""
        Me.cboxMajor.Text = ""
        Me.txtSSN.SetFocus

        Me.optViewData.Enabled = True
        ' redisplay the form
        Me.Show
    End If
End Sub

Private Sub cmdClose_Click()
    Unload Me
    Set Students = Nothing
End Sub
```

8. Enter the procedure cboxGrade_Click to control the Grade combo box located on the Exams page:

```
Private Sub cboxGrade_Click()
    YesNo = MsgBox("Enter the grade in the worksheet?", _
        vbYesNo, "Modify Grade")
    If YesNo = 6 Then
       Me.lblGrade.Caption = cboxGrade.Value
       Select Case TabStrip1.Value
        Case 0
          Range("F" & indexPlus).Value = Me.lblGrade.Caption
        Case 1
            Range("H" & indexPlus).Value = Me.lblGrade.Caption
        Case 2
            Range("J" & indexPlus).Value = Me.lblGrade.Caption
```

```
            Case 3
                Range("L" & indexPlus).Value = Me.lblGrade.Caption
            End Select
            cboxGrade.Value = ""
        End If
    End Sub
```

9. Enter the Calendar1_Click procedure, as shown below:

```
    Private Sub Calendar1_Click()
        YesNo = MsgBox("Enter the date in the worksheet?", _
            vbYesNo, "Modify Date")
        If YesNo = 6 Then
           Me.lblDate.Caption = Calendar1.Value
           Select Case TabStrip1.Value
            Case 0
                Range("G" & indexPlus).Value = Me.lblDate.Caption
            Case 1
                Range("I" & indexPlus).Value = Me.lblDate.Caption
            Case 2
                Range("K" & indexPlus).Value = Me.lblDate.Caption
            Case 3
                Range("M" & indexPlus).Value = Me.lblDate.Caption
            End Select
        End If
    End Sub
```

10. Enter the TabStrip1_Change and MultiPage1_Change procedures, as follows:

```
    Private Sub TabStrip1_Change()
        indexPlus = lboxStudents.ListIndex + 3

        With ActiveWorkbook.Worksheets("Students and Exams")
            Select Case TabStrip1.Value
                Case 0  ' English
                    Me.lblGrade.Caption = Range("F" & indexPlus).Value
                    Me.lblDate.Caption = Range("G" & indexPlus).Value
                Case 1 'French
                    Me.lblGrade.Caption = Range("H" & indexPlus).Value
                    Me.lblDate.Caption = Range("I" & indexPlus).Value
                Case 2  'Math
                    Me.lblGrade.Caption = Range("J" & indexPlus).Value
                    Me.lblDate.Caption = Range("K" & indexPlus).Value
                Case 3 'Physics
                    Me.lblGrade.Caption = Range("L" & indexPlus).Value
                    Me.lblDate.Caption = Range("M" & indexPlus).Value
            End Select
        End With
    End Sub

    Private Sub MultiPage1_Change()
        Me.lblWho.Caption = Me.txtLast.Value & ", " _
            & Me.txtFirst.Value
        Call TabStrip1_Change
    End Sub
```

Using the Students and Exams Custom Form

Now that you've prepared all of the required VBA procedures, let's see how the form responds to the user's actions.

Hands-On 19-19: Using the Students and Exams Custom Form

Step 4

1. Switch to the Microsoft Excel window and activate the Students and Exams sheet.
2. Click the **Display Form** button.

   Clicking the Display Form button will run the DoStudents procedure. This procedure displays the Students and Exams custom form. Before the form appears on the screen, Visual Basic executes each statement entered in the UserForm_Initialize procedure. The result is the form shown in Figure 19-12.

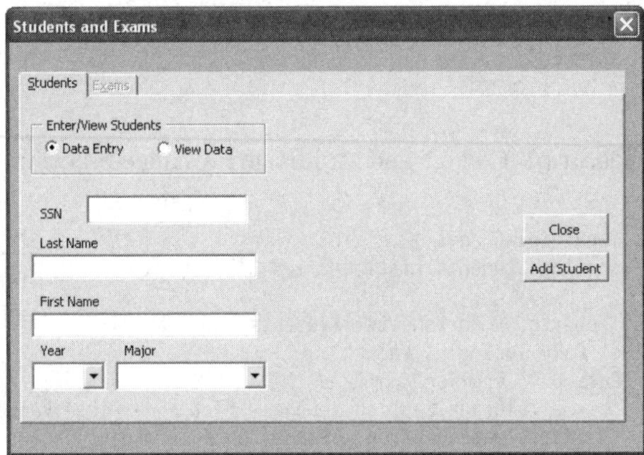

Figure 19-12: The Display Form button on the worksheet lets you quickly access the Students and Exams custom form to view or enter data. When the form is loaded, only the controls that apply to the selected option button are shown.

   After the form is displayed, you can enter a new student and click Add Student to transfer the student's data to the worksheet. When you click the Add Student button, the cmdAddStudent_Click procedure is executed. Notice that you can't enter the exams taken by the new student because the second page (Exams) of the MultiPage control is disabled at this time. Once the new student's data is written to the worksheet, the form is redisplayed. You can continue entering the data, or you can click Close to remove the form from the screen. When you click the Close button, the cmdClose_Click procedure is run.

3. Use the Students and Exams custom form to enter data for two new students.

   At any time, you can click the View Data option button and load the data for the existing students. When you click the View Data option button, the lboxStudents control and its label become visible.

4. Click the **View Data** option button, and notice that the Current Students list box displays the names of students from the worksheet.

   The selected student's data is displayed in the text and combo boxes on the left (see Figure 19-13).

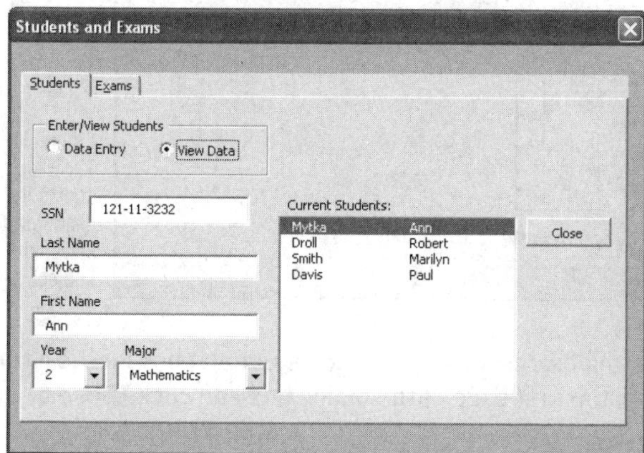

Figure 19-13: The list box on the form is automatically populated with the data stored in a worksheet.

5. Click any name in the list box, and check the student's data.
6. Click any name in the list box, and click the **Exams** tab.

The Exams page displays the name of the selected student (see Figure 19-14). The TabStrip control shows the exam subjects. If the selected student has taken any of the exams, the date and the exam grade are displayed when you click the appropriate subject tab. You can enter or change a student's grade and exam date by using the provided combo box and calendar control. Visual Basic asks that you confirm the modification of data (review the VBA code for the Calendar1_Click and cboxGrade_Click procedures). After responding **Yes** in the dialog box, the selected date or grade is written to the corresponding column in a worksheet (see Figure 19-15). The TabStrip1_Change procedure ensures that when you click the subject tab, Visual Basic displays the exam grade and date from the appropriate spreadsheet cell. The MultiPage1_Change procedure ensures that when you click the Exams page, the lblWho label control displays the last and first name of the student who is currently selected in the list box.

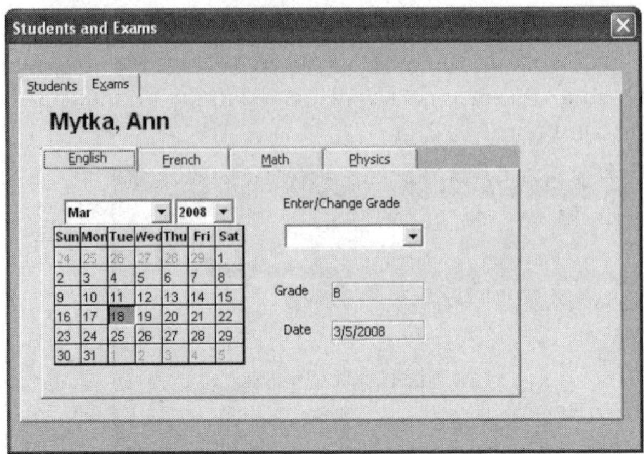

Figure 19-14: The Exams page shows the date and exam grade for the selected student and subject.

7. After entering exams for the selected student, click on the **Students** tab to return to the first page of the dialog box and click **Close** to exit.

Practice_Excel19.xlsm

	A	B	C	D	E	F	G	H	I	J	K	L	M
1		Display Form				English		French		Math		Physics	
2	SSN	Last Name	First Name	Year	Major	Grade	Date	Grade	Date	Grade	Date	Grade	Date
3	121-11-3232	Mytka	Ann	2	Mathematics	B	3/5/2008			A	2/27/2008	B	2/6/2008
4	880-36-6765	Droll	Robert	3	Chemistry								
5	980-62-0654	Smith	Marilyn	4	English	C	3/5/2008	B	1/29/2008			D	2/12/2008
6	235-32-2569	Davis	Paul	1	Computer Science			C	2/14/2008	C	3/18/2008	B	3/4/2008
7													
8													

Info Survey | Students and Exams | Sheet3

Figure 19-15: Data in columns F-M on the spreadsheet is entered via the Exams tab on the Students and Exams user form.

8. Save and close the Practice_Excel19.xlsm workbook.

Chapter Summary

Now that you've reached the end of this rather long chapter, you have the necessary skills for designing useful forms. Let's quickly summarize all that you've learned in this chapter:

- For custom VBA applications that require user input, we created a custom form. We made sure the user could move around the form in a logical order by setting the tab order (see Hands-On 19-6).
- For the form to respond to user actions, we wrote VBA procedures in a form module. We set the initial values of controls by using the Properties window or writing the UserForm_Initialize procedure. We made sure to include procedures to transfer form data to a worksheet.

In the next chapter, you will learn how to format Excel worksheets with VBA.

Chapter 20

Formatting Worksheets with VBA

Microsoft Excel has always provided users with a fairly comprehensive selection of formatting features. By applying different fonts, colors, borders, and patterns, or using conditional formatting and built-in styles, you can easily transform any raw and unfriendly worksheet data into a visually appealing and easy-to-understand document. And even if you don't care about cell appearance and your only desire is to provide a no-frills data dump, chances are that before you share your worksheet with others you will spend ample time formatting cell values. For your raw data to be understood, you will definitely want to control the format of your numerical values, dates, and times.

Excel 2007 has revamped the entire user interface, simplifying and adding new formatting features, so you can now spend less time formatting. To better highlight your information you can now apply new visual features such as data bars, color scales, and icon sets. You can produce consistent looking worksheets by using new document themes and styles. This chapter assumes that you are already a master formatter and what really interests you is how the basic and advanced formatting features can be applied to your worksheets programmatically. So, let's get going.

Performing Basic Formatting Tasks with VBA

This section focuses on cell value formatting that controls the relationship between the values that you enter in a worksheet cell and the cell's format. Cell value formatting should always be attempted prior to cell appearance formatting. Always begin your formatting tasks by checking that Excel correctly interprets the values you entered or copied over from an external data source, such as a text file, an SQL Server, or a Microsoft Access database. For example, when you copy data from an SQL Server and your data set contains date and time values separated by a space, such as 5/16/2006 11:00:04 PM, Excel displays the correct value in the formula bar, but displays 00:04.0 in the cell. When you activate the Format Cells dialog box, you will notice that Excel has applied the Custom format "mm:ss.0", and if you take a look at the General format in the same dialog box, you will notice that the value was also converted to a serial number for date and time: 38853.95838. Or perhaps your data contains five-digit invoice numbers and you want to retain the leading zeros, which Excel suppresses by default. When you enter data into a worksheet yourself, you are more likely to stop right away when Excel incorrectly interprets the data. When the data comes from an external source, it is much harder to pinpoint the cell formatting problems unless you run your custom VBA procedures that check for specific problems and automatically fix them when found. The meaning of your data largely depends on how Excel interprets your cell entries; therefore, to avoid confusing the end user, take the cell formatting control into your own hands.

Formatting Numbers

Depending on how you have formatted the cell, the number that you actually see in a worksheet can differ from the underlying value stored by Excel. As you know, each new Excel spreadsheet will have its default cell format set to the built-in number format named "General." In this format, Excel removes the leading and trailing zeros. For example, if you entered 08.40, Excel displays 8.4. In VBA, you can write the following statement to have Excel retain both zeros:

```
ActiveCell.NumberFormat = "00.00"
```

The NumberFormat property of the CellFormat object is used to set or return the format for a specific cell or cell range. The format code is the string displayed in the Format Cells dialog box (Figure 20-1) or your custom string.

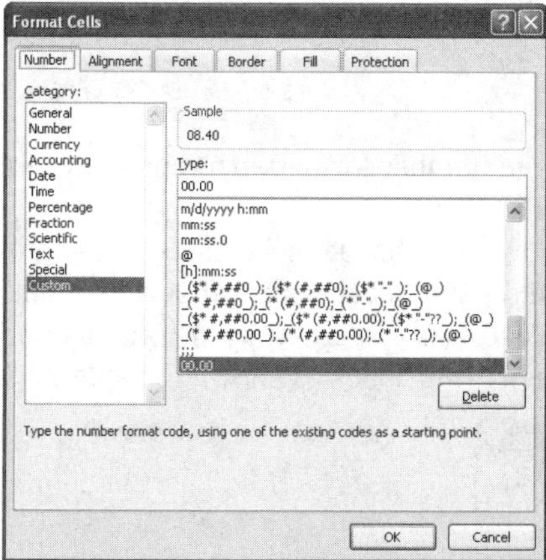

Figure 20-1: Format codes for your VBA procedures can be looked up in the Format Cells dialog box (choose Home | Format | Format Cells, or press Alt + HOE).

If the number you entered has decimal places, Excel will only display as many decimal places as it can fit in the current column width. For example, if you enter 9.34512344443 in a cell that is formatted with the General format, Excel displays 9.345123 but keeps the full value you entered. When you widen the column, it will adjust the number of displayed digits. While determining the display of your number, Excel will also determine whether the last displayed digit needs to be rounded.

You can use the NumberFormat property to determine the format that Excel applied to cells. For example, to find out the format in the third column of your worksheet, you can use the following statement in the Immediate window:

```
?Columns(3).NumberFormat
```

If all cells in the specified column have the same format, Excel displays the name of the format, such as General, or the format code that has been applied, such as $#,##0.00. If different formatting is found in different cells of the specified column, Excel prints out Null in the Immediate window.

It is recommended that you apply the same number formatting for the entire column. Whether you are doing this programmatically or manually via the Excel user interface, the formatting can be applied before or after you enter the numbers. Excel will only apply number formatting to cells containing numeric values; therefore, you do not need to be concerned if the first cell in the selected column contains text that defines the column heading.

Because the NumberFormat property sets the cell's number format by assigning a string with a valid format from the Format Cells dialog box, you can use the macro recorder to get the exact VBA statement for the format you would like to apply. For example, the following statements were generated by the macro recorder to format the values entered in cells D1 and E1:

```
Range("D1").Select
Selection.NumberFormat = "#,##0"
```

The above statement displays a large number with the thousands separator (a comma) and with no decimal places.

```
Range("E1").Select
Selection.NumberFormat = "$#,##0.00"
```

The above statement displays a large number formatted as currency with the thousands separator and two decimal places.

The Custom category in the Format Cells dialog box lists many built-in custom formats that you can use in the NumberFormat property to control how values are displayed in cells. Also, you can create your own custom number format strings by using formatting codes as shown in Table 20-1.

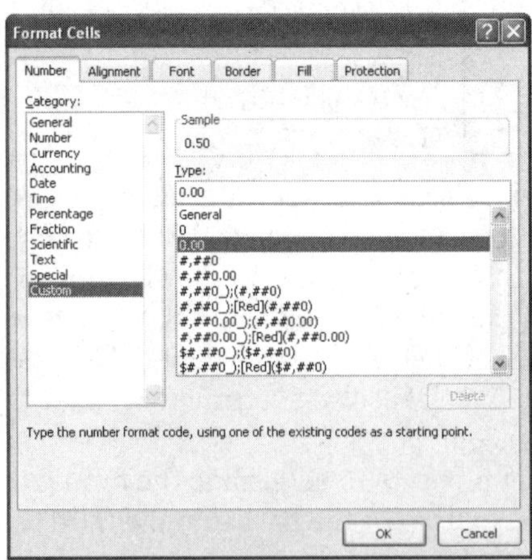

Figure 20-2: The Custom category in the Number tab of the Format Cells dialog box displays a list of ready-to-use number formats, and allows you to create a new format or edit the existing format code to suit your particular needs.

Table 20-1: Number formatting codes

Code	Description
0	Digit placeholder. Use it to force a zero. For example, to display .5 as 0.50 use the following VBA statement: `Selection.NumberFormat = "0.00"` or enter 0.00 in the Type box in the Format Cells dialog box.
#	Digit placeholder. Use it to indicate the position where the number can be placed. For example, the code #,### will display the number 2345 as 2,345.
.	Decimal placeholder. In the United States, a period is used as the decimal separator. In Germany, it is a comma.

,	Thousands separator (comma). In the United States, one thousand two hundred five is displayed as 1,205. In other countries, the thousands separator can be a period (e.g., Germany) or a space (e.g., Sweden).
	In the United States, placing a single comma after the number format indicates that you want to display numbers in thousands. To make it clear to the user that the number is in thousands, you may want to place the letter "K" after the comma:
	`Selection.NumberFormat = "#, ##0, K"`
	Use two commas at the end to display the number in millions:
	`Selection.NumberFormat = "#,##0.0,,"`
	To indicate that the number is in millions, add a backslash followed by "M":
	`Selection.NumberFormat = "#,##0.0,,\M"`
	Or surround the letter "M" with double quotes:
	`Selection.NumberFormat = "#,##0.0,,""M"""`
	This will cause the number 23093456 to appear as 23.1M.

/	Forward slash character. Used for formatting a number as a fraction. For example, to format 1.25 as 1¼ use the following statement: `Selection.NumberFormat = "# ?/?"`
_	The underscore character is used for aligning formatting codes. For example, to ensure that positive and negative numbers are aligned as shown below, apply the format as follows: `Selection.NumberFormat = "#,##0.00_);(#,##0.00)"` 234.23 (234.12)
*	The asterisk in a number format allows you to fill in the cell with the character that follows the asterisk. For example, the following VBA statement produces the output shown below: `Selection.NumberFormat = "*_0000"` __________1045 _________23455

When working with cell formatting, keep in mind that number formats have four parts separated by semicolons. The first part is applied to positive numbers, the second to negative numbers, the third to zero, and the fourth to text. For example, take a look at the following VBA statement:

```
Range("A1:A4").NumberFormat = "#,##0;[red](#,#0);""zero"";@"
```

This statement tells Excel to format positive numbers with the thousands separator, display negative numbers in red and in parentheses, display the text "zero" whenever 0 is entered, and format any text entered in the cell as text. Make the following entries in cells A1:A4:

```
2870
-3456
 0
Test text
```

When you apply the above format to cells A1:A4, you will see the cells formatted as shown below:

```
        2,870
      (3,456)
         zero
Test text
```

You can hide the content of any cell by using the following VBA statement:

```
Selection.NumberFormat = ";;;"
```

When the number format is set to three semicolons, Excel hides the display of the cell entry on the worksheet and in printouts. You can only see the actual value or text stored in the cell by taking a look at the Formula bar.

By using the number format codes it is also possible to apply conditional formats with one or two conditions. Consider the following VBA procedure:

```
Sub FormatUsedRange()
    ActiveSheet.UsedRange.Select
    Selection.SpecialCells(xlCellTypeConstants, 1).Select
    Selection.NumberFormat = "[<150][Red];[>250][Green];[Yellow]"
End Sub
```

The above procedure tells Excel to select all the values in the used range on the active sheet and display them as follows: values less than 150 in red, values over 250 in green, and all the other values in the range from 150 to 250 in yellow. Excel supports eight colors: [white], [black], [blue], [cyan], [green], [magenta], [red], and [yellow].

Later in this chapter we will learn how to use VBA to perform more advanced conditional formatting.

In addition to the NumberFormat property, Excel VBA has a Format function that you can use to apply a specific format to a variable. For example, take a look at the following procedure that formats a number prior to entering it in a worksheet cell:

```
Sub FormatVariable()
    Dim myResult, frmResult
    myResult = "1435.60"
    frmResult = Format(myResult, "Currency")
    Debug.Print frmResult
    ActiveSheet.Range("G1").FormulaR1C1 = frmResult
End Sub
```

The Format function specifies the expression to format (in this case the expression is the name of the variable that stores a specified value) and the number format to apply to the expression. You can use one of the predefined number formats such as: "General", "Currency", "Standard", "Percent", and "Fixed", or you can specify your custom format using the formatting codes from Table 20-1. For example, the following statement will apply number formatting to the value stored in the myResult variable and assign the result to the frmResult variable:

```
frmResult = Format(myResult, "#.##0.00")
```

For more information about the Format function and the complete list of formatting codes, refer to the online help. A quick way to find this topic is to enter the word Format in the Immediate window, place the insertion point within this word, and press F1.

To check whether the cell value is a number, use the IsNumber function as shown below:

```
MsgBox Application.WorksheetFunction.IsNumber(ActiveCell.Value)
```

If the active cell contains a number, Excel returns True; otherwise, it returns False.

Note: To use an Excel function in VBA, you must prefix it with "Application.WorksheetFunction." The WorksheetFunction property returns the WorksheetFunction object that contains functions that can be called from VBA.

Formatting Text

To format a cell as a text string, use the following VBA statement:

```
Selection.NumberFormat = "@"
```

To find out if a cell value is indeed a text string, use the following statement:

```
MsgBox Application.WorksheetFunction.IsText(ActiveCell.Value)
```

Use the UCase function to convert a cell entry to uppercase:

```
Range("K3").value = UCase(ActiveCell.Value)
```

Use the LCase function to convert a cell entry to lowercase if the cell is not a formula:

```
If not Range(ActiveWindow.Selection.Address).HasFormula then
    ActiveCell.Value = LCase(ActiveCell.Value)
End If
```

Use the Proper function to capitalize the first letter of each word in a text string:

```
ActiveCell.Value = Application.WorksheetFunction.Proper(ActiveCell.Value)
```

Use the Replace function to replace a specified character within text. For example, the following statement replaces a space with an underscore (_) in the active cell:

```
ActiveCell.Value = Replace(ActiveCell.Value, " ", "_")
```

To ensure that the text entries don't have leading or trailing spaces, use the following VBA functions:

LTrim — Removes the leading spaces
RTrim — Removes the trailing spaces
Trim — Removes both the leading and trailing spaces

For example, the following statement written in the Immediate window will remove the trailing spaces from the text found in the active cell:

```
ActiveCell.value = RTrim(ActiveCell.value)
```

Use the Font property to format the text displayed in a cell. For example, the following statement changes the font of the selected range to Verdana:

```
Selection.Font.Name = "Verdana"
```

You can also format parts of the text in a cell by using the Characters collection. For example, to display the first character of the text entry in red, use the following statement:

```
ActiveCell.Characters(1,1).Font.ColorIndex = 3
```

Formatting Dates

Microsoft Excel stores dates as serial numbers. In the Windows operating system, the serial number 1 represents January 1, 1900. If you enter the number 1 in a worksheet cell and then format this cell as Short Date using the Number Format drop-down in the Number section of the Ribbon's Home tab, Excel will display the date formatted as 1/1/1900 and will store the value of 1 (you can check this out by looking at the General category in the Format Number dialog box). By storing dates as serial numbers, Excel can easily perform date calculations.

To apply a date format to a particular cell or range of cells using VBA, use the NumberFormat property of the Range object, like this:

```
Range("A1").NumberFormat = "mm/dd/yyyy"
```

Table 20-2: Date and time formatting codes

Code	Description
d	Day of the month. Single-digit number for days from 1 to 9.
dd	Day of the month (two-digit). Leading zeros appear for days from 1 to 9.
ddd	A three-letter day of the week abbreviation (Mon, Tue, Wed, Thu, Fri, Sat, and Sun).
m	Month number from 1 to 12. Zeros are not used for single-digit month numbers.
mm	Two-digit month number.
mmm	Three-letter month name abbreviation (e.g., Jan, Jun, Sep).

Code	Description
yy	Two-digit year number (e.g., 08).
yyyy	Four-digit year number (e.g., 2008).
h	The hour from 0 to 23 (no leading zeros).
hh	The hour from 0 to 23 (with leading zeros).
:m	The minute from 0 to 59 (no leading zeros).
:mm	The minute from 0 to 59 (with leading zeros)
:s :s.0 :s.00	The second from 0 to 59 (no leading zeros). To add tenths of a second, follow this with a period and a zero (.0), and to add hundredths of a second, follow this code with a period and two zeros (.00).
:ss :ss.0 :ss.00	The second from 0 to 59 (with leading zeros). To add tenths of a second, follow this code with a period and a zero (.0), and to add hundredths of a second, follow this code with a period and two zeros (.00).
AM/PM am/pm A/P a/p	Use for a 12-hour clock, with AM or PM. Use for a 12-hour clock, with am or pm. Use for a 12-hour clock, with A or P. Use for a 12-hour clock, with a or p.
[ ]	Bracket the time component (hour, minute, second) to prevent Excel from rolling over hours, minutes, or seconds when they hit the 24-hour mark (hours become days) or the 60 mark (minutes become hours, seconds become minutes). For example, to display time as 25 hours, 59 minutes, and 12 seconds use the following format code: [hh]:[mm]:ss.

The following VBA procedure applies a date format to the Inspection Date column in Figure 20-3.

```
Sub FormatDateFields()
    Dim wks As Worksheet
    Dim cell As Range

    Set wks = ActiveWorkbook.ActiveSheet

    For Each cell In wks.UsedRange
      If cell.NumberFormat = "mm:ss.0" Then
         cell.NumberFormat = "m/dd/yyyy h:mm:ss AM/PM"
      End If
    Next
End Sub
```

After running the above procedure, the cells in column C are displayed as shown in Figure 20-4.

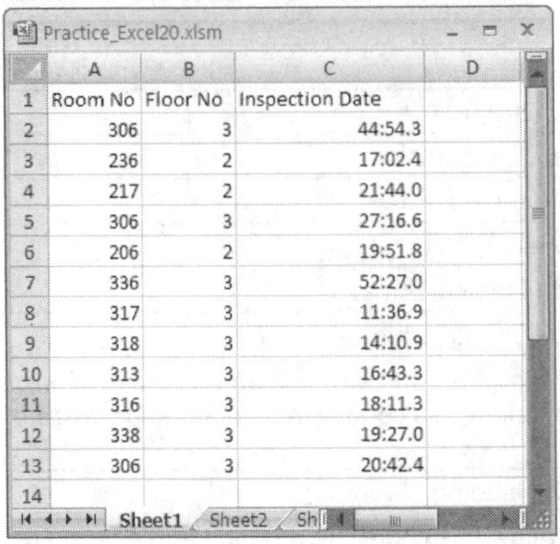

Practice_Excel20.xlsm

	A	B	C	D
1	Room No	Floor No	Inspection Date	
2	306	3	44:54.3	
3	236	2	17:02.4	
4	217	2	21:44.0	
5	306	3	27:16.6	
6	206	2	19:51.8	
7	336	3	52:27.0	
8	317	3	11:36.9	
9	318	3	14:10.9	
10	313	3	16:43.3	
11	316	3	18:11.3	
12	338	3	19:27.0	
13	306	3	20:42.4	
14				

Sheet1 Sheet2 Sh

Figure 20-3: A worksheet with an unformatted Inspection Date column.

Practice_Excel20.xlsm

	A	B	C	D
1	Room No	Floor No	Inspection Date	
2	306	3	5/16/2006 1:44:54 PM	
3	236	2	5/16/2006 2:17:02 PM	
4	217	2	5/16/2006 2:21:44 PM	
5	306	3	5/16/2006 2:27:17 PM	
6	206	2	5/31/2006 8:19:52 AM	
7	336	3	6/13/2006 4:52:27 AM	
8	317	3	6/02/2008 7:11:37 PM	
9	318	3	6/02/2008 7:14:11 PM	
10	313	3	6/02/2008 7:16:43 PM	
11	316	3	6/02/2008 7:18:11 PM	
12	338	3	6/02/2008 7:19:27 PM	
13	306	3	6/02/2008 7:20:42 PM	
14				

Sheet1 Sheet2 Sh

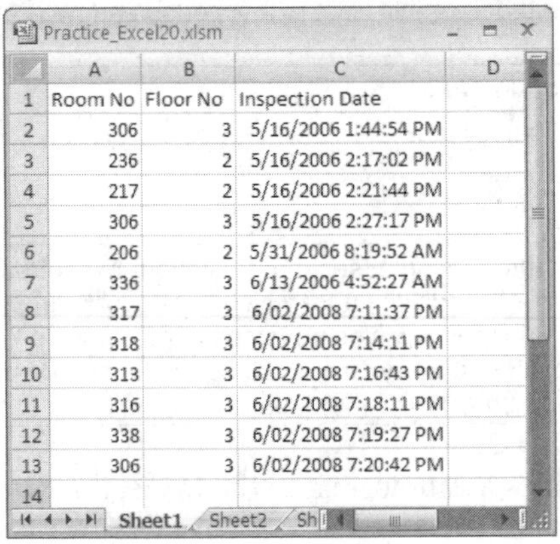

Figure 20-4: The Inspection Date column after it has been formatted with a VBA procedure.

Formatting Columns and Rows

To speed up your worksheet formatting tasks you can apply formatting to entire rows and columns instead of single cells. The best way to find the required VBA statement is by using the macro recorder (choose Developer | Record Macro). Keep in mind that Excel will record more code than is necessary for your specific task and you'll need to clean it up before copying it to your VBA procedure. For example, here's the recorded code for setting the horizontal alignment of data in row 7:

```
Rows("7:7").Select
    Range("D7").Activate
    With Selection
        .HorizontalAlignment = xlRight
        .VerticalAlignment = xlBottom
        .WrapText = False
        .Orientation = 0
        .AddIndent = False
        .IndentLevel = 0
        .ShrinkToFit = False
        .ReadingOrder = xlContext
        .MergeCells = False
    End With
```

To set the horizontal alignment for row 7 you can write a single VBA statement like this:

```
Rows(7).HorizontalAlignment = xlRight
```

Using the macro recorder is helpful in finding out the names of properties that should be used to turn on or off a specific formatting feature. Once you know the property and the required setting, you can write your own short statement to get the job done.

Here are some VBA statements that can be used to format columns and rows:

Formatting Columns and Rows	VBA Statement
To format column D as a date using the NumberFormat property:	`Columns("D").NumberFormat = "mm/dd/yyyy"`
To format column G as currency:	`Columns("G").NumberFormat = "$###,##0.00"`
To format column G as currency using the Style property:	`Columns("G").Style = "Currency"`
To set column width or row height:	`Columns(2).ColumnWidth = 21.5` `Rows(2).RowHeight = 55.55`
To auto-fit column width or row height:	`Columns(2).AutoFit` `Rows(2).Autofit`
To apply bold font to the 1st row:	`Rows(1).Font.Bold = True`
To right align data in row 1:	`Rows(1).HorizontalAlignment = xlRight`
To center data in column B:	`Columns("B").HorizontalAlignment = xlCenter`
To set the background of the column where the active cell is located to yellow:	`Columns(ActiveCell.Column).interior.color = vbYellow`
To check the width of a column, use the ColumnWidth method:	`MsgBox Columns(ActiveCell.Column).ColumnWidth`
To auto-fit all rows and colums:	`ActiveSheet.Cells.EntireRow.AutoFit` `ActiveSheet.Cells.EntireColumn.AutoFit`

Formatting Headers and Footers

Headers and footers are made of three sections each: LeftHeader, CenterHeader, and RightHeader, and LeftFooter, CenterFooter, and RightFooter. Using special formatting codes (see Table 20-3) you can customize your worksheet's header or footer according to your needs.

Table 20-3: Header and footer formatting codes

Format Code	Description
&D	Prints the current date
&T	Prints the current time
&F	Prints the name of the workbook
&A	Prints the name of the sheet tab
&P	Prints the page number
&P+number	Prints the page number plus the specified number
&P–number	Prints the page number minus the specified number

Format Code	Description
&N	Prints the total number of pages in the workbook
&Z	Prints the workbook's path
&G	Inserts an image
&&	Prints a single ampersand
&nn	Prints the characters that follow in the specified font size in points
&color	Prints the characters in the specified color using the hexadecimal color value
&"fontname"	Prints the characters that follow in the specified font
&L	Left-aligns the characters that follow
&C	Centers the characters that follow
&R	Right-aligns the characters that follow
&B	Turns bold printing on or off
&I	Turns italic printing on or off
&U	Turns underline printing on or off
&E	Turns double-underline printing on or off
&S	Turns strikethrough printing on or off
&X	Turns superscript printing on or off
&Y	Turns subscript printing on or off

Here are several VBA statements that demonstrate applying custom formatting to a header or footer:

Formatting Headers and Footers	VBA Statement (enter on one line)
To create a two-line header with bold text in the first line and italic text in the second line:	`ActiveSheet.PageSetup.LeftHeader = "&BYour Company Name" & Chr(13) & "&IYour Company Department"`
To place the workbook creation date in the footer:	`ActiveSheet.PageSetup.RightFooter = "Created on: " & ActiveWorkbook.BuiltinDocumentProperties("Creation Date")`
To place a cell's contents in the header:	`ActiveSheet.PageSetup.CenterHeader = ActiveSheet.Cells(2,2).value`
To insert the filename and path in the footer:	`ActiveSheet.PageSetup.CenterFooter = ActiveWorkbook.FullName`
To place text in the header using Arial Narrow font, bold and italic formatting, and red font color (applied to the last word):	`ActiveSheet.PageSetup.CenterHeader = "&""ArialNarrow""&IYour text goes here &I&B&KFF0000now."`
To remove the formatting and text entries from the center header:	`ActiveSheet.PageSetup.CenterHeader = ""`

Note: If you need to use a different date format in your header or footer than the date format shown in the Regional settings of the Windows Control panel, use the Format function to specify the date format string you want to use:

```
ActiveSheet.PageSetup.RightFooter = Format(Date, "mm-dd-yyyy")
```

The above statement inserts in the right footer a current system date returned by the Date function. The date is formatted as a two-digit month number followed by a dash, two-digit day number followed by a dash, and four-digit year number (see Table 20-2 for the explanation of date and time formatting codes).

Formatting Cell Appearance

As mentioned earlier, adding cosmetic touches to your worksheet such as fonts, color, borders, shading, and alignment should be undertaken after applying the required formatting to numbers, dates, and times. Formatting cell appearance makes your worksheet easier to read and interpret. By applying borders to cells, and with the clever use of font colors, background shading, and patterns, you can draw the reader's attention to particularly important information.

Use the Font object to change the font format in VBA. You can apply multiple format properties at once using the With...End With statement block as shown below:

```
Sub ApplyCellFormat()
    With ActiveSheet.Range("A1").Font
        .Name = "Tahoma"
        .FontStyle = "italic"
        .Size = 14
        .Underline = xlUnderlineStyleDouble
        .ColorIndex = 3
    End With
End Sub
```

The ColorIndex property refers to the 56 colors that are available in the color palette. Number 3 represents red. The following procedure prints a color palette to the active sheet:

```
Sub ColorLoop()
    Dim r As Integer
    Dim c As Integer
    Dim k As Integer

    k = 0

    For r = 1 To 8
        For c = 1 To 7
            Cells(r, c).Select
            k = k + 1
            ActiveCell.Value = k
            With Selection.Interior
                .ColorIndex = k
```

```
                .Pattern = xlSolid
            End With
        Next c
    Next r
End Sub
```

To change the background color of a single cell or a range of cells, use one of the following VBA statements:

```
Selection.Interior.Color = vbBlue
Selection.Interior.ColorIndex = 5
```

To change the font color, use the following VBA statement:

```
Selection.Font.Color = vbMagenta
```

The font can be made bold, italic, or underlined or a combination of the three using the following With...End With block statement:

```
With Selection.Font
        .Italic = True
        .Bold = True
        .Underline = xlUnderlineStyleSingle
End With
```

To apply borders to your cells and ranges in VBA, use the following statement examples:

```
Selection.BorderAround Weight:=xlMedium, ColorIndex:=3
Selection.BorderAround Weight:=xlThin, Color:=vbBlack
```

The BorderAround method of the Range object places a border around all edges of the selected cells. The following xlBorderWeightEnumeration constants can be used to specify the weight of the border: xlHairline, xlMedium, xlThick, and xlThin. When specifying border color, you can use either ColorIndex or Color but not both.

Instead of specifying the thickness of the border, you may want to use LineStyle as in the following example:

```
Selection.BorderAround LineStyle:=xlDashDotDot, Color:=vbBlack
```

You can use any of the following xlLineStyle enumeration constants: xlContinuous (continuous line), xlDash (dashed line), xlDashDot (alternating dashes and dots), xlDashDotDot (dash followed by two dots), xlDot (dotted line), xlDouble (double line), xlLineStyleNone (no line), and xlSlantDashDot (slanted dashes and dots). Use xlLineStyleNone to clear the border.

VBA has a Borders collection that contains the four borders of a Range or Style object. To set just a bottom border of cells A1:C1, use the following statement:

```
ActiveSheet.Range("A1:C1").Borders(xlEdgeBottom).Weight = xlThick
```

You may specify any of the following border types: xlDiagonalDown, xlDiagonalUp, xlEdgeBottom, xlEdgeLeft, xlEdgeRight, xlEdgeTop, xlInsideHorizontal, and xlInsideVertical.

You can change the appearance of cells by specifying the horizontal or vertical alignment:

```
Selection.HorizontalAlignment = xlCenter
Selection.VerticalAlignment = xlTop
```

The value of the HorizontalAlignment property can be one of the following constants: xlCenter, xlDistributed, xlJustify, xlLeft, and xlRight.

The VerticalAlignment property can be one of the following constants: xlBottom, xlCenter, xlDistributed, xlJustify, and xlTop.

Removing Formatting from Cells and Ranges

To remove cell formatting, use the ClearFormats method of the Range object. This method restores the formatting to the original General format without removing the cell's content. To remove the content of the cell, use the ClearContents method.

Performing Advanced Formatting Tasks with VBA

Having mastered basic worksheet formatting techniques that can be used with Excel 2007 and earlier, let's focus on how you can use VBA with the new and enhanced formatting features that are available in Excel 2007 in the Styles group on the Ribbon's Home tab and in the Themes group of the Page Layout tab. We will work with the FormatConditions collection of the Range object and explore new conditional formatting tools: Data Bars, Color Scales, and Icon Sets. Next, we will take a look at document themes that can be applied to a workbook, and see how they affect another formatting feature — styles.

Conditional Formatting Using VBA

To help you automatically highlight important parts of your worksheet, Excel provides a feature known as *conditional formatting*. This feature allows you to set a condition (a formatting rule), and specify the type of formatting that should be applied to cells and ranges when the condition is met. For example, you can use conditional formatting to apply different background color, font, or borders to a cell based on its value. The Conditional Formatting feature has been greatly improved in Excel 2007 by providing users with various types of common rules and the availability of new formatting tools such as Data Bars, Color Scales, and Icon Sets. The new options make it easy to highlight the top or bottom 10% of values, locate duplicate or unique values, or indicate values above or below the average. Unlike previous versions of Excel that restricted the use of conditional formatting to three criteria, you can now specify an unlimited number of conditional formats. In the user interface you now have the Conditional Formatting Rules Manager (see Figure 20-5) that simplifies the creation, modification, and removal of conditional rules. All conditional formatting features that are available in the Excel application window can be accessed via VBA.

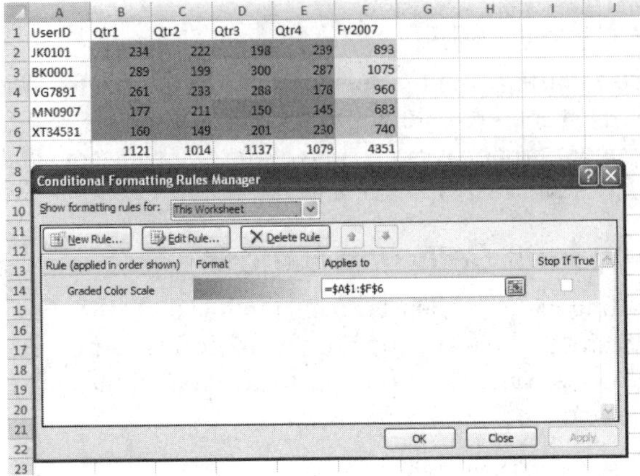

Figure 20-5: To activate the Conditional Formatting Rules Manager, choose Home | Conditional Formatting | Manage Rules.

To create a new conditional formatting rule, click the New Rule button in the Conditional Formatting Rules Manager dialog box. You will see the list of built-in rules that you can select from (Figure 20-6).

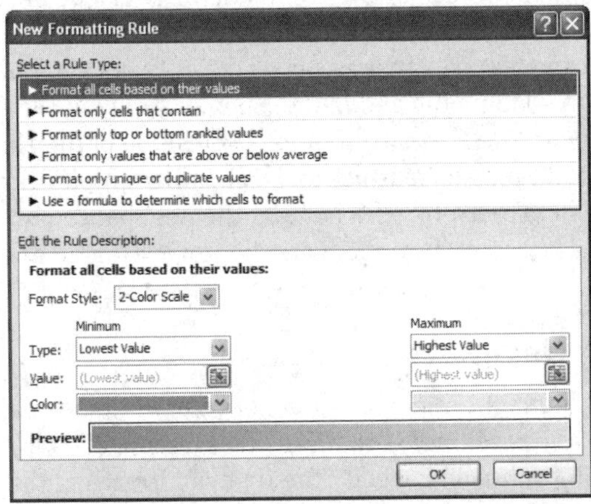

Figure 20-6: Creating a new conditional format using the Excel built-in dialog. This window appears after choosing the New Rule button in the Conditional Formatting Rules Manager (Figure 20-5), or choosing Home | Conditional Formatting | New Rule.

In VBA, use the Add method of the FormatConditions collection to create a new rule. For example, to format cells containing "Qtr" in the text string, write and then run the following VBA procedure:

```
Sub FormatQtrText()
    With ActiveSheet.UsedRange
        .FormatConditions.Delete
        .FormatConditions.Add Type:=xlTextString, String:="Qtr", _
            TextOperator:=xlContains
        .FormatConditions(1).Interior.Color = RGB(123, 130, 0)
    End With
End Sub
```

Notice that before creating and applying a new conditional format to a range of cells, it's a good idea to delete the existing format condition from the selection using the Delete method. The Add method that is used to add a new condition requires at minimum the Type argument that specifies whether the conditional format is based on a cell value or an expression. Use the xlFormatConditionType enumeration constants (see Table 20-4) to set the condition type. For example, to format cells that contain dates, use the xlTimePeriod constant in the Type argument, and specify the DateOperator using one of the following constants: xlToday, xlYesterday, xlTomorrow, xlLastWeek, xlThisWeek, xlNextWeek, xlLast7Days, xlLastMonth, xlThisMonth, or xlNextMonth:

```
Selection.FormatConditions.Add Type:=xlTimePeriod,
DateOperator:=xlLast7Days
```

Table 20-4: Conditional format Type settings

Constant	Description

xlAboveAverage
xlBelowAverage
	Above/below average condition:
	`With Selection`
	`    .FormatConditions.Delete`
	`    .FormatConditions.AddAboveAverage`
	`    .FormatConditions(1).AboveBelow = xlAboveAverage`
	`    .FormatConditions(1).Font.Bold = True`
	`End With`

xlBlanksCondition	Format cells that contain blanks:
	`With Selection`
	`    .FormatConditions.Add Type:=xlBlanksCondition`
	`End With`

xlCellValue	Format cell value:
	`With Selection`
	`    .FormatConditions.Add Type:=xlCellValue,`
	`Operator:=xlLess`
	`       Formula1:="=2000"`
	`    .FormatConditions(1).NumberFormat = "#, ##0"`
	`End With`
	You can use the following constants in the Operator argument: xlBetween, xlEqual, xlGreater, xlGreaterEqual, xlLess, xlLessEqual, xlNotBetween, or xlNotEqual.
	To specify the numeric value for the operator, use the Formula1 argument. The xlBetween and xlNotBetween operators require that you also specify a second value in Formula2.

xlColorScale	Format color scale:
	`If Selection.FormatConditions(1).Type = 3 Then`
	`    MsgBox "This selection is formatted with " & _`
	`      "ColorScale conditional format."`
	`End If`

xlDataBar	Format data bar:
	`If Selection.FormatConditions(1).Type = 4 Then`
	`    MsgBox "This selection is formatted with " & _`
	`      "DataBar conditional format."`
	`End If`

xlErrorsCondition	Format cells that contain errors: `Selection.FormatConditions.Add Type:=xlErrorsCondition`

<table>
<tr><th>Constant</th><th>Description</th></tr>
<tr><td>xlExpression</td><td>

Expression to specify a custom formula that identifies the cells that the conditional format applies to. For example, the following procedure changes the background color of alternate rows in the used range:

```
Sub HighlightAltRows()
   With ActiveSheet.UsedRange
     .FormatConditions.Add Type:=xlExpression, _
         Formula1:="=MOD(ROW(),2)=0"
     .FormatConditions(1).Interior.ColorIndex = 6
   End With
End Sub
```

To highlight every third row, use the formula:

```
= MOD(ROW(),3)=0.
```

</td></tr>
<tr><td>xlIconSet</td><td>

Format icon set:

```
If Selection.FormatConditions(1).Type = 6 Then
    MsgBox "This selection is formatted with " & _
     "IconSet conditional format."
End If
```

</td></tr>
<tr><td>xlNoBlanksCondition</td><td>

Format cells that do not contain blanks:

```
Sub HighlightNonEmptyCells()
    Range("A1:B12").Select
    Selection.FormatConditions.Add _
        Type:=xlNoBlanksCondition
    With Selection.FormatConditions(1).Interior
        .ThemeColor = xlThemeColorAccent4
        .TintAndShade = 0.399945066682943
    End With
End Sub
```

</td></tr>
<tr><td>xlNoErrorsCondition</td><td>

Format cells that do not contain errors:

```
Sub HighlightCellsWithNoErrors()
    Range("F1:F7").Select
    Selection.FormatConditions.Add _
        Type:=xlNoErrorsCondition
    With Selection.FormatConditions(1).Interior
        .ThemeColor = xlThemeColorAccent4
        .TintAndShade = 0.399945066682943
    End With
End Sub
```

Before running the above procedure, enter any number in cell F1, and enter zero (0) in cell F2. In cell F3 enter the following formula: =F1/F2. Because there is no division by zero, Excel will display the following error code: #DIV/0! When you run the procedure all cells in the selected range except for cell F2 will be shaded with the specified color.

</td></tr>
<tr><td>xlTextString</td><td>

Format cells that contain text:

```
With ActiveSheet.UsedRange
 .FormatConditions.Add Type:=xlTextString, _
     String:="es", TextOperator:=xlContains
 .FormatConditions(1).Font.Bold = True
End With
```

Other text operators you can use: xlBeginsWith, xlDoesNotContain, and xlEndsWith.

</td></tr>
</table>

<table>
<tr><th>Constant</th><th>Description</th></tr>
<tr><td>xlTimePeriod</td><td>Format cells that contain dates:<pre>With ActiveSheet.UsedRange
 .FormatConditions.Add Type:=xlTimePeriod, _
    DateOperator:=xlLastMonth
 .FormatConditions(1).Interior.ColorIndex = 6
End With</pre>Other date operators you can use: xlToday, xlYesterday, xlTomorrow, xlLastWeek, xlThisWeek, xlNextWeek, xlLast7Days, xlThisMonth, and xlNextMonth.</td></tr>
<tr><td>xlTop10</td><td>Format 10 top values:<pre>With Selection
   .FormatConditions.AddTop10
   .FormatConditions(1).TopBottom = xlTop10Top
   .FormatConditions(1).Value = 5
   .FormatConditions(1).Percent = False
   .FormatConditions(1).Interior.Color = RGB(255,0,0)
End With</pre></td></tr>
<tr><td>xlUniqueValue</td><td>Format unique values:<pre>With Selection
   .FormatConditions.AddUniqueValues
   .FormatConditions(1).DupeUnique = xlUnique
      Formula1:="=200"
End With</pre>By replacing the xlUnique constant with xlDuplicate, you can select duplicate values.</td></tr>
</table>

Conditional Formatting Rule Precedence

In Excel 2007 you can apply multiple conditional formats to a cell. For example, you can apply a conditional format to make the cell bold, and then another one to make a red border around the cell. Because these two formats do not conflict with one another, they can both be applied to the same cell. However, if you create another format that tells Excel to apply a blue border to the cell, this rule will not be applied because it conflicts with the previous rule that told Excel to apply the red border. In order to control multiple conditions applied to a range of cells, Excel uses so-called rule precedence. When rules conflict with one another, Excel applies the rule that is higher in precedence. Rules are evaluated in order of precedence by how they listed in the Conditional Formatting Rules Manager dialog box. In VBA, this is controlled by the Priority property of the FormatConditions object. For example, to assign a second priority to the first rule, use the following statement:

```
Range("B2:B17").FormatConditions(1).Priority = 2
```

You can make the rule the lowest priority with the following statement:

```
Range("B2:B17").FormatConditions(1).SetLastPriority
```

Note: In cases where the same format is applied both manually and via conditional formatting to a range of cells, the conditional formatting rule takes precedence over the manual format. Formats applied manually are not considered when determining conditional formatting rule precedence and do not appear in the Conditional Formatting Rules Manager dialog box.

Deleting Rules with VBA

You can use the following statement to delete all rules applied to a specific range of cells:

```
Range("B2:B17").FormatConditions.Delete
```

To delete a particular rule, refer to its index number before calling the Delete method of the FormatConditions collection:

```
Range("B2:B17").FormatConditions(2).Delete
```

Using Data Bars

The data visualization tool known as the data bar, new in Excel 2007, allows users to easily see how data values relate to each other. Data bars can be added via conditional formatting using the New Formatting Rule dialog box (see Figure 20-7) or by a VBA procedure.

In VBA, you can create a data bar formatting rule by using the AddDatabar or Add method of the FormatConditions collection, as shown below:

```
Range("B2:E6").FormatConditions.AddDatabar
Range("B2:E6").FormatConditions.Add Type:=xlDatabar, _
    Operator:=xlGreaterEqual, Formula1:="200"
```

The above statements will place a blue bar in the worksheet cells, as illustrated in Figure 20-8. Notice that the length of the data bar corresponds to the cell's value. If you change or recalculate the worksheet data, the data bar is automatically reapplied to the specified range. Instead of using the Lowest and Highest value to specify the Shortest and Longest bar (Figure 20-7), you can specify that the bar is based on numbers, percentages, formulas, or percentiles. For example, you can use the following statements to change the color, type, and threshold parameters of the data bar:

```
set mBar = Selection.FormatConditions.AddDatabar
mBar.MinPoint.Modify NewType:=xlConditionValuePercentile, NewValue:=20
mBar.MaxPoint.Modify NewType:=xlConditionValuePercentile, NewValue:=80
mBar.BarColor.ColorIndex = 7
```

In the above statements, the MinPoin and MaxPoint properties of the DataBar object are used to set the values of the shortest and longest bar of a range of data, and the BarColor property is used to modify the color of the bars in the data bar conditional format.

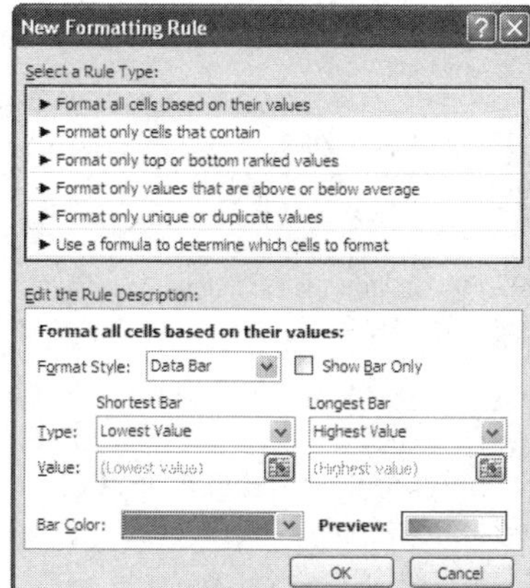

Figure 20-7: The New Formatting Rule dialog box can be accessed from the Ribbon by choosing Home | Conditional Formatting | Data Bars | More Rules.

Practice_Excel20.xlsm

	A	B	C	D	E	F
1	UserID	Qtr1	Qtr2	Qtr3	Qtr4	FY2007
2	JK0101	234	222	198	239	893
3	BK0001	289	199	300	287	1075
4	VG7891	261	233	288	178	960
5	MN0907	177	211	150	145	683
6	XT34531	160	149	201	230	740
7		1121	1014	1137	1079	4351

Sheet2 Sheet3 Sheet4

Figure 20-8: A worksheet shown with the new data bar formatting.

Using Color Scales

You can create special visual effects in your worksheet by selecting a range of values and applying a color scale. Color scales use cell shading to help you understand variation in your data. When you apply a color scale conditional format via the user interface (Home | Conditional Formatting | Color Scales | More Rules) or from your VBA procedure, Excel uses the lowest, highest, and midpoint values in the range to determine the color gradients. You can apply a two-color or a three-color scale to your data.

To create a color scale conditional formatting rule in VBA, use the AddColorScale or Add method of the FormatConditions collection:

```
set cScale = Selection.FormatConditions.AddColorScale(ColorScaleType:=2)
```

The above statement creates a two-color ColorScale object in the selected worksheet cells.

To change the minimum threshold to green and the maximum threshold to blue, use the following statements:

```
cScale.ColorScaleCriteria(1).FormatColor.Color = RGB(0, 255, 0)
cScale.ColorScaleCriteria(2).FormatColor.Color = RGB(0, 0, 255)
```

For darker color scales, it makes sense to change the font color to white:

```
Selection.Font.ColorIndex = 2
```

Practice_Excel20.xlsm

	A	B	C	D	E	F
1	UserID	Qtr1	Qtr2	Qtr3	Qtr4	FY2007
2	JK0101	234	222	198	239	893
3	BK0001	289	199	300	287	1075
4	VG7891	261	233	288	178	960
5	MN0907	177	211	150	145	683
6	XT34531	160	149	201	230	740
7		1121	1014	1137	1079	4351

Sheet2 / Sheet3 / Sheet4

Figure 20-9: This worksheet was formatted using the two-color (green/blue) color scale conditional format.

Similar to a data bar, you can change the type of threshold value for a color scale to a number, percent, formula, or percentile.

To create striking visual effects, try applying both data bar and color scale conditional formatting to the same range of data.

Using Icon Sets

Like data bars and color scales, icon sets are a new visualization feature introduced in Excel 2007. By using icon sets you can place icons in cells to make your data more comprehensive and visually appealing to the user. Icon sets allow users to easily see the relationship between data values as well as recognize trends in the data. To view the available icon choices, choose Home | Conditional Formatting | Icon Sets.

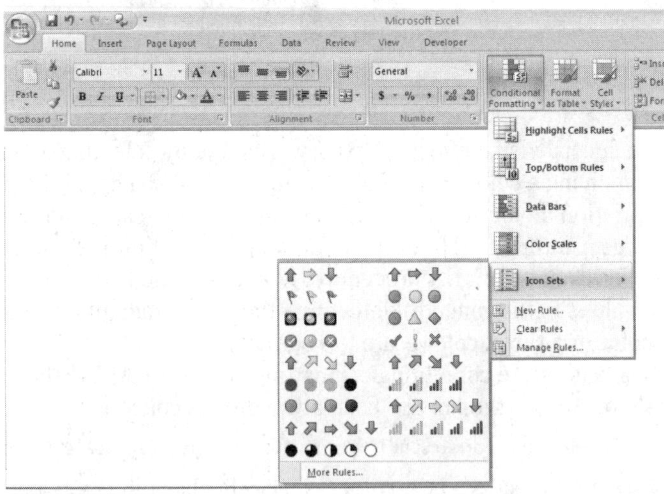

Figure 20-10: While you cannot add your own customized icons in this release of Excel, you can select from a large selection of built-in icons.

Each icon in an icon set represents a range of values. For example, in a three-icon set such as 3 Symbols (Circled), Excel uses the check mark symbol in a green circle for values that are greater than or equal to 67%, an exclamation point in an orange circle for values that are less than 67% and greater than or equal to 33%, and an x symbol in a red circle for values that are less than 33% (see Figure 20-11).

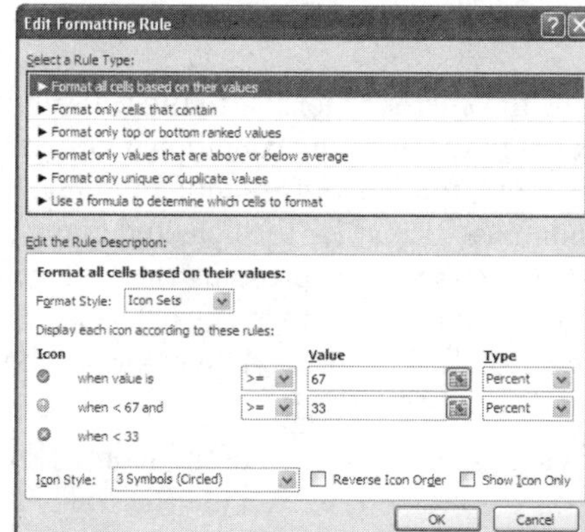

Figure 20-11: You can view or edit the details of the formatting rule in this dialog box.

Four- and five-icon sets display each icon according to which quartile or quintile the value falls into. You may change the default threshold value and its type (number, percent, formula, or percentile) for each icon in an icon set by editing the formatting rule using the dialog box shown in Figure 20-11 or with a VBA procedure as demonstrated in Hands-On 20-1.

Note: Icons can be made larger or smaller by increasing or decreasing the font size.

In VBA, the IconSet object in the IconSets collection represents a single set of icons. To create a conditional formatting rule that uses icon sets, use the IconSetCondition object. You can add criteria for an icon set conditional formatting rule with the IconCriteria collection. The following VBA procedure applies an icon set conditional formatting rule to a range of cells. The final result of this procedure is depicted in Figure 20-12.

Hands-On 20-1: Using Icon Sets Programmatically

1. Copy the **Practice_Excel20.xlsm file** from the Ex07_HandsOn folder to your **Ex07_ByExample** folder.
2. Open the **C:\Ex07_ByExample\Practice_Excel20.xlsm** workbook.
3. Switch to the Visual Basic Editor screen and insert a new module into VBAProject (Practice_Excel20.xlsm).
4. In the module's Code window, enter the following IconSetRules procedure:

```
Sub IconSetRules()
    Dim iSC As IconSetCondition

    Columns("B:B").Select
    With Selection
        .SpecialCells(xlCellTypeConstants, 23).Select
        .FormatConditions.Delete
        .NumberFormat = "$#,##0.00"
        Set iSC = Selection.FormatConditions.AddIconSetCondition
        iSC.IconSet = ActiveWorkbook.IconSets(xl3Symbols)
```

```
    End With
End Sub
```

The above procedure applies the currency format to the cell values in column B and clears the selected range from the conditional format that may have been applied earlier. Next, the IconSetCondition method is used to create an icon set conditional format for the selected range of cells. If you run the procedure in step mode by pressing the F8 key, you will notice at this time colored circles applied to the cells. The next statement actually changes the default icon set to xl3Symbols as shown in Figure 20-12.

5. Place the insertion point anywhere inside the code of the IconSetRules procedure and press F8 after each statement to execute the code in step mode.

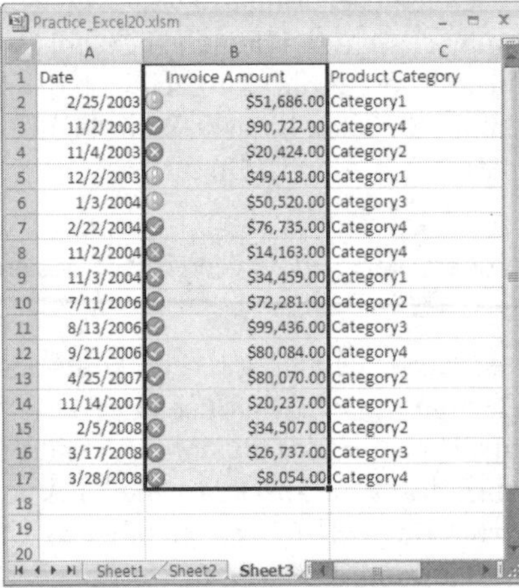

Figure 20-12: A column of data with an icon set used in the conditional format.

As mentioned earlier, you can modify the icon set conditions using the dialog box shown in Figure 20-11 or with VBA. Let's say that instead of using the default percentage distribution with the threshold of >=67, >=33, and <33, you want to use the following criteria: >=80000, >=50000, and <50000.

Let's take a look at the revised procedure that modifies the formatting rule and applies a filter by cell icon criteria:

```
Sub IconSetRulesRevised()
    Dim iSC As IconSetCondition

    Columns("B:B").Select
    Selection.SpecialCells(xlCellTypeConstants, 23).Select
    With Selection
        .FormatConditions.Delete
        .AutoFilter
        .NumberFormat = "$#,##0.00"
        Set iSC = Selection.FormatConditions.AddIconSetCondition
        iSC.IconSet = ActiveWorkbook.IconSets(xl3Symbols)
        With iSC.IconCriteria(2)
            .Type = xlConditionValueNumber
            .Value = 50000
```

```
            .Operator = xlGreaterEqual
        End With

        With iSC.IconCriteria(3)
            .Type = xlConditionValueNumber
            .Value = 80000
            .Operator = xlGreaterEqual
        End With

       .AutoFilter Field:=1, Criteria1:=iSC.IconSet.Item(3), _
               Operator:=xlFilterIcon
    End With
End Sub
```

Note that when changing the criteria for the icon set conditional format you do not need to specify the type, value, and operator for IconCriteria(1). This property is read-only. Excel determines on its own the threshold value of IconCriteria(1) and if you try to set it in your code as shown in the example procedure available in online help, you will get a run-time error. The Sort and Filter commands in Excel 2007 allow you to sort or filter data based on cell icon. The above procedure demonstrates how you can apply the filter programmatically using an icon in the specified icon set.

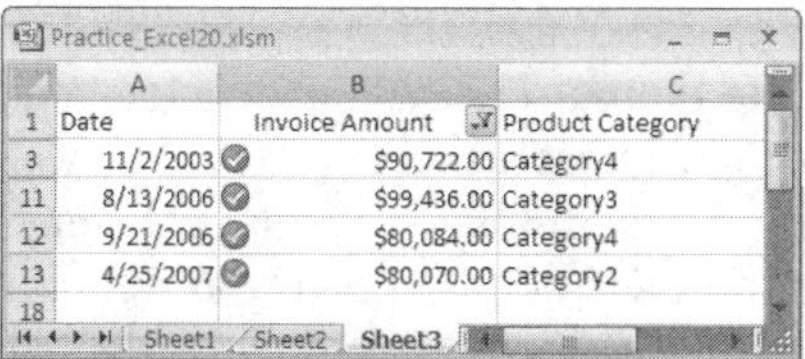

Figure 20-13: After running the IconSetRulesRevised procedure, a filter is applied to the Invoice Amount column to display only the cells with invoice values >=80000.

Formatting with Themes

If you need to change the look of the entire workbook, spend some time familiarizing yourself with document themes. A *document theme* consists of a predefined set of fonts, colors, and effects, such as lines and fills that you can apply to the workbook and also share between other Office documents. It is important to note that a theme applies to the entire workbook, not just the active worksheet. There are 20 document themes available in the user interface (choose Page Layout | Themes; see Figure 20-14), and you can also create custom themes by mixing and matching different theme elements using the three drop-down controls found in the Themes group on the Page Layout tab (Colors, Fonts, and Effects). New themes can also be downloaded from Office Online. When you change the theme, the font and color pickers on the Home tab, and other galleries such as Cell Styles or Table Styles, are automatically updated to reflect the new theme. Therefore, if you are looking to apply a cell background with a particular color, and that color is not listed in the color picker, apply a predefined theme that contains that color, or create your own custom color by choosing the More Colors option in the Font Color drop-down.

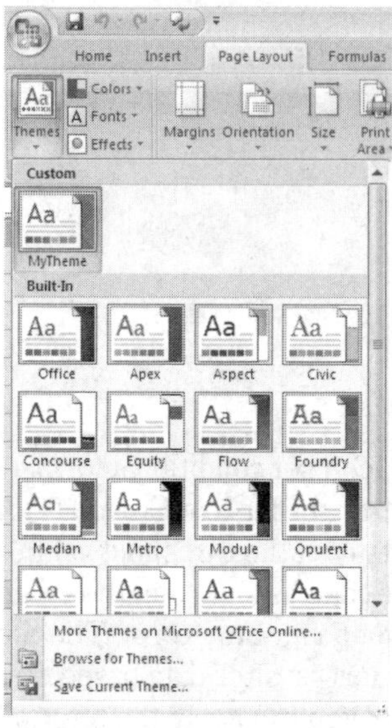

Figure 20-14: Excel 2007 built-in and custom document themes.

On the Page Layout tab, the Colors drop-down displays the color groups for each theme and gives you an option to create new theme colors. The Fonts drop-down shows a list of fonts for the theme. Theme fonts contain a heading font and a body text font, which can be changed using the Create New Theme Fonts option in the drop-down. The Effects drop-down displays the line and fill effects for each of the built-in themes and does not give you an option to create your own set of theme effects.

A theme color scheme consists of 12 base colors, as illustrated in Figure 20-15. When applying a color to a cell, the color is selected from the Fill Color drop-down as shown in Figure 20-16.

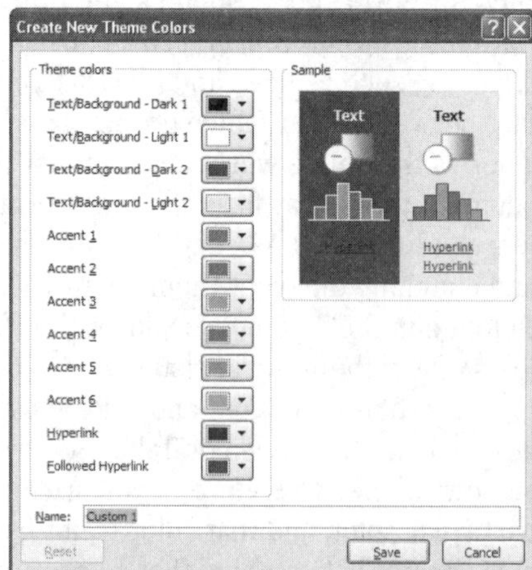

Figure 20-15: The theme colors consist of four text/background colors, six accent colors, and two hyperlink colors.

The top row in the color palette displays 10 base colors in the current color theme (the two hyperlink colors shown in the Create New Theme Colors dialog box are not included). The five rows below show various color variations of the base color. A color can be lighter or darker. The color name is shown in the tooltip.

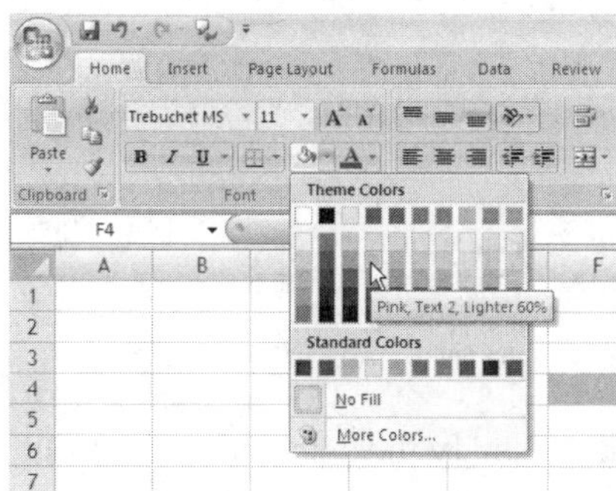

Figure 20-16: The Fill Color control is used to color the background of selected cells.

If you record a macro while applying the "Pink, Text 2, Lighter 60%" color to the cell background, you will get the following VBA code:

```
Sub Macro1()
'
' Macro1 Macro
'

'
    Range("F4").Select
    With Selection.Interior
        .Pattern = xlSolid
        .PatternColorIndex = xlAutomatic
        .ThemeColor = xlThemeColorLight2
        .TintAndShade = 0.599993896298105
        .PatternTintAndShade = 0
    End With
End Sub
```

The pattern properties refer to the cell patterns that can be set via the Format Cells dialog box (Home | Format | Format Cells | Fill). These properties can be ignored if all that's required is setting the cell background color. The above code can be modified as follows:

```
Sub Macro1()
'
' Macro1 Macro
'

'
    Range("F4").Select
    With Selection.Interior
        .ThemeColor = xlThemeColorLight2
        .TintAndShade = 0.599993896298105
    End With
End Sub
```

The ThemeColor property specifies the theme color to be used (see Figure 20-17).

XlThemeColor Enumeration

Specifies the theme color to be used.

Version Information
Version Added: Excel 2007

Name	Value	Description
xlThemeColorAccent1	5	Accent1
xlThemeColorAccent2	6	Accent2
xlThemeColorAccent3	7	Accent3
xlThemeColorAccent4	8	Accent4
xlThemeColorAccent5	9	Accent5
xlThemeColorAccent6	10	Accent6
xlThemeColorDark1	1	Dark1
xlThemeColorDark2	3	Dark2
xlThemeColorFollowedHyperlink	12	Followed hyperlink
xlThemeColorHyperlink	11	Hyperlink
xlThemeColorLight1	2	Light1
xlThemeColorLight2	4	Light2

Figure 20-17: Theme color constants and values as shown in the online help.

The TintAndShade property is used to modify the selected color. A tint (lightness) and a shade (darkness) is a value from –1 to 1. If you want a pure color, set the TintAndShade property to 0. The value of –1 will result in black, and the value of 1 will produce white. Negative values will produce darker colors, and positive values lighter colors. The TintAndShade value of 0.599993896298105 means a 60% tint (or 60% lighter than the base color). If you change this number to –0.599993896298105, you will get a 60% darker color.

The following procedure loops through the colors in themes 4 through 10 and writes the color index and color variations to a range of cells (see Figure 20-18).

```
Sub Themes4Thru10()
    Dim tintshade As Variant
    Dim heading As Variant
    Dim cell As Range
    Dim themeC As Integer
    Dim r As Integer
    Dim c As Integer
    Dim i As Integer

    heading = Array("ThemeColorIndex", "Neutral", "Lighter 80%", _
             "Lighter 60%", "Lighter 40%", "Darker 25%", "Darker 50%")
    tintshade = Array(0, 0.8, 0.6, 0.4, -0.25, -0.5)

    i = 0
    For Each cell In Range("A1:G1")
        cell.Formula = heading(i)
        i = i + 1
    Next

    For r = 2 To 8
       themeC = r + 2
         For c = 1 To 7
           If c = 1 Then
             Cells(r, c).Formula = themeC
           Else
               With Cells(r, c)
                   With .Interior
                     .ThemeColor = themeC
```

```
                    .TintAndShade = tintshade(c - 2)
                End With
            End With
        End If
    Next c
Next r
ActiveSheet.Columns("A:G").AutoFit
End Sub
```

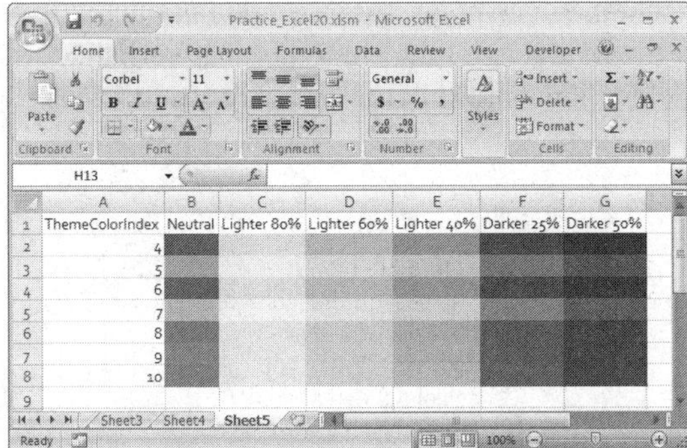

Figure 20-18: This worksheet was generated by a VBA procedure. When you apply a different document theme, the colors will be replaced by those from the new theme.

The following procedure applies the current theme colors to a range of cells in an active worksheet.

```
Sub GetThemeColors()
    Dim tColorScheme As ThemeColorScheme
    Dim colorArray(10) As Variant
    Dim i As Long
    Dim r As Long

    Set tColorScheme = ActiveWorkbook.Theme.ThemeColorScheme
    For i = 1 To 10
      colorArray(i) = tColorScheme.Colors(i).RGB
      ActiveSheet.Cells(i, 1).Value = colorArray(i)
    Next i
    i = 0
    For r = 1 To 10
      ActiveSheet.Cells(r, 2).Interior.Color = colorArray(i + 1)
      i = i + 1
    Next r
End Sub
```

In the above procedure, the ThemeColorScheme object represents the color scheme of a Microsoft Office 2007 theme. In the first For...Next loop, the Colors method and the RGB property are used to return a specific color. The color value is then stored in the colorArray array variable and entered in the specified row of the first worksheet column. The second For...Next loop applies background color to cells based on the color values stored in the colorArray variable.

The following procedure does more color work in the active sheet, this time using the Interior.ThemeColor property:

```
Sub ApplyThemeColors()
    Dim i As Integer
```

```
        For i = 1 To 10
            ActiveSheet.Cells(i, 3).Interior.ThemeColor = i
            ActiveSheet.Cells(i, 4).Value = i
        Next i
    End Sub
```

In the above procedure, we use the Interior.ThemeColor property to set the background color of cells in the third worksheet column using colors available in the current color scheme. The color scheme value is then written in the corresponding cell in the fourth column. The resulting worksheet (after running the GetThemeColors and ApplyThemeColors procedures) is shown in Figure 20-19.

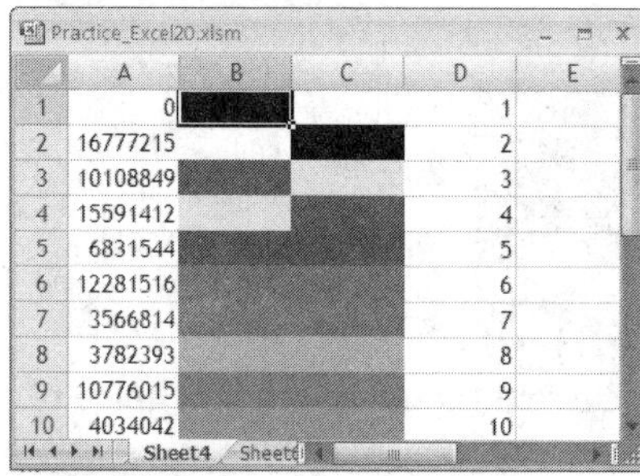

Figure 20-19: The background color of the cells was applied with VBA. When you select a different color theme, the background color of these cells (C1:C10) will automatically adjust.

Note: You may have noticed that the colors in the first four rows of the worksheet do not match. This is a bug in Excel 2007. The theme index of 0 is mapped to color 1, and theme index 1 is mapped to color 0.

Each new Excel 2007 workbook is created with a default theme named Office. The theme information is stored in a separate theme file with the extension .thmx. When you change the theme in the workbook, the workbook's theme file is automatically updated with the new settings. When you create a custom theme by selecting a new set of fonts, colors, or effects, save the theme in a file so that it can be used in any document in any Office application or shared with other users. You will find your custom theme file in the \Documents and Settings\<user name>\Application Data\Microsoft\Templates\Document Themes\ folder. The built-in themes are stored in C:\Program Files\Microsoft Office\Document Themes 12.

Use the ApplyTheme method of the Workbook object to apply the specified theme to the current workbook:

```
ActiveWorkbook.ApplyTheme "C:\Documents and Settings\username\Application
Data\Microsoft\Templates\Document Themes\MyTheme.thmx"
```

After you apply a custom theme to a workbook, the theme name appears in the Custom group of the Themes control, as illustrated in Figure 20-14. To programmatically load a color theme or font theme from a file, the following VBA statements can be used:

```
ActiveWorkbook.Theme.ThemeColorScheme.Load ("C:\Program Files\Microsoft
Office\Document Themes 12\Theme Colors\Paper.xml")
```

```
ActiveWorkbook.Theme.ThemeFontScheme.Load "C:\Documents and
Settings\username\Application Data\Microsoft\Templates\Document
Themes\PolishFonts.xml")
```

In order to customize some theme components you need to know how to work with document parts in the Office Open XML file format. You will find information on how to open, read, and modify data in Office XML files in Chapter 29. The following example procedure prints the current workbook's theme name to the Immediate window:

```
Sub GetThemeName()
    ' set a reference to the Microsoft XML, v.6.0 object library
    Dim xmlDoc As DOMDocument
    Dim xmlNode As IXMLDOMNode

    Set xmlDoc = New DOMDocument
    xmlDoc.async = False
    xmlDoc.Load ("C:\Ex07_ByExample\ZipPackage\xl\theme\theme1.xml")
    xmlDoc.setProperty "SelectionLanguage", "XPath"
    xmlDoc.setProperty "SelectionNamespaces", _
        "xmlns:a='http://schemas.openxmlformats.org/drawingml/2006/main'"

    Set xmlNode = xmlDoc.SelectSingleNode("//a:clrScheme/@name")

    Debug.Print "Current theme name is " & xmlNode.Text & "."

    Set xmlNode = Nothing
    Set xmlDoc = Nothing
End Sub
```

The above procedure requires that you first unzip your Excel 2007 workbook into the specified folder (see Chapter 29 for more information). The font, color, and effects settings can be found in a file named theme1.xml.

Formatting with Shapes

You can make your worksheets more interesting by adding various types of shapes (see Figure 20-20). When formatting shapes, you can use document theme colors as shown in the following procedure:

```
Sub AddCanShape()
    Dim oShape As Shape

    Set oShape = ActiveSheet.Shapes.AddShape(msoShapeCan, 54, 0, 54, 110)
    With oShape
        .Fill.ForeColor.ObjectThemeColor = msoThemeColorAccent4
        .Fill.Transparency = 0.5
        .Line.Visible = msoFalse
    End With
End Sub
```

In the above procedure we declare an object variable of type Shape, and then use the AddShape method of the ActiveSheet Shapes collection to add a new Shape object. This method has five required arguments. The first one specifies the type of the Shape object that you want to create. This can be one of the constants in the msoAutoShapeType enumeration (check out the online help). Excel offers a large number of shapes. The next two arguments tell Excel how far the object should be placed from the left and top corners of the worksheet. The last two arguments specify the width and height of the shape (in points). To specify the theme color of the Shape object, set the ObjectThemeColor property of the ColorFormat object to the required theme. To return the ColorFormat object, you must use the ForeColor property of the FillFormat object. The FillFormat object is returned by the Fill property of the Shape object:

```
oShape.Fill.ForeColor.ObjectThemeColor = msoThemeColorAccent4
```

Next, set the degree of transparency to make sure that the shape does not obstruct the data. The last line removes the border from the shape.

The above procedure places a Shape object over the data in column B.

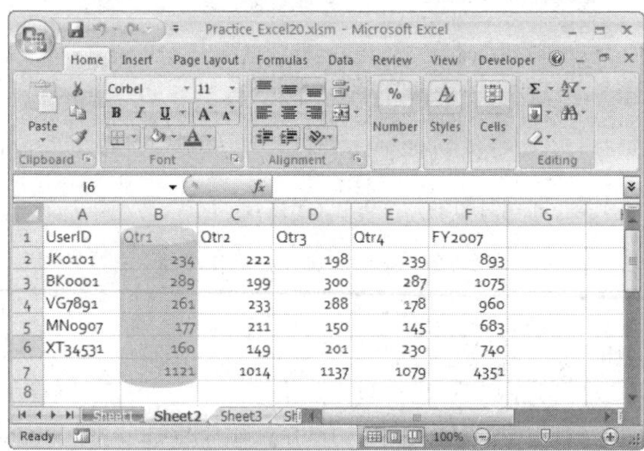

Figure 20-20: A Shape object placed on the worksheet uses the theme color scheme.

Formatting with Styles

Most people use the Format Painter tool on the Ribbon's Home tab (the paintbrush icon) to quickly copy formatting to other cells of the same worksheet or from one worksheet to another. However, when you create complex worksheets with different types of formatting, it is a good idea to save all your formatting settings in a file so you can reuse them whenever you need them. This can be done via the Styles feature. Cell styles can contain format options such as Number, Alignment, Font, Border, Fill, and Protection. If you change the style after you have applied it to your worksheet, Excel will automatically update the cells that have been formatted using that style. Styles are easier to find and apply in Excel 2007, thanks to the introduction of galleries (see Figure 20-21). To apply a style to a cell, simply select the cells you want to format with the style, and click on the appropriate style in the gallery (available by clicking Cell Styles). Styles are based on the current theme, and you can also apply them to Excel tables, PivotTables, charts, and shapes. Excel 2007 offers a large number of built-in styles. You can modify, duplicate, or delete the existing styles and add your own — simply right-click the style in the gallery and select the option you need.

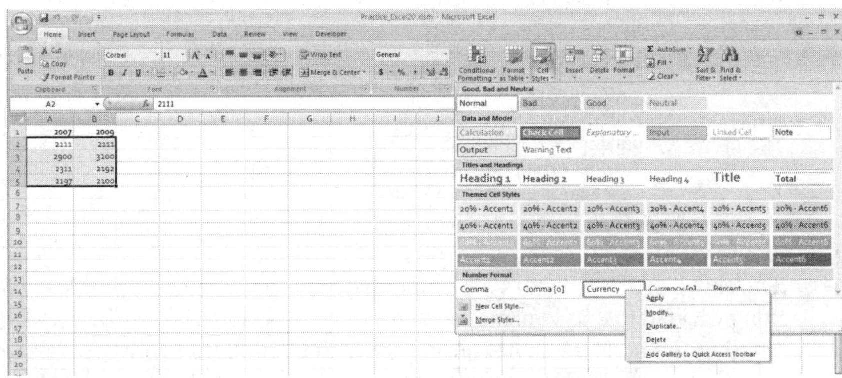

Figure 20-21: Excel 2007 offers a preview of how the style looks before you apply the style. If the built-in style does not suit your needs, you can create your own custom style.

To find out the number of styles in the active workbook, use the following statement:

```
MsgBox "Number of styles=" & ActiveWorkbook.Styles.Count
```

Excel tells us that there are 47 styles defined for a workbook. Use the Styles collection and the Style object to control the styles in a workbook. To get a list of style names, let's iterate through the Styles collection:

```
Sub GetStyleNames()
    Dim i As Integer

    For i = 1 To ActiveWorkbook.Styles.Count
        Debug.Print "Style " & i & ":" & _
            ActiveWorkbook.Styles(i).Name
    Next i
End Sub
```

The above procedure prints the names of all workbook styles into the Immediate window. The style names are listed alphabetically.

To add a style, use the Add method, as shown in the following example procedure:

```
Sub AddAStyle()
    Dim newStyleName As String
    Dim curStyle As Variant
    Dim i As Integer

    newStyleName = "SimpleFormat"
    i = 0

    For Each curStyle In ActiveWorkbook.Styles
        i = i + 1
        If curStyle.Name = newStyleName Then
            MsgBox "This style " & "(" & newStyleName & _
               ") already exists. " & Chr(13) & _
               "It's the " & i & " style in the Styles collection."
            Exit Sub
        End If
```

```
    Next

    With ActiveWorkbook.Styles.Add(newStyleName)
        .Font.Name = "Arial Narrow"
        .Font.Size = "12"
        .Borders.LineStyle = xlThin
        .NumberFormat = "$#,##0_);[Red]($#,##0)"
        .IncludeAlignment = False
    End With
End Sub
```

The above procedure adds a specified style to the workbook's Styles collection provided the style name is unique. The procedure begins by checking whether the style name has already been defined. If the workbook has a style with the specified name, the procedure ends after displaying a message to the user. If the style name does not exist, then the procedure creates the style with the specified formatting. Notice that if you do not wish to include a specific formatting feature in the style, you can set the following properties to False: IncludeAlignment, IncludeFont, IncludeBorder, IncludeNumber, IncludePatterns, and IncludeProtection. For example, a setting of False omits the HorizontalAlignment, VerticalAlignment, WrapText, and Orientation properties in the style. The default setting for these properties is True.

The custom style is added to the Styles collection. To find out the index number of the newly added style, simply rerun this procedure.

To programmatically apply your custom style to a selected range, run the following code in the Immediate window:

```
Selection.Style = "SimpleFormat"
```

To check out the settings the specific style includes, select the formatted range of cells and choose Home | Cell Styles | New Cell Style. Excel displays the dialog box shown in Figure 20-22.

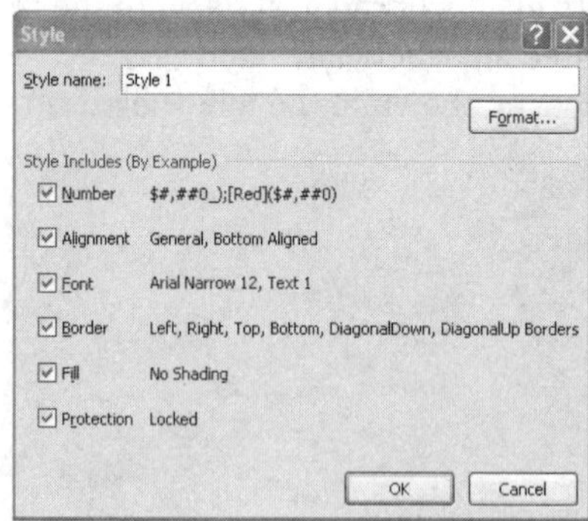

Figure 20-22: This dialog box displays the formatting settings of the SimpleFormat style that was created earlier by the above VBA procedure.

The following code removes formatting applied to the selected range:

```
Selection.ClearFormats
```

This statement returns selection formats to the original state. It does not remove the style from the Styles collection. To delete a style from a workbook, use the following statement:

```
ActiveWorkbook.Styles("SimpleFormat").Delete
```

If you have already formatted a cell, you can create a new style based on the active cell:

```
Sub AddSelectionStyle()
    Dim newStyleName As String

    newStyleName = "InvoiceAmount"
    ActiveWorkbook.Styles.Add Name:=newStyleName, _
               BasedOn:=ActiveCell
End Sub
```

By default Excel creates a new style based on the Normal style. However, if you have already applied formatting to a specific cell and would like to save the settings in a style, use the optional BasedOn argument of the Styles collection Add method to specify a cell on which to base the new style.

The custom styles you create can be reused in other workbooks. To do this you need to copy the style information from one workbook to another. In VBA, this can be done by using the Merge method of the Workbook object Styles collection:

```
ActiveWorkbook.Styles.Merge "Report2007.xlsx"
```

The above statement copies the styles found in "Report2007.xlsx" to the active workbook.

Chapter Summary

In this chapter you learned how to use VBA to apply basic formatting features to your worksheets to make your data easier to read and interpret. You also learned advanced formatting features such as conditional formatting and the utilization of new tools like Data Bars, Icon Sets, and Color Scales, as well as themes and cell styles.

The next chapter focuses on programming shortcut menus and the Excel 2007 Ribbon interface that replaces the menus and toolbars featured in earlier versions of Excel.

Chapter 21

Shortcut Menu Programming and Ribbon Customizations

Working with Shortcut Menus ■ Modifying a Built-in Shortcut Menu ■ Removing a Custom Item from a Shortcut menu ■ Disabling and Hiding Items on a Shortcut Menu ■ Adding a Shortcut Menu to a Command Button ■ Finding a FaceID Value of an Image ■ **A Quick Overview of the Ribbon Interface** ■ **Ribbon Programming with XML and VBA** ■ Creating the Ribbon Customization XML Markup ■ Loading Ribbon Customizations ■ Errors on Loading Ribbon Customizations ■ Using a Custom Fluent UI Editor ■ Using Images in Ribbon Customizations ■ Using Various Controls in Ribbon Customizations ■ Disabling a Control ■ Repurposing a Built-in Control ■ Refreshing the Ribbon ■ The CommandBar Objects and the Ribbon ■ **Customizing the Microsoft Office Button Menu** ■ **Customizing the Quick Access Toolbar (QAT)** ■ **Chapter Summary**

Users have come to expect easy ways to select commands and options in any Windows application. Therefore, after you have written VBA procedures that provide solutions to specific worksheet automation dilemmas, you should spend additional time adding features that will make your application quick and easy to use. The most desired features of the user interface (UI) in Excel 2007 are customizations of the shortcut menus and the Ribbon. While it is easy for users to get quick access to a specific command by placing it in the Quick Access toolbar located to the right of the Microsoft Office Menu button, your application's tools will need to appear either on the Ribbon or in a shortcut menu. This chapter teaches you how to work with the shortcut menus and the Fluent Ribbon interface programmatically.

Working with Shortcut Menus

A shortcut menu appears when you right-click on an object in the Microsoft Excel application window. For many years now Excel programmers have been able to customize Excel's built-in shortcut menus by using the CommandBar object. Using this object's properties and method you can create, modify, or disable shortcut menus depending on your application's needs.

Each object in the CommandBars collection is called CommandBar. In Excel 2007, the term CommandBar is used to refer to a shortcut menu only. Because in earlier versions of Excel a CommandBar object referred to various tools (toolbar, menu bar, shortcut menu), this object comes with a special Type property that can be used to return the specific type of the command bar (see Table 21-1).

Table 21-1: Types of CommandBar objects in the CommandBars collection

Type of Object	Index	Constant
Toolbar	0	msoBarTypeNormal (no longer used in Excel 2007)
Menu Bar	1	msoBarTypeMenuBar (no longer used in Excel 2007)
Shortcut Menu	2	msoBarTypePopup

Note: In previous versions of Excel, the CommandBar object was also used to programmatically work with menu bars and toolbars. Due to the major changes in the user interface, the CommandBar object is only used with shortcut menus in Excel 2007. If you attempt to use the available methods and properties of the CommandBar object to customize a menu or toolbar, your code will be ignored, as these objects no longer exist in the current version of Excel. Later on in this chapter you will find out how to customize the Ribbon, which replaces the menus and toolbars found in Excel 2003 and earlier.

Modifying a Built-in Shortcut Menu

Microsoft Excel 2007 offers 63 shortcut menus with different sets of frequently used menu options. Using VBA, you can return the exact number of the shortcut menus, as well as their names. Let's write a VBA procedure that returns the names of the shortcut menus to the Immediate window.

Hands-On 21-1: Enumerating Shortcut Menus

1. Create a new workbook and save it as **C:\Ex07_ByExample\Practice_Excel21.xlsm.**
2. Switch to the Visual Basic Editor screen and insert a new module into VBAProject (Practice_Excel21.xlsm).
3. Use the Properties window to rename the module **ShortcutMenus.**
4. In the ShortcutMenus Code window, enter the ShortcutMenus procedure as shown below:

```
Sub ShortcutMenus()
    Dim myBar As CommandBar
    Dim counter As Integer

    For Each myBar In CommandBars
     If myBar.Type = msoBarTypePopup Then
          counter = counter + 1
          Debug.Print counter & ": " & myBar.Name
     End If
    Next
End Sub
```

   Notice the use of the msoBarTypePopup constant to identify the shortcut menu in the collection of CommandBars.

5. Run the ShortcutMenus procedure.

   The result of this procedure is a list of shortcut menus as shown below:

```
1: PivotChart Menu
2: Workbook tabs
3: Cell
4: Column
5: Row
6: Cell
7: Column
8: Row
9: Ply
10: XLM Cell
11: Document
12: Desktop
13: Nondefault Drag and Drop
14: AutoFill
15: Button
16: Dialog
17: Series
18: Plot Area
19: Floor and Walls
```

```
20: Trendline
21: Chart
22: Format Data Series
23: Format Axis
24: Format Legend Entry
25: Formula Bar
26: PivotTable Context Menu
27: Query
28: Query Layout
29: AutoCalculate
30: Object/Plot
31: Title Bar (Charting)
32: Layout
33: Pivot Chart Popup
34: Phonetic Information
35: Auto Sum
36: Paste Special Dropdown
37: Find Format
38: Replace Format
39: List Range Popup
40: List Range Layout Popup
41: XML Range Popup
42: List Range Layout Popup
43: Nil
44: Filter Names
45: Excel Previewer
46: Shapes
47: Inactive Chart
48: Excel Control
49: Curve
50: Curve Node
51: Curve Segment
52: Pictures Context Menu
53: OLE Object
54: ActiveX Control
55: WordArt Context Menu
56: Rotate Mode
57: Connector
58: Script Anchor Popup
59: Canvas Popup
60: Organization Chart Popup
61: Diagram
62: Add Command
63: Built-in Menus
```

Now that you know the exact names of Excel's shortcut menus, you can easily add other frequently used commands to any of these menus. Let's see how you can add the Insert Picture command to the shortcut menu activated when you right-click a worksheet cell.

Hands-On 21-2: Adding a New Item to a Shortcut Menu

1. In the ShortcutMenus Code window that you created in the previous Hands-On, enter the following procedures:

```
Sub AddToCellMenu()
    With Application.CommandBars("Cell")
```

```
        .Reset
        .Controls.Add(Type:=msoControlButton, _
            Before:=2).Caption = "Insert Picture..."
        .Controls("Insert Picture...").OnAction = "InsertPicture"
    End With
End Sub

Sub InsertPicture()
    CommandBars.ExecuteMso ("PictureInsertFromFile")
End Sub
```

The Reset method of the CommandBar object used in the AddToCellMenu procedure prevents placing the same option in the shortcut menu again when you run the procedure more than once.

To add a built-in or custom control to a shortcut menu, use the Add method with the syntax as follows:

```
CommandBar.Controls.Add(Type, Id, Parameter, Before, Temporary)
```

The CommandBar is the object to which you want to add a control. Type is a constant that determines the type of custom control you want to add. You may select one of the following types:

msoControlButton	1
msoControlPopup	10
msoControlEdit	2
msoControlDropDown	3
msoControlComboBox	4

Id is an integer that specifies the number of the built-in control that you want to add. Parameter is used to send information to a Visual Basic procedure or to store information about the control.

The Before argument is the index number of the control before which the new control will be added. If omitted, Visual Basic adds the control at the end of the specified command bar.

The Temporary argument is a logical value (True or False) that determines when the control will be deleted. When you set this argument to True, the control will be automatically deleted when the Excel application is closed.

CommandBar controls have a number of properties that help you specify the appearance and the functionality of a control. For example, the Caption property specifies the text displayed for the control. In the above procedure, you will see the "Insert Picture..." entry in the cell shortcut menu. Note that it is customary to add an ellipsis (...) at the end of the menu option's text to indicate that the option will trigger a dialog box in which the user will need to make more selections. The OnAction property specifies the name of a VBA procedure that will execute when the menu option is selected. In this example, upon selecting the Insert Picture... option, the InsertPicture procedure will be called.

This procedure uses the ExecuteMso method of the CommandBar object to execute the Ribbon's PictureInsertFromFile command.

2. Run the AddToCellMenu procedure.
3. Switch to the Microsoft Excel application window, right-click any cell in a worksheet, and select the **Insert Picture...** command (see Figure 21-1).

   Excel displays the Insert Picture dialog box from which you can insert a picture from a file. The same dialog is displayed when you click the Picture button on the Ribbon's Insert tab.

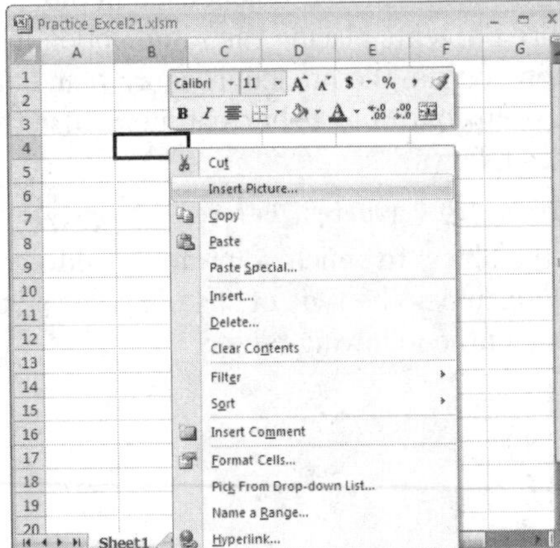

Figure 21-1: The built-in cell shortcut menu displays a new item (Insert Picture...) that was added by a VBA procedure.

Note: Custom menu items added to Excel shortcut menus are available in all workbooks. It does not matter which workbook was used to add a custom item. For this reason, it's a good idea to ensure that the custom menu item is removed when the workbook is closed. (See the section titled "Removing a Custom Item from a Shortcut Menu" later in this chapter.)

Notice that some options in the shortcut menu are preceded with a small graphic image. Let's write another version of the AddToCellMenu procedure to include an image next to the Insert Picture... command.

4. Enter the following procedure in the ShortcutMenus Code window:

```
Sub AddToCellMenu2()
    Dim ct As CommandBarButton

    With Application.CommandBars("Cell")
        .Reset
        Set ct = .Controls.Add(Type:=msoControlButton, _
            Before:=11, Temporary:=True)
    End With
    With ct
        .Caption = "Insert Picture..."
        .OnAction = "InsertPicture"
        .Picture = Application.CommandBars. _
            GetImageMso("PictureInsertFromFile", 16, 16)
        .Style = msoButtonIconAndCaption
```

```
    End With
End Sub
```

In the procedure code above, we tell Visual Basic to add our custom menu item in the 11th position on the cell shortcut menu. We also specify that this custom menu option is removed automatically when we exit Excel. This is accomplished by setting the value of the Temporary parameter to True. Next, we use the With...End With statement block to set a couple of properties for the newly created control object (ct). In addition to setting two standard properties (Caption and OnAction), we assign the imageMso image to the Picture property of our new control. To return the image you must use the CommandBars.GetImageMso method and specify the name of the image and its size (width and height). The size of the image is specified as 16 x 16 pixels. The Style property is used here to specify that the control button should display both the icon and its caption.

5. Run the AddToCellMenu2 procedure.
6. Switch to the Microsoft Excel application window, right-click any cell in a worksheet, and look for the **Insert Picture...** command (see Figure 21-2).

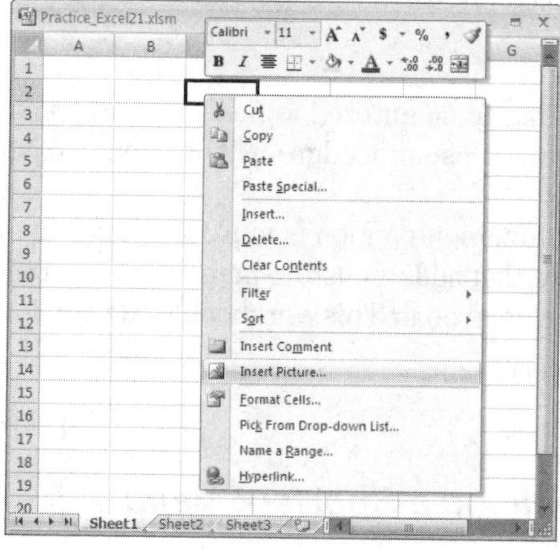

Figure 21-2: A custom Insert Picture... menu item is now identified by an icon and positioned just below the built-in Insert Comment command.

Notice that built-in shortcut menu commands have a special hot key indicated by the underlined letter. To invoke a menu option, you simply press the underlined letter after opening the menu.

7. To add a hot key to your custom menu option, modify the Caption property in the above procedure like this:

```
.Caption = "Insert Pict&ure..."
```

The "&" symbol in front of the letter "u" indicates that the lowercase "u" will serve as the hot key. Remember that hot keys are unique; you cannot use a letter that is already used by another menu item.

8. Switch to the Microsoft Excel application window, right-click any cell in a worksheet, and press the lowercase **u**. You should see the Insert Picture dialog box.

Removing a Custom Item from a Shortcut Menu

When you modify shortcut menus, your customizations will not go away when you close the workbook. Restarting Excel will remove your custom changes to the shortcut menu only if you set the value of the Temporary parameter to True when adding your custom menu item. To ensure that the custom item is removed from the menu when you need it, consider writing a delete procedure similar to the one shown below:

```
Sub DeleteInsertPicture()
    Dim c As CommandBarControl
    On Error Resume Next
    Set c = CommandBars("Cell").Controls("Insert Pict&ure...")
    c.Delete
End Sub
```

For automatic cleanup, call the above procedure from the Workbook_Before-Close event procedure like this:

```
Private Sub Workbook_BeforeClose(Cancel As Boolean)
    Call DeleteInsertPicture
End Sub
```

The above event procedure has to be entered in the ThisWorkbook code module. The Workbook_BeforeClose procedure will be executed just before the workbook is closed.

To ensure that your custom menu option is in place when you open the workbook, call the procedure that adds a custom menu item from the Work-book_Open event procedure entered in ThisWorkbook Code window:

```
Private Sub Workbook_Open()
    Call AddToCellMenu
End Sub
```

Disabling and Hiding Items on a Shortcut Menu

To disallow using a particular shortcut menu item, you may want to disable it or hide it.

When a shortcut menu item is disabled, its caption appears dimmed. When a menu item is hidden, it simply does not appear on the menu.

To disable a menu item, set the Enabled property of the control to False. For example, the following statement entered in the Immediate window will disable the Hide command on the Ply menu (this menu appears when you click a sheet tab):

```
Application.CommandBars("Ply").Controls("Hide").Enabled = False
```

To enable a disabled menu item, simply set the Enabled property of the desired control to True:

```
Application.CommandBars("Ply").Controls("Hide").Enabled = True
```

To hide a menu item, set the Visible property of the control to False:

```
Application.CommandBars("Ply").Controls("Hide").Visible = False
```

And to unhide the hidden menu item, use the following statement:

```
Application.CommandBars("Ply").Controls("Hide").Visible = True
```

A good place to use the above commands is in the Worksheet_Activate and Worksheet_Deactivate event procedures. For example, to disable the specific shortcut menu item only when Sheet1 is active, write the following event procedures in the Sheet1 code module:

```
Private Sub Worksheet_Activate()
    Application.CommandBars("Cell").Controls("Sort").Enabled = False
End Sub


Private Sub Worksheet_Deactivate()
    Application.CommandBars("Cell").Controls("Sort").Enabled = True
End Sub
```

Adding a Shortcut Menu to a Command Button

When you design your custom forms you may want to add shortcut menus to various controls placed on the form. The following set of VBA procedures demonstrates how right-clicking a command button can offer users a choice of options to select from.

Hands-On 21-3: Using Shortcut Menus on User Forms

1. In the ShortcutMenus Code window, enter the Create_ShortcutMenu procedure as shown below:

```
Sub Create_ShortcutMenu()
    Dim sm As Object

    Set sm = Application.CommandBars.Add("MyComputer", msoBarPopup)
    With sm
        .Controls.Add(Type:=msoControlButton). _
                Caption = "Operating System"
        With .Controls("Operating System")
            .FaceId = 1954
            .OnAction = "OpSystem"
        End With
        .Controls.Add(Type:=msoControlButton).Caption = "Active Printer"
        With .Controls("Active Printer")
            .FaceId = 4
            .OnAction = "ActivePrinter"
        End With
        .Controls.Add(Type:=msoControlButton).Caption = "Active Workbook"
        With .Controls("Active Workbook")
            .FaceId = 247
            .OnAction = "ActiveWorkbook"
        End With
        .Controls.Add(Type:=msoControlButton).Caption = "Active Sheet"
        With .Controls("Active Sheet")
            .FaceId = 18
```

```
            .OnAction = "ActiveSheet"
        End With
    End With
End Sub
```

The above procedure creates a custom shortcut menu named MyComputer and adds four commands to it. Notice that each command is assigned an icon. When you select a command from this shortcut menu, one of the procedures shown in step 2 will run.

2. In the ShortcutMenus Code window, enter the following procedures that are called by the Create_ShortcutMenu procedure:

```
Sub OpSystem()
    MsgBox Application.OperatingSystem, , "Operating System"
End Sub

Sub ActivePrinter()
    MsgBox Application.ActivePrinter
End Sub

Sub ActiveWorkbook()
    MsgBox Application.ActiveWorkbook.Name
End Sub

Sub ActiveSheet()
    MsgBox Application.ActiveSheet.Name
End Sub
```

3. Run the Create_ShortcutMenu procedure.

   To test the custom shortcut menu you just created, use the ShowPopup method, as shown in step 4.

4. Type the following statement in the Immediate window and press **Enter**:

```
CommandBars("MyComputer").ShowPopup 0, 0
```

   The ShowPopup method for the CommandBar object accepts two optional arguments (x, y) that determine the location of the shortcut menu on the screen. In the above example, the MyComputer shortcut menu that was added by running the Create_ShortcutMenu procedure will appear at the top left-hand corner of the screen.

   Let's make our shortcut menu friendlier by attaching it to a command button placed on a user form.

5. In the Visual Basic Editor screen, choose **Insert | UserForm** to add a new form to the current VBA project.
6. Using the CommandButton control in the Toolbox, place a button anywhere on the empty user form. Use the Properties window to change the Caption property of the command button to **System Information.** You may need to resize the button on the form to fit this text.
7. Switch to the Code window for the form by clicking the **View Code** button in the Project Explorer window or double-clicking the form background.

8. Enter the following procedure in the UserForm1 Code window:

```
Private Sub CommandButton1_MouseDown(ByVal Button _
        As Integer, _
        ByVal Shift As Integer, _
        ByVal X As Single, _
        ByVal Y As Single)
    If Button = 2 Then
        Call Show_ShortMenu
    Else
        MsgBox "You must right-click this button."
    End If
End Sub
```

The above procedure calls the Show_ShortMenu procedure (see step 9) when the user right-clicks the command button placed on the form. Visual Basic has two event procedures that are executed in response to clicking a mouse button. When you click a mouse button, Visual Basic executes the MouseDown event procedure. When you release the mouse button, the MouseUp event occurs. The MouseDown and MouseUp event procedures require the following arguments:

- The object argument specifies the object. In this example, it's the name of the command button placed on the form.
- The Button argument is the Integer value that specifies which mouse button was pressed.

Value of Button Argument	Description
1	Left mouse button
2	Right mouse button
3	Middle mouse button

- The Shift argument determines whether the user was holding the Shift, Ctrl, or Alt key when the event occurred.

Value of Shift Argument	Description
1	Shift key
2	Ctrl key
3	Shift and Ctrl keys
4	Alt key
5	Alt and Shift keys
6	Alt and Ctrl keys
7	Alt, Shift, and Ctrl keys

9. In the ShortcutMenus Code window, enter the code of the Show_ShortMenu procedure:

```
Sub Show_ShortMenu()
    Dim shortMenu As Object

    Set shortMenu = Application.CommandBars("MyComputer")
    With shortMenu
```

```
        .ShowPopup
    End With
End Sub
```

Notice that the ShowPopup method used in this procedure does not include the optional arguments that determine the location of the shortcut menu on the screen. Therefore, the menu appears where the mouse was clicked (see Figure 21-3).

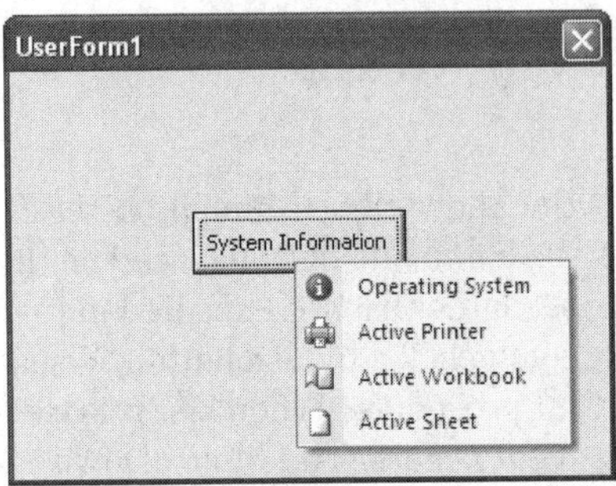

Figure 21-3: A custom shortcut menu appears when you right-click an object.

10. In the Project Explorer window, double-click **UserForm1** and press **F5** to run the form. Right-click the **System Information** button, and select one of the options from the shortcut menu.

    To delete the shortcut menu named MyComputer, enter and then run the following Delete_ShortMenu procedure in the ShortcutMenus Code window:

```
Sub Delete_ShortMenu()
   Application.CommandBars("MyComputer").Delete
End Sub
```

Finding a FaceID Value of an Image

When modifying shortcut menus, you will most likely want to include an image next to the displayed text, as we did in Hands-On 21-3 (see Figure 21-3). The good news is that the CommandBars collection has hundreds of images that you can use. Each command bar control button has a FaceID that determines the look of a control. But how do you know which ID belongs to which control button? The FaceID property returns or sets the ID number of the icon on the control button's face. In most cases, the icon ID number (FaceID) is the same as the control's ID property. The icon image can be copied to the Windows clipboard using the CopyFace method. The Images procedure demonstrated below iterates through the CommandBars collection and writes to a new workbook a list of control buttons that have a FaceID number.

```
Sub Images()
    Dim i As Integer
    Dim j As Integer
    Dim total As Integer
    Dim buttonId As Integer
    Dim buttonName As String
    Dim myControl As CommandBarControl
```

```
        Dim bar As CommandBar

        On Error GoTo ErrorHandler

        Workbooks.Add
        Range("A1").Select
        With ActiveCell
            .Value = "Image"
            .Offset(0, 1) = "Index"
            .Offset(0, 2) = "Name"
            .Offset(0, 3) = "FaceID"
            .Offset(0, 4) = "CommandBar Name (Index)"
        End With

        For j = 1 To Application.CommandBars.Count

            Set bar = CommandBars(j)
            total = bar.Controls.Count

            With bar
                For i = 1 To total
                    buttonName = .Controls(i).Caption
                    buttonId = .Controls(i).ID

                    Set myControl = CommandBars.FindControl(ID:=buttonId)

                    myControl.CopyFace ' error could occur here

                    ActiveCell.Offset(1, 0).Select
                    Sheets(1).Paste

                    With ActiveCell
                        .Offset(0, 1).Value = buttonId
                        .Offset(0, 2).Value = buttonName
                        .Offset(0, 3).Value = myControl.FaceID
                        .Offset(0, 4).Value = bar.Name & " (" & j & ")"
                    End With
    StartNext:
                Next i
            End With
        Next j

        Columns("A:E").EntireColumn.AutoFit
        Exit Sub
    ErrorHandler:
            Resume StartNext
    End Sub
```

Because you cannot copy the image of an icon that is currently disabled, Visual Basic encounters an error when it attempts to copy the button's face to the clipboard. The procedure traps this error with the On Error GoTo ErrorHandler statement. This way, when Visual Basic encounters the error, it will jump to the ErrorHandler label and execute the instructions below this label. This will ensure that the problem control button is skipped and the procedure can continue without interruption. A partial result of the procedure is shown in Figure 21-4.

Book3

	A	B	C	D	E
1	Image	Index	Name	FaceId	CommandBar Name (Index)
2		1031	&WordArt...	1031	WordArt (3)
3		2094	Edit Te&xt...	2094	WordArt (3)
4		1606	&WordArt Gallery	1606	WordArt (3)
5		962	&Object...	962	WordArt (3)
6	Aa	1063	&WordArt Same Letter Heights	1063	WordArt (3)
7		1061	&WordArt Vertical Text	1061	WordArt (3)
8		2619	&From File...	2619	Picture (4)
9		1064	&More Contrast	1064	Picture (4)
10		1065	&Less Contrast	1065	Picture (4)
11		1066	&More Brightness	1066	Picture (4)

Sheet1 Sheet2 Sheet3

Figure 21-4: A list of icon images and their corresponding FaceID values generated by the VBA procedure.

A Quick Overview of the Ribbon Interface

The Fluent Ribbon user interface replaces the system of menus and toolbars found in earlier versions of Excel. The Ribbon contains the title bar, the Microsoft Office button, the Quick Access toolbar, and the tabs. Each tab on the Ribbon provides access to features and commands related to a particular task. For example, you can use the Insert tab to quickly insert tables, illustrations, charts, links, or text (see Figure 21-5). Related commands within a tab are organized into groups. This type of organization makes it easy to locate a particular command.

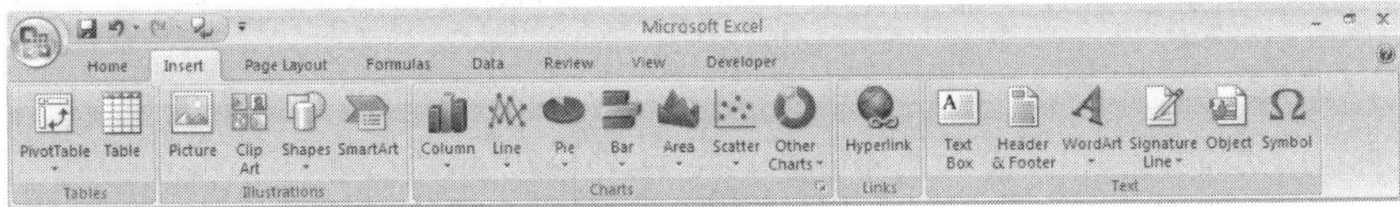

Figure 21-5: The rectangular area at the top of the Microsoft Excel 2007 window is called the Ribbon. Each tab on the Ribbon contains groups of related commands.

Various program commands are displayed as large or small buttons. A large button denotes a frequently used command, while a small button shows a specific feature of the main command that you may want to work with. Some large and small command buttons include drop-down lists of other specialized commands. For example, the small More Functions button drop-down in the Function Library group on the Formulas tab contains additional types of functions you can insert: Statistical, Engineering, Cube, and Information (Figure 21-6).

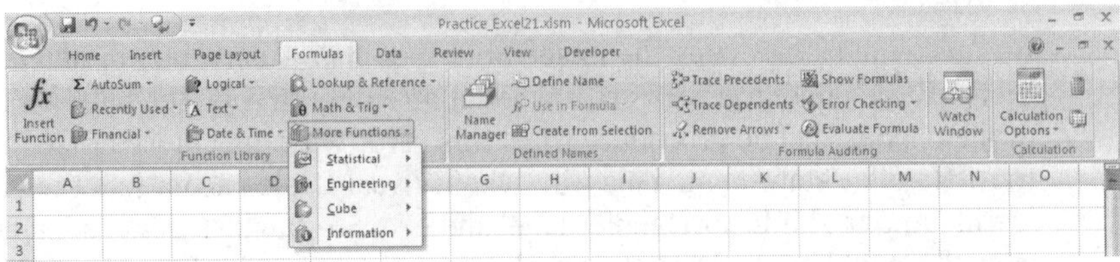

Figure 21-6: Additional commands can be accessed by clicking on the down arrow to the right of the button control.

Some controls that you find on the Ribbon do not display commands. Instead, they provide a visual clue of the output you might expect when a specific option is selected. These types of controls are known as galleries. The Gallery control is often used to present various formatting options, such as the margin settings shown in Figure 21-7.

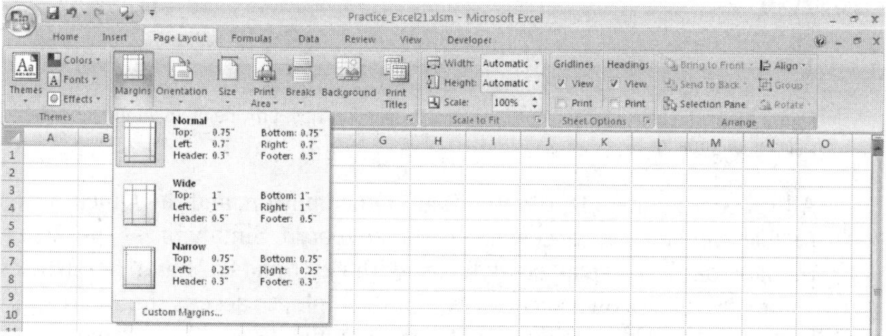

Figure 21-7: The margin layouts are displayed in a gallery control.

As mentioned earlier, the commands on the Ribbon tabs are organized into groups for easy browsing. Some tab groups have dialog box launchers in the bottom right-hand corner that display a dialog box where you can set several advanced options at once. For example, see the Charts group in Figure 21-5.

In addition to main Ribbon tabs, there are also contextual tabs that contain commands that apply to what you are doing. When a particular object is selected, the Ribbon displays a contextual tab that provides commands for working with that object. For example, when you select an image in a worksheet, the Ribbon displays a contextual tab called Picture Tools, as shown in Figure 21-8. Clicking on the Picture Tools tab activates the Format tab that has commands for dealing with a Picture object. The contextual tab disappears when you cancel the selection of the object. In other words, if you select a different cell in a worksheet, the Picture Tools tab will be gone.

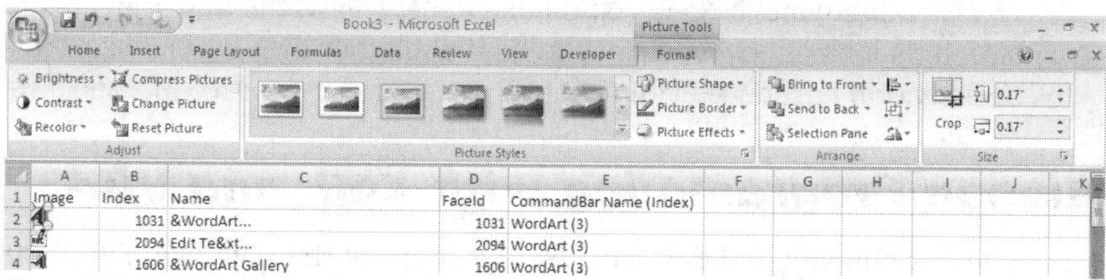

Figure 21-8: Contextual tabs will appear when you work with a particular object such as a picture, PivotTable, or chart.

When you open a workbook created in an earlier version of Excel that contains menu or toolbar customizations, the changes made in the user interface appear on an Add-Ins tab in the Ribbon.

The tooltips of the controls in Excel 2007 have been enhanced to display the name of the command, the control keyboard shortcut (where available), and a description of what the command does (see Figure 21-9).

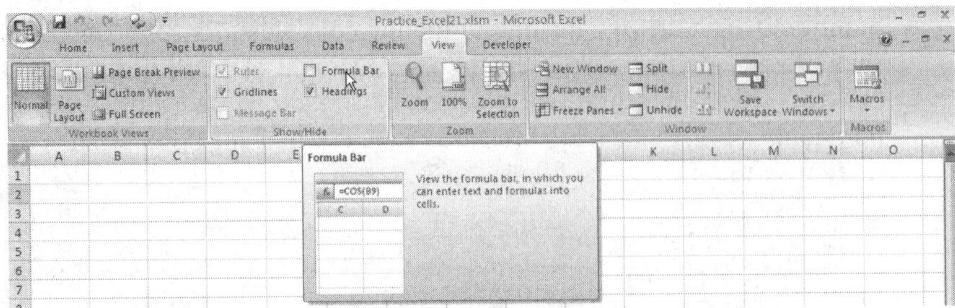

Figure 21-9: The enhanced tooltips, known as Super ToolTips, provide more information about the selected command.

All Ribbon commands, the Microsoft Office button, and the Quick Access toolbar can be easily accessed via the keyboard. Simply press the Alt key on the keyboard to display small boxes with key tips (see Figure 21-10). Every command has its own access key. For example, to access the Microsoft Office button, press Alt and then F. Within the menus you will see other key tips for every command. To view key tips for the commands on a particular tab, first select the access key for that tab. To remove the key tips, press the Alt key again.

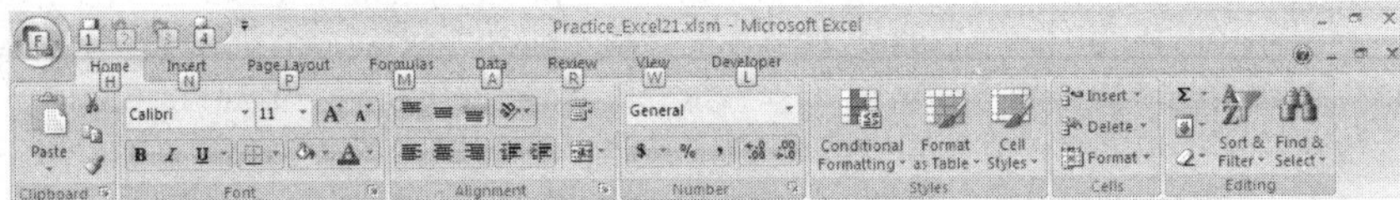

Figure 21-10: To view the Ribbon's key tips, press the Alt key.

When you are working in command mode (you have previously pressed the Alt key), you can also use the Tab key and arrow keys to move around the Ribbon. If you use an old keyboard shortcut from Excel 2003 that begins with Alt, such as Alt+V to open the View menu, you will see a message informing you that you are using an Office 2003 access key. If you know the keys, you can continue to type the Office 2003 sequence keys, or press Esc to cancel.

Now that you've reviewed the main features of the new Ribbon interface, let's look at how you can extend it with your own tabs and controls. The next section introduces you to Ribbon programming with XML and VBA.

Ribbon Programming with XML and VBA

The components of the Ribbon user interface in the Microsoft Office 2007 system can be manipulated programmatically using Extensible Markup Language (XML) or other programming languages. All Office 2007 applications that use Ribbons rely on the new programming model known as Ribbon extensibility, or RibbonX.

This section introduces you to customizing Excel 2007 ribbons by using XML markup. No special tools are required to perform these customizations. XML is plain text; therefore, you can use any text editor to create your customization files. In the examples that follow, we'll be using the simple Windows Notepad.

Note: Simple text editors such as Notepad do not provide tools for validating your XML markup. You must be extra careful to write well-formed XML or your code will fail (see Chapter 29 for an introduction to XML terms and markup). If you have access to a copy of Visual Studio 2005, you can use its editor to perform the XML validation based on the XSD schema file. You can download this file (customUI.xsd) from http://msdn.microsoft.com/office/tool/ribbon.

If you'd like to work with XML in a tree-based format, you may want to download free of charge the Microsoft XML Notepad 2006 from http://microsoft.com/downloads/. You can also download the Office 2007 Custom UI Editor from http://openxmldeveloper.org/articles/CustomUIeditor.aspx. None of these advanced tools are necessary for the completion of this chapter's Ribbon customizations. Each new tool, especially an advanced one, requires that you first familiarize yourself with its interface. To get started with XML programming without further delays, Notepad will do.

Creating the Ribbon Customization XML Markup

To make custom changes to the Ribbon user interface in Excel 2007 you need to prepare an XML markup file that specifies all your customizations. The XML markup file that we will use in the Hands-On exercise in this section is shown in Figure 21-11 and the resulting output in Figure 21-12.

Practice_Ribbon1.xml - Notepad

File Edit Format View Help

```
<customUI xmlns="http://schemas.microsoft.com/office/2006/01/customui">
  <ribbon startFromScratch="false">
    <tabs>
      <tab idMso="TabHome">
        <group idMso="GroupStyles" visible="false" />
      </tab>
      <tab id="TabJK1" label="Favorite">
        <group id="GroupJK1" label="SmallApps">
          <button id="btnNotes" label="Notepad" image="Note1" size="large" onAction="OpenNotepad"
           screentip="Open Windows Notepad"
           supertip="It is recommended that you save your notes about this worksheet in a simple text file."/>
          <button id="btnCharMap" label="CharMap"
           imageMso="SymbolInsert" size="large" onAction="OpenCharmap" />
         </group>
        <group id="GroupJK2" label="Print/Email" >
          <button idMso="FilePrintQuick" size="normal" />
          <button idMso="FileSendAsAttachment" size="normal" />
        </group>
      </tab>
    </tabs>
  </ribbon>
</customUI>
```

Figure 21-11: This XML file defines a new tab with two groups for the existing Excel 2007 Ribbon. See the output this file produces in Figure 21-12.

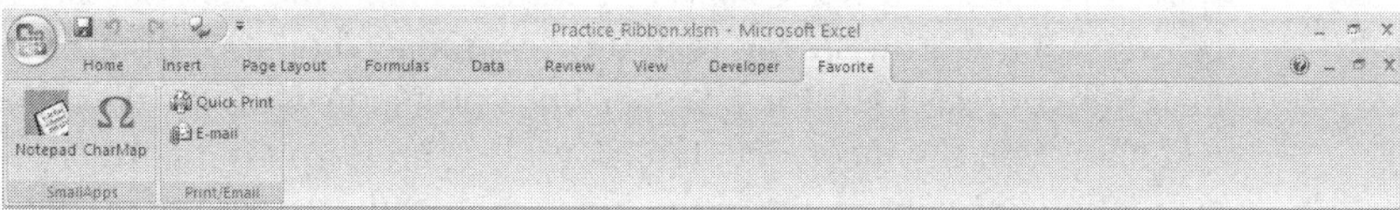

Figure 21-12: The custom Favorite tab is based on the XML markup file shown in Figure 21-11.

Hands-On 21-4: Creating an XML Document with Ribbon Customizations

1. Create a new folder named **customUI** on your C:\ drive.
2. Within the customUI folder, create two subfolders named **images** and **_rels**. Note that the name of the _rels folder must start with an underscore (_).
3. Copy the **Note.gif** file from your **C:\Ex07_HandsOn** folder to your **C:\customUI\images** folder.
4. Open Windows Notepad and type the XML markup file as shown below, or copy the code from C:\Ex07_HandsOn\Practice_Ribbon1.txt.

```
<customUI xmlns="http://schemas.microsoft.com/office/2006/01/customui">
  <ribbon startFromScratch="false">
    <tabs>
      <tab idMso="TabHome">
        <group idMso="GroupStyles" visible="false" />
      </tab>
      <tab id="TabJK1" label="Favorite">
        <group id="GroupJK1" label="SmallApps">
         <button id="btnNotes" label="Notepad" image="Note1" size="large"
          onAction="OpenNotepad" screentip="Open Windows Notepad"
          supertip="It is recommended that you save your notes about this
          worksheet in a simple text file." />
         <button id="btnCharMap" label="CharMap" imageMso="SymbolInsert"
          size="large" onAction="OpenCharmap" />
         </group>
        <group id="GroupJK2" label="Print/Email">
          <button idMso="FilePrintQuick" size="normal" />
          <button idMso="FileSendAsAttachment" size="normal" />
        </group>
      </tab>
    </tabs>
  </ribbon>
</customUI>
```

   XML is case sensitive, so make sure you enter the statements exactly as shown above.

5. Save the file as **C:\customUI\Practice_Ribbon1.xml**.

   By entering the XML extension, the text file is saved as an XML document.

6. To ensure that this XML document is well formed (it follows the formatting rules for XML; see Chapter 29 for more information), open it in a browser. If the browser can read the document, then its output should match Figure 21-13. If the browser finds problems with the document, it will show you the incorrect statement. It is up to you to figure out what correction is required. Open the file in Notepad, correct the erroneous code, save the file, and test it again by loading it in the browser.

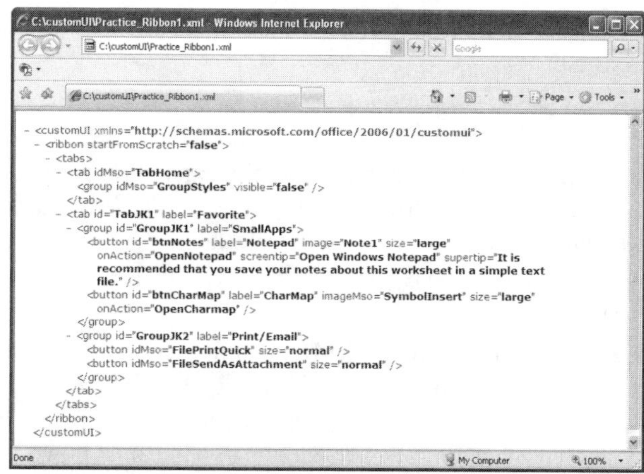

Figure 21-13: The XML file opened in the Internet Explorer browser.

7. Close the browser.

   At this point, you should have a well-formed XML document with Ribbon customizations.

Let's go over the XML document contents. As you will learn in Chapter 29, every XML document consists of a number of elements, called nodes. In any XML document there must be a root node, or a top-level element.

In the Ribbon customization file, the root tag is <customUI>. The root's purpose is to specify the Office 2007 RibbonX XML namespace:

```
<customUI xmlns="http://schemas.microsoft.com/office/2006/01/customui">
```

The xmlns attribute of the <customUI> tag holds the name of the default namespace to be used in the Ribbon customization. Notice that the root element encloses all other elements of this XML document: ribbon, tabs, tab, group, and button. Each element consists of a beginning and ending tag. For example, <customUI> is the name of the beginning tag and </customUI> is the ending tag. The actual Ribbon definition is contained within the <ribbon> tag:

```
<ribbon startFromScratch="false">
[Include xml tags to specify the required ribbon customization]
</ribbon>
```

The startFromScratch attribute of the <ribbon> tag defines whether you want to replace the built-in Ribbon with your own (true) or add a new tab to the existing Ribbon (false).

Hiding the Elements of the Excel User Interface Setting startFromScratch="true" in the <ribbon> tag will hide the default Ribbon as well as the contents of the Quick Access toolbar. The Office menu will be left with only three commands: New, Open, and Save.

To create a new tab set in the Ribbon, use the <tabs> tag. Each tab element is defined with the <tab> tag. The label attribute of the tab element specifies the name of your custom tab. The name in the id attribute is used to identify your custom tab:

```
<tabs>
<tab id="TabJK1" label="Favorite">
```

Ribbon tabs contain controls organized in groups. You can define a group for the controls on your tab with the <group> tag. The example XML markup file defines the following two groups for the Favorite tab:

```
<group id="GroupJK1" label="SmallApps">
<group id="GroupJK2" label="Print/Email">
```

Like the tab node, the group nodes of the XML document also contain the id and label attributes. Placing controls in groups is easy. The group labeled SmallApps has two custom button controls, identified by the <button> elements. The group labeled Print/Email also contains two buttons; however, unlike the SmallApps group, the buttons placed here are built-in Office System controls rather than custom controls. You can quickly determine this by looking at the id attribute for the control. Any attribute that ends with "Mso" refers to a built-in Office item:

```
<button idMso="FilePrintQuick" size="normal" />
```

Determining the Name of a Ribbon Control In the Ribbon customization XML, and when writing VBA callback procedures, you will need to reference built-in control names. Previous versions of Excel allowed you to write VBA code to loop through all the built-in toolbars and generate a list of their controls. This is no longer possible with the new Ribbon interface. To determine the name of the control you can:

- Use the Customize tab of the Excel Options dialog box (click the Microsoft Office button, choose Excel Options, and select Customize in the left pane). Find the control you need in the list box on the left and hover the mouse pointer over the name to view the control name in a screen tip.
- Download the 2007 Office System lists of control IDs from the following web site: http://www.microsoft.com/downloads/details.aspx?familyid=4329d9e9-4d11-46a5-898d-23e4f331e9ae&displaylang=eng.

Buttons placed on the Ribbon can be large or small. You can define the size of the button with the size attribute set to "large" or "normal." Buttons can have additional attributes:

```
<button id="btnNotes" label="Notepad" image="Note1" size="large"
  onAction="OpenNotepad" screentip="Open Windows Notepad" supertip="It is
  recommended that you save your notes about this worksheet in a simple
  text file." />
<button id="btnCharMap" label="CharMap" imageMso="SymbolInsert"
  size="large" onAction="OpenCharmap" />
```

The screentip and supertip attributes allow you to specify the short and longer text that should appear when the mouse pointer is positioned over the button.

The imageMso attribute denotes the name of the existing Office icon. You can use images provided by any Office application. To provide your own image, use the image attribute as shown in this Hands-On, or use the getImage attribute in the XML markup (see more information in the section "Creating a Gallery Control," later in this chapter).

The controls that you specify in the XML markup perform their designated actions via *callback procedures*. For example, the onAction attribute of a button control contains the name of the callback procedure that is executed when the button is clicked. When that procedure completes, it calls back the Ribbon to provide the status or modify the Ribbon. You will write the callback procedures for the onAction attribute in the next Hands-On.

Buttons borrowed from the Office system do not require the onAction attribute. When clicked, these buttons will perform their default built-in action.

Before finishing off the XML Ribbon customization document, always make sure that you have included all the ending tags:

```
</tab>
</tabs>
</ribbon>
</customUI>
```

Because our Ribbon customization calls upon a custom image located in the customUI\images folder, we need to create another XML file to establish the required relationship.

8. Open Notepad and enter the following XML markup:

```
<?xml version="1.0" encoding="utf-8"?>
<Relationships xmlns="http://schemas.openxmlformats.org/package/2006/
    relationships">
<Relationship Type="http://schemas.openxmlformats.org/officeDocument/2006/
    relationships/image" Target="images/Note.gif" Id="Note1" />
</Relationships>
```

   XML is case sensitive, so make sure you enter the statements exactly as shown above.

   The above markup relates the Id (Note1) used in the Practice_Ribbon1.xlm file to the corresponding image file. You will find more information about working with image files later in this chapter.

9. Save the file as **Practice_Ribbon1.xlm.rels** in the C:\customUI_rels folder that you created in step 2 of this Hands-On exercise.

About Tabs, Groups, and Controls Built-in tabs and groups can be made invisible by setting the visible property of the <tab> or <group> elements to "false". A built-in tab can contain a custom group. Built-in groups can also be added to other built-in or custom tabs. You cannot add controls to built-in groups. Also, you cannot create your own contextual tabs, but you can add your custom groups to the built-in contextual tabs using the <tabSet> element within the <contextualTabs> element, like this:

```
<contextualTabs>
   <tabSet idMso="TabSetTableTools">
      <tab idMso="TabTableToolsDesign">
         <group id="CustomTools">
            <button id="btnID1"/>
         </group>
      </tab>
   </tabSet>
</contextualTabs>
```

Now that you know how to structure an XML document for Ribbon customizations, you should find it straightforward to add other features to the Ribbon as they are discussed later in the chapter.

Loading Ribbon Customizations

The Hands-On 21-5 exercise walks you through the remaining steps that are necessary in order to integrate Ribbon customizations into your workbook.

Hands-On 21-5: Writing VBA Procedures and Setting Relationships for Use by the Ribbon Customizations

1. Create a new Excel workbook and save it as **C:\Ex07_ByExample\Practice_Ribbon.xlsm.**
2. Switch to the Visual Basic Editor window and activate **VBAProject (Practice_Ribbon.xlsm)** in the Project Explorer window. Next, choose **Insert | Module** to add a new module to the selected project.
3. In the module's Code window, enter the following procedures:

```
Public Sub OpenNotepad(ctl As IRibbonControl)
    Shell "Notepad.exe", vbNormalFocus
End Sub

Public Sub OpenCharmap(ctl As IRibbonControl)
    Shell "Charmap.exe", vbNormalFocus
End Sub
```

   OpenNotepad and OpenCharmap are the names of the callback procedures that were specified in the onAction attribute of the button (see the previous Hands-On). As mentioned earlier, a callback procedure executes some action and then notifies the Ribbon that the task has been completed. In Excel 2007, the onAction callback is handled by a VBA procedure. The callback includes the IRibbonControl parameter, which is the control that was clicked. This control is passed to your VBA code by the Ribbon.

```
Sub OpenNotepad(ctl as IRibbonControl)
Sub OpenCharmap(ctl as IRibbonControl)
```

For VBA to recognize this parameter, you must make sure that the References dialog box (Tools | References) has a reference to the Microsoft Office 12.0 object library.

The IRibbonControl Properties You can view the properties (Context, Id, and Tag) of the IRibbonControl object in the Object Browser. The Context property returns the active window that contains the Ribbon interface, in this case Microsoft Excel. The Id property contains the ID of the control that was clicked. The Tag property can be used to store additional information with the control. To use this property, you need to add a tag attribute to the Ribbon customization XML document. By using the Tag property you can write a more generic procedure to handle the callbacks.

The OpenNotepad and OpenCharMap procedures tell Excel to use the Shell function to open Windows Notepad or the Charmap application. Notice that the program's executable filename is in double quotes. The second argument of the Shell function is optional. This argument specifies the window style, that is, how the program will appear once it is launched. The vbNormalFocus constant will open the application in a normal size window with focus. If the window style is not specified, the program will be minimized with focus (vbMinimizedFocus).

4. Save and close the **Practice_Ribbon.xlsm** workbook. Keep the Excel application window open.

   Proceed to step 5 to make sure that Excel is set up to display the RibbonX errors.

5. Click the **Microsoft Office** button and choose **Excel Options.** In the Excel Options dialog box, click the **Advanced** tab and scroll down to the **General** section. Make sure that the **Show Add-in User Interface Errors** check box is selected, and click **OK.**

   When you enable Show Add-in User Interface Errors, Excel will display errors in your Ribbon customization when you load a workbook that contains errors in the custom RibbonX code. This is very helpful in the process of debugging. If you want to successfully use your custom interface you must make sure that Excel does not find any errors when loading your workbook.

6. Exit Microsoft Excel.

7. In the Windows Explorer, right-click the **Practice_Ribbon.xlsm** file in your Ex07_ByExample folder and choose **Rename** from the shortcut menu. Add the **.zip** extension to the Practice_Ribbon.xlsm file. The file should now be named **Practice_Ribbon.xlsm.zip**. Click **Yes** to the message when prompted that changing the file extension may make the file unusable.

Note: As mentioned earlier in this book, the new Excel 2007 file format is XML based. Workbook files saved with the .xlsx or .xlsm file extensions are actually zip files containing a number of XML documents, known as "XML parts." To see the structure of the file (its files and folders), all you need to do is add a zip extension at the end of the filename and open it using a zip utility such as WinZip or the compression program built into Windows XP (see step 9 below). For more information about accessing the Workbook file structure in Excel 2007, refer to Chapter 29.

8. Drag the entire **customUI** folder created in the previous Hands-On and drop it into the Practice_Ribbon.xlsm.zip archive.
9. Right-click the **Practice_Ribbon.xlsm.zip** archive and choose **Open with compressed (zipped) folders**.

   You should see the contents of the zip archive, as shown in Figure 21-14.

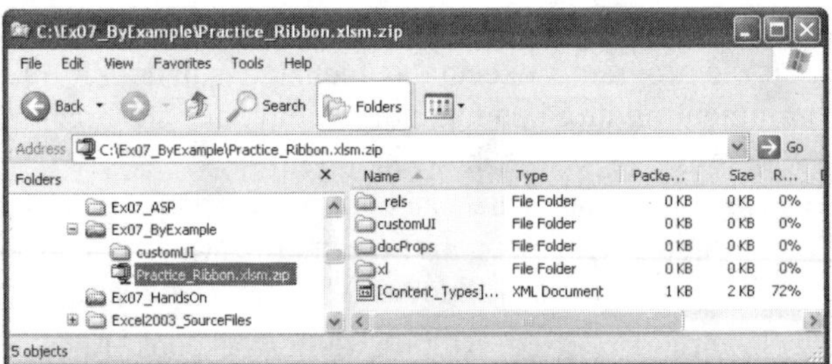

Figure 21-14: Examining the contents of the compressed folder.

In the Excel file, various document parts are related to one another using relationships. Because we have now added a new folder to the file, we need to let Excel know how the custom UI part relates to the existing parts. The _rels folder contains a relationship file named .rels that lists the default relationships already present in the Excel file. To add a new relationship, we need to extract this file from the archive and edit it with a text editor (see steps 10-13 below).

10. Open the **_rels** folder by double-clicking on it. The folder should contain one XML file named .rels. Drag this .rels file anywhere outside the zip file; for example, drop it in the C:\Ex07_ByExample folder.
11. Open the **.rels** file with Notepad or any other text editor that you have installed on your machine.

    We need to edit this file to include a reference to the Practice_Ribbon1.xml file we created in the previous Hands-On exercise.
12. Add the following statement (in bold letters) to the open .rels file:

```
<?xml version="1.0" encoding="UTF-8" standalone="yes"?>
<Relationships xmlns="http://schemas.openxmlformats.org/package/2006/relationships">
<Relationship Id="rId3"
Type="http://schemas.openxmlformats.org/officeDocument/2006/relationships/extended-properties"
Target="docProps/app.xml"/><Relationship Id="rId2"
Type="http://schemas.openxmlformats.org/package/2006/relationships/metadata/core-properties"
```

```
Target="docProps/core.xml"/><Relationship Id="rId1"
Type="http://schemas.openxmlformats.org/officeDocument/2006/relationships/officeDocument"
Target="xl/workbook.xml"/>
<Relationship Id="crId1"
Type="http://schemas.microsoft.com/office/2006/relationships/ui/extensibility"
Target="/customUI/Practice_Ribbon1.xml"/>
</Relationships>
```

The statement in bold tells Excel where to look for the Ribbon customization. XML is case sensitive, so make sure you enter the statement exactly as shown above.

13. Save the modified .rels file and close Notepad.
14. Drag the modified .rels file back into the **Practice_Ribbon.xlsm.zip** archive's **_rels** folder. Click **OK** to overwrite the original version of this file.
15. Change the Practice_Ribbon.xlsm.zip filename back to **Practice_Ribbon.xlsm**. Click **Yes** to the message that changing the file extension may render the file unusable.
16. Open the **Practice_Ribbon.xlsm** workbook.

When you open the workbook file, the Excel user interface should appear with your customizations as shown in Figure 21-12 earlier (provided the Ribbon customization is error free).

Errors on Loading Ribbon Customizations

If Excel finds any errors in the Ribbon customization markup, it displays an appropriate error message. For example, if your Practice_Ribbon1.xml document is missing a matching opening or closing tag, or you typed the name of an attribute in uppercase when lowercase was expected, you will see a message indicating a line and a column number, and the name of the attribute where the problem is located (see Figure 21-15). You must open the XML file, find and correct the error, and then try again to open the Excel file containing the Ribbon customization. Excel will bug you with error messages until the entire file is debugged.

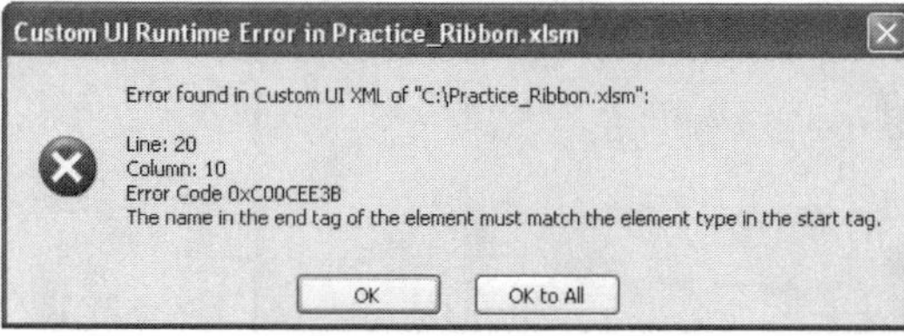

Figure 21-15: Excel displays an error message when it finds an error in Custom UI XML code of the workbook file you are attempting to open.

Some problems found within the file may cause Excel to generate an error message about unreadable content and ask you if you want to recover the contents of the workbook (see Figure 21-16). When you click No, the workbook will not open; when you click Yes, Excel will try to repair the file and let you know whether it has succeeded. Sometimes the correction will be made for you, and other times you will have to locate and fix the problem yourself.

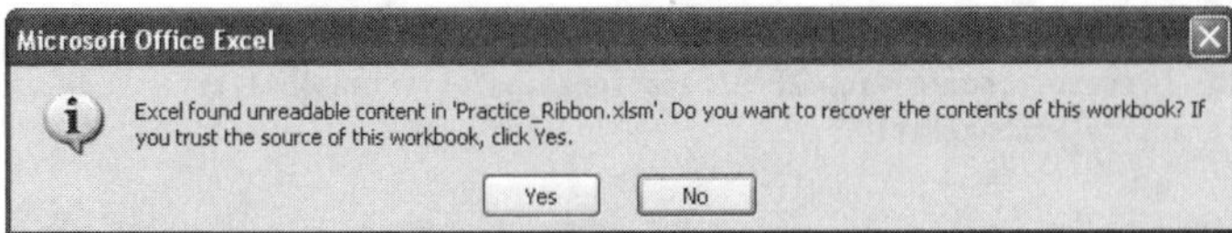

Figure 21-16: This type of error message may appear when the Ribbon's .rels file contains a conflicting relationship ID.

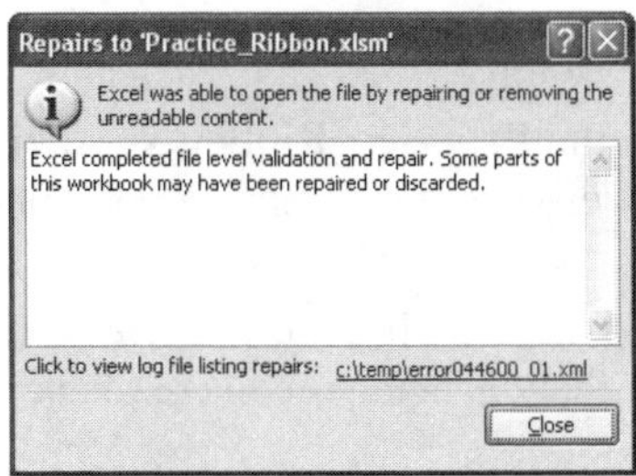

Figure 21-17: You will see this message if Excel was able to repair the file.

Using a Custom Fluent UI Editor

In previous Hands-On exercises you learned that customizing the Ribbon involves numerous steps and understanding of the Office Open XML format structure. Moreover, each time you want to add another customization or fix an error, you need to follow a multitude of steps. If you find this process much too difficult or frustrating to implement, try working with the Custom Fluent UI Editor tool, which is available for download at http://openXMLDeveloper.org/articles/CustomUIeditor.aspx.

This tool allows you to open a file, enter and validate your custom XML markup, insert the images, generate callbacks, save the file with the XML markup, and put your custom UI part into the Office Open XML document package with the required relationships.

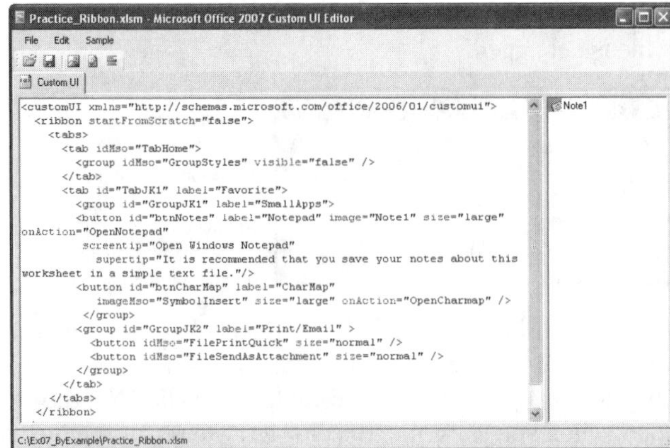

Figure 21-18: Custom UI Editor displays the Ribbon customization markup in the Practice_Ribbon.xlsm workbook file.

Using Images in Ribbon Customizations

So far in this chapter you have learned how to use built-in and custom images in your Ribbon customizations. You already know that to reuse an Office icon you must use the imageMso attribute of a control. You also know that to call your own BMP, GIF, and JPEG image files you should use the image attribute. In the example Ribbon customization, we have stored images in the customUI\images folder and created the Practice_Ribbon1.xml.rels file in a customUI_rels folder to define the relationship between the IDs used in the XML document and the image files. With this approach, the customUI \images folder had to be copied to the workbook file. But what if you store images in another folder on a local or a network drive and would like to load them at run time when you open a workbook? To implement this particular scenario, use the loadImage callback for the customUI element as shown below:

```
<customUI xmlns="http://schemas.microsoft.com/office/2006/01/customui"
loadImage="OnLoadImage">
  <ribbon startFromScratch="false">
    <tabs>
      <tab idMso="TabHome">
        <group idMso="GroupStyles" visible="false" />
      </tab>
      <tab id="TabJK1" label="Favorite">
        <group id="GroupJK1" label="SmallApps">
         <button id="btnNotes" label="Notepad" image="Note1" size="large"
          onAction="OpenNotepad" screentip="Open Windows Notepad"
          supertip="It is recommended that you save your notes about this
          worksheet in a simple text file." />
         <button id="btnCharMap" label="CharMap" imageMso="SymbolInsert"
          size="large" onAction="OpenCharmap" />
         <button id="btnCalc" label="Calculator"
              image="DownArrow.gif" onAction="OpenCalculator" />
         </group>
        <group id="GroupJK2" label="Print/Email">
          <button idMso="FilePrintQuick" size="normal" />
          <button idMso="FileSendAsAttachment" size="normal" />
        </group>
      </tab>
    </tabs>
  </ribbon>
</customUI>
```

The above shows the revised Practice_Ribbon1.xml document that we created earlier. The new statements are indicated in bold print. Notice that the first statement contains the loadImage attribute:

```
<customUI xmlns="http://schemas.microsoft.com/office/2006/01/customui"
loadImage="OnLoadImage">
```

The loadImage attribute specifies the following OnLoadImage callback procedure, which needs to be entered in a VBA module:

```
Public Sub OnLoadImage(imgName As String, ByRef image)
    Dim strImgFileName As String
    strImgFileName = "C:\Ex07_HandsOn\Extra Images\" & imgName
    Set image = LoadPicture(strImgFileName)
End Sub
```

Notice that to load a picture from a file, you need to use the LoadPicture function. This function is a member of the stdole.StdFunctions library. The library file, which is called stdole2.tlb, is installed in the System or System32 folder on your computer and is available to your VBA procedures without setting additional references. The LoadPicture function returns an object of type IPictureDisp that represents the image. You can view objects, methods, and properties available in the stdole library using the Object Browser in the Visual Basic Editor window.

The following new button control in the XML Ribbon customization document has an image control that specifies the name of the image file:

```
<button id="btnCalc" label="Calculator"
        image="DownArrow.gif" onAction="OpenCalculator" />
```

This button uses the following callback procedure entered in a VBA module:

```
Public Sub OpenCalculator(ctl As IRibbonControl)
    Shell "Calc.exe", vbNormalFocus
End Sub
```

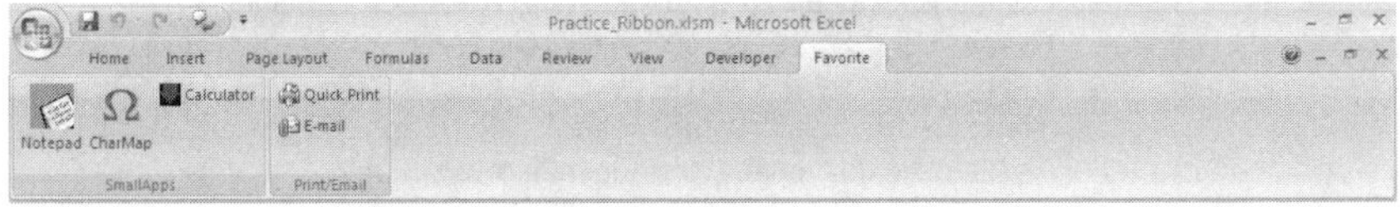

Figure 21-19: The Calculator button in the SmallApps group of the Favorite tab displays an image retrieved by the OnLoadImage callback procedure.

Using Various Controls in Ribbon Customizations

Now that you know how to go about creating the XML markup for your Ribbon customizations and applying the custom Ribbon to a workbook, let's look at other types of controls you can show in the Ribbon.

Creating Toggle Buttons

A *toggle button* is a button that alternates between two states. Many formatting features such as Bold, Italic, or Format Painter are implemented as toggle buttons. When you click a toggle button, the button will stay down until you click it again. To create a toggle button, use the <toggleButton> XML tag as shown below:

```
<toggleButton id="tglR1C1" label="Reference Style" size="normal"
          getPressed="OnGetPressed" onAction="SwitchRefStyle" />
```

You can add a built-in image to the toggle button with the imageMso attribute or use a custom image as discussed earlier in this chapter. To find out whether or not the toggle button is pressed, include the getPressed attribute in your XML markup. The getPressed callback procedure provides two arguments: the control that was clicked and the pressed state of the toggle button.

```
Sub OnGetPressed(control As IRibbonControl, _
            ByRef pressed)
    If control.ID = "tglR1C1" Then
        pressed = False
    End If
End Sub
```

The above callback procedure will ensure that the specified toggle button is not pressed when the Ribbon is loaded.

To perform an action when the toggle button is clicked, set the onAction attribute to the name of your custom callback procedure. This callback also provides two arguments: the control that was clicked and the state of the toggle button.

```
Sub SwitchRefStyle(control As IRibbonControl, _
            pressed As Boolean)
    If pressed Then
        Application.ReferenceStyle = xlR1C1
    Else
        Application.ReferenceStyle = xlA1
    End If
End Sub
```

If the toggle button is pressed, the value of the pressed argument will be True; otherwise, it will be False.

Figure 21-20 in the next section shows a custom toggle button named Reference Style. When you click this button, the worksheet headings change to display letters or numbers. For more information on using R1C1 style references instead of A1 style, see the online help.

Creating Split Buttons, Menus, and Submenus

A *split button* is a combination of a button or toggle button and a menu. Clicking the button performs one default action, and clicking the drop-down arrow opens a menu with a list of related options to select from. To create the split button, use the <splitButton> tag. Within this tag, you need to define a <button> or a <toggleButton> control and the <menu> control, as shown in the following XML markup:

```
<splitButton id="btnSplit1" size="large">
   <button id="btnGoTo" label="Navigate To..." imageMso="GoTo" />
   <menu id="mnuGoTo" label="Spreadsheet Navigation" itemSize="normal">
      <menuSeparator id="mnuDiv1" title="Formulas and Constants" />
      <button id="btnFormulas" label="Select Formulas"
       onAction="GoToSpecial" />
      <button id="btnNumbers" label="Select Numbers Only"
       onAction="GoToSpecial" />
      <button id="btnText" label="Select Text Only"
       onAction="GoToSpecial" />
      <menuSeparator id="mnuDiv2" title="Special Cells" />
```

```
        <button id="btnBlanks" label="Select blank cells"
         onAction="GoToSpecial" />
        <button id="btnLast" label="Select last cell"
         onAction="GoToSpecial" />
    </menu>
</splitButton>
```

You can specify the size of the items in the menu with the itemSize attribute. The <menuSeparator> tag can be used inside the menu node to break the menu into sections. Each menu segment can then be titled using the title attribute, as shown in the above example. You can add the onAction attribute to each menu button to specify the callback procedure or macro to execute when the menu item is clicked. The above XML markup uses the following callback procedure entered in a VBA module:

```
Sub GoToSpecial(control As IRibbonControl)
    On Error Resume Next
    Range("A1").Select

    If control.ID = "btnFormulas" Then
        Selection.SpecialCells(xlCellTypeFormulas, 23).Select
    ElseIf control.ID = "btnNumbers" Then
        Selection.SpecialCells(xlCellTypeConstants, 1).Select
    ElseIf control.ID = "btnText" Then
        Selection.SpecialCells(xlCellTypeConstants, 2).Select
    ElseIf control.ID = "btnBlanks" Then
        Selection.SpecialCells(xlCellTypeBlanks).Select
    ElseIf control.ID = "btnLast" Then
        Selection.SpecialCells(xlCellTypeLastCell).Select
    End If
End Sub
```

In addition to button controls, menus can contain toggle buttons, check boxes, gallery controls, split buttons, and other menus. Figure 21-20 displays a split button control with a menu.

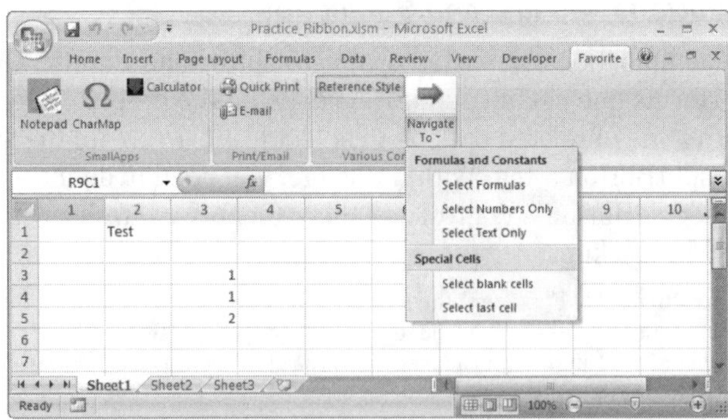

Figure 21-20: A toggle button and a custom split button control with a menu.

Creating Check Boxes

The check box control is used to show the state — either true (on) or false (off). It can be included inside a menu control or used as a separate control on the Ribbon. To create a check box, use the <checkBox> tag, as shown in the following XML:

```
<separator id="OtherControlsDiv1" />
    <labelControl id="TitleForBox1" label="Show or Hide Screen
     Elements" />
    <box id="boxLayout1">
        <checkBox id="chkGridlines" label="Gridlines" visible="true"
         getPressed="OnGetPressed" onAction="DoSomething" />
        <checkBox id="chkFormulaBar" label="Formula Bar" visible="true"
          getPressed="OnGetPressed" onAction="DoSomething" />
    </box>
```

In the above XML markup, the <separator> tag will produce the vertical bar that visually separates controls within the same Ribbon group (see Figure 21-21). The <labelControl> tag can be used to display static text anywhere in the Ribbon. In this example, we use it to place a header over a set of controls. To control the layout of various controls (to display them horizontally instead of vertically), use the <box> tag. You can define whether a check box should be visible or hidden by setting the visible attribute to true or false. To disable a check box, set the enabled attribute to false; this will cause the check box to appear grayed out.

To get the checked state for a check box, specify a callback procedure in the getPressed attribute. You can modify the OnGetPressed procedure that we used earlier with the toggle button:

```
Sub OnGetPressed(control As IRibbonControl, _
            ByRef pressed)
    If control.id = "tglR1C1" Then
        pressed = False
    End If

    If control.id = "chkGridlines" And _
        ActiveWindow.DisplayGridlines = True Then
        pressed = True
    ElseIf control.id = "chkGridlines" And _
        ActiveWindow.DisplayGridlines = False Then
        pressed = False
    End If

    If control.id = "chkFormulaBar" And _
        Application.DisplayFormulaBar = True Then
        pressed = True
    ElseIf control.id = "chkFormulaBar" And _
        Application.DisplayFormulaBar = False Then
        pressed = False
    End If
End Sub
```

The action of the check box control is handled by the callback procedure in the onAction attribute. To make this check box example work, you need to enter the following procedure in a VBA module:

```
Sub DoSomething(ctl As IRibbonControl, _
                pressed As Boolean)
    If ctl.id = "chkGridlines" And pressed Then
       ActiveWindow.DisplayGridlines = True
    ElseIf ctl.id = "chkGridlines" And Not pressed Then
```

```
            ActiveWindow.DisplayGridlines = False
        ElseIf ctl.id = "chkFormulaBar" And pressed Then
            Application.DisplayFormulaBar = True
        ElseIf ctl.id = "chkFormulaBar" And Not pressed Then
            Application.DisplayFormulaBar = False
        End If
    End Sub
```

Similar to other controls, labels for check boxes can contain static text in the label attribute as shown in the above XML, or they can be assigned dynamically using the callback procedure in the getLabel attribute.

Note: Callback procedures don't need to be named the same as the attribute they are used with. Also, you may change the callback's argument names as desired.

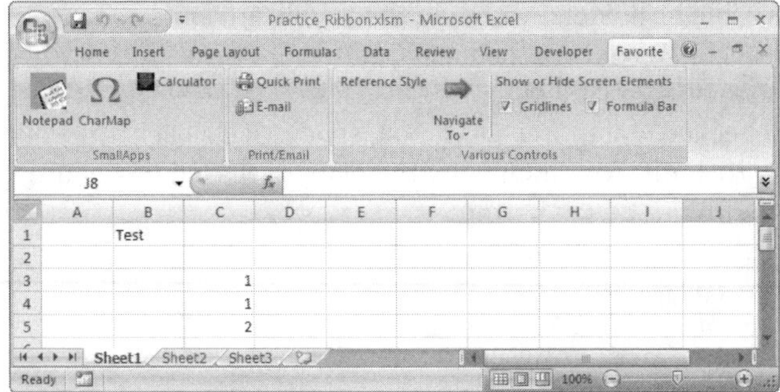

Figure 21-21: The check box controls are laid out horizontally.

Creating Edit Boxes

Use the <editBox> tag to provide an area on the Ribbon where users can type text or numbers:

```
<editBox id="txtFullName" label="First and Last Name:"
    sizeString="AAAAAAAAAAAAAAAA" maxLength="25"
    onChange="onFullNameChange" />
```

The sizeString attribute specifies the width of the edit box. Set it to a string that will give you the width you want. The maxLength attribute allows you to limit the number of characters and/or digits that can be typed in the edit box. If the text entered exceeds the specified number of characters (25 in this case), Excel automatically displays a balloon message on the Ribbon: "The entry may contain no more than 25 characters." When the entry is updated in an edit box control, the callback procedure specified in the onChange attribute is called:

```
Public Sub onFullNameChange(ctl As IRibbonControl, _
                    text As String)
    If text <> "" Then
       MsgBox "You've entered '" & text & _
         "' in the edit box."
    End If
End Sub
```

When the user enters text in the edit box, the procedure will display a message box.

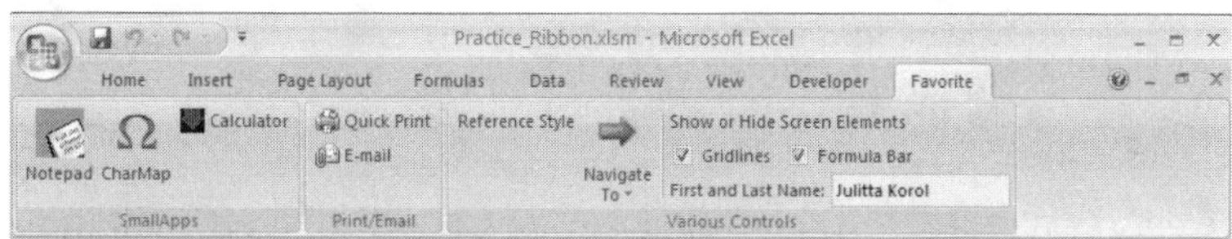

Figure 21-22: An edit box control allows data entry directly on the Ribbon.

Creating Combo Boxes and Drop-Downs

There are three types of drop-down controls that can be placed on the Ribbon: combo box, drop-down, and gallery.

These controls can be dynamically populated at run time by writing callbacks for their getItemCount, getItemID, getItemLabel, getItemImage, getItemScreentip, or getItemSupertip attributes. The combo box and drop-down controls can also be made static by defining their drop-down content using the <item> tag, as shown below:

```
<separator id="OtherControlsDiv2" />
<comboBox id="cboDepartment" label="Departments" supertip="Select
    Department" onChange="OnChangeDept">
        <item id="Marketing" label="Marketing" />
        <item id="Sales" label="Sales" />
        <item id="Personnel" label="Personnel" />
        <item id="ResearchAndDevelopment" label="Research and
             Development" />
 </comboBox>
```

To separate the combo box control from other controls in the same Ribbon group, the above example uses the <separator> tag. Notice that each <item> tag specifies a new drop-down row.

Note: A combo box is a combination of a drop-down list and a single-line edit box, allowing the user to either type a value directly into the control or choose from the list of predefined options. Use the sizeString attribute to define the width of the edit box.

The combo box control does not have the onAction attribute. It uses the onChange attribute that specifies the callback to execute when the item selection changes:

```
Public Sub OnChangeDept(ctl As IRibbonControl, _
          text As String)
     MsgBox "You selected " & text & " department."
End Sub
```

Notice that the onChange callback provides only the text of the selected item; it does not give you access to the selected index. If you need the index of the selection, use the drop-down control instead, as shown below:

```
<dropDown id="drpBoro" label="City Borough"
    supertip="Select City Borough"
```

```
        onAction="OnActionBoro">
            <item id="M" label="Manhattan" />
            <item id="B" label="Brooklyn" />
            <item id="Q" label="Queens" />
            <item id="I" label="Staten Island" />
            <item id="X" label="Bronx" />
    </dropDown>
```

The onAction callback of the drop-down control will give you both the selected item's ID and its index:

```
Public Sub OnActionBoro(ctl As IRibbonControl, _
         ByRef SelectedID As String, _
         ByRef SelectedIndex As Integer)
    MsgBox "Index=" & SelectedIndex & " ID=" & SelectedID
End Sub
```

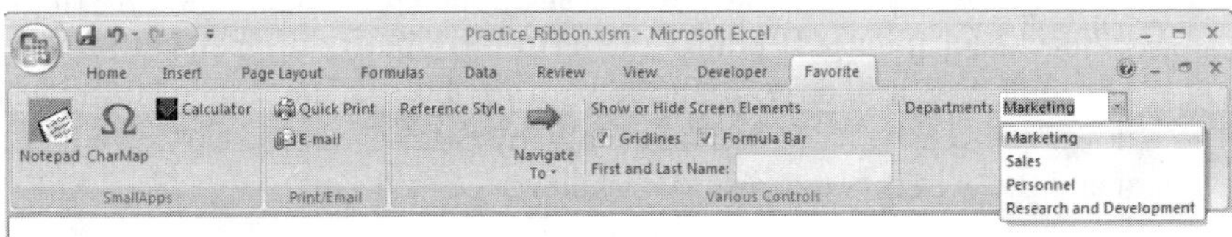

Figure 21-23: A combo box with a list of departments.

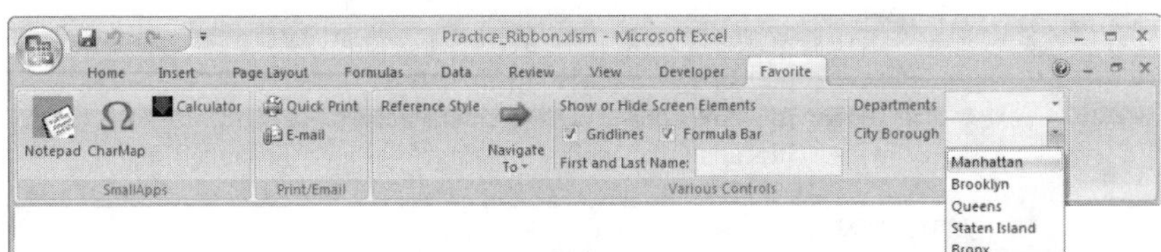

Figure 21-24: The Departments combo box and the City Borough drop-down look the same on the Ribbon.

Creating a Gallery Control

A gallery control is a drop-down control that can display a grid of images with or without a label. Built-in galleries cannot be customized, but you can build your own using the <gallery> tag. The following XML markup dynamically populates a custom gallery control at run time:

```
<gallery id="glHolidays" label="Holidays" columns="3" rows="4"
    getImage="OnGetImage" getItemCount="OnGetItemCount"
    getItemLabel="OnGetItemLabel" getItemImage="OnGetItemImage"
    getItemID="onGetItemID" onAction="onSelectedItem" />
```

In the above XML markup, the gallery control will perform the action specified in the onSelectedItem callback procedure. Notice that the gallery control has many attributes that contain static text or define callbacks. We will discuss them later. Right now, let's focus on the image loading process. The gallery control uses the getImage attribute with the OnGetImage callback procedure. This procedure will tell Excel to load the appropriate image to the Ribbon:

```
Public Sub OnGetImage(ctl As IRibbonControl, ByRef image)
    Select Case ctl.ID
      Case "glHolidays"
         Set image = LoadPicture("C:\Ex07_HandsOn\Extra
              Images\Square0.gif")
    End Select
End Sub
```

Notice that the decision as to which image should be loaded is based on the ID of the control in the Select Case statement. The gallery control also uses the OnGetItemImage callback procedure (defined in the getItemImage attribute) to load custom images for its drop-down selection list (see Figure 21-25). Use the columns and rows attributes to specify the number of columns and rows in the gallery when it is opened. If you need to define the height and width of images in the gallery, use the itemHeight and itemWidth attributes (not used in this example due to the simplicity of the utilized images). The getItemCount and getItemLabel attributes contain callback procedures that provide information to the Ribbon on how many items should appear in the drop-down list and the names of those items. The getItemImage attribute contains a callback procedure that specifies the images to be displayed next to each gallery item. The getItemID attribute specifies the onGetItemID callback procedure that will provide a unique ID for each of the gallery items.

Now let's go over other VBA callbacks that are used by the gallery control. All the VBA procedures in this section need to be added to the VBA module for the above XML markup to work:

```
Public Sub OnGetItemCount(ctl As IRibbonControl, ByRef count)
  count = 12
End Sub
```

In the above procedure we use the count parameter to return to the Ribbon the number of items we want to have in the gallery control.

```
Public Sub OnGetItemLabel(ctl As IRibbonControl, _
           index As Integer, ByRef label)
    label = MonthName(index + 1)
End Sub
```

The above procedure will label each of the gallery items. The VBA MonthName function is used to retrieve the name of the month based on the value of the index. The initial value of the index is zero (0). Therefore, index + 1 will return January. To display the month's name abbreviated (Jan, Feb, etc.), specify True as the second parameter to this function:

```
label = MonthName(index + 1, True)
```

If you are using a localized version of Microsoft Office (French, Spanish, etc.), the MonthName function will return the name of the month in the specified interface language.

The next callback procedure shows how to load images for each gallery item:

```
Public Sub OnGetItemImage(ctl As IRibbonControl, _
        index As Integer, ByRef image)
    Dim imgPath As String

    imgPath = "C:\Ex07_HandsOn\Extra Images\square"
    Set image = LoadPicture(imgPath & index + 1 & ".gif")
End Sub
```

Each item in the gallery must have a unique ID, so the onGetItemID callback uses the MonthName function to use the month name as the ID:

```
Public Sub onGetItemID(ctl As IRibbonControl, _
           index As Integer, ByRef id)
    id = MonthName(index + 1)
End Sub
```

The last procedure you need to write for the Holidays gallery control should define the actions to be performed when an item in the gallery is clicked. This is done via the following onSelectedItem callback that was specified in the onAction attribute of the XML markup:

```
Public Sub onSelectedItem(ctl As IRibbonControl, _
                selectedId As String, _
                selectedIndex As Integer)
    Select Case selectedIndex
        Case 6
            MsgBox "Holiday 1: Independence Day, July 4th", _
            vbInformation + vbOKOnly, _
            selectedId & " Holidays"
        Case 11
            MsgBox "Holiday 1: Christmas Day, December 25th", _
            vbInformation + vbOKOnly, _
            selectedId & " Holidays"
        Case Else
            MsgBox "Please program holidays for " & selectedId & ".", _
            vbInformation + vbOKOnly, _
            " Under Construction"
    End Select
End Sub
```

In the above callback procedure the selectedId parameter returns the name that was assigned to the label, while the selectedIndex parameter is the position of the item in the list. The first item in the list (January) is indexed with zero (0), the second one with 1, and so forth. In the above procedure we have just coded two holidays: one for the month of July (selectedIndex=6), and one for December (selectedIndex=11). The Case Else clause in the Select Case statement provides a message when other months are selected.

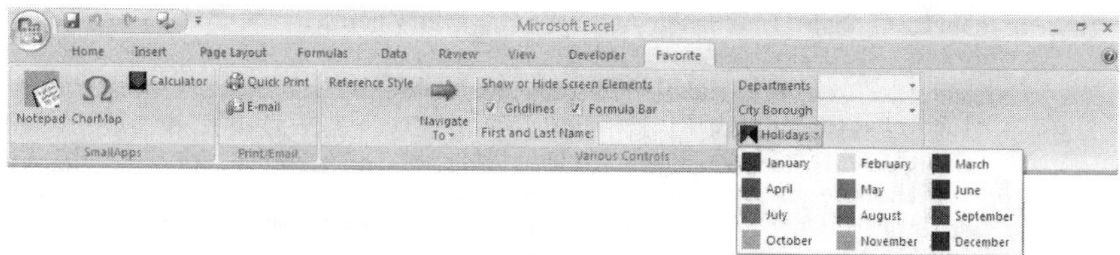

Figure 21-25: Customized Ribbon with the gallery control.

Creating a Dialog Box Launcher

On some Ribbon tabs you can see a small dialog launcher button at the bottom-right corner of a group (see Figure 21-10). You can use this button to open a special form that allows the user to set up many options at once, or you can display a form that contains specific information. To add a custom dialog launcher button to the Ribbon, use the <dialogBoxLauncher> tag, as shown below:

```
<dialogBoxLauncher>
   <button id="Launch1" screentip="Show Auto Correct Dialog"
    onAction="OnActionLaunch" />
</dialogBoxLauncher>
```

The dialog box launcher control must contain a button. The onAction attribute for the button contains the callback procedure that will execute when the button is clicked:

```
Public Sub OnActionLaunch(ctl As IRibbonControl)
    Application.Dialogs(xlDialogAutoCorrect).Show
End Sub
```

The dialog box launcher control must appear as the last element within the containing group element. The XML code below contains the entire definition of the Ribbon customization discussed so far in this chapter and depicted in Figure 21-26:

```
<customUI xmlns="http://schemas.microsoft.com/office/2006/01/customui"
      loadImage="OnLoadImage">
  <ribbon startFromScratch="false">
    <tabs>
      <tab idMso="TabHome">
        <group idMso="GroupStyles" visible="false" />
      </tab>
      <tab id="TabJK1" label="Favorite">
        <group id="GroupJK1" label="SmallApps">
          <button id="btnNotes" label="Notepad" image="Note1" size="large"
              onAction="OpenNotepad" screentip="Open Windows Notepad"
              supertip="It is recommended that you save your notes about this
              worksheet in a simple text file." />
          <button id="btnCharMap" label="CharMap"
            imageMso="SymbolInsert" size="large" onAction="OpenCharmap" />
          <button id="btnCalc" label="Calculator"
            image="DownArrow.gif" onAction="OpenCalculator" />
        </group>
        <group id="GroupJK2" label="Print/Email">
          <button idMso="FilePrintQuick" size="normal" />
```

```
  <button idMso="FileSendAsAttachment" size="normal" />
</group>
<group id="GroupJK3" label="Various Controls">
  <toggleButton id="tglR1C1" label="Reference Style" size="normal"
      getPressed="OnGetPressed" onAction="SwitchRefStyle" />
  <splitButton id="btnSplit1" size="large">
   <button id="btnGoTo" label="Navigate To..." imageMso="GoTo" />
   <menu id="mnuGoTo" label="Spreadsheet Navigation" itemSize="normal">
   <menuSeparator id="mnuDiv1" title="Formulas and Constants" />
     <button id="btnFormulas" label="Select Formulas"
         onAction="GoToSpecial" />
     <button id="btnNumbers" label="Select Numbers Only"
         onAction="GoToSpecial" />
     <button id="btnText" label="Select Text Only"
         onAction="GoToSpecial" />
   <menuSeparator id="mnuDiv2" title="Special Cells" />
     <button id="btnBlanks" label="Select blank cells"
         onAction="GoToSpecial" />
     <button id="btnLast" label="Select last cell" onAction="GoToSpecial" />
   </menu>
 </splitButton>
 <separator id="OtherControlsDiv1" />
   <labelControl id="TitleForBox1" label="Show or Hide Screen Elements" />
  <box id="boxLayout1">
    <checkBox id="chkGridlines" label="Gridlines" visible="true"
        getPressed="OnGetPressed" onAction="DoSomething" />
    <checkBox id="chkFormulaBar" label="Formula Bar" visible="true"
        getPressed="OnGetPressed" onAction="DoSomething" />
   </box>
  <editBox id="txtFullName" label="First and Last Name:"
      sizeString="AAAAAAAAAAAAAAAA" maxLength="25"
      onChange="onFullNameChange" />
  <separator id="OtherControlsDiv2" />
  <comboBox id="cboDepartment" label="Departments" supertip="Select
      Department" onChange="OnChangeDept">
    <item id="Marketing" label="Marketing" />
    <item id="Sales" label="Sales" />
    <item id="Personnel" label="Personnel" />
    <item id="ResearchAndDevelopment" label="Research and Development" />
  </comboBox>
  <dropDown id="drpBoro" label="City Borough" supertip="Select City Borough"
      onAction="OnActionBoro">
    <item id="M" label="Manhattan" />
    <item id="B" label="Brooklyn" />
    <item id="Q" label="Queens" />
    <item id="I" label="Staten Island" />
    <item id="X" label="Bronx" />
  </dropDown>
 <gallery id="glHolidays" label="Holidays" columns="3" rows="4"
    getImage="OnGetImage" getItemCount="OnGetItemCount"
    getItemLabel="OnGetItemLabel" getItemImage="OnGetItemImage"
    getItemID="onGetItemID" onAction="onSelectedItem" />
 <dialogBoxLauncher>
 <button id="Launch1" screentip="Show Auto Correct Dialog"
     onAction="OnActionLaunch" />
  </dialogBoxLauncher>
</group>
```

```
      </tab>
    </tabs>
  </ribbon>
</customUI>
```

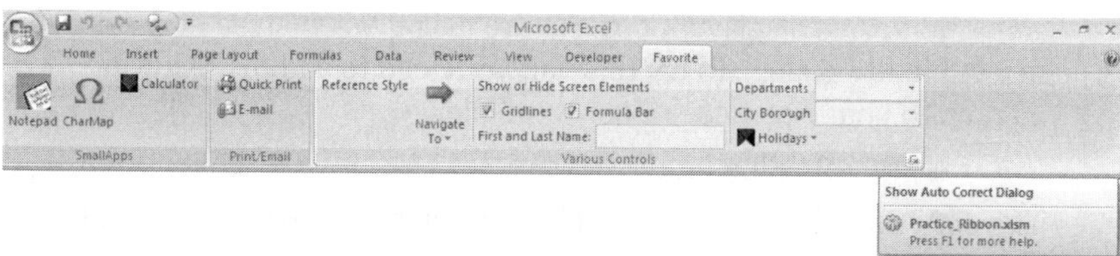

Figure 21-26: A dialog box launcher control on the Ribbon.

Disabling a Control

You can disable a built-in or custom Ribbon control by using the enabled or getEnabled attribute. Here's how we can disable our custom check box control that we created earlier:

```
<checkBox id="chkGridlines" label="Gridlines" visible="true"
getPressed="OnGetPressed" enabled="false" onAction="DoSomething" />
```

Use the getEnabled attribute to disable a control based on some conditions or simply display a "not authorized" message. The following XML code shows how to disable the built-in Name Manager button on the Ribbon's Formulas tab:

```
<!-- Built-in commands section -->
<commands>
<command idMso="NameManager" onAction="DisableNameManager" />
</commands>
```

To make your XML code more readable, you can include comments between the <!-- and --> characters. The <command> tag can be used to refer to any built-in command. This tag must appear in the <commands> section of the XML code. To see how this works, simply add the above code fragment to the XML code shown in the previous section just before the line:

```
<ribbon startFromScratch="false">
```

The onAction attribute contains the following callback procedure that will display a message when the Name Manager button is clicked:

```
Sub DisableNameManager(ctl As IRibbonControl, _
                       ByRef cancelDefault)
    MsgBox "You are not authorized to use this function."
    cancelDefault = True
End Sub
```

You can add more code to the above procedure if you need to cancel the control's default behavior only when certain conditions have been satisfied.

Repurposing a Built-in Control

It is possible to change the purpose of a built-in Ribbon button. For example, when the user clicks the Picture button on the Insert tab when Sheet1 is active you could display a Copy Picture dialog box instead of the default Insert Picture dialog. To try this out, you need to add the following XML markup to your Practice_Ribbon1.xml file:

```
<command idMso="PictureInsertFromFile" onAction="CopyPicture" />
```

The onAction attribute has the following callback procedure in a VBA module:

```
Public Sub CopyPicture(ctl As IRibbonControl, _
                ByRef cancelDefault)
    If ActiveSheet.Name = "Sheet1" Then
        ' display the CopyPicture dialog box instead
        Application.Dialogs(xlDialogCopyPicture).Show
    Else
        cancelDefault = False
    End If
End Sub
```

Only simple buttons that perform an action when clicked can be repurposed. You cannot repurpose advanced controls such as combo boxes, drop-downs, or galleries.

Refreshing the Ribbon

So far in this chapter you've seen how to use callback procedures to specify the values of control attributes at run time. But what if you need to update your custom Ribbon or the controls placed in the Ribbon based on what the user is doing in your application? The good news is that you can change the attribute values at any time by using the InvalidateControl method of the IRibbonUI object. To use this object, start by adding the onLoad attribute to the customUI element in your Ribbon customization XML:

```
<customUI xmlns="http://schemas.microsoft.com/office/2006/01/customui"
      loadImage="OnLoadImage" onLoad="RefreshMe">
```

The onLoad attribute points to the callback procedure that will give you a copy of the Ribbon that you can use to refresh anytime you want. In this example, the onLoad callback procedure name is RefreshMe. Let's say that upon entry you want the text of the edit box to appear in uppercase. To implement the onLoad callback, start by declaring a Public module-level variable of type IRibbonUI:

```
Public objRibbon As IRibbonUI
```

The above statement should appear in the declaration section at the top of the VBA module. To keep track of the state of the edit box control, declare a Private module-level variable:

```
Private strUserTxt As String
```

Next, enter the callback procedure that will store a copy of the Ribbon in the objRibbon variable:

```
'callback for the onLoad attribute of customUI
Public Sub RefreshMe(ribbon As IRibbonUI)
    Set objRibbon = ribbon
End Sub
```

When the Ribbon loads, you will have a copy of the IRibbonUI object saved for later use. Now let's take a look at the XML markup used in this scenario:

```
<editBox id="txtFullName" label="First and Last Name:"
sizeString="AAAAAAAAAAAAAAAAAA" maxLength="25"
getText="getEditBoxText" onChange="onFullNameChangeToUcase" />
```

This edit box control was introduced earlier in this chapter (see Figure 21-22). You need to modify the original XML markup for the edit box by adding the getText attribute, which points to the following callback:

```
Public Sub getEditBoxText(control As IRibbonControl, _
           ByRef text)
    text = UCase(strUserTxt)
End Sub
```

The above callback uses the VBA built-in UCase function to change the text that the user entered in the edit box to uppercase letters. When text is updated in the edit box, the procedure in the onChange attribute is called (be sure to change the procedure name in your original XML markup):

```
Public Sub onFullNameChangeToUcase(ByVal control As IRibbonControl, _
               text As String)
    If text <> "" Then
        strUserTxt = text
        objRibbon.InvalidateControl "txtFullName"
    End If
End Sub
```

The above callback begins by checking the value of the text parameter provided by the Ribbon. If this parameter contains a value other than an empty string (""), the text the user entered is stored in the strUserTxt variable. Before a change can occur in the Ribbon control, you need to mark the control as invalid. This is done by calling the InvalidateControl method of the IRibbonUI object that we have stored in the objRibbon variable:

```
objRibbon.InvalidateControl "txtFullName"
```

The above statement will tell the txtFullName control to refresh itself next time it is displayed. When the control is invalidated, it will automatically call its callback functions. The onFullNameChangeToUcase callback procedure in the onChange attribute will execute, causing the text entered in the txtFullName edit box control to appear in uppercase letters.

Note: The IRibbonUI object has only two methods: InvalidateControl and Invalidate. Use the InvalidateControl method to refresh an individual control. Use the Invalidate method to refresh all controls in the Ribbon.

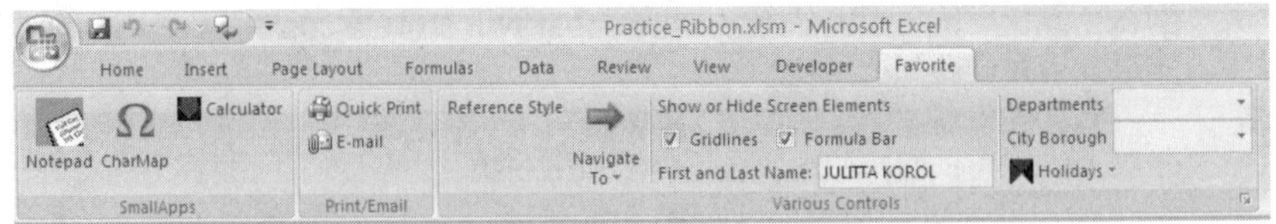

Figure 21-27: The first and last name entry now appears in uppercase letters.

The CommandBar Objects and the Ribbon

You can make your custom Ribbon button match any built-in button by using the CommandBar object. In Office 2007, this object has been extended with several get methods that expose the state information for the built-in controls: GetEnabledMso, GetImageMso, GetLabelMso, GetPressedMso, GetScreentipMso, GetSupertipMso, and GetVisibleMso. Use these methods in your callbacks to check the built-in control's properties. For example, the following statement will return False if the Ribbon's built-in Cut button is currently disabled (grayed out) or True if it is enabled (ready to use):

```
MsgBox Application.CommandBars.GetEnabledMso("Cut")
```

Notice that the GetEnabledMso method requires that you provide the name of the built-in control. To see the result of the above statement, simply type it in the Immediate window and press Enter.

The GetImageMso method is very useful if you'd like to reuse any of the built-in button images in your own controls. This method allows you to get the bitmap for any imageMso tag. For example, to retrieve the bitmap associated with the Cut button on the Ribbon, enter the following statement in the Immediate window:

```
MsgBox Application.CommandBars.GetImageMso("Cut", 16, 16)
```

The GetImageMso method above uses three arguments: the name of the built-in control, and the width and height of the bitmap image in pixels. Because this method returns the IPictureDisp object, it is very easy to place the retrieved bitmap onto your own custom Ribbon control by writing a simple VBA callback for your control's getImage attribute.

In addition to the methods that provide information about the properties of the built-in controls, the CommandBar object also includes a handy ExecuteMso method that can be used to trigger the built-in control's default action. This method is quite useful when you want to perform a click operation for the user from within a VBA procedure or want to conditionally run a built-in feature.

Let's take a look at the example implementation of the GetImageMso and ExecuteMso methods. Here's the XML definition for a custom Ribbon button:

```
<button id="btnWordWizard" label="Use Thesaurus" size="normal"
getImage="onGetBitmap" onAction="DoDefaultPlus" />
```

The above XML code can be added to the custom Ribbon definition you've worked with in this chapter. Now let's look at the VBA part. You want the button to use the same image as the built-in button labeled ResearchPane. When the button is clicked, you'd like to display the built-in Research pane set to Thesaurus only when a certain condition is true. Here is the code you need to add to your VBA module:

```
Sub onGetBitmap(ctl As IRibbonControl, ByRef image)
   Set image = Application.CommandBars. _
     GetImageMso("ResearchPane", 16, 16)
End Sub
```

When the Ribbon is loaded, the onGetBitmap callback automatically retrieves the image bitmap from the ResearchPane button's imageMso attribute and assigns it to the getImage attribute of your button. When your button is clicked and the active cell contains a text entry, the Thesaurus opens up in the Research pane; if the active cell is empty or it contains a number, the user will see a message box:

```
Sub DoDefaultPlus(ctl As IRibbonControl)
    If Not IsNumeric(ActiveCell.Value) Then
        Application.CommandBars.ExecuteMso "Thesaurus"
    Else
        MsgBox "To use Thesaurus, select a cell " & _
        "containing text.", _
        vbOKOnly + vbInformation, "Action Required"
    End If
End Sub
```

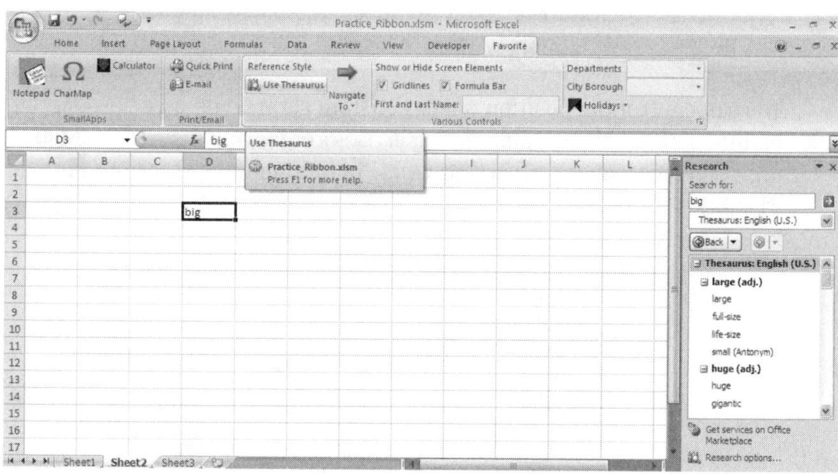

Figure 21-28: A custom button can conditionally trigger a built-in control's action.

Customizing the Microsoft Office Button Menu

While the Microsoft Office button menu cannot be removed, it can be easily customized. You can show, hide, add, or reposition any commands in the menu by preparing Ribbon customization markup. Your menu customization must appear between the <officeMenu> and </officeMenu> tags, just below <ribbon startFromScratch="false">:

```
<ribbon startFromScratch="false">
   <!-- Office Button Menu section -->
   <officeMenu>
        <control idMso="MenuPublish" visible="false" />
        <menu idMso="FileSaveAsMenu">
            <button idMso="FileSaveAsWebPage" />
        </menu>
            <button id="btnNotes1" label="Open Notepad"
            image="Note1" insertBeforeMso="FileSave"
            onAction="OpenNotepad" />
   </officeMenu>
   <!--Other Ribbon Customization section -->
</ribbon>
```

In the above XML, we hide one default command in the Microsoft Office button menu by setting the value of its visible attribute to False. We also add a new option to the FileSaveAs command:

```
<menu idMso="FileSaveAsMenu">
   <button idMso="FileSaveAsWebPage" />
</menu>
```

You can also include your own custom buttons as commands in the Microsoft Office button menu:

```
<button id="btnNotes1" label="Open Notepad"
image="Note1" insertBeforeMso="FileSave"
onAction="OpenNotepad" />
```

You can control the position of your custom commands with respect to other built-in commands by using the insertBeforeMso and insertAfterMso attributes. The customized Microsoft Office button menu is shown in Figure 21-29.

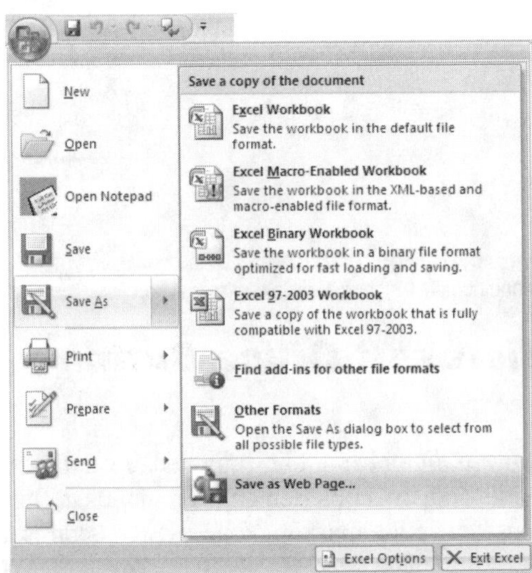

Figure 21-29: The customized Microsoft Office button menu.

Customizing the Quick Access Toolbar (QAT)

The Quick Access toolbar that appears to the right of the Microsoft Office button has been created to give application users quick access to tools they use most frequently. These tools can be easily added to the toolbar by selecting More Commands from the Customize Quick Access Toolbar drop-down menu. The QAT can only be customized in the start from scratch mode by setting the startFromScratch attribute to true in the Ribbon XML customization file:

```
<ribbon startFromScratch="true">
```

When you load a workbook that contains the above setting, Excel hides all built-in tags. In addition, all the Microsoft Office button menu commands are hidden except for New, Open, Exit, Excel Options, and the custom options that you've added to the XML Ribbon markup.

QAT modifications are specified using the <qat> element. Within this element you should use the <sharedControls> element to include controls that are shared by all open workbooks, and the <documentControls> element to specify the controls that should appear in the Quick Access toolbar when the workbook has the focus:

```
<ribbon startFromScratch="true">
  <qat>
    <sharedControls>
      <button idMso="FilePrintQuick" />
    </sharedControls>
    <documentControls>
      <button id="btnCalc2" label="Calculator"
      image="DownArrow.gif" onAction="OpenCalculator" />
    </documentControls>
  </qat>
```

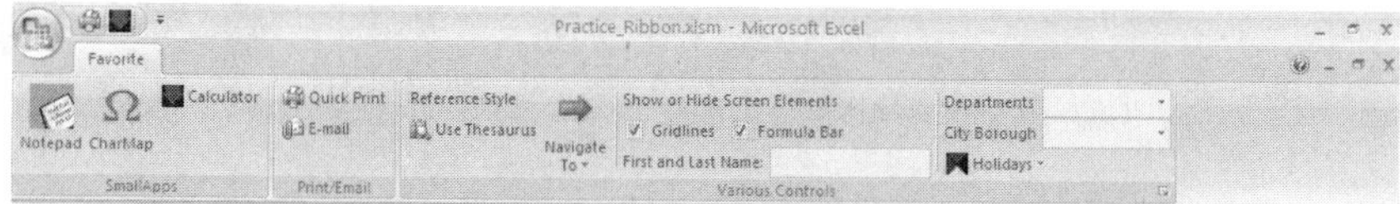

Figure 21-30: A basic UI with a custom tab and the customized Quick Access toolbar.

Chapter Summary

In this chapter, you learned how to use VBA to work with built-in shortcut menus and customize the new Ribbon interface using a combination of XML and VBA. While working with shortcut menus you learned about various properties and methods of the CommandBar object. Next, you learned how to create XML Ribbon customization markup and modify the .rels file to let Excel know about your customization. Then you learned the steps required to drop your customization file into the zip container of your macro-enabled workbook. You spent quite a bit of time in this chapter familiarizing yourself with various controls that can be added to the Ribbon and writing VBA callback procedures in order to set your controls' attributes at run time. In addition to Ribbon customizations, you learned how to modify the Microsoft Office button menu and the Quick Access toolbar. While this chapter covered many controls and features of the Ribbon, it did not attempt to cover all there is to know about this interface. The knowledge and experience you gained in this chapter can be used to make similar customizations in all of the Microsoft Office 2007 applications that use the Ribbon interface.

In the next chapter, we focus on writing VBA code that handles printing and sending emails.

Part VIII

Programming Excel Special Features

Some Excel 2007 features are used more frequently than others; some are only used by Excel power users and developers.

In this part of the book, you start by writing code that automates printing and e-mailing. Next, you gain experience in programming advanced Excel features such as PivotTables, PivotCharts, and Excel tables. You are also introduced to a number of useful Excel 2007 objects and learn how to program the Visual Basic Editor (VBE) itself.

Chapter 22

Printing and Sending E-mail from Excel

Controlling the Page Setup ■ Controlling the Settings on the Page Layout Tab ■ Controlling the Settings on the Margins Tab ■ Controlling the Settings on the Header/Footer Tab ■ Controlling the Settings on the Sheet Tab ■ Retrieving Current Values from the Page Setup Dialog Box ■ **Previewing a Worksheet** ■ **Changing the Active Printer** ■ **Printing a Worksheet** ■ **Disabling Printing and Print Previewing** ■ **Using Printing Events** ■ **Sending E-mail from Excel** ■ Sending E-mail Using the SendMail Method ■ Sending E-mail Using the MsoEnvelope Object ■ Sending Bulk E-mail from Excel via Outlook ■ **Chapter Summary**

After you set up your spreadsheet, you will want people to see it. Excel provides easy-to-use commands and buttons for printing and e-mailing your workbooks. Excel also allows programmers to control these tasks with VBA code. This chapter demonstrates how you can automate Excel's printing and e-mailing features.

Controlling the Page Setup

You can control the look of your printed worksheet pages via the Page Layout tab on the Ribbon. The Page Layout tab is divided into groups that include settings related to page setup (margins, orientation, and size), scaling, and sheet options.

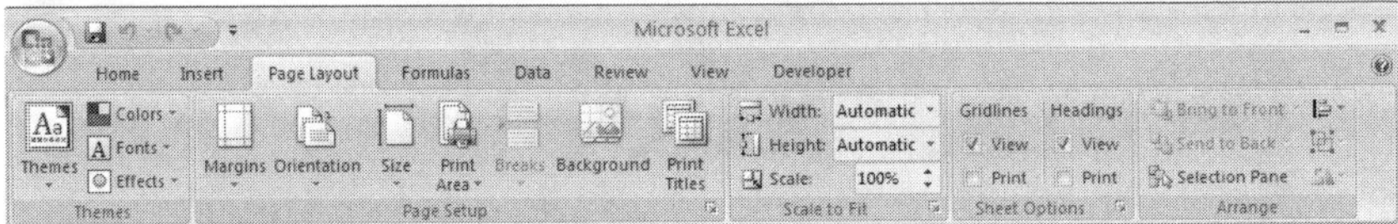

Figure 22-1: The Page Layout tab allows you to specify the page margins, orientation, paper size, and scaling and sheet options along with other settings.

You may programmatically access these settings via the Page Setup dialog box, using the properties of the PageSetup object. To display the Page Setup dialog box, type the following statement in the Immediate window and press Enter:

```
Application.Dialogs(xlDialogPageSetup).Show
```

The above statement uses the Show method of the Dialogs object to display the built-in Page Setup dialog box. You can include a list of arguments after the Show method. To set initial values in the Page Setup dialog box, use the arguments in Table 22-1.

Table 22-1: Show method arguments for the Dialogs object

Argument Number	Argument Name
Arg1	head
Arg2	foot
Arg3	left
Arg4	right
Arg5	top
Arg6	bot
Arg7	hdng
Arg8	grid
Arg9	h_cntr
Arg10	v_cntr
Arg11	orient
Arg12	paper_size
Arg13	scale

Argument Number	Argument Name
Arg14	pg_num
Arg15	pg_order
Arg16	bw_cells
Arg17	quality
Arg18	head_margin
Arg19	foot_margin
Arg20	notes
Arg21	draft

If you don't specify the initial settings, the Page Setup dialog box appears with its default settings. How should you use the above arguments? If you want to display the Page Setup dialog box with the page orientation set to landscape use the following statement:

```
Application.Dialogs(xlDialogPageSetup).Show Arg11:=2
```

Excel uses 1 for portrait and 2 for landscape orientation.

The following statement displays the Page Setup dialog box in which the Center on page Horizontally setting is selected on the Margins tab (Arg9:=1), and the Page tab has the Orientation option set to Portrait (Arg11:=1):

```
Application.Dialogs(xlDialogPageSetup).Show Arg9:=1, Arg11:=1
```

You can also set the initial values in the Page Setup dialog box by using the PageSetup object with its appropriate properties. For example, to set the page orientation as landscape, type the following statement on one line in the Immediate window and press Enter:

```
ActiveSheet.PageSetup.Orientation = 2 : Application.Dialogs
          (xlDialogPageSetup).Show
```

The following sections describe various page settings (and the corresponding properties of the PageSetup object) you may want to specify prior to printing your worksheets.

Controlling the Settings on the Page Layout Tab

The settings on the Page Layout tab (see Figure 22-1) are grouped into five main areas: Themes, Page Setup, Scale to Fit, Sheet Options, and Arrange. The Orientation settings in the Page Setup group indicate whether the page will be printed in portrait or landscape view (Orientation property). The Size setting lets you select one of the common paper sizes such as Letter, Legal, Executive, A4, and so on (PaperSize property). The Scale to Fit settings make it possible to adjust the printout according to your needs. You can reduce or enlarge the worksheet by using the Scale setting in the Scale to Fit group of the Page Layout tab. Excel can automatically scale a printout to fit a specified number of pages with the Width and Height settings.

To render this into VBA:	Use this statement:
Set Sheet1 to be printed in landscape orientation.	Worksheets("Sheet1").PageSetup.Orientation = xlLandscape
Scale Sheet1 for printing by 200%.	Worksheets("Sheet1").PageSetup.Zoom = 200
Scale the worksheet so it prints exactly one page tall and wide.	With Worksheets("Sheet1").PageSetup .FitToPagesTall = 1 .FitToPagesWide = 1 End With
Set the paper size to legal for Sheet1.	Worksheets("Sheet1").PageSetup.PaperSize = xlPaperLegal
Return current setting for the horizontal and vertical print quality.	Debug.Print "Horizontal Print Quality = " & Worksheets("Sheet1").PageSetup.PrintQuality(1) Debug.Print "Vertical Print Quality = " & Worksheets("Sheet1").PageSetup.PrintQuality(2)

Controlling the Settings on the Margins Tab

The settings available on the Margins tab of the Page Setup dialog box (shown in Figure 22-2) allow you to specify the width of the top, bottom, left, and right margins (TopMargin, BottomMargin, LeftMargin, and RightMargin properties). The Header and Footer settings allow you to determine how far you'd like the header or footer to be printed from the top or bottom of the page (HeaderMargin and FooterMargin properties). The print area can be centered on the page horizontally and vertically (CenterHorizontally and CenterVertically properties).

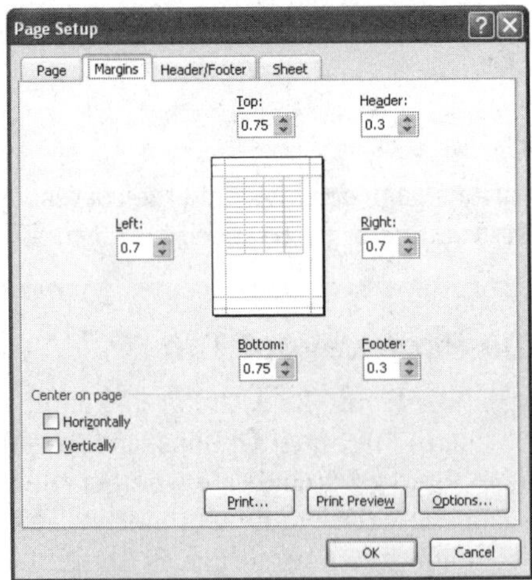

Figure 22-2: The settings on the Margins tab of the Page Setup dialog box determine the margins around the print area and the manner in which the print area should be centered on the printed page.

To render this into VBA:	Use this statement:
Set all page margins (left, right, top, and bottom) to 1.5 inches.	With Worksheets("Sheet1").PageSetup .LeftMargin = Application.InchesToPoints(1.5) .RightMargin = Application.InchesToPoints(1.5) .TopMargin = Application.InchesToPoints(1.5) .BottomMargin = Application.InchesToPoints(1.5) End With
Set header and footer margin to 0.5 inch.	With Worksheets("Sheet1").PageSetup .HeaderMargin = Application.InchesToPoints(0.5) .FooterMargin = Application.InchesToPoints(0.5) End With
Center Sheet1 horizontally when it's printed.	With Worksheets("Sheet1").PageSetup .CenterHorizontally = True .CenterVertically = False End With

Controlling the Settings on the Header/Footer Tab

The settings on the Header/Footer tab (shown in Figure 22-3) allow you to add built-in or custom headers and footers to your printed worksheets. You can use the Custom Header and Custom Footer buttons to design your own format for headers and footers.

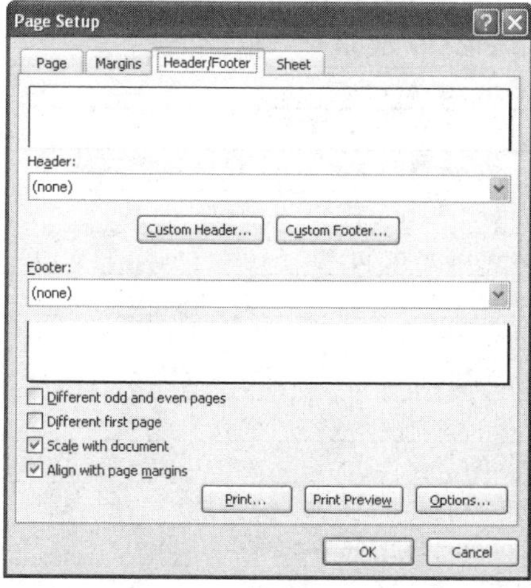

Figure 22-3: The Header/Footer tab of the Page Setup dialog box allows you to select one of the built-in headers or footers or create your own custom header and footer formats.

The PageSetup object has the following properties for setting up and controlling the creation of headers and footers: RightHeader, LeftHeader, RightFooter, LeftFooter, CenterHeader, CenterFooter, RightHeaderPicture, RightFooterPicture, LeftHeaderPicture, LeftFooterPicture, CenterHeader-Picture, and CenterFooterPicture.

In version 2007, the following new settings are available on the Header/Footer tab of the Page Setup dialog box:

- Different odd and even pages — Use the PageSetup.OddAndEvenPages-HeaderFooter property. This property returns True if the specified

PageSetup object has different headers and footers for odd-numbered and even-numbered pages.

- Different first page — Use the PageSetup.DifferentFirstPageHeaderFooter property. This property returns True if a different header or footer is used on the first page.
- Scale with document — Use the PageSetup.ScaleWithDocHeaderFooter property. This property returns true if the header and footer should use the same font size and scaling as the worksheet.
- Align with page margins — Use the PageSetup.AlignMarginsHeaderFooter property. This property returns True for Excel to align the header and the footer with the margins set in the page setup options.

Special formatting codes can be used in the header and footer text, as shown in Table 22-2.

Table 22-2: Formatting codes for headers and footers

Format Code	Description
&L	Left aligns the characters that follow.
&C	Centers the characters that follow.
&R	Right aligns the characters that follow.
&E	Turns double-underline printing on or off.
&X	Turns superscript printing on or off.
&Y	Turns subscript printing on or off.
&B	Turns bold printing on or off.
&I	Turns italic printing on or off.
&U	Turns underline printing on or off.
&S	Turns strikethrough printing on or off.
&D	Prints the current date.
&T	Prints the current time.
&F	Prints the name of the document.
&A	Prints the name of the workbook tab.
&P	Prints the page number.
&P+number	Prints the page number plus the specified number.
&P-number	Prints the page number minus the specified number.
&&	Prints a single ampersand.
& "fontname"	Prints the characters that follow in the specified font. Be sure to include the double quotation marks.
&nn	Prints the characters that follow in the specified font size. Use a two-digit number to specify a size in points.
&N	Prints the total number of pages in the document.
&G	Enables the image to show up in the header or footer.

To render this into VBA:	Use this statement:
Print the full path of the workbook in the upper-right corner of every page when Sheet1 is printed.	Worksheets("Sheet1").PageSetup.RightHeader = ActiveWorkbook.FullName
Print the date, page number, and number of pages on the left at the bottom of each page when Sheet1 is printed.	Worksheets("Sheet1").PageSetup.LeftFooter = "&D page &P of &N"
Display a watermark in the center section of the header on Sheet1.	Sub ShowWaterMark() With Worksheets("Sheet1").PageSetup.CenterHeaderPicture .Filename = "C:\Ex07_HandsOn\cd.bmp" .Height = 75 .Width = 75 .Brightness = 0.25 .ColorType = msoPictureWatermark .Contrast = 0.45 End With ' Display the picture in the center header. Worksheets("Sheet1").PageSetup.CenterHeader = "&G" End Sub

Controlling the Settings on the Sheet Tab

The settings available on the Sheet tab of the Page Setup dialog box (shown in Figure 22-4) determine what types of data you would like to include in the printout and the order in which Excel should proceed to print data ranges if the printout will span multiple pages.

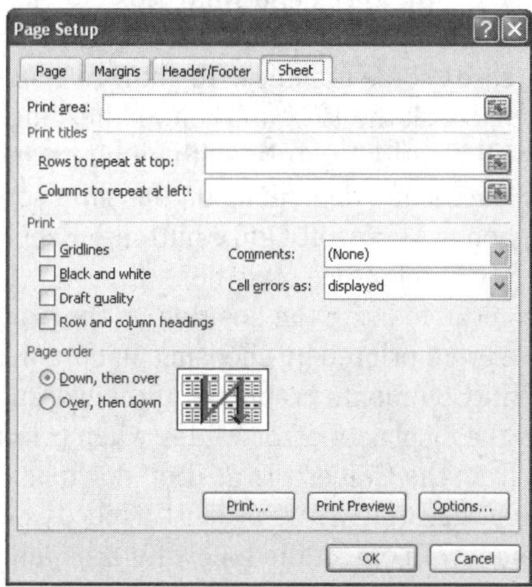

Figure 22-4: The Sheet tab of the Page Setup dialog box allows you to specify headings and ranges of data to appear on your printout and adjust the appearance of each page.

The print area is a special range that defines the cells you want to print. You can decide how much of the worksheet data you'd like to print. Excel prints the entire worksheet by default. You can print only what you actually want by defining a print area. You can specify the range address to print in the Print area setting. If you do not specify a print area, Excel will print all the data in the current worksheet. If you specify the range of cells to print in the Print area setting and then choose the Selection option in the Print dialog box, Excel will print the current selection of cells in the worksheet instead of the range of cells specified in the Print area setting of the Print Setup dialog box. Use the PrintArea property of the PageSetup object to programmatically return or set the range of cells to be printed. Setting the PrintArea property to False or to an empty string ("") will set the print area to the entire sheet.

The Print titles area on the Sheet tab allows you to specify workbook rows that should be printed at the top of every page or workbook columns that should be printed on the left side of every page. These settings are especially useful for printing very large worksheets. By default, Excel prints your row and column titles only on the first page, making it very difficult to understand data on subsequent pages. To fix this problem, you can tell Excel to print the specified row and column headings on every page. Specify the rows that contain the cells to be repeated at the top of each page in the Rows to repeat at top setting (PrintTitleRows property), and specify the columns that contain cells to be repeated on the left side of each page in the Columns to repeat at left setting (PrintTitleColumns property). You should specify both of these settings for extremely large worksheets. To turn off the title rows or title columns, set the corresponding property (PrintTitleRows or PrintTitleColumns) to False or to an empty string ("").

The Print settings control the look of your printed pages. To print the worksheet with gridlines, check the Gridlines box (PrintGridlines property). To print colors as shades of gray, select the Black and white box (BlackandWhite property). Draft quality printing will be faster since Excel does not print gridlines and suppresses some graphics. To show row and column headings on the printed pages, check the Row and column headings box (PrintHeadings property). Excel will identify the rows with numbers and worksheet columns with letters or numbers, depending on the style setting in the Excel Options dialog box (choose Microsoft Office button | Excel Options | Formulas, and see the R1C1 Reference style box). If your worksheet contains comments, you can indicate the position on the printed page where you would like to have them printed by choosing an option from the Comments drop-down box (PrintComments property). If the worksheet contains errors, you can suppress the display of error values when printing a worksheet by making a selection from the Cell errors as drop-down box (PrintErrors property). When using the PrintErrors property, specify how you would like errors to be displayed with one of the following constants: xlPrintErrorsBlank, xlPrintErrorsDash, xlPrintErrorsDisplayed, or xlPrintErrorsNA.

The settings in the Page order area of the Sheet tab allow you to specify how Excel should print and number pages when printing large spreadsheets. The default printing order is from top to bottom. You may request that this order be changed to left to right, which is a convenient way to print wide tables. Use the OrderProperty of the PageSetup object to set or return the print order. The page order can be one of the following constants: xlDownThenOver or xlOverThenDown.

To render this into VBA:	Use this statement:
Set the print area as cells A2:D10 on Sheet1.	Worksheets("Sheet1").PageSetup.PrintArea = _ "$A$2:$D$10"
Specify row 1 as the title row and columns A and B as title columns.	ActiveSheet.PageSetup.PrintTitleRows = _ ActiveSheet.Rows(1).Address ActiveSheet.PageSetup.PrintTitleColumns = _ ActiveSheet.Columns("A:B").Address
Print gridlines and column headings on Sheet1.	With Worksheets("Sheet1").PageSetup .PrintHeadings = True .PrintGridlines = True End With
Number and print worksheet starting from the first page to the pages to the right, and then move down and continue printing across the sheet.	Worksheets("Sheet1").PageSetup.Order = _ xlOverThenDown

Retrieving Current Values from the Page Setup Dialog Box

Now that you are familiar with the many settings available in the Page Setup dialog box and know the names of the corresponding properties that can be used in VBA to write code that sets up your worksheets for printing, it's time for a complete procedure. The following procedure prints some page setup settings to the Immediate window.

Hands-On 22-1: Printing Page Setup Settings to the Immediate Window

1. Open a new workbook and save it as **Practice_Excel22.xlsm.**
2. On Sheet1 of Practice_Excel22.xlsm, enter the data shown in Figure 22-5. The bonus values are calculated using the following formula: Months Employed * 3. Enter **=C2*3** in cell D2, **=C3*3** in cell D3, and so on.

Practice_Excel22.xlsm

	A	B	C	D	E
1	First Name	Last Name	Months Employed	Bonus	
2	Kevin	Blanc	10	$ 30.00	
3	Sylvia	Cohen	14	$ 42.00	
4	Martha	Pilchman	34	$102.00	
5	Robert	Almirez	27	$ 81.00	
6	Mayumi	Nagasaki	18	$ 54.00	
7	Mathew	Roder	60	$180.00	
8	Myrna	Takum	16	$ 48.00	
9					

Sheet1 Sheet2 Sheet3

Figure 22-5: Sample worksheet data.

3. Press **Alt+F11** to switch to the Visual Basic Editor. Select **VBAProject (Practice_Excel22.xlsm)** in the Project Explorer window and choose **Insert | Module.**
4. In the Module1 Code window, enter the ShowPageSettings procedure as shown below.

```
Sub ShowPageSettings()
    With ActiveSheet.PageSetup
        Debug.Print "Orientation = "; .Orientation
        Debug.Print "Paper Size = "; .PaperSize
        Debug.Print "Print Gridlines = "; .PrintGridlines
        Debug.Print "Horizontal Print Quality = "; .PrintQuality(1)
        Debug.Print "Print Area = "; .PrintArea
    End With
End Sub
```

5. Run the ShowPageSettings procedure.

   The results of the procedure are printed to the Immediate window. Because we have not changed any settings in the Page Setup dialog box, the values you see after the equal signs are the default values.
6. Modify the ShowPageSettings procedure as follows:

```
Sub ShowPageSettings()
    With ActiveSheet.PageSetup
        Debug.Print "Orientation = "; .Orientation
        Debug.Print "Paper Size = "; .PaperSize
        Debug.Print "Print Gridlines = "; .PrintGridlines
        Debug.Print "Horizontal Print Quality = "; .PrintQuality(1)
        Cells(1, 1).Select
        .PrintArea = ActiveCell.CurrentRegion.Address
        Debug.Print "Print Area = "; .PrintArea;
        .CenterHorizontally = True
        .CenterVertically = True
        .CenterHeader = "Bonus Information Sheet"
    End With
    Application.Dialogs(xlDialogPrintPreview).Show
End Sub
```

7. Run the modified ShowPageSettings procedure.

   Now, in addition to writing selected settings to the Immediate window, the test worksheet is formatted and displayed in the Print Preview window.

When printing worksheets that contain a large number of rows, it is a good idea to separately set the print titles and print area so that each page is printed with the column titles. The following procedure demonstrates this particular scenario. Notice how the CurrentRegion property of the Range collection is used together with the Offset and Resize properties to resize the print area so that it does not include the header row (Row 1). The procedure sets the header row using the PrintTitleRows property of the PageSetup object.

```
Sub FormatSheet()
    Dim curReg As Range
```

```
        Set curReg = ActiveCell.CurrentRegion

        With ActiveSheet.PageSetup
            .PrintTitleRows = "$1:$1"
            Cells(1, 1).Select

            .PrintArea = curReg.Offset(1, 0). _
                Resize(curReg.Rows.Count - 1, _
                curReg.Columns.Count).Address

            Debug.Print "Print Area = "; .PrintArea;
            .CenterHeader = "Bonus Information Sheet"
            .CenterHorizontally = False
            .CenterVertically = False
            .PrintGridlines = True
        End With
        Application.Dialogs(xlDialogPrintPreview).Show
    End Sub
```

Previewing a Worksheet

In versions of Excel prior to 2007 you needed to use the Print Preview option to examine how the selected settings such as margins, headers, and footers would look when the worksheet was printed. With the Page Layout view in Excel 2007 (View | Page Layout), users can now easily see how the worksheet will print and add headers and footers while in this view.

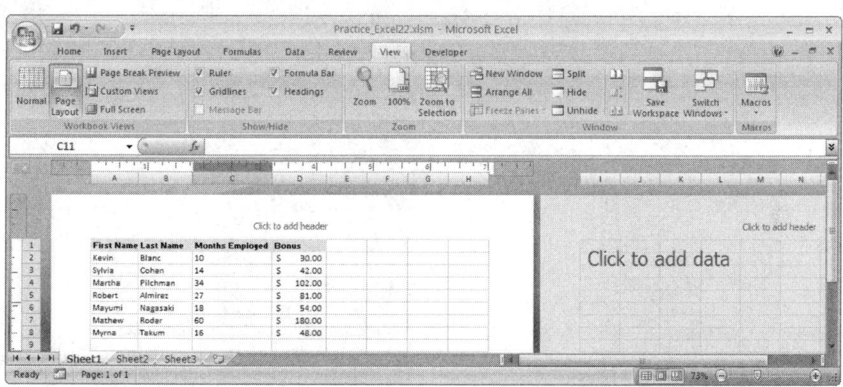

Figure 22-6: To view the worksheet as it would look when printed, choose View | Page Layout.

To add a header, simply click the area labeled "Click to add header" and type your text or simply click the appropriate buttons in the Design tab of the Header & Footer Tools on the Ribbon (Figure 22-7). For example, to add today's date, click the Current Date button. To add the footer, scroll down to the bottom of the page and click the area labeled "Click to add footer."

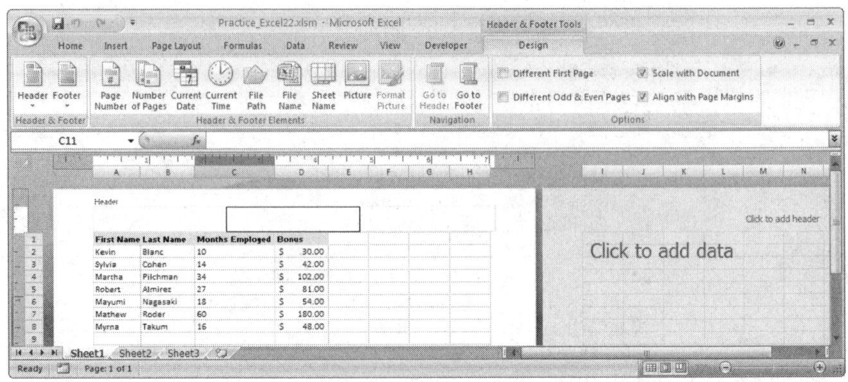

Figure 22-7: To create the header or footer, use any of the buttons contained in the Design tab of the Header & Footer Tools.

Use the following VBA statement to activate the Page Layout view:

```
ActiveWindow.View =xlPageLayoutView
```

You can also display your worksheet in the Print Preview window by typing either one of the following statements in the Immediate window or in your VBA procedure:

```
Application.Dialogs(xlDialogPrintPreview).Show
```

or

```
Worksheets("Sheet1").PrintPreview
```

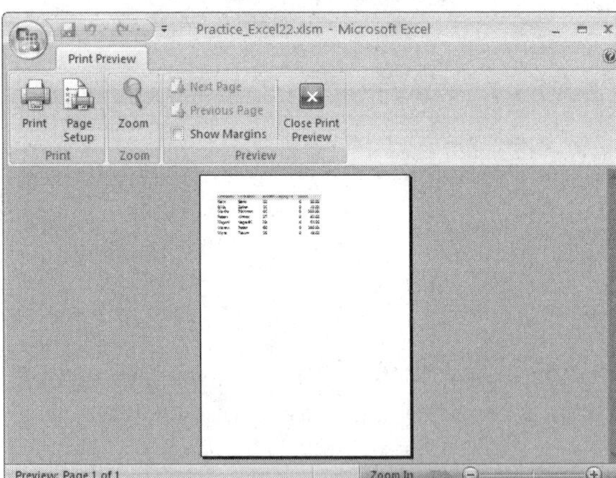

Figure 22-8: Excel's Print Preview window displays a scaled-down version of the worksheet pages.

There are buttons at the top of the Print Preview window that allow you to move between individual pages of your printout, make adjustments to the page setup and margins, get a closer look at the data or any part of the printout (Zoom button), and print your worksheet. If the worksheet has more than one page you can display other pages in the Print Preview by clicking on the Next and Previous buttons or by using the keyboard (down arrow, up arrow, End, and Home keys). You can use the Zoom button in the Print Preview window to change the Print Preview magnification, and you can adjust your page margins and column widths visually by using the mouse (to do this, select the Show Margins check box on the Preview area of the Ribbon). You can also print using the Print button and can easily access the Page Setup dialog box to make changes in the desired layout of your printout.

Sometimes you may want to prevent users from modifying the page setup or printing from the Print Preview window. This can be accomplished programmatically. You can disable the Show Margins and Page Setup buttons in the Print Preview in one of the following ways:

```
Application.Dialogs(xlDialogPrintPreview).Show False
```

or

```
Worksheets("Sheet1").PrintPreview enableChanges:=False
```

or

```
Worksheets("Sheet1").PrintPreview False
```

Changing the Active Printer

Before printing, you may want to display a list of printers for the users to select or force a print job to go to a specific printer. The Printer Setup dialog box is shown in Figure 22-9. This dialog box can be displayed with this statement:

```
Application.Dialogs(xlDialogPrinterSetup).Show
```

To find out the name of the active printer, use the ActivePrinter property of the Application object:

```
MsgBox Application.ActivePrinter
```

To change the active printer, use the following statement, replacing the printer name and port with your own:

```
Application.ActivePrinter = "Canon Pixma ip4000 on LPT1:"
```

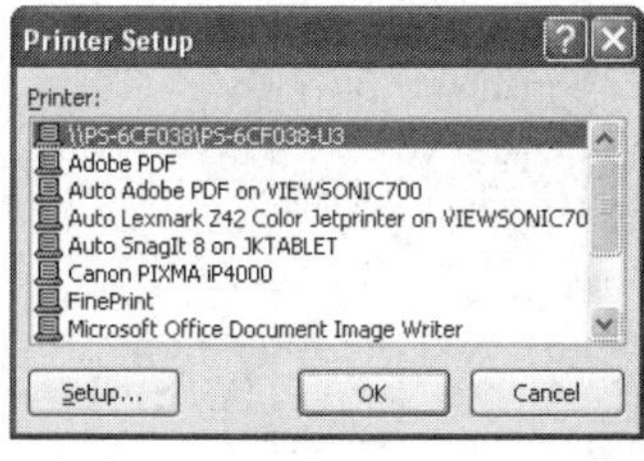

Figure 22-9: Printer Setup dialog box.

You can tell Excel to set your default printer on opening a specific workbook by writing a simple Auto_Open macro.

Hands-On 22-2: Setting a Default Printer When Opening a Specific Workbook

1. In the Practice_Excel22.xlsm workbook, switch to the Visual Basic Editor screen and choose **Insert | Module.**

2. In the module Code window, enter the Auto_Open procedure as shown below, replacing the printer name with the name of your own printer:

```
Sub Auto_Open()
    Application.ActivePrinter = "Lexmark Optra M412 (MS) on Ne05:"
    MsgBox Application.ActivePrinter
End Sub
```

Note: The printer needs to be connected for this code to execute.

3. Save the Practice_Excel22.xlsm workbook and close it. Do not exit Excel.
4. Reopen the **Practice_Excel22.xlsm** workbook.

   Excel will run the Auto_Open macro and display the active printer name in the message box.

Printing a Worksheet

If prior to printing you need to set print options such as print ranges, collation, or the number of copies to print, click the Microsoft Office button and choose Print to display the Print dialog box, shown in Figure 22-10. If you want to print your worksheet immediately to the default printer without going through the Print dialog box, click the Quick Print button.

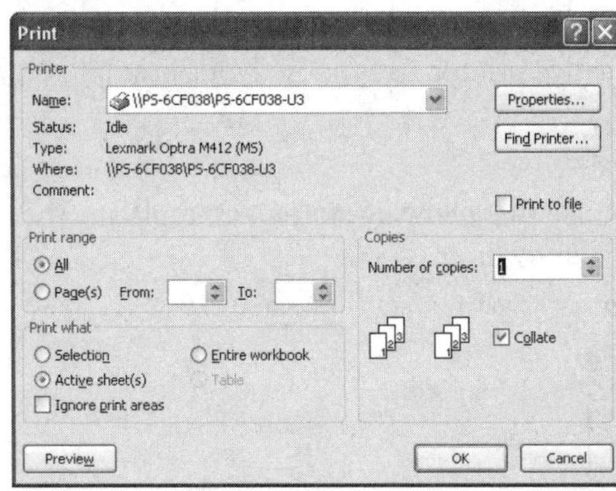

Figure 22-10: The Print dialog box allows you to specify the print options.

To display the Print dialog box programmatically, use the following statement:

```
Application.Dialogs(xlDialogPrint).Show
```

You can include a list of arguments after the Show method. To set initial values in the Print dialog box, use the arguments shown in Table 22-3.

Table 22-3: Show method arguments for the Print dialog

Argument Number	Argument Description
Arg1	range_num
Arg2	from

Argument Number	Argument Description
Arg3	to
Arg4	copies
Arg5	draft
Arg6	preview
Arg7	print_what
Arg8	color
Arg9	feed
Arg10	quality
Arg11	y_resolution
Arg12	selection
Arg13	printer_text
Arg14	print_to_file
Arg15	collate

For example, the following statement will print pages 1 to 2 of the active worksheet (assuming that the worksheet consists of two or more pages):

```
Application.Dialogs(xlDialogPrint).Show Arg1:=2, Arg2:=1, Arg3:=2
```

The first argument specifies the Page(s) option button in the Print range area of the Print dialog box. To select the All option button in the Print range area, set Arg1 to 1.

The second and third arguments specify the pages you want to print (the beginning page number and the last page number to print should be specified).

To send your worksheet directly to the printer (without going through the Print dialog box), use the following statement:

```
ActiveSheet.PrintOut
```

The PrintOut method can take the following arguments:

Table 22-4: PrintOut method arguments

Argument Name	Argument Description
From	The number of the first page to print. If omitted, printing will start from the first page.
To	The number of the last page to print. If omitted, printing will end with the last page.
Copies	The number of copies to print. If omitted, one copy will be printed.
Preview	If set to True, Excel will display the Print Preview window before printing. If omitted or set to False, printing will begin immediately.
ActivePrinter	Sets the name of the active printer.
PrintToFile	If True, the worksheet is printed to a file. This is convenient when you want to print a worksheet on an off-site printer such as a PostScript printer. You should supply the filename in the PrToFileName argument.

Argument Name	Argument Description
Collate	Set this argument to True to collate multiple copies.
PrToFileName	Specifies the name of the file you want to print to if the PrintToFile argument is set to True.

Disabling Printing and Print Previewing

At times you may not want your users to print or print preview the worksheet. In Excel 2007 you can remove these features by customizing the Office Button menu (see Chapter 21). Another way to disable printing and print previewing is by writing the Workbook_BeforePrint event procedure, as demonstrated in the next section.

Using Printing Events

Before the workbook is printed (and before the Print dialog appears), Excel triggers the Workbook_BeforePrint event. You can use this event to perform certain formatting or calculating tasks prior to printing or to cancel printing and print previewing entirely when these features are requested via the menu options or toolbar buttons. The code for the Workbook_BeforePrint event procedure must be placed in the ThisWorkbook Code window (Figure 22-11).

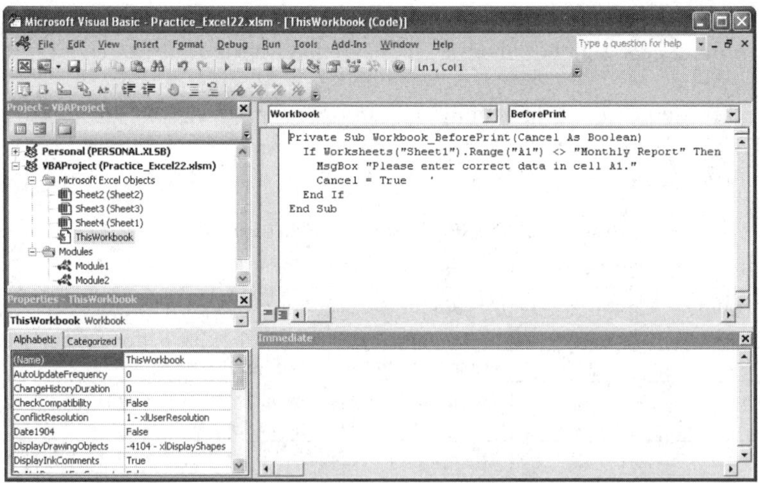

Figure 22-11: Writing the Workbook_BeforePrint event procedure in the ThisWorkbook Code window.

The ThisWorkbook Code window can be accessed by double-clicking the appropriate workbook name in the Project Explorer window of the Visual Basic Editor screen and double-clicking the ThisWorkbook object. Next, at the top of the ThisWorkbook Code window, select Workbook from the drop-down Object list on the left. The Procedure drop-down list on the right will display the names of the events that the Workbook object can respond to. Select the BeforePrint event name and Excel will place the skeleton of this procedure in the Code window. Type your VBA code between the Sub and End Sub lines. The next time you print, Excel will run your code first and then proceed to print the worksheet. The Workbook_BeforePrint event code is triggered whether you have requested printing via Excel's built-in tools or have written your own VBA procedure to control printing.

The following tasks can be performed via the VBA code placed in the Workbook_BeforePrint event procedure:

- Disabling printing and print previewing.

```
Private Sub Workbook_BeforePrint(Cancel As Boolean)
   If Weekday(Date, vbSunday) = 7 Then Cancel = True
End Sub
```

  When you set the Cancel argument to True, the worksheet isn't printed when the procedure ends. The above procedure disallows printing on Saturdays (the seventh day of the week). The Weekday function specifies that Sunday is the first day of the week.

- Placing the full workbook's name in the page footer (see the procedure in Hands-On 17-14 in Chapter 17).
- Changing worksheet formatting prior to printing.
- Validating data upon printing.

```
Private Sub Workbook_BeforePrint(Cancel As Boolean)
  If Worksheets("Sheet1").Range("A1") <> "Monthly Report" Then
    MsgBox "Please enter correct data in cell A1."
    Cancel = True
  End If
End Sub
```

- Calculating all worksheets in the active workbook.

```
Private Sub Workbook_BeforePrint(Cancel As Boolean)
    Dim sh as Variant
    For Each sh in Worksheets
        sh.Calculate
    Next
End Sub
```

If you need to perform certain formatting tasks for all your workbooks prior to printing, you need to create the WorkbookBeforePrint event procedure for the Application object. You've already worked with Excel's application-level events in Chapter 17. The following example demonstrates how to have Excel automatically print in the footer the full path and filename of all existing and new workbooks. This technique requires that you understand the use of the Personal.xlsb workbook, class modules, and the WithEvents keyword (see Chapters 1, 9, and 17).

Hands-On 22-3: Automatically Adding a Footer to Each Workbook

1. Switch to the Visual Basic Editor screen. In the Project Explorer window, click the plus sign (+) next to Personal (Personal.xlsb).

   Recall that the Personal macro workbook loads automatically in the background each time you start Excel. This file is located in one of the following folders:

   ```
   C:\Documents and Settings\username\Application Data\Microsoft\Excel\
   XLStart
   ```

   or

   ```
   C:\Program Files\Microsoft Office\Office12\XLStart
   ```

2. Choose **Insert | Class Module**.

   Excel inserts a module named Class1 in the Class Modules folder in the Personal (Personal.xlsb) workbook.

3. In the Properties window, rename Class1 **clsFooter**.
4. Enter the following declaration line and event procedure code in the clsFooter Code window:

   ```
   Public WithEvents objApp As Application

   Private Sub objApp_WorkbookBeforePrint(ByVal Wb As Workbook, Cancel As
   Boolean)
       With Wb.ActiveSheet
           .PageSetup.RightFooter = Wb.FullName
       End With
   End Sub
   ```

   Recall from Chapter 17 that the WithEvents keyword is used in a class module to declare an object variable that points to the Application object. In this procedure, objApp is the variable name for the Application object. The Public statement before the WithEvents keyword allows the objApp variable to be accessed by all modules in the VBA project.

   Once you've declared the object variable, you can select objApp in the Object drop-down list in the clsFooter module's Code window, and select the WorkbookBeforePrint event in the Procedure drop-down list in the top-right corner of the Code window. When you start writing your event procedures using this technique (by choosing options from the Object and Procedure drop-down lists), Excel always inserts the procedure skeleton (the start and end of the procedure) in the Code window. This way you can be sure that you always start with the correct procedure structure and the definition of the parameters that the particular event can utilize. All that's left to do is write some VBA code to specify tasks that should be performed. The above procedure simply tells Excel to place the full path and filename in the right footer of the workbook's active sheet.

   After writing the event procedure code in the class module, we need to write some code in the ThisWorkbook class module.

5. In the Project Explorer window, double-click the **ThisWorkbook** object located in the Microsoft Excel object folder under the Personal (Personal.xlsb) project.
6. Type the following declaration and event code in the ThisWorkbook Code window:

```
Dim clsFullPath As New clsFooter

Private Sub Workbook_Open()
    Set clsFullPath.objApp = Application
End Sub
```

   The first line above declares a variable named clsFullPath, which points to the object (objApp) in the clsFooter class module. The New keyword indicates that a new instance of the object should be created the first time the object is referenced. We do this in the Workbook_Open event procedure by using the Set keyword. This statement connects the object located in the clsFooter class module with the object variable objApp representing the Application object.

   The code placed in the Workbook_Open event procedure is run whenever a workbook is opened. Therefore, when a workbook (an existing one or a new one) is opened, Excel will know that it must listen to the Application events; in particular it must track events for the objApp object and execute the code of the WorkbookBeforePrint event procedure when a request for print or print preview is made through the Excel user interface or via the VBA code that is placed inside a custom printing procedure.

   Before Excel can perform the programmed tasks, you must save the changes to the Personal.xlsb file and exit Excel.

7. Choose **Debug | Compile Personal** to ensure that Excel will be able to execute the VBA code you've added to the Personal.xlsb macro workbook. If Excel finds any errors, it will highlight the statement that you need to examine. Make any appropriate corrections and repeat the Debug | Compile Personal command. When there are no errors in the Personal.xls project, the Compile Personal command on the Debug menu is grayed out.
8. Close the Practice_Excel22.xlsm workbook file and any other workbooks that you may have opened.
9. Exit Microsoft Excel. When Excel asks whether you'd like to save changes to the Personal.xlsb file, click **Yes**.
10. Restart Microsoft Excel. Open a new workbook and type anything in any cell on any sheet of this new workbook, then save the file as **TestFooter.xlsx**.
11. Click the **Microsoft Office** button and choose **Print | Print Preview**. Notice that Excel automatically displays the path and filename in the right footer. Close the Print Preview window and TestFooter.xlsx workbook.

12. Open any existing workbook that did not have footers set up. Choose **File | Print Preview**. Notice that a complete filename appears in the right footer.
13. Close the TestFooter.xlsx workbook and any other workbook you have opened.

Note: You can modify the WorkbookBeforePrint event procedure to automatically perform other tasks as needed prior to printing. Save yourself time by delegating as many tasks as possible to Excel.

Sending E-mail from Excel

You can share your Excel workbooks with others by e-mailing them. To send e-mail from Excel you need one of the following programs:

- Microsoft Outlook
- Microsoft Outlook Express
- Microsoft Exchange Client
- Any MAPI-compatible e-mail program (MAPI stands for Messaging Application Programming Interface)

Excel workbooks can be sent as attachments or embedded in the body of a message. The latter is convenient when you want your recipient to view only a range of data or a chart and not the entire workbook. Embedding your data can keep your e-mails smaller. When you send an e-mail with a workbook attachment, the file is larger but the recipient can open and edit the workbook in Excel. It is recommended that you attach workbooks when sending e-mail to recipients using Microsoft Office 97 or earlier. When you send data in the body of a message, the recipients may have trouble understanding the data as the worksheet formatting is lost.

Excel offers the Send command in the Microsoft Office button menu, as shown in Figure 22-12.

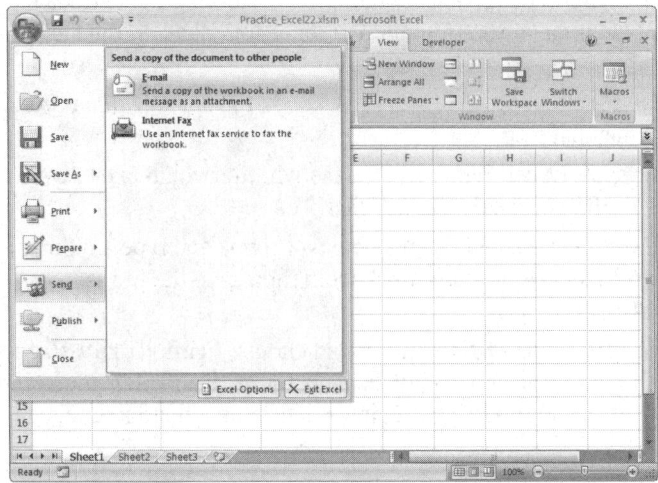

Figure 22-12: Send options allow you to send e-mails from Excel.

When you select the E-mail option, Excel displays an e-mail message window as shown in Figure 22-13.

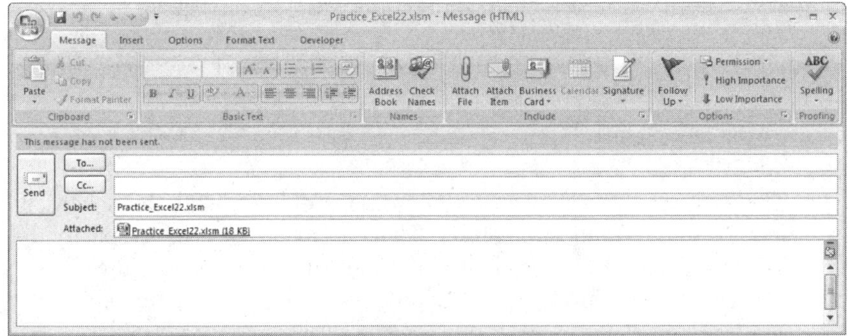

Figure 22-13: Sending a workbook as an e-mail attachment from Excel.

You can invoke the e-mail message window programmatically with the following statement:

```
Application.Dialogs(xlDialogSendMail).Show
```

You can include the arguments shown in Table 22-5 after the Show method.

Table 22-5: Show method arguments for the e-mail message window

Argument Number	Argument Description
Arg1	recipients
Arg2	subject
Arg3	return_receipt

For example, the following statement displays the e-mail message window with the recipient's e-mail address filled in and the specified text in the subject line:

```
Application.Dialogs(xlDialogSendMail).Show
Arg1:="YourName@YourProvider.com", Arg2:="New workbook file"
```

To check out the above statement, you can type the text on one line in the Immediate window and press Enter, or you can place it inside a VBA procedure.

Sending E-mail Using the SendMail Method

Before you begin sending e-mails from your VBA procedures, it's a good idea to determine what e-mail system is installed on your computer. You can do this with the MailSystem property of the Application object. This is a read-only property that uses the xlMAPI, xlPowerTalk, and xlNoMailSystem constants to determine the installed mail system. MAPI stands for Messaging Application Programming Interface and is used for interfacing with e-mail systems. PowerTalk is a Macintosh e-mail system.

The Discover_EmailSystem procedure below demonstrates how to use the MailSystem property.

```
Sub Discover_EmailSystem()
    Select Case Application.MailSystem
        Case xlMAPI
            MsgBox "You have Microsoft Mail installed."
        Case xlNoMailSystem
            MsgBox "No mail system installed on this computer."
        Case xlPowerTalk
            MsgBox "Your mail system is PowerTalk"
    End Select
End Sub
```

The easiest way to send an e-mail from Excel is by using the SendMail method of the Application object. This method allows you to specify the e-mail address of the recipient, the subject of your e-mail, and whether you'd like a return receipt. Let's create an e-mail and send it to ourselves.

Hands-On 22-4: Using the SendMail Method to Send E-mail

1. Open the **Practice_Excel22.xlsm** workbook, switch to the Visual Basic Editor screen, and insert a new module in VBAProject (Practice_Excel22.xlsm).
2. In the module's Code window, enter the following procedure:

```
Sub SendMailNow()
    Dim strEAddress As String

    On Error GoTo ErrorHandler

    strEAddress = InputBox("Enter e-mail address", _
                "Recipient's E-mail Address ")

    If IsNull(Application.MailSession) Then
        Application.MailLogon
    End If

    ActiveWorkbook.SendMail Recipients:=strEAddress, Subject:="Test Mail"

    Application.MailLogoff
    Exit Sub

ErrorHandler:
    MsgBox "Some error occurred while sending e-mail."
End Sub
```

   If Microsoft Mail isn't already running, you must use the MailSession property of the Application object to establish a mail session in Excel before sending e-mails. The MailSession property returns the MAPI mail session number as a hexadecimal string or Null if the mail session hasn't been established yet. The MailSession property isn't used on PowerTalk mail systems. To establish a mail session, use the MailLogon method of the Application object. To close a MAPI e-mail session established by Microsoft Excel, use the MailLogoff method.

3. Run the SendMailNow procedure to e-mail the active workbook. Type your e-mail address when prompted and click **OK**.

When you see the message shown in Figure 22-14, click the **Allow** button to allow sending the e-mail.

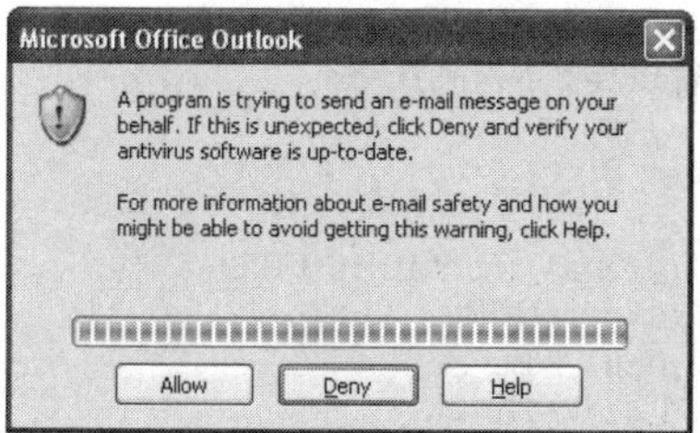

Figure 22-14: Microsoft Office Outlook displays a warning message when you try to send e-mail from Excel.

4. Open your e-mail program and check the received mail.

When the recipient receives an e-mail with an attached workbook, he or she will need Excel 97 or later to open the file. To view Excel data embedded in the body of a message, all that's needed is a web browser or an e-mail program such as Microsoft Outlook.

Sending E-mail Using the MsoEnvelope Object

You can send e-mails directly from Microsoft Excel and other Microsoft Office applications via the MsoEnvelope object, which is included with the Microsoft Office 12.0 object library. To return an MsoEnvelope object, use the MailEnvelope property of the Worksheet object. You also need to set up a reference to the MailItem object in the Microsoft Outlook 12.0 object library to access its properties and methods that format the e-mail message. The following procedure demonstrates sending e-mail from Excel using the MsoEnvelope object. Instead of attaching the entire workbook, we will only embed the data shown in Sheet1 (see Figure 22-5 earlier in this chapter).

Hands-On 22-5: Sending E-mail Using the MsoEnvelope Object

1. Activate Sheet1 in the Practice_Excel22.xlsm workbook file. This sheet contains the data shown earlier in Figure 22-5.
2. Press **Alt+F11** to switch to the Visual Basic Editor screen.
3. Set up a reference to the Microsoft Outlook 12.0 and Microsoft Office 12.0 object libraries using the **Tools | References** dialog box.
4. In the Visual Basic Editor screen, insert a new module in VBAProject (Practice_Excel22.xlsm).
5. In the module's Code window, enter the following procedure:

```
Sub SendMsoMail(ByVal strRecipient As String)
    Dim objMailItem As MailItem

    ' use MailEnvelope property of the worksheet to return the
    ' msoEnvelope object
    With ActiveSheet.MailEnvelope

    ' Add introductory text at the top of the e-mail
```

```
        .Introduction = "Please see the list of employees " & _
                     "who are to receive a bonus."

          ' Set up a reference to the MailItem to access
          ' Outlook MailItem properties and methods
            Set objMailItem = .Item
            ' Set up the Mailtem
            With objMailItem
                ' Make sure the e-mail format is HTML
                .BodyFormat = olFormatHTML
                ' Add the recipient name
                .Recipients.Add strRecipient
                ' Add the subject
                .Subject = "Employee Bonuses"
                ' Send Mail
                .Send
            End With
      End With
End Sub
```

6. Run the SendMsoMail procedure by typing the following statement in the Immediate window (be sure to replace the e-mail address with your own):

   ```
   SendMsoMail("YourName@YourProvider.com")
   ```

   When you press **Enter**, Excel calls the SendMsoMail procedure, passing to it the recipient's e-mail address.

Sending Bulk E-mail from Excel via Outlook

At times you may need to send individualized e-mail messages to people whose e-mail addresses and the information you want to send have been entered in a worksheet. The following procedure demonstrates how to process this kind of request from Excel via objects, properties, and methods provided by the Microsoft Outlook 12.0 object library.

Hands-On 22-6: Sending Bulk E-mail from Excel

1. Prepare the worksheet as shown in Figure 22-15. Enter the valid e-mail addresses of your own contacts in Column D.

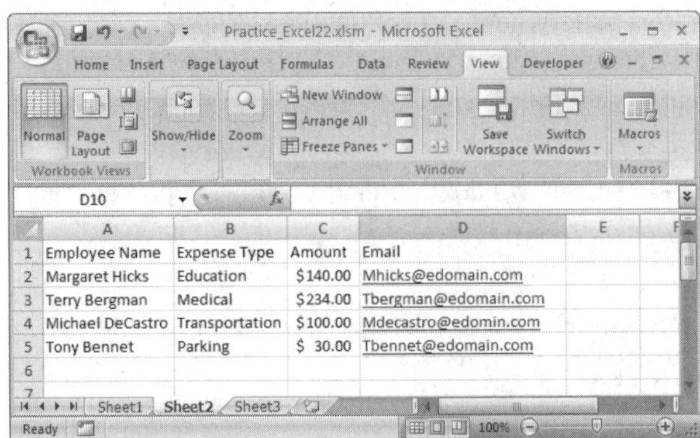

Figure 22-15: Sample worksheet for bulk e-mailing demo.

2. Switch to the Visual Basic Editor screen and choose **Tools | References**. Ensure that there is a checkmark next to **Microsoft Outlook 12.0 Object Library**. If the library is not yet selected, click the box next to its name. Click **OK** to close the References dialog box.
3. Choose **Insert | Module** to add a new module to VBAProject (Practice_Excel22.xlsm).
4. In the module Code window, enter the code of the SendBulkMail procedure as shown below:

```
Sub SendBulkMail(EmailCol, BeginRow, EndRow, SubjCol, AmountCol)
    Dim objOut As Outlook.Application
    Dim objMail As Outlook.MailItem
    Dim strEmail As String
    Dim strSubject As String
    Dim strBody As String
    Dim r As Integer

    On Error Resume Next

    Application.DisplayAlerts = False

    Set objOut = New Outlook.Application

    For r = BeginRow To EndRow
        Set objMail = objOut.CreateItem(olMailItem)
        strEmail = Cells(r, EmailCol)
        strSubject = Cells(r, SubjCol) & " reimbursement"

        strBody = "We have approved your request for " & _
                   LCase(strSubject)
        strBody = strBody & " in the amount of " & Cells(r, _
                   AmountCol).Text & "."
        strBody = strBody & vbCrLf & "Please allow 3 business " & _
                    "days for this"
        strBody = strBody & " amount to appear on your bank statement."
        strBody = strBody & vbCrLf & vbCrLf & " Employee Services"

        With objMail
            .To = strEmail
            .Body = strBody
            .Subject = strSubject
            .Send
        End With
    Next
    Set objOut = Nothing
    Application.DisplayAlerts = True
End Sub
```

The above procedure requires the following parameters: EmailCol, BeginRow, EndRow, SubjCol, and AmountCol. The EmailCol parameter is the number of the column on the worksheet where the e-mail address has been entered. In this example, it's the fourth column. The BeginRow and EndRow parameters specify the first and last rows of your data range. In this example, the first row we want to process is 2 and the last row is 5. SubjCol is the column number where the e-mail subject is entered. In this example, it's the second column (Expense Type). AmountCol is the column number where the expense amount has been entered. In this example, it's the third column.

The statement Application.DisplayAlerts = False will cause Excel to stop displaying alert messages; however, this will not prevent Outlook's messages from appearing. Prior to specifying the details of the e-mail, we must set up a reference to the Outlook application with the following statement:

```
Set objOut = New Outlook.Application
```

Next, we need to get data for each person to whom we need to send e-mail. The procedure uses the For…Next loop to iterate through the worksheet data starting at row 2 and ending at row 5. Each time in the loop we set a reference to an Outlook MailItem and place the data we need for our e-mail message in various variables. Once the procedure knows where the data is in the worksheet, we can go ahead and set the required properties of Microsoft Outlook:

```
With objMail
    .To = strEmail
    .Body = strBody
    .Subject = strSubject
    .Send
End With
```

The To property returns or sets a semicolon-delimited string list of display names for the To recipients for the Outlook item. In this example we use one recipient for each e-mail we send. The Body property returns or sets a string representing the text message we want to send in the e-mail. The Subject property is used to specify the e-mail subject. Finally, the Send method sends the e-mail message.

5. Enter the Call_SendBulkMail procedure in the same module where you entered the code of the SendBulkMail procedure:

```
Sub Call_SendBulkMail()

    SendBulkMail EmailCol:=4, _
        BeginRow:=2, _
        EndRow:=5, _
        SubjCol:=2, _
        AmountCol:=3
End Sub
```

The above procedure calls the SendBulkMail procedure and passes it the parameters indicating the column number of the recipient's address (4), the beginning and ending rows of the data (2, 5), the column where the e-mail subject is located (2), and the column number with the amount of reimbursement (3).

6. Run the Call_SendBulkMail procedure.

Excel VBA begins to execute the specified procedure. Your first recipient listed in the worksheet should receive an e-mail similar to the one shown in Figure 22-16.

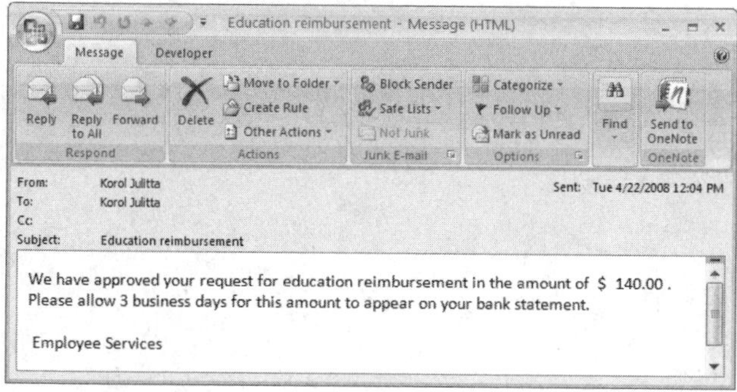

Figure 22-16: Sample e-mail message viewed in Microsoft Outlook.

Chapter Summary

This chapter has shown you how to print and use various e-mailing techniques for the presentation and distribution of Excel workbooks. You learned how to programmatically set page and print options, set up printers, and use printing events to perform formatting or data calculation tasks prior to printing.

You also practiced various methods of sending your workbooks through electronic e-mail as attachments or embedded as the body of a message.

In the next chapter, you will learn how to program two Microsoft Excel objects that are used for data analysis: PivotTable and PivotChart.

Chapter 23

Programming PivotTables and PivotCharts

Introduced in Excel 5, PivotTables continue to serve millions of Microsoft Office applications users as powerful tools for organizing and presenting information from various sources. If you are not familiar with this feature, now is the time to get your feet wet. Using PivotTables and PivotCharts, you can analyze your data from multiple perspectives. PivotTables make it possible to drag headings around a table to rearrange them so that your data is displayed dynamically any way you (or your users) want it. Similar to PivotTables, PivotCharts are interactive and allow you to view data in different ways by changing the position or detail of the PivotChart fields. Both PivotTables and PivotCharts allow you to focus on understanding your data rather than on organizing it.

Creating a PivotTable Report

Before you can create a PivotTable, you need to prepare the data. You can get the data from one of the following sources:

- A range on an Excel worksheet (you can type in your data or paste it from other sources)
- An external data source (you can connect to a Microsoft Access file or an SQL Server database and get data directly)

Figure 23-1 displays the data that was dumped into a Microsoft Excel worksheet from an SQL Server database. The downloadable workbook file is named EquipmentList.xlsx. This file contains approximately 1,500 rows of data that would be difficult to summarize if it weren't for the built-in Excel PivotTable feature.

EquipmentList.xlsx

	A	B	C	D	E	F	G	H
1	Vendor	Equipment Type	Equipment Id	WarrExpDate	WarrYears	WarrParts	Warranty Type	Total Units
2	Expert Installers	Laptop	102	7/26/2004	3	2	Parts & Labor	1
3	Expert Installers	Laptop	102	8/31/2004	3	2	Parts & Labor	1
4	ABC Hardware	MiniTower Monitor	4	7/21/2001	3	2	Non-Warranty	1
5	ABC Hardware	MiniTower Monitor	4	7/22/2001	3	2	Non-Warranty	1
6	ABC Hardware	MiniTower Monitor	4	7/23/2001	3	2	Non-Warranty	1
7	ABC Hardware	MiniTower Monitor	4	7/29/2001	3	2	Non-Warranty	1
8	ABC Hardware	MiniTower Monitor	4	7/30/2001	3	2	Non-Warranty	1
9	ABC Hardware	MiniTower Monitor	4	8/17/2001	3	2	Non-Warranty	1
10	ABC Hardware	MiniTower Monitor	4	8/27/2001	3	2	Non-Warranty	1
11	ABC Hardware	MiniTower Monitor	4	9/17/2001	3	2	Non-Warranty	1
12	ABC Hardware	MiniTower Monitor	4	9/18/2001	3	2	Non-Warranty	1
13	ABC Hardware	MiniTower Monitor	4	10/9/2001	3	2	Non-Warranty	1
14	ABC Hardware	Monitor	79	11/1/1991	3	2	Non-Warranty	1
15	ABC Hardware	Monitor	86	2/22/2002	3	2	Non-Warranty	1
16	ABC Hardware	Monitor	94	2/1/2002	3	2	Non-Warranty	1
17	Expert Installers	Monitor	5	5/8/2004	3	2	Parts & Labor	1
18	Expert Installers	Monitor	5	5/9/2004	3	2	Parts & Labor	1
19	Expert Installers	Monitor	5	5/10/2004	3	2	Parts & Labor	1
20	Expert Installers	Monitor	5	5/14/2004	3	2	Parts & Labor	1

Source Data / Sheet2 / Sheet3

Figure 23-1: Source data for the PivotTable.

Let's start our encounter with PivotTables by using built-in Ribbon commands.

Hands-On 23-1: Creating a PivotTable

1. Copy the **C:\Ex07_HandsOn\EquipmentList.xlsx** workbook to your **Ex07_ByExample** folder, and then open the copied file in Microsoft Excel.
2. Select any cell anywhere in the data range. For example, select cell A2 in the source data worksheet.
3. Choose **Insert | PivotTable | PivotTable.**

   The Create PivotTable dialog box appears, as shown in Figure 23-2.

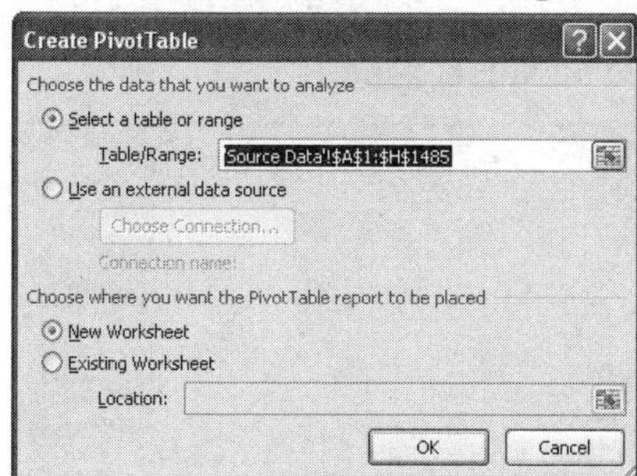

Figure 23-2: Create PivotTable dialog box.

   Notice that there are two sections in the Create PivotTable dialog box. In the top section, you need to choose the data source for your report. This can be a table or range within a Microsoft Excel worksheet or data accessed from an external data source. The bottom section of the Create PivotTable dialog box lets you choose between placing the PivotTable report in the current worksheet or a new worksheet.

4. Make sure the **Select a table or range** and **New Worksheet** option buttons are selected.

   Ensure that the range displayed in the Table/Range box incorporates all the data on which you want to report. The range will appear automatically if the active cell is within the data range. If the currently selected cell is outside of the data range, you will need to make your own selection.

5. Click **OK.**

   A blank PivotTable report is inserted in a new sheet and the PivotTable Field List pane is displayed, as shown in Figure 23-3.

Figure 23-3: The PivotTable report waits for you to make field selections.

The PivotTable user interface has been redesigned in Excel 2007 to make it easier to work with the data. Notice that all the fields are listed in the PivotTable Field List pane to the right of the worksheet. Each field has a check box so you can easily indicate which fields to include in the report. The report is built as you make field selections. For example, when you check the box next to Vendor, you will notice that the Vendor field is automatically added to the Row Labels box at the bottom of the PivotTable Field List pane and the PivotTable updates to show your selection. By default, text fields are placed in the Row Labels list and numeric fields appear in the Values list (see Figure 23-4). You can easily adjust the position of the fields by dragging them between areas in the PivotTable Field List pane.

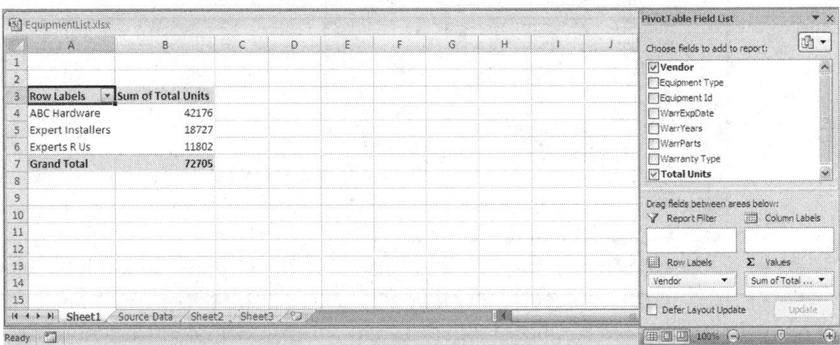

Figure 23-4: Adding Vendor and Total Units fields to the PivotTable

You can change the view of the PivotTable Field List pane by clicking on the button at the top of the pane.

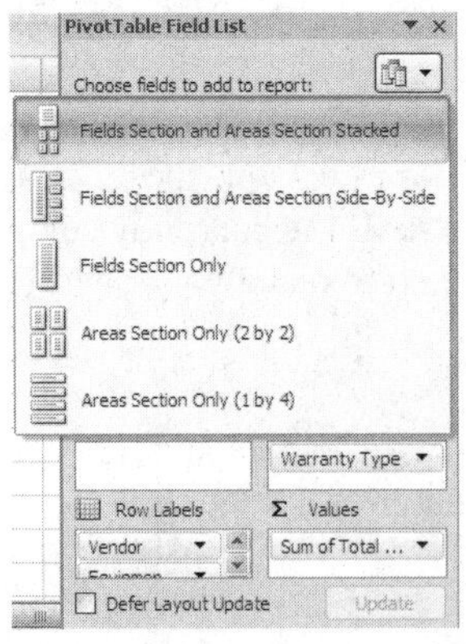

Figure 23-5: You can choose what sections should appear in the PivotTable Field List pane.

At the bottom of the PivotTable Field List pane there are four areas where you can place the fields:

- The **Row Labels** area should contain the fields that you want to display your data "by." For example, if you want to produce the report by vendor, drag the Vendor field onto the Row Labels area. The Row Labels area can contain more than one field. In the example report that you will create, we also want to see the report by equipment type, so the Equipment Type field will be placed in the Row Labels area as well. If you position the Equipment Type field below the Vendor field in the Row Labels area, the data will be grouped first by vendor and then by equipment type within those vendors. Fields listed in the Row Labels area can be moved into desired position by dragging.

- The **Column Labels** area should contain fields that answer the question "what." For example, What type of information do you want to display for each of the fields in the Row Labels area? Our example PivotTable will report on the warranty type. Because we want to see all types of warranties for each vendor and equipment type, we will place the Warranty Type field in the Column Labels area. However, if you want to view your data from a different perspective, you can place the fields from the Row Labels area in the Column Labels area and vice versa. It is up to you.
- The **Values** area displays the data that you want to analyze. In our example, we want to find out the total number of units (equipment type) covered by each of the warranty types. The Values area must contain a field that has numeric data. Once we place the field containing numeric data in the Values area, we can choose what calculation (sum, count, average, and so on) we want to perform on the data.
- The **Report Filter** area is optional. Filter fields add a third dimension to your data analysis. For example, if you want to look at the total units under each warranty type for a particular equipment ID, you would place the Equipment Id field in the Report Filter area. This would allow you to drill down your PivotTable by the equipment ID or show the data for all the equipment.

Later on in this chapter, when you generate a PivotTable programmatically, you will add a field to the Report Filter area so you can experiment with the data.

Note that you do not have to place all the fields from your data source in the PivotTable. Place only those fields that you need; you can easily add other fields later.

6. Make field selections as shown in Figure 23-6.

Sum of Total Units	Column Labels				
Row Labels	Full Warranty	Non-Warranty	Parts & Labor	Parts Only	Grand Total
ABC Hardware		42176			42176
Laptop		6933			6933
MiniTower Monitor		41			41
Monitor		10251			10251
Scanner		110			110
Server Monitor		61			61
WS		24780			24780
Expert Installers	5369		2923	10435	18727
Laptop			344		344
Monitor	1398		23	15	1436
Scanner	42				42
Server	19		20	15	54
Server Monitor	9		76		85
WS	3901		2460	10405	16766
Experts R Us			102	11700	11802
Monitor				5888	5888

Figure 23-6: Completed PivotTable report

While the PivotTable is selected, the PivotTable Field List pane is visible on the right-hand side so that you can easily modify the PivotTable by adding or removing fields. You can temporarily remove the PivotTable Field List pane by clicking outside the PivotTable selection in the worksheet. For example, if you click any cell in row 1 or 2 the pane will disappear. Click again anywhere in the area containing the pivot data and the pane reappears.

PivotTables are used for data analysis and presentation only. This means that you are not permitted to enter data directly into a PivotTable. To make any changes or additions to the data, you must do this in the underlying source data and then use the Refresh button on the PivotTable Tools area of the Ribbon (see the Options tab in Figure 23-7) to update the PivotTable. If you added new rows to the source data, you must use the Change Data Source button in the Data group of the Options tab to expand the data range.

Figure 23-7: When the PivotTable is selected you can use commands available on the PivotTable Tools context Ribbon.

7. To see the data from a different point of view, reposition the selected fields in the PivotTable Field List as shown in Figure 23-8.

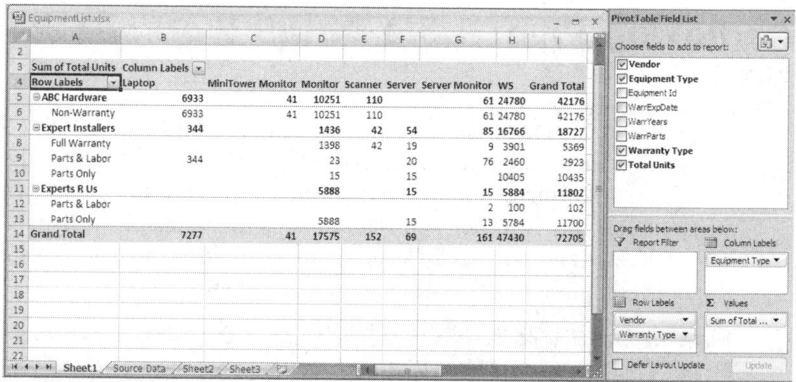

Sum of Total Units	Column Labels							
Row Labels	Laptop	MiniTower Monitor	Monitor	Scanner	Server	Server Monitor	WS	Grand Total
ABC Hardware	6933	41	10251	110		61	24780	42176
Non-Warranty	6933	41	10251	110		61	24780	42176
Expert Installers	344		1436	42	54	85	16766	18727
Full Warranty			1398	42	19	9	3901	5369
Parts & Labor	344		23		20	76	2460	2923
Parts Only			15		15		10405	10435
Experts R Us			5888		15	15	5884	11802
Parts & Labor						2	100	102
Parts Only			5888		15	13	5784	11700
Grand Total	7277	41	17575	152	69	161	47430	72705

Figure 23-8: PivotTable report – another view of the source data.

You can examine the contributing data by double-clicking any cell containing a total.

8. Double-click any cell that displays total units. For example, double-click **I14**.

   Excel will add a new worksheet to the active workbook showing all the records that contributed to the selected total value (see Figure 23-9).

9. Save the changes in the EquipmentList.xlsx workbook.

Vendor	Equipment Type	Equipment Id	WarrExpDate	WarrYears	WarrParts	Warranty Type	Total Units
Expert Inst	Monitor	46	9/19/2005	5	NULL	Full Warranty	1
Expert Inst	Monitor	46	9/21/2005	5	NULL	Full Warranty	1
Expert Inst	Monitor	46	9/27/2005	5	NULL	Full Warranty	1
Expert Inst	Monitor	46	9/28/2005	5	NULL	Full Warranty	1
Expert Inst	Monitor	46	9/29/2005	5	NULL	Full Warranty	1
Expert Inst	Monitor	46	10/3/2005	5	NULL	Full Warranty	1
Expert Inst	Monitor	46	10/5/2005	5	NULL	Full Warranty	1
Expert Inst	Monitor	46	10/10/2005	5	NULL	Full Warranty	1
Expert Inst	Monitor	46	10/11/2005	5	NULL	Full Warranty	1
Expert Inst	Monitor	34	12/21/2005	5	NULL	Full Warranty	5
Expert Inst	Monitor	33	2/28/2005	5	NULL	Full Warranty	20
Expert Inst	Monitor	33	3/1/2005	5	NULL	Full Warranty	20
Expert Inst	Monitor	33	3/2/2005	5	NULL	Full Warranty	20
Expert Inst	Monitor	33	3/3/2005	5	NULL	Full Warranty	20
Expert Inst	Monitor	33	3/7/2005	5	NULL	Full Warranty	20
Expert Inst	Monitor	33	10/6/2005	5	NULL	Full Warranty	39
Expert Inst	Monitor	33	10/12/2005	5	NULL	Full Warranty	42
Expert Inst	Monitor	33	9/18/2005	5	NULL	Full Warranty	54
Expert Inst	Monitor	33	9/29/2005	5	NULL	Full Warranty	58

Figure 23-9: You can obtain details of any summary figure by double-clicking on a data field in the PivotTable.

Drilling down on the data is a nice feature except for the fact that if you do a lot of double-clicking you will end up with many additional and most likely unwanted worksheets in your workbook. You may want to delete the drill-down worksheet after examining the detail data. You can do this manually, or you can perform the cleanup programmatically by writing VBA event procedures as described in the next section.

Removing PivotTable Detail Worksheets with VBA

In the previous Hands-On, Excel added to the EquipmentList.xlsx workbook a new worksheet displaying the detailed data that contributed to the selected total. The following example demonstrates two event procedures that allow you to determine whether you want to keep the detailed worksheet or you'd rather delete it automatically after you've examined the data. This exercise requires completion of the steps outlined in Hands-On 23-1.

Hands-On 23-2: Writing VBA Procedures to Remove a PivotTable Detail Worksheet

1. In the EquipmentList.xlsx workbook, rename the sheet with your PivotTable **PivotReport**.
2. Save the workbook in the Excel macro-enabled format as **C:\Ex07_ByExample\EquipmentPivot.xlsm.**
3. Press **Alt+F11** to switch to the Visual Basic Editor screen.
4. In the Project Explorer window, double-click the **ThisWorkbook** object in the Microsoft Excel object folder under VBAProject (EquipmentPivot.xlsm).
5. In the EquipmentList.xlsx - ThisWorkbook Code window, enter the global variable declaration and two event procedures as shown below:

```
' Global variables
Dim flag As Boolean            ' Boolean variable to indicate whether
                               ' to delete a drill-down worksheet
Dim strPivSheet As String      ' String to hold the name of the sheet
                               ' containing the PivotTable
Dim strDrillSheet As String    ' String to hold the name of the drill-down
                               ' sheet
Dim strPivSource As String     ' String to hold the name of the worksheet
                               ' with the PivotTable source data

Private Sub Workbook_SheetActivate(ByVal Sh As Object)
    If strPivSheet = "" Then Exit Sub
    If Sh.Name <> strPivSheet Then
      If InStr(1, strPivSource, Sh.Name) = 0 Then
        If MsgBox("Do you want to Delete " & Sh.Name & _
            " from the workbook" & vbCrLf _
            & "upon returning to PivotTable report?", _
             vbYesNo + vbQuestion, _
             "Sheet: Delete or Keep") = vbYes Then
              flag = True
              strDrillSheet = Sh.Name
        Else
          flag = False
          Exit Sub
        End If
      End If
    End If
```

```
    If ActiveSheet.Name = strPivSheet And flag = True Then
        Application.DisplayAlerts = False
        Worksheets(strDrillSheet).Delete
        Application.DisplayAlerts = True
        flag = False
    End If
End Sub

Private Sub Workbook_SheetBeforeDoubleClick(ByVal Sh As Object, _
            ByVal Target As Range, Cancel As Boolean)
    With ActiveSheet
        If .PivotTables.Count > 0 Then
            strPivSource = ActiveSheet.PivotTables(1).SourceData
            If ActiveCell.PivotField.Name <> "" And IsEmpty(Target) Then
                MsgBox "There is no data in the selected cell " & _
                  "- cannot drill down."
                Cancel = True
                Exit Sub
            End If
            strPivSheet = ActiveSheet.Name
        End If
    End With
End Sub
```

The first event procedure above (Workbook_SheetActivate) will ask the user whether the drill-down worksheet should be deleted when the user returns to the worksheet containing the PivotTable report. If the user answers "Yes" in the message box, the Boolean variable flag will be set to True. Because by default Excel displays a confirmation message whenever the worksheet is about to be deleted, the procedure code turns off the application messages so the deletion can be performed without further user intervention. After the deletion, don't forget to turn the alerts back on.

The second event procedure (Workbook_SheetBeforeDoubleClick) will disable the drill-down if the user clicks on a PivotTable cell that is empty. If the double-clicked cell is not empty, the name of the worksheet containing the PivotTable will be written to the global variable strPivSheet. Also, because we do not want to delete the worksheet containing the PivotTable source data, we will use the SourceData property of the PivotTables collection to store the name of the source data worksheet and the underlying data range in the global variable strPivSource.

To find out exactly how these two event procedures work together, use some of the debugging skills that you acquired in Chapter 10.

6. Double-click cell **D8** on the PivotTable worksheet.

   Excel will execute the code inside the Workbook_SheetBefore-DoubleClick event procedure and proceed to execute the code inside the Workbook_SheetActivate procedure. Because cell D8 is not empty, Excel will ask you whether you want to delete the drill-down worksheet upon returning to the PivotTable worksheet.

7. Click the **Yes** button in the message box.
   Nothing happens at this point. Excel simply has set the flag to delete this drill-down worksheet when you are done viewing it.
8. Click the **PivotReport** worksheet tab.
   At this point, Excel deletes the drill-down worksheet and activates the PivotTable worksheet.
9. Click cell **C8** in the PivotTable worksheet.
   Excel displays the message that the drill-down is not allowed because there is no data in this cell. Recall that this message was coded inside the Workbook_SheetBeforeDoubleClick event procedure.
10. Save the EquipmentPivot.xlsm workbook and then close it.

Creating a PivotTable Report Programmatically

Although the creation process of PivotTables has undergone many improvements in Excel 2007, some users may still find the process of creating PivotTable reports confusing. For those users, you may want to generate PivotTables via VBA code. Also with VBA, you can make many formatting changes to the existing PivotTables. This section demonstrates how you can work with PivotTables programmatically. We will start by creating the PiviotTable report shown earlier in Figure 23-6 using the data source presented in Figure 23-1.

Hands-On 23-3: Creating a PivotTable Report with VBA

1. Open the **C:\Ex07_ByExample\EquipmentList.xlsx** workbook.
2. Right-click the **Source Data** sheet tab in the EquipmentList.xlsx workbook and choose the **Move or Copy** option from the pop-up menu.
3. In the Move or Copy dialog box, choose the **(new book)** entry from the To book drop-down list. Indicate that you want to make a copy of the selected sheet by clicking the check box next to **Create a copy label**. Click **OK** to proceed with the copy operation.
   Excel creates a new workbook with one sheet named Source Data. This sheet has been copied from the EquipmentList.xlsx file.
4. Save this new workbook in the Excel macro-enabled format as **C:\Ex07_ByExample\ Practice_Excel23.xlsm**.
5. Insert three new sheets into the Practice_Excel23.xlsm file and save the changes made to the workbook.
6. Close the **EquipmentList.xlsx** workbook. Leave the Practice_Excel23.xlsm file open.
7. Press **Alt+F11** to switch to the Visual Basic Editor screen.
8. In the Project Explorer window, highlight **VBAProject (Practice_Excel23.xlsm)** and choose **Insert | Module**.

9. In the Practice_Excel23.xlsm - Module1 Code window, enter the CreateNewPivot procedure as shown below:

```
Sub CreateNewPivot()
    Dim wksData As Worksheet
    Dim rngData As Range
    Dim wksDest As Worksheet
    Dim pvtTable As PivotTable

    ' Set up object variables
    Set wksData = ThisWorkbook.Worksheets("Source Data")
    Set rngData = wksData.UsedRange
    Set wksDest = ThisWorkbook.Worksheets("Sheet2")

    ' Create a skeleton of a PivotTable

    Set pvtTable = wksData.PivotTableWizard(SourceType:=xlDatabase, _
       SourceData:=rngData, TableDestination:=wksDest.Range("B5"))

    ' Close the PivotTable Field List that appears automatically
    ActiveWorkbook.ShowPivotTableFieldList = False

    ' Add fields to the PivotTable
    With pvtTable
       .PivotFields("Vendor").Orientation = xlRowField
       .PivotFields("Equipment Type").Orientation = xlRowField
       .PivotFields("Warranty Type").Orientation = xlColumnField
       With .PivotFields("Total Units")
            .Orientation = xlDataField
            .Function = xlSum
       End With
       .PivotFields("Equipment Id").Orientation = xlPageField
    End With

    ' Autofit columns so all headings are visible
    wksDest.UsedRange.Columns.AutoFit
End Sub
```

The CreateNewPivot procedure shown above creates a new PivotTable report using the PivotTableWizard method of a Worksheet object. This method takes a few arguments that specify the type of the data source, its location, and the location where the PivotTable reports should be placed. All of these arguments are optional; however, it is a good idea to use them as we did in our example code. Because you can create a PivotTable from various sources of data by using the xlDatabase constant in the SourceType argument, the code specifically says that the data comes from an Excel range. If you want to create a PivotTable report from another PivotTable, use xlPivotTable for this argument. If your data is to be pulled from an external database (as shown in a later example), specify xlExternal as the SourceType. The SourceData argument in the above example procedure is a reference to the used range on the worksheet containing the source data. The TableDestination argument has a reference to cell B5 on Sheet2 in the current workbook. This is where the upper left-hand corner of the report will be placed.

The code assumes that Sheet2 exists in the workbook. If you don't have Sheet2, it's easy enough to add one via the VBA code prior to setting the reference. It is important to understand that when you call the PivotTableWizard method, you create a blank PivotTable report. All the fields from the data source are hidden. To make the fields visible, you need to add them to appropriate areas of the PivotTable Field List pane. As you recall, there are four such areas: Row Labels, Column Labels, Values, and Report Filter. While creating the PivotTable report the PivotTable Field List pane appears automatically on the right-hand side of the worksheet. However, because you are creating a PivotTable programmatically, there is no need to display that list on the screen. By setting the ShowPivotTableFieldList property to False, the PivotTable Field List pane will not be displayed.

For each field that you want to display in the PivotTable report, set the Orientation property of the PivotField object. Use the following constants for the Orientation property: xlRowField, xlColumnField, xlDataField, and xlPageField. Note that for the Total Units field placed in the Values area, the procedure sets the Function property of the PivotField object to xlSum.

When you are creating a PivotTable report via code, you may need to check whether a PivotTable already exists in the destination worksheet. You can place the following code just below the code that sets up object variables (see the CreateNewPivot procedure above):

```
' Check if PivotTable already exists
If wksDest.PivotTables.Count > 0 Then
    MsgBox "Worksheet " & wksDest.Name & _
        " already contains a pivot table."
    Exit Sub
End If
```

10. Run the CreateNewPivot procedure.

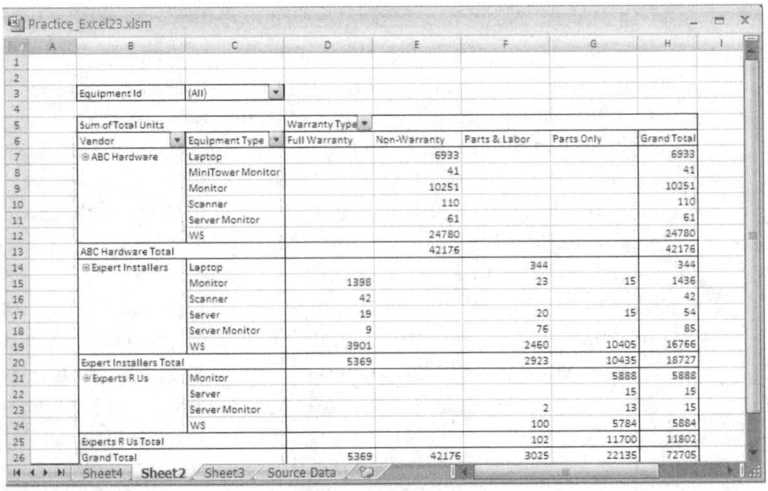

Practice_Excel23.xlsm

Equipment Id	(All)					
Sum of Total Units		Warranty Type				
Vendor	Equipment Type	Full Warranty	Non-Warranty	Parts & Labor	Parts Only	Grand Total
ABC Hardware	Laptop		6933			6933
	MiniTower Monitor		41			41
	Monitor		10251			10251
	Scanner		110			110
	Server Monitor		61			61
	WS		24780			24780
ABC Hardware Total			42176			42176
Expert Installers	Laptop			344		344
	Monitor	1398		23	15	1436
	Scanner	42				42
	Server	19		20	15	54
	Server Monitor	9		76		85
	WS	3901		2460	10405	16766
Expert Installers Total		5369		2923	10435	18727
Experts R Us	Monitor				5888	5888
	Server				15	15
	Server Monitor			2	13	15
	WS			100	5784	5884
Experts R Us Total				102	11700	11802
Grand Total		5369	42176	3025	22135	72705

Sheet4 | Sheet2 | Sheet3 | Source Data

Figure 23-10: PivotTable report created with VBA code.

When you switch to the Microsoft Excel application window, Sheet2 should contain the PivotTable report shown in Figure 23-10.

Creating a PivotTable Report from an Access Database

You can use the same PivotTableWizard method of the Worksheet object (demonstrated in Hands-On 23-3) to create a PivotTable report from an external data source. Let's start by creating a PivotTable report from a Microsoft Access sample database. We will use a Microsoft Access driver to connect to the Northwind database and then call the PivotTableWizard method of the Worksheet object to create an empty PivotTable. We will populate the PivotTable report with the data by setting the Orientation property of the PivotField objects.

Hands-On 23-4: Creating a PivotTable Report from Access with VBA

1. Add a new module to VBAProject (Practice_Excel23.xlsm) and enter the PivotTable_External1 procedure as shown below:

```
Sub PivotTable_External1()
    Dim strConn As String
    Dim strQuery_1 As String
    Dim strQuery_2 As String
    Dim myArray As Variant
    Dim destRange As Range
    Dim strPivot As String

    strConn = "Driver={Microsoft Access Driver (*.mdb)};" & _
          "DBQ=" & "C:\Ex07_ByExample\" & _
          "Northwind.mdb;"

    strQuery_1 = "SELECT Customers.CustomerID, Customers.CompanyName," & _
          "Orders.OrderDate, Products.ProductName, Sum([Order " & _
          "Details].[UnitPrice]*[Quantity]*(1-[Discount])) AS Total " & _
          "FROM Products INNER JOIN ((Customers INNER JOIN Orders " & _
          "ON Customers.CustomerID = "

    strQuery_2 = "Orders.CustomerID) INNER JOIN [Order Details] " & _
          "ON Orders.OrderID = [Order Details].OrderID) ON " & _
          "Products.ProductID = [Order Details].ProductID " & _
          "GROUP BY Customers.CustomerID, Customers.CompanyName, " & _
          "Orders.OrderDate, Products.ProductName;"

    myArray = Array(strConn, strQuery_1, strQuery_2)
    Worksheets.Add

    Set destRange = ActiveSheet.Range("B5")
    strPivot = "PivotFromAccess"

    ActiveSheet.PivotTableWizard _
         SourceType:=xlExternal, _
```

```
            SourceData:=myArray, _
            TableDestination:=destRange, _
            TableName:=strPivot, _
            SaveData:=False, _
            BackgroundQuery:=False

    ' Close the PivotTable Field List that appears automatically
    ActiveWorkbook.ShowPivotTableFieldList = False

    ' Add fields to the PivotTable
    With ActiveSheet.PivotTables(strPivot)
       .PivotFields("ProductName").Orientation = xlRowField
       .PivotFields("CompanyName").Orientation = xlRowField
       With .PivotFields("Total")
            .Orientation = xlDataField
            .Function = xlSum
            .NumberFormat = "$#,##0.00"
       End With
       .PivotFields("CustomerID").Orientation = xlPageField
       .PivotFields("OrderDate").Orientation = xlPageField
    End With

    ' Autofit columns so all headings are visible
    ActiveSheet.UsedRange.Columns.AutoFit
End Sub
```

When using the PivotTableWizard method of the Worksheet object to create a PivotTable report from an external data source, you need to specify at a minimum the following arguments:

SourceType	Use the xlExternal constant to indicate that the data for the PivotTable comes from an external data source.
SourceData	Specify an array containing two or more elements. The first element of the array must be a connection string to the database. The second argument is the SQL statement for querying an external database. If the SQL statement is longer than 255 characters, break up the statement into several strings and pass each string as a separate element of the array. In the example procedure above, the SQL statement necessary for obtaining the required data from an external database is longer than 255 characters; therefore, the SQL string is broken into two strings: strQuery_1 and strQuery_2. Next, the connection string and the SQL statement are placed in an array like this: myArray = Array(strConn, strQuery_1, strQuery_2) myArray is then used as the SourceData argument of the PivotTableWizard method.
TableDestination	Specify a worksheet range where the PivotTable should be placed.
TableName	Specify the name of the PivotTable that you want to create.

In addition to the above arguments, the example procedure shown above uses the optional SaveData and BackgroundQuery arguments.

SaveData	This argument tells Visual Basic whether to save the PivotTable when the workbook file is saved. By setting the SaveData argument to False, the PivotTable will not be saved. This setting allows you to save space on disk.
BackgroundQuery	When set to False, this argument tells Visual Basic to refrain from executing other operations in Excel in the background until the query is complete.

After creating a PivotTable, the procedure specifies where the fields returned by the SQL statement should be placed in the PivotTable report.

2. Run the PivotTable_External1 procedure to generate the PivotTable.

   The resulting PivotTable report is illustrated in Figure 23-11.

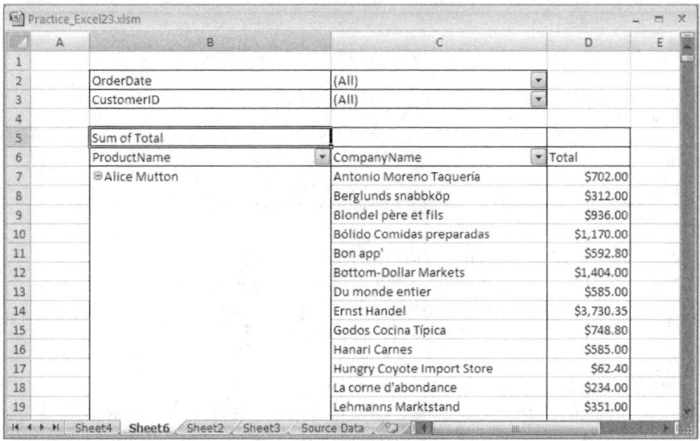

Figure 23-11: A PivotTable report can be created programmatically from an external data source such as a Microsoft Access database.

Using the CreatePivotTable Method of the PivotCache Object

When you use the macro recorder to generate the code for creating a PivotTable programmatically, Excel uses the Add method of the PivotCaches collection to create a new PivotCache. A PivotCache object represents the data behind a PivotTable. It is an area in memory where data is stored and accessed as required from a data source. Use the PivotCache when you need to generate multiple PivotTables from the same data source. By using a PivotCache, you can gain a high level of control over your external data source. The PivotCache object can also be used to change and refresh data stored in the cache.

The example procedure in Hands-On 23-5 connects to the Microsoft Access Northwind 2007 database using the Microsoft.ACE.OLEDB.12.0 provider. To use this type of connection, you must set up a reference to the Microsoft ActiveX Data Objects (ADO) in the References dialog box located in the Microsoft Excel Visual Basic Editor screen.

Hands-On 23-5: Creating a PivotTable Report Using the PivotCache Object

1. In the Visual Basic Editor screen, choose **Tools | References**. In the Available References list box, select the **Microsoft ActiveX Data Objects 2.8 Library** and click **OK.**
2. Add a new module to VBAProject (Practice_Excel23.xlsm) and enter in the Code window the Pivot_External2 procedure as shown below:

```
Sub Pivot_External2()
    Dim objPivotCache As PivotCache
    Dim conn As New ADODB.Connection
    Dim rst As New ADODB.Recordset
    Dim dbPath As String
    Dim strSQL As String

    dbPath = "C:\Ex07_HandsOn\Northwind 2007.accdb"

    conn.Open "Provider=Microsoft.ACE.OLEDB.12.0;" _
            & "Data Source=" & dbPath & _
            "; Persist Security Info=False;"

    strSQL = "SELECT Products.[Product Name], " & _
             "Orders.[Order Date], " & _
             "Sum([Unit Price]*[Quantity]) AS Amount " & _
             "FROM Orders INNER JOIN (Products INNER JOIN " & _
             "[Order Details] ON Products.ID = " & _
             "[Order Details].[Product ID]) ON " & _
             "Orders.[Order ID] = [Order Details].[Order ID] " & _
             "GROUP BY Products.[Product Name], " & _
             "Orders.[Order Date], Products.[Product Name]" & _
             "ORDER BY Sum([Unit Price]*[Quantity]) DESC , " & _
             "Products.[Product Name];"

    Set rst = conn.Execute(strSQL)

    ' Create a PivotTable cache and report
    Set objPivotCache = ActiveWorkbook.PivotCaches.Add( _
        SourceType:=xlExternal)
    Set objPivotCache.Recordset = rst

    Worksheets.Add
    With objPivotCache
        .CreatePivotTable TableDestination:=Range("B6"), _
            TableName:="Invoices"
    End With

    ' Add fields to the PivotTable
    With ActiveSheet.PivotTables("Invoices")
        .SmallGrid = False
        With .PivotFields("Product Name")
            .Orientation = xlRowField
            .Position = 1
        End With
        With .PivotFields("Order Date")
            .Orientation = xlRowField
```

```
            .Position = 2
            .Name = "Date"
        End With
        With .PivotFields("Amount")
            .Orientation = xlDataField
            .Position = 1
            .NumberFormat = "$#,##0.00"
        End With
    End With

    ' Autofit columns so all headings are visible
    ActiveSheet.UsedRange.Columns.AutoFit

    ' Clean up
    rst.Close
    conn.Close
    Set rst = Nothing
    Set conn = Nothing

    ' Obtain information about PivotCache
    With ActiveSheet.PivotTables("Invoices").PivotCache
        Debug.Print "Information about the PivotCache"
        Debug.Print "Number of Records: " & .RecordCount
        Debug.Print "Data was last refreshed on: " & .RefreshDate
        Debug.Print "Data was last refreshed by: " & .RefreshName
        Debug.Print "Memory used by PivotCache: " & .MemoryUsed & _
            " (bytes)"
    End With
End Sub
```

After establishing a connection with a database and executing the SQL statement to obtain the data, the procedure creates a PivotCache using the following line of code:

```
Set objPivotCache = ActiveWorkbook.PivotCaches.Add( _
     SourceType:=xlExternal)
```

The code then places the data from the external data source in the PivotCache by assigning a Recordset object to the PivotCache object, like this:

```
Set objPivotCache.Recordset = rst
```

Next, the code uses the CreatePivotTable method of the PivotCache object to create an empty PivotTable:

```
With objPivotCache
    .CreatePivotTable TableDestination:=Range("B6"), _
            TableName:="Invoices"
End With
```

Once the skeleton of the PivotTable is created, the code adds appropriate fields to the PivotTable. The last several lines of the example procedure demonstrate how to find out information about the PivotCache.

To force the PivotCache to refresh automatically when a workbook containing the PivotTable is opened, set the RefreshOnFileOpen property to True. To do this, you may want to add the following statement at the end of the Pivot_External2 procedure:

```
ActiveSheet.PivotTables("Invoices").PivotCache.RefreshOnFileOpen = True
```

3. Run the Pivot_External2 procedure to generate the PivotTable.

   The resulting PivotTable report is illustrated in Figure 23-12.

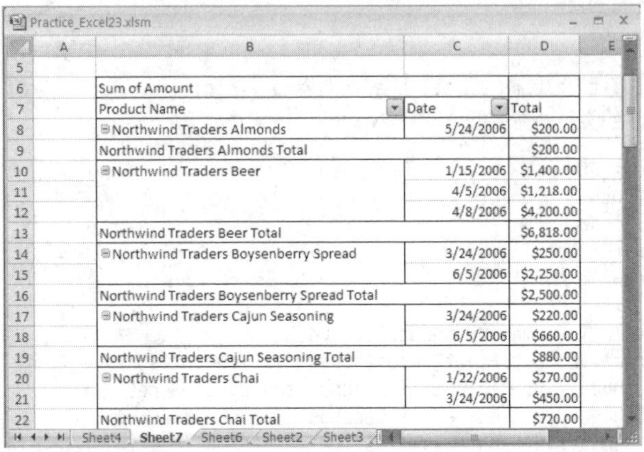

Practice_Excel23.xlsm

	A	B	C	D
5				
6		Sum of Amount		
7		Product Name	Date	Total
8		Northwind Traders Almonds	5/24/2006	$200.00
9		Northwind Traders Almonds Total		$200.00
10		Northwind Traders Beer	1/15/2006	$1,400.00
11			4/5/2006	$1,218.00
12			4/8/2006	$4,200.00
13		Northwind Traders Beer Total		$6,818.00
14		Northwind Traders Boysenberry Spread	3/24/2006	$250.00
15			6/5/2006	$2,250.00
16		Northwind Traders Boysenberry Spread Total		$2,500.00
17		Northwind Traders Cajun Seasoning	3/24/2006	$220.00
18			6/5/2006	$660.00
19		Northwind Traders Cajun Seasoning Total		$880.00
20		Northwind Traders Chai	1/22/2006	$270.00
21			3/24/2006	$450.00
22		Northwind Traders Chai Total		$720.00

Sheet4 Sheet7 Sheet6 Sheet2 Sheet3

Figure 23-12: A PivotTable report created using the CreatePivotTable method of the PivotCache object.

Formatting, Grouping, and Sorting a PivotTable Report

You can modify the display and format of a PivotTable programmatically by using a number of different properties of the PivotTable object. For example, you may want to reposition the fields within the PivotTable report, sort the data by a specific field, or group your data by years, quarters, months, and so on. The example procedure below reformats the PivotTable report shown in Figure 23-11 to look like the one shown in Figure 23-13.

Hands-On 23-6: Formatting a PivotTable Report

1. Add a new module to VBAProject (Practice_Excel23.xlsm) and enter the FormatPivotTable procedure as shown below:

```
Sub FormatPivotTable()
    Dim pvtTable As PivotTable
    Dim strPiv As String

    If ActiveSheet.PivotTables.Count > 0 Then
        strPiv = ActiveSheet.PivotTables(1).Name
        Set pvtTable = ActiveSheet.PivotTables(strPiv)
    Else
        Exit Sub
    End If

    With pvtTable
        .PivotFields("OrderDate").Orientation = xlRows
        .PivotFields("CompanyName").Orientation = xlHidden
```

```
        ' use this statement to group OrderDate by year
        .PivotFields("OrderDate").DataRange.Cells(1).Group _
            Start:=True, End:=True, _
            periods:=Array(False, False, False, False, False, False, _
            True)

        ' use this statement to group OrderDate both by quarter and year
        ' .PivotFields("OrderDate").DataRange.Cells(1).Group _
            Start:=True, End:=True, _
            periods:=Array(False, False, False, False, False, True, True)

        .PivotFields("OrderDate").Orientation = xlColumns
        .TableRange1.AutoFormat Format:=xlRangeAutoFormatColor2
        .PivotFields("ProductName").DataRange.Select

        ' sort the Product Name field in descending order based on the
        ' Sum of Total
        .PivotFields("ProductName").AutoSort xlDescending, "Sum of Total"
        Selection.IndentLevel = 2
        With Selection.Font
            .Name = "Times New Roman"
            .FontStyle = "Bold"
            .Size = 10
        End With
        With Selection.Borders(xlInsideHorizontal)
            .LineStyle = xlContinuous
            .Weight = xlThin
            .ColorIndex = xlAutomatic
        End With
    End With
End Sub
```

By studying the code of the procedure presented above, you can easily conclude that:

- To change the layout of a PivotTable, you should set the Orientation property of the required field to a different constant. The example code above moves the OrderDate field from the Report Filter area to the Row Labels area of the PivotTable.
- To display a PivotTable without a particular field, you need to set the Orientation property of the required field to xlHidden.
- To group the OrderDate field by year, you should use the Group method of the Range object. For example, the code uses the following statement to group the data in the OrderDate field by year:

```
.PivotFields("OrderDate").DataRange.Cells(1).Group Start:=True, _
    End:=True, periods:=Array(False, False, False, False, False, _
    False, True)
```

- The Start and End arguments specify the start and end date to be included in the grouping. By setting these arguments to True, all dates are included. The periods argument is an array of Boolean values that specifies the period for the group, as shown in the following table:

Array Element	Period
1	Seconds
2	Minutes
3	Hours
4	Days
5	Months
6	Quarters
7	Years

Note: The following statement will ungroup the dates:

```
ActiveSheet.PivotTables(1).PivotFields("OrderDate").LabelRange.Ungroup
```

- You can apply automatic formatting to the entire PivotTable report by using the AutoFormat property of the Range object. The TableRange1 property returns a Range object that represents the range containing the entire PivotTable report without the page fields:

  ```
  .TableRange1.AutoFormat Format:=xlRangeAutoFormatColor2
  ```

- You can select the data items in a particular field by using the DataRange property and the Select method, like this:

  ```
  .PivotFields("ProductName").DataRange.Select
  ```

- You can sort a particular field in descending or ascending order. The example procedure uses the following statement to sort the ProductName field in descending order based on the Sum of Total:

  ```
  .PivotFields("ProductName").AutoSort xlDescending, "Sum of Total"
  ```

- You can change the text indentation, font name, size, and style, as well as the borders of the selected range, as demonstrated in the last statements of the example procedure shown above.

2. Switch to the Microsoft Excel application window and activate the sheet containing the PivotTable report as shown in Figure 23-11 earlier in this chapter.
3. Press **Alt+F8** to open the Macro dialog box. Highlight the Format-PivotTable procedure and click **Run**.

The resulting reformatted PivotTable report is illustrated in Figure 23-13.

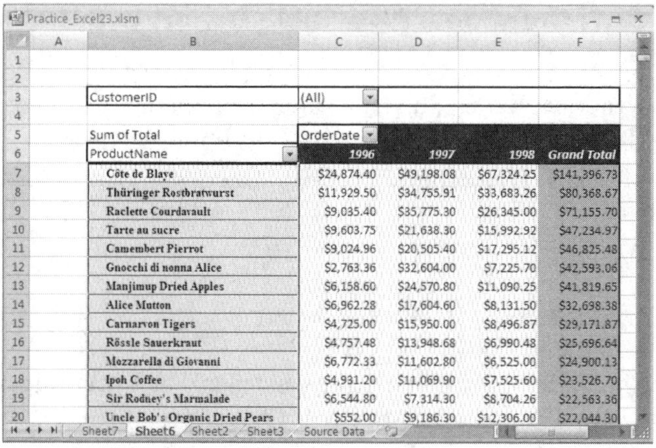

Practice_Excel23.xlsm

CustomerID	(All)			
Sum of Total	OrderDate			
ProductName	1996	1997	1998	Grand Total
Côte de Blaye	$24,874.40	$49,198.08	$67,324.25	$141,396.73
Thüringer Rostbratwurst	$11,929.50	$34,755.91	$33,683.26	$80,368.67
Raclette Courdavault	$9,035.40	$35,775.30	$26,345.00	$71,155.70
Tarte au sucre	$9,603.75	$21,638.30	$15,992.92	$47,234.97
Camembert Pierrot	$9,024.96	$20,505.40	$17,295.12	$46,825.48
Gnocchi di nonna Alice	$2,763.36	$32,604.00	$7,225.70	$42,593.06
Manjimup Dried Apples	$6,158.60	$24,570.80	$11,090.25	$41,819.65
Alice Mutton	$6,962.28	$17,604.60	$8,131.50	$32,698.38
Carnarvon Tigers	$4,725.00	$15,950.00	$8,496.87	$29,171.87
Rössle Sauerkraut	$4,757.48	$13,948.68	$6,990.48	$25,696.64
Mozzarella di Giovanni	$6,772.33	$11,602.80	$6,525.00	$24,900.13
Ipoh Coffee	$4,931.20	$11,069.90	$7,525.60	$23,526.70
Sir Rodney's Marmalade	$6,544.80	$7,314.30	$8,704.26	$22,563.36
Uncle Bob's Organic Dried Pears	$552.00	$9,186.30	$12,306.00	$22,044.30

Sheet7 Sheet6 Sheet2 Sheet3 Source Data

Figure 23-13: A PivotTable report can be reformatted to view data from a different perspective.

Hiding Items in a PivotTable

In the previous example procedure, you grouped the data in the PivotTable by year based on the OrderDate field. To hide some of the grouped data, you can set the Visible property of the PivotItem object to False. For instance, the following procedure demonstrates how to hide the 1996 column of data in the PivotTable report presented in Figure 23-13:

```
Sub Hide1996Data()
    Dim myPivot As PivotTable
    Dim myItem As PivotItem
    Dim strFieldLabel As String

    strFieldLabel = "1996"

    Set myPivot = ActiveSheet.PivotTables(1)
    For Each myItem In myPivot.PivotFields("OrderDate").PivotItems
        If myItem.Name <> strFieldLabel Then
            myItem.Visible = True
        Else
            myItem.Visible = False
        End If
    Next
End Sub
```

Adding Calculated Fields and Items to a PivotTable

You can customize a PivotTable report by defining calculated fields and items. Using the contents of other numeric fields in a PivotTable, you can create a calculated field that performs the required calculation. For example, let's create a procedure with two calculated fields named Change: 2001/2000 and Change: 2000/1999 to calculate the difference in number of products sold from year to year.

Hands-On 23-7: Creating a PivotTable Report with Calculated Fields

1. Copy the **Practice_Excel23b.xlsm** workbook from the C:\Ex07_HandsOn folder to your **C:\Ex07_ByExample** folder.
2. Open the **C:\Ex07_ByExample\Practice_Excel23b.xlsm** workbook.

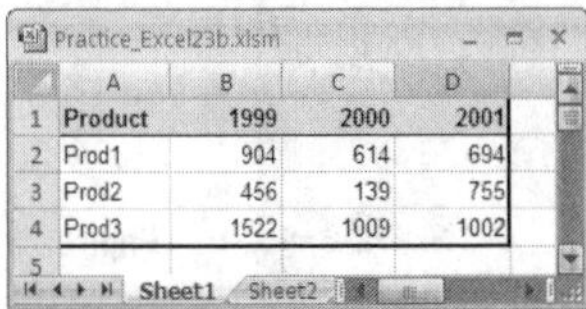

	A	B	C	D
1	Product	1999	2000	2001
2	Prod1	904	614	694
3	Prod2	456	139	755
4	Prod3	1522	1009	1002

Figure 23-14: Sample data for the PivotTable report.

3. Switch to the Visual Basic Editor screen and highlight **VBAProject (Practice_Excel23b.xlsm)** in the Project Explorer.
4. Choose **Insert | Module** to add a new module and enter the PivotWithCalcFields procedure as shown below:

```
Sub PivotWithCalcFields()
    ActiveWorkbook.PivotCaches.Add( _
        SourceType:=xlDatabase, _
        SourceData:="Sheet1!R1C1:R4C4").CreatePivotTable _
        TableDestination:="'[Practice_Excel23b.xlsm]Sheet1'!R4C7", _
        TableName:="Piv1", _
        DefaultVersion:=xlPivotTableVersion10

    With ActiveSheet.PivotTables("Piv1").PivotFields("Product")
        .Orientation = xlRowField
        .Position = 1
    End With

    ActiveSheet.PivotTables("Piv1").AddDataField _
        ActiveSheet.PivotTables("Piv1").PivotFields("2001"), _
        "Sum of 2001", xlSum
    ActiveSheet.PivotTables("Piv1").AddDataField _
        ActiveSheet.PivotTables("Piv1").PivotFields("2000"), _
        "Sum of 2000", xlSum
    ActiveSheet.PivotTables("Piv1").AddDataField _
        ActiveSheet.PivotTables("Piv1").PivotFields("1999"), _
        "Sum of 1999", xlSum
    ActiveSheet.PivotTables("Piv1").CalculatedFields.Add _
        "Change: 2001/2000", "='2001' -'2000'", True
    ActiveSheet.PivotTables("Piv1").CalculatedFields.Add _
        "Change: 2000/1999", "='2000' -'1999'", True
    ActiveSheet.PivotTables("Piv1"). _
        PivotFields("Change: 2001/2000"). _
        Orientation = xlDataField
    ActiveSheet.PivotTables("Piv1"). _
        PivotFields("Change: 2000/1999"). _
        Orientation = xlDataField
    ActiveSheet.PivotTables("Piv1"). _
        PivotFields("Data").Orientation = xlColumnField
End Sub
```

Notice that calculated fields are defined by using the Add method of the CalculatedFields object and supplying the name for the new field and a formula:

```
ActiveSheet.PivotTables("Piv1").CalculatedFields.Add _
    "Change: 2001/2000", "='2001' -'2000'", True
ActiveSheet.PivotTables("Piv1").CalculatedFields.Add _
    "Change: 2000/1999", "='2000' -'1999'", True
```

The third (optional) argument set to True indicates that the strings in field names will be interpreted as having been formatted in standard U.S. English instead of using local settings. The default setting is False.

A calculated field uses a formula that refers to other pivot fields that contain numeric data. This can be a simple formula, such as addition (+), subtraction (–), multiplication (*), or division (/), or an Excel function. In the procedure example above, we created the two calculated fields shown below:

Calculated Field Name	Formula Used
Change: 2001/2000	='2001' -'2000'
Change: 2000/1999	='2000' -'1999'

"2001," "2000," and "1999" are the names of the fields placed in the Data area of the PivotTable. When you use multiple pivot fields in the Data area, Excel creates a new pivot field named Data (see Figure 23-15). The labels for the multiple pivot fields in the Data area can be displayed going down the rows or across columns. You can specify the orientation of the labels by setting the Orientation property of the Data field to xlRowField or xlColumnField.

Once you define a calculated field, the field is added to the PivotTable Field List and maintained in the PivotTable cache.

Note: You can add a calculated field manually by using the Options tab of the PivotTable Tools context Ribbon. Click Options | Formulas | Calculated field.

5. Run the PivotWithCalcFields procedure.

   The resulting PivotTable report is shown in Figure 23-15.

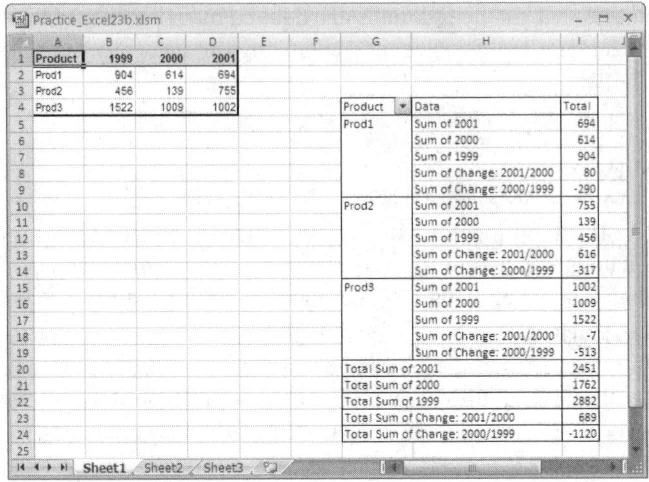

Product	1999	2000	2001
Prod1	904	614	694
Prod2	456	139	755
Prod3	1522	1009	1002

Product	Data	Total
Prod1	Sum of 2001	694
	Sum of 2000	614
	Sum of 1999	904
	Sum of Change: 2001/2000	80
	Sum of Change: 2000/1999	-290
Prod2	Sum of 2001	755
	Sum of 2000	139
	Sum of 1999	456
	Sum of Change: 2001/2000	616
	Sum of Change: 2000/1999	-317
Prod3	Sum of 2001	1002
	Sum of 2000	1009
	Sum of 1999	1522
	Sum of Change: 2001/2000	-7
	Sum of Change: 2000/1999	-513
Total Sum of 2001		2451
Total Sum of 2000		1762
Total Sum of 1999		2882
Total Sum of Change: 2001/2000		689
Total Sum of Change: 2000/1999		-1120

Figure 23-15: You can add additional calculations to a PivotTable by defining additional fields, such as Change: 2001/2000 and Change: 2000/1999 depicted here.

By adding the following statement at the end of the PivotWithCalcFields procedure, deleting rows F:I in Sheet1, and rerunning the procedure, the PivotTable depicted in Figure 23-15 will look like the one shown in Figure 23-16.

```
ActiveSheet.PivotTables("Piv1"). _
     PivotFields("Data").Orientation = xlColumnField
```

	Data				
Product	Sum of 2001	Sum of 2000	Sum of 1999	Sum of Change: 2001/2000	Sum of Change: 2000/1999
Prod1	694	614	904	80	-290
Prod2	755	139	456	616	-317
Prod3	1002	1009	1522	-7	-513
Grand Total	2451	1762	2882	689	-1120

Figure 23-16: Changing the orientation of the PivotTable data.

You must not confuse a calculated item with a calculated field. A calculated item is a custom item you define in a PivotTable field to perform calculations using the contents of other fields and items in the PivotTable.

Let's say you have created a report showing the total product sales for each of your salespeople by country. Then you want to look at the data differently and show the sales made by each salesperson on three continents. You will need three new (calculated) items under the Country field. These items will be named North America, South America, and Europe. After you create these items, you can change the name of the Country field to Continent (see Figure 23-17) to make your data easier to read. The following procedure retrieves the data for this demonstration example from the Microsoft Access sample Northwind database. The code of this procedure was generated by a macro recorder.

Hands-On 23-8: Creating a PivotTable Report with Calculated Items

1. Open a new workbook file and save it as **C:\Ex07_ByExample\Practice_Excel23c.xlsm**.
2. Switch to the Visual Basic Editor screen and highlight **VBAProject (Practice_Excel23c.xlsm)** in the Project Explorer.
3. Choose **Insert | Module** to add a new module and enter the PivotWithCalcItems procedure as shown below:

```
Sub PivotWithCalcItems()
    Dim strConn As String
    Dim strSQL As String
    Dim myArray As Variant
    Dim destRng As Range
    Dim strPivot As String

    strConn = "Driver={Microsoft Access Driver (*.mdb)};" & _
              "DBQ=" & "C:\Ex07_ByExample\" & _
              "Northwind.mdb;"

    strSQL = "SELECT Invoices.Customers.CompanyName, " & _
             "Invoices.Country, Invoices.Salesperson, " & _
             "Invoices.ProductName, Invoices.ExtendedPrice " & _
             "FROM Invoices ORDER BY Invoices.Country"

    myArray = Array(strConn, strSQL)
    Worksheets.Add

    Set destRng = ActiveSheet.Range("B5")
    strPivot = "PivotTable1"

    ActiveSheet.PivotTableWizard _
        SourceType:=xlExternal, _
        SourceData:=myArray, _
        TableDestination:=destRng, _
        TableName:=strPivot, _
        SaveData:=False, _
        BackgroundQuery:=False

    With ActiveSheet.PivotTables(strPivot).PivotFields("CompanyName")
        .Orientation = xlPageField
        .Position = 1
    End With

    With ActiveSheet.PivotTables(strPivot).PivotFields("Country")
        .Orientation = xlRowField
        .Position = 1
    End With

    ActiveSheet.PivotTables(strPivot).AddDataField _
        ActiveSheet.PivotTables(strPivot).PivotFields("ExtendedPrice"), _
        "Sum of ExtendedPrice", xlSum
```

```
With ActiveSheet.PivotTables(strPivot).PivotFields("Salesperson")
    .Orientation = xlRowField
    .Position = 1
End With

With ActiveSheet.PivotTables(strPivot).PivotFields("Salesperson")
    .Orientation = xlPageField
    .Position = 1
End With

With ActiveSheet.PivotTables(strPivot).PivotFields("Salesperson")
    .Orientation = xlColumnField
    .Position = 1
End With

ActiveSheet.PivotTables(strPivot).PivotFields("Country"). _
    CalculatedItems.Add "North America", "=USA+Canada", True
ActiveSheet.PivotTables(strPivot).PivotFields("Country"). _
    CalculatedItems.Add "South America", _
    "=Argentina+Brazil+Venezuela ", True
ActiveSheet.PivotTables(strPivot).PivotFields("Country"). _
    CalculatedItems("North America").StandardFormula = _
    "=USA+Canada+Mexico"
ActiveSheet.PivotTables(strPivot).PivotFields("Country"). _
    CalculatedItems.Add "Europe", _
    "=Austria+Belgium+Denmark+Finland+" & _
    "France+Germany+Ireland+Italy+Norway+Poland+" & _
    "Portugal+Spain+Sweden+Switzerland+UK", True

With ActiveSheet.PivotTables(strPivot).PivotFields("Country")
    .PivotItems("Argentina").Visible = False
    .PivotItems("Austria").Visible = False
    .PivotItems("Belgium").Visible = False
    .PivotItems("Brazil").Visible = False
    .PivotItems("Canada").Visible = False
    .PivotItems("Denmark").Visible = False
    .PivotItems("Finland").Visible = False
    .PivotItems("France").Visible = False
    .PivotItems("Germany").Visible = False
    .PivotItems("Ireland").Visible = False
    .PivotItems("Italy").Visible = False
    .PivotItems("Mexico").Visible = False
    .PivotItems("Norway").Visible = False
    .PivotItems("Poland").Visible = False
    .PivotItems("Portugal").Visible = False
    .PivotItems("Spain").Visible = False
    .PivotItems("Sweden").Visible = False
    .PivotItems("Switzerland").Visible = False
    .PivotItems("UK").Visible = False
    .PivotItems("USA").Visible = False
    .PivotItems("Venezuela").Visible = False
End With

ActiveSheet.PivotTables(strPivot).PivotFields("Country").Caption = _
    "Continent"

With ActiveSheet.PivotTables(strPivot). _
```

```
        PivotFields("Sum of ExtendedPrice").NumberFormat = "$#,##0.00"
    End With

    With ActiveSheet.PivotTables(strPivot).PivotFields("ProductName")
        .Orientation = xlRowField
        .Position = 2
    End With

    ActiveSheet.PivotTables(strPivot). _
      PivotFields("ProductName").Orientation = xlHidden
End Sub
```

A calculated item uses a formula that refers to other items in the specified PivotTable field. For example, a PivotTable that contains a Country field listing a number of different country items (Austria, UK, Brazil, Argentina, etc.) could have a calculated item named "South America" defined as the sum of countries located on the South American continent:

Calculated Item	Formula
South America	=Argentina+Brazil+Venezuela

All of the calculated items in the specified PivotTable are members of the CalculatedItems collection. Calculated items are defined by using the Add method of the CalculatedItems object and supplying two arguments — the name for the new item and a formula as shown below:

```
ActiveSheet.PivotTables(strPivot).PivotFields("Country"). _
    CalculatedItems.Add "South America", "=Argentina+Brazil+Venezuela",
True
```

The third (optional) argument set to True indicates that the strings in field names will be interpreted as having been formatted in standard U.S. English instead of using local settings. The default setting is False.

4. Run the PivotWithCalcItems procedure.

   The resulting PivotTable report is shown in Figure 23-17.

Practice_Excel23c.xlsm

CompanyName	(All)									
Sum of ExtendedPrice	Salesperson									
Continent	Andrew Fuller	Anne Dodsworth	Janet Leverling	Laura Callahan	Margaret Peacock	Michael Suyama	Nancy Davolio	Robert King	Steven Buchanan	Grand Total
North America	33279.5	18191.51	48798.09	28022.68	57916.98	21229.78	57710.18	37793.07	16421.15	319362.94
South America	13428.51	3232.5	20758.16	23769.38	27209.92	9830.99	39398.45	14911.7	19315.9	171855.51
Europe	119829.74	55884.03	133256.57	75070.21	147763.93	42852.36	94998.93	71863.45	33055.2	774574.42
Grand Total	166537.75	77308.04	202812.82	126862.27	232890.83	73913.13	192107.56	124568.22	68792.25	1265792.9

Sheet4 Sheet1 Sheet2 Sheet3

Figure 23-17: By defining new items in a PivotTable report, you can present information summaries according to specific needs. Here the Country field has been renamed Continent to present information summarized by continent. North America, South America, and Europe are calculated items in this PivotTable report.

You can modify the PivotWithCalcItems procedure by defining new calculated items in the Salesperson PivotTable field to generate the output shown in Figure 23-18.

```
ActiveSheet.PivotTables(strPivot).PivotFields("Salesperson"). _
      CalculatedItems.Add "Male", _
```

```
        "=Michael Suyama+Andrew Fuller+Robert King+" & _
        "Steven Buchanan", True

    ActiveSheet.PivotTables(strPivot).PivotFields("Salesperson"). _
        CalculatedItems.Add "Female", _
        "=Anne Dodsworth+Laura Callahan+Janet Leverling+" & _
        "Margaret Peacock+Nancy Davolio", True

    With ActiveSheet.PivotTables("PivotTable1").PivotFields("Salesperson")
        .PivotItems("Andrew Fuller").Visible = False
        .PivotItems("Anne Dodsworth").Visible = False
        .PivotItems("Janet Leverling").Visible = False
        .PivotItems("Laura Callahan").Visible = False
        .PivotItems("Margaret Peacock").Visible = False
        .PivotItems("Michael Suyama").Visible = False
        .PivotItems("Nancy Davolio").Visible = False
        .PivotItems("Robert King").Visible = False
        .PivotItems("Steven Buchanan").Visible = False
    End With
```

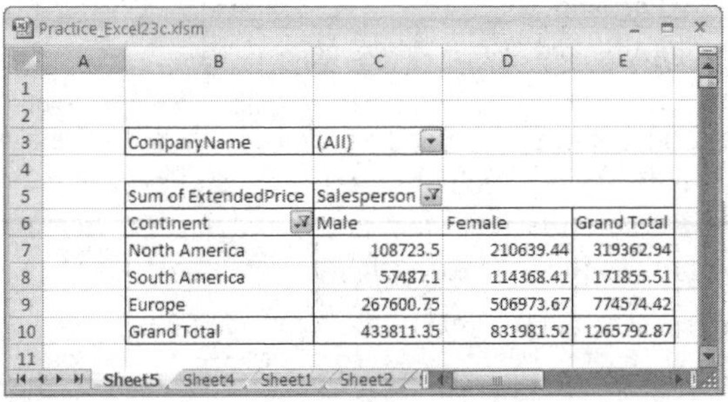

Practice_Excel23c.xlsm

CompanyName	(All)		
Sum of ExtendedPrice	Salesperson		
Continent	Male	Female	Grand Total
North America	108723.5	210639.44	319362.94
South America	57487.1	114368.41	171855.51
Europe	267600.75	506973.67	774574.42
Grand Total	433811.35	831981.52	1265792.87

Sheet5 Sheet4 Sheet1 Sheet2

Figure 23-18: By defining new calculated items in a PivotTable report, you can present information summaries according to specific needs. Here the Northwind employees were grouped by gender.

You can find out if the PivotField or PivotItem is calculated by using the IsCalculated property of the PivotField or PivotItem object. The procedure below prints a list of fields and items in the PivotTable to the Immediate window, indicating whether the field or item is calculated. In addition, this procedure prints the names of all calculated items and their formulas to Sheet2 of the current workbook.

```
Sub ListCalcFieldsItems()
    Dim pivTable As PivotTable
    Dim fld As PivotField    ' field enumerator
    Dim itm As PivotItem     ' item enumerator
    Dim r As Integer         ' row number

    Set pivTable = Worksheets(1).PivotTables(1)

    On Error Resume Next

    ' print to the Immediate window the names of fields
    ' and calculated items
    For Each fld In pivTable.PivotFields
        If fld.IsCalculated Then
           Debug.Print fld.Name & ":" & _
             fld.Name & vbTab & "-->Calculated field"
        Else
```

```
                Debug.Print fld.Name
            End If
            For Each itm In pivTable. _
                PivotFields(fld.Name).CalculatedItems
                    Debug.Print fld.Name & ":" & _
                        itm.Name & vbTab & "-->Calculated item"
                    ' enter information about Calculated items
                    ' in a worksheet
                    r = r + 1
                    With Worksheets("Sheet2")
                        .Cells(r, 1).Value = itm.Name
                        .Cells(r, 2).Value = Chr(39) & itm.Formula
                    End With
            Next
        Next
End Sub
```

Creating a PivotChart Report Using VBA

A PivotChart represents the data in a PivotTable report. Using VBA code you can create a PivotChart based on an existing PivotTable report, and you can change the layout and data displayed in a PivotChart just as easily as you can reformat a PivotTable report.

A PivotChart report is linked to a PivotTable report. This means that when you rearrange the data in a PivotTable report, the PivotChart report displays the same view of the data, and vice versa. The default chart type for a PivotChart is a stacked column chart. This type of chart is useful for comparing the contribution of each value to a total across categories. You can generate any type of PivotChart report except XY (Scatter), Stock, or Bubble.

You can create a PivotChart manually by choosing Insert | PivotTable | PivotChart. Creating a PivotChart report programmatically boils down to using the SetDataSource method of the PivotChart object and specifying a reference to the PivotTable range. The PivotTable object has the following two properties that return ranges representing part or all of the PivotTable report:

- TableRange1 — Returns a range representing the PivotTable report without page fields
- TableRange2 — Returns a range representing the entire PivotTable report

The procedures in Hands-On 23-9 generate a PivotTable report from the Microsoft Access sample Northwind database. Another procedure in this Hands-On will set up a PivotChart based on the PivotTable's data.

Hands-On 23-9: Creating a PivotTable and PivotChart Reports

1. Open a new workbook file and save it as **C:\Ex07_ByExample\Practice_Excel23d.xlsm**.

2. Switch to the Visual Basic Editor screen and highlight **VBAProject (Practice_Excel23d.xlsm)** in the Project Explorer.
3. Choose **Insert | Module** to add a new module and enter the Generate-PivotReport procedure as shown below:

```
Sub GeneratePivotReport()
    Dim strConn As String
    Dim strSQL As String
    Dim myArray As Variant
    Dim destRng As Range
    Dim strPivot As String

    strConn = "Driver={Microsoft Access Driver (*.mdb)};" & _
            "DBQ=" & "C:\Ex07_ByExample\Northwind.mdb;"

    strSQL = "SELECT Invoices.Customers.CompanyName, " & _
             "Invoices.Country, Invoices.Salesperson, " & _
             "Invoices.ProductName, Invoices.ExtendedPrice " & _
             "FROM Invoices ORDER BY Invoices.Country"

    myArray = Array(strConn, strSQL)
    Worksheets.Add

    Set destRng = ActiveSheet.Range("B5")
    strPivot = "PivotTable1"

    ActiveSheet.PivotTableWizard _
            SourceType:=xlExternal, _
            SourceData:=myArray, _
            TableDestination:=destRng, _
            TableName:=strPivot, _
            SaveData:=False, _
            BackgroundQuery:=False

    With ActiveSheet.PivotTables(strPivot).PivotFields("ProductName")
        .Orientation = xlPageField
        .Position = 1
    End With


    With ActiveSheet.PivotTables(strPivot).PivotFields("Country")
        .Orientation = xlRowField
        .Position = 1
    End With

    With ActiveSheet.PivotTables(strPivot).PivotFields("Salesperson")
        .Orientation = xlColumnField
        .Position = 1
    End With

    ActiveSheet.PivotTables(strPivot).AddDataField _
        ActiveSheet.PivotTables(strPivot).PivotFields("ExtendedPrice"), _
        "Sum of ExtendedPrice", xlSum

    With ActiveSheet.PivotTables(strPivot). _
       PivotFields("Sum of ExtendedPrice").NumberFormat = "$#,##0.00"
```

```
    End With
End Sub
```

4. Run the GeneratePivotReport procedure.

   Excel adds a new worksheet with a PivotTable to the current workbook, as shown in Figure 23-19.

Practice_Excel23d.xlsm

ProductName	(All)

Sum of ExtendedPrice	Salesperson									
Country	Andrew Fuller	Anne Dodsworth	Janet Leverling	Laura Callahan	Margaret Peacock	Michael Suyama	Nancy Davolio	Robert King	Steven Buchanan	Grand Total
Argentina	477	944.5	319.2	2750.5	1329.4	76	686.7	1535.8		8119.1
Austria	16603.08	8967.8	23941.35	10970.59	17959.66	6728.93	17087.27	25745.15		128003.83
Belgium	2866.5	2808.37	295.38		13597.2	1209	732.6	4641.5	7674.3	33824.85
Brazil	9985.03	1910	9192.59	11118.58	17770.57	6581.47	29459.37	6200.2	14707.97	106925.78
Canada	9034.5	966.8	12156.73	1278.4	4826.05	3412.83	8801.41	9719.56		50196.28
Denmark	2345.7		1684.27	1814.35	17291.81	736	6674	2114.88		32661.01
Finland	5878.03	1590.56	957.86	4131.8	2117.7	270	1828.9	642	1393.2	18810.05
France	9434.28	3828.73	15471.13	5356	24340.8	4470.38	12487.44	2985.9	2983.65	81358.31
Germany	53627.17	15753.53	45978.81	26497.97	38341.32	9816.93	24611.38	7608.93	8048.54	230284.58
Ireland	10604.98	7403.9	16615.04	1313.82	1366.4	7558	2519	2598.76		49979.9
Italy	5422.05	583.8	88	2078.86	3686	55.2	1138.44	1025	1692.8	15770.15
Mexico	2190.65		3076.9	988.8	6706.1		5147.46	4223.06	1249.1	23582.07
Norway	622.35		2684.4				1728.4	700		5735.15
Poland				686	1019.1	808	858.85		160	3531.95
Portugal		57.8	987.5	2893.4	4454.58		1519.24	285.12	1274.72	11472.36
Spain	977.5	224	3375.25	206	7729.89		1241	1861.1	2368.46	17983.2
Sweden	8036.7	4879.75	11520.4	9303.52	1826.3	3240.62	7491.18	6395.44	1801.23	54495.14
Switzerland		2949.24	5049.08	498.1	5282.06	3431.8	4135.5	9790.24	556.62	31692.64
UK	3411.4	6836.55	4608.1	9319.8	8751.11	4527.5	10945.73	5469.43	5101.68	58971.3
USA	22054.35	17224.71	33564.46	25755.48	46384.83	17816.95	43761.31	23850.45	15172.05	245584.59
Venezuela	2966.48	378	11246.37	9900.3	8109.95	3173.52	9252.38	7175.7	4607.93	56810.63
Grand Total	166537.75	77308.04	202812.82	126862.27	232890.83	73913.13	192107.56	124568.22	68792.25	1265792.87

Sheet4 Sheet1 Sheet2 Sheet3

Figure 23-19: This PivotTable report is used to graph data in the PivotChart report.

5. In the same code module where you entered the GeneratePivotReport procedure, enter the code of the CreatePivotChart procedure as shown below:

```
Sub CreatePivotChart()
    Dim shp As Shape
    Dim rngSource As Range
    Dim pvtTable As PivotTable
    Dim r As Integer

    Set pvtTable = Worksheets("Sheet4").PivotTables(1)

    ' set the current page for the PivotTable report to the
    ' page named "Tofu"
    pvtTable.PivotFields("ProductName").CurrentPage = "Tofu"

    Set rngSource = pvtTable.TableRange2
    Set shp = ActiveSheet.Shapes.AddChart

    shp.Chart.SetSourceData Source:=rngSource
    shp.Chart.SetElement (msoElementChartTitleAboveChart)
    shp.Chart.ChartTitle.Caption = _
       pvtTable.PivotFields("ProductName").CurrentPage

    r = ActiveSheet.UsedRange.Rows.Count + 3

    With Range("B" & r & ":E" & r + 15)
        shp.Width = .Width
        shp.Height = .Height
        shp.Left = .Left
        shp.Top = .Top
```

```
    End With
End Sub
```

The CreatePivotChart procedure changes the current page for the PivotTable report to display information about the product named Tofu. The AddChart method of the Shapes collection is used to create a Chart object. The SetSourceData method of the Chart object is then used to specify the PivotTable range as the chart's data source. It's always a good idea to add a chart title, so the next two lines of code make sure that the title is positioned above the chart area and its text is set to the current product name in the PivotTable:

```
shp.Chart.SetElement (msoElementChartTitleAboveChart)
shp.Chart.ChartTitle.Caption = _
    pvtTable.PivotFields("ProductName").CurrentPage
```

To ensure that the chart appears just below the PivotTable report, we calculate the used range on the active worksheet and add to it three rows. The Top, Left, Width, and Height properties are used to position the chart over the specified range:

```
r = ActiveSheet.UsedRange.Rows.Count + 3

    With Range("B" & r & ":E" & r + 15)
        shp.Width = .Width
        shp.Height = .Height
        shp.Left = .Left
        shp.Top = .Top
    End With
```

6. Run the CreatePivotChart procedure.

   The resulting PivotChart report is shown in Figure 23-20.

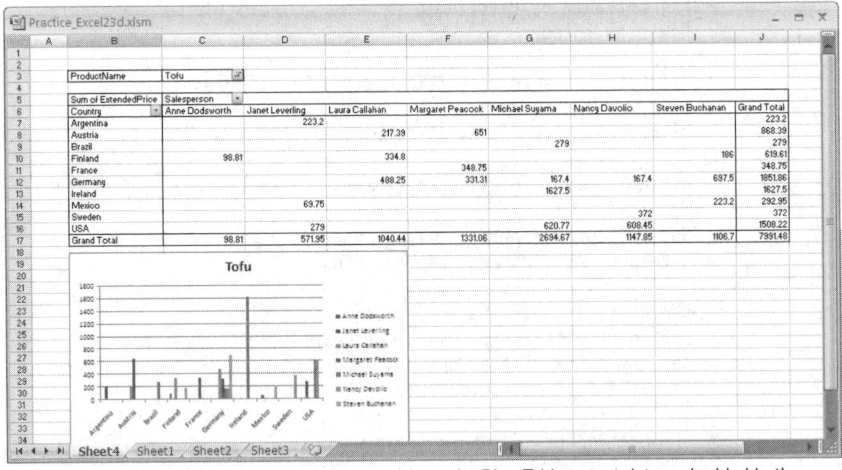

ProductName	Tofu							
Sum of ExtendedPrice	Salesperson							
Country	Anne Dodsworth	Janet Leverling	Laura Callahan	Margaret Peacock	Michael Suyama	Nancy Davolio	Steven Buchanan	Grand Total
Argentina		223.2						223.2
Austria			217.39	651				868.39
Brazil					279			279
Finland	98.81		334.8				186	619.61
France				348.75				348.75
Germany			488.25	331.31	167.4	167.4	697.5	1851.86
Ireland					1627.5			1627.5
Mexico		69.75					223.2	292.95
Sweden						372		372
USA		279			620.77	608.45		1508.22
Grand Total	98.81	571.95	1040.44	1331.06	2694.67	1147.85	1106.7	7991.48

Figure 23-20: The PivotChart report is generated from the PivotTable report data embedded in the same worksheet.

To ensure that the chart title changes when you select a different product in the Product Name field of the PivotTable report, you must create the Worksheet_PivotTableUpdate event procedure in the Sheet4 module.

7. In the Project Explorer window, double-click **Sheet4** under VBAProject (Practice_Excel23d.xlsm) and enter the following event procedure in the Code window:

```
Private Sub Worksheet_PivotTableUpdate(ByVal Target As PivotTable)
    Dim strPivotPage As String
    Dim r As Integer

    strPivotPage = Target.PivotFields("ProductName").CurrentPage.Value

    If ActiveSheet.ChartObjects.Count > 0 Then
        ActiveSheet.ChartObjects(1).Activate
        ActiveChart.ChartTitle.Text = strPivotPage

        r = ActiveSheet.UsedRange.Rows.Count + 3

        With Range("B" & r)
            ActiveSheet.ChartObjects(1).Top = .Top
        End With
    End If
End Sub
```

The above event procedure will be triggered automatically each time you update the PivotTable report.

8. In Sheet4, select another product name from the PivotTable ProductName field.

Notice that as you select a different product, the chart data and the chart title adjust to reflect your selection.

Chapter Summary

In this chapter you have worked with two powerful Microsoft Excel objects that are used for data analysis: PivotTable and PivotChart. You have learned how to use VBA to manipulate these two objects to quickly produce reports that allow you or your users to easily examine large amounts of data pulled from an Excel worksheet range or from an external data source such as a Microsoft Access database.

The next chapter focuses on using and programming data lists known in Excel 2007 as tables.

Chapter 24

Using and Programming Excel Tables

Understanding Excel Tables ■ Creating a Table ■ Creating a Table Using VBA ■ Understanding Column Headings in the Table ■ Multiple Tables in a Worksheet ■ Working with the Excel ListObject ■ Deleting Worksheet Tables ■ Chapter Summary

Over the years people have used spreadsheets for storing and extracting data from databases. In Microsoft Excel 2007, a single worksheet database allows users to store as many as 1,048,576 rows by 16,384 columns (compare this to 65,536 records and 256 fields you had available in Excel 2003). Furthermore, the data can be easily sorted, filtered, summarized, and validated. If you need to create any kind of a table and store it in a spreadsheet, this chapter's tour of Excel table management will be helpful. We will look at the user interface for the table ranges and learn how to access and work with the table feature programmatically.

Understanding Excel Tables

Tables are groups of cells that store related data and are managed separately from data in other cells on the worksheet. Tables aren't a new feature in Excel 2007; however, they were known as lists when they were introduced in Excel 2003. You can have one or more tables in a worksheet, but a table cannot overlap another table. Each table is treated as a single entity and can be sorted, filtered, or shared. Tables can be easily recognized in worksheets as Excel automatically enables filtering in the header row for each column (see Figure 24-1). You can use this feature to sort data in ascending or descending order or create a custom view of your data.

When you create a table from a cell range and don't specify that your table contains column headers, Excel automatically adds column headers (Column1, Column2, etc.) to the range.

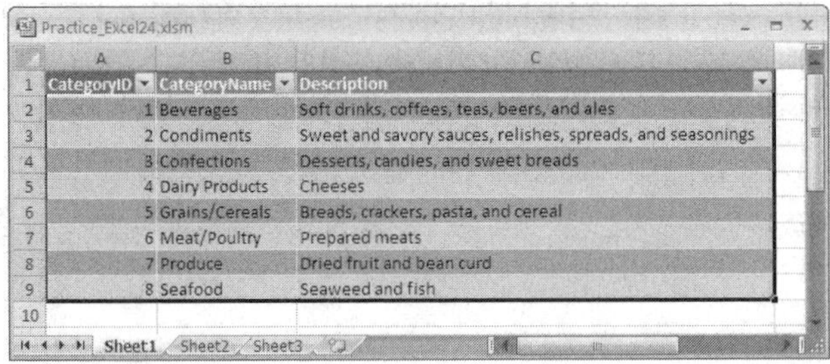

CategoryID	CategoryName	Description
1	Beverages	Soft drinks, coffees, teas, beers, and ales
2	Condiments	Sweet and savory sauces, relishes, spreads, and seasonings
3	Confections	Desserts, candies, and sweet breads
4	Dairy Products	Cheeses
5	Grains/Cereals	Breads, crackers, pasta, and cereal
6	Meat/Poultry	Prepared meats
7	Produce	Dried fruit and bean curd
8	Seafood	Seaweed and fish

Figure 24-1: A table in an Excel worksheet.

Note: In Excel 2003 data lists had a special row at the bottom marked with an asterisk (*). This row was used to add new records to the list. When you typed information in this row, the list range automatically expanded, adding this row to your data. This special row has been removed in Office Excel 2007. To add new records to the Excel 2007 table, all you have to do is select any cell in the last row of the table, and then press Enter, or you can press Tab in the last cell of the last row to add a blank row at the end of the table.

To subtotal data in the Excel 2007 table, you need to take the following steps:

1. Convert an Excel table into a standard worksheet range. To do this, click the **Design** tab and select **Convert to Range** in the Tools group. Click **Yes** in the dialog box that appears.
2. Sort the data according to your needs. Select any cell in the column you want to sort by and click **Sort & Filter** in the Editing group on the Home tab. Select the desired option from the Sort & Filter menu.
3. Now to add a subtotal, click anywhere within the worksheet, and then click **Subtotal** in the Outline group on the Data tab. You will see the Subtotal dialog box, as shown in Figure 24-2.

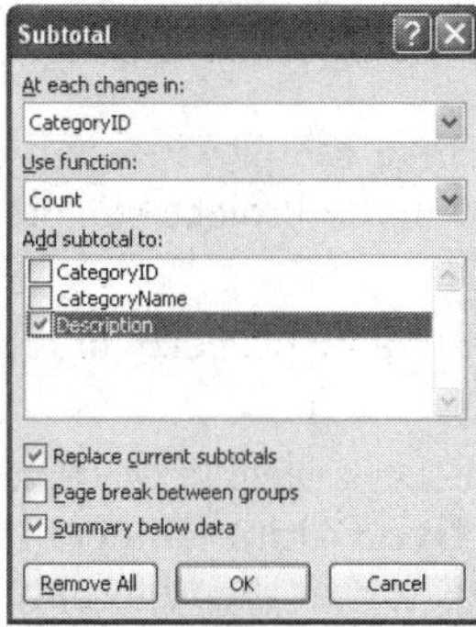

Figure 24-2: Use the Subtotal dialog box to subtotal Excel 2007 tables.

4. In the Subtotal dialog box, make appropriate selections:
   - In the At each change in drop-down box, choose the column by which you want to subtotal.
   - In the Use function drop-down, select the Sum function, or another function that is appropriate for the type of summary you want to produce.
   - In the Add subtotal to drop-down, check the appropriate column.
5. Click **OK** to finish adding subtotals.

Excel cells belonging in the table can be formatted using the formatting options you are already familiar with (applying bold, underline, font color, pattern, shading, conditional formatting, and so on). Data in the table may be validated via the Data Validation button in the Data Tools group on the Data tab.

Excel tables can be shared with others via Microsoft SharePoint Services, which is part of Windows 2003 Server. Shared lists are parts of documents stored on SharePoint. To share a table, you simply publish it by selecting any cell in a table and then choosing Design | Export | Export Table to SharePoint list. Lists on the SharePoint can also be imported to or linked with Excel.

Creating a Table

To create a table in Excel, select a range of cells containing the data you want to include in the table and then choose Insert | Table. Excel displays a Create Table dialog box where you can accept the current selection of cells for the table or change the range of data for your table (see Figure 24-3). To see how this is actually done, we will start by writing a VBA procedure that gets data from the Microsoft Access Northwind database.

Hands-On 24-1: Obtaining Table Data from a Microsoft Access Database

1. Open a new workbook and save it as **C:\Ex07_ByExample\Practice_Excel24.xlsm.**
2. Press **Alt+F11** to switch to the Visual Basic Editor window, highlight **VBAProject (Practice_Excel24.xlsm)** in the Project Explorer window, and choose **Insert | Module.**
3. Use the Properties window to change the Name property of Module1 to **Tables.**
4. Choose **Tools | References** and in the list of available references, select the check box next to the **Microsoft ActiveX Data Objects Library** (2.8 or an earlier version). Next, click **OK** to exit the References dialog box.
5. In the Tables module Code window, enter the GetCategories procedure as shown below:

```
Sub GetCategories()
    Dim conn As New ADODB.Connection
    Dim rst As ADODB.Recordset
    Dim strPath As String
    Dim wks As Worksheet
    Dim j As Integer

    strPath = "C:\Ex07_ByExample\Northwind.mdb"

    Set wks = ThisWorkbook.ActiveSheet

    conn.Open "Provider=Microsoft.Jet.OLEDB.4.0;" _
              & "Data Source=" & strPath & ";"

    ' Create a Recordset from data in the Categories table

    Set rst = conn.Execute(CommandText:="Select CategoryID," & _
                "CategoryName, Description from Categories", _
                Options:=adCmdText)

    rst.MoveFirst

    ' transfer the data to Excel
    ' get the names of fields first
      With wks.Range("A1")
```

```
            .CurrentRegion.Clear
            For j = 0 To rst.Fields.Count - 1
                .Offset(0, j) = rst.Fields(j).Name
            Next j
            .Offset(1, 0).CopyFromRecordset rst
            .CurrentRegion.Columns.AutoFit
            .Cells(1, 1).Select
        End With
        rst.Close
        conn.Close

        Set rst = Nothing
        Set conn = Nothing
    End Sub
```

6. Switch to the Microsoft Excel application window and select **Sheet1**.
7. Press **Alt+F8** to display the Macro dialog box. Highlight the **GetCategories** procedure and click **Run**.

    The data is retrieved from the Categories table and placed in Sheet1.
8. Choose **Insert | Table**.

    Microsoft Excel displays the Create Table dialog box and highlights the range of cells identified as a table (see Figure 24-3). You may change the range by making your own range selection in the worksheet.

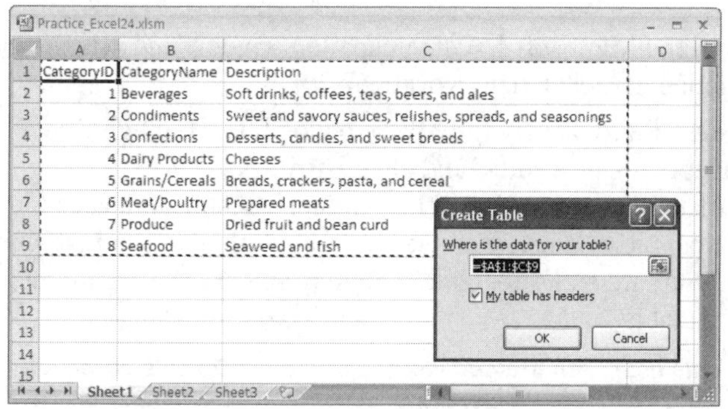

Figure 24-3: Converting a range of cells into an Excel table.

9. Click **OK** to exit the Create Table dialog box.

    Your table is now ready to use or share with others (see Figure 24-1).

Creating a Table Using VBA

To programmatically create an Excel table, use the ListObject object, which represents a list object in a worksheet. The ListObject object is a member of the ListObjects collection. This collection contains all the list objects on the worksheet. As mentioned earlier, you can have one or more tables in a single worksheet.

In the previous section, you learned how to retrieve data from Access and convert it into an Excel table using the built-in Ribbon commands. In this section, we will modify the GetCategories procedure so that it automatically creates a table out of the Access data.

Hands-On 24-2: Creating a Table Using VBA

1. In the Tables module Code window, modify the GetCategories procedure as follows:
   - Add the following declaration to the procedure declaration section:

     ```
     Dim rng As Range
     ```

   - Type the following statements just before the End Sub keywords:

     ```
     'create a table in Excel

     Set rng = wks.Range(Range("A1").CurrentRegion.Address)
     wks.ListObjects.Add xlSrcRange, rng
     ```

   The first statement that follows the comment will set the object variable (rng) to point to the range of cells that we want to convert into a table. The second statement uses the Add method of the ListObjects collection to create a table out of a specified range of cells. The xlSrcRange constant specifies that the source of the table is an Excel range, while the rng object variable indicates a Range object representing the data source.
2. Switch to the Microsoft Excel application window and activate Sheet2 in the Practice_Excel24.xlsm workbook.
3. Press **Alt+F8** to display the Macro dialog box. Highlight the **GetCategories** procedure and click **Run**.

   The data is retrieved from the Categories table and placed in Sheet2 as an Excel table. When you use the Add method of the ListObjects collection to create an Excel table, you may specify the arguments as shown in Table 24-1.

Table 24-1: Arguments used with the Add method of the ListObjects collection

Argument Name	Description
SourceType (optional)	Indicates the type of data for the list. You can use one of the following source types: ■ External data (xlSrcExternal) ■ Excel range (xlSrcRange) ■ XML data (xlSrcXML) If omitted, SourceType will default to xlSrcRange.

Argument Name	Description
Source (optional when SourceType = xlSrcRange) (required when SourceType = xlSrcExternal)	This argument can be one of the following: ■ An array of String values specifying a connection to the source: Use 0 to indicate the SharePoint URL. Use 1 to indicate the name of the list. Use 2 to indicate the ViewGUID (identifies the view for a list on SharePoint site). ■ A Range object representing the data source. If this argument is omitted, Source is the range returned by list range detection code.
LinkSource (optional)	Indicates whether an external data source is to be linked to the ListObject object. The SourceType argument must be set to xlSrcExternal.
HasHeaders (optional)	Indicates whether the data to be used for the list has column labels. You can use one of the following constants for this argument: xlGuess, xlNo, or xlYes. If Source does not have column headings, Excel automatically generates headers as Column1, Column2, etc.
Destination (required when SourceType = xlSrcExternal) (ignored when SourceType = xlSrcRange)	Indicates the top-left corner of the new list object. Use a Range object with a single-cell reference. You cannot reference more than one cell. If the destination range is not empty, new columns will be added to fit the new list (existing data will not be overwritten).

Notice that the arguments of the ListObject object's Add method are optional. If you omit the arguments, Excel will use its own logic to identify the range of cells for the table and will determine whether the table contains column headings. Contiguous cells containing data are always assumed to be a part of a table. If the first row of the identified data range contains text, Excel assumes that this is a header row.

Understanding Column Headings in the Table

When creating a table, Excel automatically adds column headings to the table. Depending on the type of data Excel finds in the first row of the data range, the first row may be designated as column headings or a new row may need to be inserted, causing other rows of data to shift down. Because you will not know exactly what Excel will do in a particular situation given a particular set of data, it is a good idea to supply the value for the HasHeaders argument in your VBA code (see Table 24-1). Let's look at how we can control the location of the column headings in the Excel table.

Hands-On 24-3: Adding Headings to a Table

1. Activate Sheet3 in the Practice_Excel24.xlsm workbook and type the sample data shown in Figure 24-4.

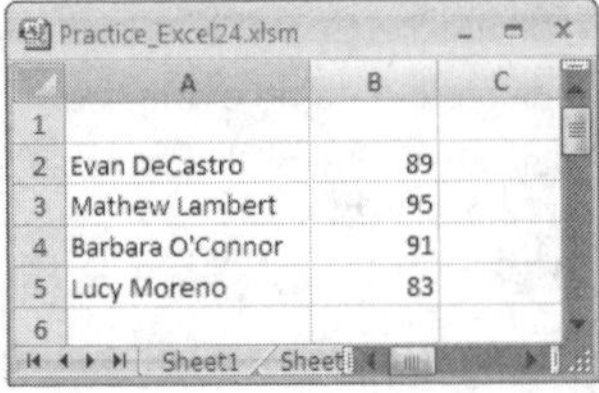

Figure 24-4: Data in a spreadsheet prior to conversion into a table.

2. Switch to the Visual Basic Editor screen and enter the following procedure in the Tables module:

```
Sub List_Headers()
    Dim rng As Range
    Dim wks As Worksheet

    Set wks = ActiveWorkbook.Worksheets(3)
    Set rng = wks.Range("A2:B5")

    wks.ListObjects.Add SourceType:=xlSrcRange, _
                        Source:=rng, _
                        XlListObjectHasHeaders:=xlNo
End Sub
```

Because the data in Figure 24-4 does not have column headings, we have specified xlNo for the HasHeaders argument. When Excel executes this procedure, it will add default headers (Column1, Column2) in row 2 and will shift the range down one row (see Figure 24-5).

3. Position the insertion point anywhere within the List_Headers procedure and press **F5** to run it.
4. Switch to the Microsoft Excel application window to view the result of running the procedure.

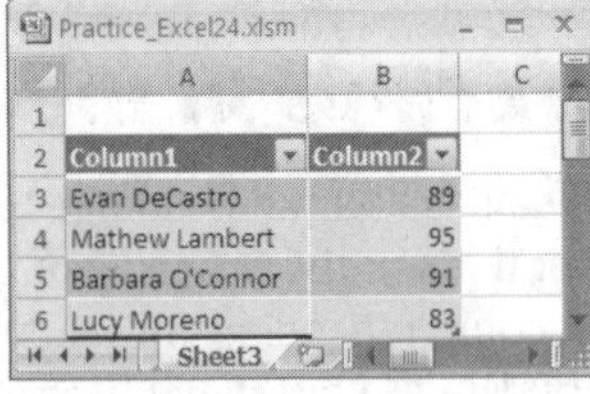

Figure 24-5: A range of data after conversion to an Excel table. Notice that Excel has added default column headings in row 2 and shifted the data range one row down.

Sometimes you may not want Excel to shift data down when your table does not include column headings. To prevent this, it is recommended that you specify for your table a range of data in which the first row is blank. For example, to prevent Excel from shifting the data down one row, specify A1:B5 as the range and use xlYes for the HasHeaders parameter. Before trying this out, let's convert the Excel table we have just created back to a normal range.

5. Select any cell within the table on the worksheet, and choose **Design | Convert to Range**. Click **Yes** when Excel displays a confirmation message.

   Notice that after Excel creates a normal range out of a table, the default column headings are preserved.
6. Delete row 2 from this worksheet and save your changes.
7. Switch back to the Visual Basic Editor screen and, in the Tables module, enter the following List_Headers2 procedure:

```
Sub List_Headers2()
    Dim rng As Range
    Dim wks As Worksheet

    Set wks = ActiveWorkbook.Worksheets(3)
    Set rng = wks.Range("A1:B5")

    wks.ListObjects.Add SourceType:=xlSrcRange, _
                        Source:=rng, _
                        XlListObjectHasHeaders:=xlYes
End Sub
```

8. Run the List_Headers2 procedure and view its results on Sheet3, shown in Figure 24-6.

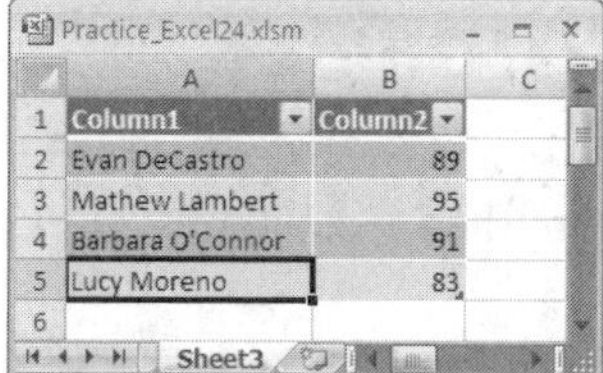

Figure 24-6: A range of data after conversion to an Excel table. Notice that Excel has added default column headings in row 1, which was empty when we specified the range of data for the table.

Multiple Tables in a Worksheet

You have seen in the previous section how Excel shifts the cells down when the data range specified for your table does not have column headings. Because you may have more than one table in a particular worksheet, this behavior may cause problems when another table is placed right below the first table. Also, when you add new rows to the table, the table expands, so a conflict may occur if another table is placed in the rows below. Therefore, it is a good idea to avoid placing any data in the rows below a table.

When you have more than one table in a worksheet and want to manipulate these tables programmatically, you may want to assign names to your tables so you can easily refer to them in your code.

While you can always refer to a table by using its index number, names are more meaningful and easier to understand. By default Excel assigns the names Table1, Table2, Table3, etc., to the tables in a worksheet. To name a table or retrieve the name of an existing table, use the Name property of the

ListObject object. For example, the following statement entered in the Immediate window returns the name of the table in the active sheet:

```
?ActiveSheet.ListObjects(1).Name
Table1
```

To rename Table1, we can simply type the following statement in the Immediate window and press Enter:

```
ActiveSheet.ListObjects(1).Name = "Student Scores"
```

Now you can refer to the first table in the active sheet as Student Scores.

The DefineTableName procedure shown below uses the ListObjects property to get a reference to the first table on Sheet3. Next, the Name property is used to assign a name to the referenced table.

```
Sub DefineTableName()
    Dim wks As Worksheet
    Dim lst As ListObject

    Set wks = ActiveWorkbook.Worksheets(3)

    Set lst = wks.ListObjects(1)
    lst.Name = "1st Qtr. 2008 Student Scores"
End Sub
```

Working with the Excel ListObject

The ListObject object represents a table on a worksheet. You can manipulate the table via the properties and methods of the ListColumns and ListRows collections.

- The ListColumns collection contains all the ListColumn objects in the specified ListObject object. Each ListColumn object is a column in the table.
- The ListRows collection contains all the ListRow objects in the specified ListObject object. Each ListRow object is a row in the table.

You can perform various operations on Excel tables using properties and methods of the ListObject object as shown in Tables 24-2 and 24-3.

Table 24-2: Properties of the ListObject object

Property Name	Description

Active	Indicates whether a list in a worksheet is currently active.
	Returns True or False. For example:
	`IsTblActive = ActiveSheet.ListObjects(1).active`
	`Debug.Print IsTblActive`
	Note: There is no Activate method for the ListObject object. To activate a table, you must activate a cell range within a table. For example:
	`ActiveSheet.ListObjects(1).Range.Activate`
	The above statement selects the entire range for the list.

Property Name	Description

DataBodyRange	Returns a Range object that represents the range of cells without the header row in a table. For example:
	`ActiveSheet.ListObjects(1).DataBodyRange.Select`
	or
	`dataRng = ActiveSheet.ListObjects(1).DataBodyRange .Address Debug.Print dataRng`

HeaderRowRange	Returns a Range object that represents the range of the header row for a table. For example, use the following statement to select the header row in the table: `ActiveSheet.ListObjects(1).HeaderRowRange.Select`
InsertRowRange	In Excel 2003, this property returns a Range object representing the insert row. This property is not supported in Excel 2007: `ActiveSheet.ListObjects(1).InsertRowRange.Activate`

ListColumns	Returns a ListColumns collection that represents all the columns in a ListObject object. For example, the following procedure deletes the last column from the table:
	`Sub DeleteLastCol()`
	`    Dim myList As ListObject`
	`    Dim lastCol As Integer`
	
	`    Set myList = ActiveSheet.ListObjects(1)`
	`    lastCol = myList.ListColumns.Count`
	`    myList.ListColumns(lastCol).Delete`
	`End Sub`

ListRows	Returns a ListRows object that represents all the rows of data in the ListObject object. For example, the following procedure prints to the Immediate window the total number of rows in the table:
	`Sub CountListRows()`
	`    Dim objRows As ListRows`
	`    Set objRows = ActiveSheet.ListObjects(1).ListRows`
	`    Debug.Print objRows.Count`
	`End Sub`

Name	Returns or sets the name of the ListObject object. For example, use the following statement to assign a name to the first table in the active worksheet: `ActiveSheet.ListObjects(1).Name = "Student Scores"`
QueryTable	Returns the QueryTable object that provides a link for the ListObject object to the SharePoint site server.
Range	Returns a Range object that represents the range to which the specified list object applies. For example, the following statement prints to the Immediate window the range address of the entire list: `Debug.Print ActiveSheet.ListObjects(1).Range.Address`

SharePointURL	Returns a String representing the URL of the SharePoint list. Use it to find the address of the shared list after it has been published:
	`listURL = ActiveSheet.ListObjects(1).SharePointURL`
	`Debug.Print listURL`

Property Name	Description
ShowAutoFilter	Indicates whether the AutoFilter will be displayed in the header row (True or False). Use the following statement to turn off the AutoFilter mode for a given table: `ActiveSheet.ListObjects(1).ShowAutoFilter = False`
ShowTotals	Indicates whether the Total row is visible (True) or hidden (False). The following statement turns on the display of the Total row: `ActiveSheet.ListObjects(1).ShowTotals = True`
SourceType	Returns one of the XlListObjectSourceType constants indicating the current source of the table (xlSrcRange, xlSrcExternal, or xlSrcXML). See Table 24-1.
TotalsRowRange	Returns a range representing the Total row for the specified ListObject object: `Debug.Print ActiveSheet.ListObjects(1).TotalsRowRange.Address`
XmlMap	Returns an XmlMap object that represents the schema map used for the specified table. See Chapter 29 for more information.

Table 24-3: Methods of the ListObject object

Method Name	Description
Delete	Deletes the ListObject object and clears the cell data from the worksheet. If the list is linked to a SharePoint site, deleting it does not remove data on the server that is running Windows SharePoint Services. Any uncommitted changes not sent to the SharePoint list are lost when the list is deleted in Excel.
Publish	Publishes the ListObject object to a server that is running Microsoft Windows SharePoint Services. Returns a String indicating the URL of the published list on the SharePoint site. The Publish method requires two arguments. ■ Target — This is a three-element string array that specifies the address of the SharePoint server (element 0), the name of the list (element 1), and an optional description of the list (element 2). ■ LinkSource — A Boolean value (True or False) If the ListObject object is not currently linked to a list on a SharePoint site: ■ LinkSource = True (creates a new list on the specified SharePoint site) ■ LinkSource = False (leaves the list object unlinked) If the ListObject object is currently linked to a SharePoint site: ■ LinkSource = True (replaces the existing link – only one link to the list is allowed on the SharePoint site) ■ LinkSource = False (keeps the ListObject object linked to the current SharePoint site)
Refresh	This method can be used only with tables that are linked to a SharePoint site. Retrieves the current data and schema for the table from the SharePoint server.

Method Name	Description
Resize	Allows a ListObject object to be resized over a new range. You must provide the range address as the argument to the Resize method. Assuming that the current table range is "A1:B6," we can specify the new range for the table as: `ActiveSheet.ListObjects(1).Resize Range("A1:B3")`
Unlink	Removes the link to a SharePoint Services site from a list. For example: `ActiveSheet.ListObjects(1).Unlink`
Unlist	Converts an Excel table back to a regular range of data. For example, the table on the active sheet is turned into a normal range like this: `ActiveSheet.ListObjects(1).Unlist`
UpdateChanges	Updates the list on a Microsoft Windows SharePoint Services site with the changes made to table in the worksheet. You can specify how list/table conflicts should be resolved by using one of the xlListConflict resolution constants: xlListConflictDialog (default), xlListConflictRetry-AllConflicts, xlListConflictDiscardAllConflicts, or xlListConflictError. For example: `ActiveSheet.ListObjects(1).UpdateChanges xlListConflictDialog`

The following procedure demonstrates how to use selected properties from Table 24-2.

Hands-On 24-4: Defining Table Names

1. Enter the following procedure in the Tables module of VBAProject (Practice_Excel24.xlsm):

```
Sub DefineTableName2()
    Dim wks As Worksheet
    Dim lst As ListObject
    Dim col As ListColumn
    Dim c As Variant

    Set wks = ActiveWorkbook.Worksheets(3)

    Set lst = wks.ListObjects(1)
    With lst
        .Name = "1st Qtr. 2008 Student Scores"
        .ListColumns(1).Name = "Student Name"
        .ListColumns(2).Name = "Score"
        Set col = .ListColumns.Add
        col.Name = "Previous Score"
        Debug.Print "Header Address = " & .HeaderRowRange.Address
        Debug.Print "Data Range = " & .Range.Address
        Debug.Print "Data Body Range = " & .DataBodyRange.Address

        For Each c In wks.Range(.HeaderRowRange.Address)
            Debug.Print c
        Next
    End With
End Sub
```

2. Activate Sheet3 of the Practice_Excel24.xlsm workbook.
3. Press **Alt+F8** to display the Macro dialog box. Highlight the **DefineTableName2** procedure and click **Run**.
4. Check the Immediate window for the procedure results.

Deleting Worksheet Tables

You can delete an Excel table using one of the following methods:

User Interface

- Select the table on the worksheet and choose Home | Delete | Delete Cells.
- If you don't need the sheet with the table, delete the entire worksheet.

VBA Code

- Use the Delete method to delete the worksheet table and its data.
- Use the Unlist method to convert the worksheet table to a normal data range.
- Use the Unlink method to remove the link between the worksheet table and the list on the SharePoint site. An unlinked list cannot be relinked.

Note: The SharePoint lists can only be deleted on the SharePoint site or by using the Lists web service provided by SharePoint Services.

Chapter Summary

This chapter has introduced you to Excel tables. You have learned how to retrieve information from a Microsoft Access database, convert it into a table, and enjoy database-like functionality in the spreadsheet. You've also learned how tables are exposed through Excel's object model and manipulated via VBA.

The biggest selling point for Excel tables is that the information contained in a table can be easily shared with others as long as you have access to Microsoft Windows SharePoint Services. If you have Windows 2003 Server, these services are free and can be downloaded from the Microsoft web site. If you don't have access to Windows 2003 Server, there are many SharePoint hosting providers on the Internet that offer these services for a monthly fee.

The next chapter covers programming special features in Excel.

Chapter 25

Programming Special Features

Tab Object ■ Speech Object ■ SpellingOptions Object ■ CellFormat Object ■ Characters Object ■ AutoCorrect Object ■ FormatCondition Object ■ Graphic Object ■ CustomProperty Object ■ Sort Object ■ Excel8CompatibilityMode Property ■ Chapter Summary

The Excel 2007 object model contains hundreds of objects, allowing you to control various aspects of the Excel application. For this chapter, I have selected a number of objects from the Excel 2007 object library to give you a feel for what can be accomplished by calling upon them.

Tab Object

Sheet tabs at the bottom of an Excel chart sheet or worksheet are represented by the Tab object. You can change the color of sheet tabs by using the Color or ColorIndex properties of the Tab object. The Color property requires that you use the RGB function to create a color value. For example, to set the Sheet1 tab color to purple, you could enter the following statement in the Immediate window:

```
ActiveWorkbook.Worksheets(1).Tab.Color = RGB(128, 0, 255)
```

The following example demonstrates a procedure that changes the tab color of all the worksheets in the current workbook.

Hands-On 25-1: Changing the Color of the Tabs on Current Worksheets

1. Open a new workbook and save it as **Practice_Excel25.xlsm** in your **C:\Ex07_ByExample** folder.
2. Press **Alt+F11** to switch to the Visual Basic Editor window, highlight **VBAProject (Practice_Excel25.xlsm)** in the Project Explorer window, and choose **Insert | Module.**
3. Use the Properties window to change the Name property of Module1 to **TabObject**.
4. In the TabObject Code window, enter the ColorTabs procedure as shown below:

```
Sub ColorTabs()
    Dim wks As Worksheet
    Dim i As Integer

    i = 5

    For Each wks In ThisWorkbook.Worksheets
        If wks.Tab.ColorIndex = xlColorIndexNone Then
            wks.Tab.ColorIndex = i
            i = i + 1
        End If
    Next
End Sub
```

5. Run the ColorTabs procedure.

   When you switch to the Microsoft Excel application window, each worksheet tab will shine with a different color.

Speech Object

Microsoft Office comes with a speech recognition feature that makes it possible to read text on demand. The text can be read automatically on data entry by clicking the Speak Cells on Enter button. You can add this button to the Quick Access toolbar by clicking the Microsoft Office button and choosing Excel Options | Customize. Next, choose Commands Not in the Ribbon from the left-hand drop-down box and scroll down in the list to locate the Speak Cells on Enter button. Click Add, and then OK.

You can also control the speech feature via the Speech object from a VBA procedure. This object has the Speak method that causes the text to be spoken by Excel. The Speech object is accessed via the Application object. To cause the active cell to be spoken on entry or when it is finished being edited, set the SpeakCellOnEnter property of the Speech object to True:

```
Application.Speech.SpeakCellOnEnter = True
```

The example below demonstrates a procedure that reads aloud only the cell values in the specified range.

Hands-On 25-2: Reading Cell Values Aloud

1. In Sheet1 of the Practice_Excel25.xlsm workbook, enter the data shown in Figure 25-1.

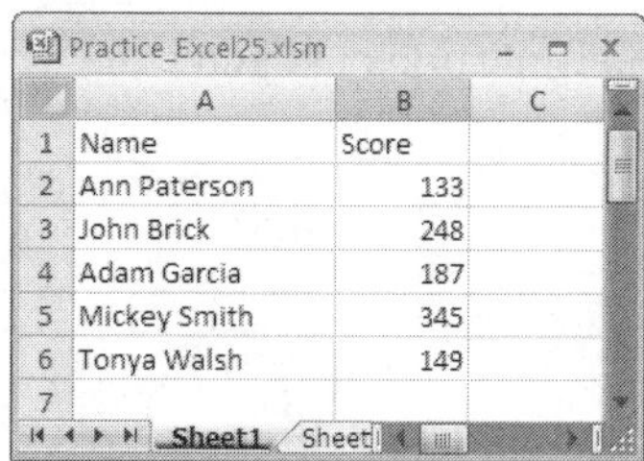

Figure 25-1: Example data.

2. Press **Alt+F11** to switch to the Visual Basic Editor window.
3. Highlight **VBAProject (Practice_Excel25.xlsm)** in the Project Explorer window and choose **Insert | Module.**
4. Use the Properties window to change the Name property of Module1 to **SpeechObject**.
5. In the SpeechObject Code window, enter the ReadNamesWithHighScores procedure as shown below:

```
Sub ReadNamesWithHighScores()
    Dim v As Integer
    Dim cell As Variant

    v = InputBox("Enter the minimum expected score:", "Approved Minimum")

    For Each cell In ActiveSheet.UsedRange.Columns("B").Cells
        If IsNumeric(cell.Value) And cell.Value >= v Then
```

```
            Application.Speech.Speak "Congratulations " & _
            cell.Offset(0, -1).Text
            Application.Speech.Speak " your score is " & cell.Text
        End If
    Next
End Sub
```

6. Run the ReadNamesWithHighScores procedure. When prompted for the minimum expected score, enter **200** and click **OK**.

   If your computer speaker is on or you have connected a headphone, you will be able to hear the names and scores of people who met the minimum score criteria.

SpellingOptions Object

The SpellingOptions object represents the various spell-checking options for a worksheet. Spelling options can also be set manually on the Proofing tab in the Options dialog box (click the Microsoft Office button and choose Excel Options | Proofing). The following procedure sets some spelling options and adds a new dictionary named Special.dic, where you can add correct words found during the spell check.

Hands-On 25-3: Setting Spelling Options and Adding a New Dictionary

1. In Sheet2 of the Practice_Excel25.xlsm workbook, enter the data shown in Figure 25-2.

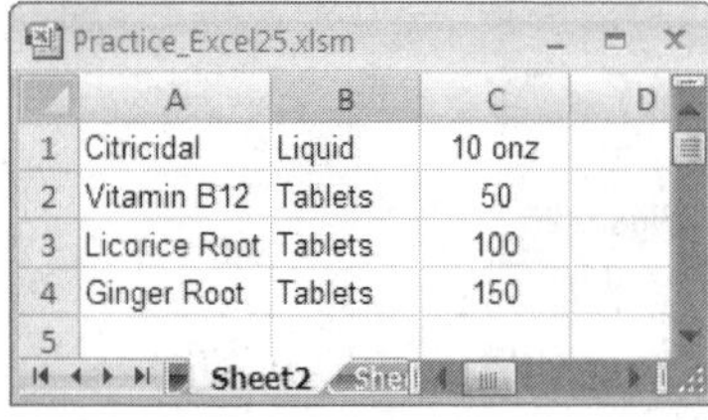

	A	B	C	D
1	Citricidal	Liquid	10 onz	
2	Vitamin B12	Tablets	50	
3	Licorice Root	Tablets	100	
4	Ginger Root	Tablets	150	
5				

Figure 25-2: Example data.

2. Press **Alt+F11** to switch to the Visual Basic Editor window.
3. Highlight **VBAProject (Practice_Excel25.xlsm)** in the Project Explorer window and choose **Insert | Module.**
4. Use the Properties window to change the Name property of Module1 to **SpellingOptionsObject**.
5. In the SpellingOptionsObject Code window, enter the SpellCheck procedure as shown below:

```
Sub SpellCheck()
    ' set spelling options
    With Application.SpellingOptions
        .IgnoreCaps = True
        .IgnoreMixedDigits = True
        .SuggestMainOnly = False
        .IgnoreFileNames = True
        .UserDict = "Special.dic"
```

```
        End With

        ' run a spell check
        Cells.CheckSpelling
    End Sub
```

6. Run the SpellCheck procedure.

   After setting the spelling options, Excel displays the Spelling dialog box, indicating that the word "Citricidal" is not in the dictionary.

7. Press the **Add to Dictionary** button.

   The word "Citricidal" will be added to the custom user dictionary Special.dic as specified in the SpellCheck procedure. In Microsoft Windows 2000 and later, this custom dictionary is stored by default in the \Documents and Settings\<username>\Application Data\Microsoft\Proof folder. A custom dictionary is a simple text file that you can open and edit. Each dictionary entry appears on a separate line.

8. Click **Cancel** to exit the Spelling dialog box.

CellFormat Object

The FindFormat and ReplaceFormat properties of the Application object return the CellFormat object that represents the search criteria for the cell format.

- FindFormat property — Sets or returns the search criteria for the type of cell formats to find
- ReplaceFormat property — Sets the replacement criteria to use in replacing cell formats

The following example procedure replaces the regular Arial font style with Tahoma Bold, makes some of the cell borders darker, and performs other formatting changes in the worksheet.

Hands-On 25-4: Changing Fonts and Worksheet Formatting

1. In Sheet1 of the Practice_Excel25.xlsm workbook, change the font face in cells A1:B6 to Arial and specify 10 for the font size.
2. Press **Alt+F11** to switch to the Visual Basic Editor window.
3. Highlight **VBAProject (Practice_Excel25.xlsm)** in the Project Explorer window and choose **Insert | Module**.
4. Use the Properties window to change the Name property of Module1 to **CellFormatObject**.
5. In the CellFormatObject Code window, enter the Reformat procedure as shown below:

```
Sub Reformat()
    ' Set search criteria
    With Application.FindFormat.Font
        .Name = "Arial"
        .FontStyle = "Regular"
```

```
        .Size = 10
    End With

    ' Set replacement criteria
    With Application.ReplaceFormat.Font
        .Name = "Tahoma"
        .FontStyle = "Bold"
        .Size = 11
    End With

    With Application.ReplaceFormat.Borders(xlEdgeBottom)
        .LineStyle = xlContinuous
        .Weight = xlThick
    End With

    ' Perform the replace
    Sheets(1).UsedRange.Replace _
        What:="", _
        Replacement:="", _
        SearchFormat:=True, _
        ReplaceFormat:=True

    ' Reset the Find and Replace formats
    Application.FindFormat.Clear
    Application.ReplaceFormat.Clear
End Sub
```

6. Run the Reformat procedure.

   Excel formats Sheet1 data as shown in Figure 25-3.

Figure 25-3: Example data reformatted with VBA.

Characters Object

The Characters object allows you to modify individual characters in a text string. To return a Characters object, use Characters (start, length), where start is the start character number and length is the number of characters. The following procedure changes the font color of the first letter of every word found in the UsedRange.

Hands-On 25-5: Changing Font Color in the UsedRange

1. Press **Alt+F11** to switch to the Visual Basic Editor window.
2. Highlight **VBAProject (Practice_Excel25.xlsm)** in the Project Explorer window and choose **Insert | Module.**
3. Use the Properties window to change the Name property of Module1 to **CharactersObject**.

4. In the CharactersObject Code window, enter the Format1stLetters procedure as shown below:

```
Sub Format1stLetters()
    Dim myChr As Characters
    Dim cell As Variant
    Dim i As Integer

    For Each cell In Sheets(1).UsedRange
        If Not IsNumeric(cell) Then
            Set myChr = cell.Characters(1, 1)
            myChr.Font.Color = RGB(128, 0, 255)
            For i = 1 To Len(cell.Text)
                If Asc(Mid(cell, i, 1)) = 32 Then
                    Set myChr = cell.Characters(i + 1, 1)
                    myChr.Font.Color = RGB(255, 0, 0)
                End If
            Next
        End If
    Next
End Sub
```

5. Run the Format1stLetters procedure.

   When you switch to Sheet1 you will notice the color change in the first letter of every word.

AutoCorrect Object

The AutoCorrect object has properties and methods that allow you to work with Excel's AutoCorrect features. The following two procedures will get you started working with AutoCorrect programmatically. The first procedure uses the ReplacementList method to retrieve commonly misspelled words and their automatic replacements into an array. The procedure then reads the values of this array and enters them into a worksheet so that you can print them out easily. If you need to update your AutoCorrect list with a number of new entries, you may want to enter them in a worksheet instead of working with the provided dialog box. The first column would hold the misspelled words, and the next column would contain the corrected words. You could then use the second VBA procedure shown below to update the AutoCorrect list with your new entries quickly and easily.

Hands-On 25-6: Using the ReplacementList Method to Update the AutoCorrect List

1. Press **Alt+F11** to switch to the Visual Basic Editor window.
2. Highlight **VBAProject (Practice_Excel25.xlsm)** in the Project Explorer window and choose **Insert | Module.**
3. Use the Properties window to change the Name property of Module1 to **AutoCorrectObject**.

4. In the AutoCorrectObject Code window, enter the two procedures shown below:

```
' this procedure generates a list of AutoCorrect entries
Sub Auto_Correct()
    Dim myList As Variant
    Dim i As Integer

    myList = Application.AutoCorrect.ReplacementList
    ActiveSheet.Cells(1, 1).Select
    For i = LBound(myList) To UBound(myList)
        With ActiveCell
            .Offset(0, 0).Value = myList(i, 1)
            .Offset(0, 1).Value = myList(i, 2)
            .Offset(1, 0).Select
        End With
    Next
    ActiveSheet.Columns("A:B").AutoFit
    Cells(1, 1).Select
End Sub

' this procedure adds new worksheet entries to the AutoCorrect list
Sub Auto_Correct_Batch_Add()
    Dim myRange As Range
    Dim myList As Variant
    Dim strReplaceWhat As String
    Dim strReplaceWith As String
    Dim i As Integer

    ' prompt user to select data for processing
    ' the Type argument ensures that the return value is
    ' a valid cell reference (a Range object).
    Set myRange = Application.InputBox( _
        Prompt:="Highlight the range containing your list", _
        Title:="List Selection", _
        Type:=8)
    If myRange.Columns.Count <> 2 Then Exit Sub

    ' save all the values in the selected range to an array
    myList = myRange.Value

    ' retrieve the values from the array and
    ' add them to the AutoCorrect replacements
    For i = LBound(myList) To UBound(myList)
        strReplaceWhat = myList(i, 1)
        strReplaceWith = myList(i, 2)
        If strReplaceWhat <> "" And strReplaceWith <> "" Then
            Application.AutoCorrect.AddReplacement _
                    strReplaceWhat, strReplaceWith
        End If
    Next
End Sub
```

5. Activate Sheet3 in the current workbook and press **Alt+F8** to activate the Macro dialog box. Choose **Auto_Correct** and click **Run**.

   Excel enters all AutoCorrect list entries in the worksheet.

6. To add new entries to the AutoCorrect list, type your entries in any two columns of the worksheet (as shown below). For example, enter the following words in cells E11:F12:

derfore	therefore
acess	Access

7. Run the Auto_Correct_Batch_Add procedure. When asked to highlight the range containing your list, select cells **E11:F12** and click **OK**.

   Excel adds your entries to the AutoCorrect list. To view the new additions, simply rerun the Auto_Correct procedure.

FormatCondition Object

You can add conditional formatting to your spreadsheet by using the FormatCondition object. Conditional formatting is associated with a particular range of cells. The FormatCondition object is a member of the FormatConditions collection. This collection can contain up to three FormatCondition objects for a given range. Use the Count method of the FormatConditions collection to return the number of objects in the collection. Use the Add method of the FormatConditions collection to create a new conditional format. This method requires that you specify the Type constant (xlCellValue, xlExpression) to indicate whether the conditional format is based on a cell value or an expression. The Add method has three optional arguments (Operator, Formula1, and Formula2) that allow you to specify the condition. Use the Modify method to modify a formatting condition. Use the Delete method to delete a formatting condition.

The following example procedure creates a conditional format to be applied to all non-numeric cells in the active sheet when the cell value is greater than or equal to 150. Notice how the cell with a value of 150 is formatted with white font color and colored background.

Hands-On 25-7: Applying Conditional Formatting to a Worksheet Range

1. Press **Alt+F11** to switch to the Visual Basic Editor window.
2. Highlight **VBAProject (Practice_Excel25.xlsm)** in the Project Explorer window and choose **Insert | Module**.
3. Use the Properties window to change the Name property of Module1 to **FormatConditionObject**.
4. In the FormatConditionObject Code window, enter the ApplyConditionalFormat procedure as shown below:

```
Sub ApplyConditionalFormat()
    Dim objFormatCon As FormatCondition
    Dim objFormatColl As FormatConditions
    Dim myRange As Range
```

```
    ' select range containing numeric cells only
    Set myRange = ActiveSheet.UsedRange. _
        SpecialCells(xlCellTypeConstants, 1)
    Set objFormatColl = myRange.FormatConditions

    ' find out if any conditional formatting already exists
    If objFormatColl.Count > 0 Then
        MsgBox "There are " & objFormatColl.Count & " conditions " & _
            "defined for the used range."
    End If

    ' remove existing conditions if they exist
    For Each objFormatCon In objFormatColl
        objFormatCon.Delete
    Next

    ' add first condition
    Set objFormatCon = objFormatColl.Add(Type:=xlCellValue, _
        Operator:=xlGreaterEqual, _
        Formula1:="150")
    With objFormatCon
        .Font.Bold = True
        .Font.ColorIndex = 2 ' white
        .Interior.Pattern = xlSolid
        .Interior.Color = RGB(0, 0, 255) ' blue
    End With
End Sub
```

5. Activate Sheet2 in the Practice_Excel25.xlsm workbook and press **Alt+F8** to activate the Macro dialog box. Choose **ApplyConditional-Format** and click **Run**. Cell C4 should now be formatted with white font and blue background.

Graphic Object

Use the Graphic object to place a picture in the header or footer area of an Excel worksheet. There are six properties of the PageSetup object (Center-FooterPicture, CenterHeaderPicture, LeftFooterPicture, LeftHeaderPicture, RightFooterPicture, and RightHeaderPicture) that can return the Graphic object.

The following procedure displays the File Picker dialog box where the user can select a picture file. Next, the file is inserted in the left header of the active sheet. Notice that to make the picture visible, you must set the LeftHeader property to the following string: "&G."

Hands-On 25-8: Displaying the File Picker and Inserting a File in the Worksheet Header

1. Press **Alt+F11** to switch to the Visual Basic Editor window.
2. Highlight **VBAProject (Practice_Excel25.xlsm)** in the Project Explorer window and choose **Insert | Module**.

3. Use the Properties window to change the Name property of Module1 to **GraphicObject**.
4. In the GraphicObject Code window, enter the AddWatermarkImage procedure as shown below:

```
Sub AddWatermarkImage()
    Dim strFilename As String

    With Application.FileDialog(msoFileDialogFilePicker)
        .Title = "Custom image selection"
        .AllowMultiSelect = False
        .Filters.Add "Pictures", "*.gif; *.jpg; *.jpeg; *.bmp", 1
        .InitialView = msoFileDialogViewThumbnail
        If .Show = -1 Then
            strFilename = .SelectedItems(1)
            With ActiveSheet.PageSetup
                With .LeftHeaderPicture
                    .Filename = strFilename
                    .Brightness = 0.85
                    .ColorType = msoPictureWatermark
                    .Contrast = 0.15
                    .Height = 72
                    .Width = 72
                End With
                .TopMargin = Application.InchesToPoints(1.25)
                .LeftHeader = "&G"
            End With
        End If
    End With
End Sub
```

5. Activate Sheet1 in the current workbook and press **Alt+F8** to activate the Macro dialog box. Choose **AddWatermarkImage** and click **Run.**
6. Excel will present a Custom image selection dialog box where you can specify your image. Switch to the folder containing the picture you want to include, select the image, and click **OK.**
7. Click the **Microsoft Office** button and choose **Print | Print Preview** to view the image placed in the worksheet's header.

CustomProperty Object

When you write VBA procedures, you often need to store specific information regarding a worksheet. Excel offers many ways to preserve information for later use. For example, you can store information in worksheet-level range names or hidden worksheets, or you can write it directly to the registry. The fourth method is storing information using custom properties. A CustomProperty object can store information with a worksheet or smart tag. Use the Add method of the CustomProperties collection to add custom property information and return a CustomProperty object. You must specify the name and value of the custom property.

The following example procedure demonstrates how to store student names and scores as custom properties.

Hands-On 25-9: Storing Data as Custom Properties

1. Press **Alt+F11** to switch to the Visual Basic Editor window.
2. Highlight **VBAProject (Practice_Excel25.xlsm)** in the Project Explorer window and choose **Insert | Module.**
3. Use the Properties window to change the Name property of Module1 to **CustomPropertyObject**.
4. In the CustomPropertyObject Code window, enter the StoreScores procedure as shown below:

```
Sub StoreScores()
    Dim mySheet As Worksheet
    Dim custPrp As CustomProperty
    Dim i As Integer
    Dim rng As Range
    Dim totalCount As Integer

    Set mySheet = ThisWorkbook.Sheets(1)

    ' find out if custom properties exist
    If mySheet.CustomProperties.Count > 0 Then
        ' Display custom properties
        totalCount = mySheet.CustomProperties.Count

        For i = 1 To totalCount
            With mySheet.CustomProperties(1)
                Debug.Print .Name & vbTab; .Value
                Set rng = mySheet.Range("A:A").Find(what:=.Name)
                ' Delete the custom property
                 If Not rng Is Nothing Then .Delete
            End With
        Next
    End If

    mySheet.Activate
    Cells(2, 1).Select
    Do While ActiveCell <> ""
        If Not IsEmpty(ActiveCell) Then
            Set custPrp = mySheet.CustomProperties.Add( _
            Name:=ActiveCell.Text, _
            Value:=ActiveCell.Offset(0, 1).Text)
            Debug.Print custPrp.Name & vbTab & custPrp.Value
            ActiveCell.Offset(1, 0).Select
        End If
    Loop

    If mySheet.CustomProperties.Count > 0 Then
        ' Display custom properties
        For i = 1 To mySheet.CustomProperties.Count
            With mySheet.CustomProperties(i)
                Debug.Print .Name & vbTab; .Value
            End With
```

```
        Next
    End If
End Sub
```

5. Run the StoreScores procedure.

   Excel writes the names and values of the custom properties to the Immediate window.

Sort Object

Use the Sort object to sort data in a range in the active workbook. This is a new object in Excel 2007. The Sort object contains a SortFields collection in which you can use SortFields to define as many sort fields as you need. Use the Clear method to clear all the SortFields objects. If you record the sorting process you will notice the SortMethod property set to xlPinYin. This property is only used for Asian languages; therefore it is omitted in the example code below. Use the SetRange method to specify the data range to sort. This method can only be used to apply sorting to a sheet range; it cannot be used if the range is within a table. After configuring all the sort options, use the Apply method to execute the sort. You can try out the code below to sort the data entered on Sheet1 of the Practice_Excel25.xlsm workbook.

```
Sub SortData()
    Range("A2").Select
    With ActiveWorkbook.Worksheets(ActiveSheet.Name).Sort
        .SortFields.Clear
        .SortFields.Add Key:=Range("A2:A6"), _
            SortOn:=xlSortOnValues, _
            Order:=xlDescending, _
            DataOption:=xlSortNormal
        .SetRange Range("A1:B6")
        .Header = xlYes
        .MatchCase = False
        .Orientation = xlTopToBottom
        .Apply
    End With
    MsgBox "Data has been sorted.", vbInformation
End Sub
```

Excel8CompatibilityMode Property

As you already know, due to the file format changes, new Excel 2007 features will not work in Excel 97-2003 workbooks. In compatibility mode some features are disabled or work differently. For this reason, it is more important than ever for your VBA code to check whether the workbook is opened in compatibility mode. The Excel8CompatibilityMode property provides a way to perform this check. The IsCompatible function in HandsOn 25-10 returns True if the active workbook is in compatibility mode and False if it is not.

Hands-On 25-10: Checking if the Workbook Is in Compatibility Mode

1. Open the **Assets.xls** file located in your **C:\Ex07_HandsOn** folder.
2. Press **Alt+F11** to switch to the Visual Basic Editor window.
3. Highlight **VBAProject (Practice_Excel25.xlsm)** in the Project Explorer window and choose **Insert | Module**.
4. Use the Properties window to change the Name property of Module1 to **Compatibility**.
5. Enter the following procedures in the Compatibility module:

```
Function IsCompatible() As Boolean
    If Application.Version = "12.0" Then
        If ActiveWorkbook.Excel8CompatibilityMode Then
            IsCompatible = False
        Else
            IsCompatible = True
        End If
    End If
End Function


Sub CheckCompatibility()
    Windows("Assets.xls").Activate
    If Not IsCompatible Then
        MsgBox "Excel 2007 features will not work " & _
            "in this workbook.", vbCritical, _
            "Excel 97-2003 Compatibility Workbook"

    End If
End Sub
```

6. Run the CheckCompatibility procedure.

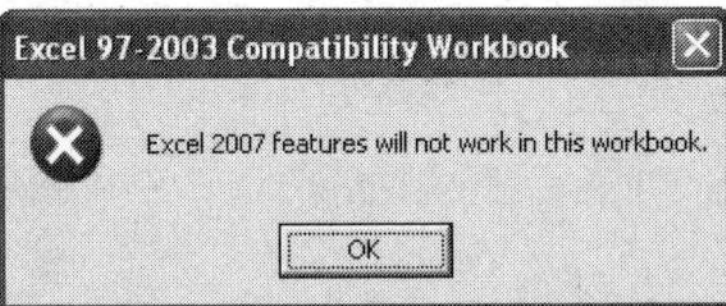

Figure 25-4: You can use a custom function to inform the user that certain features will not work when a workbook is opened in Excel 97-2003 Compatibility mode.

Chapter Summary

This chapter has shown you how to take advantage of many of the Microsoft Excel 2007 objects. The Excel objects presented here (Tab, CellFormat, Characters, FormatCondition, and Graphic) showed you how to make your worksheets more attention grabbing by applying special formatting. Other objects, such as Speech, SpellingOptions, and AutoCorrect, demonstrated how you can make sure that the worksheets your users distribute contain as few errors as possible. This chapter has also demonstrated how to apply a sort to a sheet range and check if the workbook is in compatibility mode.

The next chapter focuses on programming the Visual Basic Editor.

Chapter 26

Programming the Visual Basic Editor (VBE)

The Visual Basic Editor Object Model ■ Understanding the VBE Objects ■ Accessing the VBA Project ■ Finding Information about a VBA Project ■ VBA Project Protection ■ **Working with Modules ■** Listing All Modules in a Workbook ■ Adding a Module to a Workbook ■ Removing a Module ■ Deleting All Code from a Module ■ Deleting Empty Modules ■ Copying (Exporting/Importing) a Module ■ Copying (Exporting/Importing) All Modules ■ **Working with Procedures ■** Listing All Procedures in All Modules ■ Adding a Procedure ■ Deleting a Procedure ■ Creating an Event Procedure ■ **Working with UserForms ■** Creating and Manipulating UserForms ■ Copying UserForms Programmatically ■ **Working with References ■** Creating a List of References ■ Adding a Reference ■ Removing a Reference ■ Checking for Broken References ■ **Working with Windows ■ Working with VBE Menus and Toolbars ■** Generating a Listing of VBE CommandBars and Controls ■ Adding a CommandBar Button to the VBE ■ Removing a CommandBar Button from the VBE ■ **Chapter Summary**

Having worked through 25 chapters of this Microsoft Excel 2007 programming book, you have already acquired a working knowledge of many tools available in the Visual Basic Editor (VBE) to create, modify, and troubleshoot Visual Basic for Applications (VBA) procedures. VBA also allows you to program its own development environment known as the Visual Basic Integrated Design Environment (VBIDE). For instance, you can:

- Control Visual Basic projects
  - Get or set project properties
  - Add/remove individual components
- Control Visual Basic code
  - Add, delete, and modify code
  - Save code to a file/insert code from a file
  - Search for specific information in the code
- Control UserForms
  - Programmatically design a UserForm
  - Dynamically add/remove controls from a form
- Work with references
- Add a reference to an external object library
  - Check for broken references
- Control the VBIDE user interface
  - Control various windows
  - Add/change menus and toolbars

This chapter introduces you to objects, methods, and properties that you can use to automate the VBE.

The Visual Basic Editor Object Model

To program and manipulate the Visual Basic Editor (VBE) in code, you need to access objects contained in the Microsoft Visual Basic for Applications Extensibility 5.3 library. To ensure that you can run the procedures in this chapter, perform the steps as outlined below.

Hands-On 26-1: Trusting Access to the VBA Project Object Model

1. Open a new workbook and save it as **C:\Ex07_ByExample\Practice_Excel26.xlsm.**
2. To trust the Visual Basic project, click the **Developer** tab and then choose **Macro Security.** Excel displays the Trust Center dialog box with various macro settings (Figure 26-1). Select the **Trust access to the VBA project object model** check box and click **OK.**

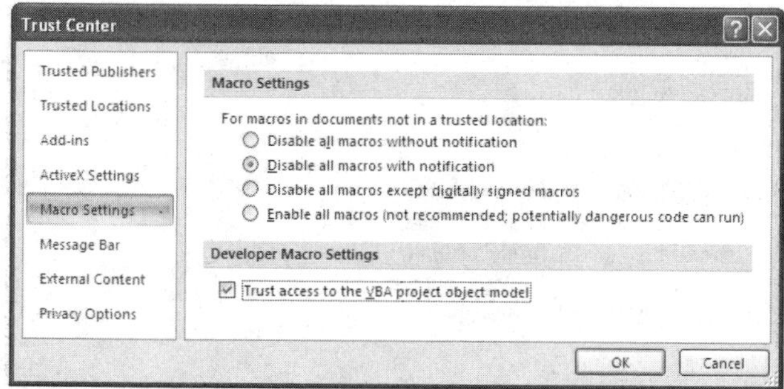

Figure 26-1: You must set access to the VBA project object model to allow for programming the Visual Basic Editor.

Note: If access to the VBA project object model is not enabled, an attempt to run a VBA procedure that accesses objects from the Microsoft Visual Basic for Applications Extensibility 5.3 library results in the following error run-time error message: "Programmatic access to Visual Basic Project is not trusted."

3. To create a reference to the Microsoft Visual Basic for Applications Extensibility 5.3 library, choose **Tools | References** in the Visual Basic Editor window. Check the **Microsoft Visual Basic for Applications Extensibility 5.3** reference, and click **OK**.

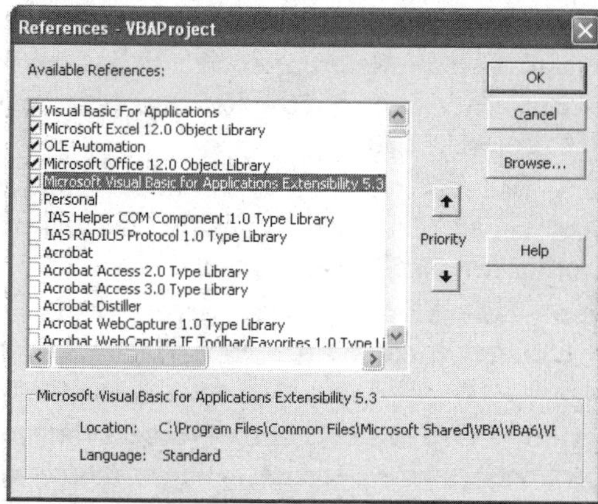

Figure 26-2: Setting a reference to the Microsoft Visual Basic for Applications Extensibility 5.3 library.

Understanding the VBE Objects

In the Object Browser the Microsoft Visual Basic for Applications Extensibility 5.3 library is referred to as VBIDE. You will use this name when referencing this library in code. The VBIDE object library is located in the VBE6EXT.OLB file and is stored in the \Program Files\Common Files\Microsoft Shared\VBA\VBA6 folder.

The top-level object in the VBE object model is the VBE object, which represents the Visual Basic Editor itself (as shown in Figure 26-3).

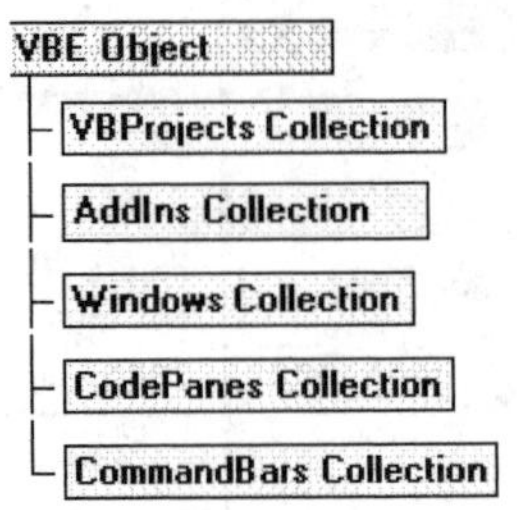

Figure 26-3: The VBE object model contains five collections of objects.

The VBE object model contains five collections of objects as follows:

- **VBProjects collection** — Contains each VBProject object that is currently open in the development environment. Use the VBProject object to set properties for the project. The VBProject object also allows you to access the VBComponents collection and the References collection.
  - Use the VBComponents collection to access, add, or remove components in a project. A component can be a form, a standard module, or a class module contained in a project.
  - Use the References collection to add or remove references in the VBA project. Each VBA project can reference one or more type libraries or projects. Use the Reference object to find out what references are currently selected in the References dialog box for the specific VBA project.
- **AddIns collection** — Use this collection to access the AddIn objects. Add-ins are programs that add extended capabilities and features to Microsoft Excel or other Microsoft Office products.
- **Windows collection** — Use this collection to access window objects such as the Project Explorer window, Properties window, or currently open Code windows.
- **CodePanes collection** — Use this collection to access the open code panes in a project. A Code window can contain one or more code panes. A code pane contained in a Code window is used for entering and editing code.
- **CommandBars collection** — Contains all of the command bars in a project, including command bars that support shortcut menus.

Accessing the VBA Project

Beginning with version 2002, Microsoft Excel added an additional level of security that controls the access to the Visual Basic project in a workbook. By default this access is not trusted and it cannot be changed via code. The only way to determine the current setting for Trust access to the VBA project object model in the Trust Center (see Figure 26-1) is via error trapping.

The following procedure displays a message if access to the VBA project is not trusted. Instructions on how to change the security settings are then displayed in a text box placed in a new workbook.

Hands-On 26-2: Checking Access to the VBA Project Using VBA

Note: All VBA code presented in this chapter will fail unless you followed the steps in Hands-On 26-1.

1. Switch to the Visual Basic Editor window and insert a new module into VBAProject (Practice_Excel26.xlsm).
2. In the Code window, enter the AccessToVBProj procedure as shown below:

```
Sub AccessToVBProj()
    Dim objVBProject As VBProject
    Dim strMsg1 As String
    Dim strMsg2 As String
    Dim response As Integer

    On Error Resume Next

    If Application.Version >= "12.0" Then
        Set objVBProject = ActiveWorkbook.VBProject

        strMsg2 = "The access to the VBA "
        strMsg2 = strMsg2 + " project must be trusted for this "
        strMsg2 = strMsg2 + "procedure to work."
        strMsg2 = strMsg2 + vbCrLf + vbCrLf
        strMsg2 = strMsg2 + " Click 'OK' to view instructions,"
        strMsg2 = strMsg2 + "  or click 'Cancel' to exit."

        If Err.Number <> 0 Then
            strMsg1 = "Please change the security settings to "
            strMsg1 = strMsg1 & "allow access to the VBA project:"
            strMsg1 = strMsg1 & Chr(10) & "1. "
            strMsg1 = strMsg1 & "Choose Developer | Macro Security."
            strMsg1 = strMsg1 & Chr(10) & "2. "
            strMsg1 = strMsg1 & "Check the 'Trust access to the VBA " _
                 & "project object model'. "
            strMsg1 = strMsg1 & Chr(10) & "3. Click OK."

            response = MsgBox(strMsg2, vbCritical + vbOKCancel, _
                        "Access to VB Project is not trusted")

                If response = 1 Then
                    Workbooks.Add
                    With ActiveSheet
                      .Shapes.AddTextbox(msoTextOrientationHorizontal, _
                         Left:=0, Top:=0, Width:=300, _
                         Height:=100).Select
                      Selection.Characters.Text = strMsg1
                      .Shapes(1).Fill.PresetTextured _
                           PresetTexture:=msoTextureBlueTissuePaper
```

```
                .Shapes(1).Shadow.Type = msoShadow6
              End With
          End If
        Exit Sub
      End If

      MsgBox "There are " & objVBProject.References.Count & _
          " project references in " & objVBProject.Name & "."
    End If
End Sub
```

The procedure begins by checking the application version currently in use. If the Trust access to the VBA project object model setting is turned off in the Trust Center dialog box's Developer Macro Settings area, the attempt to set the object variable objVBProject will cause an error. The procedure traps this error with the On Error Resume Next statement. If the error occurs, the Err object will return a non-zero value. At this point we can tell the user that security settings must be adjusted for the procedure to run. Instead of simply displaying the instructions in the message box, we print them to a worksheet so users can follow them easily while accessing the necessary options. They can also print them out if they want to make this change later (see Figure 26-4).

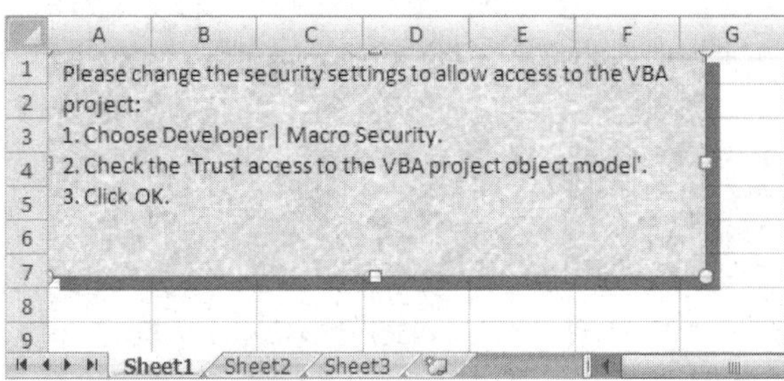

Figure 26-4: Instructions for allowing access to the VBA project object model are generated by the example procedure.

3. Run the above procedure.

   If the Trust access to the VBA project object model setting is turned on, the procedure displays the number of references that are set for the active workbook's VB project; otherwise, you get a message prompting you to click OK to view instructions on how to make the change.

Finding Information about a VBA Project

As you already know, each new workbook in the Microsoft Excel user interface has a corresponding workbook project named VBAProject. You can change the project name to a more meaningful name by supplying a new value for the Name property in the Properties window or by accessing the VBAProject properties dialog box via the Tools menu in the Visual Basic Editor screen. You can also perform this change programmatically. If the project you want to edit is currently highlighted in the Project Explorer window, simply type the following statement in the Immediate window to replace the default VBA project name with your own:

```
Application.VBE.ActiveVBProject.Name = "Chap26SourceCode"
```

If the VBA project you want to change is not active, the following statement can be used:

```
Workbooks("Practice_Excel26.xlsm").VBProject.Name = "Chap26SourceCode"
```

To change the description of the VBProject object, use the following statement:

```
Workbooks("Practice_Excel26.xlsm").VBProject.Description = "Programming
Visual Basic Editor"
```

You can find out if the project has been saved by using the Saved property of the VBProject object:

```
MsgBox Application.VBE.ActiveVBProject.Saved
```

Visual Basic returns False if the changes to the project have not been saved.

To find out how many component objects are contained within a specific VBA project, use the code like this:

```
MsgBox Workbooks("Practice_Excel26.xlsm").VBProject.VBComponents.Count
```

And to find out the name of the currently selected VBComponent object, type the following lines of code in the Immediate window:

```
Set objVBComp = Application.VBE.SelectedVBComponent
MsgBox objVBComp.Name
```

You can also quickly find out the number of references defined in the References dialog box by typing the following statement in the Immediate window:

```
?Application.VBE.ActiveVBProject.References.Count
```

VBA Project Protection

To prevent users from viewing code, you can lock each VBA project. To lock a VBA project, you will need to perform the following tasks:

1. In the Project Explorer, right-click the project you want to protect, and then click **ProjectName Properties** on the shortcut menu.
2. In the Project Properties dialog box, click the **Protection** tab and select the **Lock project for viewing** check box. Enter and confirm the password, and then click **OK**.

The next time you open the workbook file you will be prompted to enter the password when attempting to view code in the project. There is no way to programmatically specify a password for a locked VBA project.

You should check whether the project is protected before you attempt to edit the project or run code that accesses information about the project's components. To determine if a VBA project is locked, check the Protection property of the VBProject object. The following function procedure demonstrates how to check the Protection property of the VBA project in an Excel workbook.

Hands-On 26-3: Using VBA to Determine whether the VBA Project Is Protected

1. In the same module where you entered the procedure from Hands_On 26-2, enter the IsProjProtected function procedure as shown below:

```
Function IsProjProtected() As Boolean
    Dim objVBProj As VBProject

    Set objVBProj = ActiveWorkbook.VBProject

    If objVBProj.Protection = vbext_pp_locked Then
        IsProjProtected = True
    Else
        IsProjProtected = False
    End If
End Function
```

2. To test the above function, type **MsgBox IsProjProtected()** in the Immediate window and press **Enter**.

   The MsgBox function displays False for a project that is not protected and True if protection is turned on.

Note: If a project is protected and you attempt to run a procedure that needs to access information in this project without first checking whether the protection is turned on, run-time error 50289 appears with the following description: "Can't perform operation since the project is protected."

Working with Modules

All standard modules, class modules, code modules located behind worksheets and workbooks, and UserForms are members of the VBComponents collection of a VBProject object. To determine the type of the component object, use the Type property of the VBComponent object as shown in Figure 26-5. The code of each VBComponent is stored in a CodeModule. The UserForm component has a graphical development interface called ActiveX Designer.

The **Type** property settings for the **VBComponent** object are described in the following table:

Constant	Value	Description
vbext_ct_StdModule	1	Standard module
vbext_ct_ClassModule	2	Class module
vbext_ct_MSForm	3	Microsoft Form
vbext_ct_ActiveXDesigner	11	ActiveX Designer
vbext_ct_Document	100	Document Module

Figure 26-5: Type property setting for the VBComponent object (see the online help for more information).

The following sections demonstrate several procedures that access the VBComponents collection to perform the following tasks:

- Listing all modules in a workbook
- Adding a module

- Removing a module
- Removing all code from a module
- Removing empty modules
- Copying (exporting and importing) modules

Listing All Modules in a Workbook

The procedure below generates a list of all modules contained in the Practice_Excel26.xlsm workbook. The name of each module and the description of the module type are placed in a two-dimensional array and then written to a worksheet. Because the Type property of the VBComponent object returns a constant or a numeric value containing the type of object (see Figure 26-5), the procedure uses a function to show the corresponding description of the object.

Hands-On 26-4: Listing All Workbook Modules

1. Insert a new module into the current VBA project in the Practice_Excel26.xlsm workbook.
2. In the Code window, enter the following procedure and function:

```
Sub ModuleList()
    Dim objVBComp As VBComponent
    Dim listArray()
    Dim i As Integer

    If ThisWorkbook.VBProject.Protection = vbext_pp_locked Then
       MsgBox "You must unprotect the project to run this procedure."
       Exit Sub
    End If

    i = 2

    For Each objVBComp In ThisWorkbook.VBProject.VBComponents
        ReDim Preserve listArray(1 To 2, 1 To i - 1)
        listArray(1, i - 1) = objVBComp.Name
        listArray(2, i - 1) = GetModuleType(objVBComp)
        i = i + 1
    Next

    With ActiveSheet
        .Cells(1, 1).Resize(1, 2).Value = Array("Module Name", _
            "Module Type")
        .Cells(2, 1).Resize(UBound(listArray, 2), UBound(listArray, _
            1)).Value = Application.Transpose(listArray)
        .Columns("A:B").AutoFit
    End With

    Set objVBComp = Nothing
End Sub

Function GetModuleType(comp As VBComponent)
    Select Case comp.Type
        Case vbext_ct_StdModule
```

```
                GetModuleType = "Standard module"
            Case vbext_ct_ClassModule
                GetModuleType = "Class module"
            Case vbext_ct_MSForm
                GetModuleType = "Microsoft Form"
            Case vbext_ct_ActiveXDesigner
                GetModuleType = "ActiveX Designer"
            Case vbext_ct_Document
                GetModuleType = "Document module"
            Case Else
                GetModuleType = "Unknown"
        End Select
    End Function
```

3. Run the ModuleList procedure and then switch to the Microsoft Excel application window to view the results.

If the VBA project is not protected, Sheet1 will show the following information:

Module Name	Module Type
ThisWorkbook	Document module
Sheet1	Document module
Sheet2	Document module
Sheet3	Document module
Module1	Standard module
Module2	Standard module

If the VBA project is protected when you execute this procedure, you will see a message box advising you to unprotect the project before attempting to run this procedure.

Adding a Module to a Workbook

Use the Add method of the VBComponents collection to add a new module to ThisWorkbook. The CreateModule procedure shown below prompts the user for the module name and the type of module. When this information has been provided, the AddModule procedure is called.

Hands-On 26-5: Adding a Module to a Workbook

1. Insert a new module into the current VBA project in the Practice_Excel26.xlsm workbook.
2. In the Code window, enter the following procedures:

```
Sub CreateModule()
    Dim modType As Integer
    Dim strName As String
    Dim strPrompt As String

    strPrompt = "Enter a number representing the type of module:"
    strPrompt = strPrompt & vbCr & "1 (Standard Module)"
    strPrompt = strPrompt & vbCr & "2 (Class Module)"
```

```
    modType = Val(InputBox(prompt:=strPrompt, Title:="Insert Module"))
    If modType = 0 Then Exit Sub
    strName = InputBox("Enter the name you want to assign to " & _
              "new module", "Module Name")
    If strName = "" Then Exit Sub
    AddModule modType, strName
End Sub


Sub AddModule(modType As Integer, strName As String)
    Dim objVBProj As VBProject
    Dim objVBComp As VBComponent

    If InStr(1, "1, 2", modType) = 0 Then Exit Sub

    Set objVBProj = ThisWorkbook.VBProject
    Set objVBComp = objVBProj.VBComponents.Add(modType)
    objVBComp.Name = strName

    Application.Visible = True

    Set objVBComp = Nothing
    Set objVBProj = Nothing
End Sub
```

3. Run the CreateModule procedure. Enter **1** for a standard module when prompted and click **OK**. Enter **TestModule** as the module name and click **OK**. When the procedure finishes executing you should see a new module named TestModule in the Project Explorer window. Do not delete this module, as we will need it for the next example.

Removing a Module

Use the following procedure to delete the module you added in the previous section.

Hands-On 26-6: Removing a Module from the Workbook

1. Insert a new module into the current VBA project in the Practice_Excel26.xlsm workbook.
2. In the Code window, enter the following procedure:

```
Sub DeleteModule(strName As String)
    Dim objVBProj As VBProject
    Dim objVBComp As VBComponent

    Set objVBProj = ThisWorkbook.VBProject

    Set objVBComp = objVBProj.VBComponents(strName)

    objVBProj.VBComponents.Remove objVBComp

    Set objVBComp = Nothing
    Set objVBProj = Nothing
End Sub
```

3. Run the DeleteModule procedure by typing the following statement in the Immediate window and pressing **Enter** to execute:

```
DeleteModule "TestModule"
```

At this point VBAProject (Practice_Excel26.xlsm) should contain four standard modules with the VBA procedures entered so far in this chapter.

Deleting All Code from a Module

Use the CountOfLines property of the CodeModule object to return the number of lines of code in a code module. Use the DeleteLines method of the CodeModule object to delete a single line or a specified number of lines. The DeleteLines method can use two arguments. The first argument, which specifies the first line you want to delete, is required. The second argument is optional and specifies the total number of lines you want to delete. If you don't specify how many lines you want to delete, only one line will be deleted. The following procedure deletes all code from the specified module.

Hands-On 26-7: Deleting a Module's Code

1. Insert a new module into the current VBA project in the Practice_Excel26.xlsm workbook.
2. In the Code window, enter the following procedure:

```
Sub DeleteModuleCode(strName As String)
    Dim objVBProj As VBProject
    Dim objVBCode As CodeModule
    Dim firstLn As Long
    Dim totLn As Long

    Set objVBProj = ThisWorkbook.VBProject
    Set objVBCode = objVBProj.VBComponents(strName).CodeModule
    With objVBCode
        firstLn = 1
        totLn = .CountOfLines
        .DeleteLines firstLn, totLn
    End With

    Set objVBProj = Nothing
    Set objVBCode = Nothing
End Sub
```

3. Insert a new module in the current VBA project and rename it **DeleteTest**.
4. Copy the first procedure you created in this chapter (in Hands-On 26-2) into the DeleteTest module.
5. In the Immediate window, enter the following statement:

```
DeleteModuleCode "DeleteTest"
```

When you press **Enter**, all the code in the DeleteTest module is removed.

Do not delete the empty DeleteTest module. We will remove it programmatically in the next example.

Deleting Empty Modules

In the course of writing your VBA procedures you may have inserted a number of new modules in your VBA project. While most of these modules contain valid code, there are probably a couple of empty modules that were left behind. You can remove all the unwanted empty modules in one sweep with a VBA procedure. To remove a module, use the Remove method of the VBComponents collection. This method requires that you specify the type of component you want to remove. Use the enumerated constants shown in Figure 26-5 earlier in this chapter to indicate the type of component. The following procedure iterates through the VBComponents collection and checks whether the retrieved component is a standard module or a class module. If the module contains less than three lines, we assume that the module is empty and okay to delete. We write the information about the deleted modules into the Immediate window.

Hands-On 26-8: Deleting an Empty Module

1. Insert a new module into the current VBA project in the Practice_Excel26.xlsm workbook.
2. In the Code window, enter the following procedure:

```
Sub DeleteEmptyModules()
    Dim objVBComp As VBComponent

    Const vbext_ct_StdModule As Long = 1
    Const vbext_ct_ClassModule As Long = 2

    For Each objVBComp In ActiveWorkbook.VBProject.VBComponents
      Select Case objVBComp.Type
        Case vbext_ct_StdModule, vbext_ct_ClassModule
          If objVBComp.CodeModule.CountOfLines < 3 Then
            Debug.Print "(deleted) " & objVBComp.Name & vbTab & _
                 "declarations: " & objVBComp.CodeModule. _
            CountOfDeclarationLines & vbTab & "Total code Lines: " & _
                 objVBComp.CodeModule.CountOfLines
            ActiveWorkbook.VBProject.VBComponents.Remove objVBComp
           End If
      End Select
    Next
    Set objVBComp = Nothing
End Sub
```

3. Run the DeleteEmptyModules procedure.

   The DeleteTest module that we created in Hands-On 26-7 should now be removed from the current VBA project. Check the Immediate window for information about the deleted module.

Copying (Exporting/Importing) a Module

Sometimes you may want to copy modules between VBA projects. There is no single method to perform this task. To copy a module you must perform the following two steps:

1. Export a module to an external text file.

   The Export method of the VBComponent object saves the component as a separate text file. You must specify the name of the file to which you want to export the component. The filename must be unique or an error will occur.

2. Import a module from an external text file.

   The Import method of the VBComponent object adds the component to a project from a file. You must specify the path and filename of the file from which you want to import the component. The workbook file that will receive the imported component must be open.

Let's assume that you want to copy Module1 from the Practice_Excel26.xlsm workbook to another workbook file named Practice_Excel26b.xlsm. The procedure that follows requires three arguments for the copy operation: the name of the workbook containing the module you want to copy, the name of the workbook that will receive the copied module, and the name of the module you will be copying.

Hands-On 26-9: Exporting/Importing a Module

1. Insert a new module into the current VBA project in the Practice_Excel26.xlsm workbook.
2. In the Code window, enter the following procedure:

```
Sub CopyAModule(wkbFrom As String, _
                wkbTo As String, _
                strFromMod As String)
    Dim wkb As Workbook
    Dim strFile As String

    Set wkb = Workbooks(wkbFrom)

    strFile = wkb.Path & "\vbCode.bas"
    wkb.VBProject.VBComponents(strFromMod).Export strFile

    On Error Resume Next
    Set wkb = Workbooks(wkbTo)
    If Err.Number <> 0 Then
        Workbooks.Open wkbTo
        Set wkb = Workbooks(wkbTo)
    End If

    wkb.VBProject.VBComponents.Import strFile
    wkb.Save

    Set wkb = Nothing
End Sub
```

3. Create a new workbook and save it as **Practice_Excel26b.xlsm** in your **Ex07_ByExample** folder. You will use this workbook in the CopyAModule procedure.
4. In the Immediate window, enter the following statement to run the procedure:

```
CopyAModule "Practice_Excel26.xlsm", "Practice_Excel26b.xlsm", "Module1"
```

   When you press **Enter**, the CopyAModule procedure exports Module1 from Practice_Excel26.xlsm to a file named vbCode.bas. Next, the vbCode.bas file is imported into the Practice_Excel26b.xlsm workbook and the workbook is saved. You may want to add an additional statement to this procedure to remove the vbCode.bas file from your computer (use the Kill statement you learned earlier in this book).
5. Activate VBAProject (Practice_Excel26b.xlsm) and notice Module1 in the Modules folder. Module1 should contain the same procedure as Module1 in the Practice_Excel26.xlsm workbook.

Copying (Exporting/Importing) All Modules

Sometimes you may want to transfer all your VBA code from one project to another. The procedure shown below exports all the modules in the specified workbook file to an external text file and then imports them into another workbook. An error occurs if the receiving workbook cannot be activated. The procedure traps this error by executing the code that opens the required workbook. If the text file with the same name already exists in the same folder, the procedure ensures that the file is deleted before the specified project modules are exported.

Hands-On 26-10: Exporting/Importing All Modules

This Hands-On exercise assumes that the Practice_Excel26b.xlsm workbook created in the previous Hands-On is open.

1. Insert a new module into the current VBA project in the Practice_Excel26.xlsm workbook.
2. In the Code window, enter the following procedure:

```
Sub CopyAllModules(wkbFrom As String, _
                   wkbTo As String)

    Dim objVBComp As VBComponent
    Dim wkb As Workbook
    Dim strFile As String

    Set wkb = Workbooks(wkbFrom)

    On Error Resume Next
    Workbooks(wkbTo).Activate
    If Err.Number <> 0 Then Workbooks.Open wkbTo

    strFile = wkb.Path & "\vbCode.bas"
```

```
    If Dir(strFile) <> "" Then Kill strFile

    For Each objVBComp In wkb.VBProject.VBComponents
        If objVBComp.Type <> vbext_ct_Document Then
            objVBComp.Export strFile
            Workbooks(wkbTo).VBProject.VBComponents.Import strFile
        End If
    Next

    Set objVBComp = Nothing
    Set wkb = Nothing
End Sub
```

3. In the Immediate window, enter the following statement to run the procedure:

```
CopyAllModules "Practice_Excel26.xlsm", "Practice_Excel26b.xlsm"
```

When you press **Enter**, the CopyModules procedure will copy all the modules from the Practice_Excel26.xlsm workbook to the Practice_Excel26b.xlsm workbook that was created in Hands-On 26-9. Because a module with the same name may already exist in the receiving workbook, you may want to modify this procedure to only copy modules that do not have conflicting names. See the CopyAllModulesRevised procedure below.

Note: When you copy a module whose name is the same as the name of a module in the receiving workbook, Excel assigns a new name to the inserted module following its default naming conventions.

```
Sub CopyAllModulesRevised(wkbFrom As String, _
                    wkbTo As String)

    Dim objVBComp As VBComponent
    Dim wkb As Workbook
    Dim strFile As String

    Set wkb = Workbooks(wkbFrom)

    On Error Resume Next
    Workbooks(wkbTo).Activate
    If Err.Number <> 0 Then Workbooks.Open wkbTo

    strFile = wkb.Path & "\vbCode.bas"
    If Dir(strFile) <> "" Then Kill strFile

    For Each objVBComp In wkb.VBProject.VBComponents
        If objVBComp.Type <> vbext_ct_Document Then
            objVBComp.Export strFile

          With Workbooks(wkbTo)
            If Len(.VBProject.VBComponents(objVBComp.Name).Name) = 0 Then
              Workbooks(wkbTo).VBProject.VBComponents.Import strFile
            End If
          End With
        End If
```

```
        Next

        Set objVBComp = Nothing
        Set wkb = Nothing
    End Sub
```

Working with Procedures

Code modules contain procedures, and at times you may want to:

- List all the procedures contained in a module or in all modules
- Programmatically add or remove a procedure from a module
- Programmatically create an event procedure

The following sections demonstrate how to perform the above tasks.

Listing All Procedures in All Modules

Code modules contain declaration lines and code lines. You can obtain the number of lines in the declaration section of a module with the CountOfDeclarationLines property of the CodeModule object. Use the CountOfLines property of the CodeModule object to get the number of code lines in a module. Each code line belongs to a specific procedure. Use the ProcOfLine property of the CodeModule object to return the name of the procedure in which the specified line is located. This property requires two arguments: the line number you want to check and the constant that specifies the type of procedure to locate. All subprocedures and function procedures use the vbext_pk_Proc constant. The following procedure prints to the Immediate window a list of all modules and all procedures within each module in the current VBA project.

Hands-On 26-11: Listing Procedures in Modules

1. Insert a new module into the VBA project in the Practice_Excel26.xlsm workbook.
2. In the Code window, enter the following procedure:

```
Sub ListAllProc()
    Dim objVBProj As VBProject
    Dim objVBComp As VBComponent
    Dim objVBCode As CodeModule
    Dim strCurrent As String
    Dim strPrevious As String

    Dim x As Integer

    Set objVBProj = ThisWorkbook.VBProject

    For Each objVBComp In objVBProj.VBComponents
    If InStr(1, "1, 2", objVBComp.Type) Then
        Set objVBCode = objVBComp.CodeModule
        Debug.Print objVBComp.Name
```

```
            For x = objVBCode.CountOfDeclarationLines + 1 To _
                    objVBCode.CountOfLines
               strCurrent = objVBCode.ProcOfLine(x, vbext_pk_Proc)

               If strCurrent <> strPrevious Then
                  Debug.Print vbTab & objVBCode.ProcOfLine(x, vbext_pk_Proc)
                  strPrevious = strCurrent
               End If
            Next
        End If
        Next

        Set objVBCode = Nothing

        Set objVBComp = Nothing
        Set objVBProj = Nothing
    End Sub
```

3. Run the ListAllProc procedure.

   When this procedure finishes executing, the following list can be found in the Immediate window:

```
Module1
    AccessToVBProj
    IsProjProtected
Module2
    ModuleList
    GetModuleType
Module3
    CreateModule
    AddModule
Module4
    DeleteModule
Module5
    DeleteModuleCode
Module6
    DeleteEmptyModules
Module7
    CopyAModule
Module8
    CopyAllModules
    CopyAllModulesRevised
Module9
    ListAllProc
```

Adding a Procedure

It is fairly easy to write procedure code into a module. Use the InsertLines method of the CodeModule object to insert a line or lines of code at a specified location in a block of code. The InsertLines method requires two arguments: the line number at which you want to insert the code and the string containing the code you want to insert.

The following example writes a simple procedure that opens a new workbook and renames it Sheet1. The procedure is inserted at the end of the specified module code.

Hands-On 26-12: Adding a Procedure to a Module Using VBA

1. Insert a new module into the VBA project in the Practice_Excel26.xlsm workbook.
2. In the Code window, enter the following procedure:

```
Sub AddNewProc(strModName As String)
    Dim objVBCode As CodeModule
    Dim objVBProj As VBProject
    Dim strProc As String

    Set objVBProj = ThisWorkbook.VBProject

    Set objVBCode = objVBProj.VBComponents(strModName).CodeModule

    strProc = "Sub CreateWorkBook()" & Chr(13)
    strProc = strProc & Chr(9) & "Workbooks.Add" & Chr(13)
    strProc = strProc & Chr(9) & "ActiveSheet.Name = ""Test"" " & Chr(13)
    strProc = strProc & "End Sub"

    Debug.Print strProc

    With objVBCode
        .InsertLines .CountOfLines + 1, strProc
    End With

    Set objVBCode = Nothing
    Set objVBProj = Nothing
End Sub
```

3. In the Immediate window, enter the following statement to run the above procedure and press **Enter**:

```
AddNewProc "Module6"
```

   When the procedure finishes executing, Module6 will contain a new procedure named CreateWorkBook.

Deleting a Procedure

Use the DeleteLines method of the CodeModule object to delete a single line or a specified number of lines. The DeleteLines method has two arguments: one required and one optional. You must specify the first line you want to delete. Specifying the total number of lines you want to delete is optional. Before deleting an entire procedure you need to locate the line at which the specified procedure begins. This is done with the ProcStartLine property of the CodeModule object. This property requires two arguments: a string containing the name of the procedure and the kind of procedure to delete. Use the vbext_pk_Proc constant to delete a subprocedure or a function procedure.

The following procedure deletes a specified procedure from a specified module.

Hands-On 26-13: Deleting a Procedure from a Module Using VBA

1. Insert a new module into the current VBAProject in the Practice_Excel26.xlsm workbook.
2. In the Code window, enter the following procedure:

```
Sub DeleteProc(strModName As String, strProcName As String)
    Dim objVBProj As VBProject
    Dim objVBCode As CodeModule
    Dim firstLn As Long
    Dim totLn As Long

    Set objVBProj = ThisWorkbook.VBProject
    Set objVBCode = objVBProj.VBComponents(strModName).CodeModule
    With objVBCode
      firstLn = .ProcStartLine(strProcName, vbext_pk_Proc)
      totLn = .ProcCountLines(strProcName, vbext_pk_Proc)
     .DeleteLines firstLn, totLn
    End With

    Set objVBProj = Nothing
    Set objVBCode = Nothing
End Sub
```

3. In the Immediate window, enter the following statement to run the above procedure and press **Enter**:

```
DeleteProc "Module6", "CreateWorkBook"
```

   When the procedure finishes executing, Module6 will no longer contain the CreateWorkBook procedure that was created in the previous Hands-On exercise.

   Before attempting to delete a procedure from a specified module, it is recommended that you check whether the module and the procedure with the specified name exist. Consider creating two separate functions that return this information. You can call these functions whenever you need to test for the existence of a module or a procedure.

4. Enter the following function procedure in the Code window:

```
Function ModuleExists(strModName As String) As Boolean
    Dim objVBProj As VBProject

    Set objVBProj = ThisWorkbook.VBProject

    On Error Resume Next

    ModuleExists = Len(objVBProj.VBComponents(strModName).Name) <> 0
End Function
```

   The above function will return True if the length of the module name is a number other than zero (0); otherwise, it will return False.

5. Enter the following function procedure in the Code window:

```
Function ProcExists(strModName As String, _
                    strProcName As String) As Boolean

    Dim objVBProj As VBProject

    Set objVBProj = ThisWorkbook.VBProject

    On Error Resume Next

    ' first find out if the specified module exists
    If ModuleExists(strModName) = True Then
        ProcExists = objVBProj.VBComponents(strModName) _
            .CodeModule.ProcStartLine(strProcName, vbext_pk_Proc) <> 0
    End If
End Function
```

6. On your own, modify the DeleteProc procedure in step 2 so that it checks the existence of the procedure prior to its deletion. Include the call to the ProcExists function.

Creating an Event Procedure

While you could create an event procedure programmatically by using the InsertLines method of the CodeModule object as you've done earlier in the "Adding a Procedure" section, there is an easier way. Because event procedures have a specific structure and usually require a number of parameters, Visual Basic offers a special method to handle this task. The CreateEventProc method of the CodeModule object creates an event procedure with the required procedure declaration and parameters. All you need to do is specify the name of the event you want to add and the name of the object that is a source of the event. The CreateEventProc method returns the line at which the body of the event procedure starts. Use the InsertLines method of the CodeModule object to insert the code in the body of the event procedure.

The following procedure adds a new worksheet to the current workbook and writes the Worksheet_SelectionChange event procedure to its code module.

Hands-On 26-14: Creating an Event Procedure with VBA

1. Insert a new module into the VBA project in the Practice_Excel26.xlsm workbook.
2. In the Code window, enter the following procedure:

```
Sub CreateWorkSelChangeEvent()
    Dim objVBCode As CodeModule
    Dim wks As Worksheet
    Dim firstLine As Long

   ' Add a new worksheet
   Set wks = ActiveWorkbook.Worksheets.Add
```

```
    ' create a reference to the code module of the inserted sheet
    Set objVBCode = wks.Parent.VBProject.VBComponents(wks.Name).CodeModule

    ' create an event procedure and return the line at which the body of
    ' the event procedure begins
    firstLine = objVBCode.CreateEventProc("SelectionChange", "Worksheet")

    Debug.Print "Procedure first line: " & firstLine

    ' proceed to add code to the body of the event procedure
    objVBCode.InsertLines firstLine + 1, _
        Chr(9) & "Dim myRange As Range"
     objVBCode.InsertLines firstLine + 2, _
        Chr(9) & "On Error Resume Next"
    objVBCode.InsertLines firstLine + 3, _
        Chr(9) & "Set myRange = Intersect(Range(""A1:A10""), Target)"
    objVBCode.InsertLines firstLine + 4, _
        Chr(9) & "If Not myRange Is Nothing Then"
    objVBCode.InsertLines firstLine + 5, _
         Chr(9) & Chr(9) & _
         "MsgBox ""Data entry or edits are not permitted."""
    objVBCode.InsertLines firstLine + 6, _
        Chr(9) & "End If"

  Set objVBCode = Nothing
  Set wks = Nothing
End Sub
```

3. Run the CreateWorkSelChangeEvent procedure.

   As soon as the procedure finishes executing, the newly inserted Sheet module is activated and displays the following event procedure code:

```
Private Sub Worksheet_SelectionChange(ByVal Target As Range)
    Dim myRange As Range
    On Error Resume Next
    Set myRange = Intersect(Range("A1:A10"), Target)
    If Not myRange Is Nothing Then
        MsgBox "Data entry or edits are not permitted."
    End If

End Sub
```

4. To test the newly inserted event procedure, switch to Sheet4 and click on any cell in the A1:A10 range. The event procedure will cause a message to appear.

Working with UserForms

Earlier in this book you learned how to create and work with UserForms. Creating UserForms is done most easily by utilizing the manual method; however, at times you may find it necessary to use VBA to create a quick form on the fly and display it correctly on the user's screen.

To programmatically add a UserForm to the active project, use the Add method of the VBComponents collection and specify vbext_ct_MSForm for the type of component to add:

```
Dim objVBComp As VBComponent
Set objVBComp = Application.VBE.ActiveVBProject.VBComponents.Add(vbext_
     ct_MSForm)
```

To change the name of the UserForm, use the Name property of the VBComponent object. To change other properties of the UserForm, use the VBComponent's Properties collection. For example, to change the Name and Caption of the UserForm, use the following statement block:

```
With objVBComp
   .Name = "ReportGenerator"
   .Properties("Caption") = "My Report Form"
   End With
```

Here's a complete procedure:

```
Sub ReportGeneratorForm()
    Dim objVBComp As VBComponent

    Set objVBComp = Application.VBE.ActiveVBProject. _
        VBComponents.Add(vbext_ct_MSForm)
    With objVBComp
        .Name = "ReportGenerator"
        .Properties("Caption") = "My Report Form"
    End With
    Set objVBComp = Nothing
End Sub
```

To delete the UserForm from the project, use the Remove method of the VBComponents collection:

```
Set objVBComp =
Application.VBE.ActiveVBProject.VBComponents("ReportGenerator")
Application.VBE.ActiveVBProject.VBComponents.Remove objVBComp
```

Creating and Manipulating UserForms

The following procedure creates a simple UserForm as shown in Figure 26-6 and writes procedures for each of the form's controls.

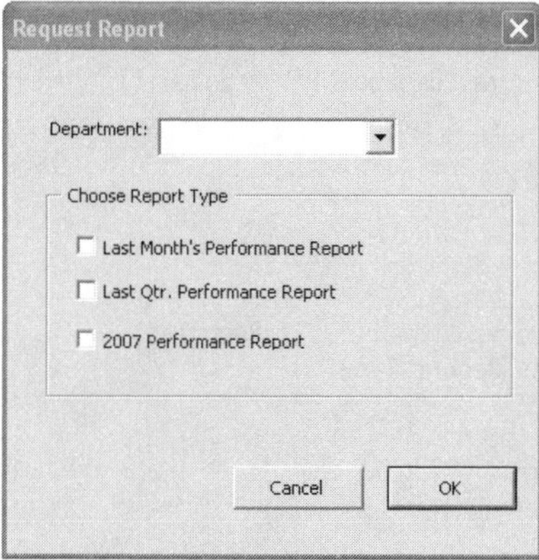

Figure 26-6: UserForm created programmatically.

Hands-On 26-15: Creating a Custom UserForm with VBA

1. Insert a new module into the VBA project in the Practice_Excel26.xlsm workbook.
2. In the Code window, enter the following procedure:

```
Sub AddUserForm()
    Dim objVBProj As VBProject
    Dim objVBComp As VBComponent
    Dim objVBFrm As UserForm
    Dim objChkBox As Object
    Dim x As Integer
    Dim sVBA As String

    Set objVBProj = Application.VBE.ActiveVBProject
    Set objVBComp = objVBProj.VBComponents.Add(vbext_ct_MSForm)

    With objVBComp
    ' read form's name and other properties
        Debug.Print "Default Name " & .Name
        Debug.Print "Caption: " & .DesignerWindow.Caption
        Debug.Print "Form is open in the Designer window: " &
             .HasOpenDesigner
        Debug.Print "Form Name " & .Name
        Debug.Print "Default Width " & .Properties("Width")
        Debug.Print "Default Height " & .Properties("Height")

    ' Set form's name, caption and size
        .Name = "ReportSelector"
        .Properties("Width") = 250
        .Properties("Height") = 250
        .Properties("Caption") = "Request Report"
    End With

      Set objVBFrm = objVBComp.Designer
      With objVBFrm
           With .Controls.Add("Forms.Label.1", "lbName")
                .Caption = "Department:"
                .AutoSize = True
                .Width = 48
                .Top = 30
                .Left = 20
            End With

            With .Controls.Add("Forms.Combobox.1", "cboDept")
                .Width = 110
                .Top = 30
                .Left = 70
            End With

            ' add frame control
            With .Controls.Add("Forms.Frame.1", "frReports")
                .Caption = "Choose Report Type"
                .Top = 60
                .Left = 18
                .Height = 96
```

```
        End With

        ' add three check boxes
        Set objChkBox = .frReports.Controls.Add("Forms.CheckBox.1")
        With objChkBox
            .Name = "chk1"
            .Caption = "Last Month's Performance Report"
            .WordWrap = False
            .Left = 12
            .Top = 12
            .Height = 20
            .Width = 186
        End With

        Set objChkBox = .frReports.Controls.Add("Forms.CheckBox.1")
        With objChkBox
            .Name = "chk2"
            .Caption = "Last Qtr. Performance Report"
            .WordWrap = False
            .Left = 12
            .Top = 32
            .Height = 20
            .Width = 186
        End With

        Set objChkBox = .frReports.Controls.Add("Forms.CheckBox.1")
        With objChkBox
            .Name = "chk3"
            .Caption = Year(Now) - 1 & " Performance Report"
            .WordWrap = False
            .Left = 12
            .Top = 54
            .Height = 20
            .Width = 186
        End With

        ' Add and position OK and Cancel buttons
          With .Controls.Add("Forms.CommandButton.1", "cmdOK")
              .Caption = "OK"
              .Default = "True"
              .Height = 20
              .Width = 60
              .Top = objVBFrm.InsideHeight - .Height - 20
              .Left = objVBFrm.InsideWidth - .Width - 10
          End With

            With .Controls.Add("Forms.CommandButton.1", "cmdCancel")
                .Caption = "Cancel"
                .Height = 20
                .Width = 60
                .Top = objVBFrm.InsideHeight - .Height - 20
                .Left = objVBFrm.InsideWidth - .Width - 80
            End With
End With

 'populate the combo box
```

```
With objVBComp.CodeModule
   x = .CountOfLines
   .InsertLines x + 1, "Sub UserForm_Initialize()"
   .InsertLines x + 2, vbTab & "With Me.cboDept"
   .InsertLines x + 3, vbTab & vbTab & ".addItem ""Marketing"""
   .InsertLines x + 4, vbTab & vbTab & ".addItem ""Sales"""
   .InsertLines x + 5, vbTab & vbTab & ".addItem ""Finance"""
   .InsertLines x + 6, vbTab & vbTab & ".addItem ""Research &
        Development"""
   .InsertLines x + 7, vbTab & vbTab & ".addItem ""Human Resources"""

   .InsertLines x + 8, vbTab & "End With"
   .InsertLines x + 9, "End Sub"

   ' write a procedure to handle the Cancel button

   Dim firstLine As Long
   With objVBComp.CodeModule
        firstLine = .CreateEventProc("Click", "cmdCancel")
       .InsertLines firstLine + 1, "    Unload Me"
   End With

   ' write a procedure to handle OK button
   sVBA = "Private Sub cmdOK_Click()" & vbCrLf
   sVBA = sVBA & "    Dim ctrl As Control" & vbCrLf
   sVBA = sVBA & "    Dim chkflag As Integer" & vbCrLf
   sVBA = sVBA & "    Dim strMsg As String" & vbCrLf
   sVBA = sVBA & "    If Me.cboDept.Value = """" Then " & vbCrLf
   sVBA = sVBA & "       MsgBox ""Please select the Department.""" &
                               vbCrLf
   sVBA = sVBA & "       Me.cboDept.SetFocus " & vbCrLf
   sVBA = sVBA & "       Exit Sub" & vbCrLf
   sVBA = sVBA & "    End If" & vbCrLf
   sVBA = sVBA & "    For Each ctrl In Me.Controls " & vbCrLf
   sVBA = sVBA & "       Select Case ctrl.Name" & vbCrLf
   sVBA = sVBA & "         Case ""chk1"", ""chk2"", ""chk3""" &
                               vbCrLf
   sVBA = sVBA & "           If ctrl.Value = True Then" & vbCrLf
   sVBA = sVBA & "             strMsg = strMsg & ctrl.Caption &
                                   Chr(13)" & vbCrLf
   sVBA = sVBA & "             chkflag = 1" & vbCrLf
   sVBA = sVBA & "           End If" & vbCrLf
   sVBA = sVBA & "       End Select" & vbCrLf
   sVBA = sVBA & "    Next" & vbCrLf
   sVBA = sVBA & "    If chkflag = 1 Then" & vbCrLf
   sVBA = sVBA & "      MsgBox ""Run the following Report(s) for ""
                           & _ " & vbCrLf
   sVBA = sVBA & "      Me.cboDept.Value & "":"" & Chr(13) & Chr(13)
                           & strMsg" & vbCrLf
   sVBA = sVBA & "    Else" & vbCrLf
   sVBA = sVBA & "      MsgBox ""Please select Report type.""" &
                           vbCrLf
   sVBA = sVBA & "    End If" & vbCrLf
   sVBA = sVBA & "End Sub"

   .AddFromString sVBA
```

```
    End With
End Sub
```

In the above procedure, the following statement creates a blank UserForm:

```
Set objVBComp = objVBProj.VBComponents.Add(vbext_ct_MSForm)
```

Next, the form's default name and other properties (Caption, Width, and Height) are written to the Immediate window and then reset with new values.

Before we can access the content of the UserForm, we need a reference to the VBComponent's Designer object, like this:

```
Set objVBFrm = objVBComp.Designer
```

Several With...End With statement blocks are used to add controls (label, combo box, frame, check boxes, and command buttons) to the blank UserForm and position them within the form by using the Top and Left properties. The InsideHeight and InsideWidth properties are used to move the OK and Cancel buttons to the bottom of the UserForm. These properties return the height and width, in points, of the space that's available inside the form.

The remaining code in the procedure creates various event procedures for the UserForm and its controls. The first one is the UserForm_Initialize() procedure that will populate the combo box control with department names before the form is displayed on a user's screen. Next, the event procedures for command buttons (OK and Cancel) are created. The cmdCancel_Click() event procedure unloads the form, and the cmdOK_Click() procedure displays a message box with information about the types of reports selected via the check boxes. Code for the event procedure can be added with several techniques. One technique is using the InsertLines statement of the CodeModule. Another is creating a string to hold the code and adding this string to the code module with the AddFromString method. The code added by the AddFromString method is inserted on the line preceding the first procedure in the module. The AddFromFile method can be used for adding code that is stored in a text file.

Note: The CreateEventProc method automatically adds the Private Sub and the End Sub statements and a space between these lines. All you need to do is add the actual code using the InsertLines statements. The CreateEventProc method returns the number of the line in the module where the Private Sub statement was added.

3. Run the AddUserForm procedure.

   When the procedure finishes its execution, the Visual Basic Editor screen will display the form shown in Figure 26-6.

4. Choose **View | Code** or press **F7** and review the procedures that were programmatically created for the form by the AddUserForm procedure.

5. Choose **Run | Run Sub/UserForm** or press **F5** to display and work with the form.

If you'd like to display your custom UserForm in a specific location on the screen, consider adding the following event procedure to the AddUserForm procedure. You must code this procedure by using one of the techniques described earlier.

```
Private Sub UserForm_Activate()
  With ReportSelector
    .Top = 100
    .Left = 25
  End With
End Sub
```

Copying UserForms Programmatically

If you need to add an existing UserForm to another workbook, you can simply export the form to disk by choosing File | Export File in the Visual Basic Editor screen. Excel will create a form file (identified with a .frm extension) that you can then import to another VBA project by choosing the File | Import File command.

You can also automate the export/import process of UserForms by writing VBA code. The following example procedure exports the form created in the previous section. After the form is imported, a procedure is written to a standard module of the Practice_Excel26b.xlsm file to display the form.

Hands-On 26-16: Copying a UserForm with VBA

1. Insert a new module into the VBA project in the Practice_Excel26.xlsm workbook.
2. In the Code window, enter the following procedure:

```
Sub UserFormCopy(strFileName As String)
    Dim objVBComp As VBComponent
    Dim wkb As Workbook

    On Error Resume Next
        Set wkb = Workbooks(strFileName)
        If Err.Number <> 0 Then
            Workbooks.Open ActiveWorkbook.Path & "\" & strFileName
            Set wkb = Workbooks(strFileName)
        End If

    For Each objVBComp In ThisWorkbook.VBProject.VBComponents
        If objVBComp.Type = 3 Then  ' this is a UserForm
            ' export the UserForm to disk
            objVBComp.Export Filename:=objVBComp.Name
            ' import the UserForm to a specific workbook
            wkb.VBProject.VBComponents.Import Filename:=objVBComp.Name
            ' delete two form files created by the Export method
            Kill objVBComp.Name
            Kill objVBComp.Name & ".frx"
        End If
```

```
    Next

    ' add a standard module to the workbook
    ' and write code to show the UserForm
    Set objVBComp = wkb.VBProject.VBComponents.Add(vbext_ct_StdModule)

    objVBComp.CodeModule.AddFromString _
        "Sub ShowReportSelector()" & vbCrLf & _
        "    ReportSelector.Show" & vbCrLf & _
        "End Sub" & vbCrLf

    ' close the Code pane
    objVBComp.CodeModule.CodePane.Window.Close

    ' run the ShowReportSelector procedure to display the form
    Application.Run wkb.Name & "!ShowReportSelector"

    Set objVBComp = Nothing
    Set wkb = Nothing
End Sub
```

3. Run the UserFormCopy procedure by entering the following statement in the Immediate window and pressing **Enter**:

```
UserFormCopy "Practice_Excel26b.xlsm"
```

Recall that the Practice_Excel26b.xlsm workbook was created earlier in this chapter. When you execute the above statement, the UserForm is imported into this workbook and displayed on the user's screen.

Working with References

When you write VBA procedures you often need to access objects that are stored in external object libraries. For example, in this chapter you have used objects defined in the Microsoft Visual Basic for Applications Extensibility 5.3 library. In other chapters of this book you have worked with objects exposed by the Microsoft Word 12.0 object library or Microsoft Outlook 12.0 object library, Microsoft Access 12.0 object library, Microsoft ActiveX Data Objects 2.8 library, and so on.

There are two ways to expose an object model to your Excel application: early binding and late binding.

You use early binding when you expose the object model at design time. This is done by choosing Tools | References in the Visual Basic Editor screen. The References dialog box lists files with which you can bind. Binding means exposing the client object model to the host application, in this case Microsoft Excel. To manipulate a specific application in your Excel VBA project, you must select the check box next to the name of the library you want to use.

You perform late binding when you bind the object library in code at run time. Instead of using the References dialog box, you use the GetObject or CreateObject functions as discussed in Chapter 15.

By adding a reference to the external object library via the Tools | References dialog box (early binding), you are able to get on-the-fly programming assistance for the objects you need to include in your VBA code, consequently avoiding many syntax errors. You can also view the application's object model via the Object Browser and have access to the application's built-in constants. In addition, your code runs faster because the references to the external libraries are checked and compiled at design time. The problems arise, however, when you move your code to other computers that do not have the external libraries installed. The procedures that ran perfectly well on your computer suddenly begin to display compile-time errors that cannot be trapped using standard error-handling techniques. To ensure that the end users have the required references and object libraries you must write code that checks not only whether these libraries are present but also that they are the correct version. This section shows how to:

- List references to the external object libraries that have been selected in the References dialog box
- Add a reference to a specific library on the fly
- Remove missing library references
- Check for broken references

Creating a List of References

The Reference object in the References collection represents a reference to a type library or a VBA project. You can use various properties of the Reference object to:

- Find out whether the reference is built in or added by a developer (BuiltIn property)
- Determine if the reference is broken (IsBroken property)
- Find out the reference version number (Major and Minor properties)
- Get the description of the reference as it appears in the Object Browser (Description property)
- Return the full path to the workbook, DLL, OCX, TLD, or OLB file that is a source of the reference (FullPath property)
- Return the globally unique identifier for the reference (Guid property)
- Determine the reference type (Type property)

The following procedure prints to the Immediate window the names of all VBA projects, the names and full paths of selected references for each VBA project, and the names of each project's components.

Hands-On 26-17: Listing VBA Project References and Components Using VBA

1. Insert a new module into the VBA project in the Practice_Excel26.xlsm workbook.
2. In the Code window, enter the following procedure:

```
Sub ListPrjCompRef()
  Dim objVBPrj As VBIDE.VBProject
  Dim objVBCom As VBIDE.VBComponent
  Dim vbRef As VBIDE.Reference

    ' List VBA projects as well as references and
    ' component names they contain
    For Each objVBPrj In Application.VBE.VBProjects
        Debug.Print objVBPrj.Name
        Debug.Print vbTab & "References"
        For Each vbRef In objVBPrj.References
            With vbRef
               Debug.Print vbTab & vbTab & .Name & "---" & .FullPath
            End With
        Next
        Debug.Print vbTab & "Components"
        For Each objVBCom In objVBPrj.VBComponents
            Debug.Print vbTab & vbTab & objVBCom.Name
        Next
    Next
    Set vbRef = Nothing
    Set objVBCom = Nothing
    Set objVBPrj = Nothing
End Sub
```

3. Run the ListPrjCompRef procedure.

   When the procedure finishes executing, the Immediate window displays information about all the VBA projects that are currently open in Excel. For example:

```
Personal
    References
        VBA---C:\Program Files\Common Files\Microsoft
              Shared\VBA\VBA6\VBE6.DLL
        Excel---C:\Program Files\Microsoft Office\Office12\EXCEL.EXE
        stdole---C:\WINDOWS\system32\STDOLE2.TLB
        Office---C:\Program Files\Common Files\Microsoft
                 Shared\OFFICE12\MSO.DLL
    Components
        ThisWorkbook
        Sheet1
        Switches
Chap26SourceCode
    References
        VBA---C:\Program Files\Common Files\Microsoft
              Shared\VBA\VBA6\VBE6.DLL
        Excel---C:\Program Files\Microsoft Office\Office12\EXCEL.EXE
        stdole---C:\WINDOWS\system32\STDOLE2.TLB
        Office---C:\Program Files\Common Files\Microsoft
                 Shared\OFFICE12\MSO.DLL
        VBIDE---C:\Program Files\Common Files\Microsoft
                Shared\VBA\VBA6\VBE6EXT.OLB
        MSForms---C:\WINDOWS\system32\FM20.DLL
    Components
        ThisWorkbook
        Sheet1
        Sheet2
```

```
Sheet3
Module1
Module2
Module3
Module4
Module5
Module6
Module7
Module8
Module9
Module10
Module11
Module12
Sheet4
Module13
ReportSelector
Module14
Module15
```

4. On your own, modify the ListPrjCompRef procedure to list procedures in each module. Refer to the "Listing All Procedures in All Modules" section earlier in this chapter for related code examples.

Adding a Reference

The AddFromFile method of the References collection is used to add a reference to a project from a file. You must specify the project library filename, including its path. The following procedure adds a reference to the Microsoft Scripting Runtime library, which is stored in the scrrun.dll (dynamic link library) file.

Hands-On 26-18: Adding a Project Reference with VBA

1. Insert a new module into the VBA project in the Practice_Excel26.xlsm workbook.
2. In the Code window, enter the following procedure:

```
Sub AddRef()
    Dim objVBProj As VBProject

    Set objVBProj = ThisWorkbook.VBProject

    On Error GoTo ErrorHandle
    objVBProj.References.AddFromFile "C:\Windows\System32\scrrun.dll"
    MsgBox "The reference to the Microsoft Scripting Runtime was set."
    Application.SendKeys "%tr"

ExitHere:
    Set objVBProj = Nothing
    Exit Sub
ErrorHandle:
    MsgBox "The reference to the Microsoft Scripting Runtime" & _
        " already exists."
    GoTo ExitHere
End Sub
```

3. Run the AddRef procedure.

   When a message box appears, click **OK**. If the reference to the Microsoft Scripting Runtime was set during the procedure execution, the References dialog box will appear with a check mark next to Microsoft Scripting Runtime.
4. Close the References dialog box if it is open.

Every type library has an associated globally unique identifier (GUID) that is stored in the Windows registry. If you know the GUID of the reference, you can add a reference by using the AddFromGuid method. This method requires three arguments: a string expression representing the GUID of the reference, the major version number of the reference, and the minor version number of the reference. The AddFromGuid method searches the registry to find the reference you want to add.

The following procedure prints to the Immediate window the names, GUIDs, and version numbers of the libraries that are already installed in the active workbook's VBA project. The procedure also adds a reference to the Microsoft DAO 3.6 object library if this library has not yet been added.

Hands-On 26-19: Obtaining Information about Installed VBA Libraries from the Registry

1. In the Code window where you entered the previous procedure, enter the AddRef_FromGuid procedure as shown below:

```
Sub AddRef_FromGuid()
    Dim objVBProj As VBProject
    Dim i As Integer
    Dim strName As String
    Dim strGuid As String
    Dim strMajor As Long
    Dim strMinor As Long

    Set objVBProj = ActiveWorkbook.VBProject

    ' Find out what libraries are already installed
    For i = 1 To objVBProj.References.Count
          strName = objVBProj.References(i).Name
          strGuid = objVBProj.References(i).GUID
          strMajor = objVBProj.References(i).Major
          strMinor = objVBProj.References(i).Minor
          Debug.Print strName & " - " & strGuid & _
            ", " & strMajor & ", " & strMinor
    Next i

    ' add a reference to the Microsoft DAO 3.6 Object library
    On Error Resume Next
    ThisWorkbook.VBProject.References.AddFromGuid _
       "{00025E01-0000-0000-C000-000000000046}", 5, 0
End Sub
```

2. Run the AddRef_FromGuid procedure.

The procedure produces the following list of references in the Immediate window:

```
VBA - {000204EF-0000-0000-C000-000000000046}, 4, 0
Excel - {00020813-0000-0000-C000-000000000046}, 1, 6
stdole - {00020430-0000-0000-C000-000000000046}, 2, 0
Office - {2DF8D04C-5BFA-101B-BDE5-00AA0044DE52}, 2, 4
VBIDE - {0002E157-0000-0000-C000-000000000046}, 5, 3
MSForms - {0D452EE1-E08F-101A-852E-02608C4D0BB4}, 2, 0
Scripting - {420B2830-E718-11CF-893D-00A0C9054228}, 1, 0
DAO - {00025E01-0000-0000-C000-000000000046}, 5, 0
```

Removing a Reference

To remove an unwanted reference from the VBA project, use the Remove method of the References collection. The following procedure removes the reference to the Microsoft DAO 3.6 object library that was added by the AddRef_FromGuid procedure in the previous section.

Hands-On 26-20: Removing a Reference Using VBA

1. In the Code window where you entered the previous procedure, enter the RemoveRef procedure as shown below:

```
Sub RemoveRef()
    Dim objVBProj As VBProject
    Dim objRef As Reference
    Dim sRefFile As String

    Set objVBProj = ActiveWorkbook.VBProject

    ' Loop through the references and delete the reference to DAO library
    For Each objRef In objVBProj.References
        If InStr(1, objRef.Description, "DAO 3.6") > 0 Then
            objVBProj.References.Remove objRef
            Exit For
        End If
    Next objRef
End Sub
```

2. Run the RemoveRef procedure. When the procedure finishes executing, open the References dialog box to verify that the reference to the Microsoft DAO 3.6 object library is no longer selected.

In addition to removing references to external object libraries, you can remove any existing references to other VBA projects. This is done by checking the BuiltIn property of the Reference object and removing the reference when the BuiltIn property is not True:

```
For Each objRef in objVBProjReferences
    If Not objRef.BuiltIn Then objVBProj.References.Remove objRef
Next objRef
```

The BuiltIn property of the Reference object returns False if the particular reference isn't a default reference. When a reference is not built in, it can be removed. Default references cannot be removed.

Checking for Broken References

If the required object libraries are not installed on a user's computer or aren't the correct version, the culprit references are marked as "missing" in the References dialog box. You can use the IsBroken property to find these invalid references. The IsBroken property returns a Boolean value True if the Reference object no longer points to a valid reference in the registry. If the reference is valid, False is returned. The code to check for broken references should be included or called from the Workbook_Open event procedure before attempting to add any new references via code.

The following example procedure checks for broken references.

Hands-On 26-21: Checking for Broken References in a VBA Project

1. In the ThisWorkbook module of VBAProject (Practice_Excel26.xlsm), enter the following Workbook_Open event procedure:

```
Private Sub Workbook_Open()
   Dim objVBProj As VBProject
   Dim objRef As Reference
   Dim refBroken As Boolean

   Set objVBProj = ThisWorkbook.VBProject

   ' Loop through the selected references in
   ' the References dialog box
   For Each objRef In objVBProj.References
   ' If the reference is broken, get its name and its GUID
      If objRef.IsBroken Then
         Debug.Print objRef.Name
         Debug.Print objRef.GUID
         refBroken = True
      End If
   Next
   If refBroken = False Then
        Debug.Print "All references are valid."
   End If
End Sub
```

2. Save and close the Practice_Excel26.xlsm workbook. Do not exit Microsoft Excel.
3. Reopen the **Practice_Excel26.xlsm** workbook.
   When the workbook opens, Excel executes the code in the Workbook_Open event procedure.
4. Switch to the Visual Basic Editor window and activate the Immediate window. If broken references are found in the active project, you will see the reference name and its GUID; otherwise, a message is displayed that all references are valid.

If you'd like to test whether a specific reference is valid, insert a new module into the active VBA project and write a function procedure like this:

```
Function IsBrokenRef(strRef As String) As Boolean
    Dim objVBProj As VBProject
    Dim objRef As Reference

    Set objVBProj = ThisWorkbook.VBProject

    For Each objRef In objVBProj.References

    If strRef = objRef.Name And objRef.IsBroken Then
        IsBrokenRef = True
        Exit Function
    End If
    Next

    IsBrokenRef = False
End Function
```

To test the above function, you could enter the following statements in the Immediate window:

```
ref = IsBrokenRef("OLE Automation")
?ref
```

If True, the reference is invalid; if False, it is valid.

Working with Windows

As you know, the VBE screen contains numerous windows. Each window (VBE main window, Project Explorer, Properties window, Immediate and Watch windows, open Code window, Designer windows, and so on) is represented by the Window object. Each Window object is a member of the VBIDE.Windows collection. Use the Type property of the Window object to determine the window type.

Table 26-1: Window types available in the VBA project

Window Description	Constant	Value
Code window	vbext_wt_CodeWindow	0
Designer	vbext_wt_Designer	1
Object Browser	vbext_wt_Browser	2
Watch window	vbext_wt_Watch	3
Locals window	vbext_wt_Locals	4
Immediate window	vbext_wt_Immediate	5
Project Explorer window	vbext_wt_ProjectWindow	6
Properties window	vbext_wt_PropertyWindow	7
Find dialog box	vbext_wt_Find	8
Search and Replace dialog box	vbext_wt_FindReplace	9
Toolbox	vbext_wt_Toolbox	10
Linked window frame	vbext_wt_LinkedWindowFrame	11
Main window	vbext_wt_MainWindow	12
Tool window	vbext_wt_ToolWindow	15

The following procedure loops through all the open windows in the VBE, closes the Immediate window, and displays a dialog box with the names of open windows.

Hands-On 26-22: Closing the Immediate Window and Listing All Open Windows in the VBE Screen

1. Insert a new module into the VBA project in the Practice_Excel26.xlsm workbook.
2. In the Code window, enter the following procedure:

```
Sub Close_ImmediateWin()
    Dim objWin As VBIDE.Window
    Dim strOpenWindows As String

    strOpenWindows = "The following windows are open:" & _
           vbCrLf & vbCrLf

    For Each objWin In Application.VBE.Windows
        Select Case objWin.Type
            Case vbext_wt_Immediate
                MsgBox objWin.Caption & " window was closed."
                objWin.Close
            Case Else
                strOpenWindows = strOpenWindows & _
                    objWin.Caption & vbCrLf
        End Select
    Next
    MsgBox strOpenWindows
    Set objWin = Nothing
End Sub
```

3. Run the Close_ImmediateWin procedure.

Working with VBE Menus and Toolbars

In Chapter 21, you learned how to write VBA code to create or modify shortcut menus, or create Excel old style menus (prior to Excel 2007) for display in the Add-Ins tab of the Ribbon. Using the same CommandBar object that you are already familiar with, you can now customize menus and toolbars in the Visual Basic Editor. To work with the CommandBars collection, you need to ensure that a reference to the Microsoft Office 12.0 object library is set in the References dialog box. If the reference to this library is not set, Excel displays a "User-defined type not defined" error message when the code attempts to access the CommandBars collection.

Generating a Listing of VBE CommandBars and Controls

The following procedure lists all the CommandBars that can be found in the Visual Basic Editor. Each command bar is defined as a menu bar, toolbar, or pop-up menu via the Type property of the CommandBar object. Each

CommandBar object has a number of controls assigned to it. The procedure lists all these controls for each CommandBar, including the control IDs.

Hands-On 26-23: Listing VBE CommandBars and Controls

1. Insert a new module into the VBA project in the Practice_Excel26.xlsm workbook.
2. In the Code window, enter the following procedure:

```
Sub ListVBECmdBars()
    Dim objCmdBar As CommandBar
    Dim strCmdType As String
    Dim c As Variant

    Workbooks.Add
    Range("A1").Select

    With ActiveCell
        .Offset(0, 0) = "CommandBar Name"
        .Offset(0, 1) = "Control Caption"
        .Offset(0, 2) = "Control ID"
    End With

    For Each objCmdBar In Application.VBE.CommandBars
        Select Case objCmdBar.Type
            Case 0
                strCmdType = "toolbar"
            Case 1
                strCmdType = "menu bar"
            Case 2
                strCmdType = "popup menu"
        End Select

        ActiveCell.Offset(1, 0) = objCmdBar.Name & _
                  " (" & strCmdType & ")"

        For Each c In objCmdBar.Controls
            ActiveCell.Offset(1, 0).Select
            With ActiveCell
                .Offset(0, 1) = c.Caption
                .Offset(0, 2) = c.ID
            End With
        Next
    Next

    Columns("A:C").AutoFit

    Set objCmdBar = Nothing
End Sub
```

3. Run the ListVBECmdBars procedure.

   The procedure adds a new workbook and writes to it the information about all the CommandBars and controls found in the Visual Basic Editor (see the partial listing in Figure 26-7).

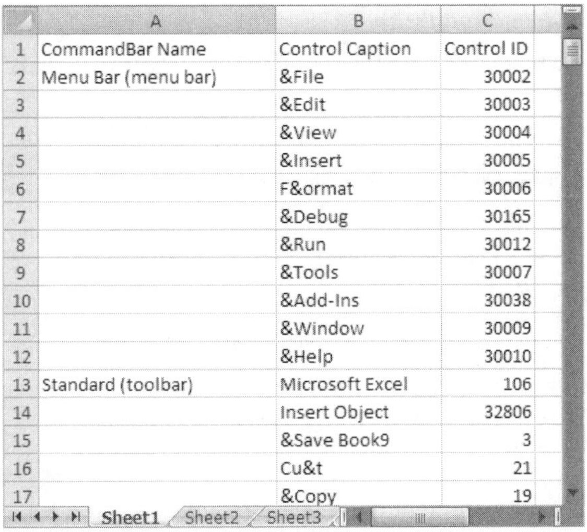

	A	B	C
1	CommandBar Name	Control Caption	Control ID
2	Menu Bar (menu bar)	&File	30002
3		&Edit	30003
4		&View	30004
5		&Insert	30005
6		F&ormat	30006
7		&Debug	30165
8		&Run	30012
9		&Tools	30007
10		&Add-Ins	30038
11		&Window	30009
12		&Help	30010
13	Standard (toolbar)	Microsoft Excel	106
14		Insert Object	32806
15		&Save Book9	3
16		Cu&t	21
17		&Copy	19

Sheet1 Sheet2 Sheet3

Figure 26-7: You can list all the CommandBars available in the Visual Basic Editor by running the custom ListVBECmdBars procedure as demonstrated in this section.

Adding a CommandBar Button to the VBE

The following procedure adds a new command button to the end of the Tools menu in the Visual Basic Editor.

Hands-On 26-24: Modifying the VBE Tools Menu

1. In the same module where you entered the ListVBECmdBars procedure (see the previous section), type the following procedure:

```
Sub AddCmdButton_ToVBE()
    Dim objCmdBar As CommandBar
    Dim objCmdBtn As CommandBarButton

   ' get the reference to the Tools menu in the VBE
    Set objCmdBar = Application.VBE.CommandBars.FindControl _
            (ID:=30007).CommandBar

    ' add a button to the Tools menu
    Set objCmdBtn = objCmdBar.Controls.Add(msoControlButton)

    ' set the new button's properties
    With objCmdBtn
        .Caption = "List VBE menus and toolbars"
        .onAction = "ListVBECmdBars"
     End With
End Sub
```

Please do not run this procedure yet, as it is not complete. To run a custom procedure assigned to any VBE menu item, you need to raise the Click event of the CommandBarButton. Use the CommandBarEvents object to trigger the Click event when a control on the CommandBar is clicked. This is done in a class module.

2. Choose **Insert | Class Module.**
3. In the Properties window, change the name of the Class1 module to **clsCmdBarEvents.**
4. In the clsCmdBarEvents module Code window, enter the following code:

```
Public WithEvents cmdBtnEvents As CommandBarButton

Private Sub cmdBtnEvents_Click(ByVal Ctrl As Office.CommandBarButton, _
                CancelDefault As Boolean)
    On Error Resume Next

    ' run the procedure specified in the onAction property
    Application.Run Ctrl.onAction

    ' specify that we already handled this event
    CancelDefault = True
End Sub
```

   Notice that the first statement in the class module uses the WithEvents keyword to declare an object called cmdBtnEvents of the type CommandBarButton whose events we want to handle. Next, we specify that this object (cmdBtnEvents) is to receive the Click event when the menu item is selected. The first statement in the cmdBtnEvents_Click event procedure will prevent an error message from appearing in case the procedure specified in the onAction property doesn't exist. The next statement will run the procedure specified in the control's onAction property. Because the onAction property of the controls located on the VBE CommandBars does not cause the specified procedure code to execute, you must call the required procedure with the Run method of the Application object.

   Now that you've told Visual Basic that you'd like it to handle the Click event for the menu item, you need to connect the class module with the standard module containing the code of the AddCmdButton_ToVBE procedure that you created in step 1.

5. Enter the following declaration line at the very top of the module that contains the AddCmdBtn_ToVBE procedure:

```
Dim myClickEvent As clsCmdBarEvents
```

   In the above declaration statement, the myClickEvent is a module-level variable defined by the class clsCmdBarEvents. This variable will serve as a link between the menu item and the clsCmdBarEvents class module.

   The final step requires that you add additional code to the AddCmdButton_ToVBE procedure so that Visual Basic knows that it needs to handle the Click event for the menu item.

6. Enter the following code at the very end of the AddCmdButton_ToVBE procedure:

```
    ' create an instance of the clsCmdEvents class
    Set myClickEvent = New clsCmdBarEvents

    ' hook up the class instance to the newly added button
    Set myClickEvent.cmdBtnEvents = objCmdBtn

    Set objCmdBtn = Nothing
    Set objCmdBar = Nothing
```

The modified AddCmdButton_ToVBE procedure should look as follows:

```
Sub AddCmdButton_ToVBE()
    Dim objCmdBar As CommandBar
    Dim objCmdBtn As CommandBarButton

   ' get the reference to the Tools menu in the VBE
    Set objCmdBar = Application.VBE.CommandBars.FindControl _
            (ID:=30007).CommandBar

    ' add a button to the Tools menu
    Set objCmdBtn = objCmdBar.Controls.Add(msoControlButton)

    ' set the new button's properties
    With objCmdBtn
        .Caption = "List VBE menus and toolbars"
        .onAction = "ListVBECmdBars"

     End With

    ' create an instance of the clsCmdEvents class
    Set myClickEvent = New clsCmdBarEvents

    ' hook up the class instance to the newly added button
    Set myClickEvent.cmdBtnEvents = objCmdBtn

    Set objCmdBtn = Nothing
    Set objCmdBar = Nothing
End Sub
```

7. Run the AddCmdButton_ToVBE procedure.

   The procedure places a new menu item on the Tools menu and connects this item with the event handler located in the class module.

8. Choose **Tools | List VBE menus and toolbars**.

   Visual Basic triggers the Click event of the selected menu item and runs the procedure code specified in the onAction property. When you switch to the Microsoft Excel application window, you should see a new workbook with a complete listing of the VBE CommandBars and their controls.

Removing a CommandBar Button from the VBE

The following procedure removes the custom menu item that was added to the Tools menu by the procedure in the previous section.

Hands-On 26-25: Removing a Custom Option from the VBE Menu

1. In the same module where you entered the AddCmdButton_ToVBE procedure (see the previous section), type the following procedure:

```
Sub RemoveCmdButton_FromVBE()
    Dim objCmdBar As CommandBar
    Dim objCmdBarCtrl As CommandBarControl

    ' get the reference to the Tools menu in the VBE
    Set objCmdBar = Application.VBE.CommandBars("Tools")

    ' loop through the Tools menu controls
    ' and delete the control with the matching caption
    For Each objCmdBarCtrl In objCmdBar.Controls
        If objCmdBarCtrl.Caption = "List VBE menus and toolbars" Then
            objCmdBarCtrl.Delete
        End If
    Next

    Set objCmdBarCtrl = Nothing
    Set objCmdBar = Nothing
End Sub
```

2. Run the RemoveCmdButton_FromVBE procedure.

   Upon the procedure's completion, the Tools menu in the VBE screen no longer displays our custom item "List VBE menus and toolbars."

Chapter Summary

In this chapter you have used numerous objects, properties, and methods from the Microsoft Visual Basic for Applications Extensibility 5.3 object library to control the Visual Basic Editor (VBE).

In the next chapter, we will switch our focus to using Excel with Internet technologies. You will learn the basics of HTML programming and web queries.

Part IX

Excel and Web Technologies

Thanks to the Internet and intranets, your spreadsheet data can be easily accessed and shared with others 24/7. Excel 2007 is capable of both capturing data from the web and publishing it to the web.

In this part of the book, you are introduced to using Excel with web technologies. You learn how to retrieve live data into worksheets with web queries and use Excel VBA to create and publish HTML files. You also learn how to retrieve and send information to Excel via Active Server Pages (ASP). Programming XML and Smart Tags is also thoroughly discussed and practiced.

Chapter 27

HTML Programming and Web Queries

Creating Hyperlinks Using VBA ■ Creating and Publishing HTML Files Using VBA ■ Web Queries ■ Creating and Running Web Queries with VBA ■ Web Queries with Parameters ■ Static and Dynamic Parameters ■ Dynamic Web Queries ■ **Refreshing Data ■ Chapter Summary**

The dramatic growth of the Internet over the past several years has made it possible to gain access to enormous knowledge archives scattered all over the world. Thanks to the Internet, we now have at our fingertips databases covering various industries and fields of knowledge, dictionaries and encyclopedias, stock quotes, maps, weather forecasts, and a great deal of other types of information stored on millions of web servers. Often, the information retrieved from web pages becomes a subject of further analysis by computer programs. Thanks to its file structure (rows and columns), Microsoft Excel 2007 is a preferred tool for working with table data found on the Internet. Using Excel, you can easily create, publish, review, and analyze data. This chapter demonstrates the built-in tools available in Excel 2007 for retrieving data from the web and publishing Excel spreadsheets on the web. You will find many Visual Basic statements here that will allow you to obtain and publish data using custom Visual Basic procedures. To maximize your benefit from this chapter, you should have a connection to the Internet.

Creating Hyperlinks Using VBA

Excel 2007, like other applications in Microsoft Office, allows you to create hyperlinks in your spreadsheets. After clicking on a cell that contains a hyperlink, you can open a document located on a network server, an intranet, or the Internet. Hyperlinks can be created manually by choosing Insert | Hyperlink (as shown in Figure 27-1) or programmatically using VBA.

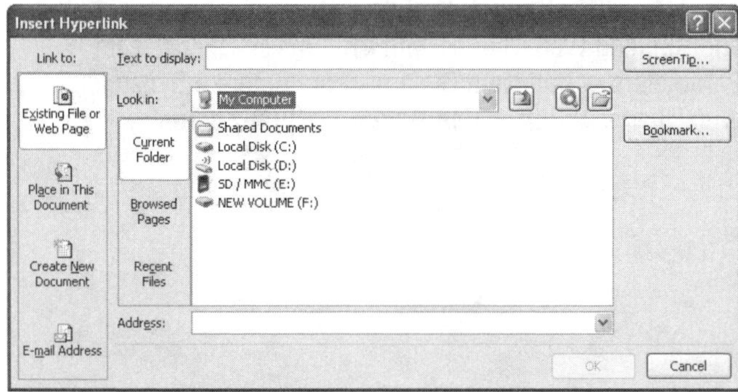

Figure 27-1: The Insert Hyperlink dialog box is used to insert a hyperlink in a Microsoft Excel spreadsheet.

In VBA, each hyperlink is represented by a Hyperlink object. To create a hyperlink to a web page, use the Add method of the Hyperlinks collection. This method is shown below:

```
Expression.Hyperlinks.Add(Anchor, Address, [SubAddress], [ScreenTip], _
    [TextToDisplay])
```

The arguments in square brackets are optional. Expression denotes a worksheet or range of cells where you want to place the hyperlink. Anchor is an object to be clicked. This can be either a Range or Shape object. Address points to a local network or a web page. SubAddress is the name of a range in the Excel file. ScreenTip allows the display of a screen label. TextToDisplay is the name that you'd like to display in a spreadsheet cell for a specific hyperlink.

Let's see how you can programmatically place a hyperlink in a worksheet cell. The hyperlink you are going to create should take you to the Yahoo! site when clicked.

Hands-On 27-1: Using VBA to Place a Hyperlink in a Worksheet Cell

1. Open a new workbook and save it as **C:\Ex07_ByExample\Practice_Excel27.xlsm.**
2. Switch to the Visual Basic Editor screen and insert a new module into VBAProject (Practice_Excel27.xlsm).
3. In the Code window, enter the code of the FollowMe procedure shown below:

```
Sub FollowMe()
    Dim myRange As Range
    Set myRange = Sheets(1).Range("A1")

    myRange.Hyperlinks.Add Anchor:=myRange, _
       Address:="http://search.yahoo.com/", _
       ScreenTip:="Search Yahoo", _
       TextToDisplay:="Click here"
End Sub
```

4. Run the FollowMe procedure.

   When you run the FollowMe procedure, cell A1 in the first worksheet will contain a hyperlink titled "Click here" with the screen tip "Search Yahoo" (see Figure 27-2). If you are now connected to the Internet, clicking on this hyperlink will activate your browser and load the Yahoo! search engine, as shown in Figure 27-3.

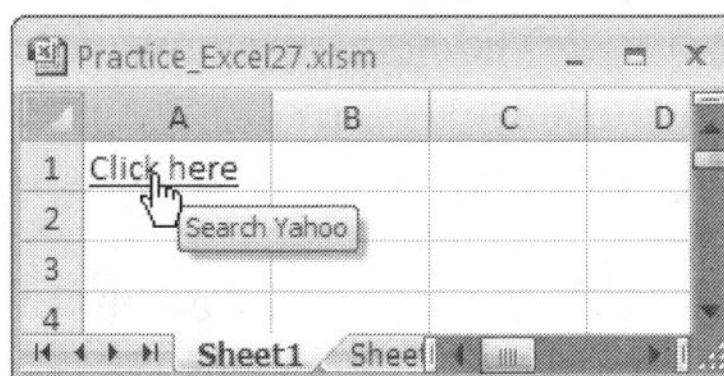

Figure 27-2: This hyperlink was placed in a worksheet by a VBA procedure.

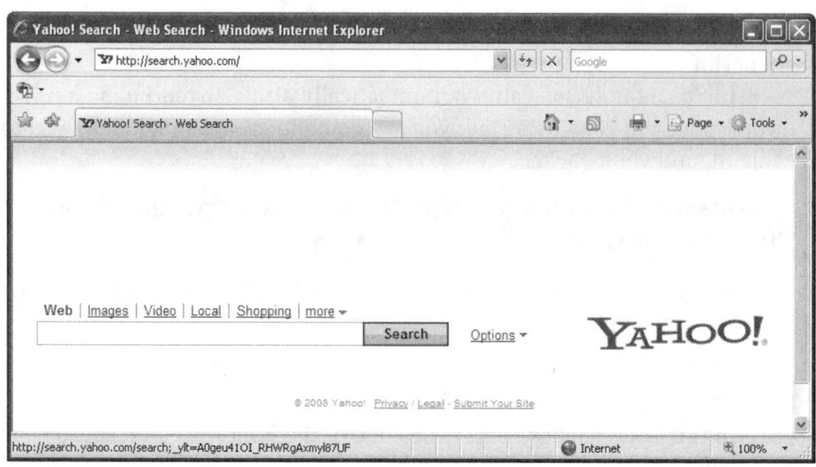

Figure 27-3: The main page of the Yahoo! search engine was activated by clicking on the hyperlink placed in a worksheet cell.

If you'd rather not place hyperlinks in a worksheet but want to make it possible for a user to reach the required Internet pages directly from an Excel worksheet, you can use the FollowHyperlink method. This method allows you to open the required web page without the need to place a hyperlink object in a worksheet. The FollowHyperlink method looks like this:

```
Expression.FollowHyperlink(Address, [SubAddress], [NewWindow], _
    [AddHistory], [ExtraInfo], [Method], [HeaderInfo])
```

Again, the arguments in square brackets are optional. Expression returns a Workbook object. Address is the address of the web page that you want to activate. SubAddress is a fragment of the object to which the hyperlink address points. This can be a range of cells in an Excel worksheet. NewWindow indicates whether you want to display the document or page in a new window; the default setting is False. The next argument, AddHistory, is not currently used and is reserved for future use. ExtraInfo gives additional information that allows jumping to the specific location in a document or on a web page. For example, here you can specify the text for which you want to search. Method specifies the method in which the additional information (ExtraInfo) is attached. This can be one of the following constants: msoMethodGet or msoMethodPost. When you use msoMethodGet, ExtraInfo is a string that's appended to the URL address. When using msoMethodPost, ExtraInfo is posted as a string or byte array. The last optional argument, HeaderInfo, is a string that specifies header information for the HTTP request. The default value is an empty string.

Let's use the FollowHyperlink method in a VBA procedure. The purpose of this procedure is to use the AltaVista search engine to find pages containing the text entered in a worksheet cell.

Hands-On 27-2: Using a Search Engine to Find Text Entered in a Worksheet Cell

1. In the Visual Basic Editor window, activate the Project Explorer window and double-click the **Sheet2 (Sheet2)** object in the Microsoft Excel Objects folder located in VBAProject (Practice_Excel27.xlsm).
2. In the Sheet2 Code window, enter the Worksheet_BeforeDoubleClick event procedure shown below (you may want to review Chapter 17 on creating and using event procedures in Excel):

```
Private Sub Worksheet_BeforeDoubleClick(ByVal Target As Range, _
            Cancel As Boolean)
    Dim strSearch As String

    strSearch = Sheets(2).Range("C3").Formula
    If Target = Range("C3") Then
        Cancel = True
        ActiveWorkbook.FollowHyperlink _
        Address:="http://www.altavista.com/cgi-bin/query", _
        ExtraInfo:="q=" & strSearch, _
        Method:=msoMethodGet
    End If
End Sub
```

3. Switch to the Microsoft Excel application window. In cell C3 on Sheet2, enter any word or term about which you want to find information (see Figure 27-4).

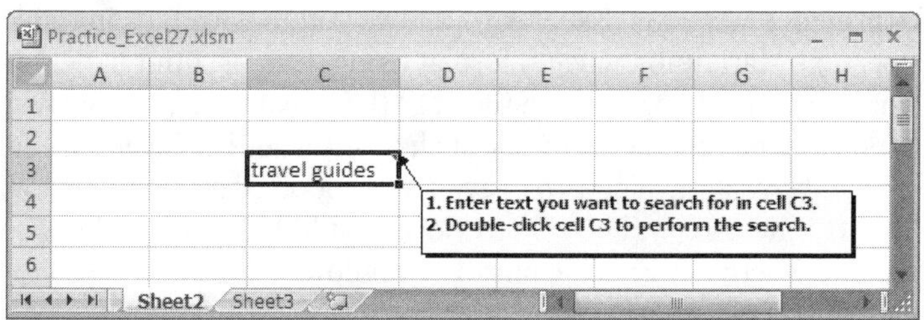

Figure 27-4: A Microsoft Excel worksheet can be used to send search parameters to any search engine on the Internet.

4. Make sure that you are connected to the Internet. Double-click cell **C3**. This will cause the text entered in cell C3 to be sent to the AltaVista search engine. The screen should show the index to found topics with the specified criteria (see Figure 27-5).

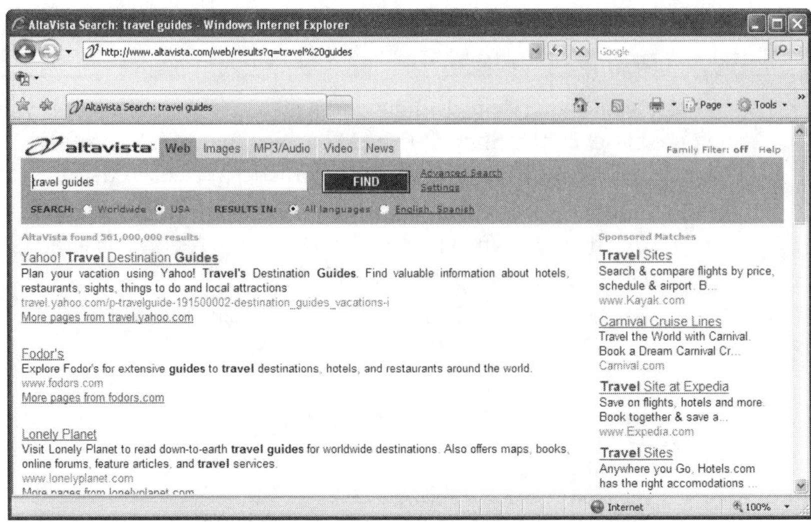

Figure 27-5: A web page opened from a Microsoft Excel worksheet lists topics that were found based on the criteria entered in a worksheet cell (see Figure 27-4).

Creating and Publishing HTML Files Using VBA

Like previous versions, Excel 2007 allows you to save files in the HTML (Hypertext Markup Language) format using .htm or .html file extensions. When you save an Excel file in the HTML format, you can view your spreadsheets using an Internet browser such as Internet Explorer, FireFox, or Netscape Navigator. When you save a workbook or a portion of a workbook as HTML, the user will be able to view the file either in the browser or inside the Microsoft Excel application window.

Note: Unlike previous versions, Excel 2007 is not capable of saving data and charts as interactive web pages. While saving an entire workbook or its worksheets in HTML format in Excel 2003, you were able to choose between creating a static or interactive HTML document.

You can save your HTML files directly to the web server, a network server, or a local computer. To do this, simply click the Microsoft Office button, choose Save As, and click Other Formats. In the Save as type drop-down box, select Web Page (*.htm; *.html). Working with nothing other than the user interface (see Figures 27-6 and 27-7), you can place an entire workbook or selected sheets on the web page. Detailed instructions on how to go about placing an entire workbook or any worksheet (or its elements — such as charts or PivotTables) on a web page can be found in the Excel online help. Because this book is about programming, we will focus only on the way these tasks are performed via VBA code.

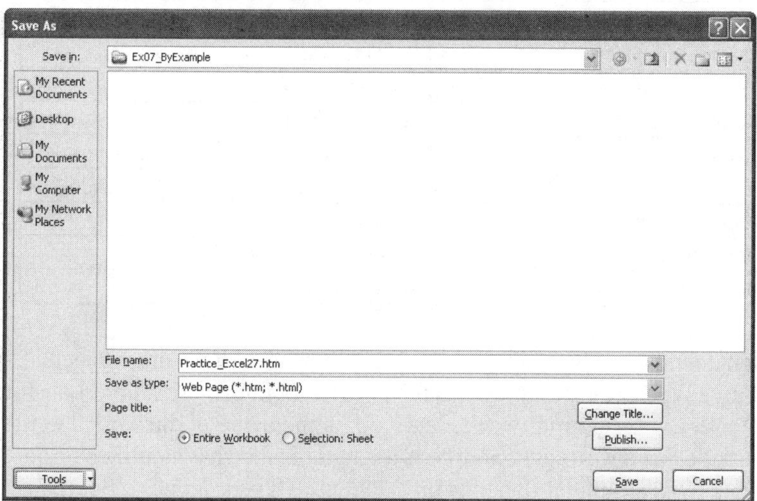

Figure 27-6: The Save As dialog box that appears after choosing Save As and clicking Other Formats allows saving the workbook as a web page.

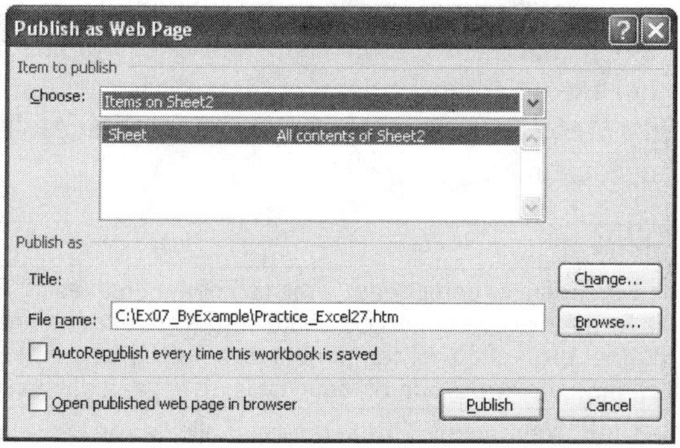

Figure 27-7: The Publish as Web Page dialog box appears after clicking the Publish button on the Save As dialog box (see Figure 27-6).

The Visual Basic for Applications (VBA) object library in Excel 2007 offers objects for publishing worksheets on web pages. To programmatically create and publish Excel files in the HTML format, you should become familiar with the PublishObject object and the PublishObjects collection.

PublishObject represents a worksheet element that was saved on a web page, while PublishObjects is a collection of all PublishObject objects of a specific workbook. To add a worksheet element to the PublishObjects collection, use its Add method. This method will create an object representing a specific worksheet element that was saved as a web page. The format of the Add method looks like this:

```
Expression.Add(SourceType, Filename, Sheet, Source, HtmlType, _
    [DivID], [Title])
```

The arguments in square brackets are optional. Expression returns an object that belongs to the PublishObjects collection. SourceType specifies the source object using one of the following constants:

Constant	Value	Description
xlSourceAutoFilter	3	An AutoFilter range
xlSourceChart	5	A chart
xlSourcePivotTable	6	A PivotTable report
xlSourcePrintArea	2	A range of cells selected for printing
xlSourceQuery	7	A query table (an external data range)
xlSourceRange	4	A range of cells
xlSourceSheet	1	An entire worksheet
xlSourceWorkbook	0	A workbook

Filename is a string specifying the location where the source object (SourceType) was saved. This can be a URL (Uniform Resource Locator) or the path to a local or network file. Sheet is the name of the worksheet that was saved as a web page. Source is a unique name that identifies a source object. This argument depends on the SourceType argument. Source is a range of cells or a name applied to a range of cells when the SourceType argument is the xlSourceRange constant. If the SourceType argument is a constant such as xlSourceChart, xlSourcePivotTable, or xlSourceQuery, Source specifies the name of a chart, PivotTable report, or query table. HtmlType specifies whether the selected worksheet element is saved as an interactive Microsoft Office Web Component or static text and images. This can be one of the following constants:

Constant	Description
xlHTMLCalc	Use the Spreadsheet component. This component makes it possible to view, analyze, and calculate spreadsheet data directly in an Internet browser. This component also has options that allow you to change the formatting of fonts, cells, rows, and columns.
xlHTMLChart	Use the Chart component. This component allows you to create interactive charts in the browser.
xlHTMLList	Use the PivotTable component. This component allows you to rearrange, filter, and summarize information in a browser. This component is also able to display data from a spreadsheet or a database (for instance, Microsoft Access, SQL Server, or OLAP servers).
XlHTMLStatic	(default value) Use static (non-interactive) HTML for viewing only. The data published in an HTML document does not change.

Note: The Office Web Components (OWC) are ActiveX controls that provide four components: Spreadsheet, Chart, PivotTable, and Data Source Control (DSC). In prior releases of Office (XP/2003/2000), these components allow you to use Excel analytical options in an Internet browser. In Office 2007, the Office Web Components have been discontinued. If you need the OWC components to support older applications, you will need to reinstall these components or allow users to download and install them on the fly when the document that requires their use is opened in a browser.

DivID is a unique identifier used in the HTML DIV tag to identify the item on the web page. Title is the title of the web page.

Before we look at how you can use the Add method from a VBA procedure, you also need to learn how to use the Publish method of the PublishObject object. This method will allow you to publish an element or a collection of elements in a particular document on the web page. This method is quite simple and looks like this:

```
Expression.Publish([Create])
```

Expression is an expression that returns a PublishObject object or PublishObjects collection. The optional argument, Create, is used only with a PublishObject object. If the HTML file already exists, setting this argument to True will overwrite the file. Setting this argument to False inserts the item or items at the end of the file. If the file does not yet exist, a new HTML file is created, regardless of the value of the Create argument.

Now that you've been introduced to VBA objects and methods used for creating and publishing an Excel workbook in HTML format, you can begin programming. In the following Hands-On you will create and publish an Excel worksheet with embedded chart as static HTML.

Hands-On 27-3: Creating and Publishing an Excel Worksheet with an Embedded Chart

1. Create a worksheet and chart, as shown in Figure 27-8.

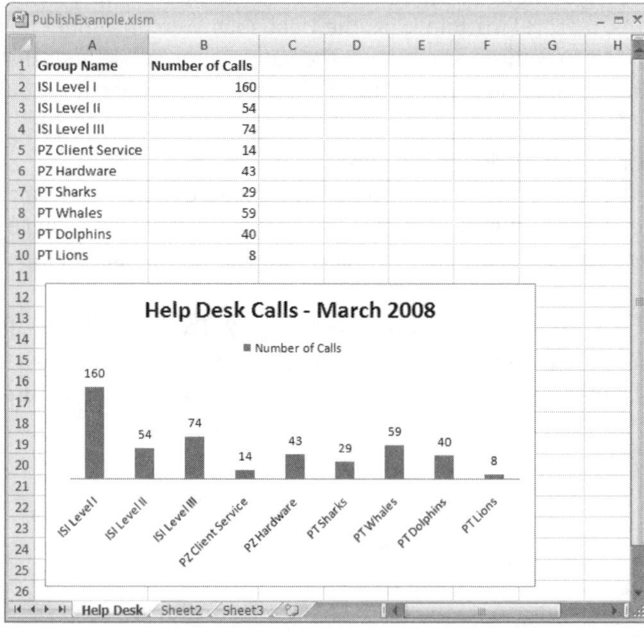

Group Name	Number of Calls
ISI Level I	160
ISI Level II	54
ISI Level III	74
PZ Client Service	14
PZ Hardware	43
PT Sharks	29
PT Whales	59
PT Dolphins	40
PT Lions	8

Figure 27-8: A worksheet like this one with an embedded chart can be placed on a web page by using Save As and clicking on Other Formats, and choosing the Web Page format or via a VBA procedure.

2. Right-click the worksheet name and choose **Rename**. Type **Help Desk,** and then press **Enter**. Save the workbook in a file named **C:\Ex07_ByExample\PublishExample.xlsm**.
3. Activate the Visual Basic Editor window and insert a new module into VBAProject (PublishExample.xlsm).
4. In the Code window, enter the two procedures shown below:

```
' The procedure below will publish a worksheet
' with an embedded chart as static HTML

Sub PublishOnWeb(strSheetName As String, _
                strFileName As String)

    Dim objPub As Excel.PublishObject
    Set objPub = ThisWorkbook.PublishObjects.Add( _
       SourceType:=xlSourceSheet, _
       Filename:=strFileName, Sheet:=strSheetName, _
       HtmlType:=xlHtmlStatic, Title:="Calls Analysis")
    objPub.Publish True
End Sub

Sub CreateHTMLFile()
    Call PublishOnWeb("Help Desk", _
         "C:\Ex07_ByExample\WorksheetWithChart.htm")
End Sub
```

   The first procedure above, PublishOnWeb, publishes a web page with a worksheet containing an embedded chart as static HTML. The second procedure, CreateHTMLFile, calls the PublishOnWeb procedure and feeds it the two required arguments: the name of the worksheet that you want to publish and the name of the HTML file where the data should be saved.

5. Run the CreateHTMLFile procedure.

   When this procedure finishes, a new file called C:\Ex07_ByExample\WorksheetWithChart.htm is created on your hard drive. Also, there will be a folder named WorksheetWithChart_files for storing supplemental files.

6. In Windows Explorer, double-click the **C:\Ex07_ByExample\WorksheetWithChart.htm** file created in step 5. This action will cause the published worksheet to appear in your Internet browser (see Figure 27-9).

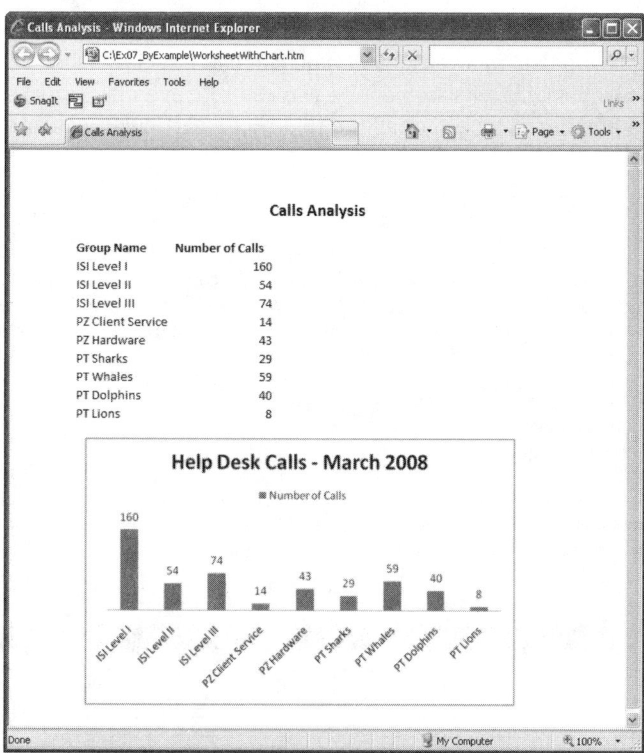

Figure 27-9: Excel worksheet published as a static (non-interactive) web page.

Web Queries

If you are planning to retrieve data from a web page for use or analysis in Excel, simply select the Data tab and choose From Web in the Get External Data group. Excel will display the New Web Query dialog box, as shown in Figure 27-10.

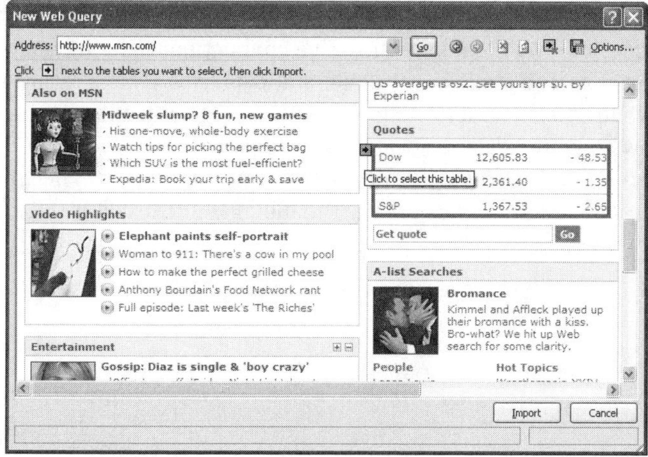

Figure 27-10: This dialog box allows you to create a web query without knowing anything about programming.

Web queries allow you to retrieve data from the web directly into Microsoft Excel. After placing data in a worksheet, you can use Excel tools for performing data analysis. Using a web query, you can retrieve into a worksheet a single table, a number of tables, or all the text that a particular web site contains.

Ready-to-Use Web Queries

Microsoft Excel 2007 comes with several built-in web queries. They are installed in the C:\Program Files\Microsoft Office\Office12\Queries folder, and can be opened in Excel by choosing the Query Files in the Files of type drop-down box in the Open dialog box. The names of these queries are:

MSN MoneyCentral Investor Currency Rates.iqy
MSN MoneyCentral Investor Major Indicies.iqy
MSN MoneyCentral Investor Stock Quotes.iqy

If your C:\Program Files\Microsoft Office\Office12\Queries folder is empty, you may need to update your current installation of Excel (use the Control Panel's Add/Remove Programs dialog box) and indicate that you want these features to be installed.

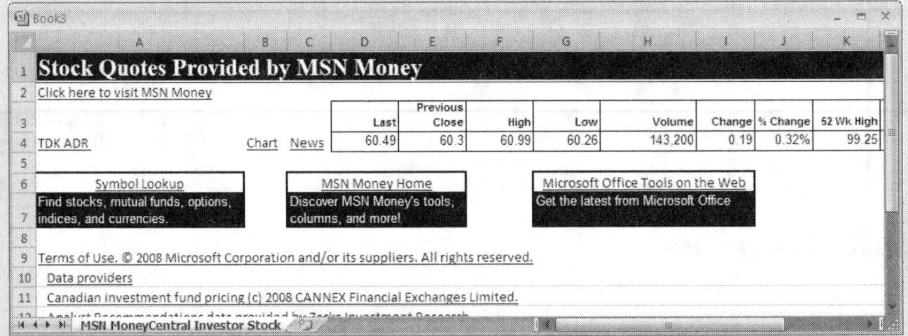

Figure 22-11: TDK corporation stock quotes were retrieved from the web using the built-in web query MSN MoneyCentral Investor Stock Quotes.iqy after typing "TDK tickler" in a dialog box displayed upon activating this query.

To run web queries, you must have an active connection to the Internet.

Web queries can be static or dynamic. Static queries always return the same data, while dynamic queries allow the user to specify different parameters to narrow down the data returned from the web page.

Web queries are stored in text files with the .iqy extension. The content of the .iqy file can be viewed by opening the file in any text editor (for example, Windows Notepad).

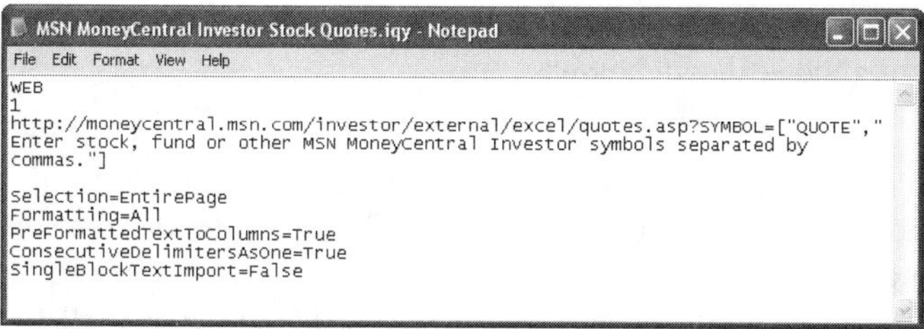
```
WEB
1
http://moneycentral.msn.com/investor/external/excel/quotes.asp?SYMBOL=["QUOTE","
Enter stock, fund or other MSN MoneyCentral Investor symbols separated by
commas."]

Selection=EntirePage
Formatting=All
PreFormattedTextToColumns=True
ConsecutiveDelimitersAsOne=True
SingleBlockTextImport=False
```

Figure 27-12: The web query file references the page from which you want to retrieve data, and specifies parameters to define how data should be imported and any special instructions for the web server.

The .iqy files contain the following parts:

Section Name	Description/Example
Query Type (optional section)	Set to WEB when you use Version Section: WEB
Query Version (optional section)	Allows you to set the version number of a web query. For example: 1.
URL (required)	The URL of the web page where you will get your data. For example: http://www.computers.us.fujitsu.com/ http://www.lsjunction.com/facts/missions.htm
POST Parameters (optional section)	You can send parameters to the web server using the POST or GET method. This section is used for sending parameters with the POST method. These parameters need to be entered on a separate line, as in the following example: http://www.xe.net/cgi-bin/ucc/convert From=USD&Amount=1&To=CAD From, Amount, and To are the names of parameters, while the values that follow the equal (=) signs are the parameter settings. Parameters are separated from one another with the ampersand (&) symbol. **Note:** When sending parameters using the GET method, the parameters are attached to the URL address using the question mark, as shown below: http://moneycentral.msn.com/investor/external/excel/quotes.asp?SYMBOL=GOOG SYMBOL is a parameter name. GOOG is a stock symbol (a parameter value) you want to retrieve from the specified URL.

Creating and Running Web Queries with VBA

In the previous section you learned that a web query can be created by using a command on the Excel Ribbon or typing special instructions in a text editor such as Notepad. The third method of creating a web query is through a VBA statement.

To programmatically create a web query, use the Add method of the QueryTables collection. This collection belongs to the Worksheet object and contains all the QueryTable objects for a specific worksheet. The Add method returns the QueryTable object that represents a new query. The format of this method is shown below:

```
Expression.Add(Connection, Destination, [Sql])
```

Expression is an expression that returns the QueryTable object. Connection specifies the data source for the query table. The data source can be one of the following:

- A string containing the address of the web page in the form "URL; <url>". For example:

  ```
  "URL; http://home.nyc.gov/portal/site/nycgov"
  ```

- A string indicating the path to the existing web query file (.iqy) using the form "FINDER; <data finder file path>". For instance:

  ```
  "FINDER; C:\Program Files\Microsoft Office\Office12\Queries\ _
       MSN MoneyCentral Investor Currency Rates.iqy"
  ```

- A string containing an OLEDB or ODBC connection string. The ODBC connection string has the form "ODBC; <connection string>". For instance:

  ```
  "ODBC; DSN=MyNorthwind;UID=NorthUser;PWD=UserPass;Database=Northwind"
  ```

- An ADO or DAO Recordset object. Microsoft Excel retains the recordset until the query table is deleted or the connection is changed. The resulting query table cannot be edited.
- A string indicating the path to a text file in the form "TEXT; <text file path and name>". For instance:

  ```
  "TEXT; C:\Ex07_HandsOn\myTextFile.txt"
  ```

Destination is the cell in the upper-left corner of the query table destination range (this is where the resulting query table will be placed). This cell must be located in the worksheet containing the QueryTable object used in the expression. The optional argument, Sql, is not used when a QueryTable object is used as the data source.

The example procedure shown below creates a new web query in the active workbook. The data retrieved from a web page is placed in a worksheet as static text.

Hands-On 27-4: Creating a Web Query in an Active Workbook

1. Open a new workbook and save it as **C:\Ex07_ByExample\MyWebQueries.xlsm**.
2. Switch to the Visual Basic Editor window and insert a new module in VBAProject (MyWebQueries.xlsm).
3. In the Code window, enter the NewBooks_Wordware procedure, which retrieves a list of new books from the Wordware Publishing web site.

```
Sub NewBooks_Wordware()
    ' create a web query in the current worksheet
```

```
    ' connect to the web, retrieve data, and paste it
    ' in the worksheet as static text

  With ActiveSheet.QueryTables.Add _
       (Connection:="URL; http://www.wordware.com/computer/ _
         whats_new.shtml", Destination:=Range("A1"))
         .BackgroundQuery = True
         .WebSelectionType = xlSpecifiedTables
         .WebTables = "7"
         .WebFormatting = xlWebFormattingNone
         .Refresh BackgroundQuery:=False
         .SaveData = True
  End With
End Sub
```

4. Switch to the Microsoft Excel application window and choose **Developer | Macros.**
5. In the Macros dialog box, highlight the **NewBooks_Wordware** procedure and click **Run**.

   While the procedure executes, the following tasks occur: (a) a connection is established with the specified web page, (b) data from a web page is retrieved, and (c) data is placed in a worksheet. When the procedure finishes executing, the active worksheet displays a list of new books from Wordware Publishing (Figure 27-13).

MyWebQueries.xlsm

	A	B
1		
2		
3	What's New?	
4		
5	These are the Wordware titles that were published in the past three months:	
6		
7	Advanced 3D Game Programming with DirectX 10	
8	by Peter Walsh	
9	ISBN: 1-59822-054-3	
10	Price: $49.95	
11		
12	Access 2007 Programming by Example with VBA, XML, and ASP	Camtasia Studio 5: The Definitive Guide
13	by Julitta Korol	by Daniel Park
14	ISBN 1-59822-042-X	ISBN 1-59822-057-8
15	Price: $44.95	Price: $39.95

Figure 27-13: This data was retrieved from a web page using the web query in a VBA procedure.

Notice that this worksheet does not contain any hyperlinks because we set the WebFormatting property of the query table to xlWebFormattingNone in the procedure code. This property determines how much formatting from a web page, if any, is applied when you import the page into a query table. You can use one of the following constants: xlWebFormattingAll, xlWebFormattingNone (this is the default setting), or xlWebFormattingRTF.

Setting the BackgroundQuery property of the QueryTable object to True allows you to perform other operations in the worksheet while the data is being retrieved from the web page. The WebSelectionType property determines whether an entire web page, all tables on the web page, or only specific tables on the web page are imported into a query table. The WebSelectionType property can be one of the following constants: xlAllTables, xlEntirePage, or xlSpecifiedTables. The WebTables property specifies a comma-delimited list of table names or table index numbers when you import a web page into a query table. After retrieving data from the web page, you must use the Refresh method of the QueryTable object in order to display the data in a worksheet. If you omit this method in your procedure code, the data retrieved from the web page will be invisible. By setting the SaveData property to True, the table retrieved from the web page will be saved with the workbook.

6. Right-click anywhere within the data placed by the web query in the worksheet. Choose **Edit Query** from the shortcut menu.

   You will see the Edit Web Query dialog box.

7. Click the **Options** button located on this dialog box's toolbar to access the Web Query Options dialog box, as shown in Figure 27-14.

   Notice that the option button None is selected in the Formatting area. This option button represents the xlWebFormattingNone setting of the WebFormatting property in the procedure code.

Figure 27-14: The Web Query Options dialog box.

Web Queries with Parameters

You often need to specify parameters in order to retrieve data from a web page. To send parameters to the web server in your web query, use the POST or GET method after checking to see which of these methods the particular web server uses. You can find this information as instructed below.

Hands-On 27-5: Checking for POST and GET Methods in Web Pages

1. Activate your browser and enter the address of a web page from which you want to retrieve information. For example, enter: **http://www.xe.net/ucc/**.

Figure 27-15: This web page allows you to convert one type of currency into another type.

2. Right-click anywhere in the text area of the web page and choose **View Source** from the shortcut menu. The underlying code for this web page appears in Notepad, as shown in Figure 27-16.

```
border="0" cellspacing="0" cellpadding="0" class="bgHeader">
          <tr>
            <td><a href="/"><img src="/gen/images/logoText.gif" class="logoText"
alt="XE.com The World's Favorite Currency Site" title="XE.com The World's Favorite
Currency Site" /></a></td>
            <td class="search"><div id="search">
      <form name="xesearch" action="http://xesearch-ext.xe.com/xe/search.php"
method="post" onsubmit="SearchSub()" target="_self">
          <input type="hidden" name="id" value="78955197" />
    <input type="hidden" name="pageid" value="r" />
    <input type="hidden" name="mode" value="all" />
    <input type="hidden" name="nsb" value="true" />
    <input type="hidden" name="n" value="0" />
    <input type="hidden" name="query" value="" />
                  <table width="100%" cellpadding="0" cellspacing="0"
align="right">
                      <tr>
                        <td><table cellpadding="3" cellspacing="0" align="right">
                            <tr>
                                                  <td align="right">
<div class="menuOne">
<div class="menu">
<ul>
<li class="language">
<![if !IE]>
      <a href="/languages.php"><img src="/gen/images/ico_map_65x30.gif" width="65"
height="30" class="alignBottom" alt="World Map" />English</a>
```

Figure 27-16: You can view the source of the underlying data for a particular web page by selecting View Source from your browser's shortcut menu. The underlying code will appear in Notepad.

3. While the source code is open in Notepad, choose **Edit | Find** and type **METHOD="POST"** as the text to search for.

   If the parameters are being sent to the web server using the POST method, the search string should appear highlighted, as shown in Figure 27-16. Just before the POST method, there is a URL of the web server that supplies the data (see the action property).

   Now that you know which method is used to send the parameters, you need to find out how the parameters are called.

Note: A web page can contain more than one form; therefore you will find more than one occurrence of the POST method. Each form may require different parameters.

4. While the source code remains open in Notepad, choose **Edit | Find** and type **NAME=** as the search string. Next to the word NAME you should see text in quotation marks. This text is the name of the first parameter. After the word VALUE=, you should see the current value of a parameter. For example:

```
<INPUT TYPE="text" NAME="Amount" VALUE="1" SIZE=10>
```

   In the above HTML statement, the word "Amount" is the name of a parameter and "1" is the current value of this parameter. A value of the parameter can also be one of the options located in the HTML <option> tag. For example:

```
<select class="uccinpts" name="From" size=5 onChange="CheckMore()">
        <option value="EUR" SELECTED>Euro - EUR</option>
        <option value="USD">United States Dollars - USD</option>
        <option value="GBP">United Kingdom Pounds - GBP</option>
        <option value="CAD">Canada Dollars - CAD</option>
        <option value="AUD">Australia Dollars - AUD</option>
        <option value="JPY">Japan Yen - JPY</option>
...
...
</select>
```

   In the above HTML code segment, the word "From" is the name of a parameter. This parameter can have one of the following values: EUR, USD, GBP, CAD, AUD, JPY, and so on.

   If a web server receives parameters using the GET method, you can see the parameter names and their values in your browser's address bar:

```
http://www.wordware.com/Merchant2/merchant.mv?Screen=PROD&Store_Code=wwpub
&Product_Code=159822042x
```

   Notice that the first parameter (Screen) is preceded by a question mark. Parameters are separated from one another with the ampersand symbol (&).

Static and Dynamic Parameters

Web query parameters can be static or dynamic. When you use static parameters, you do not need to enter any values when running a web query (see the code of the Portfolio procedure in Hands-On 27-6). A static web query always returns the same data. If you use dynamic parameters, you can specify one or more values as criteria for your data retrieval while executing your web query (see the Portfolio2 procedure in Hands-On 27-7). A dynamic web query returns data based on the supplied parameters.

In the following example you will see how to create a static web query programmatically. This web query will send parameters to the web server using the GET method. These parameters are static because you are not prompted to supply their values when the web query is run. The values of the parameters that the web server expects to receive are coded inside the VBA procedure.

Hands-On 27-6: Using the GET Method to Send Parameters to the Web Server

1. In the Visual Basic Editor window, insert a new module into VBAProject (MyWebQueries.xlsm).
2. In the Code window, enter the code of the Portfolio procedure as shown below:

```
Sub Portfolio()
   Dim sht As Worksheet
   Dim qryTbl As QueryTable

   ' insert a new worksheet in the current workbook
   Set sht = ThisWorkbook.Worksheets.Add
   ' create a new web query in a worksheet
   Set qryTbl = sht.QueryTables.Add(Connection:="URL; http:// _
   moneycentral." & "msn.com/investor/external/excel/quotes.asp?SYMBOL= _
   GOOG&SYMBOL=YHOO", Destination:=sht.Range("A1"))
   ' retrieve data from web page and specify formatting
   ' paste data in a worksheet
   With qryTbl
       .BackgroundQuery = True
       .WebSelectionType = xlSpecifiedTables
       .WebTables = "1"
       .WebFormatting = xlWebFormattingAll
       .Refresh BackgroundQuery:=False
       .SaveData = True
   End With
   ' delete unwanted rows/columns
   With sht
       .Rows("2").Delete
       .Columns("B:C").Delete
       .Rows("5:16").Delete
   End With
End Sub
```

3. Switch to the Microsoft Excel application window and choose **Developer | Macros.**
4. In the Macro dialog box, highlight the **Portfolio** procedure and click **Run.**

   The result of this procedure is shown in Figure 27-17. Notice that the Portfolio procedure shown above imports data contained in the first table of the specified web site (see the WebTables property setting). To retrieve data from two or more tables, separate their indices or names with commas. When setting the WebTables property, you must surround the table names or indices with quotation marks. To view the explanations of other properties used in this procedure, see the NewBooks_Wordware procedure in Hands-On 27-4.

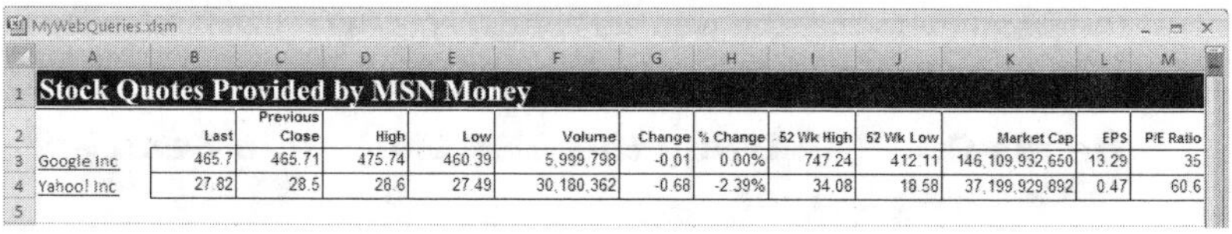

MyWebQueries.xlsm

Stock Quotes Provided by MSN Money

	Last	Previous Close	High	Low	Volume	Change	% Change	52 Wk High	52 Wk Low	Market Cap	EPS	P/E Ratio
Google Inc	465.7	465.71	475.74	460.39	5,999,798	-0.01	0.00%	747.24	412.11	146,109,932,650	13.29	35
Yahoo! Inc	27.82	28.5	28.6	27.49	30,180,362	-0.68	-2.39%	34.08	18.58	37,199,929,892	0.47	60.6

Figure 27-17: A web query can retrieve data from a specific table on a web page.

When sending several values using the same parameter name, instead of repeating the parameter name (as shown in the Portfolio procedure), you can separate parameter values with the plus sign (+), like this:

```
http://moneycentral.msn.com/investor/external/excel/quotes.asp?SYMBOL=GOOG + YHOO
```

You can also use a comma as a separator:

```
http://moneycentral.msn.com/investor/external/excel/quotes.asp?SYMBOL=GOOG,YHOO
```

Which Table Should I Import?

Web pages may contain many tables. Tables allow you to organize the content of the page. When viewing the HTML source code in Notepad, you can easily recognize tables by the following tags: <TABLE> (beginning of table) and </TABLE> (end of table). The <TD> tag indicates table data. This data will be placed in a worksheet cell when retrieved by Excel. Every new table row begins with the <TR> tag and ends with the </TR> tag. Many times, one table is placed inside another table (referred to as table nesting). Because tables are usually numbered in the HTML code, finding the correct table number containing the data you want to place in the worksheet usually requires experimentation. The New Web Query dialog box provides a visual clue to which tables a particular page contains (see Figure 27-10 earlier in this chapter). By clicking on the arrow pointing to the table, you can mark a particular table for selection. You can then click the Save Query button to save the query to a file. When you open the prepared .iqy file in Notepad, you will see the number assigned to the selected table (as shown below). You can now use this number in your VBA procedure.

```
WEB
1
http://money.cnn.com/quote/quote.html?
shownav=false&symb=MET&symb=TDK
Selection=5
Formatting=None
PreFormattedTextToColumns=False
ConsecutiveDelimitersAsOne=False
SingleBlockTextImport=False
DisableDateRecognition=False
DisableRedirections=True
```

Important Note: Web pages undergo frequent modifications. It's not uncommon to find out that a web query you prepared a while ago suddenly stops working because the web page address or parameters required to process the data have changed. If you plan on using web queries in your applications, you must watch for any changes introduced on web sites that supply you with vital information. Particularly watch for table references. A reference to table "13" from a while ago could now be a totally different number, causing your query to retrieve data that you don't care about or no data at all.

Dynamic Web Queries

Instead of hard coding the parameter values in the code of your VBA procedures, you can create a dynamic query that will prompt the user for the parameter setting when the query is run. The Portfolio2 procedure shown below uses the GET method for sending dynamic parameters. This procedure displays a dialog box prompting the user to enter stock symbols separated by spaces.

Hands-On 27-7: Using the GET Method for Sending Dynamic Parameters

1. In the Code window of VBAProject (MyWebQueries.xlsm), enter the following Portfolio2 procedure below the code of the Portfolio procedure:

```
Sub Portfolio2()
   Dim sht As Worksheet
   Dim qryTbl As QueryTable

   ' insert a new worksheet in the current workbook
   Set sht = ThisWorkbook.Worksheets.Add
   ' create a new web query in a worksheet
   Set qryTbl = sht.QueryTables.Add(Connection:= _
   "URL; http://moneycentral." & "msn.com/investor/external/excel/ _
   quotes.asp?SYMBOL=[""Enter " & "symbols separated by spaces""]", _
   Destination:=sht.Range("A1"))
   ' retrieve data from web page and specify formatting
   ' paste data in a worksheet
   With qryTbl
       .BackgroundQuery = True
       .WebSelectionType = xlSpecifiedTables
       .WebTables = "1"
       .WebFormatting = xlWebFormattingAll
       .Refresh BackgroundQuery:=False
       .SaveData = True
   End With
   ' delete unwanted rows/columns
   With sht
       .Rows("2").Delete
       .Rows("6:18").Delete
       .Columns("B:C").Delete
  End With
End Sub
```

2. Switch to the Microsoft Excel application window and choose **Developer | Macros.**
3. In the Macro dialog box, highlight the **Portfolio2** procedure and click **Run.**

   When the web query is activated, a dialog box appears. Here the user may specify any stock symbols in which he or she is interested.
4. Enter the stock symbols in the dialog box as shown in Figure 27-18 and click **OK.**

   The data is retrieved from the specified web page and placed in a worksheet.

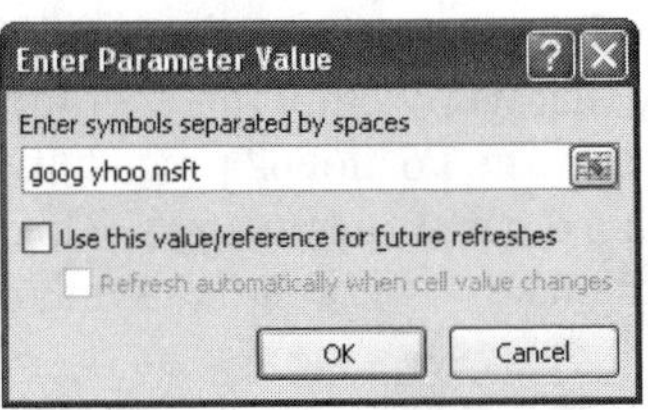

Figure 27-18: Dynamic web queries request parameter values from the user.

The next example demonstrates a web query that uses the POST method with dynamic parameters:

Hands-On 27-8: Using the POST Method for Sending Dynamic Parameters

1. In the Visual Basic Editor window, insert a new module into VBAProject (MyWebQueries.xlsm).
2. In the Code window, enter the the Currency_Exchange_POST procedure as shown below:

```
Sub Currency_Exchange_POST()
    Dim sht As Worksheet

   ' insert a new worksheet in the current workbook
   Set sht = ThisWorkbook.Worksheets.Add
  With ActiveSheet.QueryTables.Add(Connection:= _
       "URL; http://www.xe.NET/cgi-bin/ucc/convert", _
        Destination:=Range("B1"))
    .PostText = "From=[""Enter the currency symbol from which " & _
      "you want to convert""]&Amount=[""Enter amount you wish " & _
      "to convert""]&To=[""Enter the currency symbol you want " & _
      "to obtain""]"
    .BackgroundQuery = True
    .WebSelectionType = xlSpecifiedTables
    .WebTables = "11"

    .WebFormatting = xlWebFormattingAll
    .RefreshStyle = xlOverwriteCells
    .AdjustColumnWidth = True
    .Refresh BackgroundQuery:=False
    .SaveData = True
  End With
End Sub
```

The Currency_Exchange_POST procedure uses the PostText property of the QueryTable object for sending dynamic parameters to the web server. A web query can use a combination of static and dynamic parameters, as shown in the following code fragment:

```
"From=[""Enter the currency symbol from which " & _
"you want to convert ""]&Amount="1"& To=[""Enter the currency " & _
"symbol you want to obtain""]"
```

Because Amount is a static parameter, the user will only be prompted for the From and To currency symbols.

3. Switch to the Microsoft Excel application window and choose **Developer | Macros.**
4. In the Macro dialog box, highlight the **Currency_Exchange_POST** procedure and click **Run**. Enter **USD** when prompted for the currency symbol to convert from. Enter **100** when prompted for the amount to convert, and enter **PLN** when prompted for the currency to convert to.

   The data retrieved from the specified web page is shown in Figure 27-19.

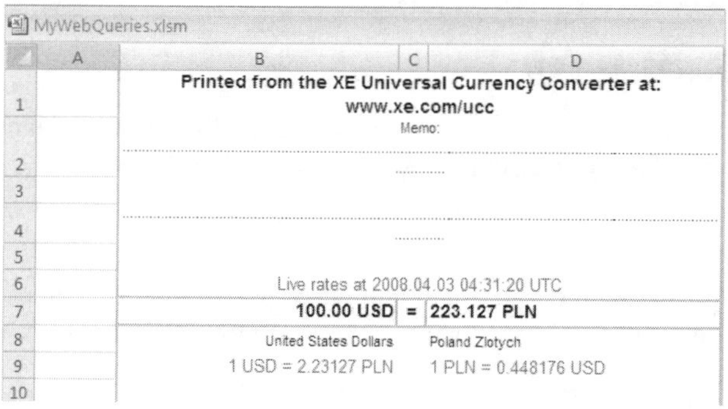

Figure 27-19: This worksheet's data has been generated by the Currency_Exchange_POST procedure.

Refreshing Data

You can refresh data retrieved from a web page by using the Refresh option on the shortcut menu. To access this menu, right-click any cell in the range where the data is located. Try this out using the data placed in a worksheet by the Currency_Exchange_POST procedure in the previous section of this chapter. When the dialog box appears, prompting you for currency symbols and amount, specify USD as the From currency and CAD as the To currency. Enter any amount you want to convert.

The Refresh option is also available from the Ribbon's Data tab. Data can be refreshed in the background while performing other tasks in the worksheet, when the file is being opened, or at specified time intervals. You can specify when the data should be refreshed in the External Data Range Properties dialog box; right-click anywhere in the data range and choose Data Range Properties from the shortcut menu.

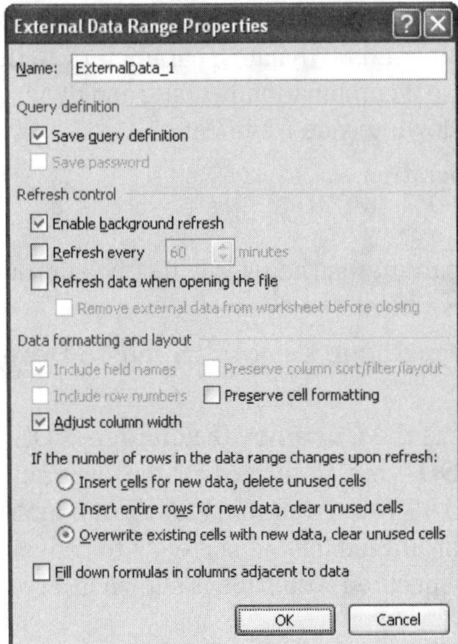

Figure 27-20: After retrieving data from a particular web page using the web query, you can use the External Data Range Properties dialog box to control when data is refreshed and how it is formatted.

Chapter Summary

In this chapter, you were introduced to using Excel with the Internet. Let's quickly summarize the information we've covered here:

- Hyperlinks allow you to activate a specified web page from a worksheet cell.
- HTML files can be created and published from Excel by selecting the Web Page (*.htm; *.html) format type in the Save As dialog box or via VBA procedures.
- Web queries allow you to retrieve "live" data from a web page into a worksheet. These queries can be created using built-in Ribbon commands or programmatically with VBA. Web queries let you retrieve an entire web page or specific tables that a particular web page contains. The retrieved data can be refreshed as often as required. There are two types of web queries: static and dynamic.

The next chapter demonstrates how you can retrieve or send information to Excel via Active Server Pages.

Chapter 28

Excel and Active Server Pages

You already learned various methods of retrieving data from a Microsoft Access database and placing this data in an Excel worksheet. This chapter explores another technology, known as Active Server Pages (ASP), that you can use for accessing and displaying data stored in databases.

Active Server Pages (ASP) — also referred to as "classic" ASP (this version of ASP preceded a newer technology known as ASP.NET) — is a web development technology developed by Microsoft that enables you to combine HTML, scripts, and reusable ActiveX server components to create dynamic web applications.

ASP is platform independent. This means that you can view ASP pages in any browser (Internet Explorer, Netscape Navigator, Firefox, Safari, Opera, and others). The current ASP version is 3.0, and it is available with Internet Information Services (IIS) 5.0 or higher. While HTML (Hypertext Markup Language), which is used for creating web pages, contains text and formatting tags, ASP pages are a collection of HTML standard formatting elements, text, and embedded scripting statements. You can easily recognize an ASP page in a browser by its .asp extension in the URL address:

http://www.asptutorial.info/learn/Forms.asp

Simply put, ASP pages are text files with the .asp extension. ASP code is processed entirely by the web server and sent to the user browser as pure HTML code. Users cannot view the script commands that created the page they are viewing. All they can see is the HTML source code for the page. However, if you have access to the original ASP file, and open this file in any text editor, you will be able to view the ASP code. Because the default scripting language for ASP is VBScript, a subset of Visual Basic for Applications, you should find it easy to create ASP pages that address your specific needs.

Note: ASP.NET (pronounced ASP dot net) is a newer, more advanced, and feature-rich web development technology from Microsoft that requires the Microsoft .NET Framework installed on users' computers. Unlike classic Active Server Pages (ASP), which is limited to scripting languages, .NET technology provides cross-language support (you can write and share code in many different .NET languages such as Visual Basic .NET, C#, Managed C++, JScript.NET, and J#). ASP files prepared in .NET end in .aspx, .ascx, or .asmx. ASP.NET is not an upgrade to the classic ASP; it is an entirely new infrastructure for web development that requires learning new concepts behind building web applications and "unlearning" the concepts learned and utilized in programming classic ASP applications. Because programming in .NET languages is quite different from writing programs in Visual Basic for Applications, it is not covered here. Instead, this chapter concentrates on ASP classic programming, which is more related to Visual Basic for Applications via its subset, VBScript.

The ASP Object Model

ASP has its own object model consisting of the objects shown in Table 28-1 that provide functionality to the web pages.

Table 28-1: The ASP object model

ASP Object Name	Object Description
Request	Obtains information from a user
Response	Sends the information to the client browser
Application	Shares information for all the users of an application
Server	Creates server components and server settings
Session	Stores information pertaining to a particular visitor

The ASP objects have methods, properties, and events that can be called to manipulate various features. For example, the Response object's Write method allows you to send the output to the client browser. The Create-Object method of the Server object is used to create a link between a web page and other applications such as Microsoft Excel or Access. You will become familiar with some of the above ASP objects and their properties and methods as you create the example ASP pages in this chapter.

Note: Complete coverage of the ASP object model is beyond the scope of this book. This chapter's objective is to demonstrate how your VBA skills can be used with other Internet technologies (HTML, VBScript, and ASP) to programmatically access spreadsheet data in the Internet browser or place web data in Excel.

HTML and VBScript

Hypertext Markup Language (HTML) is a simple, text-based language that uses special commands known as *tags* to create a document that can be viewed in a browser. HTML tags begin with a less-than sign (<) and end with a greater-than sign (>). For example, to indicate that the text should be displayed in bold letters, you simply type your text between the begin bold and end bold tags (<b> and </b>) like this:

```
<b>This text will appear in bold letters</b>
```

Using plain HTML, you can produce static web pages with text, images, and hyperlinks to other web pages. A good place to start learning HTML is the Internet. For easy, step-by-step tutorials and lessons, check out the following web site addresses:

http://www.htmlgoodies.com
http://www.htmltutorials.ca/

Microsoft Visual Basic Scripting Edition (VBScript) is a scripting language based on Microsoft Visual Basic for Applications (VBA). Because this is just a subset of VBA, some of the VBA features have been removed. For example,

VBScript does not support data types — every variable is a Variant. Like VBA, VBScript is an event-driven language; that is, the VBScript code is executed in response to an event caused by a user action or the web browser itself. VBScript is the default language for classic ASP pages. Another built-in scripting language that can be used in ASP pages is JScript, which is Microsoft's proprietary implementation of JavaScript.

To create an ASP file, you need a simple text editor such as Notepad. However, if you are planning to create professional Internet applications using classic ASP, it's worthwhile to purchase Microsoft Visual InterDev 6.0, which offers many tools for creating and debugging ASP scripts and viewing HTML.

Before creating your first ASP page, let's go over the script delimiters and HTML tags listed in Table 28-2.

Table 28-2: Script delimiters and HTML tags used in the first example procedure

Delimiters/tags	Description
<% and %>	Beginning and end of the ASP script fragment. The script code between the <% and %> delimiters will be executed on the server before the page is delivered to the user browser.
<html> and </html>	You should place the <html> tag at the beginning of each web page. To indicate the end of a web page, use the closing tag: </html>.
<body> and </body>	The text you want to display on the web page should be placed between these tags.
<table> and </table>	Indicate the beginning and end of a table.
<table border = "1">	The border parameter specifies the width of the table border.
<th> and </th>	Place table headings between these tags.
<tr> and </tr>	The <tr> tag begins a new row in a table. Each table row ends with the </tr> tag.
<td> and </td>	Table data starts with the <td> tag and ends with the </td> tag.

Creating an ASP Page

In this section you will create your first ASP page using HTML and Microsoft Visual Basic Scripting Edition (VBScript). Suppose that you want to retrieve some data from a Microsoft Access database and make it available to users as an Excel worksheet. The following procedure creates an ASP page that retrieves data from the Shippers table.

Hands-On 28-1: Creating an ASP Page that Retrieves Data from a Database Table into an Excel Worksheet

1. Open Notepad and enter the following ASP script:

```
<% @Language = VBScript %>
<%
```

```
' Send the output to Excel

Response.ContentType = "Application/vnd.ms-excel"
Response.AddHeader "Content-Disposition", _
     "attachment;filename = Shippers.xls"

' declare variables
Dim accessDB
Dim conn
Dim rst
Dim sql

' name of the database
accessDB = "Northwind 2007.accdb"


' prepare connection string
conn = "Provider = Microsoft.ACE.OLEDB.12.0;" & _
    "Data Source = " & Server.MapPath(accessDB) & _
    "; Persist Security Info = False;"


' Create a Recordset
Set rst = Server.CreateObject("ADODB.Recordset")

' select records from Shippers table
sql = "SELECT ID, Company, Address, City FROM Shippers"

' Open Recordset (and execute SQL statement above)
' using the open connection

rst.Open sql, conn

%>
<html>
<body>
<Table Border = "1">

    <%
    For Each fld in rst.Fields
    %>
        <th>
            <% Response.Write fld.Name %>
        </th>
            <%
            Next
            rst.MoveFirst
            Do While Not rst.EOF
            %>
        <tr>
            <%
            For Each fld in rst.Fields
            %>
                <td>
                    <% Response.Write fld.Value %>
                </td>
                <% Next %>
```

```
        </tr>
        <% rst.MoveNext
        Loop
        %>
</table>
</body>
</html>
<%

' close the Recordset
rst.Close
Set rst = Nothing
%>
```

2. Save the file as **C:\Ex07_ByExample\AccessTbl.asp**.
3. Close Notepad.

The AccessTbl.asp file shown above begins by specifying a scripting language for the page with the Active Server Page directive <% @Language = VBScript %>. The script contained between the <% and %> delimiters is Visual Basic script code that is executed on the web server. Similar to VBA procedures, the first step in scripting is the declaration of variables. Because in VBScript all variables are of the Variant type, you don't need to use the As keyword to specify the type of variable. To declare a variable, simply precede its name with the Dim keyword:

```
Dim accessDB
Dim conn
Dim rst
Dim sql
```

Similar to VBA, you can declare all your variables on one line, like this:

```
Dim accessDB, conn, rst, sql
```

To tell the browser that the code that follows should be formatted for display in Excel, we need to use the following directive:

```
Response.ContentType = "Application/vnd.ms-excel"
```

The ContentType property of the ASP Response object specifies which format should be used for displaying data obtained from a web server. If you don't set this property, the data will be presented in the browser in text/HTML format.

To ensure that the workbook file is created with the specific filename, use the following directive:

```
Response.AddHeader "Content-Disposition","attachment;filename = Shippers.xls"
```

Note: In the above directive, notice the use of the old Excel file extension (.xls). If you use the new file extension (.xlsx), Excel 2007 will generate the following error message when you attempt to open the file: *Excel cannot open the file "Shippers.xlsx" because the file format or extension is not valid. Verify that the file has not been corrupted and that the file extension matches the format of the file.* This is a known problem with Excel 2007. Excel no longer recognizes the HTML format the way previous versions of the product did. By saving the file as .xls, you will be able to view the file in Excel 2007. (For additional information, please refer to "Suppressing Error Messages when Opening XLS Files in Office 2007" later in this chapter.)

To connect with the Access database, we specify a connection string like this:

```
conn = "Provider = Microsoft.ACE.OLEDB.12.0;" & _
  "Data Source = " & Server.MapPath(accessDB) & _
  "; Persist Security Info = False;"
```

The exact path will be supplied by the MapPath method of the Server object:

```
Server.MapPath(accessDB)
```

You can also connect to your Access database by using the OLE DB data provider as follows:

```
conn = "DRIVER = {Microsoft Access Driver (*.mdb, *.accdb)};"
conn = conn & "DBQ = " & Server.MapPath(accessDB)
```

The DRIVER parameter specifies the name of the driver that you are planning to use for this connection (Microsoft Access Driver (*.mdb, *.accdb)). The DBQ parameter indicates the database path. Similar to the previous example, the exact path will be supplied by the MapPath method of the Server object.

To connect to an SQL Server database, use the following format:

```
Set conn = Server.CreateObject("OLEDB.Connection")
conn.Open "Provider = "SQLOLEDB;" & _
"Data Source = YourServerName;" & _
"Initial Catalog = accessDB;" & _
"UID = yourId; Password = yourPassword;"
```

To gain access to database records, we create the Recordset object using the CreateObject method of the Server object:

```
Set rst = Server.CreateObject("ADODB.Recordset")
```

After creating the recordset, we open it using the Open method, like this:

```
rst.Open sql, conn
```

The above statement opens a set of records. The sql variable is set to select four columns from the Shippers table. The conn variable indicates how you will connect with the database.

The next part of the ASP page contains HTML formatting tags that prepare a table. These tags are summarized in Table 28-2 earlier in this chapter. The table headings are read from the Fields collection of the Recordset object using the For Each...Next loop. Notice that all instructions that need to be executed on the server are enclosed by the <% and %> delimiters. To enter the data returned by the server in the appropriate worksheet cells, use the Write method of the ASP Response object:

```
Response.Write fld.Name
```

The above statement will return the name of a table field. Because this instruction appears between the <th> and </th> HTML formatting tags, the names of the table fields will be written in the first worksheet row in table heading type.

After reading the headings, the next loop reads the values of the fields in each record:

```
Response.Write fld.Value
```

Because the above statement is located between the <td> and </td> formatting tags, the values retrieved from each field in a particular record will be written to table cells.

The script ends by closing the recordset and releasing the memory used by it:

```
rst.Close
Set rst = Nothing
```

Because the web server reads and processes the instructions in the ASP page every time your browser requests the page, the information you receive is highly dynamic. ASP allows the page to be built or customized on the fly before the page is returned to the browser.

We are not ready yet to view the data. Before you can run this script, you must perform the following tasks:

1. Install Microsoft Internet Information Services (IIS) 5.0 or a newer version. The installation instructions are presented in the next section.
2. Create a virtual folder (see the section following the IIS installation instructions).

Installing Internet Information Services (IIS)

To perform all of the examples in this chapter, let's proceed to set up Internet Information Services on your computer if you are using Windows 2000 or Windows XP. If you are running Windows Vista, please see the link on the website www.wordware.com/files/Excel2007 for the Vista instructions for this Hands-On.

Hands-On 28-2: Installing Internet Information Services (Windows XP/2000)

1. Insert the Windows 2000 or XP Professional CD-ROM into a drive.
2. Click **Start** and select **Control Panel**.
3. Double-click **Add or Remove Programs**.

4. Click the **Add/Remove Windows Components** button in the left-hand panel.
5. Click the box beside **Internet Information Services (IIS)**.
6. Click **Next** to start the installation.
7. When the installation is complete, click **Finish** to close the wizard.

After successful installation of the IIS, there should be an Inetpub folder on your computer (see Figure 28-1).

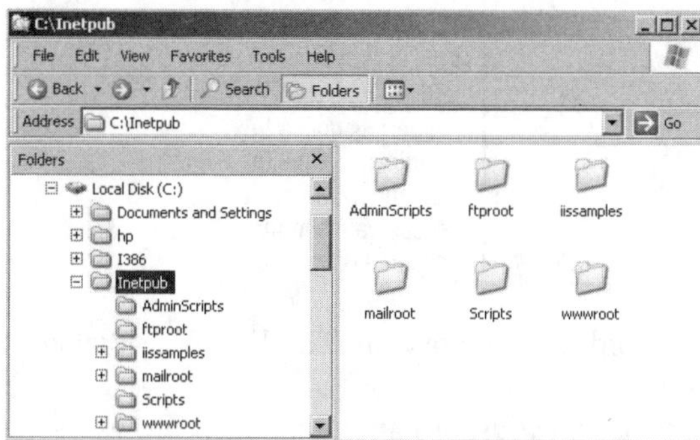

Figure 28-1: Once you have installed Internet Information Services, you should see the Inetpub folder on your computer.

Creating a Virtual Directory

The default home directory for the World Wide Web (WWW) service is \Inetpub\wwwroot. Files located in the home directory and its subdirectories are automatically available to visitors to your site. If you have web pages in other folders on your computer and you'd like to make them available for viewing by your web site visitors, you can create virtual directories. A virtual directory appears to client browsers as if it were physically contained in the home directory.

For the purposes of this chapter, you will create a directory called ASPClassicWithExcel on your computer and designate it as a virtual directory.

Hands-On 28-3: Creating a Virtual Directory

1. Create a new folder named **ASPClassicWithExcel** for this chapter's example files.
2. Right-click the **ASPClassicWithExcel** folder and choose **Properties** from the shortcut menu.
3. In the ASPClassicWithExcel Properties dialog box, click the **Web Sharing** tab (Figure 28-2). The dialog box may look slightly different if you are using Windows 2000. Note that the Web Sharing tab only appears if Internet Information Services (IIS) has been installed.

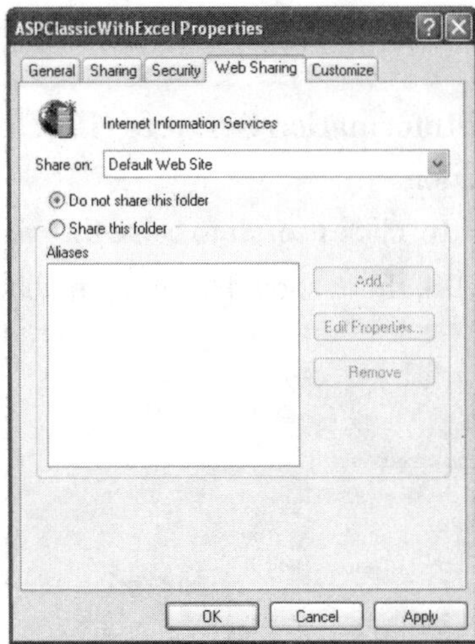

Figure 28-2: You can use the Properties dialog box to quickly set up an alias users will use to access pages in the specified directory.

4. Click the **Share this folder** option button. The Edit Alias dialog box will appear, as shown in Figure 28-3.

   A virtual directory has an *alias*, or name that client browsers use to access that directory. An alias is often used to shorten a long directory name. In addition, an alias provides increased security. Because users do not know where your files are physically located on the server, they cannot modify them.

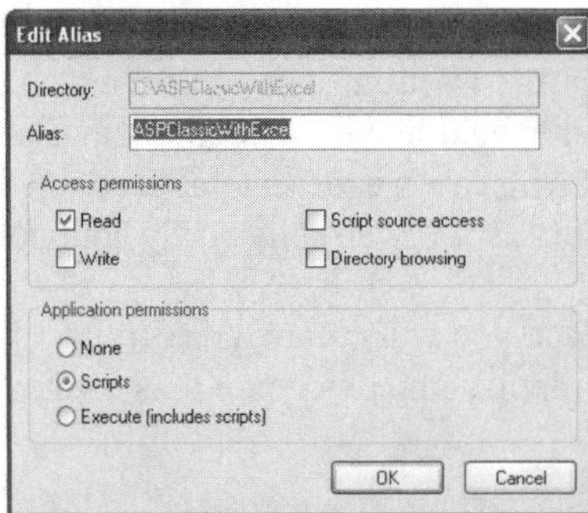

Figure 28-3: The Edit Alias dialog box can be accessed from the Properties dialog box by choosing the Share this folder option button (see Figure 28-2). The directory name is automatically entered as the suggested name for the virtual directory alias.

5. Enter **TASP** in the Alias box, as shown in Figure 28-4. In the Access permissions area, make sure that the **Read** and **Write** permissions are selected. When you select the Write permission, Excel displays a Web Warning dialog box. Click **Yes** to this message. In the Application permissions area, ensure that the **Scripts** option button is selected.

   When you set up a virtual directory, it is important to specify the access permissions for that directory. The Read permission allows users to access web pages. It is turned on by default. In addition, the Scripts permission should be turned on in the Application permissions area for all virtual directories that will contain ASP files.

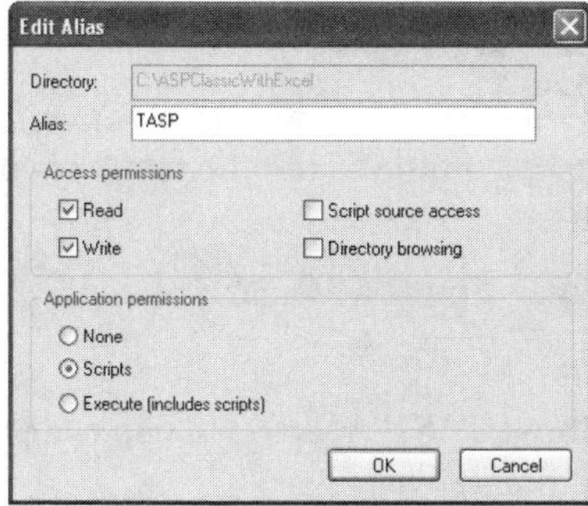

Figure 28-4: You can change the suggested name of the virtual directory by typing your own entry in the Alias box.

6. Click **OK** to close the Edit Alias dialog box.

   When you click OK, you will see the alias TASP listed in the Aliases box in the Properties dialog box for ASPClassicWithExcel (Figure 28-5).

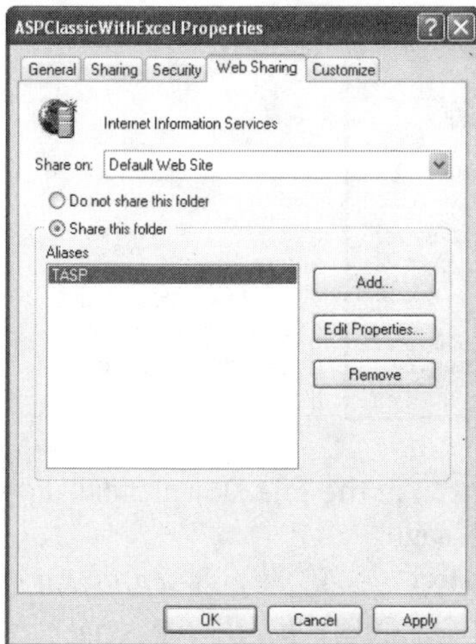

Figure 28-5: The physical folder named ASPClassicWithExcel will be shared over the web as TASP.

7. Click **OK** to close the Properties dialog box.
8. To ensure that all of the components you need for this chapter's examples can be quickly accessed, copy the sample **Northwind 2007.accdb** database file from the C:\Ex07_HandsOn folder to your **ASPClassicWithExcel** folder.
9. Copy the **AccessTbl.asp** file that you created earlier in this chapter (see HandsOn 28-1) to the **C:\ASPClassicWithExcel** folder.

Running Your First ASP Script

Now that you've prepared the ASP file and set up the virtual directory, including the necessary permissions, it's time to see the result of your efforts.

Hands-On 28-4: Running Your First ASP Script

1. Open your Internet browser.
2. Type the address **http://localhost/TASP/AccessTbl.asp** and press **Enter** to execute the script in the .asp file.

   Localhost is the name of the web server installed on your computer, and TASP is the name of the virtual folder where the ASP script file named AccessTbl.asp is stored.
3. When the File Download dialog box appears, click the **Open** button.

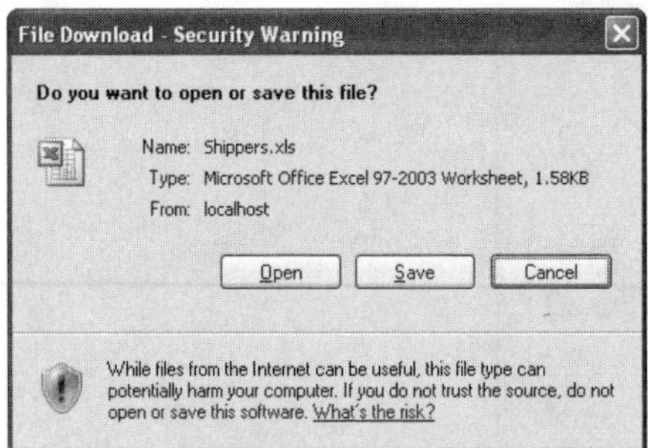

Figure 28-6: The File Download dialog box appears when you request an ASP page in the browser.

   When you click the Open button in the File Download dialog box, you may see the following error message:

   The file you are trying to open, 'Shippers.xls', is in a different format than specified by the file extension. Verify that the file is not corrupted and is from a trusted source before opening the file. Do you want to open the file now?

   Note: This error occurs because you are trying to open an Excel workbook in the old XLS file format with Excel 2007. You can suppress this message by inserting a key in the Registry Editor (see the sidebar at the end of this Hands-On exercise).

   Clicking the Save button in the File Download dialog box will allow you to download the file to your computer or network drive so that you can work with it later.
4. Click **Yes** in the message box to open the XLS file.

   The data from the Microsoft Access Northwind 2007 database's Shippers table appears in a Microsoft Excel workbook opened in a new Excel application window.

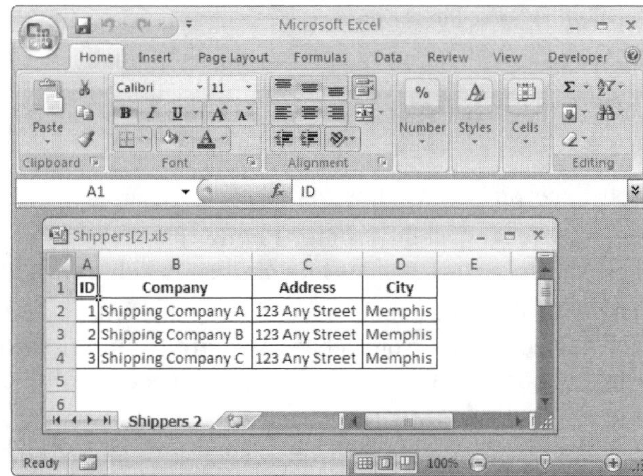

Figure 28-7: The Excel application window opened by the ASP script displays a table of data retrieved from an Access database.

Note: In previous versions of Microsoft Office, Excel opened in the Internet browser window, with its menu bar merged with your browser's menu. The default behavior in Office 2007 is for documents to open in their own application windows.

5. Save the workbook file in the XLSX format by clicking the **Microsoft Office** button and selecting **Save As | Excel Workbook**.

Suppressing Error Messages when Opening XLS Files in Office 2007

To disable the message that appears when you click the Open button in the File Download dialog box, you will need to insert a new key in the Registry Editor. Editing the registry is a serious matter, so make sure you know what you are doing before performing the following steps:

1. Choose **Start | Run**, then type **regedit**, and click **OK**.
2. When the Registry Editor opens, navigate to HKEY_CURRENT USER\Software\Microsoft\Office\12.0\Excel\Security.
3. Choose **Edit | New** and select **DWORD Value**.
4. Type **ExtensionHardening** to specify the key name.
5. Choose **File | Exit** to exit the Registry Editor.

Sending Data from an HTML Form to an Excel Workbook

An ASP script can contain a form that is used for collecting data. Assume that you need to gather information about patients visiting an urgent care center in your town. It's been requested that your data entry/display screen have a web interface. Normally, when you collect data on a web page, the information is saved into some sort of a database, like SQL Server or Microsoft Access. However, your client particularly requested that the data from your web form's input fields be saved directly to an existing Excel workbook file. To meet this requirement, we will take the following steps:

- Create an Excel workbook file for data collection purposes.
- Create an ASP page for collecting and processing user input.

Hands-On 28-5: Sending Data from an HTML Form to an Excel Workbook

1. Start Microsoft Excel and open a new workbook.
2. In cell A1, enter **Patient**. In cell B1, enter **Phone**.

   These labels will serve as headings for your two-field Excel database.
3. Select columns **A:B**. With the columns A and B highlighted, choose **Formulas**. In the Defined Names group, choose **Create from Selection**. When the Create Names from Selection dialog box appears with the Top row check box selected, click **OK**.

   These tasks result in creating two named ranges in your workbook: Patient and Phone.
4. Choose **Formulas | Name Manager** to open the Name Manager dialog box.

   You should see that the Patient range refers to cells =Sheet1!$A$2:$A$1048576, and the Phone range references cells =Sheet1!$B$2:$B$1048576.

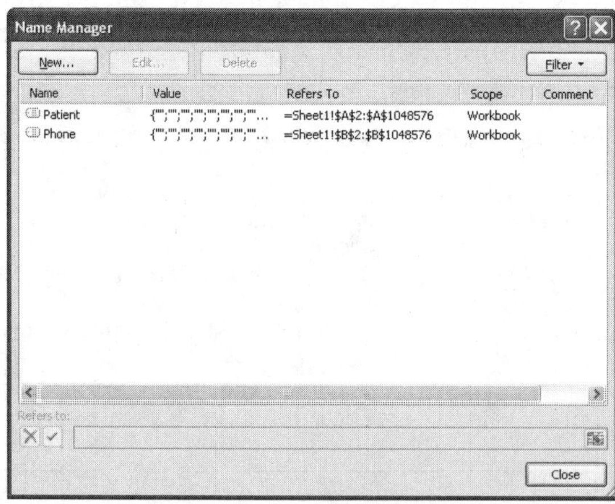

Figure 28-8: Viewing named ranges in an Excel workbook.

5. Close the Name Manager dialog box.
6. Save this workbook file as **C:\ASPClassicWithExcel\ExcelDb.xlsx**.
7. Close the file and exit Microsoft Excel.

Now that we have a workbook file for data collection purposes, let's proceed to create a web user interface for data input and processing.

Hands-On 28-6: Creating a Web User Interface for Data Input and Processing

1. Open Notepad and enter the ASP script code as shown below:

```
<% @Language = VBScript %>
<%
' Variable Declarations
Dim con         ' The ADODB connection object
Dim rst         ' The ADODB recordset object
Dim strCon      ' Variable to hold connection string to Excel database
Dim strSQL      ' Variable to hold SQL query string to perform the insert
Dim name        ' Variable to hold patient's name
Dim phone       ' Variable to hold patient's phone number
Dim key         ' Iterator (dummy variable) in the For Each loop
Dim goAhead     ' The flag to indicate whether we can proceed
Dim myStr       ' Variable to hold the message to display in
                ' the right-hand side table


' ADODB Constants
' ---- CursorTypeEnum Value ----
Const adOpenKeyset = 1

' ---- LockTypeEnum Value ----
Const adLockPessimistic = 2

On Error Resume Next
name = Request("txtPatientName")
phone = Request("txtPhone")

  For Each key In Request.Form
   If Request.Form(key) = "" Then
     If key = "txtPatientName" Then
       Response.Write "<font color = 'blue'>"
       Response.Write "Please enter the Patient name.</font>"
     Else
       Response.Write "<font color = 'red'>"
       Response.Write "Please enter the Phone number.</font>"
     End If
     goAhead = False
     Exit For
   End If
  GoAhead = True
 Next


If goAhead = True Then
name = Replace(Request("txtPatientName"),"'","''")
  If Len(name) <> 0 Or _
    Len(phone) <> 0 Then
      Set con = Server.CreateObject("ADODB.Connection")
      strCon = "Provider = Microsoft.ACE.OLEDB.12.0;Data Source = "
      strCon = strCon & server.MapPath("ExcelDb.xlsx") & ";"
      strCon = strCon & "Extended Properties = Excel 12.0"
      If Request("cmdSubmit") = "Enter Data in Excel" Then
        strSQL = "INSERT INTO [Sheet1$] (Patient, Phone)"
```

```
          strSQL = strSQL & " VALUES ('" & name & "'"
          strSQL = strSQL & ",'" & Phone & "')"
        End If
        With con
           .Open strCon
           If Request("cmdDelete") <> "Delete Data" Then
              .Execute(strSQL)
           Else
              set rst = Server.CreateObject("ADODB.Recordset")
              rst.Open "Select * from [Sheet1$] Where Patient = '" & _
                 name & "'" & _
                 " AND phone = '" & phone & "'", _
                 con, adOpenKeyset, adLockPessimistic
              rst.fields(0).value = ""
              rst.fields(1).value = ""
              rst.Update
              rst.Close
            End If
         End With
         If err.Number = 3021 Then
            Response.Write "The information you entered "
            Response.Write "cannot be deleted." & "<BR>"
            Response.Write "Either name or phone number "
            Response.Write "is incorrect. " & "<p>"
         Else
            name = ""
            phone = ""
            set rst = Server.CreateObject("ADODB.Recordset")
            rst.Open "Select * from [Sheet1$]", con
            Response.Write "<table border = ""1"">"
            For Each fld in rst.Fields
              Response.Write "<th>" & fld.Name & "</th>"
            Next
            rst.MoveFirst
            Do While Not rst.EOF
              Response.Write "<tr>"
            For Each fld in rst.Fields
              Response.Write "<td>" & fld.Value & "</td>"
              Next
              Response.Write "</tr>"
              rst.MoveNext
            Loop
            Response.Write "</table>"
            rst.Close
            Set rst = Nothing
            con.Close
            Set con = Nothing
         End If
      End If
    End If
%>

</hr>
<html>
<head>
   <title>Patient Data Entry Screen</title>
</head>
```

```
<body>
  <form action = "ExcelEntry.asp" method = "POST" Name = "form1">
  <P>
  <table border = "1" cellpadding = "2" cellspacing == "4">
    <tr>
      <td>
        <table border = "1" cellpadding = "2" cellspacing == "3">
        <tr>
          <td>Patient Name: </td>
          <td>
             <input type = "text1" name = "txtPatientName"
             value = "<% = name%>" size = "30">
          </td>
        </tr>
        <tr>
          <td>Phone: </td>
          <td>
           <input type = "text2" name = "txtPhone" value = "<% = phone%>">
          </td>
        </tr>
          <input type = "Submit" name = "cmdSubmit" value = "Enter Data in
                      Excel">
          <input type = "Submit" name = "cmdDelete" value = "Delete Data">
      </table>
      </td>
  <td>
  <%
    If err.number = 0 Then
     If (Request("cmdSubmit") = "Enter Data in Excel" or _
        Request("cmdDelete") = "Delete Data") and _
        Request.Form(key) <> "" Then
          myStr = "The following data has been successfully "
        If Request("cmdSubmit") = "Enter Data in Excel" Then
          Response.Write "<i><font color = 'green'>" & _
          myStr & "added: </i></font><hr>"
        ElseIf Request("cmdDelete") = "Delete Data" Then
          Response.Write "<i><font color = 'green'>" & _
          myStr & "deleted:</i></font></hr>"
        End If
     End If
     If Request("txtPatientName") <>"" or _
           Request("txtPhone") <>"" Then
      Response.Write "Patient Name: <b>" & _
          Request("txtPatientName") & "</b></p>"

      Response.Write "Phone Number: <b>" & _
          Request("txtPhone") & "</b>"
     End If
    End If
  %>
  </td>
 </tr>
</table>
</form>
</body>
</html>
```

2. Save the above ASP script code in the C:\ASPClassicWithExcel folder as **ExcelEntry.asp.**

   Because forms are used to gather information from users, you will often want to place the information from the form's fields into variables. Instead of constantly calling Request.Form (variablename) to get the content of each variable, you can use an iterator (dummy variable) in a For Each loop. The ExcelEntry.asp script shown above uses the following code to display a message when a form's input field has been left empty:

```
For Each key In Request.Form
   If Request.Form(key) = "" Then
     If key = "txtPatientName" Then
       Response.Write "<font color = 'blue'>"
       Response.Write "Please enter the Patient name.</font>"
     Else
       Response.Write "<font color = 'red'>"
       Response.Write "Please enter the Phone number.</font>"
     End If
     goAhead = False
     Exit For
   End If
  GoAhead = True
 Next
```

   The above code fragment checks for any blanks in the form. Next, if the user has filled in the two text boxes, the code uses the Microsoft Jet database engine to access data in other database file formats, such as Excel workbooks. Notice that to connect to a Microsoft Excel file (ExcelDb.xlsx) that serves as our database, you need to specify the database type in the extended properties for the connection. You should use the Excel 12.0 source database type for Microsoft Excel 2007. Therefore, the connection string looks like this:

```
strCon = "Provider = Microsoft.ACE.OLEDB.12.0;Data Source = "
strCon = strCon & server.MapPath("ExcelDb.xlsx") & ";"
strCon = strCon & "Extended Properties = Excel 12.0"
```

Note: When you use Excel as a database, the first row is considered the header unless you specify HDR=No in the extended properties in your connection string.

   Depending on which button the user has clicked, either an SQL INSERT INTO statement or the Recordset's Update method is executed. When inserting data into an Excel spreadsheet, we use the sheet name followed by a dollar sign (Sheet1$):

```
If Request("cmdSubmit") = "Enter Data in Excel" Then
        strSQL = "INSERT INTO [Sheet1$] (Patient, Phone)"
        strSQL = strSQL & " VALUES ('" & name & "'"
        strSQL = strSQL & ",'" & Phone & "')"
      End If
```

It is also possible to reference data in a range with a defined name or a specific address. For example, if your spreadsheet contains the Patient list in cells A1:B15, you can use the following statement to select data based on what the user has entered in the web form's text boxes:

```
rst.Open "Select * from [Sheet1$A1:B15] Where Patient = '" & name & "'" _
   & " AND phone = '" & phone & "'", con, adOpenKeyset, adLockPessimistic
```

Or, if you assign the name PatientList to cells A1:B15, you can refer to the named range as follows:

```
rst.Open "Select * from PatientList Where Patient = '" & name & "'" & _
    " AND phone = '" & phone & "'", con, adOpenKeyset, adLockPessimistic
```

To remove data from the Excel spreadsheet, the example code uses the Execute method of the ADO connection:

```
If Request("cmdDelete") <> "Delete Data" Then
   .Execute(strSQL)
Else
   set rst = Server.CreateObject("ADODB.Recordset")
   rst.Open "Select * from [Sheet1$] Where Patient = '" & name & "'" & _
      " AND phone = '" & phone & "'", con, adOpenKeyset, adLockPessimistic
   rst.fields(0).value = ""
   rst.fields(1).value = ""
   rst.Update
   rst.Close
End If
```

The Else clause in the code fragment above locates the data in an Excel workbook file based on the user's input. Once found, the data is cleared from the spreadsheet cells using the Recordset's Value method, and the change is saved with the Recordset's Update method. When using ADO from ASP, you are not allowed to delete entire rows in a spreadsheet. The SQL statement DELETE FROM will not work. To get rid of the existing data in a spreadsheet, you can only blank it out. This, of course, will cause empty lines within your data range. To delete these empty lines, you can write some code in the Open event for the workbook.

If the data the user wants to remove from the Excel file cannot be located, error 3021 will occur, and we display the user-friendly message:

```
Response.Write "The information you entered cannot be deleted." & "<br>"
Response.Write "Either name or phone number is incorrect. " & "<p>"
```

Every time the user clicks any of the provided buttons, we want to keep him posted about the data currently contained in the Excel database by building a table on the fly:

```
   set rst = Server.CreateObject("ADODB.Recordset")
   rst.Open "Select * from [Sheet1$]", con
   Response.Write "<table border = ""1"">"
   For Each fld in rst.Fields
     Response.Write "<th>" & fld.Name & "</th>"
   Next
```

```
rst.MoveFirst
Do While Not rst.EOF
  Response.Write "<tr>"
For Each fld in rst.Fields
  Response.Write "<td>" & fld.Value & "</td>"
  Next
  Response.Write "</tr>"
  rst.MoveNext
Loop
Response.Write "</table>"
rst.Close
Set rst = Nothing
con.Close
Set con = Nothing
```

The above code fragment writes the data contained in an Excel spreadsheet to an HTML table. Notice that the first For Each…Next loop iterates through the Recordset object's Fields collection to write out the names of column headings. The second For Each…Next loop places the actual data in table cells.

The remaining code of the ASP script creates an HTML table within another HTML table to provide a user interface. The table on the right-hand side will advise the user whether or not the requested operation (insert or delete) was successfully completed.

3. Close Notepad.
4. Open your Internet browser and enter the following address in the address bar: **http://localhost/tasp/ExcelEntry.asp**.

   When you press **Enter** or click the **Go** button, you should see the data entry form shown in Figure 28-9.
5. Enter some information in the provided text boxes and press the **Enter Data in Excel** button.

   Your screen should resemble Figure 28-10.

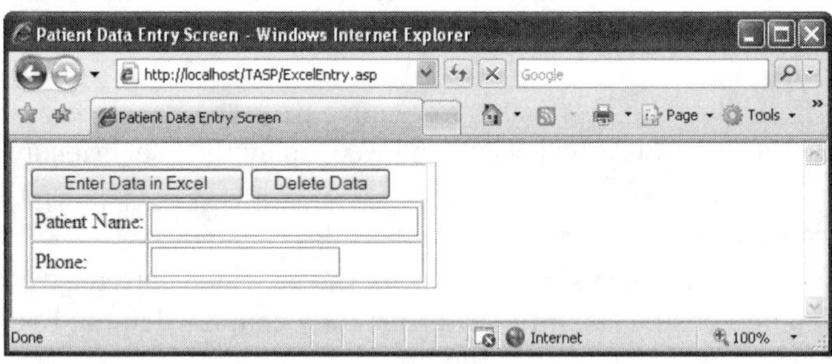

Figure 28-9: An HTML form can be used for collecting data from a user.

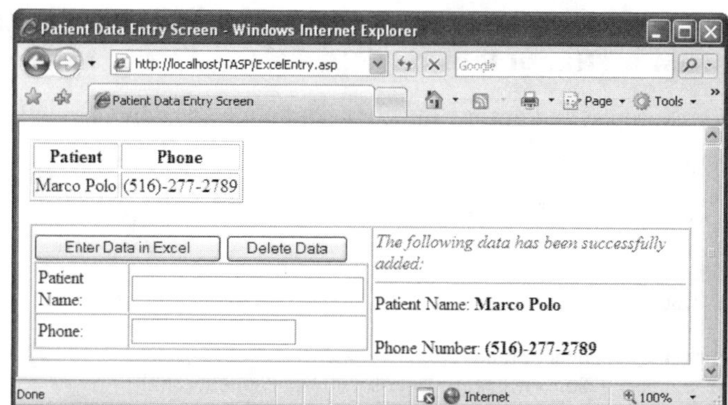

Figure 28-10: Entering data into Excel via an HTML form. The top table displays data that was retrieved from an Excel worksheet.

6. Add data for another patient.
7. Remove the data for the patient that you entered in step 5 by typing it in the text boxes and pressing the **Delete Data** button.
8. Try to delete the data entered in step 6 by supplying only the patient name. The screen should prompt you to enter the phone number.
9. Try to delete data that does not exist.
10. Close your Internet browser.

Sending Excel Data to the Internet Browser

Use the Recordset object's GetString method to display data contained in an Excel spreadsheet in the Internet browser. This method returns a set of records to a string and is faster than looping through the recordset. The GetString method has the following syntax:

```
variant = recordset.GetString(StringFormat, NumRows, _
    ColumnDelimiter, RowDelimiter, NullExpr)
```

- StringFormat determines the format for representing the recordset as a string.
- NumRows specifies the number of recordset rows to return. If blank, GetString will return all the rows.
- ColumnDelimiter specifies the delimiter for the columns within the row (the default is a tab character).
- RowDelimiter specifies a row delimiter (the default is a carriage return).
- NullExpr specifies an expression to represent NULL values (the default is an empty string).

The next example demonstrates using the GetString method to retrieve data from the ExcelDb.xlsx file created in an earlier example. You can also use a workbook file of your own, provided it contains data on the first sheet and the sheet name is Sheet1.

Hands-On 28-7: Using the GetString Method to Retrieve Data from an Excel File

1. Open Notepad and enter the ASP script code as shown below:

```
<% @Language = VBScript %>
<%
dim myConn
dim myExcel
dim strCon
dim mySQL

' Create the connection object
 set myConn = Server.CreateObject("ADODB.Connection")

' Specify the connection string
 strCon = "Provider = Microsoft.ACE.OLEDB.12.0;Data Source = "
      strCon = strCon & server.MapPath("ExcelDb.xlsx") & ";"
      strCon = strCon & "Extended Properties = Excel 12.0"

' Open the connection
 myConn.Open strCon

' Create the Recordset
 set myExcel = Server.CreateObject("ADODB.Recordset")
 mySQL = "Select * from [Sheet1$]"

' Open the Recordset
 myExcel.Open mySQL, myConn

' Show data in a table
 Response.Write "<table border = 1><tr><td>"

' Get the column names
  For Each fld in myExcel.Fields
   Response.Write fld.Name & "<td>"
  Next
 Response.Write "</tr><tr><td>"

' Get the actual data
 Response.Write myExcel.GetString(, -1, "</tr><td>", _
       "</td></tr><tr><td>", nbspace)

' Close the Recordset and release the object
  myExcel.Close
  set myExcel = Nothing

' Close the connection
  myConn.Close
  set myConn = Nothing
%>
</table>
```

2. Save the above ASP script code in the C:\ASPClassicWithExcel folder as **GetExcel.asp**.

   The above ASP script connects to the specified Excel workbook file and retrieves the data located in Sheet1. After reading the column names from the recordset's Fields collection, the code uses the GetString method to pull the data:

```
Response.Write myExcel.GetString(, -1, "</tr><td>", _
              "</td></tr><tr><td>", nbspace)
```

Notice that –1 indicates that all rows should be read, the </tr><td> tags are used for delimiting columns, and the </td></tr><tr><td> tags specify the row delimiter. If the cell does not contain any data, a non-breaking space will be entered (nbspace) so that there are no gaps in the table structure.

3. Close Notepad.
4. Open your Internet browser and enter the following address in the address bar: **http://localhost/tasp/GetExcel.asp**.

   When you press **Enter** or click the **Go** button, you should see the HTML table of data retrieved from Sheet1 of the specified workbook.
5. Close your Internet browser.

Creating Charts in ASP

When you present dynamic data in web pages, you can make the data easier for the user to comprehend by providing a nice chart. The example shown below demonstrates how to use an Active Server page to create a chart based on data pulled dynamically from the Microsoft Access sample Northwind.mdb database.

Hands-On 28-8: Creating and Displaying a Chart

1. Open Notepad and enter the ASP script as shown below:

```
<% @Language = VBScript %>
<%
' Constant declaration
 Const adOpenStatic = 3
 Const adLockReadOnly = 1
 Const xlColumnClustered = 51
 Const xlRows = 1
 Const xlLocationAsObject = 2
 Const xlCategory = 1
 Const xlPrimary = 1
 Const xlValue = 2
 Const xlHtml = 44

 ' Variable declaration
 Dim myExcel     ' Object variable representing Excel application.
 Dim fso         ' Object variable representing the FileSystemObject.
 Dim path        ' Folder location.
 Dim strFile     ' String variable to hold the name of the chart file.
 Dim filename    ' String variable to hold the full name of the chart
                 ' file.
 Dim conn        ' Object variable representing the Connection object.
 Dim rst         ' Object variable representing the Recordset object.
 Dim wkb         ' Object variable representing the Workbook object.
```

```
Dim rng        ' Object variable representing the Range object.
Dim fld        ' Dummy variable for enumerating fields.
Dim rowNum     ' Row counter.
Dim colNum     ' Column counter.
Dim varData    ' Variant to hold returned Recordset.

Set myExcel = Server.Createobject("Excel.Application")
Set fso = Server.Createobject("Scripting.FileSystemObject")

' If exists, delete the previously prepared chart
path = "c:\ASPClassicWithExcel\"
strFile = "xlsChart.htm"
filename = path & strFile

If fso.FileExists(filename) Then
    fso.DeleteFile filename, True
End If

' Release the FileSystemObject
Set fso = Nothing

' Create a new workbook
set wkb = myExcel.Workbooks.Add

' Get data to chart from Microsoft Access database
' Create and establish connection to the database
Set conn = Server.CreateObject("ADODB.Connection")

' Open the Northwind database
conn.Open "Driver = {Microsoft Access Driver (*.mdb)};" & _
          "DBQ = " & Server.MapPath("Northwind.mdb")

' Create recordset and retrieve values using the open connection
Set rst = Server.CreateObject("ADODB.Recordset")

' Open the Recordset with a static cursor (3) in read-only mode (1)
 rst.Open "SELECT CategoryName As [Product Category], " & _
        "SUM(Quantity) AS [Total Quantity Sold] " & _
        "FROM Categories " & _
        "INNER JOIN (Products INNER JOIN [Order Details] ON " & _
        "Products.ProductID = [Order Details].ProductID) ON " & _
        "Categories.CategoryID = Products.CategoryID " & _
        "GROUP BY Categories.CategoryName " & _
        "ORDER BY Categories.CategoryName", _
         conn, adOpenStatic, adLockReadOnly

' Add field names as column headers.
For fld = 0 to rst.Fields.Count - 1
  colNum = colNum + 1
  wkb.ActiveSheet.Cells(1, colNum).Value = _
     rst.Fields(fld).Name
Next

' Store the records in a variable
varData = rst.GetRows()

' Place data from the database in a worksheet.
```

```
  For rowNum = 1 To rst.RecordCount
   For colNum = 0 To UBound(varData)
    wkb.ActiveSheet.Cells(rowNum + 1, colNum + 1).Value = _
       varData(colNum, rowNum - 1)
   Next
  Next

 ' Close the Recordset and release the object
  rst.Close
  set rst = Nothing

 ' Close the Connection to the database
  conn.Close
  Set conn = Nothing

 ' Autofit the used range
  wkb.ActiveSheet.UsedRange.Columns.Autofit

 ' Set the range of the chart
  set rng = wkb.Sheets("Sheet1").Range("A1").CurrentRegion

 ' Create a chart based on pulled data
  wkb.Charts.Add

 ' Format the chart
  wkb.ActiveChart.ChartType = xlColumnClustered

 ' Specify the data source of the chart
  wkb.ActiveChart.SetSourceData rng, xlRows

 ' Place the chart on the second sheet
  wkb.ActiveChart.Location xlLocationAsObject, "Sheet2"

 ' Add chart and value axis titles
  With wkb.ActiveChart
   .HasTitle = True
   .ChartTitle.Characters.Text = "Quantity Sales by Category"
   .Axes(xlValue, xlPrimary).HasTitle = True
   .Axes(xlValue, xlPrimary).AxisTitle.Characters.Text = "Quantity"
  End With

 ' Save the workbook file as a web page (in HTML format)
  wkb.SaveAs filename, xlHtml

 ' Close the workbook
  myExcel.ActiveWorkbook.Close

 ' Shut down Excel application and release the object
  myExcel.Quit
  Set myExcel = Nothing

 ' Display the generated web page in the browser
Response.Redirect "http://localhost/TASP/" & strFile
%>
```

2. Save the above ASP script code in the C:\ASPClassicWithExcel folder as **MakeChart.asp**.

   The ASP script code shown above is well commented, so you should not have any trouble understanding the entire process. In short, we start by defining constants and variables. Constant declaration will allow you to use the intrinsic constants instead of their values and make the code easier to understand. Before creating a new workbook, the script uses the FileSystemObject to delete the previously prepared HTML file if it exists. The remaining part of the ASP script can be broken into the following main sections:

   - Creating a new workbook
   - Connecting to the Access database and obtaining the data
   - Writing out column headings and the data to a web page (notice how the GetRows method is used to store the data in a two-dimensional array)
   - Closing the recordset and connection to the Access database
   - Creating and formatting the chart. Some of the code for this section can be recorded using the macro recorder if you are not familiar with Chart objects, methods, and properties.
   - Saving the workbook as a web page. When you save a workbook file as a web page, the document is saved as an HTML file. In addition, a folder containing all the supporting files that are referenced by the HTML file is created on your hard drive. This folder is named name_files, where name is the document name. Therefore, when your ASP code saves the workbook in HTML format you should see on your computer a folder of supporting files named xlsChart_files.

     Note: If you'd rather keep the supporting files in the same folder as the HTML file, you can indicate your preference in the Excel Options dialog box. Open Excel and click the Microsoft Office button. Choose Excel Options | Advanced, and scroll down in the right pane to locate General options. Click the Web Options button. Next, click the Files tab, and clear the Organize supporting files in a folder check box. Click OK until you exit the dialog boxes.

   - Response.Redirect tells the browser to request a different page (in this case, the newly created xlsChart.htm file).

3. Close Notepad.

4. Open your Internet browser and enter the following address: **http://localhost/tasp/MakeChart.asp**.

   When you press **Enter** or click the **Go** button, you should see the xlsChart.htm file in the browser (see Figure 28-11) with Sheet1 displaying the data pulled from the Access database.

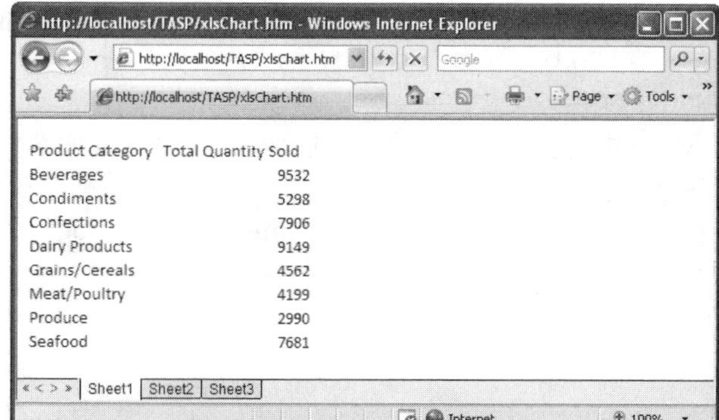

Figure 28-11: Data used for charting can be obtained dynamically from the Microsoft Access database.

5. Click the Sheet2 tab to view the chart.

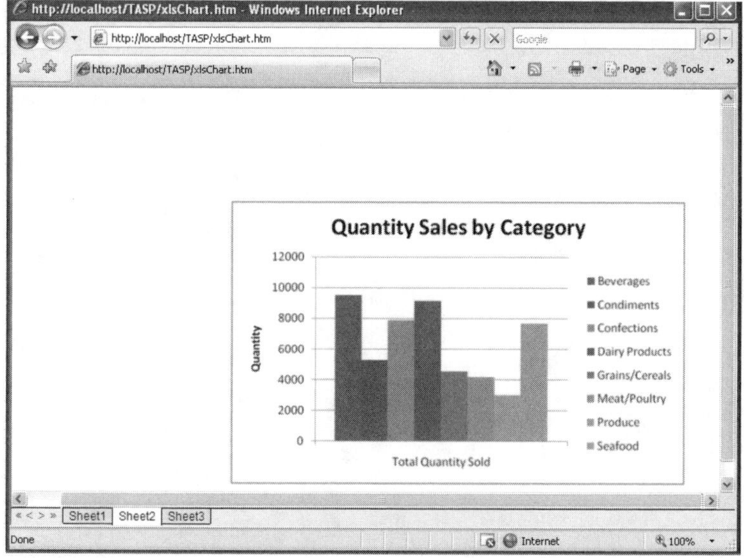

Figure 28-12: This chart has been created dynamically based on the data retrieved from the Access database (see Figure 28-11).

Chapter Summary

In this chapter, you were introduced to using Excel with Active Server Pages. Let's quickly summarize the information that we've covered here:

- Active Server Pages (ASP) is a technology from Microsoft enabled by the Internet Information Services (IIS) or Personal Web Server (on Windows 95/98/ or NT Workstation 4.0). ASP allows you to create dynamic web pages that are automatically updated when your data changes.

- You learned how to write ASP pages that open worksheets in the Microsoft Excel 2007 application, and how to get data entered in your browser into Excel.
- You also learned how to create charts dynamically based on data pulled from an Access database.

In the next chapter you will explore another Internet technology known as XML and find out how it is integrated with Microsoft Excel.

Chapter 29

Using XML in Excel 2007

What Is XML ■ Well-Formed XML Documents ■ Validating XML Documents ■ Editing and Viewing an XML Document ■ Opening an XML Document in Excel ■ Working with XML Maps ■ Working with XML Tables ■ Exporting an XML Table ■ XML Export Precautions ■ Validating XML Data ■ Programming XML Maps ■ Adding an XML Map to a Workbook ■ Deleting Existing XML Maps ■ Exporting and Importing Data via an XML Map ■ Binding an XML Map to an XML Data Source ■ Refreshing XML Tables from an XML Data Source ■ Viewing the XML Schema ■ **Creating XML Schema Files ■ Using XML Events ■ The XML Document Object Model ■ Working with XML Document Nodes ■ Retrieving Information from Element Nodes ■ XML via ADO ■** Saving an ADO Recordset to Disk as XML ■ Loading an ADO Recordset ■ Saving an ADO Recordset into the DOMDocument Object ■ **Understanding Namespaces ■ Understanding Open XML Files ■** Manipulating Open XML Files with VBA ■ **Chapter Summary**

In previous chapters you mastered several techniques of using Excel with the Internet. You've used HTML, ASP, and VBScript to put Excel worksheets on the web and retrieved data via web queries for further manipulation in Excel. This chapter expands your knowledge of Internet technologies by introducing you to XML (Extensible Markup Language). The XML functionality is not new; it was added to Excel in version 2000 and was much improved in versions 2002/2003 and 2007. Throughout the years Excel progressed from being able to read, write, and save XML data to finally obtaining a file structure based on XML rather than a binary file format. The new XML format supports all of the functionality of Excel 2007. We will look at this format in detail later on in this chapter after we've learned what XML is and how it is used in Excel.

What Is XML?

XML is a standard that provides a mechanism for designing your own custom markup language and using that language for describing the data in your own documents. Although XML was designed specifically for delivering information over the World Wide Web, it is being utilized in other areas, such as storing, sharing, and exchanging data. Like HTML, XML is a markup language; however, HTML and XML serve different functions. HTML describes web page layout by using a set of fixed non-customizable tags, while XML lets you describe data content using custom tags.

The main goal of XML is the separation of content from presentation. Because XML documents are text files, XML is independent of operating system platform, software vendor, and natural or programming language. XML makes it easy to describe any data structure (structured or unstructured) and send it anywhere across the web using common protocols, such as HTTP or FTP. As long as any two organizations can agree on the XML tag set to be used to represent the data being exchanged, it doesn't matter what back-end systems these organizations run or databases they use; the data can be interpreted and easily exchanged.

Although anyone can describe the data by creating a set of custom tags, the representatives of many industry groups have defined and published XML schemas that dictate how XML documents are formatted to represent data for their industry. XML schemas define the structure and data types that are allowed within an XML document and enforce that the document conforms to the rules.

Let's take a look at the following XML document (Courses1.xml) that was created and saved using Windows Notepad:

```
<?xml version = "1.0"?>
<Courses>
    <Course ID = "VBA1EX">
         <Title>Beginning VBA in Excel</Title>
         <Startdate>3/4/2008</Startdate>
         <Sessions>6</Sessions>
```

```
        </Course>
        <Course ID = "VBA2EX">
            <Title>Intermediate VBA in Excel</Title>
            <Startdate>4/13/2008</Startdate>
            <Sessions>8</Sessions>
        </Course>
        <Course ID = "VBA3EX">
            <Title>Advanced VBA in Excel</Title>
            <Startdate>9/7/2008</Startdate>
            <Sessions>12</Sessions>
        </Course>
    </Courses>
```

The first line of an XML document is called the XML declaration:

```
<?xml version = "1.0"?>
```

The above instruction identifies the file as an XML file. If you removed this instruction and attempted to open the XML file in Excel 2003, the file wouldn't be recognized as XML. Excel would open it as a text file. Excel 2007 is smarter; it knows how to open the structured data file even if you omit this instruction. The declaration line is also known as a processing instruction. This instruction begins and ends with a question mark (?) and contains the name of the application (in this example "xml") to which the instruction is directed, as well as additional information that needs to be passed to the XML processor such as the version number, and optionally encoding and standalone attributes:

```
<?xml version = "1.0" encoding = "UTF-8" standalone = "Yes"?>
```

The encoding attribute specifies the character style to be applied, and the standalone attribute when set to Yes tells the XML processor that the document does not reference an external file.

You can include other processing instructions in the XML file if you need the processing application to take a specific action. For example, you can specify that the file be opened by Excel by adding the following instruction to the above XML:

```
<?mso-application progid = "Excel.Sheet"?>
```

Notice the simple structure of XML. Similar to HTML, XML uses tags for data markup. However, unlike HTML, XML tags are not predefined. You can change the name of the tag to anything you want, for example, courses can become <Classes> and </Classes>. You can create custom tags that best describe data in your document. To do this right, you'll need to follow some simple XML rules so that your document is well-formed (see the next section).

An XML document contains one or more elements, data attributes, and text. The top element, in this example the element marked with the <Courses> tag, is called a root node. Every XML file must have a start root node and end root node. There can be only one root node in the file. The start tag is represented by left and right angle brackets (< >), and the end tag has a left angle bracket, forward slash, and a right angle bracket (< / >).

The names of the tags are case-sensitive. The name of the start tag and the name of the corresponding end tag must match exactly.

Elements may contain text and other elements. For example, the <Courses> element is defined to contain one or more <Course> elements. Notice that in the above example the data for the <Course> element is provided by the ID attribute:

```
<Course ID = "VBA1EX">
```

The values of attributes must be surrounded by double or single quotation marks.

Notice that the <Course> element has three other elements: <Title>, <Startdate>, and <Sessions>. The second and third <Course> elements have exactly the same structure. The structure of the XML document is very logical and easy to follow. You can quickly add more data to the file by following the same pattern.

Character Encodings in XML

When you type an XML document into Notepad and save it, you can choose from one of several supported character encodings, including ANSI, Unicode (UTF-16), Unicode (Big Endian), or UTF-8. The encoding declaration in the XML document identifies which encoding is used to represent the characters in the document. UTF-8 encoding allows the use of non-ASCII characters, regardless of the language of the user's operating system and browser or the language version of Office. When you use UTF-8 or UTF-16 character encoding, an encoding declaration is optional. XML parsers can determine automatically if a document uses UTF-8 or UTF-16 Unicode encoding.

Well-Formed XML Documents

When you create or modify an XML document, you must make sure that your XML file is well-formed. Here's what makes a document well-formed:

- An XML document must have one root element. In HTML the root element is always <HTML>, but in the XML document you can name your root element anything you want. Element names must begin with a letter or underscore character. The root element must enclose all other elements. Elements must be properly nested. The XML data must be hierarchical; the beginning and ending tags cannot overlap.

```
<Employee>
   <Employee ID>090909</Employee ID>
</Employee>
```

- All element tags must be closed. A begin tag must be followed by an end tag:

```
<Sessions>5</Sessions>
```

- You can use shortcuts, such as a single slash (/), to end the tag so you don't have to type the full tag name. For example, if the current Sessions element is empty (does not have a value), you could use the following tag:

```
<Sesssions />
```

- Tag names are case sensitive. The tags <Title> and </Title> aren't equivalent to <TITLE> and </TITLE>. For example, the following line:

```
<Title>Beginning VBA Programming</Title>
```

is not the same as:

```
<TITLE>Beginning VBA Programming</TITLE>
```

- All attributes must be in quotation marks:

```
<Course Id = "VBAEX1"/>
```

- You cannot have more than one attribute with the same name within the same element. If the <Course> element has two Id attributes, they must be written separately, as shown below:

```
<Course Id = "VBAEX1"/>
<Course Id = "VBAEX2"/>
```

The well-formedness of an XML document is similar to syntax checking in VBA. When you try to open an XML file in Excel that is not well-formed, you will receive an error message similar to the one in Figure 29-1. I forced this error by removing the ending "s" from the <Courses> in the Courses1.xml file while it was open in Notepad. Therefore, the beginning <Course> tag will not match the ending </Courses> tag. Notice that the error message specifies the type of error that was found and the name of the source file. To help you troubleshoot the error, the XML Import Error dialog box includes the Details button.

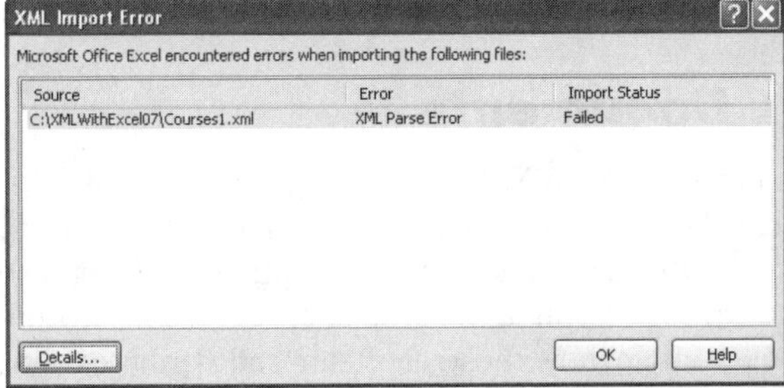

Figure 29-1: When the XML document is not well-formed, Excel displays an XML Import Error dialog box when you try to open the file.

Figure 29-2 displays the error details. You must fix all the errors before you can successfully open the file in Excel.

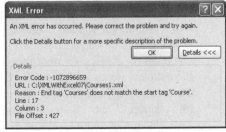

XML Error

An XML error has occurred. Please correct the problem and try again.

Click the Details button for a more specific description of the problem.

OK | Details <<<

Details

Error Code : -1072896659
URL : C:\XMLWithExcel07\Courses1.xml
Reason : End tag 'Courses' does not match the start tag 'Course'.
Line : 17
Column : 3
File Offset : 427

Figure 29-2: XML Error dialog box with error details.

You do not need to wait for Excel to discover errors in XML files. To verify that the document is well-formed, it's a good idea to open it in the browser before attempting this task with Excel. Double-click the XML filename, and it should open up in your default browser.

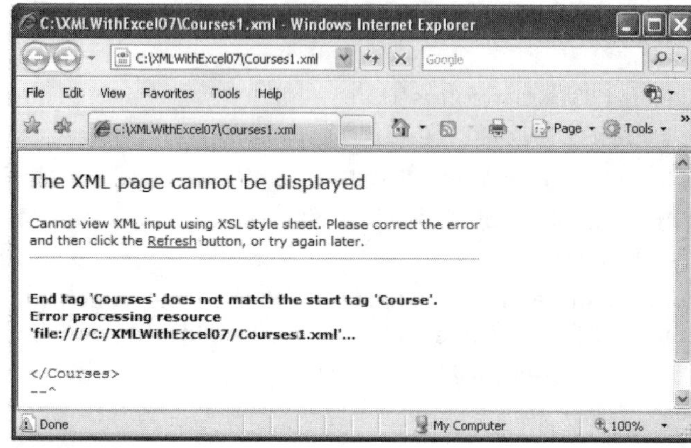

Figure 29-3: A quick way to check whether an XML document is well-formed is to open it in a browser, such as Internet Explorer.

What Is a Parser?

If you want to read, update, create, or manipulate any XML document, you will need an XML parser. A parser is a software engine, usually a dynamic link library (DLL), that can read and extract data from XML. Microsoft Internet Explorer 5 or higher has a built-in XML parser (MSXML.DLL, MSXML2.DLL, MSXML3.DLL, or MSXML4.DLL) that can read and detect all non-well-formed documents. MSXML has its own object model, known as DOM (Document Object Model), that you can use from VBA to quickly and easily extract information from an XML document (see "The XML Document Object Model" later in this chapter).

Validating XML Documents

There are two types of validation in XML. One is checking whether the document is well-formed (see the previous section). The other type of validation requires that you create a Document Type Definition (DTD) or a set of rules (known as schema) to determine the type of elements and attributes an XML document should contain, how these elements and attributes should be named, and how the element should be related.

Creating DTD or schema for an XML document is optional. Create either one only if you are planning to validate data. In XML, data validation is accomplished by comparing the document with the DTD or schema. When you open the XML document in a parser, the parser compares the DTD to the data and raises an error if the data is invalid. This book does not explore the creation and use of DTDs or schemas. These topics alone require a separate chapter. What you should remember from this section is that a valid XML document is not the same as a well-formed XML document. A valid

XML document conforms to a structure outlined in the Document Type Definition (DTD) or schema, while well-formed documents follow the basic formatting rules mentioned in the previous section, "Well-Formed XML Documents."

Editing and Viewing an XML Document

To make changes in an XML document you should open it in a text editor such as Notepad or an XML editor. There are many XML editors that you can purchase or download for free from the Internet. The advantage of using XML editors is that they come with special features that organize your XML data into an easy-to-read tree and allow you to create well-formed documents.

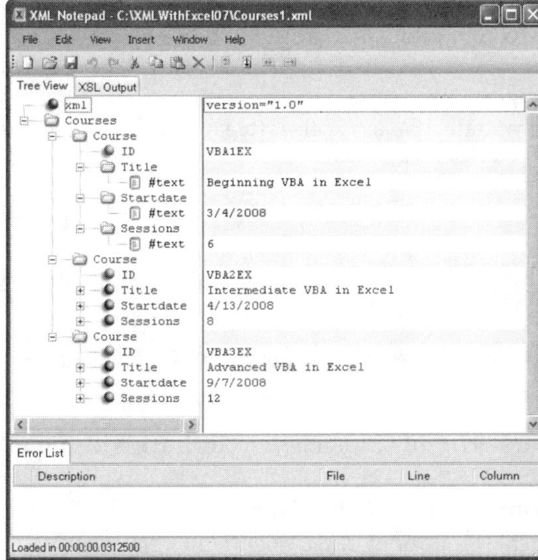

Figure 29-4: The example Courses1.xml file opened in the Microsoft XML Notepad.

You can make your XML documents legible and clear by using comments. The XML processor ignores all commented text. A comment begins with the <! -- characters and ends with the --> characters. Within your comment you can use any characters except for a double hyphen (--). A comment can be placed anywhere within an XML document provided that it's outside (not within) other markup tags. Let's add a comment to the Courses1.xml document that we discussed earlier.

Hands-On 29-1: Adding a Comment to an XML Document

1. In Windows Explorer, create a new folder named **XMLWithExcel07**.
2. Copy the **Courses1.xml** file from the **C:\Ex07_HandsOn** folder to your **XMLWithExcel07** folder.

3. Right-click the **Courses1.xml** file, choose **Open with** and then select **Notepad.** If Notepad is not listed, select **Choose Program** and then locate and select **Notepad** in the list.
4. Type the following comment between the <Courses> and <Course ID = "VBA1EX"> tags:

```
<!-- You can add more courses to this list -->
```

The beginning of the file should now look like this:

```
<Courses>
<!-- You can add more courses to this list -->
   <Course ID = "VBA1EX">
```

5. Save the changes to the **Courses1.xml** file and exit Notepad.

Comments can also be used to disable a particular processing instruction or an XML node. For example, you could prevent the display of the information about a specific course by commenting out the section of code like this:

```
<!--
     <Course ID = "VBA2EX">
          <Title>Intermediate VBA in Excel</Title>
          <Startdate>4/13/2008</Startdate>
          <Sessions>8</Sessions>
     </Course>
-->
```

Now that you've edited the file, let's open it in the browser to ensure that you have a well-formed XML document.

Hands-On 29-2: Viewing an XML Document in the Internet Browser

1. Double-click the **Courses1.xml** document in your **XMLWithExcel07** folder.

   The file opens up in your Internet browser (Figure 29-5). Here you can see the hierarchical layout of an XML document very clearly. Internet Explorer automatically places a plus sign (+) to the left of each element so you can expand the XML data layout. Once expanded, the plus changes to a minus (–) and you can click it to collapse the XML data layout.

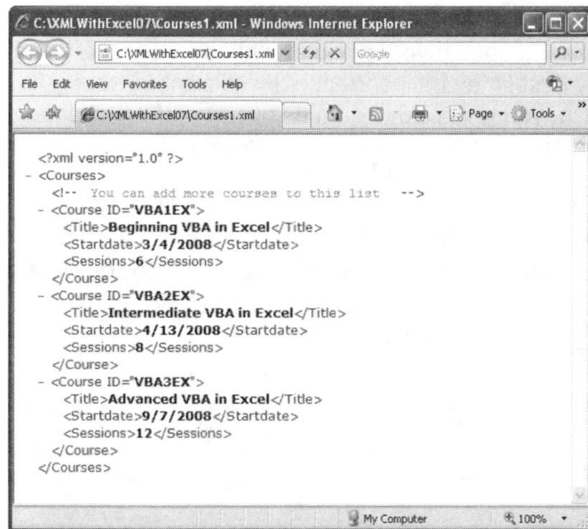

Figure 29-5: Unformatted XML data file opened in Internet Explorer.

2. Close the Internet browser.

Opening an XML Document in Excel

Once you've checked that you have a well-formed XML document by opening it with your browser, you can open it directly in Excel. Let's familiarize ourselves with this process in Hands-On 29-3.

Hands-On 29-3: Opening an XML Document in Excel

1. Start Excel and open the **C:\XMLWithExcel07\Courses1.xml** file.

   Excel displays the Open XML dialog box.

2. In the Open XML dialog box, select the **As an XML table** option button and click **OK**.

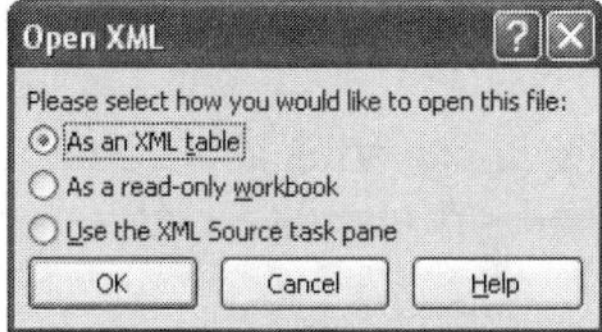

Figure 29-6: Excel displays the Open XML dialog box when you open an XML document that does not have a stylesheet associated with it.

   When you select the first option button, Excel tells you that it could not find the schema for the XML document. A schema will be automatically created for you when you click OK.

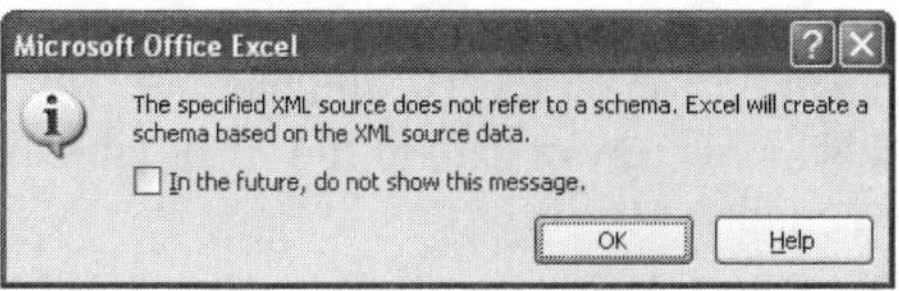

Figure 29-7: A schema file provides the rules for the XML document. If it is missing, Excel will infer the schema from the XML data file.

Note: If you are trying to open a very complex XML document, a schema file created by Excel may be incorrect or insufficient for your needs. If this is the case, you will need to create your own XML Schema Description file (XSD) or ask someone else to create it for you.

3. Click **OK** to have Excel create a schema and open the file.

   Excel imports the contents of the XML document into an XML table. The cells in the worksheets are mapped to the XML elements in the source file and can be refreshed at any time by clicking the Refresh button on the Design tab (Figure 29-8).

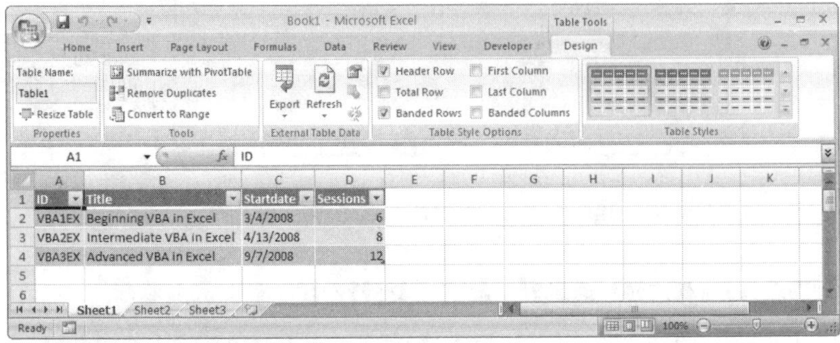

Figure 29-8: An XML document opened in Excel.

   When Excel creates a schema based on the contents of your XML document, your XML source file becomes read-only. This means that you cannot make changes to the file by editing the XML table in Excel. Excel refers to the schema files it creates as XML maps. Only by creating your own map can you write back to your XML document from Excel. The next section of this chapter demonstrates how to work with XML maps.

4. Leave Excel open with the data as shown in Figure 29-8, and open the **Courses1.xml** in **Notepad.**

5. Modify the file by adding the following information about another course to the end of the file just before the end </Courses> tag:

```
<Course ID = "VBA3Word">
    <Title>Advanced VBA in Word</Title>
    <Startdate>10/9/2008</Startdate>
    <Sessions>12</Sessions>
</Course>
```

6. Save the file and close Notepad.

7. In Excel, click the **Refresh** button on the Design tab.

   Notice that Excel adds a new row of data to the XML table listing the VBA3Word course you added in step 5.

8. Save the workbook as **C:\Ex07_ByExample\Practice_Excel29.xlsm,** and then close it.

XSL Stylesheets

Earlier in this chapter you saw how the XML data is displayed in a browser. While it was very easy to identify the XML elements, the data appeared in the raw format, quite unattractive to the end user. The XML formatting problem can be addressed via the Extensible Stylesheet Language (XSL). Using XSL you define a stylesheet that describes the way the XML data should be formatted and displayed. The XSL document is just another XML document that contains HTML instructions for formatting the elements in your XML document. This book does not cover XSL; however, if you'd like to see an example of an XSL document from the previous 2003 edition of this book, I have included it in the downloadable files. The file is called Courses.xsl. Copy this file to your C:\XMLWithExcel07 folder, and then open the Courses1.xml file in Notepad. Next, enter the following instruction below the XML declaration line:

```
<?xml-stylesheet type = "text/xsl" href
= "Courses.xsl"?>
```

The above line will tell the XML processor to format the data with the specified XSL stylesheet. Now when you double-click the Courses1.xml file, it should appear formatted as shown in Figure 29-9.

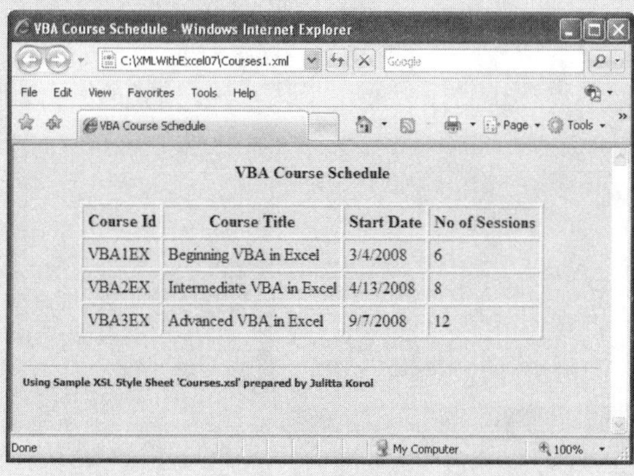

Figure 29-9: The XML document formatted with a stylesheet.

Working with XML Maps

XML schemas in Excel are called XML maps. You can associate one or more schemas with a workbook and then map all or some of the schema elements to various cells or ranges on a worksheet. Using XML mapping makes it relatively easy to import and export data into and out of Excel. In the following Hands-On exercise you will learn how to:

- Work with the XML Source task pane
- Add a schema to your workbook
- Map cells to elements in an XML map
- Populate the XML map with XML data

Hands-On 29-4: Mapping Schema Elements to Worksheet Cells

1. Copy the **Employees.xml** and **Employees.xsd** downloaded files from the **C:\Ex07_HandsOn** folder into your **ExcelWithXML** folder.
2. Open a new workbook in Microsoft Excel.
3. Click the **Source** button in the XML group on the Developer tab.

   Excel displays the XML Source task pane, as shown in Figure 29-10.

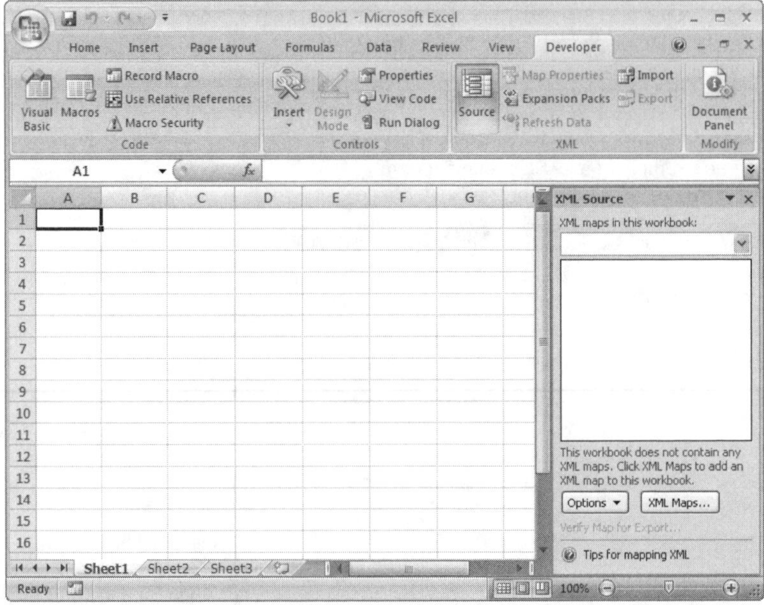

Figure 29-10: The XML Source task pane.

The XML Source task pane is used for displaying XML maps found in the XML data or schema documents and mapping XML elements to cells or ranges on a worksheet. If the current worksheet doesn't have any XML maps associated with it, the XML Source task pane is blank. The XML Source task pane includes two buttons (Options and XML Maps) and one hyperlink (Verify Map for Export).

4. In the XML Source task pane, click the **XML Maps** button.

   Excel displays the XML Maps dialog box.

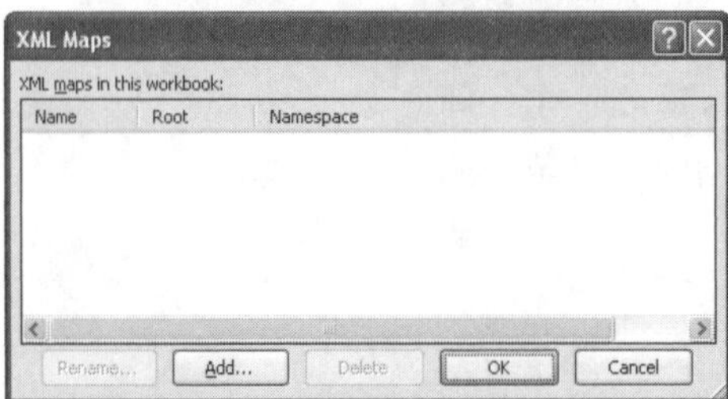

Figure 29-11: Use the XML Maps dialog box to add, delete, or rename an XML map associated with the workbook.

5. Click the **Add** button in the XML Maps dialog box.
6. In the Select XML Source dialog box, switch to the **ExcelWithXML** folder, select the **Employees.xsd** schema file, and click **Open.**

   Excel displays the Multiple Roots dialog box shown in Figure 29-12.

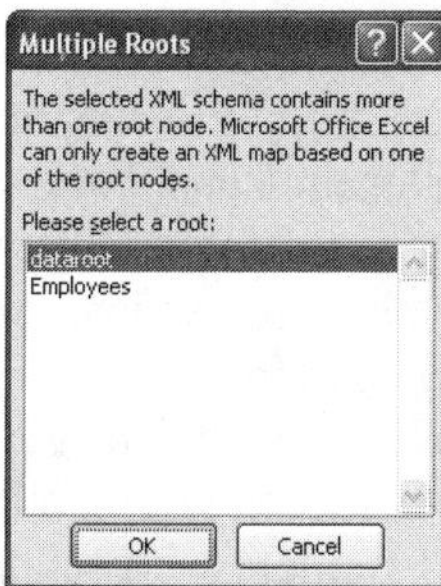

Figure 29-12: If the XML data or schema file contains more than one root node, you must indicate which root node should be used.

7. In the Multiple Roots dialog box, select **dataroot** and click **OK.**

   Excel displays the XML map name in the XML Maps dialog box (Figure 29-13). The name of the map consists of the schema's root element followed by an underscore and the word "Map." You can change the map name by clicking the Rename button.

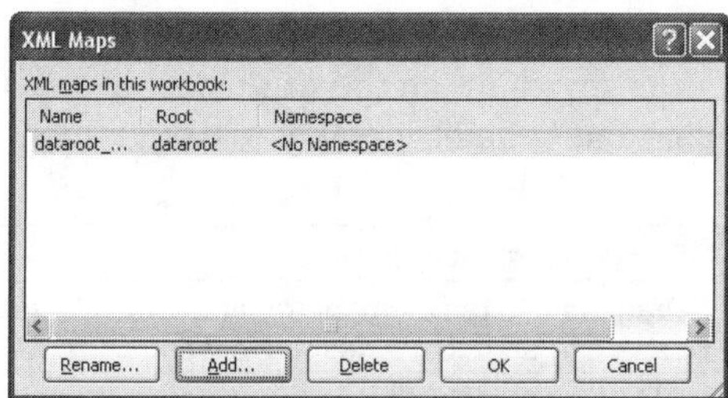

Figure 29-13: The XML Maps dialog box now displays the XML map (dataroot_Map) that was added to the workbook.

   You cannot update an existing XML map. Excel only allows you to create new maps or delete existing ones using the XML Maps dialog box. Because of this, you must recreate the XML table created from an XML map any time the source XML schema changes.

8. Click **OK** to close the XML Maps dialog box and return to Excel.

   The XML Source task pane now displays the structure of the XML map, as shown in Figure 29-14.

   Notice that the name of the XML map appears in the list box at the top of the XML Source task pane. If the workbook contains more than one XML map, you will use this list box

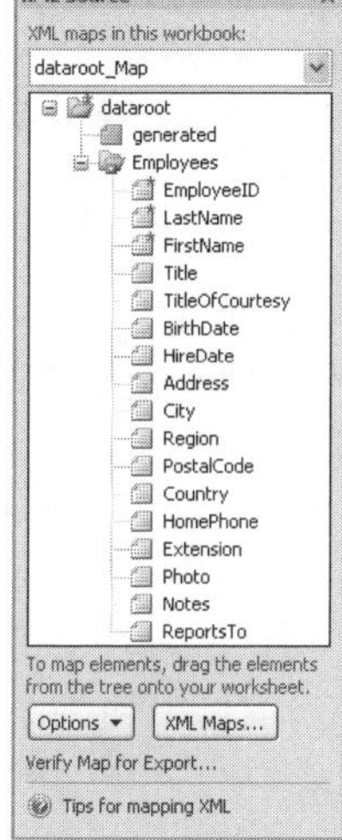

Figure 29-14: The XML Source task pane displays the XML map generated from the XML schema file (Employees.xsd).

to select the map you want to work with. Excel obtains the map information from the schema that the XML file references and, when the schema is not available, the map is generated based on the content of the XML data file as you have seen earlier in this chapter while opening the Courses1.xml document.

The XML map is displayed as a tree and can be expanded or collapsed by clicking the plus and minus buttons to the left of the element names. Elements in the tree are represented by different icons. For example, the folder icon with a red asterisk in front of the dataroot element (see Figure 29-14) represents a required parent element. An icon that looks like a piece of paper with a corner folded down in front of the element name indicates a child element. The child element labeled "generated" stores the date the schema was generated. The icon in front of Employees tells us that this is the repeating parent element with children. The elements below the Employees element are child and required child elements. Required elements have a red asterisk in the icon image. To get the list and images of all the icons that can appear in the XML map, click on "Tips for mapping XML" in the XML Source task pane.

Now that you've got the XML map, you can use it to map XML elements to your worksheet. Mapping is done by selecting the elements or entire nodes in the XML map and then dragging them onto a worksheet. You can drag mapped cells anywhere on the worksheet in any order you require. You can only map one schema element to one location in a workbook at a time.

XML Mapping	Follow This Procedure...
Single element	Drag the desired element from the XML Source task pane and drop it in a desired location on a worksheet.
Multiple elements	Select the first desired element in the XML Source task pane and hold down the Ctrl key while selecting other elements. Next, drag the selection to a desired location on a worksheet.
Entire node	Click on the parent node. All the child items will be highlighted. Drag the selection to a desired location on a worksheet.

9. In the XML Source task pane, select the **Employees** folder and drag it to cell **A1** on the worksheet.

   Excel maps XML elements to a range of cells (Figure 29-15).

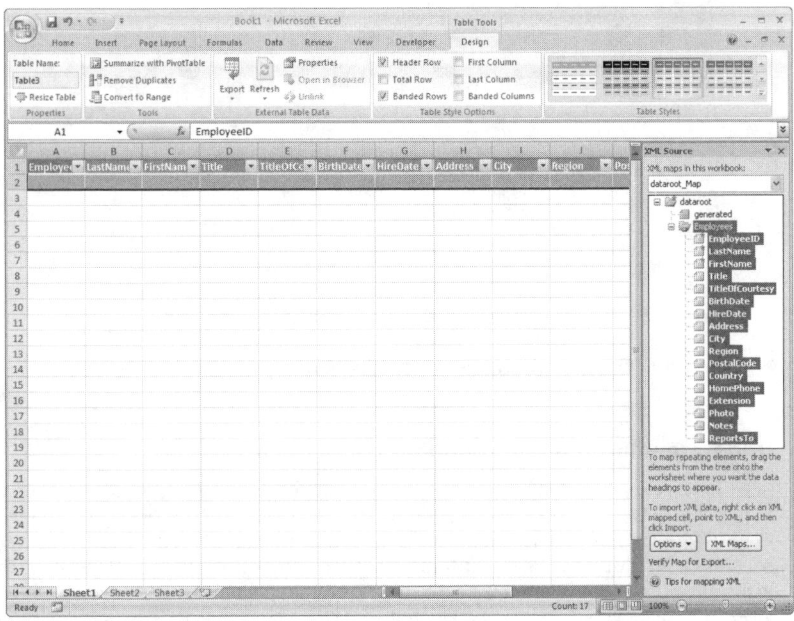

Figure 29-15: Mapping XML elements to cells in a worksheet.

Notice that the XML elements are laid out in the order they appear in the XML Source task pane. Excel generates a structure called an XML table when you drag the repeating elements from the XML Source task pane to a worksheet. At this point, the generated table contains a header row with the AutoFilter option enabled. You can adjust the size of the table by dragging the resize handle found at the bottom-right corner of the table border.

In this example we have placed all of the XML elements on the worksheet by dragging them from the XML Source task pane and dropping them at a specific cell. When you don't require all the elements, simply drag those you need and leave out those you do not need. Mapped elements appear in bold type in the XML Source task pane.

Note: Recall that you've already been introduced to the table feature in Chapter 24. XML tables are described in the next section.

10. To populate the table with data, right-click anywhere within the table and choose **XML | Import** (or click the Import button on the Developer tab).
11. In the Import XML dialog box, select **Employees.xml** and click **Import**.

    The table on the worksheet is now populated with the data from the selected XML document.

EmployeeID	LastName	FirstName	Title	TitleOfCourtesy	BirthDate	HireDate	Address	City	Region	PostalCode
1	Davolio	Nancy	Sales Representative	Ms.	12/8/1968 0:00	5/1/1992 0:00	507 - 20th Ave. E. Apt. 2A	Seattle	WA	98122
2	Fuller	Andrew	Vice President, Sales	Dr.	2/19/1952 0:00	8/14/1992 0:00	908 W. Capital Way	Tacoma	WA	98401
3	Leverling	Janet	Sales Representative	Ms.	8/30/1963 0:00	4/1/1992 0:00	722 Moss Bay Blvd.	Kirkland	WA	98033
4	Peacock	Margaret	Sales Representative	Mrs.	9/19/1958 0:00	5/3/1993 0:00	4110 Old Redmond Rd.	Redmond	WA	98052
5	Buchanan	Steven	Sales Manager	Mr.	3/4/1955 0:00	10/17/1993 0:00	14 Garrett Hill	London		SW1 8JR
6	Suyama	Michael	Sales Representative	Mr.	7/2/1963 0:00	10/17/1993 0:00	Coventry House Miner Rd.	London		EC2 7JR
7	King	Robert	Sales Representative	Mr.	5/29/1960 0:00	1/2/1994 0:00	Edgeham Hollow Winchester Way	London		RG1 9SP
8	Callahan	Laura	Inside Sales Coordinator	Ms.	1/9/1958 0:00	3/5/1994 0:00	4726 - 11th Ave. N.E.	Seattle	WA	98105
9	Dodsworth	Anne	Sales Representative	Ms.	7/2/1969 0:00	11/15/1994 0:00	7 Houndstooth Rd.	London		WG2 7LT

Sheet1 Sheet2 Sheet3

Figure 29-16: A table populated with the data from the XML document.

12. Save the workbook as **C:\ExcelWithXML\Employees.xlsm.**

Understanding the XML Schemas

Schema files describe XML data using the XML Schema Definition (XSD) language and allow the XML parser to validate the XML document. An XML document that conforms to the structure of the schema is said to be *valid*. The Employees.xsd schema file that we worked with in Hands-On 29-4 was generated in Microsoft Access 2007 using built-in menu options.

Here are some examples of types of information that can be found in an XML schema file:

- Elements that are allowed in a given XML document
- Data types of allowed elements
- Number of occurrences of a given element that are allowed
- Attributes that can be associated with a given element
- Default values for attributes
- Elements that are child elements of other elements
- Sequence and number of child elements

If you open the Employees.xsd file in Notepad, you will notice a number of declarations and commands that begin with the <xsd> tag followed by a colon and the name of the command. You will also notice the names of the elements and attributes that are allowed in the Employees.xml file as well as the data types for each element. The names of the data types are preceded with the "od" prefix followed by a colon. For example:

od:jetType = "text"	Defines the Jet data type for an element.
od:sqlSType = "nvarchar"	Defines the Microsoft SQL Server data type for an element.
od:autounique = "yes"	Defines a Boolean data type for an auto-incremented identity column.
od:nonNullable = "yes"	Indicates whether or not a column can contain a null value.

The schema file also specifies the number of times an element can be used in a document based on the schema. This is done via the minOccurs and maxOccurs attributes.

Working with XML Tables

An XML table is a table in Excel that has been mapped to one or more XML elements. In other words, each column in the XML table represents an element in your XML document. In this chapter you've already created two

XML tables based on the Courses1.xml and Employees.xml documents (see Hands-On 29-3 and 29-4).

After placing your XML data in an XML table in a workbook, you can work with this data just like any other Excel workbook file. This means you can add new columns and rows to your data, include formulas and functions, create charts, and perform various formatting tasks. You can even change the column headings that were automatically created from the XML element names. It is important to keep in mind that even when you change the column headings in the worksheet, the original XML element names will be used to export data from the mapped cells.

The changes you make to the data in the XML table will not affect the XML data that is stored in the original XML data file. Once you are done working with the XML table, you can save it as a standard Excel spreadsheet (.xlsx file) or in any other file format that is available in the Save As dialog box. You can also export the contents of mapped cells. The XML export feature is explained in the next section.

If the original XML data file has changed, you can easily update the data in your XML table by clicking the Refresh Data button on the Developer tab.

When you use the Refresh command, the data is read from the original XML document into the mapped locations on the worksheet. If you have another XML file that uses the same mapping, you can import the data from that file into your XML table by clicking the Import button on the Developer tab. Simply said, refreshing updates the XML table with the most current data from the original XML file, while importing gets the data from another XML file that follows the same schema.

When refreshing or importing data you can:

- Overwrite existing data with new data.
- Append new data to an existing XML table.

These options can be specified via the XML Map Properties dialog box.

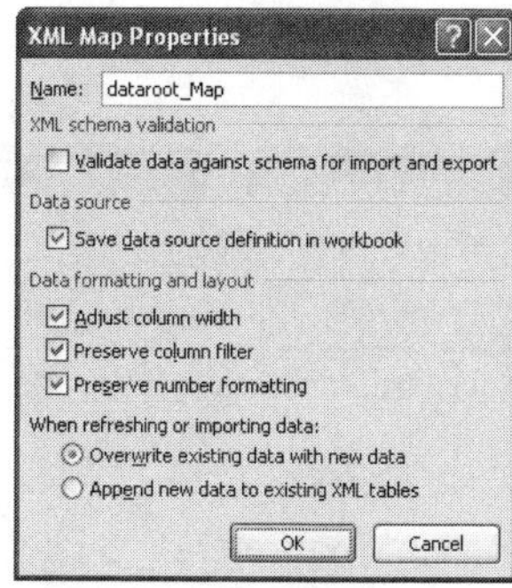

Figure 29-17: The XML Map Properties dialog box.

The XML Map Properties dialog box allows you to set certain properties that relate to working with XML maps. This dialog can be accessed using any of the techniques listed below:

- Click the Map Properties button on the Developer tab.

- Right-click anywhere in the XML table and choose XML | XML Map Properties.

Each XML table in a workbook can be independently manipulated via the XML Map Properties dialog. The following properties can be set:

XML Property	Description
Name	The name of the active XML map.
Validate data against schema for import and export	If selected, Excel will validate XML data against its schema while importing and exporting.
Save data source definition in workbook	Specifies whether your table is dynamic or static. If selected, the XML data is linked to the XML file and can be refreshed. If not selected, the data is static and cannot be refreshed.
Adjust column width	If selected, Excel will automatically adjust the width of table columns to fit the data.
Preserve column filter	If selected, Excel will preserve the selected column sorting, filtering, and layout.
Preserve number formatting	If selected, Excel will preserve the specified formatting of numbers in the table.
Overwrite existing data with new data	If selected, new data from the XML file will replace old data during a refresh or import.
Append new data to existing XML tables	If selected, new data from the XML file will be added at the bottom of the XML table during a refresh or import.

Exporting an XML Table

You can preserve the data in your XML table in two ways:

- Save your data to an XML data file.

  To do this, click the Microsoft Office button. Click the arrow next to Save As and select Other Formats. In the File name box, type a name for the XML data file. In the Save As type list, select XML Data (*.xml) and click OK. Before proceeding with the save operation, Excel will display the message shown in Figure 29-18:

  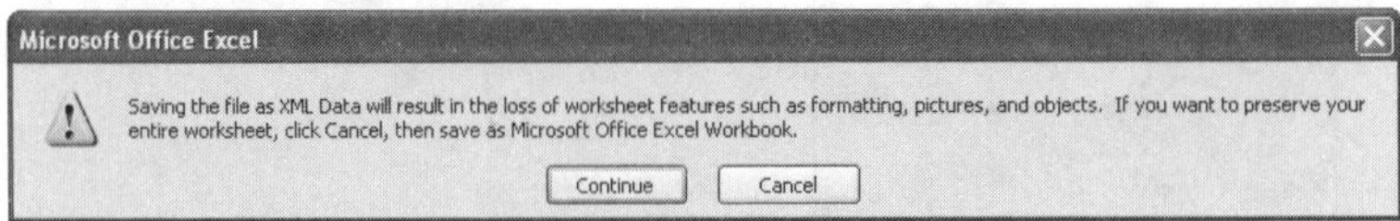

  Figure 29-18: Excel displays a message about the loss of certain worksheet features prior to saving data in an XML data file.

  To save the data as an XML document, click Continue. If you keep working with this file and make any data and formatting changes, only the data will be saved during subsequent save operations.

- Save your data by exporting it through the XML map.

We will see how this feature is used in the following hands-on exercise. You should be working with the XML table that was created in Figure 29-16 earlier in this chapter.

Hands-On 29-5: Exporting XML Data in Mapped Worksheet Cells

1. Make sure that the **Employees.xlsm** file you created in Hands-On 29-4 is currently open in the Microsoft Excel application window. The XML Source task pane should be visible on the right side of the worksheet. If it is missing, click the **Source** button on the Developer tab.
2. Click the **Verify Map for Export** hyperlink at the bottom of the XML Source task pane.

   If the map is valid for export, Excel displays the message that the map is exportable. If the map is invalid for export, a message is displayed with information about why the map isn't exportable. A map is invalid for export when:

   - It contains more than one level of data. Although Excel can import data using multilevel maps, when it comes to exporting, only single-level maps such as the dataroot_Map that we've worked with in prior sections (see Figure 29-14) can be exported.
   - It is *denormalized*. A map becomes denormalized when non-repeating items from an XML map are included in the XML table on the worksheet. Denormalized elements appear multiple times on the worksheet. If the user changes a non-repeating item in one row, that item will become inconsistent with other rows that should be showing the same data. Because Excel does not know how to reconcile the differences, the table can't be exported. To avoid denormalization of data, always create separate XML tables for non-repeating and repeating nodes.
3. Click **OK** when Excel displays the message that the dataroot_Map is exportable.
4. Click the **Export** button on the Developer tab.

   If the workbook contains more than one XML map, you will be prompted to choose the map to use. You can export data using only one XML map at a time. Excel proceeds to display the Export XML dialog box.
5. In the Export XML dialog box, specify the name for your XML file and the folder where it should be saved. Select your **ExcelWithXML07** folder and enter **Northwind_Employees.xml** in the File name box. Click the **Export** button to complete the export operation.
6. You can view the contents of the Northwind_Employees.xml document in Notepad. Simply double-click the filename in Windows Explorer to open it. The structure of this file is shown below.

```
<?xml version = "1.0" encoding = "UTF-8" standalone = "yes"?>
<dataroot>
    <Employees>
          <EmployeeID>1</EmployeeID>
          <LastName>Davolio</LastName>
          <FirstName>Nancy</FirstName>
          <Title>Sales Representative</Title>
          <TitleOfCourtesy>Ms.</TitleOfCourtesy>
          <BirthDate>1968-12-08T00:00:00.000</BirthDate>
          <HireDate>1992-05-01T00:00:00.000</HireDate>
          <Address>507 - 20th Ave. E. Apt. 2A</Address>
          <City>Seattle</City>
          <Region>WA</Region>
          <PostalCode>98122</PostalCode>
          <Country>USA</Country>
          <HomePhone>(206) 555-9857</HomePhone>
          <Extension>5467</Extension>
          <Photo>EmpID1.bmp</Photo>
            <Notes>Education includes a BA in psychology from Colorado
            State University. She also completed "The Art of the Cold
            Call." Nancy is a member of Toastmasters
            International.</Notes>
          <ReportsTo>2</ReportsTo>
    </Employees>
    <Employees>
          <EmployeeID>2</EmployeeID>
          <LastName>Fuller</LastName>
          <FirstName>Andrew</FirstName>
          <Title>Vice President, Sales</Title>
          <TitleOfCourtesy>Dr.</TitleOfCourtesy>
          <BirthDate>1952-02-19T00:00:00.000</BirthDate>
          <HireDate>1992-08-14T00:00:00.000</HireDate>
          <Address>908 W. Capital Way</Address>
          <City>Tacoma</City>
          <Region>WA</Region>
          <PostalCode>98401</PostalCode>
          <Country>USA</Country>
          <HomePhone>(206) 555-9482</HomePhone>
          <Extension>3457</Extension>
          <Photo>EmpID2.bmp</Photo>
            <Notes>Andrew received his BTS commercial and a Ph.D. in
            international marketing from the University of Dallas. He
            is fluent in French and Italian and reads German. He joined
            the company as a sales representative, was promoted to sales
            manager and was then named vice president of sales. Andrew
            is a member of the Sales Management Roundtable, the Seattle
            Chamber of Commerce, and the Pacific Rim Importers
            Association.</Notes>
    </Employees>
    <Employees>
    ...
    ...
    </Employees>
</dataroot>
```

7. Close Notepad.

Note: After exporting XML data in mapped cells to an XML data file, the name of your active workbook does not change. You can continue working with the data in this workbook. However, if you make changes to existing data or add new rows of data, you should re-export the data to the Northwind_Employees.xml file.

XML Export Precautions

When exporting data, be aware of the fact that only the data included in the XML table will be saved; XML elements that were not mapped will not be exported. If you don't want to lose any content during export, always place all the elements from the XML map on the worksheet.

If the XML table contains a formula, the result of the formula (and not the formula itself) will be exported with the other data in the XML table. Formulas that you place in an XML table column must reference XML data elements that contain either a number, time, or date value.

If you add a new column to your XML table and then export the data, the data from this new unmapped column will not be saved. The reason for this is that Excel exports a table as XML using the schema stored in the workbook. The generated XML file must match the XML source file from which the XML table was created. Because the added column is not in the XML source file, Excel cannot save it. Therefore, if you need to add data to the existing XML table, do the following:

- Open the appropriate schema file in Notepad and add a new element with the name for your new column.
- Save the modified schema file and close Notepad.
- Because the XML schema has changed, and Excel does not allow you to modify an existing XML map, you will need to create a new XML map and drag the required XML elements to your worksheet. You are already familiar with this process, as it was a part of the Hands-On exercise in the section titled "Working with XML Maps" earlier in this chapter. After mapping your XML elements to cells in a worksheet, simply refresh your XML table. There will be no data in the optional column that you've added to the schema file. You can now proceed to enter the data or formula you need in this empty column. Formulas can be copied as required. When you export your data to the XML file, the data in the new column will be exported together with the other data in your XML table.

Validating XML Data

To have Excel validate XML data upon import or export, you need to follow these steps:

1. Select any cell within your XML table on the worksheet and click the **Map Properties** button on the Developer tab.

Excel displays the XML Map Properties dialog box shown earlier in Figure 29-17.

2. Select **Validate data against schema for import and export.**
3. Click **OK** to close the dialog box.

If you enter an invalid value in any column of your XML table, Excel will not automatically validate your entry. However, all of the entries will be validated when you click the Export button on the Developer tab to export the data. If any data is found to be invalid, Excel displays an error message similar to the one shown in Figure 29-19.

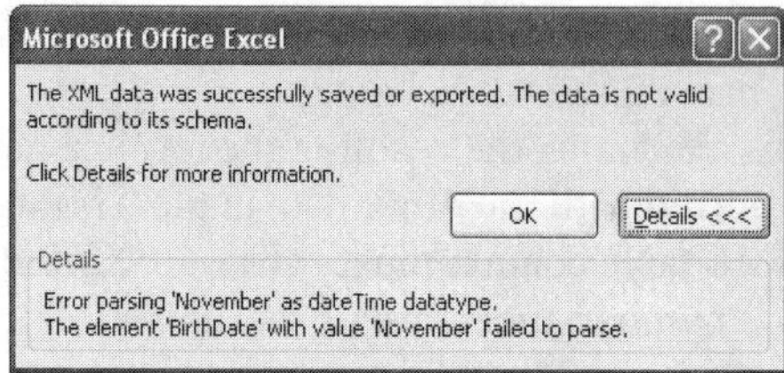

Figure 29-19: Excel displays a message when data is found to be invalid according to its schema during the export or refresh operation.

Notice that the error in validating the data does not prevent Excel from saving or exporting. The Details section in the error message dialog will give you a hint why data is invalid, so that you can correct the data and re-export it. You may want to define your own data validation rules that comply with the XML schema by using the Data Validation button on the Data tab. Then Excel will validate your data as you work in the worksheet. An example of such a validation technique is presented in Figure 29-20.

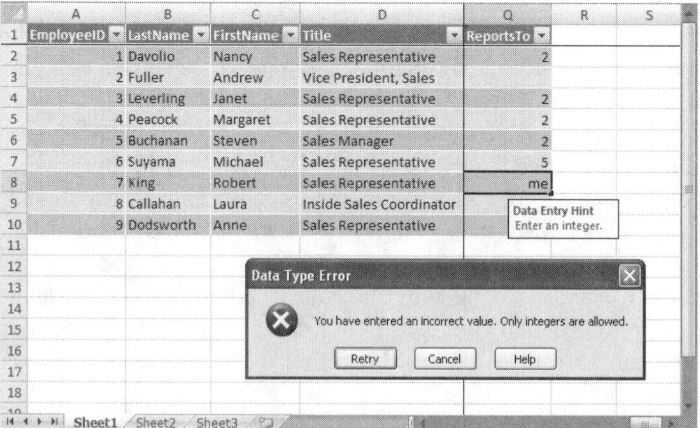

Figure 29-20: You can define custom validation rules that follow the XML schema by using the built-in Validation command on the Data tab. Once the validation rules have been specified for desired cells in your XML table, Excel will display your custom-designed hints to simplify the data entry and a custom-designed error message will be displayed on an attempt to enter invalid data.

Programming XML Maps

Earlier in this chapter you learned that a workbook can contain more than one XML map. These maps can be from the same schema or different schemas. When mapping XML elements to cells and ranges on the worksheet, keep in mind that mapped cell ranges cannot overlap.

In this section, we will add another XML map to the current workbook, but instead of using a manual method we'll perform this task programmatically. Excel provides specific objects to deal with programming its XML features such as the XmlMap object in the XmlMaps collection and the XmlNamespace object in the XmlNamespaces collection.

The XmlMaps collection contains the XmlMap object, which can be used to perform the programming tasks described in the following sub-sections. You can try out the example code in the Immediate window. I assume that you have the Employees.xlsm workbook open and your active worksheet contains the XML table displaying Northwind employees. This table was created earlier in this chapter from the dataroot_Map based on the Employees.xsd schema (see Hands-On 29-4).

Adding an XML Map to a Workbook

You can add an XML map to a workbook using the Add method of the XmlMaps collection. This method requires that you specify the location of an XML schema file. If the schema file is not available, you can specify the XML source data file and Excel will create a schema based on that source data. Earlier in this chapter you worked with the Courses1.xml document. Let's create an XML map using this file. Press Alt+F11 to switch to the Visual Basic Editor screen. Type the following statement in the Immediate window:

```
ActiveWorkbook.XmlMaps.Add("C:\XMLWithExcel07\Courses1.xml")
```

When you press Enter, Excel will display the message shown earlier in this chapter in Figure 29-7.

Click OK to the message. When you switch back to the Excel application window, you will notice that the Courses_Map is added to the XML maps in the workbook drop-down list at the top of the XML Source task pane. When Excel creates a new map it uses the name of the root node for its name, followed by an underscore and the word "Map." Sometimes a newly added map may have the same root node name as an existing map. To differentiate one map from another, Excel will add a number following the word "Map." So, if you already have a dataroot_Map in the workbook and you are adding another map whose root node is also named dataroot, Excel will assign the name "dataroot_Map2" to the new map.

Deleting Existing XML Maps

To delete an existing XML map from the workbook, use the Delete method of the XmlMap object. The Delete method requires that you specify the name of the map to delete. Let's delete the Courses_Map that you added in the previous section. Type the following statement in the Immediate window:

```
ActiveWorkbook.XmlMaps("Courses_Map").Delete
```

When you press Enter, Excel deletes the specified map. This map's name no longer appears in the XML Source task pane. When you delete the map using the Delete button in the XML Maps dialog box (see Figure 29-13 earlier), Excel displays a message informing you "If you delete the specified XML map, you will no longer be able to import or export XML data using this XML map." You don't get this warning message when you delete the XML map programmatically.

Exporting and Importing Data via an XML Map

Use the XmlMap object to export and import XML data. Use the XmlMap object's Export method for exporting and the Import method for importing. For example, to export the XML table data through the dataroot_Map that the Northwind employees XML table is mapped to, type the following statement on one line in the Immediate window:

```
ActiveWorkbook.XmlMaps("dataroot_Map").Export
"C:\XMLWithExcel07\InternalContacts.xml"
```

When you press Enter, Excel creates the specified XML document in your XMLWithExcel07 folder. Excel also offers the ExportXml method for those situations when you'd rather export your XML data to a String variable instead of to a file as is done with the simple Export method. The following procedure demonstrates this:

```
Sub ExportToString()
    Dim strEmpData As String

    ActiveWorkbook.XmlMaps("dataroot_Map").ExportXml Data: = strEmpData
    Debug.Print strEmpData
End Sub
```

To import new XML data into an XML map, copy the Davolio.xml document from the Ex07_HandsOn folder to your XMLWithExcel07 folder, then in the Immediate window, enter the following statement on one line:

```
ActiveWorkbook.XmlMaps("dataroot_Map").Import
      URL: = "C:\XMLWithExcel07\Davolio.xml", Overwrite: = True
```

The Overwrite parameter specifies whether or not the newly imported data should overwrite existing data. The Davolio.xml file holds only data for one Northwind employee named Nancy Davolio. After running the above statement, the XML table in the worksheet will contain only one record.

Binding an XML Map to an XML Data Source

Each XML map is bound to an XML data source. Use the DataBinding property of the XMLMap object to find out the name of the data source that is used in the XML map. For example, when you type the following statement in the Immediate window:

```
Debug.Print ActiveWorkbook.XmlMaps("dataroot_Map").DataBinding
```

Excel returns the following data source: C:\XMLWithExcel07\Davolio.xml. And, if you haven't run the statement in the previous section, you should see C:\XMLWithExcel07\Employees.xml as the data source.

It is possible to change the data source used by the XML map with the LoadSettings method of the DataBinding property as shown below. Be sure to enter this on one line in the Immediate window.

```
ActiveWorkbook.XmlMaps("dataroot_Map").DataBinding.LoadSettings
    ("C:\XMLWithExcel07\Employees.xml")
```

After changing the data source used by the XML map, you should refresh the data in your XML table either via the user interface by clicking the Refresh Data button on the Developer tab or from code using the Refresh method (as shown in the next section).

Refreshing XML Tables from an XML Data Source

Use the Refresh method of the DataBinding property of the XmlMap object to refresh the XML table in your worksheet. The following statement can be used:

```
ActiveWorkbook.XmlMaps("dataroot_Map").DataBinding.Refresh
```

After running the above statement, the XML table in the worksheet should display all of the Northwind employee records.

Viewing the XML Schema

To see the schema that is used by an XML map, use the Schemas collection of the XmlMap object. The Schemas property of the XmlMap object is used to return the XmlSchemas collection. The XmlSchemas collection contains XmlSchema objects. By using the XML property of the XmlSchema object, it is possible to return the string representing the content of the specified schema. Try out this code in the Immediate window:

```
Set objMap = ActiveWorkbook.XmlMaps(1)
Debug.Print objMap.Name
Debug.Print objMap.Schemas(1).Xml
```

If you'd like to use the above code fragment inside a VBA procedure, don't forget to declare the objMap variable with the following statement:

```
Dim objMap As XmlMap
```

Note: By saving the text of the generated schema in a file, you can create a schema file for future use. To do this, open Notepad and paste the data returned by the Debug.Print objMap.Schemas(1).Xml statement. Next, save the Notepad file using any name you wish, but be sure to use the ".xsd" file extension.

Now that you've acquired a useful vocabulary for programming tasks related to XML maps, let's write a full-fledged VBA procedure that will add an XML map to the current workbook, perform the mapping, and refresh the data. You can work with the current workbook that already has the dataroot_Map, or you can create a new workbook file for this example.

Hands-On 29-6: Using VBA to Program XML Maps

1. In the Visual Basic Editor screen, insert a new module in VBAProject (Employees.xlsm).
2. In the module's Code window, enter the AddNew_XMLMap procedure as shown below:

```
Sub AddNew_XMLMap()
    Dim lstCourses As ListObject
    Dim lstCol As ListColumn
    Dim objMap As XmlMap
    Dim mapName As String
    Dim strXPath As String

    On Error GoTo ErrorHandler

    ' Create a new XML map
    ActiveWorkbook.XmlMaps.Add _
      ("C:\XMLWithExcel\Courses.xml", "Courses").Name = "Courses_Map"

    Set objMap = ActiveWorkbook.XmlMaps("Courses_Map")
    Range("B20").Select

    ' Create a new List object
    Set lstCourses = ActiveSheet.ListObjects.Add

    ' Bind the first XML element to the first table column
    strXPath = "/Courses/Course/@ID"
    With lstCourses.ListColumns(1)
       .XPath.SetValue objMap, strXPath
       .Name = "ID"
    End With

    ' Add a column to the table
    ' and bind it to an XML node
    Set lstCol = lstCourses.ListColumns.Add
    strXPath = "/Courses/Course/Title"
    With lstCol
      .XPath.SetValue objMap, strXPath
      .Name = "Title"
    End With
```

```
    ' Add a column to the table
    ' and bind it to an XML node
    Set lstCol = lstCourses.ListColumns.Add

    strXPath = "/Courses/Course/Startdate"
    With lstCol
      .XPath.SetValue objMap, strXPath
      .Name = "Start Date"
    End With

    ' Add a column to the table
    ' and bind it to an XML node
    Set lstCol = lstCourses.ListColumns.Add

    strXPath = "/Courses/Course/Sessions"
    With lstCol
      .XPath.SetValue objMap, strXPath
      .Name = "Sessions"
    End With

    ' Set some XML properties
    With ActiveWorkbook.XmlMaps("Courses_Map")
      .ShowImportExportValidationErrors = False
      .AdjustColumnWidth = True
      .PreserveColumnFilter = True
      .PreserveNumberFormatting = True
      .AppendOnImport = False
    End With

    ' Refresh the XML table in the worksheet
    ActiveWorkbook.XmlMaps("Courses_Map").DataBinding.Refresh
Exit Sub

ErrorHandler:
    MsgBox "The following error has occurred: " & vbCrLf _
        & Err.Description
End Sub
```

The above code begins by creating the XML map named "Courses_Map" using the Courses1.xml data file. Next, a new XML table is created in a worksheet. At this time, the table will contain just one column with the default name "Column1." We bind this column with the first item in the XML map — ID. The XPath object's SetValue method is used to bind data from an XML map to a table column. This method has two required arguments, Map and XPath. Map is the XML map that has been added to the workbook. In this example, it's the object variable named objMap. XPath is the XPath statement in the form of a String variable (strXPath) that specifies the XML map data you want to bind to the specified table column. Because the ID is an attribute, you must precede it with the "@" character. Once the ID is mapped to the table column, we replace the default column name with our own (ID), using the Name property of the ListColumn object:

```
strXPath = "/Courses/Course/@ID"
With lstCourses.ListColumns(1)
    .XPath.SetValue objMap, strXPath
    .Name = "ID"
End With
```

Next, we proceed to add another column to the table using the Add method of the ListColumns collection:

```
Set lstCol = lstCourses.ListColumns.Add
```

This column is then bound to the next item in the XML map — Title. Again, we use the SetValue method of the XPath object to do the binding:

```
strXPath = "/Courses/Course/Title"
With lstCol
    .XPath.SetValue objMap, strXPath
    .Name = "Title"
End With
```

In the same manner, we add two more columns to our table and bind each column to the remaining elements in the XML map. Next, we set some XML map properties and proceed to refresh the list. The empty table is now populated with the data from the source XML file (Courses1.xml).

3. Switch to the Microsoft Excel application window and press **Alt+F8** to activate the Macro dialog box.
4. In the Macro dialog box, select **AddNew_XMLMap** and click the **Run** button.

   Excel displays a message informing you that the specified XML source document does not have a schema and Excel will create one on the fly using the XML source data (see Figure 29-7 earlier in this chapter).
5. Click **OK** to the message.

   Excel adds the specified columns and performs the required data mappings; however, it stops and displays a message about incompatible formatting when it gets to the mapping of the Session element (see Figure 29-21).

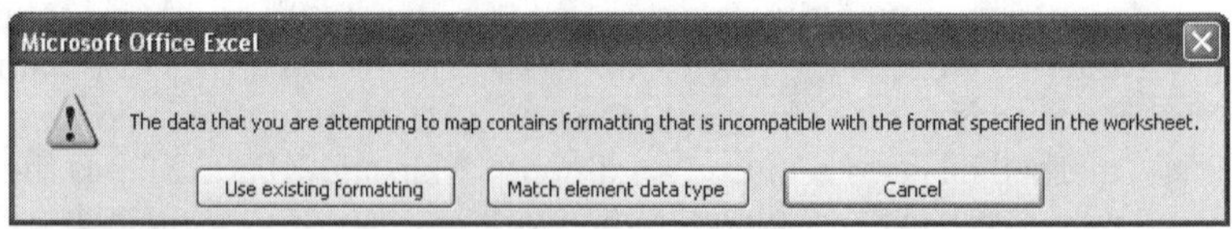

Figure 29-21: This warning message appears when the data type of the data being mapped is not compatible with the cell formatting.

When Excel determines that the cell formatting is not compatible with the data type specified in the XML Schema Definition (XSD) for the requested data element, you receive a warning message as shown in Figure 29-21. This dialog box contains the following buttons:

Use existing formatting	Click this button to ignore the data type in the XSD file.
Match element data type	Click this button to change the cell formatting to the appropriate type.
Cancel	Click this button to cancel mapping of this data element.

6. Click the **Match element data type** button to proceed with the data mapping.

   The resulting XML table and XML map are shown in Figure 29-22.

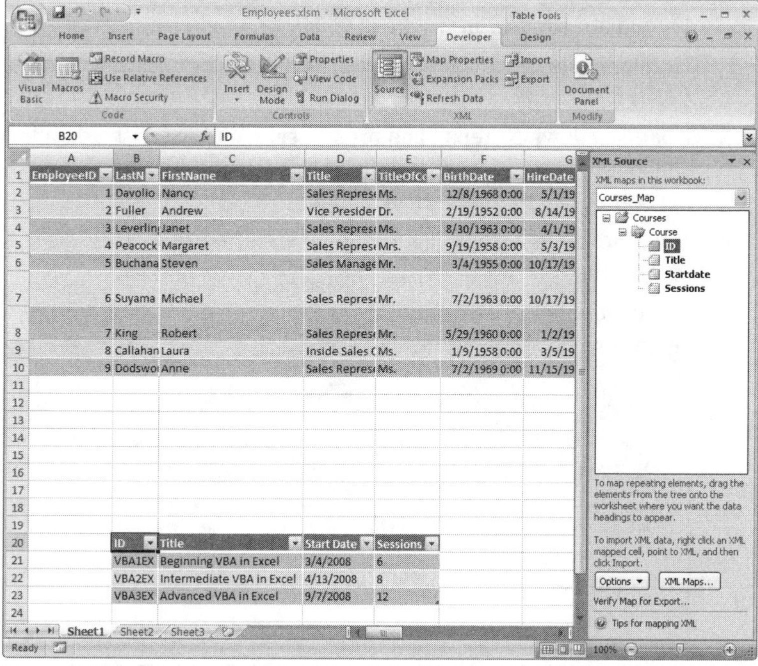

Figure 29-22: The Excel worksheet with two XML tables. The upper table was created via the user interface; the one at the bottom was generated programmatically. The XML Source task pane displays the Courses_Map with mapped data elements.

What Is XPath?

XML Path Language (XPath) is a query language used to create expressions for finding data in the XML file. These expressions can manipulate strings, numbers, and Boolean values. They can also be used to navigate an XML tree structure and process its elements with XSL Transformations (XSLT) instructions. With XPath expressions, you can easily identify and extract from the XML document specific elements (nodes) based on their type, name, values, or the relationship of a node to other nodes (this is covered later in this chapter).

Creating XML Schema Files

When you request that Excel create an XML map based on the specified XML data file, Excel informs you that the specified XML source data does not refer to a schema and therefore Excel will create a schema based on the XML source data. To obtain the schema information that Excel has generated during the XML mapping process, do the following:

1. Open the Immediate window and type the following statement:

   ```
   ? ThisWorkbook.XMLMaps(1).Schemas(1).Xml
   ```

   When you press **Enter**, the content of the schema appears in the Immediate window in the form of a very long string.

2. Highlight the retrieved schema text in the Immediate window, and press **Ctrl+C** to copy it to the clipboard.
3. Open Windows Notepad and press **Ctrl+V** to paste the data from the clipboard. You may want to format the data as shown in Figure 29-23 to make it easier to understand.
4. Save the file using any name, but be sure to specify the ".xsd" file extension.
5. Close Notepad.

Courses1.xsd - Notepad

File Edit Format View Help

```
<xsd:schema xmlns:xsd="http://www.w3.org/2001/XMLSchema">
<xsd:element nillable="true" name="Courses">
<xsd:complexType>
<xsd:sequence minOccurs="0">
<xsd:element minOccurs="0" maxOccurs="unbounded" nillable="true" name="Course" form="unqualified">
<xsd:complexType>
<xsd:sequence minOccurs="0">
<xsd:element minOccurs="0" nillable="true" type="xsd:string" name="Title" form="unqualified">
</xsd:element>
<xsd:element minOccurs="0" nillable="true" type="xsd:string" name="Startdate" form="unqualified">
</xsd:element>
<xsd:element minOccurs="0" nillable="true" type="xsd:integer" name="Sessions" form="unqualified">
</xsd:element>
</xsd:sequence>
<xsd:attribute name="ID" form="unqualified" type="xsd:string">
</xsd:attribute>
</xsd:complexType>
</xsd:element>
</xsd:sequence>
</xsd:complexType>
</xsd:element>
</xsd:schema>
```

Figure 29-23: This XML schema was generated by Excel during the XML mapping of the XML data file.

Using XML Events

Chapter 17 of this book is devoted to event-driven programming. This section expands your knowledge of Excel events by introducing you to events that occur before and after data is exported, imported, or refreshed via the XML map.

The Workbook object provides the following events: AfterXMLExport, AfterXMLImport, BeforeXMLExport, and BeforeXMLImport. By writing code for these events in the ThisWorkbook code module, you can fully control what happens before and after import, export, and refresh operations.

<table>
<tr><th>Event Name</th><th>AfterXMLExport</th></tr>
<tr><th>Event Description</th><th>Example 1</th></tr>
<tr><td>This event applies to the Workbook object. It occurs after Microsoft Excel saves or exports XML data from the specified workbook.

The following parameters are required:

Map — The schema map that was used to save or export data.

Url — The location of the XML file that was exported.

Result — A constant indicating the result of the save or export operation. Use one of the following xlXmlExportResult constants:

■ xlXmlExportSuccess — specifies that the XML data file was successfully exported.
■ xlXmlExportValidationFailed — specifies that the content of the XML data file does not match the specified schema map.</td><td><pre>Private Sub Workbook_AfterXMLExport _
    (ByVal Map As XmlMap, _
    ByVal Url As String, _
    ByVal Result As xlXmlExportResult)
  If Result = xlXmlExportSuccess Then
    MsgBox ("XML export succeeded.")
  Else
    MsgBox ("XML export failed.")
  End If

End Sub</pre></td></tr>
</table>

<table>
<tr><th>Event Name</th><th>AfterXMLImport</th></tr>
<tr><th>Event Description</th><th>Example 2</th></tr>
<tr><td>This event applies to the Workbook object. It occurs after an existing XML data connection is refreshed or after new XML data is imported into the specified Microsoft Excel workbook.

The following parameters are required:

Map — The XML map that will be used to import data.

IsRefresh — A Boolean value (True/False). True if the event was triggered by refreshing an existing connection to XML data; False if the event was triggered by importing from a different data source.

Result — A constant indicating the result of the refresh or import operation. Use one of the following xlXmlImportResult constants:

■ xlXmlImportElementsTruncated — specifies that the content of the specified XML data file has been truncated because the XML data file is too large for the worksheet.</td><td><pre>Private Sub Workbook_AfterXMLImport(ByVal _
    Map As XmlMap, _
    ByVal IsRefresh As Boolean, _
    ByVal Result As xlXmlImportResult)
  If Result = xlXmlImportSuccess Then
    MsgBox ("XML import succeeded.")
    ActiveSheet.ListObjects(1).Range.Select
    Selection.Interior.ColorIndex = 35
    ActiveCell.Select
  Else
    MsgBox ("XML import failed.")
  End If

End Sub</pre></td></tr>
</table>

Event Name	AfterXMLImport
Event Description	**Example 2 (Cont.)**

- xlXmlImportSuccess — specifies that the XML data file was successfully imported.
- xlXmlImportValidationFailed — specifies that the content of the XML data file does not match the specified schema map.

Event Name	BeforeXMLExport
Event Description	**Example 3**

This event applies to the Workbook object. It occurs before Microsoft Excel saves or exports XML data from the specified workbook. This event occurs only when saving to an XML data file format; it does not occur when you are saving to the XML spreadsheet file format.

The following parameters are required:

Map — The XML map that will be used to save or export data.

Url — The location where you want to export the resulting XML file.

Cancel — A Boolean value (True/False). Set to True to cancel the save or export operation.

```
Private Sub Workbook_BeforeXMLExport _
    (ByVal Map As XmlMap, _
    ByVal Url As String, _
    Cancel As Boolean)

  If (Map.IsExportable) Then
    If MsgBox("Microsoft Excel is about" & _
      " to export XML from the" & _
      " Map.Name & "." & vbCrLf & "Do" & _
      " you want to continue?", _
      vbYesNo + vbQuestion, _
      "XML Export Process") = 7 Then _
      Cancel = True
  End If
End Sub
```

Event Name	BeforeXMLImport
Event Description	**Example 4**

This event applies to the Workbook object. It occurs before an existing XML data connection is refreshed or before new XML data is imported into a Microsoft Excel workbook.

The following parameters are required:

Map — The XML map that will be used to import data.

Url — The location of the XML file to be imported.

IsRefresh — A Boolean value (True/False). True if the event was triggered by refreshing an existing connection to XML data; False if the event was triggered by importing from a different data source.

Cancel — A Boolean value (True/False). Set to True to cancel the import or refresh operation.

```
Private Sub Workbook_BeforeXMLImport _
    (ByVal Map As XmlMap, _
    ByVal Url As String, _
    ByVal IsRefresh As Boolean, _
    Cancel As Boolean)

  If MsgBox("Microsoft Excel is about" & _
    " to import XML into the workbook." & _
    " Continue with importing?", _
    vbYesNo + vbQuestion, _
    "XML Import Process") = 7 Then _
    Cancel = True
  End If
End Sub
```

The XML events are also available for the Application object. These events are listed below. Recall from Chapter 17 that event procedures for the Application object require that you create a new object using the WithEvents keyword in a class module.

- **WorkbookBeforeXmlExport** — Occurs before Microsoft Excel saves or exports XML data from the specified workbook. Use this event if you want to capture XML data that is being exported or saved from a particular workbook.
- **WorkbookAfterXmlExport** — Occurs after Microsoft Excel saves or exports XML data from the specified workbook. Use this event if you want to perform an operation after XML data has been exported from a particular workbook.
- **WorkbookBeforeXmlImport** — Occurs before an existing XML data connection is refreshed or new XML data is imported into any open Microsoft Excel workbook. Use this event if you want to capture XML data that is being imported or refreshed to a particular workbook.
- **WorkbookAfterXmlImport** — Occurs after an existing XML data connection is refreshed or new XML data is imported into any open Microsoft Excel workbook. Use this event if you want to perform an operation after XML data has been imported into a particular workbook.

The XML Document Object Model

You can create, access, and manipulate XML documents programmatically via the XML Document Object Model (DOM). The DOM has properties, methods, and constants for interacting with XML documents. The XML DOM is supplied free with Internet Explorer. To use the XML DOM from your VBA procedures, you need to set up a reference to the MSXML object library.

Hands-On 29-7: Setting up a Reference to DOM

1. In the Visual Basic Editor window of VBAProject (Empoyees.xlsm), choose **Tools | References.**
2. In the References dialog box, locate and select **Microsoft XML, v5.0** or **6.0** (see Figure 29-24).

   If you are still using Microsoft Internet Explorer 5.0, you'll need to choose the version 3.0 type library (or upgrade your browser to the higher version).

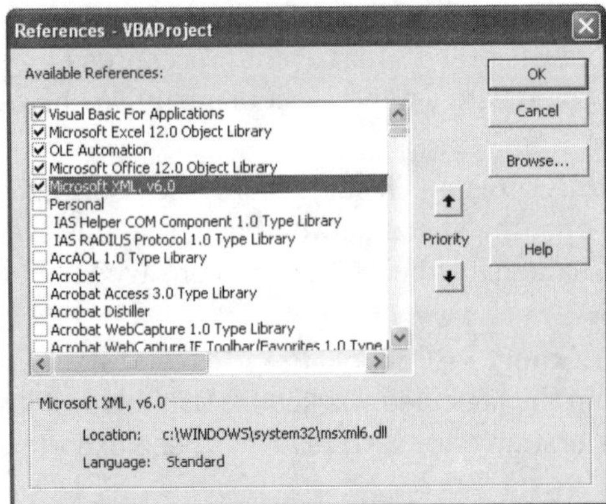

Figure 29-24: To work with XML documents programmatically, you need to establish a reference to the Microsoft XML type library.

3. Click **OK** to close the References dialog box.
4. Now that you have the reference set, open the Object Browser and examine the XML DOM's objects, methods, and properties.

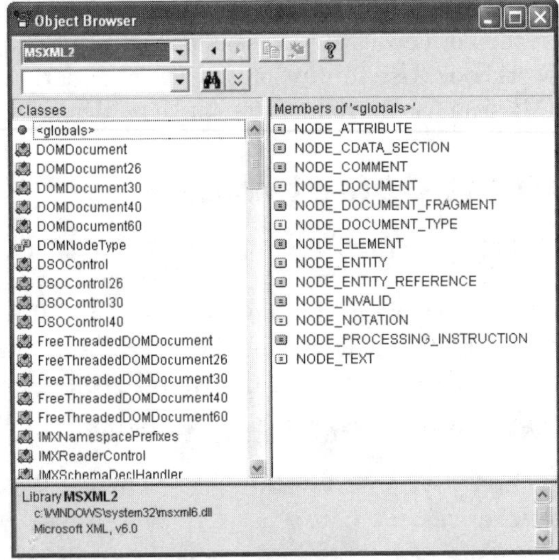

Figure 29-25: To see objects, properties, and methods exposed by the DOM (Document Object Model), open the Object Browser after setting up a reference to the Microsoft XML type library (see Figure 29-24).

5. Close the Object Browser.

The DOMDocument object is the top level of the XML DOM hierarchy. This object represents a tree structure composed of nodes. You can navigate through this tree structure and manipulate the data contained in the nodes by using various methods and properties. The DOMDocument object is the parent for all other elements in the DOM hierarchy. Because every XML object is created and accessed from the document, the DOMDocument object must be created first.

To work with an XML document, you need to create an instance of the DOMDocument object, as in the following example:

```
Dim myXMLDoc As MSXM2.DOMDocument60
Set myXMLDoc = New MSXML2.DOMDocument60
```

To make the instantiated DOMDocument object useful, you should load it with some data. The following example VBA procedure demonstrates how to get started with the XML DOM. You will perform the following tasks:

- Create an instance of the DOMDocument.
- Load XML information from a file using the Load method.
- Use the DOMDocument object's XML property to retrieve the raw data.
- Use the DOMDocument object's Text property to retrieve the text stored in nodes.

Hands-On 29-8: Reading an XML Document with DOM

1. Enter the following Load_ReadXMLDoc procedure in a new module of VBAProject (Employees.xlsm):

```
Sub Load_ReadXMLDoc()
    Dim xmldoc As MSXML2.DOMDocument60

    ' Create an instance of the DOMDocument
    Set xmldoc = New MSXML2.DOMDocument60

    ' Disable asynchronous loading
    xmldoc.async = False

    ' Load XML information from a file
    If xmldoc.Load("C:\XMLWithExcel07\Courses1.xml") Then
        ' Use the DOMDocument object's XML property to
        ' retrieve the raw data
        Debug.Print xmldoc.XML
        ' Use the DOMDocument object's Text poperty to
        ' retrieve the actual text stored in nodes
        Sheets(2).Range("A1").Value = xmldoc.Text
    End If
End Sub
```

The XML DOM has two methods for loading XML information: Load and LoadXML. Use the Load method to load XML information from a text file. Use the LoadXML method when loading from a string in memory.

MSXML uses an asynchronous loading mechanism by default for working with documents. Asynchronous loading allows you to perform other tasks during long database operations, such as providing feedback to the user as MSXML parses the XML file or giving the user the chance to cancel the operation. Before calling the Load method, however, it's a good idea to set the Async property of the DOMDocument object to False to ensure that when the load returns, the entire document has finished loading. The Load method returns True if it successfully loaded the data and False otherwise.

Having loaded the data into a DOMDocument object, you can use the XML property to retrieve the raw data or use the Text property to obtain the text stored in document nodes.

2. Run the Load_ReadXMLDoc procedure and examine its results in the Immediate window and in Sheet2 of the Employees.xlsm workbook.

Working with XML Document Nodes

As you already know, the XML DOM represents a tree-based hierarchy of nodes. An XML document can contain nodes of different types. Some nodes represent comments and processing instructions in the XML document, and others hold the text content of a tag. To determine the type of node, use the nodeType property of the IXMLDOMNode object. Node types are identified either by a text string or a constant. For example, the node representing an element can be referred to as NODE_ELEMENT or 1, while the node representing the comment is named NODE_COMMENT or 8. See the MSXML2 library in the Object Browser (Figure 29-25 earlier in this chapter) for the names of other node types.

In addition to node types, nodes can have parent, child, and sibling nodes. The hasChildNodes method lets you determine if a DOMDocument object has child nodes. There's also a childNodes property for retrieving a collection of child nodes. Before you start looping through the collection of child nodes, it's a good idea to use the Length property of the IXMLDOMNode to determine how many elements the collection contains.

The LearnAboutNodes procedure shown below will get you working with nodes programmatically in no time. The following example demonstrates how to experiment with XML document nodes.

Hands-On 29-9: Working with XML Document Nodes

1. In the Visual Basic Editor window of VBAProject (Employees.xlsm), insert a new module and enter the LearnAboutNodes procedure, as shown below:

```
Sub LearnAboutNodes()
    Dim xmldoc As MSXML2.DOMDocument60
    Dim xmlNode As MSXML2.IXMLDOMNode

    ' Create an instance of the DOMDocument
    Set xmldoc = New MSXML2.DOMDocument60

    xmldoc.async = False

    ' Load XML information from a file
    xmldoc.Load ("C:\XMLWithExcel07\Courses1.xml")

    ' find out the number of child nodes in the document
    If xmldoc.hasChildNodes Then
        Debug.Print "Number of Child Nodes: " & _
                    xmldoc.childNodes.Length

        ' iterate through the child nodes to gather information
        For Each xmlNode In xmldoc.childNodes
            Debug.Print "Node Name: " & xmlNode.nodeName
```

```
            Debug.Print vbTab & "Type: " & _
                    xmlNode.nodeTypeString & _
                    "(" & xmlNode.nodeType & ")"
            Debug.Print vbTab & "Text: " & xmlNode.Text
        Next xmlNode
    End If
End Sub
```

2. Run the LearnAboutNodes procedure in step mode by pressing **F8**.

   The LearnAboutNodes procedure prints to the Immediate window the information about child nodes found in the Courses1.xml document. Notice that the Text property of a node returns all the text from all the node's children in one string (see the text for the Courses node below).

```
Number of Child Nodes: 3
Node Name: xml
    Type: processinginstruction(7)
    Text: version = "1.0"
Node Name: xml-stylesheet
    Type: processinginstruction(7)
    Text: type = "text/xsl" href = "Courses.xsl"
Node Name: Courses
    Type: element(1)
    Text: Beginning VBA in Excel 3/4/2008 6 Intermediate VBA in Excel
4/13/2008 8 Advanced VBA in Excel 9/7/2008 12
```

Retrieving Information from Element Nodes

Let's assume that you want to read only the information from the text element nodes and place it in an Excel worksheet. Use the getElements-ByTagName method of the DOMDocument object to retrieve an IXMLDOMNodeList object containing all the element nodes.

The getElementsByTagName method takes one argument specifying the tag name for which to search. To look for all the element nodes, use "*" as the tag to search for (as illustrated in the procedure below). The following example demonstrates how to obtain data from an XML document's element nodes.

Hands-On 29-10: Obtaining Data from Element Nodes

1. In the Visual Basic Editor window of VBAProject (Employees.xlsm), insert a new module and enter the IterateThruElements procedure, as shown below:

```
Sub IterateThruElements()
    Dim xmldoc As MSXML2.DOMDocument60
    Dim xmlNodeList As MSXML2.IXMLDOMNodeList
    Dim xmlNode As MSXML2.IXMLDOMNode
    Dim myNode As MSXML2.IXMLDOMNode

    ' Create an instance of the DOMDocument
    Set xmldoc = New MSXML2.DOMDocument60
    xmldoc.async = False
```

```
    ' Load XML information from a file
    xmldoc.Load ("C:\XMLWithExcel07\Courses1.xml")

    ' Find out the number of child nodes in the document
    Set xmlNodeList = xmldoc.getElementsByTagName("*")

    ' Open a new workbook and paste the data
    Workbooks.Add
    Range("A1:B1").Formula = Array("Element Name", "Text")
    For Each xmlNode In xmlNodeList
      For Each myNode In xmlNode.ChildNodes
        If myNode.nodeType = NODE_TEXT Then
          ActiveCell.Offset(0, 0).Formula = xmlNode.nodeName
          ActiveCell.Offset(0, 1).Formula = xmlNode.Text
        End If
      Next myNode
      ActiveCell.Offset(1, 0).Select
    Next xmlNode
    Columns("A:B").AutoFit
End Sub
```

2. Run the above procedure in step mode by pressing **F8**.

   The IterateThruElements procedure fills in two worksheet columns with the XML element name and the corresponding text for all the text elements in the Courses1.xml document (see the procedure result in Figure 29-26). Notice that this procedure uses two For Each...Next loops. The first one (outer For Each...Next loop) iterates through the entire collection of element nodes. The second one (inner For Each...Next loop) uses the nodeType property to find only those element nodes that contain a single text node.

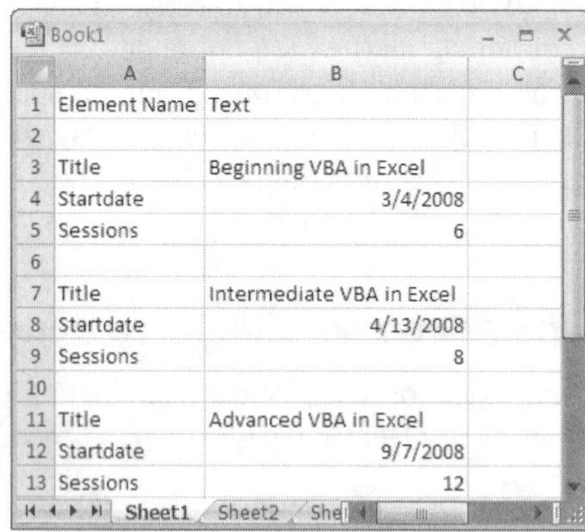

Figure 29-26: You can programmatically retrieve information about element nodes from the XML document. The IterateThruElements procedure was used to create this worksheet.

To list all the nodes that match a specified criterion, use the selectNodes method. The next example demonstrates how to return to the Immediate window the text for all Title nodes in the Courses1.xml file.

Hands-On 29-11: Obtaining Data from an Element Node Based on a Condition

1. In the Visual Basic Editor window of VBAProject (Employees.xlsm), insert a new module and enter the SelectNodes_SpecifyCriterion procedure, as shown below:

```
Sub SelectNodes_SpecifyCriterion()
    Dim xmldoc As MSXML2.DOMDocument60
    Dim xmlNodeList As MSXML2.IXMLDOMNodeList
    Dim myNode As Variant

    ' Create an instance of the DOMDocument
    Set xmldoc = New MSXML2.DOMDocument60
    xmldoc.async = False

    ' Load XML information from a file
    xmldoc.Load ("C:\XMLWithExcel07\Courses1.xml")

    ' Retrieve all the nodes that match the specified criterion
    Set xmlNodeList = xmldoc.selectNodes("//Title")
    If Not (xmlNodeList Is Nothing) Then
       For Each myNode In xmlNodeList
         Debug.Print myNode.Text
       Next myNode
    End If
End Sub
```

   In the SelectNodes_SpecifyCriterion procedure, the "//Title" criterion of the selectNodes method looks for the element named "Title" at any level within the tree structure of the nodes.

2. Run the above procedure in step mode by pressing **F8**.

   Excel prints to the Immediate window only the names of the courses:

```
Beginning VBA in Excel
Intermediate VBA in Excel
Advanced VBA in Excel
```

The criterion in the selectNodes method can be more complex. Let's assume that you are only interested in the title for the Course element with an ID of "VBA2EX." To retrieve this information, use the following statement:

```
Set xmlNodeList = xmldoc.selectNodes("//Course[@ID = 'VBA2EX']//Title")
```

The above statement tells the XML processor to search for an element named "Course" at any level within the tree structure of nodes, find only the course element whose ID attribute contains the value of "VBA2EX," and return the Title element. If all you want to do is retrieve the first node that meets the specified criterion, use the selectSingleNode method of the XML document. As the argument of this method, specify the string representing the node that you'd like to find. In the next example you will find the first node that matches the criterion "//Title" in the Courses1.xml document.

Hands-On 29-12: Finding a Specific Node

1. In the Visual Basic Editor window of VBAProject (Employees.xlsm), insert a new module and enter the Select_SingleNode procedure, as shown below:

```
Sub Select_SingleNode()
    Dim xmldoc As MSXML2.DOMDocument60
    Dim xmlSingleN As MSXML2.IXMLDOMNode

    ' Create an instance of the DOMDocument
    Set xmldoc = New MSXML2.DOMDocument60
    xmldoc.async = False

    ' Load XML information from a file
    xmldoc.Load ("C:\XMLWithExcel07\Courses1.xml")

    ' Retrieve the reference to a particular node
    Set xmlSingleN = xmldoc.selectSingleNode("//Title")
    Debug.Print xmlSingleN.Text
End Sub
```

2. Run the above procedure in step mode by pressing **F8**.

   The result of this procedure is the text "Beginning VBA in Excel" written to the Immediate window.

The following statements will retrieve the first Course node with the ID attribute:

```
Set xmlSingleN = xmldoc.selectSingleNode("//Course//@ID")
Debug.Print xmlSingleN.Text
```

If you replace the last two lines in the Select_SingleNode procedure with the above statements and run the procedure again, you should see the text "VBA1EX" in the Immediate window.

Once you find the correct node to work with, you can easily modify its value. For example, to change the text of the first Course element with the ID attribute, use the following lines of code:

```
Set xmlSingleN = xmldoc.selectSingleNode("//Course//@ID")
xmlSingleN.Text = "VBA1EX2007"
xmldoc.Save "C:\XMLWithExcel07\Courses1.xml"
```

Notice that to make a permanent change in the XML document, you must save it using the Save method.

When using the selectSingleNode method, you should use the Is Nothing conditional expression to determine whether a matching element was found in the loaded XML document, as demonstrated in the next example.

Hands-On 29-13: Using a Conditional Expression with an Element Node

1. In the Visual Basic Editor window of VBAProject (Employees.xlsm), insert a new module and enter the Select_SingleNode_2 procedure, as shown below:

```
Sub Select_SingleNode_2()
    Dim xmldoc As MSXML2.DOMDocument60
    Dim xmlSingleN As MSXML2.IXMLDOMNode

    ' Create an instance of the DOMDocument
    Set xmldoc = New MSXML2.DOMDocument60
    xmldoc.async = False

    ' Load XML information from a file
    xmldoc.Load ("C:\XMLWithExcel07\Courses1.xml")

    ' Retrieve the reference to a particular node
    Set xmlSingleN = xmldoc.SelectSingleNode("//Course//@ID")
    If xmlSingleN Is Nothing Then
       Debug.Print "No nodes selected."
    Else
       Debug.Print xmlSingleN.Text
       xmlSingleN.Text = "VBA1EX2007"
       Debug.Print xmlSingleN.Text
       xmldoc.Save "C:\XMLWithExcel07\Courses1.xml"
    End If
End Sub
```

2. Run the procedure in step mode by pressing **F8**.

   Excel prints to the Immediate window the text of the node before and after modification.

3. Replace the XPath expression "//Course//@ID" with "//**Cours**//@**ID**" and run the procedure again.

   You should see the text "No nodes selected" in the Immediate window.

XML DOM provides a number of other methods that make it possible to programmatically add or delete elements. Covering all of the details of the XML DOM is beyond the scope of this chapter. When you are ready for more information on this subject, visit the following web sites: http://www.w3.org/DOM/ and http://www.w3.org/XML/.

XML via ADO

Earlier in this book you learned how to retrieve external data using the ActiveX Data Objects (ADO). This section will show you what you can do with XML and ADO. Since the release of ADO version 2.5 (in 2000), you can save all types of recordsets as XML to disk. You can also save any type of ADO recordset to XML in memory using the ADO Stream object; however, that is not covered here.

Saving an ADO Recordset to Disk as XML

To save an ADO recordset as XML to a disk file, use the Save method of the Recordset object with the adPersistXML constant. The following example procedure demonstrates how to create XML files from ADO recordsets.

Hands-On 29-14: Saving an ADO Recordset as an XML Document

1. In the Visual Basic Editor window of VBAProject (Employees.xlsm), insert a new module.
2. Choose **Tools | References**. In the References dialog box, find and select the reference to the **Microsoft ActiveX Data Objects 2.8 Library** or earlier.
3. Click **OK** to close the References dialog box.

Note: ADO is part of Microsoft Data Access Components (MDAC). You can download the latest version of MDAC from the Microsoft web site. ADO 2.8, released in 2007, is the current version of ADO.

4. In the Code window of the new module you added in step 1, enter the SaveRst_ADO procedure, as shown below:

```
Sub SaveRst_ADO()
    Dim rst As ADODB.Recordset
    Dim conn As New ADODB.Connection
    Const strConn = "Provider = Microsoft.Jet.OLEDB.4.0;" _
       & "Data Source = C:\Ex07_HandsOn\Northwind.mdb"

    ' Open a connection to the database
    conn.Open strConn

    ' Execute a select SQL statement against the database
    Set rst = conn.Execute("SELECT * FROM Products")

    ' Delete the file if it exists
    On Error Resume Next
    Kill "C:\XMLWithExcel07\Products.xml"

    ' Save the recordset as an XML file
    rst.Save "C:\XMLWithExcel07\Products.xml", adPersistXML
End Sub
```

The procedure shown above establishes a connection to the sample Northwind.mdb database using the ADO Connection object. Next, it executes a select SQL statement against the database to retrieve all of the records from the Products table. Once the records are placed in a recordset, the Save method is called to store the recordset to a disk file. If the disk file already exists, the procedure deletes the existing file using the VBA Kill statement. The On Error Resume Next statement allows bypassing the Kill statement if the file that you are going to create does not yet exist.

5. Run the SaveRst_ADO procedure.
6. Use Notepad to open the **C:\XMLWithExcel07\Products.xml** file created by the SaveRst_ADO procedure.

The file content is depicted in Figure 29-27. XML files can be element-based or attribute-based. The XML files produced by ADO 2.5 or higher are all attribute-based.

XML files generated by ADO are self-describing objects that contain data and metadata (information about the data). If you take a look at the Products.xml file in Figure 29-27, you will notice that below the XML document's root tag there are two children nodes: <s:Schema> and <rs:data>. The schema node describes the structure of the recordset, while the data node holds the actual data.

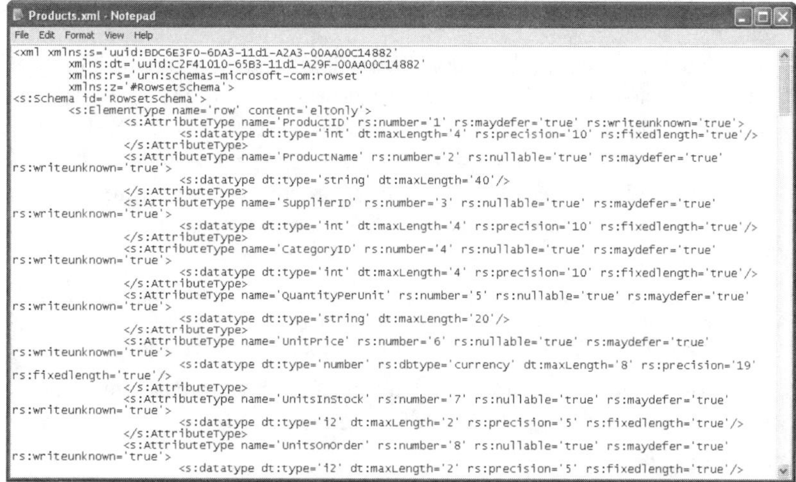

Figure 29-27: Saving a recordset to an XML file with ADO 2.5 or above produces an attribute-based XML file.

Between the <s:Schema id ="RowsetSchema"> and </s:Schema> tags, ADO places information about each column, including field name, position, data type and length, nullability, and whether the column is writable. Take a look at the following code fragement:

```
<s:Schema id="RowsetSchema">
    <s:ElementType name="row" content="eltOnly">
    <s:AttributeType name="ProductID" rs:number="1" rs:maydefer="true"
        rs:writeunknown="true">
        <s:datatype dt:type="int" dt:maxLength="4" rs:precision="10"
            rs:fixedlength="true"/>
     </s:AttributeType>
    <s:AttributeType name="ProductName" rs:number="2" rs:nullable="true"
        rs:maydefer="true" rs:writeunknown="true">
        <s:datatype dt:type="string" dt:maxLength="40"/>
</s:AttributeType>
    <s:AttributeType name="SupplierID" rs:number="3" rs:nullable="true"
        rs:maydefer="true" rs:writeunknown="true">
        <s:datatype dt:type="int" dt:maxLength="4" rs:precision="10"
            rs:fixedlength="true"/>
</s:AttributeType>
    <s:AttributeType name="CategoryID" rs:number="4" rs:nullable="true"
```

```
        rs:maydefer="true" rs:writeunknown="true">
        <s:datatype dt:type="int" dt:maxLength="4" rs:precision="10"
           rs:fixedlength="true"/>
</s:AttributeType>
 <s:extends type="rs:rowbase"/>
 </s:ElementType>
</s:Schema>
```

Notice that each field is represented by the <s:AttributeType> element. The value of the name attribute is the field name. The <s:AttributeType> element also has a child element, <s:datatype>, which holds information about its data type (integer, number, string, etc.) and the maximum field length.

Below the schema definition, you will find the actual data. The ADO schema represents each record using the <z:row> tag. The fields in a record are expressed as attributes of the <z:row> element. Every XML attribute is assigned a value that is enclosed in a pair of single or double quotation marks; however, if the value of a field in a record is NULL, the attribute on the <z:row> is not created. Notice that each record is written out in the following format:

```
<z:row ProductID='1' ProductName='Chai' SupplierID='1' CategoryID='1'
QuantityPerUnit='10 boxes x 20 bags' UnitPrice='18' UnitsInStock='39'
UnitsOnOrder='0' ReorderLevel='10' Discontinued='False'/>
```

The above code fragment is an attribute-based XML document. However, you may want to have each record written out as follows:

```
<Product>
<ProductID>1</ProductID>
<ProductName>Chai</ProductName>
<SupplierID>1</SupplierID>
<CategoryID>1</CategoryID>
<QuantityPerUnit>10 boxes x 20 bags</QuantityPerUnit>
<UnitPrice>18</UnitPrice>
<UnitsInStock>39</UnitsInStock>
<UnitsOnOrder>0</UnitsOnOrder>

<ReorderLevel>10</ReorderLevel>
<Discontinued>False</Discontinued>
</Product>
```

The above code fragment represents an element-based XML. Each record is wrapped in a <Product> tag, and each field is an element under the <Product> tag. You can write a stylesheet to transform attribute-based XML into element-based XML. Writing stylesheets and using XSL transformations is not covered in this book.

Loading an ADO Recordset

After saving an ADO recordset to an XML file on disk, you can load it back and read it as if it were a database. To gain access to the records saved in the XML file, use the Open method of the Recordset object and specify the filename including its path and the persisted recordset service provider as

"Provider=MSPersist". Let's look at an example that demonstrates opening a persisted recordset.

Hands-On 29-15: Opening a Persisted Recordset with XML Data

1. In the Visual Basic Editor window of VBAProject (Employees.xlsm), insert a new module and enter the procedure OpenAdoFile, as shown below:

```
Sub OpenAdoFile()
    Dim rst As ADODB.Recordset
    Dim StartRange As Range
    Dim h As Integer

    ' Create a recordset and fill it with
    ' the data from the XML file
    Set rst = New ADODB.Recordset
    rst.Open "C:\XMLWithExcel07\Products.xml", _
             "Provider=MSPersist"

    ' Display the number of records
    MsgBox rst.RecordCount

    ' Open a new workbook
    Workbooks.Add

    ' Copy field names as headings to the first row
    ' of the worksheet
    For h = 1 To rst.fields.Count
      ActiveSheet.Cells(1, h).Value = rst.fields(h - 1).Name
    Next

    ' Specify the cell range to receive the data (A2)
    Set StartRange = ActiveSheet.Cells(2, 1)

    ' Copy the records from the recordset
    ' beginning in cell A2
    StartRange.CopyFromRecordset rst

    ' Autofit the columns to make the data fit
    Range("A1").CurrentRegion.Select
    Columns.AutoFit

    ' Close the workbook and save the file
    ActiveWorkbook.Close SaveChanges:=True, _
       Filename:="C:\Ex07_ByExample\Products.xlsx"
End Sub
```

The example procedure shown above creates a Recordset object and fills it with the data from the Products.xml file. After displaying the number of records in the file, the procedure opens a new workbook and fills the first worksheet row with field names. Next, the CopyFromRecordset method is used to retrieve all the records into the worksheet. After adjusting the size of the columns to fit the data, the workbook is saved using the default Excel 2007 file format (.xlsx).

2. Run the OpenAdoFile procedure.
3. Open the **Products.xlsx** file that was created by the OpenAdoFile procedure in your XMLWithExcel07 folder.

   You should see all of the records from the Products.xml document nicely arranged in rows and columns and therefore easy to analyze and make changes to.
4. Close the **Products.xlsx** file. Do not close the Employees.xlsm workbook as we will continue to use it in the next section.

Saving an ADO Recordset into the DOMDocument Object

You can save an ADO recordset directly into an XML DOMDocument object using the following code:

```
Set xmlDoc = New MSXML2.DOMDocument30
rst.Save xmlDoc, adPersistXML
```

The next Hands-On exercise demonstrates how you can use DOM to modify XML data in the recordset generated by the ADO Save method.

Hands-On 29-16: Modifying a Recordset Saved into the XML DOMDocument Object

1. In the Visual Basic Editor window of VBAProject (Employees.xlsm), insert a new module and enter the SaveToDOM procedure, as shown below:

```
Sub SaveToDOM()
    Dim conn As ADODB.Connection
    Dim rst As ADODB.Recordset
    Dim xmlDoc As MSXML2.DOMDocument60
    Dim myNode As IXMLDOMNode
    Dim strCurValue As String

    ' Declare constant used as database connection string
    Const strConn = "Provider=Microsoft.Jet.OLEDB.4.0;" _
      & "Data Source=C:\Ex07_ByExample\Northwind.mdb"

    ' Open a connection to the database
    Set conn = New ADODB.Connection
    conn.Open strConn

    ' Open the Shippers table
    Set rst = New ADODB.Recordset
    rst.Open "Shippers", conn, adOpenStatic, adLockOptimistic

    ' Create a new XML DOMDocument object
    Set xmlDoc = New MSXML2.DOMDocument60

    ' Add the default namespace declaration
    ' to the Namespace names of the DOMDocument object
```

```
    ' using the setProperty method of the DOMDocument object

    xmlDoc.setProperty "SelectionNamespaces", _
        "xmlns:rs='urn:schemas-microsoft-com:rowset'" & _
        " xmlns:z='#RowsetSchema'"


    ' Save the recordset directly into
    ' the XML DOMDocument object
    rst.Save xmlDoc, adPersistXML
    Debug.Print xmlDoc.XML

    ' Modify shipper's phone
    Set myNode = xmlDoc.selectSingleNode( _
        "//z:row[@CompanyName='Speedy Express']/@Phone")
    strCurValue = myNode.Text
    Debug.Print strCurValue
    myNode.Text = "(508)" & Right(strCurValue, 9)
    Debug.Print myNode.Text

    xmlDoc.Save "C:\XMLWithExcel07\Shippers_Modified.xml"

    ' Cleanup
    Set xmlDoc = Nothing
    Set conn = Nothing
    Set rst = Nothing
    Set myNode = Nothing
End Sub
```

After saving the recordset into the XML DOMDocument object, the procedure locates a node matching a specified search string by using the selectSingleNode method. Notice that the XPath expression used as an argument of this method searches for the Phone attribute in the z:row element nodes that have a CompanyName attribute set to "Speedy Express":

```
Set myNode = xmlDoc.selectSingleNode( _
     "//z:row[@CompanyName='Speedy Express']/@Phone")
```

Once the required phone number is located, the procedure modifies the area code, as follows:

```
strCurValue = myNode.Text
myNode.Text = "(508)" & Right(strCurValue, 9)
```

If you'd rather remove the Phone entry completely, you could use the following code:

```
Set myNode = xmlDoc.selectSingleNode( _
   "//z:row[@CompanyName='Speedy Express']")
myNode.Attributes.removeNamedItem "Phone"
```

The removeNamedItem method removes an attribute from the attributes of a given node. This method requires one parameter: a string specifying the name of the attribute to remove from the collection.

2. Run the procedure in step mode by pressing **F8**. Make sure the Immediate window is open so you can see at once the results of various Debug.Print statements that the example procedure contains.
3. Use Notepad to open the **C:\XMLWithExcel07\Shippers_Modified.xml** file created by the SaveToDOM procedure.

   Notice the modified phone number for the Speedy Express record.
4. Close the Notepad.
5. Close the Employees.xlsm workbook, saving changes when prompted.

Understanding Namespaces

As mentioned earlier, XML is a markup language that uses custom tags. Because XML allows you to invent your own tag names to describe your data, how can you ensure that your tags will not conflict with someone else's tags when two or more XML documents are combined? The <TABLE> tag will certainly have a different meaning and content in an Excel XML document than the <TABLE> element used to describe different types of tables listed in a catalog for a furniture store. Fortunately, there is a way to differentiate elements and attributes that have the same name. The XML Namespaces specification ensures that element names do not conflict with one another and are unique within a particular set of names (a namespace).

A *namespace* is a collection of names in which all names are unique. The namespace is identified by a Uniform Resource Identifier (URI) — either a Uniform Resource Locator (URL) or a Uniform Resource Name (URN). Usually the namespace declaration is placed at the beginning of the XML document. There is no requirement for the specified URI to be valid or for it to conform to any sort of specification. Most namespaces use URIs for the namespace names because URIs are guaranteed to be unique.

Take a look at the following lines in the Shippers_Modified.xml file that was created in Hands-On 29-16:

```
<xml xmlns:s="uuid:BDC6E3F0-6DA3-11d1-A2A3-00AA00C14882"
xmlns:dt="uuid:C2F41010-65B3-11d1-A29F-00AA00C14882"
xmlns:rs="urn:schemas-microsoft-com:rowset"
xmlns:z="#RowsetSchema">
```

Namespaces can be declared in any element by using the xmlns attribute. A namespace whose xmlns attribute is not followed by a prefix is referred to as a "default namespace." In the above example, there are four namespaces, each of which is associated with a particular prefix ("s", "dt", "rs", and "z"). In the XML document these prefixes are used in front of element and attribute names to indicate which namespace they are referencing. In other words, anything with an "s" in front of it applies to the uuid:BDC6E3F0-6DA3-11d1-A2A3-00AA00C14882 namespace, and anything marked with the "z" prefix references the RowsetSchema namespace. When a namespace xmlns attribute is not followed by a prefix, that namespace is said to be a "default namespace." Therefore, elements or attributes with no prefix will be assumed to be part of the default namespace.

What you should remember from this section is that namespaces don't really exist. They are arbitrary names that allow you to distinguish between tags with the same names that need to be processed differently. Namespaces prevent naming conflicts that might arise in XML documents.

Understanding Open XML Files

Excel 2007, like other applications of the 2007 Office system (such as Word and PowerPoint), saves its data in an XML file format by default. This new file format known as Open XML uses four-letter file extensions (.xlsx, .xlsm, .xltx, .xltm, and .xlam).

The first two letters of the file extension refer to the application, in this case, xl=Excel. The third letter (s/t/a) indicates the specific file type: s=spreadsheet; t=template; and a=add-in. The last letter (x/m) specifies whether the file format supports macros: x=macro-free file; m=macro-enabled file.

In Chapter 21 you learned that the Open XML file is actually a compressed zip file. A zip file contains one or more files that have been compressed to reduce their file size. By changing the Excel 2007 file extension to ".zip," you can take a look inside the zip container using WinZip or another zip-aware tool, or use the built-in compressed folders feature in Windows XP/Vista. If you worked through Chapter 21 you should already be familiar with changing the file extension to .zip and manipulating the contents of the zip archive in order to apply customizations to the Ribbon.

The Open XML file format for the first time ever gives users the ability to directly edit the workbook without the need to open Excel. This means that you can work with the file content without having an Excel application installed on your computer. The same applies to Word and PowerPoint documents that follow the same Open Packaging Conventions (OPC) specification. You can easily insert new data, edit existing data, modify document properties, and add or remove specific XML parts.

This section takes a detailed look inside the compressed file, known as a "package." Figure 29-28 shows the contents of the Practice_Excel19.xlsm workbook file you created in Chapter 19. Figure 29-29 depicts the same file opened with the Windows compressed (zipped) folder feature.

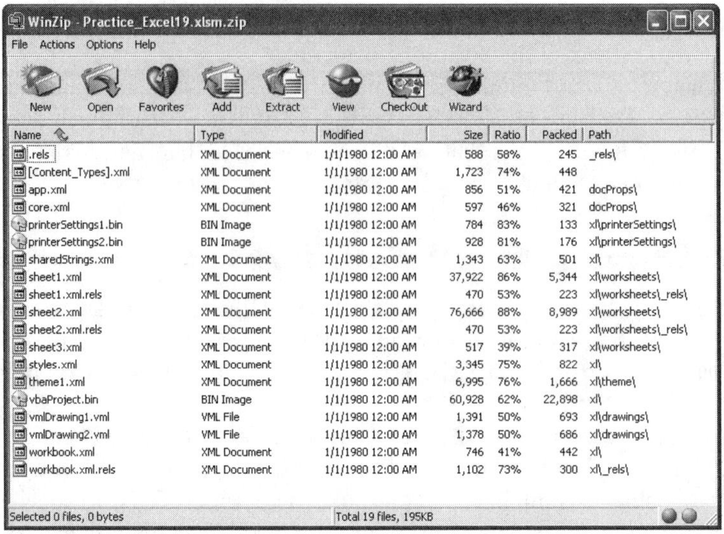

WinZip - Practice_Excel19.xlsm.zip

Name	Type	Modified	Size	Ratio	Packed	Path
.rels	XML Document	1/1/1980 12:00 AM	588	58%	245	_rels\
[Content_Types].xml	XML Document	1/1/1980 12:00 AM	1,723	74%	448	
app.xml	XML Document	1/1/1980 12:00 AM	856	51%	421	docProps\
core.xml	XML Document	1/1/1980 12:00 AM	597	46%	321	docProps\
printerSettings1.bin	BIN Image	1/1/1980 12:00 AM	784	83%	133	xl\printerSettings\
printerSettings2.bin	BIN Image	1/1/1980 12:00 AM	928	81%	176	xl\printerSettings\
sharedStrings.xml	XML Document	1/1/1980 12:00 AM	1,343	63%	501	xl\
sheet1.xml	XML Document	1/1/1980 12:00 AM	37,922	86%	5,344	xl\worksheets\
sheet1.xml.rels	XML Document	1/1/1980 12:00 AM	470	53%	223	xl\worksheets_rels\
sheet2.xml	XML Document	1/1/1980 12:00 AM	76,666	88%	8,989	xl\worksheets\
sheet2.xml.rels	XML Document	1/1/1980 12:00 AM	470	53%	223	xl\worksheets_rels\
sheet3.xml	XML Document	1/1/1980 12:00 AM	517	39%	317	xl\worksheets\
styles.xml	XML Document	1/1/1980 12:00 AM	3,345	75%	822	xl\
theme1.xml	XML Document	1/1/1980 12:00 AM	6,995	76%	1,666	xl\theme\
vbaProject.bin	BIN Image	1/1/1980 12:00 AM	60,928	62%	22,898	xl\
vmlDrawing1.vml	VML File	1/1/1980 12:00 AM	1,391	50%	693	xl\drawings\
vmlDrawing2.vml	VML File	1/1/1980 12:00 AM	1,378	50%	686	xl\drawings\
workbook.xml	XML Document	1/1/1980 12:00 AM	746	41%	442	xl\
workbook.xml.rels	XML Document	1/1/1980 12:00 AM	1,102	73%	300	xl_rels\

Selected 0 files, 0 bytes — Total 19 files, 195KB

Figure 29-28: A sample Excel 2007 workbook is shown here after renaming the file with a .zip extension and opening it with the WinZip utility.

The package file contains a number of documents called "parts" grouped into various folders. Every part has a defined content type that describes whether it's a worksheet, image, sound, or other binary object. Some types of parts are shared across all Office 2007 applications; others are unique to the application. For example, a worksheet part can only be found in an Excel file. While most parts are XML documents, some parts such as images, VBA projects, or embedded OLE objects are stored in their native format as binary files. Every part within a container package is connected to at least one other part using a special part referred to as a relationship. A relationship file is an XML document with a ".rels" extension.

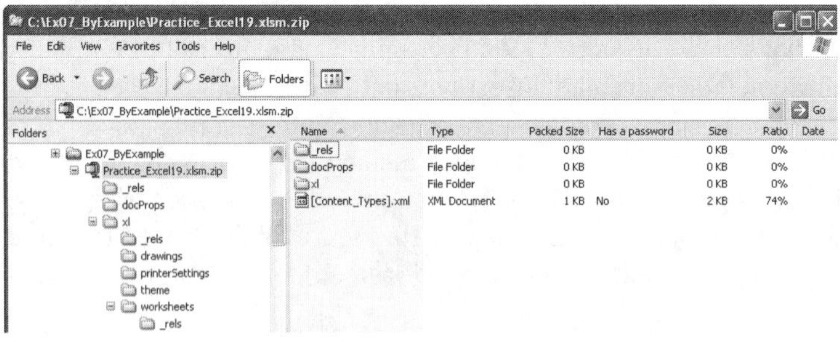

C:\Ex07_ByExample\Practice_Excel19.xlsm.zip

Name	Type	Packed Size	Has a password	Size	Ratio	Date
_rels	File Folder	0 KB		0 KB	0%	
docProps	File Folder	0 KB		0 KB	0%	
xl	File Folder	0 KB		0 KB	0%	
[Content_Types].xml	XML Document	1 KB	No	2 KB	74%	

Figure 29-29: A sample Excel 2007 file opened with compressed folders.

At the root level (see Figure 29-29), you will notice three folders named _rels, docProps, and xl, and an XML file called [Content_Types].xlm.

- The [Content_Types].xlm file — This XML file lists the types of files that are included in the package. The example Excel file package contains the following content types:

```
"application/vnd.openxmlformats-officedocument.spreadsheetml.printerSet-
    tings"
"application/vnd.openxmlformats-officedocument.theme+xml"
"application/vnd.openxmlformats-officedocument.spreadsheetml.styles+xml"
"application/vnd.ms-excel.sheet.macroEnabled.main+xml"
"application/vnd.ms-office.vbaProject"
"application/vnd.openxmlformats-package.relationships+xml"
"application/xml"
"application/vnd.ms-excel.sheet.macroEnabled.main+xml"
"application/vnd.openxmlformats-officedocument.extended-properties+xml"
"application/vnd.openxmlformats-officedocument.spreadsheetml.worksheet+
    xml"
"application/vnd.openxmlformats-officedocument.vmlDrawing"
"application/vnd.openxmlformats-officedocument.spreadsheetml.sharedStrings
    +xml"
"application/vnd.openxmlformats-package.core-properties+xml"
```

- The _rels folder — The parts listed in the Excel package are linked together via relationships. The .rels file in the _rels folder defines the package relationships. You will see here relationships between document properties files, docProps/app.xml and docProps/core.xml, and the xl/workbook.xml file. Parts that are related to other parts contain a _rels subfolder. Within this subfolder you will find a .rels file that describes the relationships. The name of the relationship consists of the filename of the original part and the .rels extension. For example, for the Workbook.xml file in the xl folder there is a relationship file named Workbook.xml.rels in the xl_rels folder.
- The docProps folder — This folder contains two document properties files that were referenced in the .rels file: app.xml and core.xml. These properties files store information that you enter in Excel when you click the Microsoft Office button and choose Prepare | Properties. The core.xml part consists of properties such as the document title, subject, and author. The app.xml part stores application-specific properties such as the name and the version of the application, company name, and others, as shown below:

```
<?xml version="1.0" encoding="UTF-8" standalone="yes" ?>
<Properties xmlns="http://schemas.openxmlformats.org/officeDocument/2006/
    extended-properties"
xmlns:vt="http://schemas.openxmlformats.org/officeDocument/2006/
    docPropsVTypes">
<Application>Microsoft Excel</Application>
<DocSecurity>0</DocSecurity>
<ScaleCrop>false</ScaleCrop>
<HeadingPairs>
<vt:vector size="2" baseType="variant">
<vt:variant>
<vt:lpstr>Worksheets</vt:lpstr>
</vt:variant>
<vt:variant>
<vt:i4>3</vt:i4>
</vt:variant>
</vt:vector>
```

```
</HeadingPairs>
<TitlesOfParts>
<vt:vector size="3" baseType="lpstr">
<vt:lpstr>Sheet1</vt:lpstr>
<vt:lpstr>Sheet2</vt:lpstr>
<vt:lpstr>Sheet3</vt:lpstr>
</vt:vector>
</TitlesOfParts>
<Company/>
<LinksUpToDate>false</LinksUpToDate>
<SharedDoc>false</SharedDoc>
<HyperlinksChanged>false</HyperlinksChanged>
<AppVersion>12.0000</AppVersion>
</Properties>
```

- The xl folder — This is the application folder for the program that was used to create the file, in this case, Excel. This folder contains application-specific document files organized in various subfolders. The root level of the xl folder contains the workbook part, sharedStrings part, vbaProject part, and the styles part (see Figure 29-30). The sharedStrings.xml part stores all of the strings used in the entire workbook. If you change a string in this file, the change will be applied to every occurrence of the string in your workbook.

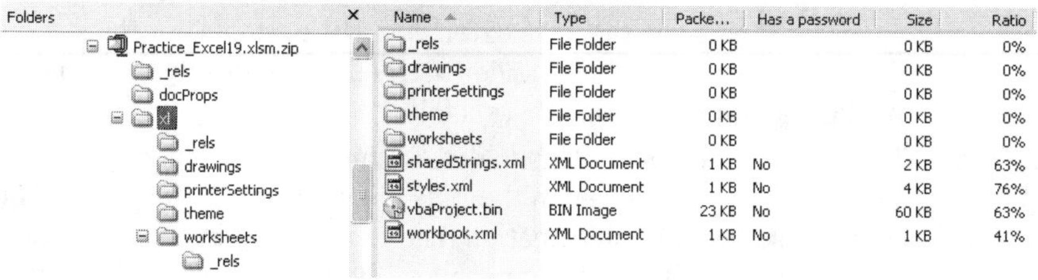

Folders
- Practice_Excel19.xlsm.zip
  - _rels
  - docProps
  - xl
    - _rels
    - drawings
    - printerSettings
    - theme
    - worksheets
      - _rels

Name	Type	Packe...	Has a password	Size	Ratio
_rels	File Folder	0 KB		0 KB	0%
drawings	File Folder	0 KB		0 KB	0%
printerSettings	File Folder	0 KB		0 KB	0%
theme	File Folder	0 KB		0 KB	0%
worksheets	File Folder	0 KB		0 KB	0%
sharedStrings.xml	XML Document	1 KB	No	2 KB	63%
styles.xml	XML Document	1 KB	No	4 KB	76%
vbaProject.bin	BIN Image	23 KB	No	60 KB	63%
workbook.xml	XML Document	1 KB	No	1 KB	41%

Figure 29-30: The contents of the xl folder.

The worksheets folder within the xl folder contains a separate XML part for every worksheet, in this case sheet1.xml, sheet2.xml, and sheet3.xml.

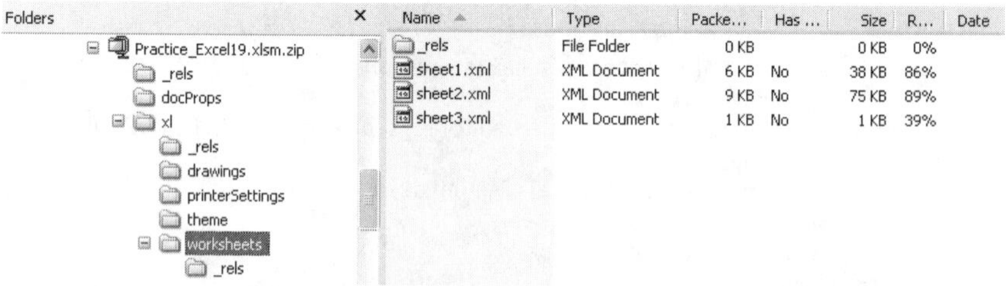

Folders
- Practice_Excel19.xlsm.zip
  - _rels
  - docProps
  - xl
    - _rels
    - drawings
    - printerSettings
    - theme
    - worksheets
      - _rels

Name	Type	Packe...	Has ...	Size	R...	Date
_rels	File Folder	0 KB		0 KB	0%	
sheet1.xml	XML Document	6 KB	No	38 KB	86%	
sheet2.xml	XML Document	9 KB	No	75 KB	89%	
sheet3.xml	XML Document	1 KB	No	1 KB	39%	

Figure 29-31: The contents of the worksheets folder.

Figure 29-32 shows the contents of the sheet1.xml part. Notice that all the sheet data is contained within the <sheetData> element. Each data row has its own <row> element and an index (r attribute). Rows use a span attribute to indicate the number of cells occupied. Other attributes may be used to indicate row style or custom formatting. Cell values are stored in the <c>

element. The r attribute holds the cell address using the A1 reference style notation (e.g., "A2", "B2"); the s attribute indicates which style was used. The numbers used in the style attribute are described in the xl/styles.xml part. The t attribute indicates a data type (String, Number, or Boolean). For example, t="s" denotes that the underlying value is a string, not a number. String values are not stored in cells unless they are the result of a calculation. They are stored in the sharedStrings.xml part. Each unique text value found within a workbook is listed only once in this part. This prevents duplication of information, saves space, and speeds up loading and saving workbooks. If the cell value is textual, then the numeric value inside the <v> element is an index to a particular string in the sharedStrings.xml document.

```
  <?xml version="1.0" encoding="UTF-8" standalone="yes" ?>
- <worksheet xmlns="http://schemas.openxmlformats.org/spreadsheetml/2006/main"
    xmlns:r="http://schemas.openxmlformats.org/officeDocument/2006/relationships">
    <sheetPr codeName="Sheet4" />
    <dimension ref="A1:K9" />
  - <sheetViews>
    - <sheetView workbookViewId="0">
        <selection activeCell="E10" sqref="E10" />
      </sheetView>
    </sheetViews>
    <sheetFormatPr defaultRowHeight="12.75" />
  + <cols>
  - <sheetData>
      <row r="1" spans="1:11" s="2" customFormat="1" />
    - <row r="2" spans="1:11" ht="97.5" customHeight="1" thickBot="1">
      - <c r="A2" s="8" t="s">
          <v>18</v>
        </c>
      - <c r="B2" s="7" t="s">
          <v>17</v>
        </c>
      - <c r="C2" s="7" t="s">
          <v>16</v>
        </c>
      - <c r="D2" s="7" t="s">
          <v>15</v>
        </c>
      - <c r="E2" s="7" t="s">
          <v>14</v>
        </c>
      - <c r="F2" s="7" t="s">
          <v>13</v>
        </c>
      - <c r="G2" s="6" t="s">
          <v>19</v>
        </c>
      - <c r="H2" s="6" t="s">
          <v>12</v>
        </c>
      - <c r="I2" s="6" t="s">
          <v>11</v>
        </c>
      - <c r="J2" s="6" t="s">
          <v>10</v>
        </c>
        <c r="K2" s="5" />
      </row>
    + <row r="3" spans="1:11" ht="13.5" thickTop="1">
    + <row r="4" spans="1:11">
    + <row r="5" spans="1:11">
    + <row r="6" spans="1:11">
    + <row r="7" spans="1:11">
    + <row r="8" spans="1:11">
    + <row r="9" spans="1:11">
    </sheetData>
    <pageMargins left="0.75" right="0.75" top="1" bottom="1" header="0.5" footer="0.5" />
    <pageSetup orientation="portrait" horizontalDpi="300" verticalDpi="300" r:id="rId1" />
    <headerFooter alignWithMargins="0" />
    <legacyDrawing r:id="rId2" />
  </worksheet>
```

Figure 29-32: The contents of the sheet1.xml file in the Practice_Excel29.xlsm workbook.

You can easily replace the sharedStrings file in the package with a file containing strings from another language, thus providing multiple language support for your spreadsheet users.

After this short overview of the internals of the Open XML file format, let's spend some time putting this newfound knowledge to practical use. Now that you know how to navigate the package, you can easily alter, replace, or add parts to the Excel container. The next section will introduce you to working with XML document parts programmatically.

Manipulating Open XML Files with VBA

Earlier in this chapter you learned how to work with XML document nodes using the XML DOM. In this section, you will learn how to use the DOM objects, properties, and functions, and XPath expressions to augment some of the XML parts found in the Excel workbook. Working with the XML document parts requires that you first learn how to programmatically zip and unzip Excel 2007 files.

Hands-On 29-17: Unzipping an Excel 2007 File with VBA

1. Copy the **C:\Ex07_HandsOn\SupportedEquipment.xlsx** workbook to your **Ex07_ByExample** folder.
2. Open a new Microsoft Excel workbook and save it as **C:\Ex07_ByExample\ManipulateXMLParts.xlsm**.
3. Press **Alt+F11** to activate the Visual Basic Editor, and select **VBAProject (ManipulateXMLParts.xlsm)** in the Project Explorer window.
4. Choose **Insert | Module**.
5. Choose **Tools | References**. In the Available References list box, select **Microsoft XML, v6.0** or earlier object library, and click **OK** to exit the References dialog box.
6. In the Code window of VBAProject (ManipulateXMLParts.xlsm), enter the following UnizpExcelFile procedure:

```
Public blnIsFileSelected As Boolean 'Module level variable

Sub UnzipExcelFile()
    Dim objShell As Object
    Dim ZipFile, ZipFolder, SourceFile, objFile
    Dim strStartDir As String

    strStartDir = "C:\Ex07_ByExample"
    'change folder
    If ActiveWorkbook.Path <> strStartDir Then
        ChDir strStartDir
    End If

    ' get Excel 2007 file to unzip
    SourceFile = Application.GetOpenFilename _
        (FileFilter:="Excel Files (*.xlsx; *.xlsm), *.xlsx; *.xlsm", _
```

```
        Title:="Select Excel 2007 file you want to unzip")

    'exit if file was not selected
    If SourceFile = False Then
        blnIsFileSelected = False
        Exit Sub
    End If

    blnIsFileSelected = True
    ZipFile = SourceFile & ".zip"

    'create the zip file
    FileCopy SourceFile, ZipFile

    'Create new folder to store unzipped files
    ZipFolder = "C:\Ex07_ByExample\ZipPackage"
    On Error Resume Next
    MkDir ZipFolder

    'Copy package files to the ZipPackage folder
    Set objShell = CreateObject("Shell.Application")

    For Each objFile In objShell.Namespace(ZipFile).items
        objShell.Namespace(ZipFolder).CopyHere (objFile)
    Next objFile

   'Activate Windows Explorer
    Shell "Explorer.exe /e," & ZipFolder, vbNormalFocus

    'remove the zip file and release resources
    Kill ZipFile
    Set objShell = Nothing
End Sub
```

The above example procedure asks the user for an Excel file to unzip using the GetOpenFilename method of the Application object. After the file is selected, the FileCopy statement copies this file to another file with a .zip extension. This way, you can work with the temporary zip file without changing the original file. Next, the procedure uses the MkDir statement to create a destination folder for the zip archive. A Shell.Application object is then created and used for accessing the Windows file system. Its CopyHere method copies files to the zip folder returned by the Namespace method. Once all the files have been copied, the procedure activates the Windows Explorer. The "/e" parameter of the Shell function is used to display the files in the list view. The procedure ends by deleting the temporary zip file using the VBA Kill statement.

7. Run the UnzipExcelFile procedure. When prompted to select the file to unzip, choose the **SupportedEquipment.xlsx** workbook from your C:\Ex07_ByExample folder. The Explorer window will pop up automatically when the unzip process is complete.

After making changes to the XML parts (as shown in subsequent Hands-On exercises), you will need to zip the files back into the Excel container before you can open the modified file in Excel. The next Hands-On procedure demonstrates how you can perform the zip operation with VBA.

Hands-On 29-18: Zipping Files to Create an Excel 2007 Package Container

1. In the same module where you entered the UnzipExcelFile procedure in the previous Hands-On exercise, enter the following two procedures: CreateEmptyZipFile and ZipToExcel:

```
Sub CreateEmptyZipFile(strFileName As String)
    Dim strHeader As String
    Dim fso As Object

    strHeader = Chr$(80) & Chr$(75) & Chr$(5) & Chr$(6) & String(18, 0)

    ' delete the file if it already exists
    If Len(Dir(strFileName)) > 0 Then
        Kill strFileName
    End If

    ' add a required header
    Set fso = CreateObject("Scripting.FileSystemObject")
    fso.CreateTextFile(strFileName).Write strHeader

End Sub
```

The above procedure uses the CreateTextFile method of the Scripting.FileSystemObject to create an empty zip container. The Write method is used to add a required header to the file so Windows can recognize the file as a zip archive. The next procedure (ZipToExcel) will fill the file with the files found in the specified folder.

```
Sub ZipToExcel()
    Dim objShell As Object
    Dim ZipFile, ZipFolder, SourceFile, objFile
    Dim strStartDir As String
    Dim ExcelFile As String
    Dim mFlag As Boolean

    ZipFolder = "C:\Ex07_ByExample\ZipPackage"
    ZipFile = "C:\Ex07_ByExample\PackageModified.zip"
    mFlag = False

    'check if folder is empty
    If Len(Dir(ZipFolder & "\*.*")) < 1 Then
        MsgBox "There are no files to zip."
        Exit Sub
    End If

    ' check if a VBA project exists
    If Len(Dir(ZipFolder & "\xl\vbaProject.bin")) > 0 Then
        mFlag = True
    End If

    'Create an empty zip file
```

```
    CreateEmptyZipFile (ZipFile)

    'Copy files from ZipFolder to the ZipFile
    On Error Resume Next
    Set objShell = CreateObject("Shell.Application")

    For Each objFile In objShell.Namespace(ZipFolder).items
        objShell.Namespace(ZipFile).CopyHere (objFile)
        Application.Wait (Now + TimeValue("0:00:10"))
    Next objFile

    'Create Excel file name
    If mFlag Then
        ExcelFile = Replace(ZipFile, ".zip", ".xlsm")
    Else
        ExcelFile = Replace(ZipFile, ".zip", ".xlsx")
    End If

    'Rename the ZipFile
    Name ZipFile As ExcelFile

    Set objShell = Nothing
    Set objFile = Nothing

    MsgBox "Zipping files completed."
End Sub
```

The above procedure starts by designating ZipPackage as the zip folder name and PackageModified.zip as the target zip file. Before we go ahead with the copy operation, we perform two checks. First, we want to exit the procedure if there are no files in the zip folder. Second, we check for the existence of the vbaProject.bin file in the xl folder of the zip folder. Based on this test we will assign a macro-free or macro-enabled Excel 2007 format to the destination file later in the procedure when we rename the zip archive. If there are files in the zip folder, we call the CreateEmptyZipFile procedure to create an empty zip container. Next, we use the CopyHere method of the Shell.Application object (discussed in Hands-On 29-17) to copy files into the zip archive. Copying and compressing files can take some time, so we use the Application.Wait statement to wait 10 seconds between each copy operation. If the procedure ends before the files are copied, you may end up with a corrupt file when you try to open it in Excel. When the files have been copied into a zip container, we rename the file with the .xlsx or .xlsm extension.

2. Run the ZipToExcel procedure.

   When the procedure has executed, you should see the PackageModified.xlsx workbook file in your Ex07_ByExample folder. Because we have not yet made any changes to the XML parts contained in the SupportedEquipment.xlsx file that was unzipped in Hands-On 29-17, the PackageModified.xlsx file should contain the same content as this file.

3. Open **PackageModified.xlsx** in Microsoft Excel to ensure that the file is not corrupted. If you get a message saying the file is corrupted, you will need to pause the ZipToExcel procedure for a couple of seconds longer to allow each file to be completely compressed and saved.
4. If open, close PackageModified.xlsx.
5. In Windows Explorer, delete PackageModified.xlsx.

In the next three Hands-On examples, we will utilize both the zip and unzip procedures from Hands-On 29-17 and 29-18 to modify some XML parts in the Excel zip archive. The procedure in Hands-On 29-19 demonstrates how you can retrieve to a worksheet the unique text values that are stored in the sharedStrings.xml part (Figure 29-33).

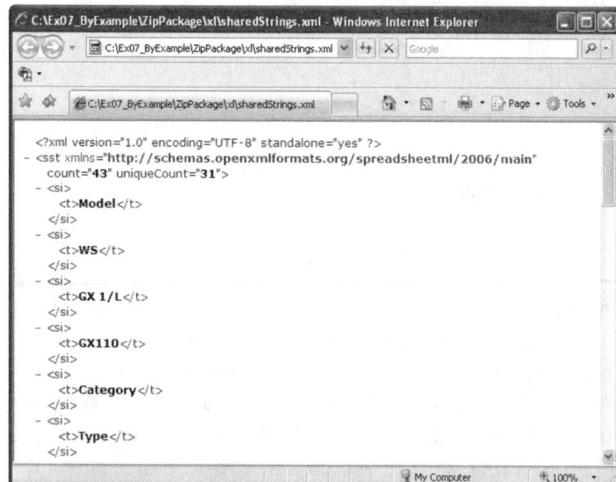

Figure 29-33: Partial content of the sharedStrings.xml part in the SupportedEquipment.xlsx workbook.

Hands-On 29-19: Retrieving Unique Text Values from the sharedStrings XML File

1. Insert a new module in VBAProject (ManipulateXMLParts.xlsm), and in the Code window, enter the following ListUniqueValues procedure:

```
Sub ListUniqueValues()
    Dim xmlDoc As DOMDocument
    Dim myNodeList As IXMLDOMNodeList
    Dim i As Integer
    Dim iLen As Integer

    Set xmlDoc = New DOMDocument
    xmlDoc.async = False
    xmlDoc.Load ("C:\Ex07_ByExample\ZipPackage\xl\sharedStrings.xml")
    Set myNodeList = xmlDoc.SelectNodes("//t")
    iLen = myNodeList.Length

    Worksheets(1).Activate
    For i = 0 To iLen - 1
```

```
        Range("A" & i + 1).Formula = myNodeList(i).Text
    Next
    Columns("A").AutoFit

    Set myNodeList = Nothing
    Set xmlDoc = Nothing
End Sub
```

The above procedure uses the Load method of the DOMDocument object to open the sharedStrings.xml file. For this procedure to run, you must set a reference to the Microsoft XML object library (choose Tools | References in the Visual Basic Editor screen). Next, the procedure retrieves all the nodes that match the specified XPath query and determines the number of entries found:

```
Set myNodeList = xmlDoc.SelectNodes("//t")
iLen = myNodeList.Length
```

With this information, we can start writing the myLoadList content to the worksheet.

2. Ensure that the Ex07_ByExample folder contains the folder named ZipFolder with XML parts. If the folder is missing, run the procedure in Hands-On 29-17.
3. Run the ListUniqueValues procedure.

   The result of the procedure is the list of unique text values that were originally entered in the SupportedEquipment.xlsx workbook and stored in the sharedStrings.xml part (see Figure 29-34).

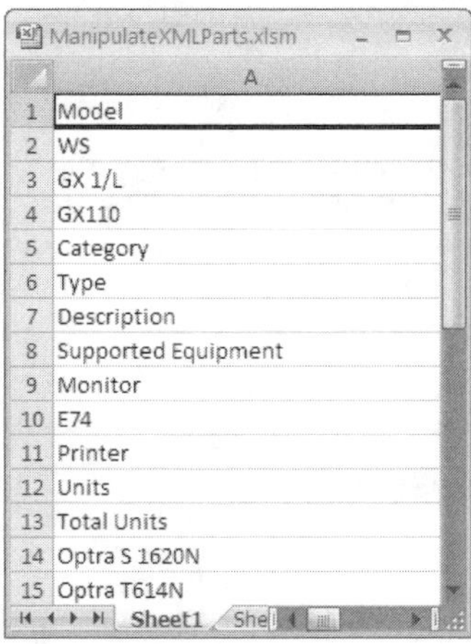

Figure 29-34: Partial content of the sharedStrings.xml part for the SupportedEquipment.xlsx workbook.

Now that you know how to read text values stored in the sharedStrings.xml part, how about editing this file. Let's say we'd like to replace the worksheet's text entry "Monitor" with "Flat Panel Monitor" without opening the Excel application. The procedure in the next Hands-On exercise does this.

Hands-On 29-20: Modifying the sharedString XML File

1. Insert a new module in VBAProject (ManipulateXMLParts.xlsm), and in the Code window, enter the following Text_Replace procedure:

```
Sub Text_Replace()
    Dim xmlDoc As DOMDocument
    Dim myNode As IXMLDOMNode
    Dim srchStr As String
    Dim newStr As String
    Dim strFileToEdit As String

    strFileToEdit = "C:\Ex07_ByExample\ZipPackage\xl\sharedStrings.xml"

    Call UnzipExcelFile
    If blnIsFileSelected = False Then Exit Sub

    Set xmlDoc = New DOMDocument
    xmlDoc.async = False
    xmlDoc.Load (strFileToEdit)

    srchStr = InputBox("Please enter the string to find:", "Search for
            String")

    If srchStr <> "" Then
        ' find the text that needs to be replaced
        Set myNode = xmlDoc.SelectSingleNode("//t[text()='" + _
            srchStr + "']")
        If myNode Is Nothing Then Exit Sub
    Else
        Exit Sub
    End If

    ' replace text
    newStr = InputBox("Please enter the replacement string for " _
            & srchStr, "Replace with String")
    If newStr <> "" Then
       myNode.Text = newStr
       xmlDoc.Save strFileToEdit
    Else
        Exit Sub
    End If

    ' zip the files in the package
    Call ZipToExcel

    Set xmlDoc = Nothing
    Set myNode = Nothing

End Sub
```

In the above procedure we prompt the user to enter the string to find using the InputBox function. If text was specified, then we use the following statement to find the node with the specified text entry:

```
Set myNode = xmlDoc.SelectSingleNode("//t[text()='" + srchStr + "']")
```

In the above statement we use the XPath text() function to retrieve the text value of a node. The XPath expression tells the XML parser to look at the si element node and select the t node (see Figure 29-33 earlier) where the text content is equal to the value of the srchStr variable. Instead of using the XPath text() function, you can examine the t node using the dot operator, like this:

```
Set myNode = xmlDoc.SelectSingleNode("//t[.='" + srchStr + "']")
```

If the node with the text entry was not found, we exit the procedure. If the node was found, we prompt the user for the replacement text. When we get the new string, we write it to the node and save the file:

```
myNode.Text = newStr
xmlDoc.Save strFileToEdit
```

Next, we need to zip the files back into an Excel container, so we call the ZipToExcel procedure that we created earlier.

2. Run the Text_Replace procedure. When prompted for the string to find, enter **Monitor** and click **OK**. When prompted for the new text, enter **Flat Panel Monitor** and click **OK**.
3. When the procedure completes, open the **PackageModified.xlsx** file in Excel. Each cell entry that previously had "Monitor" as the underlying text value should now show "Flat Panel Monitor."

Note: To check the current unique values in the sharedStrings.xml part, you can rerun the ListUniqueValues procedure from Hands-On 29-19.

4. Close the PackageModified.xlsx workbook and then delete this workbook using Windows Explorer.

Sometimes you may be interested in retrieving all text values from a particular worksheet and placing them in exact positions in a new worksheet. The procedure in Hands-On 29-21 recreates the worksheet's text by reading the content of the sharedStrings.xml and sheet1.xml parts.

Hands-On 29-21: Retrieving All Text Values from the XML Part to a Worksheet

1. Insert a new module in VBAProject (ManipulateXMLParts.xlsm), and in the Code window, enter the following RetrieveAllTextValues procedure:

```
Sub RetrieveAllTextValues()
    Dim xmlDoc As DOMDocument
    Dim myNodeList1 As IXMLDOMNodeList
    Dim myNodeList2 As IXMLDOMNodeList
    Dim myNodeList3 As IXMLDOMNodeList
    Dim strArray() As String
    Dim i As Integer
    Dim iLen As Integer
```

```
    Set xmlDoc = New DOMDocument
    xmlDoc.async = False

    xmlDoc.Load ("C:\Ex07_ByExample\ZipPackage\xl\sharedStrings.xml")
    Set myNodeList1 = xmlDoc.SelectNodes("//t")

    iLen = myNodeList1.Length
    ReDim strArray(iLen)

    For i = 0 To iLen - 1
        strArray(i) = myNodeList1(i).Text
    Next

    xmlDoc.async = False
    xmlDoc.Load ("C:\Ex07_ByExample\ZipPackage\xl\worksheets\sheet1.xml")
    Set myNodeList2 = xmlDoc.SelectNodes("//sheetData/row/c[@t='s']/@r")
    Set myNodeList3 = xmlDoc.SelectNodes("//sheetData/row/c[@t='s']/v")

    Worksheets(2).Activate
    i = 0

    For i = 0 To myNodeList2.Length - 1
        With Range(myNodeList2(i).Text)
          .Value = strArray(myNodeList3(i).Text)
        End With
    Next

    Range("A1").CurrentRegion.Select
    Selection.EntireColumn.AutoFit

    Set myNodeList1 = Nothing
    Set myNodeList2 = Nothing
    Set myNodeList3 = Nothing
    Set xmlDoc = Nothing
End Sub
```

The above procedure begins by loading the sharedStrings.xml part into the DOMDocument object and then retrieving its unique text values into an array variable named strArray. Notice how the Length property of the nodeList object is used to obtain the number of unique values and to redimension the array. Next, the procedure loads the sheet1.xml part into the DOMDocument object. In order to retrieve the values from the worksheet, we need to look for nodes whose cell element has a "t" attribute set to "s," indicating that this is a text value. We also need to find the "r" attribute value for each cell with the text value. We do this using the following statement with the XPath expression:

```
Set myNodeList2 = xmlDoc.SelectNodes("//sheetData/row/c[@t='s']/@r")
```

The attribute name is denoted by the "@" character. The above statement says that we want to find the value of the "r" attribute for cell elements that have the "t" attribute set to "s" for each row element found in the sheetData element. We also want to obtain values from the <v> elements for cells holding text values:

```
Set myNodeList3 = xmlDoc.SelectNodes("//sheetData/row/c[@t='s']/v")
```

The <v> elements for cells with the "t" attribute set to "s" point to indexes in the sharedStrings.xml part.

Next, the procedure uses the For...Next loop to write all found text values to appropriate cells in a worksheet. Text is entered in the same cell range as in the original worksheet.

2. Run the RetrieveAllTextValues procedure.

   When the procedure completes, Sheet2 in the current workbook should contain the entries shown in Figure 29-35.

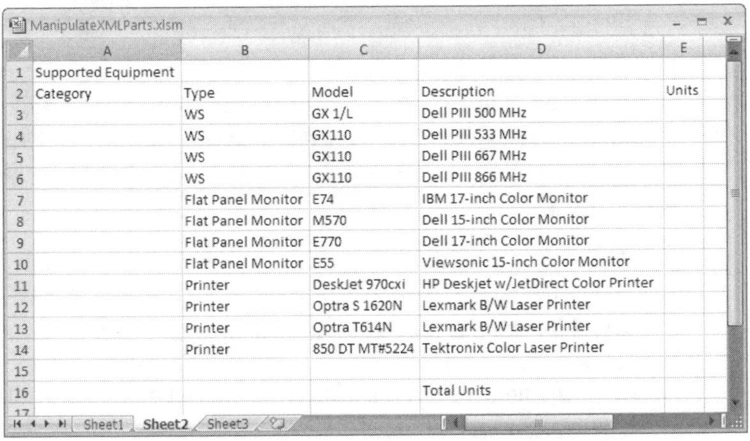

ManipulateXMLParts.xlsm

	A	B	C	D	E
1	Supported Equipment				
2	Category	Type	Model	Description	Units
3		WS	GX 1/L	Dell PIII 500 MHz	
4		WS	GX110	Dell PIII 533 MHz	
5		WS	GX110	Dell PIII 667 MHz	
6		WS	GX110	Dell PIII 866 MHz	
7		Flat Panel Monitor	E74	IBM 17-inch Color Monitor	
8		Flat Panel Monitor	M570	Dell 15-inch Color Monitor	
9		Flat Panel Monitor	E770	Dell 17-inch Color Monitor	
10		Flat Panel Monitor	E55	Viewsonic 15-inch Color Monitor	
11		Printer	DeskJet 970cxi	HP Deskjet w/JetDirect Color Printer	
12		Printer	Optra S 1620N	Lexmark B/W Laser Printer	
13		Printer	Optra T614N	Lexmark B/W Laser Printer	
14		Printer	850 DT MT#5224	Tektronix Color Laser Printer	
15					
16				Total Units	

Sheet1 Sheet2 Sheet3

Figure 29-35: Text data retrieved directly from two XML parts in an Excel zip container.

The next Hands-On procedure demonstrates how to change the size of the left margin and remove the entire node from the sheet1.xml part.

Hands-On 29-22: Changing and Removing Elements in an XML Part

1. Insert a new module in VBAProject (ManipulateXMLParts.xlsm), and in the Code window, enter the following ChangeLeftMargin_RemovePageSetup procedure:

```
Sub ChangeLeftMargin_RemovePageSetup()
   Dim xmlDoc As DOMDocument
   Dim myNode As IXMLDOMNode

   Set xmlDoc = New DOMDocument
   xmlDoc.async = False
   xmlDoc.Load ("C:\Ex07_ByExample\ZipPackage\xl\worksheets\sheet1.xml")
   Set myNode = xmlDoc.SelectSingleNode("/worksheet/pageMargins/@left")

   Debug.Print "previous left margin = " & myNode.Text
   myNode.Text = "0.50"
   Set myNode = xmlDoc.SelectSingleNode("//pageSetup")
   On Error Resume Next
   myNode.ParentNode.RemoveChild myNode
   xmlDoc.Save ("C:\Ex07_ByExample\ZipPackage\xl\worksheets\sheet1.xml")
```

```
    Set myNode = Nothing
    Set xmlDoc = Nothing
End Sub
```

In the above procedure we begin by loading the sheet1.xml part into the DOMDocument object. To change the left margin, we need to read the value of the left attribute of the <pageMargins> element, which is a child of the <worksheet> element. We can achieve this using the following statement:

```
Set myNode = xmlDoc.SelectSingleNode("/worksheet/pageMargins/@left")
```

Once we have located the node with the required attribute, we set the node's text to the new value:

```
myNode.Text = "0.50"
```

The remaining part of the procedure locates the <pageSetup> element inside the sheet1.xml part and uses the RemoveChild method to remove this node:

```
Set myNode = xmlDoc.SelectSingleNode("//pageSetup")
On Error Resume Next
myNode.ParentNode.RemoveChild myNode
```

In case the node is not found (for example, you may have mistyped the element name in the XPath expression), On Error Resume Next will skip over the node removal statement. The last statement will save the changes in the sheet1.xml part.

Note: You may want to add to this procedure statements that call the zipping and unzipping procedures that you created in this chapter.

2. Run the ChangeLeftMargin_RemovePageSetup procedure.

Now that you know how to write procedures that manipulate XML parts, you probably will come up with many uses for the newfound knowledge. You will definitely need to pick up a good book on writing XPath expressions or use free online resources to get a better understanding of this subject matter.

Chapter Summary

This chapter has only scratched the surface of what's possible with XML. You learned here what XML is and how it is structured. While HTML consists of markup tags that define how the information should be formatted for display in a web browser, XML allows you to invent your own tags in order to define and describe data stored in a wide range of documents. XML supplies you with numerous ways to accomplish a specific task. Because XML is stored in plain text files, it can be read by many types of applications, independent of the operating system or hardware.

This chapter has shown you how to perform many tasks using XML and Excel together. You learned how to view and edit XML documents and open them in Excel. You also used XML maps and XML tables and learned how to program these features with VBA. You were introduced to working with the Document Object Model in your VBA procedures and wrote procedures that saved XML data in an ADO recordset. Finally, this chapter has shown you how you can read and manipulate Open XML files with VBA.

It's understandable that the methods and techniques that you've studied here will need time to sink in. XML is not like VBA. It is not very independent, needing many supporting technologies to assist it in its work. So don't give up if you don't understand something right away. Learning XML requires learning many other new concepts (like XSLT, XPath, schemas, etc.) at the same time. Take XML step by step by experimenting with it. The time that you invest in studying this new technology will not be in vain. XML is here to stay. Here are four main reasons why you should really consider XML:

- XML separates content from presentation. This means that if you are planning to design web pages, you no longer need to make changes to your HTML files when the data changes. Because the data is kept in separate files, it's easy to make modifications.
- XML is perfect for sharing and exchanging data. This means that you no longer have to worry if your data needs to be processed by a system that's not compatible with yours. Because all systems can work with text files (and XML documents are simply text files), you can share and exchange your data painlessly.
- XML can be used as a database. This means that you no longer need a separate database application.
- XML is now the default file format for Excel.

In the next chapter, you learn how to use and program a special feature known as SmartTags.

Chapter 30

Using and Programming Smart Tags

Checking Smart Tag Options in an Excel Workbook ■ Creating Your First Simple Smart Tag ■ Storing Smart Tag List Definition Files ■ Using Custom Smart Tags ■ Information Lookups via ASP Pages ■ Dynamic Recognition of Smart Tag Terms ■ Manipulating Smart Tags with VBA ■ SmartTag Object ■ SmartTagAction Object ■ SmartTagOptions Object ■ SmartTagRecognizer Object ■ **Chapter Summary**

When you enter certain text into a Microsoft Excel spreadsheet cell, you may notice a small purple triangle that appears in the lower-right corner of that cell. This feature is a result of a technology called *smart tags*, which was introduced in Office XP (2002). When you move your mouse pointer over text that has been tagged, you will see a button identified by a circle with a lowercase "i" inside it. When clicked, this smart tag button displays a list of available actions that are relevant to the marked text (Figure 30-1).

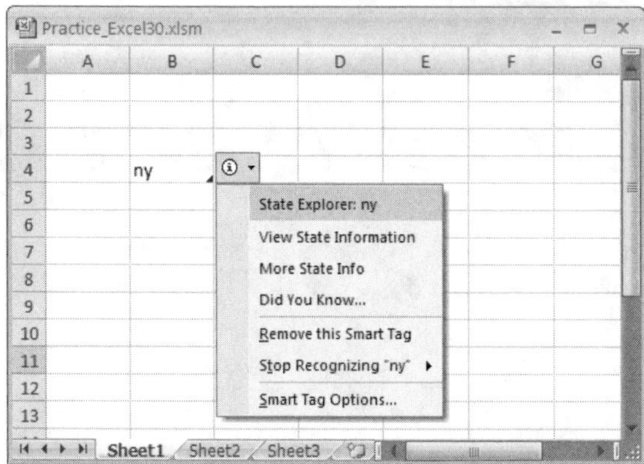

Figure 30-1: A custom smart tag implemented in the Microsoft Excel 2007 worksheet.

The purpose of smart tags is to recognize frequently accessed data, such as stock symbols, zip codes, customer names, part numbers, dates, and so on, and make it easy for users to perform actions on those pieces of data regardless of what application they are currently using. For example, a smart tag could check warranty information on a specific part number entered in a spreadsheet or check prices for specific products. Or it could retrieve flight information when an airline and flight number are recognized. With the implementation of smart tag technology, your spreadsheet applications can become more intelligent and user friendly. Users will no longer need to manually launch other applications, as smart tags can return data from any data source or open a browser and navigate to a web site — all automatically. In summary, smart tags allow you to eliminate extra steps that you would normally have to take to perform a certain action.

At this point, you are probably anxious to get started. So, how can you create your own smart tags? There are two ways to develop smart tags: with XML or ActiveX DLLs. After studying XML in Chapter 29, you already have the necessary skills to develop some simple smart tags. With XML, you can define a set of terms that smart tags will recognize and create a list of actions to display whenever a term from the list is encountered in a worksheet or another Microsoft Office document. If you require more dynamic and powerful smart tags, you must develop ActiveX DLLs (dynamic link libraries) using development environment tools provided within Microsoft Visual Basic 6.0, Microsoft Visual Basic .NET, or Microsoft Visual C++ . Smart tags are currently available for Microsoft Excel 2007, Microsoft Word 2007, Microsoft

Outlook 2007, Microsoft Access 2007, Microsoft PowerPoint 2007, and Internet Explorer.

This chapter expands your knowledge of XML by showing you how to get started creating smart tag lists. If you are interested in learning more about developing your own smart tags (using either the XML or DLL approach), you can download a free Smart Tag Software Development Kit (Smart Tag SDK) from the Microsoft web site.

Checking Smart Tag Options in an Excel Workbook

Let's start by checking whether your workbook is set to recognize smart tags.

Hands-On 30-1: Turning On Smart Tags

1. Start Microsoft Excel, click the **Microsoft Office** button, and then click **Excel Options**.
2. Click the **Proofing** category, and then click **AutoCorrect Options**.
3. In the AutoCorrect dialog box, click the **Smart Tags** tab.

Figure 30-2: Configuring smart tags.

Both built-in and custom smart tags are listed as groups in the Recognizers section. Microsoft Excel 2007 comes with the Financial Symbol smart tag that allows you to check the latest stock prices. So if you enter a financial symbol, such as "MSFT," in a spreadsheet cell and the smart tag lists are selected as shown in Figure 30-2, you will be presented with a list of actions allowing you to insert a refreshable stock price, obtain a stock quote on MSN MoneyCentral, look at the company report on MSN MoneyCentral, or read recent news on MSN MoneyCentral. The Smart Tags tab allows you to turn off the display of smart tags, label data with smart tags, configure how you want to display a smart tag on a per-workbook basis, save the smart tags with the workbook, and search for more smart tags on the web. You will learn how to create and use a custom smart tag in the next section.

4. Make sure that the **Label data with smart tags** check box is selected as shown in Figure 30-2.
5. Click **OK** to exit the AutoCorrect dialog box, and then click **OK** to exit Excel Options.

Creating Your First Simple Smart Tag

Smart tags are based on *actions* and *recognizers*. Recognizers check whether the term entered by the user belongs to the list of stored terms. When the user has entered a term that has been recognized, the action associated with the term is executed. Each term can have one or more actions associated with it. Actions are also called *verbs*. Your first tag will recognize certain state abbreviations as smart-tag actionable. For example, when you enter "ny," "ca," or another state abbreviation included in your list of terms in a spreadsheet cell, you will be presented with smart tag actions as shown in Figure 30-1 earlier in this chapter. We will call this smart tag State Explorer. By default, smart tags are case-sensitive; therefore, if you enter state names in uppercase, such as NY or CA, or type state abbreviations that are not included in your smart tag list of terms (see the State.xml file in Figure 30-3), they will not be recognized by the smart tag.

Now let's proceed to write some XML code to define the list of terms and the actions for our State Explorer smart tag.

Hands-On 30-2: Creating a Custom Smart Tag

1. Open Notepad.
2. Type the XML document as shown in Figure 30-3. When you are done, save the file as **C:\Ex07_ByExample\State.xml** anywhere on your hard drive. Later on, you will move this file to the appropriate location on your disk to put your smart tags to work.

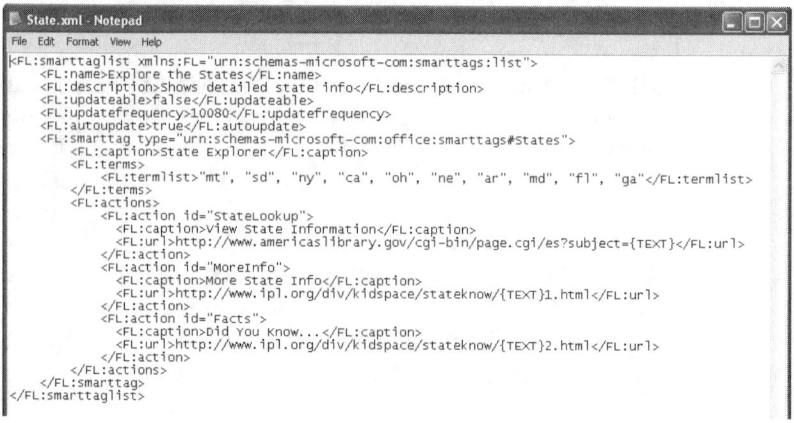

State.xml - Notepad

File Edit Format View Help

```
<FL:smarttaglist xmlns:FL="urn:schemas-microsoft-com:smarttags:list">
    <FL:name>Explore the States</FL:name>
    <FL:description>Shows detailed state info</FL:description>
    <FL:updateable>false</FL:updateable>
    <FL:updatefrequency>10080</FL:updatefrequency>
    <FL:autoupdate>true</FL:autoupdate>
    <FL:smarttag type="urn:schemas-microsoft-com:office:smarttags#States">
        <FL:caption>State Explorer</FL:caption>
        <FL:terms>
            <FL:termlist>"mt", "sd", "ny", "ca", "oh", "ne", "ar", "md", "fl", "ga"</FL:termlist>
        </FL:terms>
        <FL:actions>
            <FL:action id="StateLookup">
              <FL:caption>View State Information</FL:caption>
              <FL:url>http://www.americaslibrary.gov/cgi-bin/page.cgi/es?subject={TEXT}</FL:url>
            </FL:action>
            <FL:action id="MoreInfo">
              <FL:caption>More State Info</FL:caption>
              <FL:url>http://www.ipl.org/div/kidspace/stateknow/{TEXT}1.html</FL:url>
            </FL:action>
            <FL:action id="Facts">
              <FL:caption>Did You Know...</FL:caption>
              <FL:url>http://www.ipl.org/div/kidspace/stateknow/{TEXT}2.html</FL:url>
            </FL:action>
        </FL:actions>
    </FL:smarttag>
</FL:smarttaglist>
```

Figure 30-3: Custom smart tag XML document.

The XML code that you have just entered describes your smart tag using a specific syntax defined by Microsoft. Recall from Chapter 29 that an XML document begins by specifying a root element and declaring a namespace. The namespace is stated in the form of the Uniform Resource Identifier (URI) to uniquely identify a group of XML tags belonging to a logical category. For smart tags, the "urn:schemas-microsoft-com:smarttags:list" URI is used. Notice that this name is preceded by the alias FL — a short name for this namespace. The root element is named smarttaglist. This element is contained within the FL namespace. Therefore, each smart tag list that you develop using XML should begin with:

```
<FL:smarttaglist xmlns:FL="urn:schemas-microsoft-com:smarttags:list">
```

and end with a closing tag:

```
</FL:smarttaglist>
```

Once you've declared a smart tag, you need to specify certain properties, such as a user-friendly name for the smart tag recognizer:

```
<FL:name>Explore the States</FL:name>
```

The name element is required. The optional description element is a longer string describing the smart tag:

```
<FL:description>Shows detailed state info</FL:description>
```

The optional elements, such as updateable, updatefrequency, and autoupdate, as well as lastcheckpoint, lastupdate, and updateurl (not specified here), tell if the smart tag list can be updated, and if so, how often the update should occur, when the last update occurred, and which URL should be checked for updates to the smart tag list. The default value of updatefrequency is 10,080 minutes (seven days). The State Explorer smart tag uses some of these elements for demonstration only. Our term list will not be updatable as coded here. To recognize more states, you will have to manually add new state abbreviations to the term list, save the modified XML file, and relaunch Excel before your changes can take effect. To find out how you can replace one smart tag list with another on a scheduled basis, check this topic in the Smart Tag SDK.

A smart tag type is defined by a unique namespace in the form of a URI and a tag name, as in the following line of code:

```
<FL:smarttag type="urn:schemas-microsoft-com:office:smarttags#States">
```

The smart tag element is absolutely required. In the above line, "urn:schemas-microsoft-com:office:smarttags" is the name of the namespace and "States" is the tag name. The tag name is always preceded by the # symbol. The tag name can be any unique string.

After defining the smart tag type, you need to define the caption and terms for the tag type. For example:

```
<FL:caption>State Explorer</FL:caption>
<FL:terms>
   <FL:termlist>"mt", "sd", "ny", "ca", "oh", "ne", "ar", "md", "fl",
```

```
        "ga"</FL:termlist>
</FL:terms>
```

The caption is what will appear at the top of the Smart Tag Actions menu when the user clicks the smart tag button. The terms element can be either a termlist or a termfile. A *termlist* is a comma-delimited list of terms. Double quotes denote that the listed terms are case-sensitive. The specified state abbreviations will be recognized only when typed in lowercase. In this particular example, we must use the lowercase letters as this is required by the web pages that our custom smart tag is associated with.

A *termfile* is a special binary file (.bin) containing your terms. Microsoft offers two utilities (MakeTrie and TestTrie) that can be used to prepare such a file. You may download these advanced tools from the Microsoft web site. Once you have defined the terms, you need to specify the actions that will show up when the user clicks on the smart tag button. In this example, we have defined three actions, as shown below:

```
<FL:actions>
   <FL:action id="StateLookup">
      <FL:caption>View State Information</FL:caption>
      <FL:url>http://www.americaslibrary.gov/cgi-bin/page.cgi/
          es?subject={TEXT} </FL:url>
   </FL:action>
   <FL:action id="MoreInfo">
      <FL:caption>More State Info</FL:caption>
      <FL:url>http://www.ipl.org/div/kidspace/stateknow/
          {TEXT}1.html</FL:url>
   </FL:action>
   <FL:action id="Facts">
      <FL:caption>Did You Know...</FL:caption>
      <FL:url>http://www.ipl.org/div/kidspace/stateknow/
          {TEXT}2.html</FL:url>
   </FL:action>
</FL:actions>
```

Notice that each action has an action ID, a caption, and the URL that should be activated when the user selects a smart tag menu item. The first action, View State Information, will open the browser, navigate to the americaslibrary.gov web site, and invoke the CGI application named page.cgi located in the cgi-bin folder. Once there, it will run the script named es, passing to it the name of the term as the subject argument. Note that {TEXT} will be substituted with the term that caused the smart tag to be invoked. The other two actions, MoreInfo and Facts, will navigate to other web addresses and run appropriate HTML files. Notice that the name of the HTML file includes the name of the term. Before you define your smart tag actions, you need to investigate which arguments are required to get the information you need from a specific web site.

3. Close Notepad.

Storing Smart Tag List Definition Files

Before you or your users can take advantage of the State Explorer tag you've just defined, you must save the XML smart tag list definition code in the proper location on your computer.

Hands-On 30-3: Placing a Smart Tag List in a Specific Directory

1. Move the State.xml file that you prepared in the previous section into the \Program Files\Common Files\Microsoft Shared\Smart Tag\Lists\ folder.

   Smart tag lists placed in the above directory will be available to all users.

Note: If the smart tag has been designed for a specific user, you should place it in the following folder:

`\Documents and Settings\username\Application Data\Microsoft\Smart Tag Lists`

Placing the smart tag list in the above directory will ensure that the list roams with the user. Smart tag lists created with XML use the MOFL.DLL file included with Microsoft Office XP. This file is installed in the C:\Program Files\Common Files\Microsoft Shared\Smart tag folder.

Using Custom Smart Tags

Before you distribute your smart tag solutions to other users, be sure to test the solution on your computer to ensure that it performs as desired. Let's see how the State Explorer smart tag is recognized in an Excel spreadsheet.

Hands-On 30-4: Using Custom Smart Tags

1. Ensure that the smart tag definition file State.xml is currently located in the **\Program Files\Common Files\Microsoft Shared\Smart Tag\Lists**\ folder on your computer.
2. Restart Microsoft Office Excel.
3. Open a new workbook and save it as **C:\Ex07_ByExample\Practice_Excel30.xlsm.**

Note: This workbook will later on contain VBA code; therefore you need to save it in the macro-enabled format.

4. Click in any cell and type one of the terms that you defined in the State.xml file. For example, type **ny** in cell B4 as shown in Figure 30-1 in the beginning of this chapter. Recall that the State Explorer smart tag will only recognize state abbreviations written in lowercase letters.

When you press **Enter**, Excel displays a small purple triangle in the lower-right corner of cell B4 and displays a small button (a circle with a lowercase "i").

5. Move the mouse pointer over cell B4 and click the smart tag button.
6. Excel displays a list of smart tag actions as shown earlier in Figure 30-1.

   The action items View State Information, More State Info, and Did You Know… come from the State.xml file and activate a specific web page when clicked (see Figure 30-4).

Figure 30-4: This web site was activated by a smart tag.

7. Test all three actions in the State Explorer smart tag.

   If you find that your smart tag does not perform as planned, you should quit Excel and edit your XML file. Resave the XML file with the newly made changes and relaunch Excel.

Note: You must restart Excel each time you make changes to the smart tag list definition files because the workbooks are scanned for smart tag recognizers only when the Excel application starts.

Information Lookups via ASP Pages

In earlier sections of this chapter you learned how to create smart tag actions that navigate to a specific web site when a user enters a term that is stored in the XML term list. Instead of sending users to public or commercial web sites, you may want to program actions that link to your own ASP pages and return appropriate data from your database. The XML smart tag list description file can call the ASP script and pass to it the required term to look up, as well as other arguments that you may find necessary for your script. To illustrate how you can provide information lookups via ASP pages, let's create a new XML smart tag list definition file that will display information related to some customers in the Microsoft Access sample Northwind database. We will call this new smart tag Customer Information. Figure 30-5 displays smart tag actions that we will implement for this smart tag.

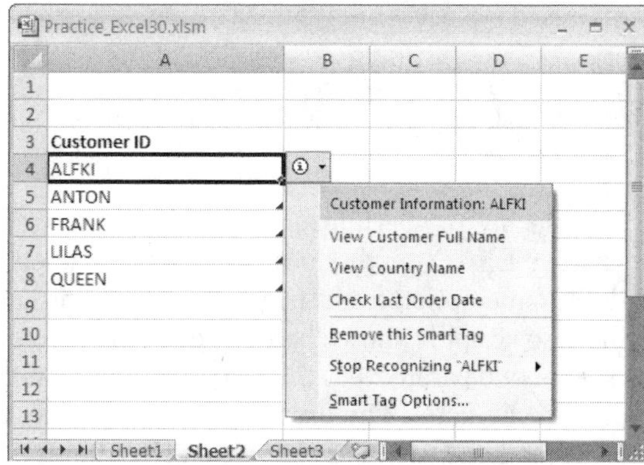

Figure 30-5: This custom smart tag will access customer information from the Northwind database.

Hands-On 30-5: Using an ASP Page with Smart Tags

1. Open Notepad and prepare the XML document as shown in Figure 30-6.

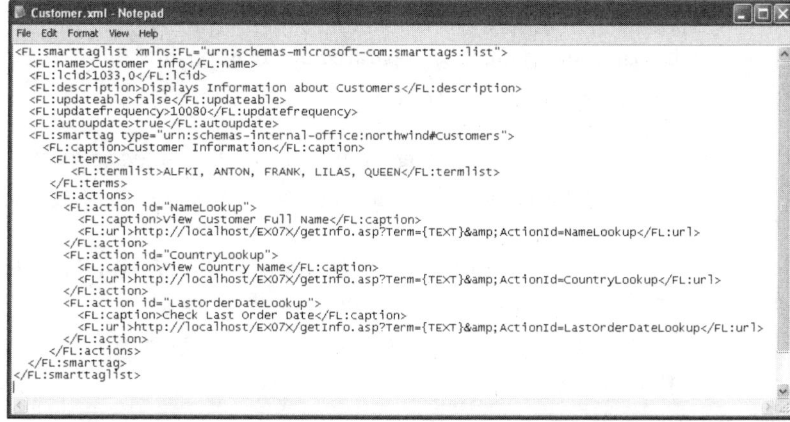

```
<FL:smarttaglist xmlns:FL="urn:schemas-microsoft-com:smarttags:list">
  <FL:name>Customer Info</FL:name>
  <FL:lcid>1033,0</FL:lcid>
  <FL:description>Displays Information about Customers</FL:description>
  <FL:updateable>false</FL:updateable>
  <FL:updatefrequency>10080</FL:updatefrequency>
  <FL:autoupdate>true</FL:autoupdate>
  <FL:smarttag type="urn:schemas-internal-office:northwind#Customers">
    <FL:caption>Customer Information</FL:caption>
     <FL:terms>
        <FL:termlist>ALFKI, ANTON, FRANK, LILAS, QUEEN</FL:termlist>
     </FL:terms>
     <FL:actions>
       <FL:action id="NameLookup">
         <FL:caption>View Customer Full Name</FL:caption>
         <FL:url>http://localhost/EX07X/getInfo.asp?Term={TEXT}&amp;ActionId=NameLookup</FL:url>
       </FL:action>
       <FL:action id="CountryLookup">
         <FL:caption>View Country Name</FL:caption>
         <FL:url>http://localhost/EX07X/getInfo.asp?Term={TEXT}&amp;ActionId=CountryLookup</FL:url>
       </FL:action>
       <FL:action id="LastOrderDateLookup">
         <FL:caption>Check Last Order Date</FL:caption>
         <FL:url>http://localhost/EX07X/getInfo.asp?Term={TEXT}&amp;ActionId=LastOrderDateLookup</FL:url>
       </FL:action>
     </FL:actions>
  </FL:smarttag>
</FL:smarttaglist>
```

Figure 30-6: The XML smart tag list definition file can link to an ASP script.

Note: The above code references EX07X, which is the virtual directory for the XMLWithExcel07 folder that we created in Chapter 29.

2. Save the file as **Customer.xml** in the \Program Files\Common Files\Microsoft Shared\Smart Tag\Lists\ folder.

3. Exit Notepad.

   The XML code in the Customer.xml document uses the same elements as the State Explorer smart tag that you prepared in Hands-On 30-4. This time, however, the termlist contains the customer IDs that you would like to look up in a database on your server. Because the customer IDs are not enclosed in double quotes, they will be recognized whether they are typed in upper- or lowercase letters. Let's take a closer look at the defined actions as they differ a bit from what you've seen in the State Explorer smart tag. To query a database, you need to reference your ASP script in the URL element, as follows:

```
<FL:action id="NameLookup">
   <FL:caption>View Customer Full Name</FL:caption>
   <FL:url>http://localhost/EX07X/getInfo.asp?Term= {TEXT}&amp;ActionId=
        NameLookup</FL:url>
</FL:action>
```

The above code will execute the getInfo.asp script (which is located in the virtual directory named EX07X on the local server) upon selection of the View Customer Full Name option from the smart tag actions list. The code of the getInfo.asp script is shown below (see step 5). Notice that this script file expects two parameters that are provided at the end of a URL following the "?" character. The first parameter will pass the Customer ID, and the second one will pass the Action ID. The Action ID will allow the script to decide which SQL statement should be run to return the data. This way, you can have one Active Server Page handle all of your smart tag actions. Recall that when you pass parameters to ASP pages, they are separated by the ampersand (&). In your XML code, however, to ensure proper parsing and interpretation of values passed, the parameters must be separated by "&" like this:

```
<FL:url>http://localhost/EX07X/getInfo.asp?Term={TEXT}
     &amp;ActionId=NameLookup</FL:url>
```

When you call the ASP page, the URL will be parsed as follows:

http://localhost/EX07X/getInfo.asp?Term=ALFKI&ActionId=NameLookup

4. Copy the **Northwind.mdb** file from the **C:\Ex07_HandsOn** folder to the **XMLWithExcel07** folder on your computer.
5. Open Notepad and enter the ASP script shown below:

```
<%@ Language=VBScript %>
<%
Dim conn
Dim strSearch
Dim strstrSQL

strSearch = Request.QueryString("Term")
strAction = Request.QueryString("ActionID")

' Establish connection to the database
conn="Provider=Microsoft.Jet.OleDB.4.0; Data Source=" & _
    Server.Mappath("Northwind.mdb")

' Build SQL statement
Select Case strAction
   Case "NameLookup", "CountryLookup"
      strSQL = strSQL & "SELECT * FROM Customers"
```

```
      strSQL = strSQL & " WHERE Customers.CustomerID = "
      strSQL = strSQL & "'" & strSearch & "'"
   Case "LastOrderDateLookup"
      strSQL = strSQL & "SELECT Customers.CustomerID,"
      strSQL = strSQL & " Max(Orders.OrderDate) AS LastDate"
      strSQL = strSQL & " FROM Customers INNER JOIN Orders ON"
      strSQL = strSQL & " Customers.CustomerID = Orders.CustomerID"
      strSQL = strSQL & " GROUP BY Customers.CustomerID"
      strSQL = strSQL & " HAVING (((Customers.CustomerID)="
      strSQL = strSQL & "'" & strSearch & "'))"
End Select

' Create a recordset
Set rst = CreateObject("ADODB.Recordset")

' Open a static (3) Recordset (and execute the SQL
' statement above) using the open connection
rst.Open strSQL, conn, 3

' Display information if found
If not rst.EOF then
 Response.Write strSearch & ": "
 Select Case strAction
   Case "NameLookup"
       Response.Write "<B>" & rst("CompanyName").value & "</B>"
   Case "CountryLookup"
       Response.Write "<B>" & rst("Country").value & "</B>"
   Case "LastOrderDateLookup"
      Response.Write "<B>" & rst("LastDate").value & "</B>"
  End Select
Else
   Response.Write "No match for the specified ID: "
   Response.Write strSearch
End if

' Close the recordset
rst.close
Set rst = Nothing
Set conn = Nothing
%>
```

6. Save the ASP file as **getInfo.asp** in your **XMLWithExcel07** folder.

   The ASP script that you've just created begins by retrieving the required parameters. Notice that this is done through the QueryString collection of the ASP Request object:

```
strSearch = Request.QueryString("Term")
strAction = Request.QueryString("ActionId")
```

   Next, a connection to the Northwind database is established using the Microsoft Jet OLEDB.4.0 Provider. For this connection to work properly, you had to place the Northwind.mdb file in the virtual directory that you created earlier (EX07X), or change the connection string to point to a different location where this file is located. To look up a Customer ID and return a different type of information from the database depending on a selected smart tag action, you need to build appropriate SQL statements.

The first two actions will use the same SQL statement, as the information that you want to return is located in the same table. This SQL statement simply says to select all fields from the Customers table where CustomerID is the ID (term) that the user typed:

```
strSQL = strSQL & "SELECT * FROM Customers"
strSQL = strSQL & " WHERE Customers.CustomerID = "
strSQL = strSQL & "'" & strSearch & "'"
```

In the above statement, the strSearch variable holds the value of the CustomerID that was typed by the user in a worksheet cell. The date lookup will require a different, more complex SQL statement.

The following statement says to select the CustomerID field and a calculated field named LastDate obtained by applying the Max function to the OrderDate field in the Orders table. The two tables (Customers and Orders) necessary to obtain this information are to be joined on the CustomerID field. All information will be grouped by CustomerID. The HAVING clause will limit the returned records to the one record meeting our criteria — the CustomerID (term) provided by the user in a worksheet:

```
strSQL = strSQL & "SELECT Customers.CustomerID,"
strSQL = strSQL & " Max(Orders.OrderDate) AS LastDate"
strSQL = strSQL & " FROM Customers INNER JOIN Orders ON"
strSQL = strSQL & " Customers.CustomerID = Orders.CustomerID"
strSQL = strSQL & " GROUP BY Customers.CustomerID"
strSQL = strSQL & " HAVING (((Customers.CustomerID)="
strSQL = strSQL & "'" & strSearch & "'))"
```

The Select Case statement will allow you to build an SQL statement based on the ActionID. The next statements in the code create and open the recordset based on the SQL statement using the open connection to the database. The remaining code deals with the display of data. If the returned recordset is not empty, we will read the value of the CompanyName, Country, or LastDate field, depending on the type of action the user has selected. Otherwise, we will display a message that the data for the specified ID was not found. This ASP script is pretty straightforward.

Now that you have both the XML smart tag description file (Customer. xml) and the ASP script file (getInfo.asp) ready and placed in the appropriate directories, let's test the Customer Information smart tag that you've created.

7. Restart Microsoft Excel.
8. Open the **C:\Ex07_ByExample\Practice_Excel30.xlsm** workbook file.
9. Activate **Sheet2** and enter the data shown in Figure 30-5 earlier. Notice that we are using the terms (Customer IDs) defined in the Customer.xml file as shown in Figure 30-6 earlier.
10. When the smart tag button appears, click it and select one of the actions. You should see the requested information appear in your browser.

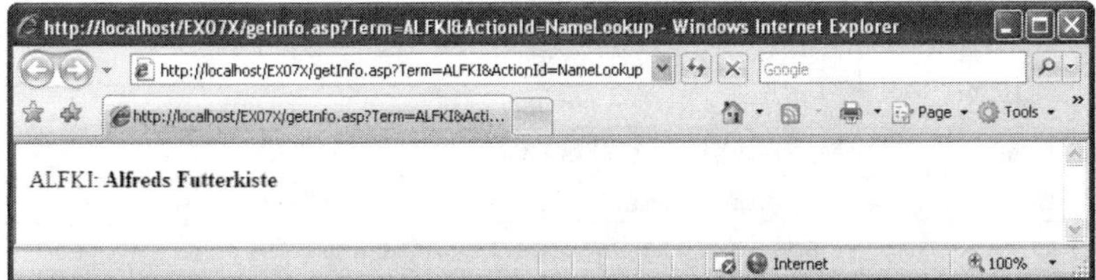

Figure 30-7: A simple smart tag can pull the requested information from a database and display it in a browser.

Note: If you are looking for the ability to feed information that you have looked up back into Microsoft Excel, you will need to take the DLL approach to creating smart tags. You can find examples on how to do this in the Microsoft Smart Tag SDK.

11. Close the browser.

Dynamic Recognition of Smart Tag Terms

One of the new features introduced in the previous version of Microsoft Office (2003) is a dynamic recognition of smart tag terms via regular expressions. A regular expression allows you to match strings based on a provided search pattern. You are already familiar with pattern matching using wildcards. Think of how many times in the course of working with computer files you used search patterns like *.xls, *.doc, or *.*.

Regular expressions can be just as simple or they can be very complex. Many books and technical articles are devoted to using regular expressions. Table 30-1 shows examples of characters you can use in creating regular expression search patterns.

Table 30-1: Special characters used in regular expressions

Character	Meaning
^	Forces the search expression to match at the beginning of the line. When the ^ symbol is the first symbol in the bracket expression, the characters following it will be excluded from the search. When used outside the brackets, it means to start from the first character.
. (period)	Matches any single character
$	Forces the search expression to match at the end of the line
|	Provides alternate matches like the OR operator. For example, x|y will match either x or y.
( )	Groups characters or patterns
[ ]	Matches any one of the enclosed characters. Ranges can be specified by using a hyphen, such as [0-9] or [A-Z].
*	Matches zero or more instances of the preceding character
+	Matches one or more instances of the preceding character
?	Matches zero or one instance of the preceding character
\	Escape character. Indicates that the next character should not be interpreted as a regular expression special character.

Character	Meaning
{n}	Matches exactly n times
{n,}	Matches at least n times
{n,m}	Matches at least n but no more than m times
\w	Any "word" character (alphanumeric and the underscore)
\s	Finds white space (space, tab, or punctuation)
\d	Matches a single digit (0-9)
\b	Matches a word boundary, such as a space
\r	Matches a carriage return
\t	Matches a tab
\v	Matches a vertical tab

Here are some examples of creating regular expressions:

[^A|H]	Matches any character that is NOT a capital A or a capital H.
\d{1,2}	Matches any number consisting of one or two digits; e.g., 1, 10, or 99.
DOA[0|1]\d	Searches for the letters "DOA" followed by a 0 or 1, followed by any single digit.

Let's say that in the State Explorer smart tag that you created earlier in this chapter you'd like to recognize all of the U.S. Postal Service state abbreviations. The following regular expression could be used:

```
[a-w][a-z]
```

This expression will recognize two-letter combinations in which the first letter is a lowercase a through w, and the second letter is any lowercase letter from a to z.

In the XML document, the regular expression pattern is defined in the <FL:exp> tag, which is a member of the <FL:re> tag:

```
<FL:caption>US State Explorer</FL:caption>
    <FL:re>
        <FL:exp>([a-w][a-z])</FL:exp>
    </FL:re>
```

Figure 30-8 shows the above code segment inside the XML smart tag definition file.

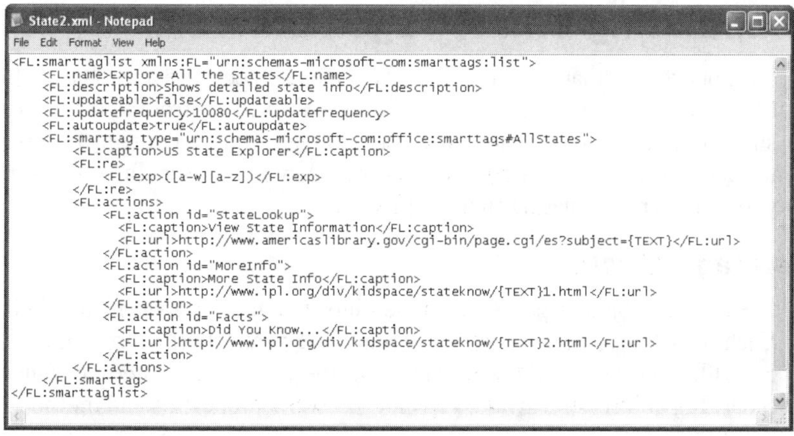

```
State2.xml - Notepad
File Edit Format View Help
<FL:smarttaglist xmlns:FL="urn:schemas-microsoft-com:smarttags:list">
    <FL:name>Explore All the States</FL:name>
    <FL:description>Shows detailed state info</FL:description>
    <FL:updateable>false</FL:updateable>
    <FL:updatefrequency>10080</FL:updatefrequency>
    <FL:autoupdate>true</FL:autoupdate>
    <FL:smarttag type="urn:schemas-microsoft-com:office:smarttags#AllStates">
        <FL:caption>US State Explorer</FL:caption>
        <FL:re>
            <FL:exp>([a-w][a-z])</FL:exp>
        </FL:re>
        <FL:actions>
            <FL:action id="StateLookup">
              <FL:caption>View State Information</FL:caption>
              <FL:url>http://www.americaslibrary.gov/cgi-bin/page.cgi/es?subject={TEXT}</FL:url>
            </FL:action>
            <FL:action id="MoreInfo">
              <FL:caption>More State Info</FL:caption>
              <FL:url>http://www.ipl.org/div/kidspace/stateknow/{TEXT}1.html</FL:url>
            </FL:action>
            <FL:action id="Facts">
              <FL:caption>Did You Know...</FL:caption>
              <FL:url>http://www.ipl.org/div/kidspace/stateknow/{TEXT}2.html</FL:url>
            </FL:action>
        </FL:actions>
    </FL:smarttag>
</FL:smarttaglist>
```

Figure 30-8: XML smart tag definition file that uses regular expression pattern matching.

Let's create the State2.xml smart tag definition file.

Hands-On 30-6: Creating Smart Tag Definition File with Regular Expressions

1. Open Notepad and enter the code shown in Figure 30-8.
2. Save the file as **State2.xml** in the \Program Files\Common Files\Microsoft Shared\Smart Tag\Lists\ folder.
3. Restart Microsoft Excel.

> **Note:** Remember that if an Excel application is open, you must close it and reopen it so a new smart tag will be recognized.

4. Follow the steps in Hands-On 30-1 to display the AutoCorrect dialog box with the Smart Tags tab.

   The dialog box displays the list of available smart tag recognizers. You should see the U.S. State Explorer smart tag selected in this list along with other built-in and custom smart tags that were created earlier in this chapter.
5. Close the AutoCorrect dialog box.
6. Open the **C:\Ex07_ByExample\Practice_Excel30.xlsm** workbook.
7. Activate **Sheet1** and enter any U.S. state abbreviation in any cell on the active worksheet. Remember to use lowercase letters. When the term is recognized, click the smart tag button and choose one of the actions in the list.

Manipulating Smart Tags with VBA

To support the smart tag functionality, special objects are available in the Microsoft Excel object model. You can use VBA to control the display of smart tags, add a smart tag to a worksheet cell, and execute any of the smart tag actions. The following sections introduce you to SmartTag objects and get you started manipulating them with VBA.

SmartTag Object

A SmartTag object represents an identifier assigned to a worksheet cell. Each SmartTag object belongs to a SmartTags collection. To return a SmartTag object, use the Add method of the SmartTags collection. Once the SmartTag object is returned, you can access its properties and methods (Figure 30-9).

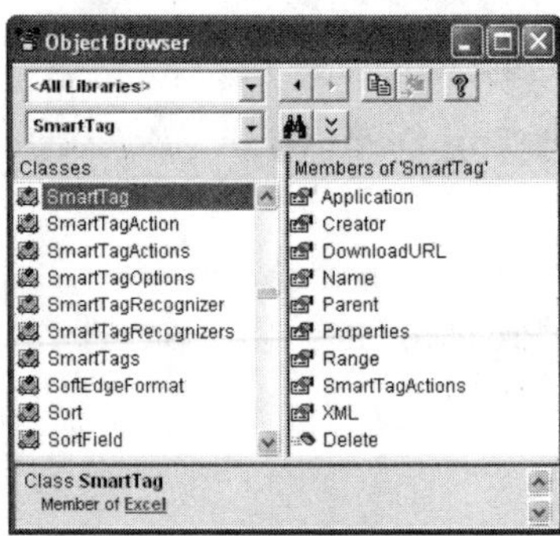

Figure 30-9: The properties and methods of the SmartTag object.

SmartTagAction Object

Use the SmartTagAction object to access actions that can be performed with smart tags. Each SmartTagAction object is a member of a SmartTagActions collection. Use the Item property of the SmartTagActions collection to return the SmartTagAction object. This object has several properties and one method, as illustrated in Figure 30-10. Use the Execute method to invoke a smart tag action.

Figure 30-10: The properties and the method of the SmartTagAction object.

SmartTagOptions Object

You can control options that can be performed with smart tags using the SmartTagOptions object.

- Use the SmartTagOptions property of the Workbook object to return a SmartTagOptions object.
- Use the EmbedSmartTags property of the SmartTagOptions object to turn on or off the embedding of smart tags in a workbook.
- Use the DisplaySmartTags property of the SmartTagOptions object to control the display features of the smart tags.

SmartTagRecognizer Object

In Microsoft Excel, if the data is recognized by the installed recognition engine, you will see a purple triangle in the lower-right corner of the cell. Use the SmartTagRecognizer object to determine if tag recognizers are enabled for the entire application. The SmartTagRecognizer is a member of the SmartTagRecognizers collection. You can return a single SmartTagRecognizer via the Item property of the SmartTagRecognizers collection.

Now let's spend a few minutes working with the above-mentioned objects, properties, and methods.

Hands-On 30-7: Obtaining Information about Smart Tags from the Immediate Window

1. Type **MSFT** in cell B5 in any worksheet.
2. Switch to a Visual Basic Editor window.
3. Press **Ctrl+G** to activate the Immediate window.
4. In the Immediate window, enter the following statements and observe the results:

```
?Range("B5").SmartTags(1).Name
?Range("B5").SmartTags(1).SmartTagActions(1).Name
?Range("B5").SmartTags(1).SmartTagActions(2).Name
?Range("B5").SmartTags(1).SmartTagActions(2).Parent
Range("B5").SmartTags(1).SmartTagActions(2).Execute
?Range("B5").SmartTags(1).XML
```

The following example procedure relates to the Customer Information smart tag that was created in an earlier section. The procedure illustrates how, by using VBA, you can recognize a Customer ID typed into a worksheet cell, even though that particular ID is not stored in the smart tag list definition file that was created using the Extensible Markup Language (XML). Recall that the Customer.xml file contains just a few customer IDs.

Hands-On 30-8: Using VBA to Add and Execute a Smart Tag

1. Open a new workbook and save it as **C:\Ex07_ByExample\SmartTags_VBA.xlsm.**
2. Switch to the Visual Basic Editor window and insert a module into VBAProject (SmartTags_VBA.xlsm).
3. In the Code window, enter the following AddNExecute_SmartTag procedure:

```
Sub AddNExecute_SmartTag()
    Dim strValue
    Dim strLink

    strLink = "urn:schemas-internal-office:northwind#Customers"

    ' Get Customer Id from the user
    strValue = InputBox("Enter an ID of a Northwind customer " _
       & "that is not in the Customer.xml " _
       & "smart tag list definition file:", "Enter: Customer ID")

    ' Exit if user clicked Cancel
    If strValue = "" Then Exit Sub

    ' Set Smart Tag options to embed and recognize smart tags
    ActiveWorkbook.SmartTagOptions.EmbedSmartTags = True
    Application.SmartTagRecognizers.Recognize = True

    With Range("B6")
      .Formula = strValue
      .SmartTags.Add(strLink).SmartTagActions(1).Execute
    End With
End Sub
```

   The above procedure will prompt you for a customer ID that does not exist in Customer.xml. To recognize values that are not listed in the smart tag list definition file, you must set the EmbedSmartTags property of the SmartTagOptions object to True and tell Excel to label data as a smart tag using the Recognize property of the SmartTagRecognizers collection. After setting the smart tag options, the procedure will enter the customer ID stored in the strValue variable in cell B6 on the active worksheet and will proceed to execute the first smart tag action, which returns the customer's full name.

4. Switch to the Microsoft Excel application window and press **Alt+F8** to display the Macro dialog box.
5. Select the **AddNExecute_SmartTag** macro and click the **Run** button. When prompted for the customer ID, enter **WOLZA** and click **OK.**

   Excel enters WOLZA in cell B6 on the active worksheet and displays the customer's name in the browser.

6. In the worksheet, move the mouse pointer over cell **B6** and click the smart tag button. Select another action from the list. For example, check the last order date for this customer.
7. Try this procedure with other IDs such as: LAZYK, OCEAN, TORTU, or VINET.

Chapter Summary

In this chapter you have seen how smart tags can help Excel users get instant, context-sensitive access to information stored in external sources such as web pages or databases.

You learned how to create simple XML smart tag definition files containing a list of terms and search patterns that can be recognized when typed in a cell on an Excel worksheet. You also learned how the smart tag definition files can call ASP scripts and how you can manipulate smart tags with VBA.

Index

Q

R